The Oxford Handbook of Identity Development

OXFORD LIBRARY OF PSYCHOLOGY

EDITOR-IN-CHIEF

Peter E. Nathan

AREA EDITORS:

Clinical Psychology
David H. Barlow

Cognitive Neuroscience
Kevin N. Ochsner and Stephen M. Kosslyn

Cognitive Psychology
Daniel Reisberg

Counseling Psychology
Elizabeth M. Altmaier and Jo-Ida C. Hansen

Developmental Psychology
Philip David Zelazo

Health Psychology
Howard S. Friedman

History of Psychology
David B. Baker

Methods and Measurement
Todd D. Little

Neuropsychology
Kenneth M. Adams

Organizational Psychology
Steve W. J. Kozlowski

Personality and Social Psychology
Kay Deaux and Mark Snyder

OXFORD LIBRARY OF PSYCHOLOGY

Editor in Chief PETER E. NATHAN

The Oxford Handbook of Identity Development

Edited by
Kate C. McLean
and Moin Syed

OXFORD
UNIVERSITY PRESS

Oxford University Press is a department of the University of Oxford.
It furthers the University's objective of excellence in research,
scholarship, and education by publishing worldwide.

Oxford   New York
Auckland   Cape Town   Dar es Salaam   Hong Kong   Karachi
Kuala Lumpur   Madrid   Melbourne   Mexico City   Nairobi
New Delhi   Shanghai   Taipei   Toronto

With offices in
Argentina   Austria   Brazil   Chile   Czech Republic   France   Greece
Guatemala   Hungary   Italy   Japan   Poland   Portugal   Singapore
South Korea   Switzerland   Thailand   Turkey   Ukraine   Vietnam

Oxford is a registered trademark of Oxford University Press
in the UK and certain other countries.

Published in the United States of America by
Oxford University Press
198 Madison Avenue, New York, NY 10016

© Oxford University Press 2015

First issued as an Oxford University Press paperback, 2016

All rights reserved. No part of this publication may be reproduced, stored in
a retrieval system, or transmitted, in any form or by any means, without the prior
permission in writing of Oxford University Press, or as expressly permitted by law,
by license, or under terms agreed with the appropriate reproduction rights organization.
Inquiries concerning reproduction outside the scope of the above should be sent to the
Rights Department, Oxford University Press, at the address above.

You must not circulate this work in any other form
and you must impose this same condition on any acquirer.

Library of Congress Cataloging-in-Publication Data
The Oxford handbook of identity development / edited by Kate C. McLean and Moin Syed.
    pages cm.—(Oxford library of psychology)
Includes index.
ISBN 978–0–19–993656–4 (hardcover : alk. paper); 978-0-19-046923-8 (paperback : alk. paper)
1. Identity (Psychology)   2. Group identity.
I. McLean, Kate C., editor of compilation.   II. Syed, Moin U., editor of compilation.
BF697.O94 2014
155.2'5—dc23
2014022202

This book is dedicated to Herold Jones, Mark "Cutback" Davis, and Bob "Jungle Death" Gerrard.

SHORT CONTENTS

Oxford Library of Psychology   ix

About the Editors   xi

Contributors   xiii

Contents   xvii

Chapters   1–574

Index   575

OXFORD LIBRARY OF PSYCHOLOGY

The *Oxford Library of Psychology*, a landmark series of handbooks, is published by Oxford University Press, one of the world's oldest and most highly respected publishers, with a tradition of publishing significant books in psychology. The ambitious goal of the *Oxford Library of Psychology* is nothing less than to span a vibrant, wide-ranging field and, in so doing, to fill a clear market need.

Encompassing a comprehensive set of handbooks, organized hierarchically, the *Library* incorporates volumes at different levels, each designed to meet a distinct need. At one level are a set of handbooks designed broadly to survey the major subfields of psychology; at another are numerous handbooks that cover important current focal research and scholarly areas of psychology in depth and detail. Planned as a reflection of the dynamism of psychology, the *Library* will grow and expand as psychology itself develops, thereby highlighting significant new research that will impact on the field. Adding to its accessibility and ease of use, the *Library* will be published in print and, later on, electronically.

The *Library* surveys psychology's principal subfields with a set of handbooks that capture the current status and future prospects of those major subdisciplines. This initial set includes handbooks of social and personality psychology, clinical psychology, counseling psychology, school psychology, educational psychology, industrial and organizational psychology, cognitive psychology, cognitive neuroscience, methods and measurements, history, neuropsychology, personality assessment, developmental psychology, and more. Each handbook undertakes to review one of psychology's major subdisciplines with breadth, comprehensiveness, and exemplary scholarship. In addition to these broadly-conceived volumes, the *Library* also includes a large number of handbooks designed to explore in depth more specialized areas of scholarship and research, such as stress, health and coping, anxiety and related disorders, cognitive development, or child and adolescent assessment. In contrast to the broad coverage of the subfield handbooks, each of these latter volumes focuses on an especially productive, more highly focused line of scholarship and research. Whether at the broadest or most specific level, however, all of the *Library* handbooks offer synthetic coverage that reviews and evaluates the relevant past and present research and anticipates research in the future. Each handbook in the *Library* includes introductory and concluding chapters written by its editor to provide a roadmap to the handbook's table of contents and to offer informed anticipations of significant future developments in that field.

An undertaking of this scope calls for handbook editors and chapter authors who are established scholars in the areas about which they write. Many of the nation's and world's most productive and best-respected psychologists have agreed to edit *Library* handbooks or write authoritative chapters in their areas of expertise.

For whom has the *Oxford Library of Psychology* been written? Because of its breadth, depth, and accessibility, the *Library* serves a diverse audience, including graduate students in psychology and their faculty mentors, scholars, researchers, and practitioners in psychology and related fields. Each will find in the *Library* the information they seek on the subfield or focal area of psychology in which they work or are interested.

Befitting its commitment to accessibility, each handbook includes a comprehensive index, as well as extensive references to help guide research. And because the *Library* was designed from its inception as an online as well as a print resource, its structure and contents will be readily and rationally searchable online. Further, once the *Library* is released online, the handbooks will be regularly and thoroughly updated.

In summary, the *Oxford Library of Psychology* will grow organically to provide a thoroughly informed perspective on the field of psychology, one that reflects both psychology's dynamism and its increasing interdisciplinarity. Once published electronically, the *Library* is also destined to become a uniquely valuable interactive tool, with extended search and browsing capabilities. As you begin to consult this handbook, we sincerely hope you will share our enthusiasm for the more than 500-year tradition of Oxford University Press for excellence, innovation, and quality, as exemplified by the *Oxford Library of Psychology*.

Peter E. Nathan
Editor-in-Chief
Oxford Library of Psychology

ABOUT THE EDITORS

Kate C. McLean
Kate C. McLean is an associate professor at Western Washington University. Her research centers on the development of narrative identity in adolescence and emerging adulthood, particularly as it develops in social contexts and as it relates to individual differences in personality and psychological adjustment.

Moin Syed
Moin Syed is an associate professor of psychology at the University of Minnesota, Twin Cities. His research focuses broadly on identity development among ethnically diverse youth and the implications of identity development for educational experiences.

CONTRIBUTORS

Jeffrey Jensen Arnett
Clark University
Department of Psychology
Worcester, Massachusetts

Margarita Azmitia
University of California, Santa Cruz
Department of Psychology
Santa Cruz, California

Joan Chiao
Northwestern University
Department of Psychology
Evanston, Illinois

Jeffrey T. Cookston
San Francisco State University
Department of Psychology
San Francisco, California

Catherine R. Cooper
University of California, Santa Cruz
Department of Psychology
Santa Cruz, California

James Côté
The University of Western Ontario
Department of Sociology
London, Ontario, Canada

Elisabetta Crocetti
Utrecht University
Research Centre Adolescent Development
Utrecht, The Netherlands

Elizabeth A. Daniels
Oregon State University-Cascades
Department of Psychology
Bend, Oregon

Kyle Eichas
Tarleton State University
Department of Psychology and Counseling
Waco, Texas

Robyn Fivush
Emory University
Department of Psychology
Atlanta, Georgia

Hanoch Flum
Ben-Gurion University
Department of Education
Beer Sheva, Israel

Mark Freeman
College of the Holy Cross
Department of Psychology
Worcester, Massachusetts

Meghan M. Gillen
Pennsylvania State University
Division of Social Sciences
Abington, Pennsylvania

Elizabeth Gonzalez
University of California, Santa Cruz
Department of Psychology
Santa Cruz, California

Tilmann Habermas
Goethe University
Department of Psychology
Frankfurt, Germany

Phillip L. Hammack
University of California, Santa Cruz
Department of Psychology
Santa Cruz, California

Tokiko Harada
National Institute for Physiological Sciences
Aichi, Japan

Ruthellen Josselson
The Fiedling Institute
School of Psychology
Baltimore, Maryland

Adam M. Kasmark
Connecticut College
Department of Psychology
New London, Connecticut

Christin Köber
Goethe University
Department of Psychology
Frankfurt, Germany

Neill Korobov
University of West Georgia
Department of Psychology
Carrollton, Georgia

Jane Kroger
University of Tromsø
Department of Psychology
Tromsø, Norway
Western Washington University
Department of Psychology
Bellingham, Washington

E. Saskia Kunnen
University of Groningen
Department of Developmental Psychology
Groningen, The Netherlands

William Kurtines
Florida International University
Department of Psychology
Miami, Florida

Jack Lam
University of Minnesota
Department of Sociology
Minneapolis, Minnesota

Shi-Rong Lee
University of Minnesota
Department of Sociology
Minneapolis, Minnesota

Leslie D. Leve
University of Oregon
Department of Counseling Psychology
    and Human Services
Eugene, Oregon

Jennifer Pals Lilgendahl
Haverford College
Department of Psychology
Haverford, Pennsylvania

Koen Luyckx
Katholieke Universiteit Leuven
School Psychology and Adolescent
    Development
Faculty of Psychology
Leuven, The Netherlands

Adriana M. Manago
Assistant Professor
Department of Psychology
Western Washington University

Dan P. McAdams
Northwestern University
Department of Psychology
Evanston, Illinois

Kate C. McLean
Western Washington University
Department of Psychology
Bellingham, Washington

Alan Meca
Florida International University
Department of Psychology
Miami, Florida

Wim Meeus
Utrecht University
Research Centre Adolescent Development
Utrecht, The Netherlands
Tilburg University
Department of Developmental Psychology
Tilburg, The Netherlands

Marijke Metz
University of Groningen
Department of Developmental Psychology
Groningen, The Netherlands

Marilyn J. Montgomery
Capella University
Minneapolis, Minnesota

Jeylan Mortimer
University of Minnesota
Department of Sociology
Minneapolis, Minnesota

Frosso Motti-Stefanidi
University of Athens
Department of Psychology
Athens, Greece

Alissa J. Mrazek
Northwestern University
Department of Psychology
Evanston, Illinois

Misaki N. Natsuaki
University of California, Riverside
Department of Psychology
Riverside, California

Monisha Pasupathi
University of Utah
Department of Psychology
Salt Lake City, Utah

Holly Recchia
Concordia University
Department of Education
Montreal, Quebec, Canada

Luke Remy
San Francisco State University
Department of Psychology
San Francisco, California

Onnie Rogers
University of Washington
Department of Psychology
Seattle, Washington

Wendy Rote
University of Rochester
Department of Clinical and Social Psychology
Rochester, New York

Danielle V. Samuels
University of California, Riverside
Department of Psychology
Riverside, California

Elli P. Schachter
Bar-Ilan University
School of Education
Ramat Gan, Israel

Seth Schwartz
University of Miami
Department of Public Health Sciences
Leonard M. Miller School of Medicine
Miami, Florida

Jefferson Singer
Connecticut College
Department of Psychology
New London, Connecticut

Judith Smetana
University of Rochester
Department of Clinical and Social Psychology
Rochester, New York

Moin Syed
University of Minnesota
Department of Psychology
Minneapolis, Minnesota

Cecilia Wainryb
University of Utah
Department of Psychology
Salt Lake City, Utah

Alan S. Waterman
The College of New Jersey
Department of Psychology
Ewing, New Jersey

Niobe Way
New York University
Department of Applied Psychology
New York, New York

Antoinette R. Wilson
University of California, Santa Cruz
Department of Psychology
Santa Cruz, California

Frank C. Worrell
University of California, Berkeley
Graduate School of Education
Berkeley, California

Widaad Zaman
University of Central Florida
Department of Psychology
Valencia-Osceola, Florida

Claudia Zapata-Gietl
Northwestern University
Program in Human Development and Social Policy
Evanston, Illinois

CONTENTS

Preface xxi

1. The Field of Identity Development Needs an Identity: An Introduction to *The Oxford Handbook of Identity Development* 1
   Kate C. McLean and *Moin Syed*
2. Theoretical Foundations of Identity 11
   Phillip L. Hammack

Part 1 • Debates: Identity Development Across the Lifespan

3. Gendered Narrative Voices: Sociocultural and Feminist Approaches to Emerging Identity in Childhood and Adolescence 33
   Robyn Fivush and *Widaad Zaman*
4. Identity Development from Adolescence to Emerging Adulthood: What We Know and (Especially) Don't Know 53
   Jeffrey Jensen Arnett
5. Identity Development Through Adulthood: The Move Toward "Wholeness" 65
   Jane Kroger
6. Three Strands of Identity Development Across the Human Life Course: Reading Erik Erikson in Full 81
   Dan P. McAdams and *Claudia Zapata-Gietl*

Part 2 • Debates: Identity Status Perspectives on Processes of Identity Development

7. The Identity Statuses: Strengths of a Person-Centered Approach 97
   Elisabetta Crocetti and *Wim Meeus*
8. Commitment and Exploration: The Need for a Developmental Approach 115
   Saskia E. Kunnen and *Marijke Metz*
9. Identity Status: On Refinding the People 132
   Ruthellen Josselson and *Hanoch Flum*

Part 3 • Debates: Narrative Perspectives on Processes of Identity Development

10. Autobiographical Reasoning is Constitutive for Narrative Identity: The Role of the Life Story for Personal Continuity 149
    Tilmann Habermas and *Christin Köber*

11. Autobiographical Reasoning and My Discontent: Alternative Paths from Narrative to Identity   166
    Monisha Pasupathi
12. Discerning Oneself: A Plea for the Whole   182
    Mark Freeman

Part 4 • Debates: Internal, External, and Interactional Approaches to Identity Development

13. Identity as Internal Processes: How the "I" Comes to Define the "Me"   195
    Alan S. Waterman
14. Identities as an Interactional Process   210
    Neill Korobov
15. Integrating "Internal," "Interactional," and "External" Perspectives: Identity Process as the Formulation of Accountable Claims Regarding Selves   228
    Elli P. Schachter

Part 5 • Debates: Culture and Identity Development

16. Culture as Race/Ethnicity   249
    Frank C. Worrell
17. "[T]hey Say Black Men Won't Make It, But I Know I'm Gonna Make It": Ethnic and Racial Identity Development in the Context of Cultural Stereotypes   269
    Niobe Way and *Onnie Rogers*
18. Reflections on the Cultural Lenses of Identity Development   286
    Margarita Azmitia

Part 6 • Applied Issues in Identity Development

19. Identities, Cultures, and Schooling: How Students Navigate Racial-Ethnic, Indigenous, Immigrant, Social Class, and Gender Identities on Their Pathways Through School   299
    Catherine R. Cooper, Elizabeth Gonzalez, and *Antoinette R. Wilson*
20. Transformation, Erosion, or Disparity in Work Identity?: Challenges During the Contemporary Transition to Adulthood   319
    Jeylan T. Mortimer, Jack Lam, and *Shi-Rong Lee*
21. Identity and Positive Youth Development: Advances in Developmental Intervention Science   337
    Kyle Eichas, Alan Meca, Marilyn J. Montgomery, and *William M. Kurtines*
22. A Translational Research Approach to Narrative Identity in Psychotherapy   355
    Jefferson A. Singer and *Adam M. Kasmark*
23. Youths' Constructions of Meanings About Experiences with Political Conflict: Implications for Processes of Identity Development   369
    Cecilia Wainryb and *Holly Recchia*

Part 7 • Extensions

24. Puberty, Identity, and Context: A Biopsychosocial Perspective on Internalizing Psychopathology in Early Adolescent Girls   389
    Misaki N. Natsuaki, Danielle Samuels, and *Leslie D. Leve*
25. Body Image and Identity: A Call for New Research   406
    Elizabeth A. Daniels and *Meghan M. Gillen*
26. Cultural Neuroscience of Identity Development   423
    Alissa J. Mrazek, Tokiko Harada, and *Joan Y. Chiao*
27. Parenting, Adolescent–Parent Relationships, and Social Domain Theory: Implications for Identity Development   437
    Wendy M. Rote and *Judith G. Smetana*
28. Who Am I If We're Not Us? Divorce and Identity Across the Lifespan   454
    Jeffrey T. Cookston and *Luke Remy*
29. Identity Development in the Context of the Risk and Resilience Framework   472
    Frosso Motti-Stefanidi
30. The Dynamic Role of Identity Processes in Personality Development: Theories, Patterns, and New Directions   490
    Jennifer Pals Lilgendahl
31. Identity Development in the Digital Age: The Case of Social Networking Sites   508
    Adriana M. Manago

Part 8 • Reflections, Conclusions, and the Future

32. Identity Formation Research from a Critical Perspective: Is a Social Science Developing?   527
    James E. Côté
33. What Have We Learned Since Schwartz (2001)?: A Reappraisal of the Field of Identity Development   539
    Seth J. Schwartz, Koen Luyckx, and *Elisabetta Crocetti*
34. The Future of Identity Development Research: Reflections, Tensions, and Challenges   562
    Moin Syed and *Kate C. McLean*

Index   575

PREFACE

This book started with a dinner reservation.

We had known each other for several years because we both completed our doctoral work in developmental psychology at UC Santa Cruz. We are also family, as Kate's husband's brother's wife's sister is Moin's best friend. However, it was not until the 2008 Society for Research on Adolescence Biennial meeting that the seeds for this book were sowed. Moin helped organize a dinner for Santa Cruz students and alumni. Due to his "unusual name" Moin used his pseudonym "Ronald Johnson" for the reservation. When the other attendees discovered this, most were perplexed. Kate, however, immediately recognized the reference to *Fast Times at Ridgemont High*. That conversation opened the door for many more conversations that night and ever since. In addition to our intellectual exchanges, we discovered our mutual love for San Francisco Giants baseball—leading us to believe that we could trust each other on just about all judgments in life.

When Kate was approached by Oxford in the summer of 2011 to take on this project, she called Moin to discuss. Our discussion immediately turned to how we could do something different, something that would break from the traditional mold of the Handbook. We recount these discussions a bit in our opening chapter.

Once we had settled on a concept for the book, we had to develop a timeline and recruit authors. The timeline was the easy part: we just checked to see when the 2012 baseball season would be over and arranged to have first drafts due then (good thing, as the Giants went home champions that year).

Recruiting authors proved to be remarkably easy as well. We were struck by the enthusiasm with which potential authors responded, most of whom directly commented on the exciting and innovative style for the Handbook.

This enthusiasm was likely dampened quite a bit after submitting their first drafts, however, as the authors may not have been prepared for what was to come. We were definitely "hands on" editors. Nearly all chapters were sent out for peer review, and all chapters were read and commented on by both Kate and Moin. The requests for revisions were substantial for each and every chapter. We then both read the revised chapters, and, in almost every case, we requested additional substantial revisions. For some, this happened a third time. One contributor, who will remain nameless, said he groaned when he saw our email in his inbox. All of this is to say that we asked a great deal of our contributors, and they came through in a big way. We are so grateful for their dedication to this Handbook and to our vision. Obviously, this Handbook would not exist without them, and we felt it was necessary to make public just how much work went into the chapters. We also publicly acknowledge each other here, as this was a co-editorship in full, despite the need for an order of editors on the cover of this book.

We thank those we worked with at Oxford University Press: Sarah Harrington who initially approached us and encouraged our ideas, and the team who put the book together – Anne Dellinger, Jen Vafidis, Alixandra Gould, Andrea Zekus, and Kumudhavalli Narasimhan.

We thank those individuals who provided insightful reviews of these chapters. They include most of the authors in the volume who reviewed other chapters, along with Rebecca Goodvin, Kelly Marin, Lisa Sontag, Natalie Sabik, Carla Rice, Jon Adler, Linda Juang, Andrea Greenhoot, Michael Chandler, Krista Aronson, Anthony Burrow, Fred Vondracek, Andrea Breen, Eva Telzer, and Koen Luyckx.

We hope you enjoy the book as much as we enjoyed making it happen.

– Kate C. McLean and Moin Syed

CHAPTER 1

The Field of Identity Development Needs an Identity: An Introduction to *The Oxford Handbook of Identity Development*

Kate C. McLean *and* Moin Syed

Abstract

This chapter introduces *The Oxford Handbook of Identity Development*. The authors detail their rationale for the need for such a handbook, which primarily rests on their concern that the field of identity development is in need of greater integration and coherence. To push the field into new territory, the authors also emphasize that the handbook chapters are meant to be "forward" focused, rather than simple reviews of past research. They provide a brief history of the field, as well as a discussion of what develops in terms of the processes and contents of identity. Finally, the authors describe the volume's three sections, all of which were designed to provide greater integration to the field and to push the field in new directions: debates, applications, and extensions.

Key Words: identity development

Several years ago, we were approached by Oxford University Press to consider writing a Handbook on identity development. Although the idea was certainly interesting, we spent a good deal of time pondering two questions: (1) did we want to take on such a large project? And (2) did the field need such a handbook? Regarding the first question, we decided that we would take on the project only if we could shake up the usual format of a handbook, which would certainly make the project more fun for us. More importantly, we thought such a break with tradition would be more useful to the field. Answering the second question—does the field need such a handbook—was more of a challenge, particularly given the proliferation of handbooks of late.

Of course, we are biased as scholars who study identity development, but we think that identity is one of the most interesting and important aspects of the human experience. Still, despite the importance, depth, and centrality of the topic to human functioning, we both felt that there were some issues in the field that a handbook could begin to address. In particular, the dawn of the millennium ushered in some important new ideas in the field (see Schwartz et al., this volume), as well as real growth in established areas, yet these new ideas and areas of growth have been largely disconnected from each other. Within the field we saw various groups of scholars who were not in dialogue with each other, resulting in a degree of incoherence in the literature. We also saw the field as somewhat insular, as many probably are. Yet, such insularity is problematic, because it can prohibit creative growth. These issues—disconnection and insularity—suggested to us that a handbook on identity development could be coming at an opportune time.

Our broadest aim was to facilitate growth and movement in the field by creating structures in this handbook to encourage discussion between scholars who did not appear to be in dialogue with each other. Metaphorically, we saw the field of identity development as comprising various cultural groups who seemed to be on different continents. For example, some of the researchers in this book—most of them experts on the same subject—had never read each other's work. This kind of cultural disconnect is problematic within the field, of course, but it is also quite problematic for those outside the field. How does one enter into a field that has distinct cultures, with distinct languages and norms? So, we wanted to try to create a common culture and language, providing an opportunity for scholars talk to each other and to begin to consider how each other's work fit together. Furthermore, we hoped to bring in some "outsiders" to encourage scholars of identity development to consider how our field applies to other areas, again working toward finding some integration within the field that could then be projected outward. With these goals, we hoped that this volume would look forward more than it would look backward and would provide a more coherent, stronger, and more integrated identity for the field of identity development.

A Brief History: From Erikson to a Cultural Disconnect

We review Erikson's theory in more detail below, but to clarify the need for integration in the field we offer a brief history of the field as we see it. Erikson constructed a comprehensive theory that was first taken on, empirically, by James Marcia (1966). Since Marcia's elaboration of the identity statuses, this has been the dominant approach to studying identity development, with some important variants (see Meeus, 2011; Schwartz, 2001; Syed, 2012), and it has often been called an "Eriksonian" approach to identity development. Indeed, the treatment of identity development in nearly any introductory textbook on general psychology or developmental psychology traces the history of identity from Erikson to Marcia, featuring the identity status model as *the* developmental approach to understanding identity. Recent reviews of the identity development literature have synthesized the considerable knowledge gained through nearly fifty years of scholarship based on the identity status model (Kroger, Martinussen, & Marcia, 2010; Meeus, 2011). Thus, someone new to the field would likely get the impression that the identity status model represents the dominant approach to the study of identity development.

However, almost thirty years ago, another approach to identity development was being nurtured by Dan McAdams (1985). Building very much on Erikson, but also on the tradition of the Study of Lives, which is based on the work of Alfred Adler, Henry Murray, Silvan Tompkins, and others, McAdams proposed a theory of identity development focused on narrative. Around the same time, Katherine Nelson (e.g., Nelson, 1989; see also Nelson & Fivush, 2004) and her students were developing theories of early narrative development that have since been linked to McAdams' theory of narrative identity (e.g., McLean, Pasupathi, & Pals, 2007; Reese, Yan, Jack, & Hayne, 2010). McAdams' theory is established in the field of personality and personality development, as noted by review articles in prominent journals (McAdams & Pals, 2006; McAdams & McLean, 2013; McLean et al., 2007; Singer, 2004; Thorne, 2000). Moreover, empirical work on narrative identity has recently gained attention in developmental journals; the following citations are papers that appeared in the past ten years on narrative identity in *Developmental Psychology* alone: Bauer & McAdams (2010); Dumas, Lawford, Tieu, & Pratt (2009); McLean (2005; 2008); McLean & Breen (2009); McLean & Mansfield (2011); McLean & Pratt (2006); McLean & Thorne (2003); Nosko, Tieu, Lawford, & Pratt (2011); Pasupathi & Hoyt (2009); Pasupathi & Mansour (2006); Pasupathi & Wainryb (2010); Rice & Pasupathi (2010); Syed (2010); Syed & Azmitia (2008; 2010); and Tavernier & Willoughby (2012). However, McAdams's theory and developmentally oriented narrative approaches have been largely ignored by identity status researchers, who represent the traditional, and dominant, paradigm within the field. Indeed, scholars who are trained in narrative approaches are generally the ones to have initiated the few empirical studies examining links between these approaches (Alisat & Pratt, 2012; McLean & Pratt, 2006; Pasuapthi, Wainryb, & Twali, 2012; Syed & Azmitia, 2008; 2010; cf., Schachter, 2004). We do not think this is intentional, but that this is what happens when fields become comfortable (dominant) and insular.

Thus, we have the two cultures—status and narrative. We argue here that this division not only does a disservice to the breadth of Erikson's theory, which is not entirely captured by either approach, but it also does a disservice to the spirit of engagement, debate, and collaboration that often provides the foundation for lasting and strong fields of inquiry. One way of creating space for engagement is to put scholars together to talk it out to first see the variation in approaches, and then to attempt to see where these approaches overlap and where they differ—what they share and what is unique.

A good example of the kind of discussion that we had hoped would happen in this volume occurs in the section focused on age-related issues in identity development. First, a broad range of approaches to identity development is covered here—including status and narrative approaches (Arnett, Fivush & Zaman; Kroger). However, because these authors all begin with Erikson, but focus on different parts of his theory, interpret him quite differently, and use different language to some extent, we see the disconnection we referenced above, and it can be confusing. In their commentary on these chapters, Dan McAdams and Claudia Zapata-Gietl remarked that Erikson's theory is somewhat like a Rorschach test. But, to their credit, they were able to take these three disparate approaches and provide an integrative model for what is developing, which is exactly the kind of work we hope to see continue.

Although status and narrative approaches are certainly the primary ways of studying identity, as represented in prominent developmental psychology journals, there are certainly other perspectives on identity development (e.g., Bamberg, 2004; Côté, 2002) some of which are covered in this volume. Yet we raise the issue of status and narrative approaches here for two reasons. First, we were entirely intentional in including a full representation of both approaches in this volume; offering both sets of scholars an equal seat at the table was one of the reasons we wanted to do the Handbook. Second, more broadly, along with Côté (this volume), we offer a plea for desegregating the field of identity for ourselves—the identity researchers—and for others who desire to apply and use the important and substantial research that is done on this topic. Ironically, given Erikson's focus on the very word "integration," we see the task for identity researchers as fulfilling Erikson's vision of healthy identity development by exploring the tensions between us and working toward an integrated and coherent approach to identity development (Syed, 2012)—we need an identity for the field of identity. We now turn to a discussion of what exactly is developing and then to a brief review of the three sections of the volume—debates, applications, and extensions.

Identity Development: What Develops?

In his seminal lifespan theory of development, Erikson (1950) proposed that individuals must negotiate qualitatively distinct tasks at each life stage. The successful navigation of these tasks not only reflects successful adaptation for the current stage, but also prepares individuals to navigate subsequent stages. For example, the successful navigation of the first stage—developing trust in a caregiver—sets toddlers up to explore their own autonomy with the support of that secure base. The stage that Erikson spent the most time exploring, both personally and intellectually, was identity versus role confusion. Once children have been able to develop trust in a caregiver, a sense of autonomy, initiative, and industry, the stage is set for personal exploration of the self.

Drawing from the rich psychobiographical work that he conducted, as well as work with World War II veterans, Erikson (1950; 1968) viewed developing a sense of identity fidelity as critical to psychological health. In the leaders he studied, such as Gandhi, he saw a deep sense of purpose that defined the kind of rich identity he viewed as so critical to psychosocial development. In the veterans with posttraumatic stress disorder (PTSD), he saw what happened when individuals lost a sense of identity. From these studies and observations, Erikson constructed a theory of identity development that was broad, multidimensional, and, for healthy development, required an engagement at three levels of identity work.

The first level is *ego identity*, which entails a focus on personal continuity and is found when one is able to integrate one's most important, basic, and private beliefs about the self to create a sense of personal sameness across time. This level is well-captured in the approaches to identity that center on narrative as the primary vehicle for identity development, emphasizing making sense of the self across time via reflection on past events (see the following chapters in this volume: Fivush & Zaman; Habermas & Köber; Lilgendahl; McAdams & Zapata-Gietl; Pasupathi).

Personal identity centers on how one defines one's beliefs or goals, which is represented in the negotiation of culturally relevant roles and positions (e.g., sex roles, political affiliation). This level is best captured in the current approach of examining identity statuses, based on the processes of exploring options for these roles, and then committing to them (see the following chapters in this volume: Crocetti & Meeus; Kroger; Kunnen & Metz; Lilgendahl).

Interestingly, status researchers have coined the term "ego identity statuses," not "personal identity statuses." Our read of Erikson, however, has led us to this distinction because ego identity centers on a coherence developed by seeing personal continuity through time, and personal identity centers on coherence across values, roles, and the like. We imagine, of course, that some will balk at this formulation, but this what we arrived at after a careful read of Erikson (see also McLean, Syed, Yoder, & Greenhoot, under review; Syed & McLean, in preparation).

The third level is *social identity*, which places emphasis on the connection one has to a larger group, such as ethnic background, gender, and country of origin (see the following chapters in this volume: Azmitia; Cooper et al.; Fivush & Zaman; Wainryb & Recchia; Way & Rogers, Worrell). In this way, one is defined not only by the personal or individual aspects of self, but also by the larger groups to which one belongs.

For Erikson, the culmination of the engagement with these three levels is "identity synthesis." He viewed identity synthesis as a process of reworking childhood identifications into a current self-representation that is coherent across time and contexts and is also represented by a commitment to adult roles that are valued in one's given society. Interestingly, historical and contemporary approaches to Erikson have not fully captured the totality of this process (nor do they claim to), and this is particularly apparent in the lack of attention to how these levels interact with each other. As the readers will see, however, researchers are "rediscovering" Erikson and focusing attention on the complexities of his original theory.

In terms of development, the authors in this volume address the idea that although identity development is said to take center stage in adolescence and emerging adulthood, there are developmental implications for identity development in childhood (e.g., this volume: Fivush & Zaman; Rote & Smetana), and identity continues to be a developmental consideration in adulthood (this volume: Cookston & Remy; Kroger; Lilgendahl). More specifically, whereas self-concept emerges in infancy and is viewed as a precursor to identity (this volume: Fivush & Zaman; Hammack), identity is something that is unique to adolescence, in that it begins to develop in adolescence. There are three good reasons for this assertion: (1) the emergence of cognitive abilities that allow for the kinds of complex thought processes needed to construct an identity, (2) increased choices and/or responsibilities that individuals take on in adolescence and emerging adulthood, and (3) the accumulation of experiences that foster and demand a personal identity to be brought into existence.

So then, what develops? Certainly, cognitions about oneself and the world shift with changes in experiences and opportunities for exploration (Harter, 2012; Piaget, 1965), along with greater fluctuation in emotional experiences (Larson & Richards, 1994; Rosenblum & Lewis, 2003) and associated neurological development (Choudhury, Blakemore, & Charman, 2006). Perhaps most importantly, adolescents begin to be able to recognize and reconcile contradictions in the self (Harter, 2012), which allows them to develop a sense of personal continuity in the context of unavoidable change (Chandler, Lalonde, Sokol, & Hallett, 2003; Pasupathi, Brubaker, & Mansour, 2007).

Embedded within these statements about what develops are two central constructs: process and content. Although we asked authors to consider both process and content in this volume, as the reader will see the great majority of the authors have focused on processes of identity development—that is, how people go about constructing an identity. Much of the discussion of process concerns how individuals explore various roles and possibilities for self-definitions (this volume: Crocetti & Meeus; Kunnen & Metz), how individuals reflect on important life experiences (this volume: Fivush & Zaman; Habermas & Köber; Lilgendahl), or how individuals enact themselves in identity-relevant contexts (this volume: Pasupathi; Korobov). Some also examine the process of commitment, or how people make choices about which contents are important to them (this volume: Crocetti & Meeus; Kunnen & Metz).

Although these processes are critical to understanding identity development, the overwhelming focus on them has been to the neglect of the *content* of identity—what identity actually looks like. This imbalance is reflected in this volume and in the field at large (McLean et al., under review; Syed & McLean, in preparation). Simplistically, the content of identity can be viewed as the kinds of domains in which one is exploring (e.g., religion), the specifics within an identity domain (e.g., Christianity vs. atheism), or the kinds of experiences one is reflecting on (e.g., parental divorce). However, there is so little discussion of content that we, as editors, are not sure how to define content more comprehensively. For example, several authors in this volume examine the content of ethnic identity, but this seems different from the content of narrative identity. And is ethnic identity akin to a content domain like occupation, or is it different? How do we distinguish these kinds of contents? The identity status researchers have articulated a set of content domains in which they expect people to be engaged that center on the ideological realm (occupation, values, religion, politics) and relational realm (family, friends, dating, sex roles, recreation), but we know from our recent data that these do not comprehensively cover what emerging adults spontaneously report as self-defining in using narrative methods (McLean et al., under review). Thus, our current knowledge of identity content is limited at best, and we return to these issues of process and content in the closing chapter.

A Rationale for the Structure of This Handbook

A multitude of handbooks on identity exist in the literature, so why this one? First, the two most recent and comprehensive handbooks edited by Seth Schwartz, Koen Luyckx, and Vivian Vignoles (2011), and Mark Leary and June Tangney (2012) are excellent and broad volumes, but these handbooks are not explicitly developmental. The Schwartz et al. handbook is a two-volume comprehensive review of identity theory and research that goes beyond the confines of developmental psychology. The Leary and Tangney handbook pertains to self and identity from a social psychological perspective. Second, both of these handbooks involve a "traditional" handbook structure, wherein authors provide broad reviews on the state of the knowledge of a particular aspect of identity. So, beyond our view that a handbook addressing identity *development* was critical, we also saw a need for a handbook that went beyond reviews of the field. With the latter aim in mind we designed this book to include debates, applications, and extensions of theory and research on identity development.

The debates section includes two to three chapters on a given topic, with scholars emphasizing different approaches. These chapters are then accompanied by a commentary on the various approaches taken. The applications section includes chapters on how to use research on identity development in practical and applied settings, such as psychotherapy and school. The final section examines how identity development relates to other topics important in developmental psychology, such as puberty, neuroscience, and culture.

The Argument for Debate, Which Turned into an Invitation for Fika

In our view, there are several tensions in the field of identity development, which partly arise from researchers who are essentially studying the same thing but from different perspectives and who do not frequently interact with one another; scholars entrenched in their own cultures. In this section on debates, we wanted to shed a light on these underlying tensions in the field. Importantly, not all of these tensions are active "debates," but rather reflect researcher's choices to examine one aspect of identity at the expense of others. That is, most of us tend to favor one view or approach over another, whether or not we explicitly say so. However, when scholars do not acknowledge the various approaches one could take, incoherence festers. For example, within the narrative identity field there are scholars who focus more on the internalized processes of identity development and those who focus more on the sociocultural settings in which narratives are told and socially shaped. Both processes are critical to the development of narrative identity, but scholars tend to use one or the other without addressing why. In this volume, we created a space for this discussion of why one might favor one approach over the other (this volume: Habermas & Köber; Pasupathi) and how we might integrate these approaches (Freeman, this volume; see also Thorne, 2004).

We asked authors not to do extensive literature reviews or to rehash familiar arguments but to venture outside of the normal approaches and put more effort into articulating what their approach to identity is and why they have adopted it. Although we used the word "debate," we were not asking the authors to debate in the literal sense. That is, we did not have a common set of questions for the authors from which they would construct arguments and rebuttals. Rather, we framed the context of the debate and asked the authors to go about the business of describing and explaining their approach. The authors of the debate chapters read each other's drafts, which in some cases led to major changes in the chapters and in some cases not. We then invited another person to write a commentary chapter in response. The commentary chapter was not meant to declare a winner in the debate, but rather the commentators were to use the chapters as source material to discuss the issues at hand and to chart a way forward. We intentionally chose groups of authors who are not always in conversation with each other to provoke more variety in the discussions. Thus, this section reflects not only our explicit structure to encourage conversation, but also our desire for the conversation to go beyond the intimates in the field, the latter of which is a theme extended throughout the volume.

Initially, we found that authors reacted strongly to the term "debate," with many, frankly, resisting it. It made some of them become oddly conciliatory in their chapters. This may reflect the camaraderie and collegiality in the field. However, although making nice is good for one's relationships, it may not be good for a field of research, which needs tension and challenge to work through the difficult stuff. Like the individual wrestling with identity, the field must wrestle too.

In our conversations with each other (as editors), we began referring to this section as "*fika*," which turned out to be a better model of what we were up to in creating this section. Notably, this happened after the chapters were under construction and we had already defined the task to our authors. Nevertheless, we offer our new name here to encourage the spirit of what we hope will occur for the readers. *Fika* was a new term we learned when one of us (MS) first visited the University of Gothenburg in Sweden. *Fika* is a Swedish cultural practice, which is meant to be a time to take a pause from the daily grind and maintain social connection with others. At the University of Gothenburg, *fika* typically occurs twice a day—in the morning and afternoon—and is a time when professors and students gather in a common place for coffee, pastries, and conversation. The idea is to get researchers out of their offices and to encourage conversation, whether personal or professional. This is the spirit in which we asked authors to engage in these debate chapters. Our idea was to facilitate communication between these various cultural groups and to avoid essentialized, and insular, discussion. The definition of debate can include a focus on right and wrong, but we embrace the definition that includes a conversation of different points of view. In some ways, we asked our authors to have coffee and pastries together and discuss various approaches to specific aspects of identity development.

The debates we chose to focus on are certainly not the only debates in the field, but they do represent some important tensions and areas ripe for creative approaches to empirical study.

IDENTITY ACROSS THE LIFESPAN

In the first section, we asked developmental psychologists who focus on different parts of the lifespan to discuss identity process and content at different life stages. Robyn Fivush and Widaad Zaman are scholars of self and identity development in the context of families and storytelling, particularly in childhood and adolescence. Jeff Arnett is the architect of the theory of emerging adulthood, in which identity development is a central developmental task of this stage. Jane Kroger is an eminent identity researcher, with an expertise in status approaches across the lifespan, particularly in adulthood. Dan McAdams has written eloquently and at length about narrative identity development, but from a personality perspective. His commentary, written with Claudia Zapata-Gietl, elegantly integrates the content of the three chapters. This is the least debate-like of the groupings in this section, but each of these authors has a very different vantage point on identity, as we mentioned earlier. Furthermore, due to the common belief that identity both begins and ends in adolescence, we felt it was important to highlight the lifespan significance of identity.

PROCESSES VERSUS PERSONS IN THE IDENTITY STATUS MODEL

In terms of status approaches to identity development, we asked several scholars of contemporary research on identity statuses to contribute to a discussion of how to best study identity development from the status approach. Within identity status studies, some researchers focus on the continuous processes of exploration and commitment (as well as subprocesses of each), whereas other researchers place greater emphasis on the categorization of these processes (e.g., identity achievement). Elisabetta Crocetti and Wim Meeus have studied the processes of identity development, particularly as they unfold over time in adolescence and emerging adulthood. Meeus, in particular, has pioneered a revision to traditional views of exploration to include several forms of exploratory processing. Saskia Kunnen and Marijke Metz use a dynamic systems approach to studying the processes of identity development. These authors debated the issue of using identity status categories or the processes of exploration and commitment as the constructs of interest in a given study design. Ruthellen Josselson and Hanoch Flum offered a commentary on these chapters. Josselson is clinical psychologist, psychotherapist, and an expert on personological approaches to identity, and Flum focuses on social and cultural contexts of identity development. This section highlights the diversity of approaches to examining identity development using the constructs of exploration and commitment.

AUTOBIOGRAPHICAL REASONING AND ALTERNATIVES IN NARRATIVE APPROACHES

The primary way that scholars have approached identity development from a narrative perspective is to examine processes of autobiographical reasoning, or how people reflect on and make sense of their pasts. Many studies have shown not only that these processes increase in prominence across adolescence, but that they are also associated with a variety of beneficial outcomes. Given the prominence of this approach, we thought it would be timely to engage a discussion about why this process seems so important and what alternatives we might consider. We asked Tilmann Habermas and Christin Köber to argue in favor of autobiographical reasoning as a primary mode of narrative identity development and Monisha Pasupathi to argue for alternatives. Habermas, along with Susan Bluck (Habermas & Bluck, 2000), provided a theoretical foundation to the study of autobiographical reasoning, and Monisha Pasupathi (e.g., 2001) is a pioneer in bridging the fields of conversational remembering and narrative identity. Mark Freeman, who has written extensively about narrative and self, often from a more philosophical than empirical perspective, provided the commentary. This section highlights the strengths of existing approaches to narrative identity development, as well as alternative approaches to be further investigated.

INTERVAL VERSUS EXTERNAL IN IDENTITY DEVELOPMENT

Somewhat related to the above discussion, scholars of identity development tend to privilege internal approaches to their questions, meaning that they examine thoughts, emotions, reflections, and other processes that appear to be "in the head." However, there are alternatives to these approaches. We thought it would be a worthy venture to ask two scholars who employ an internal and external, or interactional, approach to articulate their positions around why they have chosen to examine identity from their respective standpoints. Alan Waterman has written extensively on identity development and eudaimonic theories of human functioning. Neil Korobov has employed discursive approaches to his work on identity development. Elli Schachter, who has bridged multiple approaches to questions of identity development, responded to these chapters. These scholars have shed clear light on why they have taken their chosen paths to the study of identity development and provide us with excellent rationale for these two paths.

CONCEPTUALIZATIONS OF CULTURE AND IDENTITY

Finally, we included a section on culture and identity. When thinking about the relation between these two constructs, one of the issues that seemed primary to us was how to define culture when asking questions about identity development. Again, there are a variety of definitions, and the definition one uses surely impacts the questions one asks, the methods one uses and, thus, the results one gets. We asked Niobe Way and Onnie Rogers, who focus on various contextual nuances of adolescent socio-emotional development to make the argument for culture as context. Frank Worrell, who examines adolescent development, particularly with at-risk youth and in educational contexts, argued for the representation of culture as categories of ethnicity. Margarita Azmitia investigates relational aspects of adolescent development, and she wrote the commentary for this section. This section accentuates the complexity in defining culture and the various ways that researchers might do so as they examine identity development.

In the end, the authors and commentators took on this task beautifully, and we hope that the lively discussion in these pages inspires future discussion and pointed research on some of these issues. Moreover, we hope that this framing will challenge each of us to think more clearly and deeply about the approaches we take to the study of identity development and why we take them.

The Argument for Applications

The need for a discussion of the application of identity research is simple: this is *the* psychosocial task of adolescence and emerging adulthood, and it matters for healthy (and unhealthy) development. The chapters in this section make clear that identity matters for a variety of concerns relevant to adolescents and emerging adults themselves, their teachers, counselors, and parents, and the culture at large.

In terms of healthy adjustment, broadly defined, we had two chapters in this topic area. Kyle Eichas, Alan Meca, Marilyn Montgomery, and Bill Kurtines all investigate positive youth development and how outreach programs can successfully apply scholarly work in developmental science to meet the needs of youth from varied backgrounds. In their chapter, they detail their work on positive identity interventions across various ages, samples, and outcomes. From a psychotherapy perspective, Jefferson Singer and Adam Kasmark drew from their program of research that examines how narrative theories can be translated to psychotherapeutic settings. This section highlights the importance of identity development in aiding and encouraging psychological health and functioning.

Moving toward contexts of development, we asked scholars to elaborate on school, work, and political conflict as three specific contexts in which adolescents are developing identities. Catherine Cooper, Elizabeth Gonzalez, and Antoinette Wilson examine identity development in the context of "multiple worlds" of influences, such as parents, peers, and, especially, schools; they addressed how educational environments influence identity development processes. Jeylan Mortimer, Jack Lam, and Shi-Rong Lee are sociologists who tackle a complementary context to school—work—focusing on the role of identity development in the transition to working life. Finally, Cecilia Wainryb and Holly Recchia are developmental psychologists who focus on moral development. They took on the issue of the personal reconstruction of political conflict and violence in the identities of youth affected by these kinds of traumas. These chapters highlight the importance of considering and comparing specific contexts in which adolescents are developing to the ways in which they define themselves.

We argue that coherence of the field is critical not only for those working within it, but also for those trying to apply it to various "outcomes." Thus, researchers need to both provide a coherent approach to the construct under study and explain to others why it matters. In an era in which grant funds are dwindling, biological and neurological approaches are privileged, and practical outcomes and translational research are increasingly required for obtaining funds and for publication, we need to make the case for the importance of the work. Beyond issues of funding and publication, we believe that challenging ourselves to consider why identity matters in a practical sense will lead to deeper and clearer theorizing about identity itself. The authors in this section have made these arguments strongly and persuasively. We hope that the rest of us can follow suit as we design our studies and communicate our findings to varied audiences.

The Argument for Extensions

In many ways, the authors in this section had the most challenging task because most of these authors are explicitly *not* identity researchers. We asked researchers in other fields to discuss how identity researchers should consider their respective fields for a fuller, more integrated understanding of this developmental phenomenon. We also asked these authors to consider how they might integrate the study of identity into their fields. The aim here was to broaden scholars' perspectives on identity development and to consider new directions for the field. This was the most explicit way of encouraging "forward thinking" in the volume because these connections have not been readily made. The speculations about the possible connections provided by these authors, however, provide fertile ground for new studies.

In terms of relationships, Wendy Rote and Judi Smetana are developmental psychologists who are focus on parenting, primarily from a moral development perspective. They examined the interplay between parenting authority and adolescent autonomy in identity development from the perspective of social domain theory. From a different angle, Jeff Cookston and Luke Remy are developmental psychologists who study co-parenting, fathering, and divorce. They focused on the impact of divorce on personal identity, examining issues around the roles played in divorce, as well as how parenting identities and identities within new relationships may be affected by divorce. Although the study of relationships in identity development is not new, these chapters provide a different lens for thinking about how relationships may impact identity development processes by focusing on a specific context—moral development, and a specific experience—divorce.

We include a series of chapters broadly focused on the body and biology. Alissa Mrazek, Tokiko Harada, and Joan Chiao examine the intersection of culture and biology, addressing identity development processes from this cultural neuroscience perspective. Beth Daniels and Meghan Gillen investigate gender and body image issues in adolescence and emerging adulthood, concentrating on the role that body image plays in identity processes. Misaki Natsuaki, Danielle Samuels, and Leslie Leve are scholars of the biological and psychological process of puberty. They focused on adolescent girls, in particular, and how pubertal timing relates to gender role identity and risks for internalizing problems. Although extant research explicitly linking identity development to the body or physiological processes is rare, these chapters provide an excellent foundation, with provocative speculations, for future research in the area.

Finally, we have three chapters that link identity development to other broad approaches that are prominent within developmental psychology. Frosso Motti examines child and adolescent resilience, particularly in the context of immigration. She addressed individual differences in identity development from the lens of risk and resilience. Jennifer Lilgendahl's program of research centers on personality and identity development. She focused on the role of individual differences in identity processes for personality functioning across the adult lifespan. Finally, Adriana Manago is a cultural developmental psychologist who examined the sociocultural changes relevant to identity development that have come about from the use of the internet and social media. Overall, these chapters highlight the diversity of areas in which identity development is relevant.

To our knowledge, extensions are new to the handbook format. We included this section to avoid insularity, to push us, the authors, and the audience, to think more deeply about identity and to facilitate a broader discussion that we hope will continue beyond this volume. Furthermore, for the field of identity development research to continue its long and rich tradition, the extension of research into other areas is critical. Our aim here was to ensure that identity is well-represented and coherent for other fields to draw from, as well as to make sure that we, as identity researchers, are incorporating these issues into our work. As good developmentalists should, we hope to see bidirectionality in the field.

The Big Picture: Theoretical Orientations and Commentaries on the Field

To provide context to the volume, we also include three chapters that orient the reader to the theoretical approaches in the field and provide critical perspectives on the state of the scholarly work. To open the volume, Phil Hammack, who examines identity development from multiple perspectives including cultural, social, and political vantage points, provided a framework for understanding the various theoretical approaches to identity. In closing the volume, James Côté, a sociologist and scholar of identity development, offered a critique of the field from an interdisciplinary perspective, asking the question: Is a social science of identity developing? Finally, in 2001, Seth Schwartz wrote an integrative review piece on Eriksonian and neo-Eriksonian approaches to identity development. We asked him to close the volume, with colleagues Koen Luyckx and Elisabetta Crocetti, by revisiting that paper and reflecting on what we have learned about identity development since then. The final chapter is our musings on the volume as a whole, what we have learned as editors, and future directions.

In Closing This Chapter…We Invite You into the Volume

There have been many advances in theory and research on identity development since Erikson's initial writings more than fifty years ago, and the time has come to consolidate that knowledge and set an agenda for future research. We view this volume as beginning to meet that need by including the varied and disconnected approaches to empirically articulating Erikson's theory under one roof, setting the stage for a deeper and more inclusive understanding of the construct. The conversations between us and the authors of this volume have been lively, and we hope to see and hear more conversations erupting. As editors, we have learned a lot from our authors, and we hope you, the reader, will too.

Acknowledgments

We are appreciative of the comments and critiques of Kelly Gola, Madeline Kerrick, Cade Mansfield, Lauren Mitchell, Sarah Morrison-Cohen, Monisha Pasupathi, and Avril Thorne on an earlier draft of this chapter.

References

Alisat, S., & Pratt, M. W. (2012). Characteristics of young adults' personal religious narratives and their relation with the identity status model: A longitudinal, mixed methods study. *Identity: An International Journal of Theory and Research, 12*, 29–52.

Bamberg, M. (2004). Form and functions of "slut bashing" in male identity constructions in 15-year-olds. *Human Development, 47*, 331–353.

Bauer, J. J., & McAdams, D. P. (2010). Eudaimonic growth: Narrative growth goals predict increases in ego development and subjective well-being three years later. *Developmental Psychology, 46*, 761–772.

Chandler, M. J., Lalonde, C. E., Sokol, B. W., & Hallett, D. (2003). Personal persistence, identity development, and suicide: A study of Native and non-Native North American adolescents. *Monographs of the Society for Research in Child Development, 68*(2).

Choudhury, S. Blakemore, S. -J., & Charman, T. (2006). Social cognitive development during adolescence. *Social Cognitive and Affective Neuroscience 1*, 165–174

Côté J. E., Levine, C. G. (2002). *Identity formation, agency, and culture: A social psychological perspective*. Erlbaum: Mahwah, NJ.

Dumas, T M., Lawford, H. L., Tieu, T., & Pratt, M. W. (2009). Positive parenting in adolescence and its relation to low point life story narration and identity status in emerging adulthood: A longitudinal analysis. *Developmental Psychology, 45*, 1531–1544.

Erikson, E. (1968). *Identity, youth and crisis*. New York: Norton.

Erikson, E. H. (1950). *Childhood and society*. New York: Norton.

Habermas, T., & Bluck, S. (2000). Getting a life: The development of the life story in adolescence. *Psychological Bulletin, 126*, 748–769.

Harter, S. (2012). *The construction of self: A developmental perspective* (2nd edition). New York: Guilford Press.

Kroger, J., Martinussen, M., & Marcia, J. E. (2010). Identity stat change during adolescence and young adulthood: A meta-analysis. *Journal of Adolescence, 12*, 683–98.

Larson, R. W., & Richards, M. H. (1994). Family emotions: Do young adolescents and their parents experience the same states? *Journal of Research on Adolescence, 4*(4), 567–583.

Leary, M. R., & Tangney, J. P. (Eds.). (2012). *Handbook of self and identity*. New York: Guilford.

Marcia, J. E. (1966). Development and validation of ego-identity status. *Journal of Personality and Social Psychology, 5*, 551–558.

McAdams, D. P. (1985). *Power, intimacy, and the life story: Personological inquiries into identity*. Homewood, IL: Dorsey Press.

McAdams, D. P., & McLean, K. C. (2013). Narrative Identity. *Current Directions in Psychological Science, .22*, 233–238.

McAdams, D. P., & Pals, J. L. (2006). A new Big Five: Fundamental principles for an integrative science of personality. *American Psychologist, 61*(3), 204–217.

McLean, K. C. (2005). Late adolescent identity development: Narrative meaning-making and memory telling. *Developmental Psychology, 41*, 683–691.

McLean, K. C. (2008). Stories of the young and the old: Reflections on self-continuity. *Developmental Psychology, 44*, 254–264.

McLean, K. C., & Breen, A. (2009). Gender differences in adolescent meaning-making. *Developmental Psychology, 45*, 702–710.

McLean, K. C., & Mansfield, C. (2011). The co-construction of adolescent narrative processes: Narrative processing as a function of adolescent age, gender, and maternal scaffolding. *Developmental Psychology, 5*, 1–12.

McLean, K. C., Pasupathi, M., & Pals, J. P. (2007). Selves creating stories creating selves: A process model of self-development. *Personality and Social Psychology Review, 11*, 262–280.

McLean, K. C., & Pratt, M. W. (2006). Life's little (and big) lessons: Identity statuses and meaning-making in the turning point narratives of emerging adults. *Developmental Psychology, 42*, 714–722.

McLean, K. C., Syed, M., Yoder, A., & Greenhoot, A. F. (under review). Identity integration: The importance of domain content in linking narrative and status approaches to emerging adult identity development.

McLean, K. C., & Thorne, A. (2003). Adolescents' self-defining memories about relationships. *Developmental Psychology, 39*, 635–645.

Meeus, W. (2011). The study of adolescent identity formation 2000–2010: A review of longitudinal research. *Journal of Research on Adolescence, 21*, 75–94.

Nelson, K. (1989). *Narratives from the crib*. Boston, MA: Harvard University Press.

Nelson, K., & Fivush, R. (2004). The emergence of autobiographical memory: A social cultural developmental theory. *Psychological Review, 111*, 486–511.

Nosko, A., Tieu, T., Lawford, H., & Pratt, M. W. (2011). How do I love thee? Let me count the ways: Family parenting, attachment styles, interpersonal trust, and romantic narratives in emerging adulthood. *Developmental Psychology, 47*, 645–657.

Pasupathi, M. (2001). The social construction of the personal past and its implications for adult development. *Psychological Bulletin, 127*, 651–672.

Pasupathi, M., Brubaker, J., & Mansour, E. (2007). Developing a life story: Constructing relations between self and experience in autobiographical narratives. *Human Development, 50*, 85–110.

Pasupathi, M., & Hoyt, T. (2009). The development of narrative identity in late adolescence and emergent adulthood: The continued importance of listeners. *Developmental Psychology, 45*, 558–574.

Pasupathi, M., & Mansour, E. (2006). Adult age differences in autobiographical reasoning in narratives. *Developmental Psychology, 42*, 798–808.

Pasupathi. M., & Wainryb, C. (2010). On telling the whole story: Facts and interpretations in autobiographical memory narratives from childhood through mid-adolescence. *Developmental Psychology, 46*, 735–746.

Pasupathi, M., Wainryb, C., & Twali, M. (2012). Narrative construction of group-based differential treatment: Implications for ethnic identity development. *Identity: An International Journal of Theory and Research, 12*, 53–73.

Piaget, J. (1965). *The moral judgment of the child*. New York: Free Press.

Reese, E., Yan, C., Jack, F., & Hayne, H. (2010). Emerging identities: Narrative and self from early childhood to early adolescence. In K. C. McLean & M. Pasupathi (Eds.), *Narrative development in adolescence: Creating the storied self* (pp. 23–43). New York: Springer.

Rice, C., & Pasupathi, M. (2010). Reflecting on self-relevant experiences: Adult age differences. *Developmental Psychology, 46*, 479–490.

Rosenblum, G. D., & Lewis, M. (2003). Emotional development in adolescence. In G. R. Adams & M. D. Berzonsky (Eds.), *Blackwell handbook of adolescence* (pp. 269–289). Oxford, UK: Blackwell Publishing.

Schachter, E. P. (2004). Identity configurations: A new perspective on identity formation in contemporary society. *Journal of Personality* 72(1), 167–200.

Schwartz, S. J. (2001). The evolution of Eriksonian and neo-Eriksonian identity theory and research: A review and integration. *Identity: An International Journal of Theory and Research, 1*, 7–58.

Schwartz, S. J., Luyckx, K., & Vignoles, V. L. (Eds.). (2011). *Handbook of identity theory and research*. New York: Springer.

Singer, J. A. (2004). Narrative identity and meaning-making across the lifespan: An introduction. *Journal of Personality, 72*, 437–460.

Syed, M. (2010). Developing an integrated self: Academic and ethnic identities among ethnically-diverse college students. *Developmental Psychology, 46*(6), 1590–1604.

Syed, M. (2012). The past, present, and future of Eriksonian identity research: Introduction to the special issue. *Identity: An International Journal of Theory and Research, 12*, 1–7.

Syed, M., & Azmitia, M. (2008). A narrative approach to ethnic identity in emerging adulthood: Bringing life to the identity status model. *Developmental Psychology, 44*, 1012–1027.

Syed, M., & Azmitia, M. (2010). Narrative and ethnic identity exploration: A longitudinal account of emerging adults' ethnicity-related experiences. *Developmental Psychology, 46*, 208–219.

Syed, M., & McLean, K. C. (in preparation). *Identity content domains reveal the link between status and narrative approaches to identity.*

Tavernier, R., & Willoughby, T. (2012). Bidirectional associations between sleep (quality and duration) and psychosocial adjustment among emerging adults across the first three years of university. *Developmental Psychology, 48*, 1058–68.

Thorne, A. (2000). Personal memory telling and personality development. *Personality and Social Psychology Review, 4*, 45–56.

Thorne, A. (2004). Putting the person into social identity. *Human Development, 253*, 1–5.

CHAPTER 2

Theoretical Foundations of Identity

Phillip L. Hammack

Abstract

Across the social sciences and humanities, identity is a conceptual tool to think about sameness and difference, both in terms of individual continuity and change over time and social categorization or group affiliation. This chapter traces the theoretical lineage of the identity concept, focusing on the foundational theories of William James and George Herbert Mead. In contrast to the relative emphasis on the exterior world of social meaning found in Mead's perspective, James's theoretical emphasis on the interior experience of self-sameness and continuity inspired a distinct line of theory, including Erikson's theory of identity crisis, identity status theory and its derivatives, theories of racial and ethnic identity development, and narrative theories of identity development that emphasize life-story construction. The chapter reviews these distinct lines of theoretical development in the social sciences and concludes with a discussion of pluralism, identity politics, and social ethics in an increasingly interconnected and globalized world.

Key Words: identity, theory, development

Identity, Sameness, and Difference

In the twenty-first century, we inhabit a world of fluid borders, of rapidly moving ideas, of swift and seamless migration, of ever-expanding connectivity (Arnett, 2002). Yet, as our bodies and our words are transported, they remain subject to the universal human process of categorization. They may be *English, Arabic,* or *Chinese* language words; the product of *American, Palestinian,* or *Taiwanese* hands. I may be an *American gay man,* she a *Kurdish artist* living in *Australia,* he a *secular-minded Pakistani Muslim,* or she a *Black South African lesbian feminist.* We inhabit a world of meaning in which people are in constant states of identification, or naming and categorizing, what or who one is and to which larger categories he or she may belong, categories like gender, class, race, ethnicity, nationality, sexual identity, occupation, and the like.

Identity is the anchoring concept for thinking about difference and sameness in our time. It is not a concept confined to the jargon of the social sciences or the humanities; it permeates our everyday conversations, our moment-to-moment cognitive processes of sense-making in a world increasingly characterized by human diversity. In an era of appreciation for cultural pluralism—an era in which difference is no longer automatically considered a ground for oppression, colonization, or enslavement—identity is the tool we have to render the world of difference sensible and to confer rights through recognition (Mohanty, 2010; Taylor, 1994; Verkuyten, 2006). Identity is also the tool we have to think about conflict and continuity within an individual person at a time of rapid social change and challenges to local cultural views of self (Arnett, 2002; Hermans & Dimaggio, 2007; Jensen, Arnett, & McKenzie, 2011; Kinnvall, 2004).

Identity is thus concerned with sameness and difference at the level of social categorization, group affiliation, and intergroup relations, as well as at the level of individual consciousness or subjectivity.

The purpose of this chapter is to provide a brief sketch of the theoretical foundations of identity. Identity is a concept of study in philosophy, history, anthropology, sociology, psychology, cultural studies, gender and sexuality studies, politics, economics, literature—truly an idea that spans the borders of disciplinary thought and inquiry. This multidisciplinary conceptual "ownership" is reflected in the numerous and diverse handbooks of identity that have begun to proliferate (e.g., Elliott, 2011; Leary & Tangney, 2012; Schwartz, Luyckx, & Vignoles, 2011; Wetherell & Mohanty, 2010). It is not possible to do justice in this chapter to the incredibly vast and rich theoretical work on identity in these fields. I anchor my review both in the two disciplines with which I most closely associate (psychology and sociology) and in the intended focus of the current handbook on identity *development*. My aim is to be as integrative as possible and to link major theoretical strands in psychology and sociology to discussions in other disciplines, to provoke cross-disciplinary analysis and conversation.

The chapter is organized to reflect the historical arc of the identity concept. I begin by situating the concept in intellectual history and particularly European philosophy of the Enlightenment era—the intellectual origins of the disciplines of psychology and sociology themselves. I then focus on how these philosophical ideas were imported into the early theories of William James and George Herbert Mead. The next sections of the chapter trace the distinct theoretical strands inspired by Mead and James, respectively. I conclude the chapter with a discussion of identity politics, social ethics, and pluralism in a global context of increasing interconnectivity and inequality.

Two issues warrant explicit discussion at the outset: (1) the terminological distinction between *self* and *identity*, and (2) my own theoretical position on identity. The terms *self* and *identity* have frequently been used interchangeably, and they share a conceptual history (Baumeister, 1987; Taylor, 1989). Few have attempted to clearly distinguish the terms (e.g., Owens, 2006), although many theorists do distinguish the concepts (e.g., McAdams, 2013). The distinction I propose here centers on the relative emphasis placed on the *interior* world of perception or cognition and the *exterior* world of social meaning. In my view, *identity* deals explicitly with properties of sameness and distinction that link the interior world of psychological experience and the exterior world of language and categorization. *Self* deals chiefly with the interior world and one's perception of it (or "consciousness"). This distinction is reflected in definitions of these terms offered in the *Oxford English Dictionary* (Identity, 2013). Owens (2006) distinguishes the concepts by positing self as an individual psychological "process" and identity as a social-relational "tool" through which individuals and groups understand the social and psychological world. McAdams (2013) views identity as one aspect of self or the self-development process ("self as author"). It is through identity that the self becomes presented to the exterior world. Theories of identity are thus relatively more concerned with the exterior or the link between the interior and the exterior—the personal and the social (see also Bamberg, 2011). My focus in this chapter is concretely on identity as a concept that links individual cognition with the social world of meaning and categorization.

My own theoretical position integrates many of the perspectives I review in this chapter. In my view, the identity concept evokes the dialogic idea of sameness and difference, in that identity provides a sense of internal coherence and continuity for the person in a particular social context but also serves to divide the social world into meaningful categories. Identity thus operates at both the level of individual psychology and social organization. This perspective is influenced by James's (1890) emphasis on personal coherence but also Mead's (1934) view of the self as socially constructed and Tajfel's (1981) view of social identities as significant determinants of thought, feeling, and action. Poststructural approaches provide a framework for thinking about the relationship among power, social categories, and individual subjectivity (e.g., Foucault, 1978). My emphasis on the role of language as the mediational mechanism through which identity develops leads me to posit narrative theories as central to the study of identity development (e.g., Bruner, 1990; McAdams, 2001), and my work has viewed continuity in personal identity and the social construction of identity through a narrative theoretical framework (e.g., Hammack, 2008, 2011a). My framework is also highly influenced by cultural psychological ideas of learning through guided activity or social practice (e.g., Vygotsky, 1978) and dialogism (e.g., Bakhtin, 1981), which have historically had less to say explicitly about the identity concept (cf. Hermans, 2001; Pasupathi, 2001). Nonetheless, my work seeks to bring these theoretical perspectives into dialogue through a commitment to the study of individual lives in social and political context.

Historical and Philosophical Foundations of Identity

The fundamental concepts that underlie self and identity have distant historical roots. Whereas Burkitt (2011) traces these concepts to Greco-Roman ideas of *persona* and later Stoic emphasis on self-mastery, Harbus (2002) emphasizes ideas of self in early medieval English literature. Earlier historical treatments connected concerns with selfhood and identity to Augustine's *Confessions* (Taylor, 1989) and to the Protestant Reformation, which linked ideas of personhood and agency through the concept of a "calling" or vocational mission (Baumeister, 1986).

Prior to the formation of the social sciences in the nineteenth and early twentieth centuries, questions about selfhood and identity were the domain of philosophy. The modern idea of identity emerged from Enlightenment-era philosophical perspectives on memory and perception, which were later appropriated by the first generation of psychologists and sociologists. Probably the earliest statement related to identity came from Rene Descartes (1637/2000), whose famous dictum "cogito, ergo sum" ("I think, therefore I am") prized the role of self-conscious cognition in human existence. John Locke (1694/1998) viewed identity and diversity as concepts concerned with sameness or distinction of perception. He emphasized that similar properties of objects or persons create coherence in consciousness, providing a sense of unity to our experience of the sensory world.

In the eighteenth century, philosophers such as David Hume and Immanuel Kant challenged the idea that the sense of identity resided in the properties of persons or objects themselves, suggesting instead that the *memory process* creates this unity (e.g., Hume, 1739/1986; Kant, 1781/2007). In other words, identity entails the perception of sameness or invariability constructed in memory. Kant emphasized that we can only know the self in relation to the world. Hence, our engagement with the material world is rendered sensible as we stitch together perceptions from various experiences (Baumeister, 1986).

In the transition from philosophy to psychology proper in the late nineteenth century, Wilhelm Dilthey argued for the centrality of meaning in his articulation of a hermeneutic approach to psychology (e.g., Dilthey, 1923/1988, 1976). He suggested that we make meaning through perceiving unity in events and that we use language to construct a unified account of who we are in the social world. This view presaged later narrative theories of identity and hermeneutic approaches in the social sciences (Tappan, 1997).

Early philosophical perspectives thus emphasized the significance of *memory, meaning, relationality*, and the perception of *sameness* or *difference* in the identity concept. These conceptual emphases would go on to greatly influence the theories of William James and George Herbert Mead, foundational theorists whose ideas continue to form the core of contemporary theoretical approaches (e.g., Hammack, 2011*a*; McAdams, 2013; Serpe & Stryker, 2011; Thorne, 2000). In the next section, I review the perspectives of these foundational theorists.

James and Mead: The Foundational Theorists

The two most prominent early theorists of identity in the social sciences were William James and George Herbert Mead. James, an American philosopher and psychologist, defined personal identity as a "consciousness of personal sameness" (James, 1890, p. 331), consistent with earlier philosophical perspectives emphasizing individual cognition and self-reflection. James's view emphasized perception of continuity and unity in mind, as well as a somatic sense of "warmth," providing a positive physiological sensation. James thus sought to integrate cognition, emotion, and physiological response in his view of identity. As he put it, "resemblance among the parts of a continuum of feelings (especially around bodily feelings) experienced along with things widely different in all other regards, thus constitutes the real and verifiable 'personal identity' which we feel" (James, 1890, p. 336).

As psychology and sociology emerged from philosophy as distinct fields of social science inquiry, the theoretical foundations of identity shifted from a largely private, interior view to one in which the private and public were considered in tandem. In psychology, James (1890) famously spoke of the social self, positing that "*a man [sic] has as many social selves as there are individuals who recognize him* and carry an image of him [sic] in their mind" (p. 294). Charles Horton Cooley (1902) coined the term "looking glass self" to refer to the self as constructed in the reflections provided in social interaction. Although these scholars preferred the term *self* to *identity* in these articulations, we can see an opening of the identity concept from a largely private, interior view to a public, distributed view in which identities are made in social acts.

George Herbert Mead (1934) offered one of the earliest systematic treatments of the idea of self as socially constructed, positing that "the self is something which has a development; it is not initially there, at birth, but arises in the process of social experience and activity" (p. 135). Laying the foundation for the theoretical perspective in sociology that came to be known as "symbolic interactionism" (Blumer, 1969), Mead argued for an early, radical form of social constructionism in which mind, self, and society emerge through small-scale social interactions. The sense of sameness and difference that underlies "identities" arises as we participate in what Mead (1934) called the "conversation of gestures" (p. 43). Hence, we can only comprehend ideas and concepts through our engagement with the symbolic—the gesture, the word, the representation.

Both James and Mead theorized an *I*/*me* distinction. For James (1890), the *me* represents the "empirical self," or the self as object: "*The words* ME, *then, and* SELF, *so far as they arouse feeling and connote emotional worth, are* OBJECTIVE *designations, meaning* ALL THE THINGS *which have the power to produce in a stream of consciousness excitement of a certain peculiar sort*" (p. 319). The *me* represents the apparent, visible identity that arouses a response in others. The *I*, by contrast, represents the private, interior sense of self: "…[P]ersonality implies the incessant presence of two elements, an objective person, known by a passing subjective Thought and recognized as continuing in time. *Hereafter let us use the words* ME *and* I *for the empirical person and the judging Thought*" (James, 1890, p. 371). If the *me* is the empirical object, the *I* is the cognitive process that constructs it as possessing meaning and unity in perception (see McAdams & Cox, 2010; McAdams, 2013).

Whereas James' *I*/*me* distinction implies a social world in which identity is negotiated in individual cognition, Mead (1934) is more explicit in the significance of the community in self-perception and self-construction: "The 'I' is the response of the organism to the attitudes of the others; the 'me' is the organized set of attitudes of others which one himself assumes" (p. 175). For Mead (1934), the *me* embodies the "generalized other"—"the organized community or social group which gives to the individual his [sic] unity of self" (p. 154). It is the version of self identifiable to a larger community of shared meaning. The *I* represents individual agency to operate within that community to either uphold or challenge its system of symbolic meaning: "The 'I' is his [sic] action over against that social situation" (Mead, 1934, p. 175). Hence, Mead's version of the *I* retains the interpretive freedom of James's, but it diverges in the degree to which it explicitly theorizes a link between cognition and social action.

As they translated foundational philosophical ideas about identity for social science inquiry, both James and Mead retained the centrality of internal psychological processes seeking unity and coherence. But their theories of identity diverged in the extent to which they either privileged the private world of interior thought (in James' case) or the public world of symbolic meanings (in Mead's case), thus also constructing divergent pathways for the study of identity in psychology and sociology over the twentieth century. In the next two sections of the chapter, I trace these divergent pathways in theoretical formulations of identity.

Mead's Lineage: Identities in Interaction

Mead's focus on the development of self in social interaction inspired theoretical perspectives that placed a relative emphasis on the public, exterior world. Compared with theoretical perspectives more linked to James, these perspectives place less emphasis on individual cognition and agency and more on the constraints of social context. Consistent with Kant's emphasis on *relationality* as the basis for the memory process, these perspectives placed greater weight on the relational basis of identities in interaction. Most notably, Goffman's (1963) theory of stigma, McCall and Simmons's (1966) role-identity model, Stryker's (1968) identity theory, and Tajfel and Turner's (1979, 1986) social identity theory (SIT) are situated in this theoretical lineage.

Stigma and Identity Management

Goffman's (1963) theory of stigma emphasizes the idea of identities as performances managed in social interaction. Rooted in his dramaturgical theory of self-presentation (Goffman, 1959), in which he uses the metaphor of the theater to explain social interaction, Goffman (1963) argues that an individual with a stigmatized identity (e.g., a disabled person or a minority) constantly engages in practices of identity management in social interaction. These practices control the impressions of others through control of what aspects of one's biography are revealed, a process Goffman (1959) calls *impression management*.

Goffman (1963) distinguishes among *personal*, *ego*, and *social* identity. He defines *ego identity* as "the subjective sense of [one's] own situation and [one's] own continuity" (Goffman, 1963, p. 105). Both *social* and *personal* identity, unlike ego identity, are concerned with the perceptions of others with whom one interacts. *Social identity* is linked to social role and status and informs the interaction in terms of whether those interacting view themselves as part of the same group. *Personal identity* represents aspects of biography that are shared or available in social interaction, and thus is the product of intentional self-presentation. Stigmatized individuals engage in *information control* as they decide what aspects of their personal identity to disclose in interaction. These decisions have implications for the nature of the interaction and its consequences for our ego identities.

Goffman's (1963) theory of identity and stigma thus views identity as a tripartite construct reflecting (1) societal definitions of roles, statuses, and categories; (2) an individual's self-presented biography; and (3) a subjective sense of self. His view of identity is ambitiously integrative of the social and psychological, and he maintains that identity is not simply a matter of ascription but rather an agentic process of information control and impression management. Key to the symbolic interactionist frame, though, is the idea that the social process produces or reproduces society at large and that the psychological experiences involved in this process support that social structure (e.g., Mead, 1934). This idea would become even more prominent in other theoretical perspectives on identity influenced by Mead.

Role-Identity Theory

Like Goffman, McCall and Simmons (1966) emphasize the significance of identity in social interaction. In their role-identity model, they argue that all human behavior is characterized by intentional action to achieve some end. The decisions we make in behavior require that we identify persons as both known (i.e., *personal identity*) and classified into some social category (i.e., *social identity*). They define *role-identity* as "the character and the role that an individual devises for himself [sic] as an occupant of a particular social position" (McCall & Simmons, 1966, p. 67). Similar to Stryker's (2007) later view of identities as self-schemas, McCall and Simmons (1966) view role-identities as "imaginative views" of the self that confer meaning to daily interaction. Foreshadowing perspectives that would later develop in cultural psychology and narrative identity (e.g., Bruner, 1990; McAdams, 2013; McAdams & Pals, 2006), they view role-identities as variants of "culturally established them" (McCall & Simmons, 1966, p. 70). In other words, we appropriate role-identities and rely on them in interaction as the product of a socialization process in which we have internalized the matrix of social positions and the meaning of particular social categories.

Role-identity theory thus integrates earlier perspectives on both personal and social identity from James and Mead but emphasizes the way in which social interaction represents a site of role performance. Ideas about personal identity are maintained, but the relative emphasis of role-identity theory is on the significance of social categories, social positions, and their relative value and meaning in context. Anticipating later perspectives that would emphasize cognition (e.g., Stryker, 2007) and intentional action based on interpretation (e.g., Bruner, 1990), role-identity theory represented an early integrative treatment of the identity concept.

Identity Theory and Structural Symbolic Interactionism

Mead's (1934) focus on social interaction and the meanings provided by the social world is central to Stryker's (1968, 2007) identity theory. Stryker (1968, 1980) emphasizes that roles in interaction reflect positions in a larger social structure and that identities exist in a salience hierarchy determined by specific social situations. Identities in this framework reflect various social positions determined by linguistic classifications of roles (e.g., occupational, familial, political), and Stryker's identity theory is most concerned with explaining "the choices persons make in situations in which they have the possibility of enacting alternative role-related actions" (Stryker, 2007, p. 1084). In his later articulations of the theory, Stryker (2007) endorses a social cognitive view of identities as "self-cognitions" or "internalized role expectations attached to positions" (p. 1084). Rather than these choices being purely agentic, Stryker views our self-cognitions as closely linked to social structural positions enacted in social life. How we think about our identities and which identities become prominent in social interaction are determined by the way in which our social world is constructed with regard to relative meaning and position.

Structural symbolic interactionism hence views society as shaping self, which in turn shapes social interaction (Stryker, 2008). This perspective diverges from Mead's (1934) original formulation in that society and its symbolic scheme of identity and meaning is a priori, and the self acts in such a way as to structure cognition according to this received social structure. Mead's theory of self places greater emphasis on society as emergent in social interactions, but Stryker (2008) sees interactions as determined by society and self as the mediator of this process. Identities are self-cognitions tied to roles determined by society (Stryker, 2008). The structural perspective is not purely deterministic with regard to social structure, however. Agency (or Mead's *I*) is maintained through the concepts of identity commitment and role choice in specific interactions (Serpe & Stryker, 2011).

Social Identity Theory

Social identity theory emerged in the 1970s in British social psychology as a new lens through which to understand ingroup bias and its real-world analogue, ethnocentrism (e.g., Tajfel & Turner, 1979; see Hornsey, 2008). Although more explicitly linked to cognitive views about categorization posited by Allport (1954), SIT can nonetheless be viewed as a descendant of Mead's theoretical emphasis on self-development in social interaction, for it places primacy on how social categorization influences behavior.

The concept of identity in SIT is both *social* and *cognitive* and is rooted in the social psychological idea of *categorization*. Tajfel and Turner (1986) define social identity as "those aspects of an individual's self-image that derive from the social categories to which he [sic] perceives himself [sic] as belonging" (p. 16). They include an important evaluative dimension to the concept, positing that social identities are "associated with positive or negative value connotations" and that individuals "strive for a positive self-concept" (p. 16). A fundamental assumption of SIT is that individuals act in ways that either maintain or enhance a positive self-concept with regard to social identity.

According to social identity theorists, we inhabit a world of social categories that can range from nationality, race, or ethnicity to small-scale community groups or, in the "minimal group" experimental paradigm pioneered by SIT, any arbitrary group assignment (Tajfel, 1981, 1982). In the experimental work of social identity theorists, the consistent finding was that random assignment to an arbitrary social identity in the lab (e.g., "underestimators" vs. "overestimators") was sufficient to activate ingroup bias (Tajfel, 1970). Thus, even when social categorization has little or no real-world relevance, the experience of group affiliation seems to influence behavior related to the distribution of resources. The mere experience of belonging to a particular group may be all that is needed for individuals to act in ways that are unequal or unjust. The later terminological emphasis on "categorization," as opposed to "identity," reflects the desire to emphasize cognitive processes related to group formation (e.g., Turner, Hogg, Oakes, Reicher, & Wetherell, 1987).

The findings of SIT research have profound implications for how we think about conflict, social relations, social injustice, and ethnocentrism, racism, and prejudice. Rather than rooted in competition over material resources (e.g., Sherif, 1958), hostile social relations and unjust and violent actions may rather be viewed as the *product of identity itself* (Tajfel & Turner, 1986). That is, if all that is needed to produce hostility is that individuals think of themselves as belonging to a group, identity may represent *the* tool of conflict and tension across the globe.

Social identity theory goes beyond the mere explanation of conflict and intergroup relations through processes of categorization and differentiation toward an explanation of social change through social identity processes (Spears, 2011). If individuals are motivated to enhance or maintain their sense of positive social identity, then SIT helps to explain why and how groups will work for social change. Tajfel and Turner (1986) outline specific strategies low-status groups use to change status hierarchies, such as individual mobility, social creativity, and direct social competition with high-status groups.

The identity concept in the SIT tradition is thus chiefly concerned with how social categorization and its cognitive internalization impact social behavior. Although SIT researchers have posited key processes related to social identity formation (e.g., "differentiation"; Tajfel, 1978), they are less concerned with the development of "identity cognition" (i.e., how individuals make meaning of group affiliation) than are personality and developmental psychologists. Rather, they are concerned with how group assignment or affiliation impacts intergroup behavior, including collective action (e.g., Reicher, 2004). Proponents of SIT's major offshoot, self-categorization theory (Turner et al., 1987), place greater emphasis on individual cognitive processes related to social categorization and have generated considerable research on social cognition (for review, see Hornsey, 2008).

Mead's theoretical lineage thus placed primary emphasis on the relational basis of identity and the significance of social interaction and the exterior world of meaning and social categories. This emphasis can be linked to Mead's relative emphasis on the significance of the exterior world in the construction of self. By contrast, the line of theory that more explicitly traces itself to James has been chiefly concerned with the *interior* experience and *interior-exterior* negotiation of identity and more explicitly concerned with identity *development* at the level of the individual person.

James's Lineage: Identity, Personality, and Human Development

James's (1890) focus on identity as a sense of self-sameness and continuity in self-perception forms the theoretical foundation of much contemporary empirical work in developmental and personality psychology (e.g., McAdams, 2013), as well as in versions of social and cultural psychology that emphasize narrative (e.g., Hammack, 2008). James's views inspired Erikson's (1959, 1968) landmark theory of identity crisis and the several paradigms that followed, including identity status theory (Marcia, 1966). In this section, I review the theoretical lineage from James and Erikson to Marcia's paradigm and its derivatives (for an extended exceptional review, see Schwartz, 2001), as well as to theories of racial and ethnic identity development and narrative identity development. These theoretical approaches to identity share a concern with person-level processes of interior-exterior negotiation over time. That is, they seek to describe how individuals develop and maintain a sense of coherence and continuity in relation to the external world of social meaning, thus providing a closer focus on the individual as unit of analysis, in contrast to approaches inspired by Mead (1934).

Erik Erikson and Identity Crisis

Perhaps no scholar is more associated with the identity concept in the social sciences than Erik Erikson. Erikson's theory of identity was likely inspired by his personal experience with identity confusion (see Erikson, 1970), and his theory was so influential that one biographer dubbed him "identity's architect" (Friedman, 1999). The central premise of Erikson's (1950, 1959, 1968) theory of identity is that, in adolescence, we experience a normative identity "crisis" in which we ultimately determine the trajectory of our adult lives. Central to his theory—and a novel departure from philosophical and early psychological approaches to the concept—is the idea of identity *development*.

Erikson (1950, 1959, 1968) views identity as a process and an outcome of human development—across the lifespan but assuming centrality in the developmental stage of adolescence.

Identity is the centerpiece of Erikson's (1950) broader developmental theory, characterized by a series of successive psychosocial tasks to be successfully mastered if one is to proceed to the next stage of development. The fifth stage of development in Erikson's (1950) scheme, which occurs in adolescence, is concerned explicitly with the formation of identity. With the "physiological revolution" of puberty, adolescents become increasingly concerned with their social roles and "how to connect their earlier cultivated roles and skills with the ideal prototypes of the day" (Erikson, 1959, p. 94). He defines *ego identity* as "the accrued confidence that one's ability to maintain inner sameness and continuity . . . is matched by the sameness and continuity of one's meaning for others" (Erikson, 1959, p. 94). Hence, Erikson integrates James's (1890) cognitive perspective with Mead's (1934) emphasis on the self as a social product, all the while subsuming these within a psychoanalytic view of mind emphasizing the ego.

Erikson (1959) views adolescence as a moment of *psychosocial moratorium*—a transitional moment in which "the individual through free role experimentation may find a niche in some section of his [sic] society, a niche which is firmly defined and yet seems to be uniquely made for him [sic]" (p. 120). Identity is the term Erikson uses to explain this process, both for the individual and his or her sense of inner psychological understanding and the meaning he or she has for others in the form of some identifiable role.

The developmental process of identity may result in one of several outcomes in Erikson's (1959) view. Successful navigation of this process may result in a "healthy personality," in which one has "achieved" an identity that provides a sense of continuity, self-sameness, and meaning for others. Alternatively, the inability to master the demands of this stage may result in *diffusion* or *role confusion*, in which the individual struggles to perceive a sense of continuity and place in the world. Erikson's notions of identity development would inspire the identity status model developed by James Marcia (1966) to classify individuals according to their place in this process.

Although he theorized identity as a universal psychosocial process, the idea of an identity "crisis" was in many ways linked to the concerns of Erikson's time, as he himself acknowledged. Erikson theorized identity as a central developmental process at a time of heightened attention to adolescence as a period of inevitable rebellion. As technological changes and industrialization created a longer gap between childhood and the assumption of adult roles in much of the world, adolescence increasingly became a "problem" of social scientific inquiry (Kett, 1977; see Arnett, 1999). G. Stanley Hall (1904) famously proclaimed the inevitability of "storm and stress" during this period, but others argued that rebellion during adolescence represents a cultural phenomenon unique to the industrialized world (e.g., M. Mead, 1928). On the one hand, Erikson identified with this latter approach, grounding his theory of identity in an explicit cultural-historical moment. On the other, he presented his theory of development as a universal, sequential model (see Arnett, this volume).

For Erikson, adolescence represents the moment at which the inner and outer worlds converge to create a person whose sense of self is grounded in an ideological moment—a point at which "the resources of tradition fuse with new inner resources to create something potentially new—a new person, and with that a new era" (Erikson, 1958, p. 20). The problem of identity is thus a project for psychosocial reconciliation at a particular moment in the life course and entails not just a proximal concern with one's family or community but rather an entire historical moment—an era in which youth are compelled to either reproduce or repudiate a status quo.

The developmental aspect of Erikson's theory was novel in two ways. First, earlier perspectives had emphasized identity as a momentary cognitive experience (e.g., James, 1890) or a product of social interaction (e.g., Mead, 1934). Erikson introduced the idea that this process, although anchored in psychological experiences (i.e., identifications, interactions) of childhood, was particularly pivotal at a moment in the development of an individual (i.e., adolescence). Second, Erikson's theory offered a broader and more integrative perspective on the relationship between individual psychology and social change. Whereas Mead's (1934) theory had theorized mind, self, and society as dynamically co-constructed through social acts, Erikson's theory conceived identity as the psychological process through which social orders are made, remade, or crushed. Hence, his theory was developmental not only in the sense of the psychological makeup of an individual but also of the ideological structure of a society. Erikson (1968) viewed identity as the key to understanding social and political change.

Identity Status Theory and Its Derivatives

While Erikson laid the theoretical foundation for attention to identity in developmental psychology, Marcia's (1966) identity status theory came to generate an extraordinary amount of empirical work in the late twentieth and early twenty-first centuries (for review, see Kroger, 2012; Kroger & Marcia, 2011; Meeus, 2011; Schwartz, 2001). Central to identity status theory is the idea that individuals may be classified according to one of four statuses with regard to dimensions of exploration and commitment in identity development—achievement, moratorium, foreclosure, and diffusion (see Crocetti & Meeus, this volume).

According to Marcia (1966), individuals high in both exploration and commitment are in a state of identity *achievement*. They reveal a high degree of exploration but are committed to a particular identity in terms of occupation and ideology. Individuals high in exploration but low in commitment are classified as in a state of identity *moratorium*. They are exploring possibilities in terms of occupation and ideology but have not made commitments. Individuals low in exploration but high in commitment are in a state of identity *foreclosure*. They have committed to an occupation and ideology before fully exploring options. Finally, individuals in a state of identity *diffusion* are low in both exploration and commitment. They are uncommitted and uninterested in matters of occupation and ideology.

Marcia's (1966, 1967) original studies and many that followed revealed a link between particular identity statuses and authoritarianism, self-esteem, and performance on conceptual tasks (for a review of early studies, see Bourne, 1978a; for more recent review, see Meeus, 2011), and the extraordinary amount of empirical work that the identity status paradigm inspired has examined various antecedent and consequent factors associated with particular statuses (see Kroger & Marcia, 2011). Inspired by identity status theory, more recent theoretical innovations have proposed that identity formation is a "dual-cycle" process and that two cycles (one emphasizing "commitment-formation" and one emphasizing "commitment-evaluation") may more accurately reflect the complexity of identity formation (e.g., Luyckx, Goossens, & Soenens, 2006). Exploration and commitment are thus multidimensional, and recent theoretical and empirical work has revealed the utility of "unpacking" these processes (e.g., Crocetti, Rubini, Luyckx, & Meeus, 2008; Crocetti, Rubini, & Meeus, 2008; Luyckx,

Goossens, Soenens, & Beyers, 2006; Luyckx, Goossens, Soenens, Beyers, & Vansteenkiste, 2005; see also Kunnen & Metz, this volume).

Given the amount of empirical work that the identity status paradigm has generated, it is not surprising that it has come under close scrutiny among identity theorists. The first critique emerged in 1978, with Bourne's (1978b) contention that the paradigm fails to address fundamental aspects of Erikson's theory, such as ego synthesis, temporal continuity, and role stability. Bourne (1978b) also raised concerns about the external validity of identity status research, given its reliance on US college students. A decade later, Côté and Levine (1988) argued that identity status theory significantly underrepresented Erikson's notion of identity and used much of Erikson's terminology inappropriately. Côté and Levine (1988) also raised concerns about the limited attention to social context, including historical and cultural factors, which were central to Erikson's original formulations. The idea of identity "status" also problematically categorizes individuals in such a way as to reify identity development processes as "outcomes," thus failing to appropriately conceive of identity as a process of temporal-spatial continuity consistent with Erikson's theory (Côté & Levine, 1988). More recent critiques of identity status theory have focused on the lack of attention paid to issues of race and ethnicity or to theories of racial and ethnic identity development (Sneed, Schwartz, & Cross, 2006).

Proponents of identity status theory and its derivatives have countered critics by arguing that the theory was not intended to capture all aspects of Erikson's original theory but that it is appropriate to view Eriksonian theory as foundational to the identity status approach (e.g., Berzonsky & Adams, 1999; Waterman, 1988, 1999). Kroger and Marcia (2011) suggested that identity status research became too focused on measurement at the expense of theoretical richness (see also Kroger, this volume). Theoretical offshoots of identity status theory have continued to emphasize the importance of clear operationalization and measurement but have focused on social-cognitive processes related to identity exploration and commitment. For example, Berzonsky and colleagues proposed the idea of *identity style* to describe information-processing approaches with regard to identity development processes (Berzonsky, 1989; Berzonsky & Neimeyer, 1988). Grotevant (1987) proposed a process model of identity development rooted in Eriksonian theory and emphasizing developmental contexts, individual differences, and a broader range of domains (e.g., values, relationships) than the identity status paradigm (see also Grotevant, Thorbecke, & Meyer, 1982). Common among all theoretical offshoots of identity status theory has been a concern with the measurement of identity processes, suggesting a more nomothetic approach to identity than Erikson (Waterman, 1988).

Research inspired by the identity status paradigm has undergone a significant empirical shift in the twenty-first century, with an abundance of longitudinal studies designed to address unresolved theoretical issues. In his comprehensive review of these studies, Meeus (2011) concludes that identity formation may represent a less "dynamic" process than previously considered, as studies reveal more continuity at the person-level than conflict. Identity status research thus has increasingly suggested an identity formation process marked by coherence and continuity and less by the "crisis" Erikson (1968) emphasized. In addition, theoretical refinements to the identity status paradigm have revealed exploration and commitment to be multidimensional processes revealing the complexity of identity formation (Meeus, 2011).

Theories of Racial and Ethnic Identity Development

Early theorists of identity, including Erikson, did not emphasize a distinct developmental process with regard to racial and ethnic identity, beyond the notion that minorities had to navigate the potential experience of a "negative identity" (Erikson, 1968). Beginning in the 1970s,[1] psychologists began to formulate theoretical approaches to race and ethnic identity, recognizing the way in which racial and ethnic minorities underwent a unique psychological experience (for review, see Quintana, 2007). Compared to the identity status paradigm and its derivatives, these theoretical perspectives more explicitly integrated concern with the interior world of psychological experience and the exterior world of social meaning with regard to social identity (see Way & Rogers, this volume). Their aim was to provide an account of the distinct psychological process minorities undergo as they navigate a social world characterized by racial and ethnic hierarchy. Unlike social psychological approaches that focused more on identity processes in social interaction (e.g., Goffman, 1963), these perspectives were more person-centered and explicitly concerned with identity development as a sequential process.

Cross (1971) posited a stage-based theory of black identity development in which African Americans gradually come to internalize and commit to a strong black identity, having gone through previous stages of encounter with white majority culture in the United States. Cross (1971) describes this process as a "Negro-to-black conversion" experience (or *nigrescence*), in which a once devalued and negative identity (the "Negro") becomes ultimately transformed into a positive, meaningful social identity as a black person (see also Cross, 1978; Parham, 1989; Worrell, this volume). Cross's (1971) theory is rooted in a particular historical moment for African Americans in the post-Civil Rights Movement era in which political activism called for a rejection of former assimilationist models of black identity and politics in favor of the formation of a distinct and positive counter-identity.

Although identity status theory and its derivatives have been criticized for lack of attention to theories of racial and ethnic identity development (e.g., Sneed et al., 2006), it is noteworthy that Phinney's (1989) theory of ethnic identity has its origins in the identity status model. Based on research with ethnic minority youth in the United States, she proposed a three-stage model of ethnic identity development in which youth have either not explored their ethnic minority identities (*diffusion/foreclosure*), are in an active process of exploration (*moratorium*), or have committed to an ethnic identity (*achievement*) (Phinney, 1989). She subsequently developed a measure of ethnic identity development that has been widely adopted in the literature as the primary tool to assess ethnic identity (Phinney, 1992; for review, see Phinney & Ong, 2007; for a critique, see Gjerde, 2014). The measure emphasizes an individual's level of affiliation with an ethnic group with which he or she identifies, assessing factors such as sense of belongingness and ingroup pride. This approach to ethnic identity development has recently been integrated with narrative approaches (Syed & Azmitia, 2008, 2010), providing a richer account of the content involved in identity development processes for ethnic minorities (McLean & Pasupathi, 2012).

In the 1990s, Sellers and colleagues developed the multidimensional model of racial identity (MMRI) and accompanying measure to assess identity among African Americans in a more global way than did previous approaches (Sellers, Rowley, Chavous, Shelton, & Smith, 1997; Sellers, Smith, Shelton, Rowley, & Chavous, 1998). Tracing the intellectual origins of their approach to identity theory in structural symbolic interactionism (Stryker & Serpe, 1994), they argue that African Americans possess multiple social identities and must make decisions about salience in the context of social interaction. Their concept and measure posits four dimensions of African-American racial identity: salience, centrality, regard, and ideology (Sellers et al., 1998). The idea of *salience* comes directly from identity theory in symbolic interactionism, suggesting that African Americans' racial identity may assume significance to self-concept depending on the particular social setting of interaction. The related notion of *centrality* speaks to the extent to which African Americans may or may not view their racial identities as of central importance to their overall sense of self. The idea of *regard* brings an evaluative, affective dimension to identity, referring to the extent of positive or negative sentiment an African American has about his or her racial identity. Finally, *ideology* speaks to the content of beliefs about the ingroup and its political stance that African Americans may endorse. Hence, Sellers and colleagues (1998) attempt to bridge the literature on the uniqueness of black identity and the black self-concept (e.g., Smith, 1980) with broader theoretical perspectives on identity from sociology.

Another theoretical approach to racial identity development emerged in the 1990s, in the work of Helms and colleagues on white racial identity development (e.g., Helms, 1995; Helms & Carter, 1990). Like the work of Phinney and Sellers and colleagues, a central aim of this theoretical development was to establish a measure of white racial identity for use in the United States. Based on Cross's (1971) theory of black racial identity development, Helms (1984) proposed a five-stage model of white racial identity development. Her theoretical model posited that, like blacks, whites develop a racial consciousness through a stage-based progression based on their encounter with members of other racial groups. Unlike racial minorities, whites have the privilege to decide whether they will undergo this process of racial consciousness and may, as a member of the racial majority in the United States, not develop a sense of white racial identity consciousness. Those who do develop this consciousness proceed from initial *contact* with non-whites to stages of *disintegration* (acknowledgment of white identity), *reintegration* (hostility toward non-whites), *pseudo-independence* ("an intellectual acceptance and curiosity" about race and race relations; Helms, 1984, p. 156), and ultimately *autonomy* (acknowledgment of and acceptance of racial differences).

Psychometric studies of the theoretical model revealed that individuals can be classified according to their stage of white racial identity development using a measure of racial attitudes (Helms & Carter, 1990). Although her theoretical model was not rooted in identity status theory, Helms (1995) later adopted the language of identity *status* to describe the developmental stage a white individual may be in at the time of assessment, and she also linked identity development status to *information processing* approaches, implicitly linking her theoretical model to the work of identity status theorists such as Berzonsky (1989).

In sum, theories of race and ethnic identity development that emerged in psychology in the 1970s and 1980s attempted to characterize the progression of both minorities (e.g., Cross, 1971) and majorities (e.g., Helms, 1984) through a process of consciousness and were largely concerned with classification and measurement of individuals along a sequential trajectory. These theories derived from diverse traditions in psychology and sociology, including the identity status paradigm (e.g., Phinney, 1989) and identity theory in sociology (e.g., Sellers et al., 1998). Theories of racial and ethnic identity development placed a greater emphasis on the individual's interior navigation of the world of social meaning than identity status theory and its derivatives. Their relative emphasis on identity as a developmental, stage-based process of interior navigation situates these theoretical approaches in the theoretical lineage typically traced to Erikson and James, compared with approaches emphasizing identity in interaction (e.g., Goffman, 1963; Tajfel & Turner, 1986), with the work of Sellers and colleagues (1998) representing an approach that bridges theoretical lineages.

Narrative Identity Development

Inspired by approaches in philosophy that emphasized the narrative structure of meaning making (e.g., Ricoeur, 1984), theorists in psychology began to argue in the 1980s that the defining feature of identity is the formation of a personal narrative (e.g., Cohler, 1982; Freeman, 1984; McAdams, 1988, 1990; Polkinghorne, 1988) and that we make meaning of the social world through narrative processes (e.g., Bruner, 1986, 1990). In the narrative perspective, the sense of sameness, continuity, and coherence James (1890) identified as the defining feature of identity develops over time, across the life course, as we link events and experiences in a personal narrative or life story (Cohler, 1982; McAdams, 1988, 1990).

The earliest theoretical perspectives on narrative identity development challenged the anchoring ontogenetic paradigm in developmental psychology that viewed individuals as progressing through universal sequential stages (Cohler, 1982; Freeman, 1984). Cohler (1982) argued that human development is better characterized as a process of *narrative development* in which individuals construct and reconstruct their identities across the life course. Human development is an interpretive process chiefly concerned with meaning making (intelligibility) in context; the aims of developmental science are interpretive rather than explanatory (Cohler, 1982; see also Bruner, 1986). Cohler (1982) placed emphasis on the significance of generation cohort in the construction of personal narratives, and his later work was particularly concerned with how the personal narrative varies as a function of generation cohort (e.g., Cohler, 2007, 2008; Cohler & Hammack, 2006; Cohler & Hostetler, 2003).

McAdams proposed an integrative theory of personality with narrative identity at its conceptual center (McAdams, 1988, 1995, 1996, 2001; McAdams & Pals, 2006). He defines identity as "an internalized and evolving life story" (McAdams, 2001, p. 117) and acknowledges the origins of his theory in Erikson's (1959) view of identity. McAdams (1996, 2013) also explicitly links his theory to James's (1890) *I/me* distinction, arguing that the *I* represents the process of personal narrative construction, whereas the *me* represents the personal narrative as an object or product ("the self that the I constructs"; McAdams, 1996, p. 295; see also McAdams & Cox, 2010). Consistent with Cohler's (1982) view, McAdams (1988, 1990, 1996, 1997) posits that life stories function to provide a sense of unity, purpose, and coherence, which may assume particular psychological significance in the context of modern or late modern social organization (Giddens, 1991; McAdams, 1996, 2001; Schachter, 2005). Life stories can be studied for their tone, imagery, structure or form, thematic content, and ideological setting, among other components (McAdams, 1988, 1990, 1996), all of which may evolve within a person over time and vary according to historical time and place (McAdams, 1996, 2008; McAdams & Cox, 2010; McAdams & Pals, 2006; Nelson, 2003).

Since the life story represents an evolving personal narrative concerned with the reconstructed past and anticipated future, it stands to reason that different processes are at work at different developmental moments in the course of an individual life (McAdams, 1996, 2001). Autobiographical memory begins to develop in childhood (Nelson & Fivush, 2004), but life-story construction requires particular cognitive and social skills not present until adolescence in most societies (Habermas & Bluck, 2000). In adolescence and early adulthood, establishing the ideological setting for the life story becomes central as the individual develops awareness about the social and political surround (McAdams, 1996). This perspective on the significance of ideology in personal narrative development can be linked to Erikson's (1958, 1968) theory of identity and has been further examined among narrative psychologists working with youth in settings of political conflict (e.g., Hammack, 2008, 2010, 2011a). The life story continues to develop in adulthood, as self-event connections shift over time (Pasupathi, Mansour, & Brubaker, 2007). In midlife, narrative identity development becomes more concerned with harmony and reconciliation (McAdams, 1996), as well as generativity (i.e., care for the next generation; McAdams, 2006; McAdams, Diamond, de St. Aubin, & Mansfield, 1997) and a satisfying ending for the life story (McAdams, 1996).

In a similar line of theoretical development, Schachter (2004, 2005) revived Erikson's (1959) concept of *identity configuration*. Erikson (1959) argued that the identity formation process is characterized as "an *evolving configuration*..., integrating *constitutional givens, idiosyncratic libidinal needs, favored capacities, significant identification, effective defenses, successful sublimations, and consistent roles*" (p. 125). Schachter (2004) seeks to revitalize this aspect of Eriksonian theory to explain the individual's negotiation of multiple and competing identifications and roles, particularly in the context of late modernity, in which multiplicity abounds (Schachter, 2005). Schachter's (2004, 2005) empirical work examining narrated accounts of identifications and commitments among modern Orthodox Jews in Israel provides examples of identity formation as a process of evolving configurations, addressing the need in identity research for a renewed emphasis on process rather than outcome (Grotevant, 1987, 1997).

In a recent theoretical formulation, McAdams (2013) subsumes his life story theory of identity development within a broader perspective on self-development across the lifespan (see also McAdams & Cox, 2010; McAdams & Zapata-Gietl, this volume). Again anchoring his theory in James's (1890) I/me distinction, McAdams (2013) posits that the self progresses in the course of development from a "social actor" to "motivated agent" by the end of childhood, then to "autobiographical author" in adolescence and emerging adulthood. He refers to this process as a "developing I-me configuration" (McAdams, 2013, p. 272). The *self as actor* develops in early childhood and is primarily concerned with self-regulation. The contents of self at this stage are characterized by social roles, skills, and traits. The *self as agent* develops in mid to late childhood and is primarily concerned with self-esteem. The contents of self at this stage are characterized by personal goals, plans, values, hopes, and fears. Finally, the *self as author* develops in adolescence and emerging adulthood and is primarily concerned with self-continuity (see also Habermas & Köber, this volume). The life narrative characterizes the content of self at this stage. Like his integrative theory of personality, McAdams's (2013) theory of self-development is rooted in ideas about the self as both process and product of development, which can be traced to both James (1890) and Erikson (1959). Positing identity as a life narrative, McAdams (2013) suggests that identity development is chiefly concerned with the integration of interior and exterior meaning through intentional autobiographical work.

Whereas narrative theorists like Cohler and McAdams are chiefly concerned with "big stories," in the sense of whole autobiographical narratives, other theorists have emphasized the role of "small stories" and storytelling as a situated process in identity development (for review, see Thorne & Nam, 2009; see also Bamberg, 2011; Korobov, this volume). This line of theory in narrative identity development is more explicit in its emphasis on the co-constitutive or social basis of narrative, thus making links to Mead's (1934) theoretical emphasis on self and society as co-constructed. For example, Thorne (2000) views personality development through the lens of the personal memory telling process. She views narrative not as a private process of personal formation but rather as developing in interaction, and she places greater emphasis on storytelling as *process* rather than the life narrative as a *product* (see also Thorne & Nam, 2007). Similarly, Pasupathi (2001; this volume) suggests that autobiographical memories are socially constructed, and Bamberg (2004) argues that narratives develop in small-scale social interaction as interlocutors collectively construct meaning. McLean, Pasupathi, and Pals (2007) argue that storytelling is central to self-development and that situated stories have a reciprocal impact on the developing self-concept and life story. These perspectives on narrative identity development place relatively more emphasis on the socially constructed nature of self (e.g., Mead, 1934) than on identity development as an interior process of perceptual continuity (e.g., James, 1890).

Another line of narrative theory emphasizes the cultural and political situatedness of autobiographical memory and personal narrative. These theorists recognize the socially constructed nature of identity, suggesting that individuals appropriate cultural themes and are also constrained by the received system of social categories and version of collective memory (e.g., Fivush, 2010; Hammack, 2008, 2010; Nelson, 2003). The relative emphasis in these perspectives is on narrative identity development as a cultural process highly influenced by the relative value of one's social identity and on the negotiation between dominant and resistance narratives in interaction (e.g., Fivush, 2010; Hammack, 2010). For example, subordinate status on the basis of gender, sexual identity, ethnic identity, or the like may create unique processes for personal narrative development, and concordance between personal and collective ("master") narratives may be linked to social status (e.g., Fivush, 2010; Hammack, 2008, 2010, 2011b; Thorne & McLean, 2003).

Although many narrative theorists do not directly engage with poststructural social theory (e.g., Butler, 1990), the narrative turn in psychological understandings of identity can be viewed as part of the broader turn toward language and discourse in the social sciences (Hammack & Pilecki, 2012). A theoretical alliance thus exists between poststructural theories emphasizing the production of identities through language (e.g., Butler, 1990; Foucault, 1977, 1978) and narrative theories in psychology. In both theoretical traditions, individual self-understandings are conceived as products of historical moments, although poststructural theorists are more likely to emphasize the political context of these processes than are narrative psychologists (for exceptions, see Fivush, 2004, 2010; Hammack, 2011a; Hammack & Cohler, 2011).

In sum, narrative theories of identity posit that individuals construct coherent life stories that provide a sense of meaning and purpose across the life course (Cohler, 1982; McAdams, 1990, 1996, 1997), that this process is especially salient in adolescence and emerging adulthood (Habermans & Bluck, 2000; McAdams, 2001; McLean, 2005), and that this process involves engagement with "master narratives" or dominant storylines about the meaning of social categories (Fivush, 2010; Hammack, 2008, 2011b; McLean, 2008; Thorne & McLean, 2003). A growing movement in developmental, personality, and social psychology has come to see human development and autobiographical memory as guided by story-making (Hammack, 2008, 2010; McLean et al., 2007; Pasupathi et al., 2007; Thorne, 2000). At both the individual and collective levels, identities are not simply descriptive labels but rather prescriptive storylines that inform human motivation and action. Narrative theories thus privilege the idea that cognition involves a process of linking concepts and events into a story form (Bruner, 1987, 1991) and that this process is inherently social and co-constitutive (Hammack, 2008; Pasupathi, 2001; Thorne, 2000).

The emergence of narrative theories of identity development speaks to a continuing concern with personal coherence and selfsameness expressed initially by James (1890) and Erikson (1959). Social, personality, and cultural psychologists who take a narrative approach also link their work to Mead's (1934) ideas about the social construction of self in interaction (Pasupathi, 2001; Thorne, 2000) and social identity theory (Hammack, 2010) and thus link the anchoring theoretical perspectives on identity posited by James and Mead. In this way, narrative theories of identity development have the potential to bridge theoretical traditions across the social sciences and humanities that emphasize individual cognition, social cognition, social categorization, and the power of language and discourse.

Pluralism, Identity Politics, and the Postmodern Challenge

As noted at the start of this chapter, the identity concept is not strictly the intellectual purview of psychology or sociology. Rather, it has come to dominate how we think about difference and social organization in an era characterized by a global ethic of pluralism (Gutmann, 2003; Taylor, 1994). The social movements of the postwar, postcolonial era propelled a concern with identity to disciplines beyond psychology and sociology (Hammack, 2010; Sampson, 1993). Beyond psychology and sociology, identity emerged as a theoretical concern within the humanities, in new fields like cultural studies and in revolutions within established fields like literature and philosophy. The idea of *identity politics*—that self-understandings are linked to political forces that attempt to control and regulate persons, bodies, and minds, and that political claims can and should be made on the basis of these self-understandings (see Bernstein, 2005; Sampson,

1993)—began to permeate numerous fields within the academy.

The postwar, postcolonial era witnessed a global ideological transition in which received notions of the status associated with particular identities (e.g., colonial subjects, women, minorities) were called into question. The psychological effects of colonialism and systemic forms of oppression such as racism and anti-Semitism became a major concern for scholars across a number of fields (e.g., Fanon, 1952, 1961; Memmi, 1965; Said, 1978; Sartre, 1948). Gradually, the theoretical emphasis of this line of work became concerned with interrogating how social categories influence "subjectivity," understood through the lens of theorists such as Foucault (1982) as both sense of self-consciousness and sense of subjection through control and dependence.

Through this line of theory and research, the identity concept became increasingly viewed as a product of modernity and a tool for control and domination, particular along the lines of identities based on race (e.g., Memmi, 2000) and sexual identity (e.g., Foucault, 1978). The postmodern challenge to identity emerged in the 1980s and 1990s in philosophy (e.g., Lyotard, 1984), cultural studies (e.g., Sarup, 1996), and, eventually, psychology (e.g., Kvale, 1992) and sociology (e.g., Bauman, 1988). In brief, postmodern theorists argued that the nature of late modern life commanded a reconsideration of the assumed stability of self and identity (e.g., Gergen, 1991, 1994). Technology now made discontinuity in time and space the norm, and the idea of a coherent self or social category was rendered dubious as a result (cf. Smith, 1994). The postmodern emphasis on multiplicity and discontinuity, whether in communication, art, literature, or architecture, challenged the theoretical foundations of identity in a romantic and rationalist vision of individual unity (Gergen, 1991). In place of this romantic vision, Gergen (1991, 2009) proposes a more radical form of social constructionism emphasizing the self as constructed in relation ("relational being"; Gergen, 2009), harkening back at least to some extent to Mead's (1934) theory of self.

One problem with the postmodern critique of identity is that it undermines the basis upon which individuals continue to make meaning of themselves and the basis upon which historically subordinated groups make claims for recognition (Hammack, 2010). In other words, claims about the constructed, relative, and discontinuous nature of identity may unwittingly support those groups withholding recognition of minorities and minority rights in numerous contexts. Recent theoretical perspectives have sought to recognize the constructed and historical basis of identity categories while arguing that this recognition does not obviate the need to acknowledge identity-based claims. For example, the recognition that contemporary Palestinian national identity is a product of the encounter with Zionism and the failure of pan-Arabism in the postcolonial Middle East (Khalidi, 1997), as opposed to some primordial index of identity, does not delegitimize the individual or collective experience of Palestinian identity or the national aspirations of Palestinians for their own state. Recognizing identities as products of time and place does not make them any less psychologically or politically salient (Hammack, 2010). Social organization across the globe continues to be characterized along the lines of various social identities, be they termed nationalities, ethnicities, races, cultures, or the like, and hence the claims of postmodern theorists of identity may have prematurely predicted the demise of identity. It is also noteworthy that postmodern theoretical claims about the fragmented, discontinuous nature of self or identity have not received clear empirical support.

Because identity has become an anchoring concept for the understanding of sameness and differences across human communities, scholars in political philosophy have argued for identity as the basis for a global ethic of social justice and respect for cultural pluralism. Taylor (1994) has argued that recognition is the basis for a just social ethics in the context of a multicultural, pluralistic world. Gutmann (2003) has argued that democracies must manage identity politics in ways that address the legitimate needs for security and recognition of all groups. Sen (2006) has argued that identity (understood broadly as affiliation) is not a singular matter and that violence in the name of identity is the product of injustice in matters of diversity and recognition. Finally, Appiah (2005, 2006) has argued for a "cosmopolitan" code of identity ethics in which individuals recognize the value of pluralism, diversity, and hybridity in matters of identity.

Although the emergence of identity as a critical concept in political philosophy and related fields speaks to its continued and expanding relevance, it is noteworthy that this body of work does not link to theory and empirical research in either psychology or sociology (Hammack, 2008; Moshman, 2007). As a consequence, identity is generally conceived in these works as both affiliation (in the individual psychological sense) and ascription (in the social psychological sense), with little or no attention paid to the way in which processes of identity development unfold in political context. Greater connections between disciplinary perspectives on identity would be beneficial and likely result in enhanced theoretical work.

Prospects for Theory and the Identity of Identity

In this chapter, I have argued that identity represents the key way in which we understand sameness, difference, and categories in the twentieth and twenty-first centuries. I traced our contemporary concern with identity to the theories of William James and George Herbert Mead, and I charted the distinct and sometimes overlapping trajectories these theories took in sociology and psychology. I briefly illustrated the way in which identity is now being mobilized as a valuable concept beyond these disciplines, especially in fields in the humanities such as cultural studies and political philosophy.

If one views the historical arc of this theoretical work, two observations come immediately to mind. First, since most of the twentieth century saw the project of disciplinary differentiation in the social sciences as key (Wallerstein, 2001), identity theory "split" into two branches that only occasionally referred to one another. Hence, there was significant theoretical fragmentation in identity over the course of the twentieth century, and theories of identity began to have different identities. Questions of recognition, legitimacy, and differentiation abounded (e.g., Côté & Levine, 1988; Waterman, 1988). Theoretical perspectives beyond psychology and sociology (e.g., in the humanities), in fact, rarely called on the theoretical work conducted in psychology and sociology and hence contributed to insular disciplinary conversations about the concept (Hammack, 2008; Moshman, 2007). Second, although there is evidence of an interest in theoretical integration (e.g., Hammack, 2010, 2011a; McAdams & Cox, 2010; McLean & Pasupathi, 2012; Syed & Azmitia, 2008, 2010), the fragmentary nature of the knowledge production industry endures and, hence, can support both continued fragmentation and enhanced integration.

In other words, identity theories themselves are the products of scholars who inhabit social identities that prescribe a set of parameters within the knowledge production industry. Like all social identities, disciplinary identities command distinctiveness, and this need for distinctiveness has created relative emphases within different theoretical approaches. For example, identity theories can be categorized according to their relative emphasis on the private interior world of individual cognition (a greater concern within psychology) or the public exterior world of marked affiliation (a greater concern within sociology, political philosophy, and cultural studies) (see Schachter, this volume). Because Enlightenment philosophy and its intellectual descendant, the discipline of psychology, is the product of a cultural milieu that privileged individualism, it stands to reason that the earliest theories of identity were more concerned with individual perception (e.g., Locke, 1694/1998), memory (e.g., Hume, 1739/1986), meaning making through language (e.g., Dilthey, 1928/1988), and cognition (e.g., James, 1890). These theoretical perspectives were the product of privileged European and American men whose social identities were unproblematic and hence less likely to concern them in their intellectual inquiry.

The US context of identity pluralism and the rapid differentiation of the social sciences in the early twentieth century (Wallerstein, 2001) can likely be credited with the emergence of new identities for identity theory, with Mead's (1934) "social behaviorism" (later termed "symbolic interactionism"; Blumer, 1969) shifting concern away from the interior world of cognition toward the social act as unit of analysis. Over the course of the century, "identity" would move from margin to center in both the scholarly and popular discourse. It came to provide a vocabulary with which to make meaning of the social and political challenges and changes of the time, as well as the individual's attempt to navigate an increasingly complex world (e.g., Erikson, 1968).

The identity of identity in the twenty-first century has in many ways demonstrated coherence with earlier formulations. Scholars in the social sciences and humanities continue to consider many of the same dimensions of identity posited by early theorists. They understand identity as an aspect of the person that develops over time (e.g., McLean & Pasupathi, 2012); a tool for individual and collective meaning-making (e.g., Hammack, 2010); a product of the modern project of social organization on the basis of categories such as race, ethnicity, gender, nationality, sexual identity, religion, and the like (e.g., Warnke, 2008); and an opportunity for unity and division. In other words, identity transcends disciplines, levels of analysis, and planes of human experience in ways that bring sensibility and intelligibility to the muddle of human existence.

The narrative arc of identity theories holds hope for integration and cross-disciplinary conversation, provided the various social identities that make up the knowledge production industry of our time are comfortable enough in their own positive distinctiveness to acknowledge the benefits of that conversation. This handbook represents an important attempt at theoretical integration.

Acknowledgments

This chapter was completed in part while the author was supported by a National Academy of Education/Spencer Foundation Postdoctoral Fellowship. The author thanks Jonathan Muro for assistance with the preparation of this chapter. Correspondence may be addressed to Phillip L. Hammack, University of California, Santa Cruz, Department of Psychology, 1156 High Street, Santa Cruz, CA 95064 USA. Email: hammack@ucsc.edu.

Note

1. Du Bois's (1903) early notion of "double consciousness" with regard to the psychological experience of African Americans represents an important contribution that was unfortunately not widely adopted in psychological theories of identity. He argued that African Americans construct two different senses of self—one reflecting the dominant white majority and one reflecting their own experience as racial minorities. This idea has been somewhat revived by recent theorists in social psychology examining the psychological experience of "hyphenated" identities (Fine & Sirin, 2007).

References

Allport, G. W. (1954). *The nature of prejudice*. Reading, MA: Addison-Wesley.

Appiah, K. A. (2005). *The ethics of identity*. Princeton, NJ: Princeton University Press.

Appiah, K. A. (2006). *Cosmopolitanism: Ethics in a world of strangers*. New York: Norton.

Arnett, J. J. (1999). Adolescent storm and stress, reconsidered. *American Psychologist, 54*, 317–326.

Arnett, J. J. (2002). The psychology of globalization. *American Psychologist, 57*, 774–783.

Bakhtin, M. M. (1981). *The dialogic imagination* (C. Emerson & M. Holquist, Trans.). Austin: University of Texas Press.

Bamberg, M. (2004). "I know it may sound mean to say this, but we couldn't really care less about her anyway": Form and functions of "slut bashing" in male identity constructions in 15-year-olds. *Human Development, 47*(6), 331–353.

Bamberg, M. (2011). Who am I? Narration and its contribution to self and identity. *Theory & Psychology, 21*(1), 3–24.

Bauman, Z. (1988). Sociology and postmodernity. *Sociological Review, 36*(4), 790–813.

Baumeister, R. F. (1986). *Identity: Cultural change and the struggle for self*. New York: Oxford University Press.

Baumeister, R. F. (1987). How the self became a problem: A psychological review of historical research. *Journal of Personality and Social Psychology, 52*(1), 163–176.

Bernstein, M. (2005). Identity politics. *Annual Review of Sociology, 31*, 47–74.

Berzonsky, M. D. (1989). Identity style: Conceptualization and measurement. *Journal of Adolescent Research, 4*, 267–281.

Berzonsky, M. D., & Adams, G. R. (1999). Reevaluating the identity status paradigm: Still useful after 35 years. *Developmental Review, 19*(4), 557–590.

Berzonsky, M. D., & Neimeyer, G. J. (1988). Identity status and personal construct systems. *Journal of Adolescence, 11*, 195–204.

Blumer, H. (1969). *Symbolic interactionism*. Englewood Cliffs, NJ: Prentice-Hall.

Bourne, E. (1978a). The state of research on ego identity: A review and appraisal. Part I. *Journal of Youth and Adolescence, 7*(3), 223–251.

Bourne, E. (1978b). The state of research on ego identity: A review and appraisal. Part II. *Journal of Youth and Adolescence, 7*(4), 371–392.

Bruner, J. (1986). *Actual minds, possible worlds*. Cambridge, MA: Harvard University Press.

Bruner, J. (1987). Life as narrative. *Social Research, 54*(1), 11–32.

Bruner, J. (1990). *Acts of meaning*. Cambridge, MA: Harvard University Press.

Bruner, J. (1991). The narrative construction of reality. *Critical Inquiry, 18*, 1–21.

Burkitt, I. (2011). Identity construction in sociohistorical context. In S. J. Schwartz, K. Luyckx, & V. L. Vignoles (Eds.), *Handbook of identity theory and research* (pp. 267–283). New York: Springer.

Butler, J. (1990). *Gender trouble: Feminism and the subversion of identity*. New York: Routledge.

Cohler, B. J. (1982). Personal narrative and life course. In P. Baltes & O. G. Brim (Eds.), *Life span development and behavior* (Vol. 4, pp. 205–241). New York: Academic Press.

Cohler, B. J. (2007). *Writing desire: Sixty years of gay autobiography*. Madison: University of Wisconsin Press.

Cohler, B. J. (2008). Two lives, two times: Life-writing after Shoah. *Narrative Inquiry, 18*(1), 1–28.

Cohler, B. J., & Hammack, P. L. (2006). Making a gay identity: Life story and the construction of a coherent self. In D. P. McAdams, R. Josselson, & A. Lieblich (Eds.), *Identity and story: Creating self in narrative* (pp. 151–172). Washington, D. C.: American Psychological Association Press.

Cohler, B. J., & Hostetler, A. (2003). Linking life course and life story: Social change and the narrative study of lives over time. In J. T. Mortimer & M. J. Shanahan (Eds.), *Handbook of the life course* (pp. 555–576). New York: Kluwer/Plenum.

Cooley, C. H. (1902). *Human nature and the social order*. New York: Scribners.

Côté, J. E., & Levine, C. G. (1988). A critical examination of the ego identity status paradigm. *Developmental Review, 8*, 147–184.

Crocetti, E., Rubini, M., Luyckx, K., & Meeus, W. (2008). Identity formation in early and middle adolescents from various ethnic groups: From three dimensions to five statuses. *Journal of Youth and Adolescence, 37*, 983–996.

Crocetti, E., Rubini, M., & Meeus, W. (2008). Capturing the dynamics of identity formation in various ethnic groups: Development and validation of a three-dimensional model. *Journal of Adolescence, 31*, 207–222.

Cross, W. E. (1971). Negro-to-Black conversion experience. *Black World, 20*, 13–27.

Cross, W. E. (1978). The Thomas and Cross models of psychological nigrescence: A review. *Journal of Black Psychology, 5*(1), 13–31.

Descartes, R. (2000). *Discourse on method and related writings* (D. M. Clarke, Trans.). New York: Penguin. (Original work published 1637)

Dilthey, W. (1976). *Selected writings*. New York: Cambridge University Press.

Dilthey, W. (1988). *Introduction to the human sciences: An attempt to lay a foundation for the study of society and history* (R. J. Betanzos, Trans.). Detroit, MI: Wayne State University Press. (Original work published 1923)

Du Bois, W. E. B. (1996). *The souls of black folk*. New York: Penguin. (Original work published 1903)

Elliott, A. (Ed.). (2011). *Routledge handbook of identity studies*. New York: Routledge.

Erikson, E. H. (1950). *Childhood and society*. New York: Norton.

Erikson, E. H. (1958). *Young man Luther: A study in psychoanalysis and history*. New York: Norton.

Erikson, E. H. (1959). *Identity and the life cycle*. New York: Norton.

Erikson, E. H. (1968). *Identity: Youth and crisis*. New York: Norton.

Erikson, E. H. (1970). Autobiographical notes on the identity crisis. *Deadalus*, *99*(4), 730–759.

Fanon, F. (1952). *Black skin, white masks* (C. L. Markmann, Trans.). New York: Grove.

Fanon, F. (1961). *The wretched of the earth* (R. Philcox, Trans.). New York: Grove.

Fine, M., & Sirin, S. R. (2007). Theorizing hyphenated selves: Researching youth development in and across contentious political contexts. *Social and Personality Psychology Compass*, *1*(1), 16–38.

Fivush, R. (2004). Voice and silence: A feminist model of autobiographical memory. In J. M. Lucariello, J. A. Hudson, R. Fivush, & P. J. Bauer (Eds.), *The development of the mediated mind: Sociocultural context and cognitive development* (pp. 79–99). Mahwah, NJ: Erlbaum.

Fivush, R. (2010). Speaking silence: The social construction of silence in autobiographical and cultural narratives. *Memory*, *18*(2), 88–98.

Foucault, M. (1977). *Discipline and punish: The birth of the prison* (A. Sheridan, Trans.). New York: Pantheon.

Foucault, M. (1978). *The history of sexuality, Vol. 1: An introduction* (R. Hurley, Trans.). New York: Pantheon.

Foucault, M. (1982). The subject and power. *Critical Inquiry*, *8*, 777–795.

Freeman, M. (1984). History, narrative, and life-span developmental knowledge. *Human Development*, *27*(1), 1–19.

Friedman, L. J. (1999). *Identity's architect: A biography of Erik H. Erikson*. Cambridge, MA: Harvard University Press.

Gergen, K. J. (1991). *The saturated self: Dilemmas of identity in contemporary life*. New York: Basic Books.

Gergen, K. J. (1994). Exploring the postmodern: Perils or potentials? *American Psychologist*, *49*(5), 412–416.

Gergen, K. J. (2009). *Relational being: Beyond self and community*. New York: Oxford University Press.

Giddens, A. (1991). *Modernity and self-identity: Self and society in the late modern age*. Stanford, CA: Stanford University Press.

Gjerde, P. F. (2014). An evaluation of ethnicity research in developmental psychology: Critiques and recommendations. *Human Development*, *57*, 176–205.

Goffman, E. (1959). *The presentation of self in everyday life*. Garden City, NY: Doubleday Anchor.

Goffman, E. (1963). *Stigma: Notes on the management of spoiled identity*. New York: Simon & Schuster.

Grotevant, H. D. (1987). Toward a process model of identity formation. *Journal of Adolescent Research*, *2*(3), 203–222.

Grotevant, H. D. (1997). Identity processes: Integrating social psychological and developmental approaches. *Journal of Adolescent Research*, *12*(3), 354–357.

Grotevant, H. D., Thorbecke, W., & Meyer, M. L. (1982). An extension of Marcia's Identity Status Interview into the interpersonal domain. *Journal of Youth and Adolescence*, *11*, 33–47.

Gutmann, A. (2003). *Identity in democracy*. Princeton, NJ: Princeton University Press.

Habermas, T., & Bluck, S. (2000). Getting a life: The emergence of the life story in adolescence. *Psychological Bulletin*, *126*(5), 748–769.

Hall, G. S. (1904). *Adolescence: Its psychology and its relation to physiology, anthropology, sociology, sex, crime, religion, and education*. Englewood Cliffs, NJ: Prentice-Hall.

Hammack, P. L. (2008). Narrative and the cultural psychology of identity. *Personality and Social Psychology Review*, *12*(3), 222–247.

Hammack, P. L. (2010). Identity as burden or benefit? Youth, historical narrative, and the legacy of political conflict. *Human Development*, *53*, 173–201.

Hammack, P. L. (2011a). *Narrative and the politics of identity: The cultural psychology of Israeli and Palestinian youth*. New York: Oxford University Press.

Hammack, P. L. (2011b). Narrative and the politics of meaning. *Narrative Inquiry*, *21*(2), 311–318.

Hammack, P. L., & Cohler, B. J. (2011). Narrative, identity, and the politics of exclusion: Social change and the gay and lesbian life course. *Sexuality Research and Social Policy*, *8*, 162–182.

Hammack, P. L., & Pilecki, A. (2012). Narrative as a root metaphor for political psychology. *Political Psychology*, *33*(1), 75–103.

Harbus, A. (2002). The medieval concept of self in Anglo-Saxon England. *Self and Identity*, *1*, 77–97.

Helms, J. E. (1984). Toward a theoretical explanation of the effects of race on counseling: A Black and White model. *Counseling Psychologist*, *12*, 153–165.

Helms, J. E. (1995). An update of Helms's White and People of Color racial identity models. In J. G. Ponterotto, J. M. Casas, L. A. Suzuki, & C. M. Alexander (Eds.), *Handbook of multicultural counseling* (pp. 181–198). Newbury Park, CA: Sage.

Helms, J. E., & Carter, R. T. (1990). Development of the White Racial Identity Attitude Inventory. In J. E. Helms (Ed.), *Black and White racial identity: Theory, research, and practice* (pp. 67–80). Westport, CT: Greenwood.

Hermans, H. J. M. (2001). The dialogical self: Toward a theory of personal and cultural positioning. *Culture and Psychology*, *7*(3), 243–281.

Hermans, H. J. M., & Dimaggio, G. (2007). Self, identity, and globalization in times of uncertainty: A dialogical analysis. *Review of General Psychology*, *11*(1), 31–61.

Hornsey, M. J. (2008). Social identity theory and self-categorization theory: A historical review. *Social and Personality Psychology Compass*, *2*(1), 204–222.

Hume, D. (1986). *A treatise of human nature*. New York: Penguin. (Original work published 1739)

Identity. (2013). In *Oxford English dictionary online* (3rd ed.). Retrieved July 26, 2013 from http://www.oed.com.oca.ucsc.edu/view/Entry/91004?redirectedFrom=identity-eid

James, W. (1890). *The principles of psychology*. New York: Henry Holt.

Jensen, L. A., Arnett, J. J., & McKenzie, J. (2011). Globalization and cultural identity. In S. J. Schwartz, K. Luyckx, & V. L. Vignoles (Eds.), *Handbook of identity theory and research* (pp. 285–301). New York: Springer.

Kant, I. (2007). *Critique of pure reason* (M. Weigelt, Trans.). New York: Penguin. (Original work published 1781)

Kett, J. F. (1977). *Rites of passage: Adolescence in America, 1790 to the present*. New York: Basic Books.

Khalidi, R. (1997). *Palestinian identity: The construction of modern national consciousness*. New York: Columbia University Press.

Kinnvall, C. (2004). Globalization and religious nationalism: Self, identity, and the search for ontological security. *Political Psychology, 25*(5), 741–767.

Kroger, J. (2012). The status of identity: Developments in identity status research. In P. K. Kerig, M. S. Schulz, & S. T. Hauser (Eds.), *Adolescence and beyond: Family processes and development* (pp. 64–83). New York: Oxford University Press.

Kroger, J., & Marcia, J. E. (2011). The identity statuses: Origins, meanings, and interpretations. In S. J. Schwartz, K. Luyckx, & V. L. Vignoles (Eds.), *Handbook of identity theory and research* (pp. 31–53). New York: Springer.

Kvale, S. (Ed.). (1992). *Psychology and postmodernism*. Thousand Oaks, CA: Sage.

Leary, M. R., & Tangney, J. P. (Eds.). (2012). *Handbook of self and identity* (2nd ed.). New York: Guilford.

Locke, J. (1998). *An essay concerning human understanding* (2nd ed.). New York: Penguin. (Original work published 1694)

Luyckx, K., Goossens, L., & Soenens, B. (2006). A developmental contextual perspective on identity construction in emerging adulthood: Change dynamics in commitment formation and commitment evaluation. *Developmental Psychology, 42*, 366–380.

Luyckx, K., Goossens, L., Soenens, B., & Beyers, W. (2006). Unpacking commitment and exploration: Preliminary validation of an integrative model of late adolescent identity formation. *Journal of Adolescence, 29*, 361–378.

Luyckx, K., Goossens, L., Soenens, B., Beyers, W., & Vansteenkiste, M. (2005). Identity statuses based upon four rather than two identity dimensions: Extending and refining Marcia's paradigm. *Journal of Youth and Adolescence, 34*, 605–618.

Lyotard, J. (1984). *The postmodern condition: A report on knowledge* (G. Bennington & B. Massumi, Trans.). Minneapolis: University of Minnesota.

Marcia, J. E. (1966). Development and validation of ego-identity status. *Journal of Personality and Social Psychology, 3*(5), 551–558.

Marcia, J. E. (1967). Ego identity status: Relationship to change in self-esteem, "general maladjustment," and authoritarianism. *Journal of Personality, 35*, 118–133.

McAdams, D. P. (1988). *Power, intimacy, and the life story: Personological inquiries into identity*. New York: Guilford.

McAdams, D. P. (1990). Unity and purpose in human lives: The emergence of identity as a life story. In A. I. Rabin, R. A. Zucker, R. A. Emmons, & S. Frank (Eds.), *Studying persons and lives* (pp. 148–200). New York: Springer.

McAdams, D. P. (1995). What do we know when we know a person? *Journal of Personality, 63*(3), 365–396.

McAdams, D. P. (1996). Personality, modernity, and the storied self: A contemporary framework for studying persons. *Psychological Inquiry, 7*(4), 295–321.

McAdams, D. P. (1997). The case for unity in the (post)modern self: A modest proposal. In R. D. Ashmore & L. Jussim (Eds.), *Self and identity: Fundamental issues* (pp. 46–80). New York: Oxford University Press.

McAdams, D. P. (2001). The psychology of life stories. *Review of General Psychology, 5*, 100–122.

McAdams, D. P. (2006). *The redemptive self: Stories Americans live by*. New York: Oxford University Press.

McAdams, D. P. (2008). Personal narratives and the life story. In O. P. John, R. W. Robins, & L. A. Pervin (Eds.), *Handbook of personality: Theory and research* (3rd ed., pp. 242–262). New York: Guilford.

McAdams, D. P. (2013). The psychological self as actor, agent, and author. *Perspectives on Psychological Science, 8*, 272–295.

McAdams, D. P., & Cox, K. S. (2010). Self and identity across the lifespan. In M. E. Lamb, A. M. Freund, & R. M. Lerner (Eds.), *Handbook of life-span development, Vol. 2: Social and emotional development* (pp. 158–207). Hoboken, NJ: Wiley.

McAdams, D. P., Diamond, A., de St. Aubin, E., & Mansfield, E. D. (1997). Stories of commitment: The psychosocial construction of generative lives. *Journal of Personality and Social Psychology, 72*, 678–694.

McAdams, D. P., & Pals, J. L. (2006). A new Big Five: Fundamental principles for an integrative science of personality. *American Psychologist, 61*(3), 204–217.

McCall, G. J., & Simmons, J. L. (1966). *Identities and interactions: An examination of human associations in everyday life*. New York: Free Press.

McLean, K. C. (2005). Late adolescent identity development: Narrative meaning making and memory telling. *Developmental Psychology, 41*(4), 683–691.

McLean, K. C. (2008). The emergence of narrative identity. *Social and Personality Psychology Compass, 2*(4), 1685–1702.

McLean, K. C., & Pasupathi, M. (2012). Processes of identity development: Where I am and how I got there. *Identity: An International Journal of Theory and Research, 12*, 8–28.

McLean, K. C., Pasupathi, M., & Pals, J. L. (2007). Selves creating stories creating selves: A process model of self-development. *Personality and Social Psychology Review, 11*(3), 262–278.

Mead, G. H. (1934). *Mind, self and society*. Chicago: University of Chicago Press.

Mead, M. (1928). *Coming of age in Samoa*. New York: Harper.

Meeus, W. (2011). The study of adolescent identity formation 2000–2010: A review of longitudinal research. *Journal of Research on Adolescence, 21*(1), 75–94.

Memmi, A. (1965). *The colonizer and the colonized*. Boston: Beacon.

Memmi, A. (2000). *Racism* (S. Martinot, Trans.). Minneapolis: University of Minnesota Press.

Mohanty, C. T. (2010). Social justice and the politics of identity. In M. Wetherell & C. T. Mohanty (Eds.), *The SAGE handbook of identities* (pp. 529–540). Thousand Oaks, CA: Sage.

Moshman, D. (2007). Social identity and its discontents. *Journal of Applied Developmental Psychology, 28*, 184–187.

Nelson, K. (2003). Self and social functions: Individual autobiographical memory and collective narrative. *Memory, 11*(2), 125–136.

Nelson, K., & Fivush, R. (2004). The emergence of autobiographical memory: A social cultural developmental theory. *Psychological Review, 111*(2), 486–511.

Owens, T. J. (2006). Self and identity. In J. Delameter (Ed.), *Handbook of social psychology* (pp. 205–232). New York: Springer.

Parham, T. A. (1989). Cycles of psychological nigrescence. *Counseling Psychologist, 17*, 187–226.

Pasupathi, M. (2001). The social construction of the personal past and its implications for adult development. *Psychological Bulletin, 127*, 651–672.

Pasupathi, M., Mansour, E., & Brubaker, J. R. (2007). Developing a life story: Constructing relations between self and experience in autobiographical narratives. *Human Development, 50*, 85–110.

Phinney, J. S. (1989). Stages of ethnic identity development in minority group adolescents. *Journal of Early Adolescence, 9*, 34–49.

Phinney, J. S. (1992). The Multigroup Ethnic Identity Measure: A new scale for use with diverse groups. *Journal of Adolescent Research, 7*(2), 156–176.

Phinney, J. S., & Ong, A. D. (2007). Conceptualization and measurement of ethnic identity: Current status and future directions. *Journal of Counseling Psychology, 54*(3), 271–281.

Polkinghorne, D. (1988). *Narrative knowing and the human sciences*. Albany, NY: State University of New York Press.

Quintana, S. (2007). Racial and ethnic identity: Developmental perspectives and research. *Journal of Counseling Psychology, 54*, 259–270.

Reicher, S. (2004). The context of social identity: Domination, resistance, and change. *Political Psychology, 25*(6), 921–945.

Ricoeur, P. (1984). *Time and narrative, vol. 1* (K. McLaughlin & D. Pellauer, Trans.). Chicago: University of Chicago Press.

Said, E. W. (1978). *Orientalism*. New York: Vintage.

Sampson, E. E. (1993). Identity politics: Challenges to psychology's understanding. *American Psychologist, 48*(12), 1219–1230.

Sartre, J. (1948). *Anti-Semite and Jew: An exploration of the etiology of hate*. New York: Schocken.

Sarup, M. (1996). *Identity, culture and the postmodern world*. Athens: University of Georgia Press.

Schachter, E. P. (2004). Identity configurations: A new perspective on identity formation in contemporary society. *Journal of Personality, 72*(1), 167–200.

Schachter, E. P. (2005). Context and identity formation: A theoretical analysis and a case study. *Journal of Adolescent Research, 20*(3), 375–395.

Schwartz, S. J. (2001). The evolution of Eriksonian and neo-Eriksonian identity theory and research: A review and integration. *Identity: An International Journal of Theory and Research, 1*(1), 7–58.

Schwartz, S. J., Luyckx, K., & Vignoles, V. L. (Eds.). (2011). *Handbook of identity theory and research*. New York: Springer.

Sellers, R. M., Rowley, S. A. J., Chavous, T. M., Shelton, J. N., & Smith, M. A. (1997). Multidimensional Inventory of Black Identity: A preliminary investigation of reliability and construct validity. *Journal of Personality and Social Psychology, 73*(4), 805–815.

Sellers, R. M., Smith, M. A., Shelton, J. N., Rowley, S. A. J., & Chavous, T. M. (1998). Multidimensional model of racial identity: A reconceptualization of African American racial identity. *Personality and Social Psychology Review, 2*(1), 18–39.

Sen, A. (2006). *Identity and violence: The illusion of destiny*. New York: Norton.

Serpe, R. T., & Stryker, S. (2011). The symbolic interactionist perspective and identity theory. In S. J. Schwartz, K. Luyckx, & V. L. Vignoles (Eds.), *Handbook of identity theory and research* (pp. 225–248). New York: Springer.

Sherif, M. (1958). Superordinate goals in the reduction of intergroup conflict. *American Journal of Sociology, 63*(4), 349–356.

Smith, M. B. (1994). Selfhood at risk: Postmodern perils and the perils of postmodernism. *American Psychologist, 49*(5), 405–411.

Smith, W. D. (1980). The Black self-concept: Some historical and theoretical reflections. *Journal of Black Studies, 10*(3), 355–366.

Sneed, J. R., Schwartz, S. J., & Cross, W. E. (2006). A multicultural critique of identity status theory and research: A call for integration. *Identity: An International Journal of Theory and Research, 6*(1), 61–84.

Spears, R. (2011). Group identities: The social identity perspective. In S. J. Schwartz, K. Luyckx, & V. L. Vignoles (Eds.), *Handbook of identity theory and research* (pp. 201–224). New York: Springer.

Stryker, S. (1968). Identity salience and role performance: The relevance of symbolic interaction theory for family research. *Journal of Marriage and the Family, 30*, 558–564.

Stryker, S. (1980). *Symbolic interactionism: A social structural version*. Menlo Park, CA: Benjamin/Cummings.

Stryker, S. (2007). Identity theory and personality theory: Mutual relevance. *Journal of Personality, 75*(6), 1083–1102.

Stryker, S. (2008). From Mead to a structural symbolic interactionism and beyond. *Annual Review of Sociology, 34*, 15–31.

Stryker, S., & Serpe, R. T. (1994). Identity salience and psychological centrality: Equivalent, overlapping, or complementary concepts? *Social Psychology Quarterly, 57*(1), 16–35.

Syed, M., & Azmitia, M. (2008). A narrative approach to ethnic identity in emerging adulthood: Bringing life to the identity status model. *Developmental Psychology, 44*(4), 1012–1027.

Syed, M., & Azmitia, M. (2010). Narrative and ethnic identity exploration: A longitudinal account of emerging adults' ethnicity-related experiences. *Developmental Psychology, 46*(1), 208–219.

Tajfel, H. (1970). Experiments in intergroup discrimination. *Scientific American, 223*(5), 96–102.

Tajfel, H. (Ed.). (1978). *Differentiation between social groups: Studies in the social psychology of intergroup relations*. New York: Academic Press.

Tajfel, H. (1981). *Human groups and social categories: Studies in social psychology*. Cambridge, UK: Cambridge University Press.

Tajfel, H. (Ed.). (1982). *Social identity and intergroup relations*. Cambridge, UK: Cambridge University Press.

Tajfel, H., & Turner, J. (1979). An integrative theory of intergroup conflict. In W. G. Austin & S. Worchel (Eds.), *The social psychology of intergroup relations* (pp. 33–47). Monterey, CA: Brooks/Cole.

Tajfel, H., & Turner, J. (1986). The social identity theory of intergroup behavior. In S. Worchel & W. Austin (Eds.), *Psychology of intergroup relations* (pp. 7–24). Chicago: Nelson-Hall.

Tappan, M. B. (1997). Interpretive psychology: Stories, circles, and understanding lived experience. *Journal of Social Issues, 53*(4), 645–656.

Taylor, C. (1989). *Sources of the self: The making of the modern identity*. Cambridge, MA: Harvard University Press.

Taylor, C. (1994). *Multiculturalism: Examining the politics of recognition*. Princeton, NJ: Princeton University Press.

Thorne, A. (2000). Personal memory telling and personality development. *Personality and Social Psychology Review, 4*(1), 45–56.

Thorne, A., & McLean, K. C. (2003). Telling traumatic events in adolescence: A study of master narrative positioning. In R. Fivush & C. Haden (Eds.), *Autobiographical memory and the construction of a narrative self* (pp. 169–185). Mahwah, NJ: Erlbaum.

Thorne, A., & Nam, V. (2007). The life story as a community project. *Human Development, 50,* 119–123.

Thorne, A., & Nam, V. (2009). The storied construction of personality. In P. Corr & G. Matthews (Eds.), *Cambridge handbook of personality* (pp. 491–505). New York: Cambridge University Press.

Turner, J. C., Hogg, M. A., Oakes, P. J., Reicher, S. D., & Wetherell, M. S. (1987). *Rediscovering the social group: A self-categorization theory.* Oxford: Blackwell.

Verkuyten, M. (2006). Multicultural recognition and ethnic minority rights: A social identity perspective. *European Review of Social Psychology, 17*(1), 148–184.

Vygotsky, L. S. (1978). *Mind in society: The development of higher psychological processes.* Cambridge, MA: Harvard University Press.

Wallerstein, I. (2001). *Unthinking social science: The limits of nineteenth-century paradigms* (2nd ed.). Philadelphia, PA: Temple University Press.

Warnke, G. (2008). *After identity: Rethinking race, sex, and gender.* New York: Cambridge University Press.

Waterman, A. S. (1988). Identity status theory and Erikson's theory: Communalities and differences. *Developmental Review, 8*(2), 185–208.

Waterman, A. S. (1999). Identity, the identity statuses, and identity status development: A contemporary statement. *Developmental Review, 19*(4), 591–621.

Wetherell, M., & Mohanty, C. T. (Eds.). (2010). *The SAGE handbook of identities.* Thousand Oaks, CA: Sage.

PART 1

Debates: Identity Development Across the Lifespan

CHAPTER 3

Gendered Narrative Voices: Sociocultural and Feminist Approaches to Emerging Identity in Childhood and Adolescence

Robyn Fivush *and* Widaad Zaman

Abstract

This chapter develops a sociocultural and feminist theoretical framework for exploring the process of constructing a gendered narrative identity within family reminiscing from preschool through adolescence. Families that engage in more elaborated and emotionally expressive reminiscing have children who provide more elaborated and emotionally expressive narratives of self across development. Moreover, mothers are more elaborative and emotionally expressive when reminiscing than fathers, and parents are more elaborative and emotionally expressive when reminiscing with daughters than sons. Increasingly across development, girls provide more elaborative and emotionally expressive personal narratives than boys. Gender is also expressed in models of narrative identity, such as the intergenerational stories that parents tell their children about their own childhoods. Intergenerational narratives about mothers are more elaborative and emotionally expressive than those about fathers. Intriguingly, relations between personal and intergenerational narratives and emerging self-concept and identity suggest that girls are situating their identity within family stories more so than boys.

Key Words: autobiographical memory, narrative, gender, reminiscing, self, identity, sociocultural theory, feminist theory, intergenerational narratives

In response to a request to talk about the best thing that ever happened to her, a 16-year-old girl responded with a narrative about her first day in her new high school:

Well, um I remember thinking, with all my friends, like how weird it would be 'cause we were just eighth graders like at the top of the school and now we were going to the bottom and we thought it was going to be so scary. And um I had really never been inside the school except for the um registration day and then the first day of school it was... I mean I was... I was so nervous, and you know, I picked out my outfit like two days before. It was all ready and um my dad picked up one of my best friends at the time and we... we went together and he dropped us off like across the street from the school. I don't know why. So we had to walk into the school on the senior hallway and we had no idea where we were. And it was just fun because like it was all my friends and we were all happy together. Like even though I hated going to class and it was just fun because everyone was together and we were in high school. It was a huge deal to me at the time. (Chuckles) That's pretty much it.

In this short narrative about her first day in her new school, this adolescent expresses much more than the events of the day; she describes her innermost thoughts and feelings, her relationships with peers and parents, the excitement and anxiety, essentially painting a picture of who she is and her place in the world. Indeed, in these everyday stories that all of us tell all the time, over the dinner table, over the phone, and over the internet, we create a sense of our selves through sharing our personal experiences with others. These personal narratives both embody and create identity (McAdams, 2001; McLean, Pasupathi, & Pals, 2007). It is through the very act of sharing ourselves with others through our stories that we construct a sense of self (Fivush, 2008).

In this chapter, we examine the social construction of narrative identity as it emerges within the process of family reminiscing. We argue that individual identity is constructed within sociocultural narrative interactions that foreground particular ways of being in the world and background others. Identity as a process has its roots early in development, as parents and children co-construct narratives of personal experience that facilitate the child's nascent understanding of self. These early understandings are not yet coherently organized into a sense of identity that is consistent and coherent across time, but they reflect the beginning understanding of a sense of subjective perspective, an understanding that one has a unique perspective on one's own experiences (Fivush & Nelson, 2006, and Kroger, this volume). From this early foundation of a subjective self, children begin to construct a more continuous sense of self across time, a sense of self-continuity that provides the basis for an enduring sense of identity as formed in adolescence (Erikson, 1968; Kroger, this volume, McAdams, 1992). We further argue that the process of creating a continuous self is, at heart, a narrative process, and thus identity is at core the story we tell about ourselves, constructed and reconstructed in countless social narrative interactions (McAdams, 1992).

We review research conducted over the past 20 years that demonstrates that the ways in which families help preschoolers and preadolescents to understand and narrate their experiences is a critical site for the emergence of a sense of self and identity. We show the early emergence of self understanding within these parent-preschool reminiscing contexts, how this process is both internalized across childhood and adolescence, and how it continues to be forged within family reminiscing as adolescents begin to construct a more continuous sense of self across time. Moreover, this process is gendered in ways that underscore the sociocultural construction of identity and how social interactions are internalized by individuals in creating their own sense of self. To foreshadow, we argue that gender itself is a process. Following from the theoretical work of Deaux and Major (1987), we argue that gender is enacted in particular social contexts in which gender becomes a salient aspect of identity. Importantly, this conceptualization of gender focuses on the ways in which gender is activated and performed in particular social contexts in order to achieve particular goals, and we argue that reminiscing is just such a context. Within reminiscing contexts, in which individuals construct self through narrative interactions, certain aspects of self are highlighted, or "voiced," and thus become an integral part of individual identity.

We note from the outset that gender is a complex multifaceted construct. Perhaps more than any other social category, gender encompasses biological and culturally constructed ways of being in the world (Owen-Blakemore, Berenbaum, & Liben, 2009). Whereas biological sex may confer some differences in physical, cognitive, and social domains (Halpern, 2000), cultures build and expand on these differences in ways that often lead to wide variability both between and within genders in construal of self and other (Gergen, 2001; Gilligan, 1982; Golombok & Fivush, 1994). Moreover, gender continues to be a critical social category, in that, even decades after the second wave of the women's movement, it is still associated with strong stereotypes about roles, behaviors, and traits (Prentice & Carranza, 2002). Framing our arguments within sociocultural and feminist theories, we argue that identity more broadly, and gender identity more specifically, is a fluid and dynamic process of self-understanding, constructed within socially mediated interactions in ways that lead to particular gendered expressions of self through narrative. In the very act of narrating, we create gendered selves.

We first place our arguments in a theoretical framework stemming from sociocultural and feminist theories and discuss more specifically how these theories provide a lens onto the process of constructing a gendered narrative identity. With this as a framework, we provide a review of how gender is constructed in socially mediated narratives of self and other at two critical developmental time points. First, we discuss the preschool years, when autobiographical memory emerges. We then turn to adolescence, a key developmental period for the construction of a healthy adult identity (Erikson, 1968; Kroger, 1996; McLean & Pasupathi, 2010). We show how family reminiscing is critical in emerging self and identity and how this is internalized across development in the narratives that children and adolescents tell about their own personal experience. We further argue that the sociocultural construction of identity extends beyond self to include familial history and that adolescents define themselves at least partially through family stories that situate them within larger cultural frameworks. In particular, we argue that intergenerational narratives, stories adolescents know about their families, especially their parents growing up, are a critical means for understanding self (Fivush, Bohanek, & Duke, 2008; Pratt & Fiese, 2004; Zaman & Fivush, 2011). As Kroger argues (this volume) the ways in which the younger generation represents the experiences of the older generations carries the generational future. Thus, these kinds of intergenerational narratives provide frameworks and models for adolescents facing the challenge of understanding who they are and who they should be within complex social worlds.

Theoretical Frameworks
Sociocultural Theory

Stemming from Vygotsky's (1978) sociocultural theory of development, Nelson and Fivush (2004) presented a sociocultural model of the development of autobiographical memory and narrative that posits that children learn the forms and functions of autobiographical memory through parentally structured interactions. Vygotsky posited that development is a process whereby children are drawn into activities that allow them to learn the critical skills they will need to be competent members of their culture. A good example is literacy. In industrialized cultures, literacy is a necessary skill. In these cultures, well before infants can understand the meaning of these signs and symbols, they are surrounded by the forms of literacy: letters and numbers on crib mobiles and refrigerator magnets, in picture books and on clothing, alphabet songs and rhymes. Being embedded in culturally saturated interactions with these symbols both provides familiarity and informs the developing child of the importance of these forms. As children get older, they are drawn more and more into activities in which they participate and learn about literacy.

Autobiographical narratives are similarly a critical sociocultural skill, perhaps especially in industrialized cultures (McAdams, 1992; Nelson, 2003). In industrialized cultures, families are more likely to move multiple times for education or work, are more likely to live far apart from other family members, and thus need to create new communities with shared understandings. Whether it is a college entrance essay, a job interview, or meeting a potential romantic partner, individuals must be able to provide a coherent account of who they are through their autobiography. Children are drawn into learning these skills very early in development. Preschoolers are asked to tell Mommy what happened at daycare and tell Daddy about the visit to Grandma; school-aged children are expected to "show and share" special objects and outings, describing their family weekend and summer adventures, and, by middle childhood, children are expected to be able to write their autobiography. Thus, it is through the process of narrative interaction in constructing stories of personal experiences that children learn the forms and functions of autobiography. We note that this is very much a cultured process (Wang & Ross, 2007), and that, indeed, as argued by Arnett (this volume) the "crisis" of identity may be a very modern phenomenon.

THE ROLE OF NARRATIVE

Obviously, language and narrative are critical in this development. From a Vygotskian perspective, language is the prototypical cultural tool in that it is through language that children internalize the social and cultural world (Nelson, 2006). Language does not determine thought, but language helps shape thought in particular ways that facilitate meaning-making. Specific to narrative, language modulates memories of events by moving beyond descriptions of external actions to include what Bruner (1990) has called the "landscape of consciousness." By including the inner workings of mind, thoughts, and emotions; explication of intentions and motivations; and the consequences of actions for self and other, narratives move beyond a simple chronology of what happened to describe human encounters that are significant and meaningful. Autobiographical narratives afford a sense of self by linking past, present, and future together, in a way that creates a narrative identity of one's life as continuous and whole, set against the backdrop of numerous discrete experiences (Habermas & Bluck, 2000; McAdams, 1992; Ricoeur, 1991). Thus, our self is greatly defined by the way in which we remember and reconstruct our past, and creating a narrative of the past simultaneously creates a narrative of the self (Fivush, Habermas, Waters, & Zaman, 2010; Habermas & Bluck, 2000; McAdams 2001; McLean et al., 2007).

The ability to construct subjective, reflective narratives about self develops gradually across childhood and adolescence, constructed within socially mediated narrative interactions culminating in the development of a narrative identity. It is elaborated and evaluative narratives that shape self (McLean et al., 2007), and children learn these narrative forms through participating in adult-structured narrative interactions. Moreover, the way in which language helps to shape how we understand our experiences further suggests that socially mediated narratives allow for certain experiences to be voiced and others silenced, an idea that stems from feminist theories.

Feminist Theories of Voice and Silence

Although there are many flavors of feminist theory (Rosser & Miller, 2000), these theories share several basic assumptions. First, knowledge is never completely objective in the sense that it is always known by an individual in some context. This does not mean that we cannot approach objectivity or accuracy, only that any one individual perspective will always be contextualized. Objectivity is thus best obtained when multiple perspectives are considered and coordinated (Bordo, 1990; Code, 1993). Second, and following from this first assumption, knowledge is dynamic. Depending on the context in which it is used, different aspects of knowledge will be brought to bear and coordinated with other perspectives in different ways, depending on the interactants and their goals. The question is, who knows for what purpose? The formulation that knowledge is particularized in specific contexts leads to the concept of voice, that certain aspects of knowledge will be articulated, and thus, by definition, some aspects will be silenced. The very act of stating one aspect of or perspective on an event, by definition, means that some other aspect or perspective will not be voiced. This idea clearly resonates with sociocultural approaches that privilege language as a tool for the social construction of shared knowledge.

Fivush (2004; 2010) has articulated a model of the development of autobiographical memory based on an integration of sociocultural and feminist theories. She posits that, through parentally structured reminiscing, parents privilege some aspects of children's experiences through explicitly elaborating on certain aspects and/or validating the child's perspective in ways that allow for narrative voice. In contrast, parents can silence other aspects or interpretations of events through lack of elaboration and/or validation of the child's perspective. In this way, some children and/or some aspects of experience are given voice and others are silenced. Voice confers power (Belenky, Clinchey, Goldberger, & Tarule, 1986; Griscom, 1992). For personal narratives, the power to tell one's own story, to author one's own autobiography (Brison, 2002; Gergen, 2001), provides the basis for a secure sense of identity (Fivush et al., 2008). Parents who help their children develop their own autobiographical voice thus help their children achieve a healthy identity.

NARRATIVE VOICE AND GENDER IDENTITY

The concept of voice and silence resonates with sociocultural approaches that posit that the process of creating an identity involves the internalization of cultural activities and values through participation in structured interactions that highlight the importance of some activities over others. If identity is at least partly constructed through narrative, then the ways in which parentally structured narrative interactions help young children to learn particular narrative voices will influence both the development of personal narratives and identity. In a very real sense, it is the process of engaging in co-constructing narratives within social interactions that provides a base for the internalization of a narrative identity.

We argue that this process is gendered. There is substantial evidence that, as adults, females narrate longer, more elaborated, and more emotionally expressive narratives about their past experiences than do males and that these narratives are more focused on connection to others and relationships, whereas males' narratives tend to be more focused on themes of autonomy and independence (Bauer, Stennes, & Haight, 2003; Cross & Madsen, 1997; Fivush & Buckner, 2003; Niedzwienska, 2003; Thorne & McLean, 2002). These differences reflect larger stereotypes of gendered selves that posit females to be more emotional, relational, and connected and males to be more autonomous and independent (Chodorow, 1978; Gilligan, 1982). Importantly, there is not a great deal of evidence for essential differences between males and females across contexts and behaviors (see Owen-Blakemore et al., 2009, for a review); rather, gender differences emerge in particular behavioral and relational contexts, especially those contexts that make gender more salient (Deaux & Major, 1987). Thus, gender is best conceptualized as a process by which individuals express particular kinds of selves in particular situations (Fivush, 1998; Fivush & Zaman, in press; Gergen, 2001).

Reminiscing is just such a gendered context. First, overall, females talk more than do males, and they especially talk more about emotions and relationship than do males (Fischer, 2000; Newman, Groom, Handelman, & Pennebaker, 2008). Thus, elaborated emotional reminiscing is an extension of more general gender differences in conversational style. Second, when female friends interact, they are more likely than males to spend time talking together, especially about the events of their day and of their lives, whereas males are more likely to engage in activities together (Aries & Johnson, 1983; Rose & Smith, 2009), again providing more contexts and opportunities for females to engage in, practice, and ultimately come to value reminiscing. By narrating the personal past in more elaborated ways, and especially by focusing on emotions, females are creating personal narratives that allow for greater empathic access to their own past than are males (Fivush & Zaman, in press; Schectman, 2003). It is through connecting previous emotional states and reactions to current emotions that individuals create a sense of a connected self over time: "These are not just experiences that happened to me; this is what they meant then and what they mean now in creating a linked self across time." Further, by focusing on relationships, female narratives more fully embody others in their own personal history thus creating a sense of self as part of a web of interpersonal experiences.

This is not to argue that males do not do this; they do. Rather, it is an argument about frequency, practice, and skill. The argument, stemming from sociocultural theory, is that engaging in these activities allows for practice, thus leading to becoming more skilled. Activities that young children are drawn into both model for them appropriate behavior and provide opportunities for them to practice those behaviors. The more practiced, and the more skilled, the more one comes to value these activities as important (Liben & Bigler, 2002). Essentially, when one engages frequently and deeply in particular types of activities, one comes to value those activities. Thus, integrating across sociocultural and feminist theories, the argument is that females are drawn into more elaborated and emotionally expressive reminiscing than are boys beginning very early in development, both because mothers and fathers model different gendered behaviors and because mothers and fathers elicit different gendered behaviors from girls than boys; through these early experiences, females become more skilled at elaborated emotionally expressive reminiscing than males and therefore come to value this activity to a greater extent. Thus, for females, their personal past is more clearly and frequently voiced than for males, and the expectation is therefore that females are more embodied in their past as defining self than are males. It is this process that we explicate in the rest of this chapter.

We first describe the early emergence of gendered reminiscing in parent-preschooler narrative interactions. We provide an overview of how mothers and fathers differ from each other when reminiscing with their preschoolers, and we focus on how both mothers and fathers reminisce differently with daughters and with sons. Through participating in these parentally structured gendered reminiscing interactions, children are learning gendered voices. As they develop into adolescents, females and males already demonstrate gendered autobiographies. With adolescence and the motivation to construct a healthy adult identity, the way in which gender is expressed becomes related to adolescent's emerging sense of self and identity, and this is the issue we examine in the subsequent section. We further explore how adolescents define themselves within larger family frames, stories they know about their parents' growing up, or what we have termed intergenerational narratives. We explore how gender is expressed in all three contexts, family reminiscing, personal narratives, and intergenerational narratives. Especially provocative, it is possible that, because females define themselves more in relation to others, for female adolescents, the stories of others provide more powerful models for their own identities than they do for male adolescents. After exploring these questions, we return in the final section to pull together the developmental trajectory of gendered narrative identity across childhood and adolescence.

Parental Reminiscing Style and the Emergence of a Gendered Self

If it is the case that children are initially learning how to tell and how to value reminiscing through participating in co-constructed narrative interactions, then individual differences in how parents structure these narrative interactions with their young children should be related to individual differences in how children come to narrate their own past. If more elaborated narratives focusing on the "landscape of consciousness," the thoughts and feelings of self and others, are speculated to be related to a more elaborated understanding of self, then parents who help their young children to create more elaborative and emotionally expressive narratives about their past experiences should have children who both come to tell more elaborated and emotionally expressive narratives about themselves and to have a more coherent and elaborated sense of self. Moreover, theoretically posited interactions among sociocultural stereotypes, biological inclinations, and ongoing family interactions (see Owen-Blakemore et al., 2009, for a review) would predict that parental reminiscing with daughters would be more elaborative and emotionally expressive than parental reminiscing with sons, leading to girls developing a more elaborated and emotionally expressive narrative self than boys.

Substantial research has confirmed individual differences in maternal reminiscing style, such that some mothers are more highly elaborative and evaluative than other mothers (see Fivush, Haden, & Reese, 2006, and Reese, 2002, for reviews). Fathers also vary along a dimension of elaboration, but there is much less research with fathers (Fivush & Zaman, in press). Mothers who are highly elaborative talk in more detail and create more coherent, evaluative, and explanatory narratives with their children than mothers who are less elaborative. Importantly, mothers are consistent over time in their reminiscing style; mothers who are more highly elaborative with their young preschoolers continue to be more highly elaborative than their less elaborative counterparts as their children grow older. Mothers are also consistent in their reminiscing style across siblings; mothers who are more highly elaborative with one of their children are also more highly elaborative when reminiscing with their other children.

But it is not the case that some mothers simply talk more. Mothers who are highly elaborative during reminiscing are not more talkative when book-reading or during free play or care giving activities (Haden & Fivush, 1996; Hoff-Ginsburg, 1991). Rather, elaborative reminiscing seems to be a conversational strategy specific to the reminiscing context. Indeed, mothers self-report engaging in reminiscing for very specific purposes, including helping their child understand themselves better and to create and maintain emotional bonds with their child (Kulkofsky, Wang, & Koh, 2009). Individual differences in parental reminiscing style indicate that parents are actively engaged in helping their children construct narratives of their personal experiences. Again, this reinforces our arguments about context; reminiscing is a specific context that calls for learning specific skills in order to engage in sharing the past, an activity that may be differentially valued within different families.

Gender Differences in Parent-Preschool Reminiscing

Importantly, there are gender differences in parent-child reminiscing. Mothers differ from fathers in how they reminisce with their children, and both mothers and fathers reminisce differently with daughters as compared to sons. Overall, mothers are more elaborative than fathers with their preschool children while reminiscing about the child's past experiences (Reese, Haden, & Fivush, 1996; Zaman & Fivush, in press). Mothers also employ more emotion words and a greater variety of emotion words than fathers do during reminiscing (Adams, Kuebli, Boyle, & Fivush, 1995; Kuebli, Butler, & Fivush, 1995; Kuebli & Fivush, 1992), and they discuss the causes of emotions with children in greater detail than fathers (Fivush, Brotman, Buckner, & Goodman, 2000).

Parents also reminisce differently with daughters as compared to sons. Both mothers and fathers are more elaborative with their daughters than sons across the preschool years (Reese & Fivush, 1993; Reese, Haden & Fivush, 1996), and mothers of daughters in particular are more elaborative than mothers of sons (Reese & Newcombe, 2007). Both mothers and fathers use more emotion words and a greater variety of emotion words with preschool daughters than sons (Adams et al., 1995; Kuebli et al., 1995; Kuebli & Fivush, 1992), and both discuss sadness in greater detail with daughters than sons, sending the message that sadness is an appropriate emotion for girls to express and dwell on, but not for boys (Adams et al., 1995; Kuebli & Fivush, 1992). With respect to narrative theme, parents discuss the experiences of preschool girls in more social-relational contexts but in more autonomous contexts for boys (Buckner & Fivush, 2000; Fivush et al., 2000).

To illustrate these differences, Table 3.1 presents some excerpts from conversations between mothers and fathers and their 4-year-old daughters or sons. Mothers in these conversations engage in more sophisticated and richer discussions about the past with their young child than do fathers. Both mother-child conversations are saturated with open-ended questions (e.g., "Do you remember why?" "Why did they say that?") and statements that elaborate on the child's independent contributions (e.g., "You're right. And we didn't wanna go to Fernbank if you were having an accident." "Oh, that's right, at lunch time."). When mothers do ask directive questions, they are often in the service of maintaining and extending the conversation when the child fails to remember the events (e.g., "And do you know what else there was?... What did Daddy really want to do yesterday?"). On the other hand, both fathers consistently ask yes-no, leading, and directive questions (e.g., "Did that make you sad

Table 3.1 Parent-child conversation excerpts by gender of parent and child

Mother-daughter	Mother: What were you telling me… that your only friend was Christy? Child: Yeah. Mother: And that none of the other girls liked you? Why… why do you think that is? What happened? Child: Because they said they didn't want me in class anymore. Mother: Why did they say that? Child: Because I spilled Ali's milk. Mother: Oh, that's right… at lunchtime? Child: No. Breakfast. Mother: Oh, at breakfast. That's right. Well, that wasn't a very nice thing to say, huh? How did that make you feel? Child: Sad.
Mother-son	Mother: Who was keeping you? Child: Elan. Mother: Elan kinda overslept on his nap, right? Child: Yeah. Mother: And by the time he got up it was late, so we didn't have time to really get lunch before. Child: And I had an accident. Mother: You had an accident. You're right. And we didn't wanna go to Fernbank if you were having an accident. And do you know what else there was? Child: What? Mother: What'd Daddy really want to do yesterday? Child: I don't know. Mother: What did Daddy do all afternoon? Child: Daddy wanted to watch football. Mother: Daddy really wanted to watch the football game didn't Daddy? (Chuckles) Was it kinda fun watchin' with Daddy? Child: Yeah. Mother: Yeah, but it made us sad that we didn't get to go.
Father-daughter	Father: Do you remember the last time you were very sad? This morning you said you were sad, remember? Because of one of your dolls. What happened to one of your dolls this morning that made you sad? Child: Baby Alice. Father: What about baby Alice? Child: It scared me because her neck was open. Father: Her neck broke, right. What happened? What were you doing with her that her neck broke? Child: Ian was holding her in the store, he was holding her and he, and he decided to throw her. Father: He threw baby Alice and that's what broke her neck so her head was not on? What did we do then? Child: We fixed her neck. Father: We did? Did that make you sad that she lost her neck? Child: Yes.
Father-son	Father: What about sometime when you're sad? Child: (Unintelligible) Father: When xxxx bites you, you're sad? Child: Yes. Father: What else makes you sad? Child: I dunno. Father: What about when you have to leave your friends? Does that make you sad? Child: Yes. Father: But then you get to see your friends again. Does that make you happy? Child: Yes. Father: So your friends make you happy and sad? Child: Yes. Father: What about when you go to bed? Are you sad at night when you have to go to bed? Child: Uh huh.

that she lost her neck?" "So your friends make you happy and sad?"), and there is a distinct sense that the father-son conversation is a mere list of events that make the child sad rather than an elaboration of any one specific episode.

Thus, what we see in early parentally structured narrative interactions is that children are participating in gendered ways of reminiscing about the personal past. Differences between mothers and fathers model that females are more elaborative and emotionally expressive than males. Differences in how parents structure these interactions with daughters as compared to sons indicates that children are being asked to participate differently in these narrative interactions, with daughters being encouraged to narrate their past in more elaborated and emotionally expressive ways than sons.

Importantly, longitudinal studies confirm that maternal reminiscing style early in the preschool years predicts children's developing autobiographical narratives (there is simply not enough research with fathers to draw any conclusions). Mothers who are more highly elaborative early in development have children who, by the end of the preschool years, are telling more coherent and elaborated narratives of their own personal past (Fivush, 1991; Reese et al., 1993), and mothers who focus more on emotional aspects of experiences when co-constructing narratives with their young preschoolers have children who, 1 to 2 years later, are imbuing their own personal narratives with more emotion (Fivush, 1989; Fivush & Haden, 2005; Haden, Ornstein, Rudeck, & Cameron, 2009; Kuebli et al., 1995). Only one study has extended these longitudinal findings into adolescence. Reese and colleagues found that mothers who were more highly elaborative when their children were preschoolers had 12-year-olds who expressed higher levels of internal state language, including emotion, in their personal narratives (Reese, Yan, Jack, & Hayne, 2010). Although these studies did not explicitly examine gender, we can speculate that because mothers are co-constructing more elaborative and emotionally expressive narratives with their preschool girls—and the more that mothers use this kind of narration, the more their children do—it is highly likely that girls are learning to construct more elaborative emotionally expressive narratives through participating in more highly elaborative emotionally expressive reminiscing with their mothers. Obviously, these links need to be empirically demonstrated in further longitudinal work. But it seems that through both modeling of parents and participation of children, girls are learning that elaborated emotionally expressive personal narratives are voiced in a way that males are not learning. Moreover, both boys and girls are learning that more elaborated emotionally expressive personal narratives are associated with being female as opposed to male.

Parental Reminiscing Style and the Emergence of Self-Understanding

It is quite clear that maternal reminiscing style is a critical factor in children's developing autobiographical skills. The question is whether this also matters for children's developing sense of self. There is some evidence that this is the case. We must be cautious because, at this early age, children are just beginning to develop a coherent or consistent sense of self; it is only in middle childhood that individuals begin to have a fully organized self-concept based mostly on self-descriptions of typical behaviors and some emerging recognition of psychological traits (Harter, 1990), and it is not until adolescence, as discussed later, that individuals develop a sense of identity that involves not just self-description but also values, commitments, and goals (Erikson, 1968). Thus, the question is whether maternal reminiscing style is related to this nascent self-understanding in preschoolers.

Preschool children of more highly elaborative mothers display a more differentiated and coherent nascent self-concept than children of less elaborative mothers (Bird & Reese, 2006; Welch-Ross, Fasig, & Farrar, 1999). More specifically, using a self-concept scale that asks preschoolers to indicate behaviors that do and do not describe them, children of more highly elaborative mothers provide self descriptions that are more coherent across behaviors (i.e., endorsing both "When I get angry, I feel like hitting someone" and "I get mad a lot") and more differentiated between traits (i.e., not endorsing both "I mostly do things that are easy" and "I climb really high things"). In addition, mothers who use more internal state language, which includes discussion of emotions, when reminiscing with their preschoolers have children who endorse a more coherent self-concept (Wang, Doan, & Song, 2010). This research is based on concurrent measures. Moreover, studies linking maternal reminiscing style to child self-concept have not fully examined gender differences in these relations, usually because these studies rely on fairly small samples. Examining developing relations between parental reminiscing styles and child self-concept by both gender of parent and gender of child is an important avenue for future research.

The Emergence of Gendered Personal Narratives

Although the empirical links need further investigation, it does appear that gender differences in parental reminiscing are related to emerging gender differences in children's own personal autobiographies. Girls and boys learn to focus on different aspects of their experiences and self, and, from an early age, they begin to narrate their past in gendered ways. Four-year-old girls tell longer, more emotional personal narratives than do boys (Fivush, Haden, & Adam, 1995). By age 7 years, girls are telling more emotional, social-relational narratives than boys, whereas boys are narrating more autonomously themed autobiographies (Buckner & Fivush, 1998; Fivush et al., 2000). Similar gender patterns continue to persist throughout development. Middle-childhood girls narrate longer, more elaborate positive and negative past experiences than boys, and intriguingly, these gender differences accentuate over time to become more pronounced during adolescence (Pasupathi & Wainryb, 2010). Hence, leading up to adolescence, when identity achievement becomes critical, pervasive gender differences in early parent-child reminiscing and similar and consistent gender differences in early independent autobiographical narratives set the stage for the emergence of a gendered identity.

Adolescence and the Construction of a Gendered Narrative Identity

Erikson (1968) argued that the task of identity development becomes foregrounded during adolescence, when the quest becomes committing to a stable adult identity. With the social and cognitive advances of adolescence, individuals become able to fully construct narratives that express reflection on self and links among life experiences into an overarching story of "me" (Fivush et al., 2008; Habermas & Bluck, 2000; McAdams, 2001). In adolescence, personal narratives begin to take on a richer, more organized form, as single events are connected to create a more coherent story with an overarching theme (Habermas, 2007; McAdams, 2001), and individuals become increasingly able to engage in narrative meaning-making and autobiographical reasoning, in which single events that are meaningful to understanding the self are selected and organized into a story format structured around specific life goals. From this, the beginnings of a life story emerge, allowing adolescents to integrate past identities with current ones to develop a sense of self as continuous and enduring through time (Habermas & Bluck, 2000; McLean & Pratt, 2006; Negele & Habermas, 2010; see also Habermas, this volume; Pasupathi, this volume). Importantly, adolescents who have a more organized life story report higher levels of self-esteem (Reese et al., 2010), and those who engage in more sophisticated meaning-making and create more coherent narratives of their lives are more advanced in their identity development in that they are less likely to be diffused or foreclosed and more likely to report a mature identity (McLean & Pratt, 2006). In general, adolescents higher in identity development also show higher levels of self-esteem (see Kroger, 2003, for a review). Thus, adolescent autobiographical narratives are one of the cornerstones to successful identity exploration and commitment.

Consistent with our frame of sociocultural and feminist theories focusing on the critical role of parentally structured narrative interaction for the emergence of autobiographical narratives and self in the preschool years, we argue that family reminiscing continues to be a critical site for the emergence of a temporally extended narrative identity in adolescence. Over the past several years, we have been examining three aspects of the process of narrative identity in pre- and early adolescents in The Emerging Identity Project (see Fivush, Bohanek, & Marin, 2010; Fivush, Bohanek, & Zaman, 2011 for reviews). More specifically, following directly from the research with parent-preschooler narrative interaction, we have examined the ways in which families reminisce about the shared past as children develop into adolescents. We posit that family narrative interaction will continue to play a role in adolescents' developing personal narratives and that this process will continue to be gendered. Thus, we examine both family reminiscing and adolescent's own personal narratives. We further speculate that, as adolescents enter larger social worlds, stories not just of their own experience, but those of others will begin to play a more important role. In particular, intergenerational narratives, stories adolescents may know about their parents' childhoods, should be critical filters for adolescents to understand both self and other. Intergenerational narratives place the individual in a social context that defines identity across generations; shapes an understanding of how the world does, or should, work; provides a sense of security and resilience that others have weathered the storms of life; and models how the individual can do so as well (Fiese & Bickham, 2004; Fiese, Hooker, Kotary, Schwagler, & Rimmer, 1995; Fivush, Bohanek, & Duke, 2008).

Family Reminiscing in Preadolescence

Our first question centered on how families engage in reminiscing as children enter adolescence. We studied 40 diverse, broadly middle-class, two-parent opposite-gender parent families with a child just entering adolescence, between 10 and 12 years of age. Most of these families had other children as well, but we focused our measures of self on this target child. Although the research was based on that with preschool children, we also wanted to obtain a more spontaneous assessment of family reminiscing, so we asked families to tape record a typical dinnertime conversation when the whole family was chatting around the table, and, from these data, we ascertained the number and types of narratives about past experiences that emerged and how these narratives were structured. We also elicited family reminiscing, asking the family as a whole to sit together and talk about a time that was highly positive for the family and a time that was highly stressful. Thus, in contrast to the preschool data, in these data, it is not a dyadic interaction, but one that involves the whole family. Still, there were remarkable consistencies, both across age and context.

FAMILY NARRATIVE INTERACTION

Looking first at the dinner conversations, narratives emerged quite frequently, an average of about six narratives per family, across a 30-minute dinnertime, so about one narrative every 5 minutes (see Bohanek et al., 2009). The majority of these narratives were stories of the day—what each family member did—but about a third of the stories were family narratives, narratives about the more remote past. Of these, most were the shared family past, stories of past vacations, visiting relatives, and so on, and these stories were just as likely to be initiated by a child as by a parent, suggesting that children are highly engaged and invested in sharing family stories. About half of the families also told at least one intergenerational story over a typical dinner table. These stories were about the experiences of one of the parents when he or she was growing up, and, intriguingly, these stories were also just as likely to be initiated by one of the children as by a parent, indicating that these stories are known and told again and again. Further indication of this is that, once initiated, children contributed as much to the ongoing story as did the parents. This finding was an impetus for a more detailed study of intergenerational narratives that we describe later.

In addition to cataloguing the narratives, we were interested in the process of family storytelling and coded all the narratives in ways similar to the preschool data, examining the number of elaborations and the number of emotions expressed and explained within the story by each family member (Bohanek et al., 2009). Mothers were, overall, more elaborative and emotionally expressive than fathers or children, who did not differ from each other. This held across all narrative types.

Remarkably similar effects were found for the elicited narratives, when families were specifically asked to talk about highly positive and highly negative family experiences (Fivush, Marin, McWilliams, & Bohanek, 2009). Again, mothers were overall more elaborative and more emotionally expressive than fathers. Thus, what we see across spontaneous dinnertime family narrative interactions and elicited family narrative interactions is a continuation of the parental gender differences demonstrated in the preschool data. Mothers are more elaborative and emotionally expressive than fathers.

FAMILY REMINISCING AND GENDERED IDENTITY

Within these family reminiscing contexts, we did not find any differences in how daughters compared to sons interacted. However, there was a hint in these data that family reminiscing may have different consequences for daughters and sons for developing self and identity. When the family was considered holistically, coding for the overall story constructed by all family members together, two types of family styles emerged (Bohanek, Marin, Fivush, & Duke, 2006). Collaborative families engaged in producing a single coherent narrative, in which each family member contributed to the evolving story, with all contributions woven together into a single thread. More individually centered families, in contrast, engaged in a process whereby each family member told his or her part of the story and then the conversation moved to the next family member. Although each family member participated and was listened to, no single coherent story emerged. Intriguingly, daughters in collaborative families showed higher levels of self-esteem, but sons in individually centered families showed higher levels of locus of control, a measure of self-efficacy. These patterns suggest that daughters may benefit from more collaborative family reminiscing that integrates family members into a cohesive unit, leading to a higher sense of self-worth, whereas sons may benefit more from a more independent storytelling style, in which each family member is seen as an independent agent, leading to a higher sense of self-efficacy. Unfortunately, we did not collect any personal narratives from the preadolescents themselves in this study. It was to a consideration of this question that we turned in the next study.

Gendered Identity in Adolescents' Narratives

In a second study in the Emerging Identity Project, we focused on adolescents' narratives. We asked 65 racially diverse, broadly middle-class adolescents, 13 to 16 years old, to narrate highly emotional life events. We also asked the adolescents to complete the Rosenberg self-esteem scale (Rosenberg, 1965) and the Ego Identity Scale (Tan, Kendis, Fine, & Porac, 1977), which provides a continuous measure of where the adolescent is in his or her identity journey from diffused through foreclosed through achieved. Stemming from previous findings, we were particularly interested in if and how we might see gender differences in how girls and boys narrate their own personal experiences as they move into middle adolescence and how these narratives might be related to emerging concepts of self and identity. We were also interested in how adolescents' personal narratives might be situated in larger narratives of family. Thus, we also asked these same adolescents to tell us stories they might know about their parents' childhood. Before we explicate the rationale and findings for this part of the study, we first describe the personal narratives.

Adolescents' narratives about highly positive and negative personal experiences were coded for elaboration and internal state language (see Bohanek & Fivush, 2010, and Fivush, Bohanek, Zaman, & Grapin, 2011, for full details). Elaboration was coded on a 4-point dimensional scale, with 0 representing little to no elaboration and 4 representing high elaboration, defined as narrating multiple actions related to an event that are linked by causal connections, expanded upon with adjectives and adverbs, and include background information, quoted speech, and information about characters' thoughts and feelings. Internal states were defined as specific mentions of both emotions and cognitions. Emotions were captured by use of specific emotion words, both positive (e.g., happy, excited) and negative (e.g., sad, angry), as well as by more general statements reflecting affect, again both positive (e.g., that was the best thing ever) and negative (e.g. that was so hard on me). Cognitions were captured by language referring to thoughts at the time of the event (e.g., I thought I had failed the test; I was not sure if she was my friend). To give a better sense of these narratives, we present positive and negative experiences as narrated by a female and a male in Table 3.2.

Although the positive narrative of the adolescent girl is about an experience of achievement and success, she imbues her narrative with her inner thoughts and feelings about the experience and even embeds her achievement in a relational context, one of being afraid of not making any friends. Interestingly, although the adolescent girl's negative narrative captures the depth of her emotions and thoughts regarding the loss of her pet, she specifically includes the emotional and cognitive perspective of her brother as well, making for a much more extended and elaborated experience. This is in stark contrast to the less elaborate, far less emotional and relational narratives of the adolescent boys, in which the little mention of an emotion, cognition, or another individual occurs primarily in passing.

As shown on Table 3.3, statistical analyses confirmed that girls told more elaborated narratives than boys that included more of every category of internal state language, cognitive words, specific positive and negative emotion words, and more general positive and negative affect, and this effect held for both positive and negative event narratives. These results indicate that early emerging gender differences in parent-child reminiscing are mirrored in adolescents' narratives. That mothers are more elaborative and emotionally expressive than fathers and that both mothers and fathers are more elaborative and emotionally expressive with daughters than with sons resonates with adolescent females telling more elaborative and emotionally expressive narratives than adolescent males.

However, surprisingly, when we examine relations between these narrative dimensions and self-esteem and identity status, there are virtually no relations (however, see Reese et al., 2010, for relations between adolescents' life stories and self-worth). Correlations conducted separately for males and females on positive and negative events showed only one significant correlation, such that girls who told negative narratives with more negative affect had lower self-esteem. Given a total of 32 correlations, with only one achieving significance, we really cannot draw any conclusions. We return to this finding in our conclusions.

Table 3.2 Positive and negative autobiographical narratives of adolescent girls and boys

Female Positive Narrative	When I got accepted into this um SEMA program. It's Science, Engineering, Mathematics and Aerospace Academy. It's sponsored by NASA. I was in the second grade. I was, one out of I think three kids in my school or something like that and it was a random out-of-a-hat thing and I got picked for it and I was so excited (Emotion) and I've been doing it ever since. It's really just like a day camp thing on Saturdays, science based. I was really happy (Emotion). I was going like "Whoa, that's cool" (Affect). And I think (Cognition) it's really fun (Affect), but they only go up to um, I'm not sure what grade they go up to. Well, I remember I was in second grade and my second grade teacher came up to me and asked me if it would be okay if she nominated me for it. And I said, "Oh. Well what is it?" And she told me about it and I thought (Cognition) it was cool (Affect) so she nominated me, but I didn't expect (Cognition) it would happen. I think I was up against another fifth grader and I think maybe a third or fourth grader. And I remember, on the announcements, hearing um my name being called as the one who had gotten accepted into it. They, for some reason, took one person from each school in DeKalb County or something. And it's at Fernbank Science Center and I remember I went there and it was just really fun (Affect). We learned about this stuff; it all ties into space somehow. Like um we like learned about food that the astronauts eat or something. And I remember I went to it and I thought (Cognition) it was so cool (Affect) even though it did take up like the whole morning of my Saturdays, but it was almost…it was like completely worth it (Affect). And I took it always in the winter and then I took it once in the summer and I didn't like it (Emotion) in the summer. But, from then on, I took it in the winter and only this past year have I started taking it in the fall. I was so happy (Emotion) and I was so proud (Emotion) of myself for actually beating those two older students for it. And I remember being so scared (Emotion) because we went to the planetarium and then they herded us out into our classrooms. I was so scared (Emotion) that I wouldn't make any friends or anything and I made one friend and that was really cool (Affect) and it was just so fun (Affect). And the kids in there were really nice. Some of the boys were a little xxxx. Other than that, they were really nice. It was just so cool (Affect). And then, also, that my teacher would nominate me for that, I felt really good (Emotion) that I'd like accomplished something." Elaboration: 3
Male Positive Narrative	Uh my dad, this summer, bought Jet Skis for our lake house and uh every time we went up to our lake house we uh ride them. And I can remember (Cognition) this one time that um my friend Sean and I uh were up there and there was a big cruise boat and it put off this wake about uh three to four feet high and it was really big and we hit it straight on and…and we went really like about four feet of air or five and there was a wave right in front of it and we hit it dead on and we both flew off the uh back of the Jet Ski 'cause it was an impact. And that's all I have to say about that. Elaboration: 1
Female Negative Narrative	He was our first dog my brother and I have ever had and he…we've had 'im since he was like a puppy and it was so short, his lifespan, like it really hurt (Emotion) Ben a lot 'cause he…he wanted (Cognition) the dog in the first place. So that kinda did a chain reaction on all of us. Um so like he…he had already shown like he was mister lovable little dog and uh he really strengthened our family in showin' how much fun (Affect) we could have. And then um we had a feeling (Cognition) someone got to 'im in our backyard. He must have been just barkin' at 'im and…and they must have terrorized 'im or something and he started getting really mean and he almost got a couple of people that came to our door and stuff. And so that was really kinda stressin' us out (Affect) and my mom uh made the decision (Cognition) that we couldn't deal if he bit someone and that wouldn't be good or anything. So it would just mess it all up. Uh, he was a year and a half old when we had to put 'im down and that was really sad (Emotion) 'cause it was our first dog and everything and so it affected us a lot (Affect). (Chuckles) But we kinda got over it (Affect) since we have Spanky now and he's so lovable. Elaboration: 3
Male Negative Narrative	I wanted (Cognition) to get a paintball gun. I've been trying to get one for a really long time and then I made a "C," which was so close to being a "B" 'cause it was 79 and then I couldn't get it. Well, I was trying really hard because I wanted (Cognition) it, but then at the last, like towards the end of the nine weeks, I didn't turn in a grade, which made it go really low now. So it was like an 85 or 86, but since I didn't turn that in it lowered it a lot. And I had a good grade everywhere else but that in the end. So it made me really mad (Emotion), yeah. And I still didn't get it even though it was a 79. So I didn't get it. That made me really mad (Emotion). Elaboration: 2

Table 3.3 Means (and standard deviations) for variables in adolescents' personal stories

	Negative Narratives		Positive Narratives	
	Girls	Boys	Girls	Boys
Elaboration	1.81 (.85)	1.37 (.61)	1.84 (.77)	1.34 (.66)
Cognitive Words	3.48 (3.72)	2.03 (2.45)	4.11 (4.42)	2.05 (2.55)
Positive Affect	1.39 (1.73)	.34 (.60)	3.94 (3.74)	1.89 (1.43)
Positive Emotion	.69 (1.05)	.10 (.24)	1.55 (1.59)	.79 (.80)
Negative Affect	4.29 (5.86)	2.15 (2.64)	2.24 (1.60)	1.29 (.96)
Negative Emotion	3.02 (3.96)	1.69 (2.31)	2.05 (2.66)	1.02 (1.81)

Intergenerational Narratives as Frames for Gendered Identity

Family reminiscing provides frames for adolescent narrative identity development in at least two ways. First, the very process of engaging in narrative construction within the family helps adolescents learn new forms and functions of narrating, and this family reminiscing context may directly benefit the adolescents' sense of family belonging and identity, thus facilitating higher levels of self-esteem and identity development. In addition, family stories can provide frames for adolescents to understand their own experiences and make sense of their own identities. This process expands family reminiscing beyond experiences of the self to include family stories of generations past that provide narrative models of ways of being in the world.

THEORIZING INTERGENERATIONAL NARRATIVES

There is sparse research on intergenerational stories. We do know that parents begin telling their children narratives of their own childhood experiences long before children attain the language to fully engage in these conversations (Fiese et al., 1995). These kinds of narratives, although not personally experienced, may still provide a powerful frame from which to understand personal experiences, particularly when those stories involve the parents with whom children identify (Fivush et al., 2008). The types and structure of stories that parents tell their children about their own experiences may become the model for children's organization of their own experiences into story form. For example, mothers who narrate more dramatic and negative personal experiences to their children have children who tell their own personal experiences with an emphasis on negative content and dramatic expressions (see Miller, Cho, & Bracey, 2005, for a review). Thus, the stories that parents narrate about their own experiences may serve as an example of adult identity for adolescents to emulate when constructing their own identity.

Furthermore, intergenerational narratives from parents to children are often gendered, in that fathers narrate childhood stories with stronger themes of autonomy and achievement than mothers, whereas mothers narrate childhood stories with stronger social and affiliation themes (Fiese & Bickham, 2004; Fiese & Skillman, 2000). In addition, just like they do during reminiscing, parents differentiate between daughters and sons in the types of intergenerational narratives they tell. Both mothers and fathers focus their childhood narratives on social events more with girls than with boys, but sons are more likely to hear stories with themes of autonomy than are daughters (Buckner & Fivush, 2000; Fiese & Skillman, 2000).

To date, however, no study had examined how adolescents themselves internalize these stories and use them to help frame their own identities. We were somewhat surprised in our previous study that stories of the intergenerational past emerged as a reasonably frequent occurrence in a typical family dinnertime conversation. As described, about half of the families studied told at least one such story during a 30-minute or so dinnertime conversation. We became intrigued by these kinds of stories. Do most families tell intergenerational narratives? And, how do adolescents understand these stories? Might these stories help adolescents in forming their own personal stories and identities? Thus, in the Emerging Identity Project, we asked the adolescents to tell us two stories they knew about their mother when she was growing up and two stories about their father (all narratives were counterbalanced).

GENDER DIFFERENCES IN ADOLESCENTS' INTERGENERATIONAL NARRATIVES

Almost all adolescents were able to narrate two stories about each parent, indicating that these stories are told and heard. We were particularly interested in how adolescents might use these stories as models for their own gendered identity. Thus, we coded these narratives in the same way that we coded the personal narratives, for elaboration and internal state language. Note, however, that for these narratives, internal states were of the parents, not the adolescents. Thus, adolescents who use more internal state language in these narratives are essentially taking the perspective of their parent, integrating what the parent thought and felt at the time of experience into the narrative (Zaman & Fivush, 2011). Again, illustrations make this clear.

Table 3.4 shows examples of intergenerational narratives told by females and males about mothers and fathers.

In both examples, the narratives about mothers' childhoods are far more detailed than the narratives about fathers'. In fact, both maternal intergenerational narratives describe elaborate social experiences, imbued with rich background information and internal states language, suggesting the ability of the adolescent, both male and female, to more easily take the perspective of the mother ("She was really upset." "She looked at them and she thought..."). Both paternal intergenerational narratives focus on light and funny experiences, and both are narrated in a more matter-of-fact manner, focusing primarily on just what the events of the experience were and less on the thoughts and emotions of those involved.

Table 3.4 Intergenerational narratives of adolescent girls and boys

Female Narrative about Mother	When she was younger she was really smart so she didn't have a lot of friends and then I think she went to high school early or something and so she was the youngest and so everybody was, you know, veered around her because she was like different from everybody else. And then I think there was this girl who was the smartest person in school until she came, so they had to take like a big test or something and my mom like did really good on it. But the girl, just to get my mom in trouble, said that my mom cheated. So they got like all upset (Emotion) and made her take the test over again. So my mom went home to my grandma and was like crying (Emotion) and stuff. So she went back to school the next day and she had to take the test in between like these two teachers and it was really formal and stuff. And she like studied really hard for that test and when they got the scores back it was basically the same as before. So they said it was because she remembered the scores [sic], so she was just really upset (Emotion) because nobody believed her (Cognition) and nobody trusted her (Cognition). So she transferred schools and never went back. Elaboration: 3
Male Narrative about Mother	She said that she remembered some people driving around and calling her a "dirty Mexican" but that fact wasn't true because my mom is um mostly Caucasian and she doesn't believe that she has any roots in Mexico. When she was a teenager, which she...well, actually, more (unintelligible)...so she kind of wondered (Cognition), "Hm, are Mexicans really dirty?" So then she went over to a friend's house at first, which, of course, they were Spanish, so she kind of wondered (Cognition) whether or not they were dirty. She looked at them and she thought (Cognition), "Hm, they don't look very dirty." And she checked out the bathrooms. Apparently, they had been using the shower. Well, I know the person who drove by and told her was some teenage guy in some weird car. And he was just making assumptions. Elaboration: 2
Female Narrative about Father	Once, my dad and Rick came home from being somewhere and Rick's dog was kind of like propped up by the table and he was like this (demonstrates) and then he turns around and looks at my dad and Rick and gave them this look like...oopsy. (Chuckles) And then they just like busted out laughing (Emotion) and the dog ran away. Elaboration: 1
Male Narrative about Father	Well, I know once when he was camping a snake crawled into his sleeping bag. Well, he said he was pretty scared (Emotion) and he ran right out of the sleeping bag and that's it. I think he was fifteen or sixteen. Elaboration: 1

Table 3.5 Means (and standard deviations) for variables in intergenerational stories

Narrative Variables	Narratives about Mothers		Narratives about Fathers	
	Boys	Girls	Boys	Girls
Elaboration	1.44(0.82)	1.79(0.93)	1.71(0.76)	1.32(0.82)
Affective States	0.78(0.89)	1.29(1.53)	0.64(0.80)	0.68(0.84)
Emotion Words	0.83(0.90)	1.21(1.48)	0.63(0.75)	0.66(0.93)
Cognitive States	0.73(0.97)	1.05(1.14)	0.56(0.83)	0.79(1.05)

The means for each of the intergenerational narrative variables are shown in Table 3.5. Note that these are the same adolescents who demonstrated large gender differences in how they narrated their personal experiences. Yet, when telling intergenerational studies, there were no differences between boys and girls. Instead, both boys and girls told stories about their mothers that were more elaborated and contained more cognitive states and emotional expressions. In essence, both male and female adolescents are telling stories about their mothers that conform to the female narrative gender type (more elaborate and emotionally expressive) and stories about their fathers that conform to the male narrative gender type (less elaborative and emotionally expressive). This finding is striking for at least two reasons.

First, that boys and girls are telling narratives that reflect the gender of their parent and not of themselves indicates that both boys and girls are capable of telling both female and male gender typed narratives. That is, they both know the narrative forms appropriate to each gender. Of course, much of this may represent how the story was told to them by their parents, but this story has been filtered through the adolescents' lens. Second, it suggests that both boys and girls are telling their own personal stories from their own gendered perspective. It is not that boys cannot tell highly elaborated and emotionally expressive stories because they do tell these kinds of stories about their mothers. In fact, boys' stories about their mothers contain more internal state language than do the stories about themselves (see Zaman & Fivush, 2011, for details)! Thus, boys choose to tell less elaborated and emotionally expressive narratives about themselves, suggesting that they are selecting to voice a particular gendered narrative identity in their personal narratives. And, of course, the same can be said of girls.

Finally, these findings suggest that boys and girls may be modeling their own personal narratives on their same gender parent. Indeed, girls are telling personal narratives that are correlated with how they tell narratives about their mother on elaboration (r = .42), overall affect (r = .36), and cognitive states (r = .60), but there are no correlations between girls' personal narratives and their paternal intergenerational narratives (see Peterson & Roberts, 2003, for similar findings on narratives that mothers and daughters tell about the child's experiences). For boys, there are no relations between their personal narratives and their maternal intergenerational narratives, and the only correlation to achieve significance between personal and paternal intergenerational narratives was for elaboration (r = .37). So, it seems that girls are using their maternal stories as a model for their own narratives to a greater extent that boys are using their paternal stories.

INTERGENERATIONAL CONNECTIONS

One of the interesting things that emerged in the stories adolescents told about their parents' experiences growing up were the specific connections adolescents made between themselves and their parents. Some adolescents simply extracted a general lesson from the parent's experience (e.g., "I learned not to smoke"; "I learned to wear seatbelts"), with no relation to the parent or self, whereas some took a step back from the events and reflected more on what the parent's actions suggested about his or her personality or family life (e.g., "My mother's family was crazy"; "My dad likes to play pranks"), and some adolescents even went so far as to draw parallels between the parent's and their own experiences (e.g., "She told me that because there was a time when I felt guilty about hitting my brother too"; "It's funny because she yells at us when we make a C when she used to make Cs too").

Thus, we explicitly coded for the number of times that the adolescent made a connection between self and parent (Fivush, Zaman, Waters, & Merrill, 2010). An intergenerational connection was defined as the spontaneous provision of ideas connecting the beliefs, actions, values, and identity of the adolescent to some aspect of the parent or the parent's experiences described in the intergenerational story. Accordingly, this coding scheme focused on the ways in which adolescents created personal meaning from their intergenerational narratives. The scores were assigned on a scale of 0–3, with higher scores reflecting greater connection between the parent and the self.

Adolescent girls who made higher levels of intergenerational connections in their narratives about their mothers showed higher levels of identity development on the Ego Identity Scale ($r = .38$) and self-esteem ($r = .33$), and girls who made higher levels of intergenerational connections in narratives about their fathers also showed higher levels of identity development ($r = .27$), but there were no relations to self-esteem ($r = .14$). For boys, the results indicate that, unlike their female counterparts, the level of intergenerational connection made in narratives about their mothers' childhood was not related to ego identity ($r = .07$) or self-esteem ($r = -.01$). Surprisingly, boys who made higher levels of intergenerational connections in narratives about their fathers showed lower identity development ($r = -.36$) and lower self-esteem ($r = -.29$), suggesting that, unlike girls, boys may have a greater need to differentiate from the parental identity.

Conclusions and Implications: Gendered Voices

In this chapter, framed by sociocultural and feminist theories, we have argued that narrative identity emerges from early parentally structured reminiscing about children's past experiences. Moreover, these interactions are gendered in ways that allow females to have a more elaborative and emotionally expressive autobiographical voice than males. Both by modeling gendered autobiographical voices in their own narrative constructions, and by eliciting gendered voices from their children, mothers and fathers highlight that girls voice their experiences differently than boys. These early experiences continue into adolescence and lead to enduring gender differences in autobiographical narratives, such that, through adolescence and adulthood, females narrate more elaborated and emotional autobiographical narratives than do males.

Returning to the theoretical framework laid out at the beginning of this chapter, we posit that children are learning how to narrate the events of their lives through participating in parentally structured narrative interactions. Family narrative interactions provide both models and values for reminiscing about the personal and familial past and thus facilitate children's developing narrative identity. Importantly, this process is gendered. Across development, mothers are more elaborative and emotionally expressive when reminiscing with their children than are fathers. Thus, parents are modeling gendered ways of understanding personal experience. Indeed, the research on intergenerational narratives further suggests, in accord with existing research on parental familial storytelling, that mothers tell their children more elaborative and emotionally expressive stories about their own childhood than do fathers. What is most intriguing about this finding is that adolescents tell narratives from the gendered lens of the protagonist; when narrating their own personal past, girls tell more elaborated and emotionally expressive stories than do boys, but both boys and girls tell more elaborative and emotionally expressive narratives about their mothers than about their fathers.

This finding underscores our assertion that gender is a process and that a critical site for the expression of gender is personal and familial narratives. In the process of narrating experience, gender becomes a lens into understanding the world in certain ways and giving voice to certain experiences. Thus, the argument is that boys and girls come to understand their own experiences, as well as others' experiences, through gendered narrative lenses. In line with feminist theory, we argue that gender is contextually dynamic. In the context of narrating their own autobiographies, individuals take on their own gendered lens, whereas in narrating others' stories, they take on the gendered lens of the other. With continued practice at narrating one's own experiences, one comes to understand one's self as gendered in this way. Thus, females come to understand their experiences in more elaborative and emotional ways than do males and thus develop a more elaborated, emotionally laden autobiographical voice than do males. Moreover, for girls, the maternal narrative frame seems to be adopted into their own storytelling; for boys, the results are not as clear-cut. Exactly how this process unfolds over developmental time is an important area for future research.

Perhaps somewhat surprisingly, adolescents' personal narratives are not related to either their self-esteem or their identity development (although they are related to psychological well-being; Bohanek & Fivush, 2010). Perhaps elaboration and emotional expression are not critical dimensions for identity at this developmental point. We note that research has shown relations between narrative dimensions of reflection and growth, with identity in adolescence (see McLean & Pasupathi, 2010, for an overview). However, our results suggest a complementary interpretation. It may be that, as postulated by sociocultural theory, it is the social narrative interactions that are critical for children's and adolescents' emerging self and identity. We see relations between family reminiscing and preschoolers' early emerging self-concepts, and we continue to see relations between family reminiscing and adolescent's self-understanding, although these latter findings are only suggestive at this point. Furthermore, although we do not see relations between adolescents' personal narratives and identity, we do see relations between adolescents' intergenerational narratives and identity, at least for girls. This pattern suggests that the sociocultural frames through which adolescents are learning to understand their own experiences may be more important, at least through middle adolescence, than individual construction of personal experience. It is likely that adolescents are still in the process of learning how to create more coherent, meaningful narratives of their own experiences and thus are still at the developmental point of relying on familial models, both in terms of structuring reminiscing about the adolescent's own experiences in family reminiscing and through modeling narrative forms through intergenerational narratives. Clearly, this is speculative, but provocative, and begs for longitudinal research to examine the developmental process in greater detail.

Moreover, this process is gendered. Adolescent females who make more intergenerational connections with both their mothers' and their fathers' childhood stories show higher levels of identity achievement and higher self-esteem, with more connection to mothers' childhood stories. In contrast, for boys, there are no relations to mothers' childhood stories, but boys who make more connections to their fathers' childhood stories show lower identity achievement and self-esteem. This pattern suggests that girls who identify and connect with their parents, and especially their mothers, using their stories as models to understand self, are doing better than girls who do not. Boys, on the other hand, who are showing more connections and identification with their father are actually showing less progress in their identity work. This needs to be interpreted in the context of relations between the ways in which girls tell their mothers' stories and their own, suggesting that girls who are connecting their own autobiographical voice with others, especially their mothers, may be better able to construct a healthy identity. Boys may be striving for more autonomy rather than connection, and thus they not only tell their own stories in different ways from their parents' stories, but, if they connect to their parents' stories, especially their fathers', they may have more difficulty achieving a healthy independent identity. Hence, it may be that females are able to achieve a healthy identity through connection whereas boys need to separate or differentiate to a greater extent (as similarly argued by Grotevant & Cooper, 1998).

These interpretations remain speculative. Obviously, longitudinal research with more diverse samples is needed. But our research across preschool and adolescence reinforces the need to include gender in any discussion of emerging self and identity and further demonstrates that identity is situated within larger social networks, especially the family. Stories of self and stories of family are contextually gendered from early in development, and gender continues to influence self and identity throughout our lives.

References

Adams, S., Kuebli, J., Boyle, P. A., & Fivush, R. (1995). Gender differences in parent-child conversations about past emotions: A longitudinal investigation. *Sex Roles*, 33 (5–6), 309–323.

Aries, E., & Johnson, F. (1983). Close friendship in adulthood: Conversational content between same-sex friends. *Sex Roles*, 9, 1183–1196.

Bauer, P. J., Stennes, L., & Haight, J. C. (2003). Representation of the inner self in autobiography: Women's and men's use of internal states language in personal narratives. *Memory*, 11, 27–42.

Belenky, M. F., Clinchy, B. M., Goldberger, N. R., & Tarule, J. M. (1986). *Women's ways of knowing: The development of self, voice and mind.* New York: Basic Books.

Bird, A., & Reese, E. (2006). Emotional reminiscing and the development of an autobiographical self. *Developmental Psychology*, 42, 613–626.

Bohanek, J. G., & Fivush, R. (2010). Personal narratives, well-being, and gender in adolescence. *Cognitive Development*, 25, 368–379

Bohanek, J., Fivush, R., Zaman, W., Thomas-Lepore, C., Merchant, S., & Duke, M. (2009). Narrative interaction in family dinnertime interactions. *Merrill-Palmer Quarterly*, 55, 488–515.

Bohanek, J. G., Marin, K. A., Fivush, R., & Duke, M. P. (2006). Family narrative interaction and children's sense of self. *Family Processes*, 45, 39–54.

Brison, S. J. (2002). *Aftermath: Violence and the remaking of a self.* Princeton, NJ: Princeton University Press

Bruner, J. S. (1990). *Acts of meaning.* Cambridge, MA: Harvard University Press.

Bordo, S. (1990). Feminism, postmodernism and gender skepticism. In L. Nicholson (Ed.), *Feminism/Postmodernism* (pp. 133–156). New York: Routledge.

Buckner, J. P., & Fivush, R. (1998). Gender and self in children's autobiographical narratives. *Applied Cognitive Psychology, 12*, 407–429.

Buckner, J. P., & Fivush, R. (2000). Gendered themes in family reminiscing. *Memory, 8*, 401–412.

Chodorow, N. J. (1978). *The reproduction of mothering: Psychoanalysis and the socialization of gender*. Berkeley: University of California Press.

Code, L. (1993). Take subjectivity into account. In L. Alcoff & E. Potter (Eds.), *Feminist epistemologies* (pp. 15–48). New York: Routledge.

Cross, S. E., & Madson, L. (1997). Models of the self: Self-construals and gender. *Psychological Bulletin, 122*, 5–37.

Deaux, K., & Major, B. (1987). Putting gender into context: An interactional model of gender-related behavior. *Psychological Review, 94*, 369–389.

Erikson, E. H. (1968). *Identity: Youth and crisis*. New York: Norton.

Fiese, B. H., & Bickham, N. L. (2004). Pin-curling grandpa's hair in the comfy chair: Parents' stories of growing up and potential links to socialization in the preschool years. In M. W. Pratt & B. H. Fiese (Eds.), *Family stories and the life course*. (pp. 259–277). Mahwah, NJ: Lawrence Erlbaum Associates.

Fiese, B. H., Hooker, K. A., Kotary, L., Scwagler, J., & Rimmer, M. (1995). Family stories in the early stages of parenthood. *Journal of Marriage and the Family, 57*, 763–770.

Fiese, B. H., & Skillman, G. (2000). Gender differences in family stories: Moderating influence of parent gender role and child gender. *Sex Roles, 43*, 267–283.

Fischer, A. H. (2000). *Gender and emotion: Social psychological perspectives*. New York: Cambridge University Press.

Fivush, R. (1989). Exploring sex differences in the emotional content of mother-child conversations about the past. *Sex Roles, 20* (11–12), 675–691.

Fivush, R. (1991) The social construction of personal narratives. *Merrill-Palmer Quarterly 37*, 59–82.

Fivush, R. (1998). Interest, gender and personal narrative: How children construct self-understanding. In A. Karp, A. Renninger, J. Baumeister, & L. Hoffman (Eds.), *Interest and gender in education*. (pp. 58–73). Kiel, Germany: Institute for Science Education.

Fivush, R. (2004). Voice and silence: A feminist model of autobiographical memory. In J. M. Lucariello, J. A. Hudson, R. Fivush, & P. J. Bauer (Eds.), *The development of the mediated mind* (pp. 79–100). Mahwah, NJ: Lawrence Erlbaum.

Fivush, R. (2008). Remembering and reminiscing: How individual lives are constructed in family narratives. *Memory Studies, 1*, 45–54.

Fivush, R. (2010). The development of autobiographical memory. *Annual Review of Psychology, 62*, 2.1–2.24.

Fivush, R., Bohanek, J. G., & Duke, M. (2008). The intergenerational self: Subjective perspective and family history. In F. Sani (Ed.), *Individual and collective self-continuity* (pp. 131–144). Mahwah, NJ: Erlbaum.

Fivush, R., Bohanek, J. G., & Marin, K. (2010). Patterns of family narrative co-construction in relation to adolescent identity and well-being. In K. C. McLean and M. Pasupathi (Eds.), *Narrative development in adolescence: Creating the storied self* (pp. 45–64). New York: Springer.

Fivush, R., Bohanek, J. G., & Zaman, W. (2011). Personal and intergenerational narratives in relation to adolescents' well-being. In T. Habermas (Ed.), *The development of autobiographical reasoning in adolescence and beyond. New Directions in Child and Adolescent Development* 131, 45–57. doi: 10.1002/cd.288

Fivush, R., Bohanek, J. G., Zaman, W., & Grapin, S. (2011). Gender differences in adolescent's autobiographical narratives. *Journal of Cognitive Development. 13*, 295–319.

Fivush, R., Brotman, M. A., Buckner, J. P., & Goodman, S. H. (2000). Gender differences in parent-child emotion narratives. *Sex Roles, 42*, 233–253.

Fivush, R., & Buckner, J. P. (2003). Constructing gender and identity through autobiographical narratives. In R. Fivush & C. Haden (Eds.), *Autobiographical memory and the construction of a narrative self: Developmental and cultural perspectives* (pp. 149–168). Mahwah, NJ: Erlbaum.

Fivush, R., Habermas, T., Waters, T. E. A., & Zaman, W. (2010). The making of autobiographical memory: Intersections of culture, narratives and history. *International Journal of Psychology, 46*, 321–345.

Fivush, R., & Haden, C. A. (2005). Parent-child reminiscing and the construction of a subjective self. In B. D. Homer & C. S. Tamis-LeMonda (Eds.), *The development of social cognition and communication* (pp. 315–335). Mahwah, NJ: Erlbaum.

Fivush, R., Haden, C., & Adam, S. (1995). Structure and coherence of preschoolers' personal narratives over time: Implications for childhood amnesia. *Journal of Experimental Child Psychology, 60*, 32–56.

Fivush, R., Haden, C. A., & Reese, E. (2006). Elaborating on elaborations: Maternal reminiscing style and children's socio-emotional outcome. *Child Development, 77*, 1568–1588

Fivush, R., Marin, K., McWilliams, K., & Bohanek, J. G. (2009). Family reminiscing style: Parent gender and emotional focus in relation to child well-being. *Journal of Cognition and Development, 10* (3), 210–235.

Fivush, R., & Nelson, K. (2006). Parent-child reminiscing locates the self in the past. *British Journal of Developmental Psychology, 24*, 235–251.

Fivush, R., & Zaman, W. (in press). Gender, subjectivity and autobiography. In P. J. Bauer & R. Fivush (Eds.), *Handbook of the development of children's memory*. New York: Wiley-Blackwell.

Fivush, R., Zaman, W., Waters, T. E. O., & Merrill, N. (June, 2010). *Situating self in family stories. Adolescent narrative workshop*. University of Frankfurt, Frankfurt, Germany.

Gergen, M. (2001). *Feminist reconstructions in psychology: Narrative gender and performance*. New York: Sage.

Gilligan, C. (1982). *In a different voice: Psychological theory and women's development*. Cambridge, MA: Harvard University Press.

Golombok, S., & Fivush, R. (1994). *Gender development*. New York: Cambridge University Press.

Griscom, J. L. (1992). Women and power: Definitions, dualism and difference. *Psychology of Women Quarterly, 16*, 389–414.

Grotevant, H. D., & Cooper, C. R. (1998). Individuality and connectedness in adolescent development: Review and prospects for research on identity, relationships, and context. In E. E. A. Skoe & A. L. von der Lippe (Eds.), *Personality development in adolescence: A cross national and life span perspective* (pp. 3–37). London: Routledge.

Habermas, T. (2007). How to tell a life: The development of the cultural concept of biography across the lifespan. *Journal of Cognition and Development, 8*, 1–31.

Habermas, T., & Bluck, S. (2000). Getting a life: The emergence of the life story in adolescence. *Psychological Bulletin, 126*, 748–769.

Haden, C. A., & Fivush, R. (1996). Contextual variation in maternal conversational styles. *Merrill-Palmer Quarterly, 42*, 200–227.

Haden, C. A., Ornstein, P. A., Rudek, D. J., & Cameron, D. (2009). Reminiscing in the early years: Patterns of maternal elaborativeness and children's remembering. *International Journal of Behavioral Development, 33* (2), 118–130.

Halpern, D. (2000). *Sex differences in cognitive abilities.* New York: Taylor & Francis.

Harter, S. (1990). Processes underlying adolescent self-concept formation. In R. Montemayor, G. R. Adams, & T. P. Gullotta (Eds.), *From childhood to adolescence: A transitional period? Advances in adolescent development, 2,* (pp. 205–239). Thousand Oaks, CA: Sage.

Hoff-Ginsburg, E. (1991). Mother-child conversations in different social classes and communicative settings. *Child Development, 62,* 782–796.

Kroger, J. (1996). Identity, regression, and development. *Journal of Adolescence, 10,* 317–337.

Kroger, J. (2003). Identity development during adolescence. In G. R. Adams & M. D. Berzonsky (Eds.), *Blackwell handbook of adolescence.*(pp. 204–226). Malden, MA: Blackwell Publishing.

Kuebli, J., Butler, S., & Fivush, R., (1995). Mother-child talk about past events: Relations of maternal language and child gender over time. *Cognition and Emotion, 9,* 265–293

Kuebli, J., & Fivush, R. (1992). Gender differences in parent-child conversations about past emotions. *Sex Roles, 27* (11–12), 683–698.

Kulkofsky, S., Wang, Q., & Koh, J. B. K. (2009). Functions of memory sharing and mother-child reminiscing behaviors: Individual and cultural variations. *Journal of Cognition and Development, 10* (1–2), 92–114.

Liben, L. S., & Bigler, R. S. (2002). The developmental course of gender differentiation: Conceptualizing, measuring and evaluating constructs and pathways. *Monographs of the Society for Research in Child Development, 67,* serial no. 269.

McAdams, D. P. (1992). Unity and purpose in human lives: The emergence of identity as a life story. In R. A. Zucker, A. I. Rabin, J. Aronoff, & S. J. Frank (Eds.), *Personality structure in the life course: Essays on personology in the Murray tradition.* (pp. 323–375). New York: Springer Publishing Company.

McAdams, D. P. (2001). The psychology of life stories. *Review of General Psychology, 5,* 100–122.

McLean, K., & Pasupathi, M. (2010). *Narrative development in adolescence: Creating the stories self.* New York: Springer.

McLean, K., Pasupathi, M., & Pals, J. (2007). Selves creating stories creating selves: A process model of self-development. *Personality and Social Psychology Review, 11,* 262–278.

McLean, K. C., & Pratt, M. W. (2006). Life's little (and big) lessons: Identity statuses and meaning-making in the turning point narratives of emerging adults. *Developmental Psychology, 42,* 714–722.

Miller, P. J., Cho, G. E., & Bracey, J. R. (2005). Working class children's experience through the prism of personal story-telling. *Human Development, 48,* 115–135.

Negele, A., & Habermas, T. (2010). Self-continuity across developmental change in and of repeated life narratives. In K. C. McLean and M. Pasupathi (Eds.), *Narrative development in adolescence: Creating the storied self* (pp. 1–22). New York: Springer.

Nelson, K. (2003). Narrative and self, myth and memory. In R. Fivush & C. Haden (Eds.), *Autobiographical memory and the construction of a narrative self: Developmental and cultural perspectives,* (pp. 3–28). Mahwah, NJ: Erlbaum.

Nelson, K. (2006). *Young minds in social worlds.* Boston: Harvard University Press.

Nelson, K., & Fivush, R. (2004). The emergence of autobiographical memory: A social cultural developmental theory. *Psychological Review, 111,* 486–511.

Newman, M. L., Groom, C. J., Handelman, L. D., & Pennebaker, J. W. (2008). Gender differences in language use: An analysis of 14,000 text sample. *Discourse Processes 45,* 211–236.

Niedzwienska, A. (2003). Gender differences in vivid memories. *Sex Roles, 49,* 321–331.

Owen-Blakemore, J. E., Berenbaum, S. A., & Liben, L. S. (2009). *Gender Development.* New York: Psychology Press.

Pasupathi, M., & Wainryb, C. (2010). On telling the whole story: Facts and interpretations in autobiographical memory narratives from childhood through midadolescence. *Developmental Psychology, 46* (3), 735–746.

Peterson, C., & Roberts, C. (2003). Like mother, like daughter: Similarities in narrative style. *Developmental Psychology, 39,* 551–562.

Pratt, M. W., & Fiese, B. H. (2004). *Family stories and the life course: Across time and generations.* Mahwah, NJ: Erlbaum.

Prentice, D. A., & Carranza, E. (2002). What women and men should be, shouldn't be, are allowed to be and don't have to be: The contents of prescriptive gender stereotypes. *Psychology of Women Quarterly, 26,* 269–281.

Reese, E. (2002). A model of the origins of autobiographical memory. In J. W. Fagen & H. Hayne (Eds.), *Progress in infancy research* (vol. 2, pp. 215–260). Mahwah NJ: Erlbaum.

Reese, E., & Fivush, R. (1993). Parental styles of talking about the past. *Developmental Psychology, 29,* 596–606.

Reese, E., Haden, C. A., & Fivush, R. (1993). Mother-child conversations about the past: Relationships of style and memory over time. *Cognitive Development, 8* (4), 403–430.

Reese, E., Haden, C. A., & Fivush, R. (1996). Mothers, fathers, daughters, sons: Gender differences in autobiographical reminiscing. *Research on Language and Social Interaction, 29* (1), 27–56.

Reese, E., & Newcombe, R. (2007). Training mothers in elaborative reminiscing enhances children's autobiographical memory and narrative. *Child Development, 78,* 1153–1170.

Reese, E., Yan, C., Jack, F., & Hayne, H. (2010). Emerging identities: Narrative and self from early childhood to early adolescence. In K. McLean & M. Pasupathi (Eds.), *Narrative development in adolescence: Creating the storied self.* (pp. 23–43). New York: Springer.

Ricoeur, P. (1991). Life in quest of narrative. In D. Wood (Ed.), *On Paul Ricoeur: Narrative and interpretation* (pp. 20–33). London: Routledge.

Rose, A. J., & Smith, R. L. (2009). Sex differences in peer relations. In K. H. Rubin, W. M. Bukowski, & B. P. Laursen (Eds.), *Handbook of peer interactions* (pp. 379–393). New York: Guilford.

Rosenberg, M. (1965). *Society and the adolescent self-image.* Princeton, NJ: Princeton University Press.

Rosser, S. V., & Miller, P. J. (2000). Feminist theories: Implications for developmental psychology. In P. Miller & E. Scholnick (Eds.), *Towards a feminist developmental psychology* (pp. 11–28). New York: Cambridge University Press.

Schectman, M. (2003). Empathic access: The missing ingredient in personal identity. In R. Martin & J. Barresi (Eds.), *Personal identity,* (pp. 238–259). Oxford: Oxford press.

Tan, A. L., Kendis, R. J., Fine, J. T., & Porac, J. (1977). A short measure of the Eriksonian Ego Identity. *Journal of Personality Assessment, 41*(3), 279–284.

Thorne, A., & McLean, K. C. (2002). Gendered reminiscence practices and self-definition in late adolescence. *Sex Roles, 46*, 262–277.

Vygotsky, L. S. (1978). *Mind in society: The development of higher psychological processes.* Cambridge, MA: Harvard University Press.

Wang, Q., Doan, S. N., & Song, Q. (2010). Talking about internal states in mother-child reminiscing influences children's self-representations: A cross-cultural study. *Cognitive Development, 25*, 380–393.

Wang, Q., & Ross, M. (2007). Culture and memory. In S. Kitayama & D. Cohen (Eds.), *Handbook of cultural psychology* (pp. 645–667). New York: Guilford.

Welch-Ross, M. K., Fasig, L., & Farrar, M. J. (1999). Predictors of preschoolers' self-knowledge: Reference to emotion and mental states in mother-child conversation about past events. *Cognitive Development, 14*, 401–422.

Zaman, W., & Fivush, R. (2011). When my mom was a little girl…: Gender differences in adolescents' intergenerational and personal narratives. *Journal of Research on Adolescence*. doi: 10.1111/j.1532-7795.2010.00709.x

CHAPTER 4

Identity Development from Adolescence to Emerging Adulthood: What We Know and (Especially) Don't Know

Jeffrey Jensen Arnett

Abstract

A critical analysis is presented of Erikson's theory of identity development and the field of identity development research. Erikson's proposal of identity development as a human universal is critiqued by examining the applicability of this idea in human phylogenetic history and across world regions today, with a focus on adolescence and emerging adulthood. The current state of research in identity develop is also critiqued, with the conclusion that, because most research to date has been based on the identity status model, and because this model and the methods used to investigate it are of dubious validity, much remains to be known about the most basic, fundamental questions of identity development. The narrative approach is advocated as a more promising model for future investigations, and the questions to be addressed by this approach are summarized.

Key Words: emerging adulthood, identity status, narrative method, Erikson, culture

---

Of the eight stages Erikson proposed in his lifespan theory of development, it is his concept of the adolescent stage, identity versus role confusion, that has been the most influential. In recent decades, an entire field has sprung up devoted to identity research and its many permutations, including ethnic identity, cultural identity, and sexual identity. Erikson himself seemed partial to identity among his concepts. He devoted an entire book to the topic, *Identity: Youth and Crisis* (Erikson, 1968), and his psychobiographies of Martin Luther and Mohandas Gandhi focused on identity issues.

Perhaps his preoccupation with identity issues arose from the ways his own identity was a complicated stew of influences. Born in Germany in 1902 as Erik Salomonsen to a Jewish mother from Denmark, he became Erik Homberger at age 9 when his mother remarried, lived as an artist in Austria as a young man, then became a psychoanalyst. After the Nazis came to power in 1933, he and his new wife immigrated to the United States. In effect, he remade his identity during his twenties and thirties as he chose a new profession, a new country, a new religion (he converted to Christianity from Judaism), and a new name: Erik Homberger Erikson.

Like many theorists in the psychology of his time, and like his mentors in psychoanalysis, Erikson sought human universals, principles of psychology that would apply to all people in all cultures in all times. His lifespan theory was proposed as a universal stage theory, although he recognized the possibility of cultural variations. In *Childhood and Society* (Erikson, 1950), where he first presented his lifespan theory, he drew on his ethnographic experiences among the Sioux and Yurok cultures of Native Americans, but he was less interested in their cultural distinctiveness than in finding evidence for the universal validity of the life stages he proposed. His psychobiographies, in particular his analysis of the life of Luther (Erikson, 1958), implied that his life stages applied across historical eras as well, in particular the special salience of the "identity crisis" as the major issue to be confronted and resolved on the threshold of adulthood.

Erikson's emphasis on universals of human development is sometimes downplayed in current summaries of his theory. According to the standard version of twentieth-century psychology, it was Freud who proposed universals, in his psychosexual theory. Erikson, in contrast, presented a *psychosocial* theory of development, which rejected Freud's psychosexual theory and underlined the importance of social, historical, and cultural contexts. In fact, however, Erikson presented his theory as a supplement to psychoanalytic theory, not as an alternative. In both his first book, *Childhood and Society* (1950), and his final book, *The Life Cycle Completed* (Erikson & Erikson, 1997), he placed the psychosexual and psychosocial stages side by side, as mutually important human universals.

Moreover, in *The Life Cycle Completed*, written near the end of his life, Erikson uncritically endorsed the whole panoply of Freudian nonsense—oral and anal stages in infancy and toddlerhood, the Oedipus complex in early childhood, even penis envy. Erikson not only believed in the validity of these ideas but regarded them as universal and biologically based, arguing that "psychoanalysis discovered the pregenital stages of sexuality" (p. 27) much as the early biologists discovered stages of embryonic development. He developed the analogy further as he described his psychosocial stages, likening them, too, to the "epigenetic" stages of the embryo. There would be historical and cultural variations, yes, but they would be variations on the same universal themes.

However, like the would-be universal stage theories proposed by Freud, Piaget, and Kohlberg in the twentieth century, Erikson's claims of the universality of his lifespan theory of development have proven difficult to sustain. From the perspective of a more empirically based twenty-first-century psychology, the universal ambitions of the twentieth-century theorists seem far-fetched, to say the least, based as they were on such tiny slices of humanity: for Freud, upper-class Jews in Vienna; for Piaget, his own three children and a handful of Swiss boys; for Kohlberg, a small sample of boys in Chicago; and for Erikson, the children he saw in his psychoanalytic practice along with his brief experiences among the Sioux and Yurok. Nevertheless, the success of Erikson's identity concept in generating a large body of research in the past several decades, and its continued vitality as an inspiration to theoretical conversations and new research, suggest that it remains an idea that has the potential to enlighten our understanding of human development.

In this chapter, the focus will be on the cultural and historical contexts of identity development in adolescence and emerging adulthood. I will not attempt to summarize the existing research, as this has been done well recently by several authors (Meeus, 2011; Kroger & Marcia, 2011; Schwartz et al., 2013). Rather, I provide a critical analysis of Erikson's theory and the research based on it. First, I take a fresh look at the question of cultural and historical variation in the scope of identity options and how recognizing this variation alters our understanding of Erikson's ideas. Second, I look at what we know—and, mostly, do not know—about the development of identity from adolescence through emerging adulthood. Third, and finally, I critically evaluate the methods that have been used in identity research on adolescents and emerging adults and advocate the narrative method as the most promising approach to revivifying the identity paradigm.

The Rise of Identity: Cultural and Historical Considerations

For all his attention to historical figures in his psychobiographies, Erikson was surprisingly quiet on the larger question of the human evolutionary past. Perhaps he was deterred by Freud's evolutionary misadventures in proposing the "primal horde," which must have seemed preposterous, to put it gently, even by the time Erikson was proposing his theory. Whatever the reason, Erikson's neglect of the human past is a major omission in his theory. Any theory of human development that purports to be universal must address not only ontogenetic development but phylogenetic development; that is, it must explain how the elements of the theory can be seen to arise in the course of our development as a species and thereby became a characteristic that all humans possess.

This test is not one that Erikson's theory of identity development survives very well. Erikson proposed identity as having three domains, love, work, and ideology, and he believed that exploration of possibilities led, by the end of adolescence, to choices in all three domains that would form the structure of an adult life: a marriage partner, stable work, and a worldview. There is a consensus among evolutionary anthropologists that *Homo sapiens* first took its modern form about 200,000 years ago (Wrangham, 2010). The earliest humans apparently relied on a hunter-gatherer way of life, hunting whatever animals were available and gathering edible plants. They controlled fire, which they used for warmth, light, and to cook their food, but their other tools were limited mainly to sharpened stones used to cut their meat and to make pointed sticks for hunting and defense against animal and human attackers.

It is difficult to find any evidence of identity as a salient issue in this way of life. With regard to work, what options were there to explore? They hunted, they gathered; the goal was survival, not the development of the individual's unique abilities. With regard to love, exploration followed by individual choice seems equally unlikely. Early human communities were small, usually only 100–150 persons. We know nothing about how they regarded love and marriage, but from what we know about modern hunter-gatherer cultures of similar size, marriage was most likely a community and family transaction in which the young people involved had little say.

As for ideology, from what the archeological record shows, this appears to have arisen more recently, about 40,000 years ago, during the Upper Paleolithic period (Diamond, 1992; Gazzaniga, 2008). This was when a variety of cultural objects that may have symbolized ideologies first appeared, including jewelry, musical instruments, painting, and sculpture. For the first time, humans buried their dead, and they often buried them with artifacts and objects from daily life, which implies that they held a worldview that included afterlife beliefs. Ideological expression may have been led in some groups by a shaman, such as those depicted in European cave paintings some 30,000–40,000 years old (Wilson, 2012). Still, it seems unlikely that the people of that era had a range of ideologies to explore and select from. These small human communities must have shared in common the ideology they had developed.

The next major shift in human phylogenetic history took place from 10,000 to 5,000 years ago, known as the Neolithic period (Taylor, 2010). Agriculture began as people cultivated the plants they had once gathered, and, at the same time, they began raising domestic animals so that they would not have to hunt constantly. Dwellings were built because people stayed in settled communities to tend their plants and animals, rather than living nomadically as people in hunter-gatherer cultures tend to do. Although the archeological record of this period is limited, it can be surmised that here, too, there must have been little in the way of what we now think of as identity development in love, work, and ideology. Marriages were probably family-based transactions arranged by elders, work was farming and raising domestic animals almost exclusively, and ideological variation was limited (Ember, Ember, & Peregrine 2011).

With the development of civilizations about 5,000 years ago, the story of our phylogenetic identity development becomes more complex, and perhaps it is here that it truly begins. For the first time, there was a range of occupations, including priests, soldiers, craftsmen, government workers, and slaves (Ember, Ember, & Peregrine, 2011). Ideologies became systematized and recorded in written languages for the first time and were represented and celebrated in monuments such as the Egyptian pyramids. Did people begin to have a range of identity choices in love, work, and ideology for the first time? Perhaps some did. We know little about how they regarded love and marriage, but as human populations began to cluster in cities rather than small agricultural communities, there may have been a greater potential range of marriage partners. Whether or not young people were allowed to choose from among them is another question, one that is difficult to answer. Perhaps some young men had the opportunity to choose whether to be a priest, soldier, craftsman, or government worker, but young women were entirely excluded from professions. Furthermore, it is important to note that even as these professions developed, most people, men and women alike, remained dependent on farming and raising domestic animals. As for ideology, with the development of civilizations, people were exposed to a wider range of ideologies as a consequence of trade, migration, and war. Some were converted to new ideologies; others were forced to convert once they were conquered. Still, for most people in most places during this era, it seems unlikely that they ever became aware of any worldview beyond their own local version.

Over the past 5,000 years, even until recent times, this pattern of severely limited identity options has continued (Ridley, 2010). With regard to love, most cultures developed a custom of arranged marriage that allowed young people little or no individual choice in the selection of a marriage partner. Even after the idea of love-based marriage became accepted in Western societies in recent centuries, this meant that a young man was allowed to court and then propose marriage to a young woman. It would not have been acceptable for either young men or young women to explore their options in love by having a series of relationships with romantic partners. Even after work became more diverse as economies grew and became more complex following the Industrial Revolution several centuries ago, most people remained farmers until about 200 years ago, even in "industrialized" societies. Whether they were farmers or not, few people had the freedom to consider and explore a range of possible occupational paths. Young men generally did what their fathers did; young women were wives and mothers, as they had been throughout human history, and those in farm families contributed farm work. Even after ideologies developed into religious and political systems, few people would have known much about any ideologies except what they were taught locally, within their families and communities.

This whirlwind tour of human phylogenetic history has been necessarily brief, but it serves to highlight and underscore just how modern Erikson's theory of identity is, just how specific it is to our time, and just how little it seems to describe a human universal. In developing and presenting his ideas about identity development in adolescence, Erikson was describing the world as he found it in the mid-twentieth-century in European and American societies. The idea of an "identity crisis" in adolescence was quickly embraced by scholars and in the general public because, for people in these societies, Erikson's description matched what they witnessed in the young people around them. Scores of scholars conducted hundreds of studies on identity development among adolescents in these societies, and the results seemed to these scholars to validate the insights Erikson had proposed, that forming an identity is a crucial challenge of development in the adolescent stage of life.

Erikson's theory of identity development has thus served as a productive and fruitful paradigm for understanding adolescents in developed countries today, but it can only be sustained in our time if it is shorn of his proposition of universality. It is only in recent times, really only since the early twentieth century, that young men and women have been encouraged or even allowed to have a series of romantic partners in order to explore their options in love prior to making a marriage commitment. It is only since the early twentieth century that young men have had a range of work options to choose from, and really only since the late twentieth century for young women. It is only since the late twentieth century that an ethic of tolerance has become dominant in developed countries, allowing young people to choose for themselves what their religious and political beliefs, and their social attitudes, shall be. Human societies have had a mix of ideologies for centuries, but it is only in recent times that choosing an ideology different from what was dominant in the family and community did not result in ostracism or even execution.

Adolescent identity development, then, is a modern idea, suitable for the modern world, not a universal and eternal stage of ontogenetic human development. However, even in our time, it has only limited application outside the Western societies that gave it birth, as we will see in the following section.

Adolescent Identity Development: What Do We Know?

Although scholarship on identity development has generally ignored the phylogenetic history just reviewed and the way Erikson's theory depends on conditions that have come to exist only recently, a substantial body of research has accumulated in recent decades on identity in adolescence (Meeus, 2011; Kroger & Marcia, 2011; Schwartz et al., 2013). For many decades, the dominant paradigm for mainstream identity development research has been the identity status paradigm. Originally proposed by James Marcia (1966), it operationalized Erikson's theory of adolescent identity development into two dimensions, exploration and commitment. The various combinations of these two dimensions resulted in four identity statuses: foreclosure (low exploration, high commitment), diffusion (low exploration, low commitment), moratorium (high exploration, low commitment), and achievement (high exploration, high commitment).

Research using the identity status model has yielded a number of consistent findings (Berzonsky & Adams, 1999; Meeus, 2011). Perhaps most prominently, it has shown that adolescents' identity status tends to be related to other aspects of their development. For example, the "achievement" and "moratorium" statuses are notably related to favorable development. Adolescents classified in these categories of identity development are more likely than adolescents in the "diffusion" or "foreclosure" categories to be self-directed, cooperative, and good at problem solving. Diffusion is considered to be the least favorable of the identity statuses and is viewed as predictive of later psychological problems. Compared with adolescents in the achievement or moratorium statuses, adolescents in the diffusion status are lower in self-esteem and self-control. Diffusion status is also related to high anxiety, apathy, and disconnected relationships with parents.

Yet a critical analysis of the existing research reveals that we still know surprisingly little about identity development. First, identity research has focused almost entirely on a narrow proportion of humanity: adolescents living in developed countries. Second, the main framework for identity research has been the identity status paradigm, which has serious limitations, and the focus of this research has been on the relation of identity statuses in adolescence to other aspects of functioning. Third, there has been little research establishing identity as the central crisis or challenge of adolescence, as Erikson proposed.

Identity Research and the Neglected 95 Percent

One obligation of proponents of a universal theory is to establish that it actually exists universally, among all or at least a broad and diverse range of the human population. This is something that scholars devoted to Erikson's theory of identity development in adolescence have not done. In fact, the vast majority of the research on adolescent identity development so far has been conducted in the United States, Canada, and Western Europe. What I have called "the neglected 95 percent"—the vast human population that lives outside the United States—has been almost entirely neglected by research on adolescent identity development (Arnett, 2008). In this case, it is more accurately a neglected 90 percent, as a substantial amount of research on adolescent identity has taken place in Western Europe, and, added together, the United States, Canada, and Western Europe currently comprise about 10 percent of the human population. But most studies on "adolescent" identity development have actually taken place among students at four-year colleges and universities, constraining further the range of what is known so far.

This neglect of 90 percent of the world's population poses a serious challenge to the universal claims of identity theory because the conditions of adolescence in the neglected 90 percent are dramatically different from the 10 percent living in developed countries, in ways that have important implications for identity development. Two key differences are in income and education. Nearly half the world's population lives on less than US$2 per day, and 80 percent of the world's population lives on a family income of less than US$6,000 per year (United Nations Development Program [UNDP], 2012). It seems likely that, among this 80 percent, the focus for adolescents would be on contributing work that would help their families survive from day to day, not on the pursuit of a self-chosen identity.

With regard to education, a sharp contrast exists between developed and developing countries. In developed countries, virtually all children obtain primary and secondary education, and 50 percent go on to tertiary education (college or other post-secondary training). In contrast, only about half of adolescents in developing countries are enrolled in secondary school (UNDP, 2012). Tertiary education is only for the wealthy elite. Education is the basis of identity development in work for adolescents in developed countries because it provides them with an introduction to a variety of occupational paths from which they may choose. For adolescents in developing countries, limited education means limited work options, chiefly in agriculture or manufacturing.

Not only in work but in love and ideology, identity options for adolescents are much more restricted in developing countries than in developed countries. In developed countries, for the most part, it is assumed—even encouraged—that adolescents will have a series of romantic partners beginning in their late teens and that their romantic relationships will include some sexual play. Most emerging adults in developed countries have more serious and enduring romantic relationships than in adolescence, culminating in an enduring commitment in the late twenties, usually marked by marriage. However, in most developing countries, including in Asia, Africa, and Latin America, having a series of love partners is discouraged or prohibited (Hatfield & Rapson, 2006; Schlegel & Hewlett, 2011). Courtship is allowed—the expression of a serious interest in a potential marriage partner—but not "dating"; that is, not casual relationships that are understood to be transient, as a kind of practice for a relationship that will eventually involve a commitment. Consequently, for adolescents in most of the world, there is no identity exploration of possible love partners of the kind that is accepted and normative in developed countries.

In the area of ideology as well, the contrast between developed and developing countries is stark. Across developed countries, it is an accepted principle that a diverse range of ideological views is allowed, expressed in politics, religion, and the arts, including views that expressly contradict the views held by the majority. However, in most developing countries, the question of the acceptability of ideological diversity is contested, and in some cases it is actively suppressed. For example, in China, the most populous country in the world, any attempts to advocate a democratic alternative to the dominant communist ideology quickly land the proponents in a labor camp, without trial. With regard to religion, more than 90 percent of the Latin American continent is Catholic (Galambos & Martinez, 2007). It seems unlikely that the people of this continent have all gone through a period of considering religious alternatives during adolescence and happened to end by choosing Catholicism. Rather, for most, the Catholic religion is the only alternative presented, and, by adolescence, they have been thoroughly socialized to believe and practice this faith. Erikson's theory, as well as the identity status model based on it, assume that adolescents have a range of alternatives and the freedom to explore and choose among them, but this assumption has never applied to most adolescents, not in love, work, or ideology.

Of course, adolescents in developing countries almost certainly form an identity despite these restrictions on explorations in love, work, and ideology. It seems likely that they would have a ready answer to the central identity question, "Who are you?" The answer would likely be based on ascribed social roles: son/daughter; grandchild/cousin/nephew niece; member of this ethnic group, that geographic group, this religion; perhaps (already in adolescence) worker in a particular job. But this is not what Erikson meant in describing an adolescent "crisis" of identity versus role confusion. For Erikson, identity was not only a consciousness of "who you are" but also the outcome of a period of "free role experimentation" in adolescence that would entail "choices and decisions" that would "lead to commitments for life" (1968, pp. 156, 155). But it is as difficult to detect anything resembling "free role experimentation" for adolescents in developing countries as it is to find it in our evolutionary history.

In short, with respect to identity development, the conditions of life for most adolescents in developing countries today more closely resemble the conditions of our phylogenetic past than they resemble the lives of adolescents in developed countries today: an economy with a severely limited range of work options, tightly restricted conditions of mate selection, and little variation in ideological options, as well as little tolerance for choosing a non-normative ideology. Like the phylogenetic review that preceded it, this overview of identity in developing countries has necessarily been presented in broad strokes, and there is of course a substantial amount of variability within both developed and developing countries. Furthermore, in some ways, adolescent identity development in developing countries is changing rapidly and becoming more complex than ever, as we will see in the following section.

Globalization and Identity Development

The gap between living conditions in developed countries and developing countries is wide, and it has profound implications for identity development. However, developing countries are indeed developing economically, and, along with their economic development, the pace of cultural change is accelerating and the challenges of forming an identity in adolescence and beyond is becoming more formidable even as options for identity formation broaden.

The influence of globalization on identity formation may be particularly salient in adolescence and emerging adulthood. By 2008—for the first time in human history—more people were living in urban than rural areas (Population Reference Bureau, 2008), and this migration has been led mainly by emerging adults (Hugo, 2005). According to projections by the United Nations, by 2050, 70 percent of the human population will be urban; a combination of increased total population (to at least 9 billion) plus rural–urban migration will result in an urban population of more than 6 billion (United Nations Department of Economic and Social Affairs, 2012). In urban areas, young people come into contact with the ideology and values promoted by the global economy, including independence, consumerism, and individual choice (Arnett, 2011). Recent media technologies make it possible for young people to connect with the whole world, even if they remain at home (see Manago, this volume).

Furthermore, adolescence and emerging adulthood are stages of life with a pronounced openness to diverse cultural beliefs and behaviors. Research has noted that, in many ways, adolescents and emerging adults have not yet settled on particular beliefs and behaviors (Arnett, 2000, 2004, 2011). Some research with immigrants to the United States has also shown that adolescents change their behaviors, beliefs, values, and identifications more than adults do (Phinney, Ong, & Madden, 2000). This phenomenon may apply not only to immigrants but also more generally to adolescents and emerging adults who are exposed to globalization.

Especially in places where economic and social changes are occurring rapidly, young people may decide in the course of growing up that their local culture has little or nothing to offer them (Liechty, 1995). They may see the global culture, not the local culture, as where their future will be found. Consequently, as soon as they are able—usually in adolescence or emerging adulthood—they may leave behind the ways of their local culture as much as possible for the ways of the global culture.

One example of this pattern can be seen in the lives of young women in China. In her book *Factory Girls*, Leslie Chang (2008) describes a massive migration in recent years from rural villages to booming urban industrial centers led by young women in their late teens and early twenties. When they first arrive in the city, they are often tentative and reserved. They work in a strenuous factory job for long hours and little pay. They send a substantial part of their pay home to their family in the village. Their limited social life is spent with other girls whom they already know from the village or with others who are from their region.

Gradually, however, many of them gain more confidence and begin to learn and adopt the ways of the city. Many embrace the values of the global culture as presented to them in city life: individualism, consumerism, and self-development. They learn that there is a wide range of jobs available, and they switch jobs frequently for better pay, better working conditions, and greater opportunity to learn and advance themselves. They begin to send less of their income back home and spend more of it on themselves, for example on clothes, make-up, technological products such as cell phones, and a nicer place to live. Many seek out additional education and training—including training in how to speak English—so that they can compete for better jobs in not only Chinese but also international companies. Some undergo a dramatic change in values because they learn that, in the global culture, values of assertiveness, self-confidence, and initiative are rewarded, not the traditional Chinese values of humility, self-sacrifice, and self-denial. The lives and identities of these young Chinese women, then, in many ways fit with a pattern of assimilation to global values even as they also experience the competing demands of the patriarchal family and socialist state (Ngai, 2005).

However, so far, it appears that for adolescents and emerging adults in developing countries, globalization does not typically result in a wholesale assimilation to global (usually Western) values. More common is that young people maintain their identification with their culture of origin even as they also seek to adapt to the ways of the global cultural influences. This response has also been termed *bicultural* in the literature on ethnic identity (Phinney, 1990). Applying the concepts of integration and biculturalism more broadly, they may pertain to anybody who has been exposed to and has internalized two cultures (Nguyen & Benet-Martinez, 2010). Applied to globalization, the integration response means that, in addition to their local identity, young people may develop a global identity that gives them a sense of belonging to a worldwide culture and includes an awareness of the events, behaviors, styles, and information that are part of the global culture. (However, there are alternative definitions of global identity, as noted below.) Their global identity allows them to communicate with people from diverse places when they travel from home, when others travel to where they live, and when they communicate with people in other places via media technology (see Manago, this volume).

Alongside their global identity, adolescents and emerging adults in developing countries continue to develop a local identity as well, based on the local circumstances, local environment, local traditions, and local language of the place where they grew up. This is the identity they are likely to use most in their daily interactions with family, friends, and community members. For example, India has a growing, vigorous high-tech economic sector, led largely by young people. However, even the better educated young people who have become full-fledged members of the global economy still tend to prefer to have an arranged marriage, in accordance with Indian tradition (Verma & Saraswathi, 2002). They also generally expect to care for their parents in old age, again in accord with Indian tradition. This suggests that they may have one identity for participating in the global economy and succeeding in the fast-paced world of high technology, and another identity, rooted in Indian tradition, that they maintain with respect to their families and their personal lives. However, it remains to be investigated whether young Indians view their identities in this bicultural way.

Although developing a bicultural identity means that a local identity is retained alongside a global identity, there is no doubt that local cultures everywhere are being modified by globalization, specifically by the introduction of global media, free market economics, democratic institutions, increased length of formal schooling, and delayed entry into marriage and parenthood. These changes greatly alter traditional cultural practices and beliefs. In fact, individuals who integrate two or more cultures into their identities are taking part in an active process of constructing and co-constructing their social milieu in a multicultural world (Chao & Hong, 2007). Such changes may, in effect, lead less to a bicultural identity than to a *hybrid identity*, combining local culture and elements of the global culture in ways that lead to entirely new concepts and practices (Hermans & Dimaggio, 2007).

The concept of a global identity is intriguing and shows great potential for understanding identity development in the twenty-first century, but thus far this area has been richer in theoretical proposals than in empirical investigation. A variety of basic questions have yet to be answered. First, how should "global identity" be defined? Is it primarily a consumer identity, reflected in one's interest in purchasing products from around the world (Tu, Khare, & Zhang, 2012)? Does it require the individual to consider the interests and welfare of humanity as a whole (Karlberg, 2008)? Does it mean embracing Western values such as independence, personal choice, and hedonism (Arnett, 2011)? Or is it, rather, a subjective sense of being a member of a world community, capable of social interactions with people anywhere (Arnett, 2002)? Second, how do we know that a large number of people worldwide are developing a global identity? Are adolescence and emerging adulthood periods when people are most likely to develop a global identity? Third, to what extent can a global identity co-exist with other aspects of identity, such as ethnic identity, national identity, or local identity? When people develop both a global identity as well as a local identity, does that enhance their prospects for success in the globalized world economy, or does it result in greater anxiety, frustration, and depression when the bright world promised by global media fails to appear in the lives of the individual adolescent or emerging adult? These are questions to challenge researchers for many years to come.

The Limitations of Conventional Identity Development Research

Mainstream identity development research has mostly ignored issues of global and cultural identity and has focused on American and European adolescents and emerging adults. The body of this research was recently summarized by Jane Kroger and James Marcia (2011). Because identity research has accumulated over nearly a half century, they were able to report a wide range of meta-analyses, mostly performed by Kroger and her colleagues. For the most part, the identity statuses of achievement and (to a lesser extent) moratorium were associated with more favorable characteristics than were foreclosure and diffusion. For example, with regard to *concurrent personality variables*, achievement was associated with higher self-esteem, "postconventional" moral reasoning, and "postconformist" ego development; achievement and moratorium were associated with lower authoritarianism. With regard to *antecedent conditions*, achievement was associated with secure attachment "style." For *consequent conditions*, achievement and moratorium were associated with high intimacy status.

Meta-analyses were also conducted on developmental changes in identity status from adolescence (13–19 years) to what they called "young adulthood" (20–36 years). It was hypothesized that there would be mostly "progressive rather than regressive developmental movements" (p. 46); that is, from diffusion and foreclosure to moratorium and achievement, and from moratorium to achievement. In general, "progressive" patterns were found, but the effect sizes were small and there was also a substantial proportion of "regressive" patterns.

These conclusions seem like a rather paltry result for hundreds of studies using the identity status model, spanning a half century. What happened to the richness of Erikson's theory of identity development, with its compelling proposal of identity as a process of integrating past identifications with the adolescent's sense of his or her talents, abilities, and desires, leading to a motivating vision of an adult future? Like so much in psychology, it fell victim before long to the discipline's focus on quantification and statistics.

Actually, the original basis of the identity status model was Marcia's (1966) Identity Status Interview, but because the interview was used only to establish the individual's identity classification, it was soon superseded by questionnaires that served the same purpose (e.g., Adams, 1999; Berzonsky, 1989). The identity status model inspired a large number of studies in relation to a wide range of variables, even though the questionnaires did not do justice to the complexity of identity but provided only a surface view.

If this conclusion seems harsh, it is one shared by Kroger and Marcia (2011), even though Marcia is the originator of the identity status model:

> A number of questionnaire measures assessing identity status have been developed in the service of "efficiency" and "objectivity." These measures could

be acceptable to the extent that they correspond closely to identity status categorization using the interview. However, because of their closed-ended form, they all lack the opportunity to probe, in depth, the genuineness and extensiveness of a person's exploratory process and the depth of subsequent commitment... What can be, and, to some extent, has been lost with questionnaire methods is the original theoretical grounding of the construct. (pp. 38–39)

Is Identity a Crisis of Adolescence?

Even if we were to limit our focus to the 10 percent of the world's adolescents who reside in Europe and North America, and even if we were to accept the validity of the legions of questionnaire studies of identity development despite the limitations detailed in the previous section, it would have to be recognized that there is surprisingly little evidence of any kind on the question that lies at the heart of Erikson's theory: Is identity a crisis that is central to adolescence? That is, do most adolescents experience it, and is it more likely to occur in adolescence than in any other life stage?

In Erikson's lifespan theory, he proposed that each of the eight stages is characterized by a distinctive "psychosocial crisis" (Erikson, 1950. By "crisis" Erikson meant "[not] impending catastrophe" but "a necessary turning point, a crucial moment, when development must move one way or another, marshaling resources of growth, recovery, and further differentiation" (Erikson, 1968, p. 16). However, few studies have even addressed directly the question of whether an identity crisis is normative in adolescence because the identity status model that became so dominant did not examine whether a crisis occurred. The Identity Status Interview, and later questionnaires based on it, looked for a more gradual "exploration" of identity options as a signifier of identity development, rather than a dramatic "turning point," the "crucial moment" proposed by Erikson.

Nevertheless, Kroger and Marcia (2011) and other identity researchers (e.g., Waterman, 1999) view the progression from the diffusion and foreclosure statuses to the moratorium status to the achievement status as consistent with Erikson's theory of identity development. In this model, "moratorium" represents the exploration stage, in lieu of Erikson's "crisis." In a meta-analysis by Kroger, Martinussen, and Marcia (2010), the overall conclusion was that longitudinal and cross-sectional studies generally show this kind of progression, with the diffusion, foreclosure, and moratorium statuses decrease proportion from the teens through the late and early thirties, while the achievement proportion increases. However, in studies using the identity status model, it does not appear to be normative to experience the progression diffusion/foreclosure → moratorium → achievement. On the contrary, there is a great diversity of patterns, including about 15 percent that show a "regression" going the other way.

If studies using the identity status model do not show that an identity crisis is normative in adolescence, do they at least show that identity is a more salient issue in adolescence than at other life stages? The answer to this question depends on how "adolescence" is defined. Erikson (1950, 1968) never specified an age range for adolescence or any of his other life stages. Identity researchers have generally viewed university students as being in "late adolescence" (and some still do; e.g., Kroger & Marcia, 2011). I have proposed that the age period from 18–25 in developed countries is better understood as emerging adulthood, a life stage distinguished from adolescence, and the life stage when identity explorations mainly take place. Meta-analyses of research using the identity status model have found that the proportion of people in the moratorium status rises in the teens, peaks at age 18–19, and then declines, which might be taken to indicate support for the notion that identity explorations peak in the early part of emerging adulthood (Kroger et al., 2010; Waterman, 1999). However, given the inadequacies of the identity status model described earlier, this conclusion should be viewed as preliminary at best.

Few studies of identity development compare children in middle childhood (ages 6–9) to adolescents, either cross-sectionally or longitudinally. Research by Susan Harter (1999) and others has examined changes in self-concept from childhood through adolescence and emerging adulthood, but more should be done to connect these findings to identity development theory and research. Similarly, few studies have compared emerging adults to young adults in their thirties. Are identity issues resolved once enduring choices have been made in love and work? Or do people continually assess their identities through their thirties and beyond, and make changes in their adult lives as their identities change? Is it true, as Erikson proposed, that "A sense of identity is never gained nor maintained once and for all... It is continually lost and regained" (1959, p. 118)? Narrative research by Dan McAdams (McAdams, Josselson, & Lieblich, 2001) indicates that "turns in the road" in self-concept and identity can take place throughout the lifespan, but more research is needed on identity development beyond emerging adulthood.

Given that (1) the identity status model has dominated research on identity; (2) this model is a highly questionable framework for identity research, both conceptually and in how it has been operationalized; and (3) few studies have been done that compare middle childhood to adolescence or emerging adulthood to young adulthood with regard to identity development, it must be concluded that, with regard to the question of whether identity is central to development in either adolescence or emerging adulthood, the answer is: we still do not know. In fact, the question has not yet been addressed at all in a conceptually and empirically persuasive way.

The Future of Identity Research: The Promise of the Narrative Approach

Fortunately, in recent years, research on identity development in adolescence and emerging adulthood has begun to supplement the paradigm of the identity status model with more in-depth approaches, using the narrative method. This method emphasizes the stories people tell, to themselves and others, as they seek to make sense of their lives and create meaning (McAdams, 2006). The narrative approach is a perfect methodological fit for the topic of identity development because it enables researchers to investigate identity development in the depth the topic requires (Hammack, 2008). The narrative method also provides a vivid sense of individual variation in identity development, in contrast to the questionnaire method that classifies people into a few discrete categories. By allowing people to tell their stories, researchers are able to discern how people perceive the parts of themselves—in love, work, and ideology—fit together into a coherent self. The narrative approach has the potential to fulfill Erikson's original vision of identity development as taking place through adolescents and emerging adults reflecting on the important people they have identified with throughout childhood, evaluating their abilities and interests, and seeking to find a match between the adult life they wish to build for themselves and the range of opportunities available to them in their society.

Use of the narrative method in research on identity development has expanded greatly in the past two decades. However, much remains to be learned about identity development in adolescence and emerging adulthood from a narrative perspective.

Many of the studies taking the narrative approach have focused on adults in midlife and beyond, examining how their autobiographical accounts reflect their identity development (e.g., McAdams, 2006; Wang & Conway, 2004). Narrative studies of adolescents and emerging adults have focused mostly on Americans (e.g., McLean, 2005; McAdams et al., 2006; Syed & Azmitia, 2010). Consequently, many of the most important questions are wide open for further investigation. I end this chapter with a list of those questions, as a stimulus to what will hopefully be an expanding body of narrative research on identity development.

Is identity development primarily focused on adolescence and emerging adulthood? Just as in studies using the identity status model, narrative studies have so far insufficiently addressed this key question. Notably, one narrative study has investigated identity among 8- to 20-year-olds (Habermas & de Silveira, 2008) and showed a progression with age in *causal coherence* (understanding of how one autobiographical event led to another) and *thematic coherence* (integration of multiple life events into a coherent conception of the self). Also, as noted, McAdams (2006; McAdams et al., 2001) has shown that identity issues can arise in life stages beyond emerging adulthood. But more narrative studies that compare emerging adulthood to later development are needed.

How is identity development in adolescence different from identity development in emerging adulthood? Which represents the apex of identity development? So far, few narrative studies of identity have compared adolescents to emerging adults, perhaps because the theoretical proposition that the heart of identity development lies in emerging adulthood has been advanced only recently. It seems likely, theoretically, that identity development intensifies during adolescence and reaches its apex in emerging adulthood, when most people make enduring choices in love, work, and ideology (Arnett, 2004). However, this promising question remains to be investigated.

Does identity development follow a coordinated path across the three major domains (love, work, and ideology)? With some exceptions (e.g., Frisen & Wangqvist, 2011), narrative studies using the autobiographical approach have not systematically explored the three domains of identity proposed by Erikson (e.g., McAdams, 2006). In fact, most narrative studies do not examine identity in terms of love, work, and ideology, but are more focused on general issues of self-development and self-concept (e.g., McAdams, 2006). This is a potentially important extension of narrative research.

Is identity development primarily a phenomenon of developed countries? Narrative identity studies have focused so far mostly on Americans. Is identity development mainly possible in developed countries, where many options are available to most people in terms of love, work, and ideology? Or are identity paths even more complicated for people in developing countries because their societies are changing so rapidly? Are people in developing countries commonly developing bicultural or hybrid identities that include components of a global identity, or not?

What is the intersection of personal identity and cultural identity? In all countries and cultures, it is important to understand identity development as not just a process within the self but of the self in the context of a culture. This is how Erikson originally postulated identity formation. Phillip Hammack (2008) has provided an expansion and updating of Erikson's theory, explaining the interaction between the *master narrative* of the culture and the *personal narrative* of the individual, and Hammack's ideas would be an excellent basis for narrative research.

Jensen (2011) also provides a model for cultural–developmental research that could be applied to identity research. In her model of moral development, Jensen (2011) proposes a developmental template that is modified according to cultural context and individual characteristics. That is, there may be age-related tendencies across cultures (e.g., children are more self-oriented than adults) that are then modified by cultural context (e.g., some cultures promote individualism, others emphasize obligations to others). It may be that a similar interaction of development and culture takes place for identity development.

Conclusion

Erikson's ideas about identity development were conceived in an early-twentieth-century context of theorizing in psychology that sought to propose universals of human development that would underlie any cultural structure that might be built on them. From the perspective of the early twenty-first century, it is easy to see how his theory of identity development was not simply conceived but misconceived and made claims of universal validity that have not held up well in the succeeding decades. However, Erikson's insights regarding identity remain valuable and continue to inspire new theorizing and research. Although it is necessary to concede that, at this point, little is actually known about the most important questions in identity development despite a half century of empirical investigations, the rise of the narrative method in identity research holds out the promise that a very different conclusion will be made a half century hence.

References

Arnett, J. J. (2000). Emerging adulthood: A theory of development from the late teens through the twenties. *American Psychologist*, 55, 469–480.

Arnett, J. J. (2002). The psychology of globalization. *American Psychologist*, 57, 774–783.

Arnett, J. J. (2004). *Emerging adulthood: The winding road from the late teens through the twenties*. New York: Oxford University Press.

Arnett, J. J. (2008). The neglected 95%: Why American psychology needs to become less American. *American Psychologist*, 63, 602–614.

Arnett, J. J. (2011). Emerging adulthood(s): The cultural psychology of a new life stage. In Jensen, L. A. (Ed.), *Bridging cultural and developmental approaches to psychology: New Syntheses in theory, research and policy* (pp. 255–275). New York: Oxford University Press.

Berzonsky, M. D. (1989). Identity style: Conceptualization and measurement. *Journal of Adolescent Research*, 4, 268–282.

Berzonsky, M. D., & Adams, G. R. (1999). Reevaluating the identity status paradigm: Still useful after all these years. *Developmental Review*, 19, 557–590.

Chang, L. (2008). *Factory girls: From village to city in a changing China*. New York: Spiegel & Grau.

Chao, M. M., & Hong, Y. Y. (2007). Being a bicultural Chinese: A multilevel perspective to biculturalism. *Journal of Psychology in Chinese Societies*, 8, 141–157.

Diamond, J. (1992). *The third chimpanzee: The evolution and future of the human animal*. New York: Harper Perennial.

Ember, C. R., Ember, M., & Peregrine, P. N. (2011). *Anthropology* (13th ed.). New York: Pearson.

Erikson, E. H. (1950). *Childhood and society*. New York: Norton.

Erikson, E. H. (1958). *Young man Luther*. New York: Norton.

Erikson, E. H. (1968). *Identity: Youth and crisis*. New York: Norton.

Erikson, E. H., & Erikson, J. M. (1997). *The life cycle completed*. New York: Norton.

Frisen, A., & Wangqvist, M. (2011). Emerging adulthood in Sweden: Identity formation in the light of love, work, and ideology. *Journal of Adolescent Research*, 26, 200–221.

Gazzaniga, M. (2008). *Human: The science behind what makes your brain unique*. New York: Ecco.

Galambos, N., & Martinez, M. L. (2007). Poised for emerging adulthood in Latin America: A pleasure for the privileged. *Child Development Perspectives*, 1, 109–114.

Habermas, T., & de Silveira, C. (2008). The development of global coherence in life narratives across adolescence. *Developmental Psychology*, 44, 707–721.

Harter, S. (1999). *The construction of the self: A developmental perspective*. New York: Guilford.

Hammack, P. L. (2008). Narrative and the cultural psychology of identity. *Personality and Social Psychology Review*, 12, 222–247.

Hatfield, E., & Rapson, R. L. (2006). *Love and sex: Cross-cultural perspectives*. New York: University Press of America.

Hermans, H. J. M., & Dimaggio, G. (2007). Self, identity, and globalization in times of uncertainty: A dialogical analysis. *Review of General Psychology*, 11, 31–61.

Hugo, G. (2005). A demographic view of changing youth in Asia. In F. Gale and S. Fahey (Eds.), *Youth in transition: The challenge of generational change in Asia* (pp. 59–88). Canberry, Australia: Association of Asian Social Science Research Councils.

Jensen, L. A. (2011). *Bridging cultural and developmental approaches to psychology: New syntheses in theory, research and policy*. New York: Oxford University Press.

Karlberg, M. (2008). Discourse, identity, and global citizenship. *Peace Review*, 20, 310–320.

Kroger, J., & Marcia, J. E. (2011). The identity statuses: Origins, meanings, and interpretations. In S. J. Schwartz, K. Luyckx, & V. L. Vignoles (Eds.), *Handbook of identity theory and research* (vol. 1, pp. 31–53). New York: Springer.

Kroger, J., Martinussen, M., & Marcia, J. E. (2010). Identity status change during adolescence and young adulthood: A meta-analysis. *Journal of Adolescence*, 33, 683–698.

Liechty, M. (1995). Media, markets, and modernization: Youth identities and the experience of modernity in Kathmandu, Nepal. In V. Amit-Talai & H. Wulff (Eds.), *Youth cultures: A cross-cultural perspective* (pp. 166–201). New York: Routledge.

Marcia, J. (1966). Development and validation of ego identity status. *Journal of Personality and Social Psychology*, 3, 551–558.

McAdams, D. P. (2006). *The redemptive self: Stories Americans live by*. New York: Oxford University Press.

McAdams, D. P., Bauer, J. J., Sakaedo, A. M., Anyidoho, N. A., Machado, M. A., & Magrino, K., et al. (2006). Continuity and change in the life story: A longitudinal study of autobiographical memories in emerging adulthood. *Journal of Personality*, 74, 1371–1400.

McAdams, D. P., Josselson, R. E., & Lieblich, A. E. (2001). *Turns in the road: Narrative studies of lives in trnsition*. Washington, DC: APA Press.

McLean, K. C. (2005). Late adolescent identity development: Narrative meaning making and memory telling. *Developmental Psychology*, 41, 683–691.

Meeus, W. (2011). The study of identity formation, 2000-2010: A review of longitudinal research. *Journal of Research on Adolescence*, 21, 75–94.

Ngai, P. (2005). *Made in China: Women factory workers in a global workplace*. Durham, NC: Duke University Press.

Nguyen, A. M. D., & Benet-Martinez, V. (2010). Multicultural identity: What it is and why it matters. In R. Crisp (Ed.), *The psychology of social and cultural diversity* (pp. 87–114). Oxford, UK: Wiley-Blackwell.

Phinney, J. S. (1990). Ethnic identity in adolescents and adults: A review of research. *Psychological Bulletin*, 108, 499–514.

Phinney, J. S., Ong, A., & Madden, T. (2000). Cultural values and intergenerational value discrepancies in immigrant and non-immigrant families. *Child Development*, 71, 528–539.

Population Reference Bureau. (2008). *World population data sheet*. Washington, DC: Author.

Ridley, M. (2010). *The rational optimist: How prosperity evolves*. New York: Harper.

Schlegel, A., & Hewlett, B. L. (2011). Contributions of anthropology to the study of adolescence. *Journal of Research on Adolescence*, 21 (1), 281–289.

Schwartz, S. J., Zamoanga, B. L., Luyckx, K., Meca, A., & Ritchie, R. A. (2013). Identity in emerging adulthood: Reviewing the field and looking forward. *Emerging Adulthood*, 1, 96–113. doi: 10.1177/2167696813479781

Syed, M., & Azmitia, M. (2010). Narrative and ethnic identity exploration: A longitudinal account of emerging adults' ethnicity-related experiences. *Developmental Psychology*, 46, 208–219.

Taylor, T. (2010). *The artificial ape: How technology changed the course of human evolution*. New York: Palgrave Macmillan.

Tu, L., Khare, A., & Zhang, Y. (2012). A short 8-item scale for measuring consumers' local-global identity. *International Journal of Research in Marketing*, 29, 35–42.

United Nations Department of Economic and Social Affairs. (2012). *World urbanization prospects, 2011 revision*. New York: Author.

United Nations Development Programme (UNDP). (2012). *Human development report*. New York: Author.

Verma, S., & Saraswathi, T. S. (2002). Adolescents in India: Street urchins or Silicon Valley millionaires? In R. Larson, & T. S. Saraswathi (Eds.), *The world's youth: Adolescence in eight regions of the globe*. New York: Cambridge University Press.

Wang, Q., & Conway, M. A. (2004). The stories we keep: Autobiographical memory in American and Chinese middle-aged adults. *Journal of Personality*, 72, 911–938.

Waterman, A. S. (1999). Issues of identity formation revisited: United States and the Netherlands. *Developmental Review*, 19, 462–479.

Wilson, E. O. (2012). *The social conquest of earth*. New York: Liveright.

Wrangham, R. (2010). *Catching fire: How cooking made us human*. New York: Basic Books.

CHAPTER 5

Identity Development Through Adulthood: The Move Toward "Wholeness"

Jane Kroger

Abstract

How does identity commonly evolve over adulthood, and in what way is identity related to other psychosocial tasks of normative adult development? This chapter uses an Eriksonian framework to address these questions. The chapter begins by reviewing the meanings of identity, according to Erikson, and proceeds to models by Marcia, Whitbourne, Berzonsky, and McAdams that suggest how different dimensions of identity develop over the adulthood years. A discussion of cross-sectional and longitudinal research on the course of identity through early, mid, and late adulthood follows, with findings pointing to considerable scope for identity development in the years beyond its initial formation in adolescence. Theory and research on identity in relation to Eriksonian tasks of Intimacy versus Isolation, Generativity versus Stagnation, and Integrity versus Despair are also reviewed, and suggestions for further research are offered. The chapter concludes with notes on how identity is both reshaped and maintained through the years of adult life.

Key Words: identity, adulthood, intimacy, generativity, integrity

---

There's some core in me that I still recognize from the obstinate 5-year-old child that became a determined, bolshie adolescent and a protective young mother to oppose the destruction I see large industry inflicting on our planet in pursuit of corporate greed. Life has brought a lot of hard knocks to this 50-year-old body, and I'm probably a bit more realistic now about how to channel my energies for change. But somewhere deep inside... there's still the same me, changed in shape and circumstance... meeting whatever life sends my way.

– *Sharon, midlife environmental activist*

Integrity simply means a willingness not to violate one's identity.

– *Erich Fromm*

Identity is that entity which enables one to move with direction and effectiveness, to find meaningful outlets for the actualization of one's interests, talents, and values within a social milieu. Identity is shaped and reshaped by contextual forces as it mediates or is mediated by them. Identity's normative time of ascendance as an issue of primary concern is during adolescence and young adulthood, when decisions about the foundations on which one will enter adult life press for clarification and resolution. Much theory and research over the past five decades has been devoted to understanding the process and contents of identity development through adolescence and emerging adulthood. Identity, however, is not a static entity, remaining fixed once initial resolutions are made. Changing life circumstances, coupled with changing biological and psychological needs, will likely spur ongoing identity developments over the course of adulthood years.

How does identity commonly evolve over adulthood, and in what ways is identity related to other psychosocial tasks of normative adult development? In attempting to address these questions here, I have organized this chapter through the framework of identity's "architect," Erik Erikson (1959, 1963, 1968; E. H. Erikson & J. M. Erikson, 1981, 1997; E. H. Erikson, J. M. Erikson, & Kivnick, 1986). From the consolidation of identity in young adulthood, this chapter defines what identity actually *is* from a psychosocial perspective and traces its normative evolutionary course through young, middle, and later adulthood years. Here, normative identity development and its modifications are considered through the Eriksonian psychosocial adulthood tasks of Intimacy versus Isolation, Generativity versus Stagnation, and Integrity versus Despair as they exist throughout life but come particularly to the forefront during specific spans of adulthood.

This chapter begins with a theoretical focus on the meaning Erikson gives to identity and its evolution during adulthood. I attend primarily to the *process* of identity development through the adulthood years and how this process broadens and deepens over time. I examine identity's normative movements through adulthood via existing longitudinal and cross-sectional studies that point to various patterns of stability and change over time. Through further studies, I present factors that have been associated with each phenomenon. I also address how the identity formed at adolescence becomes reshaped by the Eriksonian tasks of Intimacy versus Isolation, Generativity versus Stagnation, and Integrity versus Despair during early, middle, and later adulthood, respectively, and offer thoughts regarding ongoing theoretical and research needs in the area of adult identity development.

Studies reviewed here draw from a variety of methodological traditions, although all have foundations in Erikson's writings. Ultimately, the researchers' leading questions should determine the methodology most appropriate to drive their research; the studies reviewed here raise key questions that social scientists have asked and sought to answer over the past three decades about identity development throughout adulthood. New questions arising from this review and others will undoubtedly stimulate a variety of research approaches to issues of adult identity development. All are valuable in detailing different dimensions of identity and identity's complexities during adult life.

Identity Development in Adulthood: Theory

> [I]dentity formation neither begins nor ends with adolescence.
> – Erikson (1959), *Identity and the Life Cycle*

Erikson's Psychosocial Approach

Erikson (1963) was first to consider the form and function of identity, as well as ongoing psychosocial developments during adulthood. Erikson's interests in identity were spurred by his clinical work with veterans returning from World War II and suffering from the loss of a sense of sameness and continuity in their lives. Through its absence, Erikson (1968, p. 50) tentatively began to detail the parameters of ego identity: "Ego identity then, in its subjective aspect, is the awareness of the fact that there is a self-sameness and continuity to the ego's synthesizing methods, the *style of one's individuality*, and that this style coincides with the sameness and continuity of one's *meaning for significant others* in the immediate community." Erikson's notions of self-sameness and continuity are the result of the identity revision and maintenance processes described later in this chapter.

Erikson (1968) outlined key elements of ego identity in his fifth psychosocial task of *Identity versus Role Confusion*, normatively pressing for resolution during adolescence: identity's origins in the *introjections* of infancy, the *identifications* of childhood, leading to the culmination of identity synthesis during adolescence with the emergence of a new identity configuration that is uniquely one's own; the biological, psychological, and social components of ego identity; both the conscious and unconscious foundations of ego identity; common social domains for identity's expression (meaningful work roles, ideological values, relationships, and sexuality); identity's epigenetic nature (whereby resolutions to each preceding stage set the foundations for psychosocial tasks that follow); and the roles of exploration and commitment in the formation of ego identity. A key outcome of optimal resolution to the adolescent task of Identity versus Role Confusion is *fidelity*, the capacity to make identity-defining commitments and follow them over time. On the identity formation process, Erikson (1959, p. 125) describes an evolving configuration, "gradually integrating *constitutional givens, idiosyncratic libidinal needs, favored capacities, significant identifications, effective defenses, successful sublimations, and consistent roles.*"

With regard to ongoing identity development during adulthood, Erikson (1968) uses the epigenetic principle to show how resolutions to the crisis of Identity versus Role Confusion during adolescence are reworked in subsequent psychosocial stages of adult development as the individual moves from a focus on the "I" to the "We." Generally, in Erikson's (1968) view, young adulthood is primarily a time of identity consolidation, as previous identity explorations and decisions are actualized within social contexts. The identity work of adolescence is commonly actualized through vocational and ideological undertakings and relational commitments to a long-term partner and friends (see Arnett, this volume).

E.H. Erikson, J. M. Erikson, and Kivnick (1986, p. 130) note ongoing identity development among midlife adults because life's vicissitudes often spark a reconsideration of previous identity-defining values and commitments: "During adulthood, the individual struggles to balance a faithfulness to some commitments with an inevitable confusion and abandonment of others, all the while living a life that, in turn, both represents and reflects an underlying sense of self." Identity development in later adulthood years is grounded in the reality that there are no living elders to provide assistance for traversing the final task of "Integrity versus Despair." Although identity development through early and mid- adulthood could be guided by older role models, it is only one's own remembered heroes, life experiences, and expectations from younger generations that aid the identity redefinitions of late adulthood. "The sense of identity in old age rests not only on recollection and evaluation of the personal past but also on members of younger generations and on their representation of the generational future" (Erikson et al., 1986, p. 130).

In 1970, Erikson, aged 68, retired from his professorship at Harvard University to focus on the question of what it means to be a mature adult. Hoare (2002) has provided an invaluable documentation of Erikson's final writing years, in which he produced numerous unpublished manuscripts (mostly held by Harvard University) about adult development, including ongoing identity development. As Erikson (1959) had earlier noted, identity remains an active ingredient of adult development, although the foci for its expression likely change from those of adolescents. From "Fragments" (Erikson, various dates, as cited in Hoare, 2002, p. 31), . . . "[I]t is a sense of identity that presides over adulthood. Identity is the 'integrator' that moves one toward 'wholeness.'" Erikson also said in a succinct, handwritten note, "Fidelity—to go back on it, weakens; to carry it forward, strengthens" (Erikson, undated, as cited in Hoare, 2002, p. 32). Through adulthood themes of prejudice toward others, morality and spirituality, play, historical and cultural relativity, insight, and wisdom, Hoare (2002) traces Erikson's ideas of what it means to be a mature adult, engaged in ongoing psychological developments during adulthood. And, indeed, many of Erikson's unpublished documents illustrate how it is identity that potentially enables the adult to negotiate personal and communal conflicts to develop a heightened insight into and understanding of both self and others, as well as an ever-increasing sense of "wholeness" through the adult years.

From Erikson's groundbreaking ideas on identity formation and ongoing psychological developments of adulthood, some have attempted elaborations of his basic tenets. Some, for example, have proposed modifications to Erikson's (1968) psychosocial tasks of adulthood (e.g., Franz & White, 1985; Gilligan, 1982; Vaillant & Milofsky, 1980), whereas others have criticized Erikson for failing to clearly catalogue the ongoing developments of identity during adulthood (Friedman, 2001).

Several contemporary writers have elaborated Eriksonian concepts of identity developments during adulthood; however, it is the work of James Marcia that has, to date, been the most widely used model to actually trace structural dimensions of identity development during and beyond adolescence. Marcia's approach has been successfully applied in a variety of Western and non-Western settings, including North America and a variety of countries in Western Europe, New Zealand (within Maori and Pakeha cultures), Nigeria, Japan, India, Ghana, South Korea, Egypt, Israel (with Bedouin and oriental Jewish participants), Russia, Jordan, Lebanon, Iran, and the Cameroons, with adaptations appropriate for specific cultural contexts (see Marcia, Waterman, Matteson, Archer, & Orlofsky, 1993, for a partial review of this work). This approach will be described later. Several more recent models for addressing additional dimensions of adult identity development (e.g., Whitbourne's Identity Processing Theory [Whitbourne, Sneed, & Skultety, 2002], Berzonsky's [1992; 2011] Identity Styles, and McAdams' [1985, 2011] Narrative Identity approach) are also used in some of the studies cited in this chapter. However, these latter approaches have not yet charted their respective dimensions of identity development longitudinally through adulthood, and, thus, they are only briefly reviewed here.

Marcia's Views of Adult Identity Development

James Marcia is well known for his elaborations to Erikson's stage of Identity versus Role Confusion during late adolescence and young adulthood (Kroger & Marcia, 2011; Marcia, 1966, 1967; Marcia et al., 1993). Rather than conceptualizing resolution to Identity versus Role confusion as a place on the continuum between Identity and Role Confusion (so that identity is something one has "more or less of"), Marcia used Erikson's identity elements of exploration and commitment to identify four different configurations (the identity statuses) based on two processes by which late adolescents make identity-defining decisions that set the foundation for entry into adult life (see Crocetti & Meeus, this volume; Kunnen, this volume). Although Erikson had proposed that an exploration process was central to attaining a sense of one's psychosocial identity, Marcia (1966, 1967) showed that identity acquisition is possible without identity exploration.

Marcia (1966, 1967) used the narratives of late adolescents, with their stories of a search for directions into adult life, to develop the Identity Status Interview; from the stories he heard in interviews, Marcia catalogued various approaches to the identity formation process. Those in the *identity achieved* status have undertaken meaningful identity explorations before committing themselves to personally important adult work roles and ideological values, whereas the adult identity commitments of those in the *foreclosed* status are based on identifications with significant others, adopted without significant identity exploration. Although Erikson had also proposed that the lack of identity commitments defined identity diffusion (or, later, role confusion), Marcia proposed that both the *moratorium* and *diffusion* identity statuses described youths who had not made firm identity commitments. However, those in the moratorium status were struggling to find meaningful, identity-defining roles and values as they prepared to enter adult life, whereas those in the diffusion status were not. Marcia's identity status paradigm (with additional instruments developed for identity status assessment) has generated numerous developmental studies of identity through the adolescent and adulthood years that will be detailed in a subsequent section (and see Crocetti & Meeus, this volume; Kunnen, this volume). Here, I focus on Marcia's (2002) theoretical proposal of repeated cycles of foreclosure/diffusion to moratorium to achievement movements throughout each of Erikson's adult phases of psychosocial development.

Marcia (2002) asks the question of how identity changes in the Eriksonian phases of adulthood, beyond the time at which identity formation normatively occurs in adolescence. Marcia proposes that, for those attaining an optimal resolution to the identity formation task of adolescence, each subsequent Eriksonian psychosocial stage of development involves a disequilibration of the existing identity structure, both in response to the normative psychosocial demands of Intimacy versus Isolation, Generativity versus Stagnation, and Integrity vs Despair, as well as in response to critical life events (such as job loss or promotion, relationship loss, significant financial loss or gain). Each of these normative psychosocial tasks or critical life events is likely associated with an identity reformulation period. It is also likely that, during a time of identity reformulation, one will experience some type of regression to a previous identity status and concomitant approach to dealing with the world.

There will be individual variation in the extent of the identity regression. Some identity-achieved adults may experience moratorium-achievement-moratorium-achievement (MAMA cycles; Stephen, Fraser, & Marcia, 1992) as new identity options are considered prior to undertaking new, identity-defining commitments. Other identity-achieved adults may experience periods of identity diffusion, feeling shattered and confused in response to new normative or critical adult life demands. Following a time of diffusion, one may return to the safety of earlier identity commitments that may ultimately give way to the exploration of new identity possibilities via a moratorium process, prior to undertaking new identity commitments. Marcia (2002) notes that although the reformulated identity is "new," it also will hold important elements reintegrated from the past (see also Pasupathi, this volume).

There will also be individuals entering adulthood who are not identity achieved, and their passage through Erikson's psychosocial tasks of adult development is likely more limited in terms of potential resolution. The foreclosed adult has developed a personality structure that resists disequilibration. If life events do destabilize the foreclosed adult, identity restructuring is likely to be a shattering experience; adults who are identity diffuse will also be resistant to identity disequilibrium because they lack a solid identity structure from the start (Marcia, 2002).

Social-Cognitive Approaches

Whitbourne and her colleagues (Jones, Whitbourne, & Skultety, 2006; Whitbourne et al., 2002) have developed a model to trace identity development from adolescence through adulthood based on the Eriksonian concept of identity and Piagetian concepts of schemata, assimilation, accommodation, and equilibrium. In Whitbourne's *identity processing model* (IPT), identity is defined as one's self-representations (or schemas) in physical, psychological, and social functioning. The IPT model suggests that identity development is best understood via the interrelationships among three identity processes: identity assimilation, identity accommodation, and identity balance.

Identity assimilation refers to the process of interpreting new, identity-relevant experiences in terms of one's existing schemas about the self. Individuals use this process to maintain identity consistency, even in the face of discrepant information about the self.

Identity accommodation refers to the process of changing one's identity schemas to incorporate new information about the self that is incongruent with one's current self-perceptions. Identity accommodation thus enables one to approach changing biological, psychological, or social experiences in ways that evoke more adaptive responses. The IPT model assumes that the individual strives to reach a state of identity equilibrium or balance. Those experiencing identity equilibrium will maintain that sense of self-sameness and continuity that Erikson (1963) describes, while also being able to adjust self-representations to changing biological, psychological, and social circumstances. Indeed, identity balance resulting from use of both identity assimilation and accommodation processes has been associated with optimal aging (Whitbourne & Connolly, 1999).

Berzonsky (1992, 2011) draws from Erikson and social cognitive theory to conceptualize identity as an implicit theory of oneself, about who one thinks one is and what one thinks one wants. Berzonsky further proposes that there are differences in the social-cognitive processes that individuals use to deal with identity-related issues and that Marcia's (1966) identity statuses, in fact, reflect three stylistic differences in approach to identity-related decisions. An individual using the *informational processing style* is open to new experiences, seeks out relevant information, and considers and evaluates this information to make a decision. This style is characteristic of the identity achieved and moratorium statuses, in Marcia's (Marcia et al. 1993) terms. O the *normative-avoidant processing style* ass goals and values of significant others and imp tant reference groups without question or critical evaluation; these individuals furthermore disregard information that may threaten their existing belief or value systems. This style has been associated with the foreclosure identity status. Last, those using the diffuse-avoidant processing orientation generally procrastinate or in other ways avoid dealing with important identity-related decisions, allowing external circumstances to determine their identity directions. This group has been associated with Marcia's diffusion identity status. When examined longitudinally over the years of adolescence, several studies have shown an increase in use of the informational processing style (see Berzonsky, 2011, for a review); however, longitudinal work has not yet extensively been undertaken through adulthood years.

McAdams's Narrative Identity Approach

The field of narrative identity began with McAdams's (1985) work that built on Erikson's (1963) concept of ego identity and Murray's (1938) personological approach to the study of individual lives. The field has now grown to encompass a wide range of approaches, but nearly all attempt to provide an integrative theory of selfhood across the lifespan. McAdams (1985, 2006, 2011) has examined how individuals use narratives or life stories to develop a sense of personal unity, purpose, and meaning from the diversity of their life experiences. Central to a narrative identity approach is understanding how individuals build stories from their life experiences, relate these stories to others, and ultimately apply these stories to their understanding of the self, others, and the world at large. The process is heavily impacted by the immediate social and cultural contexts in which one lives.

By late adolescence, the individual begins to work on the story of his or her life, complete with settings and scenes, characters, plots, and themes. A narrative identity approach, in general, focuses on an individual's reconstruction of his or her personal past, integrated with an anticipated future. One's life story is important because it informs the self and/or audience of how a person came to be who she is and can shed light on factors associated with various developmental pathways. But autobiographical memory is reconstructive and fallible, and thus one's life story also provides insights into the personal meanings of the present, rather than an objective measure of past "facts." McAdams's (1985, 2011) model of narrative identity suggests that one's life story is dynamic and evolves from late adolescence through late adulthood; narrative identity provides one with that sense of self-sameness and continuity that Erikson described as the function of ego identity.

Reflections on Erikson and Marcia Concepts in Adult Identity Development Theory

Erikson (1968, p. 50) has stressed the issue of sameness and continuity of the ego's synthesizing methods in the process of identity development through adolescent and young adult years, and he has illustrated the ways in which one's "style of individuality" has remained constant through the course of ongoing identity development via his individual case studies. Beyond these illustrations, however, Erikson does little to articulate what he actually means by continuity and how the individual organizes his or her life to best meet those needs. Longitudinal use of narrative methods with individual life stories could be one method particularly well-suited to address identity continuity in the face of structural change (see Kroger, 2003, for examples of such methodology).

Erikson et al. (1986, pp. 129–130) has also noted how identity issues resurface in old age, with one's last chance to deal with existential identity concerns: "Old age's reconciling of the tension between identity and identity confusion reinvolves the individual in the psychosocial process that dominated adolescence... [the elder] faces a last opportunity to make... commitments that best reflect the 'I' in the totality of life." In seeking to detail that final push toward "wholeness" or reintegration of important identity elements from the past within the context of the present, identity theory might examine how important identity elements (or contents, such as important relational, physical ability, ideological commitments, coupled with societal circumstances) may, at best, serve to reshape the structure of identity itself or, at least, press for more satisfying resolution and closure.

Expansions to Erikson's (1968) work by Marcia (1966, 1967; Marcia et al., 1993) have been used to test and interpret some dimensions of identity development throughout adulthood. My comments here focus on Marcia's (1966; Marcia et al., 1993) identity status model, although they may also be applicable to the other identity approaches noted earlier.

First, a note of caution. Misconceptions of Marcia's (1967, Marcia et al., 1993) identity status model abound, including (a) that the statuses are an oversimplified way of addressing identity development, (b) that the identity statuses reflect static end states, (c) that identity achievement is the endpoint of identity development, and (d) that "domains" to assess identity status are fixed across time and place. In response, Marcia (personal communication, March, 2004) has likened his identity status interview to the process a geologist uses to anticipate where to probe for oil. One surveys the geological features of the terrain to anticipate what may lie underneath. The identity statuses, similarly, are useful when one's focus lies in the underlying structure of identity by which one comes to interpret, make sense of, and act on one's life experiences. Like the geologist, the identity researcher must identify elements in the terrain (i.e., domains that are culturally relevant to the interviewees in question, the interviewee's exploration and commitment processes) that best point to what may lie below the surface.

Marcia's identity status model was developed to document a complex developmental process, commonly but not exclusively experienced during adolescence—the movement from an identity structure based on identification (i.e., the foreclosure status) through restructuring to a new configuration, greater than the sum of its identificatory elements (i.e., identity achievement; Erikson, 1968). "Identity formation, finally, begins where the usefulness of identification ends" (Erikson, 1968, p. 159). Like Erikson, Marcia (Marcia et al., 1993) recognized the life-long process of identity development.

One needs to exercise some caution, however, in the application of the identity status model to the study of adult identity development. As noted earlier, the model was developed for use with late adolescents to capture the movement from an identity based on childhood identifications to a more individuated state of self-chosen goals and values. However, what do these identity statuses reflect in the years beyond identity's initial formation? What does it mean if a midlife nurse, achieved in identity after many satisfying years in the profession, begins to feel increasingly discontent and cynical at the long hours and low pay of the profession but finds herself "trapped" by life circumstances and unable to make changes? Can this previously identity-achieved individual still be regarded in the same identity-achieved way? What does it mean if a midlife adult, married to his initial childhood sweetheart, leaves this marriage of many years to enter into a new relationship to "find where he will really be loved," as his former wife begins to explore new vocational interests of her own? Has anything fundamentally changed about the nature of this man's foreclosed identity, despite his change of partners? (See Kroger, 2003, for a further discussion of these issues.)

There may be a need to develop new ways to expand the identity statuses in order to capture the structural changes of adult development. For example, the identity achievement status may need further differentiation to distinguish those remaining open and able to follow new identity-defining directions from those seemingly "stuck" in dissatisfying identity-defining roles and value commitments of the past (e.g. "open" versus "closed" identity achievement, differentiated by Valde, 1996). Does identity formation in adult life reflect the same underlying change in identity organization that was present during adolescence (e.g., the movement from an identity based on identifications to a new, integrative configuration)? It may or may not. There may be a need to differentiate "characterological" or "ruminative" moratoriums from those experiencing a renewed and time-limited reconsideration process (Luyckx et al., 2008; Marcia et al., 1993). There may be new forms of underlying ego organization in mid and late adulthood that cannot be adequately captured by the identity status model (see, for example, Kegan's 1994 subject-object balances of adult life). I encourage researchers to explore new questions that application of the identity statuses to adult life may bring.

The Development of Identity in Adulthood: Research
Identity Development

Erikson (1968) has described identity development during adolescence, and both longitudinal and cross-sectional research on the course of identity through early, middle, and later phases of adult development has burgeoned in recent decades. A number of studies now have utilized Marcia et al.'s (1993) identity status approach to examine patterns of stability, progression, and regression in identity status movements over time. Research on factors and contexts associated with these varied identity trajectories during adulthood is in its infancy, and the need for further investigations of such issues will be addressed.

One recent and comprehensive study examines trajectories of identity status change from adolescence through mid-adulthood through techniques of meta-analysis (Kroger, Martinussen, & Marcia, 2010). Drawing from publications and doctoral dissertations between 1966 and 2005, this investigation examined the likelihood of identity status progression, stability, and regression trajectories in longitudinal studies of identity status change over an average of about 3 years among late adolescents and young adults. We predicted that the presence of progressive identity status change would significantly exceed that of regressive identity status change. Results showed that the mean proportion of progressive identity status movements was .36, more than twice the mean proportion of regressive movements at .15. However, the likelihood of remaining stable in any identity status was high at .49 (with the mean proportion of F–F at .53 and D–D at .36)

From cross-sectional studies in a further meta-analysis from this database, we also obtained predicted results showing a steady increase in the mean proportion of identity achievement over time (from .17 at age 18 years to .47 by age 36). Patterns for foreclosure and diffusion identity statuses were more varied, with the mean proportion of foreclosures remaining relatively constant over this time period at around .20, and the mean proportion of diffusions dropping only in the 30- to 36-year interval to .14.

Both cross-sectional and longitudinal results from this study point to relatively large mean proportions of young adults who are not identity achieved by age 36 years. Results from these two meta-analyses are particularly interesting, given Erikson's (1963, 1968) emphasis on adolescence as the critical time for identity formation. The high probability of identity status stability and relative lack of identity achievement by young adulthood suggests the potential for considerable identity development in the years beyond late adolescence. (Alternatively, these findings may also indicate that many will remain stable with foreclosed or diffuse identity resolutions over their adult lives.)

Several additional studies of identity status change from late adolescence through mid-adulthood that could not be included in meta-analyses for various reasons have produced similar findings. Cramer (2004) examined men and women from the Institute of Human Development's Intergenerational Study over a period of 24 years, from young adulthood (around ages 30–37), through mid-adulthood (ages 40–47) and late middle age (ages 54–61).

Results indicated an increase in achievement, moratorium, and foreclosure identity statuses over time, alongside a decrease in the diffusion identity status. Fadjukoff, Kokko, and Pulkkinen (2010) examined identity status changes longitudinally for Finnish men and women sampled initially from the general population. Measures of identity status were obtained at ages 27, 36, 42, and 50 years. The authors found patterns of identity development in the areas of occupation and politics to change markedly over this time for both men and women, in association with changing economic conditions in Finland. In prosperous economic times, movements were in the direction of identity achievement, whereas in difficult economic times, movements were in the direction of foreclosure.

A further study examined cohort effects on identity status change from young adulthood through middle age. Helson, Stewart, and Ostrove (1995) assessed three cohorts of women who had been young adults in the 1950s, early 1960s, and late 1960s through mid-adulthood, using a Q-sort measure of identity status. Although analyses do not enable one to follow individual identity status trajectories over time, the study does reveal high stability in all of the different identity status vectors from the women's early 40s throughout mid-adulthood. Josselson (1996) has conducted a narrative examination of identity status change and stability among a sample of women from late adolescence through midlife. Of special interest was the diversity of identity pathways found among the women. Over the first decade of the study, most of the women were busy establishing themselves in work and family roles. Over the next decade, varying life circumstances produced large challenges to many, requiring integration into evolving identities. Achievement and foreclosure statuses tended to be the most stable over time.

In assessing other Eriksonian dimensions of identity over time, Stewart, Ostrove, and Helson (2001) found an increase in "identity certainty" in a retrospective study of highly educated women from age 30 to age 50. Using cross-sectional methodology with samples of college-educated young, mid, and late adulthood women, Zucker, Ostrove, and Stewart (2002) also found increases in identity certainty through late adulthood. The evolution of identity through young, mid, and late adulthood seems to bring increasingly higher levels of self-knowledge and understanding, at least among women. Whitbourne, Sneed, and Sayer (2009) also report results for two cohorts of college alumni (leading edge and trailing edge Baby Boomers) followed over 34 years with a measure of Eriksonian psychosocial development. Growth toward more optimal resolution to Identity versus Role Confusion increased steadily across adulthood, although deceleration of the growth curve was most prominent from early to mid adulthood for both samples. In combination, these findings show slow, steady growth toward identity achievement, identity certainty, and more optimal identity resolution over time, although maximum velocity toward favorable resolutions appeared from late adolescence through young adulthood, and social context likely plays a role in impacting these identity dimensions.

Two further pieces of research have focused on the process of identity integration and coherence over the adulthood years. Josselson (2009) also used a longitudinal analysis of a single case study to examine how autobiographical memory changes over 35 years of adulthood. "Maria" was interviewed at ages 21, 33, 43, and 55 years of age. What changes in Maria's recollections are not the facts of her life, but rather her interpretations of these facts, as well as her perspective on the various dimensions of her self that were present in those previous life experiences. From Maria's life and Josselson's analysis, one sees how identity development is an ongoing process featuring continuous elements but with a change in their arrangements and a dominance or de-emphasis of particular elements at different times. One thus learns from this single case study about the process of identity integration or that general "move" toward wholeness that Erikson has described.

McLean's (2008) research also focused on integrative identity processes in comparing late adolescents/young adults to individuals over age 65 years in terms of three self-defining memories. Interviews were coded according to several features of autobiographical reasoning: self–event connections evidencing self-stability or self-change, event–event connections, reflective processing, and thematic coherence. Although younger and older age groups did not differ in terms of their frequencies of self–event connections or their levels of reflective processing, there were major differences in other memory features. The older age group had more thematic coherence to their self-defining memories and more stories that reflected stability. This study suggests that the manner in which identity-defining events are integrated over adulthood differs by age; identity appears to become increasingly stable and coherent over time.

Change and Stability

From E. H. Erikson and J. M. Erikson's (1981) comments on the adult identity formation process, several interesting questions have been asked in recent decades. Among these is, what precipitates changes in identity structure during adult development, and how does such change occur? A concomitant question is what conditions are associated with identity stability? Both of these issues are addressed in studies reviewed here.

Helson and Roberts (1994) point to the importance of an "optimal level of accommodative challenge" or life stimulation to adult ego development (using Loevinger's, 1976, measure of ego development). An adult life high in accommodative challenge would be one high in both positive and negative disruptions, such as finding or losing a partner, and success in or loss of employment. In addition to personality variables, such as psychological mindedness and verbal skills, a high level of accommodative challenge was associated with more complex levels of ego development during adulthood. It may be that life challenges and conflicts are also important spurs to ongoing identity development during adulthood. Conversely, low levels of accommodative challenge may be linked with less mature identity resolutions.

Anthis (2002a, 2002b) explored the roles of stressful life events and sexist discrimination in women's adult identity development, respectively. Findings from the two studies suggest that the recent experience of some critical life event and/or sexist discrimination provoke increased levels of identity exploration; for the study of critical life events, psychosocial identity commitments also decreased, although that finding was not replicated in the study of sexist discrimination. Anthis and La Voie (2006) further examined the role of "readiness to change" in identity development in adulthood. Scores on a contemplation of change measure were significant predictors of increased identity exploration some 5 months later. It appears that increases in adult identity exploration are precipitated by a circumstance presenting conflict to the individual that may, in turn, give impetus to a readiness for change.

Kunnen and Wassink (2003) attempted to distinguish different steps in Whitbourne et al.'s (2002) identity accommodation process during adulthood. The authors used a single case study of a young adult, aged 27 years and undergoing treatment at a drug rehabilitation center, to identify a series of phases that were undertaken in his initial desire to become "clean": identity assimilation; withdrawal from the situation; exploration of one's feeling, thoughts, experiences; exploration of his script; exploration of conflict in the script and conflicting components; experience of the primary emotion; and identity accommodation. Exploring these movements in larger samples of individuals throughout adult life will be an important step toward the understanding of adult identity revision and maintenance processes.

Based on Erikson's (1963, 1968) and Marcia's (1966, 1967; Marcia et al., 1993) identity exploration and commitment processes to describe initial identity formation during adolescence, I began to examine parallel processes of identity revision and maintenance processes among 14 New Zealand late adulthood men and women, aged 65–85 years (Kroger, 2002). Among important *identity revision processes* in the early years of late adulthood were reintegrating important identity elements from the past. Sometimes setting aside, sometimes ignoring or denying important identity elements for many years, a number of the "younger old" found that niggling, back-burner identity issues did not go away but rather pressed more urgently for attention and reintegration in the early years of late adulthood, while action was still possible. Other *identity revision processes* among the younger old included readjustments following physical and/or social loss, rebalancing vocational roles (exiting some, trying out new), and rebalancing relationships, including shifting investments of time. *Identity maintenance processes* for this group included "tying up the package" (packing important identity elements into one physical, creative product), establishing visible forms of continuity with phases of their earlier lives, and retaining important identity elements through loss. Among the "older old," finding life meanings was an *identity revision process* commonly expressed, in addition to those also seen among the "younger old," and maintaining a predictable, daily life structure as well as living more fully in the present were additional *identity maintenance processes* found among the very old, in addition to those that appeared among the "younger old."

While conducting this study, I became curious about the ways in which people often used cherished possessions to help maintain identity continuity during later life, particularly in the face of many losses. Thus, in a second qualitative study, my colleague Vivienne Adair and I examined the role that cherished possessions played in helping to maintain identity continuity for a group of 20 late life adults (aged 65–89 years) living in one of two New Zealand adult residential facilities (Kroger & Adair, 2008). All participants had moved from their family homes in the preceding 18 months and were prescreened for lack of cognitive impairment. Through interviews, we identified a number of identity maintenance functions that these cherished possessions served, including the provision of links to cherished relationships, links to the family across generations, links with significant past events, links to the self in previous life phases, links with previous social status, and links with past historical eras. Having cherished possessions from a previous life era seemed to provide much comfort for participants; these objects also seemed to serve as "identity anchors" through the many changes that living into late adulthood often brought.

Reflections on Identity Development Research During Adulthood

One issue of particular importance in the study of adult identity development is the impact that historical events have on identity for individuals born in a particular era (cohort effect). Ideal research designs would attempt to follow individuals of different birth cohorts over a period of their adult lives to untangle individual developmental processes of aging from the impact of historical circumstances. The works of Helson et al. (1995) and Whitbourne et al. (2009) are examples of the very few investigations of identity development in adulthood that have employed this type of design; future investigations of identity development during the adulthood years could benefit greatly from use of such methodology.

Without access to large, extant databases, however, this type of design is likely difficult to undertake for many identity researchers. In this event, attention to variation in the social contexts of participants over time will be extremely valuable in understanding the adult identity development process. In a post hoc analysis in Kroger et al. (2010), there was evidence that identity development in contexts that were classified as "open" or "closed" were associated with different identity status patterns from late adolescence through mid-adulthood. Open contexts consisted of environments that were shared by a broad range of individuals, providing diversity in study, work, recreation, and/or social exchange opportunities. Closed contexts were often small religious schools or community social or living centers that restricted membership to those holding similar values, promoted narrow curricula, and generally discouraged a questioning attitude toward the status quo. In closed contexts, the mean proportion of foreclosed individuals was generally high, and the mean proportion of the identity achieved was generally low. Similarly, Helson and Roberts (1994), cited earlier, have pointed to the importance of contexts offering some optimal level of accommodative challenge for optimal levels of ego development by midlife. Longitudinal studies of identity development among adults who have made different lifestyle choices in terms of work-family balances or residential and working environments are likely to provide important insights into the relationship between developmental processes of identity formation and contextual effects.

In addition, data collection at frequent time intervals over the course of adulthood will vastly improve our understanding of the ongoing nature of identity development during this time. From the few existing longitudinal studies of identity development in adulthood, data collection frequently occurs with intervals of a decade or more. Although these studies show identity development to be a gradually evolving process, many changes are still likely to take place over the course of a decade that may not be registered at the times of data input. More intensive analyses of the identity development process are essential, particularly at times of crisis or major identity transition during adulthood years. It is likely that qualitative/narrative methodologies will be particularly valuable in this type of undertaking. Such efforts will also likely be an aid to the structuring of any subsequent intervention programs.

Identity in Relation to Intimacy, Generativity, and Integrity: Theory and Research

Erikson (1963) describes three psychosocial tasks of adult life: Intimacy versus Isolation, Generativity versus Stagnation, and Integrity versus Despair. The study of each of these adult life phases has generated a number of measures for assessment, as well as for research with associated personality variables and mental health outcomes. Indeed, McAdams's Loyola Generativity Scale (McAdams & St. de Aubin, 1992) has been an important instrument used to assess the degree of generativity an individual reports, and numerous empirical studies have focused, for example, on various mental health outcomes associated with optimal resolutions to Generativity versus Stagnation. As noted in the introduction, however, the focus of theory and research here will be on the way in which identity resolutions impact subsequent psychosocial tasks of adult development, in what Erikson has described as that move toward "wholeness" or integration. Thus, the research here focuses on those studies that examine relationships between varied identity resolutions and their associations with resolutions to subsequent Eriksonian tasks of adulthood, a test of Erikson's epigenetic principle.

Identity and Intimacy Versus Isolation

The task of Intimacy versus Isolation represents the primary psychological challenge of young adulthood, and it comes to the fore, in Erikson's (1968) view, once identity questions have found some initial resolutions. True intimacy, according to Erikson, is a counterpointing as well as a fusing of identities, a feat simply not possible if identity foundations are weak. Intimacy involves the desire to commit oneself to a relationship, and it can take a variety of forms—in same- and opposite-sex friendships, in love, in partnerships, and even with one's self. Sexuality is an important expression of intimacy, but not its determinant. Intimacy's counterpoint, isolation, describes a phenomenon whereby the individual isolates him- or herself, or at best engages in stereotypic or highly formal relationships with others that have little warmth or spontaneity. The optimal resolution to this task is the ability to love, to experience mutual devotion and respect both toward a partner and a few selected others, as well as toward oneself.

One of Erikson's controversial positions (1968) was on "womanhood and the inner space"—his view that women find their identities through a partner who is allowed into the "inner space." This view generated much anger among feminist writers at the time but also generated research through the following decades on the relationship between Identity versus Role Confusion and Intimacy versus Isolation. Some argued that men and women may follow different pathways in identity and intimacy development and that Erikson's (1968) epigenetic model may characterize psychosocial development for men only (e.g., Franz & White, 1985; Gilligan, 1982). One approach to understanding the epigenetic nature of the relationship between identity and intimacy during young adulthood comes from a further meta-analytic investigation by Årseth, Kroger, Martinussen, and Marcia (2009).

In this analysis, strong support was found for Erikson's theorized epigenetic relationship between identity and intimacy for men—high identity status (moratorium and achievement) was positively associated with high intimacy status (intimate and pre-intimate), whereas low identity status (foreclosure and diffusion) was positively related to low intimacy status (pseudo intimate, stereotypic, and isolate). Among women, however, the relationship was more complicated. Some 65 percent of high identity status women were also high in intimacy status; however, low identity status women were almost equally distributed between high and low intimacy status groups. A stronger relationship between identity status and intimacy status was found for men compared with women ($p < .001$).

A further meta-analysis in this study examined identity statuses for men and women on scale measures of intimacy. For men, women, and the combined sample, high identity status individuals scored higher on measures of intimacy than low identity status individuals, with low to moderate effect sizes in all analyses. It may be that identity and intimacy co-develop for some women, whereas for men and some other women, identity and intimacy do show an epigenetic relationship. In sum, foreclosed or diffuse identity development in young adulthood appears associated with more restricted relationship forms for men and some women. Contemporary long-term longitudinal research, conducted in contexts that offer differing adult role opportunities for men and women, may help to clarify the relationship between these two important developmental tasks.

Researchers have used additional measures of identity resolution to examine links between identity and intimacy in young adulthood. A recent longitudinal investigation into the relationship between identity and intimacy in German young adults used Loevinger's (1976) measure of ego development, as well as Marcia et al.'s (1993) identity status approach (Beyers & Seiffge-Krenke, 2010). These authors, too, questioned the epigenetic nature of identity and intimacy, asking whether identity achievement in the transition to adulthood may mediate any potential link between ego development in mid-adolescence and intimacy in romantic relationships at age 25 for both men and women. Findings showed that intimacy at age 25 was strongly predicted by ego development in mid-adolescence for both genders. Furthermore, relational identity achievement mediated the association between ego development and later intimacy. Results strongly support the epigenetic relationship of identity to intimacy for both genders.

Similarly, Beaumont and Pratt (2011) used a measure of identity style to examine potential links between identity and intimacy. They asked both young and midlife men and women to complete Berzonsky's (1992) Identity Style Measure and Domino and Affonso's (1990) Inventory of Psychosocial Balance (measuring positive and negative dimensions of Erikson's eight psychosocial tasks). Results indicated that both the informational (comparable to identity achievement) and normative (comparable to foreclosure) identity styles were positively associated with intimacy resolutions for both men and women, whereas the diffuse-avoidant (comparable to identity diffusion) identity style negatively predicted intimacy. An additional study by Seaton and Beaumont (2011) again found similar results for both men and women, again supporting Erikson's (1968) epigenetic notion of the relationship between identity and intimacy.

Identity and Generativity Versus Stagnation

Erikson's (1968) seventh psychosocial task of Generativity versus Stagnation generally becomes a primary focus for psychosocial development during mid-adulthood. Here, as well as in the preceding stage, questions arise as to whether or not to parent, to serve in mentor work and community roles, and to contribute one's time and financial resources to voluntary organizations or objectives that one wishes to support. Generativity refers to the desire to guide and care for the next as well as future generations. Its counterpoint is stagnation, denoting self-absorption and self-indulgence in one's relationship to others. The Eriksons (E. H. Erikson & J. M. Erikson, 1981) elaborated the theme of stagnation, referring both to rejectivity, or the exclusion of others different from oneself from one's focus of care, as well as authoritism, or the use of power alone for regimenting others. An optimal resolution to this task involves the ability to genuinely care for others, both near and far in place and time.

Much research has explored generativity at midlife in relation to mental health outcomes and its most likely time of emergence, but research on the direct relationship between identity and generativity has been far more limited. Beaumont and Pratt (2011) used structural equation modeling to examine Berzonsky's (1992) identity styles in relation to balances in the Eriksonian stages of Intimacy versus Isolation and Generativity versus Stagnation. Using cross-sectional methods to sample young and midlife adults, they found that the informational identity style (associated with identity achievement) positively predicted the capacity for both intimacy and generativity. However, the normative identity style (associated with the foreclosure identity status) did not predict generativity. The diffuse-avoidant style negatively predicted generativity, and midlife adults reported significantly higher scores than did younger adults on the measure of generativity balance. Christiansen and Palkovitz (1998) studied fathers and their involvement in childcare, along with measures of paternal and psychosocial identity, intimacy, and generativity, The father's paternal identity best predicted the level of generativity; however, psychosocial identity and intimacy also predicted the father's level of generativity. These studies all suggest that identity resolutions are directly related to generativity resolutions, in accordance with Erikson's epigenetic principle.

Researchers have also examined issues that impinge on identity and generativity at midlife. Bradley and Marcia (1998) investigated the relationship between ego development and generativity in attempting to differentiate five generativity styles. In general, they found the generative style to be modestly positively associated with a rising level of ego development, whereas the conventional group (caring involvement with others "like them," but lacking tolerance and concern for those who differ) was moderately negatively related to level of ego development. Contrary to expectation, the stagnant group was unrelated to level of ego development. Pulkkinen, Lyyra, Fadjokoff, and Kokko (2012) collected data from Finnish adults aged 27, 36, 42, and 50 years on a number of measures including parental identity, general identity, generativity, and integrity. Generativity, as well as psychological and social well-being, were highest if parental identity was achieved by age 42. Thus, from the scant research on the relationship between psychosocial stages of Identity versus Role Confusion and Generativity versus Stagnation, Erikson's (1968) epigenetic principle is generally supported; there is also preliminary evidence that limitations in identity resolution will also limit the capacity for optimal generativity resolution.

Identity and Integrity Versus Despair

Erikson's (1963) final psychosocial task of late adulthood is Integrity versus Despair. Questions regarding the meaning that one's own life has held arise, and reflections over opportunities missed or taken are common. Integrity refers to the ability to accept and reconcile with the decisions one has made over one's own life course, whereas Despair refers to a general attitude of dissatisfaction or despondence at the meaning of one's life and dread at the way it is ending. Optimal resolution to this late adulthood task results is *wisdom*, the integration of mature forms of all previous psychosocial stage resolutions. Optimal resolution also involves an appreciation of the general human condition and the feeling of comradeship with those of different times and pursuits, without fear of death.

Following her husband's death, Joan Erikson used her husband's annotations to an earlier edition of *The Life Cycle Completed* to propose a ninth stage of psychosocial development, capturing the tasks that arise from living into very old age (E. H. Erikson & J. M. Erikson, 1997). In late life, growing mental and physical declines present daily challenges for many. Although this ninth-stage psychosocial task does not receive a new label, Integrity versus Despair in very late adulthood is centered primarily on the body and retaining a sense of identity despite decline. Preliminary research into this Integrity stage distinction has differentiated two sets of integrity concerns by age group (60s versus 80s and 90s; Brown & Lowis, 2003); the older age group was preoccupied with concerns of physical and mental decline noted by E. H. Erikson & J. M. Erikson (1997), whereas the younger age group was primarily focused on traditional integrity concerns (Erikson et al., 1983).

Several longitudinal and cross-sectional studies have examined the relationship between identity and integrity in late adult years. Hearn et al. (2012) investigated Marcia's (1966; Marcia et al., 1993) identity statuses in relation to a newly developed measure of integrity status, the Self-Examination Interview. Results for these late adulthood participants showed a significant relationship between identity status and integrity status; some 86 percent of integrated persons were identity achieved, whereas no despairing persons were. Individuals in nonexploring (those who had not examined questions of personal meaning in their lives), pseudointegrated (those who fit the world into simplistic templates and clichéd meanings), and despairing integrity statuses tended to be in the foreclosed identity status. This study again provides support for Erikson's epigenetic principle in psychosocial development; those experiencing less-than-optimal resolutions to Identity versus Role Confusion appear limited in their resolutions to Integrity versus Despair.

Hannah, Domino, Figuedo, and Hendrickson (1996) investigated predictors of Integrity versus Despair in a sample of elders. The most predictive and parsimonious model for Integrity versus Despair included generativity, trust, intimacy, identity, and autonomy, with no meaningful gender differences. Additionally, James and Zarrett (2005) looked at predictors and concomitants of ego integrity in a sample of older women. Among findings, identity in 1951 predicted generativity some 45 years later in 1996, whereas generativity in 1996 predicted integrity in 1996, and integrity in 1996 negatively predicted depression in that same year. Again, strong support was found for Erikson's (1968) epigenetic principle; the authors additionally noted that all women grew through their young adulthood years under tremendous pressures to be homemakers and raise children. In this context, findings regarding the importance of individual identity development to both generativity and integrity in late adulthood is remarkable. The authors observed that, as young adults, these mothers had a clear sense of themselves, despite cultural pressures, and this identity certainty enabled them to meet subsequent life challenges very effectively. Thus, resolutions to the Eriksonian task of Identity versus Role Confusion has also been linked to Integrity versus Despair resolutions in all of the published studies I have located in this area of research.

Conclusion

Theory and research into adult identity development all point to considerable scope for change during the years beyond the initial identity consolidations of late adolescence/emerging adulthood. What is the nature of this movement? Researchers have approached this question in varied ways; however, some common threads connect their findings. Longitudinal, cross-sectional, and retrospective investigations of identity change from early through middle adulthood years point to a slow, ongoing transition of development toward identity achievement, identity certainty, greater self-knowledge, cohesion, and stability of commitments over time. The maximum period of acceleration for identity development appears to be from late adolescence through young adulthood, although various dimensions of identity continue to develop through mid and late adulthood years. Trajectories of identity development during adulthood appear associated with contextual factors. That which precipitates identity change in adulthood is the experience (rather than denial) of an identity conflict coupled with a readiness for change. The capacities for both identity assimilation and ultimately identity accommodation are essential to the ongoing process of identity development during adulthood. A dearth of research appears in the area of identity development during late adulthood, and much opportunity remains for the study of identity revision and maintenance processes during this phase of the lifespan.

Identity development through adulthood is inevitably "flavored" by Erikson's key psychosocial tasks of Intimacy versus Isolation, Generativity versus Stagnation, and Integrity versus Despair. Research to date has supported the epigenetic nature of Erikson's scheme and has begun to point out specific ways in which limited resolutions to identity are linked with limited resolutions in all subsequent adult stages. However, ongoing longitudinal research into identity resolutions and their ramifications to generativity and integrity are sorely needed. Further qualitative and quantitative studies over the course of adulthood may detail those increasingly complex moves toward integration and self-certainty that identity may ultimately strive to attain.

I conclude with Hannah's story, the tale of a prolonged identity formation crisis, impacted by context and historical epoch, and providing evidence of identity's integrative powers in that move toward wholeness that Hannah's courage and determination allowed. I met Hannah, at the age of 72, volunteering to be interviewed in one of my studies of identity in late adulthood. Hannah reported growing up in a conventional New Zealand family, doing all the conventional things that being a conventional farmer's daughter demanded. There was no thought of an education for her, beyond what was required by law. There was no thought during her late adolescence of doing anything other than marrying a local farm boy from the countryside who could provide more labor for her father and brothers and their families on adjoining farm properties. Hannah's life proceeded according to the family plan, as her brothers returned from the war and she married a local farm boy and had three children in close succession. But, gradually, a severe depression set in, initially written off as postpartum blues by the local doctor, but eventually leaving Hannah unable to get out of bed. To the consternation of all of her extended family, Hannah was admitted to a psychiatric hospital.

Life had certainly not gone according to the family plan for Hannah, and Hannah had no sense of a self beyond those family plans: "It was like my 'I' just didn't exist—I didn't even know I had one, just never stopped to listen—I just didn't know there was anything there." Life from that time for Hannah was a very long and slow series of moves through hope and despair, but even in those darkest of times Hannah persevered. Through therapy and sheer determination, Hannah began to find a small voice, a voice from the "very back of some closet somewhere" that reminded her of her love of learning, her love of music, her joy in reading the literature her fifth-form English syllabus had required. Love and rage dominated Hannah's emotional life over the following years. Through therapeutic support, Hannah continued to follow her interests in music and literature at the university, while returning "home" to continual family arguments. "It was like my life was almost the template for Nora in Ibsen's *The Doll House*, and I was just like some Raggedy Ann doll, not able to move unless someone else jerked me!"

Ultimately, Hannah's marriage did not survive, although she shared joint custody of her children as they grew through childhood and adolescence. At the time of my interview with Hannah, many years later, she was living as a widow in the countryside and able to reflect over a "life well lived," including remarriage to an established musician who shared many of her interests in music and literature, an eventual career as a high school teacher of English, and joy in the role of grandmother to her children's children. "What a life! I can't believe I made it, with most of 'me' still intact. No that's not quite right—'me' was really born in my mid 20s even though my physical birth was long past. These days there just is a feeling of contentment and peace after the battle of my earlier years, and now I can really say 'I' and mean it."

References

Anthis, K. S. (2002a). On the calamity theory of growth: The relationship between stressful life events and changes in identity over time. *Identity: An International Journal of Theory and Research, 2*, 229–240.

Anthis, K. S. (2002b). The role of sexist discrimination in adult women's identity development. *Sex Roles, 47*, 477–484.

Anthis, K. S., & La Voie, J C. (2006). Readiness to change: A longitudinal study of changes in adult identity. *Journal of Research in Personality, 40*, 209–219.

Årseth, A. K., Kroger, J., Martinussen, M., & Marcia, J. E. (2009). Meta-analytic studies of identity status and the relational issues of attachment and intimacy. *Identity: An International Journal of Theory and Research, 9*, 1–32.

Beaumont, S. L., & Pratt, M. M. (2011). Identity processing styles and psychosocial balance during early and middle adulthood: The role of identity in intimacy and generativity. *Journal of Adult Development, 18*, 172–183.

Berzonsky, M. D. (1992). Identity style inventory (ISI3) revised version. Unpublished measure. Available from the author.

Berzonsky, M. D. (2011). A social-cognitive perspective on identity construction. In S. J. Schwartz, K. Luyckx, and V. L. Vignoles (Eds.), *Handbook of identity theory and research, vol. 1*. New York: Springer.

Beyers, W., & Seiffge-Krenke, I. (2010). Does identity precede intimacy? Testing Erikson's theory on romantic development in emerging adults of the 21st century. *Journal of Adolescent Research, 25*, 387–415.

Bradley, C. L., & Marcia, J. E. (1998). Generativity-stagnation: A five-category model. *Journal of Personality, 66*, 39–64.

Brown, C., & Lowis, M. J. (2003). Psychosocial development in the elderly: An investigation into Erikson's ninth stage. *Journal of Aging Studies, 17*, 415–426.

Christiansen, S. L, & Palkovitz, R. (1998). Exploring Erikson's psychosocial theory of development: Generativity and its relationship to paternal identity, intimacy, and involvement in childcare. *Journal of Men's Studies, 7*, 133–156.

Cramer, P. (2004). Identity change in adulthood: The contribution of defense mechanisms and life experiences. *Journal of Research in Personality, 38*, 280–316.

Domino, G., & Affonso, D. (1990). The IPB: A personality measure of Erikson's life cycle stages. *Journal of Personality Assessment, 54*, 576–588.

Erikson, E. H. (1959). *Identity and the life cycle*. Psychological Issues [Monograph 1]. New York: International Universities Press.

Erikson, E. H. (1963). *Childhood and society* (2nd ed.). New York: W. W. Norton.

Erikson, E. H. (1968). *Identity, youth and crisis*. New York: W. W. Norton.

Erikson, E. H., & Erikson, J. M. (1981). On generativity and identity: From a conversation with Erik and Joan Erikson. *Harvard Educational Review, 51*, 249–269.

Erikson, E. H., & Erikson, J. M. (1997). *The life cycle completed (Extended version)*. New York: W. W. Norton.

Erikson, E. H., Erikson, J. M., & Kivnick, H. Q. (1986). *Vital involvement in old age*. New York: W. W. Norton.

Fadjukoff, P., Kokko, K., & Pulkkinen, L. (2010). Changing economic conditions and identity formation in adulthood. *European Psychologist, 15*, 293–303.

Franz, C. E., & White, K. M. (1985). Individuation and attachment in personality development: Extending Erikson's theory. *Journal of Personality, 53*, 224–256.

Friedman, L. J. (2001). Erik Erikson on identity, generativity, and pseudospeciation: A biographer's perspective. *Psychoanalysis and History, 3*, 179–192.

Gilligan, C. (1982). *In a different voice: Psychological theory and women's development*. Cambridge, MA: Harvard University Press.

Hannah, M. T., Domino, G., Figueredo, A. J., & Hendrickson, R. (1996). The prediction of ego integrity in older persons. *Educational and Psychological Measurement, 56*, 930–950.

Hearn, S., Saulnier, G., Strayer, J., Glenham, M., Koopman, R., & Marcia, J. E. (2012). Between integrity and despair: Toward construct validation of Erikson's eighth stage. *Journal of Adult Development, 19*, 1–20.

Helson, R., & Roberts, B. W. (1994). Ego development and personality change in adulthood. *Journal of Personality and Social Psychology, 66*, 911–920.

Helson, R., Stewart, A., & Ostrove, J. (1995). Identity in three cohorts of midlife women. *Journal of Personality and Social Psychology, 69*, 544–557.

Hoare, C. H. (2002). *Erikson on development in adulthood: New insights from the unpublished papers*. New York: Oxford University Press.

James, J. B., & Zarrett, N. (2005). Ego integrity in the lives of older women: A follow-up of mothers from the Sears, Maccoby, and Levin (1951) Patterns of Childrearing Study. *Journal of Adult Development, 12*, 155–167.

Jones, K. M., Whitbourne, S. K., & Skultety, K. M. (2006). Identity processes and the transition to midlife among baby boomers. In S. K. Whitbourne & S. L. Lewis (Eds.), *The baby boomers grow up: Contemporary perspectives on midlife* (pp. 149–164). Mahwah, NJ: Lawrence Erlbaum Associates.

Josselson, R. (1996). *Revising herself: The story of women's identity from college to midlife*. New York: Oxford University Press.

Josselson, R. (2009). The present of the past: Dialogues with memory over time. *Journal of Personality, 77*, 647–668.

Kegan, R. (1994). *In over our heads*. Cambridge, MA: Harvard University Press.

Kroger, J. (2002). Identity processes and contents through the years of late adulthood. *Identity: An International Journal of Theory and Research, 2*, 81–99.

Kroger, J. (2003). What transits in an identity status transition? *Identity: An International Journal of Theory and Research, 3*, 291–304.

Kroger, J., & Adair, V. (2008). Symbolic meanings of valued personal objects in identity transitions of late adulthood. *Identity: An International Journal of Theory and Research, 8*, 5–24.

Kroger, J., & Marcia, J. E. (2011). The identity statuses: Origins, meanings, and interpretations. In S. J. Schwartz, K. Luyckx, V. L. Vignoles (Eds.), *Handbook of identity theory and research, vol. 1* (pp. 31–53). New York: Springer.

Kroger, J., Martinussen, M., & Marcia, J. E. (2010). Identity status change during adolescence and young adulthood. *Journal of Adolescence, 33*, 683–698.

Kunnen, E. S., & Wassink, M. E. K. (2003). An analysis of identity change in adulthood. *Identity: An International Journal of Theory and Research, 3*, 347–366.

Loevinger, J. (1976). *Ego development*. San Francisco: Jossey-Bass.

Luyckx, K., Schwartz, S. J., Berzonsky, M. D., Soenens, B., Vantsteenkiste, M., & Smits., et al. (2008). Capturing ruminative exploration: Extending the four dimensional model of identity formation in late adolescence. *Journal of Research in Personality, 42*, 58–82.

Marcia, J. E. (1966). Development and validation of ego identity status. *Journal of Personality and Social Psychology, 3*, 551–558.

Marcia, J. E. (1967). Ego identity status: Relationship to change in self-esteem, "general maladjustment," and authoritarianism. *Journal of Personality, 35*, 118–133.

Marcia, J. E. (2002). Identity and psychosocial development in adulthood. *Identity: An International Journal of Theory and Research, 2*, 7–28.

Marcia, J. E., Waterman, A. S., Matteson, D. R., Archer, S. L., & Orlofsky, J. L. (Eds.), (1993). *Ego identity: A handbook for psychosocial research*. New York: Springer Verlag.

McAdams, D. P. (1985). *Power, intimacy, and the life story: Personological inquiries into identity*. New York: Guilford Press.

McAdams, D. P. (2008). Personal narratives and the life story. In O. John, R. Robbins, & L. Pervin (Eds.), *Handbook of personality: Theory and research* (3rd ed., pp. 242–262). New York: Guilford Press.

McAdams, D. P. (2011). Narrative identity. In S. J. Schwartz, K. Luyckx, & V. L. Vignoles (Eds.), *Handbook of identity theory and research, vol. 1.* (pp. 99–116). New York: Springer.

McAdams, D. P., & de St. Aubin, E. (1992). A theory of generativity and its assessment through self-report, behavioral acts, and narrative themes in autobiography. *Journal of Personality and Social Psychology, 62,* 1003–1015

McLean, K. (2008). Stories of the young and the old: Personal continuity and narrative identity. *Developmental Psychology, 44,* 254–264.

Murray, H. A. (1938). *Explorations in personality.* New York: Oxford University Press.

Pulkkinen, L., Lyyra, A. L., Fadjukoff, P., & Kokko, K. (2012, July). Parental identity in relation to social and psychological functioning in early middle age. Paper presented at the Biennial Meeting of the International Society for the Study of Behavioral Development, Edmonton, Canada.

Seaton, C. L., & Beaumont, S. L. (2011). The link between identity style and intimacy: Does emotional intelligence provide the key? *Identity: An International Journal of Theory and Research, 11,* 311–332.

Stephen, J., Fraser, E., & Marcia, J. E. (1992). Moratorium-achievement (MAMA) cycles in life-span identity development: Value orientations and reasoning systems correlates. *Journal of Adolescence, 15,* 283, 300.

Stewart, A. J., Ostrove, J. M., & Helson, R. (2001). Middle aging in women: Patterns of personality change from the 30s to the 50s. *Journal of Adult Development, 8,* 23–37.

Vaillant, G. E., & Milofsky, E. (1980). Natural history of male psychological health: IX. Empirical evidence for Erikson's model of the life cycle. *American Journal of Orthopsychiatry, 137,* 1348–1359.

Valde, G. A. (1996). Identity closure: A fifth identity status. *Journal of Genetic Psychology, 157,* 245–254.

Whitbourne, S. K., & Connelly, L. A. (1999). The developing self in midlife. In S. L. Willis & J. D. Reid (Eds.), *Life in the middle: Psychological and social development in middle age* (pp. 25–45). San Diego, CA: Academic Press.

Whitbourne, S. K., Sneed, J. R., & Sayer, A. (2009). Psychosocial development from college through midlife: A 34-year sequential study. *Developmental Psychology, 45,* 1328–1340.

Whitbourne, S. K., Sneed, J. R., & Skultety, K. M. (2002). Identity processes in adulthood: Theoretical and methodological challenges. *Identity: An International Journal of Theory and Research, 2,* 29–45.

Zucker, A. N., Ostrove, J. M., & Stewart, A. J. (2002). College educated women's personality development in adulthood: Perceptions and age differences. *Psychology and Aging, 17,* 236–244.

CHAPTER 6

Three Strands of Identity Development Across the Human Life Course: Reading Erik Erikson in Full

Dan P. McAdams *and* Claudia Zapata-Gietl

Abstract

This chapter synthesizes perspectives on identity development in childhood, adolescence, and adulthood in terms of a broad conceptual model that identifies three strands of identity development across the human life course. The first strand of identity development involves the performance of traits and roles, eventuating in the establishment of a reputation as a *social actor*. The second strand begins with the consolidation of theory of mind in early childhood and the development of identity as a goal-directed, *motivated agent*. Beginning with the emergence of autobiographical reasoning in adolescence, identity development also follows the third strand of the *autobiographical author* who reconstructs the past and imagines the future in terms of an evolving and internalized life narrative. A person's life story provides that sense of temporal sameness and continuity that Erikson imagined to be a defining feature of identity. A full understanding of identity requires a consideration of how all three strands – the self as actor, agent, and author – develop and interact over the human life course.

Key Words: life story, traits, roles, agency, goals, values, self-continuity

Erik Erikson himself is one of psychology's greatest projective tests. To make sense of what he wrote about the concept of identity, for example, is not altogether different from responding to a Rorschach inkblot. What I see may be a projection of what I want or need to see and (appropriately enough) of who I am. From *Childhood and Society* (Erikson, 1950) to his late-life writings on aging and integrity (Erikson, Erikson, & Kivnick, 1986), Erikson produced a rich corpus of theoretical texts, clinical case studies, biographical analyses, and personal observations that demand the kind of exegesis historically given to sacred texts, great literature, and Freud. There are many different ways to read Erikson because his writings are both extraordinarily generative and maddeningly ambiguous. In the three chapters that precede ours, each of the authors reads Erikson in a very different way (Arnett, this volume; Fivush & Zaman, this volume; Kroger, this volume).

In this chapter, we clarify and delineate what we see to be these different readings of Erikson. We argue that, taken together, the readings converge on a broad and integrative framework for understanding in full the development of identity across the human life course (McAdams, 2013a; McAdams & Cox, 2010). Our life-course framework proposes that identity may be construed from three different standpoints of the self—the self as a *social actor*, a *motivated agent*, and an *autobiographical author*.

What Is Identity?

To begin with, let us identify what most readings of Erikson's concept of identity, including the three very different chapters preceding ours, do indeed *have in common*. After all, there is a particular inkblot there, with certain specific features that nearly everybody will detect. We might consider these to be the core or defining characteristics of identity as Erikson conceived it to be—those aspects of the concept that most readers agree differentiate it, if only by matter of emphasis, from other related concepts in psychology and the social sciences, concepts such as "ego," "self," and "personality."

The core of Erikson's meaning regarding identity is about sameness and continuity over time and about how that constructed sameness and continuity situates a developing person in a complex and multivalent social world. What nearly everybody sees in reading Erikson on identity appears clearly, we believe, in these two oft-quoted passages:

> The integration now taking place in the form of ego identity is, as pointed out, more than the sum of the childhood identifications. It is the accrued experience of the ego's ability to integrate all identifications with the vicissitudes of the libido, with the aptitudes developed out of endowment, and with the opportunities offered in social roles. The sense of ego identity, then, is the accrued confidence that the inner sameness and continuity of one's meaning in the past are matched by the sameness and continuity of one's meaning for others.
> *(Erikson, 1963, p. 261)*

> [Identity formation] begins where the usefulness of identification ends. It arises from the selective repudiation and mutual assimilation of childhood identifications and their absorption in a new configuration, which in turn, is dependent on the process by which a *society* (often through subsocieties) *identifies the young individual*, recognizing him as somebody who had to become the way he is, and who, being the way he is, is taken for granted.
> *(Erikson, 1959, p. 113)*

For Erikson, identity is something that the *ego* does. The ego integrates different things—identifications from childhood, one's libidinal history, natural aptitudes or skills, and opportunities to be found in social roles—into a particular configuration that provides the developing person with a sense that he or she is the same continuing person over time and across social space. In terms made famous by William James (1892/1963), the ego is the "I" (the subjective self), and identity is a feature of the "Me" (the objective self, the self as construed by the I). Beginning in adolescence, to the extent that the I is able to construe and arrange the Me into a configuration that assures personal sameness and continuity, the developing person experiences identity. Identity, therefore, is not my entire "personality" (whatever that may be) but rather only those features that are part of the patterning or arrangement (the configuration) whereby I come to see Me as continuous over time. Critically, moreover, the configuration must be recognized and affirmed by society. The I's meaning of itself (the Me) and the attendant sense of sameness and continuity must be matched by the sameness and continuity of one's meaning for others. As Erikson described it in other passages, identity provides the young person with a psychosocial niche in the broad and dynamic world of adulthood. It situates the young person within a social world that now recognizes the young person as somebody who had to become the way he [or she] is—that is, somebody whose life choices and life trajectory now make sense to those people in society and to those societal arrangements whose stamp of recognition matters.

So far, so good. Now, we encounter the differences.

In their chapter on gendered narrative voice in children and their families, Fivush and Zaman (this volume) bring a sociocultural and feminist frame to the activity of telling stories about the self. Beginning in the preschool years, girls and boys tell stories about their personal experiences, supported by the scaffolding efforts of parents, siblings, and other storytellers in their social world. Invoking the concept of *narrative identity*, Fivush and Zaman submit that even in childhood human beings construe sameness and continuity in the self through reminiscing and storytelling and that this builds autobiographical memories and the growing individuated sense of a temporally extended Me. The process of developing a narrative identity is highly gendered, they suggest. Mothers engage in more elaborative reminiscing with their children than do fathers, and both mothers and fathers engage in more elaborative reminiscing with their daughters than with their sons. In adolescence, daughters develop narrative identities that draw from the stories told by and about their mothers, but sons do not seem to use either parent as a model for their own life stories. Recalling a point made forcefully by the feminist theorist Nancy Chodorow (1978), boys seem to become men through a great deal of guess work and experimentation. As *autobiographical authors* of identity, they seem to gather surprisingly little material from the stories that originate in their families.

In his discussion of identity in emerging adulthood, Arnett (this volume) adopts a broad historical and evolutionary perspective to consider the societal arrangements whereby identity might indeed arise as a salient concern in the life course. Arnett questions the universality of Erikson's concept of identity and suggests that it is mainly under conditions of cultural modernity that young people experience the luxuries of choosing a job, a mate, and an ideology—the very choices whereby identity in adolescence and emerging adulthood is made. In traditional premodern societies, going back all the way to our hunting-and-foraging forebears, human beings may not typically struggle very much to discern sameness and continuity in their lives. As *social actors* who perform well-established and tightly circumscribed roles, they know who they are already. Even today, certain societies may not offer the behavioral opportunities and dilemmas that give identity its distinctive Eriksonian meanings.

Like Arnett, Kroger (this volume) examines the life choices that human beings make to define themselves in social groups. Kroger follows Marcia's (1966) classic conceptualization of the *identity status*. In the conventional scenario for identity achievement, adolescents and young adults explore various occupational, ideological, and interpersonal options available to them and eventually make commitments that ideally situate them in a productive and fulfilling psychosocial niche. Those who continue to explore but who have yet to commit are said to be in the status of *moratorium*; those who never explored but committed anyway are in *foreclosure*; and those who neither explore nor commit manifest *identity diffusion*. In Marcia's reading of Erikson, identity is mainly about the decisions that human beings make as motivated agents in the world. In adulthood, sameness and continuity are affirmed through the occupational, ideological, and interpersonal goals, plans, values, and investments that agents set out to pursue. According to Erikson (1963), the virtue of the identity stage in the human life cycle is *fidelity*—staying true to the choices one has made as a free moral agent, choices that are surely shaped by society but whose origins nonetheless lie in the decision-making powers of an agential ego.

The three different readings of Erikson's concept of identity correspond roughly to what our own conceptual framework suggests are three lines or strands of identity development across the human life course (McAdams, 2013a; McAdams & Cox, 2010). Each of the three pertains to a corresponding deep metaphor for the self—the self as actor, agent, and author. A full reading of Erikson, we believe, implicates all three metaphors.

As Arnett (this volume) states, human beings evolved to live as actors in social groups. The corresponding metaphor of the self as a social actor suggests a conception of identity that privileges social roles and the idiosyncratic styles that actors display in their performance of roles (Goffman, 1959). Even in premodern societies, we would argue, the problem of sameness and continuity still arises in the life course, as actors construe identity in the roles and self-attributed traits through which they are recognized by other members of the group.

Human beings also operate as motivated agents, increasingly so from late childhood onward. We come to define ourselves, in part, through the plans, goals, values, and commitments we make as we envision our lives projected into the future. As motivated agents who make self-defining life choices, we construe sameness, continuity, and purpose in ways that Kroger (this volume) and others have traditionally captured through the construct of identity status.

Finally, human beings connect their reconstructed pasts to their imagined futures by constructing and living according to integrative stories of the self, the narrative identities that Fivush and Zaman (this volume) trace back to early childhood years. From the standpoint of the autobiographical author, narrative identity becomes an especially compelling psychological challenge in emerging adulthood and beyond. As authors, we gather material for our narrative identities from our personal experiences and conversations and from the menu of favored images, themes, motifs, and plots that prevail in culture. At the end of the developmental day, narrative may represent the most powerful tool for achieving temporal sameness and continuity in life and the most important psychosocial arena wherein culture and the self come to terms with each other.

Self + Society

The Social Actor: Identity Through Roles and Traits

Following Arnett (this volume), we might wonder what meaning the concept of identity could possibly have had among the hunting and foraging tribes of *Homo sapiens* who lived on the African savannah between 200,000 and 50,000 years ago. And even after—with the technological and cultural innovations that paved the way for agriculture—what relevance might Erikson's idea regarding personal sameness and continuity have for human beings who lived (and continue to live) under those social arrangements that predate urban life? For example, the concept of identity status (Kroger, this volume; see also Crocetti & Meeus, this volume)—with its emphasis on ideological and occupational exploration—does not seem to fit well with what we imagine to be the exigencies of life in hunting and gathering societies. In many traditional agrarian societies, moreover, people may not perceive the human life course as a series of agential commitments to be made amid a plethora of life choices. Nonetheless, we believe that a rudimentary form of identity does indeed arise as a psychological challenge in nearly all human societies, even in those we might imagine to have existed 200,000 years ago. It is that form of identity that speaks directly to the nature of performing as a social actor in a human group.

As cognitively gifted, bipedal organisms, human beings evolved to live in complex, multigenerational groups, cooperating and competing to achieve group and individual goals (Wilson, 2012). Different group members assume different social roles in the group, and roles change with development. To a certain extent, one's social role specifies a particular identity in the group—as a mother, for example, as a hunter, as a defender of the tribe, as a group leader, as one who has the greatest expertise in and responsibility for preparing group meals, and so on. Striving to get along with other actors and to get ahead in the face of limited resources, individual group members develop particular social reputations, which differentiate them from each other (Hogan, 1982). Reputations may be linked to social roles. Group members may perceive a particular person, for instance, as an especially caring mother, a brave warrior, an irresponsible son, or a failed leader. Reputations may also apply more generally, as perceived characteristics of the person that transcend social roles. One may be perceived as especially honest, conscientious, gullible, modest, irritable, or gregarious. For the most part, reputations refer to important qualities attributed to the person as a social actor in the group. Actors are aware of their reputations, and they may seek to burnish or develop them, managing the impressions of others in order to garner acceptance or status in the group (Goffman, 1959; Hogan, 1982).

Shakespeare captured what may be the most basic feature of human nature when he wrote: "All the world's a stage, and all the men and women merely players." As actors on a social stage, human beings enact their roles and display their traits as they move from one social performance to the next, over the long course of human development. Even infants play (unwittingly) to an audience, as caregivers monitor assiduously their emotional expressions and behavioral displays, attributing states and traits along the way: This baby is happy right now! This one is a fussy baby. This one seems to like people.

By the time they hit their second birthday, most human infants recognize themselves in mirrors and other reflecting devices (Lewis & Brooks-Gunn, 1979). A developmental landmark for the human species, self-recognition begins in the literal perception of oneself as an embodied social actor moving through space. Around the same period, toddlers begin to use self-referential words—such as "I," "me," and "mine"—and begin to show social emotions such as pride and embarrassment, which indicates a nascent realization that they are indeed actors on a social stage, social actors whose performances are observed and critiqued by others (Tangney, Stuewig, & Mashek, 2007). For social actors, there is no getting away from an audience: other group members are nearly always observing what the actor does, a phenomenon that ultimately results, Mead (1934) argued, in the child's astute apprehension of a *generalized other*. As actors learn to anticipate how their audiences will react, and as they develop the powers of empathy for other group members, they develop a conscience (Kochanska & Aksan, 2006), which ideally promotes self-regulation and enhances the actor's reputation as a "good" member of the group.

For social actors in human groups, identity is defined by the roles they play and the traits they consistently display. Studies that trace the development of the self-concept show that young children (age 3–6) typically describe themselves in the simple language of fleeting states and physical appearance, but by late childhood (age 8–11) they attribute broad personality traits to the self (Harter, 2006). A ten-year old girl may see herself as "outgoing," "spontaneous," "a very good listener," "lacking confidence in new situations," and "happy with my girlfriends but shy around boys." Her explicit trait attributions may capture general tendencies that she (the I) reflexively sees in herself (the Me) as a social actor (outgoing, spontaneous), as well as more conditional ascriptions that seem to depend on the exigencies of social situations (happy with my girlfriends but shy around boys).

Research suggests that people continue to refine and expand the discourse of traits as they move across the adolescent years. According to Harter (2006), early adolescence is marked by a proliferation of self-ascribed traits and the construction of multiple versions of the Me, as the I struggles to accommodate the increasing complexity of social life. The teenaged I may now begin to see how the various roles and traits attributed to the Me do not coalesce very well. Like Holden Caulfield in *The Catcher in the Rye*, a young man may note the jarring discontinuity between the social performances that seem to define him in the presence of good friends and those that characterize his behavior with his parents. Do his wildly discordant social performances suggest that he is what Caulfield famously described as a phony? More cognizant now of how their social actions may contradict their inner thoughts and feelings, adolescents may begin to wonder: "Who am I?" "What links together my many different social performances?" "In what sense am I the same person from one situation to the next and across time?" "And how do others *really* see me?"

Amid the increasing, and increasingly contradictory, social demands that actors encounter as they move toward adulthood, young men and women may now find themselves face to face with the Eriksonian problem of identity. In the rudimentary terms of the social actor, however, identity is not so much about vocation, ideology, or even exploration and commitment. It is instead about coming to terms with my social reputation in a social world that places competing demands on me. It is about settling on what I want my audiences to see and know about me, even as I change over time and perform differently from one social scene to the next. It is about the character traits and the social roles that I believe define me, and that I want other people to ascribe to me when they define me, for their definitions of me—my social reputation in their eyes—will go a long way in determining how well I am able, as an adult, to get along and get ahead in the group.

The psychological and social dynamics that determine how social actors develop identities in human groups may not have changed all that much in the last 200,000 years. Then as now, social actors fashion reputations as they strive to get along and get ahead in the group. Then and now, a sense of inner sameness and continuity—as experienced by the actor and formulated by the audience through social reputation—may draw heavily on the attribution of traits and roles. These kinds of attributions about social actors capture what Erikson (1968, p. 50) describes as the "style of one's individuality," a phrase that he (along with Kroger, this volume) repeatedly invokes in characterizing the concept of identity.

As they perform their various roles in the group, social actors observe their own behavior, and they observe the responses to their behavior displayed by others. Relying on these observations, social actors attribute traits to themselves (Bem, 1972), in a manner not unlike how audiences observe actors in order to make trait attributions about them. As identity develops, the style of a particular social actor's individuality is conveyed through the trait attributions and role characterizations that the I ultimately formulates through repeated observations of the Me. Going back 200,000 years, gender has probably always exerted a strong impact on the kinds of roles and traits that actors attribute to themselves, shaped by group expectations regarding how female and male actors should behave, feel, and think. In contemporary modern societies, class and ethnicity are likely to be important factors, as well. Working-class communities may embrace different value systems and manifest different adaptive concerns than their counterparts in the upper middle class, which may shape the characteristic manner in which corresponding social actors perform their roles.

For certain ethnic groups, moreover, the self may be split between the performative demands associated with two contrasting cultures. Going back to DuBois's (1903/1989) characterization in *The Souls of Black Folk*, social scientists have analyzed the challenges faced by African-American adults who must often adapt to the norms of behavior among white Americans while staying true to their identities as people of color. Research with bilingual Mexican Americans and Latina and Latino groups suggests that ethnic minorities in the United States often feel torn between different self-representations. In one study, for example, bilingual Mexican Americans tended to endorse different personality traits when thinking about themselves in English compared with thinking about themselves in Spanish (Ramirez-Esparza, Gosling, Benet-Martinez, Potter, & Pennebaker, 2006). Accordingly, social-psychological research on *bicultural identity integration* examines the extent to which bicultural individuals are able to combine the self-attributions they associate with their different cultures into a coherent whole (Benet-Martinez & Haritatos, 2005). Similar identity challenges may confront immigrants and other social actors who cross group, class, and cultural boundaries, as Arnett's (this volume) example of Chinese factory girls makes clear (see also Way & Rogers, this volume; Worrell, this volume).

As social actors grow up, their style of individuality may begin to crystallize. The traits that they attribute to themselves as a way of affirming and explaining psychological sameness and continuity may show increasing stability as social actors move through their twenties and thirties and into middle age. As indexed in research on self-report scales of dispositional traits, the basic trait dimensions that capture the gamut of psychological individuality show increasing interindividual stability across the adult life course (Roberts & Del Vecchio, 2000; see also Lilgendahl, this volume). At the same time, research on mean-level changes in these self-attributions reveals gradual increases in positive traits regarding conscientiousness and agreeableness across the adult life course and gradual decreases in the negative self-attributions associated with the broad trait of neuroticism (Roberts, Walton, & Viechtbauer, 2006). On average, social actors come to see themselves as increasingly dutiful, self-disciplined, competent, industrious, caring, altruistic, and socially responsible as they age, at least through midlife, and decreasingly irritable, anxious, depressive, vulnerable, and prone to hostility. These well-established trends, supported by a large and growing body of empirical research, are linked to developmental changes in social roles and experiences (Neyer & Lehnart, 2007). As social actors take on mature adult roles, such as spouse and parent, and assume generative responsibilities in a social community, they change how they see themselves, and others change their views of them, as well. Social reputations, as encoded in the minds of actors and in their audiences, may change gradually over the life course, following an arc of maturation.

The well-established developmental trends in self-attributions across the adult life course signal the kind of maturation in identity that Kroger (this volume) depicts as "the move toward wholeness." Whereas Kroger (this volume) couches this move in the agential language of identity status, researchers in the field of personality psychology would explain it all in terms of the maturation of dispositional traits. Our view is more consistent with the latter perspective than with Kroger (this volume). However, we interpret personality change in this case as reflective of identity change, too—for the putative traits that comprise personality are represented in the minds of actors as explicit self-attributions. In other words, *self-attributed* personality traits, along with associated social roles, are the basic stuff of identity for the social actor. They are the categories of self that the I draws on to affirm sameness and continuity of the Me as an actor who performs on the social stage of life. And, given the foundational fact that human beings evolved to live in complex social groups, the traits and roles that define an actor's social reputation have been the most fundamental dimensions of Eriksonian identity for 200,000 years and remain so today. They are the most basic psychological elements of a human being's unique style of individuality.

The Motivated Agent: Identity Through Goals, Values, and Life Projects

Although Erikson (1950; 1968) articulated a seminal theory of identity development across the life course, he was not the first social scientist to discuss the problem of identity. William James (1892/1963) got to the heart of the matter in this famous passage:

> I am often confronted by the necessity of standing by one of my empirical selves and relinquishing the rest. Not that I would not, if I could, be both handsome and fat and well-dressed, and a great athlete, and make a million a year, be a wit, a *bon vivant*, and a lady killer, as well as a philosopher; a philanthropist, statesman, warrior, and African explorer; as well as a "tone poet" and saint. But the thing is simply impossible. The millionaire's work would run counter to the saint's; the *bon vivant* and philanthropist would trip each other up; the philosopher and lady-killer could not well keep house in the same tenement of clay. Such different characters may conceivably at the outset of life be alike *possible* to a man. But to make any one of them actual, the rest must more or less be suppressed. So the seeker of his truest, strongest, deepest self must review the list carefully, and pick out the one on which to stake his salvation. All other selves thereupon become unreal, but the fortunes of this self are real. Its failures are real failures, its triumphs real triumphs, carrying shame and gladness with them. (p. 174)

Living in a modern world wherein some men (and a few women) enjoyed the luxury of choosing from a list of many different selves, James asserted that one must ultimately commit to a single life vocation, or at most a small set of possibilities, and theretofore "stake" one's "salvation" on the choice. The man (or woman) who seeks his (or her) "truest, strongest, deepest self" must make a self-defining decision. In Kroger's (this volume) language of identity status, the individual must explore the various possibilities that present themselves in the world and eventually commit to a subset of them.

In terms of identity, the passage from James is less about developing a social reputation as an actor in the group than it is about exerting human agency. Looking to the future, the motivated agent surveys the possibilities in life and eventually commits to a plan, a set of goals and values, a life project that will orient the agent as he or she moves purposely into the future. Of course, the social context supremely matters: the African explorer needs to acquire funding for the expedition and the tone poet needs to win approval (and financial remuneration) for his or her talent. Identity choice(s) must be validated by society. But the key point here is that identity involves more than the social actor's achievement and maintenance of a good social reputation in the group. It also involves making life choices, developing plans, articulating goals and values, and making long-term commitments as a motivated agent.

Erikson's major contribution to social science discourse on the concept of identity was to explore the intricate dialectic between self and society in the formation of an identity and to identify a stage in the human life course wherein the dialectic appears to become most dynamically salient. Erikson defined the fifth stage in his famous model of psychosocial development as *identity versus role confusion*. Although he often linked the stage to the adolescent years (Erikson, 1963), it is clear that concerted work on establishing an identity often, if not nearly always, extends well into what Arnett (2000, this volume) characterizes as the developmental period of emerging adulthood. In Erikson's (1958) classic study of Martin Luther's identity development, for example, the struggle to reconcile self and society runs from Luther's teenaged-years into his thirties—his years as not only an adolescent but also a "young man," signaling the book's title: *Young Man Luther*.

Luther began the period as an idealistic and obsessive Catholic monk and emerged, two decades later, as a radical church reformer. Whereas few young men and women experience the kind of dramatic upheaval that Luther experienced, and fewer yet make identity decisions that alter the course of history, Luther's sixteenth-century adventure in exploration and commitment serves as a model, Erikson believed, for the decisions that twentieth-century young people must also make. Ideally, young men and women should sample life's occupational, ideological, and interpersonal options within a developmental period of low-risk experimentation, trying on different identity possibilities before m long-term commitments. Erikson (1959) ima such a period as a time of *psychosocial moratorium*.

> The period can be viewed as a psychosocial moratorium during which the individual through free role experimentation may find a niche in some section of his society, a niche which is firmly defined and yet seems to be uniquely made for him. In finding it the young adult gains an assured sense of inner continuity and social sameness which will bridge what he was as a child and what he is about to become, and will reconcile his conception of himself and his community's recognition of him. (p. 111)

Ever since Marcia (1966) translated the idea of a moratorium period in life to a categorical status, researchers have used interview and questionnaire methods to classify young people as having either (1) identity achievement (explored options, made commitments), (2) moratorium (exploring options, not made commitments yet), (3) foreclosure (never explored options, made commitments anyway), or (4) diffusion (never explored options, never made commitments). Kroger (this volume) reviews notable research in the study of identity statuses. Her review shows that the concept of identity status hedges its bets when it comes to the question of whether identity should be located within a demarcated developmental stage. Early studies focused on Erikson's fifth psychosocial stage, suggesting that young adults should explore occupational, ideological, and interpersonal options in life before making long-term commitments—like Martin Luther, in a sense, and consistent with Erikson's belief that successful resolution of the identity versus role confusion stage should solidify the human virtue of fidelity. More recent studies, however, seem to suggest that individuals may recycle through the statuses at any point in the adult life course, reexploring options (pertaining to occupational, ideological, and interpersonal goals) and making new (and seemingly more provisional) commitments. In principle, then, a particular person might be located in the status of identity achievement at age twenty-five, but move (backward or forward, it is not clear) to moratorium by age forty. The flexibility with which the researchers employ the identity status concept likely reflects the fact that motivated agents living in modern societies continue to make new life choices, formulate new goals and projects, and alter their motivational agendas, often in dramatic ways, as they respond to on-time and off-time developmental demands and as their life circumstances invariably change, often unpredictably, from one period to the next (Elder, 1995).

The strand of identity development that ultimately results in the exploration of and commitment to life goals, values, and projects begins with the child's realization, around the age of four or five years, that he or she is, like all other people, a motivated agent. Developmental research has shown that most children acquire a *theory of mind* shortly before the kindergarten years, when they come to understand that human beings have desires and beliefs in their minds and that these desires and beliefs *motivate* human behavior (Wellman, 1993). By age five, then, most children have acquired a folk psychology of the mind that says people do things because they *want* to do them and because they *believe* certain things: Jessica looks for the cookie in the kitchen cabinet because (1) she *wants* the cookie and (2) she *believes* that that is where the cookie is. In the short-term, Jessica's *goal* is to find the cookie. Jessica is, therefore, a motivated agent: her behavior is self-determined and goal-directed, ultimately motivated by desire and belief.

It is critical to note that theory of mind is not about what children can do but rather about how they think about what they do. Research conclusively shows that even human infants act in a goal-directed manner. Like all other children, therefore, Jessica has been behaving in accord with implicit goals nearly all her life—going back to the first few weeks of life. But she does not realize that she is doing so until she acquires a theory of mind. In other words, she does not know that she is a motivated agent until she realizes that people have desires and beliefs in their heads, upon which they act—people like *Me*! In the same sense, then, that the Jamesian I does not see itself (the Me) as a social actor until self-recognition kicks in (around eighteen months of age), the I's conception of the Me as a motivated agent—the watershed realization that I am the source of my own behavior, that I act on my own desires and beliefs in order to make things happen in the world—awaits the preschool emergence of theory of mind.

As children move through elementary school, they come to attribute goals, plans, projects, and values to themselves. Along with the personal traits and social roles that children, as social actors, ascribe to their own social reputations, the I begins to define itself in teleological terms, too, in terms of what it wants to accomplish in the future, what it values, what it plans to do to actualize wants and values, what it is "working on" these days in order to achieve desired ends. Research and theory on what is often called *the age five to seven shift* suggest that most children become increasingly planful, goal-directed, and future-oriented as they move through the early grade school years (Sameroff & Haith, 1996). The development of concrete operational thought during this time (Piaget, 1970) ushers in a more rational and systematic understanding of how the world works, which, along with the effects of schooling, may confer on consciousness a greater sense of order and planfulness. Fourth- and fifth-graders wake up in the morning with goals and plans on their minds. As motivated agents, they structure their time in order to accomplish their goals or at least they respond to the structures established for them by teachers, parents, and other socializing authorities. They learn to value certain goals, and the means whereby goals are accomplished, over other goals and means (Rokeach, 1973). The I eventually attributes the most psychologically salient goals and values to the Me.

As Erikson (1959; 1963; 1968) made abundantly clear, the identity struggle that many adolescents and emerging adults experience often centers, as it did for Luther, on life goals and values. *Who am I?* (identity) is tied up with *What do I want to do with my life?* (goals) and *What do I believe to be true and good?* (values). It should come as no surprise, therefore, that Marcia's (1966; Kroger, this volume) paradigm for assessing identity statuses emphasizes the domains of occupational and ideological choice—how motivated agents decide what their (occupational) goals and their (ideological) values are to be going forward in life, aiming toward the future. To the extent that the exploration of and commitment to life goals and values affirm a sense of inner sameness and temporal continuity, and to the extent that society recognizes that particular configuration of desire and belief, the young person is able to consolidate a sense of identity as a motivated agent.

Outside the framework of identity status, many well-regarded lines of research in personality, developmental, social, and cultural psychology have examined the vicissitudes of such motivational constructs as goals, plans, and values as they relate to identity and the self. For example, Markus and Nurius (1986) launched a fruitful line of empirical inquiry around the concept of *possible selves*, which refer to the "hopes, fears, goals, and threats" that give "meaning, organization, and direction" to human life (p. 954). At any given time in life, the I may construe the Me in terms of multiple possible selves (see also King & Hicks, 2006). Each possible self exists as a concretely articulated and highly personalized motivational image of the Me. Motivational features of identity have also been examined in studies of personal strivings (Emmons, 1986), personal projects (Little, 1999), and life longings (Schiebe, Freund, & Baltes, 2007). Cultural differences in identity often track different priorities in strivings, projects, longings, and values. Among individualistic cultures, for example, priority is given to the goals of individual achievement and differentiating the self from others, whereas more collectivist cultures value social harmony and the goal of finding one's secure place in a hierarchical social order (Markus & Kitayama, 1991). As another example, research has shown that Asian Americans, Koreans, and Russians tend to endorse more *avoidance* goals, compared to European Americans (Elliot, Chirkov, Kim, & Sheldon, 2001). By contrast, European Americans show more goals aimed at *approaching* positive states.

Lifespan studies document developmental shifts in the motivational content and structure of identity. For example, younger adults prioritize life goals regarding the acquisition of knowledge and skills, intimacy, friendships, and careers; midlife adults find their psychosocial niches in goals regarding the future of their children and securing what they have already attained; for older adults, goals related to health, retirement, leisure, and understanding current events in the world structure their self-conceptions and provide them with a sense of inner sameness and continuity (Freund & Riediger, 2006). Goals indicative of prosocial engagement—generativity, civic involvement, improving one's community—become more pronounced as people move into midlife and remain relatively strong for many adults into their retirement years (McAdams, de St. Aubin, & Logan, 1993; Peterson & Duncan, 2007). Compared to younger adults, moreover, midlife adults appear to approach goals in a more realistic and prudent manner, realizing their limitations and conserving their resources to focus on those few goals in life they consider to be most central to identity (Wrosch, Heckhausen, & Lachman, 2006).

The Autobiographical Author: Identity Through Life Narrative

Picking up on intellectual movements in philosophy and literary studies (e.g., MacIntyre, 1981; Ricoeur, 1984), psychologists began to connect the concept of identity to life narrative in the 1980s and 1990s (e.g., Bruner, 1986; Freeman, 1993; Shotter & Gergen, 1989). The most explicit linkage was articulated in the *life-story model of identity*, initially presented by this paper's first author in his book, *Power, Intimacy, and the Life Story: Personological Inquiries into Identity* (McAdams, 1985). The book proposed that the psychological configuration best designed to confer a sense of inner sameness and continuity in a person's life is an internalized story of the self—an evolving narrative in the mind of an autobiographical author serving to integrate the reconstructed past, experienced present, and anticipated future. Stories effectively make sense of human time by expressing how motivated agents move across landscapes of consciousness and action, ordering events into meaningful sequences, from beginning to middle to end (Bruner, 1986). In fiction and in life, stories show how people change over time, and how they stay the same. For a reflexive autobiographical narrator (the I), who serves as the protagonist in his or her own constructed life story (the Me), the narrative conveys the subjective understanding of how the protagonist came to be, underscoring the deep temporal continuity of an individual life even as circumstances, characters, and the protagonist him- or herself continue to change.

Beginning in late adolescence, McAdams (1985) asserted, people discover who they are and how they fit into the broader adult world of work and love by finding and/or creating a story that fits their understanding of how they have developed over time and what their lives may mean. Strongly shaped by both culture and personal experience, the life story is situated within a particular ideological setting, or backdrop of belief and value, and it is punctuated by key scenes, or autobiographical episodic memories that stand out as self-defining high points, low points, and turning points in the story. The most salient content themes running through the texts of people's life stories, as projected back to the past and forward to the future, are those related to agency (power, achievement, the expansion of the self) and communion (intimacy, love, the surrender of the self).

Although Erikson never explicitly construed identity to be an integrative and evolving story of the self, he came close. In his two great psychobiographies—*Young Man Luther* (Erikson, 1958) and *Gandhi's Truth* (Erikson, 1969)—Erikson described the kinds of stories that these men told themselves about themselves as they struggled to figure out who they were (identity) and what kind of legacy they would leave in their world (generativity). In both cases, Erikson aimed to account for how these monumental figures in history came to understand themselves *as adults*. What does it mean to be an adult? In this revealing passage, Erikson suggests that it means, among other things, constructing a story for life:

> To be [an] adult means among other things to see one's own life in continuous perspective, both in retrospect and prospect. By accepting some definition as to who he is, usually on the basis of a function in an economy, a place in the sequence of generations, and a status in the structure of society, the adult is able to selectively reconstruct his past in such a way that, step for step, it seems to have planned him, or better he seems to have planned it. In this sense, psychologically we do choose our parents, our family history, and the history of our kings, heroes, and gods. By making them our own, we maneuver ourselves into the inner position of proprietors, of creators.
>
> *(Erikson, 1958, pp. 111–112)*

The origins of narrative identity may be traced back to the early childhood years. In the second and third years of life, children begin to show evidence of autobiographical memory (Fivush, 2011). Shortly after the I becomes aware of itself as a Me (around age two), it begins to attach to the Me simple episodic memories of everyday life. Children begin to collect memories of personal events, putting together what happened to them in a given situation with how they, as a social actor, responded. With the consolidation of theory of mind, moreover, children may inject agency, desire, and belief into their memories. With the help of their parents and others, they begin to tell stories about their experiences as social actors and motivated agents. By the age of five or six, children typically know how a good telling of a story—any story—should unfold, displaying their deep appreciation of what Mandler (1984) calls a *story grammar*. Grade-school children know, for example, that stories typically are set in a particular time and place and that they involve the actions of a motivated agent/protagonist. The protagonist acts to achieve an end, and other characters respond in turn, or else the protagonist encounters some sort of obstacle along the way, and it all gets worked out eventually, as the sequence of events that make up the story terminate in a satisfying ending.

As Fivush and Zaman (this volume) make clear, a broad range of social forces shape children's inclinations and abilities to construct stories about their personal experiences and about themselves. In the preschool years, parents encourage children to tell stories about events in their lives. They may prompt children with questions about what happened in a given event and what they were thinking and feeling. They may help children fill in the details of the event or explore what the event may mean. They may relate their own experiences to those of their children. Research on parent–child conversations reveals marked individual differences in the ways parents approach the task of self-storytelling. Mothers tend to encourage daughters, more than sons, to explore the emotional dynamics of autobiographical memories, especially memories involving sadness. Early on, girls use more emotion words than boys in their autobiographical recollections. When parents consistently engage their children in an elaborative conversational pattern, asking children to reflect and elaborate on their feelings and thoughts, children develop richer autobiographical memories and tell more detailed stories about themselves. Conversely, a more constricted style of conversation on the part of parents is associated with less articulated personal narratives in children.

The full expression of narrative identity requires more, however, than telling coherent stories about individual episodes in one's life. Autobiographical authors must be able to string events together into extended narratives that explain the development of the self over time. They must be able to draw conclusions about themselves from recollected events, deriving personal themes that summarize how they believe themselves to be similar to and different from others in their world, themes that articulate what Erikson depicted as one's style of individuality. In sum, they must be able to engage in *autobiographical reasoning* (see Habermas, this volume; Pasupathi, this volume), which refers to a wide range of cognitive operations whereby authors draw on their storied accounts of life to make inferences about who they are and what their lives may mean (Habermas & Bluck, 2000; McLean & Fournier, 2008).

Developmental research shows that autobiographical reasoning skills begin to emerge in late childhood and continue to grow through the adolescent years. Older adolescents and young adults show more facility than their younger counterparts in (1) deriving organizing themes in their lives; (2) sequencing personal episodes into causal chains in order to explain their development; (3) illustrating personal growth over time; (4) identifying clear beginnings and endings in their life narrative accounts; and (5) incorporating foreshadowing, retrospective reflection, and other markers of mature self-authorship (Habermas & Bluck, 2000; Habermas & de Silveira, 2008; McAdams et al., 2006; McLean & Breen, 2009; Pasupathi & Wainryb, 2010). The development of narrative identity is contoured, furthermore, by normative expectations regarding the life course—cultural knowledge that young people gather regarding when people typically get married, for example, have children, move into and out of jobs, care for aging parents, retire, and so on (Thomsen & Bernsten, 2008). Gender, ethnicity, and social class strongly shape these identity expectations (McAdams, 2013b; Syed & Azmitia, 2010).

Research suggests that young people construct narrative identity through a protracted process of experiencing events, narrating those experiences to others (such as friends and parents), monitoring the reactions to those narrations, editing the narrations in response to the reactions, experiencing new events, narrating those new events in light of past narrations, and on and on. Over developmental time, selves create stories, which in turn create new selves (McLean, Pasupathi, & Pals, 2007). Narrative identity emerges gradually, through daily conversations and social interactions, through introspection, through decisions that people make regarding work and love, and through normative and serendipitous passages in life, as when a high-school senior composes a college admissions essay, a young couple write their marriage vows, or a person meets with a vocational counselor to discuss "What do I want to do with my life?"

Narrative identity continues to develop, furthermore, for much of the rest of the life course. Cross-sectional studies show that middle-aged adults construct more interpretive and psychologically nuanced life narratives than do younger adults (Bluck & Gluck, 2004; Pasupathi & Mansour, 2006). Older adults also tend to tell life stories that are more emotionally positive (Singer, Rexhaj, & Baddeley, 2007) and more focused on stable rather than changing aspects of the self (McLean, 2008). Findings like these dovetail with Pennebaker and Stone's (2003) demonstration, based on laboratory studies of language use and analyses of published fiction, that adults use more positive and fewer negative affect words and demonstrate greater levels of cognitive complexity as they age, at least up through midlife. The findings are also consistent with a broader literature in lifespan developmental psychology showing that middle-aged adults tend to express the most complex, individuated, and integrated self-conceptions, and with research on episodic memory and aging showing a positive memory bias among older adults (Kennedy, Mather, & Carstensen, 2004).

The ultimate arbiter for determining the psychological and moral legitimacy of narrative identity is *culture* (Hammack, 2008; McAdams, 2006). A growing research literature documents important cultural differences in autobiographical memory and self-storytelling. Examining self-defining autobiographical memories among Chinese and American adults, for example, Wang and Conway (2004) found that Americans provide more memories of individual experiences and one-time events, focusing mainly on their own roles and emotions, whereas Chinese adults are more inclined to recall memories of social and historical events, and they placed more emphasis on social interactions and significant others in their stories. Culture, moreover, provides the *master narratives* for what it means to live a good and worthy life, invoking favored images, plots, and characters from which developing persons sample and appropriate as they make meaning out of their own lives. In research on Israeli and Palestinian adolescents, for instance, Hammack (2008) has shown how the form and content of individual life stories often reflect cultural morality stories of persecution and triumph for the Israeli youth and the tragedy of a lost land and stolen identity for young Palestinians.

McAdams (2013b) has identified a set of *redemptive narratives* that appear again and again in favored cultural expressions and in individual life stories told by American men and women at midlife, including stories of atonement, upward social mobility, personal emancipation, and recovery. Whereas individual variations on the theme of redemption tend to characterize the narrative identities constructed by highly generative and well-functioning American adults today (e.g., McAdams, Diamond, de St. Aubin, & Mansfield, 1997), the cultural sources for these stories may be traced back to the spiritual testimonials of seventeenth-century New England Puritans, Benjamin Franklin's iconic autobiography, nineteenth-century narratives of escaped African-American slaves, Horatio Alger stories, and the burgeoning twentieth- and twenty-first-century literature of self-help, twelve-step programs, and Oprah (McAdams, 2013b). For Americans, redemptive narratives come in contrasting liberal and conservative variations, reflected at the level of political discourse itself and in the actual life narratives told by politically liberal and politically conservative adults (McAdams et al., 2008). Indeed, there may be no clearer illustration of the power of redemptive narratives to integrate lives and inspire others than the life stories fashioned by the two most recent presidents of the United States: George W. Bush (McAdams, 2011) and Barack Obama (McAdams, 2013b).

Conclusion

Across the life course, human beings develop identity through the social reputations they establish, the vocational and ideological choices they make, and the stories they project and internalize to comprehend their changing lives in time. A full reading of Erikson's concept of identity suggests that there are at least three primary ways whereby human beings consolidate the sense of inner sameness and temporal continuity that he identified to be the hallmark of identity. Through reputation, choice, and narrative, the developing person configures the self to express a unique style of individuality that is recognized and affirmed by society.

Arnett (this volume) is correct, we believe, in suggesting that certain features of Erikson's identity concept do not readily apply to traditional, premodern societies, and to the hunting and foraging tribes of *Homo sapiens* who populated the African savannah in the late Paleolithic period and before. However, because we lived then, and continue to live now, in complex social groups, cooperating and competing in the face of limited resources, human beings care deeply about our reputations as social actors in the group. From the standpoint of the social actor, identity refers to the dispositional traits and the characteristic roles that people attribute to each other, and to themselves, through repeated observations of social performance. Among our evolutionary forebears and for modern men and women today, one's style of individuality is recognized and expressed through those traits and roles that capture, albeit in simple psychosocial terms, how an actor remains the same person from one situation to the next and over time. Identity begins with the actor's social reputation.

But in contemporary society, identity does not end there. Kroger (this volume) summarizes decades of research on the concept of identity status, which captures the sense in which young people need to explore different options in ideology, vocation, and interpersonal relationships and then commit to a delimited set of them, in order to achieve a second sense of identity—identity from the standpoint of a motivated agent. Ideally, such an achievement, Erikson argued, affirms the virtue of fidelity. Fidelity suggests faithfulness to the identity commitments one has made. The motivated agent chooses those life goals to pursue, those values to personify, and those relationships to cultivate and then, if all goes according to the Eriksonian plan, sticks with the choices. Of course, all rarely goes according to plan, as Kroger (this volume) seems to suggest when she shows that people often recycle through the statuses as they move through adulthood. Here, it seems that the concept of identity status is too static to capture fully the dynamic nature of identity change in the adult years. Outside what we judge to be the rather parochial viewpoint of the identity status tradition, researchers in personality and social psychology have extensively examined this developmental process through such constructs as life goals, life tasks, life longings, personal strivings, personal projects, and the development of human values.

A third strand of identity development captures the sense in which human beings construe inner sameness and temporal continuity in their lives through the construction of self-defining life stories. The origins of narrative identity lie in the emergence of autobiographical memory and early parent–child conversations about personal experiences (Fivush & Zaman, this volume). Erikson hinted at the importance of narrative identity in his psychobiographies of Luther and Gandhi, wherein he imagined how these two protagonists struggled to make narrative sense of their own lives—in full retrospect and prospect—as they moved into and through adulthood. From the standpoint of the autobiographical author, identity is the story that one tells (to oneself and to others) about the reconstructed past and imagined future, complete with setting, scenes, characters, plot, and themes. It is the I's integrative narrative about the Me, an evolving tale that reflects prevailing cultural norms as much as it reflects the self. As those features of identity that correspond to the social actor and the motivated agent develop over the life course, the autobiographical author aims to make sense of it all through narrative. At the end of the developmental day, narrative identity offers a storied explanation of why the actor does what it does and why the agent wants what it wants, and what it all may mean—past, present, and future—for one particular person moving through time and social space, over the long course of a human life.

References

Arnett, J. J. (2000). Emerging adulthood: A theory of development from the late teens through the twenties. *American Psychologist, 55,* 469–480.

Arnett, J. J. (this volume). Identity development from adolescence to emerging adulthood. In K. C. McLean & M. Syed (Eds.), *The Oxford handbook of identity development*.

Bem, D. J. (1972). Self-perception theory. In L. Berkowitz (Ed.), *Advances in experimental social psychology* (vol. 6, pp. 1–62). New York: Academic Press.

Benet-Martinez, V., & Haritatos, J. (2005). Bicultural identity integration (BII): Components and psychosocial antecedents. *Journal of Personality, 73,* 1015–1050.

Bluck, S., & Gluck, J. (2004). Making things better and learning a lesson: Experiencing wisdom across the lifespan. *Journal of Personality, 72,* 543–572.

Bruner, J. S. (1986). *Actual minds, possible worlds*. Cambridge, MA: Harvard University Press.

Chodorow, N. (1978). *The reproduction of mothering*. Berkeley: University of California Press.

DuBois, W. E. B. (1903/1989). *The souls of black folk*. New York: Penguin.

Elder, G. H., Jr. (1995). The life course paradigm: Social change and individual development. In P. Moen, G. H. Elder, Jr., & K. Luscher (Eds.), *Examining lives in context: Perspectives on the ecology of human development* (pp. 101–139). Washington, DC: American Psychological Association Press.

Elliot, A. J., Chirkov, V. I., Kim, Y., & Sheldon, K. M. (2001). A cross-cultural analysis of avoidance (relative to approach) personal goals. *Psychological Science, 12,* 505–510.

Emmons, R. A. (1986). Personal strivings: An approach to personality and subjective well-being. *Journal of Personality and Social Psychology, 51,* 1058–1068.

Erikson, E. H. (1950). *Childhood and society*. New York: Norton.

Erikson, E. H. (1958). *Young man Luther*. New York: Norton.

Erikson, E. H. (1959). Identity and the life cycle: Selected papers. *Psychological Issues, 1,* 5–165.

Erikson, E. H. (1963). *Childhood and society* (2nd Ed.). New York: Norton.

Erikson, E. H. (1968). *Identity: Youth and crisis*. New York: Norton.

Erikson, E. H. (1969). *Gandhi's truth*. New York: Norton.

Erikson, E. H., Erikson, J. M., & Kivnick, H. Q. (1986). *Vital involvements in old age*. New York: Norton.

Fivush, R. (2011). The development of autobiographical memory. In S. T. Fiske, D. L. Schacter, & S. E. Taylor (Eds.), *Annual review of psychology* (vol. 62, pp. 559–582). Palo Alto, CA: Annual Reviews.

Fivush, R., & Zaman, W. (this volume). Gendered narrative voice: Sociocultural and feminist approaches to identity. In K. C. McLean & M. Syed (Eds.), *The Oxford handbook of identity development*.

Freeman, M. (1993). *Rewriting the self: History, memory, narrative*. London: Routledge.

Freund, A. M., & Riediger, M. (2006). Goals as building blocks of personality and development in adulthood. In D. K. Mroczek & T. D. Little (Eds.), *Handbook of personality development* (pp. 353–372). Mahwah, NJ: Erlbaum.

Goffman, E. (1959). *The presentation of self in everyday life*. Garden City, NY: Doubleday.

Habermas, T., & Bluck, S. (2000). Getting a life: The emergence of the life story in adolescence. *Psychological Bulletin, 126,* 748–769.

Habermas, T., & de Silveira, C. (2008). The development of global coherence in life narrative across adolescence: Temporal, causal, and thematic aspects. *Developmental Psychology, 44,* 707–721.

Hammack, P. L. (2008). Narrative and the cultural psychology of identity. *Personality and Social Psychology Review, 12,* 222–247.

Harter, S. (2006). The self. In N. Eisenberg (Ed.) and W. Damon & R. M. Lerner (Series Eds.), *Handbook of child psychology: Vol. 3. Social, emotional, and personality development* (pp. 505–570). New York: Wiley.

Hogan, R. (1982). A socioanalytic theory of personality. In M. Paige (Ed.), *Nebraska symposium on motivation* (vol. 29, pp. 55–89). Lincoln, NE: University of Nebraska Press.

James, W. (1892/1963). *Psychology*. Greenwich, CT: Fawcett.

Kennedy, Q., Mather, M., & Carstensen, L. L. (2004). The role of motivation in age-related positivity effect in autobiographical memory. *Psychological Science, 15,* 208–214.

King, L. A., & Hicks, J. A. (2006). Narrating the self in the past and future: Implications for maturity. *Research in Human Development, 3,* 121–138.

Kochanska, G., & Aksan, N. (2006). Children's conscience and self-regulation. *Journal of Personality, 74,* 1587–1617.

Kroger, J. (this volume). Identity development through adulthood: The move toward "wholeness." In K. C. McLean & M. Syed (Eds.), *The Oxford handbook of identity development*.

Lewis, M., & Brooks-Gunn, J. (1979). *Social cognition and the acquisition of self*. New York: Plenum.

Little, B. R. (1999). Personality and motivation: Personal action and the conative evolution. In L. A. Pervin & O. P. John (Eds.), *Handbook of personality: Theory and research* (2nd Ed., pp. 501–524). New York: Guilford Press.

MacIntyre, A. (1981). *After virtue*. Notre Dame, IN: University of Notre Dame Press.

Mandler, J. M. (1984). *Stories, scripts, and scenes: Aspects of schema theory*. Hillsdale, NJ: Erlbaum.

Marcia, J. E. (1966). Development and validation of ego identity status. *Journal of Personality and Social Psychology, 3,* 551–558.

Markus, H., & Kitayama, S. (1991). Culture and the self: Implications for cognition, emotion, and motivation. *Psychological Review, 98,* 224–253.

Markus, H., & Nurius, P. (1986). Possible selves. *American Psychologist, 41,* 954–969.

McAdams, D. P. (1985). *Power, intimacy, and the life story: Personological inquiries into identity*. Homewood, IL: Dorsey Press.

McAdams, D. P. (2006). The problem of narrative coherence. *Journal of Constructivist Psychology, 19,* 109–125.

McAdams, D. P. (2011). *George W. Bush and the redemptive dream: A psychological Portrait*. New York: Oxford University Press.

McAdams, D. P. (2013a). The psychological self as actor, agent, and author. *Perspectives on Psychological Science, 8,* 272–295.

McAdams, D. P. (2013b). *The redemptive self: Stories Americans live by* (revised and expanded edition). New York: Oxford University Press.

McAdams, D. P., Albaugh, M., Farber, E., Daniels, J., Logan, R. L., & Olson, B. (2008). Family metaphors and moral intuitions: How conservatives and liberals narrate their lives. *Journal of Personality and Social Psychology, 95,* 978–990.

McAdams, D. P., Bauer, J. J., Sakaeda, A., Anyidoho, N. A., Machado, M. A., Magrino, K., White, K. W., & Pals, J. L.

(2006). Continuity and change in the life story: A longitudinal study of autobiographical memories in emerging adulthood. *Journal of Personality, 74,* 1371–1400.

McAdams, D. P., & Cox, K. S. (2010). Self and identity across the life span. In A. Freund & R. Lerner (Eds.), *Handbook of life-span development: Vol. 2* (pp. 158–207). New York: Wiley.

McAdams, D. P., de St. Aubin, E., & Logan, R. L. (1993). Generativity among young, midlife, and older adults. *Psychology and Aging, 8,* 221–230.

McAdams, D. P., Diamond, A., de St. Aubin, E., & Mansfield, E. D. (1997). Stories of commitment: The psychosocial construction of generative lives. *Journal of Personality and Social Psychology, 72,* 678–694.

McLean, K. C. (2008). Stories of the young and the old: Personal continuity and narrative identity. *Developmental Psychology, 44,* 254–264.

McLean, K. C., & Breen, A. V. (2009). Process and content in narrative identity development in adolescence: Gender and well-being. *Developmental Psychology, 45,* 702–710.

McLean, K. C., & Fournier, M. A. (2008). The content and process of autobiographical reasoning in narrative identity. *Journal of Research in Personality, 42,* 527–545.

McLean, K. C., Pasupathi, M., & Pals, J. L. (2007). Selves creating stories creating selves: A process model of self-development. *Personality and Social Psychology Review, 11,* 262–278.

Mead, G. H. (1934). *Mind, self, and society.* Chicago: University of Chicago Press.

Neyer, F. J., & Lehnart, J. (2007). Relationships matter in personality development: Evidence from an 8-year longitudinal study across young adulthood. *Journal of Personality, 75,* 535–568.

Pasupathi, M., & Mansour, E. (2006). Adult age differences in autobiographical reasoning in narratives. *Developmental Psychology, 42,* 798–808.

Pasupathi, M., & Wainryb, C. (2010). On telling the whole story: Facts and interpretations in autobiographical memory narratives from childhood through midadolescence. *Developmental Psychology, 46,* 735–746.

Pennebaker, J. W., & Stone, L. D. (2003). Words of wisdom: Language use over the life span. *Journal of Personality and Social Psychology, 85,* 291–301.

Peterson, B. E., & Duncan, L. E. (2007). Midlife women's generativity and authoritarianism: Marriage, motherhood, and 10 years of aging. *Psychology and Aging, 22,* 411–419.

Piaget, J. (1970). Piaget's theory. In P. H. Mussen (Ed.), *Carmichael's manual of child psychology* (2nd Ed., vol. *1,* pp. 703–732). New York: Wiley.

Ramirez-Esparza, N., Gosling, S., Benet-Martinez, V., Potter, J. P., & Pennebaker, J. (2006). Do bilinguals have two personalities? A special case of cultural frame switching. *Journal of Research in Personality, 40,* 99–120.

Ricoeur, P. (1984). *Time and narrative* (vol. 1). (K. McGlaughlin & D. Pelauer, trans.). Chicago: University of Chicago Press.

Roberts, B. W., & Del Vecchio, W. F. (2000). The rank-order consistency of personality traits from childhood to old age. *Psychological Bulletin, 126,* 3–25.

Roberts, B. W., Walton, K. E., & Viechtbauer, W. (2006). Patterns of mean-level change in personality traits across the life course: A meta-analysis of longitudinal studies. *Psychological Bulletin, 132,* 1–25.

Rokeach, M. (1973). *The nature of human values.* New York: The Free Press.

Sameroff, A. J., & Haith, M. M. (Eds.). (1996). *The five to seven year shift.* Chicago: University of Chicago Press.

Schiebe, S., Freund, A. M., & Baltes, P. B. (2007). Toward a developmental psychology of Sehnsucht (life longings): The optimal (utopian) life. *Developmental Psychology, 43,* 778–795.

Shotter, J., & Gergen, K. J. (Eds.). (1989). *Texts of identity.* London: Sage.

Singer, J., Rexhaj, B., & Baddeley, J. (2007). Older, wiser, happier? Comparing older adults' and college students' self-defining memories. *Memory, 15,* 886–898.

Syed, M., & Azmitia, M. (2010). Narrative and ethnic identity exploration: A longitudinal account of emerging adults' ethnically-related experiences. *Developmental Psychology, 46,* 208–219.

Tangney, J. P., Stuewig, J., & Mashek, D. J. (2007). Moral emotions and moral behavior. In S. Fiske & D. Schacter (Eds.), *Annual review of psychology* (vol. *58,* pp. 345–372). Palo Alto, CA: Annual Reviews.

Thomsen, D. K., & Bernsten, D. (2008). The cultural life script and life story chapters contribute to the reminiscence bump. *Memory, 16,* 420–435.

Wang, Q., & Conway, M. A. (2004). The stories we keep: Autobiographical memory in American and Chinese middle-aged adults. *Journal of Personality, 72,* 911-938.

Wellman, H. M. (1993). Early understanding of mind: The normal case. In S. Baron-Cohen, H. Tager-Flusberg, & D. J. Cohen (Eds.), *Understanding other minds: Perspectives from autism* (pp. 10–39). New York: Oxford University Press.

Wilson, E. O. (2012). *The social conquest of earth.* New York: Liveright.

Wrosch, C., Heckhausen, J., & Lachman, M. E. (2006). Goal management across adulthood and old age: The adaptive value of primary and secondary control. In D. K. Mroczek & T. D. Little (Eds.), *Handbook of personality development* (pp. 399–421). Mahwah, NJ: Erlbaum.

PART 2

Debates: Identity Status Perspectives on Processes of Identity Development

CHAPTER 7

The Identity Statuses: Strengths of a Person-Centered Approach

Elisabetta Crocetti *and* Wim Meeus

Abstract

This chapter discusses how a better understanding of identity formation can be achieved by integrating person-centered and variable-centered approaches, particularly how the person-centered approach might be more suitable for capturing identity development. To support this thesis, exemplars are drawn from the identity literature rooted in Erikson's psychosocial theory, in Marcia's identity status paradigm, and in its recent extensions. In the person-centered approach, the starting point is groups of people, defined by the fact that individuals share similar characteristics with members of their group and differ from members of other groups. Thus, the first step for adopting a person-centered approach is the classification of respondents into groups, each of which corresponds to one identity status. The chapter discusses shortcomings and strengths of various methods used to classify individuals into identity statuses and also highlights future lines of research.

Key Words: identity statuses, person-centered approach, variable-centered approach, classification, methodology, developmental trajectories, longitudinal

George Gray
I have studied many times
The marble which was chiseled for me—
A boat with a furled sail at rest in a harbor.
In truth it pictures not my destination
But my life.
For love was offered me and I shrank from its disillusionment;
Sorrow knocked at my door, but I was afraid;
Ambition called to me, but I dreaded the chances.
Yet all the while I hungered for meaning in my life.
And now I know that we must lift the sail
And catch the winds of destiny
Wherever they drive the boat.
To put meaning in one's life may end in madness,
But life without meaning is the torture
Of restlessness and vague desire—
It is a boat longing for the sea and yet afraid.
   – Edgar Lee Masters, Spoon River Anthology (1915)

We open this chapter with a poem from the *Spoon River Anthology*. In this epitaph, Edgar Lee Masters captures the identity path of George Gray. The author describes a man who has avoided the identity formation task, delaying until the end of his life the enactment of meaningful commitments in various domains of his experience, such as love and career.

The leading question of this chapter is how an identity path like that of George Gray can be empirically studied. In the identity literature, two approaches—namely, variable-centered and person-centered—have been proposed to study identity formation. In this chapter, we will discuss the characteristics of variable-centered and person-centered approaches; show how they have been applied and integrated in the identity field; and support our thesis that the person-centered approach can provide, in some cases, a more comprehensive understanding of identity stories.

Identity Matters

"Who am I?" is the core question that accompanies each human being throughout his or her entire life (Erikson, 1950, 1968). Addressing this question implies both a bright and a dark side: on the one hand, it is an exhilarating process because it corresponds to the human need to search for and find a personal identity; but, on the other hand, it is often painful since choosing one alternative requires giving up other possibilities that also might be attractive. As a consequence, individuals might oscillate between the wish to clearly define themselves and the fear of making wrong choices, as it was the case for George Gray.

Moreover, answering the question "Who am I?" is particularly challenging since it implies the synthesis of a number of different answers related to multiple life domains. In fact, the question "Who am I?" entails a number of subquestions, such as "What kind of occupation do I want to pursue? What are my religious values? What are my political opinions? In which interpersonal relationships do I want to invest? To which social groups do I belong? How do I feel in relationship to my ethnicity?" and so on (Marcia, Waterman, Matteson, Archer, & Orlofsky, 1993). Therefore, identity formation implies choosing commitments in a number of relevant different life domains.

Briefly, to fully answer the question "Who am I?" is a great challenge for each individual throughout his or her entire lifespan. Given this complexity, unraveling identity processes through empirical research is even more challenging. Every complex object of analysis, such as identity, requires it to be examined from different angles and through different lenses. Therefore, to grasp identity complexity, it is mandatory to adopt multiple approaches and methods of data collection.

In this chapter, we discuss how a better understanding of identity formation can be achieved by integrating two different approaches: the person-centered and the variable-centered. In particular, we discuss when a person-centered approach might be more suitable for capturing identity development. To support our thesis, we provide exemplars drawn from the identity literature rooted in Erikson's (1950, 1968) psychosocial theory. Thus, we also examine Marcia's (1966) identity status paradigm and its recent extensions (Meeus, 2011).

Finally, we focus on overall identity processes (e.g., commitment) without referring to specific identity contents (e.g., religious commitment, political commitment). Although examination of interconnections between identity processes and identity contents is of great importance (e.g., Berzonsky, Macek, & Nurmi, 2003), the interplay of overall identity processes can provide a framework for unraveling identity formation across several content domains (e.g., religion, politics, ethnicity, education, relationships) whose importance can vary widely according to contextual (e.g., ethnic identity is more salient for minority than for majority groups; Branch, Tayal, & Triplett, 2000) and individual (e.g., interpersonal identity is more important for females than for males; Crocetti, Sica, Schwartz, Serafini, & Meeus, 2013) factors. Thus, considerations on identity processes can be generalized to multiple identity contents.

Person-Centered and Variable-Centered Approaches: Defining Characteristics

Person- and variable-centered approaches have been applied, in a parallel or integrated fashion, in a variety of research fields (von Eye & Bogat, 2006). Before discussing in detail the contributions that these approaches can provide to the identity literature, here, we present their defining characteristics. This preliminary step is necessary for understanding strengths and limitations of each approach before moving to their applications in the identity research field.

Person- and variable-centered approaches represent two distinct strategies of examining psychological phenomena. In the variable-centered approach concepts or variables are the key units, both in theory construction and statistical analyses. The basic assumption is that populations are homogeneous, and, therefore, each individual within a certain population is interchangeable with another individual belonging to the same population (von Eye & Bogat, 2006).

On the contrary, in the person-centered approach, the individual is regarded as a dynamic system of interwoven components that is best understood in terms of whole-system properties. Person-oriented research is based on the notions that (1) distinct subgroups may exist within a certain population and (2), if they exist, aggregate-level parameters may contradict parameters estimated for groups or individuals (von Eye & Bogat, 2006). To investigate the patterns of characteristics that are shared within a specific subgroup, person-oriented methods determine relationships at the individual level rather than the variable level. In this way, person-oriented methods emphasize the potential uniqueness of individuals (Bergman, Magnusson, & El Khouri, 2003).

Magnusson and Allen (1983, p. 372) summarized the essence of the person-centered approach, stating that: "The person oriented approach to research (in contrast to the variable centered approach) takes a holistic and dynamic view; the person is conceptualized as an integrated totality rather than as a summation of variables."

Earlier precursors of the person-centered approach can be found in differential psychology and in the conceptualization of psychology as an idiographic science (cf. von Eye & Bogat, 2006). The person-oriented strategy as applied today can be traced back to Block's (1971) distinction between variable and person approaches (see also Carlson, 1971). Specifically, in personality research, adopting a variable-centered approach means paying attention to how personality dimensions (e.g., the Big Five: extroversion, agreeableness, conscientiousness, emotional stability, and openness to experience; cf. McCrae & Costa, 1987) are related to other variables (e.g., internalizing problems, risk behaviors); whereas adopting a person-centered approach implies focusing on the patterning and organization of personality dimensions within a person (i.e., personality types).

Thus, the basic assumption of the person-centered approach is that individuals are unique. Strictly speaking, this assumption would require separate psychological models for each individual. However, as suggested by Block (1971), although every person is unique, he or she is not so exquisitely unique as to define his or her own personality type. Thus, it is possible to find a finite (instead of infinite) number of typical patterns that can properly describe groups of individuals. Random variations and fluctuations do not need to be modeled. For instance, in personality research, three widely studied personality types are resilients, overcontrollers, and undercontrollers (cf. Robins, John, Caspi, Moffitt, & Stouthamer-Loeber, 1996).

Variable- and person-centered approaches address different research questions. Therefore, like two different pairs of lenses, they can provide new insights on different issues of the same phenomenon. For this reason, there are increasing examples (e.g., Bamaca-Colbert & Gayles, 2010; Bogat, Levendosky, & von Eye, 2005; Van Leeuwen, Mervielde, Braet, & Bosmans, 2004) of studies in which these two approaches are integrated to gain a more comprehensive understanding of a topic.

Methodological Considerations

From a methodological point of view, to adopt a variable- or person-centered approach necessitates the application of a different statistical strategy of analysis. In a variable-centered approach, differences on the scores of a variable can be tested through analysis of variance, and associations between variables can be analyzed using correlations, regression analyses, and structural equation modeling. In all of these cases, the starting point is the variable. On the contrary, in the person-centered approach, the starting point is groups of people, defined by the fact that individuals share similar characteristics with members of their group and differ from members of other groups. Thus, the first step of the person-centered approach is the classification of respondents into groups.

We can differentiate methods of classifications in two classes: methods that employ a-priori criteria and those that are empirically based. Methods that use a-priori criteria define a set of rules (e.g., respondents are assigned to groups according to their scores, higher or lower on certain cutoffs) used to assign participants to groups. In this case, the groups are predefined and it follows that a main advantage of methods that use a priori criteria is that they provide consistent classifications of individuals across different samples.

Conversely, empirically based methods of classification do not work with predefined groups; rather, they model the data to find the best classification. Empirically based methods include cluster analysis, latent class analysis, latent class growth analysis, and growth mixture modeling. All of these statistical techniques share the fact that the number of clusters/classes/groups is unknown. Therefore, different solutions are compared to detect the one that fits the data significantly better. This method is sensitive to characteristics of the sample and, as a shortcoming, is likely to yield classifications that might change across samples (i.e., decreasing replicability of the classification). However, this problem is counterbalanced by the fact that the decision about the optimal number of groups that should be retained does not rely exclusively on statistical results (e.g., percentage of explained variance by each cluster solution, significant differences between cluster solutions with different number of classes), but also takes into consideration parsimony and theoretical issues. It means that a cluster solution that is more parsimonious and consistent with theoretical expectations is preferred to cluster solutions in which higher complexity does not entail an added theoretical value (i.e., new detected clusters represent only slight variations of already existing groups and are not theoretically meaningful). The main strength of empirically based methods of classification is that they are useful to demonstrate if hypothesized group differences are supported by the data or if new configurations provide a better understanding of classes existing in the population being studied.

Once the classification has been performed and participants have been assigned to distinct groups, either with a-priori criteria or with empirically based methods, their profile becomes the object of analysis. Thus, the main focus of the research becomes the external validity of the classification and the specific pattern of characteristics reported by individuals belonging to distinct groups.

Applications of the Person- and Variable-Centered Approaches in Identity Research

After having presented the main characteristics of person- and variable-centered approaches, we are now going to see how these approaches have been applied in the identity field. Our analysis here focuses on the identity literature rooted in the pioneering contribution of Erik Erikson.

Erikson (1950, 1968) proposed an epigenetic theory of psychological development that embraced the entire lifespan. According to his theory, the life course can be divided into eight qualitatively distinct phases or stages. In each stage, individuals face a core developmental conflict, and the extent to which they succeed in resolving this conflict determines the likelihood of transitioning smoothly to subsequent developmental tasks.

In adolescence, the core conflict is *identity versus identity confusion*. In this period, individuals undergo radical physical, cognitive, and social changes that stimulate their reflections on what gives them a sense of continuity. Erikson conceptualized ego identity both as a conscious sense of individual uniqueness and as an unconscious striving for continuity of experience. Identity achieved individuals have combined and integrated relevant earlier identifications in a unique and personal way. On the contrary, young people in a status of identity confusion have not chosen their own commitments, and they do not hold meaningful identifications that could provide them with a sense of direction.

Marcia's Identity Status Paradigm

Marcia's (1966) identity status paradigm is the most well-known and widely used elaboration of Erikson's (1950, 1968) views on identity formation. Marcia shared the notion that adolescence is a period of crisis in which important commitments need to be assumed. From his clinical work, Marcia understood that, in addition to the two poles proposed by Erikson (i.e., identity vs. identity confusion), other statuses should be considered. Specifically, these statuses could be meaningfully differentiated by taking into account two dimensions: *exploration* (i.e., the active questioning and weighing of various identity alternatives before making decisions about the values, beliefs, and goals that one will pursue) and *commitment* (i.e., making a relatively firm choice about an identity domain and engaging in significant activities geared toward the implementation of that choice).

Four identity statuses can be obtained by crossing exploration and commitment (Marcia, 1966; see Table 7.1). Specifically, in the *achievement* status, adolescents have made a commitment following a period of active exploration; in the *foreclosure* status, adolescents have made a commitment with little or no prior exploration; in the *moratorium* status, adolescents are actively exploring various alternatives and have not yet made a commitment; finally, in the *diffusion* status, adolescents have not engaged in a proactive process of exploration of different alternatives nor have they made a commitment. Thus, consistently with a person-centered approach, Marcia conceptualized identity statuses as a combination of commitment and exploration aimed at representing an individual's style of coping with the identity crisis (Marcia, 1966).

In line with this conceptualization, research inspired by Marcia's paradigm has sought to detect interindividual differences among youth classified into the various identity statuses. Consistent evidence has indicated that the identity statuses could be clearly differentiated in terms of personality characteristics and psychosocial problems (for an extensive review, see Kroger & Marcia, 2011; Kroger, this volume). Specifically, adolescents in the *achievement* status are characterized by a highly adaptive personality profiles: in fact, they are highly extrovert, emotionally stable, conscientious, and open to experience (Clancy & Dollinger, 1993);

Table 7.1 Identity statuses

		Commitment	
		Present	Absent
Exploration	Present	*Achievement*	*Moratorium*
	Absent	*Foreclosure*	*Diffusion*

Reprinted with permission from Marcia, 1966

they demonstrate high achievement motivation and self-esteem (Orlofsky, 1978), high internal locus of control (Abraham, 1983), and low authoritarianism (Marcia, 1966, 1993); they use planned decision-making strategies (Blustein & Phillips, 1990) and exhibit a high level of moral reasoning (Skoe & Marcia, 1991). Regarding psychosocial problems, youth in the achievement status display a healthy adjustment characterized by low anxiety and depression and high satisfaction with life (Marcia, 1980; Meeus, Iedema, Helsen, & Vollebergh, 1999). Adolescents in the *foreclosure* status are characterized by personality features such as high levels of conformity and authoritarianism (Marcia, 1966, 1980) and low openness to new experiences (Clancy & Dollinger, 1993; Tesch & Cameron, 1987). Regarding adjustment, they demonstrate low anxiety, low depression, and high satisfaction with life, equal to their peers in the achievement status (Meeus et al., 1999). Adolescents in the *moratorium* status on the one hand are comparable to their peers in the achievement status in terms of personality features because they are highly open to new experiences. On the other hand, they are different from identity-achieved adolescents since they demonstrate lower extroversion, emotional stability, and conscientiousness (Clancy & Dollinger, 1993; Tesch & Cameron, 1987). A key characteristic of moratorium individuals is their high level of anxiety: these adolescents are looking for satisfying commitments they cannot find, and this generates anxiety (Marcia, 1980; Meeus et al., 1999). They also report high depression and low well-being (later in this chapter, we discuss in more detail these two facets of the moratorium status). Finally, adolescents in the *diffusion* status demonstrate low emotional stability and conscientiousness and moderate levels of openness to experience (Clancy & Dollinger, 1993; Tesch & Cameron, 1987). Moreover, they report low autonomy and self-esteem (Marcia, 1966), a low sense of personal integration (Berzonsky, Rice, & Neimeyer, 1991), low levels of moral reasoning (Skoe & Marcia, 1991), and inadequate approaches to decision-making processes (Blustein & Phillips, 1990). Regarding well-being, individuals in the diffusion status report moderate levels of adjustment when compared to their peers in the other statuses (Meeus et al., 1999).

Methodological Issues

As discussed earlier, researchers inspired by Marcia's paradigm were mainly interested in documenting interindividual differences among youth classified in one of the four identity statuses. Consequently, from a methodological point of view, they needed a reliable way of classifying participants into the various identity statuses. To this end, Marcia (1964) developed a semistructured interview, and various identity researchers (e.g., Adams, Shea, & Fitch, 1979; Balistreri, Bush-Rossnagel, & Geisinger, 1995; Dellas & Jernigan, 1981) developed self-report scales. We briefly present the most common instruments, highlighting for each of them their strengths and shortcomings.

IDENTITY STATUS INTERVIEW

Marcia (1964) proposed using a semistructured interview, the *Identity Status Interview*, to establish individuals' identity statuses (for the scoring manual, see Marcia et al., 1993). The first interview employed by Marcia (1964) with male college students covered three identity domains: occupation, religion, and politics. Afterward, when the interview was used with females, additional domains were investigated: family and careers conflicts (Marcia & Friedman, 1970) and attitudes toward premarital intercourse (Schenkel & Marcia, 1972). Moreover, other scholars have added further identity domains so that a distinction can be made between core and supplemental domains (Waterman, 1993).

For each domain, specific identity issues were investigated in order to determine interviewee's identity status. For instance, a sample question in the religious domain was: "Have you ever had any doubts about your religious beliefs?" Examples of typical answers for the four identity statuses were (Marcia, 1966; p. 553): "Yeah, I even started wondering whether or not there was a god. I've pretty much resolved that now, though. The way it seems to me is…" (identity achievement); "Yes, I guess I'm going through that now. I just don't see how there can be a god and yet so much evil in the world…" (moratorium); "No, not really, our family is pretty much in agreement on these things" (foreclosure); "Oh, I don't know. I guess so. Everyone goes through some sort of stage like that. But it really doesn't bother me much. I figure one's about as good as the other" (diffusion). Thus, using the identity status interview, individuals were classified into four groups, corresponding to one of the four identity statuses.

The benefit of using the Identity Status Interview is that it is a useful tool for gathering rich and abundant information about an individual's personal story. For instance, this instrument has been used by Josselson (1987) to shed light on identity paths of young women. In her classic work conducted in the 1970s, Josseleson provided new insight on the identity specifics of women in a period in which most research was on male samples and little was known on normative (in opposition to clinical) female identity development. In this case, the Identity Status Interview was the most appropriate tool for getting rich information and unravelling (understudied) feminine pathways to identity.

Nevertheless, the Identity Status Interview also entails some shortcomings. In particular, the administration of this instrument is highly time-consuming and interviewers need to be trained to provide reliable classifications. Therefore, since investigation in large and/or different samples, can be difficultly managed by means of Marcia's interview, scholars have developed identity self-report scales.

SELF-REPORT QUESTIONNAIRES

Among the first self-report questionnaires developed to measure identity statuses were the Dellas Identity Status Inventory-Occupation (DISI-O; Dellas & Jernigan, 1981; later expanded to measure identity statuses also in religious [DISI-R] and political [DISI-P] domains; Dellas & Jernigan, 1990), and the Objective Measure of Ego-Identity Status (OM-EIS; Adams et al., 1979; later extended into the Extended Objective Measure of Ego-Identity Status [EOM-EIS]; Bennion & Adams, 1986). Both measures included items referring directly to the identity statuses. For instance, EOM-EIS sample items are (Bennion & Adams, 1986): "It took me a while to figure it out, but now I really know what I want for a career" (occupation/achievement); "My ideas about men's and women's roles are identical to my parents'. What has worked for them will obviously work for me" (sex role/foreclosure); "I'm looking for an acceptable perspective for my own 'life style' view, but I haven't really found it yet" (philosophical life-style/moratorium); "I don't have any real close friends, and I don't think I'm looking for one right now" (friendship/diffusion). From continuous scores on achievement, foreclosure, moratorium, and diffusion, respondents are assigned to only one identity status according to classification rules defined by the authors of these instruments. For instance, for the DISI-O, scoring instructions indicated that one status was assigned to a participant if he or she had chosen the option "most like me" for at least four out of the eight items for this status. As a consequence of this procedure, some participants did not fit any status and were "unclassified." Therefore, these classification rules presented two main criticisms: (a) they were defined a-priori (instead of being empirically derived), and (b) they produced a high number of participants who were "unclassified." A further shortcoming of questionnaires developed to measure identity statuses was, especially for the EOM-EIS, the rather low reliability (Cronbach's α <.70) of identity status factors (Schwartz, Adamson, Ferrer-Wreder, Dillon, & Berman, 2006).

Successively, Balistreri et al. (1995) developed the Ego Identity Process Questionnaire (EIPQ) to assess directly commitment and exploration. Sample items are: "I've definitely decided on the occupation I want to pursue" (commitment); and "I have considered different political views thoughtfully" (exploration). The EIPQ provides both continuous scores of commitment and exploration, as well as allowing categorization of individuals into Marcia's four identity statuses using the median scores of commitment and exploration as the cutoff points. Thus, respondents scoring high on both commitment and exploration are assigned to the achievement status; those high on commitment but low on exploration are assigned to the foreclosure status; and so on. In this way, the criticisms of having many participants being unclassified is overcome. However, it remained a problem that the classification of participants into one of the four identity statuses was "imposed" through the classification rule, instead of being empirically derived.

To summarize, Marcia's identity status paradigm implies a person-centered approach to identity. In this paradigm, the focus is on interindividual differences exhibited by respondents classified in the identity statuses of achievement, foreclosure, moratorium, and diffusion. From a methodological point of view, adoption of the person-centered approach requires reliable ways of classifying participants into one and only one of the identity statuses. However, most common methods present relevant criticisms. The Identity Status Interview allows collection of rich personal stories, but these stories are rarely used beyond extracting the status classification, thus leading to loss of their richness. Recently, Frisén and Wängqvist (2011) provided an exception to this way of administering the ISI. They enriched the identity status classification with quotes from the interviews that provided good examples of the voices of the emerging adults themselves (see also Arnett, this volume). An additional criticism of the ISI is that it is difficult to administer and requires trained interviewers. Conversely, self-report questionnaires can be administered easily, but they fail on classifying a large number of participants (i.e., DISI; EOM-EIS) or they rely on a-priori criteria (i.e., EIPQ) of classification that are not empirically tested.

Extensions of the Identity Status Paradigm: Identity Process Models

Identity status research has been guided by the intent of providing a classification of individuals rather than studying the process of identity development (Bosma, 1985). The identity statuses were conceived as various outcomes of the adolescent period described by Erikson's theory (Meeus, Iedema, & Maassen, 2002). However, Grotevant (1987), Stephen, Fraser and Marcia (1992), and Marcia (1993) himself recognized the importance of studying the process of identity formation rather than focusing exclusively on its outcomes (see also Kunnen & Metz, this volume).

Bosma (1985) and Meeus (1996) took up this challenge, working on the meaning and function of commitment and exploration. Specifically, Bosma distinguished between commitment making and the extent to which one identifies with a commitment. He further underlined that a commitment may contribute to a clear sense of identity only when adolescents have identified themselves with that commitment. Meeus (1996) introduced a new conceptualization of exploration, in-depth exploration, which represents the extent to which adolescents actively reflect on and gather information about current commitments. Thus, whereas in Marcia's theory exploration involves weighing up various alternatives *before* a choice is made, Meeus (1996) emphasized the relevance of exploration *after* a choice is made, which is a "sine qua non" condition to maintain and validate existing commitments.

Building upon Bosma's (1985) and Meeus's (1996) contributions, two extensions of Marcia's (1966) identity status paradigm were proposed in the past decade. We refer to the process models of Luyckx and colleagues (Luyckx, Goossens, Soenens, & Beyers, 2006; Luyckx et al., 2008) and Meeus, Crocetti, and collaborators (Crocetti, Rubini, & Meeus, 2008; Meeus, van de Schoot, Keijsers, Schwartz, & Branje, 2010). Both models proposed a process-oriented approach to identity. In fact, whereas Marcia conceptualized commitment as the outcome of exploration, these models assume that commitments are formed and revised in an iterative process of choosing commitments, evaluating, and questioning them (Meeus, 2011;

Meeus et al., 2010). As we shels have advanced identity grating variable- and pers
(b) applying modern, en classifying respondents into i
(c) modeling identity over time studies with multiple waves.

Luyckx's et al. Integrative Identity Mode

Luyckx et al. (2006b) have integrated Marcia's (1966) theory with the extensions proposed by Bosma (1985) and Meeus (1996). Thus, Luyckx et al. (2006b) proposed a four-dimensional identity model comprising commitment making, identification with commitment, exploration in breadth, and in-depth exploration. Specifically, *commitment-making* covers Marcia's original concept and indicates whether adolescents have made choices in relevant life domains. *Identification with commitment*, as proposed by Bosma (1985), indexes the degree to which adolescents internalize and feel certain about their commitments. *Exploration in breadth* captures Marcia's original concept and indicates the exploration of various alternative commitments before choosing one. *In-depth exploration* refers to Meeus's (1996) conceptualization and indicates whether adolescents evaluate and maintain their commitments in an active manner after choosing them.

Luyckx and colleagues integrated the four dimensions into a dual-cycle model of identity formation (Luyckx, Goossens, & Soenens, 2006a). The first cycle represents identity formation, in that adolescents make commitments after exploration in breadth. The second cycle represents identity-evaluation and maintenance, in that in-depth exploration of current commitments serves to verify their validity and to enhance identification with commitment. Thus, the tentative order of both cycles is exploration in breadth → commitment making → exploration in depth → identification with commitment. Subsequently, Luyckx et al. (2008) expanded this model by adding ruminative exploration. This latter dimension captures a dysfunctional form of exploration, typical of individuals who continuously doubt and mull over available possibilities without being able to commit to any of them.

After having used a combination of existing measures (i.e., the EIPQ for assessing commitment making and exploration in breadth and the U-GIDS for measuring identification with commitment and in-depth exploration), Luyckx developed a new ment for assessing the five dimensions: the Dimensions of Identity Development Scale (DIDS; Luyckx et al., 2008). Sample items read: "I have decided on the direction I want to follow in my life" (commitment making), "I sense that the direction I want to take in my life will really suit me" (identification with commitment), "I regularly think over a number of different plans for the future" (exploration in breadth), "I regularly talk with other people about the plans for the future I have made for myself" (exploration in depth), and "It is hard for me to stop thinking about the direction I want to follow in my life" (ruminative exploration). Thus, the DIDS include five factors, each of them indexing one identity dimension.

Luyckx's et al. model was applied in variable-centered studies in which the goal was to examine how identity dimensions (i.e., commitment making, identification with commitment, exploration in breadth, in-depth exploration, and ruminative exploration) were related to identity correlates (for an extensive review, see Luyckx, Schwartz, Goossens, Beyers, & Missotten, 2011). In particular, identification with commitment and ruminative exploration came out as the strongest (positively and negatively, respectively) correlates of positive functioning.

Applications of Luyckx's et al. model in person-centered studies, along with use of empirically based methods of classification, shed more light on ways in which individuals can resolve the identity task. Using cluster analysis, Luyckx et al. found six identity statuses (Luyckx et al., 2008; Schwartz et al., 2011). Three of these statuses recalled Marcia's original statuses: achievement (high on commitment making, identification with commitment, exploration in depth, and exploration in breadth, and low on ruminative exploration); foreclosure (high on both commitment dimensions and low on the three exploration factors); moratorium (low on both commitment dimensions and high on the three exploration factors). Furthermore, two forms of diffusion were found: adolescents in the carefree diffusion status reported low scores on all the five identity processes, whereas adolescents in the diffused diffusion status reported similar low scores, except for a high score on ruminative exploration. Finally, an undifferentiated cluster with moderate scores on all the identity dimensions was identified.

These "new" identity statuses exhibited a distinct profile in terms of psychosocial functioning (e.g., Luyckx et al., 2008; Schwartz et al., 2011). The achievement and foreclosure statuses reported positive profiles, characterized by high well-being, and low internalizing and externalizing problem behaviors (with the main difference that achieved adolescents reported higher need satisfaction than their foreclosed counterparts). The moratorium, diffused diffusion, and carefree diffusion statuses displayed more negative profiles, characterized by low well-being, high internalizing and externalizing problem behaviors, and low need satisfaction. Finally, the undifferentiated status tended to show an intermediate profile.

Thus, these results pointed out that, considering more identity dimensions and applying more refined ways of classifying individuals into identity statuses, it was possible to further extend Marcia's theory. In particular, differential combinations of the five dimensions highlighted a distinction between two forms of diffusion: carefree and diffused diffusion. Although members of the diffused diffusion cluster scored high on ruminative exploration and maladjustment, those in the carefree diffusion were characterized by an untroubled approach toward identity, and they did not appear to be distressed by their current lack of identity commitments. This recalls a distinction that earlier researchers (Archer & Waterman, 1990; Marcia, 1989) had proposed between different types of diffusion. Therefore, with an empirically based method of deriving identity statuses it was possible to differentiate between two forms of diffusion hypothesized in previous theoretical contributions.

Meeus, Crocetti, and Colleagues' Three-Factor Model

Meeus, Crocetti, and colleagues (Crocetti et al., 2008b; Meeus et al., 2010), building on previous work by Meeus (1996; Meeus et al., 1999; Meeus et al., 2002), have expanded the identity status paradigm by proposing a three-factor identity model aimed at capturing the dynamic by which identity is formed and modified over time. This model takes into account three pivotal identity processes. *Commitment* refers to enduring choices that individuals have made with regard to various developmental domains and to the self-confidence they derive from these choices; *in-depth exploration* represents the extent to which individuals think actively about the commitments they have enacted (e.g., reflecting on their choices, searching for additional information, talking with others about their commitments); and *reconsideration of commitment* refers to the comparison of present commitments with possible alternative commitments because the current ones are no longer satisfactory. This conceptualization of reconsideration of commitment is, on the one hand, similar to Marcia's (1966) definition of exploration because it encompasses the investigation of possible new commitments. On the other hand, it differs from exploration in that it taps into adolescents' present attempts to change current commitments because they are no longer satisfied with their prior choices. Thus, reconsideration of commitment represents an evaluation of various alternatives that starts from the basis of present commitments, rather from a lack of commitment, as originally hypothesized by Marcia. In fact, in this three-factor model, in contrast to Marcia's (1966) conceptualization, it is assumed that individuals approach adolescence with a set of commitments (generally internalized from parents or other authority figures) of at least minimal strength in various identity domains and can decide to maintain or revise them (Meeus et al., 2010).

The three-factor model includes a dual-cycle process (Meeus, 2011). Adolescents explore their commitments in depth and decide whether they provide a good fit with their overall talents and potentials (the identity formation and maintenance cycle). If the current commitments are not satisfying or do not provide a good fit, they may be reconsidered in favor of other commitments (the identity revision cycle). Thus, by including commitment, in-depth exploration, and reconsideration, this model sought to capture Erikson's (1968) dynamic of identity versus identity confusion. Commitment and in-depth exploration, on the one hand, and reconsideration, on the other hand, are conceptualized as the two opposing forces within this dynamic. Whereas commitment and in-depth exploration imply attempts to develop and maintain a sense of self (i.e., identity coherence or synthesis), reconsideration represents questioning and rethinking this sense of self (identity confusion).

To assess these three identity processes, Meeus developed a self-report instrument, the Utrecht-Management of Identity Commitments Scale (U-MICS; Crocetti et al., 2008b). The U-MICS items can be used to assess identity dimensions in different domains: educational, job, relational (friendship, romantic relationship), and the like. Thus, the U-MICS can be employed to assess identity processes in one specific domain or to measure global identity, obtained by combining at least one ideological domain (e.g., educational or job identity) and one relational domain (e.g., peer or romantic relationship). Sample items read: "My education/best friend gives me certainty in life" (commitment), "I think a lot about my education/best friend" (in-depth exploration), and "I often think it would be better to try to find a different education/best friend" (reconsideration of commitment).

Validation studies conducted with Dutch (Crocetti et al., 2008b), Italian (Crocetti, Schwartz, Fermani, & Meeus, 2010), and Swiss French-speaking (Zimmermann, Biermann, Mantzouranis, Genoud, & Crocetti, 2012) participants have indicated that the three-factor model (including commitment, in-depth exploration, and reconsideration of commitment) provided a significantly better fit to the data compared to alternative one-factor (in which all identity processes were collapsed on the same latent variable) and two-factor (consisting of commitment and global exploration, obtained combining in-depth exploration and reconsideration of commitment) models. Furthermore, the three-factor model fit equally well for different age and gender groups and also for both autochthons and ethnic minority adolescents (Crocetti et al., 2008b, Crocetti et al., 2010; Crocetti, Fermani, Pojaghi, & Meeus, 2011). Interestingly, results of a cross-cultural study (Crocetti et al., 2014) highlighted that the U-MICS has very strong psychometric properties in a variety of European (i.e., Italy, the Netherlands, Poland, Portugal, Romania, and Switzerland) and non-European (i.e., China, Japan, Taiwan, Turkey) nations.

The three-factor model has been used in variable- and person-centered studies, as well as in studies integrating the two approaches. Variable-centered studies have pointed out that the three identity processes were meaningfully related to personality dimensions, psychosocial problems, and aspects of parent–adolescent relationships (Crocetti et al., 2008b; 2010; Crocetti, Rubini, Berzonsky, & Meeus, 2009). Specifically, commitment was positively related to extraversion and emotional stability; it was positively linked to nurturing parent–adolescent relationships; it was negatively associated with internalizing symptoms such as depression and anxiety; and it was positively associated with both informational and normative identity styles and negatively linked to a diffuse-avoidant identity orientation. In-depth exploration was positively associated with agreeableness, conscientiousness, openness to experience and to an informational style, but also negatively related to emotional stability and positively to internalizing symptoms. Finally, reconsideration of commitment was negatively associated with agreeableness, conscientiousness, and openness to experience; it was linked to poor family relationships; positively associated with both internalizing and externalizing behaviors; and associated with an avoidant identity style. Summing up, commitment appeared to serve as an indicator of identity consolidation and of successful identity development; in-depth exploration was associated with curiosity but also with confusion and distress; and reconsideration of commitment appeared to be intertwined with disequilibrium and distress, assuming the character of an identity crisis.

Person-centered studies have highlighted that using commitment, in-depth exploration, and reconsideration of commitment, as well as empirically based methods of deriving identity statuses (i.e., cluster analysis or latent class analysis), it was possible to reliably classify participants into identity statuses (Crocetti, Rubini, Luyckx, & Meeus, 2008; Crocetti, Schwartz, Fermani, Klimstra, & Meeus, 2012; Klimstra, Crocetti, Hale, Kolman, Fortanier, & Meeus, 2011; Meeus et al., 2010). Importantly, by applying empirically based methods of deriving identity statuses, it was possible to assign a status to *all* respondents. Thus, it overcame the criticism of identity studies using the EOM-EIS or the DISI-O, which resulted in a large number of participants being unclassified. In addition, indexes of classification accuracy further pointed to the reliability of status classification obtained with the U-MICS by means of empirically based methods. For instance, Meeus et al. (2010, 2012) reported values of entropy (i.e., a standardized measure of classification of individuals into classes based on the posterior class probabilities; it ranges from 0 to 1, with values of .70 or higher indicating good classification accuracy; Reinecke, 2006) higher than .80.

Results showed that by combining the three identity processes it was possible to empirically derive five clusters (Crocetti et al., 2008a; Crocetti, Schwartz et al., 2012). As expected, four of these clusters (achievement, foreclosure, diffusion, and moratorium) strongly resembled Marcia's classical identity statuses and reported a profile that was comparable to that found in interview-based studies. Furthermore, a fifth identity cluster emerged, labeled as searching moratorium. Specifically, the *achievement* status consists of adolescents who scored high on commitment and in-depth exploration but low on reconsideration of commitment. The *early closure* status includes individuals with moderately high scores on commitment and low scores on both in-depth exploration and reconsideration of commitment. The *moratorium* status consists of individuals who scored low on commitment, medium on in-depth exploration, and high on reconsideration of commitment. The *diffusion* status comprises individuals with low scores on commitment, in-depth exploration, and reconsideration of commitment. Finally, the *searching moratorium* status is represented by adolescents high on commitment, in-depth exploration, and reconsideration of commitment (Table 7.2).

This evidence points out that by applying a person-centered approach by means of empirical methods of classification it is possible to shed further light on how people develop their identities. In particular, the distinction between two types of moratorium signaled a significant improvement in the identity field, offering a key of understanding for contradictory findings reported in previous literature. In fact, studies conducted within Marcia's framework have systematically revealed two contrasting facets of the moratorium status. Moratorium was defined, theoretically, as a positive or adaptive status in the developmental trajectory from diffusion to achievement (Marcia, 1980). Consistent with this view, adolescents in moratorium are actively weighing different identity alternatives in order to commit themselves to one of them, adopt an informational processing orientation, and actively seek out and evaluate self-relevant information in an analytical fashion (e.g., Berzonsky, 2004). This positive aspect of moratorium is also consistent with findings demonstrating that individuals in this status were similar to their peers in the achievement status on a number of variables, such as autonomy, moral reasoning, and low authoritarianism (for a review, see Meeus, 1992). On the other hand, moratorium is defined as the status indicative of an "identity crisis." These adolescents are aware that they do not have strong commitments but that they need to find them. Consequently, being in the moratorium status is accompanied by some negative characteristics, such as depression and anxiety (for a review, see Meeus et al., 1999), fear of success (Orlofsky, 1978), nervousness (Adams, Ryan, Hoffman, Dobson, & Nielsen, 1984; Côté & Levine, 1983), and self-destructiveness (Rotheram-Borus, 1989).

Research conducted with the three-factor model has clarified that these two facets can be captured by two different types of moratorium status (Crocetti et al., 2008a; Crocetti, Schwartz, et al. 2012). The (classical) moratorium status (characterized by low commitment, medium in-depth exploration, and high on reconsideration of commitment) captures

Table 7.2 Identity statuses based on three identity processes

Identity processes	Identity statuses				
	Achievement	Early closure	Moratorium	Searching moratorium	Diffusion
Commitment	High	Moderate or High	Low	High	Low
In-depth exploration	High	Low	Low or moderate	High	Low
Reconsideration of commitment	Low	Low	High	High	Low

Reprinted with permission from Crocetti, Rubini, Luycxk, & Meeus, 2008

the dark side of moratorium documented in extant literature. On the contrary, the searching moratorium status (characterized by high levels of commitment, in-depth exploration, and reconsideration of commitment) captures the bright side of moratorium. The two moratorium statuses differ in terms of the base from which reconsideration is attempted: adolescents in the *moratorium* cluster have few commitments and are evaluating alternatives in order to find satisfying identity-related commitments; their peers in the *searching moratorium* group, however, are seeking to revise commitments that have already been enacted, and they are able to do so from the secure base provided by their current commitments.

Meeus, van de Schoot, Keijsers, and Branje (2012) reported that adolescents in the five identity statuses report different levels of adjustment over time. In particular, adolescents in the high commitment statuses (i.e., achievement and early closure) exhibit positive psychosocial adjustment, whereas those in the low commitment statuses (i.e., moratorium and diffusion) report higher levels of depressive symptoms and delinquency over time. The searching moratorium status seems to be a more adaptive identity status trajectory than moratorium, as adolescents in searching moratorium showed less depressive symptoms than their counterparts in moratorium. This suggests that adolescent indecision about commitments does not seem to be overly maladaptive. This is especially true in less structured contexts in which identity revisions can be acceptable for a longer time (cf. Crocetti, Schwartz et al., 2012, for evidence of this derived from a comparison of meaning of the searching moratorium status in Dutch and Italian adolescents).

Furthermore, these findings indicate that a person-centered approach is useful for gaining a more comprehensive understanding of identity correlates. In this respect, the strong power of commitment in predicting individual psychosocial functioning and adjustment (Berzonsky, 2003) could suggest that the variable-centered approach provides a more parsimonious framework for unraveling identity correlates. This position is supported by results of variable-centered studies showing that commitment is consistently associated with optimal psychosocial functioning and by findings of person-centered studies showing that, overall, those with high commitment statuses perform better than do those with low commitment statuses (Kroger & Marcia, 2011; Meeus, 2011). However, an examination of the profile of searching moratorium indicates that such a position is only partially correct. Indeed, when high commitment is combined with high reconsideration (as happens in the searching moratorium group), the positive effect of commitment is lessened, as shown by empirical evidence indicating that youth in the searching moratorium cluster perceive lower levels of personal control (Crocetti, Sica et al., 2013) and exhibit more internalizing problems (Crocetti et al., 2008a; Crocetti, Schwartz et al., 2012) than their achieved counterparts. Thus, examination of commitment alone (as in the variable-centered approach) provides only a partial understanding of identity correlates, whereas investigation of interplay of commitment and reconsideration (obtained in the person-centered approach) offers a more complete picture.

Integration of Variable- and Person-Centered Approaches

The variable- and person-centered approach can be fruitfully integrated to gain a better understanding of a topic. For instance, Crocetti et al. (2011) integrated the two approaches to compare identity formation in adolescents from autochthonous, mixed, and migrant families. The variable-centered approach highlighted that adolescents from migrant families reported significantly higher levels of reconsideration of commitment than did their peers from autochthonous and mixed families. However, this result provides a partial picture; indeed, we do not know if higher levels of reconsideration occur in a status of classical moratorium (the more negative variant of the moratorium) or in a status of searching moratorium (the more positive variant of the moratorium) or in both. This information can be gathered through a person-centered approach. In this example, the person-centered approach strategy shows that adolescents from migrant families were more represented in the searching moratorium status (whereas there were no differences in the classic moratorium status) than their counterparts from autochthonous and mixed families. Overall, these results indicate that migrant adolescents are actively revising their personal identity and are involved in comparisons between the commitments they have already enacted and other alternatives. Commonly, this process consists of a dialectic between maintaining traditional family values and/or embracing the values of the hosting society (e.g., Berry, 2001).

In a further study, Crocetti, Jahromi, and Meeus (2012) integrated the two approaches to examine the links between identity and adolescent civic engagement (volunteer and political participation). First, using a person-centered approach, they found that achieved adolescents were more involved in volunteer activities, reported higher civic efficacy, and had stronger aspirations to contribute to their communities than did their diffused counterparts. Second, by means of a variable-centered approach, they demonstrated that the link between identity processes (i.e., commitment and in-depth exploration) and volunteer and political participation was mediated by social responsibility. In this example, the person-centered approach highlighted strong differences in rates of civic engagement reported by adolescents in the various identity statuses, and the variable-centered approach completed the picture by clarifying the mechanisms by which identity affects civic participation (i.e., through the mediating effect of feeling a sense of social responsibility).

Disentangling Identity Formation over Time

Identity scholars are mainly interested in unraveling how identity develops over time and in finding predictors and outcomes of identity transitions (cf. Schwartz, 2005). To address these research interests, longitudinal designs are needed. Nonetheless, up to now, few longitudinal studies have been conducted. Thus, key assumptions of Marcia's (1966) identity status paradigm have remained speculative or have received only partial empirical support.

Tests of Marcia's Developmental Assumptions

A key assumption of Marcia's model was that individuals enter adolescence in the diffusion or foreclosure statuses (i.e., that, according to Marcia, represent low-level statuses) and then transition to achievement through moratorium (Marcia, 1976; Waterman, 1999). Thus, this hypothetical sequence diffusion/foreclosure → moratorium → achievement should capture most healthy individual identity trajectories. Al-Owidha, Green, and Kroger (2009) have examined the plausibility of this developmental order using the Rasch model threshold and scale statistics, and they have provided preliminary support to the expected optimal category status order. Further longitudinal tests of this developmental sequence require studies with at least three waves of data collection. However, as highlighted in the meta-analytic review conducted by Kroger, Martinussen, and Marcia (2010), from the 1960s to 2000, eleven longitudinal studies on identity statuses have been conducted. Ten of these studies included only two assessments. Thus, they did not allow a test of the sequence hypothesized by Marcia. Further criticisms regarded the fact that most of these studies employed the Identity Status Interview applied with small samples; only one study (Cramer, 1998) used the EOM-EIS, but it resulted in anomalous findings and, because of this, it was excluded from the meta-analytic review; only six studies (including a total of 496 participants who were mainly university students) reported identity transitions from one identity status to another.

Results of these six studies provided only partial support to Marcia's assumptions. First, they pointed out that 49% of the participants remained in the same identity status. Among the most stable statuses were achievement (66% of the participants remained in this status) and foreclosure (53% remained in this status). This last result contradicted Marcia's assumption, according to which the foreclosure status is a lower level status that individuals abandon at the beginning of adolescence to move to higher level statuses after a period of exploration. Second, Kroger et al.'s (2010) meta-analytic results indicated that, among those who did not remain in the same status, progressive movements were more common than regressive movements (36% and 15%, respectively). The most typical regressive transition implied a return to the foreclosure status from the moratorium or achievement statuses. These results are consistent with Marcia's (2002) hypothesis that individuals are likely to go back to a status of foreclosure as a result of a disequilibrium in an existing identity structure. Taken together, these findings suggest that foreclosure, more than a starting point, often represents an endpoint of identity formation (Meeus et al., 1999) and that Marcia's model has somehow failed in providing a suitable model for studying identity development over time.

Insights from Recent Longitudinal Studies

In the past decade, there has been an increase in more complex longitudinal studies (for a review, see Meeus, 2011), with multiple waves of data collection and covering different age periods (adolescence, emerging adulthood, or early adulthood). Reviewing these studies, we can further clarify specifics of variable- and person-centered approaches.

Longitudinal studies focused on identity dynamics in early to late adolescents were mainly conducted with the three-factor model of Meeus, Crocetti, and colleagues (Crocetti et al., 2008a, 2008b, Meeus et al., 2010). Adopting a variable-centered perspective, Klimstra, Hale, Raaijmakers, Branje, and Meeus (2010) found that commitment was stable over time (i.e., the linear slope was nonsignificant); in-depth exploration was stable in early to middle adolescence, whereas it slightly increased in middle to late adolescence. Further, development of reconsideration of commitment, explained by a combination of linear and quadratic growth factors, was moderated by gender. Specifically, for boys, a decrease in reconsideration from 12 to 16 years was followed by an increase in reconsideration from 16 to 18, followed by another decrease in reconsideration (from 18 to 20); for girls, a more linear pattern was detected, with a slight decrease in reconsideration from 12 to 16, followed by a slight increase from 16 to 20.

Furthermore, these developmental trends can vary not only for boys and girls but also for different groups of adolescents. In particular, adolescents with high levels of internalizing (Crocetti et al., 2009) and externalizing (Crocetti, Klimstra et al., 2013) problem behaviors have been found to face more difficulties in developing a firm sense of identity. For instance, adolescents who reported high levels of anxiety over the course of adolescence also reported decreasing levels of commitment and increasing levels of reconsideration of commitment, thus showing increasing uncertainty in identity formation.

It is worth integrating longitudinal studies using annual identity assessments with more intensive designs (Lichtwarck-Aschoff, van Geert, Bosma, & Kunnen, 2008) aimed at capturing identity stability-instability on a daily basis (see also Kunnen & Metz, this volume). Klimstra, Luyckx, Hale, Frijns, van Lier, and Meeus (2010) provided an example of this new line of research by examining how the short-term dynamics of identity formation impact long-term paths. They found evidence for a certainty–uncertainty (i.e., commitment–reconsideration) dynamic that operated on a daily basis and predicted long-term identity formation. More specifically, their results are in line with Erikson's (1950, 1968) conceptualization of identity formation as a search for sameness and continuity. In fact, Klimstra, Luyckx, et al. (2010) found that experiencing daily continuity on identity (i.e., low fluctuations) was predictive of a more robust identity in the long term. Future longitudinal studies integrating short- and long-term analyses could further clarify identity dynamics over time.

But which are the most common identity transitions that young people undertake during adolescence? To address this question, a person-centered approach is needed to examine in which identity statuses individuals are classified at various moments of their adolescent years and toward which statuses they are more likely to move. To unravel this issue, Meeus et al. (2010) applied a person-centered approach to a five-wave longitudinal study conducted with a large sample of Dutch early to middle and middle to late adolescents. Latent class analysis indicated the emergence of the five identity statuses (i.e., achievement, early closure, moratorium, searching moratorium, diffusion) across waves. Furthermore, latent transition analysis was used to test the probability of moving from one status to another. Findings revealed that 63% of respondents stayed in the same status, whereas 37% changed statuses. Additionally, findings revealed very clearly identity maturation: over time, prevalence of diffusion and searching moratoriums decreased and prevalence of achievement increased. Among the adolescents changing identity status, the majority (about 80%) made only one transition in a four-year period suggesting that changes in identity status tend to be decisive and that there is an extremely low probability of additional identity status transitions. This study was the first person-centered study to show systematic identity maturation across the whole period of adolescence, that is between ages 12 and 20.

Longitudinal studies on identity in emerging adulthood have mainly been conducted with the integrative model of Luyckx et al. (2006a, 2008). Within a variable-centered approach, Luyckx et al. (2006a) found only limited empirical support for a core assumption of Marcia's model. Specifically, Marcia hypothesized that individuals explore in breadth various alternatives *before* commitment making. However, Luyckx et al. (2006a) found that initial levels (i.e., intercept) of exploration in breadth do not predict changes (i.e., slope) in commitment making over time. They further added that this over-time link between intercept of exploration in breadth and slope of commitment making was significant only in a subgroup of university students reorientating their educational choices after a failure.

In a further study, Luyckx, Schwartz, Goossens, Soenens, and Beyers (2008) examined through a person-centered approach identity trajectories undertaken by female university students. They found that females pathways could be captured by four identity developmental trajectories: pathmakers (high on all four dimensions, with growth over time of commitment making and a downward trend for exploration in breadth), consolidators (high on both commitment dimensions and exploration in depth, and lowest of all trajectories on exploration in breadth), guardians (moderate on both commitment dimensions, low on both exploration dimensions with a small growth over time of exploration in breadth), and finally searchers (low on both commitment dimensions, high and increasing over time on exploration in breadth, and moderate on in-depth exploration). Three of these trajectories are consistent with typologies identified in qualitative studies conducted with young women by Josselson (1996) and with Marcia's identity statuses. In fact, the pathmakers recall individuals in the achievement status, the guardians those in foreclosure (the consolidator can represent a subtype of foreclosure), and the searchers those in the moratorium status. In this study, the expected developmental trajectory of the drifters (i.e., the equivalent of the diffusion status) was not empirically found.

In brief, longitudinal studies conducted both with adolescents and emerging adults clearly reveal that a person-centered approach is the most suitable strategy for capturing individual developmental trajectories, empirically identified from the combination of various commitment and exploration dimensions. Furthermore, a person-centered approach allows the testing of transitions more likely to occur in these stages of the lifespan. A future avenue for research consists in further unraveling the predictors and consequences of these transitions (Meeus, 2011).

Conclusions and Directions for Future Research

The main take-home message of this chapter is that to capture the complexity of individual identity it is necessary to look at identity using different "lenses." In this respect, variable- and person-centered approaches can be fruitfully integrated, as shown in the examples we have reviewed. That said, we have also shown that, in the identity literature, modern application of the person-centered approach offers powerful instruments for capturing identity complexity. In particular, we have seen that extensions of Marcia's identity status paradigm, such as the integrative model of Luyckx et al. (2006a, 2006b, 2008) and the three-factor model of Meeus, Crocetti, and collaborators' (Crocetti et al., 2008b; Meeus et al., 2010), applied using rigorous and empirically based method of classifications (e.g., cluster analysis, latent class analysis) have provided new insights in the identity literature. In particular, recent studies have shed light on differentiation within identity statuses that have clarified contrasting findings reported in earlier literature (e.g., the distinction between classic moratorium and searching moratorium statuses have disentangled the dark and bright side of Marcia's moratorium status; Crocetti et al., 2008a; Crocetti, Schwartz et al., 2012; Meeus et al., 2010, 2012) and through multiple-wave longitudinal studies have detected patterns of identity transitions over time (Meeus et al., 2010).

In this chapter, we focused on identity processes and statuses without referring to specific content domains. At this point, it is worthwhile noting that the literature reviewed so far was based on different content domains. For instance, a main difference between Luyckx's et al. integrative model and Meeus, Crocetti et al.'s three-factor model refers to the domains taken into account. In particular, Luyckx et al.'s integrative model has been used to evaluate identity related to general future plans. In fact, the DIDS (Luyckx, Schwartz, Berzonsky et al., 2008) measures a unique identity domain that is based on extent to which individuals explore future-related goals and commit themselves to future plans. In contrast, Meeus, Crocetti et al.'s three-factor model has been adopted to study how individuals deal with identity domains that are relevant for their present experience. In more specific terms, the U-MICS (Crocetti et al., 2008b) measures multiple identity domains that can be grouped into ideological (e.g., educational identity) and relational domains.

What are the implications of considering different identity domains? The empirical evidence revealing that the profile of identity processes and statuses is similar, despite different domains taken into account, strongly supports our initial claim about the fact that the interplay of overall identity processes provides a valuable framework for uncovering identity formation across different content domains. This means that, for instance, achieved adolescents are happier than their diffused counterparts, and this holds true whether we consider as content domain future life plans or current educational and relational choices.

On the other hand, it is still largely unexplored how congruence in identity statuses reached across multiple identity domains impacts self-definition and adjustment (Crocetti, Scrignaro, Sica, & Magrin, 2012). To further unravel this issue, scholars need to assess identity processes and statuses in several identity domains. However, they also need to address a key issue: which domains to take into account? To repeat the same scale for measuring several domains (e.g., eight domains) might result in questionnaires that are too long, repetitive, and burdensome. A selection based on the most important identity domains is definitely not an easy task, since the importance of various identity domains changes across time, cultural/ethnic groups, and special populations (Marcia, 2001). Therefore, to select identity domains that can be shared by individuals from various cohorts and, within the same cohort from various groups, is challenging. A viable solution to this caveat could be the one proposed by Marcia (2001), which is to study the identity domains that are most *important* for the participant. However, this makes it difficult to rigorously compare identity development across individuals. At present, there is no straightforward solution to this issue. Therefore, further reflections on intersections between identity processes/statuses and identity contents are needed.

Suggestions for Future Research

Today, identity researchers have various reliable instruments in their "toolbox." From a theoretical point of view, they can count on process models that have renewed Marcia's identity status paradigm (Meeus, 2011). From a methodological point of view, they have two main resources: (a) reliable instruments for assessing identity, such as the U-MICS, which has very strong psychometric properties and is currently being used in various cultural contexts (Crocetti et al., 2014); and (b) sophisticated statistical strategies of analysis and empirically based methods of classifications. With these available tools, identity scholars can now take off, digging more in depth in the identity arena. So, how could they further advance identity literature?

First, it would be worthwhile to unravel identity formation from early adolescence to late adulthood, adopting a lifespan approach. In this way, it would be possible to monitor identity in different stages, when life transitions (e.g., marriage, parenthood, retirement) stimulate the search of new identity structures (Marcia, 2002).

Second, a future line of research that should become the priority in scholars' agenda is the need to integrate various identity literatures. As we have suggested in the opening of this chapter, identity formation is a complex process because it entails making relevant choices in multiple domains. Given this complexity, identity is one of the most important constructs in the social sciences (Vignoles, Schwartz, & Luyckx, 2011). Multiple disciplines and subdisciplines have focused on identity, each of them unraveling various identity facets: personal identity, ethnic identity, racial identity, social identity, collective identity, national identity, cultural identity, and more. Up to now, these literatures have mainly proceeded on parallel tracks, each of them leading to articulated conceptualizations. Nonetheless, an integration of these literatures is strongly urged (e.g., Schwartz, Vignoles, & Luyckx, 2011) for attaining a better comprehension of identity complexity.

Finally, in closing this chapter, we can still draw inspiration from the poem with which we have started. The story of George Gray is an illustration of how unresolved identity issues are sources of distress and threat to individual mental health. Therefore, it is of utmost importance to clarify conditions that can support identity formation and promote positive youth development. Improving our understanding of psychosocial factors that underpin healthy identity formation is necessary to inform evidence-based interventions aimed at supporting the achievement of a mature identity (Schwartz & Pantin, 2006).

Acknowledgments

Elisabetta Crocetti was supported by a Marie Curie fellowship (FP7-PEOPLE-2010-IEF).

References

Abraham, K. G. (1983). The relation between identity status and locus of control among rural high school students. *Journal of Early Adolescence, 3,* 257–264.

Adams, G. R., Ryan, J. H., Hoffman, J. J., Dobson, W. R., & Nielsen, E. C. (1984). Ego identity status conformity behaviour, and personality in late adolescence. *Journal of Personality and Social Psychology, 47,* 1091–1104.

Adams, G. R., Shea, J., & Fitch, S. A. (1979). Toward the development of an objective assessment of ego-identity status. *Journal of Youth and Adolescence, 8,* 223–237.

Al-Owidha, A., Green, K. E., & Kroger, J. (2009). On the question of an identity status category order: Rasch model step and scale statistics used to identify category order. *International Journal of Behavioral Development, 33,* 88–96.

Archer, S. L., & Waterman, A. S. (1990). Varieties of identity diffusions and foreclosures: An exploration of subcategories of the identity statuses. *Journal of Adolescent Research, 5,* 96–111.

Balistreri, E., Busch-Rossnagel, N. A., & Geisinger, K. F. (1995). Development and preliminary validation of the Ego Identity Process Questionnaire. *Journal of Adolescence, 18,* 179–192.

Bamaca-Colbert, M. Y., & Gayles, J. G. (2010). Variable-centered and person-centered approaches to studying Mexican-origin mother-daughter cultural orientation dissonance. *Journal of Youth and Adolescence, 39,* 1274–1292.

Bennion, L. D., & Adams G. R (1986). A revision of the extended version of the objective measure of ego identity status: An identity instrument for use with late adolescents. *Journal of Adolescent Research, 1,* 183–198.

Bergman, L. R., Magnusson, D., & El Khouri, B. M. (2003). *Studying individual development in an inter individual context. A person-oriented approach.* Mahwah, N.J.: Lawrence Erlbaum Associates.

Berry, J. W. (2001). A psychology of immigration. *Journal of Social Issues, 57,* 615–631.

Berzonsky, M. D. (2003). Identity style and well-being: Does commitment matter? *Identity: An International Journal of Theory and Research, 3,* 131–142.

Berzonsky, M. D. (2004). Identity processing style, self-construction, and personal epistemic assumptions: A social-cognitive perspective. *European Journal of Developmental Psychology, 1,* 303–315.

Berzonsky, M. D., Macek, P., & Nurmi, J. (2003). Interrelationships among identity process, content, and structure: A cross-cultural investigation. *Journal of Adolescent Research, 18,* 112–130.

Berzonsky, M. D., Rice, K. G., & Neimeyer, G. J. (1991). Identity status and self-construct systems: Process X structure interactions. *Journal of Adolescence, 13,* 251–263.

Block, J. (1971). *Lives through time.* Berkeley, CA: Bancroft Books.

Blustein, D. L., & Phillips, S. D. (1990). Relation between ego identity statuses and decision-making styles. *Journal of Counseling Psychology, 37,* 160–168.

Bogat, G. A., Levendosky, A. A., & von Eye, A. (2005). The future of research on intimate partner violence: Person-oriented and variable-oriented perspectives. *American Journal of Community Psychology, 36,* 49–70.

Bosma, H. A. (1985). *Identity development in adolescents: Coping with commitments.* Unpublished doctoral dissertation, University of Groningen, The Netherlands.

Branch, C. W., Tayal, P., & Triplett, C. (2000). The relationship of ethnic identity and ego identity status among adolescents and young adults. *International Journal of Intercultural Relations, 24,* 777–790.

Carlson, R. (1971). Where is the person in personality research? *Psychological Bulletin, 75,* 203–219.

Clancy, S. M., & Dollinger, S. J. (1993). Identity, self, and personality: I. Identity status and the five-factor model of personality. *Journal of Research on Adolescence, 3,* 227–245.

Cramer, P. (1998). Freshman to senior year: A follow-up study of identity, narcissism, and defense mechanisms. *Journal of Research in Personality, 32,* 156–172.

Côté, J. E., & Levine, C. (1983). Marcia and Erikson: The relationships among ego identity status, neuroticism, dogmatism and purpose in life. *Journal of Youth and Adolescence, 12,* 43–53.

Crocetti, E., Cieciuch, J., Gao, C. H., Klimstra, T., Lin, C. L., Matos, P. M., Morsünbül, Ü., Negru, O., Sugimura, K., Zimmermann, G., & Meeus, W. (2014). National and gender measurement invariance of the Utrecht-Management of Identity Commitments Scale (U-MICS): A ten-nation cross-cultural study. Manuscript under review.

Crocetti, E., Fermani, A., Pojaghi, B., & Meeus, W. (2011). Identity formation in adolescents from Italian, mixed, and migrant Families. *Child & Youth Care Forum, 40,* 7–23

Crocetti, E., Klimstra, T. A., Hale III, W. W., Koot, H. M., & Meeus, W. (2013). Impact of early adolescent externalizing problem behaviors on identity development in middle to late adolescence: A prospective 7-year longitudinal study. *Journal of Youth and Adolescence, 42* (11), 1745-1758.

Crocetti, E., Jahromi, P., & Meeus, W. (2012). Identity and civic engagement in adolescence. *Journal of Adolescence, 35,* 521–532.

Crocetti, E., Rubini, M., Berzonsky, M. D., & Meeus, W. (2009). Brief report: The Identity Style Inventory—Validation in Italian adolescents and college students. *Journal of Adolescence, 32,* 425–433.

Crocetti, E., Rubini, M., Luyckx, K., & Meeus, W. (2008a). Identity formation in early and middle adolescents from various ethnic groups: From three dimensions to five statuses. *Journal of Youth and Adolescence, 37,* 983–996.

Crocetti, E., Rubini, M., & Meeus, W. (2008b). Capturing the dynamics of identity formation in various ethnic groups: Development and validation of a three-dimensional model. *Journal of Adolescence, 31,* 207–222.

Crocetti, E., Schwartz, S. J., Fermani, A., Klimstra, T., & Meeus, W. (2012). A cross-national study of identity status in Dutch and Italian adolescents: Status distributions and correlates. *European Psychologist, 17,* 171–181.

Crocetti, E., Schwartz, S. J., Fermani, A., & Meeus, W. (2010). The Utrecht-Management of Identity Commitments Scale (U-MICS): Italian validation and cross-national comparisons. *European Journal of Psychological Assessment, 26,* 172–186.

Crocetti, E., Scrignaro, M., Sica, L. S., & Magrin, M. E. (2012b). Correlates of identity configurations: Three studies with adolescent and emerging adult cohorts. *Journal of Youth and Adolescence, 41,* 732–748.

Crocetti, E., Sica, L. S., Schwartz, S. J., Serafini, T., & Meeus, W. (2013). Identity styles, processes, statuses, and functions: Making connections among identity dimensions. *European Review of Applied Psychology, 63,* 1–13.

Dellas, M., & Jernigan, L. P. (1981). Development of an objective instrument to measure identity status in terms of occupation crisis and commitment. *Educational and Psychological Measurement, 41,* 1039–1050.

Dellas, M., & Jernigan, L. P. (1990). Affective personality characteristics associated with undergraduate ego identity formation. *Journal of Adolescent Research, 5*, 306–324.

Erikson, E. (1950). *Childhood and society.* New York: Norton.

Erikson, E. (1968). *Identity, youth and crisis.* New York: Norton.

Frisén, A., & Wängqvist, M. (2011). Emerging adults in Sweden: Identity formation in the light of love, work and family. *Journal of Adolescent Research, 26*, 200–221

Grotevant, H. D. (1987). Toward a process model of identity formation. *Journal of Adolescent Research, 2*, 203–222.

Klimstra, T. A., Crocetti, E., Hale, W. W., Kolman, A. I. M., Fortanier, E., & Meeus, W. H. J. (2011). Identity formation in juvenile delinquents and clinically referred youth. *European Review of Applied Psychology, 61*, 123–130.

Klimstra, T. A., Hale III, W. W., Raaijmakers, Q. A. W., Branje, S. J. T., & Meeus, W. H. J. (2010). Identity formation in adolescence: Change or stability? *Journal of Youth and Adolescence, 39*, 150–162.

Klimstra, T. A., Luyckx, K., Hale, W. W., Frijns, T., van Lier, P. A. C., & Meeus, W. H. J. (2010). Short-term fluctuations in identity: Introducing a micro-level approach to identity formation. *Journal of Personality and Social Psychology, 99*, 191–202.

Kroger, J., & Marcia, J. E. (2011). The identity statuses: Origins, meanings, and interpretations. In S. J. Schwartz, K. Luyckx, & V. L. Vignoles (Eds.), *Handbook of identity theory and research* (pp. 31–53). New York: Springer.

Kroger, J., Martinussen, M., & Marcia, J. E. (2010). Identity status change during adolescence and young adulthood: A meta-analysis. *Journal of Adolescence, 33*, 683–698.

Josselson, R. (1987). *Finding herself: Pathways to identity development in women.* San Francisco, London: Jossey-Bass Inc.

Josselson, R. (1996). *Revising herself: The story of women's identity from college to midlife.* Oxford: Oxford University press.

Lichtwarck-Aschoff, A., van Geert, P., Bosma, H., & Kunnen, S. (2008). Time and identity: A framework for research and theory formation. *Developmental Review, 28*, 370–400.

Luyckx, K., Goossens, L., & Soenens, B. (2006a). A developmental contextual perspective on identity construction in emerging adulthood: Change dynamics in commitment formation and commitment evaluation. *Developmental Psychology, 42*, 366–380.

Luyckx, K., Goossens, L., Soenens, B., & Beyers, W. (2006b). Unpacking commitment and exploration: Preliminary validation of an integrative model of late adolescent identity formation. *Journal of Adolescence, 29*, 361–378.

Luyckx, K., Schwartz, S. J., Berzonsky, M. D., Soenens, B., Vansteenkiste, M., Smits, I., & Goossens, L. (2008). Capturing ruminative exploration: Extending the four-dimensional model of identity formation in late adolescence. *Journal of Research in Personality, 42*, 58–82.

Luyckx, K., Schwartz, S., Goossens, L., Beyers, W., Missotten, L. (2011). Processes of personal identity formation and evaluation. In S. J. Schwartz, K. Luyckx, & V. L. Vignoles (Eds.), *Handbook of identity theory and research* (pp. 77–98). New York: Springer.

Luyckx, K., Schwartz, S. J., Goossens, L., Soenens, B., & Beyers, W. (2008). Developmental typologies of identity formation and adjustment in female emerging adults: A latent class growth analysis approach. *Journal of Research on Adolescence, 18*, 595–619.

Magnusson, D., & Allen, V. L. (Eds.). (1983). *Human development: An interactional perspective.* Orlando, FL: Academic Press.

Marcia, J. E. (1964). *Determination and construct validity of ego identity status.* Unpublished doctoral dissertation, Ohio State University.

Marcia, J. E. (1966). Development and validation of ego-identity status. *Journal of Personality and Social Psychology, 3*, 551–558.

Marcia, J. E. (1976). Identity six years after: A follow up study. *Journal of Youth and Adolescence, 5*, 145–160.

Marcia, J. E. (1980). Identity in adolescence. In J. Adelson (Ed.), *Handbook of adolescent psychology* (pp. 159–187). New York: Wiley.

Marcia, J. E. (1989). Identity diffusion differentiated. In M. A. Luszcz & T. Nettelbeck (Eds.), *Psychological development: Perspectives across the life-span* (pp. 123–137). Dordrecht, the Netherlands: Elsevier.

Marcia, J. E. (1993). The status of the statuses: Research review. In J. E. Marcia, A. S. Waterman, D. R. Matteson, S. L. Archer, & J. L. Orlofsky (Eds.), *Identity: A handbook for psychosocial research* (pp. 22–41). New York: Springer-Verlag.

Marcia, J. E. (2001). A commentary on Seth Schwartz's review of identity theory and research. *Identity: An International Journal of Theory and Research, 1*, 59–65.

Marcia, J. E. (2002). Identity and psychosocial development in adulthood. *Identity: An International Journal of Theory and Research, 2*, 7–28.

Marcia, J. E., & Friedman, M. L. (1970). Ego identity status in college women. *Journal of Personality, 38*, 249–263.

Marcia, J. E., Waterman, A. S., Matteson, D. R., Archer, S. L., & Orlofsky, J. L. (1993). *Identity: A handbook for psychosocial research.* New York: Springer-Verlag.

Masters, E. L. (1915). *Spoon River Anthology.* New York: McMillan Company.

McCrae, R. R., & Costa, P. T. (1987). Validation of the 5-factor model of personality across instruments and observers. *Journal of Personality and Social Psychology, 52*, 81–90.

Meeus, W. (1992). Toward psychosocial analysis of adolescent identity. In W. Meeus, M. de Goede, W. Kox, & K. Hurrelmann (Eds.), *Adolescence, careers and cultures* (pp. 55–76). Berlin, de Gruyter.

Meeus, W. (1996). Studies on identity development in adolescence: An overview of research and some new data. *Journal of Youth and Adolescence, 25*, 569–598.

Meeus, W. (2011). The Study of Adolescent Identity Formation 2000–2010: A Review of Longitudinal Research. *Journal of Research on Adolescence, 21*, 75–94.

Meeus, W., Iedema, J., Helsen, M., & Vollebergh, W. (1999). Patterns of adolescent identity development: Review of literature and longitudinal analysis. *Developmental Review, 19*, 419–461.

Meeus, W., Iedema, J., & Maassen, G. H. (2002). Commitment and exploration as mechanisms of identity formation. *Psychological Reports, 90*, 771–785.

Meeus, W., van de Schoot, R., Keijsers, L., & Branje, S. (2012). Identity statuses as developmental trajectories: A five-wave longitudinal study in early-to-middle and middle-to-late adolescents. *Journal of Youth and Adolescence, 41*, 1008–1021.

Meeus, W., van de Schoot, R., Keijsers, L., Schwartz, S. J., & Branje, S. (2010). On the progression and stability of adolescent identity formation: A five-wave longitudinal study in early-to-middle and middle-to-late adolescence. *Child Development, 81*, 1565–1581.

Orlofsky, J. L. (1978). Identity formation, achievement, and fear of success in college men and women. *Journal of Youth and Adolescence, 7*, 49–63.

Reinecke, J. (2006). Longitudinal analysis of adolescent's deviant and delinquent behavior. *Methodology, 2*, 100–112.

Robins, R. W., John, O. P., Caspi, A., Moffitt, T. E., & Stouthamer-Loeber, M. (1996). Resilient, overcontrolled, and undercontrolled boys: Three replicable personality types. *Journal of Personality and Social Psychology, 70*, 157–171.

Rotheram-Borus, M. J. (1989). Ethnic differences in adolescents' identity status and associated behavior problems. *Journal of Adolescence, 12*, 361–374.

Schenkel, S., & Marcia, J. E. (1972). Attitudes toward premarital intercourse in determining ego identity status in college women. *Journal of Personality, 3*, 472–482.

Schwartz, S. J. (2005). A new identity for identity research: Recommendations for expanding and refocusing the identity literature. *Journal of Adolescent Research, 20*, 293–308.

Schwartz, S. J., Adamson, L., Ferrer-Wreder, L., Dillon, F. R., & Berman, S. L. (2006). Identity status measurement across contexts: Variations in measurement structure and mean levels among white American, Hispanic American, and Swedish emerging adults. *Journal of Personality Assessment, 86*, 61–76.

Schwartz, S. J., Beyers, W., Luyckx, K., Soenens, B., Zamboanga, B. L., Forthun, L. F.,...Waterman, A. S. (2011). Examining the light and dark sides of emerging adults' identity: A study of identity status differences in positive and negative psychosocial functioning. *Journal of Youth and Adolescence, 40*, 839–859.

Schwartz, S. J., & Pantin, H. (2006). Identity development in adolescence and emerging adulthood: The interface of self, context, and culture. In A. Prescott (Ed.), *The concept of self in psychology* (pp. 45–85). Hauppage, NY: Nova Science Publishers.

Schwartz, S. J., Vignoles, V. L., & Luyckx, K. (2011). Epilogue: What's next for identity theory and research. In S. J. Schwartz, K. Luyckx, & V. L. Vignoles (Eds.), *Handbook of identity theory and research* (pp. 933–938). New York: Springer.

Skoe, E. E., & Marcia, J. E. (1991). A care-based measure of morality and its relation to ego identity. *Merrill-Palmer Quarterly, 37*, 289–304.

Stephen, J., Fraser, E., & Marcia, J. E. (1992). Moratorium-achievement (Mama) cycles in lifespan identity development: Value orientations and reasoning system correlates. *Journal of Adolescence, 15*, 283–300.

Tesch, S. A., & Cameron, K. A. (1987). Openness to experience and development of adult identity. *Journal of Personality, 55*, 615–630.

Van Leeuwen, K. G., Mervielde, I., Braet, C., & Bosmans, G. (2004). Child personality and parental behavior as moderators of problem behavior: Variable- and person-centered approaches. *Developmental Psychology, 40*, 1028–1046.

Vignoles, V. L., Schwartz, S. J., & Luyckx, K. (2011). Introduction: Toward an integrative view of identity. In S. J. Schwartz, K. Luyckx, & V. L. Vignoles (Eds.), *Handbook of identity theory and research* (pp. 1–27). New York: Springer.

Von Eye, A., & Bogat, G. A. (2006). Person-oriented and variable-oriented research: Concepts, results, and development. *Merrill-Palmer Quarterly-Journal of Developmental Psychology, 52*, 390–420.

Waterman, A. S. (1993). Overview of the identity status scoring criteria. In J. E. Marcia, A. S. Waterman, D. R. Matteson, S. L. Archer, & J. L. Orlofsky (Eds.), *Identity: A handbook for psychosocial research* (pp. 156–176). New York: Springer-Verlag.

Waterman, A. S. (1999). Identity, the identity statuses, and identity status development: A contemporary statement. *Developmental Review, 19*, 591–621.

Zimmermann, G., Mahaim, E. B., Mantzouranis, G., Genoud, P. A., & Crocetti, E. (2012). Brief report: The Identity Style Inventory (ISI-3) and the Utrecht-Management of Identity Commitments Scale (U-MICS): Factor structure, reliability, and convergent validity in French-speaking university students. *Journal of Adolescence, 35*, 461–465.

CHAPTER
8
Commitment and Exploration: The Need for a Developmental Approach

E. Saskia Kunnen *and* Marijke Metz

Abstract

This chapter addresses identity development from a process perspective, with specific focus on commitment and exploration as core processes of identity development. It begins with an overview of the theory on identity development. Via Erikson and Marcia, the authors discuss the recent models of Meeus and colleagues, as well as of Luyckx and colleagues, demonstrating that a process approach is becoming increasingly salient in thinking about identity development and arguing that, to understand the developmental processes, one needs to study the development of individuals. Next, the authors present a process model that describes how identity emerges from real-time events. Finally, the authors elaborate how, based on a dynamic systems perspective, researchers could set up studies that gain insight into the processes of emergence, stability, and change of commitments, and they discuss some simple techniques that can be used to study developmental processes on an individual level.

Key Words: identity development, exploration, commitments, developmental processes, dynamic systems

---

Erikson began publishing his work on ego-identity approximately fifty years ago (1959; 1963; 1968). His ideas have inspired many researchers, but his writings are so broad and all-encompassing that not all ideas have been picked up by later researchers. In particular, the interest in Erikson's notions concerning developmental process and the role of context are fairly recent, although the interest in process-oriented and contextualized perspectives on identity development in adolescence and adulthood is growing rapidly. In this chapter, we address identity development from a process perspective, and, more specifically, we focus on commitment and exploration as core processes of identity development. Our aim is to develop a model that describes the mechanisms of change in identity development, a model that helps to answer questions about how identity changes and stabilizes on a developmental long-term level as a consequence of daily experience on a microlevel. The leading questions throughout this chapter are: "How does an individual's identity emerge, change and stabilize over time?" And, "How can we explain differences in this developmental process between individuals?"

We start with an overview of the theories on identity development. Based on Erikson and Marcia, we argue that exploration and commitment are well suited concepts for our enquiry but that the identity status model is not truly a developmental model. We discuss recent models that address identity processes more specifically (Berzonsky, Luyckx, and colleagues and Meeus and colleagues). Based on these models, we specify our general leading questions and specify which questions can be answered with help of these models and which questions are still open. We conclude that the unanswered questions are those that address the developmental mechanisms in detail. We argue that, in order nd these mechanisms and processes of development, we need to study the development of individuals and how long-term identity development emerges from daily life. We elaborate on how dynamic systems theory can be helpful in studying these processes. As a first step in understanding individual development, we need to gain knowledge about the different types of identity trajectories possible. As a next step, we need to analyze how, on the level of daily events, identity measures and contextual measures interact over time. Finally, we discuss some simple techniques that can be used to study developmental processes on an individual level.

The Founding Fathers: Erikson and Marcia

Literature concerning identity development goes back to Erikson (1959) and Marcia (1966). The first definition of identity is usually ascribed to Erikson (1959), who incorporated the concept of identity into his theory about developmental stages. Erikson (1963) distinguishes eight stages of psychosocial development. Each stage is related to a developmental task that belongs to a specific period in the human lifespan. For each of these tasks, the basic process is the same: as a consequence of different changes and new demands (both in the person and in the context), the old ways of functioning become inadequate, and this results in a crisis. Such a crisis can be seen as a kind of turning point, in which development either proceeds in the direction of increasing integration on a higher level or gets stuck. The eight stages can be described by the two possible outcomes of each stage: (1) a sense of basic trust/basic mistrust during infancy, (2) autonomy/shame during early childhood, (3) a sense of initiative/guilt during play age, (4) a sense of industry/inferiority during school age, (5) a sense of identity/identity confusion during adolescence, (6) a sense of intimacy/isolation in young adulthood, (7) a sense of generativity/stagnation during later adulthood, and finally (8) a sense of integrity/despair in old age.

Each stage is centered around a specific conflict or crisis; for adolescence, this is the "identity crisis." Erikson defined "identity" as follows: "The conscious feeling of having a personal identity is based on two simultaneous observations: the perception of the selfsameness and continuity of one's existence in time and space and the perception of the fact that others recognize one's sameness and continuity" (Erikson, 1968, p. 50). Thus, although development implies change, there is also the feeling that one stays the same person (Lichtwarck-Aschoff, Van Geert, Bosma, & Kunnen, 2008). Moreover, this sameness is perceivable to others.

In this chapter, we focus on the fifth stage. That this stage is related to adolescence does not mean that identity development starts in adolescence. According to Erikson (1968), identity development begins in childhood with the processes of introjection and identification. "Introjection" refers to the internalization of the mother's image. The integration of this image depends on the mutuality and trustworthiness of the mother–infant relationship. Identifications are derived from the available role models in childhood (e.g. "I want to be like my father, teacher," etc.). This process is embedded in interactions with others. From the very first beginnings, identity development therefore emerges from the interactions of the individual with significant others. Identification becomes less useful for identity development in adolescence, and this is where the process of (active) identity formation starts. Equipped with new physical and sexual abilities, enabled by their new cognitive skills, and encouraged to become more autonomous and independent (a push and pull resulting from the interaction of maturational processes and social/cultural expectations), adolescents begin to build their own identity configuration by actively selecting and discarding earlier and new identifications in the light of their own interests, talents, and values and the demands and affordances offered by society. Next to the interactions with significant others, the mutuality between the individual and the wider social and cultural context becomes essential in the process of identity formation.

In his discussion of identity formation, Erikson focused on two processes: crisis and commitment. Erikson's (1968) use of the term *identity crisis* referred to a period during the lifespan when someone is struggling to make decisions about who he wishes to be, for oneself and for one's interactions with family, peers, and community. The term implies a sense of struggle, even distress. Given the normative nature of such experiences and the fact that not everyone going through the process experiences it as distressing, later identity researchers have preferred the term *exploration* rather than *crisis*. As pointed out by Marcia (1993), the optimal outcome of this process is a kind of dialectic balance in which the so-called *syntonic* pole of identity integration is predominant over the *systonic* pole of identity diffusion. Such an identity outcome consists of personally meaningful identity commitments that help the person successfully resolve the demands of everyday life and of subsequent developmental stages. To serve such purposes, commitments have to be firmly held, elaborated (detailed), and realistic; that is, capable of being implemented within the person's sociohistorical context.

The complexity of the identity construct as conceptualized by Erikson made it difficult for those seeking to study identity to develop operational definitions for use in empirical research. To overcome this difficulty, Marcia developed the identity status paradigm (Marcia, 1966; 1980; Marcia, Waterman, Matteson, Archer, & Orlofsky, 1993). This paradigm focuses on the two processes that were discussed by Erikson, crisis (exploration) and commitment. Marcia's (1966) status theory offers a differentiation of the bipolar outcome of the identity crisis in adolescence described by Erikson. According to the status model, individuals can be classified into one of four statuses on the basis of the two process variables "crisis" (later "exploration") and "commitment" in various content domains. Both exploration and commitment are behavioral variables. Exploration (or "crisis") refers to an individual's "period of engagement in choosing among meaningful alternatives," whereas the concept of commitment refers to the presence of a stable set of goals, values, and beliefs that provide a direction, purpose, and meaning to life. It indicates an individual's "degree of personal investment the individual exhibits" (Marcia, 1966, p. 551). These two processes amount to four statuses: achievement (previous high exploration and current strong commitments), diffusion (no current exploration and weak commitments), moratorium (current high exploration and weak commitments), and foreclosure (no current or past exploration and strong commitments). Thus, Erikson's polar outcomes are the two ends of the continuum; we see diffusion and identity achievement as synonymous with Erikson's concepts of identity diffusion and identity integration, and foreclosure and moratorium are placed between these two statuses.

Later research has elaborated on the original four-status paradigm by adding substatuses. Kroger (1995) found longitudinal evidence for two types of foreclosure, namely "firm" and "developmental" foreclosure statuses. The "firm foreclosures" show a very stable pathway, whereas the "developmental foreclosures" progress toward the more mature statuses moratorium and achievement. Marcia (1989) reported a comparable differentiation with regard to the diffusion status: stability versus progressive developmental change. Flum (1994) found a new type of trajectory. In a study with high school adolescents, he discovered a distinct group that displayed a so-called *evolutive style* of identity formation. This group showed a gradual, step-by-step exploration of identity issues. Contrary to the other statuses, in this status, no moratorium phase is present: the commitment remains strong.

Since Marcia's publication in 1966, the identity status paradigm has developed into the dominant approach in identity research. It generated many studies, in which much knowledge has been gathered about identity and the relations between identity statuses and other variables. An issue in identity research has been the implicit assumption that Marcia's statuses reflect a progressive order of less to more advanced stages of identity, which proceeds from identify diffused, to foreclosure, to moratorium, to the achieved status. Meeus and colleagues (Meeus, 1996; 1999; Meeus, Van de Schoot, Keijsers, Schwartz, & Branje, 2010) conducted several analyses to inspect whether a progressive development through Marcia's identity statuses could be found. These studies, as well as the meta-analysis of Kroger, Martinussen, and Marcia (2010), showed that progressive shifts in identity development are more common than regressive shifts. In addition, Meeus and colleagues (2010) found that more than half of the adolescents had stable identity statuses during the five waves of the study.

However, Marcia's theory about identity is not a developmental theory (Bosma & Kunnen, 2008; Vleioras & Bosma, 2005; Waterman, 1982). First, the main aim of the theory is to offer a typology, not to describe a developmental process (cf., Kroger, this volume). And although the sequence from foreclosed or diffused via moratorium is the most common one, all other sequences have been found to be possible as well, and therefore the theory does not offer a model to describe the process over time. Finally, as will be elaborated later in this chapter, the theory distinguishes between only four broad statuses. This means that a lot of change can be happening but, as long as it does not result in a status shift, it remains invisible. Therefore, this theory offers no answers to our questions "How does an individual's identity emerge, change, and stabilize over time?" and "How can we explain differences in this developmental process between individuals?," nor to more specifics of these basic questions such as: "Why do some people develop from their initial diffused or foreclosed status to an achieved status and while others don't?" "How do the identity components exploration and commitments develop over time?," and "How are they related to each other?" In the past two decades, more attention has been directed toward issues related to these questions. The identity status model became the basis of new models that aimed to address the developmental process and the mechanisms of change (see, e.g., Bosma & Kunnen, 2001a; Crocetti, Rubini, & Meeus, 2008; Crocetti & Meeus, this volume; Klimstra, 2012; Kroger, 2003; Luyckx, 2006) and the role of the context in identity development (see, e.g., Bosma & Kunnen, 2008; Luyckx, Goossens, & Soenens, 2006a). In the following section we discuss models that address these issues.

New Models of Identity Development

One of the most elaborated models is that developed by Luyckx and colleagues. Luyckx, Goossens, and Soenens (2006)a developed a model of identity development in which they distinguished between two types of exploration and two types of commitment. Exploration in breadth plays a role during the formation of commitments and refers to the exploration of different alternatives, whereas exploration in depth is relevant in the process of maintaining commitments; it refers to the in-depth exploration of current commitments. Moreover, the concept of commitment is distinguished in two separate processes: the process of making a commitment and the extent to which people identify with the commitment. Luyckx and colleagues deduced the following sequence of identity development from a sample consisting of freshmen psychology students (mean age 18.8 years): exploration in breadth is followed by commitment making, after which exploration in depth occurs, leading to a stronger identification with commitment. This cycle can be reactivated if commitments turn out to be unsatisfactory. This model is called the *dual-cycle model* (Luyckx, Goossens, Soenens, & Beyers, 2006b). The first cycle (the commitment formation cycle) consists of commitment making and exploration in breadth; the second cycle (commitment evaluation) consists of exploration in depth and identification with commitment.

Through structural equation modeling, it was demonstrated that a model including these four dimensions provided a better fit than simpler models that included two or three dimensions. Moreover, they found that the four dimensions were significantly related to variables such as self-esteem, depressive symptoms, and social and academic adjustment at university (Luyckx, Goossens, Soenens, et al., 2006b). In addition, life events were found to influence identity development. For example, students who experienced a challenge of their commitment in their studies, such as having to repeat their freshman year or changing their major, showed both cycles—commitment evaluation and commitment formation—whereas for students who proceeded from the first to the second year of their studies, the cycle of commitment evaluation was the core cycle in their identity development.

In later research, Luyckx and colleagues (Luyckx, Schwartz, Berzonsky, et al., 2008) added a fifth dimension to their model. This dimension is labeled as ruminative (or maladaptive) exploration, and it was added as a complement to two forms of reflective (or adaptive) exploration already included in the model. Ruminative exploration may be characterized by indecision, and it was found to be positively related to distress and self-rumination.

Another model was developed by Meeus and colleagues (Crocetti et al., 2008; Meeus et al., 2010), differentiating Marcia's concept of exploration into in-depth exploration and reconsideration (which serve to maintain and change commitments). Their approach focuses on the management of commitments and describes the process of identity formation by means of three dimensions. First, commitment refers to strong choices that adolescents have, along with the self-confidence that they derive from these choices. Second, in-depth exploration refers to the ways in which adolescents maintain their present commitments, especially to the extent to which adolescents actively explore the commitments that they have already made by reflecting on their choices, searching for information about these commitments, and talking with others about them. This in-depth exploration resembles the in-depth exploration in the model of Luyckx and colleagues. Finally, reconsideration of commitment refers to the willingness to discard one's commitments and search for new commitments. It refers to the comparison of present commitments with possible alternative commitments when the present ones are no longer satisfactory.

The model assumes that identity is formed in a process of continuous interplay between commitment, in-depth exploration, and reconsideration. Adolescents are assumed to manage their commitments in two ways: through in-depth exploration and through reconsideration. Confirmatory factor analyses on cross sectional data of ten- to nineteen-year-old adolescents showed that the three-factor model provided a better fit than alternative one- and two-factor models (Crocetti et al., 2008). The model applied to the whole adolescent sample and also to the early and middle adolescent age groups separately. A later study (Meeus et al., 2010) that used the three factors in a longitudinal study found evidence for both a sequence of progressive transitions over time and a high level of stability.

Theoretically, the main difference between these models is the conceptualization of the initial commitment formation. Luyckx et al. assume that commitment formation starts with a broad exploration of different possibilities, whereas Meeus et al. suggest that identity development starts with more or less strong commitments that can be reconsidered (or not). Commitment making is not included as a separate dimension in the Meeus model, probably because the model describes the process of reconsideration of existing commitments instead of the process of emergence of commitments. Empirically, both models have been tested on different samples: the sample in the Crocetti et al. study was cross-sectional and consisted of a very broad age group (10–19 years), and the Luyckx et al. study used a longitudinal design and a much older sample (mean age 18.8 at the start of the studies). Thus, it may be that the models describe identity development in different age periods.

However, both models provide a set of concepts that are considered to be important in describing identity development processes. The models describe how exploration and commitment are related to each other, and how they change over time during adolescence. They offer insight into the possible pathways of commitment development over time and into the way the relevant variables affect each other in the emergence of these different pathways during the developmental process. Important questions that are addressed by these models are: "Which concepts or factors do we need to describe identity development?," "How do these factors develop over time?," and "How are they related to each other?" The models do not elaborate, however, on what may cause interindividual differences in identity development.

A model that specifically addresses the question of individual differences is that of Berzonsky (1990; 1992). He elaborated a detailed view of the mechanisms of the identity formation process in his studies on "identity styles." The concept of "identity style" refers to stable interindividual differences in short-term processes—in the way individuals construct and revise or maintain their sense of identity (Berzonsky, 1992). Although the different styles are related to identity statuses, Berzonsky does not perceive identity development as a sequence of stages but as a long-term process that has different forms, depending on an individual's (stable) processing style. People with an "information-oriented style" actively explore and evaluate relevant information before committing themselves. These people have either a moratorium or achieved status. People in the foreclosed status focus on normative expectations of significant others and are called "norm oriented." People in the diffusion status tend to delay and procrastinate until hedonic cues in the immediate situation dictate a course of behavior. Their "diffuse orientation" involves attempts to avoid confronting problems for as long as possible (Berzonsky, 1990). Berzonsky stresses that people are capable of using all styles, but that there are interindividual differences in the preferred (and most used) style.

So, the identity style theory may give some first answers to the question: "Why do some people develop from their initial diffused or foreclosed status to an achieved status while others don't?" The answer is that the first group probably uses an information-oriented identity style. However, still more important in our eyes is that the model explicitly connects short-term processes (i.e., the way in which people cope with specific events) to long-term identity development. Interindividual differences between developmental trajectories are related to the ways in which individuals cope with concrete identity challenges.

This insight draws attention to specific characteristics of short-term processes and the factors that play a role in the way people cope. Therefore, to understand how identity develops over time, we need research that focus on identity development in more detail. Most longitudinal research into identity development focuses on changes on a long-term time scale: the time between two waves is six months (Luyckx, et al., 2006a) or one year (as in the Meeus study). This is a general characteristic of longitudinal studies (see, e.g., Block & Block, 2006; Cairns & Cairns, 1994). However, we do not know what happens between two measurement points and what drives the eventual changes that we observe between one measurement point and the next. Berzonsky's model offers a general idea about the role of short-term mechanisms and real-time events, but to grasp the mechanisms of development, we need to take a closer look. Identity develops in daily life. It is driven by the day-to-day experiences of adolescents. The following questions then arises: what happens on a day-to-day basis?

Microlevel Processes in Identity Development

We know of only one study that has investigated changes in commitment on a day-to-day basis. Klimstra et al. (2010) conducted a study investigating the day-to-day iterations of these cycles. They measured identity for five days in a row at three-month intervals during one year (mean age of participants was 13.2 years). Klimstra and colleagues found evidence for the commitment evaluation cycle in the domain of interpersonal relationships (i.e., friendship). Thus, commitment strength on day one negatively predicted the level of consideration next day, and the level of consideration on day one negatively predicted the next day's commitment strength. The authors conclude that reconsideration of commitments drives the reformulation of commitments; thus, adolescents first start to compare their commitments to possible alternatives before actually reshaping their commitment, and this happens on a day-to-day basis. Further, Klimstra and colleagues (2010) found that adolescents who show many fluctuations in their levels of commitment and reconsideration generally have weaker commitments and higher levels of reconsideration than do adolescents who show fewer fluctuations. The authors suggest that fluctuations in reconsideration may be a part of the moratorium status.

Returning to our leading questions "How does an individual's identity emerge, change, and stabilize over time?" and "How can we explain differences in this developmental process between individuals?," we see that these questions into the developmental process are becoming more central in recent research. The focus on process is advocated by several scholars (Bosma & Kunnen, 2001a; 2008; Kunnen, Bosma, Van Halen, & Van der Meulen, 2001; Lichtwarck-Aschoff et al., 2008). With the increasing focus on short-term processes, the interactional character of identity development also receives more attention because real-time events can hardly be studied without considering the context (see Korobov, this volume). This fits with Erikson's notion that the interactions with significant others and the mutual relation between the individual and the context are highly relevant in identity development. This conceptualization of context differs from the way in which context is often operationalized in empirical research. Most studies that investigate contextual factors focus on broad, stable characteristics of the macroenvironment, such as differences in gender, ethnicity, or social class. This means we need to consider how the role of the context can be included in our thinking about identity development.

Identity Development as an Interactional Process

In both Erikson's and Marcia's theories, commitments do not refer to some characteristic that can be located inside the person but to a characteristic of the relation between the person and the context (see also Korobov, this volume). Commitments are about how a person sees his or her position in the world and about how he or she is perceived by the world (Kunnen et al., 2001).

From the notion that commitments refer to the relation between a person and the world, it follows that the development of commitments is a process that unfolds in the continuous interaction between person and context. A commitment can be seen as a kind of agreement between the person and the world about the identity of the person. This agreement is at stake in every interaction that is relevant with regard to the commitment (Bosma & Kunnen, 2001a; Kunnen et al., 2001). Take, for example, a master student who has a strong commitment toward her studies. She aims to become a researcher, performs well, and is highly motivated. Her teachers and fellow students perceive her as a competent and motivated student, and they recognize her ambition to become a researcher. This commitment has emerged and is maintained during a long series of interactions, such as receiving high grades, questions she posed during class, and discussions she has with teachers and other students.

Thus, a trajectory of commitment development consists of a sequence of interactions, or behavioral manifestations of a commitment, across many subsequent events. The outcome of each interaction affects the commitment. Imagine, for example, what could happen if the master student failed an important exam. This would challenge her commitment in her own eyes and in those of the people around her. Most likely, just one bad exam would not have much effect. Both the student and other people may attribute this outcome to some external variable factor, such as illness. Therefore, the situation would be given meaning in such a way that the existing commitment is not challenged, but a series of failures on subsequent exams can be expected to have a negative effect on the commitment. However, systematic empirical evidence for the mechanisms described earlier is still scarce. We found in a longitudinal diary study (Kunnen, 2006) that, for students who experienced conflicts in a specific domain, the strength of the commitments decreased. In diary research (van der Gaag & Kunnen, 2012), we found evidence for the earlier assumptions: negative events were followed by a decrease in commitment strength. The study by Luyckx, Goossens, and Soenens et al. (2006b) also clearly demonstrated that the event of failure in studies affects the process of identity development. In the next section, we discuss a model (Bosma & Kunnen, 2001a) that describes mechanisms of change in commitments based on the interactional principles described earlier.

Processes of Identity Development: Proposed Theoretical Mechanisms

In 2001, we (Bosma and Kunnen) developed a model that describes how individual long-term commitment development emerges from real-time interactions (Figure 8.1). It integrates theories of several scholars (e.g. Berzonsky, 1990; 1992; Grotevant, 1987; Kerpelman & Lamke, 1997). The model is based on the theories of disequilibrium, assimilation, and accommodation that were introduced into developmental psychology by Jean Piaget (e.g., 1985) and applied later by many other scholars, such as Block (1982). The model focuses on the real-time processes of identity development. Each cycle in the model depicts an event in which there is a transaction between a person's commitment and the context/environment. This transaction results in a fit or a misfit. A fit confirms and strengthens the commitment. A misfit or conflict means that the outcome of an interaction challenges the existing commitment, which then triggers action aimed toward solving the conflict. The first step in the actions to solve the conflict is assimilation, which means that people try to solve the conflict by changing their interpretation of the situation or possibly the situation itself. If assimilation fails, this results in a weakening of the commitment because the commitment is at odds with what is happening. Repeated failure to assimilate results in increasing conflict and in further weakening of the commitment. The prolonged conflict situation forces the individual to take more rigorous steps: this can be either withdrawal or accommodation of the now very weak commitment.

Withdrawal is seen in the model as a kind of escape. The person may, for example, quit his or her

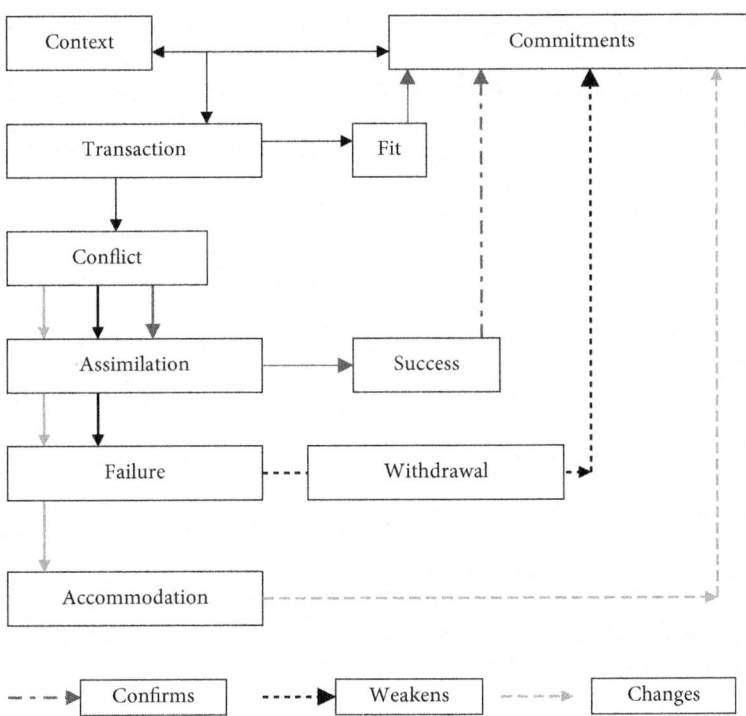

Fig. 8.1 A schematic representation of the development of commitments (Bosma & Kunnen, 2001a, p. 60).

job, leave his or her university, or end his or her relationship. Accommodation implies an adjustment of one's identity. If the accommodation of the commitment is successful, conflicts will disappear, and this will result in a strengthening of the new commitment. Accommodation can be seen as a developmental step because it is aimed toward a better adjustment and may result in a more complex and strong, yet flexible, commitment (Kunnen & Bosma, 2003).

It is assumed that assimilation is always the first reaction to conflict, mainly because, in our complex and fuzzy world, people are continuously confronted with nonfitting information. Take, for example, the good student who receives a bad grade once. It is very probable that, in that case, the bad grade is attributed to some external and variable factor, such as a miscommunication, a bad test, or having the flu. It is only if the conflict persists and becomes very salient that accommodation may be necessary.

An important assumption in the model is that people differ in how persistent they are in using assimilation. Bosma and Kunnen (2001a) assume that people in a diffuse identity status accommodate very rapidly, whereas people in a foreclosed identity status continue to assimilate even when confronted with strong and repeated nonfitting information. People in an identity achieved status show a balance between assimilating if possible and accommodation if necessary. This interindividual difference in tendency to accommodate resembles the concept of Berzonsky's identity style: a diffuse style resembles a very strong tendency to accommodate, whereas the normative style resembles a strong tendency to assimilate.

Long series of cycles in this model result in developmental trajectories. The model describes how the commitment strength may change over time as a function of daily events. The model illustrates that the "fit" between context and person and the resulting conflict could be a driving force behind the development of identity. The processes of assimilation and accommodation are illustrations of mechanisms that can explain changes in commitment strength and explorative behavior.

All models discussed so far describe identity development as a process, and all are based on the same concepts. Bosma and Kunnen's model offers a microlevel insight into processes that, on a larger time scale, may result in the cycles as proposed in the model of Luyckx and colleagues. However, at this moment, the model is mainly theoretical and based on assumptions concerning the processes within an individual. In the next section, we argue that the findings of Meeus et al. and Luyckx et al., which are based on group-level analyzed empirical data, cannot be used to test a model of individual processes without further analysis concerning the comparability of the underlying processes in both models.

The question of the relation between the different models is, in fact, part of a broader discussion: what are the processes underlying the long- and short-term changes in identity (i.e., in the levels of exploration and commitment)? Or, in other words, why and how do individuals exhibit particular temporal changes and stabilizations? What determines the specific pathway that is followed by an individual? The answers to such questions remain largely unknown. They require a process-focused type of research. Studying processes of development calls for a new framework of research in which systems, rather than variables and relationships, are studied (Bosma & Kunnen, 2008; Lichtwarck-Aschoff et al., 2008). Dynamic systems theory (DST) is the framework that has received most attention in this regard. The following section discusses the necessity to study developmental process from this perspective and the principles underlying this theory.

Identity Development from a Dynamic Systems Perspective

Dynamic systems theory aims to study the mechanisms of change (Kunnen & Van Geert, 2011a). An important assumption is that growth or development cannot exist without its environment and that development unfolds over time (Thelen & Smith, 1994). Van Geert (1991; 1994) puts forward that relations between the different aspects of a person's experience are not linear and causal, but should be understood in terms of a complex dynamic system of factors that are related to one another. In identity development, for example, cognitions, emotions, behavior, and context can be viewed as a complex, interacting network (Bosma & Kunnen, 2001b).

An important characteristic of DST is that it distinguishes between the types of development on different time scales and describes how these types of development on these different scales are related to each other. Theoretically, a large number of time scales can be distinguished, from the time scale on the level of microseconds, to a time scale on the level of ages (Kunnen & Van Geert, 2011b). In most psychological research, the lowest order time scale is the real-time scale: the scale of current behavior, of what happens in seconds or minutes. Developmental time is a higher order time scale and describes processes that cover months or even years. Developmental change as described by the models of Luyckx et al. and Meeus et al. are examples of the developmental time scale.

As argued, real-time interactions are the building blocks of development at the scale of developmental time. Thus, what happens on the real-time level both shapes and constrains the possibilities of the developmental process on a higher order time scale. Thus, a commitment can be perceived as a higher order construct that emerges in the self-organization of more basic elements of the real-time event. Empirical evidence for this type of processes is still scarce because, as mentioned, we have very few studies that focus on identity development on a day-to-day basis.

The interaction between the different time scales is mutual: the higher order constructs that emerge on a developmental time scale also affect the real-time events. These are the top-down processes. Top-down processes refer to the influence that the higher level characteristics have on actual real-time behavior. People's commitments influence the way they behave in real time. For example, a student with a strong commitment to her studies will most probably choose not to attend information meetings about other types of study. But her strong commitment may also manifest itself in interactions with, for example, her teachers and her fellow students. They will perceive her strong commitment and react to it. For example, her teacher may offer her challenging tasks and spend extra time answering her questions. For these top-down processes, empirical evidence can be found in many studies that demonstrate relations between identity (e.g., different statuses) and behavioral measurements such as coping styles, attribution patterns, and autonomous behavior (e.g., see Marcia, 1993). This mutual relation between real-time events and higher order constructs contributes to the complexity of developmental processes.

Another assumption within DST is that a system is at any moment affected by its own previous state and by its environment (Van Geert, 2003). This is called *iterativity*: every step (i.e., development or change) depends on the previous step (i.e., the previous state of the system). This process is depicted in Figure 8.2, representing the development of commitments in the interaction between a person and the context. Every step in the developmental process, thus every cycle in the model, changes both the person and the environment, and the starting point of the next developmental step is the changed individual and the changed environment. Take the example of a high school student who is in the process of making a choice for her major as a first part in the trajectory of developing a career commitment. Once she tells her friends that she thinks about choosing law as a major, the friends may draw her attention to television programs or movies about law or discuss law-related topics. This changed environment may affect the student's developing commitment and so on, in a long sequence of real-time interactions or steps in the process. Research into the impact of turning points demonstrate how specific events may affect the sequence of events by affecting both the person and the context (Docan-Morgan, 2011). The relevance of iterativity is also demonstrated in the model of self-development developed by McLean, Pasupathi, and Pals (2007). They stress how the act of telling a story changes over time as a direct consequence of the stories that were told the previous time.

Most developmental processes do not proceed as a steady, gradual rise or fall, but show bumps, sudden changes, and irregularities (e.g., Kunnen, 2009). The principles of interactions between time scales and of iterativity explain why development is often nonlinear. The mutual interactions may, for example, result in positive feedback loops that suddenly

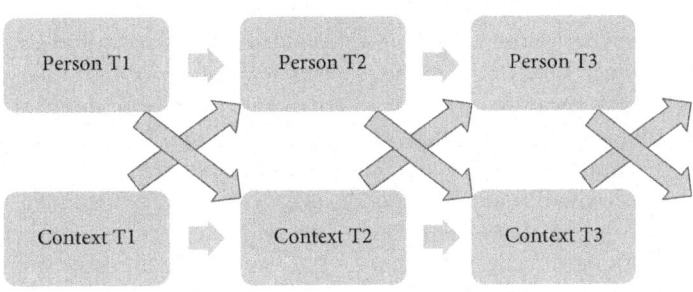

Fig. 8.2 The mutual interactions between person and context over time.

speed up a process that started slowly. For example, it takes time before a teacher recognizes a student as being motivated. But once he does so, and starts to provide her with extra challenges, the whole system may show a rapid development in which the student develops strong commitments and becomes embedded in a commitment-supporting context. Dynamic systems theory helps to explain these characteristics as inherent to the processes of change by approaching developing individuals as systems that do not necessarily follow a linear pattern of change.

Dynamic systems theory seems to be well suited as a theoretical framework from which we can study the mechanisms and processes of identity development and address our questions concerning an individual's identity emerging, changing, and stabilizing over time and the explanation of interindividual differences in this developmental process. However, as mentioned, empirical evidence is needed to elaborate the application of a dynamic approach to identity development, and that empirical evidence is still scarce. As we argue in the next section, research into these mechanisms differs in fundamental ways from the common research, and that implies that available research often cannot be used to test assumptions from a process perspective.

The Need for New Types of Research

To find empirical evidence for theories concerning developmental processes, we need a different type of research for three different reasons. First, Lichtwarck-Aschoff and others (2008) point out that it is generally not possible to generalize research from static approaches (such as linear regression modeling) to dynamic processes of development. The static approach identifies structural relationships between two different variables, whereas dynamic approaches aim to describe the evolution of a system over time. Static approaches do not aim to identify mechanisms of change and, therefore, these findings cannot be used in this regard.

Second, as put forward by these researchers, relationships that have been found at the level of developmental time cannot be assumed to operate on the level of real time. Take, for example, autonomy. Autonomy is often measured by means of questionnaires picturing the reflective aspect of autonomy. On this aggregated level, autonomy is rather stable and changes slowly. But autonomy is not an internal executive structure that operates in the head of the adolescent and directly influences his or her behavior during a real-time event, such as a conflict with the parents. In a real-time conflict, the adolescent's expression of autonomy is governed by immediate, short-term mechanisms and context, like the importance of the goal threatened during the conflict, the course of the interaction, and the accompanying emotions and thoughts. Thus, the first important step in dealing with the conceptualization of constructs such as autonomy or identity is to keep the dynamics on differing time scales separate; that is, distinct but linkable.

A third important point that is made by several authors is that developmental processes should be studied at the individual level (e.g., Lichtwarck-Aschoff et al., 2008). The reason for this is the so-called *ergodicity problem*. The two conditions of ergodicity are homogeneity within a population ("each subject in the population has to obey the same statistical model," Molenaar & Campbell, 2009, p. 113) and stationarity ("a psychological process should have constant statistical characteristics in time," Molenaar & Campbell, 2009, p. 115). As Molenaar and Campbell point out, developmental processes are "prime examples" (p. 115) of processes in which the condition of stationarity is violated. Thus, empirical results that are found in group data, and therefore based on analyses of differences between people, cannot be the basis of knowledge of changes within one individual between different points in time. Molenaar (2004) carried out research that shows the results of interindividual variability generally do not correctly portray intraindividual variability. The only instance in which variance in groups can be generalized to the individual level is if the ergodicity principle is met.

Molenaar (2004) suggests the use of idiographic time series analyses (i.e., multiple measurements within the same person) to obtain valid results regarding developmental processes. In their overview of existing research on identity, Lichtwarck-Aschoff and others (2008) conclude that research into processes is especially lacking. The studies discussed so far in this chapter are based on aggregated group data and are therefore not capable of uncovering mechanisms of change in individuals. Also, the studies cannot be categorized as dynamic. Even the studies by Luyckx and others (2006) are not truly dynamic, since no mechanisms of change were identified, and their findings are based on correlations between aggregated group data. Furthermore, one of our studies (Kunnen, 2006), in which we demonstrated the relation between conflict and a decrease in commitment strength, although focusing on mechanisms, was based on averages and did not take into account the sequence of events or the microlevel processes of change. The same is true for the study by Klimstra and colleagues. Even though these authors uncovered a mechanism of change (i.e., reconsideration of commitment leads to change in commitments), those results pertain to group data, which cannot be generalized to the individual level and hence cannot be interpreted as true mechanisms of change. This means we need a new type of research.

Another consideration with regard to the framework of DST is the inclusion of the context because the context is part of the system and all elements in the system mutually influence each other. None of the earlier studies discussed includes explicit measures of the environment as one of the interacting factors. This is striking, since identity is explicitly perceived as occurring in a context (Kunnen et al., 2001; Lichtwarck-Aschoff et al., 2008; Korobov, this volume). We will come back later to the question of how context could be included in research.

Developing a New Type of Research: Analyzing Trajectories

As argued by Lichtwarck et al., research into developmental processes should focus on individual trajectories. A first step in the study of trajectories is the question: what do individual trajectories look like? There are some studies that address the question concerning the different types of trajectories that describe the changes in exploration and commitment on the individual level. The first studies using longitudinal designs to examine the course of identity development involved the Identity Status Interview (ISI; Marcia et al., 1993). In these studies, changes in status revealed that, during the college years, consistent with expectations, there were proportionally more progressive than regressive developmental shifts, although stability of status assignment over time was observed more frequently than status shifts in either direction (Waterman, 1982). However, as argued before, the status approach is not a developmental theory and uses a typology that is based on a dichotomous representation of exploration and commitment: it can be high or low. Thus, the commitment strength or the amount of exploration may increase or decrease, but it is only notified as a change when the value crosses the border between "low" and "high." For example, assume that an adolescent's commitment strength increases gradually over a period of five years. Every year, an identity interview is administered. The developmental pattern will show stability until somewhere in those five years the border is crossed. There, a sudden change will be visible, followed again by stability. Thus, the status approach is not sensitive to small changes, and statuses may not be the best concepts for investigating developmental change. Continuous assessment of exploration and commitment is better suited for such research because it is more sensitive to detecting smaller quantitative changes in the extent of exploration or the strength of commitment.

Recently, cluster and latent class analyses based on such dimensional measures have been used to analyze longitudinal dimensional data. Variations in change and stability of the dimensions were analyzed to differentiate developmental trajectories (Luyckx, Schwartz, Goossens, Soenens, & Beyers, 2008; Meeus et al., 2010). Although based on dimensional measures, the different types of trajectories found in these studies resemble the Marcia statuses, and most studies found one or two additional statuses. Meeus et al. (2010) distinguished diffusions, moratoriums, searching moratoriums, and two variants of a [fore]closed identity—"early closure" and "closure"—and achievement. Following Josselson (1996), Luyckx et al. (2008*b*) distinguished pathmakers (achieved), guardians (foreclosed), searchers (moratorium), and consolidators. This latter class consisted of individuals characterized by a strong focus on strengthening their current identity commitments at the expense of a thorough exploration of alternative options.

We used still another approach (Kunnen, 2009; 2010). We categorized individual trajectories consisting of at least five commitment and exploration scores over at least two years by means of theoretically based criteria. Based on whether trajectories showed fluctuating or stable high and low patterns of exploration and commitment strength, we classified almost all trajectories into types that could be described by means of Marcia's statuses (stable foreclosed, diffused, achieved, or moratorium). The methods used in the studies of Meeus et al., Luyckx et al., and Kunnen are different in the sense that Meeus and Luyckx and colleagues based the clustering on a group-level analysis, whereas Kunnen and colleagues grouped all individual trajectories on the basis of predefined criteria. The results of the study of Luyckx et al. (2008*b*) are based on the same data that resulted in the model described earlier (Luyckx et al. 2006*a,b*). Moreover, the typologies were described in terms of the concepts that Luyckx et al. proposed in their model.

The finding that the outcomes of these three studies are rather comparable is highly relevant. In a previous section, we discussed that the lack of ergodicity in developmental processes does not allow us to compare processes on an individual level and on a group level. Now we see that developmental trajectories of identity development that are found by means of group-based analysis and by means of individually based analysis are rather comparable. The comparability of the trajectories does not yet prove that the underlying dynamics in groups are the same as the intraindividual dynamics. However, the fact that the trajectories found by Luyckx et al. are found on the individual level as well allows us to address the question of how the microlevel model of Bosma and Kunnen may generate the trajectories as described in the model of Luyckx et al. In addition, the findings discussed here demonstrate the robustness of the theory and the typologies as distinguished by Marcia (1966). They demonstrate that these typologies—with some additions—are applicable in distinguishing trajectories as well.

These studies into the shapes of trajectories are an important first step because they give insight into the type of trajectories possible. However, they merely provide a sequence of time points; they are snapshots of identity at different times, not a movie of the unfolding of identity. Understanding developmental processes implies answering questions such as: how do individuals change from one time point to the next? What causes the changes in commitment in this specific individual at this time point? Thus, these questions are entirely different from questions such as: what does the sequence over time of commitment and exploration levels look like? Or, how does variable X affect commitment formation?

Developing a New Type of Research: Intensive Time Series

As argued in the previous section, knowledge about developmental mechanisms cannot be derived from analysis of group data. To understand developmental processes means that we have to focus on the developmental trajectories and that we have to use the individual trajectory as a unit of analysis. If we want to understand how levels of commitment development change in daily life, we need long and rather dense time series of measurements. Only that type of data may reveal how levels of commitment strength and exploration may change as a function of each other, of the value of other variables, and as a function of events. In such a study, the first step would be to define which variables should be included in the study. For example, based on the four-factor model of Luyckx et al. (2008*a*) that we discussed earlier, exploration in breadth and in depth, commitment making, and identification with commitment could be included. In addition, depending on the research question, contextual factors could be included. For example, if we study a program that aims to stimulate identity development, the relevant variables could consist of the tasks or events offered in the program.

Previously, we mentioned that context is seldom included in studies into identity status development. The approach advocated here has major consequences for the role of the context in research. In the dynamic systems approach, identity is seen as embedded in the context, as relational, and therefore as emerging from continuous interactions between the person and the context. Both the context and the person may change in each interaction (see Figure 8.2).

Thus, context is not included as one stable independent variable, such as the socioeconomic (SES) level, but instead the researcher defines which part of the context is relevant and repeatedly assesses those aspects of the context as well. A point for consideration is whether context should be included as a measure that is assessed independently from the person or as an event as it is perceived by the person. For example, in Kunnen (2006) we used the subjects' description of events as indications of the context. Because it is the perceived context that affects identity development, we think the latter option may be preferable, although, for some research questions, independently assessed events, such as exam marks if one studies vocational commitments, may be relevant as well.

A practical—and we think not yet completely solved—issue if one aims to assess identity repeatedly and frequently concerns the manner in which to assess it. As Korobov (this volume) states, empirical work detailing the relationship between social interactions and identity development has been scarce, especially within the identity status model research paradigm. Klimstra et al. (2010) used a single-item version of the two Utrecht-Management of Identity Commitments (U-MIC) Scales for commitment and reconsideration: "Today, I felt confident about my education/best friend" and "Today, I felt I could better look for a different education/best friend." By means of mentioning the name of the best friend they made sure that the answers were about the same person. Van der Gaag (in preparation) started her data collection with an extensive identity interview by means of the Groningen Identity Development Scale (Bosma, 1985). During this interview, a commitment is formulated by the respondent. In her subsequent weekly assessments, Van der Gaag used this commitment as a basis to ask whether the participant felt confident about the commitment and whether he or she was exploring the commitment (exploration in depth) or alternatives (exploration in breadth).

In both these approaches the data collection started with a detailed assessment of commitment and exploration that was used as an anchor for the subsequent short assessments. However, the disadvantage of these two methods is that the participants are directly asked about their commitments. If this is done repeatedly, the assessment may affect the developmental process. Other, unobtrusive methods could be developed. One could think of free reports in which participants describe how they feel about a specific topic, such as education, or observations concerning which friends the adolescents choose to associate with. For example, Spithorst (2012) used weekly diaries in which students reported about the event that had been most important with regard to their studies and answered some questions concerning the way they felt about their studies. Free reports of events has another advantage because it takes to into account that individual and context define each other, instead of trying to measure each separately (see also Korobov, this volume). Korobov pleads for an ethnomethodological approach to identities by seeing them as relationally responsive categorizations that are claimed, resisted, and otherwise used in communicative contexts to conduct social and personal life. In the model on self-development by McLean, Pasupathi, and Pals (2007) elaborate how the analysis of storytelling could be used to analyze the process of self-development. Their overview of research suggests that storytelling analysis may be very fruitful. Especially, assimilative and accommodative solutions for a conflict may become visible in discourse and storytelling. People tend to tell stories about unexpected, negative events, and one of the functions of telling stories about these events is that it helps people make sense of the event in the light of their existing view of themselves. So, repeated storytelling about what we called a conflict or crisis may be a life report of accommodation and assimilation at work.

Developing a New Type of Research: New Techniques for Analysis

Research into developmental processes that is based on individual data sequences needs not only different types of assessment, but also different types of analysis. Although in the recent literature we observed an increasing attention to dynamic systems, self-organization, processes, and process characteristics, the attention is still mainly conceptual. Often, research questions concern processes, and the data are interpreted in terms of processes, but the analysis of the data does not allow for conclusions concerning process characteristics (Bosma & Kunnen, 2008). This is not surprising because many standard statistical tools are not well suited for the analysis of processes. Most statistical techniques are sample based and focus on differences between groups or, in longitudinal studies, changes in groups over time. In the conclusions of papers reporting about such research, the changes that are found are often assumed to hold for individuals as well. As discussed before, this is based on the often incorrect assumption that ergodicity is present in the phenomena under study.

We do not have the space here to discuss the different possible techniques in detail, but we will sketch some possibilities. If we want to study developmental processes from a dynamic systems perspective, intraindividual variability, and especially changes in variability, are considered as relevant. By variability we mean the fluctuations in individual time series of data (i.e., the changes between each individual data point and the next point). For example, increase of intraindividual variability is an indicator of increasing instability of the system and one of the first signs of a transition (Granic & Patterson, 2006; van der Maas & Molenaar, 1992). In addition, shortly before a transition, a system tends to react more strongly to perturbations, and it takes more time to return to the stable position. These changes in variability in individual time series require specific techniques to analyze them. The variability in the value of one single variable in individual time series can sometimes be expressed in a simple way by means of (changes in) the standard deviation. However, to test differences in standard deviations one needs long data series. Moreover, a standard deviation is not the best way to measure individual variability, because in the standard deviation the sequence of the data points is not taken into account. To demonstrate what that means, we show two time series of data in Figure 8.3. Imagine that these two series represent the individual developmental trajectories of two different adolescents. At first sight, they are very different. One series shows a steady growth, whereas the other fluctuates quite chaotically. Most probably, the two trajectories demonstrate important differences in the developmental process of the

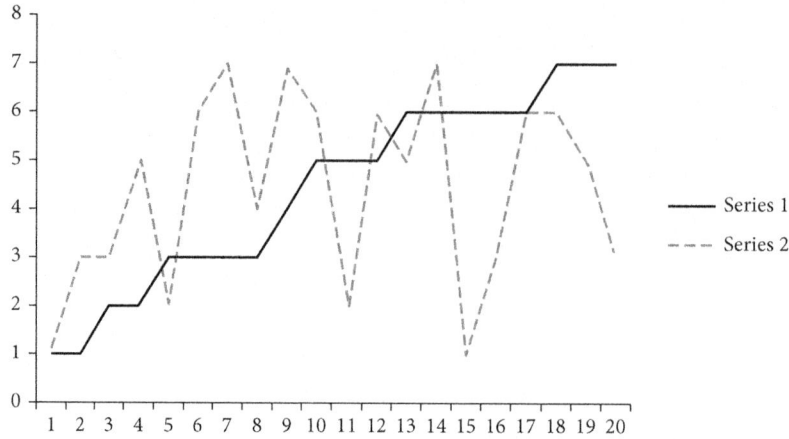

Fig. 8.3 Two individual time series of data with identical standard deviation but different variability.

two adolescents. However, both series have the same standard deviation, 1.96, because they consist of the same data points, and it is only the sequence that differs. Thus, standard deviations do not grasp relevant differences in individual time series.

A better solution may be to calculate the absolute difference between the values at each measurement point and the next and use the sum of these distances as an indication of variability. If we use that technique, the variability of series 1 is 6, and that of series 2 is 44 (for more explanation see Kunnen, 2011a). If we want to investigate changes in variability over time, we can use the technique of a moving window. We will calculate the variability in a window of, for example, six data points. We start to calculate the variability between the first six data points. Next, we move the window one point and calculate the variability over points 2 to 7, then points 3 to 8, and so on, until we have reached the end of the series. In our example the last window includes data points 15 to 20. This results in a series of variability values. In case of increasing variability, we should see an increase in these values. For other types of variability, standard deviations are not applicable at all. For example, in complex processes, variability often means that different variables (such as different emotions, cognitive styles, behaviors) occur together in different constellations, and one may want to know whether there are differences between individuals or over time in the amount of variability of these patterns.

In Kunnen (2011a) we elaborated different techniques to explore variability and process characteristics in general. For example, we demonstrated a technique to find evidence that, following a specific event, sudden change occurred in individual trajectories that consisted of only four or five measurement points. We also described techniques that address the question of whether a specific aspect of early language development is a continuous or discontinuous process and to assess the level of variability in a series of emotional reactions in which the number of emotions and the intensity of each emotion may be different for each data point.

A rather simple technique that can be used to analyze a variety of process characteristics is the State Space Grid (SSG) (Hollenstein, 2011). In their most common form, SSGs are used to describe the changes of a system that consists of two dimensions. These dimensions are represented in a two-dimensional graph, or space. Each data point of an individual time series can be described as a point in that graph, and the changes of a two-dimensional system over time can be made visible as movements through the two-dimensional space. In an exploratory study, we applied the SSG technique in a dataset that consisted of a series of assessments of the levels of exploration and commitment (Post, 2012). Each data point in the space describes a specific level of commitment and exploration. By means of SSG, one can analyze whether dominant patterns can be found, whether there are so-called attractors (specific states or sets of values to which the system tends to return after perturbations), and whether specific changes in one variable are followed by changes in the other, and the like.

In addition, many techniques are being developed to analyze the structure in individual data series (De Roover et al., 2012; Timmerman, 2006). De Roover et al. (2012) describe how factor analysis can be applied on individual data series where it is assumed that the structure differs between individuals. Timmerman (2006) describes how factor analysis can be applied on longitudinal data series in which it is assumed that the intraindividual structure may differ from the interindividual structure, but in which no differences in structure between individuals are expected. The most famous example of such a situation—although not psychological—is that if we study the relation between the speed of machine typing and the number of errors that are made in a randomly chosen group of people, there is a negative relation between speed and number of errors: professional typists type faster and make fewer errors than the amateur two-finger typists. This, therefore, tells us something about differences in a population. However, if we study individual time series of performances over time, we find a positive relation between speed and number of errors. This relation tells us something about the process: trying to work faster makes people less careful.

A more advanced method to investigate developmental processes is quantitative dynamic modeling. In Kunnen (2011*b*), a dynamic systems model of commitment development is presented. Building a dynamic systems model means that, based on a conceptual model of the developmental process, a mathematical model is made that represents the theoretical assumptions. Such a model can be used to test the theoretical assumptions, to predict development in different conditions, and to compare the developmental processes between different groups.

But even very simple techniques based on techniques that are generally used for analysis of group data sometimes can be used to analyze intraindividual data sequences. For example, intraindividual correlations between time series of measurements of two variables within one individual may provide information about how different variables relate to each other. Bosman (2009) studied the relation between commitment strength and exploration within individuals. Each individual in her studies had been administered six to eight identity interviews, with six months between each interview. For each individual, she calculated the correlation between commitment strength and exploration. She found strong negative correlations. In the same way, changes in autocorrelations (i.e., the correlation between each data point and the next of the same variable within one individual) may indicate developmental changes.

In conclusion, although methods for individual time series are still less common than those for group data and may demand more creativity and active searching for the best method, their availability and diversity are rapidly increasing, and with this increase, analysis of individual data sequences is increasingly within the reach of all researchers.

Limitations

Research based on the methods described here will reveal knowledge concerning the dynamics involved in the development of exploration and commitment strength and in the processes that keep commitments stable or result in change. Starting from the assumption that exploration and commitment formation are the basic processes in identity formation, this will provide relevant knowledge concerning identity development. However, we do not assume that levels of exploration and commitment strength offer a complete insight into identity development. The notion that commitments may change in order to adjust to the changing wishes of the person and changing demands and challenges in the environment do raise the question of whether the type or quality of commitments may change over time. We (Kunnen & Bosma, 2003) addressed changes in the quality of commitments in a discussion with Kroger (2003). We suggested that changes in quality of commitment might be described in terms of flexibility or complexity. Changes in quality may occur in developmental trajectories that are characterized by changes in commitments. That is, trajectories that show periods of reconsideration (Meeus et al., 2010) or moratorium-achievement-moratorium- achievement (MAMA) cycles as described by Stephen, Fraser, and Marcia (1992). Reconsideration of commitments and MAMA cycles occur only after the initial commitment formation. It seems plausible therefore that developmental change in terms of changing quality may be relevant, especially in trajectories after adolescence.

Conclusion

Starting from the questions "How does an individual's identity emerge, change, and stabilize over time?," and "How can we explain differences in this developmental process between individuals?," we aim to develop a model that may help to answer these questions. We thus plead for more research into the developmental processes that drive identity development. The increasing focus on longitudinal studies and the rapidly growing interest in process studies does show that this type of research is widely seen as promising in generating a new understanding of development. Although we have some insight into the different long-term shapes of identity development, we do not yet know whether this development occurs gradually, in steps, or with peaks and regressions. More knowledge about this process is also practically relevant. It may help teachers, counselors, and other people who monitor and guide the identity development of adolescents and (emerging) adults. To give an example, if identity development proceeds in a continuous and gradual way, a period of stability despite attempts to stimulate development may be a cause for worry. But if the developmental process takes place in steps, then a stable period is normal. In that case, knowledge of the duration of steps and of the conditions that may stimulate the "jump" to the next step would be extremely useful. Another insight that can be gained especially from model building is the nonlinear relation between (change in) influencing factors and the changes in development. For example, time delay is an important concept when one studies the effect of an intervention. Also, dynamic systems models may show how a specific variable sometimes affects identity development, whereas at other times it does not seem to have any effect at all. By means of process analysis and dynamic modeling, we may start to unravel such phenomena.

References

Berzonsky, M. D. (1990). Self-construction over the life span: A process perspective on identity formation. In G. J. Neimeyer & R. A. Neimeyer (Eds.), *Advances in personal construct psychology* (vol. 1; pp. 155–186). Greenwich, CT: JAI Press.

Berzonsky, M D. (1992). Identity style and coping strategies. *Journal of Personality*, 60, 771–788.

Block, J. (1982). Assimilation, accommodation, and the dynamics of personality development. *Child Development*, 53, 281–295.

Block, J., & Block, J. H. (2006). Venturing a 30-year longitudinal study. *American Psychologist*, 61, 315–327.

Bosma, H. A. (1985). *Identity development in adolescence. Coping with commitments.* Groningen: University of Groningen.

Bosma, H. A., & Kunnen, E. S. (2001a). Determinants and mechanisms in ego identity development: A review and synthesis. *Developmental Review*, 21, 39–66.

Bosma, H. A., & Kunnen, E. S. (2001b). *Identity and emotion*. Cambridge: Cambridge University Press.

Bosma, H. A., & Kunnen, E. S. (2008). Identity-in-context is not yet identity development-in-context. *Journal of Adolescence*, 31, 281–289.

Bosman, K. (2009). *De rol van exploratie en emoties in commitmentonwikkeling [The role of exploration and emotions in commitment development].* Master thesis. Groningen: University of Groningen.

Cairns, R. B., & Cairns, B. D. (1994). *Lifelines and risks: Pathways of youth in our times.* Cambridge: Cambridge University Press.

Crocetti, E., Rubini, M., & Meeus, W. J. (2008). Capturing the dynamics of identity formation in various ethnic groups: Development and validation of a three-dimensional model. *Journal of Adolescence*, 31, 207–227.

Crocetti, E., & Meeus, W. J. (this volume) The Identity Statuses: Strengths of a Person-Centered Approach. *Oxford Handbook of Identity Development.*

De Roover, K., Ceulemans, E., Timmerman, M. E., Vansteelandt, K., Stouten, J., & Onghena, P. (2012). Clusterwise simultaneous component analysis for analyzing structural differences in multivariate multiblock data. *Psychological Methods*, 17, 100–119.

Docan-Morgan, T. (2011). "Everything changed": Relational turning point events in college teacher–student relationships from teachers' perspectives. *Communication Education*, 60, 20–50.

Erikson, E. H. (1959). *Identity and the life cycle*. New York: International University Press.

Erikson, E. H. (1963). *Childhood and society* (2nd ed.). New York: Norton.

Erikson, E. H. (1968). *Identity: Youth and crisis.* New York: Norton.

Flum, H. (1994). The evolutive style of identity formation. *Journal of Youth and Adolescence*, 23, 489–498.

Granic, I., & Patterson, G. R. (2006). Toward a comprehensive model of antisocial development: A dynamic systems approach. *Psychological Review*, 113, 101–131.

Grotevant, H. D. (1987). Toward a Process Model of Identity Formation. *Journal of Adolescent Research*, 2, 203–222.

Hollenstein, T. (2011). Using state space grids for understanding processes of change and stability in adolescence. In E. S. Kunnen (Ed.), *A dynamic systems approach to adolescent development* (pp. 73–90). London: Routledge.

Josselson, R. (1996). *Revising herself: The story of women's identity from college to midlife.* New York: Oxford University Press.

Kerpelman, J. L., & Lamke, L. K. (1997). Anticipation of future identities : A control theory approach to identity development within the context of serious dating relationships. Personal Relationships, 4, 47–62.

Klimstra, T. A. (2012). The dynamics of personality and identity in adolescence. *European Journal of Developmental Psychology*, 9, 472–484.

Klimstra, T. A., Luyckx, K., Hale, W. A., Frijns, T., Van Lier, P. A. C., & Meeus, W. J. (2010). Short-term fluctuations in identity: Introducing a micro-level approach to identity formation. *Journal of Personality and Social Psychology*, 99, 191–202.

Korobov, N. (this volume). Identities as an Interactional Process. *Oxford Handbook of Identity Development.*

Kroger, J. (1995). The differentiation of "firm" and "developmental" foreclosure statuses: A longitudinal study. *Journal of Adolescent Research*, 10, 317–337.

Kroger, J. (2003). What transits in an identity status transition? *Identity: An International Journal of Theory and Research*, 3, 37–41.

Kroger, J. (this volume) Identity Development through Adulthood: The Move Toward "Wholeness." *Oxford Handbook of Identity Development.*

Kroger, J., Martinussen, M., & Marcia, J. E. (2010). Identity status change during adolescence and young adulthood: A meta-analysis. *Journal of Adolescence*, 33(5), 683–698.

Kunnen, E. S. (2006). Are conflicts the motor in identity change? *Identity*, 6, 169–186.

Kunnen, E. S. (2009). Qualitative and quantitative aspects of commitment development in psychology students. *Journal of Adolescence*, 32, 567–584.

Kunnen, E. S. (2010). Characteristics and prediction of identity conflicts concerning career goals among first-year university students. *Identity: An International Journal of Theory and Research*, 10, 222–231.

Kunnen, E. S., & Bosma, H. A. (2003). Fischer's skill theory applied to identity development: A response to Kroger. *Identity*, 3, 247–270.

Kunnen, E. S., Bosma, H. A., Van Halen, C. P. M., & Van der Meulen, M. (2001). A self-organizational approach to identity and emotions: An overview and implications. In H. A. Bosma & E. S. Kunnen (Eds.), *Identity and emotion* (pp. 202–230). Cambridge: Cambridge University Press.

Kunnen, E. S., & Van Geert, P. L. C. (2011a). A dynamic systems approach to adolescent development. In S. Kunnen (Ed.), *A dynamic systems approach to adolescent development* (pp. 3–14). London: Psychology Press.

Kunnen, E. S., & Van Geert, P. L. C. (2011b). General characteristics of a dynamic systems approach. In E. S. Kunnen (Ed.), *A dynamic systems approach to adolescent development* (pp. 15–34). London: Psychology Press.

Lichtwarck-Aschoff, A., Van Geert, P. L. C., Bosma, H. A., & Kunnen, E. S. (2008). Time and identity: A framework for research and theory formation. *Developmental Review*, 28, 370–400.

Luyckx, K. (2006). *Identity formation in emerging adulthood. developmental trajectories, antecedents, and consequences*. Leuven: Catholic University of Leuven.

Luyckx, K., Goossens, L., & Soenens, B. (2006a). A developmental contextual perspective on identity construction in emerging adulthood: Change dynamics in commitment formation and commitment evaluation. *Developmental Psychology*, 42, 366–380.

Luyckx, K., Goossens, L., Soenens, B., & Beyers, W. (2006b). Unpacking commitment and exploration: Preliminary validation of an integrative model of late adolescent identity formation. *Journal of Adolescence*, 29, 361–378.

Luyckx, K., Schwartz, S. J., Berzonsky, M. D., Soenens, B., Vansteenkiste, M., Smits, I., & Goossens, L. (2008). Capturing ruminative exploration: Extending the four-dimensional model of identity formation in late adolescence. *Journal of Research in Personality*, 42, 58–82.

Luyckx, K., Schwartz, S. J., Goossens, L., Soenens, B., & Beyers, W. (2008). Developmental typologies of identity formation and adjustment in female emerging adults: A latent class growth analysis approach. *Journal of Research on Adolescence*, 18, 595–619.

Marcia, J. E. (1966). Development and validation of ego-identity status. *Journal of Personality and Social Psychology*, 3, 118–133.

Marcia, J. E. (1980). Identity in adolescence. In J. Adelson (Ed.), *Handbook of adolescent psychology* (pp. 159–187). New York: Wiley.

Marcia, J. E. (1989). Identity diffusion differentiated. In M. A. Luszez & T. Nettelbeck (Eds.), *Psychological development: Perspectives across the life-span*. Amsterdam: North-Holland Elsevier Science.

Marcia, J. E. (1993). The status of the statuses: Research review. In J. E. Marcia, A. S. Waterman, D. R. Matteson, S. L. Archer, & J. L. Orlofsky (Eds.), *Ego identity. A handbook for psychosocial research* (pp. 22–41). New York: Springer Verlag.

Marcia, J. E., Waterman, A. S., Matteson, D. R., Archer, S. L., & Orlofsky, J. L. (1993). *Ego Identity: A handbook for psychosocial research*. New York: Springer verlag.

McLean, K. C., Pasupathi, M., & Pals, J. L. (2007). Selves creating stories creating selves: A process model of self-development. *Personality and Social Psychology Review*, 11, 262–278.

Meeus, W. J. (1996). Studies on identity development in adolescence: An overview of research and some new data. *Journal of Youth and Adolescence*, 25, 569–598.

Meeus, W. J. (1999). Patterns of adolescent identity development: review of literature and longitudinal analysis. *Developmental Review*, 19, 419–461.

Meeus, W. J., Van de Schoot, R., Keijsers, L., Schwartz, S. J., & Branje, S. (2010). On the progression and stability of adolescent identity formation: A five-wave longitudinal study in early-to-middle and middle-to-late adolescence. *Child Development*, 81, 1565–1581.

Molenaar, P. C. M. (2004). A manifesto on psychology as idiographic science: Bringing the person back into scientific psychology, this time forever. *Measurement*, 2(4), 201–218.

Molenaar, P. C. M., & Campbell, C. G. (2009). The new person-specific paradigm in psychology. *Psychological Science*, 18, 112–117.

Piaget, J. (1985). *The equilibration of cognitive structures: The central problem of intellectual development*. Chicago: University of Chicago Press.

Post, J. M. (2012). *Korte termijn veranderingen in de identiteitsontwikkeling [Short term changes in identity development]*. Master thesis. Groningen: University of Groningen.

Spithorst, H. (2012). *Study commitment of first-year students. Do experiences affect study commitment?* Groningen: University of Groningen.

Stephen, J., Fraser, E., & Marcia, J. E. (1992). Moratorium-achievement (MAMA) cycles in lifespan identity development: Value orientations and reasoning system correlates. *Journal of Adolescence*, 15, 283–300.

Thelen, E., & Smith, L. B. (1994). *A dynamic systems approach to the development of cognition and action*. Cambridge, MA: MIT Press.

Timmerman, M. E. (2006). Multilevel component analysis. *British Journal of Mathematical and Statistical Psychology*, 59, 301–320.

Van der Gaag, M., & Kunnen, E. S. (2012). Short term vocational development. Presentation at the EARA, August 29–September 1, Spetses.

Van der Maas, H. L., & Molenaar, P. C. (1992). Stagewise cognitive development: An application of catastrophe theory. *Psychological Review*, 99, 395–417.

Van Geert, P. L. C. (1991). A dynamic systems model of cognitive and language growth. *Psychological Review*, 98, 3–53.

Van Geert, P. L. C. (1994). *Dynamic systems of development. Change between complexity and chaos*. New York: Harvester Wheatsheaf.

Van Geert, P. L. C. (2003). Dynamic systems approaches and modeling of developmental processes. In J. Valsiner & K. J. Connoly (Eds.), *Handbook of developmental psychology* (pp. 640–672). London: Sage.

Vleioras, G., & Bosma, H. A. (2005). Are identity styles important for psychological well-being? *Journal of Adolescence*, 28, 397–409.

Waterman, A. S. (1982). Identity development from adolescence to adulthood: An extension of theory and a review of research. *Developmental Psychology*, 18, 341–358.

CHAPTER 9

Identity Status: On Refinding the People

Ruthellen Josselson *and* Hanoch Flum

Abstract

Erikson conceptualized ego identity as the focus of a stage of psychosocial development and, for more than half a century, researchers have utilized various approaches to make this complex concept researchable. James Marcia's delineation of four major identity statuses as pathways of identity formation has led to a particularly robust body of research. The departure point for this commentary are chapters by Crocetti and Meeus and by Kunnen and Metz who have extended identity status research in particular directions. This chapter contextualizes these papers within a broad overview of the history of identity status research, from Eriksonian theory to interview-based classification to psychometric classification, and assesses the understandings that have been created by these research programs and where identity status research might proceed. Although psychometric approaches have been fruitful to an extent, the authors argue for the integration of a phenomenological approach to augment the accumulating understandings of identity processes.

Key Words: identity formation, identity statuses, narrative inquiry, identity exploration, identity commitment

---

Psychology is truly itself only when it can deal with individuality. It is vain to plead that other sciences do not do so, that they are allowed to brush off the bothersome issue of uniqueness. The truth is that psychology is assigned the task of being curious about human persons, and persons exist only in concrete and unique patterns.
– *Allport, 1961 (p. 573)*

A young man, call him O, a college senior who transferred from a California university to Columbia in his junior year, spends a lot of time walking the streets of New York, just taking in what he sees, writing in a journal. He is in what he calls an "ascetic" phase, trying to be serious about himself, having given up smoking pot and partying. He has no clear goals for himself, reads a lot, plays some basketball, talks to friends. He'd like to have some impact on the world, but how to do this eludes him. What is most on his mind is his confusion over his biraciality. Having grown up in a family consisting of his white mother and grandparents, and meeting his African father only briefly once at the age of ten, he is confused about the inevitably of being regarded as "black" in America. He remembers a very meaningful conversation with one of his few black friends in high school, an argument about white racism, about its relative absence in Hawaii where they lived, about the freedom they had to live as they wished, about the acceptance and love they got from their white teammates. He had urged his friend to "give the bad-assed nigger pose a rest." His friend replied, "A pose, huh? Speak for your own self." But, the young man writes, now in retrospect fifteen years later, "I was different, after all, potentially suspect. And I had no idea who my own self was" (p. 82). Can there be a clearer statement about the experience of what Erikson called "identity confusion?"

Researching Identity

Erikson (1956; 1968) conceptualized ego identity as a stage of psychosocial development more than half a century ago. Identity is, as Erikson underscored, a complex concept, and identity formation an evasive process to study. In this chapter, we present a broad overview of the history of identity status research, from Eriksonian theory to interview-based classification to psychometric classification and assess where it is now and where it might go. We consider the chapters by Crocetti and Meeus and by Kunnen and Metz as a departure point for reflecting on the direction that identity research might follow. Although, in our view, psychometric approaches have been fruitful, we want to argue for the integration of a phenomenological approach that would augment the accumulating understandings of identity pathways.

The one thing that all identity researchers agree on is that the identity concept and its attendant phenomena is complex and multifaceted. Erikson returned again and again over his career to refining and reformulating his understanding of the identity stage, changing his mind (unlike with any of the other developmental stages) about whether its negative pole ought to be called "role confusion," "role diffusion," or "identity confusion." He struggled with the ambiguities of the relationship of identity to role and of whether its absence was a form of confusion or diffusion. Although he offered many attempts to "define" identity, one of his clearest statements on the complexity of the process of identity formation is,

> In psychological terms, the process of identity formation employs a process of simultaneous reflection and observation, a process…by which the individual judges himself in the light of what he perceives to be the way in which others judge him in comparison to themselves and to a typology significant to them; while he judges their way of judging him in the light of how he perceives himself in comparison to them and to types that have become relevant to him. The process is…for the most part unconscious except where inner conditions and outer circumstances combine to aggravate a painful, or elated, "identity-consciousness." (1968, pp. 22–23)

Indeed, he defines identity in what Kunnen and Metz call dynamic systems terms. Given his sensitivity to the vagaries and varieties of the processes in the development and formation of identity, Erikson was not sanguine about the idea of measuring it. "'Identity' and 'identity crisis' popular and scientific usage become terms alternately circumscribe something so large and so seemingly self-evident that to demand a definition would almost seem petty, while at other times they designate something made so narrow for purposes of measurement that the overall meaning is lost, and it could just as well be called something else" (1968, p. 15). Identity is an ongoing process, he emphasized: it is "always changing and developing…never…static or unchangeable" (1968, pp. 23–24), and yet also marked by "two simultaneous observations: the perception of the selfsameness and continuity of one's existence in time and space and the perception of the fact that others recognize one's sameness and continuity" (p. 50). At the same time, it also includes, on a different level, "the *style of one's individuality*, and that this style coincides with the sameness and continuity of one's *meaning for significant others* in the immediate community" (Erikson, 1968, p. 50, emphasis in original)

Jim Marcia (2007) took it as a challenge to "measure the unmeasurable" (p. 4) by using a semi-structured interview in which college students were asked to narrate their efforts to create an identity. From this, he observed patterns that eventually became the identity status model (Marcia, 1966), a model that has provided a conceptual platform for hundreds of studies. Recognizing that one cannot directly assess the internal configuration that Erikson called identity, Marcia was in search of indicators of its nature. In Marcia's reading of Erikson and in his analysis of the interviews he conducted, two independent dimensions seemed at the heart of both Erikson's discussions of identity and the phenomenological experience of the participants: exploration (crisis in the earliest formulation) and commitment. That is, some young people (who he called Foreclosures), simply carry forth ideological, relational, and occupational commitments bequeathed to them by significant others in their lives thus foreclosing without consideration other possibilities, indicating a fairly rigid identity structure. Other people make commitments following a period in which they have considered, even experimented with, other ways of being or believing, and these Marcia referred to as Identity Achievements (even while recognizing that Erikson did not think that identity could ever be finally "achieved"). Interview data suggested flexibility in a reasonably firm identity structure, a structure that, being unconscious, could be thus indirectly suggested. Still other young people were found in periods of flux in identity (labelled Moratoriums), without commitments but trying to forge them, whereas yet others were without commitments and seemed not to be trying to create them (Diffusions), indicating an identity structure without discernible boundaries. These latter were close to what Erikson described as people diffuse (or confused) in regard to their identity formation.

Marcia created a coding manual for his semistructured interview (the Identity Status Interview [ISI]) as a way of classifying emerging adults into one or another of these pathways. The interview allowed for "sometimes probing conversation" (Marcia, 2007, p. 6) with participants that would allow trained raters to classify people, with relatively high agreement, into one of the four identity statuses. Raters had to make sense of the life narratives told by participants, assessing the presence or absence of exploration and commitment in various domains of experience, finally weighting whichever aspects of a participant's life (even ones spontaneously offered by participants outside the standard protocol) were most salient for the participant. Subsequent studies developed construct validity for the identity statuses by demonstrating that the statuses behaved in theoretically consistent ways on other indicators of ego development (see Kroger & Marcia, 2011, for a review).

As Crocetti and Meeus (this volume) say, the process of interviewing people is time-consuming, requires trained interviewers and raters, and is too labor-intensive for other than small numbers of participants. Over the past thirty years, a number of self-report questionnaires that can be administered faster and can reach larger samples easily (Crocetti & Meeus, this volume) have been developed to assess identity status. Results of studies using these questionnaires has dominated identity status research (cf., Kroger, this volume; see also Schwartz, 2001). At the same time, as Crocetti and Meeus mention, using self-report measures for the classification of identity statuses has its own shortcomings. Among them, we do not hear the voice of the individual person because items are determined a priori by the researcher, many participants remain unclassified, and the classification itself has low reliability across measures. Although early researchers used the ISI for classification purposes, their conversations about identity with the participants nevertheless sensitized them to the particularities of the identity formation experience and contexts. And researchers recognized that these categories had fuzzy boundaries, with people having characteristics of more than one status, commitments that were more committed than not but still somewhat tentative, and exploration that may or may not have been in earnest—and people often follow quite different processes in the various areas in which identity could be staked. The ISI is sensitive to the cultural times or issues of the day (in contrast to survey questionnaires, which are static). This was recently rediscovered by Frisén and Wängqvist (2011) who turned to the ISI to investigate identity specifically in the Swedish context, adding another interview to augment their understanding and providing excerpts from both interviews in their published study to locate Swedish identity formation in its cultural specificity.

As Marcia (2007) pointed out, the effort to measure exploration and commitment through self-report scales tended to dislodge the identity concept out of the psychoanalytic soil in which Erikson located it and to reinvent it in more social psychological terms (see Erikson, 1968; Kroger & Marcia, 2011) disconnected from internal psychic structure.[1] Given that few studies actually presented the voices of the participants in the process (or not) of identity formation, the recognition of the inner complexity of the identity challenge gave way to the study of identity as scores on scales and the search for covariates of the statuses.

Crocetti and Meeus present a review of strategies in the measurement of identity statuses. An important distinction is made (following von Eye & Bogat, 2006) between a variable-centered approach and a person-centered approach. In the variable-centered approach, the basic assumption is that populations are homogeneous; in the person-centered approach, the assumption is that each individual is unique, although individuals are treated in research as sharing certain typical characteristics and hence viewed as a group with "variations and fluctuations" regarded as random. These two strategies imply the application of different techniques of statistical analysis.

Crocetti and Meeus detail in a lucid and thorough way the various attempts to categorize people into Marcia's theoretically derived "statuses" of identity development. Although the initial aim of researchers was to find ways to classify people into the statuses, recent efforts have been trying to detail identity development as a process. Recently, researchers (primarily in the Netherlands and Belgium) have extended the understanding of the four statuses to recognize different processes of exploration and of forming and maintaining identity commitments. Crocetti and Meeus join this effort, and their declared intent is to extend the identity status paradigm by focusing on identity process models rather than on the classification outcome. Exploration might occur "in breadth," choosing from a wide range of possibilities or "in depth," re-evaluating the suitability of commitments made. Commitments, once made, can be reconsidered because they no longer feel satisfying (as opposed to representing a solution to a noncommitted state). Crocetti and Meeus describe two models: one in which Luyckx and colleagues refer to four dimensions in a dual-cycle model that can be summarized in the following order: exploration in breadth → commitment making → exploration in depth → identification with commitment. Later, Luyckx et al. (2008) expanded this model by adding the possibility of a dysfunctional form of exploration termed *ruminative exploration*. Meeus, Crocetti, and colleagues offer a three-factor model comprised of commitment, in-depth exploration, and reconsideration of commitment. Both models are assessed psychometrically. Luyckx and colleagues identify two different identity diffusion statuses, whereas Meeus, Crocetti, and colleagues describe two types of moratoriums. Crocetti and Meeus show how the variable-centered approach and the person-centered approach can be integrated to address a variety of developmental issues. However, the application of a person-centered approach in longitudinal studies is underscored.

Kunnen and Metz (this volume) join with various scholars including Meeus and colleagues, Luycks and colleagues, and Berzonsky, in the recent interest in process-oriented and contextualized perspectives on identity development in adolescence and adulthood. They also build on the recent models of Meeus and colleagues and Luyckx and colleagues (as well as Berzonsky). Although these models refer to exploration and commitment as the core processes in identity development, they fall short—in Kunnen and Metz's view—of explaining what may cause interindividual differences in identity development.

Kunnen and Metz follow a microlevel approach to identity formation, with a focus on daily events, short-term processes, and their translation to the individual's developmental trajectories. Insights from Bosma and Kunnen's model of commitment development lead them to a dynamic systems perspective and an emphasis on mechanisms of change. Kunnen and Metz wrestle with fundamental issues such as how to include the context in their mode of inquiry. Can the researcher define the relevant part of the context and incorporate it in the measure (independent of the person)? Or might one need free reports, as from diaries or storytelling, to view context as it is defined by the individual? Kunnen and Metz recognize that individual and context define each other. They discuss the ways in which the interpretation of statistical analyses used in psychometric research does not allow for the process interpretation that they seek. In their paper, they debate with themselves how to best bring context into the research.

The approaches of both papers grow out of the same conceptual ground, but each one of them branches in a somewhat different direction. While Crocetti and Meeus's focus is macrolevel, group-based analysis, Kunnen and Metz lead to the individual, with a focus on microlevel developmental change. Terms like *process*, *context*, and *dynamic* appear in both chapters, but their meanings are not the same. Indeed, the difference in meaning becomes clearer when Kunnen and Metz bring these terms to the forefront of the discussion. Both chapters advocate longitudinal studies to investigate identity development, but the application of the term is different, with Crocetti and Meeus interested in group-based changes over months or several years and Kunnen and Metz advocating a daily investigation of events in individuals' lives.

Interestingly, in both chapters, the *complexity* of identity development is recognized and limitations of measurement are apparent. At the same time, the qualitative approach—whether Marcia's interview approach, storytelling, or diaries—is highlighted as a "rich" and "fruitful," way to study identity development

The Long View

In trying to take the long view of the progress of the investigation of identity status and in asking what we have learned from these massive research programs, we wonder, first of all, about the relationship between identity and context, including relational, social, and cultural contexts. We also have questions related to what brings about change in identity status: what circumstances, what triggers, within what time frames—and how this relates to where the individual begins the identity formation process.

The primary question we wish to raise in this commentary is: Have we gone as far as we can go solely relying on aggregated group studies using prefabricated questionnaires? Perhaps more sophisticated measurement is not going to answer our questions, and it is time to examine the possibilities of other modes of inquiry in order to return the people and the particularities of their identity formation, both in terms of content and process, to the discussion of the questions raised here.

Indeed, to be without identity commitments during the identity formation stage entails different forms and manifestations of uncertainty, anxiety, perhaps depression, even despair. As Erikson described it, identity confusion is painful. The new subcategories of identity diffusion and moratorium identified by these authors seem to reflect the degree of distress involved in the experience of noncommitment to identity choices.

We might wonder how the young man described at the beginning of this commentary (who the reader may recognize as Barack Obama writing in his memoir, *Dreams from My Father*), might have responded on the questionnaires that are under consideration in these papers. If he had filled out the questionnaires in college, he likely would have looked like one of the moratoriums or diffusions. He had made no commitments to occupation or belief systems—or even to relationships. He would not have endorsed the item (on the Dimensions of Identity Development Scale [DIDS], cited in Crocetti and Meeus, this volume), "I have decided on the direction I want to follow in my life," but he might have endorsed "I regularly think over a number of different plans for the future" depending on how he interpreted "regularly" and "plans." At the time, he was filled with anxiety and sometimes despair. But would knowing simply his identity status classification have helped us to understand the quite profound identity challenges that faced him—and that he details so eloquently? If we noted his confusion, or his lack of effort (in the terms of the questionnaire) to resolve his identity confusion in college, would we have any idea of what might have been creating such confusion? Would there be any way to learn about this without asking him directly and then listening closely to his response?

What Crocetti and Meeus, following established methodological tradition, call a person-centered model would, in our view, better be termed a group-centered model. There are no individual persons represented, only covariates or properties of groups of people, the groupings of identity status. Ipsative measures are still aggregated, and such an approach cannot detail the contextualized psychological organization within the person (see Carlson, 1971). Kunnen (2006) is well aware that the process of identity formation has been left out of identity status research and, in the current chapter, she and Metz grapple with how to explore these processes—while still looking in psychometric (and highly sophisticated) statistical directions. Might there be other strategies of investigation that could better address questions of individuals in context, forming identity over time within dynamic systems? Can we adapt the research strategy to suit the question rather than the questions to fit the strategy?

Identity, in Eriksonian terms, is both a structure and a process, both the outcome of developmental progress and a consistent way of being in the world. Each identity is unique and, in that sense, resides in the individual. Erikson further described identity as a *psychosocial* challenge and necessity that is arrived at through different processes and constructed in a variety of forms that in part reflect the exigencies of the society that the individual is joining. In that sense, identity is beyond the individual, a bridge between the individual and a place in society. It is always under construction, foreshadowed in the earlier stages of development, revised in later ones, and, in the identity stage itself, refined or amended continuously. Indeed, commitments may be explored further and discarded or changed (identification with commitment or reconsideration of commitment in the terms of these authors), and it is just these phenomena to which all four authors of the current papers address themselves. These are intricate and highly individualized processes. With the current research approaches, we can demonstrate that they indeed exist, but we may need to explore them in some depth, phenomenologically, before we can advance our theoretical understanding of *how* they unfold. Crocetti and Meeus comment on the limitations of questionnaire-based modes of investigation, recognizing that the richness of material available in interviews is lost. Questionnaire measures may tell us *that* a person is thinking deeply about his or her future or his or her commitments. Longitudinal administration of questionnaires may show that this changes over time, but we can only understand what is taking place at the most general level. We learn little about *how* these processes of exploration and commitment are unfolding.

It might be worth noting that the complexity of identity phenomena made the assessment of identity even from the up-close vantage point of the ISI a challenging task. Although high levels of interrater reliability were obtained, there were nevertheless many cases that required discussion with a third rater to resolve discrepancies—and even then some participants could not be classified into one or the other identity statuses.[2] In many cases, these rater experiences pointed less to the unreliability of rating and more to the elusiveness of the identity states. How much exploration constituted exploration: actions that "tried out" other possibilities or merely thinking that other choices could be possible? How was relevant exploratory experience processed in relation to the self? And what of commitments made that largely reproduced parental values but seemed to have involved at least some awareness of other avenues: foreclosure or achievement? Essentially, what the researcher had to do was reason from a participant's narrative of their identity decisionmaking to a determination of whether the narrative did indeed involve exploration and commitment.

Given that identity formation is a central and absorbing task for most college students, asking them to talk about these matters invites them to talk about what they and their friends are thinking about anyway, and most interviewees can offer detailed "thick" descriptions about what they are struggling with, exploring, deciding, or avoiding. The problem came not in eliciting the material but in deciding how much questioning and experimenting constitutes "exploration" and how firm and unwavering a decision had to be to qualify as "commitment." For many participants, this is far from clear—often even to them. Erikson was aware of this in pointing out that "although the psychosocial moratorium is of the utmost importance for the process of identity formation . . . it does not need to be consciously experienced as such" (1968, pp. 157–158).

The experience of exploration may be structured in idiosyncratic ways. Similarly, some late adolescents who have made identity commitments may yet retain a narrative aversion to labeling the finality of their choices. For those identity researchers who worked "up close" with college students in the midst of the identity stage, the identity statuses were understood to be loose groupings with many shades of meaning. What the interview made possible was the awareness of there being permutations of the pathways to identity formation, weaving in and out of or combining the four statuses, but in recent research much of that awareness seems to have fallen away. The questionnaire measures seem to us to declare a certainty about these categories that counter Erikson's insights. There has been, over the years, repeated concern that the various objective identity status measures do not classify people into the same categories (Schwartz, 2004) and little or no evidence that the survey instruments match the status assignments that would be made via the coding manual for the ISI. We do not doubt that the various questionnaires are measuring something in some ways related to identity, but without narrative data, it is hard to be clear on just what they are measuring—and if it is, indeed, closely related to what Erikson meant by identity. The interviews allowed for the possibility of discovering something new—for example, evolutive identity (Flum, 1994), foreclosed diffusion (Josselson, 1973), firm foreclosure (Kroger, 1995), alienated achievement (Marcia, Waterman, Matteson, Archer, & Orlofsky, 1993), and "thrill of dissonance" diffusions (Schachter, 2004), and these diffusions might have something in common with the alienated achievements Marcia found.

Crocetti and Meeus are right to point out that the early focus on validating the utility of the statuses kept researchers occupied with classifying people reliably and finding the covariates of the identity statuses; they did not mine the richness of the interview data. Nor did they reflect publicly on what the difficulties in rating were, even though such reflection may have yielded new insight into the nature of the statuses. Now that there is such widespread agreement about the meaningfulness of the identity status groupings, such reflection may be newly possible. Still, the psychometric studies of identity statuses, particularly those discussed in this Handbook, have extended a number of aspects of Marcia's original conceptualization. There seems to be *some* agreement on the identity trajectories that are possible—two or three types of achievement, if one includes the evolutive (Flum, 1994) and the alienated (Marcia et al., 1993); two forms of foreclosure; at least two forms of moratorium; and two or three forms of diffusion. That there are multiple forms of each of these statuses reveals that one can "explore" and "commit" in somewhat different ways. This gave rise to the "variable-centered approach" of directly measuring exploration and commitment as variables to see what understandings this may produce.

The research programs summarized by Crocetti and Meeus and by Kunnen and Metz pursue the possibility of describing the process of identity formation by more finely distinguishing types of exploration and commitment. They demonstrate that commitments, once chosen, are often reformulated or strengthened and that exploration can involve choosing from a number of alternatives (exploration in breadth) or thinking further about commitments (tentatively) made. Exploration can occur from a base of prior commitment or from a blank or confused state—and it can also become ruminative and, presumably, unresolvable. Taken together, whether from a variable-centered or group-centered analysis, these research programs demonstrate that the processes of exploration and commitment are more complex than previously envisioned in identity status research, thus documenting statistically what those who used to do identity status interviews saw up close. To be sure that we are indeed regarding the same processes, it would be useful to have phenomenological examples that demonstrate in a contextualized way *how* exploration in breadth or in depth—or identification with commitment—is experienced by actual participants.

Psychometric studies continue to strengthen our understanding that consolidating identity during the late adolescent years (i.e., being classified as Identity Achieved) is adaptive and indicative of general well-being and healthy development (Kroger & Marcia, 2011; Marcia et al., 1993). Such studies have also shown that foreclosure seems to be a more adaptive status than envisioned by Erikson or Marcia, although somewhat less so than achievement. And short-term longitudinal studies indicate that people can return from other statuses to foreclosure, a process still hard to theorize. Josselson (1987) has shown that, for at least some late adolescent women, the searching they seemed to be doing during college evaporates if they (choose to) return home and reintegrate themselves into their precollege familial and community environments. We also know that foreclosure can represent either a developmental byway or a characterological way of being in the world (Kroger, 1995), but we as yet know little about the differences between these types.

The emerging portraits of those in moratorium and diffusion classifications crystallize around the description of these statuses as composed of people in more or less distress. We still don't know if the distress is caused by the lack of identity resolution or whether distress not related to identity becomes a barrier to making identity commitments (see Marcia, 2006). One may need in-depth longitudinal studies to untangle this.

The study of differences between aggregated groups, whether conceived as a continuum of variables (such as forms of exploration or forms of commitment) or aggregations of people (the statuses) consistently yield not only regularities but also "error variance" or "unclassified" participants. One must wonder about the nature of the identity pathway for these unclassifiable young people who don't "fit" the conceptualization. There are perhaps yet undiscovered and unconceptualized pathways, particularly as the social world becomes more complex and adult commitments are delayed.

We might also note that in Erikson's theory successful resolution of the identity versus identity confusion stage involves a positive *balance* between commitment and confusion. Identity formation always implies both consolidation of aspects of self-in-society that feel meaningful and purposeful as well as aspects that are unformed, confused, labile, changeable, or inconstant. Erikson would likely assert that it is the very tension between what one feels committed to and what one feels uncertain about that fuels further growth. This is captured in Flum's (1994) description of the evolutive style of identity formation in which mid to late adolescents appear to be clear about their broad commitments and yet experience the tension between these commitments and specific aspects that they are motivated to focus on and gradually explore. (For example, a young person can be fairly certain that she would like to work with people but is still considering which human service occupation she would like to pursue.) Although some late adolescents appear "committed" on questionnaires, we might remain cognizant that these commitments are still likely to be flexible,[3] which may be represented in the cycle (described by Crocetti and Meeus) of exploration in breadth → commitment making → exploration in depth → identification with commitment. Marcia (2007) further reminds us that in both his and Erikson's conceptualization, individuals are admixtures of statuses and do not simply fit into one status.

Individuals and Their Contexts

Indeed, many interesting questions remain. To name just a few: What are the circumstances and experiences that lead to identity exploration and commitment? What assists the searching or identity-confused adolescent to make commitments? What experiences, internal and external, invoke identity reconsideration? What is the range of individual differences in the experience of these paths?

How are these questions best to be explored? Many scholars have maintained that identity is a narrative phenomenon, a *story* of the integration of the threads of one's commitments (explored in depth, breadth, not at all, or still in process) (e.g., McLean & Pasupathi, 2012). Who am I? What do I stand for? How did I become the person that I am, and what do I yet hope to become? These questions may require some form of phenomenological investigation in the form of narrated explication (see Habermas & Köber, this volume; Hammack, this volume; McAdams & Zapata-Gietl, this volume). This means that researchers have to engage ways of listening to, then interpreting, stories that people tell about their own becoming.

A narrated account makes possible knowing what personal story or autobiographical experience may lie behind a participant endorsing items that represent "identification with commitment" or "reconsideration of commitment." Narratives may illuminate the nature of the commitment and how it may be reconsidered. Here is one example of the issue of the schism between measurement and narrative in relation to what commitment means. In doing identity status interviews, we would routinely ask a participant who had described a firm occupational commitment, possibly following a period of exploration, "How willing do you think you would be to change if something better came along?" There were those who responded, "This is what I want, so there couldn't be something better," and those who said, "Yes, I'd change—if I thought it was better." We could then follow up and ask, "what would be better for you?" The answer might be, "I don't know, but if I thought it was better, I might do it" or "Well, if someone offered me a million-dollar job, I might change." It is difficult to know how these responses might relate to, for example, identification with commitment. It is difficult to know how to match the scales to the phenomenology.

Like Crocetti and Meeus, Kunnen and Metz call for the study of individuals, particularly if we wish to learn about change over time. They detail the argument that studies of aggregated group differences over time do not denote processes of intraindividual changes. They take very seriously the importance of context, noting that identity in Erikson's terms is psychosocial and, in being psychosocial, it goes beyond thinking about who one is or what one plans, but actually experiencing the self in social reality. Kunnen and Metz's argument for a dynamic systems view of identity is compelling and fully consonant with Erikson's theory. Indeed, identity is the link between internal and social reality, the process of an individual taking a place in the social world, finding, in Erikson's terms, some goals, values, or ways of acting that have *fidelity*, an anchor for a sense of self-continuity. Yet, one can only see the system by studying both content and process because these are inextricably interwoven.

Identity development is the process of defining, finding, and realizing oneself in the collectivity in which one lives—and doing so at both deeply emotional as well as cognitive levels of experience. As Erikson said, identity is less about who I am than what I will *stand for*. Both fidelity and "standing for" implicate the social world. As Kunnen and Metz point out, the responses of the world, even on a day-to-day basis, are determinative in the identity choices a young person makes. The young man, Obama, in the example we began with, describes this process: "When people who don't know me well, black or white, discover my background (and it is usually a discovery, for I ceased to advertise my mother's race at the age of twelve or thirteen, when I began to suspect that by doing so I was ingratiating myself to whites), I see the split-second adjustments they have to make, the searching of my eyes for some telltale sign. They no longer know who I am" (Obama, 1995, p. xv). Thus, the responses of the social world interact in complicated ways with the internal world to shape one's sense of one's place in the world. Relational psychoanalysts understand this as a process of *recognition* in which the "response from the other...makes meaningful the feelings, intentions, and actions of the self. It allows the self to recognize its agency and authorship in a tangible way" (Benjamin, 1988, p. 12). This is not simply a passive process, however. The specific sector of the world in which the person will choose to express the chosen identity (and be recognized) is also a matter (in most cases) of some choice. As Jane Kroger (1993) detailed in a rarely cited but very insightful retrospective interview study, people choose a context consistent with their identity structure. She demonstrated how foreclosures chose or created "insulated vocational, ideological and social contexts for themselves within whatever broader climate of social attitudes existed at the time" (p. 143). Moratoriums, by contrast, found contexts that expanded their range of opportunities or experiences. Over time, Identity Achievements were shown to "integrate and reintegrate disparate elements" (p. 156) by seeking new possibilities in their social world and reforming their commitments, choosing contexts that supported their need for autonomy. The foundation and expression of identity is in embeddedness, finding others to feel "like" and to be recognized by as "like"—an experience that Carson McCullers, in *Member of the Wedding*, called finding the "we of me." Thus, the "we" formed by the context is inseparable from the "me" when we consider identity.

Kunnen and Metz have a firm commitment to regarding identity contextually, stating that they wish to gain insight into the processes of emergence, stability, and change of identity. We join them in this. Despite decades of theorizing about identity, we remain at the frontier of conceptualizing the space between psychic reality and socially constructed discourses—and this is the intersection at which identity sits (see Flum & Kaplan, 2012; Gergen, 2009; Hall, 1996; Josselson, 2012). Again, inviting narratives from those in the psychosocial stage of identity formation, perhaps alongside scores on scales, might illuminate the available contexts within which young people could consider locating themselves. This would include contexts of race, class, and ethnicity (see Way & Rogers, this volume; Worrell, this volume).

Longitudinal Studies and Identity as Narrative

Most identity researchers, including those writing these chapters, inevitably call for longitudinal studies. How does identity evolve over time, they wonder, given that identity is a process and is always evolving? What are the longer term implications of being in one or another of the identity statuses? The issue is how such studies are best conducted. Like Kunnen and Metz, nearly all identity status researchers call for more person-centered studies over time. The problem is that the existing detailed in-depth studies of identity development over time are qualitative and case-based, and they remain outside the purview of measurement-oriented researchers. Josselson's (1996) longitudinal study of women in Marcia's four statuses, now spanning thirty-five years, is well-cited in the counseling and educational literature, most likely because the case studies resonate with the dilemmas faced by counselors and teachers working with students. Its detailed consideration of the dynamics of each of the identity statuses has, however, largely been overlooked by identity status researchers. Similarly, Marcia's (1976) six-year follow-up case-based study of identity statuses and Kroger's (1993) retrospective in-depth study are underutilized. This disconnect reflects the dilemmas faced by the wider field of psychology to integrate quantitative and qualitative studies; we don't yet know how to relate measures to meanings of personal experience. Where quantitative studies aim for generalizability and prediction, qualitative investigation aims for understanding in an interpretive way, generalizing about processes rather than populations. As Allport, who was no stranger to nomothetic study, says, abstractions are safe; the real test is understanding a single person. Case studies would provide identity status research with what Allport calls a "touchstone of reality" (Allport, 1942, p. 184).

Erikson specifically said that the "biographic" was one of the three modes to which he could turn to make his concept of identity more "explicit" (1980, pp. 109–110) (the others being the pathographic and the theoretical). As we understand more about the ways in which telling life stories both reflect and construct the self and identity (McLean, Pasupathi, & Pals, 2007), we might explore more fully ways of listening to, then interpreting (or even coding) stories that people tell about their own becoming. Identity and narrative are both meaning-making enterprises, and we advocate moving to explore in depth the phenomenology of these processes.

Only narrative can organize the intersection between subjectivity and social location (Bruner, 1986; 1990; Erikson, 1968; McAdams, 1993; Polkinghorne, 1988) and represent time (Ricoeur, 1984). The narrating, experiencing "I" relates, in story, those encounters between the subjective self and the social world (of others) that create and reflect a constructed "me," as well as an "I" that influences and can reshape the social world in turn. Identity narratives may reflect coherence and singularity or multiplicity and uncertainty (or, in some cases, both).

Studies of narrative identity have burgeoned in recent years (see McAdams, 2013, for a brief review, and Habermas & Köber, this volume; Pasupathi, this volume), but relatively few have looked specifically at the identity status groupings. It seems to us that investigating the narratives of people in these categories, integrating identity status and narrative identity, is the next step. McLean and Pratt (2006) tried to learn how people scoring in various statuses as assessed by the Objective Measure of Ego Identity Status (OM-EIS) describe and evaluate turning points in their lives and found that the ways in which people understand their lives are related to identity status. They present some case-based narrative examples to illustrate their measurement-based findings. In their ambitious longitudinal study, they found statistically that "narrative meaning is more important in its absence from lower identity statuses than its presence at higher statuses" (p. 720). This is an intriguing finding, one that identity status researchers could follow up on. We need to know more about how people in the various statuses are making meaning of their lives, and the best way to approach this may be to ask them. Sankey and

Young (1996) interviewed college students after classifying them into identity statuses using the OM-EIS and began to sketch out the more complex (and contradictory) aspects of how parents are experienced as influencing career identity differently in the different statuses. Identity status research needs exemplars, fully explored and analyzed.

Kunnen and Metz call for the study of individuals to analyze identity development in more detail. We strongly support this suggestion. Although statistical analysis of individual trajectories may document that change occurs over time (of course it does), it will not tell us what creates these changes. We think that the path most likely to lead to new understandings would be a form of investigation that allows the participant to detail his or her own experience of the identity formation and development process. This may involve qualitative, interpretive analysis in addition to hypothesis testing, but it would put the research focus solidly on the person developing an identity and less on the properties of questionnaires.

What seems to us important here is to invite participants to provide stories of identity-forming moments, moments that lead to reconsideration of commitments or moments that shore up commitments. Research that predefines experience into scales that reflect the researchers' meanings constrains individuals to fit their experience into prepackaged categories. This makes it difficult to discover anything new. And researchers cannot a priori define identity-changing contexts. In his memoir, Obama recounts a conversation with a fellow student as a turning point, a moment in which he moved out of his professed indifference to race and his proclivity to posture. He regards this conversation as the time he struck out on the road to finding his own "honest" voice and identity, something that could bridge his inner sense of connection to his (white) family and the future roles he could now begin to imagine (perhaps as a black man in America). Significantly, from the time of this conversation, he stopped asking people to call him "Barry," which he had always been called, and took up his given name, his father's name, "Barack," however unfamiliar it might be to American ears. In retrospect, Obama reflected that it was "strange how a single conversation can change you" (p. 103). For him, at this moment in his development, identity issues were centered on what he thought of as authenticity versus posturing, and his changing how he would be called was a step on the way toward claiming a truer voice.

The processes that Obama details in his memoir would have been missed by any existing questionnaire—except to flag his distress as aggregated in the general group indicators of anxiety or depression that are typical of those in moratorium and diffusion statuses. Although questionnaire measures can be useful for sorting large numbers of people into categories or pathways, they would be more useful if the studies were augmented by case presentations that illustrate the phenomenology of the score. Although aspects of identity (such as indicators of exploration and commitment in general terms) can be measured, even intraindividually over time, the holistic nature of identity can only be expressed narratively—in a personal story of who I am, have been, and hope to be over time and in a sociohistorical context. In addition, careful study of the narratives of individuals can only increase the possibility of more precise and experience-near measurement for those who wish to test hypotheses on large samples.

Ethnic identity has been illuminated by studying how emerging adults, in various states of ethnic identity development narrate experiences about ethnicity in their own words. Studying these narratives demonstrates how content and process are related (Syed & Azmitia, 2008). Hammack (2010), studying young people developing identities in the midst of the Israeli–Palestinian conflict, used the analysis of narratives to show how collective identity is embedded in personal identity, thus demonstrating that there is a great deal more to identity formation than exploration and commitment. The chapters under consideration here, by contrast, are themselves rather context free.

Case study also makes possible the consideration of multifaceted identities, identities fashioned not to be stable or linear but to suit an increasingly complex and uncertain world (see Josselson & Harway, 2012). Is the capacity to create what Kraus (2006) calls a complex, heterogeneous, and multivoiced identity more a phenomenon of what appears in the achievement or the moratorium status? Or perhaps would this, like Gergen's (1991) postmodern self, appear as diffusion? Does our understanding of commitment as identity researchers have room for open-endedness or multiplicity—or are we privileging stability and univocality? Case studies then, challenge not only our understanding, but demand an examination of the values we bring to this research.

The Statuses: What We Know and Don't Know

When I (RJ) was defending my dissertation, an early work on identity status, my Chair, Joe Adelson, asked me "But are these personality types or developmental stages?" I wasn't sure how to answer this question, and more than forty years later, we're collectively still not sure. It seems that they are both, and this is what the psychometric studies are picking up. Over (at least short periods of) time, identity status, as measured psychometrically, seems to be stable for most people. For others, it changes. For those who are identity achieved, whatever occurs happens outside of our window of observation and has to be narrated in retrospect. Foreclosures who don't change but just carry on being who they have always been, seem to be a personality type. Identity status measures repeated over short time periods often pick up some people's movement out of foreclosure and diffusion into a period of exploration and document movement of some people from moratorium (or diffusion) to achievement (see Kroger, Martinussen, & Marcia, 2010, for a meta-analysis regarding movement between statuses over time). The status most likely to change is moratorium, which, from a theoretical point of view, should be a way-station on the road to identity achievement. But the empirical results also find that people stay stable in this status, suggesting that identity exploration may be something like a continual state of being. As we read the meta-analysis, there are no dominant patterns, but there are quite different trajectories. We wonder, though, for those who stay in the uncommitted statuses over time whether some failure of societal response or some internal disorganization leaves these young people somewhat lost as their peers move on.

Identity status research has grown increasingly complex as studies multiply, and integrating them becomes more challenging. Taken together, this research paradigm has outlined the framework of the kinds of identity trajectories that are most common among university students. We have general outlines of the properties of each of the identity statuses and some ideas about the kinds of people to be found in each of them.

We know that those who score in some form of identity achievement (or high in exploration and commitment) on questionnaires are primarily a group of young people who are well-adjusted, well-along in ego development, and reasonably self-confident. But we know little about the factors in their background that have led them to this healthy, developmentally advantageous outcome.

The Foreclosure group has been of less interest to identity status researchers. They seem to do well without exploration and, at least on the questionnaires, do not seem to change much over time, although some do progress toward exploration. They are high in authoritarianism and therefore fairly certain of their positions in the world, cognitively rigid, and relatively free of anxiety. They are also lower in levels of moral development and lower than Achievements in intimacy (Marcia et al., 1993). We know little about the characteristics that distinguish those "firm" Foreclosures from those who seem to be occupying this status in preparation for identity exploration.

We know that identity diffusion (beyond developmental diffusion) is problematic and that this is, by and large, not ameliorated with time (Josselson, 1986). We know that among this group are those with more or less serious psychopathology, people who would be classified clinically as borderline or depressed, people who are impulsive and take risks, and we might wonder if these serious personality difficulties are cause or consequence of identity confusion. Although Kernberg (2006) sees identity diffusion as an aspect of borderline personality organization, the kind of identity diffusion that Erikson described (and later called identity confusion) may share some of the failures of internalization and personality integration characteristic of borderline personality but is less extreme and less disruptive. Put succinctly, all individuals with borderline personality disorder are identity diffuse, but all those with identity diffusion are not borderline (Marcia, 2006). Still, these quite troubled people bring down the mean scores of the diffusion group on just about any measure. Diffusions are defined by absences of exploration and commitment, but we still know little about what is present for them. McLean and Pratt (2006) conclude their study noting that "a lack of personal exploration in identity development and life stories lacking in meaning is the crux of" where identity status and narrative identity meet. When we study Diffusions in researcher-defined terms, we keep finding "lacks." We need to know more, though, about what *is* present in these young people's lives. The distinction between Diffusions and "carefree Diffusions" may indicate different longitudinal pathways and outcomes, but at this point we can only guess at what this means experientially. How can we better understand these people without investigating their experiences, personally and in depth? Are there some interventions that might be helpful for such people? Josselson's (1996) longitudinal study suggests that some Diffusions, if they find an external structure to organize them, lead reasonably satisfying and productive lives. This is consonant with Berzonsky and Ferrari's (1996) idea about Diffusion as procrastinators who avoid identity-relevant information and await the resolutions provided by circumstance. Josselson also identified many Diffusion/Drifter[4] women who wandered through many life organizations, only to return home in their forties, seeking some internal structure that they had lacked all along.

Working in a narrative research framework, Schachter (2004) was able to pinpoint some of the variance to be found among the diffusion group by detailing an identity configuration that embraces dissonance. Intriguingly, "these individuals are consciously and decisively rejecting the demand to create sameness and continuity in identity, preferring instead an alternative model of identity that enables them to achieve alternative psychological goals" (p. 192). Thus, using a narrative mode of investigation, Schachter could document and reflect on a very different form of what might seem to be identity diffusion.

We also have some ethical concerns in regard to those in states of identity diffusion. These are real people, many of whom are signaling in their questionnaire responses that they are floundering. We amalgamate scores and statistically analyze them, but we perhaps also have some ethical obligation to think about what can be done by the educational institutions in which these people are growing (but not thriving) to assist them. Perhaps it is time for identity status researchers to work in collaboration with counseling centers to develop programs for those stuck in states of identity diffusion and to find ethical ways to suggest to those who appear as diffuse on questionnaires to consider availing themselves of these programs.

It is those in the moratorium status who have most recently captured the attention of researchers. What is the nature of their exploration—broad or deep, searching or "classical?" The chapters we respond to here seem, in their focus on varieties of exploration and commitment, most interested in the processes of exploration that characterize the moratorium status. Well-documented case presentations could go a long way to clarify what these forms of exploration look like in situ, including the discomfort entailed by what Crocetti and colleagues have documented as "reconsideration of commitment" (Crocetti, Schwartz, Fermani, & Meeus (2010). The effort to study what happens to college students who fail in their studies (Luyckx, Goossens, & Soenens, 2006) is a step in this direction because failure is an external crisis that should engage identity reconsideration. But what are the different implications for identity processes when students fail their first year because they were partying too much or fail because they were not up to the academic challenges? The studies of migrants cited by Kunnen and Metz tell us that the inherent clash of cultures is reflected in the measure of commitment reconsideration, but case studies would document how this occurs. What Obama really wanted to do as he approached college graduation was to join the civil rights movement of the 1960s, but this was 1983. He got the idea of becoming a community organizer because this seemed as close as he could get to the past he romanticized, but alas, there were no such jobs to be found. So he took a job in business consulting just to pay the bills. A few years later, he happened on an ad placed by Jerry Kellman for a community organizing job in Chicago and sent in his resume. Fortunately, Kellman was interested and called him. (Kellman thought Obama, from Honolulu, was Japanese (Remnick, 2010)). Such are the fortuitous incidents that determine identity——turning points that make it possible to realize only vaguely formed potential identity commitments.

Finding the People in the Statuses

In summary, these review chapters seem to cry out for qualitative case-based study, not so much as a way of classifying people but of understanding the classifications that their scales produce. If identity status research is to have utility in the real world, then we have to move closer to the phenomenology, a suggestion also endorsed by Kroger, Martinussen, and Marcia (2010) in their conclusions to their meta-analysis of studies concerning identity development over time (see also Syed, 2012). Interview studies that follow administration of the questionnaire, perhaps using extreme cases, could shed light on this understanding. Kunnen and her students seem to be exploring the use of diary studies, which certainly moves in this direction. Mixed methods (e.g., Creswell & Clark, 2011) might be the next step in giving flesh and substance, content and narrated process, to these investigations of exploration and commitment.

Different questions call for different epistemologies and hence, different modes of inquiry. It is difficult to imagine how the complexities of content, context, and process, so individualized in their experience, could be fully captured by preformed questionnaires. If such questionnaires may help to map the landscape, some up-close phenomenological investigation would only enrich the map. What is the phenomenological experience of those who are high in breadth exploration but low in depth exploration? How do they experience their choices? We wonder what we could learn from interviewing people who, in Crocetti and Meeus's terms, score extremely high or low on "exploring in breadth" or "exploring in depth." Or what the phenomenology is of those who are "reconsidering commitments?" The danger—and opportunity—of this, of course, is discovering that scores and narratives don't match up (as was the case in the Sankey and Young (1996) study in regard to people identified as being identity diffuse on the OM-EIS but who sounded just like Foreclosures in their interviews).

We can learn a great deal about many of the questions raised by the authors of these chapters by designing interview-based or diary studies, trying to reach whatever experiences or conversations seem identity changing. And it would be important to pay attention to the research relationship in the sense of making enough of a relationship with the participants that they are willing to disclose what are deeply felt core experiences (Josselson, 2013). This would allow us to get beyond the superficialities that are inevitable with questionnaires. Frisén and Wängqvist (2011) attempted to detail the special circumstances of identity formation in Sweden and concluded that "the unique cultural and individual meanings were illustrated by the words of the participants themselves" (p. 217).

Although there are both general facets and individual elements to every identity resolution, for each person, identity formation is idiosyncratic, meaning that each person has unique elements to weave together to create an identity. The task for identity researchers, then, is to reason recursively from the general to the idiosyncratic to the general, grouping together what might fit. At present, when identity processes are constrained by prefabricated questionnaires, what is uniquely individual is simply left out of the studies. We are then left with a psychology of identity in its most abstract, generalizable form that obfuscates the particularities of what leads to or away from successful development in the identity stage. We need the singularities of *how* identity is "rooted in emotion, emerging in relationships, developing as a dynamic, self-organizing system" (Bosma & Kunnen, 2001, p. 5).

The authors of these chapters have moved the study of identity forward by detailing the ways in which exploration and commitment are both ongoing and cyclical. They raise interesting and important questions with their findings, findings that call for further investigation as to the actual experiences of their participants. Studying the evolving lives of people forming (and reforming) identity allows us to learn new things about identity processes. Some of this learning may not fit in a hypothesis-testing framework, and it would therefore become important to allow the phenomenology of identity to guide, as well as to substantiate, questionnaire-based assessments. "The stories we live by reflect subjectively recalled, specific, and vivid experiences, drawn together into a life narrative" (McLean & Pratt, 2006, p. 721). And what is identity but the stories we live by? Josselson (2009), for example, based on in-depth interviews conducted at ten- to twelve-year intervals over the course of thirty-five years, demonstrated how an identity-forming experience in adolescence remained part of identity at later ages but with very different meanings. Over time, this woman variously narrated the experience (of dating and planning to marry a man of a different race) to anchor, illuminate, counterpoint, and disavow her identity. We join other researchers (see especially Koepke & Denissenin, 2012) calling for integrative methods that will restore experience to abstraction and the phenomenology of the individual to statistical findings. (For an example of following up scale administration with interviews, see Josselson, Greenberger, and McConochie, 1977*a* and 1977*b*.) Researchers could also consider returning to the ISI and analyzing it beyond the status categorization, describing and interpreting the contextual factors that relate to exploration and commitment.

Viewing individual development in its subjective, meaning-making forms may make possible practical applications for identity status research. The study of identity development can contribute to education and the facilitation of learning. Based on insights gained from theory and research, the advantages of exploration and an emphasis on exploratory orientation in educational settings is proving to enhance engagement in learning and promote students' development. "Identity work," connecting student identity with the learning process, is especially beneficial in the context of rapid change and growing uncertainty that are so much part of the current world young people grow into (Flum & Kaplan, 2006; Kaplan & Flum, 2012; Sinai, Kaplan, & Flum, 2012). And a refined understanding of the various routes to identity formation can inform psychotherapy (see Marcia & Josselson, 2013).

Identity is a multidimensional puzzle in which commitments and exploration interact in light of the larger sociohistorical context. How are identity choices impacted by a difficult economic climate and high unemployment? How has the use of social media changed what it means to find and be oneself? It is our challenge as identity researchers to fit together the storied lives that our participants lead with the investigatory tools we may bring to them. Only from this, in our view, can theory evolve.

Notes

1. Erikson said that such efforts inevitably leave out the "more vital" aspects of the identity concept (1968, p. 16).
2. It is fascinating that Kunnen (2009), in a recent paper, reports that in an effort to code short answers to a semistructured interview about occupational commitments, disagreements about the categories "agency" and "reflection" led the researchers to decide to leave them out. If it is impossible to come to an agreement about what constitutes agency and reflection at this "up close" level, then how can we understand what constitutes agency and reflection once questionnaire items are aggregated and statistically manipulated?
3. Schwartz et al. (2013) make a similar comment.
4. In her 1994 work, Josselson changed the names of the statuses, from Achievements to Pathmakers, Foreclosures to Guardians, Moratoriums to Searchers and Diffusions to Drifters.

References

Allport, G. W. (1942). *The use of personal documents in psychological science*. Prepared for the Committee on the Appraisal of Research. Bulletin No. 49, New York: Social Science Council.

Allport, G. W. (1961). *Pattern and growth in personality*. New York: Holt, Rinehart and Winston.

Benjamin, J. (1988). *The bonds of love: Psychoanalysis, feminism, & the problem of domination*. Pantheon.

Berzonsky, M. D., & Ferrari, J. R. (1996). Identity orientation and decisional strategies. *Personality and individual differences, 20*(5), 597–606.

Bosma, H. A., & Kunnen, E. S. (2001). *Identity and emotion*. Cambridge: Cambridge University Press.

Bruner, J. (1986). *Actual minds, possible worlds*. Cambridge, MA: Harvard University Press.

Bruner, J. (1990). *Acts of meaning*. Cambridge, MA: Harvard University Press.

Carlson, R. (1971). Where is the person in personality research? *Psychological Bulletin, 75*(3), 203.

Creswell, J., & Clark, V. L. P. (2011). *Designing and conducting mixed methods research*. Thousand Oaks: Sage.

Crocetti, E., Schwartz, S. J., Fermani, A., & Meeus, W. (2010). The Utrecht-Management of Identity Commitments Scale (U-MICS). *European Journal of Psychological Assessment, 26*(3), 172–186.

Erikson, E. H. (1956). The Problem of Ego Identity. *Journal of the American Psychoanalytic Association, 4*, 56–121.

Erikson, E. H. (1968). *Identity: Youth and crisis*. W. W. Norton & Company.

Erikson, E. H. (1980). *Identity and the life cycle*. W. W. Norton & Company.

Flum, H. (1994). The evolutive style of identity formation. *Journal of Youth and Adolescence, 23*, 489–498.

Flum, H., & Kaplan, A. (2006). Exploratory orientation as an educational goal. *Educational Psychologist, 41*, 99–110.

Flum, H., & Kaplan, A. (2012). Identity formation in educational settings: A contextualized view of theory and research in practice. *Contemporary Educational Psychology, 37*, 240–245.

Frisén, A., & Wängqvist, M. (2011). Emerging adults in Sweden: Identity formation in the light of love, work, and family. *Journal of Adolescent Research, 26*(2), 200–221.

Gergen, K. J. (1991). *The saturated self: Dilemmas of identity in contemporary life*. New York: Basic Books.

Gergen, K. J. (2009). *Relational being: Beyond self and community*. New York: Oxford University Press.

Hall, S. (1996). Introduction: Who needs identity? In S. Hall & P. du Gay (Eds.), *Questions of cultural identity* (pp. 1–18). Thousand Oaks, CA: Sage Publications.

Hammack, P. L. (2010). Identity as burden or benefit? youth, historical narrative, and the legacy of political conflict. *Human Development, 53*(4), 173–201.

Josselson, R. (1973). Psychodynamic aspects of identity formation in college women. *Journal of Youth and Adolescence, 2*(1), 3–52.

Josselson, R. (1986). *Identity diffusion: A long-term follow-Up*. Adolescent Psychiatry, vol. XIV. Chicago: University of Chicago Press.

Josselson, R. (1987). *Finding herself: Pathways to identity development in women*. San Francisco: Jossey-Bass.

Josselson, R. (1996). *Revising herself: The story of women's identity from college to midlife*. New York: Oxford University Press.

Josselson, R. (2009). The present of the past: Dialogues with memory over time. *Journal of Personality, 77*(3), 647–668.

Josselson, R. (2012). The we of me: Barack Obama's search for identity. In R. Josselson & M. Harway (Eds.), *Navigating multiple identities: Race, gender, culture and roles*. New York: Oxford University Press.

Josselson, R. (2013). *Interviewing for qualitative inquiry: A relational approach*. New York: Guilford Press.

Josselson, R., Greenberger, E., & McConochie, D. (1977a). Phenomenological aspects of psychosocial maturity in adolescence. Part I: Boys. *Journal of Youth and Adolescence, 6*(1), 25–55.

Josselson, R., Greenberger, E., & McConochie, D. (1977b). Phenomenological aspects of psychosocial maturity in adolescence. Part II: Girls. *Journal of Youth and Adolescence, 6*(2), 145–167.

Josselson, R. and Harway, M. (Eds.) (2012). *Navigating multiple identities: Race, gender, culture and roles*. New York: Oxford University Press.

Kaplan, A., & Flum, H. (2012). Identity formation in educational settings: A critical focus for education in the 21st century. *Contemporary Educational Psychology, 37*, 171–175.

Kernberg, O. (2006). Identity: Recent findings and clinical implications. *Psychoanalytic Quarterly, 75*, 969–1044.

Koepke, S., &. Denissen, J. J. A. (2012). Dynamics of identity development and separation–individuation in parent–child relationships during adolescence and emerging adulthood— A conceptual integration. *Developmental Review, 32*, 67–88.

Kraus, W. (2006). The narrative negotiation of identity and belonging. *Narrative Inquiry, 16*(1), 103–111.

Kroger, J. (1993). Identity and context: How the identity statuses choose their match. In R. Josselson & A. Lieblich

(Eds.), *The narrative study of lives* (pp. 130–162). Thousand Oaks, CA: Sage.

Kroger, J. (1995). The differentiation of "firm" and "developmental" foreclosure statuses: A longitudinal study. *Journal of Adolescent Research, 10*, 317–337.

Kroger, J., & Marcia, J. E. (2011). The identity statuses: Origins, meanings, and interpretations. In S. J. Schwartz, K. Luyckx, & V. L. Vignoles (Eds.), *Handbook of identity theory and research* (pp. 31–53). New York: Springer.

Kroger, J., Martinussen, M., & Marcia, J. E. (2010). Identity status change during adolescence and young adulthood: A meta-analysis. *Journal of Adolescence, 33*(5), 683–698.

Kunnen, E. S. (2006). Are conflicts the motor in identity change? *Identity, 6,* 169–186.

Kunnen, E. S. (2009). Qualitative and quantitative aspects of commitment development in psychology students. *Journal of Adolescence, 32,* 567–584.

Luyckx, K., Goossens, L., & Soenens, B. (2006). A developmental contextual perspective on identity construction in emerging adulthood: Change dynamics in commitment formation and commitment evaluation. *Developmental Psychology, 42*, 366–380.

Luyckx, K., Schwartz, S. J., Berzonsky, M. D., Soenens, B., Vansteenkiste, M., Smits, I., & Goossens, L. (2008). Capturing ruminative exploration: Extending the four-dimensional model of identity formation in late adolescence. *Journal of Research in Personality, 42,* 58–82.

Marcia, J. E. (1966). Development and validation of ego-identity status. *Journal of personality and social psychology, 3*(5), 551.

Marcia, J. E. (1976). Identity six years after: A follow-up study. *Journal of Youth and Adolescence, 5*(2), 145–160.

Marcia, J. E. (2006). Ego identity and personality disorders. *Journal of Personality Disorders, 20*(6), 577–596.

Marcia, J. E. (2007). Theory and measure: The identity status interview. In M. Watzlawik & A. Born (Eds.), *Capturing identity: Quantitative and qualitative methods* (pp. 1–14). Lanham, MD: University Press of America.

Marcia, J. E., & Josselson, R. (2013). Eriksonian personality research and its implications for psychotherapy. *Journal of Personality, 81*(6), 617–629.

Marcia, J. E., Waterman, A. S., Matteson, D. R., Archer, S. A., & Orlofsky, J. S. (1993). *Ego identity: A handbook for psychosocial research*. New York: Springer-Verlag.

McAdams, D. P. (1993). *The stories we live by: Personal myths and the making of the self*. Guilford Press.

McAdams, D. P. (2013). The psychological self as actor, agent, and author. *Perspectives on Psychological Science, 8,* 272–295.

McCullers, C. (1946). *The member of the wedding*. Houghton-Mifflin.

McLean, K. C., & Pratt, M. W. (2006). Life's little (and big) lessons: Identity statuses and meaning-making in the turning point narratives of emerging adults. *Developmental psychology, 42*(4), 714.

McLean K. C., & Pasupathi, M. (2012). Processes of identity development: Where I am and how I got there, *Identity: An International Journal of Theory and Research, 12*(1), 8–28,

McLean, K. C., Pasupathi, M. & Pals, J. L. (2007). Selves creating stories creating selves: A process model of self-development. *Personality and Social Psychology Review, 11,* 262–278.

Obama, B. (1995). *Dreams from my father: A story of race and inheritance*. Times Books.

Polkinghorne, D. (1988). *Narrative knowing and the human sciences*. New York: State University of New York Press.

Remnick, D. (2010) *The bridge: The life and rise of Barack Obama*. New York: Knopf.

Ricoeur, P. (1984). *Time and narrative (vol. 1)*. Chicago: University of Chicago Press.

Sankey, A. M., & Young, R. A. (1996). Ego-identity status and narrative structure in retrospective accounts of parental career influence. *Journal of Adolescence, 19,* 2, 141–153.

Schachter, E. P. (2004). Identity configurations: A new perspective on identity formation in contemporary society. *Journal of Personality, 72*(1), 167–200.

Schwartz, S. J. (2001). The evolution of Eriksonian and neo-Eriksonian identity theory and research: A review and integration. *Identity: An International Journal of Theory and Research, 1,* 7–58.

Schwartz, S. J. (2004). Brief report: Construct validity of two identity status measures: The EIPQ and the EOM-EIS-II. *Journal of Adolescence 27,* 477–483.

Schwartz, S. J., Zamboanga, B. L., Luyckz, K, Meca, A., & Ritchie, R. A. (2013). Identity in emerging adulthood: Reviewing the field and looking forward. *Emerging Adulthood, 1*(2), 96–113.

Sinai, M., Kaplan, A., & Flum, H. (2012). Promoting identity exploration within the school curriculum: A design-based study in a junior high literature lesson in Israel. *Contemporary Educational Psychology, 37,* 195–205.

Syed, M. (2012). The past, present, and future of Eriksonian identity research: Introduction to the special issue. *Identity: An International Journal of Theory and Research, 12*(1), 1–7.

Syed, M., & Azmitia, M. (2008). A narrative approach to ethnic identity in emerging adulthood: Bringing life to the identity status model. *Developmental Psychology, 44*(4), 1012–1027. doi: http://dx.doi.org/10.1037/0012-1649.44.4.1012

von Eye, A., & Bogat, G. A. (2006). Person-oriented and variable-oriented research: Concepts, results, and development. *Merrill-Palmer Quarterly, 52*(3), 390–420.

PART 3

Debates: Narrative Perspectives on Processes of Identity Development

CHAPTER 10

Autobiographical Reasoning is Constitutive for Narrative Identity: The Role of the Life Story for Personal Continuity

Tilmann Habermas *and* Christin Köber

Abstract

Autobiographical reasoning relies on the life story format for linking distant parts of life with each other and with personal development. Taking the lead from Ricoeur's concept of narrative identity, the argument is developed that the emergence of the life story and the ability for autobiographical reasoning in adolescence adds a powerful tool for identity exploration and stabilization. Autobiographical reasoning especially helps explicitly bridge biographical disruptions by spelling out transformations and their motives. Weaker attempts to explain personal sameness in time or personal stability are reviewed and argued to be more limited than autobiographical reasoning in their ability to bridge personal change. Furthermore, the role of narrative as point of reference for autobiographical reasoning is highlighted, linking our concept to that of narrative identity as originally conceived. Finally, contextual and stylistic features of autobiographical reasoning are specified that render it beneficial for self-continuity and well-being.

Key Words: self-continuity, autobiographical reasoning, life story, well-being, identity claims, biographical ruptures, life transitions, life narratives, autobiographical arguments, psychosocial identity

The central contention of this chapter is that the life story format offers unique, explicit ways of establishing and re-establishing personal continuity. This is especially relevant in times of biographical upheaval and change. Once a change of identity is reflectively and explicitly integrated into the life story, simpler mechanisms of securing a sense of personal continuity will again do most of the work.

The epistemological self or I is present in the evaluating and reflecting voice of the narrator, whereas the empirical self or Me is the past, present, or future protagonist of the life story. The life story can represent different empirical selves in their temporal sequence, highlighting both thematic coherence, which stresses sameness across time, as well as causal-motivational coherence, which stresses change and development but still bridges the different self-states to form a continuous self.

We use the term "life story" as an overarching concept for the life as told, remembered, or thought about. There are two major manifestations of the life story: entire life narratives, which are linguistic products situated in time and social space, and autobiographical reasoning (AR). The term "autobiographical reasoning" designates a process of thinking or talking about the personal past that involves arguments that link distant elements of one's life to each other and to the self in an attempt to relate the present self to one's personal past and future. AR establishes a biographical perspective on events and oneself. This involves using the life as a frame of reference. In addition to hierarchically integrating events into static personality traits, more importantly, AR may also create a dynamic developmental story to link diverse events to the self (Habermas, 2011; Habermas & Bluck, 2000).

How can (life) narratives and (autobiographical) arguments both manifest the same representation—the life story schema (Bluck & Habermas, 2000)—given that arguments provide logical links between statements so that one statement supports the other, but narratives imitate sequences of events, typically introducing sentences with the phrases "and then..., and then..."? Narrative is the more encompassing text type because it contains not only narrative clauses, but also arguments, descriptions, and chronicles (summaries of events) (Labov & Waletzky, 1967). In life narratives, autobiographical arguments (i.e., arguments characteristic of AR) contribute to their global coherence. By global coherence we mean a characteristic of the entire text of a life narrative, which has different aspects such as temporal, causal-motivational, and thematic (Habermas & Bluck, 2000).

In the context of everyday storytelling, AR occurs when a specific life event is spontaneously placed in a biographical context. Therefore autobiographical arguments can be identified in naturally occurring texts such as diaries, web blogs, talk shows, or printed autobiographies. AR can also be elicited both by asking for narratives either of an entire life or of biographically significant single episodes, such as self-defining memories or turning points. Finally, AR may also be elicited by asking how personal continuity is created.

To make the point that AR is essential for the development of identity, specifically for bridging biographical disruptions to ensure self-continuity and thereby securing well-being, this chapter starts with Erikson's concept of psychosocial identity, relating a prereflective sense of identity to explicit AR about identity. We then summarize the philosophical argument that personal continuity requires the life story, establishing narrative identity. This will be contrasted with psychological positions that personal continuity is not necessary in a postmodern society and with positions that attempt to explain a sense of personal sameness in time by prereflective and nonbiographical mechanisms of memory, self-concept, social-environmental continuities, and situated identity performances. We then argue that, in adolescence, a new powerful tool for establishing and above all re-establishing personal continuity is acquired, the life story with its intertwined ability for AR. We first introduce Chandler's model of the development of arguments that establish personal continuity to complement them with other, more general autobiographical arguments. We specify why not only arguments, as suggested by Chandler, but also the life story as a narrative format is helpful in constructing personal continuity. Finally, we explore in which ways AR may be helpful for rather than detrimental to personal development by ensuring self-continuity as a basis for well-being.

Psychosocial Identity and Adolescence

The transition between childhood and adulthood requires taking on the responsibilities of an adult role in terms of gender and personal relationships, profession, and values. The commitment to and integration of the social aspect of identity are reflected in a subjective sense of identity, which is noticeable mostly when it is challenged. Erikson (1968) takes the description of this subjective sense of identity from clinical experience with states of identity diffusion and depersonalization (Federn, 1950). The subjective sense of identity is complemented by an explicit, objective view of one's identity resulting from social interaction and self-reflection. Identity-related self-reflection and exploration, most specifically AR, is activated when identity becomes problematic and needs to be revised and reintegrated.

We summarize Erikson's descriptions of psychosocial identity in six points. The first three aspects of identity require a balance, whereas the latter three tend to be healthier if one end of the dimension is achieved: (a) individuality versus belonging, (b) synchronous self-sameness versus flexible adaptation to situational requirements, (c) diachronic self-sameness versus change, (d) agency, (e) feeling at home in one's body, and (f) self-esteem. Identity diffusion is experienced as a cluster of (a) not belonging or being no-one special; (b) clumsily not adapting to situational demands, or of changing chameleon-like from situation to situation; (c) being frozen in time, as in depression, or as feeling disconnected from one's past self; (d) feeling helpless and controlled; (e) living in a strange body; and (f) being worthless.

Becoming able to construct a subjective life story in adolescence lends a diachronic dimension to the self-concept and therefore affects most the identity aspect of self-continuity. To achieve self-continuity, individuals need to find a balance between remaining the same and continuing to change and learn as they live their lives. Put in this general way, personal continuity is a lifelong task, especially at times when change is required, such as being confronted by developmental tasks or normative transitions or when change is imposed by others' actions, economic circumstances, or difficult life events.

Psychoanalysis suggests that identification is a basic mechanism that not only shapes identity, but also helps create personal continuity by linking values that motivate and direct life choices to the past. McAdams (2013) suggests a first developmental transition from mere traits and action tendencies to conscious intentions and medium-range goals in middle childhood. However, only adolescence brings the next developmental step that is decisive for identity. When becoming adults, individuals gain the autonomy and assume the responsibility necessary for making life choices, passing through a transitional phase of trying out identities. Thus, only in adolescence are children's prereflective identifications with parental values potentially questioned, critically reflected, refuted, or consciously reaffirmed. This timing is probably due both to the social attribution of responsibility as well as to the emerging social-cognitive ability to reflect on one's identity. This shows, for example, in the dawning of an awareness of one's physically defined identity in society as belonging to a specific race (Obama, 1995), being handicapped, or being extremely thin (Habermas, 1988). To sum up, the aspect of identity most affected by the advent of the life story is self-continuity.

Self-Continuity Through Narrative Identity

Here, we briefly introduce some philosophical arguments for a narrative conception of personal continuity (Thomä, 1998). These will then be compared with psychological positions and evidence that attempt to do without a narrative conception of self-continuity and with our and others' psychological evidence for a narrative conception of self-continuity.

Dilthey (1926, p. 200) assumes that life is lived with a direction that provides it with coherence. Therefore, when writing an autobiography, coherence does not have to be created out of chaos but can be based on the implicit coherence of the life lived by picking biographically salient events and explicating their relationships. Moreover, by looking back, unity in life is also created by valuing the present and looking ahead with a purpose in the mundane activity of reflecting on life (cf. Staudinger, 2001). Only MacIntyre (1981) explicitly links the unity of life to a narrative quality. He interprets life as a quest for the good life, and quests can be seen as the prototypical narrative plot (Propp, 1929). Therefore, he argues, we constantly narrate our life to ourselves, creating unity by orienting it toward an idea of the good life. This is ethically required because commitments made and debts assumed oblige the individual for the future.

Paul Ricoeur (1990, p. 246), in contrast, concedes to life as lived only a prenarrative quality, inasmuch as it is partly structured by the subject's actions. He distinguishes between concepts of personal identity as sameness versus self-sameness. The former is some form of substantial or formal identity, which is not necessary for the latter. Sameness requires something to remain the same, whereas self-sameness does not. Ricoeur (1992, p. 116) lists several possible ways to define sameness: numerical identity, qualitative sameness as extreme resemblance, developmental sameness as uninterrupted continuity, and relational sameness as permanence of an organization or Gestalt irrespective of the successive substitution of its parts. Character, as defined by lasting dispositions, appears to present an example of substantial sameness. However, character also has a history and may be based, for example, on identification with significant others of the past, thereby turning it into an example of developmental sameness. For Ricoeur, the prime instance of self-sameness is keeping one's word. Here, no substantial identity between the past self who gave the word and the present self who has to keep it is necessary. It is enough to have the morally binding obligation that bridges the temporal gap. Ricoeur introduces the concept of narrative identity as that which mediates the sameness of character and the self-sameness of the promise. Narrative links the permanence of character to the gap between the present narrator and the past protagonist, for whose actions the narrator is responsible. It is the nature of events and of their emplotment that they transform characters and link past to present self, character to narrator.

Thus, Ricoeur argues that whereas differing degrees of sameness can be constructed with different arguments, two discontinuities—the development of character and the gap between the actor and the responsible narrator—can only be bridged by life narration to create self-sameness, or, as we term it, self-continuity. Only the narrative transformations of emplotment, he argues, create self-continuity across character development and across the gap between protagonist and narrator. Before attempting to substantiate aspects of these philosophical claims with psychological evidence in the section on "Autobiographical Arguments and the Life Story Construct Self-Continuity across Change," we review some of the positions opposed to a narrative conception of self-continuity.

How Means Other than Narrative Support Sameness: Memory, Self-Concept, Relationships and Environment, and Identity Performances

A first line of arguments that attempt to explain the diachronic aspect of personal identity, reaching back to Locke (1634), derives a sense of personal sameness from the ability to remember. Along the same line, William James (1895, "I," p. 333) explained the sense of personal sameness in time by the reflecting I's judgment that remembered past selves possess a trace of that bodily "animal warmth" and familiarity that distinguishes the present Me from present Not-Me. A second line of arguments explains sameness by the assimilation of memories to the present self-concept. A third line of arguments ties sameness in time to continuities in the individual's relation to the environment. A fourth line places the establishment and maintenance of personal identity in local, situated identity performances, or even questions the necessity of diachronic identity at all. We now discuss each of these arguments in turn.

Remembering Establishes Personal Sameness in Time

For a long time, personal continuity played no role in the psychological theories of memory. Ebbinghaus (1885) rendered the experimental study of general laws of memory possible by decontextualizing remembering, counting the correct reproductions of meaningless syllables. The concept of episodic memory, originally invented to differentiate Ebbinghaus' kind of memory from knowledge, or semantic memory (Tulving, 1972), was later redefined (Tulving, 1983) by complementing what was being remembered (e.g., paired words) with the situational circumstances of a former experience and with the feeling of actually remembering and not imagining or simply knowing a past scene. Tulving (1985) characterized the immediate subjective experience of remembering a sequence of events that one had experienced as containing perceptual details and first-person experiences, like visual perspective, thoughts, and emotions. Remembering is metaphorically described as reliving (Wheeler, Stuss, & Tulving, 1997).

Tulving's concept of episodic memory implies, and Addis and Tippett (2008) spell this out, that a sense of personal sameness in time is created by remembering or imagining an event from a first-person perspective. However, the mere experience of remembering past experiences provides only a weak version of personal sameness in time for two reasons. First, the inclusion of a first-person perspective in remembering is not very reliable evidence of remembering a scene that the individual has personally experienced. Judgments of the source of one's memory rely not only on qualities inherent in the memory, but also on knowledge (Johnson, Hashtroudi, & Lindsay, 1993). For example, I might sometimes remember vividly and with detail accessible mainly from the first-person perspective a scene I have seen in the movies. Second, this kind of sense of personal sameness in time only regards the sameness of the cognizing I, but not of the person or Me. Elaborating their claim, Prebble, Addis, and Tippett (2013) limit the sameness in time rendered possible by remembering to the subjective sense of sameness (i.e., the identity of the remembering I with the former experiencing I), not the continuity of the reflected-upon, present Me with the remembered Me.

Prebble, Addis, and Tippett (2013) posit the ability to remember as an absolute precondition for a sense of continuity. They point to neurological patients who, together with losing personal memory, also lost knowledge of who they are. However, although the ability to remember past events may be a necessary precondition for a sense of continuity, it is not a sufficient condition. Even in the absence of neurological damage, individuals may feel as if memories did not reflect their own experiences. They may not feel that they were in the past experiencer's body, or they may not feel it was them who did what they remember. Such variations in the prereflective sense of Me-ness may regard both the body and the mind. If they regard the present self, they are termed self-estrangement or depersonalization. If they regard the past self, they constitute states of varying degrees of dissociation or simply a sense of personal discontinuity. This feeling of being disconnected with one's past self has been extensively described in the psychopathology literature. Erikson (1968) dealt with it as a symptom of identity diffusion, which Kernberg in turn (1984) used as a major criterion for borderline-level personality organization.

Memories are Compared to Stable Self-Concept to Create Self-Continuity

Thus, being able to remember does not necessarily entail a sense of self-continuity both because of other possible sources of first-person memories than actual personal experience and because of the unreliability of a subjective sense of personal continuity. There also needs to be some kind of similarity between the present and the remembered self.

Therefore William James located personal sameness in time not in the cognizing I, but in the remembered extended Me. It is a prereflective sense of familiarity and "animal warmth" evoked by a memory that leads the I to reidentify and appropriate the remembered experience as one's own (James, 1890, "I," p. 334). The core of this feeling is the constant perception at the fringe of consciousness of being alive in one's body. Thus, for James, in addition to the ability to remember at all, it is a prereflective awareness of sameness of the Me that is at the base of a sense of self-continuity.

Conway and Pleydell-Pearce (2000) suggest a more reflective comparison between past and present Me. Their model of autobiographical memory integrates a hierarchically nested autobiographical knowledge base with motivational states and personal goals. These select and also distort personal memories so as to render them consistent with personal goals and to thereby increase personal sameness in time. The stress on goals, however, leaves out the distortions of memories that enhance consistency with the present real and ideal self.

Therefore a revision of the model added a stable self-concept, termed "conceptual self," consisting of convictions about stable traits of the self, complementing the future-oriented personal goals (Conway, Singer, & Tagini, 2004). In the revised model, distortions of older memories serve to create consistency with the self-concept and to be consistent with stable motives (cf., Woike, 2008). Goal-related recent memories, in contrast, are freed from this bias so as to enable realistic actions for attaining goals. The added self-concept is a model component that describes what is assumed to be a constant in the individual's personality across time, thus accounting more realistically for a sense of personal continuity than did mere consistency with goals in the earlier model. The conceptual self is linked to self-defining memories (Moffitt & Singer, 1994) of situations that are typical of the central concerns and conflicts of the individual. These memories condense a variety of past events into one prototypical representation ("repisodic" memories [Neisser, 1981]; "nuclear scenes" [Tomkins, 1992]). They represent the highly stable core emotional and relationship patterns of an individual ("internal working model" [Bowlby, 1969]). They remain rather insensitive to situational requirements and new life experiences. This is what Pasupathi (this volume) terms tacit themes of narratives. In our life story model (Habermas & Bluck, 2000), these themes create thematic coherence in life by assimilating diverse experiences to central motives, both implicitly and explicitly.

In contrast to Tulving's assumption that remembering past events serves to establish personal sameness in time by the immediacy of the experience of reliving, Conway's model turns this relationship around, suggesting that the present self-concept biases remembering so as to increase self-continuity. Self-continuity is, thus, not provided by the identity of the remembering I, but by the perceived similarity of the present and past Me. However, the cost of this accomplishment is the necessity of downplaying and reducing actual differences and personal change.

Stability of Relations to Others and the Environment Safeguards Personal Continuity

Now, if the similarity of remembered self and present self-concept influences the sense of self-continuity, the actual stability of the individual in her or his context should also play a role. William James defined the empirical Me as comprising the spiritual, the social, and the material self. Thus, the stability of social relations and of the environment should contribute to a sense of self-continuity. Intimate relationships are at the core of personal continuity, which shows in the effects of the death of a loved one (Pennebaker, Mayne, & Francis, 1997). Developmentally, the basis for a subjective sense of continuity is a secure attachment to a stable (e.g., Smyke, Dumitrescu, & Zeanah, 2002) and sensitive parental figure, based on which internal working models are constructed that generalize early experiences with a caretaker to later relationships (Bowlby, 1969). Despite the internalization of stable relationships by the end of the first year of life, relationships remain a source of continuity throughout life, as is indicated by the negative effects of divorce on the development of attachment security in children (Beckwith, Cohen, & Hamilton, 1999; Cookston & Remy, this volume). Social roles and social identities also support a sense of subjective continuity. Again, this is most apparent at times of discontinuity, as during role transitions (e.g., retirement) or role loss (stroke; Haslam et al., 2008).

The stability of one's material basis, the body, and of the material environment is closely linked to the stability of social relations and also contributes to a sense of continuity. Feeling at home in one's body may be disrupted both by maturation and involuntary body modifications, such as the loss of body parts. Familiarity of place is an important buffer against separation anxiety in toddlers. Having a home (Smith, 1994) or community (Fried, 2000) remains a source of stability throughout adulthood. Place attachment and place identity are disrupted in relocations (e.g., when leaving the parental home, Chow & Healy, 2008).

Migration implies multiple discontinuities in terms of relationships, roles, place, and also linguistic and cultural environment. Socioterritorial transitions may be bridged collectively by rites of passage (van Gennep, 1910) or individually by an idealization of the past in terms of nostalgic longing (Sedikides, Wildschut, Arndt, & Routledge, 2008) or by taking along personal objects that serve as souvenirs (Habermas & Paha, 2002).

Social and material stability offers familiar surroundings, space for routine activities, and a secure foundation for exploring new environments and activities. The importance of stable others and environments translates psychologically into an attachment to or an identification with them. Whereas attachment requires the presence of its object, identification can do without it. Often, identifications result from identifying with a lost attachment object (Freud, 1923). If a sense of continuity is precarious because changes in the environment threaten it, identifications with specific others, groups, and values may stabilize it. Still, even a sense of continuity based on identifications in some instances depends on actually having a specific role or group of reference. Thus, a belief in the stability of a group one identifies with correlates with subjective well-being (Sani, Bowe, & Herrera, 2008). Similarly, attempts to create a collective past and future in native Canadian communities correlate with lower rates of suicides (Chandler, Lalonde, Sokol, Bryan, & Hallett, 2003).

Situated Narrative Performances Maintain or Establish Identity

Social relations and roles influence identity formation and maintenance at a relatively abstract level. Therefore, some authors ask which microgenetic mechanisms actually create and maintain identity in specific situations. Situated identity negotiations have been theorized by sociologists like Goffman (1959) and discourse analysts like Davies and Harré (1990). They stress the dramaturgical character of identity performances. Insofar as interactions are part of enduring relationships, they are essential for reinstating, reinterpreting, and reconfirming identities that are rooted in intimate relationships. Also, the more social aspects of identity require continuous confirmation and interpretation to remain alive. In this sense, identity performances are essential for maintaining self-continuity. More specifically, claiming identities by the way a story is told and by the depiction of the self in a story may contribute more to self-continuity because some stories of significant events tend to be retold again and again. McLean, Pasupathi, and Pals (2007) reviewed evidence of how stories are shaped by personality as well as by listeners (cf., Pasupathi, 2001; Pasupathi & Hoyt, 2009). They argue that stories that reflect stable self-aspects tend to be told more frequently.

Most situationist accounts of identity, however, lean toward a postmodern position that negates even the psychological and social necessity of self-continuity. Most radically, Kenneth Gergen (1991) criticizes concepts of an enduring personal identity and the construct of biography, confronting it with a concept of multiple situated identities. He argues that the belief in the life story as expressing a stable identity has historically given way to fleeting identifications and patchwork or pastiche identities that change with situational demands. This is supposedly due to society's recently increasing demand for lifelong flexibility on the job market, as well as in personal relationships.

In the narrative field, Michael Bamberg (2011) criticizes a life narrative approach as focusing solely on a crystallized, unambiguous version of a reflected past, missing the improvisational fluidity and interactional nature of everyday storytelling (see Korobov, this volume). Similarly, Antonino Ferro (2006) proposes a narrative model of psychoanalytic psychotherapy that focuses on the destabilizing moment of the analytic situation and the co-creation of new local narratives that are truer to the emotional experience of the dyad, thus opening up new ways of experiencing and understanding. Ferro discards the large biographical narrative as irrelevant to psychoanalysis. Thus, these situationist approaches do away with the necessity and reality of creating personal identity over time.

Limitations of these Approaches: Developmental and Other Challenges to Self-Continuity

The postmodern approaches just mentioned ignore the psychological necessity of self-continuity as evidenced by states of identity diffusion and identity disorders, by the devastating effects of dementia, and by the social psychological phenomena of enduring identification with roles and groups. They ignore the social necessity of being able to address others as continuous in order to be able to maintain relationships and a social order with actors who are responsible for their past actions.

The other approaches presented thus far do contribute to an understanding of how a sense of continuity is created and maintained. Many of them, however, require that the self does not, in fact, change. Mere remembering cannot bridge much of life change because memories tend to fade with time, as does the first-person perspective. The more remote the past self, the more likely it is described in terms of traits; that is, from an observer instead of an actor perspective (Pronin & Ross, 2006). Concordantly, a subjective field perspective gives way to a visual observer perspective the older personal memories grow (Nigro & Neisser, 1983). A visual observer perspective is also more frequent when remembering or imagining actions that are deemed atypical of the current self (Libby & Eibach, 2002) and probably even more so when questioning the validity of the specific motives or wanting to mitigate responsibility for an action. Thus, a first-person perspective that Tulving (2002) considers central for reliving the past, and Prebble, Addis, and Tippett (2013) consider the main source of a sense of self-continuity, tends to get lost with time and personal change.

Although assimilating memories to a current self-concept is more efficient than the mere phenomenal experience of remembering in bridging personal change simply by reducing the perception of change, it does not provide a mechanism to create self-continuity when change is acknowledged. The model of the autobiographical knowledge base, with its temporally and thematically defined nested structure, does permit placing memories in specific phases of life. But, again, what is not represented in the model is how the individual has changed and developed. If there is a conviction that one has changed, differences between past and present are even exaggerated in memories (Ross, 1989).

Stability of the body and the environment provide familiarity and a prereflective sense of personal sameness. Change in the body and in the environment, however, may lead to a sense of estrangement and discontinuity. Keepsakes, souvenirs, and telecommunication help bridge these disruptions. More forcefully, the mechanism of identification with the region one grew up in, one's family, and loved ones provides a strong psychological bridge to past relations and environments that have been lost.

However, not all change is a loss of significant others—change in the self, one's body, and personality cannot be bridged by identification.

Everyday stories may be repeated and may depict constant traits of the individual, but everyday storytelling by itself does not offer a mechanism for bridging personal change. One exception may be the sharing of memories of the distant past with friends, which may serve to reinforce a sense of self-continuity (e.g., Bluck, Alea, Rubin, & Habermas, 2005). Otherwise, to help bridge personal change, everyday storytelling does need a biographical perspective, a reference to the life story, as we will now argue.

Autobiographical Arguments and the Life Story Construct Self-Continuity Across Change

Adolescence is the one life phase—maybe together with very old age—in which individuals change the most and in which it is therefore most difficult to maintain a sense of personal continuity. Whereas children have an identity as children of their parents and define themselves by their looks, preferences, habits, and, beginning in early adolescence, character traits, adolescents take on the transitory identities of youth culture, to confront the question what kind of adult they want to become and what kind of life they want to lead. Primary emotional relationships change, as do occupation and often also the environment. Although foundations for adult identity are laid in late adolescence and postadolescence, more recently termed "emerging adulthood," modern societies require a continuing flexibility in terms of work identity and also of intimate relationships. Therefore adult identities also need to remain somewhat flexible to accommodate normative transitions and non-normative life events such as illness, separation, and loss of job.

Adolescents acquire a new cognitive-communicative ability, the life story format and the related ability for AR (Habermas & de Silveira, 2008; Köber, Schmiedek, & Habermas, 2014), which makes it easier to bridge discontinuities and integrate change into identity. We argue that under normal circumstances (i.e., in times of relative stability), the prereflective ways of establishing a sense of personal continuity discussed earlier suffice (if they are not undermined by primitive defense mechanisms in severe personality disorders or dissociative disorders). But in times of biographical change and rupture, a switch to the reflective mode of autobiographical reasoning may enable individuals to mend and bridge the breaks in their lives. Once this has been done and integrated into one's life story schema, the reflective mode is no longer necessary for maintaining a subjective sense of self-continuity.

We first present one form of AR that results in lay theories of personal change. We then add other autobiographical arguments that complement the development of a biographical perspective on life. Returning finally to Ricoeur, we argue that AR relies on narrative, more specifically on the life story format.

The Development of Lay Theories of Personal Continuity

Michael Chandler and colleagues have studied adolescents' reasoning about how it is possible to change over time and still remain the same person in Piagetian-style clinical interviews (Chandler, Lalonde, Sokol, & Hallett, 2003). They present biographical sketches of fictional characters and ask how the protagonists have changed, whether they are still the same person, and how that was possible. Also, participants are asked what they were like five years earlier, what they are like at present, how they have changed, and again how it is possible that they are still the same person. These questions aim to elicit the best arguments participants can provide to justify personal continuity despite change.

Chandler devised five developmental levels of increasingly adequate explanations of personal continuity, each level allowing for an essentialist and a narrativist version of the argument. Essentialist arguments assume some form of basic personal sameness in time, whereas narrativist arguments assume a sequence of diverse states related through transformations. Among the developmentally more refined ways of reasoning, level 3 sees personal development as following a predictable sequence of maturational steps, which either determine the changing surface of an unchanged core identity or which are causally related. At level 4, change is more individual, and continuity is found either in an abstract core trait or in the individual's quest for self-discovery. Level 5 offers a kind of epistemological uncertainty principle that one can never truly know, but only approximate, an individual's core or life line.

Chandler's theory is the only psychological work that has seriously grappled with the structure of reasoning about personal continuity. It was used with several hundred participants and has shown a clear cross-sectional correlation with age. Chandler offers a comprehensive view of lay philosophies of personal continuity. However, when narrating a life or constructing biographical coherence, the construction of personal continuity is usually less explicit and more partial. Therefore our analysis of textual means and single arguments complements Chandler's approach. Although the textual approach is more partial and formal, and therefore cannot offer the description of coherent philosophies, it does allow a more quantitative approach. Also, it does not depend on clinical interviews but can be applied to naturally occurring texts and to both oral and written monologues. We will take up Chandler's two strands of continuity claims, essentialist and narrativist, by distinguishing between claims of stability (i.e., sameness over time) and claims of continuity (i.e., a continuous sequence of transformations). Finally, we argue, with Ricoeur and against Chandler, for a specific advantage of narrative for bridging discontinuities.

Other Autobiographical Arguments and Their Contribution to Identity

AR involves arguments that refer to the life story as a frame of reference. Staudinger (2001) interpreted AR as the personal form of life reflection, the impersonal form of which she terms "general wisdom." In gerontology, the terms "life review" (Butler, 1963) and "integrative reminiscing" (Watt & Wong, 1991) denote a critical and evaluative look back on one's life that mostly involves AR.

The following nonexhaustive list of typical arguments used in AR draws mainly on Habermas and Paha (2001; cf. Habermas, 2011). Each of these arguments contributes to personal continuity by implying a concept of the whole life, either by stating sameness in time or bridging discontinuity. Habermas and Bluck (2000) introduced four major kinds of global coherence in life narratives: adherence to a cultural concept of biography (cf. Habermas, 2007), temporal, causal-motivational, and thematic coherence. In life narratives, autobiographical arguments tend to contribute to thematic coherence if they create similarity between different parts of life, thereby supporting sameness in time or stability. Autobiographical arguments tend to contribute to causal-motivational global coherence if they explain or motivate change, thereby contributing to self-continuity across change. Autobiographical arguments can be used within entire life narratives to contribute to their global coherence. They may be and mostly are used in other contexts, such as when narrating a specific biographically significant event. We first present arguments contributing to stability, then arguments contributing to personal continuity across change in the individual's personality and life, and finally arguments that create continuity across change in the individual's understanding of life.

ARGUMENTS CONTRIBUTING TO STABILITY

Thematic coherence is constructed hierarchically, by creating a higher level category that integrates more specific categories or instances. A major device in autobiographical narrations is *exemplification*. It mainly serves the rhetorical function of persuading the listener of a general claim by providing specific instances (Schütze, 1984), such as when a claimed aspect of one's personality is substantiated by an episode in which this trait is manifested. Also, evaluations of people ("he never really accepted me") or evaluations of extended time periods ("the first months at college were terrible") may be substantiated by exemplifications. In addition to lending depth and credibility to a biographical narrative, exemplifications also link specific events to more general statements covering extended periods of time, thereby creating stability across specific events.

A similar argument is used to *explain specific actions by the actor's personality*. Whereas exemplifications lead from a general claim to a specific instance, explanations of actions by personality follow from a specific action or reaction to general personality traits. Although individuals usually explain their own actions in terms of motives and goals, if an action appears to be problematic or a rational motive is not at hand, a trait may be adduced. This has the effect of assimilating a specific episode to a lasting personality trait, which potentially may also explain other actions at other times in life, thereby contributing to stability. Linde (1993) introduced this argument as one of two major ways of creating coherence in life narratives, the other being the reverse causal-motivational relation, which explains personality change with events (see later discussion). Pasupathi, Mansour, and Brubaker (2007) pointed to an interesting variation of the argument. Narrators may also deny that an action may be explained by a trait by stating that an action is atypical for the self, pointing to mitigating circumstances and to the exceptionality of the event. This *not me-event link* contributes to personal stability by discounting an event that does not fit the personality claimed by the narrator.

Another way to highlight stability in life is to state that an element of the narrated past event is still currently the same. Such a *past-present comparison* is used to relate the narrated story world to the present real time of narrator and listener. Still another way to construe stability in a life is to find *parallels between a specific episode and other episodes*. Thus, not infrequently, narrators state that a given kind of experience happened to them more than once or that it was a typical experience. In this case, it is not an abstract trait, but a class of episodes or pattern of experiences that is stable.

ARGUMENTS CONTRIBUTING TO CONTINUITY ACROSS CHANGE

The following biographical arguments create continuity not through sameness or stability but by bridging change. At a basic level, continuity may be created by referring to the *developmental status* of an individual in the normative course of development to explain her or his reaction, ability, or sensibility (McCabe, Capron, & Peterson, 1991), such as in "My parents' divorce didn't affect me much. I wasn't really aware of what was happening. I was still too little." This invokes a conception of the human lifespan.

In a more individual vein, specific experiences may be said to have had a *formative influence*. This kind of argument again helps to integrate a specific experience with the emergence of permanent aspects of personality. The discontinuity bridged here is a weak one because it is one between formlessness and being formed.

Whereas being formed by parents is part of the normative script of development, more individual influences of specific events on the development and change of personality can be formulated as *events causing personality change*, as in "After age 10, I became a shy person because the separation of my parents made me distrust others." Compared to explanations of actions by personality, here, the direction of causality is reversed (Linde, 1993), and the genuinely biographical argument is made that experience has shaped personality.

An experience may also have a more specific influence in creating a sensibility or motivation to react in a specific way in specific kinds of situations (Feldman, Bruner, Kalmar, & Renderer, 1993). This prototypical biographical argument is used to explain strange behaviors by reference to the *biographical background* of the individual, as in "When a car suddenly raced toward us, he panicked. He had been run over by a car when he was small."

Finally, events may also be causally related to long-term *biographical consequences*, such as changes in life circumstances, relationships, or later events. Mackavey, Malley, and Stewart (1991) identified events in written autobiographies that were explicitly named as biographically consequential, which most frequently came from early adulthood. A specific linguistic form to point out biographical consequences is a past-present comparison that states that something is different *ever since* a specified event happened.

ARGUMENTS CONTRIBUTING TO SAMENESS OR TO CONTINUITY ACROSS CHANGE IN THE NARRATOR'S SUBJECTIVE OUTLOOK

A subset of arguments regards the individual's knowledge and understanding, evaluations, and intentions. They may either state their sameness or their change across time. Here, we focus on the latter class of arguments. If the subjective outlook has changed, explaining the change by reference to an experience again creates continuity by bridging change.

A simple way for an event to change an individual's outlook is to provide new information. An *increase in knowledge* is often expressed negatively by stating that, at a specific point in life, one had not yet known something or by verbs like "finding out." Experiences in which an aspect of personality is revealed belong to this category if the assumption is that the aspect has always been there, just as the metaphor of "coming out" implies for homosexual orientation (cf., Pasupathi et al., 2007).

Other autobiographical arguments depict life as progressing not in terms of mere knowledge but of understanding. In *general insights,* the individual abstracts from a single experience to a general rule of how the world works, as in this insight of a 15-year-old: "I was really emotionally hooked up with him for a long time. Probably that's what always happens when it's the first kiss" (Bluck & Glück, 2004; McCabe et al., 1991; McLean & Thorne, 2003; Pratt, Norris, Arnold, & Filyer, 1999). *Personal insights* are provoked by specific experiences and regard the workings or depth of one's own (or another person's) personality or the validity of a higher value that should be adopted. This is the most consequential insight because it profoundly affects the view of oneself or one's basic values and therefore also the way one understands one's life story. For instance, a 20-year-old recounts that during puberty he totally withdrew into reading books, that only at age 16 did he realize he did this out of fear, and that he would not be able to develop as a person if he continued in this way. These insights are the hallmark of a life narrative or AR that aims at knowing oneself. Pasupathi termed these insights an "event-personality connection," in which an event *reveals* an aspect of one's personality (Pasupathi et al., 2007).

Finally, some autobiographical arguments depict life as progressing not in terms of knowledge or mere understanding, but also in terms of values that provide direction to life. In hindsight, experiences may motivate one to *re-evaluate an event* from bad to good or vice versa. This roughly corresponds to McAdams's (2006) redemption and contamination sequences. A still local, but more future-oriented change in outlook is brought about when the individual *learns a lesson*. An experience is related to a lasting understanding of a mechanisms and how to better deal with a specific future situation, as when a 12-year-old boy states "That's why I told myself, next time I fall in love, school work should not suffer from it." The most comprehensive autobiographical argument is a variant of personal insights; namely, when an experience leads to an *insight into higher values*. Such experiences are often constructed as turning points because they motivate rerouting life in a new direction.

These biographical arguments relating an experience to change in the subjective outlook imply an increase in understanding and insight. They help construct a life story as a continuous increase in knowledge and understanding of the world and the self. If the insights regard values, they even constitute the life story as one of moral improvement.

The Role of Narrative and the Life Story

Autobiographical arguments are more elementary than entire lay philosophies. To varying degrees, both help construct diachronic sameness or continuity across change. Essentialist lay philosophies may use autobiographical arguments that contribute to self-sameness or stability, whereas narrativist lay philosophies may use autobiographical arguments that contribute to self-continuity by bridging change in life and the self.

Arguments creating stability appear to support straightforward sameness; arguments supporting continuity support a kind of developmental sameness, in Ricoeur's sense. Arguments regarding change in the subjective outlook always involve the present narrator's relating to the past protagonist. To be accepted as responsible individuals by listeners, narrators are obliged to either endorse their past outlook or justify why they have changed their mind. This adds a moral quality to the empirically based continuity of character and therefore reminds us of Ricoeur's argument for the moral quality of what he termed self-sameness or what we term continuity. Although arguments used in life narratives do not neatly translate into Ricoeur's categories, they do reflect his distinctions.

Thus, in contrast to psychological approaches discussed before, the essentialist and narrativist lay philosophies and the corresponding autobiographical arguments can create personal sameness or continuity despite personal change. However, if autobiographical arguments suffice to create personal continuity across change, narrative might not be necessary and therefore loose talk of narrative identity may be misleading.

Three reasons indicate the indispensable role of the life story as narrative for maintaining personal continuity. First, autobiographical arguments use a concept of life, which is a temporally structured phenomenon that requires the narrative format to be put in words. Second, the second class of autobiographical arguments that bridge change is more potent in the face of massive personal change than is the first class, which always needs to find an ever more abstract concept for conceiving sameness. The second class of autobiographical arguments involves a concept of human development. Individual development again implies a narrative format because it is an ordered sequence of events. Ricoeur couches this argument in terms of the role of character in literary narrative or the novel, in which characters are transformed by emplotment (i.e., the narratively structured interplay of intentional actions with each other, with failure, and with chance). Third, autobiographical arguments involving the subjective outlook on life explain differences between present and past evaluations of life by reference to personal experiences. Thus, a change in outlook needs to be integrated into a story about how an event challenged the earlier evaluation. Again, this requires narrating the event that led to a revision of subjective outlook, contrasting earlier protagonist evaluations to later protagonist evaluations and finally also to the narrator's present evaluation. Evaluations, in turn, need to be justified by reference to values, which again may be justified by life experiences.

When and How Autobiographical Reasoning May Support Self-Continuity and Well-Being

Thus far, we have argued that the life story and its use in AR is the most potent instrument for creating personal continuity across change. In this final section, we discuss how specific contexts and forms of the actual use of AR may influence how effective AR is in securing self-continuity. Furthermore, since to date there are no studies of the relation between AR and a sense of self-continuity, we review evidence for the relation of AR to well-being. Based on the clinical literature (Kernberg, 1984), we expect an integrated identity and basic sense of self-continuity to form the necessary but not sufficient basis for well-being, although other measures such as the ability to tolerate ambivalence, a basic ability for empathy, and moral maturity to be closer correlates.

In the empirical narrative literature, the assumption prevails that well-being is related to and may be the result of a well-integrated and coherent life-story (e.g., Baerger & McAdams, 1999; Bauer & Bonanno, 2001; King, Scollon, Ramsay, & Williams, 2000; Lilgendahl & McAdams, 2011). However, recently, this has been called into question (McLean & Mansfield, 2011). Sales, Merrill, and Fivush (2013), for example, found a substantial positive correlation between learning a lesson and insights and depressiveness in 16- to 21-year-olds' narratives of worst-ever experiences. We will discuss under which life circumstances, at which ages, and which forms of AR may contribute to personal continuity and well-being.

Life Circumstances and Nature of Events Processed

If life circumstances are fairly stable and little maturation and psychological change is taking place in an individual's life, the mechanisms offered by other psychological approaches will probably suffice to safeguard a basic sense of self-continuity. Only when life or the individual changes drastically do these basic mechanisms no longer suffice, and a sense of personal discontinuity may threaten the individual's sense of identity. It is under these circumstances that switching to a reflective, explicit consideration of biographical ruptures through AR may compensate an impending loss of a sense of self-continuity. Once a rupture has been integrated into the life story schema in some benevolent way that protects one's self-esteem, explicit reasoning will no longer be necessary.

Most studies of coping deal not with bridging biographical disruptions but with strategies of eliminating the threat to continuity, buffering the effects by drawing on additional resources, compensating for the effects, and reducing the perception of the threat or by changing its evaluation (e.g.,

Zimbardo, 1999). Studies that do analyze strategies for maintaining or reestablishing continuity across severely disruptive life events without denying the discontinuity usually do imply the life story. The search for meaning after disruptive life events (e.g., Silver, Boon, & Stones, 1983) implies trying to integrate them into the wider web of one's life. Studies that explicitly look for strategies for bridging discontinuity (e.g., Klauer, Ferring, & Filipp, 1998) most often discuss narrative strategies to bridge biographical disruptions (Bury, 1982), such as losing one's partner (Bauer & Bonanno, 2001), losing work through retirement (Nuttman-Shwartz, 2008), or losing one's autonomy through a stroke (e.g., Hinojosa, Boylstein, Rittman, Hinojosa, & Faircloth, 2008).

Thus, individuals probably engage most in AR in times of biographical rupture or transitions. Therefore it is also in these times that AR is probably the most functional in contributing to self-continuity and, through this, also to well-being. In times of personal stability, there will be less motivation to spontaneously engage in AR because a subjective sense of self-continuity is sufficiently provided by the nonreflective mechanisms discussed earlier in the section on other than narrative supports of sameness. This is supported by a study of 18-year-olds. Among the respondents who could report a turning-point experience in their lives, those who said they had learned a lesson or gained an insight from that experience improved in well-being over the previous 3 years (Tavernier & Willoughby, 2012). The evidence remains indirect because it made no difference how long before a turning point had been experienced. Other indirect evidence for the relevance of AR in times of change is that although developmental embedding of low-point experiences was not related to life satisfaction (Chen, McAnally, Wang, & Reese, 2012), developmental embedding of turning-point experiences through AR was (Chen, 2011). Both studies also suggest that even if a biographical rupture has long passed, when asked to narrate it, the narrative bridging of biographical discontinuity by AR nevertheless still makes a difference for well-being.

Disruptive biographical transitions need not be negative. However, negative events usually tend to be more disruptive than positive events. Therefore negative events evoke more cognitive efforts at processing and narrating them. For positive life events, there is neither a need for explications nor for bridges with the narrator's personality. Indeed, reasoning about positive events can even reduce well-being (Lyubomirsky, Sousa, & Dickerhoof, 2006). Although positive life events are often results of enduring personal strivings and for that reason conform to one's personality, negative events are unforeseeable, unexpected, and therefore additionally stressful and challenging. Accordingly, in an adult sample, AR correlated positively with well-being only if concerning negative, but not positive events (Lilgendahl & McAdams, 2011; see the section following the next one).

Age

Some negative or null-correlations between autobiographical reasoning and well-being were observed in several studies in early to mid-adolescence. For instance, in a study of boys' (aged 11 to 18) written low-, high-, and turning-point narratives, McLean, Breen, and Fournier (2010) found a negative correlation of learning lessons and gaining insights in younger boys and no relation in the older boys. However, the presence of another autobiographical argument, explanations of personality change by events, did correlate with positive well-being in all age groups. In the study by Chen (2011; Chen et al., 2012), the relation between developmental embedding of turning-point narratives to life satisfaction was qualified by age, such that, in younger adolescents, the relation was negative, but in older adolescents positive. A study with an adult lifespan sample showed a positive correlation between AR and well-being. The correlation held even when event valence, personality, and social class were controlled (Lilgendahl & McAdams, 2011). However, in this study, AR was operationalized as any causally linked statement about self-growth, which means it was a selection of statements with positive implications about the self and therefore did not cover all of AR.

Therefore, it seems that AR only begins to become helpful in terms of well-being in the course of adolescence. This coincides with the acquisition of the ability for AR, which emerges in middle to late adolescence (Bohn & Berntsen, 2008; Habermas & de Silveira, 2008; Habermas & Paha, 2001), possibly suggesting that successful autobiographical reasoning requires a mature competence for AR.

Valence, Form, and Spontaneous Frequency

We have defined AR formally, abstracting from its content as well as from the way it is put into practice. McLean and Mansfield (2010) point out that sometimes repressing or consciously denying challenging events to protect and maintain positive self-perception might work better than AR. It is certainly possible that the repression and avoidance of very hurtful emotions have some gain (Coifman, Bonanno, Ray, & Gross, 2007), especially immediately following a severely negative, traumatizing event. But because negative events are unavoidable, the life story perspective and especially the need to maintain self-continuity suggest that, in the long run, avoidance of processing and biographically integrating negative life events may come at a cost.

However, difficult life events are double-edged swords that work both ways, either to damage and weaken the self or to motivate self-growth (Boals & Schuettler, 2010). The mere centrality of negative events to the life story is negatively related to well-being (Berntsen & Rubin, 2007). Thus, AR needs to be used to integrate turning points or negative life events into the life story in such a way that the consequences and final evaluation are positive. McAdams's (2006) redemption sequence describes in a general way the positive integration of negative events into the life story. Thus, in the study by Jennifer Pals Lilgendahl and Dan McAdams (2011), a second predictor of well-being in addition to (positively valenced) AR was if negative events had positive effects on the narrator's personal development. Earlier, Lilgendahl had demonstrated that women who narrated their most difficult and identity-challenging experiences in a pattern of coherent positive resolutions exhibited an increase of ego-resiliency from early adulthood to midlife, which later led to higher life satisfaction at age 61 (Pals, 2006a, 2006b).

Similarly, Banks and Salmon (2013) found in young adults that for low-point narratives the direction of the relation between depressiveness and AR (explanations linking events and personality) depends on the valence of the involved self-aspects. AR buffers negative effects of biographically salient negative life events if it succeeds in finding that positive traits helped manage the event or that they developed out of the negative experience.

This finding can be nicely linked to the depressive explanatory style in which negative events are explained by one's own traits, and positive events are explained by reference to external factors. The use of this particular reasoning style in autobiographical narratives correlated with depressiveness in a nonclinical adult sample (Adler, Kissel, & McAdams, 2006), and, despite comparable overall proportions of AR, was more frequent in life narratives of clinically depressed adult inpatients compared to matched controls (Habermas, Ott, Schubert, Schneider, & Pate, 2008). Depressed patients also produced less linear, less narrative memory reports, creating a sense of a life that is so stable that it seems to have come to a stop.

Ruminative thinking is a central symptom of clinical depression. *Rumination* is obsessive thinking about negative aspects of one's life in a repetitive, circular way. Typically, it involves relating negative events and self-aspects to one's character and actions. Thus, formally, some ruminative thinking may count as AR. This showed in studies with early adolescents. The self-reported frequency of problem talk with a best friend correlated with depressiveness, and extensive, repetitive, and speculative problem talk led to social contagion of depressiveness (Schwarz-Mette & Rose, 2012).

The obsessive and repetitive quality of monological and dialogical rumination indicates that for AR to be helpful both for bridging biographical disruptions and for maintaining well-being it needs to be used in specific ways. First, AR may be more helpful if individuals choose to use it voluntarily and for limited time periods. The mere amount of AR in response to life narrative tasks provides information neither about the voluntariness nor the frequency of AR in everyday life. Second, repetitiveness and circularity are characteristics that suggest that reasoning lacks a narrative quality because narrative requires a linear imitation of temporal sequences. This quality can best be measured by analyzing actual thought processes or narrative transcripts, not with self-reported frequencies. Third, linear, progressing reasoning is easier if it analyzes specific events and not generalizations. Raes and colleagues (2006) found that reduced autobiographical memory, which is a typical symptom in major depressive disorder, is mediated by rumination. Depressed patients tend to get lost in a too vast generalization of negative events.

To sum up, we have argued that AR is an exquisite instrument for maintaining a sense of self-continuity in situations of biographical disruption by bridging this disruption. Once the new view of one's biography becomes part of the life story schema, self-continuity is re-established and explicit AR is no longer required. This is compatible with possible conditions for beneficial effects or correlations of AR that our interpretation of the scarce research literature suggests: to be beneficial, AR may require a mature competence for AR; a voluntary and limited use; a linear, narrative quality; its use for understanding specific events; and a use that results in some kind of positive resolution.

Conclusion

In the preceding section, we discussed evidence for the relation of AR to well-being because its relation to self-continuity has not yet been studied. However, we argue that voluntary, temporally limited, linear AR regarding specific events and resulting in a positive retrospective (and therefore also prospective) evaluation maintains a sense of self-continuity, especially in situations in which it is threatened by abrupt life change. Thus, discontinuity in life may require autobiographical reasoning by oneself and with friends or therapists as a temporary measure to establish some explicit and positive form of self-continuity. Once the crisis or transition has passed, the activity of AR is no longer necessary because subjective self-continuity has been re-established. However, it seems that the result of this reflective activity of self-interpretation settles in the autobiographical knowledge base (Conway, Singer, & Tagini, 2004) at the level of the life story schema (Bluck & Habermas, 2000), so that later it can be readily retrieved when telling a life narrative or when biographically embedding important life events. This technique of compensating threats of self-discontinuity, we have argued, is more potent than the other more basic mechanisms that have been suggested by psychology to date because these presuppose the absence of change to varying degrees.

The relation of a sense of self-continuity to well-being, then, probably is not a straightforward one. Clinically speaking, a basic sense of self-continuity is a necessary precondition for feeling well, but not a sufficient one. Autobiographical reasoning may also contribute to other aspects of social identity, again as a precondition for well-being. A kind of reasoning that leads to positive re-evaluations of past negative events bolsters self-esteem and optimism. Autobiographical narrating and reasoning that is not contradictory but plausible supports self-consistency and self-continuity (Kernberg, 1984). And autobiographical narrating and reasoning that expresses the individual's agency (Adler, 2012) and responsibility without denying the limiting role of chance and powerful others (de Silveira & Habermas, 2011) supports a sense of being able to influence the path one's life is taking.

Finally, we acknowledge that our account has focussed on cognitive aspects of the autobiographical self-construction. We have only mentioned in passing the essential active role of others for the construction of a biography. Culture provides structure to autobiographies by providing a cultural concept of biography both with conventions of how to narrate a life and via a basic grid of normative life transitions that mark identity transformations (Habermas & Bluck, 2000), termed a "life script" by Berntsen and Rubin (2004). Institutional and informal social demands, such as doctor's appointments and job interviews, motivate individuals to engage in autobiographical self-construction. Also, intimate others shape the individual's life story not only by playing an essential part in life, but also by offering, repudiating, and validating identity attributions and biographical interpretations. In parent–child co-narrations of the children's lives, parents have the epistemological advantage of being able to tell the child's beginnings and to found character attributions on this privileged knowledge. Therefore parents' stories and attributions tend to become part of their offspring's life stories, if they do not explicitly repudiate them (Habermas, Negele, & Brenneisen Mayer, 2010; Zaman & Fivush, 2013).

Conversely, we found in these co-narrations that adolescents have a moral advantage over their parents when telling their lives because they can blame them for most of what was to their disadvantage during their childhood (Habermas et al., 2010). This observation points to the moral aspect of self-continuity as provided by the life story. Narrating one's life basically requires assuming responsibility for one's past (Schafer, 1983). It also requires narrating the past in such a way that others who were part of it find themselves being treated respectfully and recognize sufficient resemblance to their own version of the past. However, doing justice to the social and moral aspects of self-continuity through the life story requires more than this chapter can offer.

References

Addis, D. R., & Tippett, L. J. (2008). The contributions of autobiographical memory to the content and continuity of identity: A social-cognitive neuroscience approach. In F. Sani (Ed.), *Self-continuity: Individual and collective perspectives* (pp. 71–86). New York: Psychology Press.

Adler, J. M. (2012). Living into the story: Agency and coherence in a longitudinal study of narrative identity development and mental health over the course of psychotherapy. *Journal of Personality and Social Psychology, 102*, 367–389.

Adler, J. M., Kissel, E. C., & McAdams, D. P. (2006). Emerging from the CAVE: Attributional style and the narrative study of identity in midlife adults. *Cognitive Therapy and Research, 30*, 39–51.

Baerger, D. R., & McAdams, D. P. (1999). Life story coherence and its relation to psychological well-being. *Narrative Inquiry, 9*, 69–96.

Bamberg, M. (2011). Who am I? Narration and its contribution to self and identity. *Theory & Psychology, 21*, 3–24.

Banks. M. V., & Salmon, K. (2013). Reasoning about the self in positive and negative ways: Relationship to psychological functioning in young adulthood. *Memory, 21*, 10–26.

Bauer, J. J., & Bonanno, G. A. (2001). Continuity and discontinuity: Bridging one's past and present in stories of conjugal bereavement. *Narrative Inquiry, 11*, 123–158.

Beckwith, L., Cohen, S. E., & Hamilton, C. E. (1999). Maternal sensitivity during infancy and subsequent life events relate to attachment representation at early adulthood. *Developmental Psychology, 35*, 693–700.

Berntsen, D., & Rubin, D. C. (2004). Cultural life scripts structure recall from autobiographical memory. *Memory & Cognition, 32*, 427–442.

Berntsen, D., & Rubin, D. C. (2007). When a trauma becomes key to identity: Enhanced integration of trauma memories predicts posttraumatic stress disorder. *Applied Cognitive Psychology, 21*, 417–431.

Bluck, S., Alea, N., Habermas, T., & Rubin, D. C. (2005). A TALE of three functions: the self-reported uses of autobiographical memory. *Social Cognition, 23*, 91–117.

Bluck, S., & Glück, J. (2004). Making things better and learning a lesson: Experiencing wisdom across the lifespan. *Journal of Personality, 72*, 543–572.

Bluck, S., & Habermas, T. (2000). The life story schema. *Motivation & Emotion, 24*, 121–147.

Boals, A., & Schuettler, D. (2010). A double-edged sword: Event centrality, PTSD, and posttraumatic growth. *Applied Cognitive Psychology, 25* (5), 817–822.

Bohn, A., & Berntsen, D. (2008). Life story development in childhood. *Developmental Psychology, 44*, 1135–1142.

Bowlby, J. (1969). *Attachment*. London: Hogarth Press.

Bury M. (1982). Chronic illness as biographical disruption. *Sociology of Health and Illness, 4*, 167–182.

Butler, R. (1963). The life-review. *Psychiatry, 26*, 65–76.

Chandler, M. J., Lalonde, C. E., Sokol, B. W., & Hallett, C. (2003). Personal persistence, identity development, and suicide. *Monographs of the Society for Research in Child Development, 68* (2, series No. 273).

Chen, Y. (2011). Narrative identity and well-being from middle childhood to late adolescence: A developmental, cross-cultural perspective (Doctoral dissertation). University of Otago, NZ.

Chen, Y., McAnally, H. M., Wang, Q., & Reese, E. (2012). The coherence of critical event narratives and adolescents' psychological functioning. *Memory, 20*, 667–681.

Chow, K., & Healey, M. (2008). Place attachment and place identity: First-year undergraduates making the transition from home to university. *Journal of Environmental Psychology, 28*, 362–372.

Coifman, K. G., Bonanno, G. A., Ray, R. D., & Gross, J. J. (2007). Does repressive coping promote resilience? Affective-autonomic response discrepancy during bereavement. *Journal of Personality and Social Psychology, 92*, 745–758.

Conway, M. A., & Pleydell-Pearce, C. W. (2000). The construction of autobiographical memories in the self-memory system. *Psychological Review, 107*, 261–288.

Conway, M. A., Singer, J. A., & Tagini, A. (2004). The self and autobiographical memory: Correspondence and coherence. *Social Cognition, 22*, 491–529.

Davies, B., & Harré, R. (1990). "Positioning": The social construction of selves. *Journal for the Theory of Social Behaviour, 20*, 43–64.

De Silveira, C., & Habermas, T. (2011). Narrative means to manage responsibility in life narratives across adolescence. *Journal of Genetic Psychology, 172*, 1–20.

Dilthey, W. (1926). *Der Aufbau der geschichtlichen Welt in den Geisteswissenschaften. Gesammelte Schriften, Volume VII*. Göttingen: Vandenhoeck & Ruprecht.

Ebbinghaus, H. (1885). *Über das Gedächtnis: Untersuchungen zur experimentellen Psychologie [On memory: Studies in experimental psychology]*. Darmstadt: Wissenschaftliche Buchgesellschaft, 1992.

Erikson, E. H. (1968). *Identity, youth, and crisis*. New York: Norton.

Federn, P. (1950). *Ego psychology and the psychoses*. New York: International Universities Press.

Feldman, C., Bruner, J., Kalmar, D., & Renderer, B. (1993). Plot, plight, and dramatism: Interpretation at three ages. *Human Development, 36*, 327–342.

Ferro, A. (2006). *Psychoanalysis as therapy and storytelling*. London: Routledge.

Freud, S. (1923). The Ego and the Id. In S. Freud (Ed., 1953), *Standard edition, vol. 19* (pp. 1–66). London: Hogarth.

Fried, M. (2000). Continuities and discontinuities of place. *Journal of Environmental Psychology, 20*, 193–205.

Gergen, K. J. (1991). *The saturated self*. New York: Basic Books.

Goffman, E. (1959). *The presentation of self in everyday life*. New York: Anchor.

Habermas, T. (1988). Die Entwicklung sozialen Urteilens bei jugendlichen Magersüchtigen [Development of social reasoning in young anorectics]. *Acta Paedo-psychiatrica, 51*, 147–155.

Habermas, T. (2007). How to tell a life: The development of the cultural concept of biography across the lifespan. *Journal of Cognition and Development, 8*, 1–31.

Habermas, T. (2011). Autobiographical reasoning: Mechanisms and functions. In T. Habermas (Ed.), *The development of autobiographical reasoning in adolescence and beyond. New Directions for Child and Adolescent Development* (131, 1–17).

Habermas, T., & Bluck, S. (2000). Getting a life: The development of the life story in adolescence. *Psychological Bulletin, 126*, 748–769.

Habermas, T., & de Silveira, C. (2008). The development of global coherence in life narratives across adolescence: Temporal, causal, and thematic aspects. *Developmental Psychology, 44*, 707–721.

Habermas, T., & Paha, C. (2001). The development of coherence in adolescents' life narratives. *Narrative Inquiry, 11*, 35–54.

Habermas, T., & Paha, C. (2002). Souvenirs and other personal objects. In J. D. Webster & B. K. Haight (Eds.), *Critical advances in reminiscent work: From theory to application* (pp. 123–139). New York: Springer.

Habermas, T., Negele, A., & Brenneisen Mayer, F. (2010). „Honey, you're jumping about"—Mothers' scaffolding of their children's and adolescents' life narration. *Cognitive Development, 25*, 339–351.

Habermas, T., Ott, L. M., Schubert, M., Schneider, B., & Pate, A. (2008). Stuck in the past: Negative bias, explanatory style, temporal order, and evaluative perspectives in life narratives of clinically depressed individuals. *Depression and Anxiety, 25*, E121–E132.

Haslam, C, Holme, A., Haslam, S. A., Iyer, A., Jetten, J., & Williams, W. H. (2008). Maintaining group memberships: Social identity continuity predicts well-being after stroke. *Neuropsychological Rehabilitation, 18*, 671–691.

Hinojosa, R., Boylstein, C., Rittman, M., Hinojosa, M. S., & Faircloth, C. A. (2008). Constructions of continuity after a stroke. *Symbolic Interaction, 31*, 205–224.

James, W. (1890). *Principles of psychology.* New York: Dover.

Johnson, M. K., Hashtroudi, S., & Lindsay, D. S. (1993). Source monitoring. *Psychological Bulletin, 114*, 3–28.

Kernberg, O. F. (1984). *Severe personality disorders.* New Haven, CT: Yale University Press.

King, L. A., Scollon, C. K., Ramsey, C., & Williams, T. (2000). Stories of life transition: Subjective well-being and ego development in parents of children with Down Syndrome. *Journal of Research in Personality, 34*, 509–536.

Klauer, T., Ferring, D., & Filipp, S.-H. (1998). "Still stable after all this...?" Temporal comparison in coping with severe and chronic disease. *International Journal of Behavioral Development, 22*, 339–355.

Köber, C., Schmiedek, F., & Habermas, T. (2014). Characterizing lifespan development of three aspects of coherence in life narratives: A cohort-sequential study. Manuscript submitted for publication.

Labov, W., & Waletzky, J. (1967). Narrative analysis: Oral versions of personal experience. In I. Helm (Ed.), *Essays on the verbal and visual arts: Proceedings of the 1966 Annual Spring Meeting of the American Ethnological Society* (pp. 12–44). Seattle: University of Washington Press.

Libby, L. K., & Eibach, R. P. (2002). Looking back in time: Self-concept change affects visual perspective in autobiographical memory. *Journal of Personality and Social Psychology, 82*, 167–179.

Lilgendahl, J. P., & McAdams, D. P. (2011). Constructing stories of self-growth: How individual differences in patterns of autobiographical reasoning relate to well-being in midlife. *Journal of Personality, 79*, 391–428.

Linde, C. (1993). *Life stories.* Oxford, UK: Oxford University Press.

Locke, J. (1634). *Essay concerning human understanding.* Oxford, UK: Oxford University Press.

Lyubomirsky, S., Sousa, L., & Dickerhoof, R. (2006). The costs and benefits of writing, talking, and thinking about life's triumphs and defeats. *Journal of Personality and Social Psychology, 90*, 692–708.

MacIntyre, A. (1981). *After virtue.* London: Bloomsbury.

Mackavey, W. R., Malley, J., & Stewart, A. J. (1991). Remembering autobiographically consequential experiences. *Psychology and Aging, 6*, 50–59.

McAdams, D. P. (2006). *The redemptive self.* Oxford: Oxford University Press.

McAdams, D. P. (2013). The psychological self as actor, agent, and author. *Perspectives on Psychological Science, 8*, 272–293.

McCabe, A., Capron, E., & Peterson, C. (1991). The voice of experience: The recall of early childhood and adolescent memories by young adults. In C. Peterson (Ed.), *Developing narrative structure* (pp. 137–173). Mahwah, NJ: Erlbaum.

McLean, K. C., Breen, A. V., & Fournier, M. A. (2010). Constructing the self in early, midlife and late adolescent boys. *Journal of Research on Adolescence, 20*, 166–187.

McLean, K. C., & Mansfield, C. D. (2011). To reason or not to reason: Is autobiographical reasoning always beneficial? In T. Habermas (Ed.), *The development of AR in adolescence and beyond. New Directions for Child and Adolescent Development* (131,85–97).

McLean, K. C., Pasupathi, M., & Pals, J. L. (2007). Selves creating stories creating selves. *Personality and Social Psychology Review, 11*, 262–278.

McLean, K. C., & Thorne, A. (2003). Late adolescents' self defining memories about relationships. *Developmental Psychology, 30*, 635–645.

Moffitt, K. H., & Singer, J. A. (1994). Continuity in the life story: Self-defining memories, affect, and approach/avoidance personal strivings. *Journal of Personality, 62*, 21–43.

Neisser, U. (1981). John Dean's memory: A case study. *Cognition, 9*, 1–22.

Nigro, G., & Neisser, U. (1983). Point of view in personal memories. *Cognitive Psychology, 15*, 467–485.

Nuttmann-Shwartz, O. (2008). Bridging the gap: The creation of continuity by men on the verge of retirement. *Ageing and Society, 28*, 185–202.

Obama, B. (1995). *Dreams from my father.* New York: Times Books.

Pals, J. L. (2006a). Constructing the "springboard effect": Causal connections, self-making, and growth within the life story. In D. P. McAdams, R. Josselson, & A. Lieblich (Eds.), *Identity and story* (pp. 175–199). Washington, DC: American Psychological Association.

Pals, J. L. (2006b). Narrative identity processing of difficult life experiences: Path-ways of personality development and positive self-transformation in adult-hood. *Journal of Personality, 74*, 1079–1110.

Pasupathi, M. (2001). The social construction of the personal past and its implications for adult development. *Psychological Bulletin, 127*, 651–672.

Pasupathi, M., & Hoyt, T. (2009). The development of narrative identity in late adolescence and emergent adulthood. *Developmental Psychology, 45*, 558–574.

Pasupathi, M., Mansour, E., & Brubaker, J. R. (2007). Developing a life story: Constructing relations between self and experience in autobiographical narratives. *Human Development, 50*, 85–110.

Pennebaker, J. W., Mayne, T. J., & Francis, M. E. (1997). Linguistic predictors of adaptive bereavement. *Journal of Personality and Social Psychology, 72*, 863–871.

Pratt, M. W., Norris, J. E., Arnold, M. L., & Filyer, R. (1999). Generativity and moral development as predictors of value socialization narratives for young persons across the adult life span: From lessons learned to stories shared. *Psychology and Aging, 14*, 414–426.

Prebble, S. C., Addis, D. R., & Tippett, L. J. (2013). Autobiographical memory and the self. *Psychological Bulletin, 139*, 815–840.

Pronin, E., & Ross, L. (2006). Temporal differences in trait self-ascription: When the self is seen as an other. *Journal of Personality and Social Psychology, 90*, 197–209.

Propp, V. (1929/1968). *Morphology of the folktale.* Austin: University of Texas Press.

Raes, F., Hermans, D., Williams, J. M. G., Beyers, W., Brunfaut, E., & Eelen, P. (2006). Reduced autobiographical memory specificity and rumination in predicting the course of depression. *Journal of Abnormal Psychology, 115*, 699–704.

Ricoeur, P. (1990). *Time and narrative, Vol. 3.* Chicago: University of Chicago Press.

Ricoeur, P. (1992). *Oneself as another.* Chicago: University of Chicago Press.

Ross, M. (1989). Relation of implicit theories to the construction of personal histories. *Psychological Review, 96*, 341–357.

Sales, J. M., Merrill, N. A., & Fivush, R. (2013). Does making meaning make it better? Narrative meaning making and well-being in at-risk African-American adolescent females. *Memory, 21*, 97–110.

Sani, F., Bowe, M., & Herrera, M. (2008). Perceived collective continuity and social well-being. *European Journal of Social Psychology, 38*, 365–374.

Schafer, R. (1983). *The analytic attitude*. New York: Basic Books.

Schütze, F. (1984). Kognitive Figuren des autobiographischen Stegreiferzählens [Cognitive structures of improvised personal narratives]. In M. Kohli & G. Robert (Eds.), *Biographie und soziale Wirklichkeit* (pp. 78–118). Stuttgart, Germany: Metzler.

Schwartz-Mette, R. A., & Rose, A. (2012). Co-rumination mediates contagion of internalizing symptoms within youth's friendships. *Developmental Psychology, 48*, 1355–1365.

Sedikides, C. Wildschut, T., Arndt, J., & Routledge, C. (2008). Nostalgia: Past, present, future. *Current Directions in Psychological Science, 17*, 304–3007.

Silver, R. L., Boon, C., & Stones, M. H. (1983). Searching for meaning in misfortune: Making sense of incest. *Journal of Social Issues, 39*, 81–102.

Smith, S. G. (1994). The essential qualities of a home. *Journal of Environmental Psychology, 14*, 31–46.

Smyke, A. T., Dumitrescu, A., & Zeanah, C. H. (2002). Attachment disturbances in young children. *Journal of the American Academy of Child and Adolescent Psychiatry, 141*, 972–982.

Staudinger, U. (2001). Life reflection. *Review of General Psychology, 5*, 148–160.

Tavernier, R., & Willoughby, T. (2012). Adolescent turning points: The association between meaning-making and psychological well-being. *Developmental Psychology, 48*, 1059–1068.

Thomä, D. (1998). *Erzähle dich selbst* [*Narrate yourself*]. München: Beck.

Tomkins, S. S. (1992). *Affect, imagery, and consciousness, vol. IV: Cognition: Duplication and transformations of informations*. New York: Springer.

Tulving, E. (1972). Episodic and semantic memory. In E. Tulving & W. Donaldson (Eds.), *Organization of memory* (pp. 381–403). New Haven, CT: Yale University Press.

Tulving, E. (1983). *Elements of Episodic Memory*. Oxford: Clarendon.

Tulving, E. (1985). *Memory and consciousness*. *Canadian Psychology, 26*, 1–12.

Tulving, E. (2002). Episodic memory. *Annual Review of Psychology, 53*, 1–25.

Van Gennep, A. (1910/2010). *Rites of passage*. London: Routledge.

Watt, L. M., & Wong, T. P. (1991). The taxonomy of reminiscence and therapeutic implications. *Journal of Gerontological Social Work, 16*, 37–57.

Wheeler, M. A., Stuss, D. T., & Tulving, E. (1997). Toward a theory of episodic memory: The frontal lobe and autonoetic consciousness. *Psychological Bulletin, 121*, 331–354.

Woike, B. (2008). A functional framework for the influence of implicit and explicit motives on autobiographical memory. *Personality and Social Psychology Review, 12*, 99–117.

Zaman, W., & Fivush, R. (2013). Stories of parents and self: Relations to attachment. *Developmental Psychology, 49*, 2047–2056.

Zimbardo, P. G. (1999). Discontinuity theory. *Advances in Experimental Social Psychology, 31*, 345–486.

CHAPTER 11

Autobiographical Reasoning and My Discontent: Alternative Paths from Narrative to Identity

Monisha Pasupathi

Abstract

This chapter considers how narrating experiences may resolve the problem of identity. Although the conventional perspective has been that narratives serve identity via autobiographical reasoning, the focus here is on alternatives to this account. The author first articulates the problem of identity and identity development as well as how narrative approaches involving autobiographical reasoning have addressed that problem, then considers why the search for alternative pathways makes sense, given existing findings. The chapter outlines three potential pathways by which narratives and narrating can influence identity development: tacit themes, embodied narration, and relational positioning and considers the available evidence for these pathways and the alternative research agendas that they open up for narrative research.

Key Words: narrative identity, autobiographical reasoning, identity, embodied cognition, autobiographical memory

---

The perspective I take in this chapter is that identity is not something people build and then possess, but rather that it is a problem that needs to be resolved in an ongoing way throughout individuals' lives. In essence, it is a simple problem: Am I the same person now, typing this sentence, who was previously reading a paper by philosopher Marya Schechtman? Although the answer to this question seems obvious, people's substantial changes over the life course mean that the resolution of the problem isn't always simple. And the resolution matters. Establishing a sense of personal identity is important because, without it, all the relational bonds and connections people might establish are not meaningful. If I become a different person tomorrow, I no longer have the same obligations to my children or spouse that I might once have had. Resolving my identity problem, by contrast, means those obligations are maintained even in the face of substantial personal changes.

The act of narrating one's experiences offers multiple avenues by which the identity problem can be resolved, repeatedly, over the life course. One of those avenues entails the creation of a narrative identity—a life story—in which people articulate their reasoning about how the experiences of their lives have shaped them over time and where they anticipate their lives going in the future. However, I argue that there are other paths by which narrating the events of our lives may help resolve the problem of identity—paths that have been less well studied, which do not require or involve explicit reasoning processes, and which do not require, in any way, that the narrated events become important, self-defining, or parts of a life story. These paths include the repetition of tacit themes as people construct narratives about their various experiences, the way that narrating entails taking on a set of identities and roles in the moment in relation to the past and present (positioning), and the way that narrating entails the simultaneous reconstruction of bodily states from past experiences and current context (the embodied nature of narration).

Identity as Psychological Continuity: Laying out the Problem

So, how do I know I am the same person now who I was some time ago? Locke (1996) suggested that the key to resolving this question lies in continuity of consciousness between the person at one point in time and their past or future self. The continuity of a person's distinct psychological experience can be achieved via memory, but continuity in beliefs, ideological commitments, values, and desires can also foster a sense of identity across time (Schechtman, 2005). This identity is not limited to sameness over time. As Schechtman (2003) has argued quite convincingly, continuity can be achieved even in the presence of substantial changes, via both remembering prior experiences and having a perspective on them that involves a sense of ownership and a grasp of how that past person became the present person (something Schechtman refers to as empathic access). Thus, experiences of change do not render the problem of identity unsolvable, although they may pose more challenges to a person than do experiences that affirm sameness. In fact, development can pose serious challenges to resolving identity because it entails very real and dramatic changes in a person's distinctive psychological experience (Schechtman, 2003). Furthermore, some developmental changes will involve cognitive and social cognitive shifts that change whether identity is experienced as a problem to resolve and the means by which people may be capable of solving that problem (Chandler, Lalonde, Sokol, & Hallett, 2003).

A Narrative Solution: Life Stories and Autobiographical Reasoning

McAdams (1996) suggested that in creating a selective autobiography or life story people resolve the problem of identity. A good life story, from his standpoint, provides an account of how the person came to be the way he is and provides a sense of purpose and direction that guides actions going forward. Such a story would address the problem of identity quite well—by explaining how the past self is connected to the present self and by providing an account of the way the person has stayed the same and/or changed over time. This story is something people begin to construct as adolescents (Habermas & Bluck, 2000) but that they may continue to alter and develop across the lifespan.

From a theoretical standpoint, though, the life story can only achieve this identity function if it contains what researchers term *autobiographical reasoning* (see Dunlop & Walker, 2013). Autobiographical reasoning is defined as a process of considering how events have shaped who I am and how who I am, in turn, may shape the events I experience in ways that are unique to me (Habermas & Bluck, 2000). Autobiographical reasoning may also entail drawing explicit conclusions about the nature of the world or of life, such as "life is suffering," or "every cloud has its silver lining." Such themes represent distinctive elements of a person's consciousness, and drawing them out in narratives about one's life makes use of them to create continuity. Autobiographical reasoning is what makes a life story into an identity (Habermas & Bluck, 2000; McAdams, 1996) rather than disjointed events presented in sequence. Defined in this way, it makes great sense that autobiographical reasoning in the life story serves to further identity development. Autobiographical reasoning in the life story helps to link one individual's past with his or her present and future and, in the process, render that individual unique and continuous in time. Such reasoning, although linked to autobiographical experience, may take distinctive forms (see Chandler et al., 2003), but nonetheless it resolves the issue of how I came to be me in relation to my own autobiographical history (Habermas & Bluck, 2000; Habermas & de Silveira, 2008). Identity problem solved. Or at least, solvable.

In fact, there is strong emerging evidence that favors this perspective. Autobiographical reasoning does matter for identity and can be well-explored in the context of autobiographical narration, perhaps especially excerpts from the life story (Habermas & de Silveira, 2008; McLean, 2008; McLean & Pratt, 2006). Autobiographical reasoning in narratives, variously measured, increases in sophistication and prevalence from early adolescence through middle age (Fivush & Zaman, this volume; Habermas & de Silveira, 2008; Habermas, Negele, & Mayer, 2010; McLean, 2008; McLean & Fournier, 2008; McLean & Pratt, 2006; Pasupathi & Mansour, 2006; Reese, Yan, Jack, & Hayne, 2010; Weeks, in preparation). This increase coincides with the age period within which identity issues, and specifically issues of continuity, become salient and pressing (Chandler et al., 2003; Erikson, 1968; Harter, 1998). Moreover, autobiographical reasoning varies in its valence (e.g., Banks & Salmon, in press; McAdams, Reynolds, Lewis, Patten, &

Bowman, 2001; McLean, Pasupathi, & Pals, 2007) and other dimensions like stability and change (McLean & Pasupathi, 2011; Weeks & Pasupathi, 2011) and complexity and closure (e.g., Lilgendahl & McAdams, 2011; Pals, 2006), thus permitting autobiographical reasoning to resolve issues of distinctiveness and of continuity.

The concept of autobiographical reasoning also opens a number of interesting additional questions—including some important and not yet answered ones about how autobiographical reasoning comes to accomplish its identity work. Some of these have to do with how autobiographical reasoning is related to other self and identity outcomes (see McLean & Pratt, 2006) because studies sometimes take the presence of autobiographical reasoning as prima facie evidence of identity development in action. Other questions have to do with the ever-present need, in developmental psychology, for prospective and longitudinal work that is difficult and time-consuming to carry out. But emerging findings from prospective longitudinal studies are already revealing a great deal about the developmental origins and course of individuals' life stories from childhood through early adulthood, and we can expect to learn a great deal more from these ongoing projects in the very near future (Habermas & de Silveira, 2008; Habermas et al., 2010; Reese et al., 2010).

Are Life Stories and Autobiographical Reasoning Enough?

Despite my conviction that autobiographical reasoning is a good thing for identity, I am also subject to a sense of dissatisfaction—a nagging notion that this can't be all there is to narrative and identity. In grappling with that dissatisfaction, I have come to think that narratives, and the act of narrating, can also further identity development in other ways—via pathways that may be less fully explored—and lead to questions that are less well articulated within our field. In short, I think that there are ways that narrative can shape identity that do not involve autobiographical reasoning or life stories.

My concerns with overemphasizing autobiographical reasoning begin with the sense that such reasoning is a rare bird. Everyday narration—telling personal stories—is ubiquitous. Some 80–95 percent of everyday and more significant emotional experiences are told to others, often within a day of their occurrence (Pasupathi, McLean, & Weeks, 2009; Rimé, Finkenauer, Luminet, Zech, & Phillipot, 1998). Estimates from family dinner conversations suggest one narrative every five minutes or so (Bohanek et al., 2009). By contrast, however, autobiographical reasoning—variously defined—is not so likely. This is especially the case for causal and thematic types of reasoning—those types arguably most linked to identity. When people are asked to narrate everyday events and are instructed to include autobiographical reasoning, only 75 percent of narratives contain a single instance of such reasoning (Mansfield, Pasupathi, & McLean, under review). Without such instruction, rates of autobiographical reasoning drop precipitously, to less than half of narratives containing anything like autobiographical reasoning, even with fairly lenient criteria (Pasupathi, Mansour, & Brubaker, 2007). Some contexts for everyday narration entail entertainment or dramatic retelling and have no articulated autobiographical reasoning (McLean & Thorne, 2006; Pasupathi, 2006). So, people are narrating all the time, but autobiographical reasoning in those contexts is often much rarer. In terms of narrative contributions to identity development, this means one of three things.

First, perhaps only momentous and critical life events matter for identity development, and everyday narration is irrelevant for identity—although clearly important for bonding and relational connections. The pattern just outlined arises from the fact that most narration concerns everyday events that are irrelevant to identity and that therefore are less likely to contain autobiographical reasoning. The first conclusion may be tempting but is deeply unsatisfying with even momentary introspection. Although it is reasonable that the landmark events of our lives make us who we are and reflect our identities, are our routine and everyday lives—and the many narratives those ordinary lives generate—irrelevant for identity? Surely not.

A second possibility, perhaps more in line with relatively unexplored assumptions of current work in the field, could be that it is momentous events that require identity resolutions (via autobiographical reasoning). The resulting sense of identity that stems from grappling with and reasoning about such events may also, under some circumstances, be reflected in everyday narration. But everyday narration merely reflects and does not exert important influences on identity. This conclusion may seem more satisfying, in that it provides a role for everyday narration in reflecting who we are, but it seems unsatisfying to argue that something we engage in so frequently does not have anything to do with establishing who we are or our sense of being the same person over time. Moreover, it is difficult, given the longstanding findings on dissonance (Festinger, 1957) and self-perception theory (Bem, 1967), to imagine that actions we frequently engage in have no influence on our distinctive psychological continuity.

A third possibility, and the position I explore here, is that there may be ways that narrative can shape and influence identity—defined as the continuities in our psychological experience—that involve pathways other than autobiographical reasoning. To consider those pathways, we have to begin by acknowledging that a great deal is going on in narratives that is not quite explicit or the focus of conscious attention by either a narrator or his or her audience. I treat these aspects of narrative in three categories: tacit themes, relational selves, and embodied narration. Although I believe all three are important, I spend somewhat more time on embodied narration because it is the most speculative and least researched possibility of the three. To help with illustrating these aspects of narrative, I want to begin with an example narrative—one that has the advantage of conveying some explicit autobiographical reasoning as well:

> This was around two weeks ago at my in-laws house in [nearby city]. I told my husband he was being a moron. This occurred during a game of Yahtzee and, due to my somewhat overly competitive nature, I got a little carried away with myself (I was doing badly) and Derek, my husband, offered some advice. I was irritated and fed up with the game and displaced my ill-will towards it on innocent Derek. With an angry look and voice I said, "I don't need advice from a moron like you!"
>
> I felt horrible afterwards! I was somewhat shocked at what had just blurted from my mouth and I looked at him with an equally shocked expression—I could tell he was shocked too. Just a split-second later, however, he regained his normal composure and then began to laugh. In a mock-offensive tone he said, "Well *excuse* me" and put up his hands as though to ward off my anger. I was embarrassed and guilty—we were playing with his Mom and brother as well, and my loss of temper and control made me look and feel bad. They, however, shrugged it off with a laugh and we moved on with the game. Thank goodness for a forgiving, understanding husband!"

What's in This Story? Tacit Themes

In this example, the overt autobiographical reasoning involves drawing links between an overly competitive nature and the loss of temper that it caused. But the narrative offers a rich sense of the narrator in part because of other elements of the story. First, it is replete with tacit themes of an interpersonal or relational orientation within the narrator's identity. By tacit, I mean not explicitly expressed in forms like "I really value my identity as a wife" or "Family harmony means the world to me." Rather, the story implicates the narrator's concern with others' perceptions of her and with her relational obligations and values of self-control and kind behavior (and the breach represented by her behavior in this event). Some of this is conveyed via the content of the story—the details that are and are not emphasized. Other features of the story that could serve to convey these themes can be more subtle—linguistic choices such as using "we" versus "I" or framing the story in terms of back-and-forth social exchanges and using quotations to actively represent others. These elements of narratives are likely to be important in the process of identity development and maintenance, although such linguistic choices are likely less available to conscious reflection (Tausczik & Pennebaker, 2010). But, most importantly, the relational orientation for this narrator isn't something she is reflecting on overtly—it is the backdrop of assumptions within which the entire narrative makes sense. At no point does she say, "Relationships are really important to me" or "I care a lot about whether I'm fulfilling relationship obligations and roles." She *could* certainly draw this theme out of this and similar narratives—and perhaps might do so, given the right context. But, in the presented story, that conclusion is not explicit—there is no autobiographical reasoning creating identity in the form of lasting values. Rather, there is simply the taken-for-granted importance of relational roles and obligations, without which the entire narrative makes less—or indeed no—sense.

Most examinations of narrative themes do not distinguish between tacit and more overtly expressed themes, and one implication of the thinking here is that making such distinctions could be revealing. In two studies of children and adolescents, we examined narratives for conceptions of self and other (Pasupathi, Wainryb, Komolova, & Lucas, in preparation; Wainryb, Komolova, & Florsheim, 2010). Our approach was focused on tacit understandings that children might not explicitly convey—such as understanding persons as psychological agents or in terms of material possessions. For example, if a child narrates how she ended up hitting her friend because the friend called her fat, the narrative indicates a sense of persons as people who can be hurt by psychological means as well as physical ones, even when the child narrates with no reference to psychological states. We were able to show that children are tacitly making use of psychological conceptions of persons well before they begin to do so explicitly in their narratives (Pasupathi et al., in preparation). Furthermore, in an examination of a delinquent sample, delinquent adolescents likewise showed discrepancies between explicitly representing others' psychological states versus tacitly acknowledging the psychological existence of themselves and others (Wainryb et al., 2010). Delinquents were unlikely, relative to normative samples, to explicitly reference others' internal states, but their narratives frequently revealed a tacit acknowledgment of the psychological experience of others.

These findings point to the presence and meaningfulness of tacit themes in narratives, as well as how they are distinct from overt or explicit themes. How might such themes relate to identity? Consider how a person may invoke the themes of victimhood in constructing narratives about his own wrong-doing. This theme may be invoked explicitly, when someone expresses the idea that he is the victim in a situation and that all the responsibility for what happened lies elsewhere. But it also may be invoked more implicitly—as when people emphasize a preceding harm to themselves and their own suffering over that of their victim. In the latter case, when that way of narrating is repeated over many different events and experiences, it is easy to see how a particular identity arises—one of the ever-wronged (and never wrong) individual. Although the continuity of perceived victimization may not make the narrator feel efficacious or happy, it creates a particular kind of identity content—visible to others and potentially available to the exploration of the narrator—and it will certainly provide a sense of continuity of psychological experience over time. More positive pathways are also, of course, available (if less dramatic to write about). Empirical evidence for this route from narration to identity, however, will require that researchers draw clearer distinctions between explicit identity content in narratives—content in which narrators lay claim to identity features like beliefs, values, ideologies—and thematic and linguistic contents that imply beliefs, values, and ideologies that are not explicitly claimed by the narrator. At present, different approaches to narratives may capture both of these elements together. For example, some work on cultural differences in narratives is likely tapping into variations in tacit themes, such as emphases on obligations and relational responsibilities, as well as more explicit identity assertions, given the way that the data are coded (Wang, 2004). In this work, however, those thematic differences are connected to people's self-conceptions in ways that support the idea of tacit themes as routes from narrative to identity (e.g., Wang, 2004).

In the example I provided earlier, the narrator links her own emotional life quite strongly to relational bonds and obligations—both her distress and her positive emotions stem from her relations with others. As she tells many such stories, she may strengthen an identity built around links between emotions and relational bonds. Although to some extent virtually all humans experience relationships and relational events as emotionally meaningful, people show meaningful differences in the extent to which they identify themselves in relational terms (e.g., Cross, Gore, & Morris, 2003). In this example, the narrator's tacit themes build the kind of identity that is fashioned around bonds with others, even when she never considers that issue explicitly. Although there is, as yet, relatively little evidence directly testing these ideas, Philippe and colleague have begun to examine relationships between people's networked autobiographical memories and their appraisals of novel situations (Philippe, Koestner, Lecours, Beaulieu-Pelletier, & Bois, 2011). Their results suggest that characteristics of people's memory networks—which are likely to be shaped by the types of explicit autobiographical reasoning reviewed elsewhere and by the types of implicit themes just outlined—go on to affect the way people experience new situations. There is no direct testing of ideas about narrative themes fostering continuity or distinctiveness of identity as yet, but the paradigms emerging in these studies and studies of culture lay the groundwork for pursuing those ideas.

Constructing a narrative, however, is also an action that takes place in a specific context, often with a particular audience either present or at least in mind. This aspect of narrative construction raises a second path by which narrative can foster identity, one that I term *relational*.

What's in That Story? Relational Positioning and Narration

Although the example narrative presented earlier was produced in our laboratory, in a solitary, written setting, even that setting is a social context of a particular kind. As noted, the author of the example narrative was asked to write about an experience that contradicted her sense of self. She was doing so in a psychology research laboratory, fully aware that her narrative would be read (or "heard") by psychological researchers interested in her experiences and emotions—and unfamiliar with her as a person. The autobiographical reasoning in the story may have been more likely to be generated in that context than in any other—with familiar others, she might have left out that fact as a given. In fact, most narration, particularly narration of the sort where autobiographical reasoning may be less frequent, occurs in social contexts with familiar others. These contexts are characterized by established, already shared views of self and other (Hardin & Conley, 2001; Sinclair, Huntsinger, Skorinko, & Hardin, 2005; Swann, 2000), and thus the explicit meaning-making elicited by the psychological researcher audience may be less prevalent—especially outside the developmental periods in which identity creation is a predominant concern, primarily adolescence and emergent adulthood.

Everyday acts of narrating to close others, however, do involve repetition of relational selves. By relational selves, I mean something distinct from the strong interpersonal themes that characterize the example above. Rather, what I mean is the nature of the self being created within a particular interaction with a specific other person (see Korobov, this volume). In that sense, the narrator in the example makes use of relational themes, but is also clearly preoccupied with the construction of a particular self-image vis-à-vis her psychology researcher audience.

Perhaps the most elaborate consideration of this route of identity creation has taken place in sociolinguistics and related fields (Deppermann, 2007; Korobov & Bamberg, 2004; Norrick, 2000). As someone narrates, they position themselves on at least two levels: first, as a character within the story they are telling, and second, as a participant within the social context of the narration. These positions constitute temporarily adopted identities in the sense of social roles—resolving issues of distinctiveness from others. The example narrator positions herself as a generally good person with a particular foible who is appreciative of others' forgiveness and appropriately demanding of herself; her narrative is suggestive of a humorous self-deprecation.

In her case, these efforts at positioning are made without recourse to feedback from her intended audience. In more typical face-to-face narration, narrators take on positions, and their positioning acts garner responses from listeners conveyed via signals of attentiveness, agreement, and endorsement, as well as by overt acceptance or challenges (Deppermann, 2007; Korobov & Bamberg, 2004; McLean & Pasupathi, 2011; Pasupathi, 2001; Weeks & Pasupathi, 2011). In response to such signals, narrators may adapt their positioning, shifting toward a way of presenting self that is mutually acceptable.

Positioning certainly involves those qualities of the person that address distinctiveness from others—in fact, when Korobov and Bamberg (2004) examine positioning in adolescent conversations, it is clear that the adolescents involved take roles in relation to one another that highlight their distinctiveness as well as their common ties (see also Deppermann, 2007). However, theoretically, positioning-oriented researchers have not emphasized the idea of identity continuity and have indeed posited that identity is only realized in specific, momentary contexts and is not something that involves continuity over time (Korobov, this volume; Waterman, this volume). However, to think of identity in this way ignores the substantial intellectual history of the idea of identity as continuity in time. Furthermore, although positioning may be analyzed in context-specific, momentary discursive exchanges, this does not mean positioning cannot also create continuity over time—and therefore resolve the identity problem.

In fact, over time, given the continuity of social networks and relations, it is likely that such positioning interactions are repeated and thus could create continuity of identity as well. In fact, there is evidence that our relationships press for us to be stable and consistent in our presented identities (De La Ronde & Swann, 1998; McLean & Pasupathi, 2011). This notion is also consistent with the idea that shifts in social networks make room for identity changes (see, e.g., Festinger, Schachter, & Back, 1950; Swann, Bosson, & Pelham, 2002) and even open the possibility of identity discontinuities that require some resolution (Schechtman, 2003). To fully demonstrate the viability of this pathway would mean showing that shifts in social relationships change identity, but also that such changes are mediated by changes in the positions available to someone as she narrates the events of her life. Another means for testing this pathway's viability would be to examine individuals with bicultural identities and their narratives—again, to explore whether some of the differences within an individual's sense of identity continuity and distinctiveness across distinct contexts are mediated by differences in the nature of their narratives (e.g., Lilgendahl et al., 2012).

But relational pathways and people's positions within narration can also create continuity in another way. The positions in the here-and-now world of narration and those reflected in the there-and-then world of the events being narrated may also create identity continuity. For example, in talking about a flirtatious interaction with a woman, a narrator may both position himself as witty and charming in the there-and-then world of what he narrates and also as a funny and entertaining storyteller in the here-and-now world of what is being narrated. This creates an obvious continuity—via similarity—between the experience of the initial event and the present moment of narration. Furthermore, the example narrative, in which the positions of the narrator involve remorse and gratitude for others' understanding and the position of the narrator within the narrative is quite different, may also provide for continuity—but continuity with different identity implications. Discrepancies between the position of the narrator and the positions in the narrative may create identities of many different kinds. The example case suggests a person who is both impulsive and reflective, in a sequenced way. Other discrepancies are also possible—and a full exploration of them is well beyond the scope of this chapter. This type of relational continuity warrants further examination, as well as the more straightforward continuity described earlier.

This last idea about how relational positioning can foster identity continuity depends on the "time travel" aspects of narration—the fact that constructing autobiographical narratives takes place in a here-and-now context but also transports the narrator (and audience) to the there-and-then setting of the events being narrated. That transportation over time brings me to the last, and perhaps most speculative, idea about how narration might serve identity continuity. Narrating, like any other experience, is an embodied event, but one that makes reference to a previously experienced embodied event. As I consider next, this characteristic of narration suggests a third way in which narratives and the act of narration may both shape identity contents and foster a sense of continuity across time.

What Else is in the Story (or the Telling)? The Embodied Act of Narrating

A third pathway by which narratives and the act of narrating can give rise to a sense of psychological continuity—an identity—is via embodied experience associated with narration. Autobiographical reasoning as a pathway privileges verbal content and the narrative as a product. Tacit themes are not much of an exception in this regard; relational positioning does somewhat better by expanding consideration of narrative pathways to the act of narrating. Narration results in the reconstruction of past experiences within a different temporal context—the here and now—and *both the past and the present actions are embodied experiences*. Importantly, this is the case whether narratives are generated in a laboratory room on a written questionnaire/survey instrument or generated around a coffee table with friends or family.

Mapping the Body There-and-Then and the Body Right Now

In considering this pathway, I draw heavily on the work of Damasio and his many collaborators (Damasio, 1999; 2010). Experiences—both of narrating and of the original event that is now being narrated—are accompanied by a host of what Damasio (1999; 2010) has termed *feelings*. These feelings are constructed via the integration of the many mapping capacities of the brain—most particularly by the brain's capacity to map the body as well as the environment and the relationship between the two. As an experience unfolds, it is accompanied by both interoceptive (generated within the body) and exteroceptive (generated by the body in relation to the environment) signals that are integrated within the brain and give rise to feelings. In fact, Damasio has argued that it is this joint mapping that gives rise to a sense of core self for organisms with sufficient complexity.

Our brains are continually mapping bodily states and environmental conditions, and this is true for many different species. However, for human beings, the capacity for memory and for simulating the future raises an additional consideration—the fact that the embodied experience of current time may be juxtaposed with the reconstruction of other embodied states. When our example narrator constructs her story about the board game, she is sitting in the laboratory but is also engaged in mental time travel back to the board game incident. In terms of embodied states, this results in the representation of the earlier, game-related embodied state within the brain, in circuits that Damasio and colleagues refer to as a "body-as-if" loop. The body-as-if loop consists of circuits of associations among neurons that construct and reconstruct past or simulated states in terms of the same patterns of feelings that have occurred before. Both the "body-right-now" and the "body-as-if" circuitry within the brain can give rise to feelings and, ultimately, a sense of self. Moreover, Damasio posits that the links between body-right-now and body-as-if circuits constitute a kind of "meta"-level mapping between the two. The details of the neural circuitry are reviewed by Damasio (2010), but in this context, I want to take the concepts of body-right-now and body-as-if maps and the relational maps that link the two to consider the embodied nature of narratives and how that embodied nature may relate to identity without explicit autobiographical reasoning. Because I am focused on narrative about past experiences, I will consider the body-as-if maps more specifically as "body-there-and-then" maps in many cases, although when considering the broader implications of the body-as-if mapping system, I use that broader term.

Narration, as with other recollective actions, likely re-evokes the feelings of the past event being narrated. For our narrator in the example, the experience of writing her story in our lab room likely re-evoked some of the patterns of feelings associated with her anger, guilt, and relief as conveyed in her narrative. Based on peripheral nervous system indicators like blood pressure, heart rate, and skin conductance, there is substantial evidence that merely recalling the experience of a particular emotion can reinstate the physiological signatures of that emotion (Levenson, Carstensen, Friesen, & Ekman, 1991; Ray, Wilhelm, & Gross, 2008). What does this re-evocation mean for identity in terms of continuity over time?

To consider that question, we might first ask whether the re-evoked emotions involve the body-there-and-then map, the body-right-now map, or both. Keep in mind that these maps involve, to some extent, distinct circuitry at the neural level—so that the body-right-now and the body-there-and-then, although being mapped in similar regions of the brain, are engaging somewhat distinct circuitry within those regions. Given that, identity continuity might arise from the relationships between these two maps and their respective circuitry. Moreover, the relationships between those two maps may vary in ways that have implications for the experience of identity continuity. On the one extreme, one can think of a flashback in posttraumatic stress disorder (PTSD) as entailing complete immersion in the past—the body-right-now is mapping a state identical to the body-there-and-then state from a prior trauma. On the other extreme, one can imagine the recounting of a frequently told anecdote for the goal of entertaining a listener—in which case any re-evocation is likely to be primarily in the body-there-and-then map and perhaps not very intensely so. The body-right-now map, conversely, is evoking the current social reminiscing context and its associated feelings. Many cases of recollection are likely to fall between these extremes.

Speculatively, identity continuity may be best served when the body-there-and-then and body-right-now loops are moderately distinct during the act of remembering because it is this discrepancy that also creates clear continuity between the body-right-now and the body-there-and-then via the mapping of links between the two. When the two are highly overlapping, it may be difficult to experience any sense of continuity over time from that overlap because the two are indistinguishable; conversely, when the two are too disparate, there may be a sense of discontinuity in the body-right-now and body-there-and-then loops—as though the reconstructed event happened to someone else. Between these two extremes, the body-right-now has a clear relation to the body-as-if, but the two are different, which could create a sense of continuity across distinct settings. This is all by way of suggesting that the creation of enough, and not too much, space between the body-there-and-then and body-right-now maps—along with the mapping of relations between them—makes an important contribution to an embodied link between past and present, one that needs no explicit reasoning. That embodied sense may provide for continuity of experience over time.

But it is also important that the body-there-and-then loop map a state that the person feels belongs to the self, rather than to another person. Given Damasio's linking of body-as-if states to mirror neurons and their potential links to simulation, which are also engaged when people represent the states of others or of imagined experiences, the body-as-if map may not always represent the narrator's own embodied experience. Until mirror neuron circuitry is thoroughly understood, it is not clear whether distinct pathways serve the person's own body-as-if mapping and the mapping of others' states or if those pathways are distinct between body-there-and-then and body-if-in-imagined-state. In this way, the mapping of body-as-if states and body-right-now states needs to also resolve distinctiveness issues. For example, the narrator could retell a story about her husband's experience—and this may also evoke a body-as-if map that is simulating *his* experience at the time of the event. However, in such cases, she is likely aware that the body-as-if map being constructed is not one that was ever hers. In fact, Decety and colleagues have shown in a variety of studies that the brain makes clear distinctions between self and other even while employing overlapping circuits to simulate experiences for both self and other (Decety & Chaminade, 2003; Decety & Grèzes, 2006).

Any Recollection, or Is Something Special About Narrative?

Up until now, the speculations I have advanced are applicable to any way in which a person recalls his or her past (and, indeed, likely apply to simulations of imagined events as well). However, I want to suggest that narrating may be more effective than other modes of recollection in creating a body-there-and-then loop that is both recognized as belonging to the self in the past and different from the present body-right-now map. The act of narrating is one that entails communication to an audience—whether real or "in mind." As a consequence, narrating requires some distance, perspective, and transformation that isn't necessarily part of other recollective actions (Pasupathi, 2007*b*). To communicate to others about an event, a narrator must provide sufficient contextual information to orient his or her listeners to time, place, and participants. The narrator has to provide sufficient information about the order of events. He or she also must account for why a story deserves to be heard—especially in conversational settings, where storytelling entails the negotiation of a speaker's right to hold a monologue (Clark, 1996; Grice, 1957; Pasupathi, 2007*a*). And the narrator must translate a perceptual and embodied event into verbal representations. Narrative, in short, requires some attention and attunement to the present and the audience that likely ensures a difference between the body-right-now and the body-there-and-then (see also Holmes & Mathews, 2010) and a mapping of relations between the two that serves to convey the idea of the self here-and-now reflecting on the there-and-then.

Body-There-and-Then and Body-Right-Now in the Typical Narrating Situation

Those differences between the body-as-if and body-right-now maps, however, and the relations between them may take a variety of forms, and the forms of those differences may also matter for the nature of the identity implications they entail. To begin, consider the modal or typical context for narration, although we know relatively little about such contexts. When we have looked at typical contexts for narrating events among samples of college students (Pasupathi, in press), we find those contexts often involve being at home or en route to somewhere in a moving vehicle; they typically involve narrating to friends or family members. Furthermore, people typically report that they are narrating to share information or convey an experience and what it meant to them—that they are telling their story "straight" (Marsh & Tversky, 2004). These are likely to be relaxed, safe, and secure contexts in which the body-right-now map conveys precisely that secure, relaxed (relatively), and emotionally calm setting.

What we know about the things that typically get narrated suggests that this relaxed body-right-now map will contrast with a more aroused and emotional body-as-if. One of the major predictors of whether people go on to narrate events is the extent to which those events are important, emotional, and meaningful (Pasupathi et al., 2009; Rimé et al., 1998), with more emotional and important events being more likely to be narrated to others. This may be particularly true for negative experiences (McLean et al., 2007; Thorne, 2000). Furthermore, there is some evidence that emotionally negative experiences are better recalled, particularly for central or core elements, than are less emotional experiences (see, e.g., Heuer & Reisberg, 1992; Kensinger, Garoff-Eaton, & Schacter, 2007). Such vivid recall extends even to highly traumatic events and is true for both children and adults, particularly when central details of the event are at stake (Christianson, 1997; Greenhoot & Bunnell, 2009). In many cases, the body-there-and-then of the event being narrated is significantly more emotionally aroused and/ or under emotional stress than the body-right-now of narration.

Because even everyday event narration disproportionately involves the emotional events of our lives (Pasupathi et al., 2009; Rimé et al., 1998), and people typically are trying to convey those events as they felt at the time (Marsh & Tversky, 2004), the body-there-and-then map for such events is likely to convey a more intense and aroused emotional state along with many of the other features of the bodily states originally involved in the narrated event. Thus, the typical context of narration is likely to be one in which the body-right-now and body-as-if maps are distinctive, the latter is more emotionally charged than the former, and the relations between them convey the sense of a relaxed person reflecting on an emotionally aroused past. Thus, the comparatively high arousal for the "body-as-if" loop in the context of a calm, relaxed "body-right-now" map creates not only a sense of identity continuity in an embodied way—it creates a particular kind of continuity, one in which an emotional experience may be "owned" by the very same individual who has now returned to a place of safety.

Other States of the Body-There-and-Then and Body-Right-Now in Narrating

Although people do often report narrating to convey information about their experiences (Marsh & Tversky, 2004), these are not their only goals for narrating events (Dudukovic, Marsh, & Tversky, 2004; McLean, 2005; Pasupathi, 2006); moreover, even when they view themselves as primarily interested in "sharing information," they frequently edit their accounts of the past (Marsh & Tversky, 2004). These additional goals for narration have been linked to the relative prevalence of meaning-oriented content—including explicit autobiographical reasoning—concurrently (McLean & Thorne, 2006; Pasupathi, 2006), as well as in subsequent written narratives (McLean, 2005; Pasupathi, 2007a), and the accuracy of recall (Dudukovic et al., 2004).

Consider entertainment-oriented narrating in particular (McLean, 2005; McLean & Thorne, 2006; Pasupathi et al., 2006). Such narration could conceivably create body-right-now states (of enjoyment and social engagement—perhaps even social power) that are in distinct contrast to the body-there-and-then states being narrated. As one example, close calls and near-death experiences (Bavelas, Coates, & Johnson, 2000) involve a body-there-and-then mapping likely to entail fear and a host of associated embodied states (e.g., tensed musculature) due to the imminent threat such narratives involve. Then, imagine an entertainment-oriented telling of such an event. Rather than the kind of continuity created by a calmer, safer body-right-now and a fearful, aroused body-there-and-then, this scenario creates a different type of continuity—between a fearful, aroused body-there-and-then and a positively aroused body-right-now. It is possible that the experience of identity continuity and identity distinctiveness that is engendered by entertainment tellings is distinct from that which might be engendered by more meaning-oriented or social support-seeking kinds of narration involving talking about emotionally negative events in a more calm and emotionally secure setting.

Body-There-and-Then and Body-Right-Now in Memory Studies

Thus far, the considerations I am outlining are quite speculative. The sparse evidence that is available to consider issues of embodied narration is primarily not work that looked at narrative, but rather at memory or other aspects of psychological functioning. In one study, people were asked to recall memories while being placed in unusually relaxed circumstances—more so than would likely be the case in what we might construe as the modal narration case presented earlier. Exposure to relaxation or sensory deprivation changed memory retrieval toward more intensity and more pleasant recollections (Suedfeld & Eich, 1995), perhaps because of the reduction in body-right-now feedback under such circumstances.

By contrast, individuals who are suffering from current depression show deficits in their ability to recall personal experiences, with memories that lack contextual information, vividness, and emotional details—a phenomenon termed *overgeneral memory* (King et al., 2010; Williams, 1992). Furthermore, recent experimental work suggests that acute stress—that is, a body-right-now map that feels aroused and distressed—appears to influence recall of neutral past events toward more overgeneral recollection. For identity implications, this may mean that currently distressed embodied states make it difficult to recall previous experiences with a very intense body-there-and-then map. One potential consequence for identity is a disruption of continuity because the body-there-and-then map may simply not provide enough of a sense of identity continuity with past experience. Such disruptions matter because they may be associated with increased risk of suicidality (Chandler et al., 2003). In support of this idea, in fact, one study found that overgeneral memory was more likely among those who were both depressed and showing suicidal ideation compared to a depressed group without suicidal ideation (Kaviani, Rahimi, Rahimi-Darabad, & Naghavi, 2011).

Of course, these findings fall short of demonstrating that the body-right-now effects are mediated by changes in the way people narrate, which in turn change the nature of body-there-and-then mapping. There is a small body of evidence for that claim as well, however. Recently, we have shown that when people narrate their mental activity during a period of sedentary activity, they consume more calories than when they narrate their physical activity during that same time frame, suggesting that divergent ways of narrating the same twenty-minute period result in different physiological states vis-à-vis hunger and reward aspects of food, perhaps by creating different kinds of "body-as-if" maps (Pasupathi, Drews, Wainryb, & Stefanucci, in preparation). Other work has examined variations in how people recall by changing their perspective from the first-person (field perspective) to a third-person stance (observer perspective) (Berntsen & Rubin, 2006; Crawley & French, 2005; Eich, Nelson, Leghari, & Handy, 2009; Terry & Horton, 2007). A shift to a third-person perspective is associated with perceiving the recalled event as less emotionally intense and sensorially vivid, perhaps by diminishing the intensity of the body-there-and-then simulation or by altering the portion of that simulation that makes clear the self is the person being simulated by that loop—something that may be distorted by a third-person perspective. Recent findings showed that an observer (vs. field) perspective changes elements of the way people narrate their recollections and also coincides with lower activation of sensory-motor areas—essentially, observer perspectives are associated with a reduction in the intensity of the body-there-and-then map (Eich et al., 2009; see also Libby, Shaeffer, Eibach, & Slemmer, 2007 for more on visual perspective and the effects of memory).

What Does This Have to Do with Identity?

Even more than with tacit themes, there is little direct evidence examining embodied aspects of narration and issues of identity continuity and distinctiveness. However, there is substantial indirect evidence from broader work on embodied cognition. Current bodily states are known to affect judgment, pain tolerance, and language processing. Changes in skin conductance (an indicator of negative arousal) precede changes in decision strategies for participants in studies of decision making (Bechara, Damasio, Tranel, & Damasio, 1997). Ingestion of nonsteroidal anti-inflammatory (NSAID) painkillers appears to act on emotional as well as physical pain (DeWall, Pond, & Deckman, 2011). Emotional states affect a variety of perceptual judgments—distance, angles, and body size (Stefanucci, Gagnon, & Lessard, 2011). Glenberg and colleagues (Glenberg, 2008) have shown that bodily positions affect the speed and ease of a variety of language processing tasks—when the body is aligned congruently with the sentences to be processed, comprehension is faster than when the body is incongruent. Listening to a humorous narrative results in increased discomfort thresholds for pain (Cogan, Cogan, Waltz, & McCue, 1987). What these studies and others like them suggest is that the embodied experience of the "here-and-now" will certainly shape the way we narrate the "there-and-then," with possible implications for identity continuity and distinctiveness.

Before those implications can be tested, it will be important to consider how the body-as-if and body-right-now maps, and the mapping of relations between them, may be differentially examined in relation to narration. Although imaging techniques might directly contribute to this endeavor, experimental work that is carefully designed to create more and less differentiation of the body-there-and-then and body-right-now maps during narration will also be important. Finally, it will be important to consider how to link such body maps (and their relative discrepancy) to indices of identity continuity and how to establish that variations in narration are what mediates such links.

Tacit, Embodied, and Relational Pathways: Remaining Issues

My primary aim with this chapter has been to suggest some ways that narratives, and narrating, may shape identity without the presence of explicit autobiographical reasoning. In part, the rareness of explicit autobiographical reasoning in everyday narration suggests that autobiographical reasoning is not the only path to be explored. I suggested three potential paths and reviewed some of the available evidence supporting those pathways. As is likely clear, these are speculations about how narrative may serve identity functions rather than established findings, and my hope is to broaden the future horizons for research rather than to review established findings that do not yet exist. Many questions remain about the basic ideas—including whether and how different paths may interact with one another. In closing, I want to consider both some important issues that I did not address in this chapter, as well as some broader questions that cut across all three pathways.

Issues of Culture and Gender

Perhaps the most obvious omission is that I have spent virtually no time addressing issues of culture and gender, although narratives clearly vary in important ways across cultures and subcultures (e.g., Fivush & Nelson, 2004; Schacter, 2004), and there is a body of findings on gender differences as well (e.g., Bohanek, Marin, & Fivush, 2008; Fivush & Zaman, this volume). Incorporating the perspectives and findings on gender and culture within the ideas here about alternative pathways to identity from narrative requires more than a paragraph or two of cursory consideration. One issue is whether continuity of identity is a different, distinctive problem in ways that are shaped by culture and gender. For example, it could be that in cultures with more tolerance for discontinuity in people's characteristics, continuity of identity is easier to construct even in the face of change. In such a hypothetical culture, autobiographical reasoning might play an even lesser role because the circumstances in which it is fostered—when one must account for change or cope with difficult events—might be less frequent. Other, more subconscious paths to continuity may be more important in such cases, or the types of discontinuities that must be accommodated by identity resolution may vary. The possibilities are quite broad, and this represents one potentially important route for further work.

New Issues in Identity and Narrative Coherence

Identity matters for people's functioning in the world—identities help people to see themselves moving from past to future, make commitments meaningful, and find common ground with others. Problems of continuity can be understood as incoherence in identity over time—irreconcilable differences between the me-that-was and the me-that-is. When we consider different pathways by which identity development and narrative are related, it also raises questions about coherence across those different pathways.

Coherence issues in narrative work have often emphasized elements of the narrative that contribute to coherence; these range from syntactic elements that ensure coherence from phrase to phrase (Habermas & Paha, 2001) to broader elements that create coherence across the whole narrative. The latter may provide information about temporal order, the time and place of the event, and themes that link aspects of single events together (Reese et al., 2011) or themes that connect episodes within the person's life story (Habermas & de Silveira, 2008; Habermas & Paha, 2001; McAdams, 1996). However, the pathways described in this chapter raise new questions about coherence between different features of the narrative—explicit features, tacit themes, embodied states, and relational positions. People's narratives could conceivably be more or less coherent in the links between features of the narrative and body-there-and-then maps, or between explicit autobiographical reasoning and more tacit themes, or, likewise, between positioning of a relational self and tacit themes.

In previous work, narrative coherence has been linked to both well-being (Baerger & McAdams, 1999) and to a broad swath of developmental changes that shift children's perceptions of themselves, their memories, and their integrative capacities (Reese et al., 2011). It is worth considering how the types of coherence discussed earlier might contribute to a person's identity and, more broadly, to their adaptive functioning. For example, people whose narratives convey tacit themes of lack of agency, even while asserting an explicit goal to alter some feature of their lives, may be less successful at pursuing that goal than others whose narratives are more coherent across explicit and tacit content. Likewise, people whose narratives correspond more tightly to embodied states may be in a better position to create continuity over time in their experiences than those whose narratives exaggerate or minimize in words the messages of the body-there-and-then loops.

Accommodating Change While Solving the Identity Problem

In terms of their specific contents, identities don't always serve ideal purposes for individuals and, in some cases, people need to resolve identity while allowing or fostering changes in their understandings of themselves. One possibility is that change and stability in the explicit level of autobiographical reasoning may be bolstered or strengthened when similar changes occur within the other pathways. In fact, if we construe psychotherapy as a prototypical intervention to reshape dysfunctional identities, it may also operate by making people's tacit themes, relational positioning, and even embodied narrating experience more available to awareness. For example, even short-term, highly focused cognitive-behavioral therapy (CBT) makes use of exhuming thoughts and themes people may not be making explicit and pursuing explicit efforts to change those default cognitions (Dobson, 2010). Psychotherapy and self-reflection revolve around bringing implicit aspects of narration and behavior into conscious awareness and making deliberate change (Angus & McLeod, 2004; Singer & Kasmark, this volume).

Given the situated nature of narratives (McLean et al., 2007; Pasupathi, 2001), narratives are likely to shift to accommodate the current context. Thus, if someone's narratives need to change, then it is possible to change those stories by altering the context—with therapeutic contexts representing an extreme version of altered contexts. Changing context may be the most effective way to change the narratives people tell, and those changes may occur at the level of explicit autobiographical reasoning, but also at more subtle and tacit levels outlined earlier. However, it is still likely the case that narrators bring their stories and their tacit storytelling proclivities into new contexts and that may be increasingly so across adulthood. The extent to which this is true is also a question that warrants investigation.

A Plea for a More Complete Story on Stories

In closing, the goal of this chapter was not to deny the power of the concept of autobiographical reasoning for understanding how narratives can serve identity development, nor was it to suggest we should not continue to pursue important issues in the study of autobiographical reasoning. Rather, it was to ask of researchers in the field that we broaden our examination of narrative and identity development to consider the richness of narratives, perhaps especially in their multilayered aspects.

Doing so will require that we look beyond the verbal, and that we look both inward, into the body, and out into the social and relational settings in which narration takes place. We are fortunate that there are methodological approaches and technological tools that make it possible to take those steps if we choose to do so. In all of this thinking looms a possible shadow of epiphenomal status—that is, it could be that everyday narration and identity simply aren't important for one another, unless autobiographical reasoning comes into play. But surely, before we decide that autobiographical reasoning is the only account worth emphasizing, we should take a look at some of the other possible stories we could be telling.

References

Angus, L. E., & McLeod, J. (2004). *Toward an Integrative Framework for Understanding the Role of Narrative in the Psychotherapy Process*. Thousand Oaks, CA: Sage Publications.

Baerger, D., & McAdams, D. P. (1999). Life story coherence and its relation to psychological well-being. *Narrative Inquiry, 9*, 69–96.

Banks, M., & Salmon, K. (2013). Reasoning about the self in positive and negative ways: Relationships to psychological functioning in young adulthood. *Memory, 21*, 10-26.

Bavelas, J. B., Coates, L., & Johnson, T. (2000). Listeners as co-narrators. *Journal of Personality and Social Psychology, 79*, 941–952.

Bechara, A., Damasio, H., Tranel, D., & Damasio, A. R. (1997). Deciding advantageously before knowing the advantageous strategy. *Science, 275*(5304), 1293–1295. doi: 10.1126/science.275.5304.1293

Bem, D. J. (1967). Self-perception: An alternative interpretation of cognitive dissonance phenomena. *Psychological Review, 74*(3), 183–200.

Berntsen, D., & Rubin, D. C. (2006). Emotion and vantage point in autobiographical memory. *Cognition and Emotion, 20*(8), 1193–1215. doi: 10.1080/02699930500371190

Bohanek, J. G., Fivush, R., Zaman, W., Lepore, C. E., Merchant, S., & Duke, M. P. (2009). Narrative interaction in family dinnertime conversations. *Merrill-Palmer Quarterly, 55*(4), 488–515. doi: 10.1353/mpq.0.0031

Bohanek, J. G., Marin, K. A., & Fivush, R. (2008). Family narratives, self, and gender in early adolescence. *The Journal of Early Adolescence, 28*(1), 153–176.

Chandler, M. J., Lalonde, C. E., Sokol, B. W., & Hallett, D. (2003). Personal persistence, identity development, and suicide. *Monographs of the Society for Research on Child Development*. Oxford, England: Blackwell.

Christianson, S. A. (1997). On emotional stress and memory: We need to recognize threatening situations and we need to "forget" unpleasant experiences. In D. G. Payne & F. G. Conrad (Eds.), *Intersections in basic and applied memory research* (pp. 133–156). Mahwah: Erlbaum.

Clark, H. H. (1996). *Using language*. Cambridge, MA: Cambridge University Press.

Cogan, R., Cogan, D., Waltz, W., & McCue, M. (1987). Effects of laughter and relaxation on discomfort thresholds. *Journal of Behavioral Medicine, 10*(2), 139–144. doi: 10.1007/bf00846422

Crawley, S. E., & French, C. C. (2005). Field and observer viewpoint in remember-know memories of personal childhood events. *Memory, 13*(7), 673–681. doi: 10.1080/09658210444000296

Cross, S. E., Gore, J. S., & Morris, M. L. (2003). The relational-interdependent self-construal, self-concept consistency, and well-being. *Journal of Personality and Social Psychology, 85*, 933–944.

Damasio, A. (2010). *Self comes to mind: Constructing the conscious brain*. New York: Pantheon.

Damasio, A. R. (1999). *The feeling of what happens: Body and emotion in the making of consciousness*. New York: Harcourt Brace.

De La Ronde, C., & Swann, W. B. (1998). Partner verification: Restoring shattered images of our intimates. *Journal of Personality and Social Psychology, 75*, 374–382.

Decety, J., & Chaminade, T. (2003). When the self represents the other: A new cognitive neuroscience view on psychological identification. *Consciousness and Cognition: An International Journal, 12*(4), 577–596. doi: 10.1016/s1053-8100(03)00076-x

Decety, J., & Grèzes, J. (2006). The power of simulation: Imagining one's own and other's behavior. *Brain Research, 1079*(1), 4–14. doi: 10.1016/j.brainres.2005.12.115

Deppermann, A. (2007). Using the Other for Oneself—Conversational practice of representing out-group members among adolescents. In M. Bamberg, A. De Fina & D. Schiffrin (Eds.), *Selves and identities in narrative and discourse* (pp. 273–301). Amsterdamn: Benjamins.

DeWall, C. N., Pond, R. S., Jr., & Deckman, T. (2011). Acetaminophen dulls psychological pain. In G. MacDonald & L. A. Jensen-Campbell (Eds.), *Social pain: Neuropsychological and health implications of loss and exclusion.* (pp. 123–140). Washington, DC: American Psychological Association.

Dobson, K. S. (2010). *Handbook of cognitive-behavioral therapies* (3rd ed.). New York: Guilford Press.

Dudukovic, N. M., Marsh, E. J., & Tversky, B. (2004). Telling a story or telling it straight: The effects of entertaining versus accurate retellings on memory. *Applied Cognitive Psychology, 18*, 125–143.

Dunlop, W. L., & Walker, L. J. (2013). The life story: Its development and relation to narration and personal identity. *International Journal of Behavioral Development, 37*, 235–247.

Eich, E., Nelson, A. L., Leghari, M. A., & Handy, T. C. (2009). Neural systems mediating field and observer memories. *Neuropsychologia, 47*, 2239–2251.

Erikson, E. H. (1968). *Identity: Youth and crisis.* Oxford England: Norton & Co.

Festinger, L. (1957). *A theory of cognitive dissonance.* Evanston, IL: Row, Peterson.

Festinger, L., Schachter, S., & Back, K. (1950). *Social pressures in informal groups: A study of human factors in housing.* New York: Harper.

Fivush, R., & Nelson, K. (2004). Culture and language in the emergence of autobiographical memory. *Psychological Science, 15*, 586–590.

Glenberg, A. M. (2008). Toward the integration of bodily states, language, and action. In G. R. Semin & E. R. Smith (Eds.), *Embodied grounding: Social, cognitive, affective, and neuroscientific approaches* (pp. 43–70). New York: Cambridge University Press.

Greenhoot, A. F., & Bunnell, S. (2009). Trauma and Memory. In J. A. Quas & R. Fivush (Eds.), *Emotion and memory in development: Biological, cognitive, and social considerations* (pp. 86–117). New York: Oxford University Press.

Grice, H. P. (1957). Meaning. *Philosophical Review, 66*, 377–388.

Habermas, T., & Bluck, S. (2000). Getting a life: The development of the life story in adolescence. *Psychological Bulletin, 126*, 748–769.

Habermas, T., & de Silveira, C. (2008). The development of global coherence in life narratives across adolescence: Temporal, causal and thematic aspects. *Developmental Psychology, 44*, 707–721.

Habermas, T., Negele, A., & Mayer, F. B. (2010). "Honey, you're jumping about"—Mothers' scaffolding of their children's and adolescents' life narration. *Cognitive Development, 25*(4), 339–351. doi: 10.1016/j.cogdev.2010.08.004

Habermas, T., & Paha, C. (2001). The development of coherence in adolescent's life narratives. *Narrative Inquiry, 11*(1), 35–54.

Hardin, C. D., & Conley, T. D. (2001). A relational approach to cognition: Shared experience and relationship affirmation in social cognition. In G. B. Moskowitz (Ed.), *Cognitive social psychology: The Princeton symposium on the legacy and future of social cognition* (pp. 3–17). Mahwah, NJ: Lawrence Erlbaum.

Harter, S. (1998). The development of self-representations. In N. Eisenberg & W. Damon (Eds.), *Handbook of child psychology*, 5th ed. (vol. *3*, pp. 553–617). New York: John Wiley and Sons.

Heuer, F., & Reisberg, D. (1992). Emotion, arousal, and memory for detail. In S. A. Christianson (Ed.), *The handbook of emotion and memory: Research and theory* (pp. 151–180). Hillsdale, NJ: Lawrence Erlbaum.

Holmes, E. A., & Mathews, A. (2010). Mental imagery in emotion and emotional disorders. *Clinical Psychology Review, 30*, 349–362.

Kaviani, H., Rahimi, M., Rahimi-Darabad, P., & Naghavi, H. R. (2011). Overgeneral memory retrieval and ineffective problem-solving in depressed patients with suicidal ideation: Implications for therapy. *International Journal of Psychology & Psychological Therapy, 11*(3), 413–423.

Kensinger, E. A., Garoff-Eaton, R. J., & Schacter, D. L. (2007). How negative emotion enhances the visual specificity of a memory. *Journal of Cognitive Neuroscience, 19*(11), 1872–1887. doi: 10.1162/jocn.2007.19.11.1872

King, M. J., MacDougall, A. G., Ferris, S. M., Levine, B., MacQueen, G. M., & McKinnon, M. C. (2010). A review of factors that moderate autobiographical memory performance in patients with major depressive disorder. *Journal of Clinical and Experimental Neuropsychology, 32*(10), 1122–1144. doi: 10.1080/13803391003781874

Korobov, N., & Bamberg, M. (2004). Positioning a "mature" self in interactive practices: How adolescent males negotiate "physical attraction" in group talk. *British Journal of Developmental Psychology, 22*, 471–492.

Levenson, R. W., Carstensen, L. L., Friesen, W. V., & Ekman, P. (1991). Emotion, physiology, and expression in old age. *Psychology and Aging, 6*, 28–35.

Libby, L. K., Shaeffer, E. M., Eibach, R. P., & Slemmer, J. A. (2007). Picture yourself at the polls: Visual perspective in mental imagery affects self-perception and behavior. *Psychological Science, 18*, 199–203.

Lilgendahl, J. P., Benet-Martinez, V., Festa, L., Levenson, C., Roseblum, R., & Dix, E. (2012). So now, I wonder, what am I? A narrative approach to bicultural identity integration. Poster presented at the Society for Personality and Social Psychology, San Diego, CA.

Lilgendahl, J. P., & McAdams, D. P. (2011). Constructing stories of self—growth: How individual differences in patterns of autobiographical reasoning relate to well—being in midlife. *Journal of Personality, 79*(2), 391–428. doi: 10.1111/j.1467-6494.2010.00688.x

Locke, J. (1996). An essay concerning humane understanding. In K. P. Winkler (Ed.), *An essay concerning human understanding: Abridged and edited with an introduction and notes.* Indianapolis, IN: Hackett.

Mansfield, C. D., Pasupathi, M., & McLean, K. C. (under review). *Developing through Difficulty: Does narrating growth of self in stories of transgressions promote self-acceptance and self-compassion?* University of Utah. Salt Lake City.

Marsh, E. J., & Tversky, B. (2004). Spinning the Stories of our Lives. *Applied Cognitive Psychology, 18*, 491–505.

McAdams, D. P. (1996). Personality, modernity, and the storied self: A contemporary framework for studying persons. *Psychological Inquiry, 7*, 295–321.

McAdams, D. P., Reynolds, J., Lewis, M., Patten, A. H., & Bowman, P. J. (2001). When bad things turn good and good things turn bad: Sequences of redemption and contamination in life narrative and their relation to psychosocial adaptation in midlife adults and in students. *Personality & Social Psychology Bulletin, 27*, 474–485.

McLean, K. C. (2005). Late adolescent identity development: Narrative meaning-making and memory telling. *Developmental Psychology, 41,* 683–691.

McLean, K. C. (2008). Stories of the young and the old: Personal continuity and narrative identity. *Developmental Psychology, 44*(1), 254–264.

McLean, K. C., & Fournier, M. A. (2008). The content and processes of autobiographical reasoning in narrative identity. *Journal of Research in Personality, 42*(3), 527–545. doi: 10.1016/j.jrp.2007.08.003

McLean, K. C., & Pasupathi, M. (2011). Old, new, borrowed, Blue? The emergence and retention of personal meaning in autobiographical storytelling. *Journal of Personality, 79*(1), 135–164. doi: 10.1111/j.1467-6494.2010.00676.x

McLean, K. C., Pasupathi, M., & Pals, J. L. (2007). Selves creating stories creating selves: A process model of narrative self development. *Personality and Social Psychology Review, 11,* 262–278.

McLean, K. C., & Pratt, M. W. (2006). Life's Little (and Big) Lessons: Identity Statuses and Meaning-Making in the Turning Point Narratives of Emerging Adults. *Developmental Psychology, 42*(4), 714–722.

McLean, K. C., & Thorne, A. (2006). Identity Light: Entertainment stories as a vehicle for self-development. In D. McAdams, R. Josselson & A. Lieblich (Eds.), *Identity and story: Creating self in narrative* (pp. 111–128). Washington, DC: APA Books.

Norrick, N. R. (2000). *Conversational Narrative: Storytelling in Everyday Talk.* Amsterdam, The Netherlands: John Benjamins B. V.

Pals, J. L. (2006). Narrative identity processing of difficult life experiences: Pathways of personality development and positive self-transformation in adulthood. *Journal of Personality, 74,* 1079–1110.

Pasupathi, M. (2001). The social construction of the personal past and its implications for adult development. *Psychological Bulletin, 127,* 651–672.

Pasupathi, M. (2006). Silk from sows ears: Collaborative construction of everyday selves in everyday stories. In D. McAdams, R. Josselson & A. Lieblich (Eds.), *Identity and story: Creating self in narrative* (pp. 129–150). Washington, DC: APA Press.

Pasupathi, M. (2007a). Telling and the remembered self: Linguistic differences in memories for previously disclosed and previously undisclosed events. *Memory, 15*(3), 258–270.

Pasupathi, M. (2007b). Telling and the remembered self: Linguistic differences in memories for previously disclosed and undisclosed events. *Memory, 15,* 258–270.

Pasupathi, M. (in press). Constructing the good enough self: Mother-child conversations and moral development from an identity framework. In C. Wainryb & H. E. Recchia (Eds.), *Talking about right and wrong: Parent-child conversations as contexts for moral development.* New York: Oxford University Press.

Pasupathi, M., Drews, F., Wainryb, C., & Stefanucci, J. (in preparation). *Narrating sedentary actions and subsequent caloric intake.* Manuscript in preparation, University of Utah, Salt Lake City, UT.

Pasupathi, M., & Mansour, E. (2006). Adult age differences in autobiographical reasoning in narratives. *Developmental Psychology, 42*(5), 798–808.

Pasupathi, M., Mansour, E., & Brubaker, J. (2007). Developing a Life Story: Constructing relations between self and experience in autobiographical narratives. *Human Development, 50*(2/3), 85–110.

Pasupathi, M., McLean, K. C., & Weeks, T. (2009). To tell or not to tell: Disclosure and the narrative self. *Journal of Personality, 77,* 1–35.

Pasupathi, M., Wainryb, C., Komolova, M., & Lucas, S. (in preparation). *Children's and adolescents' conceptions of personhood: A narrative approach.*

Philippe, F. L., Koestner, R., Lecours, S., Beaulieu-Pelletier, G., & Bois, K. (2011). The role of autobiographical memory networks in the experience of negative emotions: How our remembered past elicits our current feelings. *Emotion, 11,* 1279–1290.

Ray, R. D., Wilhelm, F. H., & Gross, J. J. (2008). All in the mind's eye? Anger rumination and reappraisal. *Journal of Personality and Social Psychology, 94*(1), 133–145.

Reese, E., Haden, C. A., Baker-Ward, L., Bauer, P. A., Fivush, R., & Ornstein, P. (2011). Coherence of personal narratives across the lifespan: A multidimensional model and coding method. *Journal of Cognition and Development, 12*(4), 424–462. doi: 10.1080/15248372.2011.587854

Reese, E., Yan, C., Jack, F., & Hayne, H. (2010). Emerging identities: Narrative and self from early childhood to early adolescence. In K. C. McLean & M. Pasupathi (Eds.), *Narrative development in adolescence: Creating the storied self* (pp. 23–43). New York: Springer Science + Business Media.

Rimé, B., Finkenauer, C., Luminet, O., Zech, E., & Phillipot, P. (1998). Social sharing of emotion: New evidence and new questions. *European Review of Social Psychology, 9,* 145–189.

Schacter, E. P. (2004). Identity configurations: A new perspective on identity formation in contemporary society. *Journal of Personality, 72,* 167–199.

Schechtman, M. (2003). Empathic access: The missing ingredient in personal identity. In R. Martin & J. Barresi (Eds.), *Personal identity.* Malden, MA: Blackwell.

Schechtman, M. (2005). Personal Identity and the Past. *Philosophy, Psychiatry, and Psychology, 12,* 9–22.

Sinclair, S., Huntsinger, J., Skorinko, J., & Hardin, C. D. (2005). Social tuning of the self: Consequences for the self-evaluations of stereotype targets. *Journal of Personality and Social Psychology, 89,* 160–175.

Stefanucci, J. K., Gagnon, K. T., & Lessard, D. A. (2011). Follow your heart: Emotion adaptively influences perception. *Social and Personality Psychology Compass, 5*(6), 296–308. doi: 10.1111/j.1751-9004.2011.00352.x

Suedfeld, P., & Eich, E. (1995). Autobiographical memory and affect under conditions of reduced environmental stimulation. *Journal of Environmental Psychology, 15*(4), 321–326. doi: 10.1006/jevp.1995.0028

Swann, W. B., Jr. (2000). Identity negotiation: Where two roads meet. In E. T. Higgins & A. W. Kruglanski (Eds.), *Motivational science: Social and personality perspectives. Key readings in social psychology* (pp. 285–305). Philadelphia: Psychology Press.

Swann, W. B. J., Bosson, J. K., & Pelham, B. W. (2002). Different partners, different selves: Strategic verification of circumscribed identities. *Personality and Social Psychology Bulletin, 28,* 1215–1228.

Tausczik, Y. R., & Pennnebaker, J. W. (2010). The psycholoical meaning of words: LIWC and computerized text analysis methods. *Journal of Language and Social Psychology, 29,* 24–54.

Terry, W. S., & Horton, G. P. (2007). A comparison of self-rated emotion in field and observer memory perspectives. *Imagination, Cognition and Personality, 27*(1), 27–35. doi: 10.2190/IC.27.1.c

Thorne, A. (2000). Personal memory telling and personality development. *Personality and Social Psychology Review, 4*(1), 45–56.

Wainryb, C., Komolova, M., & Florsheim, P. (2010). How violent youth offenders and typically developing adolescents construct moral agency in narratives about doing harm. In K. C. McLean & M. Pasupathi (Eds.), *Narrative development in adolescence: Creating the storied self* (pp. 185–206). New York: Springer.

Wang, Q. (2004). The emergence of cultural self-constructs: Autobiographical memory and self-description in European-American and Chinese Children. *Developmental Psychology, 40*, 3–15.

Weeks, T. L. (in preparation). Mother-child conversations about self-relevant events across adolescence.

Weeks, T. L., & Pasupathi, M. (2011). Stability and change self-integration for negative events: The role of listener responsiveness and elaboration. *Journal of Personality, 79*, 469–498.

Williams, J. M. G. (1992). Autobiographical memory and emotional disorders. In S. A. Christianson (Ed.), *The handbook of emotion and memory: Research and theory* (pp. 451–477). Hillsdale, NJ: Lawrence Erlbaum.

CHAPTER
12

Discerning Oneself: A Plea for the Whole

Mark Freeman

Abstract

This chapter provides an integrative response to Tilmann Habermas and Christin Köber's claims regarding the primacy of autobiographical reasoning (AR) in the constitution of identity and Monisha Pasupathi's claims regarding the importance of alternative paths from narrative to identity. Although initially appearing irreconcilable, closer examination reveals them as complementary moments of a more comprehensive multidimensional process. By Habermas and Köber's account, AR is invoked mainly in the face of disruptions to identity; Pasupathi's account suggests that whereas AR processes remain relevant to the constitution of identity, less reflective alternative paths also play an important and formative role. Whether these two pathways to identity are equally formative remains unknown. Because both are likely involved in constituting identity, it would be useful to explore their respective roles in individuals' lives and how they work together both to provide a sense of personal continuity and to shape and reshape the distinctive beings we are.

Key Words: adolescence, autobiographical reasoning, big stories, continuity, identity, memory, narrative, narrative identity, self, small stories, time

Which Sorts of Narratives (If Any)?

In beginning this response to Tilmann Habermas and Christin Köber's chapter, as well as to Monisha Pasupathi's chapter, I should confess that I have been involved in a related debate concerning the value of "big stories" and "small stories" respectively. Without going into any great detail about the nature of this debate (but see Korobov, this volume; Schachter, this volume), the "big story" perspective—to which I generally (but by no means exclusively) subscribe—tends to privilege those narratives found in life story interviews, autobiographies, and other such larger tellings, seeing them as integral to the process of identity formation (e.g., Freeman, 2006; 2011). The "small story" perspective, on the other hand, tends to privilege those narratives found in conversational exchanges and other such in situ, on-the-ground tellings, the supposition being that the process of identity formation is a good deal more ongoing, piecemeal, and "local" than big story theorists would suggest (e.g., Bamberg, 2006; 2011; Georgakopolou, 2006). As Bamberg (2006) has argued, the kind of interpretive reflection deemed central to the big story approach is essentially about life "on holiday," wherein one steps out of the flow of experience to take stock of some larger swath of one's life. This process is relatively rare, he insists, and may take place mainly when social scientists and the like come around and require just this sort of stepping-out. Why not look at life itself, in all of its uncertainty and instability, ins and outs, twists and turns, and see how identity grows out of that rather than relying on the more rarefied, even contrived, atmosphere of the life story interview? The point is an important one, to be sure, and needs to be taken seriously.

It might be noted that a related critique has been offered as well, one that in fact intensifies the entire situation. Here, I am referring to those, such as Galen Strawson, who are quite convinced not only that big stories aren't what they are cracked up to be by the likes of MacIntyre (1981), Ricoeur (1981a), Taylor (1989), and others but that small stories aren't a whole lot better. Judging by the title of his well-known diatribe "Against Narrativity" (2004), Strawson has little patience for either because, in the end, they are nothing more than faddish and largely false attempts to privilege "Diachronics," as he calls them, over "Episodics"—that is, those who, for whatever ill-conceived reason, see their lives as stories and those (like himself) who do not. Now, Strawson would surely have more sympathy for the small story approach than the big. Story size aside, however, the very idea of narrativity as somehow being essential to life tends, at an extreme, to "close down important avenues of thought, impoverish our grasp of ethical possibilities, needlessly and wrongly distress those who do not fit their [advocates'] model, and [is] potentially destructive in psychotherapeutic contexts" (p. 429). Well, then! Where does this leave us? And can the two chapters we now have before us help to resolve some of the tensions at hand?

The (Putative) Primacy of Autobiographical Reasoning

Habermas and Köber's chapter corresponds roughly to the big story approach just identified. "The central contention of this chapter," they assert at the outset, "is that the life story offers unique, explicit ways of establishing personal continuity across change" (p. 149). As for what they mean by "life story," it is seen as "an overarching concept for the life as told, remembered, or thought about" and is manifested in the form of both "entire life narratives" and "autobiographical reasoning" (AR), which in turn refers to "a process of thinking or talking about the personal past that involves arguments that link distinct elements of one's life to each other and to the self in an attempt to relate the present self to one's personal past and future" (p. 149). There is much in these introductory words to consider as we go about determining how this approach fares in relation to Pasupathi's. Perhaps most central is the idea of the life story, which, on Habermas and Köber's account, entails some measure of interpretive *distance* (e.g., Gadamer, 1982; see also Ricoeur's [1981a] notion of "distanciation") from the events of the past as well as an attempt to link them together in some meaningful way from the vantage point of the present. Ricoeur (1981a; 1981b;

1985) has spoken in this context of the "episodic" and "configurational" dimensions of narrative, the former referring to the (remembered) events and experiences of the past and the latter referring to the synoptic process of seeing these events and experiences as integral parts of an evolving, interconnected whole. There is thus a *reflective* aspect to this version of identity formation, the assumption being that some form of narrative stock-taking—AR, essentially—is a key feature of the process of discerning who and what one is. Contra Strawson and company, one might also speak of "narrativity," understood here as that dimension of the human condition that comes into being through narrative.

There is also a *temporal* aspect to identity formation as Habermas and Köber conceptualize it. I question the idea that "narratives imitate sequences of events," such that they follow the classic "and then..., and then..." path (p. 150). Indeed, as I have suggested elsewhere (e.g., Freeman, 2010), one fascinating feature of narrative is that, even as event "a" may be said to lead to event "b," there is a very real sense in which event "b" may lead to event "a," calling forth a meaning or a significance that was unavailable at the time. As Nietzsche (1901/1968) put the matter some time ago, "In the phenomenalism of the 'inner world' we invert the chronological order of cause and effect. The fundamental fact of inner experience is that the cause is imagined after the effect takes place" (p. 265). In a related vein, Ned Lukacher (1986) has spoken of a "metaleptic" logic, "in which causes are both the causes of effects and effects of effects" (p. 35). And as Ricoeur (1988) has added, "Ordinary time can be characterized as a series of point-like 'nows,' whose intervals are measured by clocks. Defined in this way, time deserves to be called 'now time'" (p. 86). What is "unacceptable," he goes on to say, "is the claim that this representation be held to be the true concept of time" (p. 87). This mode of time, I have added, "is but one concept of time, and it does well to organize and order those features of the world characterized by linearity, by the inexorable forwardness of (certain) natural processes. But it cannot and does not do justice to those features of the human realm that go beyond linearity, that involve movement not only from past to present but from present to past, ever again" (Freeman, 2010, p. 178). So it is that we should supplement now time—basically clock time—with what Ricoeur (1981b) calls *narrative* time.

This qualification is an important one, I believe, precisely because it underscores the interconnection between narrativity and temporality. Narrating one's past does indeed interrupt the flow of ordinary time; it is a break from the action, a "time out," perhaps even a "holiday" of sorts. But, of course, we need such holidays every now and then, if only to pause and take stock of what's been going on. Is such reflective stock-taking a necessary feature of identity formation? Put differently, can identity formation go on in the *absence* of such stock-taking? There is a relatively simple answer to these questions: it all depends on what one means by "identity." This answer even has the virtue of being true. ("Identity" means quite different things to different people.) But it's not entirely satisfactory either.

Let us therefore proceed. "In the context of everyday storytelling," Habermas and Köber write, "AR occurs when a specific life event is spontaneously placed in a biographical context" and can be found in "naturally occurring texts such as diaries, web blogs, talk shows, or printed autobiographies" and "by asking for narratives either of an entire life or of biographically significant episodes such as self-defining memories or turning points" (p. 150). The notion of "naturally occurring texts" needs to be interrogated. If by "natural," one means "customary in the kinds of times and places that call for the narrativization of one's life," then there is little to question. Whether such texts should be regarded as natural outgrowths of some inherent narrativizing tendency, however, is decidedly less clear. As for the fact that AR can be elicited in interview situations and the like, we may well wonder whether the resultant processes and products are artifacts of these very situations. Could it be that Habermas and Köber's claim that "AR is essential for the development of identity" (p. 150) is a function of the fact that they and others call for AR in their narrative research? More to the point: How "naturally occurring" *is* AR? It may well seem natural enough in the interview context; when asked to engage in AR, the modern adolescent (among others) can likely do it. Moreover, he or she may be able to tell a quite compelling story of how it relates to the formation of his or her identity. None of this, however, means that they were engaged in this process before arriving at the interview situation. Or does it?

As Habermas and Köber note in their section on psychosocial identity and adolescence, "Identity-related self-reflection and exploration, most specifically AR, is activated when identity becomes problematic and needs to be revised and reintegrated" (p. 150). This sounds true enough. The question then becomes: How frequently does identity become problematic during this phase of life? If, in fact, such identity revision and reintegration is a regular feature of adolescent life (in modern Western culture at any rate), then AR may be a "naturally occurring" consequence. Does AR occur when life is going well? Is it simply part and parcel of adolescent personal growth, however it may emerge? We need not limit these questions to adolescence either. To what extent is AR simply part and parcel of being *human*? Is it a universal phenomenon? Or is it more local? *How* local? These seem to me to be empirical questions, at least in part, and we would do well to continue exploring them.

It should be emphasized that the process being considered presumes, on some level, a need for, or at least an orientation toward, personal continuity. As Habermas and Köber point out, this idea has been challenged by Gergen (e.g., 1991) and others who, in view of the demands and dynamics of contemporary culture especially, see a movement in the direction of discontinuity, heterogeneity, and multiplicity. Using Strawson's terminology, it may be that many of us are becoming Episodics and that Diachronics, in turn, are becoming a dying breed. If this is so, of course, the current debate dies away, too. Operating on the assumption that *some* measure of personal continuity remains important, perhaps the biggest challenge to Habermas and Köber's perspective comes from those who hold that "microgenetic mechanisms" of one sort or other actually *create* identity in the context of specific interactive situations. Central to this latter perspective—Habermas and Köber refer to Bamberg's (2011) work in this context—is the improvisational nature of the everyday storytelling process along with the idea that one need not invoke the existence of a reflective autobiographical subject to undergird it. Identity, from this perspective, is *performed*, interactionally, and although some measure of continuity may result, it is more a function of the situation than the person.

Habermas and Köber acknowledge that this approach, along with several others they review, does in fact enlarge our understanding of how personal continuity is fashioned and sustained. On the whole, however, these approaches stop short of offering a mechanism for bridging personal change. To do that, they assert, "everyday storytelling does need a biographical perspective, a reference to the life story" (p. 155). To support their argument, Habermas and Köber return to adolescent experience. Why? "Adolescence is the one phase—maybe together with very old age—in which individuals change the most and in which it is therefore most difficult to maintain a sense of personal continuity" (p. 155). Again, I am not sure whether to characterize adolescence in this threat-to-continuity way. And, as has been suggested, it may be that the "need" to maintain a sense of personal continuity has been overstated. It is not entirely clear, for instance, that adolescence is a phase in which individuals change the most. Nor is it entirely clear that whatever change they *do* undergo incites the need to maintain continuity. Finally, even if there does emerge such a need, it remains open to question whether it must be "sated" via AR. These are important qualifications, and we need to bear them in mind as we proceed. But, for present purposes, let us assume, with Habermas and Köber, that adolescence can in fact be characterized in the basic way they have identified. Following their line of thinking, "Adolescents acquire a new cognitive-communicative ability, the life story format and the related ability for AR . . . , which makes it easier to bridge discontinuities and integrate change into identity" (p. 155), all of which leads them to argue that "the life story and its use in AR is the most potent instrument to create personal continuity across change" (p. 159).

Taking this line of thinking one step further, Habermas and Köber go on to consider "how specific contexts and forms of the actual use of AR may influence how effective AR is in securing self-continuity" (p. 159). It is at this juncture that we return to the issue of disruption and how AR may provide a means for redressing it. In keeping with what was said earlier, if in fact one's life circumstances are generally stable and if, moreover, one has adequate psychological resources to bring to bear on whatever changes may occur, the kinds of processes found in "smaller" approaches may suffice to maintain one's sense of self-continuity. (Small stories for small disruptions.) When one's life circumstances or internal resources change radically, however, AR will likely step in to "compensate" the resultant discontinuity and restore the desired sense of continuity. (Big stories, issuing from AR, for big disruptions.) This sounds plausible. But doesn't it imply that the aforementioned "necessity" of AR in the formation of identity only emerges, or primarily emerges, in those life circumstances disruptive and disturbing enough to require compensatory measures? Indeed: "Thus, individuals probably engage most in AR in times of biographical rupture or transitions." As such, "it is also in these times that AR is probably the most functional in contributing to self-continuity, and, through this, also to well-being" (p. 160).

Seen from one angle, Habermas and Köber have made a solid, if not unassailable, case for the idea that (as their title puts it) "autobiographical reasoning is constitutive for narrative identity" and that the life story plays an important role in the process. Seen from another angle, however, their very reliance on disruption and rupture for the compensatory work of AR to ensue would seem to weaken their claims for its necessity. Although it may be necessary for some adolescents, it may not be necessary for others. Likewise, although it may be necessary at certain times, it may not be necessary at other times. The necessity at hand thus appears to be a partial and conditional one, tied to specific persons and life circumstances. Habermas and Köber say as much: "In times of personal stability," they reiterate, "there will be less motivation to spontaneously engage in AR because a subjective sense of self-continuity is sufficiently provided by the non-reflective mechanisms discussed [earlier]" (p. 160). That there may be "less motivation" to engage in AR in stable times seems likely. Here, though, I would ask: Does AR becomes completely irrelevant in such times? Is it all but absent? Or is it still (quietly) at work? There is a further, more substantive question to be raised here as well: Is the subjective sense of self-continuity to which Habermas and Köber refer to be equated with identity? It is a requisite condition of identity, to be sure; without some sense of personal continuity, there can be no identity. But insofar as we consider identity in more substantive terms, as having to do not only with the fact of my continuity but the existence of my distinctive mode of being, as *this* particular person with *this* particular history, it may be that Habermas and Köber's claims for AR's necessity are redeemed.

Extending their argument that "voluntary, temporally limited, linear AR regarding specific events and resulting in a positive retrospective (and therefore also prospective) evaluation maintains a sense of self-continuity, especially in situations in which it is threatened by abrupt life change," Habermas and Köber assert that "discontinuity in life may require autobiographical reasoning…as a temporary measure to establish some explicit and positive form of self-continuity" (p. 162). On their account, once this developmental identity work has been carried out, the need for AR has been obviated and other, less reflective mechanisms of identity maintenance can take over. At the same time, it may be that the results of such work "settle," the life story schema having become solidified further in the course of its employment.

To what extent does one bring this schema to the kinds of routine interactions highlighted by those small story/situationist theorists who downplay the role of AR in identity formation? Does everyone do so? Or only those who have suffered through abrupt life changes and who have therefore had to invoke the work of AR to restore their sense of self-continuity? Then again, it may be that this whole idea of AR has been overplayed and that, as Pasupathi puts it, "identity is not something people build and then possess, but rather, ... is a problem that needs to be resolved in an ongoing way throughout individuals' lives" (p. 166). I would guess that Habermas and Köber could sign on to at least a portion of this way of thinking: there is no final resolution to the problem of identity; it is an ongoing concern and task. The question is what role AR plays in the process.

Thinking Beyond AR

Pasupathi begins her chapter by calling the problem of identity "a simple problem": "[A]m I the same person now, typing this sentence, who was previously reading a paper by philosopher Marya Schechtman?" (p. 166). As I have already indicated, this issue of "sameness"—understood here in the sense of self-continuity amidst change—is certainly a necessary aspect of identity, and philosophers and psychologists alike have spilled lots of ink trying to think it through. This suggests to me that the issue is not so simple. What's more, and again, I would argue that the issue of identity, as psychologists especially have tended to study it, goes beyond the concern with sameness and moves into more existential terrain, having to do with the very nature and substance of one's distinctive being. I believe this distinction to be an important one. Indeed, I believe it may serve to resolve at least some of the tension between Habermas and Köber's and Pasupathi's perspectives on the formation of identity.

Traditionally, Pasupathi points out, the sameness question has been addressed by turning to the life story in one form or other. According to her, however, "there are other paths by which narrating the events of our lives may help resolve the problem of identity—paths that have been less well studied, which do not require or involve explicit reasoning processes, and which do not require, in any way, that the narrated events become important, self-defining, or parts of a life story" (p. 166). This is an interesting and provocative claim and, on the face of it, would seem to run entirely counter to Habermas and Köber's perspective. One Strawson-like question I would pose, at the outset, is whether the processes being referred to really entail *narrating* the events of our lives or whether we are considering something else entirely. Could it be that there are aspects of identity formation and maintenance that aren't narrative at all? On my reading, Pasupathi gestures in this direction, as have some other small story theorists; once one turns to the more immediate context of conversation (for instance), the narrative dimension of discourse may be somewhat less visible. Pasupathi's main question, in any case, is what kinds of practices are involved, or may be involved, in identity formation and whether AR is a necessary feature of them. As she acknowledges, AR is certainly one way in, so to speak, to the problem of identity. That is to say, there is no question but that, in some instances, AR plays the very role Habermas and Köber have argued for. However, she is also dissatisfied with this sort of blanket solution to the problem at hand and has "a nagging notion that this can't be all there is to narrative and identity" and, more specifically, "that there are ways that narrative can shape identity that do not involve autobiographical reasoning or life stories" (p. 168).

My initial response to this provocative assertion? It all depends on what one means by "autobiographical reasoning" and "life stories." As Pasupathi goes on to suggest, AR is actually a somewhat "rare bird." This idea is reminiscent of the aforementioned life-on-holiday comment Michael Bamberg sent my way some time ago when he was beginning to develop his small stories idea. There is no question but that big AR-style stories emerge when people sit down to write autobiographies or when big story researchers ask people to do some condensed variant of the same. In keeping with Habermas and Köber's approach, it also seems to happen with some regularity at certain pivotal life junctures—during adolescent or mid-life crises, for instance. But how often does explicit AR, reflecting, and meaning-making really take place? I ask again: Could it be that some of our theorizing is an artifact of our own methods—and preconceptions about how "life" actually works? From Pasupathi's perspective, "people are narrating all the time, but autobiographical reasoning in those contexts is often much rarer" (p. 168). Now, if we simply wanted to get on with it, we could just call the kinds of narrations (assuming they are) Pasupathi is referring to here as *small* autobiographical reasoning ("SAR") or some such thing. But this feels like cheating. Plus, it really doesn't resolve the relevant issues.

So, what are the possibilities? "In terms of narrative contributions to identity development," Pasupathi continues, "this means one of three things." The first is that all this quotidian in situ narrating is irrelevant for identity. She finds this "tempting" but "unsatisfying." Is it really possible that "our routine and everyday lives—and the many narratives those ordinary lives generate—[are] irrelevant for identity? Surely not." The second possibility is that identity resolutions are mainly a function of momentous events, with the small stories of daily life serving essentially as epiphenomena of these larger identity-resolving narratives. This is somewhat more tempting, "but it seems unsatisfying" still "to argue that something we engage in so frequently does not have anything to do with establishing who we are or our sense of being the same person over time." In the end, in other words, this second possibility is just a variant of the first. The third possibility is that "there may be ways that narrative can shape and influence identity—defined as the continuities in our psychological experience—that involve pathways other than autobiographical reasoning" (pp. 168–169). It is this last possibility that Pasupathi is moving toward. And, as far as I can tell, it is actually very much in keeping with Habermas and Köber's perspective. They, of course, were more concerned with the AR part of the equation, particularly as it emerges in the context of crises and disruptions. Pasupathi is more concerned with those "steadier," nondisruptive aspects of our lives that, on her account, comprise the lion's share of experience. Here, then, we would seem to have a comprehensive, two-tiered model of identity formation and development, entailing both AR-based processes and non-AR-based processes, working in tandem (see Freeman, 2011). Diachronics would be those whose lives are filled with disruptions (whether real or imagined), and Synchronics would be those more conflict-free beings who need not take the time to take stock of their lives. Case closed? Perhaps.

Let me, however, identify one additional possibility—which would essentially say, yes, the less explicit and less conscious acts of narration Pasupathi has highlighted do indeed have a bearing on identity—*if* we define identity mainly, or exclusively, in terms of continuities in our experience. The idea that these more momentary sites of narration are integral to the maintenance of identity qua self-continuity seems right. If, however, we define identity not simply in terms of self-continuity but in terms of what I earlier referred to as "the nature and substance of one's distinctive being"—that is, not just the *process* dimension of identity but its *content*—these piecemeal narrations alone may not suffice to perform the necessary identity work. William James's seminal reflections on the consciousness of self (1890/1950) would seem relevant to this issue. Following his extensive discussion of the "me," in which he considers the material, social, and spiritual aspects of the self, he moves on to the question of personal continuity via an exploration of the "I." On his account, the "me" refers to the "empirical person" and the "I" to the "judging Thought" (p. 371). Pasupathi's perspective is roughly in keeping with James's discussion of the latter, which is less about reasoning than recognition, the ability to identify certain features of the past as "one's own." Indeed, much of this section of the text is about just the sort of piecemeal narrational processes she is considering. But these alone cannot tell the whole story of personal identity, only that more "formal" aspect of it that concerns continuity.

This in no way renders such processes irrelevant, however. Nor does it render them as mere epiphenomena, as reflections or expressions of larger autobiographical reasoning processes. Rather, it may be that these smaller narrations are the very "data" upon which these larger processes are based (at least for those narrators who care about the data). This would suggest that some form of narrative "metabolization," at a higher level, would still be required for substantive identity work to take place. What this would suggest, in turn—and I believe this to be so—is that in order to understand the formation of identity, one needs to invoke *both* levels: the implicit, perhaps unconscious, level as it occurs in everyday narration and the explicit, more conscious, level as it occurs through some form or other of AR—or, as I prefer to call it, *narrative reflection* (Freeman, 2010). Although AR may not be necessary for the formation of identity qua self-continuity, in other words, it likely is necessary for the larger, more comprehensive sense of identity I have been referring to. For, insofar as one asks the "Who am I?" question (see Bamberg, 2011) in any sort of explicit way, whether it is driven by crisis or by those decidedly smaller concerns that irrupt quite regularly in the course of everyday life, one's answer, I believe, must entail some measure of narrative reflection. It may not be reflection of the full-blown sort that emerges through writing an autobiography or through a life story interview; it may be more transient and fleeting. But it is difficult to conceive of the sort of substantive identity work being considered apart from narrative reflection.

Let us leave these broader theoretical considerations aside for the time being and, following Pasupathi's lead, examine the narrative she has provided of the woman who gets annoyed at her husband during a game of Yahtzee and calls him a moron. Truthfully, I don't know quite what to make of this story. I find the event itself disturbing. The narrator confesses to having gotten "carried away" with herself and admits to her "somewhat overly competitive nature," but these admissions don't quite account for her venomous attack on poor Derek. It could be that she uttered her words tongue-in-cheek and that, in the context of it being "just a game," her words didn't come off quite as venomously as I am imagining. But calling her husband a moron—in front of his mother and brother, no less—seems excessive and quite hostile. Who *is* this woman? What's her problem, anyway? The aftermath is notable as well. She felt horrible following her outburst and was shocked at what she'd done, as was Derek. Not surprising! Shortly after, apparently, she and her family "shrugged it off with a laugh" and returned to Yahtzee. But what exactly does this mean? More to the point still: Can we *know* what it means, or what it might mean, without knowing more about *her*—whether, for instance, this sort of thing is common, whether she will revisit it further in retrospect, what her relationship with her husband is like, and so on? Plus, I suppose we should ask: *Is* he a moron? This exchange is telling, to be sure. But I am not entirely sure what it tells—and I am not entirely sure we can know what it tells unless we know more about the narrative backdrop within which the exchange occurs. This means knowing more about the relevant players, their histories, their characters, and their patterns of interaction.

Having said this, let me hasten to add that Pasupathi does well to underscore the "tacit themes" present in this scenario and also the fact that, strictly speaking, "there is no autobiographical reasoning creating identity in the form of lasting values," only "the taken-for-granted importance of relational roles and obligations, without which the entire narrative makes less—or indeed no—sense" (p. 169). But, of course, all we have here is a brief autobiographical fragment, and whether further, more deliberate AR might be involved remains an open question. Had her husband responded by saying "That's the last time you'll be calling me that. I've had it," she might well be provoked to do some soul searching about what her issues really are. The question, then, is whether this scenario would make even more sense if we knew more about the larger sociopsychological constellation within which this exchange has emerged. One way or the other, the notion that we might be more attentive to "thematic and linguistic contents that imply beliefs, values, and ideologies which are not explicitly claimed by the narrator" (p. 170) is surely important.

The second aspect of identity formation Pasupathi explores in her piece is "relational positioning," which refers to that aspect of identity emerging in and through particular interactions with others. She goes on to use the phrase "identity creation," the assumption being that, through positioning, one does more than simply "express" who one is; one engages in a creative identity-producing act. As she acknowledges, this doesn't quite get us to the issue of identity qua continuity-in-time. The challenge, therefore, is to somehow link up these more momentary in situ exchanges and this issue of continuity. And the way this seems to happen, she suggests, is through repetition, a kind of accretion or "sedimentation" of the momentary, such that something more enduring is fashioned. The main point, if I understand correctly, is again that we can in fact get to identity qua continuity without turning to explicit acts of autobiographical reflection. This is surely the case. But it's hard to imagine that there's not some form of autobiographical reasoning going on.

Some of Ricoeur's ideas about narrative identity seem relevant here. "Without leaving the sphere of everyday experience," he writes, "are we not inclined to see in a given chain of episodes in our own life something like *stories that have not yet been told*, stories that demand to be told, stories that offer points of anchorage for the narrative?" (1991, p. 30). We are "entangled" in stories, as Ricoeur puts it; narrating is a "secondary process," "grafted" onto this entanglement. "Recounting, following, understanding stories is then simply the continuation of these unspoken stories" (p. 30). As for how narrative identity enters the picture, Ricoeur suggests that, although it may well be rooted in these unspoken stories, it doesn't really come into being until there is a more explicit reflective process:

> Our life, when then embraced in a single glance, appears to us as the field of a constructive activity, borrowed from narrative understanding, by which we attempt to discover and not simply to impose from outside the *narrative identity which constitutes us*. I am stressing the expression "narrative identity" for what we call subjectivity is neither an incoherent series of events nor an immutable substantiality,

impervious to evolution. This is precisely the sort of identity which narrative composition alone can create through its dynamism. (p. 32)

I am also reminded of a wonderful little passage from Wilhelm Dilthey (1910/1976) in this context: "Between the parts we see a connection which neither is, nor is intended to be, the simple likeness of a life of so many years, but which, because understanding is involved, expresses what the individual knows about the continuity of his life" (215).

Pasupathi's point about relational continuity still stands. As such, it makes good sense to be more attentive to these interactive dimensions. I would nevertheless ask: Can identity be fashioned through momentary exchanges alone? Or does it still require some more synthetic, synoptic reflective act?

Moving on, finally, to the third aspect of identity Pasupathi addresses, having to do with embodied experience, the idea is that there is a connection set up between what she (drawing on Damasio) refers to as "body-there-and-then" maps and "body-right-now" maps and that this connection has some bearing on the formation of identity. Here, too, then, we are seeing identity-forming acts taking place without explicit acts of AR—indeed, one might even argue, without reason altogether. "Speculatively," in any case, Pasupathi continues, there is the idea that "identity continuity may be best served when the body-there-and-then and body-right-now loops are moderately distinct during the act of remembering because it is this discrepancy that also creates clear continuity between the body-right-now and the body-there-and-then via the mapping of links between the two" (p. 173). And so, "the creation of enough, and not too much, space in between the body-there-and-then and body-right-now maps"—I couldn't help but think of the three bears in this context—"along with mapping of the relations between them—makes an important contribution to an embodied link between past and present, one that needs no explicit reasoning" (p. 173).

Continuing in this speculative mode, Pasupathi goes on to suggest that, in everyday event narration, what we frequently see is a somewhat relaxed body-right-now linking up with a more intense "body-there-then," which in turn "creates a particular kind of continuity, one in which an emotional experience may be 'owned' by the very same individual who has now returned to a place of safety" (p. 26). It's a fascinating idea. Nevertheless, I would want to ask again: Isn't there a kind of autobiographical reasoning involved; that is, an *embodied* kind, wherein one lives through, in a way, what is being recollected from the vantage point of the present? This strikes me as classic narrative fare, nicely filled out by bringing the body into a picture that may too often be seen as purely cognitive. But, is this an alternative to AR or a fuller picture of how it actually works in this context of everyday narration? We could ask this another way too: Is this mode of narration different in kind from the sorts of larger processes that are being cast into question? Or is it just a "smaller" variant of these larger processes?

On the final page of her chapter, Pasupathi states that "the goal of this chapter was not to deny the power of the concept of autobiographical reasoning for understanding how narratives can serve identity development, nor," she adds, "was it to suggest we should not continue to pursue important issues in the study of autobiographical reasoning. Rather," the goal was "to broaden our examination of narrative and identity development to consider the richness of narratives, perhaps especially in their multilayered aspects" (p. 178). This is surely a laudable goal, and by all indications, it is one that Habermas and Köber would readily share. In this respect, there really is no debate between them: whereas Pasupathi is inclined toward those identity processes that go beyond AR, Habermas and Köber continue to focus their efforts on AR and clearly see it as being of primary importance. Is one of these sets of processes more important than the other?

In Service of the Whole

In my view, there is no way to answer this question in the abstract; it can only be answered in specific contexts. In the case of my mother, a 91-year-old woman with dementia who has pretty much moved beyond AR, Pasupathi's smaller, more interactive identity-maintenance processes are primary. Indeed, there is a very real sense in which my entry into my mother's world is identity-maintaining in its own right: she is lifted from the fog and suddenly becomes "Mother." There is no reflection involved, no effort after meaning, just a moment of recognition, one that serves to bring her back to herself, to some sense of who and what she is. In the case of my older daughter, a 27-year-old emerging adult who recently complained to me that she wasn't quite hitting some of the more customary life targets (husband, house, etc.) that many of her peers seemed to be hitting, she is engaging in AR regularly—and this, I should emphasize, even in the absence of overt crises or visits by narrative identity researchers. It's simply part of the fabric of her life at the moment.

Along these lines, I am not convinced that AR is a rare bird. Full-blown life narratives may be, but AR—or, again, less formally, narrative reflection (I am actually not sure how much "reasoning" is involved in these kinds of processes)—continues to strike me as part and parcel of (much of our) life as we know it. It's magnified in cases like my daughter; given the nature of her current world, she has somewhat more occasion to engage in these processes than I do or than my wife does (for instance). But we, too, engage in these processes with some regularity. Small stories frequently bring them forth: something big emerges out of something small. In addition, and as I have argued at length elsewhere, especially in my (2010) work on hindsight, so, too, do those situations in which we are incited to revisit and rework what has been going on—for instance, an event or encounter in which we may have behaved in a way that now appears shortsighted or deluded or just plain wrong. Often, there are limits to what we can know in the moment. Narrative reflection, the process of looking backward over the terrain of the past with an eye toward discerning its meaning and significance, can serve to redress these limits, giving us a new, more capacious perspective on things. This is particularly so, I have suggested, in the context of moral life, where there is a marked tendency to act first and think later.

Pasupathi closes her chapter with a qualification, perhaps even a worry. "In all of this thinking looms a possible shadow of epiphenomenal status—that is, it could be that everyday narration and identity simply aren't important for one another, unless autobiographical reasoning comes into play" (p. 178). I don't believe this would make everyday narration epiphenomenal, in the sense of being a mere reflection of larger reasoning processes. What it could mean, however, once more, is that there may still remain the need to somehow metabolize these everyday processes in some larger narrative context for significant identity work—especially *developmental* identity work—to be done. In speaking of developmental identity work, I refer back to the idea that we are considering identity not only in terms of self-continuity (which, as my mother's case well shows, need not be developmental at all), but in terms of the distinctive beings we are. What's more, in speaking developmentally—that is, in speaking of some form or other of progressive change from one mode of thinking or being to another—we are inevitably bringing some measure of narrative reflection into the process. This is because the process of development, as I am framing it here, involves what I have called the "revision of ends," that is,

> a process of reconstructing one's past and the self in which it has culminated. This is simply because for every new end that is figured in the course of one's life, old ends are superseded, which in a more general sense can be taken to mean that the "text" of one's life is being rewritten. What deserves emphasis here is that the process of development is an *interpretive* process; it always requires the reflective mediation of the experiencing individual, who is engaged in the task of taking a portion of the self as other and simultaneously identifying both its limitations and its possibilities.
> *(Freeman & Robinson, 1990, pp. 61–62)*

None of these words are meant to question Pasupathi's insistence that we broaden our perspective on narrative and identity development and that we look beyond AR as we do so. There is much to be said for examining carefully the ongoing movement of life itself and seeing in its everydayness some important sources of our sense of self. I am also struck by Pasupathi's insistence "that we look beyond the verbal, and that we look both inward, into the body, and out into the social and relational settings in which narration takes place" (p. 178). What a wonderful, provocative idea: narratives, so often thought to issue from the minds of individual persons (which, on some level, they do) also issue from bodies and from worlds beyond the perimeter of the self. However important AR may be, therefore, it is imperative that we extend our view and "take a look at some of the other possible stories we could be telling" (p. 178). One of these stories, I offer, would look at the issue of identity from the vantage point of big AR-type stories, small ones, and everything in between. It would also be on the lookout for those sources of identity that really aren't narrative at all. My purpose in saying so isn't merely to offer a plea for pluralism. Rather, it's to offer a plea for synthesis (see Freeman, 2011)—for understanding identity formation and development in all of its dimensions and for discerning how these different dimensions work together to shape the people we are. Habermas and Köber and Pasupathi are currently carrying out important work in support of this cause. I look forward to seeing what bridges might be built between their respective projects.

References

Bamberg, M. (2006). Stories: Big or small—Why do we care? *Narrative Inquiry, 16,* 139–147.

Bamberg, M. (2011). Who am I? Narration and its contribution to self and identity, *Theory & Psychology, 21,* 3–24.

Dilthey, W. (1910/1976). The construction of the historical world in the human studies. In H. P. Rickman (Ed.), *Dilthey: Selected writings* (pp. 170–245). Cambridge, UK: Cambridge University Press.

Freeman, M. (2006). Life "on holiday"? *Narrative Inquiry, 16*, 131–138.

Freeman, M. (2010). *Hindsight: The promise and peril of looking backward*. New York: Oxford University Press.

Freeman, M. (2011). Stories, big and small: Toward a synthesis, *Theory & Psychology, 21*, 114–121.

Freeman, M., & Robinson, R. E. (1990). The development within: An alternative approach to the study of lives. *New Ideas in Psychology, 8*, 53–72.

Gadamer, H.-G, (1982). *Truth and method*. New York: Crossroad.

Gergen, K. J. (1991). *The saturated self: Dilemmas of identity in contemporary life*. New York: Basic Books.

Georgakopoulou, A. (2006). Thinking big with small narrative and identity analysis. *Narrative Inquiry, 16*, 129–137.

James, W. (1890/1950). *The principles of psychology* (vol. 1). New York: Dover Publications.

Lukacher, N. (1986). *Primal scenes: Literature, philosophy, psychoanalysis*. Ithaca, NY: Cornell University Press.

MacIntyre, A. (1981). *After virtue: A study in moral theory*. Notre Dame, IN: University of Notre Dame Press.

Nietzsche, F. (1901/1968). *The will to power*. New York: Vintage.

Ricoeur, P. (1981a). *Hermeneutics and the human sciences*. Cambridge, UK: Cambridge University Press.

Ricoeur, P. (1981b). Narrative time. In W. J. T. Mitchell (Ed.), *On narrative* (pp. 165–186). Chicago: University of Chicago Press.

Ricoeur, P. (1985). *Time and narrative* (vol. 2). Chicago, IL: University of Chicago Press.

Ricoeur, P. (1985). *Time and narrative* (vol. 3). Chicago, IL: University of Chicago Press.

Ricoeur, P. (1991). Life in quest of narrative. In D. Wood (Ed.), *On Paul Ricoeur: Narrative and interpretation* (pp. 20–33). London: Routledge.

Strawson, G. (2004). Against narrativity. *Ratio*, 17, 428–452.

Taylor, C. (1989). *Sources of the self: The making of modern identity*. Cambridge, MA: Harvard University Press.

PART 4

Debates: Internal, External, and Interactional Approaches to Identity Development

CHAPTER 13

Identity as Internal Processes: How the "I" Comes to Define the "Me"

Alan S. Waterman

Abstract

In this chapter, theories of identity involving internal processes are analyzed using William James's distinction between the "I" as knower, an active, autonomous agent, and the "me" as known, the object of thoughts about one's being. The theories reviewed are psychosocial theory, the identity status paradigm, the identity style paradigm, eudaimonic identity theory, narrative approaches to identity, discursive identity theory, and post-modern/social-constructionist theory. Consideration is given to the ways in which these theories address the content of identity, the processes by which such contents are formed, and the functions identity is seen as serving. The theories reviewed are not considered to be in conflict with each other but rather as giving different emphasis to the various internal, external, and interactional processes described. Implications for future research in the field are discussed.

Key Words: discursive identity, essentialist philosophy, eudaimonic identity theory, existentialism, identity status, identity style, narrative identity, psychosocial theory, saturated self, William James

Discussions of identity as internal or external processes and/or interactional need to begin with a definition of what is meant by the term *identity* because the processes to be described follow from the definition used. For more than three decades, the definition I have employed has, with some variation, been the following: A person's self-definition, in terms of those goals, values, beliefs, and behaviors, whether chosen, established through identification, or ascribed, that provide direction, purpose, and meaning in life (Waterman, 1982; 2011). This definition contains three elements: (a) the constituents or content of identity, "what" identity is, broadly considered (i.e., goals, values, beliefs, and behaviors); (b) the processes by which those constituents originate or are formed, "how" identity comes into being (i.e., through choices made, identification, or ascription); and (c) the functions that identity serves, "why" it is needed (i.e., to provide direction, purpose, and meaning). My discussion of identity as internal processes will focus on these questions of "what," "how," and "why."

Perspectives on Identity as Internal, External, and Interactional: A Functional Analysis

When considering the nature and role of any theoretical construct, it is important to understand the purpose that construct is designed to serve, that is, what phenomena it is intended to help explain. For example, personality as a psychological construct was developed to aid in understanding (a) individual differences in the ways people think and behave; (b) broad similarities in thinking and behavior that appear to characterize nearly everyone, despite the presence of particular differences in expression of thought and action; (c) continuity/consistency/stability of thinking and behavior of individuals across time and/or contexts; and (d) inconsistency/changes in thoughts and actions over time and/or situations. Identity as a psychological construct emerged within the realm of personality theory as one among many ways to explain these phenomena and others such as coherence (or incoherence) regarding the ways in which individuals make sense of their lives, the role of purpose and meaning in life, interpersonal self-presentation, and the synthesizing of identifications with parents, peers, and other significant model figures (Adler, 2012; Syed et al., 2013; Waterman & Archer, 1990).

References to identity as internal or—as I refer to the concept in this chapter—as internal processes pertain to what it is that individuals bring to the task of identity formation, how it is experienced, and its implications for personal psychological functioning. References to identity formation as entailing external processes focus attention on the many ways in which identity is shaped by the particular social and cultural contexts within which people develop. Contexts viewed in this way are generally considered as broad and relatively stable aspects of a society, sanctioning some ways in which individuals may define themselves and placing other possibilities outside the range of what is considered acceptable. When identity is viewed as emerging from discursive, interactional contexts (see Korobov, this volume), the focus is placed on the specific and highly varied interpersonal interactions that people have because these both represent and shape individuals' identity at that moment in time.

Whether individual theorists or researchers choose to focus on internal, external, or interactional aspects of identity is largely a consequence of disciplinary training and personal interests and the particular functions of identity they are seeking to understand. For example, scholars with clinical backgrounds, interested in helping those struggling to make sense of their lives to find ways to move toward a personally meaningful future, are inclined toward exploring internal processes emphasizing individual differences with respect to the presence or absence of clear, stable, coherent knowledge of who one is and what one seeks to do in life. Theorists and researchers with a cognitive orientation are similarly oriented toward internal processes, with an emphasis on the implications for identity arising from individual differences in informational processing and decision making. Developmentalists often have a somewhat more inclusive orientation, exploring not only the ways in which internal processes change over time, but also considering the roles that parents, peers, and others may play in affecting the course of such changes. Social psychologists and sociologists concerned with identity issues generally take a perspective more comparably balanced with respect to consideration of external and internal processes, emphasizing the ways in which social and cultural variables influence (internal) thinking about identity. This is reflected in the work on ingroup/outgroup relations, racial and ethnic identity, and the role of social capital in identity functioning. More recently, scholars making use of the perspective of discourse analysis have focused their attention on changes in identity in the immediate present as a function of interactions taking place in the context in which a person is functioning at a single point in time. In sum, where scholars look when endeavoring to expand our understanding of identity functioning depends on what they are seeking to explain.

Although divisions among internal, external, and interactive contributors to identity formation and function have an appeal based in part on their correspondence to focal concerns of different fields and subfields within the social sciences, it should be understood that these contributors to identity are inextricably interconnected. From birth onward, our psyche always functions within some physical, social, and cultural context, and a great deal of our time is spent in interactions with others who comprise our extended social networks. Even when we are alone, our internal monologue in consciousness is influenced by the images we carry of the people in our life, both actual and virtual, by the language(s) in which we think, and by the cultural memes to which we have had exposure. Private consciousness when alone may well be interactional, as when we would describe ourselves as being of two (or more) minds regarding whatever it is that we are thinking. It can even be argued that virtually everything internal, external, and interactional has implications for identity functioning since, broadly speaking, that which does not challenge the ways in which we currently define ourselves contributes to the stability of the existing self-definition.

This should make clear that I consider distinctions between identity as internal, external, and interactive as artificial and likely to be misleading. It is all of these, and asserting that one set of processes is more important than the others is more likely to obscure the understanding of identity and identity functioning than to promote it. Yet, I believe the editors of this volume were correct when asking me to address internal processes because those have been the focus of my theoretical and research attention throughout my career. It would be fair to ask why, if internal, external, and interactive processes are of comparable importance, I have chosen to primarily study one set of contributors rather than others. The answer is that internal processes are of greater interest to me, and I believe I have more to contribute on that subject than I do on identity as external or interactional processes. I leave it to others in the field with a greater interest in external and interactive processes to balance the scales.

The "I" and the "Me" in the Context of Identity

As the title for this chapter suggests, I will be framing my presentation of identity as internal processes in terms of William James's distinction between the "I" as knower, as an active, autonomous agent and the "me" as known, as the object of thoughts about one's being (James, 1890). The "I" is the actor, the doer, those active aspects of the self subjectively experienced in consciousness as the locus of choosing/determining the course of activity a person takes at any given point in time and therefore responsible for the behaviors being enacted. This is the Cartesian "I," the "I" that thinks and therefore "is." And if "I" am, then the existential identity question follows inevitably: "Who am 'I'?" Answers to that question are to be found in the contents of the "me." The "me" refers to the subjective experiences regarding the nature of oneself as an entity. It is descriptive of who one is, at least in self-perception. It is the self as object to be understood. And as description, it does not have the capacity to initiate action.

It is through the lens of the distinction between the "I" and "me" that I review alternative conceptions of identity analyzing the role played by internal processes (and occasionally external and interactional processes as well). This review covers a broad range of theories: (a) psychosocial theory, (b) the identity status paradigm, (c) the identity style paradigm, (d) eudaimonic identity theory, (e) narrative approaches to identity, (f) discursive identity theory, and (g) post-modern/social-constructionist theory. Whereas some of these theories have emphasized internal processes, others have emphasized external or interactional processes. In these latter instances, I will be focusing my attention on what I see as internal elements in identity functioning embedded within those theories.

With respect to the definition of identity provided in the opening of this chapter, matters of "what" involving goals, values, beliefs, and behaviors, and "why" involving purpose and meaning in life, provide a description of who the person is and thus refers to aspects of the "me." In contrast, matters of "how" the content of goals, values, beliefs, behaviors, directions, purposes, meanings are adopted—that is, through choice, ascription, or identification—refer to active processes employed by the "I" in determining who one is to become. The nature of these processes requires some elaboration.

Choice is the most active of these processes and most often, although not necessarily, involves consideration of and deliberation about a set of potential alternatives. This process can be thought of as reflecting the "I" forcefully at work and at its most efficacious. Choice involves the "I" striving to do what it can to direct the course of one's life toward that which is perceived as most likely to promote well-being, whatever the "I" considers to represent well-being.

The most frequent identification figures in a child's life are parents, older siblings, parents of friends, friends themselves, teachers, and community figures outside of the child's immediate social circle. Given the number of people in a person's social context, many are likely to hold differing expectations about what goals should be pursued, what to value, what to believe, and what behaviors should be enacted. Like choice, identification is an active process in that the "I" must choose who is worthy to be a model with whom to identify and who is not so worthy. However, the process of identification typically involves active consideration of fewer and less varied alternatives than does the process of choice. Based on extensive interviewing on the theme of identity, I found it interesting to observe that interview respondents often use the language of choice when describing goals, values, and beliefs developed through identification. This reflects both an active "I" in the process of identification and a perception that the choices made through identification are presumed to promote well-being.

Ascription should also be considered an active process with respect to identity formation although less so when compared with choice and identification. The term reflects assignment to a category by circumstances external to the person. When constraints on choices regarding goals, values, beliefs, and behaviors are imposed due to assignment to a category, for example, on the basis of gender, race/ethnicity, religion, age, or physical or mental health status, the "I" will not likely be aware of the full range of options that are available or that could become available. Indeed, preconceptions and prejudices present within a society may act to render some options unavailable. It may seem an odd construction to refer to ascription as an active process to any extent. I do so here because I see the individual as having the capacity to accept, modify, ignore, or reject any goals, values, beliefs, or behaviors social others attempt to impose on the person. If the "I" accepts such efforts, those aspects of a person's identity can be seen as being simultaneously chosen and ascribed. As theory and research on racial identity attest, there exists a considerable variety of ways in which a person can respond to ascribed aspects of identity ranging from active acceptance, through passive acceptance, to intense opposition, and to transcending the dichotomies that others seek to impose (Constantine, Richardson, Benjamin, & Wilson, 1998; Worrell, Cross, & Vandiver, 2001).

Since it appears indisputable to assert that the locus of consciousness resides within the person, it follows that any identity process that involves the "I" and its modes of functioning is an internal process. It is certainly possible to hold the view, as some have, that the self is an illusion, but rejecting that concept entails rendering the concept of identity as a person's self-definition moot. If there is no self, there cannot be a self-definition, and whatever may be called identity is chimerical. Therefore, proceeding on the basis that the self is sufficiently real, what we need identity theories to do is elucidate the nature of processes the "I" employs when endeavoring to establish and/or recognize the nature of the "me" and selects actions through which the "me" is implemented or expressed.

Considerations of the extent to which identity processes involving the self as object (that is, the "me") are internal, external, and interactional would appear to be more ambiguous. It is certainly plausible to assert that the goals, values, and beliefs a person holds, and the behaviors expressed, may become established through processes that bypass in some manner direct awareness, that is, conscious functioning representing the "I." The Freudian unconscious (Freud, 1901/2003) and the Jungian collective unconscious (1934–1954/1981) are two examples of mechanisms for the origins and expression of identity that do not involve conscious choice, although both would be characterized as internal rather than external processes. With regard to promoting an understanding of the role of the "me" in identity functioning, theories should focus on the role played by differing identity structures within which identity content is organized, the functions identity serves, as well as the specific choices that constitute the person's identity.

The distinction between the "I" and the "me" raises numerous metaphysical issues that are beyond the scope of material I wish to address in depth in this chapter. As someone with a longstanding interest in the philosophical foundations of psychological theories, I do want to alert readers to the philosophical framework that has informed my writing, including this chapter. From my description of the "I," it should be clear that I embrace the existentialist perspective on freedom and responsibility. I am an essentialist, however, with respect to the ontology of identity, as will be evident in my presentation of eudaimonic identity theory later. This combination of perspectives has led me to recognize that I resonate with the view that consciousness is an emergent property of complex biological functioning (Broad, 1925; Jones 1972), and thus I accept a version of mind–body dualism. With respect to epistemology, I believe human freedom is not incompatible with a science of psychology. What is needed for the successful conduct of psychological research is that behavior is predictable, not determined. In principle, freely chosen goals, values, and beliefs provide a more than sufficient basis on which to predict behavior, at least behaviors associated with the pursuit and implementation of those identity elements.

I have not attempted to make truth claims about the positions referred to in the previous paragraph, nor will I do so here. Others, looking at much of the same philosophical and psychological information available have reached different conclusions. These are not matters subject to "proof," neither empirically, given the current state of our methodologies and technologies, nor philosophically, as evidenced by the multiplicity of theories that exist within philosophy on each of them. Rather, I hold them pragmatically, much as James advocated, because they have worked well for me in what I have sought to do throughout my career, including understanding internal processes associated with identity formation and its expression.

I have chosen to convey here a description of my philosophical perspective for several reasons. First, it illustrates one aspect of my identity, that is, my personal "me." It is the outcome of a long developmental and intellectual process that I have not described. Second, inclusion of the previous paragraph allows me to make the observation that, in writing it, I, that is, my personal "I," had to decide what to include and what to omit, how it should be said, how it needed to be revised (multiple times), and actively reflect upon why I wanted to include such material. Third, if readers find themselves taking issue with the analysis I present in the remainder of this chapter, it will very likely be because they hold a quite different perspective on one or more of the philosophical issues I referenced in the preceding paragraph. By summarizing my philosophical orientation, even as briefly as I have, I hope to help readers understand their reactions to what I have written and thus promote communication, not only where there is agreement, but where there is disagreement as well.

Theoretical Perspectives on Identity Formation and Its Expression

With respect to each of the theoretical perspectives of identity functioning I discuss here, it is not my intent to summarize the theories in depth nor to review the research that validates the theories or calls them into question. Rather, my goal is to focus on those elements within the theories that pertain to the nature of the processes entailed in the origins of identity elements and in their implementation. As called for with respect to the theme for this chapter, my attention is directed primarily to the internal processes posited within the theories, although, inevitably, I have occasion to address, at least in passing, external, and interactional processes as well.

Psychosocial Theory

It is generally acknowledged that the writings of Erik Erikson (1963; 1968) initiated the theoretical and empirical research attention to identity that has characterized the past half-century. Erikson was not a systematic theorist, his eight-stage theory notwithstanding. His genius was his intuitive insight into psychological dynamics and his ability to help readers glimpse inside the minds of developing individuals (and important historical innovators). In the *Prologue* to *Identity: Youth and Crisis*, Erikson (1968) provides the following descriptive statements and partial aspects of the identity construct: "a normative crisis," "a subjective sense of an invigorating sameness and continuity," "a common dynamic pattern," "a unity of personal and cultural identity," "a process of simultaneous reflection and observation," "a process of increasing differentiation," a process that is "always changing and developing," "an age-specific ethical capacity," "cultural, philosophic, and national identity elements," "economic, religious, or political; regional or national" remnants of identity, "a psychohistorical perspective," "a most central ethnic sense," "sexual identity confusion," identity "tied to the manner of his toil and of his cooperation with others," "specialized-technological identity," "universalist-humanist" identity, "criminal identity," "positive" and "negative" identity, "psychosocial identity," "a manufactured identity," "the eternal Identity," "an all-inclusive human identity," "worldwide identity bridging affluence and underdevelopment," "identity strength," "identity confusion," and "psychosocial moratorium." And that is just in the Prologue!

This catalog of identity-related constructs includes those referencing elements of the "I" (e.g., an invigorating sense of sameness and continuity; a process of simultaneous reflection and observation) and the "me" (e.g., cultural, philosophical, national identity elements; criminal identity), as well as those referencing internal processes (e.g., an age-specific ethical capacity; identity confusion) and external processes (e.g., a unity of personal and cultural identity; worldwide identity bridging affluence and underdevelopment).

With respect to the "what" or content of identity, Erikson (1968) identified concerns in the identity domains of work and ideology as among the most important for adolescents to resolve. Ideological elements of identity were broadly considered to cover both religious and political concerns. He also wrote extensively about gender, racial, ethnic, cultural, and national identities (Erikson, 1963; 1968; 1975). Although he coined the term *identity crisis*, he wrote little about how adolescents and others went about resolving identity concerns, that is, the processes involved in identity formation. His greatest emphasis would appear to have been on the "why," that is, the functions that identity concepts serve. Waterman and Archer (1990), working from the writings of Erikson, identified multiple such functions, including continuity, coherence, purpose, direction, social comparisons, communality with others, differentiation from others, synthesizing of identifications, and protection from threats of discontinuity.

Although Erikson's theory is usually described as a psychosocial theory, it is justified to view it as a biopsychosocial theory (Engel, 1980). In *The Life Cycle Competed: A Review* (Erikson, 1982) he wrote: "I...begin with the assumption that a human being's existence depends at every moment on three processes of organization that must complement each other. There is, in whatever order, the biological process of the hierarchic organization of organ systems constituting a body (*soma*); there is the psychic process organizing individual experience by ego synthesis (*psyche*); and there is the communal process of the cultural organization of the interdependence of persons (*ethos*)... In the end, all three approaches are necessary for the clarification of any intact human event" (pp. 25–26). Thus, he set identity theory and identity research on a course that is both remarkably diverse, yet which requires integrative efforts to most fully comprehend internal, external, and interactional aspects of the object of our common interest.

The Identity Status Paradigm

Starting with his earliest studies on identity, Marcia's (1966; 1967) goal was the development of a means for the empirical study of Erikson's concept of ego identity. Much of the terminology Marcia employed in creating the identity status paradigm was taken from Erikson's writings, although in formulating operational definitions of those terms, their meanings diverged from their use by Erikson. Whereas Erikson's writings served as the inspiration for the development of the paradigm, the theory on which it is based both converges and diverges from Eriksonian theory in numerous ways (Waterman, 1988; 1999). Among those employing an identity status perspective, departures from an Eriksonian perspective have only increased over time (Luyckx, Goossens, Soenens, Beyers, & Vansteenkiste, 2005; Schwartz, 2001).

With respect to identity processes, Marcia (1966; 1980; 1993) identified two dimensions that represented differences in the ways individuals handle the task of identity formation (Kunnen & Metz, this volume): exploration and commitment. *Exploration* refers to the active consideration of alternative possibilities in domains of identity concern, such as vocation, religious beliefs, or sex role expression. Such exploration may involve efforts to choose among multiple alternatives simultaneously present, as when it is said that a person reaches "a fork in the road." Alternatively, the process of exploration may be evident in a pattern of changes made over time such that the person holds very different goals now than were held at an earlier point in life (Waterman, 1993a). *Commitment* refers to the strength with which specific goals, values, and/or beliefs are held and the extent to which they are behaviorally expressed in the person's day-to-day life. Mere verbalization of a goal, value, or belief is not sufficient for considering it an aspect of a person's identity if it plays little or no role in the way the person actually lives (Waterman, 1993a).

Based on these two dimensions, Marcia (1966; 1980; 1993) identified four identity statuses (Crocetti & Meeus, this volume):

• The *identity achievement* status represents those instances in which a person has explored a range of alternative possibilities within a domain of identity concern and has subsequently established firm commitments to one or more of the possibilities considered. In doing so, the person is not looking to make changes with regard to the choices that were made.

• The *moratorium* status represents instances in which the person is currently exploring different identity options with a view to making a decision about what goals to pursue, what to value, and/or what to believe. The absence of meaningful commitments in a domain of identity concern is subjectively perceived as troubling, giving rise to a desire to reach a decision as soon as feasible.

• The *foreclosure* status is indicated by the presence of identity commitments without a history of exploration of alternative possibilities. Commitments are made to the first alternatives seriously considered and often are formed through identification with parents or other models. Foreclosure commitments may be held in an inflexible manner.

• The *identity diffusion* status is characterized by the absence of both identity commitments and efforts to form them. Decisions relating to identity concerns are made primarily on the basis of external pressures present at the time.

With respect to the "I" and the "me," an individual's identity status and the particular commitments made in various domains of identity concern can be said to represent aspects of the "me." The content of those commitments are descriptive of the person's identity functioning, constituting "what" identity is for a particular individual. Self-defining statements concerning work/career, religious beliefs, political views, sex role attitudes, and the like are internal aspects in consciousness concerning how one thinks about oneself, but they are not active psychological constituents in their own right. In contrast, the defining dimensions of the identity statuses, exploration and commitment, refer to active processes in consciousness and thus aspects of the "I." For a person to "explore" means to actively seek relevant information or experiences, to weigh the usefulness of the information obtained, to consider the likely outcomes of any decision to be made, to assign values to the possible outcomes, and ultimately to reach a conclusion concerning what to do or what to believe within the context of current circumstances. Identity formation for foreclosures is a less active process, one entailing either introjections of parental preferences or those of other authority figures, imitative or modeling influences, or more whole-hearted identification. Whether through active exploration or less active introjections, modeling, or identification, the focus is clearly on process, on "how" identities are formed. Such processes reflect the manner by which the "I" creates the "me" within the identity status paradigm.

The role of the "I" also includes commitment as an active identity process directly involved in how one lives on a day-by-day basis. Commitments to a career involve making a continuous series of conscious choices about obtaining the necessary education and credentials to enter that career; about seeking, obtaining, and maintaining employment within the field; about creating opportunities to pursue those aspects of the career that are most personally rewarding; and so on. A similar series of conscious, active, "I" decisions can be specified within every domain of identity concern. In this manner, the "I" creates the self-realization of the "me."

Although Marcia did not elaborate extensively on the role of external or interactional processes within the identity status paradigm, his discussions of identity did not envision a decontextualized self acting atomistically upon the world. His recognition of external factors in identity formation is most evident with respect to the foreclosure and identity diffusion statuses. The role played by identification process in the generation of foreclosure commitments and the responsivity to external pressures shown in instances of identity diffusion both attest to the embeddedness of the person within a social world. Similarly, with respect to the identity achievement and moratoriums statuses, the potential identity elements that may be considered in the process of exploration will be a function of options then available within the culture, opportunities for exposure to such possibilities, and interactions involving encouragement by parents, teacher, peers, and social others to consider some possibilities and discouragement of other options, among other societal and social factors. Furthermore, the preferences of others within the family and community will almost certainly be among the factors consciously considered when making identity-related decisions.

The Identity Style Paradigm

The identity style paradigm was developed as an alternative method for studying identity functioning that parallels the identity status paradigm in many respects but with a substantially greater focus on the nature of information processing related to identity formation (Berzonsky, 1989; 1990). Individuals with an *informational style* are self-reflective, actively seek out broad information on the strengths and limitations of alternative identity options they are considering and show strong commitment to their choices once they have been made. In contrast, individuals with a *normative style* are highly selective in the information they seek, focusing primarily on social norms and what is expected of them by significant others in their lives. The level of commitment shown to the identity choices they make is comparable to that evident among those with an informational style. Individuals with a *diffuse/avoidant* style tend to resist making identity decisions and, as a consequence, they do not actively seek out information that would focus attention on such matters. They are lacking in identity commitments, preferring an approach to life that involves taking things as they come without projecting into the future about what may happen.

The expected parallels between the identity statuses and identity styles have been empirically demonstrated. Those in the identity achievement and moratorium statuses score high on measures of the informational style, those in the foreclosure status score high on measures for the normative style, and those in the identity diffusion status score high on measures of the diffuse/avoidant style (Berzonsky, 2011). Like the identity statuses, the identity styles are internal, descriptive aspects of one's identity functioning and can be considered aspects of the "me." However, the focus on information processing in the identity style paradigm promotes a greater understanding of how the "I" is operating when it deals with matters of identity concern. Although the term "exploration" does imply seeking information, explicit attention to the processing of identity-related information makes salient matters pertaining to its gathering and evaluation. Moreover, whereas descriptions of the foreclosure and identity diffusion statuses may imply a relatively passive approach to identity functioning, within the identity style paradigm it is evident that the normative and diffuse/avoidant styles involve active restrictions in the processing of information. In the case of the normative style, the "I" is seeking only a limited type of information pertaining to social norms, whereas for the diffuse/avoidant style, the process of restricting information is considerably broader.

The clear emphasis within the identity style paradigm is with the "how" of identity formation, that is, the processes employed and their implications for the quality of psychological functioning. In research employing this paradigm considerably less attention has been directed to the content formed on the basis the various processes, the domains of identity concern, or the functions served by a sense of personal identity.

As with the identity status paradigm, there is an implicit recognition of the role played by the social environment in identity formation. Social others play a substantial role as sources of information relevant for making identity decisions. Social expectations constitute elements of the advantages and problems associated with various content alternatives that those with an informational style will wish to consider. Such expectations are central to the norms that those with a normative style seek to identify. And the responsiveness that those with a diffuse/avoidant style show to immediate contextual pressures makes evident the nature of the social influences involved.

Eudaimonic Identity Theory

Whereas the identity status and identity style paradigms focused primarily on the processes by which identity is formed and expressed, eudaimonic identity theory was developed to address questions pertaining to the quality of the identity decisions being made. It appears self-evident that some identity choices a person may make are better than other alternatives equally available. Given that premise, it becomes necessary to consider what is meant by "better" within the context of identity formation and how it is possible for someone endeavoring to make identity decisions to recognize which are the better alternatives (Waterman, 1992; 2011).

Within the context of eudaimonic identity theory, better identity choices are ones consistent with a person's best potentials, that is, those things a person might do more successfully and more expressively than alternatives equally available. The activities involved in these alternatives are intrinsically motivated (Deci & Ryan, 1985; 2002) and self-concordant (Sheldon & Elliott, 1999). As this theory's name suggests, it is based on the classical philosophical theory of eudaimonism, a conception of the nature of a life well-lived, discussed most notably in Aristotle's (4th century BCE/1985) *Nichomachean Ethics*. Eudaimonism, in contrast to hedonism, is an essentialist understanding of a good life that views well-being as the successful functioning of an organism given its nature. With respect to nature fulfillment, it is posited by contemporary eudaimonists such as Norton (1976) that there are potentials derived from generic human nature, characteristic of all people, and unique individual potentials derived from each person's specific nature, differing from person to person. In psychology, this idea can be found in the writings of Horney (1950), Rogers (1959), and Maslow (1968), among others. According to eudaimonic identity theory, well-being is most likely to be achieved through making identity choices pertaining to goals, values, beliefs, and behaviors consistent with one's individual nature.

Eudaimonic identity theory posits that better identity choices can be identified through the spontaneous subjective experiences occurring when engaged in activities consistent with personal potentials. Waterman (1990; 1993*b*) referred to these as feelings of personal expressiveness. For example, when engaging in some activity for the first time, there may be a reaction "Wow! Where has this been all my life? Why didn't I know about this sooner?" Broadly speaking, feelings of personal expressiveness involve a sense of connection and engagement with some activities far more than others, an impression that they feel "right" and that this is something that one was meant to do.

Waterman (2011) identified four steps in the process of identity formation from a eudaimonic identity theory perspective: (a) identifying one's best potentials, broadly conceived; (b) devoting dedicated effort to the development of those potentials into actual skills and explicit values; (c) identifying those goals toward which such skills and values should be directed; and (d) identifying opportunities afforded within one's societal context through which those goals can be pursued or changing contexts so as to increase the range of opportunities available. The difficulties entailed in negotiating these steps should not be underestimated.

These steps require an active "I" making decisions and taking action in attempts to successfully negotiate each step. Whereas the potentials referred to are latent, implicit aspects of the "me," their recognition is not automatic. Such recognition requires putting oneself into situations in which exposure to varied activities is possible. Certainly, external agents such as parents, teachers, and community organizations can and do act to increase exposure to varied alternatives, but the developing individual must also be open to those experiences, something that is a function of the "I." Similarly, external agents may encourage or discourage efforts to develop some talents or some values rather than others or the adoption of some goals rather than others. But the efforts of others are hardly determinative in this regard, as evidenced by the frequency with which individuals make identity choices to pursue courses of action at odds with those that parents and other societal representatives would prefer. Again, the functioning of an active "I" is clearly implicated.

In contrast to the identity status and identity style paradigms, the "whys" of identity-related functions are central to eudaimonic identity theory. Feelings of personal expressiveness serve as a guide for self-discovery, in the identification of personal potentials. Effort directed to the development of latent talents, the selection of self-concordant goals, and the search for opportunities to pursue such goals serve to promote self-realization. Together, self-discovery and self-realization are viewed as serving to promote both personal well-being and the well-being of others with whom a person interacts (Waterman, 1990). Self-discovery and self-realization are not only central to understanding the "whys" of identity functions, but also constitute processes representing "how" successful identity formation occurs. As with the identity status paradigm, it is recognized that self-discovery and self-realization may occur in an array of life domains including family, vocation, religion and spirituality, and leisure activities, among others.

More so than other theories of identity functioning discussed in this chapter, eudaimonic identity theory emphasizes internality with respect to an individual's self-definition. Whereas all of the theories entail an "I" acting to define the "me," eudaimonic identity theory posits the presence of an internal "me" prior to its recognition and adoption. Alternative theories leave open the matter as to where goals, values, and beliefs may originate for identity consideration, often with the implication that they are encountered based on what is afforded to the person by circumstance. In contrast, the concept of an individual nature emphasizes what the person brings to such encounters. Psychologists have long employed such a perspective when referring to aptitudes (Binet & Simon, 1915; Hollingsworth, 1916) and being temperamentally suited more for some activities rather than others (Bridges, 1923). This view of an inborn "me" is also embodied in concepts of authenticity (Benson, 1974; Sheldon, Ryan, Rawsthorne, & Ilardi, 1997) and self-concordance (Sheldon & Elliot, 1999). It can also explain individual differences in reactions to a given activity—why some people find it intrinsically motivating, whereas others are indifferent to it, and still others find it actively aversive.

But even with this emphasis on the internal in eudaimonic identity theory, the role of external and interactional influences and processes should not be disregarded. The standard for better identity choices may be internal, but societal and interpersonal factors play an important role with respect to the likelihood that someone will successfully negotiate the steps involved in identity formation and therefore the resulting level of well-being that may be achieved.

Narrative Identity Theories

In contrast with the psychoanalytic and essentialist roots of the identity theory perspectives previously discussed, narrative theories of identity can be traced to the hermeneutic philosophical tradition, particularly to the work of Paul Ricouer and Charles Taylor. These theories and their associated research methodologies vary widely, making this approach to understanding identity difficult to summarize (Singer, 2004). There are "big story" narratives verging on autobiography encompassing the totality of a person's life, stories designed to reflect the arc of one's life (Freeman, 1993; McAdams, Josselson, & Lieblich, 2006). Such "big story" theories owe much to the work of Erikson, generally emphasizing functions of continuity across time and coherence across domains. The contribution of narratives to achieving generativity is often prominent. In contrast, "small stories," as the term suggests, have a more limited scope, reflecting ways in which a person strives to make sense and give meaning to quite specific aspects of life, such as the events entailed in a particular interaction with another person (Bamberg, 2006). In "small story" theories, the focus is on the role of context and performance rather than continuity and coherence. Narrative approaches to understanding identity also differ with respect to macro- versus microlevels of analysis, whether the stories are written, oral, or even verbalized, the accuracy of autobiographical memory and associated subjective reconstructions, and the role of the listener or recipient of the stories.

What narrative theories share in common is the exploration of how individuals endeavor to make sense of their lives through creating their identity by integrating their life experiences into more or less meaningful narrative stories. Such stories are functional both in promoting self-understanding for the person creating the narrative and in facilitating communication with others about who the person is. The narrative identity stories a person constructs, like other stories, will likely contain elements of setting, characters, plot, and theme (Wang & Roberts, 2005). Among the more frequent themes analyzed in identity narratives are quest, redemption, contamination, agency, and communion (McAdams, 2001). The criteria for what constitutes a good identity narrative differ from the criteria for making good identity decisions within the framework of the identity status, identity style, or eudaimonistic identity perspectives. A good narrative story is judged by how well it fulfills the functions valued by the author of, and listener(s) to, the narrative. Among the more important identity functions of "big stories" are (a) continuity of past, present, and projected future; (b) coherence of diverse elements within the story; (c) providing understanding and meaning for the narrator regarding the nature of his or her life and/or experiences; and (d) promoting an understanding of similarities and differences with others within one's social context. Among the more important identity functions of "small stories" are (a) knowing who one is at the current moment in the immediate context (or was at an earlier moment and its associated context), (b) understanding the motives of the actor and responses of others within the specific context as these are related to the meaning of the events occurring, and (c) and taking or avoiding responsibility for what one says or does within that context.

Good stories may be, and almost certainly will be, a blend of fact and fiction. Narratives are more malleable than personal potentials (although it is in error to think of individual potentials as fixed). If one's narrative story is no longer perceived as functioning effectively, the opportunity is always present to rewrite it along other lines. However, there can be no guarantee that the intended audience will be receptive to a new narrative.

Within the Jamesian framework employed here, the narrative can be understood as the story of "me" with the "I" as author, editor, and very likely part of the intended audience. To create a narrative requires at least some self-reflective activity on the part of the author regarding what type of story one seeks to tell. External factors may play a very substantial role with respect to the available settings, themes, character types, and more, but even when there are strong ascriptive pressures on a person to tell a particular type of story, options for alternative narratives are always available. For example, in the face of strong conformity pressures from cultural institutions or significant others, a person may choose the narrative of a rebel, outsider, or loner in preference to the culturally sanctioned narrative (although under some circumstances these alternative narratives may be culturally sanctioned as well). The role of the "I" is also evident in the choice of audience to which the story of "me" is told and in the subtle, or sometimes not so subtle, differences in the content of the narrative as communicated to different audiences. (See McAdams, 2013, for an analysis of narrative perspectives of the self in terms of the Jamesian "I" and "me.")

Theorists employing narrative approaches to the understanding of identity have generally shown comparable interest in the "what," "how," and "why" of identity functioning. The narratives themselves are the content of identity; considerable attention is directed to the processes of narrative/story creation; and, as outlined earlier, the functions of personal continuity and coherence, purpose/meaning-making, and self-presentation tend to be emphasized in the writings of narrative theorists.

Although the relative emphases on internal, external, and interactional factors in identity functioning from a narrative perspective differ from those in the theories previously discussed, my principal point here is that internal, external, and interactional influences are all inevitably in play whatever perspective is employed. Furthermore, the theories discussed here are not incompatible. The creation of narrative stories to make sense of life does not negate the existence of personal potentials that incline the individual to resonate substantially more with some activities than with others. Nor is it incompatible with the importance of growth motives as a central element in narrative stories with implications for well-being (Bauer & McAdams, 2010; Bauer, McAdams, & Sakaeda, 2005). The person's individual nature and conceptualizations of growth can be seen as two, among many, influences on the type of story chosen to be told. And a person's narrative may involve the embrace of personal potentials and growth or the flight from them.

Dialogistic Identity Theories

Dialogistic theories are related to the narrative theories just discussed but focus more extensively on how people create meaning in their lives within the context of their social worlds, particularly in their interactions directly with others. Individuals come to recognize and identify themselves through the interactions they have with others, both real and imagined, and with dialogues they have with themselves. It is through such interactions that they make sense of their lives and attach meanings to it. Bell (2013) identified four presuppositions for dialogistic sense-making (a) it is dynamic, involving actions rather than states; (b) it is inherently interactive and intersubjective; (c) it is mediated, usually by language, and may also involve perceptions, habits, or artifacts; and (d) it is always contextual, changing as contexts change.

The dialogic self is conceptualized as embodied, decentralized, dynamic, social, and spatial (Hermans, 2001; 2003), involving a multiplicity of *I–other* positions (Hermans & Hermans-Jansen, 2003). With respect to the Jamesian "I," Salgado and Hermans (2005) note that despite this multiplicity, it is always "I" that is speaking with and to multiple others. Valsiner (1994), among others, adopts a co-constructionist perspective in which "others" are viewed as playing such an extensive role in dialogic interactions that their contributions warrant acknowledgment of authorship.

Bell (2013) points out that the cultural contexts within which dialogues occur are not monolithic frameworks that are the same for everyone, but rather vary from person to person, and vary from context to context, such as home, work, and school. Furthermore, dialogues by their nature are mediated by language, which in turn shapes both the dialogues themselves and the understandings that emerge from them. Within dialogistic theories, the interlocutors may be actual individuals with whom the person interacts but may also be intrapsychic representations of alternative positions/possibilities in "conversation." One way in which to envision such internal conversations is as an "I" alternately role-playing positions occupied by various actual or potential "me's" (possible selves).

Dialogistic theories, like their narrative counterparts, focus attention on the content of the dialogues (the "what"), the dialogic process itself from which meaning emerges (the "how"), and the self-related functions served by the dialogic interactions (the "why"). By incorporating interactional processes and cultural contexts into discussions of identity formation, dialogic theories bring external interactional processes into the foreground. But as the term "co-construction" implies, identity meaning-making involves both internal and external elements in ongoing interaction.

Post-Modern/Social Constructionist Theory

Arguably the greatest challenge to the concept of a coherent, stable sense of identity and to the role of internal processes in identity functioning comes from the post-modern perspective represented by Gergen's (1991) saturated self. Due to the proliferation of interactive technologies, from cell phones to personal computers to iPads, we are continually interconnected within social networks bombarding us with information. The networks include immediate family, extended family, friends, "friends" we never met but know only through media, and a host of groups, both real and virtual. All of these sources provide us with opinions, attitudes, lifestyles, and feedback that impact the multiple ways in which we come to define ourselves (see Manago, this volume). This saturation of our self-experiences results in fragmentation of our sense of self. We respond in so many different ways in our various interactions that there is no longer any stable inner core defining who we are. Instead, the self is plural rather than singular, socially constructed, malleable, and responsive to both immediate and broad contextual influences. This saturated self is parallel in many respect to the Protean self, which Lifton (1993) viewed as a necessary cultural development to counter the problems posed by ideological totalism.

This post-modern perspective does not, however, negate the relevance of the distinction between the "I" and the "me." The descriptive "me" may lack coherence across settings, but within each setting it can be said that this is who "I" am at the moment. More importantly, the executive functions of the "I" remain, for example in the process of determining what to "like" or who to "friend" or "defriend" within one's social networks. Post-modern theorists may well be correct that contemporary Western cultures have greatly increased the tendency toward distracted, diffused selves cluttered with and responsive to immediate information. However, even a casual analysis of such cultures reveals many parents dedicated to the well-being of their children, entrepreneurs dedicated to their businesses, scholars dedicated to their scholarship, believers dedicated to their religious faith, activists dedicated to their political cause, and enthusiasts dedicated to their leisure-time pursuits. All of these, and comparable pursuits, are choices the "I" consciously makes and that speak to the continuing importance of internal identity processes.

Writers on the post-modern perspective on identity focus their attention on how the saturated self emerges in response to the demands of contemporary Western societies. They pay limited attention to the content of identity, other than to note its responsiveness to the immediate context the individual is in at the moment. Similarly, they do not elaborate extensively on the functions that identity may serve, other than the self-presentational value it has in those contexts. It is interesting to note that the saturated self does not serve many of the functions identified as important by Erikson, including consistency over time, coherence across identity domains, providing purpose and meaning, and protections against experiences of sudden discontinuities.

Implications for Future Research on Identity

With respect to future research on internal identity processes, it would be highly desirable to create studies of the relationship of the "I" and the "me." However, this does not appear to be a plausible prospect given that the "I," although nearly universally identified in experience, is not publicly observable and cannot be operationally defined for research purposes in any meaningful sense. When the "I" reflects upon itself and provides verbal accounts of the processes employed, such as choice, identification or ascription, those descriptions are best considered aspects of the "me," although different from descriptions of the content of the "me" in terms of those goals, values, beliefs, and behaviors said to define a person's identity. The closest we are likely to get to investigations of the relationship of the "I" to the "me" are studies of the relationships between identity processes and identity contents as described by research participants. Such studies have the potential to be quite productive.

For example, one line of future research that should be explored involves relationships between the internal identity processes of choice, identification, and ascription attributed to the "I" and the particular identity contents that are adopted. There are strong theoretical grounds for expecting the two to be related. It can be hypothesized that the processes of ascription and identification will be associated with more culturally traditional and conservative contents than would the process of choice. "Conservative" in this context refers to the adoption of goals, values, beliefs, and behaviors consistent with the standards of the immediate social community and representatives of the social status quo. In contrast, a process of active choice is more likely to involve a willingness to question authority and to potentially come to conclusions about goals, values, beliefs, and behaviors at some variance from the expectations of one's family and community. Innovation is a more likely outcome of choice than of identification or ascription. It is certainly possible, however, that the processes of choice, identification, and ascription may lead to creation of the same specific identity content, for example, the adoption of the beliefs and practices of a particular religion.

Another direction for future studies concerns the possibility that the establishment of common identity contents through different identity processes may be associated with differences regarding the manner in which identity elements are held and expressed. For example, it can be hypothesized that members of a particular religion whose beliefs emerged through a process of choice will show greater tolerance for others holding differing views on religion than will members of the same religion, comparably committed, whose beliefs were a product of ascription or identification. Similarly, even when the same contents emerge via different processes, there may be differences in the subjective experiences associated with them and/or the manner in which they are expressed, for example, the pleasure or comfort derived from them, the strength of their advocacy to others, the rigidity with which they are held, and/or the willingness to consider contrasting perspectives.

Perhaps the most important area in which research on identity processes and contents is needed concerns the implications of the two, both separately and in combination, for well-being and other forms of psychosocial functioning. There is abundant research evidence from studies employing the identity status paradigm that the identity process of choice is related to well-being after identity commitments have been established but that the same process is negatively related to well-being while the process is ongoing; that is, before identity commitments have been made (see Marcia, Waterman, Matteson, Archer, & Orlofsky, 1993). There is conflicting evidence as to whether identity commitments formed through exploration (choice) or identification yield better psychosocial outcomes (Kroger & Marcia, 2011) suggesting that process may make less of a difference than generally supposed. However, consistent with eudaimonic identity theory, Soenens et al. (2011) and Waterman et al. (2013) have demonstrated that it is the quality of identity commitments made rather than the presence of identity commitments, per se, or the processes by which they are formed that accounts for the outcomes regarding well-being. From a eudaimonist perspective, commitment quality refers to the correspondence of the content of the identity commitments with the genuine potential strengths of the individual, a correspondence that can be achieved by choice, identification, or ascription, although the likelihood is that such an outcome is not the same for the different processes. In future research exploring the implications for psychosocial functioning and well-being associated with identity processes, identity contents, and the two in combination, considering the quality of the identity commitments present will be important to include as a variable for study.

Conclusion

In this survey of identity theories, I have not tried to argue that one perspective is better than another in the understanding of the identity functioning it advances (although I did make a minor exception to conceptual neutrality at the end of the section on post-modern theories.) Although advocates of various perspectives are often highly critical of alternative theories, as an identity theorist, I see all of the theories discussed here as compatible, at least in their broad outlines if not always in their specifics. With respect to various internal processes of identity functioning, the following statements all appear valid. People do identify with others and endeavor to integrate those identifications, both consciously and unconsciously. They may or may not explore a range of self-defining possibilities and may or may not form commitments to particular alternatives considered. They do process identity-related information in different ways. They do have differing potentials, resonating more with some activities than with others based on innate predispositions and their varied learning histories. They do create narrative stories to make sense of their lives, stories that are inevitably a blend of fact and fiction. The dialogues they have with both real and imagined others and with themselves play a substantial role in the self-stories they create. And the complex social lives that they lead in terms of the number and variety of others with whom they interact and the variety of roles they occupy each day do lead to the creation of multiple selves.

What is constant across all of these theories is self-awareness—the existence of an individual consciousness. As I observed in the opening of this chapter, identity is inextricably associated with consciousness and the Cartesian "I." Without consciousness, no concept of identity is possible. None of the theories of identity discussed here provides an inevitable answer to the question "Who am 'I'?", including the essentialist, eudaimonist theory I have advanced. Creating a self-definition, an identity, is something that each person must do individually. Some people will do so with more introspection and self-reflection than will others. Some will be more passively responsive to external influences than will others. But in every instance these will be matters of degree.

The observation that individuals differ in the relative extent to which internal, external, and interactional considerations shape the identities that are developed and expressed reinforces the point I have made throughout this chapter that internal, external, and interactional processes are integrally related, co-extensive, and of comparable importance for understanding identity functioning. It is certainly evident in the theory and research literatures on identity that individual scholars have focused more on one or the other set of constructs (historically more so on internal aspects of identity functioning). In terms of hypotheses advanced, empirically evaluated, and supported, such separation of analyses regarding internal, external, and interactional aspects of identity functioning, in whatever direction, has been undeniably productive. The integration of the various perspectives on identity is a still higher objective. Those of us who have contributed more to the literature on one particular perspective than others have, I believe, provided extensive material (knowledge) from which an integration can potentially be achieved.

In this chapter, I have emphasized the role of internal processes by which the active "I" creates the descriptive "me," both because I find those processes of particular interest and this was the focus I was asked to have in writing it. This focus was on what each person, each "I," brings to interactions with the particular physical, social, and cultural world he or she inhabits and how he or she processes the information emerging from those interactions. The capacities of the "I" and the processes that "I's" employ in the creation of identity(ies) are, or at least should be, an essential aspect of all theories of identity functioning. But that can only be one side of any identity theory. Equally essential are the many ways in which interactions with one's physical, social, and cultural world shape both the processes and contents of identity functioning. And that is a subject for a different chapter.

References

Adler, J. M. (2012). Living into the story: Agency and coherence in a longitudinal study of narrative identity development and mental health over the course of psychotherapy. *Journal of Personality and Social Psychology, 102*, 367–389.

Aristotle. (4th century BCE/1985). *Nicomachean ethics*. (T. Irwin, Trans.). Indianapolis, IN: Hackett.

Bamberg, M. (2006). Biographic-narrative research, quo vadis? A critical review of "big stories" from the perspective of "small stories." In K. Milnes, C. Horrocks, N. Kelly, B. Roberts, & D. Robinson (Eds.), *Narrative, memory and knowledge: Representations, aesthetics and contexts* (pp. 1–17). Huddersfield, UK: University of Huddersfield Press.

Bauer, J. J., & McAdams, D. P. (2010). Eudaimonic growth: Narrative growth goals predict increases in ego development and subjective well-being 3 years later. *Developmental Psychology, 46*, 761–772.

Bauer, J. J., McAdams, D. P., & Sakaeda, A. R. (2005). Interpreting the good life: Growth memories in the lives of mature, happy people. *Journal of Personality and Social Psychology, 88*, 203–217.

Bell, N. J. (2013). Dialogic processes of self-transformation: The sample case of eating disorder recovery. *Identity: An International Journal of Theory and Research, 13*, 46–72.

Benson, L. (1974). *Images, heroes, and self-perceptions: The struggle for identity-from mask-wearing to authenticity*. Oxford, UK: Prentice-Hall.

Berzonsky, M. D. (1989). Identity style: Conceptualization and measurement. *Journal of Adolescent Research, 4*, 268–282.

Berzonsky, M. D. (1990). Self-construction over the lifespan: A process perspective on identity formation. In G. J. Neimeyer & R. A. Neimeyer (Eds.), *Advances in personal construct theory* (vol. *1*, pp. 155–186). Greenwich, CT: JAI.

Berzonsky, M. D. (2011). A social-cognitive perspective on identity construction. In S. J Schwartz, K. Luyckx, & V. L. Vignoles (Eds.), *Handbook of identity theory and research*, Vol. *1*, Structures and Processes (pp. 55–76). New York: Springer.

Binet, A., & Simon, T. T. (1915). *A method of measuring the development of intelligence of young children*. (C. Harrison, Trans.). Chicago: Chicago Medical Book Co.

Bridges, J. W. (1923). Theories of temperament: An attempt at reconciliation. *Psychological Review, 30*, 36–44.

Broad, C. D. (1925). *The mind and its place in nature*. New York: Harcourt, Brace.

Constantine, M. G., Richardson, T. Q., Benjamin, E. M., & Wilson, J. W. (1998). An overview of Black racial identity theories: Limitations and considerations for future theoretical development. *Applied and Preventive Psychology, 7*, 95–99.

Deci, E. L., & Ryan, R. M. (1985). *Intrinsic motivation and self-determination in human behavior*. New York: Plenum.

Deci, E. L., & Ryan, R. M. (Eds.). (2002). *Handbook of self-determination research*. Rochester, NY: University of Rochester Press.

Engel, G. L. (1980). The clinical application of the biopsychosocial model. *American Journal of Psychiatry, 137*, 535–544.

Erikson, E. H. (1963). *Childhood and society* (2nd ed.). New York: Norton.

Erikson, E. H. (1968). *Identity: Youth and crisis*. New York: Norton.

Erikson, E. H. (1975). *Life history and the historical moment*. New York: Norton.

Erikson, E. H. (1982). *The life cycle completed: A review*. New York: Norton.

Freeman, M. (1993). *Rewriting the self: History, memory, narrative*. New York: Routledge.

Freud, S. (1901/2003). *The psychopathology of everyday life*. (A. Bell, Trans.). New York: Penguin Books.

Gergen, K. J. (1991). *The saturated self: Dilemmas of identity in contemporary life*. New York: Basis Books.

Hermans, H. J. M. (2001). The dialogic self: Toward a theory of personal and cultural positioning. *Culture and Psychology, 7*, 67–87.

Hermans, H. J. M. (2003). The construction and reconstruction of a dialogical self. *Journal of Constructivist Psychology, 16*, 243–281.

Hermans, H. J. M., & Hermans-Jansen, E. (2003). Dialogical processes and development of the self. In J. Valsiner & K. J. Connolly (Eds.), *Handbook of developmental psychology* (pp. 534–559). Thousand Oaks, CA: Sage.

Hollingsworth, H. L. (1916). The determinants of vocational aptitude. In H. L. Hollingworth (Ed.), *Vocational psychology: Its problems and methods*. New York: Appleton.

Horney, K. (1950). *Neurosis and human growth: The struggle toward self-realization*. New York: Norton.

James, W. (1890). *The principles of psychology. Vol. 1*. London, UK: Macmillan.

Jones, D. H. (1972). Emergent properties, persons, and the mind-body problem. *Southern Journal of Philosophy, 10*, 423–433.

Jung, C. G. (1934–1954/1981). The archetypes and the collective unconscious. (R. F. C. Hull, Trans.; 2nd ed., *Collected works of C. G. Jung, vol. 9*, part 1). Princeton, NJ: Bolligen.

Kroger, J., & Marcia, J. E. (2011). The identity statuses: Origins, meanings, and interpretations. In S. J. Schwartz, K. Luyckx, & V. L. Vignoles (Eds.), *Handbook of identity theory and research*. (Vol. 1. Structures and process; pp. 31–53). New York: Springer.

Lifton, R. J. (1993). *The Protean self: Human resilience in an age of fragmentation*. New York: Basic Books.

Luyckx. K., Goossens, L., Soenens, B., Beyers, W., & Vansteenkiste, M. (2005). Identity statuses based upon four rather than two identity dimensions: Extending and refining Marcia's paradigm. *Journal of Youth and Adolescence, 34*, 605–618.

Marcia, J. E. (1966). Development and validation of ego identity status. *Journal of Personality and Social Psychology, 3*, 551–558.

Marcia, J. E. (1967). Ego identity status: Relationship to change in self-esteem, "general maladjustment," and authoritarianism. *Journal of Personality, 35*, 118–133.

Marcia, J. E. (1980). Identity in adolescence. In J. Adelson (Ed.), *Handbook of adolescent psychology* (pp. 159–186). New York: Wiley.

Marcia, J. E. (1993). The ego identity status approach to ego identity. In J. E. Marcia, A. S. Waterman, D. R. Matteson, S. L. Archer, & J. L. Orlofsky, *Ego identity: A handbook for psychosocial research* (pp. 3–21). New York: Springer-Verlag.

Marcia, J. E., Waterman, A. S., Matteson, D. R., Archer, S. L., & Orlofsky, J. L. (1993). *Ego identity: A handbook for psychosocial research*. New York: Springer-Verlag.

Maslow, A. H. (1968). *Toward a psychology of being*. Princeton, NJ: Van Nostrand.

McAdams, D. P. (2001). Narrating life's turning points: Redemption and contamination. In D. P. McAdams, R. Josselson, & A. Lieblich (Eds.), *Turns in the road. Narrative studies of lives in transition* (pp. 3–34). Washington, DC: American Psychological Association.

McAdams, D. P. (2013). The psychological self as actor, agent, and author. *Perspectives on Psychological Science, 8*, 272–295.

McAdams, D. P., Josselson, R., & Lieblich, A. (2006). *Identity and story: Creating self in narrative*. Washington, DC: American Psychological Association.

Norton, D. L. (1976). *Personal destinies.* Princeton, NJ: Princeton University Press.

Rogers, C. R. (1959). A theory of therapy, personality, and interpersonal relationships as developed in the client-centered framework. In S. Koch (Ed.), *Psychology: A study of a science* (Vol. 3, Formulations of the person and the social context). New York: McGraw-Hill.

Salgado, J., & Hermans, H. J. M. (2005). The return of subjectivity: From a multiplicity of selves to the dialogical self. *Electronic Journal of Applied Psychology, Clinical section, 1,* 3–13.

Schwartz, S. J. (2001). The evolution of Eriksonian and neo-Eriksonian identity theory and research: A review and integration. *Identity: An International Journal of Theory and Research, 1,* 7–58.

Sheldon, K. M., & Elliot, A. J. (1999). Goal striving, need satisfaction, and longitudinal well-being: The self-concordance model. *Journal of Personality and Social Psychology, 76,* 482–497.

Sheldon, K. M., Ryan, R. M., Rawsthorne, L. J., & Ilardi, B. (1997). Trait self and true self: Cross-role variation in the Big-Five personality traits and its relations with psychological authenticity and subjective well-being. *Journal of Personality and Social Psychology, 73,* 1380–1393.

Singer, J. A. (2004). Narrative identity and meaning making across the adult lifespan: An introduction. *Journal of Personality, 72,* 437–459.

Soenens, B., Berzonsky, M. D, Dunkel, C., Papini, D., & Vansteenkiste, M. (2011). Are all identity commitments created equally? The importance of motives for late adolescents' personal adjustment. *International Journal of Behavioral Development, 35,* 358–369.

Syed, M., Walker, L. H. M., Lee, R. M., Umaña-Taylor, A., Zamboanga, B. L.,... Hunh, Q.-L. (2013). A two-factor model of ethnic identity exploration: Implications for identity coherence and well-being. *Cultural Diversity and Ethnic Minority Psychology, 19,* 143–154.

Valsiner, J. (1994). Culture and human development: A co-constructionist perspective. In P. van Geert, L. P. Mos, & W. J. Baker (Eds.), *Annals of theoretical psychology* (vol. 10; pp. 247–297). New York: Plenum.

Wang, Y., & Roberts, C. W. (2005). Actantial analysis: Greimas's structural approach to the analysis of self-narratives. *Narrative Inquiry, 15,* 51–74.

Waterman, A. S. (1982). Identity development from adolescence to adulthood: An extension of theory and a review of research. *Developmental Psychology, 18,* 342–358.

Waterman, A. S. (1988). Identity status theory and Erikson's theory: Communalities and differences. *Developmental Review, 8,* 185–208.

Waterman, A. S. (1990). Personal expressiveness: Philosophical and psychological foundations. *Journal of Mind and Behavior, 11,* 47–74.

Waterman, A. S. (1992). Identity as an aspect of optimal psychological functioning. In G. R. Adams, T. Gullota, & R. Montemayor (Eds.), *Identity formation during adolescence. Advances in adolescent development* (vol. 4; pp. 50–72). Newbury Park, CA: Sage.

Waterman, A. S. (1993a). Developmental perspectives on identity formation from adolescence to adulthood. In J. E. Marcia, A. S. Waterman, D. R. Matteson, S. L. Archer, & J. L. Orlofsky, *Ego identity: A handbook for psychosocial research* (pp. 42–68). New York: Springer-Verlag.

Waterman, A. S. (1993b). Two conceptions of happiness: Contrasts of personal expressiveness (eudaimonia) and hedonic enjoyment. *Journal of Personality and Social Psychology, 64,* 678–691.

Waterman, A. S. (1999). Identity, the identity statuses, and identity status development. A contemporary perspective. *Developmental Review, 19,* 591–621.

Waterman, A. S. (2011). Eudaimonic identity theory: Identity as self-discovery. In S. J. Schwartz, K. Luyckx, & V. L. Vignoles (Eds.), *Handbook of identity theory and research* (vol. *1*, Structures and processes; pp. 357–379). New York: Springer.

Waterman, A. S., & Archer, S. L. (1990). A life span perspective on identity formation: Developments in form, function, and process. In P. B. Baltes, D. L. Featherman, & R. M. Lerner (Eds.), *Life-span development and behavior* (vol. 10; pp. 29–57). New York: Lawrence Erlbaum.

Waterman, A. S., Schwartz, S. J., Hardy, S. A., Kim, S. Y., Lee, R. M., Armenta, B. E.,... & Agocha, V. B. (2013). Good choices, poor choices: Relationship between the quality of identity commitments and psychosocial functioning. *Emerging Adulthood, 1,* 163-174.

Worrell, F. C., Cross, W. E., Jr., & Vandiver, B. J. (2001). Nigrescence theory: Current status and challenges for the future. *Journal of Multicultural Counseling and Development, 29,* 201–213.

CHAPTER 14

Identities as an Interactional Process

Neill Korobov

> **Abstract**
>
> This chapter presents an interactional approach to identity development grounded in select aspects of social constructionism, ethnomethodology, and discursive positioning. An interactional approach is shaped by the nonfoundationalist social epistemology of social constructionism, which rejects the dualistic metaphysics that grounds the traditional internal/external dichotomy; the locus of knowledge is therefore not in individual minds nor extant sociocultural realities, but in interactional patterns of social relatedness. Furthermore, an interactional approach to identity borrows the ethnomethodological dictum to make the theoretical intimations of social constructionism analytically visible and tractable through a systematically detailed empirical grounding of interactional identities. Finally, discursive positioning is posited as the vanguard for an interactional view of identity development, as it involves an empirically grounded and microgenetic rendering of how people engage in discursive actions to develop identities as interactional (not mentalistic) phenomenon. Discursive positioning is illustrated; implications and limitations of an interactional approach to identity are discussed.
>
> **Key Words:** interactional, discourse, positioning, social constructionism, ethnomethodology, discursive psychology

Erikson's view of identity was multifaceted, focusing not only on the personal and intrapsychic, but also on the importance of social contexts and social interactions (see Côté, 1993, Côté & Levine, 1987, 1988; Schwartz, 2001). As a result, neo-Eriksonian researchers have, for decades, raised questions about the extent to which identity is an individual/internal project, a function of interacting in social and cultural contexts, or a combination of both. Although there is an ever-expanding amount of research on identity as an individual/internal project, as well as an increasing integration of this work with broad notions of context, empirical work detailing the relationship between social interactions and identity development has been scarce, especially within the identity status model research paradigm that has dominated psychological approaches to identity. In Schwartz's (2001) meta-review of the first half century of neo-Eriksonian work, there is a conspicuous lack of influential work mentioned that empirically addresses identity by studying social interactions. The lopsided prioritization of internal processes over interactional processes has been a noteworthy, yet unsurprising predilection of a discipline that has historically privileged the measurement of interiority.

Given the prioritization of internal models of identity, a number of well-known identity theories posit the importance of social contexts and even social interactions. For example, Grotevant and Cooper's (1985) use of the fictive family interaction task focused on the link between familial patterns of social interaction and adolescent identity exploration, discovering that different family interaction styles are related to unique styles of identity exploration for males and females. Similarly, Adams's developmental contextual model emphasizes not only macro social contexts but also dialogical microcontexts (see Adams, Dyk, & Bennion, 1987; Adams & Marshall, 1996). In addition, Côté's (Côté, 1993, Côté & Levine, 1987, 1988) social-structural identity capital model connects macrosociological factors and micro-interactional ones to psychological factors. Yet, in both Adams's and Côté's approaches, as well as in a range of others, social interactions *as empirical phenomenon* are rarely interrogated. Contexts are typically conceptualized as extant factors like "schools," "families," or "peer groups," and social interactions are rarely, if ever, addressed explicitly. And when they are, such as in Grotevenat and Cooper's (1985) work, the interactions are coded and transformed into "interaction variables" that are treated as "factors" or "forces" that individuals must integrate and differentiate from as part of their identity development. Although contexts and social interactions are ingredient in a range of mainstream theoretical claims about identity development, rarely is identity development microanalytically studied *as it is embodied* within those contexts or interactions.

For example, although Côté's social-structural identity capital model stresses that personal identity develops in negotiation with social resources (like peers, social institutions, and family members), his focus is primarily on the resources (social capital) that individuals develop as a result of these interactions. These resources are internal attributes (skills, beliefs, attitudes) that individuals use more or less successfully to navigate modern society. Similarly, Tajfel and Turner's (1986) seminal work on social identity theory, although rich in its emphasis on interpersonal social contexts, nevertheless treats identities as internal, cognitively held categorizations that are switched on during social interactions. These examples reflect a common trend of conceptualizing interactional contexts as stimuli that trigger interior mechanisms such as attribution and schema application, mechanisms which then serve particular social and psychological goals.

With respect to social contexts and social interactions, the trend in identity status research and social identity theory has been to argue that personal and social identities are embedded in micro-/macrocontexts and to treat these contexts and interactions as independent variables. Rarely do we see how identities develop—that is, how they are built, shaped, contested, and revised within actual interactional contexts. The development of identities within microinteractional contexts is rarely interrogated. Among psychologists, this likely reflects less a prejudice against studying interactions per se than it reveals conceptual and methodological resistance to studying interactional contexts in an up-close, detailed, and systematic way. Instead, contexts and interactions (and all other nods to the "external" cultural world) are usually treated as a kind of overlay or influencing factor and are methodologically reduced to factors and variables. Social interactions, as fluid and nuanced empirical sites in which identities develop, have thus had an impoverished status in psychological identity research for more than 50 years.

In Meeus's (2011) meta-review of identity research from 2000–2010, the omission is still apparent. Meeus (2011) notes that the pressing contemporary concerns in identity research have to do with the progression of identity across time, identity status continuum, empirical demonstrability of identity continuity, and relationship between identity status and psychological adjustment. Although a factors and variables measurement model for identity studies is still dominant and comprised of questionnaires and structured interviews, Meeus (2011) does point to a surge of narrative identity research over the past decade. Unfortunately, the majority of narrative identity work has not invigorated the study of interactions as sites for identity development. With very few exceptions (see Bamberg, 1997, 2003; Korobov, 2009*a*, 2009*b*, Korobov & Thorne, 2007, 2009), the bulk of narrative identity research (i.e., McAdams et al., 2006; McLean, 2005, 2008; Pasupathi & Hoyt, 2009) relies heavily on retrospective autobiographical life-story narratives that are generally procured in non-natural structured research settings. Although unquestionably a step in the right direction, the general focus of narrative identity research within mainstream psychology has been to use narratives as a window into understanding how and when continuity and coherence emerge *intrapsychically* for individuals across self-reported developmental time. Further, the extraction of narratives in mainstream psychological research is too often groomed (parsed and coded) for statistical analysis; rarely are unstructured narratives from natural contexts studied, and even rarer are in-depth analyses of narrative *interactions* undertaken.

The purpose of this chapter is to advance an interactional perspective (and methodology) for studying identity development. Studying how interactants establish a sense of self in interaction resembles what in developmental theorizing is termed "microgenesis" (see Bamberg, 2003; Korobov & Bamberg, 2004a, 2004b). This approach assumes that developmental changes emerge as individuals create and accomplish interactive tasks in everyday conversations. The interactive space is the arena in which identities are microgenetically performed and consolidated and where they can be microanalytically accessed. Here, we are borrowing from developmental (Bamberg, 2000a; Catan, 1986; Riegel, 1975; Werner, 1958; Werner & Kaplan, 1984; Wertsch & Stone, 1978), conversation-analytic (Schegloff, 1982; Sacks, 1995; Sacks, Schegloff, & Jefferson, 1974), and communities of practice approaches (Eckert, 1989, 2002; Hanks, 1996) to highlight the sociorelational nature of interaction, for the purpose of inquiring not only into the developing sense of self and others, but also into what is shared as a cultural model of sense-making.

A microgenetic view of identity development is concerned with the progressive sedimentation of interactive sense-making and identity constitutive processes—that is, how, in a myriad of different contexts, various identities get tried out, adopted, resisted, or consolidated. These negotiation processes are, in short, microgenetic identity development. The interest is in investigating social interactions as sites in which identities microdevelopmentally emerge. Martin Packer (1987, p. 267) states it nicely:

> Development consists in increasingly broadened fluency: becoming socially fluent in an increased range of situations... Multiple social worlds must be smoothly recognized, entered, and left... Accounts must be articulated, excuses made, descriptions given, reasons provided.

In this view, identities are not character types that are the result of reconciling stepwise developmental tasks, but rather reflect the burgeoning social and cultural capacity (or dexterity) to be rhetorically responsive and answerable in the midst of social interactions. In this sociocultural view, identity development does not reflect a necessary moral telos, nor must it involve the traditional idea of temporal unfolding of selves over time. Rather, identity development is akin to being socioculturally and interactively "in sync" with the myriad demands of various social and cultural demands, which reflects an increasing fluency in practical social activity.

This has exciting repercussions for the notion of development.

Interactional Identities

The interactional approach to identity presented here is motivated by a least three key streams of thought. First are the theoretical developments in *social constructionism* (see Gergen, 1994, 1999, 2009). Over the past several decades, social constructionism has emerged as a compendium of poststructural, postempiricist, and hermeneutic philosophical thought aimed at emancipating contemporary psychology from its ties to foundationalist assumptions regarding mind, identity, language, and thought. Social constructionism has become invaluable in clearing a space for a nonmimetic view of communication, which, in turn, has invigorated a discursive turn toward studying identities as interactional/contextual phenomena. Social constructionism is, however, a meta-theoretical orientation, not a methodological one. Second and third, then, are the systematically detailed empirical grounding of interactional identities in *ethnomethodological* (see Sacks, 1992) and *discursive positioning* (Korobov, 2010) approaches. Ethnomethodological and discursive positioning approaches provide an interactional vocabulary and empirical method for studying the practices by which people order their everyday lived realities, including their identities. These three pillars—social constructionism, ethnomethodology, and discursive positioning—work synergistically to form the backdrop for an interactional approach to identity.

Social Constructionism: Identity as Relationality

Social constructionism reflects the radical prioritization of relationality—a view that attempts to reverse the longstanding idea in psychology that relationships are derivative of individual minds; instead, to borrow from Vygotsky (1978), relationality precedes individuality and makes it possible. Following in the tradition of Vygotsky's social developmental theory (1978), continental phenomenology (see Schutz, 1970), the dialogism of Bakhtin (1984, 1986), and Wittgenstein's emphasis on language use/games (1978), as well as theories of the interpolated self and performativity (Austin, 1962; Butler, 1990), social constructionism posits that the interior/internal world of the individual is not only fashioned within social, cultural, and historical webs of interdependent relationality, but is a constitutive feature of relationality. Identities are not decontextualized entities that stand outside of relational contexts. It is later, in processes of reflection and abstraction, that identities appear reified and objectified as internal phenomenon that we experience and label as private and individualized.

Further, social constructionists capitalize on what Gergen (1999) refers to as a "crisis of representation," which is purportedly a failure of the traditional (mimetic, mirroring) responsibility of language, as well as on the epistemological problems of dualism, introspection, objectivity, and rationality. Constructionists view language not simply as a mirror or map of the world, but rather as the very instrument that is itself the basis for our methods of simultaneously understanding the world and constructing it. Social constructionism has thus been instrumental in undermining the basic distinction on which this chapter and Alan Waterman's chapter rests—that is, the Cartesian dichotomy in psychology of "internal" versus "external," particularly with respect to identity. For constructionists, neither the internal mind nor the external world is granted ontological status; constructionists remain ontologically mute or agnostic about issues regarding fundamentalism/ontology. Constructionists view all assumptions about "internal minds" and "external worlds" as constituents of discursive practices. Gergen (1994) thus problematizes psychology's longstanding commitment to a *dualistic metaphysics*, which assumes an external real world that both influences and is reflected by an interior mind (or vice versa). Instead, he refers to constructionism as a *social epistemology*, which collapses the distinction between "internal" and "external" and instead sees the locus of knowledge not in individual minds nor in extant sociocultural realities, but rather in patterns of social relatedness.

Constructionists thus invite psychologists to begin their search for identity within relationships/relationality, broadly construed. Relationality could be as micro as a wink or utterance between two people, or it could be a macro habitus, such as "Western democracy" or "capitalism." Relationality is essentially a moniker for interactive contexts, both small and large. Although social constructionism thus provides an emancipatory philosophical and theoretical framework for psychologists interested in interrogating both micro- and macrocontexts for the study of identity, it nevertheless has limited *analytic* mileage because it does not offer a method per se nor does it lay out a nuanced, microinteractional descriptive vocabulary for analyzing identities as interactional phenomena. Both of these needs are taken up by ethnomethodological and discursive positioning analytic programs.

Ethnomethodology: Identities as Relationally Responsive Categorizations

Ethnomethodology reflects both Harold Garfinkel's (1967) suggestion that people are continually displaying their local understandings of what is going on and Harvy Sacks's (1992) idea that such displays of local understandings are organized and visible in the details of everyday talk. Ethnomethodology approaches identities as relationally responsive categorizations that are claimed, resisted, and otherwise used in communicative contexts to conduct social and personal life. Although these processes are analytically tractable, they are not measurable vis-à-vis an experimental factors and variables approach, but rather are analyzable as a texture of orderly and repetitive linguistic, gestural, and sequential resources. Although ethnomethodology currently encompasses a variety of strands, apposite for this chapter is Sacks's early interest in membership categorization. Sacks's early work offered rich descriptive accounts of the ways people's identities are rendered visible in their displays of or ascriptions to membership in identity-relevant or feature-rich categories.

Sacks's approached identities as *practical categorical ascriptions* that people use as transactional tools for conducting social business with others. For Sacks, the truth or correctness of an identity claim or ascription is not what is central. It is not important that someone truly "has" the particular identity that he or she claimed or that was ascribed to them, nor was Sacks concerned, as many psychologists are, about correlating particular identities to people's actions or feelings. This (lack of) interest allowed Sacks to avoid the methodological problem of treating identities as variables or factors that could be quantifiably measured. What mattered for Sacks was how identity ascriptions were interactively used in live communicative exchanges and how such uses figured as parts of the architecture of personal and social lives.

Sacks approached identities as membership categorization ascriptions that are used to perform various kinds of discursive actions. A rich and nuanced descriptive vocabulary thus emerged from Sacks's writing and was taken up by a broad range of language and social interaction researchers (for a more elaborate discussion, see Antaki & Widdicombe, 1998). For example, speakers are said to directly or indirectly *occasion* (or *make relevant*) an identity category. Such indexical invocations are referred to as *occasioning(s)* that *orient to* an identity. *Making relevant* or *orienting to* an identity or the features of an identity is brought off through a range of discursive *conversational structures* (or discursive actions) that include not only direct speech, but also paralinguistic cues. Interrogating the identity-constitutive work these conversational structures do, as well as the attendant processes of *occasioning, making relevant*, and *orienting-to*, in the process of creating sociality, is the focus and contribution of ethnomethodology for the study of identity as a distinctively interactional phenomena.

Ethnomethodology additionally stresses the importance of focusing on how the *participants themselves* occasion identity-relevant categories and use them to conduct social interaction. This is in stark contrast to the prototypical psychological agenda of beginning with a priori researcher-constructed identity categories (or features thereof), usually visible as items on questionnaires or as parts of pre-established interview questions, and testing to see whether and how people respond to such categories, as if taking them up or not is an indication of whether one "has" this or that identity, which may in turn be associated/correlated with a range of behaviors, feelings, and so on. The shift to treating identities as endemic participant resources (rather than analyst categories or predictive variables) that people naturally use in the course of everyday interactions, as well as the up-close empirical investigation of such interactional work, is an additionally significant contribution of ethnomethodology to the interactional study of identity.

It is thus out of an ethnomethodological framework that the discursive moniker "identities are for talking" emerged (see Edwards, 1991, 1997; Stokoe, 2010). Given the enormous variability and flexibility by which speakers can categorize themselves and others in various interactions, analysts attend to what is demonstrably relevant to speakers at specific discursive junctures in order to see what identity ascriptions are designed to interactively accomplish. The idea is that the demands of interpersonal engagement are complex, requiring speakers to hone a certain level of discursive dexterity when it comes to managing various identity alignments. According to Wilkinson and Kitzinger (2008, p. 585), the study of how people engage in identity work of this kind in various conversational contexts is one of the "most vibrant areas" in the field of interactional studies.

Important to note, however, is that much of the ethnomethodological work on identity became (in the field of conversation and discourse analysis) a means to the larger end of examining social action. In other words, identity ascriptions have been studied, as the moniker states, as a means of engaging with the larger project of examining the intricacies of *social action*. Many conversation and discourse analysts pay attention to participants identity work as means of studying the types of discursive actions that such identity work accomplishes—i.e., patterns of turn-talking, turn design, repair, sequence formulation, and action formation. With few exceptions (see Stokoe, 2004, 2006, 2010), delimiting the social actions brought off through categorical identity ascriptions has been a central way that ethnomethodological insights about identity have been channeled into interactional research.

Discursive Positioning: From Discursive Action to Interactional Identities

For psychologists interested primarily in identity or, specifically, in an interactional approach to identity, and not simply in identity as a route to studying the architecture of discursive action, the ethnomethodological approach (and some resultant conversation/discourse analytic approaches) to identity may be limited. These approaches may seem to too quickly bypass an in-depth analysis of identities per se. A discursive positioning approach is an attempt to remedy this problem. Like ethnomethodology, and in keeping with the general spirit of the discursive project, a discursive positioning approach is committed to an up-close descriptively discursive vocabulary for the systematic and empirical identification of discursive action. But it does more. In order to serve as a uniquely qualitative discursive approach, a discursive positioning approach additionally shows how discursive actions are, at times, ingredients in the constitution of identities as interactional (not mentalistic) phenomenon that are organized as part of the social maintenance of relationships and daily life (see Wilkinson & Kitzinger, 2003). The analytic end goal of positioning is thus identities, not identities as a route to examining discursive action. The present approach thus conceptualizes positioning as the vanguard for an interactional approach to identity.

Before discussing the present approach to positioning, it is important to note that the use of the term *positioning* is not without precedent. Positioning has had a somewhat varied and complicated history. Historically, positioning has been conceptualized as either the outward expression of a world beneath the skull or as the realization of a shared societal order. For instance, Wendy Hollway's (1983) seminal work on positioning saw acts of positioning as driven by an interior psychodynamic operation of unconscious and irrational defense mechanisms. Poststructural thinkers like Althusser (1971), Mouffe (1992), and Laclau (1993) discuss positioning by theorizing that social agents are comprised of "subject positions" that are constituted by ideological and discursive regimes, making subjectivity an ideological effect (see Wetherell, 1998 for review). And, since the early 1990s, Rom Harré and his colleagues (see Davies &Harré, 1990; Harré & Moghaddam, 2003; Harré & van Langenhove, 1992, 1999) have variously advanced ethogenic and ontological constructionist discursive views of positioning, in which acts of positioning, although immanent in conversations, are fundamentally the product or expression of a extant societal realm of rules and/or social representations. These approaches to positioning tend to capitulate to interiority metaphors (psychodynamic or cognitivist) or poststructural assumptions about the relationship between our minds, our social worlds, and our discourse (for an extended discussion, see Korobov, 2010).

The present approach to positioning avoids treating discourse (and thus identities) as the product of something more primary (see Korobov, 2006, 2010; Korobov & Bamberg, 2004a, 2004b, 2007; Wilkinson & Kitzinger, 2003). The discursive positioning approach advocated for here is anchored in the *epistemological* discursive psychology of Edwards and Potter (Edwards, 1997; Edwards & Potter, 1992; Potter, 1996; Potter & Edwards, 1999, 2003). An epistemic discursive psychology (hereafter, epistemic DP) sees talk and identities as having a performative rather than referential quality. The analytic task of epistemic DP is that of *epistemic constructionism*—that is, examining how, on what occasions, and in the service of what kinds of interactional practices, discourse is identity constitutive (Edwards, 1997; Potter, 2010; Potter & Edwards, 2003). A discursive positioning orientation thus approaches identity by examining how social interactions are ordered, made relevant, and attended to by persons-in-conversations (Korobov & Bamberg, 2004a, 2004b, 2007; Wilkinson & Kitzinger, 2003).

Positioning and Identities

This mandate for an analysis of positioning provides a useful segue to the second central characteristic of the present formulation of positioning. For sustainability purposes, positioning cannot simply end up as the latest theoretical accoutrement to epistemological DP, otherwise it runs the risk of being folded in and forgotten as yet another discursive catch-all phrase. Consonant with Kitzinger's (2006) call for DP to develop its own rigorous and cumulative empirical research program, the argument here is that positioning will remain viable if it becomes a specialized analytic descriptive tool for the analysis of something *specific*. The argument here is that this "something specific" should be the analysis of identities. To that end, Bamberg's (1997, 2003) three-leveled positioning analysis has been a fruitful contribution because it is both systematic and applicable to research on narrative identity. As an analytic tool, and in keeping with the ethomethodological spirit, positioning must offer descriptive possibilities for the systematic and empirical demonstration of social, cultural, or psychological concepts (here, "identities") in ways that reveal them to be interactional (not mentalistic) phenomenon that are organized as part of the social maintenance of relationships and daily life (see Wilkinson & Kitzinger, 2003). The present approach conceptualizes positioning as a distinct method for examining identities.

To be useful for identity analysis, acts of positioning cannot be understood as simply discursive actions, at least not in the way that discourse analysts typically refer to discursive actions, like "blaming" or "disagreeing." One can show where and how a speaker is disagreeing, for instance, and what disagreeing is doing within an interaction. For decades, discourse and conversational analysts have made it their business to describe these sorts of discursive actions as bits of patterned interactional machinery that reveal the architecture or structure of human interaction. Analyses involving positioning must attend to this level of analysis of discursive action, but they must do more. Simply examining the architecture of a social activity like disagreement does not necessarily tell us anything about the way disagreement figures in the accomplishment of something beyond its immediate structure or architecture. For example, consider the following exchange, in which speaker B disagrees with speaker A.

A: Let's stop and ask for directions
B: No (.) don't stop and ask for directions

There is an enormous amount of discursive work that could be (and has been) performed on this type of adjacency pair, in which disagreement emerges as the turn-initial second-pair part to requests or suggestions. However, for the analysis to count as positioning analysis, it would need to show not only how the disagreement is interactively built, but also *how disagreement functions to position speakers as having certain kinds of identities* (or the hearable features of certain identities). Not all interactional exchanges will easily lend themselves to warrantable claims about the ways discursive actions directly or indirectly *position* identities (or the features thereof), and, to that end, positioning should be selectively applied lest it become a generic catch-all phrase for describing social action in general. Some exchanges, however, may be amenable to warrantable claims about the ways discursive actions index identities, and, when they are, positioning is apropos. For example, consider the analytic potential of the following exchange.

A: We should stop and ask for directions
B: No (.) we don't stop and ask for directions

B's recycling of (and emphasis on) "we" is stated in the iterative present tense and thus scripts the behavior of the "we" group as having the general feature of engaging in a certain action pattern, of being a member of the group of people who routinely do not stop to ask for directions. We might also note that B's use of "we" is a recycling-plus-emphasis of A's use of "we," which has a certain proscriptive force that *positions* B as a member of the "we" moral order (whatever that is). Certainly, a rich and interesting analysis could be worked up that details not simply the architecture of B's disagreement, *but also the way that B's disagreement makes relevant certain identities for A and B to take-up, amend, or resist*. Although this example is, admittedly, quite simple and stark, it makes the point that some interactions consist not only in discursive actions, but also in warrantable identity claims. Descriptions of the ways that such identities are built, amended, and resisted is the distinctive focus of positioning.

Positions are thus second-order phenomena. Although A is, at the first-level of ordering, doing something like "making a suggestion/directive" and B is doing something like "disagreeing," these discursive actions are also, at a second-level, arguably positioning the speakers as having the features of a certain kind of identity. Their positions, therefore, are the effect that certain discursive actions have for establishing the identities of participants present or imagined (see Korobov, 2006, 2010; Korobov & Bamberg, 2007). An analysis of positioning, therefore, is an analysis of the ways discursive actions directly or indirectly make relevant or index identities or the features of identities (more on this later). Acts of positioning involve not simply a description of the architecture or machinery of social interaction, but also a description of the identity work that orders together the speakers into collections of certain kinds of people with certain inferentially available identities.

This particular use of positioning to study identities in terms of categories and how they are sequentially occasioned in conversations represents an alignment with the discursive-ethnomethodological approach to identity in Antaki and Widdicombe's (1998) *Identities in Talk*, as well as the more recently developed blend of conversation analytic (CA) and membership categorization analytic work on participants' orientations to gender categories and gender category-bound activities/attributes (see Speer, 2005; Speer & Stokoe, 2011; Stokoe, 2004, 2006, 2010; Stokoe & Smithson, 2001). Close discursive analyses of membership categories have been shown to be useful in the analysis of identity and interpersonal relationship construction, which entails a focus on the ways speakers conduct interaction, claim identities, and build relationships as members of particular relational categories (see Mandelbaum, 2003; Pomerantz & Mandelbaum, 2005; Wilkinson & Kitzinger, 2008). Categories index (and are indexed by) culturally defined sets of category-bound activities, rights, obligations, and predicates that are expected for members of that category. Applied to positioning, attention is thus paid to the ways speakers' discursive actions occasion identity-implicative relational categories as part of the business of creating topic alignment and affiliation. The task of positioning analysis is to locate the central categories (and attributes of those categories) as they are sequentially oriented to by participants.

Wilkinson and Kitzinger (2003) have specified three positioning practices that are useful for further differentiating the relationship between identity construction and category use. The first positioning practice they specify is called "*naming or indexing a category*," which involves speakers either straightforwardly using categorical reference terms (like "fireman," "woman," "jock") to describe themselves or someone else, or they may index an unnamed category by using a referent like "them (as in "that's the trouble with a lot of them"). Positioning practices that index rather than directly specify an identity category are obviously doing different interactional work. The second positioning practice involves "*invoking categorical membership*," which involves indexing an unnamed identity category through certain assumptions displayed in one's talk. Wilkinson and Kitzinger's (2003) example includes a group of women talking about their husbands. Their talk about their husbands indirectly presumes membership in the category "heterosexual." Wilkinson and Kitzinger point out that normative categories (like "heterosexual") are often assumed and invoked indirectly and are thus rarely explicitly named, which is less true for non-normative categories. And, as Fivush (2010) has noted, remaining silent with respect to shared or normative understandings has the effect of naturalizing the status quo; deviations or challenges to the status quo call for explicit voice and thus an undermining of what is normative. The third positioning practice is "*invoking attributes*," which involves speakers showing us what kind of identity they have by invoking certain attributes. A speaker may claim to be "slow on the uptake," "shy," "terrible on first dates," and so on. Although an identity category is not directly named, these attributes may be treated by the interlocutors as indices of certain identity categories, and the speaker may be positioned as such. Applied to the current discussion, the take-away idea is that there are a variety of ways that categories and identities can be synced up within an interaction and that positioning is the analytic concept meant to sync these up. What follows is an attempt to illustrate positioning by looking more closely at what happens when speakers resist categories and/or their attributes.

Positioning in Action

Over the past decade, one of the more fruitful discursive arenas for identity analysis has been work that focuses on speakers orientations to category-appropriate behavior, which often feature speakers resisting the ascription of membership categories or the features conventionally associated with certain categories (see Speer, 2005; Speer & Stokoe, 2011; Stokoe, 2004, 2010; Stokoe & Smithson, 2001). Resisting an identity often directly or indirectly occasions alternative or non-normative identities, which may have the effect of making certain cultural identities (or their features) morally accountable, which may enforce or disrupt the status quo (see Hammack, 2008; Speer, 2005; Stokoe, 2010). Resistance to category-appropriate behavior has also been studied as a means of "doing differentiation" (see Edley & Wetherell, 1997; Korobov, 2004; Widdicombe & Wooffitt, 1995), which involves rejecting category membership by showing how one does not possess (or contrasts with) the conventional features of a particular identity category. Such contrasts often have the effect of establishing an identity style or dispositional preference that appears idiosyncratic, thus providing a means for the speaker to come across as having a personal or unique identity. As such, there may be an interesting point of connection between the sort of rhetorical work that contrasts to category-appropriate behavior achieve and the development of positioning as an analytic descriptor of such discursive processes.

Using positioning to describe categorical contrast work (or differentiation) squares elegantly with the spatial flexibility inherent in the concept of positioning. Positioning allows one to describe how discursive actions allow speakers to 'take a position," "resist a position," "display irony about a position" (thus both taking and not taking that position) or, more creatively, how speakers "take a position by resisting being positioned." The maneuverability options with respect to the dynamism of positioning as an analytic descriptor are enormous, making positioning very useful both in terms of providing a useful analytic term for work in membership categorization and, more generally, for the epistemic DP focus on describing what Potter (1996) refers to as the "offensive" and "defensive" rhetorical nature of talk. Acts of positioning may work *offensively* in so far as they undermine alternative identity positions; acts of positioning may work *defensively* in so far as they have the capacity to resist or deflect potential challenges or counters to one's identity ascriptions. Because talk usually encompasses a variety of rhetorical functions (both offensively and defensively), conversational positioning will vary from turn to turn and will involve the selective deployment of discursive formulations to bring off identity claims that are well-fitted or finely tuned; which is to say, identity claims that are interactively robust and not easily assailable.

An epistemic DP approach to positioning thus has a double focus. It examines both the discursive strategies used to work up identity positions, while at the same time considering the strategies used to deflect or defend against alternative versions or potential challenges. This double focus of rhetoric shades into the often cited notion of "stake and interest" management (Edwards & Potter, 1992; Potter, 1996), or what has been called the "dilemma of stake" (Potter, 1996). The dilemma refers to the ways that conversational positions may be discounted because they appear to be motivated by a concealed stake or interest on the part of the speaker, or on the part of the group to which the speaker belongs. In daily life, people often treat one another *as if* they have a stake or interest in some course of action or, in this case, in some form of identity to which their talk is directed. Because of this, speakers will often work up their identity positions in ways that avoid the obvious appearance of stake or interest, and, conversely, people will often work to position other people's identity ascriptions so that they appear motivated by stake or interest. One analytic goal of positioning, therefore, is to describe how people, in joint communicative activity, undermine self/other positions by invoking interests, and how, in turn, they design their identity positions to resist such undermining.

Illustrating Positioning for the Analysis of Gender Identity

These various features of positioning for identity analysis are best illustrated with a couple of worked examples. The following excerpts come from a study of speed-dating conversations between emerging adult men and women (see Korobov, 2011a, 2011b). Speed-dating involves romantically available individuals attending an event in which they participate in a series of uniformly short "dates" (e.g., 3- to 8-minute conversations) with other attendees. After the event, participants anonymously "yes" or "no" their dates; if two speed-daters "yes" one another, a "match" occurs, and they are allowed to contact each other to presumably arrange a more traditional date. The data presented here were derived from 36 speed-dates involving 12 participants (6 male; 6 female), with each date lasting approximately 6 minutes.

For illustrative purposes, two data excerpts are presented. Each excerpt was originally culled as part of a larger analysis of instances of "mate-preference talk," that is, instances in which speakers were asked about or volunteered any features (personality, physical, or otherwise) of actual or potential/imaginary partners that they found desirable. Since mate-preference disclosures are typically identity-implicative, they are especially amenable to an analysis of positioning. The two excerpts here represent examples of mate preferences that reflect a gender non-normative identity or identities that are resistant to traditional gender norms. In other words, they reflect men and women aligning themselves with attraction preferences that resist either stereotypically masculine or feminine cultural preferences. Examples of resistance are chosen here because they seemed to illuminate some fascinating findings with respect to what predicted affiliation between speed-daters. As the examples reveal, the more that men and women resisted appearing to have stereotypically masculine or feminine attraction preferences, the more likely it was that they would have a connection or positive affiliation. Two subtypes of resistance are presented here, each uniquely representing a distinct dimension of positioning. They are (1) self-positioned resistance to stereotypical gender preferences and (2) resistance to being positioned as complicit with stereotypical gender preferences.

Self-Positioned Resistance

One way to position an identity is to occasion one's own resistance to the stereotypical features of conventional identities. In this first excerpt, the female speaker (F) resists the gender conventional female categories of "typical clingy girl" and "cook" and instead formulates a preference for a range of identity-relevant activities (i.e., watching football with her "man") that positions an identity for her that promotes affiliation with her male (M) date.

(1)(F5M4)
1 M: so whadda' lookin'fur in a guy?
2 F: I'm not a typical clingy girl y'know (.) if my man likes
3 football then I'd sit down and watch football n'b'all
4 GO TEAM with him.
5 M: ohhhehehh that's awesome.
6 F: I'm not like >why are you watching football today?< (.)
7 no (.) let's kick it together (.) you (.) your homeboys
8 (.) me and my homegirls (.) have a party (.) that's how
9 I want my family.
10 M: hhhehaya' so you'd like t'have a party?
11 F: YEAH I wanna be 'cept I don't cook (.) we'll just have
12 t'order food haah.
13 M: WHAT (.) na' I can cook.
14 F: SEE (.) look we could get married.
15 M: I grill everything (.) I can (.) I grill everything
16 F: will you marry me?
17 ((both laugh))

Immediately apparent is that this interaction is transcribed with CA conventions (see Jefferson, 2004). This is not to suggest that positioning analysis ought to be conversation analytic, but it is meant to point out that positioning should begin with a close analysis of discursive action, which a CA transcript provides. Otherwise, it is tempting to run roughshod over a close analysis of the discursive actions that index identities and toward a quick, loosely grounded, and overly colloquial discussion of this-or-that identity that F or M is claiming. Let us begin, then, by looking at how F orients to M's initial topic proffer in line 1. Rather than taking up M's actual question about what she would prefer in a "guy," which would be the preferred second-pair part, F orients to the proffer as an open-ended invitation to position her identity as a certain type of potentially preferable item. In lines 2–4, she offers scripted descriptions (Edwards, 1995) of gender normative and non-normative activities that she would and would not generally perform. Defensively, she positions her identity as *not* the normatively ("typical") generic type "clingy girl." Instead, she uses a modal (I'd) and iterative present tense (n'b'all) to formulate a general action identity pattern of appearing to be the type of "girl" who would regularly sit down with her "guy," watch football with him, and cheer with him—all activities that are designed as contrasts to the identity "typical girl."

Her defensive rhetorical resistance to the normative or typical "girl" is further positioned as she constructs imaginary and scripted reported speech (line 6) to distance herself from a type of regularly occurring complaint ("why are you watching football today?") from a typical "girl." Rather, she comes off as someone who wants to "kick it" together with friends, which is an idiom that arguably indexes a nonchalant attitude of casual nonexclusive interaction, an idiom further bolstered by the referents "homeboys" and "homegirls." These formulations come as additional contrasts to what M might have normatively expected from the identity "typical clingy girl." In lines 11–12, she occasions yet another non-normative identity disposition (she does not cook), which, unlike the preferences mentioned earlier, may be dispreferable to a heterosexual male partner and thus more risky. That she points out this dispreference underscores the implicit assumption that it might be normative for him to expect that she might be the type of person who likes to cook.

Note, however, M's receipt of F's positioned resistance. In a way that continues the environment of affective affiliation that has been building with M's appreciations in lines 5 and 10, M positions his own non-normative, regularly occurring gendered-identity action pattern ("I can cook"), but mitigates this by qualifying the action (cooking) as a certain subcategory of cooking ("grilling") that is consonant with a traditional masculine identity. F and M are able to establish mutuality and affective affiliation around a coordinated resistance to normative gender preferences. F's hyperbolic "we could get married" and "will you marry me?" are designed as staged exaggerations that play up the way their positioning has engendered a kind of affiliation that is uncanny or remarkable.

In sum, M's initial turn is an *identity*-implicative proffer. Rather than responding to it by offering a "this-is-who-I-am" type response, F constructs a series of anti-identities, effectively signaling what she is not. She occasions and contrasts her own identity against a series of negative evaluations of an outgroup. F uses script formulations to construct a self-positioned resistance to the identity features of a certain gendered identity category. Her positioning largely entails contrast work, which in turn elicits contrast work from M. Although positioning is a method for formulating one's identity, positioning is always part of a real or imagined interaction, which is to say it is positioning-within-interaction. It is rhetorically responsive to various interactive contingencies, which, in this particular interaction, seems to involve promoting affective affiliation in ways that attend to the subject-side risks of self-presentation.

Resistance to Being Positioned as Complicit with Stereotypical Gender Preferences

In other interactions, speakers would directly or indirectly position another speaker as complicit with a disposition or behavior that might be expected from someone in his or her identity category. For instance, in speaking with a heterosexual male in a speed-dating interaction, a female might ask him from the outset what sorts of physical attributes he is attracted to, a question that assumes that physical attraction is a relevant sort of thing to ask a heterosexual man. She might assume, stereotypically, that men are drawn to physical appearance and thus that this sort of query is relevant. Interestingly, these sorts of projected positionings of complicity with stereotypical identity features were rarely met with straightforward compliance. Instead, men and women tended to respond with *resistance* in the form of denials, hedges, or qualifications. In this next excerpt, M positions F as having a certain type of female identity that may prefer a male partner who "spoils" her. M's positioning potentially indexes the traditional identity of "passive female" that enjoys being taken care of. This type of other-positioning is obviously risky and could derail the interaction. In this case, however, F playfully resists M's positioning and, in so doing, creates an environment in which stance affiliation with M occurs.

(2) (F3M2)
1 M: what kind of relationships you into?
2 F: I'm open to all sorts of things (.) >like t'be
3 treated well< (.) <u>typical</u> things.
4 M: you like to be <u>spoiled</u>?
5 [hmm?
6 F: [hehe <u>me::::</u>?
7 M: mm::hm::: hh.
8 F: <I lo::ve it>hh (.) but okay (.) for some reason guys
9 that I've dated (.) I don't know <u>what</u> happened
10 but like ya'll'l put lot of effort (.) like honestly
11 trying to make it work (.) but I've learned you can't
12 make something work if it ain't gonna work.
13 M: umhumm.
14 F: I gave up on that.
15 M: but'cha still like the spoiling?
16 F: w'l <u>ya::h</u> b'li:ke okay for <u>real</u> I <u>do</u> feel things for them,
17 M: you put effort in.
18 F: oh yah (.) like last guy was never there for me n'I was
19 for him (.) like I'm <u>there</u> for the person but he wasn't
20 for me (.) never (.) like Valentine's and whatever (.)
21 I never got nothing.
22 M: that isn't fair (.) that's cold.
23 F: yep (.) it was (.) I be the one always giving stuff
24 n'I don't care cuz' I'm not the type of the female
25 that's like you kno(h)w heheh ya'know,
26 M: yeah but ya'gotta ask for a small token'v appreciation
27 (.) that'd be easy for him,
28 F: yeah (.) well maybe you're letting me know there are
29 <u>different</u> kinds of guys out there.
30 M: oh <u>yeah</u>.
31 (1.0)
32 M: [there <u>are</u>]
33 F: [yeah ()] you're giving me [hope
34 M: [<u>me</u> heheh.
35 F: okay(ha)oka(h)y heheh that's good to know

M's first gender-identity positioning of F comes in line 4 as he treats F's "like t'be treated well" as a euphemism for "liking to be spoiled," which has gender-identity negative dispositional implications for F. Yet, instead of orienting to it as a negative identity scripting, F laughs and displays a knowing and exaggerated surprise ("me::::?"), thus treating it as a playful provocation. M shapes his reply in kind by recycling F's elongated affect with an exaggerated smile voice agreement of "mm::hm:::," which F parallels with "<I lo::ve it>hh." In effect, M's bid to position F vis-à-vis a potentially undesirable identity occasions a three-part repartee: F positions herself as playfully coy, M positions himself as playfully suspicious, and F then positions herself as playfully honest. In just the first 8 lines, there is a glut of positioning maneuvers, all brought off through scripting, innuendo, exaggeration, affect shifts, and laughter. Their positions are in the service of creating an interpersonal repartee, which creates the potential for affective affiliation.

In line 8, F's "but okay" both acknowledges the play frame and breaks with it. She shifts toward a focus on "guys" who try too hard when the relationship is not working, to which M responds by recycling the gender-identity negative dispositional tease "but'cha still like the spoiling." His recycling is yet again a risky identity-implicative move. It avoids F's shift of focus onto "guys" and thus holds her accountable to the possibility that she knowingly takes advantage of her partner's generosity. Here, again, F recycles her play frame. The opening part of F's response in line 16 ("w'l <u>ya::h</u>") is a *sine dicendo* rhetorical response that treats his question as having an obvious answer and proceeds to select that obvious answer. The obviousness is signaled colloquially through the intonation, which is hearable as a "yeah no duh" type formulation. By formulating it as obvious, she inoculates it from its ability to make her attraction preference seem aberrant, a move that does positioning work. It normalizes her preferences and thus her identity. By treating her preferences as obvious and expected, she does both subject-side work (Edwards, 2005, 2007) and interactive work; it positions the two of them as sharing obvious knowledge. Like her turn in line 8, it is after a jocular rejoinder that she turns to the second part of her turn to deflect possible negative identity inferences. Following this, M's next contribution in line 17 ("you put effort in") does *not* project negative gender dispositional inferences, but instead states the implication of her prior statement that she feels things for her partners, which negates his claim in line 15 that suggested she might be manipulative. By line 17, the two appear in sync, despite the riskiness of M's negative identity positioning of F.

Lines 18–25 are topic expansive, with F providing a relational history account in which her generosity and support were freely given but unreciprocated by her last male partner, which positions her as nonexploitative of men and desirous of a reciprocal relationship. Although M aligns with this identity position in line 22, which promotes topic expansion, he proposes closure to her relational history account by again positioning her as potentially complicit with gender-conventionality with "but ya' gotta ask for a small token'v appreciation." He adds that such appreciation would be "easy" for her previous male partners to show. The potentially negative identity inference here is that F may fit the category of being overly "docile" or "passive" because she cannot or will not ask for what she wants, when what she wants is an "easy" thing for her partner to give. As with M's previous formulations, F interestingly does not treat this as a criticism but rather as a presentation of alternative possibilities—that is, as a way that M is letting her know that there are different kinds of guys available. Given the speed-dating context, F's response positions M as perhaps having a personal stake or interest (Edwards & Potter, 1992) in making such an observation. In short, F's response treats M's negative gender-identity positioning of F not as a criticism, but as a method by which M is signaling that he may be one such alternative possibility (a possibility ratified by M in line 34). F orients to M's provocations as flirtatious bids, which are visible across the final turns of the excerpt.

The take-away from both of these excerpts is that although having conventional identity attraction preferences may be expected and projected by speakers onto one another in initial romantic encounters, they often do not promote an affective connection. Quite the contrary, a locally fashioned identity that eschews gender stereotypes seems to predict affective affiliation, at least perhaps in the kind of initial romantic encounters that approximate speed-dates. Were the context to shift, the interactional displays of identities would also likely shift, demonstrating again the central point here—that identities are dexterous and context-specific interactional doings.

Conclusion

The aim of this chapter is to address a pronounced half-century gap in psychological identity research. Although Erikson's view of identity development emphasized the importance of social contexts and social interactions, empirical demonstrations of the rich and nuanced links between personal identity development and social/interactional contexts have either been investigated too broadly or not at all. Psychologists have, unfortunately, contributed very little understanding to the ways that identities emerge and develop within social interactions. Within psychology, the closest we typically get to an analysis of identities vis-à-vis social interactions are studies modeled on a factors-and-variables approach that emphasizes extant "social contexts" (schools, peer groups, families, etc) and of the ways participation in these broad contexts *predicts* various facets of identity development. Conspicuously absent are up-close interrogations of the interplay between identities and the actual social interactions that comprise and enliven broad social contexts. The charge of this chapter is for psychologically minded identity researchers to investigate how identities are formed, contested, and revised within interactional contexts.

The interactional approach to identity presented here is an outgrowth of three interconnected theoretical and methodological approaches. Social constructionism is a metatheoretical orientation that attempts to free conceptualizations of identity from foundationalist assumptions regarding the ontological prioritization of individuality over relationality, as well as the (falsely) dualistic relationship between language/communication and minds/thoughts. Without reifying relationality as a new form of foundationalism, social constructionism stresses the Vygotskian emphasis on the inescapably constitutive force of relationality. One of the projects of social constructionism is thus to reverse the longstanding assumption that relationships are simply derivative of individuals coming together. Instead, identities (or whatever "private" sense of individuality we might have) emerge out of interdependent relational contexts and thus ought to be studied as emergent relational phenomena. As such, the classic dualistic metaphysics of "internal" and "external" collapses; the locus of identity lies neither in individual minds nor in extant sociocultural contexts but rather in patterns of emergent social relatedness. Although the gravity of this theoretical shift has been enormous in psychology, as well as in the social sciences more broadly, social scientists have not easily translated the theoretical idea of "identities as patterns of emergent social relatedness" into a methodological approach.

The second approach, ethnomethodology, makes the theoretical intimations of social constructionism analytically visible and tractable. It puts meat on the bones of a theoretical commitment to identities as emergent relational phenomenon that are used in communicative contexts to conduct personal and social life. Importantly, such processes are, for ethnomethodologists, analytically tractable, which is to say visible in the details of actual discourse and social interaction. Ethnomethodological work has generated a rich descriptive vocabulary for describing how speakers themselves orient, ascribe, make relevant, and resist identities (or identity relevant categories) in everyday interactions. This analytically rich interactional compendium of thinking has paved the way for a truly inductive (as opposed to an a priori, experimentally/researcher generated) study of emergent identities. Identities are examined as participant resources that are claimed, resisted, and amended in real-time interactional contexts. To date, much of the early ethnomethodological work on identities (and categorical identity work) has been appropriated in the field of CA and discourse studies more broadly. Yet, as ethno-inspired CA analyses have grown more dominant as well as microanalytic, discursive studies that ostensibly have "identity" as the topic tend to be less about identities per se, at least in the way social scientists think about identities, and more about showing what an occasioning of an identity category reveals about the basic architecture of social action. Simply put, understanding social action, not identities, is typically the end-goal of analysis.

The third pillar, a discursive positioning approach, has identities as its analytic end goal, not identities as a route to examining discursive action. Although not watering down a close analysis of discursive action, a discursive positioning approach attempts to additionally show not just the machinery of discursive action, but also how that discursive machinery is, at times, ingredient in the constitution of identities as interactional phenomenon that are organized as part of the social maintenance of relationships and daily life. A discursive positioning approach is thus posited as the vanguard for an interactional approach to identity. Central in a discursive positioning approach is a refusal to treat talk (and everything discursive that happens in social interactions) as simply a reflection or outpouring of what is happening in some "interior" realm of "mind." Rather, the meanings that our interactions have are primarily driven not by what we are thinking or feeling, but by what those interactions are designed to be doing as part of the social press of having an identity that is accountable within a context. The idea is that there is an interactional logic that drives identity processes, not simply a mentalistic one.

This particular view of positioning has been tied to a discursive psychological view that is epistemological rather than ontological. An epistemic DP view of positioning is interested not in *what* positioning reveals (ontologically) about the status of minds or worlds, or in the thorny problems that result from ontological views of discourse, but rather is concerned with *how*, and on what occasions, and in the service of certain interactional practices, speakers position themselves in accord with various identities to conduct some bit of relational business. In conversations of all sorts, there is a press to make sense of oneself in the context of other interlocutors, which is what is meant by accountability. Positioning is thus understood by examining the dynamism of interactional accountability; that is, *how* speakers order conversations and thus manage relationships by orienting to certain identities or identity-rich categories.

The present focus on discursive positioning has also been linked with a microgenetic view of identity development in order to broaden the general notion of identity by reconceptualizing identity development away from an internal, linear, and temporal formula and instead examine it from a social, locally interactive discursive perspective. The aim has been to examine the progressive, emergent, and incremental movement along developmental pathways within interactions. It is here where the notion of "developmental changes" becomes reconceptualized in microgenetic terms as emergent discursive positions. One central contribution thus concerns the advancement of a microgenetic view of identity development. The data extracts presented have hopefully illustrated moments in which positions emerge, where identities come into being, get batted about, claimed, and sometimes rejected. Analyses of such moments are not aimed at *explaining* how this or that identity, understood as a referential objective state of being or stage level, is evinced, but rather is aimed at *describing* how local identities microdevelopmentally emerge and (often) consolidate as contextually embedded and socially constructive processes. The description of these highly contextual processes is the ground on which ontogenetic changes can be mapped out. This coming-into-existence of identity positions in social interactions is what is central in the present contribution to identity development and, as such, invigorates the connection between identity development and interactional analyses.

Positioning is thus useful for showing not simply that a speaker is produced as having a certain identity, but also how that production is accomplished and how its accomplishment is part of local interactional aims. To date, this sort of analytic demonstration is missing in psychological analyses of identity. In everyday contexts, people rarely engage with the explicit aim of showing "this is who I am"; in everyday conversations, identity claims may be explicit, or (more likely) they may creep into interactions in piecemeal fashion, as parts of small and fleeting interactional aims. In fact, as the two examples in this chapter have shown, when people do position their identities, they often attend to the subject-side risks of self-presentation (see Edwards, 2005, 2007), which is to say they carefully avoid negative assessments that could be inferred if one subscribes to potentially problematic categorizations. At times, then, conversational identities may initially emerge as reactive sets of anti-positions nested in certain relational tit-for-tats where affiliation is at stake. To analytically accommodate these discursive processes, positioning must be a flexible analytic concept that is capable of tracking the ways social actions are discursively built so as to index identities that are not easily assailable, while also promoting the possibility of connection with others. In so doing, positioning reverses the typical ethomethodological agenda of looking at how identity claims index social actions. Instead, with positioning, the purpose is to examine how social actions index particular identities.

The excerpts from the speed-daters' conversations were meant to illustrate the discursive dexterity of positioning. The examples showed how male and female speed-daters created affective affiliation by responding to questions about their attraction preferences in ways that resisted stereotypical gender identity categories. Identities that resisted gender conventionality tended to function as a preliminary for affective affiliation. Positions of resistance to nonpreferable gendered dispositions seemed designed to elicit reciprocal rejection from the other; in this way, speakers could coordinate and affiliate around what they could agree was nonpreferable. Resistance at this level of particularity seemed to promote affective affiliation. Gender-categorical resistance allowed speakers to show how they shared stances around aspects of gender conventional preferences or behaviors that could arguably be taken to be unhealthy or undesirable. In so doing, speed-daters could position themselves as possibilities to one another that defy stereotypical gender categorizations—that is, as unique and thus desirable potential partners.

Limitations

There are limitations to the interactional approach to identity being argued for in this chapter. There are two ways to discuss the issue of limitations—theoretically/conceptually and methodologically. At the theoretical level, although the position taken in this chapter is that the internal/external dichotomy rests on a false metaphysical dualism, this dichotomy is still widely accepted and quite intuitively and theoretically useful in mainstream psychological theories of the self and identity. One of the more theoretically generative assumptions in mainstream thinking about identity is a kind of essentialism that posits that an individual's human nature ("interiority") plays a significant role in shaping expressions of identity. Were we to bracket this line of thinking, as interactional and discursive researchers generally do, vast amounts of empirical information about the influence of the brain/biology/personality would be difficult to integrate in theory building, and this would remain true even if these entities were contextualized as, for instance, brains-in-context. In discursive-interactional approaches, interior phenomena only become the topic of inquiry if they are occasioned as part of some social business in interactional discourse. If they are not, they do not become part of the theoretical conversation because they are not analytically tractable. As such, one of the enticing draws of an interiority approach grounded in essentialism is that it is more comprehensive and thus generates a broader theory base.

This resistance to an interior causal realm highlights a broader constraint of an interactional approach, which is that it is an epistemological and not ontological orientation. The ontological question of *what* constitutes an identity (or what the nature of identity is) is sidelined in favor of an investigation of *how* identities are interactively built. An interactional approach tends to avoid attributing identity to interior realms of minds, emotions, motivation, and biology/brains—especially when these realms carry with them assumptions about (causal) ontology. The focus is on how identities are interactively constructed, not what identities are or what interior mechanisms cause them to be what they are. Although considered a boon in more interpretive, qualitative approaches, this ontological agnosticism is arguably an encumbrance for many identity theorists. The ontological *what* question is hugely important for many psychologists because, without such a discussion, people are viewed quite simply as employing cultural resources in contextually variable ways to create sociality. We are thus unable to say anything specific about *them*. This results in a very thin view of the person. Although an approach that emphasizes interiority may offer a rather thin view of identity-as-sociality, it can offer a rather robust theoretically Cartesian view of individuality and person-/self-hood.

Methodologically, researching interactions is an incredibly time-consuming and nuanced job. Although interactional identities can be sped up and simplified through quantification and coding, the majority of researchers in the ethnomethodological and discursive traditions avoid exclusive coding schemes and quantifying features of interactions, which dramatically narrows the scope of their findings. The methodological goal is not concerned with correlating particular identities to actions or feelings, which means, unlike an interiority approach grounded in a commitment to measurement, an interactional approach is not equipped to predict the relationship between certain self-reported identities and a range of actions, feelings, or behaviors—all of which may be important to know, given one's field of research and one's concern with applicability or praxis.

This problem stems from a larger issue, namely, the broader commitment by interactional researchers to not operationalize identities as variables or factors that can be quantifiably measured. For many psychologists, however, a factors-and-variables approach to identity is not a problem, but a welcome solution. Interiority approaches to identity are readily armed with an ample supply of interior phenomenon (thoughts, beliefs, emotions, personalities, etc) that are all highly evolved as operationally defined mechanisms useful in the hypothetico-deductive commitment to prediction and control. In short, there is arguably a methodologically cleaner science to be had with an interiority approach than with a radical interactional approach.

Furthermore, since the interactional focus is on the multiplicity of identity constructions within interactions, it is difficult to make claims about identity coherence, stability, and transformation across contexts and across time. The issue of what stays the same and what changes has, for decades, lain at the heart of developmental research on identity. Although an interactional approach can speak about microgenetic development, this is only part of the puzzle. If the focus is on identities within local interactional contexts, it is difficult to trace the continuity of an individual's identity development across developmental time. And, even if we are careful to examine identities as always situated within a context, there are a myriad of interactional contexts that individuals participate in, contexts that can be difficult if not impossible to generalize one to another. In other words, although it may be interesting to study the ways that interactional positions are occasioned to construct local identities or to attend to issues of interactional accountability, it is arguably just as important to examine how identity claims/positions may serve quite personal functions that change across a speaker's life and transcend local contexts. In short, an interactional approach struggles to speak to both the private/personal functions as well as to the broader or macrosociocultural functions of identity positions.

Despite the limitations, a grounded and fine-grained analysis of identity positioning is meant to sharpen the ways psychologists typically talk, in broad strokes, about identity as a "contextual" phenomenon. The aim of a discursive positioning approach is to connect a sequentially grounded and fine-grained examination of discursive action with an analysis of identity categories. Acts of positioning describe more than social action. They describe the ways social actions sync up with and index inference-rich identities. A focus on positioning, therefore, bolsters the standard ethnomethodologically inspired sequential-discursive analytic project of describing the architecture or machinery of social interaction by connecting an analysis of social action with an analysis of identities. An analysis of positioning reveals the social practices and procedures through which speakers are grouped together into collections of certain kinds of people with certain inferentially available identities (see Sacks, 1992). Psychologists will, of course, continue to treat acts of positioning as windows into "minds" or as reflections of external "worlds." But the hope is that, with a more discursively grounded and epistemic view of conversational positioning, psychologists will increasingly find ways to study identities as interactional phenomenon that are organized as part of the social maintenance of relationships and daily life.

References

Adams, G. R., Dyk, P. A. H., & Bennion, L. D. (1987). Parent-adolescent relationships and identity formation. *Family Perspective, 21*, 249–260.

Adams, G. R., & Marshall, S. K. (1996). A developmental social psychology of identity: Understanding the person-in-context. *Journal of Adolescence, 19*, 429–442.

Althusser, L. (1971). *Lenin and philosophy and other essays.* London: New Left Books.

Antaki, C., & Widdicombe, S. (Eds.). (1998). *Identities in talk.* London: Sage.

Austin, J. L. (1962). *How to do things with words.* Cambridge, MA: Harvard University Press.

Bakhtin, M. M. (1984). *Problems of Dostoevsky's poetics.* Edited and translated by Caryl Emerson. Minneapolis: University of Minnesota Press.

Bakhtin, M. M. (1986). *Speech Genres and Other Late Essays.* Trans. by Vern W. McGee. Austin: University of Texas Press.

Bamberg, M. (1997). Positioning between structure and performance. *Journal of Narrative and Life History, 7*, 335–342.

Bamberg, M. (2000a). Critical personalism, language, and development. *Theory & Psychology, 10*, 749–767.

Bamberg, M. (2003). "Positioning with Davie Hogan. Stories, tellings, and identities. In C. Daiute & C. Lightfoot (Eds.), *Narrative analysis: Studying the development of individuals in society* (pp. 135–157). London: Sage.

Butler, J. (1990). *Gender trouble: Feminism and the subversion of identity.* New York: Routledge.

Catan, L. (1986). The dynamic display of process: Historical development and contemporary uses of the microgenetic method. *Human Development, 29*, 252–263.

Côté, J. E. (1993). Foundations of a psychoanalytic social psychology: Neo-Eriksonian propositions regarding the relationship between psychic structure and cultural institutions. *Developmental Review, 13*, 31–53.

Côté, J. E., & Levine, C. (1987). A formulation of Erikson's theory of ego identity formation. *Developmental Review, 7*, 273–325.

Côté, J. E., & Levine, C. (1988). A critical examination of the ego identity status paradigm. *Developmental Review, 8*, 147–184.

Davies, B., & Harré, R. (1990). Positioning: The discursive production of selves. *Journal for the Theory of Social Behaviour, 20*, 43–63.

Eckert, P. (1989). *Jocks and burnouts: Social categories and identity in the high school.* New York: Teachers College Press.

Eckert, P. (2002). Demystifying sexuality and desire. In K. Campbell-Kibler, R. Podesva, S. J. Roberts & A. Wong (Eds.), *Language and sexuality: Contesting meaning in theory and practice* (pp. 99–110). Stanford, CA: CSLI Publications.

Edley, N., & Wetherell, M. (1997). Jockeying for position: The construction of masculine identities. *Discourse & Society, 8*, 203–217.

Edwards, D. (1991). Categories are for talking: On the cognitive and discursive bases of categorization. *Theory and Psychology, 1*, 515–542.

Edwards, D. (1995). Two to tango: Script formulations, dispositions, and rhetorical symmetry in relationship troubles talk. *Research on Language and Social Interaction, 28*, 319–350.

Edwards, D. (1997). *Discourse and cognition.* London: Sage.

Edwards, D. (2005). Moaning, whinging and laughing: The subjective side of complaints. *Discourse Studies 7*, 5–29.

Edwards, D. (2007). Managing subjectivity in talk. In A. Hepburn & S. Wiggins (Eds.), *Discursive research in practice: New approaches to psychology and interaction* (pp. 31–49). Cambridge, UK: Cambridge University Press.

Edwards, D., & Potter, J. (1992). *Discursive psychology.* London: Sage.

Fivush, R. (2010). Speaking Silence: The social construction of voice and silence in cultural and autobiographical narratives. *Memory, 18*, 88–98.

Garfinkel, H. (1967). *Studies in ethnomethodology.* Englewood Cliffs, NJ: Prentice-Hall.

Gergen, K. J. (1994). *Realities and relationships: Soundings in social construction.* Cambridge, MA: Harvard University Press.

Gergen, K. J. (1999). *An invitation to social construction.* Thousand Oaks, CA: Sage.

Gergen, K. J. (2009). *Relational being: Beyond self and community.* Oxford: Oxford University Press.

Grotevant, H. D., & Cooper, C. R. (1985). Patterns of interaction in family relationships and the development of identity exploration in adolescence. *Child Development, 56*, 415–428.

Hanks, W. F. (1996). *Language and communicative practices.* Boulder, CO: Westview Press.

Hammack, P. L. (2008). Narrative and the cultural psychology of identity. *Personality and Social Psychology Review, 12*, 222–247.

Harré, R., & Moghaddam, F. (Eds.) (2003). *The self and others. Positioning individual groups in personal, political and cultural contexts.* Praeger: London.

Harré, R., & van Langenhove, L. (1992). Varieties of positioning. *Journal for the Theory of Social Behavior, 20*, 393–407.

Harré, R., & van Langenhove, L. (1999). *Positioning theory.* Oxford, UK: Blackwell Publishers.

Hollway, W. (1983). Heterosexual sex: Power and desire for the other (pp. 124–140). In S. Cartledge & R. Joanna (Eds.), *Sex and love: New thoughts on old contradictions.* London: Women's Press.

Jefferson, G. (2004). Glossary of transcript symbols with an introduction. In G. Lerner (Ed.), *Conversation analysis: Studies from the first generation* (pp. 13–31). Amsterdam: John Benjamins.

Kitzinger, C. (2006). After post-cognitivism. *Discourse Studies, 8*, 67–83.

Korobov, N. (2004). Inoculating against prejudice: A discursive approach to homophobia and sexism in adolescent male talk. *Psychology of Men & Masculinity, 5*, 178–189.

Korobov, N. (2006). The management of "nonrelational sexuality": Positioning strategies in adolescent male talk about (hetero)sexual attraction. *Men and Masculinities, 8*, 493–517.

Korobov, N. (2009a). Expanding hegemonic masculinity: The use of irony in young men's stories about romantic experiences. *American Journal of Men's Health, 3*, 286–299.

Korobov, N. (2009b). "He's got no game": Young men's stories about failed romantic and sexual experiences. *Journal of Gender Studies, 18*, 99–114.

Korobov, N. (2010). A discursive psychological approach to positioning. *Qualitative Research in Psychology, 7*, 263–277.

Korobov, N. (2011a). Gendering desire in speed-dating interactions. *Discourse Studies*, 13, 461–485.

Korobov, N. (2011b). Mate-preference talk in speed-dating conversations. *Research on Language and Social Interaction*, 44, 186–209.

Korobov, N., & Bamberg, M. (2004a). Positioning a "mature" self in interactive practices: How adolescent males negotiate "physical attraction" in group talk. *British Journal of Developmental Psychology*, 22, 471–492.

Korobov, N., & Bamberg, M. (2004b). Development as micro-genetic positioning: A response to the commentaries. *British Journal of Developmental Psychology*, 22, 521–530.

Korobov, N., & Bamberg, M. (2007). "Strip Poker! They don't show nothing": Positioning identities in adolescent male talk about a television game show (pp. 253–272). In A. De Fina, M. Bamberg, and D. Schiffrin (Eds.), *Selves and identities in narrative and discourse*. Amsterdam: John Benjamins.

Korobov, N., & Thorne, A. (2007). How late adolescent friends share stories about relationships: The importance of mitigating the seriousness of romantic problems. *Journal of Social and Personal Relationships*, 27, 971–992.

Korobov, N., & Thorne, A. (2009). The negotiation of compulsory romance in young women friends' stories about romantic heterosexual experiences. *Feminism and Psychology*, 19, 49–70.

Laclau, E. (1993). Politics and the limits of modernity. In T. Docherty (Ed.), *Postmodernism: A reader* (pp. 329–344). London: Harvester Wheatsheaf.

Mandelbaum, J. (2003). Interactive methods for constructing relationships. In P. Glenn, C. LeBaron, & J. Mandelbaum (Eds.), *Studies in language and social interaction: In honour of Robert Hopper* (pp. 207–220). Mahwah, NJ: Lawrence Erlbaum and Associates.

McAdams, D., Bauer, J., Sakaeda, A., Anyidoho, N., Machado, M., & Magrino-Failla, K. (2006). Continuity and change in the life-story: A longitudinal study of autobiographical memories in emerging adulthood. *Journal of Personality*, 74, 1371–1400.

McLean, K. (2005). Late adolescent identity development: Narrative meaning making and memory telling. *Developmental Psychology*, 41, 683–691.

McLean, K. (2008). Stories of the young and old: Personal continuity and narrative identity. *Developmental Psychology*, 44, 254–264.

Meeus, W. (2011). The study of adolescent identity formation 2000–2010: A review of longitudinal research. *Journal of Research on Adolescence*, 21, 75–94.

Mouffe, C. (1992). Feminism, citizenship and radical democratic politics. In J. Butler & J. W. Scott (Eds.), *Feminists theorize the political* (pp. 369–385). New York: Routledge.

Packer, M. (1987). Social interaction as practical activity: Implications for the study of social and moral development. In W. M. Kurtinez and J. L. Gewirtz (Eds.), *Moral development through social interaction*. New York: John Wiley.

Pasupathi, M., & Hoyt, T. (2009). The development of narrative identity in late adolescence and emerging adulthood: The continued importance of listeners. *Developmental Psychology*, 45, 558–574.

Pomerantz, A., & Mandelbaum, J. (2005). A conversation analytic approach to relationships: Their relevance for interactional conduct. In K. Fitch & R. E. Sanders (Eds.), *Handbook of language and social interaction* (pp. 149–171). Mahwah, NJ: Lawrence Erlbaum and Associates.

Potter, J. (1996). *Representing reality: Discourse, rhetoric, and social construction*. London: Sage.

Potter, J. (2010). Contemporary discursive psychology: Issues, prospects, and Concoran's awkward ontology. *British Journal of Social Psychology*, 49, 657–678.

Potter, J., & Edwards, D. (1999). Social representations and discursive psychology: From cognition to action. *Culture and Psychology*, 5 (4), 447–458.

Potter, J., & Edwards, D. (2003). Rethinking cognition: On Coulter and discourse and mind. *Human Studies*, 26, 165–181.

Riegel, K. F. (1975). Toward a dialectical theory of development. *Human Development*, 18, 50–64.

Sacks, H. (1992). *Lectures on Conversation* (2 vols., G. Jefferson, Ed.). Oxford: Blackwell.

Sacks, H. (1995). *Lectures on conversation: Volumes I and II*. Oxford: Basil Blackwell.

Sacks, H., Schegloff, E. A., & Jefferson, G. (1974). A simplest systematics of the organization of turn-taking for conversation. *Language*, 50, 696–735.

Schegloff, E. A. (1982). Discourse as an interactional achievement: Some uses of 'uh huh' and other things that come between sentences. In D. Tannen (Ed.), *Analyzing discourse: Text and talk* (pp. 71–93). [Georgetown University Roundtable on Languages and Linguistics 1981.] Washington, DC: Georgetown University Press.

Schutz, A. (1970). *On phenomenology and social relations*. Chicago: University of Chicago Press.

Schwartz, S. J. (2001). The evolution of Eriksonian and neo-Eriksonian identity theory and research: A review and integration. *Identity: An International Journal of Theory and Research*, 1, 7–58.

Speer, S. (2005). *Gender Talk. Feminism, discourse and conversation analysis*. London: Routledge.

Speer, S., & Stokoe, E. (2011). *Conversation and gender*. Cambridge, UK: Cambridge University Press.

Stokoe, E. (2004). Gender and discourse, gender and categorization: Current developments in language and gender research. *Qualitative Research in Psychology*, 1, 107–129.

Stokoe, E. (2006). On ethnomethodology, feminism, and the analysis of categorical reference to gender in talk-in-interaction. *Sociological Review*, 54, 467–494.

Stokoe, E. (2010). Gender, conversation analysis, and the anatomy of membership categorization practices. *Social and Personality Psychology Compass*, 4, 428–438.

Stokoe, E., & Smithson, J. (2001). "Making Gender Relevant: Conversation Analysis and Gender Categories in Interaction." *Discourse & Society*, 12, 217–244.

Tajfel, H., & Turner, J. (1986). The social identity theory of intergroup behavior. In S. Worchel & W. G. Austin (Eds.), *Psychology of intergroup relations* (pp. 7–24). Chicago: Nelson.

Vygotsky, L. S. (1978). *Mind and society: The development of higher mental processes*. Cambridge, MA: Harvard University Press.

Wetherell, M. (1998). Positioning and interpretative repertoires: Conversation analysis and post-structuralism in dialogue. *Discourse and Society*, 9, 387–412.

Werner, H. (1958). *Comparative psychology of mental development*. New York: International Universities Press.

Werner, H., & Kaplan, B. (1984). *Symbol formation*. Hillsdale, NJ: Lawrence Erlbaum Associates.

Wertsch, J., & Stone, C. A. (1978). Microgenesis as a tool for developmental analysis. *Quarterly Newsletter of the Laboratory of Comparative Human Cognition*, 1, 8–10.

Widdicombe, S., & Wooffitt, R. (1995). *The language of youth subcultures: Social identity in action*. New York: Harvester Wheatsheaf

Wilkinson, C., & Kitzinger, C. (2003). Constructing identities: A feminist conversation analytic approach to positioning in action. In R. Harré & F. Moghaddam (Eds.), *The self and others. Positioning individuals and groups in personal, political, and cultural contexts* (pp. 157–180). Westpoint, CT: Praeger.

Wilkinson, S., & Kitzinger, C. (2008). Using conversation analysis in feminist and critical research. *Social and Personality Psychology Compass, 2*, 585.

Wittgenstein, L. (1978). *Philosophical investigations*. Oxford: Blackwell.

CHAPTER 15

Integrating "Internal," "Interactional," and "External" Perspectives: Identity Process as the Formulation of Accountable Claims Regarding Selves

Elli P. Schachter

Abstract

This chapter presents a preliminary theoretical framework broadly integrating discursive-interactional and ego-identity perspectives. Identity process is conceptualized as involving discursive claims made about selves, geared toward eliciting affirmation for pragmatic purposes and formulated to be accountable. Claiming processes can take place internally (reflexively in thought); interactionally (in talk); and externally (between others). Based on Mead and Vygotsky, internal identity processes are described as emergent from and modeled after interactional identity processes, yet they operate somewhat autonomously and develop across the lifespan. Characterizing identity processes as claims made to be affirmed can alert researchers to the diverse criteria employed by participants in multiple, often overlapping contexts in the evaluation of self-made and interactionally performed claims, the result of which feed into subsequent iterations of identity formation. The chapter shows how such a perspective is consonant with classical Eriksonian theory. A brief empirical vignette is described and analyzed to demonstrate this approach.

Key Words: accountable identity claims, discursive identity, emergent identity, Eriksonian identity theory, interactional, positioning, psychosocial theory

This chapter suggests a preliminary conceptual framework within which two very different theoretical perspectives presented in this handbook (Waterman; Korobov, this volume) might be seen as more amenable to each other than at first glance. Let me explain. The editors of this handbook kindly invited me to respond to two chapters, at the time still on the drawing board, one on "identities as internal process" and the other on "identities as external process." The latter chapter's topic was later changed by the author to "identities as interactional process" to better reflect the particular position he wished to represent. After receiving and reading these fine chapters, I found myself in a familiar predicament—it was as if I was reading about two completely unrelated topics that just happen to connect via a shared name. Broadly speaking, Waterman characterizes identity as an individual's global, overarching self-understanding, examining it as it is formed through a lifelong developmental process guided at its best by individual internal contemplative reflection. Korobov portrays identities as locally constructed, dynamic, performed positions, constructed, invoked, claimed, and negotiated ad hoc through talk. He examines the discursive techniques used to establish such situated mundane identities within interaction so as to enable the parties involved to do the "social business" at hand. Both authors are careful not to rule out the other perspective's contribution, yet as can be expected given their assigned task, they each mostly focus on explaining and promoting their basic orientation.

My experience reading such disparate accounts echoed previous frustrating experiences reading papers that, broadly speaking, hail from the same two traditions. I often find many of the concepts discussed separately helpful because they address real phenomena of interest to those that study identity. Many arguments resonate as convincing within their own frameworks. However, it is difficult to translate insights from one perspective to the other without a common overarching framework. I decided to take this opportunity to construct one for myself and share it with others who are not by disposition inimical to one or the other of the two perspectives. I hope others find it relevant and engage my ideas critically, thus advancing clarity and fostering dialogue. The chapter is thus neither a typical handbook review of the literature nor an appraisal of previous empirical research; instead, it is an exercise in building conceptual bridges.

Before presenting my framework I ask the readers to bear with me while I make a few needed introductory remarks. First, as noted, this chapter was specifically commissioned as a response to Waterman's and Korobov's chapters. I chose, however, to approach their chapters creatively as sources of inspiration and released myself, them, and the readers from a meticulous examination of the particulars of their respective arguments and positions. Moreover, I allowed myself to use some of the terms they presented in a different manner than they did. I borrowed and adapted concepts without necessarily remaining committed to the way they were presented by the authors or to the philosophical underpinnings they attached to them. Thus, do not take my descriptions of internal and interactional concepts as faithfully representing Waterman's and Korobov's ideas. The bottom line is that I used their presentations as a convenient springboard to develop my own. Second, I have written the chapter hoping that it can be read as a standalone piece by those basically familiar with both views. I often refer to their chapters for the benefit of those who read them, and I highly recommend reading them to those who haven't yet done so. Regardless, in order to make it understandable to all, I sometimes briefly cover points they already have discussed.

Third, regarding terminology; initially, the editors framed the issue to be discussed as *internal* versus *external* perspectives on identity process. Whereas Waterman by-and-large accepts and uses these labels in his chapter—focusing on the former and acknowledging the latter—Korobov rejects these as reflecting a false internal–external split, instead contrasting this pair itself with the term *interactional*. In certain contexts, however, I found that using the word *internal* or *interactional* as a label for these two approaches might be confusing.

As an alternative, I sometimes used *ego-identity* to label the *internal* approach (including, but not limited to, the ego-identity status approach) and *discursive* to label the *interactional* approach, despite the fact that the terms in each pair are not synonymous.

Fourth, readers should be aware that personally, my academic biography is rooted in the perspective covered by Waterman. My familiarity with the discursive approach is relatively recent. In approaching the discursive perspective, I have had to step way out of my "comfort zone." Finding the ideas intriguing, I sought what I could find and "take back" to enrich my own. The result is an initial formulation written from the perspective of an *ego-identity psychologist* approaching new ideas, and not of an expert equally proficient in both intellectual spheres.

The Integrative Approach: A Justification

As noted earlier, anyone reading the two chapters, or other academic papers written in one of the two traditions they hail from, will immediately notice that there is little in common regarding the language each tradition uses, the literatures they reference, the philosophical traditions and assumptions each espouses, the empirical focus of their respective studies, and the methodologies they each employ to generate knowledge. Given this state of affairs, three principled approaches can be adopted:

1. A *disjunctive* approach: This approach would claim the two traditions address different, relatively unrelated phenomena that just happen to share the same name (e.g., Marxist and cognitive scientists' versions of "critical thinking"). The logical solution to such a state of affairs is to brand them each with distinct names so as to minimize confusion and have each continue in their own separate field.

2. An *antithetical* approach: This approach would hold that the two traditions do address the same phenomenon but have staunchly opposed theories regarding how to understand and study it. This would logically lead to the conclusion that it would be best to "fight it out" and perhaps, at the end of the day, proclaim who is right and who is wrong, if not about everything, then about specific issues.

3. An *integrative* approach: This approach conceptualizes the two traditions as covering the same or closely related phenomena, perhaps each emphasizing different parts, but that nevertheless can profitably be combined. Certain concepts, developed separately, are translatable from one system to the other despite perhaps needing to

gh some transformation. Whereas the ...ive approach emphasizes that there is not ... be gained by combining approaches, the ...ive approach views the two perspectives as interrelated or complementary and that integrating them is possibly synergetic.

Each of these three principled approaches has benefits and drawbacks. Although I chose to adopt an integrative approach, both the disjunctive and antithetical approaches are defensible regarding the two identity perspectives discussed in this chapter. Regarding the disjunctive approach, the referent of the word *identity* in each of the two approaches is indeed often different (e.g., consider Waterman's *self-understanding* and Korobov's *positioning*). Regarding the antithetical approach, indeed many assumptions are seemingly incompatible (e.g., *constructionism* vs. *foundationalism*). The benefit of the integrative approach is that it may lead to a more comprehensive theory, and the attempt at integration has a synergizing effect. The drawback is that it might lead to a blurring of real differences and to superficial understandings of concepts extracted from their original frameworks and mixed together in a disorganized fashion. In my opinion, an intelligent blend of the three approaches is optimal, applying each one according to the specific issue at hand. And yet, in this chapter, I chose to examine just how far the integrative approach can go. Attracted by the appeal of a synergizing effect, I adopted a charitable approach and chose where possible to translate concepts between the two rather than to accentuate differences. This undoubtedly was at the expense of scholarly accuracy.

Many before me have pleaded for integrating disparate identity perspectives. The most comprehensive and careful attempt to my knowledge is to be found in Côté and Levine (2002). The main focus of this work is on integrating sociological (external) and psychological (internal) perspectives, although the interactional perspective is discussed as well. Côté (2005) also edited a special issue of *Identity* devoted to this topic. I acknowledge being inspired as well by other attempts to relate to both Eriksonian and either sociocultural or symbolic interactionist perspectives (Holland & Lachicotte, 2007; Penuel & Wertsch, 1995; Thorne, 2004; Weigert, Teitge, & Teitge, 1986) and by attempts to discuss relations between interactional and internal models (Valsiner, 1997; 2007*a*; 2007*b*). Yet I do not hold them accountable for my model.

The Suggested Integrative Model: An Outline

The model combines elements from the ego-identity and discursive approaches and a third element not explicitly highlighted in most identity models (the evaluative criteria for affirming identity claims). I first outline the model as a whole so the reader can grasp the general picture, and I then elaborate on particular elements.

1. Following the discursive approach, I contend that processes of identity involve the making of *claims*, explicit or implied, about a self. A claim can be about some "essence" of a self or about the relevance of some "essence" of a self to a perceived situation. Identity claims cannot thus be understood as mere uncomplicated reports of an existing inner representation of an identity. Identity is not who a person is but *a claim* about who a person is. Furthermore, identity claims are made, within contexts, with the expectation that the claims be affirmed. This expectation is due to claims being perceived as needing such affirmation because the identity claimed has pragmatic implications within the context. In other words, having the identity claim validated (i.e., what discursive theorists refer to as "bringing off" an identity) is perceived of as setting the necessary stage for (possible) action involving the self.

2. Any identity claim *about* a self presupposes a "claimant," addressing an "evaluating and affirming addressee" in a certain form. From the claimant's perspective the addressee's role is to affirm ("take on") the claim. The addressee is attributed, at least in principle, with having some degree of power/agency to affirm the claim yet also perhaps to ignore, resist, counter-offer, or otherwise respond. If there were no option not to affirm the claim, there would be no need to make one. The *form* of the claim is how it is formulated, performed, symbolically encoded, formatted, and the like. I will here employ Valsiner's (2007*b*) concept of semiotic mediation and say that the claim is formulated using signs that mediate between "claimant" and "addressee." The discursive approach described by Korobov posits that claims are formed in certain ways assumed to have it within them the ability to bring about the addressee's affirmation of the identity claim or its relevance to the situation. I later take a slightly different approach, however, and discuss the criteria used by the addressee in evaluating the claim and in determining the response (see point 9

below). In either case, identity claims are formulated with the implicit knowledge that the claimant can be held accountable for the identity claim by the addressee.

3. Reading these specific elements taken from the discursive approach into a general identity theory, I posit that claims about selves can be described as occurring in three (not mutually exclusive) "sites": (a) within a person about his or her self (in the form of self-reflective thinking); (b) between a person and others (in the form of interactional talking about at least one of the interlocutors' selves); and (c) between others, external to the self (in the form of cultural, institutional, or other structuration of identity categories, their meanings, and the ways they should be performed and recognized). Processes of claiming and response can take different forms in these different sites due to the nature of such sites; nevertheless, the essential element of a claim—that of it being made in order to be affirmed as a basis for action and that the claimant can potentially be held accountable for the identity claim—holds for all three sites.

4. Specifically applying this framework to the internal perspective on identity, I now reinterpret the ego-identity perspective as essentially saying that identity processes involve a person *making and evaluating* claims about his or her own self, which are then either reflexively affirmed or not, as the basis for orienting the person toward potential future action. Within the ego identity status framework's terminology, these processes have been formulated through the use of, among others, the concepts of "exploration" and "commitment." Later, I discuss the sociogenetic theories of Mead and Vygotsky and attempt to show how these internal thought processes can be described as an appropriation of the tool provided by interactional talk, transformed from its original "outward" format.

5. External identity interactions create the constraints and affordances for internal and interactional identity processes. External interactions are "external," of course, only from the perspective of a subject whose identity is being "discussed" without being included as a party in the discussion. Any eventual effect on the person will necessarily involve some sort of interaction bringing the external into the interaction. However, this is done in ways that are not always perceived by those implicated as necessarily involving their identity.

6. Development: each interaction, whether internal, interactional, or external, tentatively "ends" with an identity that, once "established," can be "used" both as the basis for subsequent claims or as a criteria for evaluating subsequent claims (Côté, 1996b). When not in use, they can be deposited internally (in memory) or externally in cultural artifacts (such as laws, books, concepts, computer servers, routines, tattoos, diplomas, passports, etc.). These once-established identities might (or might not) be "picked up" and "invoked" later on by the person or by others to become part of future identity interactions. Repeated and recursive processes of this sort can result in solidification (or change) of personal or social identities, solidification (or change) of the regulatory standards by which identity claims are evaluated, and solidification (or change) of the skills and resources involved in "bringing off" identities. Different psychological identity theories present competing arguments as to what types of solidification or change qualify as "developmental."

7. I further adopt the discursivists' position that identity claims—be they internal, interactional, or external—are made in contexts and are formulated so as to be pragmatically relevant within a context. However, the definition of the locality of a context depends on the interpretations of participants as to what is relevant to the here-and-now. Thus, the discursive-interactional perspective that emphasizes localized short-term identity constructions is not incompatible with the internal—ego-identity perspective that conceives of identity process as triggered by the individual's perception that the long-term future is relevant to the present context. Moreover, multiple overlapping contexts can be seen as contemporaneously relevant by those making identity claims, each involving a different, present or future, internal or external interlocutor that can affirm or reject the identity claim. Identity claims are thus simultaneously negotiated internally and interactionally, with regards to short- and long-term goals.

8. Erikson's developmental theory posited that, for a host of psychological and social reasons, formulating a somewhat overarching identity claim in relation to domains deemed socially important—and that can be both self-affirmed and validated within the individual's society as a basis for adult functioning—becomes especially pressing during adolescence.

Therefore, identity processes regarding these domains were theorized by him to become more salient to the individual and to others in his or her surroundings. Interpreted through the discursive lens, we can say that the socially constructed image of the future, through countless social interactions before and during adolescence, is conveyed as relevant to the here-and-now interactive context. Therefore, the pragmatic need to claim and validate an identity is experienced in the present. Ego-identity status theory (Marcia, Waterman, Matteson, Archer, & Orlofsky, 1993) is the attempt to describe whether and how any one individual successfully goes about solidifying a (relatively global) identity (accepted by self and others) as a basis for regulating pragmatic decisions and interactions during adult life. Despite this focus, this perspective does not hold that other identity-forming processes do not take place, before, after, or in other domains, or that every identity-relevant process within a domain necessarily becomes part of the more global identity processing or is regulated by it.

9. As noted, the basic proposition that identity process is a claim made about the self to an addressee implies that the addressee has a range of options in responding—minimally including the options "affirm" or "reject." We need to understand why one response is given rather than another. The discursive approach, as I understand it, looks for the answer to this by examining how the identity position is "claimed" so as to achieve affirmation. I instead propose asking why an identity claim is affirmed, rejected, or otherwise responded to, not accepting that the answer to this question can be found solely in *how* the claim was formulated and performed (in this, my "why" question is similar, but different than Waterman's [this volume]). Rather, I surmise that this is done according to some kind of implicit or explicit standard or standards held by the addressee (see Thorne, 2004). Therefore, if an identity claim is self-addressed (i.e., the internal position), we need to ask the same question. What "responses" does an individual give to his or her own identity positionings and why?

10. Many identity theories posit an answer as to what standard is or should be used in judging an identity claim. Identity theories tend to present objective standards as to what makes an identity claim accountable to self and other or suggest evaluative and normative standards that, if used, supposedly bring about a better, more developed and mature identity. The theories present guidelines as to what "evidence" should be presented so as to make an identity claim in an accountable manner. Erikson (1968) suggested "sameness and continuity." Waterman's (2011) eudaemonic theory posits and privileges an evaluation standard based on whether the claimed identity is "real" or "authentic." Other examples are privileging "unity and purpose" (McAdams, 1988), "rational processing" (Berzonsky, 2011), "sociocentricity" (Côté & Levine, 2002), "relatedness" (Josselson, 1996), or whether the identity is socially and personally empowering (cf., Kincheloe, 2008). It follows that theorists and researchers need to recognize and examine the diversity of standards used in "judging" identity claims and provide justification in the case they themselves privilege particular standards.

The Suggested Integrative Model: An Elaboration

Here, I elaborate on four of the more novel and complex points from the general model because space does not allow me to develop them all: (a) identity processes can be conceptualized as claims made about a self, (b) *internal* identity development can be conceptualized as involving self-reflective claims, (c) the contexts in which identity claims take place vary in scope and can also be multiple and overlapping, and (d) the study of such identity claims needs to account for the criteria that are employed in determining whether they should be affirmed or rejected.

Identity Processes: Claims Made About Selves

Four aspects highlighted in the discursive position can be easily read into the ego-identity position. The first and central aspect is that identity processes involve the making of implicit or explicit, direct or indirect, claims about a self or about aspects of a self. A direct explicit claim a*bout my own self* might be if I state "I am an identity theorist." Such a claim can be made implicitly as well, for example by invoking my identity theorist identity, as in: "In my recent paper published in *Theory & Psychology* (Schachter, 2011), I argued that...," or even perhaps indirectly by my current act of writing a theoretical chapter on identity for this handbook. I will use the term *claim* for all these types despite it having a more direct explicit connotation than the discursivists' terms *invoking, occasioning*, or *positioning* because the main principled issue I want to take up in this discussion is that a claim is being made about a self—and to this matter it makes no difference whether this is done explicitly or not.

Characterizing identity as a *claim about* a self (rather than saying that identity *is* the self) is explicitly highlighted in the interactional-discursive approach. Applying this internally would mean an individual making a claim about her "self" addressed to her own "self." For example, I might address the following claim to my own self: "Elli, face it, you're an identity theorist." This discursive aspect of identity is actually recognized by many who are classically identified as taking the internal position. Erikson (1968, p. 19) wrote that he found a "sense of identity" aptly described by William James in a letter he wrote to his wife:

> A man's character is discernible in the mental or moral attitude in which, when it came upon him, he felt himself most deeply and intensely active and alive. At such moments there is a voice inside which speaks and says: "*This* is the real me!"

Characterizing identity as a claim need not necessarily involve describing a speaking "voice" within the head. Internal theorists use other terms as well to discuss self-reflexive characterizations. Waterman portrays identity as the "individual's self-understanding" or discusses how the *I defines* the *Me*. Understanding or defining the self implies an actor actively characterizing the self. These can be read as self-reflexive actions. I later give more examples.

The second aspect of the discursive position I wish to apply is its contention that identity claims are made with the intention that they be affirmed; this is what discursivists call to "bring off" an identity or have an identity "taken up." A claim is naturally made so as to become accepted as "true" or "relevant" to the situation, however defined, perhaps precisely because it is perceived to be somehow contested as untrue, irrelevant, or unimportant. By its very nature, a claim can be rejected, minimalized, or ignored. Weigert et al. (1986, p. 41) write: "Validation occurs when another social actor recognizes and reacts to that identity. Thus, one successfully claims an identity only if the intended behavior becomes an 'object' toward which others orient their behavior." This conceptualization of identity as a claim bent on eliciting (in this case behavioral) affirmation through recognition and orientation is thus explicitly highlighted in the interactional approach; however, I would again argue that it can easily be read into the internal approach. Back to Erikson, we can read the following on the self-reflective judging of the self (p. 22–23, emphases added):

> [I]n psychological terms, identity formation employs *a process of simultaneous reflection and observation*, a process taking place on all levels of mental functioning, *by which the individual judges himself* in the light of what he perceives to be the way in which others judge him in comparison to themselves and to a typology significant to them; while he judges their way of judging him in the light of how he perceives himself in comparison to them and to types that have become relevant to him.

Erikson here, and elsewhere, stresses the importance of the adolescent's emerging identity being (interactionally) recognized and affirmed by the community. This affirmation is crucial to the emergence of the individual's self-confidence expressed in Erikson's characterization of identity as a *subjective sense of an invigorating sameness and continuity*. The point, however, is that Erikson discusses self-judgment as well, meaning self-reflexive validation of the identity. Self-reflexivity is embedded in his use of the term *subjective sense* as well. In other words, identity is discussed by Erikson as a self-directed perception and evaluation of the veracity of a claim made about the self. Thus, if an ego-identity psychologist would want to examine my identity theorist identity, she would not ask whether I am truly an identity theorist but instead examine whether my identity theorist identity has been self-examined and self-affirmed. Thus, the internal position discusses identity as a self-reflexive position about the "Me," including a claim and a response both made by the "I."

A third aspect of the discursive argument is that identity claims are made and affirmation sought so as to set the foundation for doing impending "work." The classical symbolic interactionist perspective holds that individuals must coordinate a common definition of the situation in order to collaborate (McCall, 2003). This understanding includes the participants' respective roles (i.e., identities) within the situation as well. A claim about the self is conceptualized not as establishing an identity for its own sake but as, via agreement, establishing common norms, goals, rules, status, and the like that facilitate smoother organization of forthcoming interaction. It is the practical goal of ordering, syncing, and coordinating social lives that is seen as guiding the formulation of identity claims rather than the identity claims reflecting pre-existing inner identities. As Korobov writes (p. 213) on Sack's ethnomethodological approach: "Sacks approached identities as *practical categorical ascriptions* that people use as transactional tools for conducting social business with others." Thus, my claiming an identity theorist identity, if affirmed, can set the stage for colleagues to engage my claims seriously, or for procuring other invitations to present theoretical ideas, or will allow me to add a line to my CV and get myself promoted. If I fail to bring off this identity, I (or it) might be ignored.

This pragmatic aspect of the discursive approach can be read into the internal perspective on identity as well. The ego-identity status perspective also describes the trigger for identity development as due to its forward-looking pragmatic value—in the broad sense of the word *pragmatic*. To give one example, identity exploration has been defined as "problem-solving behavior aimed at eliciting information about oneself or one's environment in order to make a decision about an important life choice" (Grotevant, 1987, p. 204). The ability of the individual to make practical decisions (meaning the making of commitments) is viewed as dependent on his or her setting the foundation by "knowing" who he or she "is." Supposedly, if an individual needs to make a decision about an impending commitment, she needs to establish *for herself* her identity ("Who am I?") in relation to that identity domain. The internal self-categorization and affirmation of the self as of a certain type is the basis that enables the "I" to act. For example, the ability to respond to an invitation to write a theoretical chapter for a handbook on identity requires some sort of consolidated inner self-affirmation as "being" "someone who has something interesting to say about theories of internal and interactional processes of identity." If this self-affirmation is lacking, commitment becomes problematic. Commitment is perhaps also contingent on *wanting* to do so, mediated by a self-understanding of "who I am and what do I want to achieve." In other words, self-examination of how important and significant my *identity theorist* identity is in relation to other possible identities also serves as a pragmatic basis for my decisions regarding action. Thus, the ego-identity perspective also recognizes that claims made by the self, about the self, and affirmed by the self (or not) are pragmatically oriented toward providing a foundation of self-understanding that then provides meaningful orientation toward an "anticipated future" (Erikson, 1968, p. 30). These active processes are not viewed as merely a representation of something internal or of the past but as a "response" to an interaction with the world.

The fourth aspect of the discursive argument is that identity claims entail accountability. Interaction geared toward affirmation means that a person might need to be able to "back" his claims because they are to be evaluated by the addressee and thus might be challenged. Understanding the way the claim is formed entails recognizing that the claim is made to be accountable. Applying this to the internal perspective means we need to understand how self-addressed identity claims are formed in relation to how the individual evaluates her own identity claims as valid, perhaps also, but not necessarily, by bringing "evidence" from her biographical past (see Habermas, Pasupathi, this volume). I address this issue in detail later.

Sites of Discursive Claims: Internal, Interactional, and External

I previously suggested that discursive identity claims can "take place" in what are often referred to as three distinct "sites": internal, interactional, and external. Separating these sites is somewhat misleading because they are never completely distinct—however, for the purpose of clarifying certain points, I will start out by using this commonly used distinction. Broadly speaking, internal identity discourse would be when the self ("I") acts as both the agent making the claim about the self ("Me") and as the addressee of the claim. Interactional identity discourse is when either a person makes or invokes claims about his or her self ("Me") addressed to another or when claims about his or her self are being formulated by the interlocutor. External identity discourse refers to interactions to which the individual is not party but which either discuss his or her self directly or create identity categories (e.g., gender, race) or other identity-relevant regulators that are later "used" in interactions and in internal thought to position the self (see Figure 15.1).

The interactive site is the easiest to describe as discursive (Korobov, this volume). *Talk* is the prototypical manner in which this is realized, although nonlinguistic interactional discourse falls under this category as well. And so, for example, when the editors of this handbook wrote this author and requested that he write a theoretical chapter for the handbook, they attempted to invoke his *capable identity theorist* identity. The claim about the author's self was made by the editors in an attempt

The interactional identity claim (2 possibilities)

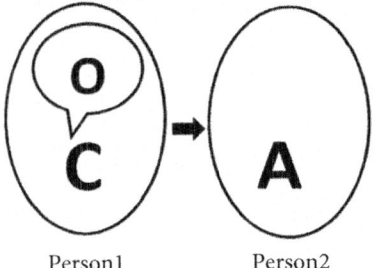
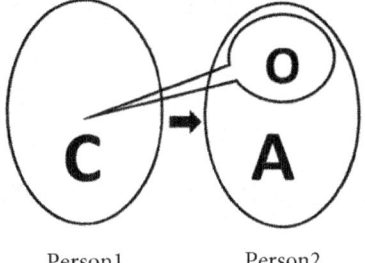

Person1 (claimant) makes identity claim to Person2 (addressee) about own self (object).

Person1 (claimant) makes identity claim to Person2 (addressee) about addressee's self (object).

The internal identity claim

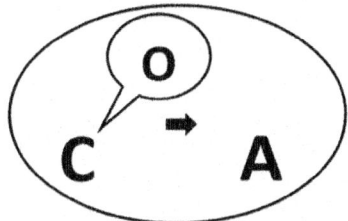

Person (claimant) makes identity claim addressed to own self (addressee) about own self (object).

The external identity claim (2 possibilities)

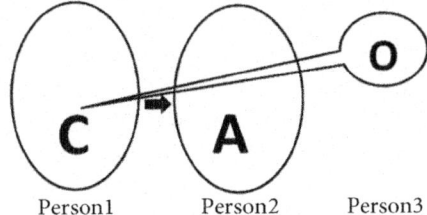
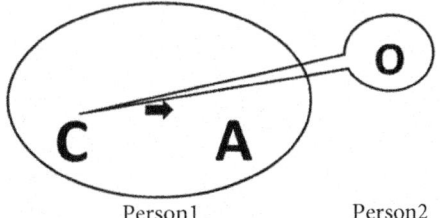

Person1 (claimant) makes identity claim to Person2 (addressee) about the self of Person3 (object).

Person1 (claimant) makes identity claim addressed to own self (addressee) about the self of Person2 (object).

Fig. 15.1 Illustration of interactional, internal, and external sites of identity claims.

to have him "take on" that identity as the basis for action (writing the chapter).

The external discursive site refers to sites wherein issues relating to identities are discussed in interaction among others, without the "subject" being part of the specific interaction. For example, a vote in parliament can establish categories that classify eligibility for citizenship or define and impact gender and racial identities. Or, certain informal norms might be put in place through countless previous external interactions that set standards for "how a handbook chapter written by an expert *should* be written." Or, cultural norms might be set in place extolling "self-consistency" as a character trait of mature adults. Although the person whose identity may be affected is not the one making the claims, nor the addressee who can currently affirm or reject these claims, issues regarding his or her identity are set in place that might become part of future interactions involving the person. Using the examples just given, when later filling out a bureaucratic government form, a person is positioned to identify herself through the categories formerly set in place by the parliamentary law. When writing a handbook chapter, an author might need to consider how to write it according to "custom" so as to "come across" as an "expert." When internally deliberating whether to take part in activities atypical to previous behaviors, an individual might shun these new "inconsistent" behaviors as demonstrating an "immature" identity. The point of all these examples being that external discourse sets in place categories and evaluation standards that can later become part of internal or interactional discourse (cf., Giddens's [1991] "cycle of structuration").

The internal discursive site refers to a person contemplating and considering claims about some object\topic made by himself or herself geared toward "reaching" a tentatively internally "agreed upon" conclusion that can be the basis for future action. Applying this way of conceptualizing inner thought to identity means a person making claims about the self with the claims being evaluated and affirmed by the same person. Thus, rather than having a model including only "I" and "Me," we should rather describe an "I" that carries out two separate functions: that of "claiming" and that of "evaluating." The discursive approach comes in handy in describing the relation between these two functions. The "claiming I" making claims about the self ("Me") addressed to the "evaluating I." In other words, the discursive approach is not used to conceptualize an "I" *addressing* the "Me"—as the "Me" just happens to be the topic of the discussion, not a participant. Note also that, in describing two functions of the "I," I am not describing supposed inner dialogue between two characters or voices (as in Hermans's theory of the dialogical self, based on Bakhtin's concept of polyphony; Hermans, 2001; Bamberg & Zielke, 2007). The two "I's" I refer to are two functions—a claiming function and an evaluating function. *Internal* identity discourse is appropriated from *interactional* identity discourse as a tool.

Conceptualizing thought as discursive, not just regarding identity, is controversial. A full discussion of this issue is beyond this chapter's scope. I will limit my analysis to aspects of this position that I believe are central to the argument pertaining to identity and refer the reader to recent treatments of the broader topic (Bamberg & Zielke, 2007; Fernyhough, 1996; Larrain & Haye, 2012; Susswein, Bibok, & Carpendale, 2007; Valsiner, 2007b). Historically, quite a few theorists have attempted to describe "internal thought processes" as emerging from social interaction (Valsiner & Van der Veer, 1996), and I briefly refer to the conceptual formulations of Mead and Vygotsky. Mead states (1934, p. 47, emphasis added):

> [O]nly in terms of gestures which are significant symbols can *thinking—which is simply an internalized or implicit conversation of the individual with himself by means of gestures*—take place. The internalization in our experience of the external conversations of gestures which we carry on with other individuals in the social process is the essence of thinking…

Thought is here described as the conversation of the individual with himself using gestures and significant symbols first used in social interaction. Serpe and Stryker (2011) describe Mead's perspective as follows (p.227): "Treating themselves as objects, humans can have conversations with and about themselves and their action plans." Mead depicts thought of this kind as a tool emerging from social interaction's need for communication through shared symbolic meanings. The individual needs to apprehend how he or she is seen by the other and "keep this in mind" when planning social (inter) action in order to coordinate with others. Following Mead, we might surmise that internal discursive conversations regarding the "Me" are emergent from social interactions in which the person learns to see the self from the other's viewpoint and needs to do so in order to coordinate social action with the other. This perspective would then describe internal thought as working alongside and in the service of interactional talk. While taking part in interaction and invoking identities in talk, we might concurrently have inner thought processes evaluating the identities we are invoking (Linell, 2009), evaluating how these are perceived by the other (coming across), and perhaps deciding how to position our next move as a result and what not to say (cf., Billig, 1999). Inner thought processes on identity emerge first to work alongside interactional identity work and in its service, yet they are still separate conversations. Even if "internal" identity thought processes emerge from interaction and are in the service of interaction, once conceptualized as separate processes, we might grant internal processes some sort of autonomy.

This idea might be better understood if we use an example taken from the type of conversations described by Korobov. In natural talk, we have interlocutors talking in face-to-face interactions. This sort of interactional context can be simulated in the lab by creating a contrived speed dating setup. We could then imagine setting up a chat platform used for such an experiment wherein the interaction is not face-to-face yet concurrent. If we spread out such turn-taking interaction even further in time and place yet still leaving the interactional dimension in, we could describe an interaction taking place by email. Going even further, we might now imagine an exchange of actual airmail letters sent between individuals living on different continents, as was customary just decades ago. Is it possible to attempt to analyze such an interactional exchange of letters without taking into account that there are thought processes in which the other, and his or her response, is imagined? While writing, the individual anticipates possible responses of the recipient to certain things written and perhaps crosses them out and considers alternatives so as to "come across" as intended. This entails the writer imagining how he or she comes across from the other's perspective—in other words, imagining how his or her identity is seen by the other. Spreading out the turn-taking makes it easier to see that interaction with the other is accompanied by interaction "within" the self that emerges from the interaction in its service. The letter writing can be conceptualized as interactive although the individual is "alone" since the identity work going on in writing and in thinking about the writing is oriented to the interaction. However, at the same time, it goes on without the presence of the other. Condensing the intercontinental time and space back to face-to-face interaction need not change this description of a simultaneous dual track of internal thought and interactional talk.

Following this, we can now describe internal identity processes as the manner in which identity issues are "worked out" internally in accompaniment of an individual's ongoing interaction with the world. Thus, in the process of writing this chapter, I can anticipate the imagined responses of particular readers or a "generalized other" reader to the positions I am formulating. In between sessions of actual writing on my laptop, while swimming laps in the pool, I have had countless "discussions" in my head with an imagined Neill Korobov, Alan Waterman, Michael Bamberg, Jim Côté, Avril Thorne, and Jaan Valsiner, to mention just a few names. I imagined how they would react to certain points made and attempted to formulate my "position" to be written in the chapter in ways that address their imagined concerns or those of others who might bring up similar ideas. However, I am not having these discussions, of course, with the "real" Michael Bamberg but with some sort of an *internalized* representation based on actual previous meetings, selective (mis)reading of his articles, and (mis)attributions of ideas I "picked up" elsewhere of his position—with the point being that we can hold to an interactional position regarding identity while at the same time acknowledging an internal position on identity. In my reading of Mead, these even necessarily go together.

Vygotsky (1986) also addresses inner thought as emergent from social interaction but in a slightly different manner. He addresses how language—first used as a tool for problem-solving while collaborating interactively—is appropriated and used in inner self-directed speech (John-Steiner, 2007; Larrain & Haye, 2012; Linell, 2009). Vygotsky stressed the self-regulating and emancipating aspects of inner thought (Larrain & Haye, 2012; Valsiner, 2007a). Language is an appropriated tool that can be used to extricate the individual from the concreteness of the situation through symbolic thought, and, when directed inward, as a way to regulate activity in the absence of the other, thus contributing to autonomous problem solving. Following this Vygotskian logic, we might further venture that internal thinking regarding identity is a way an individual extracts herself from a concrete situation of interacting with a specific person in a particular context and instead does interactive identity work autonomously. Thus, I can have discussions with the "Michael Bamberg in my head" without the actual Michael Bamberg being present (because he is not always immediately available for interaction), whereas the imagined Michael is "in" my head. I can go about clarifying my "position" regarding Michael's position to myself in private, without needing the actual public interaction. I could then later use this position in interactions with other people besides Michael. Of course, substituting the "imagined" Michael for the actual Michael has the drawback of perhaps misreading the "real" Michael's position and of missing out on his vast knowledge, his years of experience, and his sense of humor. However, I gain a measure of autonomy. Rather than settling identity issues in actual interaction, I can have identity issues worked out in imagined, private interaction.

Going yet one step further, such imagined interactions "taking place" in thought can be a model for later identity deliberations without an external or even an imagined particular interlocutor. The Vygotskian model describes how modes of interaction become appropriated or mastered. Thus, the "I," who once experienced how identity is formed through discursive interaction with others, can come to appropriate the discursive tool itself and use it, at times, internally. Just as an individual might solve a math problem on her own after first learning to do so in interaction, an individual might come to "solve" identity "problems" internally after first doing so, and learning how this should be done, in interactions.

Swimming back and forth in the pool, I am considering and testing out different positions I might take regarding identity in this chapter. Knowing that these positions, once published, might become part of my academic "identity," my pondering them and the way of expressing them becomes an identity deliberation. The "claiming I" makes a tentative claim about the "Me" position to be later "performed" in the chapter, which is addressed to an executive "evaluating I." This position might be accepted, rejected, refined, or otherwise processed according to certain appropriated standards (soon to be discussed) and returned inward for further deliberation. The external addressee might be forgotten (for the moment). The thinker is able to solve identity problems by appropriating and using the discursive, somewhat rhetorical form of identity deliberation.

The bottom line of this section is that internal identity processes can be conceptualized as emergent from interaction and in the service of interaction; they may function, however, with some manner of autonomy as well, enabling individuals to extricate themselves from immediate local interaction and perhaps "solve" some aspects of identity issues not in the context of a specific "between-person" interaction. It is this type of process that is targeted (and valued) by researchers of internal identity development. An exclusive focus on actual interaction in talk, although obviously important, misses out on internal processes going on—perhaps originating in interaction, leading toward interaction, and needed for interaction—yet also operating relatively autonomously in sites that aren't readily observable.

Contexts of Identity Interactions: "Big," "Small," and Overlapping

One of the distinctions between the internal and interactional approach that gives the impression that they deal with completely different issues can be called the *big versus small* distinction. The ego-identity status perspective tends to focus researchers' attention to "big" issues—individuals' lifespan (and even cross-domain) perspectives of self. Conversely, the discursive perspective focuses researchers' attention on "small" issues—mundane local identities dynamically created within and for specific situations. For example, the ego-identity literature addresses identity decisions of major import, such as an individual's occupational or religious identity (e.g., artist, agnostic), supposedly spanning from adolescence until retirement or death and guiding an extremely broad range of life situations. In contradistinction, interactional-discursive approaches address the individual dealing with establishing identities within specific localized and temporary situations—for example, "coming across" as "a cool gal to be with" when trying to secure a date or as "someone you wouldn't want to start a fight with" when walking at night in an unfamiliar neighborhood. This macro-micro focus has also been addressed through the topic of studying identity narratives. The discursive approach calls for the study of "small stories" supposedly told to establish identity in naturally occurring mundane interaction (Bamberg, 2011; Schachter, 2011), whereas, within the ego-identity approach, there has been a tendency to study "big stories" that establish a global identity and that are collected within research settings wherein individuals are requested to tell their life stories (Freeman, 2011; McAdams, 2013). This distinction, however, conflates a few issues: "natural" versus "invited" talk, internal versus interactional, mundane versus of import, narrative as a practice versus narrative as a mental representation, and local\short-term versus global\lifespan. These different distinctions raise different issues in the context of identity process. I specifically wish to first address the latter— local\short-term versus global\lifespan identity.

Supposedly, if we adopt an interactional approach, then we would not be dealing with "big" identity stories because identity stories are seemingly constructed locally to facilitate action within a situation. Conversely, lifespan identity issues are sometimes presented as context-free and interaction-free since they supposedly span multiple contexts and interactions. This dichotomy is false. All identity claims are made in the present and are local and context-dependent; however, the span of the "local" situation is determined by how it is perceived and defined temporally, geographically, and socially. How broad a segment of time and place is considered relevant to the situation, how large a social context is seen as bearing on the situation, and how many such contexts are contemporaneously seen as relevant depend on the perceptions and interpretations of interactionists and on cultural and institutional structuration. For example, the context of choosing a major in high school can be perceived as a local temporary decision by an adolescent and as a life-encompassing decision by her parent (or vice versa). This serves to blur the sharp distinction made between micro\macro identity processes and enables us to use some of the same terminology for both.

My reading of the discursive interactional approach presented by Korobov is that, within interaction, the individual positions herself, performing and taking on an identity—such as, using his example (p. 218), *"not a typical clingy girl"*—in order to create affiliation with a desired partner for a date (who is supposedly not interested in going out with a *"typical clingy girl"*). However, what does a "date" mean for the participants? How far ahead is the relationship envisioned (e.g., "will you marry me")? What do gender roles mean to the participants, and what future situations are imagined as possible places of interaction toward which getting this gender role issue "settled" ahead of time will help prevent problems? In other words, if the discursive approach conceptualizes identity process as establishing an identity as the basis for anticipated future action, it makes no principled difference whether such action is envisaged as five minutes from now or thirty years from now. Certain "situations" are envisaged as having small and near implications, whereas others loom larger. The broader the perceived implications, the broader the current situation will be defined. The perceived implications of a situation are socioculturally and semiotically mediated. For one person, choosing a ham and cheese sandwich rather than a salad for lunch is a decision with relatively short-term implications such as weight control, whereas for another, this might have long-term implications based on religious cultural beliefs that link dietary transgressions with the possible endangering of an everlasting afterlife.

Moreover, a local situation in which identities are being claimed can be part of many overlapping contexts, each involving different time spans and addressees. What, for example, is the interactional context of my here-and-now attempt to "bring off" the "identity theorist" identity? Am I attempting to "bring off" the "identity theorist" identity short-term, for this chapter only, for you the reader; long-term, as the basis for my adult academic career, addressed to an academic promotion committee; perhaps even longer-term, addressed to my own self, written as a contribution to a future imagined existential satisfaction in "having lived a meaningful life"; or all three? Although these three contexts (i.e., handbook chapter, career, meaningful life) differ with regards to their duration, they do not differ in their all being interactional and semiotically mediated. More importantly, it is the addressees of the identity claims that differ and the criteria that might be used by each one in evaluating it. There are three contexts operating simultaneously, with at least three targets to which I need to be accountable in formulating my claim. Thus, the discursivist approach is correct in pointing out that researchers studying lifespan identity stories need to account for the close contexts in which they are told. However, I believe the ego identity approach is correct in asserting that researchers studying local identity interactions need on their part to account for the self-perceived (and real) long-term implications of making identity claims in local contexts.

"Lifespan" identity formation is interactional to the extent that sociocultural structuration constructs the "distant" future in a manner perceived as relevant to the here-and-now of the adolescent. In such a case, constructing a "big" identity is what might be called for in, and by, the "local" interactive context. Sociological processes contribute to structuring the perceived relation between the present and the future. If modern culture or sociological contexts set up careers spanning adulthood based on adolescent choice, then the identities created or oriented toward would be of the lifelong type (Côté, 1996a; Côté & Levine, 2002). The ego-identity lifespan model is implicitly based on the premises that social contexts structure adolescent reality (through adult generativity) in ways that make the possible adult future meaningfully present in countless mundane interactions, thereby necessitating the development of skills such as identity exploration and commitment. If, however, instead the cultural zeitgeist is postmodern, and the far future is not structured as relevant to the present, then perhaps the identities formed are created ad hoc, in relation to more immediate futures (Gergen, 1991; Schachter, 2005), thereby necessitating the development of different identity skills such as identity maintenance and management (Côté, 1996a). Additionally, if in certain premodern societies lifespan identities were externally conferred with no choice given to the individual, then identity claims need not be made by the individual, and it makes sense that a "sense of personal identity" was not seen as a personal problematic issue (Baumeister, 1987) or as a major individual concern (Taylor, 1989). The importance of this discussion is in enabling a more flexible understanding of what a pragmatic orientation with regards to identity interaction really is. Rather than view the pragmatic value of having an "agreed upon" identity only with regards to the immediate and pressing context, we can conceive of a person preparing an identity for future expected social interactions by way of "exploring" his or her identity, implicitly acknowledging that an identity explored and self-validated is useful for orienting oneself across situations and across time. Thus, an adolescent examining his or her beliefs may very well be doing something very practical in Kurt Lewin's sense that *nothing is more practical than a good theory.*

To sum up to this point, the ego identity theorist's position can be read as discursive if (a) we broaden discursivity to include semiotically mediated thought processes of identity exploration, wherein the "claiming I" invokes certain claims about the "Me" in order to have them accepted (brought off) by the "evaluating I" as the basis for future agentic action; and (b) we broaden the concept of pragmatic interaction within context to include such context as defined and negotiated within culture, perhaps encompassing lifespan slices of time rather than only short-term ones and accounting for the possibility that the "local" context includes multiple contexts.

Accountability and the Criteria for Evaluating Identity

The benefit of conceptualizing identity development as involving the processing of identity claims is that it focuses our attention on identity as a claiming process bent on eliciting affirmation rather than as an uncomplicated representation of an inner identity. Viewed this way, we need to focus on the question of what gets identity affirmed. Furthermore, if the interactive model is seen as the foundation for inner identity deliberation, we could formulate the following question: How do big or small self-directed identity claims (i.e., exploration) come to be accepted as the basis for action (i.e., commitment)?

A closer look at the discursive model reveals that it attempts to focus attention on how affirmation is or is not achieved in and through interaction. This focus is clear if identity work is pragmatic; if you want to get something done, you need to know how to do it. Given that the discursive approach holds that this is done through discourse, then the obvious place to study this *how* is in studying the discursive techniques through which identity positioning is achieved. The ability to bring off an identity is supposedly to be found "contained" in the message and how it is performed in context. Gee (2007) gives the hypothetical example of his wanting (for some reason) to be recognized as a biker by another biker in a biker's bar. To do so, he must not only talk like one but also, walk, dress, drink, act, and move like a biker—if he does, he will increase the chance of being recognized as one. This assumes the addressee applies the "duck test"—if it walks like a duck and quacks like a duck—assume it's a duck. However, this approach analyzes rather simple forms of recognition. Let us instead imagine a setup in which the biker in the bar has heard that the police are planning to send an undercover agent to infiltrate the biker scene for whatever purpose. This would mean that recognizing Gee as a real biker rather than as an undercover cop might have more serious implications than if he only wanted a light for his cigarette, and the process of having the claimed identity affirmed might become more complicated and thorough. This means we also need to account for the prior knowledge, intentions, and goals of the addressee. The point is that in attempting to analyze an identity claim, examining the performance and its form are not enough. In other words, rather than exclusively focusing on *how* an identity is achieved through discourse, we should also focus on asking *why* the identity is claimed and why it is affirmed. This involves—despite methodological and other problems involved—giving more focus to the intentionality of the actors communicating and particularly to the standards they employ for evaluating positions (Thorne, 2004).

In Korobov's examples of speed-dating interactions, he demonstrates two different ways that daters resisted the appearance of having stereotypical gender attraction preferences as a means to bring about positive affiliation. The analysis, however, does not address *why* stereotypical preferences are being resisted, other than to assume that both parties are interested (or display interest) in nonstereotypical gender roles. What if one of the parties wasn't? Discursivists might attempt to show how negotiations break down and positive affiliation is not achieved, or perhaps *how* the interlocutors work to get the identity of one or both of the parties to change or get reinterpreted. But working toward affiliation or breakdown presupposes that individuals have goals regarding affiliation. The identities brought up in talk are evaluated implicitly or explicitly for their meaning according to certain standards as one precondition for deciding whether to resist, accept, or revise these identities.

The *how* issue can be analyzed only after we know (or assume we know) what the parties want and what identities they want to bring off. There is no way to analyze, in my mind, the "how" of positioning as a sensible act without assuming that (a) there is an identity that the claimant "wants," together with (b) an implicit awareness that the addressee can affirm or reject this identity according to his or her "want" (if this is significant to the addressee), which (c) represents *some implicit rule or standard employed for the occasion*. It follows therefore, that the claimant needs to formulate his or her "how" in accordance with this presumed rule or standard if he or she wants the identity to be affirmed.

So, if my writing this chapter is a positioning of my "self" as "identity theorist", I will be formulating it in accordance to the criteria I assume the addressee will employ in evaluating the position. The *how* cannot be separated from *who* the addressee is and *what* assumed criteria and evaluation processes guide the *why* of affirmation. Assuming the addressee is the reader of the chapter, one reader might say to herself something along the lines of "Well, he uses APA format; he name-drops important sounding theorists from a century ago like Mead and Vygotsky (*I wonder if he read them in the original?*); he references recent papers from the journal *Theory and Psychology*; there aren't many empirical papers cited in the chapter; and it says 'Oxford University Press' on the cover of this handbook on identity so I guess he's an identity theorist." Another reader might say "He doesn't write like a professional should with a detached demeanor, the examples he uses are often childish, and he hasn't cited *my* paper. He should have read Rom Harré. And the idea of people 'talking' to themselves in their heads is really quite ridiculous—like the discredited scientific notion of phlogiston." In other words, my positioning is being evaluated, and my "how" of writing the chapter is, up to a point, geared by my assessment of the criteria to be used by the addressee in evaluating my position and the need to be accountable to him or her, or, to my own self (cf., Shotter, 2006). Recall, however, that an identity claim might have multiple addressees (within multiple perceived contexts). This same chapter might be written for (different) readers interested in identity theory, to a promotion committee, and\or to my own imagined internal future integrity-seeking sagacious self. Each of these external and internal addressees might hold to different criteria in evaluating my identity claim and beckon me to write differently in order to get my claim affirmed.

I am suggesting here that what is important for our grasp of identity processes, be they interactional or internal, is understanding the *criteria* people employ in evaluating the "goodness" of identity claims rather than just the particular techniques used to fashion identity claims that will meet such criteria. What determines the identity being brought off is not "in" the language but in whether the claims are tailored to fit the criteria implicitly used to evaluate those claims (Larrain & Haye, 2012). In the interactional framework, this means ascertaining what criteria the addressee will employ in evaluating whether the proffered identity is affirmed. In the internal framework, this means ascertaining what criteria the individual himself or herself employs in evaluating whether a self-proffered identity is considered good. This, of course, also raises the issue of what happens when the criteria clash.

What often differentiates identity theories, from both the internal and the interactional camps, is in their positing of particular criteria used or that should be used in evaluating the "validity" of an identity claim. The distinction between the descriptive and prescriptive is important; nevertheless, I put this issue aside for the moment. In the "internal" camp, Waterman describes this issue as how a theory defines "what constitutes a good identity choice." A central criterion offered by Erikson (1968) was "sameness and continuity." Identities are internally and interactionally affirmed if they are "sensed" (and "shown") to be consistent across time and place. Neo-Eriksonians also highlighted whether an identity has been "self-explored," as opposed to being "foreclosed" or "diffuse" (Marcia et al., 1993). "Good" exploration has been further delineated as guided by openness to information and rational decision making (Berzonsky, 2011). Waterman (2011, this volume) proposes that identity claims need to be evaluated with regards to whether they are self-expressive and suggests that indicators such as experiencing "flow" can help determine whether an identity expresses a "real" self (cf., Winnicott's "true self"). Côté and Levine (2002) suggest examining the social value ("sociocentricity") of identities because identity is the basis for adult generativity; Kroger (1989) stresses a good "balance between self and other," and Josselson (1996) evaluates identities as they figure in regards to relatedness. McAdams (1988) discusses the coherence of identity claims as they are authored in life stories and as this is guided by the criteria of providing *unity and purpose*. Postmodernists often suggest criteria such as empowerment, providing the individual with the abilities to resist conferred, debilitating socially constructed identities (see Kincheloe, 2008; Schachter, 2005). Interactionists have also offered criteria. Bamberg (2011), for example, describes three tensions that identity displays need to navigate in order that they be affirmed: the tension between change and constancy, the tension between uniqueness and sameness (or belonging), and the tension between self-as-actor and self-as-acted-on. To be accountable regarding any of these chosen criteria, individuals might look toward the past to seek and display evidence backing their claims (McLean & Pasupathi, 2012).

To develop just one of these examples, the eudaemonic perspective would suggest that, within every interaction, the I subjectively evaluates the claims possibly "made" or implicated regarding the self within the interaction according to how well they "fit" a person's "potentials" with the help of criteria such as engagement, flow, or feeling right. An identity positioned within an interaction might be self-affirmed and, once tentatively established according to such criteria, become the basis for subsequent interactions. Or, if not affirmed by such criteria, it may still be adopted defensively due to external pressure (Deci & Ryan, 2000; Winnicott, 1965) thus resulting in a tentatively established identity discordant with the self (Soenens & Vansteenkiste, 2011). Such an identity might still be experienced as "mine" in subsequent interactions and defended, or perhaps not, and abandoned. Given that individuals go through recursive iterations, including experiences of both sorts, and that external sociocultural contexts differ in the importance they accord the criterion of self-expressiveness, we can expect to see quite different identity development trajectories that build up into different global identities that can, although not necessarily, be used in regulating and feeding-in to subsequent identity interactions.

So often, what identity theorists and researchers implicitly or explicitly try to accomplish in their writing is to demonstrate that the particular criteria they have posited provides a better way to evaluate identities and therefore should be adopted as the criteria for assessing a more developed identity. Hence the claim that a self-expressive identity choice is better, or that a consistent identity is better, or an agentic identity is better, or a unique identity is better, or an embedded identity is better, or a self-aware identity is better, and so on. Of course, this begs the question: Better in what way, in what context, and who determines the criteria (Raeff, 2011)? Rather than our going about in our role as theorists and researchers suggesting and endorsing such criteria, I propose we instead channel our efforts to the descriptive study of those criteria that individuals employ, and of those criteria that cultural institutions such as schools endorse employing (Schachter & Rich, 2011), in the evaluation of identities.

Giving a short example, I retrospectively and briefly reinterpret findings from my first published paper (Schachter, 2002). In it, I attempted to address the structural criteria individuals describe employing, implicitly or explicitly, in evaluating whether an identity is "good." By *structural*, I mean criteria not relating specifically to the content of the identity but to issues of, for example, how the identity under deliberation coheres with other identities. Interviewees were Jewish modern-orthodox religious youth interviewed about religious and sexual development using a life story interview methodology. Stories in which respondents discussed identity conflicts were analyzed for what I then termed *constraints* on a good identity. In the terminology I present in this chapter, these are criteria used to evaluate whether an identity should be self-affirmed. I found that individuals described quite different criteria—for example, that a good identity is consistent, that a good identity includes all significant identifications, that a good identity must be authentic, and more. Hadassah exemplifies the consistency constraint:

> I remember the first time I heard that religious boys sometimes live [cohabit] with religious girls. I was in my mid-twenties and on one of my blind dates the guy told me right off the bat, I mean this is a guy that liked me, he wanted to be straightforward, so he told me that he lived with a girl for a while. And I remember the—I almost dropped dead. "What do you mean? Weren't you religious then?," "Yes, I was." [He answered] I remember that it just didn't compute... "And how did you get along with what should be done and what is worthy?!" And the guy was calm and relaxed and said: "Yep, I wanted to be religious, and I am religious now, and I was religious then, and I will continue to be religious, and I lived

with the girl. That's that." At that point I lost focus. And of course I wouldn't go out with him again. I said whoever lives his life in such disharmony certainly isn't worthy to be my husband.

Hadassah describes her then "consistency" criterion that interprets the date's identity—cohabiting while religious—as "disharmony." This discordant identity disqualifies him as husband material.

Hagit demonstrates a different criterion, one that states that a good identity should include all significant identifications, *even if these are inconsistent*. Describing herself as cohabiting before marriage with an irreligious man she states:

[B]ut I also, more than ever before started doing things because I didn't want to give up things in my religion because of him.... Maybe because I didn't want to miss out on myself, I didn't want to forget what kind of home I came from. Even though I knew I was doing something wrong, going out with someone irreligious and entering the world of sex and things. I wanted to be the "religious girl." And I made a decision at age seventeen when it would have really been easy to say "OK I'll forget about religion, I won't go to synagogue, I'll be with him and have fun and what do I need religion for." Especially then I said to myself no matter what happens I won't throw away my religion, it's important to me.

Hagit, in contrast with Hadassah, while acknowledging the allure of a consistent identity, describes "saying to herself" that she will not "throw away" or "give up" or "miss out" on herself, bringing her in her description to balance her transgressing sexuality with heightened religious activity.

These two very abridged examples demonstrate individuals describing their employing different criteria when self-evaluating the structural qualities of identities. It is these criteria that are adopted as higher order regulators (Valsiner, 2007*b*) used to process identity claims, whether internally or interactionally. The reason I believe internal identity theorists need adopt the discursive approach for studying internal processes of identity formation is that this approach alerts us to the manner in which individuals themselves evaluate the "goodness" of their own (and others') identities according to criteria "picked up" and personalized in myriad recursive iterations of identity interactions. Recognizing and describing these personalized criteria is, in my opinion, a better option than having researchers determine what such criteria should be. This example also provides a glimpse into a possible methodology that might be used to examine the process of self-evaluating claims—although these excerpts being articulated speech in interaction raises complicated problems that, unfortunately, cannot be discussed here.

Conclusion

This chapter presented a preliminary outline of a framework that adopts certain aspects of discursivity as possibly able to describe internal, interactional, and external identity processes and the relations between them. It offers a renewed way of looking at what identity process is and where we might look in examining how it develops. It also provides an interesting way to map the theories used to study identity. The framework, of course, needs further elaboration and most probably does injustice to others' positions in the process of roughly fitting them into my own construction. The chapter also glossed over the developmental and skipped over the methodological and ontological, work that definitely still needs to be done.

The writing of this chapter can itself be seen as a good example of the interaction between internal and interactional processes. As the examples I used throughout indicate, in writing it, I was oriented interactionally and internally. These orientations fed each other within sociocultural contexts, both affording and constraining my thinking and writing.

While preparing the chapter, I re-read Erikson's preface to his book on identity. He begins with a story I choose to end with. Erikson recalls that one of his teachers in the Vienna Psychological institute was Dr. Paul Federn, who introduced a theoretical concept that students found complex. They asked him to expound on this topic as long as needed. Erikson (1968, p. 9) describes how, after holding forth for three long evenings:

[H]e folded up his papers with the air of one who has finally made himself understood and asked: "*Nun-hab ich mich verstanden*"? (*Now*-have I understood myself?).

References

Bamberg, M. (2011). Who am I? Narration and its contribution to self and identity. *Theory and Psychology*, 21, 3–24.

Bamberg, M. & Zielke, B. (2007). From dialogical practices to polyphonic thought? Developmental inquiry and where to look for it. *International Journal for Dialogical Science*, 2, 223–242.

Baumeister, R. F. (1987). How the self became a problem: A psychological review of historical research. *Journal of Personality and Social Psychology*, 52, 163–176.

Berzonsky, M. D. (2011). A social-cognitive perspective on identity construction. In S. J. Schwartz, K. Luyckx, & V. L. Vignoles (Eds.), *Handbook of identity theory and research*, vol. 1, Structures and Processes (pp. 55–76). New York: Springer.

Billig, M. (1999). *Freudian repression: Conversation creating the unconscious*. Cambridge: Cambridge University Press.

Côté, J. E. (1996a). Identity: A multidimensional analysis. In G. R. Adams, R. Montemayor, & T. P. Gullotta (Eds.), *Psychosocial development during adolescence*. (pp. 130–180). Thousand Oak, CA: Sage.

Côté, J. E. (1996b). Sociological perspectives on identity formation: The culture-identity link and identity capital. *Journal of Adolescence*, 19, 419–430.

Côté, J. E. (Ed.). (2005). The postmodern critique of developmental perspectives. [Special issue]. *Identity: An International Journal of Theory and Research*, 5(2), 95–225.

Côté, J. E., & Levine, C. G. (2002). *Identity formation, agency, and culture: A social psychological synthesis*. Mahwah, NJ: Lawrence Erlbaum.

Deci, E. L., & Ryan, R. M. (2000). The "what" and "why" of goal pursuits: Human needs and the self-determination of behavior. *Psychological Inquiry*, 11, 227–268.

Erikson, E. H. (1968). *Identity: Youth and crisis*. New York: Norton.

Fernyhough, C. (1996). The dialogic mind: A dialogic approach to the higher mental functions. *New Ideas in Psychology*, 14, 47–62.

Freeman, M. (2011). Stories, big and small: Toward a synthesis. *Theory and Psychology*, 21, 114–121.

Gee, J. P. (2007). *Social linguistics and literacies: Ideology in discourses* (3rd ed.). London: Routledge.

Gergen, K. J. (1991). *The saturated self: Dilemmas of identity in contemporary life*. New York: Basic Books.

Giddens, A. (1991). *Modernity and self-identity: Self and society in the late modern age*. Stanford, CA: Stanford University Press.

Grotevant, H. D. (1987). Toward a process model of identity formation. *Journal of Adolescent Research*, 2, 203–222.

Hermans, H. J. M. (2001). The dialogical self: Toward a theory of personal and cultural positioning. *Culture & Psychology*, 7, 243–281.

Holland, D., & Lachicotte, W. (2007). Vygotsky, Mead, and the new sociocultural studies of identity. In H. Daniels, M. Cole, & J. Wertsch (Eds.), *The Cambridge companion to Vygotsky* (pp. 101–135). New York: Cambridge University Press.

John-Steiner, V. (2007). Vygotsky on thinking and speaking. In H. Daniels, M. Cole, & J. V. Wertsch (Eds.), *The Cambridge companion to Vygotsky* (pp. 136–152). Cambridge: Cambridge University Press.

Josselson, R. (1996). *Revising herself: The story of women's identity from college to midlife*. New York: Oxford University Press.

Kincheloe, J. L. (2008). *Critical pedagogy primer*. New York: Peter Lang.

Kroger, J. (1989). *Identity in adolescence: The balance between self and other*. London: Routledge.

Larrain, A., & Haye, A. (2012). The discursive nature of inner speech. *Theory & Psychology*, 22, 3–22.

Lawrence, J. A., & Valsiner, J. (2003). Making personal sense: An account of basic internalization and externalization processes. *Theory & Psychology*, 13, 723–752.

Linell, P. (2009). *Rethinking language, mind, and world dialogically*. Charlotte, NC: Information Age Publishing.

Marcia, J. E., Waterman, A. S., Matteson, D. R., Archer, S. L., & Orlofsky, J. L. (1993). *Ego identity: A handbook for psychosocial research*. New York: Springer-Verlag.

McAdams, D. P. (1988). *Power, intimacy and the life story: Personological inquiries into identity*. New York: Guilford.

McAdams, D. P. (2013). The psychological self as actor, agent, and author. *Perspectives in Psychological Science*, 8(3), 272–295.

McCall, G. J. (2003). Interaction. In L. T. Reynolds & N. J. Herman-Kinney (Eds.), *Handbook of symbolic interactionism* (pp. 327–348). Walnut Creek, CA: Alta Mira Press.

McLean, K. C., & Pasupathi, M. (2012). Processes of identity development: Where I am, and how I got there. *Identity: An International Journal of Theory and Research*, 12, 8–28.

Mead, G. H. (1934). *Mind, self and society*. Chicago: University of Chicago Press.

Penuel, W. R., & Wertsch, J. V. (1995). Vygotsky and identity formation: A sociocultural approach. *Educational Psychologist*, 30, 83–92.

Raeff, C. (2011). Distinguishing between development and change. *Human Development*, 54, 4–33.

Schachter, E. P. (2002). Identity constraints: The perceived structural requirements of a "good" identity. *Human Development*, 45(6), 416–433.

Schachter, E. P. (2005). Erikson meets the Postmodern: Can classic identity theory rise to the challenge? *Identity: An International Journal of Theory and Research*, 5(2), 137–160.

Schachter, E. P. (2011). Narrative identity construction as a goal oriented endeavor: Reframing the issue of "Big vs. Small" story research. *Theory and Psychology*, 21(1), 107–113.

Schachter, E. P., & Rich, Y. (2011). Identity Education: A new conceptual framework for researchers and practitioners. *Educational Psychologist*, 46(4), 222–238.

Serpe, R. T., & Stryker, S. (2011). The symbolic interactionist perspective and identity theory. In S. J. Schwartz, K. Luyckx, & V. L. Vignoles (Eds.), *Handbook of identity theory and research* (pp. 225–248). New York: Springer.

Shotter, J. (2006). Vygotsky and consciousness as con-scientia, as witnessable knowing along with others. *Theory & Psychology*, 16, 13–36.

Soenens, B., & Vansteenkiste, M. (2011). When is identity congruent with the self? A self-determination theory perspective. In S. J. Schwartz, K. Luyckx, & V. L. Vignoles (Eds.), *Handbook of identity theory and research* (pp. 381–402). New York: Springer.

Susswein, N., Bibok, M. B., & Carpendale, J. I. M. (2007). Reconceptualizing internalization. *International Journal for Dialogical Science*, 2, 183–205.

Taylor, C. (1989). *Sources of the self*. Cambridge, MA: Harvard University Press.

Thorne, A. (2004). Putting the person into social identity. *Human Development*, 47(6), 361–365.

Valsiner, J. (1997). Magical phrases, human development, and psychological ontology. In B. D. Cox, & C. Lightfoot (Eds.), *Sociogenetic perspectives on internalization* (pp. 237–256). Mahwah, NJ: Erlbaum.

Valsiner, J. (2007a). Constructing the internal infinity: Dialogical structure of the internalization process. *International Journal for Dialogical Science*, 2, 207–221.

Valsiner, J. (2007b). *Culture in minds and societies*. New Delhi: Sage.

Valsiner, J., & Van der Veer, R. (1988). On the social nature of human cognition: An analysis of the shared intellectual roots of George Herbert Mead and Lev Vygotsky. *Journal for the Theory of Social Behavior*, 18(1), 117–136.

Vygotsky, L. (1986). *Thought and language*. Cambridge: MIT Press. (Original work published 1934)

Waterman, A. S. (2011). Eudaimonic identity theory: Identity as self-discovery. In S. J Schwartz, K. Luyckx, & V. L. Vignoles (Eds.), *Handbook of identity theory and research*, Vol. 1, Structures and Processes (pp. 357–379). New York: Springer.

Weigert, A. J., Teitge, J. S., & Teitge, D. W. (1986). *Society and identity: Toward a sociological psychology*. Cambridge: Cambridge University Press.

Winnicott, D. W. (1965). *The maturational processes and the facilitating environment*. New York: International Universities Press.

PART 5

Debates: Culture and Identity Development

CHAPTER
16 Culture as Race/Ethnicity

Frank C. Worrell

Abstract

This chapter makes the claim that culture can be and is used interchangeably with racial and ethnic identity and contends that these are the psychosocial manifestations of race and ethnicity, respectively. It begins with a discussion of identity development and the separation of personal and social identity into relatively independent strands of research, each with its own set of theoretical formulations. Several definitions of culture, race, ethnicity, racial identity, and ethnic identity are reviewed, and the chapter discusses how Black culture is used in both popular and academic discourse, in support of the contention of interchangeability. Racial and ethnic identity are shown to be related to cultural outcomes and dependent on culture, thus challenging the notion that racial and ethnic identity are developmental constructs and suggesting that strong evidence supports an attitudinal interpretation of both of these constructs. The chapter concludes with suggestions for the future, more precise use, definition, and operationalization of these constructs.

Key Words: culture, ethnicity, ethnic identity, race, racial identity

Culture is a term that is frequently invoked in discussions of race and ethnicity, both in the scholarly literature and in popular discourse. However, many researchers are equally adamant in distinguishing between these terms (e.g., Betancourt & Lopez, 1993; Coleman, 2008; Helms & Talleyrand, 1997). In this chapter, I argue that culture can be interpreted as race/ethnicity and, more specifically, as racial and ethnic identity, especially when we focus on all of these terms as psychological constructs. An individual's worldview—the lens through which he or she processes information and events—is determined to a large extent by his or her culture, race, and ethnicity, and the purpose of this chapter is to contend that these three ostensibly different worldviews are, in essence, the same. This similarity is due to the fact that they represent *attitudinal rather than developmental* views of the world and an acknowledgment that they describe heterogeneous rather than monolithic groups. Since much of my identity-focused scholarship is focused on African Americans, in my exposition, I draw examples primarily from research with this racial/cultural/ethnic group, although I contend that the arguments are generalizable.

In the first section, I discuss the concepts of identity and identity development, to highlight important distinctions between personal and social identities. Next, I review definitions of the three terms—culture, ethnicity, and race—and show that not only is there considerable overlap among them in the extant literature, but that also there are times when the terms are used interchangeably. In the third section, I discuss racial and ethnic identity and argue that the distinctions between these two constructs are overstated, and I relate them to the definition of culture. I then focus on the definitions of Black culture in the scholarly and more popular literature to highlight the way that all of these constructs are intertwined in both popular writing and the academic literature. Next, I discuss the evolution of racial identity models, drawing primarily but not exclusively on Cross's nigrescence theory (Cross, 1971, 1991; Cross & Vandiver, 2001; Worrell, 2012), and I review findings from recent work on nigrescence theory. I conclude with an examination of ethnic identity models and more empirical findings in support of the claim that culture can be used interchangeably with race and ethnicity (cf. Phinney, 1996).

Identity Development

Erikson's (1950, 1968) psychosocial theory is arguably the preeminent theory of identity development in psychology. As with other developmental theories, psychosocial theory conceives of development as "a process of change with direction" (Valsiner & Connolly, 2003, p. ix), and Erikson argued for the inevitability of the progression through his stages from neonates in Stage 1 (trust versus mistrust) to individuals approaching the ends of their lives in Stage 8 (ego integrity versus despair). Although Erikson contended that an achieved identity was the major positive outcome of the adolescent period in Stage 5 (identity vs. role confusion), he also acknowledged that identity is a central component of the entire psychosocial development process and hence a concern across the lifespan (see Kroger, this volume).

There are two major strands in the research on identity. The *personal* or ego identity strand is reflected in the question, "who am I?," and the *social* identity or reference group orientation strand is reflected in the question, "what group do I belong to?" Although Erikson is most often associated with personal identity, he (1950, 1968) argued that development is epigenetic in that it depends on the interaction of genetic and environmental forces, and he did not make major distinctions between personal and social identity in his writings. Indeed, Erikson discussed the development not just of ego identity in his work, but also identity development in several social groups—including African Americans and Native Americans (the Sioux and Yurok), among others—to illustrate his viewpoint. Thus, psychosocial theory acknowledges the social environment's contribution not just to personal identity but also to social identity.

Personal/Ego Identity

The growth of the two strands of research on personal or ego identity and social identity came about largely through the way the constructs were operationalized. Erikson, himself, did not operationalize his theory, and much of the empirical research on ego identity over the past half century is based on Marcia's (1966) formulation of identity development in terms of the four statuses captured in his Identity Status Interview: moratorium, achievement, foreclosure, and diffusion. The *moratorium* status describes an individual who is actively exploring identity alternatives, but has not yet committed to an identity. *Identity achievement* refers to the status in which an individual has committed to an identity after exploration. *Foreclosure* refers to commitment without exploration, and *identity diffusion* refers to individuals who have neither explored nor committed to an identity: "he is either uninterested in ideological matters or takes a smorgasbord approach in which one outlook seems as good to him as another" (Marcia, 1966, p. 552).

This status typology resulted in identity profiles, rather than stages, based on an individual's levels of exploration and commitment: moratorium (high exploration, low commitment), achievement (high exploration and commitment), foreclosure (low exploration, high commitment), and diffusion (low exploration and commitment). A full exposition of this model is beyond the scope of this chapter (but see Crocetti & Meeus, this volume; Kunnen & Metz, this volume), but it is worth noting that Marcia (1966) was originally interested in identity *within* the adolescent period (Stage 5), not across the lifespan; indeed, in his initial 1966 paper, Marcia never discussed development as an issue, although recent theorizing has focused on development from adolescence through adulthood using Marcia's typology (e.g., Kroger, 2007). Moreover, since Marcia's (1966) seminal piece, many of the assessments of ego identity also use his framework as a starting point, with a concomitant focus on adolescence and emerging adulthood (e.g., Adams, Shea, & Fitch, 1979; Grotevant & Adams, 1984; Grotevant & Cooper, 1980; Kroger, Martinussen, & Marcia, 2010; Simmons, 1970).

Social Identity

As noted previously, Erikson's (1950, 1968) writings indicate that he recognized that environmental influences on identity development included the sociocultural, political, and historical context, which differed for different social groups. For example, he commented that the Sioux have "been denied the bases for a collective identity formation and with it that reservoir of collective integrity from which the individual must derive his stature as a social being" (Erikson, 1950, p. 154). In a similar vein, he observed that in groups that were discriminated against,

> The widespread pre-occupation with identity, therefore, may be seen not only as a symptom of "alienation" but also as a corrective trend in historical evolution. It may be for this reason that revolutionary writers and writers from national and ethnic minority groups (like the Irish expatriates or our Negro and Jewish writers) have become the artistic spokesmen and prophets of identity confusion.
>
> *(Erikson, 1968, pp. 297–298)*

Thus, culture, ethnicity, and race, which are major constructs in the social identity strand, are particularly salient for groups that Erikson characterized as having an "almost total prevalence of negative identity elements" (Erikson, 1968, pp. 297–298).

Interestingly, some influential social identity theorists (e.g., Cross, 1971) took a lifespan approach to identity development rather than focusing just on adolescence. Others who adopted the status model based on exploration and commitment as a framework for examining social identity (e.g., Phinney, 1989, 1992) have been unable to provide strong empirical evidence in support of a developmental model in the context of social identities, leading Worrell (2008b, 2011) to argue that neither racial nor ethnic identity is developmental (see also Quintana, 2007). I return to this point in a subsequent section. Next, I define the major constructs in this chapter, highlighting the similarity in their definitions and use.

Culture, Ethnicity, and Race Defined
Culture

Culture has been defined in several ways (Jahoda, 2012). For example, Quijada (2008, p. 223) contended that, "historically, culture has been defined as a series of traits shared by a group of individuals," and has been "traditionally construed as a monolithic variable that is stagnant or fixed both in time and space." Alternatively, VandenBos (2007a, p. 250) defined culture as "1. The distinctive customs, values, beliefs, knowledge, art and language of a society or community [and] 2. the characteristic attitudes and behaviors of a particular group within society, such as a profession, social class, or age group." As the Quijada and VandenBos definitions imply, culture is a construct that is broad in scope and has the potential to change over time and region with changes in values, beliefs, knowledge, attitudes, and behaviors of groups (Gillespie, Howarth, & Cornish, 2012).

Moreover, culture is frequently used to refer to any and all of the aspects of VandenBos's (2007a) definition. In 1992, for example, Frisby distinguished among six connotations of culture as used in everyday language. He distinguished among culture as (a) "characteristics patterns of living, customs, traditions, values, and attitudes;" (b) "significant artistic, humanitarian, or scientific achievements" of one's racial group or of one's ancestors; (c) "race consciousness" or the "common set of attitudes and beliefs" that guide one's "feelings about, interests in, or identification with' members of one's group;" (d) "values and norms of the immediate [socialization] context;" (e) "superficial differences…in such characteristics as popular clothing or fashion styles, music or dance styles, styles of religious worship, culinary traditions, or speech and language styles;" and (f) phenotypic differences (Frisby, 1992, pp. 533–534).

Importantly, these definitions of culture suggest that one can look at culture at two levels: from an overarching level, subsuming a racial or ethnic group's accomplishments, but also from the level of the individual related to socialization, psychological functioning, and modes of expression (Psaltis, 2012). There are numerous other definitions of culture in the literature (e.g., Atkinson, 2004; Hofstede, 2001; Smith, 2003; Triandis, 1994), but the essence of all of the definitions is captured in Frisby's (1992) and VandenBos's (2007a) definitions. Moreover, when we think of culture as a trait, value, attitude, or behavior, we have left the realm of the purely anthropological, where culture is generally seen to reside, and entered the psychological realm of identity because it is through identity that culture as race and ethnicity is manifested. For example, consider what is brought to mind when we think of Jewish culture or Latino culture or the culture of any other ethnic or racial group. The embodiment of these ethnic cultural realities include what Frisby (1992) called race consciousness, as well as values of the immediate socialization context, and the characteristic patterns of living. In sum, much of what we deem as *cultural* consists of the behaviors, attitudes, and values associated with group identification, such as cuisine, music, dress, and even types of economic engagement, among other things.

Ethnicity

As with culture, there are numerous definitions of ethnicity. For example, King (2002, p. 33) defined ethnicity as "a sense of peoplehood and commonality derived from kinship patterns, a shared historical past, common experiences, religious affiliations, language or linguistic commonalities, shared values, attitudes, perceptions, modes of expression, and identity," and VandenBos (2007b, p. 345) defined ethnicity as "a social categorization based on an individual's membership of or identification with a particular ethnic group." Ethnicity has also been defined as "a social category defined by the shared historical, national, social, political and cultural heritage of a people... [and] includes a reference to shared ancestry language, customs, traditions, and similar physical characteristics among a group of people" (Coleman, 2008, p. 1137). As can be seen, these definitions of ethnicity overlap considerably with the definitions of culture, and, indeed, King's (2002) definition of ethnicity and VandenBos's (2007a) definition of culture are interchangeable (see Table 16.1 for these and other definitions).

Race

Definitions of the construct of race have evolved more than have definitions of ethnicity and culture. For many years, race was considered a biological construct. For example, Reber (1985, p. 606) defined a race as "any relatively large division of persons that could be distinguished from others on the basis of *inherited* [emphasis added] physical characteristics such as skin pigmentation, blood groups, hair texture, and the like." This view, which is predicated on race as a unitary construct, was first contested in anthropology at least a century ago (e.g., Boas, 1912), and, in 1998, the American Anthropological Association disavowed race as a biological construct (Zack, 2002). In an essay decrying the use of the term Caucasian in scientific discourse, Teo (2009 p. 94) summarized much of the recent scholarship on race, pointing out that (a) there is more within-group than between group variation in the races as they have been defined and (b) there are no "major discontinuities" between races.

Recent definitions of race indicate that it is "a socially defined concept sometimes used to

Table 16.1 Definitions of culture, race, and ethnicity

Culture
VandenBos (2007a, p. 250): "1. the *distinctive customs, values, beliefs,* knowledge, art and language of a society or community. 2. the *characteristic attitudes and behaviors* of a particular group within society, such as a profession, social class, or age group."

Ethnicity
King (2002, p. 33): "A sense of *peoplehood and commonality* derived from kinship patterns, a shared historical past, common experiences, religious affiliations, language or linguistic commonalities, *shared values, attitudes, perceptions, modes of expression,* and identity."

Race
C. E. Thompson (2008, p. 1279): "A label that is commonly ascribed to individuals in certain societies based on their *affiliation with a group of people.* Members of racial groups typically share common characteristics in physical appearance or phenotype, but more significantly, they share a *common stature within a given society...* race is a social construction."

Ethnic Identity
Phinney et al. (1994, p. 164): The "*feeling of belonging to one's group,* a clear understanding of the meaning of one's membership, positive attitudes towards the group, *familiarity with its history and culture,* and involvement with its practices."
Tran & Lee (2008, p. 1135): "a dynamic multidimensional construct that represents the part of one's self-concept that is derived from *a sense of belonging and commitment to a particular ethnic group.*"

Racial Identity
Helms (1990b, p. 3): "A sense of group or collective identity based on one's *perception* that he or she shares a common racial heritage with a particular racial group."
VandenBos (2007d, p. 765): "An individual's sense of being *a person whose identity is defined, in part, by membership of a particular race.* The strength of this sense will depend on the extent to which an individual has processed and internalized the *psychological, sociopolitical, cultural and other contextual factors related to membership of the group.*"

Note: Italicized phrases represent commonalities in the definitions.

designate a portion, or 'subdivision,' of the human population with common physical characteristics, ancestry, or language" (VandenBos, 2007c, p. 765). As can be seen, this more recent definition of race, although acknowledging that race is related to phenotype, also highlights shared ancestry and language, in keeping with the definitions of culture and ethnicity. Recent theorizing about the racialization of groups (e.g., Muslims after September, 11, 2001; Gotanda, 2011) also supports the notion that race is a social construct.

Culture Versus Race and Ethnicity

Despite the similarities articulated previously, there are several scholars who think that race should be kept distinct from culture and ethnicity, even while they are prepared to accept the intertwining of the latter two constructs. These arguments are reviewed and deconstructed below. In a 1996 article on American ethnic groups, Phinney subsumed race under ethnicity, arguing that the term "ethnicity" was preferable to race, given the contestations in defining race in the research literature. Phinney's (1996) choice elicited a pointed response from Helms and Talleyrand (1997, p. 1247), who argued that race is a "more distinctive construct" than ethnicity. Helms and Talleyrand pointed out that only 11 percent of race abstracts in the psychological literature at that time overlapped with ethnicity, whereas 29 percent of the ethnicity abstracts overlapped with race, and they invoked racial socialization and differential and discriminatory treatment of individuals on the basis of phenotypical characteristics associated with race in support of keeping race and ethnicity as distinct constructs. Helms and Talleyrand also suggested an alternative for scholars to consider: "A better solution is to say and measure ethnicity when we refer to cultural characteristics and "(socio)race" or "(psycho)race" when we refer to how a person presumably appears or perceives herself or himself as a result of racial socialization" (Helms & Talleyrand, 1997, p. 1247).

Thus, Helms and Talleyrand (1997) conceded that culture and ethnicity were interchangeable but saw race as a different construct. Despite their passionate defense of race as distinct from culture/ethnicity, Helms and Talleyrand's position can be challenged on several grounds. First, individuals from many racial and ethnic minority backgrounds, including Black, Latino and Native American, report being discriminated against on the basis of phenotypical characteristics associated with their perceived race or ethnicity and, indeed, are sometimes perceived as being of the same race. Second, Latinos of both African and European descent are included in the nondominant or marginal minority categorization (Araújo & Borrell, 2006; Bowman, 2009; Phinney, 1996), despite being members of different "races," as it were. Indeed, second- and third-generation descendants of African and Latino immigrants become indistinguishable from their nonimmigrant peers and are treated as stigmatized minorities (Ogbu & Simons, 1998; Fuligni & Hardway, 2004).

Third, although the content is not always the same, African Americans are not the only ethnic group—minority or majority—in the United States that provides racial socialization messages to children and youth (cf. Chávez & French, 2007; French, Coleman, & DiLorenzo, 2013; Hughes, 2003). Fourth, even Asian Americans, who are stereotyped as model minorities with regard to achievement (e.g., T. L. Thompson & Kiang, 2010), report being discriminated against on the basis of their ethnicity (Leong & Gupta, 2007; Mio, Nagata, Tsai, & Tewari, 2007) and sometimes report higher levels of socialization messages promoting mistrust among racial/ethnic groups (e.g., French et al., 2013).

Similarly, Coleman (2008), in arguing against using race and ethnicity interchangeably, actually supports interpreting culture as race and ethnicity. First, she claimed that ethnicity includes cultural experiences—that is, culture as ethnicity—but contended that race is limited to only three social groups (Asian, Black, and White), perhaps related to the original three racial groups in anthropology's history, and is tied to a society's political, economic, and social needs. The immigration issue, which helped decide the 2012 presidential election in the United States, was related to the political, economic, and social concerns of Latinos, invalidating the second point of this argument. Moreover, to the extent that we disavow the notion of race as unitary, biological categories, the notion of *three* distinct races and Coleman's first point is overturned. Second, Coleman also pointed out that there are far more ethnic groups than racial groups, but this argument is also untenable because the majority of racial groups in this country are *racial/ethnic* groups. African Americans include native-born, Caribbean-born, South-American-born, and Africa-born Blacks, among others; Asian Americans include Japanese, Chinese, South Korean, East Indian, Hmong, and Vietnamese, among others; European Americans include Irish Americans and Amish and German Americans, and sometimes individuals of Jewish and Arab heritage, among others; and Latinos include people from Mexico and several Caribbean, Central American, and South American countries. In sum, to claim that culture is interchangeable with ethnicity but not interchangeable with race in the United States is to use a flawed assumption that race and ethnicity are distinct concepts in the United States.

The similarities in the definitions of culture, race, and ethnicity should be apparent (see Table 16.1 for several definitions with commonalities italicized). Although the similarity between culture and ethnicity is more readily observable, accepting race as a social instead of a biological construct brings it clearly into the same sphere as culture and ethnicity. All three constructs are defined by these characteristics:

1. Ascribed membership in a specific societal group, so we can refer to Blacks in the United States and mean the Black "race," Black culture, or individuals of African descent in the United States who come from several different ethnic groups.

2. A sense of affiliation or affinity with the group, so that individuals acknowledge and accept that they are members of a group with a shared historical past.

3. Shared values and beliefs based on their group membership, an assumption that is made both by group members and by nonmembers of the group, in spite of intragroup differences.

In describing American nonmajority ethnic groups, Phinney (1996) described ethnicity as culture, identity, and minority status. Based on the arguments just given, I contend that, in the same vein, one can describe race as culture, identity, and minority status, and culture as race, ethnicity, and minority status in relation to the same groups of individuals. Moreover, the interchangeable use of these three constructs subsumes both minority and majority groups, just as Erikson (1968) noted similarities in the identity struggles among ethnic groups, some of whom were members of minority groups (e.g., African Americans and Native Americans) and some of whom were majority group members (e.g., Jews and Irish, who are often considered "White"). I further argue that the distinctions that Phinney (1996), Helms and Talleyrand (1997), Coleman (2008), and others are making *may* be useful in the context of esoteric arguments among scholars but are not particularly meaningful in everyday life or understandable to the general public.

Defining Racial and Ethnic Identity

Although I have been arguing that culture is interchangeable with race and ethnicity, a more precise statement would be that culture is interchangeable with racial identity and ethnic identity, two of the most frequently studied cultural identities in the United States. To the extent that culture consists of attitudes, values, beliefs, and traits, it is a psychosocial construct. Whereas race and ethnicity are social constructions, their psychosocial manifestations are racial and ethnic identity, respectively. Thus, culture, racial identity, and ethnic identity are members of the same family.

Research on racial identity has a longer history, dating back to the 1940s and 1950s, when the Clarks conducted their studies on African-American children (Clark & Clark, 1947, 1950). Ethnic identity began to be more systematically studied in the 1990s, with the introduction of the Multigroup Ethnic Identity Measure (MEIM; Phinney, 1992). In the paper introducing the MEIM, Phinney (1992, p. 156) argued that ethnic identity is based on an individual's "knowledge of membership in a social group (or groups) together with the value and emotional significance attached to that membership," and the MEIM was developed to be able to assess "ethnic identity as a general phenomenon that is relevant across all groups" (Phinney, 1992, p. 158).

Consider the following definition: *the feeling of belonging to one's group, a clear understanding of the meaning of one's membership, positive attitudes toward the group, familiarity with its history…involvement with its practices.* This definition is one that is potentially useful and is likely to be accepted by scholars of racial identity, ethnic identity, or culture. However, this is actually a definition of *ethnic* identity, put forward by Phinney, DuPont, Espinosa, Revill, and Sanders (1994), although, as noted earlier, it can be applied to racial identity (or cultural identity) with the simple substitution of the leading adjective without any sense of unease (Worrell & Gardner-Kitt, 2006).

The definition is also quite similar to the definitions of race, culture, and ethnicity, with several areas of commonality. Again, all five constructs—that is, culture, ethnicity, ethnic identity, race, and racial identity—are defined in terms of membership in a particular group and a sense of psychological commonality, whether referred to as values, beliefs, status in society, or the meaning of group membership. In short, all of these definitions are related to the fundamental identity questions that Erikson (1950, 1968) introduced decades ago: *Who am I, what group do I belong to, who do others say that I am,* and *how is my group perceived?* To illustrate how culture, race/racial identity, and ethnicity/ethnic identity are interchangeable, I now discuss examples of how culture is used in both everyday and academic discourse, using African Americans as the backdrop.

What Is Black Culture?
Black Culture in Everyday Discourse

When we use terms such as "Black culture" in everyday discourse, we are signaling that there are ways of being that are particular to being Black—that is, race and ethnicity as culture—and that individuals who do not act in these ways are not Black or not Black *enough*. Moreover, these ways of being Black are expected of all Black individuals. For example, consider the associations that Kwanzaa and chitlins bring to mind and the different expectations one has about going to church versus going to a Black church. Indeed, discussions of culture—whether it be Black culture, Jewish culture, or Latino culture—are often premised on extremely general claims and stereotypes about culture that are believed to be understood by all (Gillespie et al., 2012).

GENUINELY AND AUTHENTICALLY BLACK

I arrived in the United States to begin my doctoral studies in 1988, and I am still asked where I am from when people hear me speak because my accent is still not an American accent, at least within the United States. However, as I participated, with an accent that was much more distinctly foreign, in practica and internships as part of my doctoral studies, I became the "go-to" expert for issues involving African-American children and youth, simply because of my phenotype. In the minds of many teachers and administrators who knew that I was a recent arrival in the States, being Black granted me some special insight into the lives of Black children and their families. Similarly, in the 1990s, when I was on the faculty at Penn State, I was talking to an African-American friend who resided in Oakland, California. I shared with him that I had just participated in the Memorial Day Parade in Boalsburg, Pennsylvania, where I lived, as a member of a group called the Boalsburg Yard Guard, which had done a routine in the parade involving lawn mowers. My friend's response was, "we need to get you out of middle America as soon as possible; you are forgetting how to be Black." Although intended as a joke, the comment reflects the way that society, including academics, subsume race, ethnicity, and culture in their thinking. My forgetting how to be Black was simultaneously racial (of African descent), ethnic (Caribbean American), and cultural (Black American), and this monolithic viewpoint is also reflected in Frisby's (1992) scenarios about the different connotations of Black culture.

From this perspective, Black culture is related to whether one's ways of thinking and acting are in line with the "common consensus" (McWhorter, 2003b, p. xii) of the Black community. Consider that the Black bona fides of well-known African Americans such as Supreme Court Justice Clarence Thomas, former Secretary of State Condoleeza Rice, and former regent of the University of California, Ward Connerly (who led the charge to get rid of affirmative action in pubic university admissions in California) are often questioned based on actions, values, or statements that are seen as *not Black*, in large part because they are conservatives rather than liberals. Is Shelby Steele, Black conservative and opponent of affirmative action, less Black than his twin, Claude Steele, who introduced the concept of stereotype threat to social psychology?

The idea of a Black cultural litmus test is one of many that is explored in McWhorter's (2003a) book of essays entitled *Authentically Black: Essays for the Black Silent Majority*. It is also reflected in other titles, such as Copeland's (2006) *Not a Genuine Black Man: My Life as an Outsider.* In the latter book, Copeland (2006, p. xii), who is a comedian, discussed his response to receiving the following in the mail: "As an African American, I am disgusted every time I hear your voice because YOU are not a genuine Black man." In his response to this accusation, Copeland acknowledged liking stereotypically Black things such as watermelons, chitlins, and the old Motown sound, although he also points out that he likes the Beach Boys and does not "talk ghetto" (Copeland, 2006, p. xii). Copeland also reported that he has suffered many of the indignities associated with being a Black male in America, being phenotypically Black. Copeland (pp. 243–244) concluded by reclaiming his Blackness:

> When all is said and done, I AM indeed a Genuine Black Man—because I am resilient. That's what being Black in America is truly about: resilience... I have the right and ability to determine my identity regardless of what other blacks or whites say.

Of course, the right to determine one's identity is a right that can be claimed by all, but one that may be more important to members of marginalized minority groups. For example, it is manifested in some Mexican Americans' choosing to be called Chicano, as opposed to Hispanic or Latino. Similarly, the gay and lesbian community has reclaimed the term "queer," originally used to signal the group's difference from the heterosexual norm; now, the term is used as an identity moniker and in naming university departments and programs that study gay and lesbian issues around the United States. One can also see the importance of determining how a group's identity is framed in the evolution of the terms for African Americans in this country, moving from the labels Negro and Colored, to Black and African American in contemporary society (Worrell, 2005). Interestingly, the term "Black," which is now one of the predominant terms used to describe African Americans, was once considered pejorative (Morgan, 1995), until it was reclaimed by African Americans during the civil rights era with slogans such as *Black is beautiful* and *Black Power* (Smith, 2003).

BLACK SELF-SABOTAGE

McWhorter (2000) had another perspective on culture as race or ethnicity in a book written for the general public. He proposed a theory of Black self-sabotage, which subsumes all three constructs, to explain the underachievement of African American students. McWhorter (2000) identified three factors as primary causes in the ongoing academic underperformance of African Americans: victimology, separatism, and anti-intellectualism. He defined victimology as claiming to be a victim when one is not and doing so to breed resentment and alienate oneself from mainstream society, and he contended that victimology is as present in the work of Black academics as it is in the inner city. According to McWhorter (2000), victimology condones weakness and failure, hampers performance by focusing on obstacles rather than solutions, and promotes racism in White Americans.

McWhorter (2000, p. 50) argued that separatism is a "direct product of victimology" because the latter leads to interpreting mainstream culture as White. He postulated that other expressions of separatism include Black scholars limiting their scholarship to Black issues, and African Americans, in general, ignoring foreign cultures that are not Black. McWhorter (2000) suggested that separatism abrogates African Americans of responsibility by suggesting "they cannot be held responsible for immoral or destructive actions, these being 'understandable' responses to frustration and pain"

(pp. 61–62). Like victimology, he argued that separatism hinders African Americans by reinforcing the stereotype of mental inferiority, hindering the hiring and promotion of African Americans, and contributing to de facto inferiority by labeling a Black murderer a victim and an unmotivated African American a nonconformist.

Anti-intellectualism is the third pillar in McWhorter's (2000) triad (see also Way & Rogers, this volume), and he claimed that anti-intellectualism is the primary reason for the poor performance of African Americans in school. McWhorter (2000) opined that anti-intellectualism is the product of being systematically excluded from education for centuries but is maintained by separatism, which allows African Americans to label schools and books as White and "not to be embraced by the authentically 'Black' person" (p. 83), be they from poor inner-city communities or from upper-class Black communities. McWhorter (2000) noted that anti-intellectualism reveals itself in the teasing of Black students who do well in school; the lowered expectations of African-American parents; the lower participation rates in schools by Black parents, including affluent Black parents; the acceptance of low bars for acceptable performance; the classroom attitudes and behaviors of Black students; and the college dropout rates of African-American students (see also Cooper et al., this volume).

Not surprisingly, McWhorter's (2000) views have generated considerable controversy, but the purpose of including them in this chapter is neither to condemn nor endorse them. Rather, McWhorter's (2000) views provide a cogent example of the melding of the constructs in this work (see Table 16.1). His focus is on African Americans as a subgroup (*race*), as well as (a) their characteristic attitudes and behaviors (*culture*), (b) their shared values and modes of expression (*ethnicity*), (c) their involvement in group practices (*ethnic identity*), and (d) their internalized psychological, sociopolitical, and contextual factors (*racial identity*). Thus, whether conceptualized explicitly or not, these constructs are clearly interrelated and interchangeable in some discourses.

Black Culture in Academic Settings

The intertwining of culture, race, and ethnicity is not limited to books written for general audiences, however. Several scholarly models also suggest that these constructs can and should be conflated. Two of these—Black cultural learning styles and stereotype threat—are discussed in the next sections.

BLACK CULTURAL LEARNING STYLES

One potent example of culture as race and ethnicity in academic discourse is the Black cultural learning styles model (BCLS; Hale-Benson, 1986). Hale-Benson argued that "Black children grow up in a distinct culture" resulting in "certain characteristics, peculiar to Black culture" which "have their roots in West Africa and have implications for the way in which Black children learn and think" (p. 4). From the BCLS perspective, then, even if race was not originally synonymous with culture, in the sociohistorical context of the United States, being Black is both racial and cultural, and, I would argue, ethnic. Proponents of this point of view claim that being Black results in differences in worldviews, cognition, approaches to learning, communication styles, and social interactions. Although not supported by the research literature (Frisby, 1993), the idea of culturally specific learning styles is still found in the contemporary scholarly literature, not all of which is limited to the discussion of African Americans (e.g., DeVries & Golon, 2011).

STEREOTYPE THREAT

Stereotype threat (Steele, 1997; Steele & Aronson, 1995) is one of the most robust social psychological phenomena to be described in the past two decades. Researchers have shown consistently that African Americans perform less well on academic tasks when the construct of intelligence or their race is made salient before attempting the task and that this decrement in performance in testing situations due to stereotype threat does not affect their European American counterparts (Steele, 2010). Accepting the premise that race is not biological suggests that the stereotype threat effect is the result of being culturally African American, even though the stereotype invokes race.

Moreover, the phenomenon is not limited to African Americans. In one study conducted by Stone, Lynch, Sjomeling, and Darley (1999), stereotype threat had a negative impact on the athletic performance of both African-American and European-American athletes. The former performed less well when the intelligent athlete stereotype was primed and the latter performed more poorly when the natural athlete stereotype was primed. These findings suggest that both groups hold both stereotypes—that is, both African Americans and European Americans hold negative stereotypes of the intelligence of African Americans, and both groups believe that athletic ability is more natural to African Americans. Much as the intellectual stereotype is influenced by the longstanding achievement gap (Aud, Fox, & KewalRamani, 2010; Chapman, Laird, Ifill, & KewalRamani, 2011), the athletic stereotype is probably influenced by the disproportionate number of outstanding African-American athletes in the National Football League (in 2011, 67 percent of the players were Black; Lapchick, 2012a) and the National Basketball Association (in 2011–2012, 78 percent of the players were Black; Lapchick, 2012b).

In another study, Shih, Pittinsky, and Ambady (1999) examined stereotype threat and stereotype *facilitation* in a sample of females of Asian descent. In the study, US participants whose female identities were primed did significantly and meaningfully less well than participants whose Asian identities were primed, with the no prime control group's results falling in the middle. However, in Canada, where the stereotype of Asians (as a race) being quantitatively gifted is less prevalent, participants in the no prime control obtained the highest scores. Thus, the results suggest that race, as used in these studies, is really a cultural construct. The results of these stereotype threat studies, like the cultural learning styles movement, indicate that the conflating of culture and race/ethnicity is not limited to African-American groups or to popular discourse, but is also present in the academy. As may be evident, the stereotype threat studies are premised on the stereotyped group members' identification with a cultural group, which is one definition of racial and ethnic identity (Worrell & Gardner-Kitt, 2006). To make this point more explicit, in the next section, I review several of the major models of racial and ethnic identities in the extant literature and address the issue of cultural identities as attitudinal rather than developmental.

Racial Identity Models

One of the major arguments against the notion of culture as race and ethnicity is related to the apparent fluidity of culture, in contrast with the rigidity of race and ethnicity as constructs. However, an explication of the evolution of racial and ethnic identity models in the literature will show that racial and ethnic identity are similar to culture in that they are responsive to the sociohistorical context. There are several models of racial identity in the literature (Helms, 1990a, 1990d), with Cross's (1971, 1991; Cross & Vandiver, 2001) nigrescence theory and the multidimensional model of racial identity (MMRI; Sellers, Rowley, Chavous, Shelton, & Smith, 1997; Sellers, Shelton et al., 1998; Sellers, Smith, Shelton,

Rowley, & Chavous, 1998) being among the most well-known for African Americans.

Multidimensional Model of Racial Identity (MMRI)

The MMRI (Sellers et al., 1997; Sellers, Shelton et al., 1998; Sellers, Smith et al., 1998) conceptualizes Black racial identity as a set of multidimensional attitudes. This racial identity framework has been used with adolescents (Scottham, Sellers, & Nguyên, 2008), emerging adults (Hurd, Sellers, Cogburn, Butler-Barnes, & Zimmerman, 2013), and adults (Street et al., 2012), and several attitudes have been found to be related to psychological well-being (Hurd et al., 2013) and to cultural constructs (Bryant, 2011). However, to date, no studies have examined generalizable profiles using scores from the seven subscales of the Multidimensional Inventory of Black Identity (MIBI; Sellers et al., 1997), the operationalization of the MMRI.

Nigrescence Theory

The nigrescence model (Cross, 1971, 1991; Cross & Vandiver, 2001) is another well-known theoretical formulation of African-American racial identity. The utility of the nigrescence model for this analysis is the recent work describing the breadth of racial identity profiles *within* the Black community. It is also worth noting that some of these models have been used with other cultural groups. For example, the original nigrescence model (NT-O; Cross, 1971) has been adapted for other cultural identity models, including ethnicity (Arce, 1981; Kim, 1981, 2001; Phinney, 1989), gender (Downing & Roush, 1985), minority group (e.g., Atkinson, Morten, & Sue, 1998), and sexual orientation (Cass, 1979, 1984). Similarly, Sellers et al.'s model, which was developed with African Americans, has been used with a variety of other cultural groups, including both minority and majority group members (e.g., Casey-Cannon, Coleman, Knudtson, & Velazquez, 2011; Rivas-Drake, Hughes, & Way, 2009). I begin with a discussion of the developmental model of nigrescence, before turning to the more recent attitudinal conceptualization.

The evolution of nigrescence theory (Cross, 1971, 1991; Cross & Vandiver, 2001) provides us with some insight into culture as racial identity. Initially conceived of as a theory of individual development specific to African Americans, the NT-O came out of Cross's interpretation of what was happening in the Black Power movement of the 1960s (Worrell, 2008*a*), a political as well as a social and cultural phenomenon (Altman, 1987; Smith, 2003). As Cross (1971, p. 14) observed, his goal was to create a "model depicting the various stages persons traverse in becoming Black oriented. In its current form it might best be called a 'phenomenological interpretation of the Negro-to-Black conversion experience.'"

BLACK IDENTITY AS A STAGE MODEL

The NT-O (Cross, 1971) was a developmental stage theory in the vein of Piaget (1962) and Erikson (1950), with the notion of crises to be resolved or overcome. Cross (1971) postulated that African Americans went through five stages: Pre-encounter, Encounter, Immersion-Emersion, Internalization, and Internalization-Commitment. African Americans in Stage 1, Pre-encounter, were conditioned to have low or negative race salience and to use White America as the normative ideal to which they should aspire; race was considered unimportant. African Americans are propelled into Stage 2, Encounter, on the basis of some event or experience that forces them to reexamine the notion that their racial/ethnic categorization does not matter in America and confront their assumption that Blackness is something to be overcome. The resolution of Stage 2 for African Americans is fueled by a recognition, often associated with anger, that America has deceived them, and they begin Stage 3, Immersion-Emersion, by immersing themselves in the Black world (e.g., history, literature).

Whereas Stage 1 was about overcoming the fact that one is Black, Stage 3 is about being as Black as one can be and, at the same time, denigrating the White world. Stage 4, Internalization, occurs when an individual emerges from the anti-White miasma and recognizes that being pro-Black is not synonymous with being anti-White: one can accept that all human beings are equal while being pro-Black. Finally, Stage 5 is the result of recognizing that acceptance of Blackness is not enough—the individual moves beyond acceptance to planful action aimed at helping the Black community. Cross (1971) contended that an individual's movement from Pre-Encounter to Internalization also reflected a journey from Black self-hatred to Black self-acceptance.

The intertwining of racial/ethnic identity and cultural identity is evident in this model because movement through the stages is intimately connected with cultural values, beliefs about race, and identity in both an individual and societal sense. The African American in the Pre-encounter stage uses European

Americans and their culture as the norm, and progress through the stages represents changing one's cultural frame of reference, as well as one's understanding of what being of African descent means in the social context of the United States. In other words, the Negro to Black conversion process in NT-O is conceived of as both a cultural and psychological transformation: "The process should be viewed as the *Afro-American model for self-actualization under conditions of oppression*" (Cross, 1971, p. 25). As should be evident, NT-O was as dependent on the cultural zeitgeist—social, historical, political forces—of the time as it was on individual psychological development, and, in a context that was not oppressive, the model of racial identity that developed would have been a different one.

It is important to note that NT-O was not a phenomenon that was limited to the adolescent period; rather, NT-O and its revision (Cross, 1991) conceived of Black identity development as a process that began with childhood socialization and progressed into adulthood (Cross & Fhagen-Smith, 2001; Tatum, 1997), making it closer to Erikson's (1950) original psychosocial theory than to the conceptualizations of ego identity (e.g., Marcia, 1966). In 1981, Parham and Helms published the first version of the Racial Identity Attitude Scale (RIAS; see also Helms, 1990c), an operationalization of NT-O. Research using the RIAS showed that racial identity stages had differential relationships with a variety of psychological and cultural constructs, including preference for counselor race, self-actualization, and psychological well-being (e.g., Carter, 1991; Parham & Helms, 1985).

NIGRESCENCE AS A SET OF ATTITUDES

By the mid- to late-1980s, however, there was a growing recognition that a developmental stage formulation was not fully capturing racial identity as a construct (Worrell, 2012). Moreover, the developmental hypothesis was also not being supported in empirical investigations, with several studies showing no consistent relationship between racial identity attitudes and age (Neil, 2003; Parham & Williams, 1993; Plummer, 1996). Worrell (2008b) investigated the developmental hypothesis in a cross-sectional study of adolescents, emerging adults, and adults and found no support for a developmental progression of nigrescence attitudes. Worrell (2012, p. 9) summarized these findings in this way:

> Developmental change implies that the change is typical and predictable for members of a group (e.g., from babbling to one-word to two-word utterances in children; the release of hormones as individuals reach adolescence), and developmental change is often associated with a change in age. Racial identity does not fit neatly into this definition of development.

In other words, *although development involves change, not all change is developmental.*

In 1986, Helms began describing the stages as worldviews, and Cross (1991) began using terms like *attitudes* and *profiles*. This shift to racial identity as a construct consisting of attitudes and beliefs is another manifestation of the collapsing of culture, ethnicity, and race (see Frisby's [1992] definition of culture]. In the expanded nigrescence model (NT-E; Cross & Vandiver, 2001; Worrell, Cross, & Vandiver, 2001), the most recent version of this theoretical formulation, Black racial identity is conceptualized as a series of attitudes rather than a set of stages. According to NT-E, "Black racial identity refers to a set of attitudes held by individuals of African descent, and includes how these individuals view (a) themselves as Blacks, (b) other individuals of African descent, and (c) individuals from other racial and ethnic groups" (Worrell, Mendoza-Denton, Telesford, Simmons, & Martin, 2011, p. 637).

Six NT-E attitudes are operationalized using the Cross Racial Identity Scale (CRIS; Vandiver et al., 2000; Worrell, Vandiver, & Cross, 2004). The assimilation subscale assesses an individual's preference for their national identity (i.e., American) rather than a cultural or hybrid identity (i.e., African American). The miseducation subscale assesses the degree to which African Americans endorse negative stereotypes of Blacks, and the self-hatred subscale assesses an individual's unhappiness with being Black. The anti-White subscale assesses the strength of negative feelings toward European Americans, the Afrocentricity subscale assesses the degree to which individuals believe that Afrocentric principles should guide one's life, and the multiculturalist inclusive subscale assesses the degree to which individuals who are pro-Black are willing to engage with other ethnic and cultural groups.

In 2006, Worrell, Vandiver, Schaefer, Cross, and Fhagen-Smith showed that these six attitudes form profiles that generalize across samples, and, subsequently, several researchers have found that these racial identity profiles predict meaningful differences in personality (Telesford, Mendoza-Denton, & Worrell, 2013), psychopathology (Telesford et al.,

2013; Whittaker & Neville, 2010), and cultural engagement (e.g., Chavez-Korell & Vandiver, 2012). Research on racial identity profiles indicates that an individual's racial identity score on an individual subscale is less useful for interpreting their outlook than that score in relation to other subscale scores (i.e., as part of the individual's profile). For example, Worrell et al. (2011) reported generally modest correlations between the six CRIS scores and a psychopathology score ($.10 \leq r \leq .39$, Mdn $r = .13$), with only Self-Hatred's relationship being greater than .30. However, using the same sample, Telesford et al. (2013) reported percentages of individuals for racial identity profiles with clinically significant scores that ranged from 2.6 to 20.5 percent, and the mean difference between the profile with the highest and lowest scores had an effect size (Cohen's d) of 1.13.

To date, researchers have identified several profiles, including Afrocentric, Anti-White, Assimilated, Conflicted, Intense Black Involvement, Low Race Salience, Miseducated, Multiculturalist, Negative Race Salience, and Self-Hating. From the point of view of this chapter, it is important to note that all of these attitudes are general to African Americans—as a cultural/racial/ethnic phenomenon—whereas the profiles highlight the heterogeneity within the Black population.

The profile differences on personality and cultural variables, in particular, have implications for the thesis of culture as racial identity. Chavez-Korell and Vandiver (2012) found that only Assimilation ($r = -.32$) and Afrocentricity ($r = .36$) attitudes were meaningfully related to enculturation, and only anti-White attitudes ($r = -.37$) were related to attitudes toward European Americans. However, when they compared individuals in the six clusters that they found using enculturation (i.e., preference for Black culture) and social distance from mainstream culture as dependent variables, they found that individuals in the Intense Black Involvement and Afrocentric clusters reported meaningfully higher scores on preference for Black culture than individuals in the Multiculturalist, Self-Hatred, and Assimilation clusters. The findings were similar for social distance from mainstream culture, with the some profiles indicating a strong preference for mainstream culture and others indicating a preference against mainstream culture, with the Multiculturalists indicating neither preference for nor against mainstream culture.

Telesford et al. (2013) also compared the cluster groups in their study on personal rejection sensitivity (Downey & Feldman, 1996) and race-based rejection sensitivity (Mendoza-Denton, Downey, Purdie, Davis, & Pietrzak, 2002). Personal-rejection sensitivity refers to anxiety about being rejected on personal characteristics that are unique to the individual, whereas race-based rejection sensitivity refers to anxiety about being rejected on the basis of one's race, and racial identity seems to play a role in both personal and race-based rejection sensitivity. Participants in the Multiculturalist cluster—that is, those comfortable with self and with others—had lower personal rejection sensitivity than all the other groups except the Low Race Salience group; and the Conflicted group—those unhappy with self and with others—reported the highest personal rejection sensitivity. The Conflicted and Negative Race Salience groups also reported higher race-based rejection sensitivity than did the Low Race Salience group. To the extent that culture informs our attitudes toward other groups (see previous definitions of culture), these findings suggest that racial identity profiles are equivalent to cultural attitudes, thus supporting the case made in the title of this chapter.

Ethnic Identity Models

Unlike racial identity, which has been examined primarily in African Americans and European Americans, ethnic identity has been studied across many racial and ethnic groups in the United States and, perhaps not surprisingly, yields results that are similar to those found with racial identity. Much like race and racial identity, the salience of ethnicity and ethnic identity is greater in multiethnic societies (Phinney, 1990, 1996) because it is largely determined by one's sense of ingroup belonging in relation to other groups and often in response to discriminatory treatment as a result of one's ethnicity (Ghuman, 1998). Moreover, concerns can also be raised about whether one is a *genuine* member of one's ethnic group (Hunt, Moloney, & Evans, 2011).

Using a variable-centered perspective, Knight, Cota, and Bernal (1993) used a structural equation model to examine the correlates of ethnic identity in a sample of 59 Mexican-American children. Knight et al. showed that mothers' ethnic preferences and ethnic knowledge informed their teaching about ethnic culture, which predicted children's ethnic identity (consisting of ethnic knowledge, ethnic self-identification, and ethnic preferences. Children's ethnic identity in turn predicted children's resource preference allocations (individualistic, competitive, or cooperative). I contend that teaching about one ethnic heritage is directly equivalent to racial socialization in the literature on African Americans and serves the same function of preparing the child to live in a multicultural context in which discrimination is an important concern.

Like racial identity, ethnic identity scores have been used across the lifespan and are related to psychological well-being and cultural constructs (e.g., Chae & Foley, 2010; Cuéllar, Nyberg, Maldonado, & Roberts, 1997). I now discuss a developmental and an attitudinal ethnic identity model.

Phinney's Ethnic Identity Model

One of the most well-known models of ethnic identity in the literature was proposed by Phinney (1989, 1992; Phinney & Ong, 2007). In 1989, Phinney attempted to show that the ethnic identity in adolescence could be interpreted using Marcia's (1966) status framework. Based on interviews of 91 American-born adolescents aged 15–17 from different racial-ethnic backgrounds, Phinney concluded that 50 percent of the ethnic minority adolescents were in foreclosure or diffusion (no distinction could be reliably made), 25 percent were in moratorium, and 25 percent were achieved; they were unable to classify European American adolescents. In 1992, Phinney developed the MEIM to assess ethnic identity exploration and ethnic identity commitment in adolescents so that they could be classified into the four statuses on the basis of questionnaire scores rather than interviews.

Several studies (e.g., Phinney, 1992, Worrell, 2000; Worrell, Conyers, Mpofu, & Vandiver, 2006) indicated that the ethnic identity scores on the MEIM did not yield two factors. After several subsequent examinations of MEIM scores (e.g., Lee & Yoo, 2004; Roberts et al., 1999; Spencer, Icard, Harachi, Catalano, & Oxford, 2000; Yancey, Aneshensel, & Driscoll, 2001) failed to yield two consistent factors, Phinney and Ong (2007) developed a revised version of the MEIM. Psychometric analyses supported a two-factor structure for the MEIM-R—Exploration and Commitment—although the utility of this instrument's scores in yielding the four ethnic identity statuses has not yet been confirmed.

In 2006, Yip, Seaton, and Sellers used three exploration items and two commitment items from the MEIM in a sample consisting of adolescent, emerging adults, and adults. Using cluster analysis, they classified participants into the four statuses: Diffused, Foreclosed, Moratorium, and Achieved. The proportions of adolescents (6 percent, 25 percent, 42 percent, and 27 percent, respectively), emerging adults (6 percent, 20 percent, 27 percent, and 47 percent, respectively), and adults (4 percent, 16 percent, 24 percent, and 56 percent, respectively) indicated that adolescents were more likely to be in moratorium and that emerging adults and adults were more likely to be achieved; additionally, the percentages in foreclosure and moratorium decrease from adolescence to adulthood whereas the percentages who are achieved increase. These results provide the strongest support to date for a developmental conceptualization of ethnic identity, but they also need to be interpreted cautiously for several reasons. First, they used items from subscales rather than entire subscales. Second, no rigorous replications have yet emerged, even with the MEIM-R.

Finally, Meeus (2010) reviewed the longitudinal research on personal and ethnic identity. He concluded, based on the eight longitudinal studies of ethnic identity in the literature, that although there is evidence in some studies that ethnic identity progresses during adolescence, "there is no evidence for a dramatic ethnic identity crisis in adolescence" (Meeus, 2010, p. 84; see also Quintana, 2007).

The Acculturation Model of Ethnic Identity

Although there is limited evidence in support of ethnic identity development during adolescence, there is stronger evidence in support of another model of ethnic identity. Berry, Trimble, and Olmedo (1986) proposed a two-dimensional model of acculturation that allows for a person-centered approach to looking at ethnic identity. One dimension consists of identification with one's ethnic group (weak vs. strong sense of belonging) and the other is identification with majority culture (weak vs. strong). This model results in a two-by-two structure with four possibilities: Alienated (weak ethnic and weak majority group identification), Assimilated (weak ethnic and strong majority group identification), Separatist (strong ethnic and weak majority group identification), and Integrated (strong identification with both ethnic and majority group). Importantly, this is not a developmental status model. Rather, these groups parallel some of the multidimensional profiles that have been found with racial identity attitudes: the Multiculturalist profile based on the CRIS is similar to Berry et al.'s Integrated group, and the Assimilated profile is similar to Berry et al.'s (1986) group of the same name.

Berry, Phinney, Sam, and Vedder (2006) examined this model in a sample of more than 5,000 adolescents in 13 countries. Importantly, the samples subsumed youth of different ethnic-racial backgrounds. Berry et al. found four profiles—Integrated, National, Ethnic, and Diffuse—across the different nations and individuals, with different profiles differing in psychological and sociocultural adaptation outcomes. Adolescents with Integrated (or Bicultural) and National profiles perceived less discrimination than their peers with Ethnic and Diffuse profiles, with the Integrated profile perceiving the least discrimination and the Diffuse profile perceiving the most. In general, adolescents with Integrated profiles reported the healthiest psychological and sociocultural adaptation, and youth with Diffuse profiles reported the worst outcomes.

Similar results have been reported for Chinese Canadians (Chia & Costigan, 2006), Albanian immigrants in Greece (Pavlopoulos et al., 2009), and Brazilian immigrants to Japan (Scottham & Dias, 2010). Some other work suggests that ethnic identity scores and other group orientation scores from the MEIM can be used to form profiles that predict differences in attitudes toward school in ethnic groups like Latinos and African Americans (e.g., Worrell, White, & Andretta, 2010). Thus, as with studies of racial identity in African Americans, studies of ethnic identity with many different cultural groups indicate that this construct is intertwined with culture and cultural adaptation.

Future Directions

Racial and ethnic identity have also been discussed and examined in most other racial/ethnic groups in the United States, including Asian Americans (Chen, LePhuoc, Guzmán, Rude, & Dodd, 2006; Kim, 2001); European Americans (Helms, 1990*e*; Puchner, Szabo, & Roseboro, 2012), Latinos (Ferdman & Gallegus, 2001), Native Americans (Horse, 2001; Watson, 2009), and multiracial individuals (Rockquemore & Brunsma, 2002; Wijeyesinghe, 2001). Several aspects of these literatures support the integration of culture, race/racial identity, and ethnicity/ethnic identity while also highlighting the need for future research in this area.

First, many researchers are now conceptualizing the construct that they are discussing as race/ethnicity rather than just race *or* ethnicity across a variety of disciplines, including the health fields (e.g., Des Jarlais, McCarty, Vega, & Bramson, 2013; Oyserman, Kemmelmeier, Fryberg, Brosh, & Hart-Johnson, 2003; Shernock & Russell, 2012). As French, Coleman, and DiLorenzo (2013, p. 2), noted, "although the terms *racial* and *ethnic* hold different meanings, research shows that parents' efforts to teach their children about group membership cuts across racial and ethnic domains." I contend that the increasingly frequent use of the *combined* term, that is, racial/ethnic, as the construct being assessed speaks to the fact that race and ethnicity are now being used interchangeably in academic discourse. Nonetheless, to support this usage and the position taken in this chapter, researchers must clearly define what they mean by race/ethnicity in their studies and must use instruments that are intended to get at the combined construct that they are measuring.

Second, several researchers are now using subscales from instruments operationalizing larger theoretical models or items from validated subscales. For the field to move forward in terms of both status and attitudinal research, it will be important to use instruments with validated scores and instruments' scores as they have been validated. Without this consistency, generalizing findings and comparing results across studies will be difficult at best and often not possible.

Third, researchers are using ethnic identity scales to measure racial identity and racial identity scales to measure ethnic identity (e.g., Baden, 2002; Hyers, 2001). For example, there are studies in the literature in which the MEIM has been used to assess racial identity and the MIBI to assess ethnic identity in US ethnic groups other than African Americans, the group in which MIBI scores were validated. Although researchers typically report internal consistency estimates, they seldom report any type of validity information for the scores. Moreover, since the MEIM and MIBI are both based on specific theoretical models, it is not clear what constructs are being measured when they are used interchangeably. However, all of these studies provide support in favor of one of this chapter's theses—that is, that even academics who study cultural identities are now viewing racial and ethnic identities as interchangeable.

In a very recent development, the CRIS (Vandiver et al., 2000), which operationalizes NT-E, has been modified to be used with all racial and ethnic groups in the United States and in international contexts (Worrell, 2012). Preliminary examinations of recently collected data indicate that scores on the Assimilation, Miseducation, Self-Hatred, Anti-Dominant, Ethnocentricity, and Multiculturalist subscales indicate that they are reliable in samples of African-American, Asian-American, European-American, Latino,

Mixed, and Native-American adolescents, as well as samples of Asian, Maori, Pakeha (European descent), Pasifika, and Other adolescents in New Zealand. Also, Worrell (2012) showed that the profile of means for the six subscales were quite similar across samples of African Americans assessed with the CRIS and European Americans and Latinos assessed with the modified measure. If and when this instrument enters the literature, it will allow researchers to examine a wider range of ethnic identity attitudes across racial/ethnic/cultural groups with greater nuance than the MEIM allows, as well as ethnic identity attitudinal profiles, given the increased range of attitudes being assessed.

Conclusion

The basic argument in this chapter is as follows: culture = ethnicity = ethnic identity = race = racial identity. As the definitions in Table 16.1 indicate and many researchers concede, it is relatively easy to see the interchangeability of culture and ethnicity. However, those who argue that race is essentially different are arguing for race as a biological rather than a psychological construct. When one concedes that race is a social construction, its affinity with culture and ethnicity becomes much more apparent. Moving from race and ethnicity to racial and ethnic identity is more difficult only if one assumes that racial and ethnic identity are developmental constructs. If one accepts these constructs as attitudes that are developed in the crucible of cultural socialization, their similarities become more apparent. It is also important to note that there may be two separate strands of ethnic identity—one that follows the four-status model and one that is multidimensional—with the former based on the exploration and commitment processes and the latter consisting of the multiple attitudes measured by instruments such as the CRIS and the MIBI (e.g., assimilation, Afrocentricity, centrality, humanism, miseducation, multiculturalism, nationalism, oppressed minority, public and private regard, self-hatred, and so on).

What are the implications of this chapter's claims for researchers studying identity, race, ethnicity, and culture? In general, the most important outcome of this claim is that researchers need to be more cognizant of the intertwining of these constructs that we call by different names and be mindful in how we operationalize the constructs that we are studying. Philogène (2004, p. 3) observed that, "the issue of race, a dominant cultural marker guiding people's thinking and actions, tells us a lot about America."

However, as America becomes increasingly diverse, it is also becoming apparent that many of the debates that were initially characterized in terms of African Americans versus European Americans are really debates about cultural differences more broadly that apply to other racial and ethnic groups in the United States, as well as to racial and ethnic groups in other societies that are becoming more diverse (e.g., New Zealand).

In the aftermath of Trayvon Martin's shooting on February 26, 2012, there have been many discussions of what it means to be a young Black male in America. These discussions are as much cultural and ethnic markers as they are about race, and the talks that African-American, Latino, and other ethnic minority parents are having with their sons are about the cultural significance of the dark phenotype in America. According to Fischer (2007, p. 7), "culture is relational, it is elsewhere, it is in passage, it is where meaning is woven and renewed." And these meanings involve race and ethnicity and their psychological manifestations, racial and ethnic identity. It is not possible to answer the question "what is culture?" without invoking answers that draw on and involve race and ethnicity intimately. Similarly, it is naïve to think that one can study race, ethnicity, and racial and ethnic identity as variables that are independent of culture and the cultural context.

References

Adams, G. R., Shea, J. A., & Fitch, S. A. (1979). Toward the development of an objective assessment of ego-identity status. *Journal of Youth and Adolescence, 8*, 223–237. doi:10.1007/BF02087622

Altman, S. (1997). *The encyclopedia of African-American heritage*. New York, NY: Facts on File.

American Anthropological Association. (1998). AAA statement on race. *American Anthropologist, 100*, 712–713.

Araújo, B. Y., & Borrell, L. N. (2006). Understanding the link between discrimination, mental health outcomes, and life chances among Latinos. *Hispanic Journal of Behavioral Sciences, 28*, 245–266. doi:10.1177/0739986305285825

Arce, C. A. (1981). A reconsideration of Chicano culture and identity. *Daedalus, 110*, 177–192.

Atkinson, D. R. (2004). *Counseling American minorities* (6th ed.). Boston, MA: McGraw-Hill.

Atkinson, D. R. Morten, G., & Sue, D. W. (Eds.). (1989). *Counseling American minorities: A cross-cultural perspective*. (3rd ed.). Dubuque, IA: Brown.

Aud, A., Fox, M. A., & KewalRamani, A. (2010). *Status and trends in the education of racial and ethnic groups* (NCES 2010–015). Washington, DC: US Department of Education, National Center for Education Statistics.

Baden, A. L. (2002). The psychological adjustment of transracial adoptees: An application of the cultural-racial identity model. *Journal of Social Distress and the Homeless, 11*, 167–191. doi:10.1023/A:1014316018637

Berry, J., Phinney, J. S., Sam, D. L., & Vedder, P. (2006). Immigrant youth: Acculturation, identity, and adaptation. *Applied Psychology: An International Review, 55,* 302–333. doi:10.1111/j.1464-0597.2006.00256.x

Berry, J., Trimble, J., & Olmedo, E. (1986). Assessment of acculturation. In W. Lonner & J. Berry (Eds.), *Field methods in cross-cultural research* (pp. 291–324). Newbury Park, CA: Sage.

Betancourt, H., & Lopez, S. R. (1993). The study of culture, ethnicity, and race in American psychology. *American Psychologist, 48,* 629–637. doi:10.1037/0003-066X.48.6.629

Boas, F. (1912). Changes in the bodily form of descendants of immigrants. *American Anthropologist, 14,* 530–562.

Bowman, N. A. (2009). College diversity courses and cognitive development among students from privileged and marginalized groups. *Journal of Diversity in Higher Education, 2,* 182–194. doi:10.1037/a0016639

Bryant, W. E. (2011). Internalized racism's association with African American male youth's propensity for violence. *Journal of Black Studies, 42,* 690–707. doi:10.1177/0021934710393243

Carter, R. T. (1991). Racial identity attitudes and psychological functioning. *Journal of Multicultural Counseling and Development, 19,* 105–114. doi:10.1002/j.2161-1912.1991.tb00547.x

Casey-Cannon, S. L. Coleman, H; L. K., Knudtson, L. F., & Velazquez, C. C. (2011). Three ethnic and racial identity measures: Concurrent and divergent validity for diverse adolescents. *Identity: An International Journal of Theory and Research, 11,* 64–91. doi:10.1080/15283488.2011.540739

Cass, V. C. (1979). Homosexual identity formation: A theoretical model. *Journal of Homosexuality, 4,* 219–235. doi:10.1300/J082v04n03_01

Cass, V. C. (1984). Homosexual identity formation: Testing a theoretical model. *Journal of Sex Research, 20,* 143–167. doi:10.1080/00224498409551214

Chae, M. H., & Foley, P. F. (2010). Relationship of ethnic identity, acculturation, and psychological well-being among Chinese, Japanese, and Korean Americans. *Journal of Counseling Psychology, 88,* 466–476. doi:10.1002/j.1556–6678.2010.tb00047.x

Chapman, C., Laird, J., Ifill, N., & KewalRamani, A. (2011). *Trends in high school dropout and completion rates in the United States: 1972–2009* (NCES 2012-006). Washington DC: US Department of Education, National Center for Educational Statistics.

Chávez, N. R., & French, S. E. (2007). Ethnicity-related stressors and mental health in Latino Americans: The moderating role of parental racial socialization. *Journal of Applied Social Psychology, 37,* 1974–1998. doi:10.1111/j.1559-1816.2007.00246.x

Chavez-Korell, S., & Vandiver, B. J. (2012). Are CRIS cluster patterns differentially associated with African American enculturation and social distance? *The Counseling Psychologist, 40,* 755–788. doi:10.1177/0011000011418839

Chen, G. A., LePhuoc, P., Guzmán, M. R., Rude, S. S., & Dodd, B. G. (2006). Exploring Asian American racial identity. *Cultural Diversity and Ethnic Minority Psychology, 12,* 461–476. doi:10.1037/1099-9809.12.3.461

Chia, A-L., & Costigan, C. L. (2006). A person-centered approach to identifying acculturation groups among Chinese Canadians. *International Journal of Psychology, 41,* 397–412. doi:10.1080/00207590500412227

Clark, K. B., & Clark, M. P. (1947). Racial identification and preference in Negro children. In T. M. Newcomb & E. L. Hartley (Eds.), *Readings in social psychology* (pp. 169–178). New York, NY: Holt.

Clark, K. B., & Clark, M. P. (1950). Emotional factors in racial identification and preference in Negro children. *Journal of Negro Education, 19,* 341–350. doi:10.2307/2966491

Coleman, M. N. (2008). Ethnicity. In F. T. L. Leong, M. G. Constantine, & R. L. Worthington (Eds.), *Encyclopedia of counseling* (Vol. 3, pp. 1137–1139). Los Angeles, CA: Sage.

Copeland, B. (2006). *Not a genuine Black man: My life as an outsider.* San Francisco, CA: MacAdam/Cage.

Cross, W. E. Jr. (1971). The Negro-to-Black conversion experience. *Black World, 20*(9), 13–27.

Cross, W. E., Jr. (1991). *Shades of Black: Diversity in African-American identity.* Philadelphia, PA: Temple University Press.

Cross, W. E., Jr., & Fhagen-Smith, P. E. (2001). Patterns of African American identity development: A life-span perspective. In C. L. Wijeyesinghe & B. W. Jackson (Eds.), *New perspectives on racial identity development: A theoretical and practical anthology.* (pp. 243–270). New York, NY: New York University Press.

Cross, W. E., Jr., & Vandiver, B. J. (2001). Nigrescence theory and measurement: Introducing the Cross Racial Identity Scale (CRIS). In J. G. Ponterotto, J. M. Casas, L. A. Suzuki, & C. M. Alexander (Eds.), *Handbook of multicultural counseling* (2nd. ed., pp. 371–393). Thousand Oaks, CA: Sage.

Cuéllar, I., Nyberg, B., Maldonado, R. E., & Roberts, R. E. (1997). Ethnic identity and acculturation in a young adult Mexican-origin population. *Journal of Community Psychology, 25,* 535–549. doi:10.1002/(SICI)1520–6629(199711)25:6

Des Jarlais, D. C., McCarty, D., Vega, W. A., & Bramson, H. (2013). HIV infection among people who inject drugs: The challenge of racial/ethnic disparities. *American Psychologist, 68,* 274–285. doi:10.1037/a0032745

DeVries, M., & Golon, A. S. (2011). Making education relevant for gifted Native Americans: Teaching to their learning style. In J. A. Castellano & A. D. Frazier (Eds.), *Special populations in gifted education: Understanding our most able students from diverse backgrounds* (pp. 47–72). Waco, TX: Prufrock.

Downey, G., & Feldman, S. I. (1996). Implications of rejection sensitivity for intimate relationships. *Journal of Personality and Social Psychology, 70,* 1327–1343. doi:10.1037/0022-3514.70.6.1327

Downing, N. E., & Roush, K. L. (1985). From passive acceptance to active commitment: A model of feminist identity development for women. *The Counseling Psychologist, 13,* 695–709. doi:10.1177/0011000085134013

Erikson, E. H. (1950). *Childhood and society.* New York, NY: W. W. Norton & Co.

Erikson, E. H. (1968). *Identity, youth and crisis.* New York, NY: W. W. Norton & Co.

Ferdman, B. M., & Gallegos, P. I. (2001). Racial identity development and Latinos in the United States In C. L. Wijeyesinghe, & B. W. Jackson, III (Eds.), *New perspectives on racial identity development: A theoretical and practical anthology* (pp. 32–66). New York, NY: New York University Press.

Fischer, M. M. J. (2007). Culture and cultural analysis as experimental systems. *Cultural Anthropology, 22*, 1–65. doi:10.1525/can.2007.22.1.1

French, S. E., Coleman, B. R., & DiLorenzo, M. L. (2013). Linking racial identity, ethnic identity, and racial-ethnic socialization: A tale of three race-ethnicities. *Identity: An International Journal of Theory and Research, 13*, 1–45. doi:10.1080/15283488.2012.747438

Frisby, C. L. (1992). Issues and problems in the influence of culture on the psychoeducational needs of African-American children. *School Psychology Review, 21*, 532–551.

Frisby, C. L. (1993). One giant step backward: Myths of Black cultural learning styles. *School Psychology Review, 22*, 535–557.

Fuligni, A. F., & Hardway, C. (2004). Preparing diverse adolescents for the transition to adulthood. *The Future of Children 14*(2), 99–119. Retrieved from http://futureofchildren.org/futureofchildren/publications/docs/14_02_06.pdf

Ghuman, P. A. S. (1998). Ethnic identity and acculturation of South Asian adolescents: A British perspective. *International Journal of Adolescence and Youth, 7*, 227–247. doi:10.1080/02673843.1998.9747826

Gillespie, A., Howarth, C. A., & Cornish, F. (2012). Four problems for researchers using social categories. *Culture & Psychology, 18*, 391–402. doi:10.1177/1354067X12446236

Gotanda, N. (2011). The racialization of Islam in American law. *Annals of the American Academy of Political and Social Science, 637*, 184–195. doi:10.1177/0002716211408525

Grotevant, H. D., & Adams, G. R. (1984). Development of an objective measure to assess ego-identity in adolescence: Validation and replication. *Journal of Youth and Adolescence, 13*, 419–438. doi:10.1007/BF02088639

Grotevant, H. D., & Cooper, C. R. (1980). *Assessing adolescent identity in the areas of occupation, religion, politics, friendships, dating, and sex roles: Manual for the administration and coding of the interview*. Washington, DC: American Psychological Association.

Hale-Benson, J. (1986). *Black children: Their roots, culture, and learning styles* (Rev. ed.). Baltimore, MD: Johns Hopkins University Press.

Helms, J. E. (1990a). *Black and White racial identity: Theory, research and practice*. New York, NY: Greenwood.

Helms, J. E. (1990b). Introduction: Review of racial identity terminology. In J. E. Helms (Ed.), *Black and White racial identity: Theory, research and practice* (pp. 3–8). New York, NY: Greenwood.

Helms, J. E. (1990c). The measurement of Black racial identity attitudes. In J. E. Helms (Ed.), *Black and White racial identity: Theory, research and practice* (pp. 34–47). New York, NY: Greenwood.

Helms, J. E. (1990d). An overview of Black racial identity theory. In J. E. Helms (Ed.), *Black and White racial identity: Theory, research and practice* (pp. 9–32). New York, NY: Greenwood.

Helms, J. E. (1990e). Toward a model of White racial identity development. In J. E. Helms (Ed.), *Black and White racial identity: Theory, research and practice* (pp. 49–66). New York, NY: Greenwood.

Helms, J. E., & Talleyrand, R. M. (1997). Race is not ethnicity. *American Psychologist, 52*, 1246–1247. doi:10.1037/0003-066X.52.11.1246

Hofstede, G. (2001). *Culture's consequences: Comparing values, behaviors, institutions, and organizations across nations*. Thousand Oaks, CA: Sage.

Horse, P. G. (2001). Reflections on American Indian identity. In C. L. Wijeyesinghe, & B. W. Jackson, III (Eds.), *New perspectives on racial identity development: A theoretical and practical anthology* (pp. 91–107). New York, NY: New York University Press.

Hughes, D. (2003). Correlates of African American and Latino Parents' messages to children about ethnicity and race: A comparative study of racial socialization. *American Journal of Community Psychology, 31*, 15–33. doi:10.1023/A.1023066418688

Hunt, G., Moloney, M., & Evans, K. (2011). "How Asian am I?": Asian American youth cultures, drug use, and ethnic identity. *Youth & Society, 43*, 2740304. doi:10.1177/0044118X10364044

Hurd, N. M., Sellers, R. M., Cogburn, C. D., Butler-Barnes, S. T., & Zimmerman, M. A. (2013). Racial identity and depressive symptoms among Black emerging adults: The moderating effects of neighborhood racial composition. *Developmental Psychology, 49*, 938–950. doi:10.1037/a0028826

Hyers, L. L. (2001). A secondary survey analysis study of African American ethnic identity orientations in two national samples. *Journal of Black Psychology, 27*, 139–171. doi:10.1177/0095798401027002001

Jahoda, G. (2012). Critical reflections on some recent definitions of "culture." *Culture & Psychology, 18*, 289–303. doi:10.1177/1354067X12446229

Kim, J. (1981). *Processes of Asian-American identity development: A study of Japanese American women's perceptions of their struggle to achieve positive identities as Americans of Asian ancestry*. Dissertation Abstracts International, 42(4-A), 1551.

Kim J. (2001). Asian American identity development theory. In C. L. Wijeyesinghe, & B. W. Jackson, III (Eds.), *New perspectives on racial identity development: A theoretical and practical anthology* (pp. 67–90). New York, NY: New York University Press.

King, E. W. (2002). Ethnicity. In D. L. Levinson, P. W. Cookson, Jr., & A. R. Sadowski (Eds.), *Education and sociology: An encyclopedia* (pp. 247–253). New York, NY: Routledge.

Knight, G. P., Cota, M. K., & Bernal, M. E. (1993). The socialization of cooperative, competitive, and individualistic preferences among Mexican-American children: The mediating role of ethnic identity. *Hispanic Journal of Behavioral Sciences, 15*, 291–309. doi:10.1177/07399863930153001

Kroger, J. (2007). *Identity development: Adolescence through adulthood* (2nd ed.). Thousand Oaks, CA: Sage.

Kroger, J., Martinussen, M., & Marcia, J. E. (2010). Identity status change during adolescence and young adulthood: A meta-analysis. *Journal of Adolescence, 33*, 683–698. doi:10.1016/j.adolescence.2009.11.002

Lapchick, R. (with Costa, P., Sherrod, T., & Anjorin, R.). (2012a). *The 2012 racial and gender report card: National Football League*. Retrieved from http://www.tidesport.org/RGRC/2012/2012_NFL_RGRC.pdf

Lapchick, R. (with Lecky, A., & Trigg, A.). (2012b). *The 2012 racial and gender report card: National Basketball Association*. Retrieved from http://www.tidesport.org/RGRC/2012/2012_NBA_RGRC[1].pdf

Lee, R. M., & Yoo, H. C. (2004). Structure and measurement of ethnic identity for Asian American college students. *Journal of Counseling Psychology, 51*, 263–269. doi:10.1037/0022-0167.51.2.263

Leong, F. T. L., & Gupta, A. (2007). Career development and vocational behaviors of Asian Americans. In F. T. L. Leong,

A. G. Inman, A. Ebreo, L. H. Yang, L. Kinoshita, & M. Fu (Eds.), *Handbook of Asian American psychology* (2nd ed.; pp. 159–178). Thousand Oaks, CA: Sage.

Marcia, J. E. (1966). Development and validation of ego-identity status. *Journal of Personality and Social Psychology, 3,* 551–558. doi:10.1037/h0023281

McWhorter, J. (2000). *Losing the race: Self-sabotage in Black America.* New York, NY: HarperCollins.

McWhorter, J. (2003a). *Authentically Black: Essays for the silent Black majority.* New York, NY: Gotham Books.

McWhorter, J. (2003b). Preface. In J. McWhorter (Ed.), *Authentically Black: Essays for the silent Black majority.* New York, NY: Gotham Books.

Meeus, W. (2010). The study of adolescent identity formation 2000–2010. A review of longitudinal research. *Journal of Research on Adolescence, 21,* 75–94. doi:10.1111/j.1532-7795.2010.00716.x

Mendoza-Denton, R., Downey, G., Purdie, V. J., Davis, A., & Pietrzak, J. (2002). Sensitivity to status-based rejection: Implications for African American college students' college experience. *Journal of Personality and Social Psychology, 83,* 896–918. doi:10.1037/0022-3514.83.4.896

Mio, J. S., Nagata, D. K., Tsai, A. H., & Tewari, N. (2007). Racism against Asian/Pacific Island Americans. In F. T. L. Leong, A. G. Inman, A. Ebreo, L. H. Yang, L. Kinoshita, & M. Fu (Eds.), *Handbook of Asian American psychology* (2nd ed.; pp. 341–361). Thousand Oaks, CA: Sage.

Morgan, H. (1995). *Historical perspectives on the education of Black children.* Westport, CT: Praeger.

Neil, D. M. (2003). *Racial integration history and ego-identity status: Predicting student racial attitudes* (Doctoral dissertation). Available from ProQuest Dissertations and Theses database. (UMI No. 3064273)

Ogbu, J. U., & Simons, H. D. (1998). Voluntary and involuntary minorities: A cultural-ecological theory of school performance with some implications for education. *Anthropology & Education Quarterly, 29,* 155–188.

Oyserman, D., Kemmelmeier, M., Fryberg, S., Brosh, H., & Hart-Johnson, T. (2003). Racial-ethnic self-schemas. *Social Psychology Quarterly, 66,* 333–347. doi:10.2307/1519833

Parham, T. A., & Helms, J. E. (1981). The influence of Black students' racial identity attitudes on preference for counselor's race. *Journal of Counseling Psychology, 28,* 250–258. doi:10.1037/0022-0167.28.3.250

Parham, T. A., & Helms, J. E. (1985). The influence of Black students' racial identity attitudes on preference for counselor's race. *Journal of Counseling Psychology, 32,* 431–440. doi:10.1037/0022-0167.32.3.431

Parham, T. A., & Williams, P. T. (1993). The relationship of demographic background variables to racial identity attitudes. *Journal of Black Psychology, 19,* 7–24. doi:10.1177/00957984930191002

Pavlopoulos, V., Dalla, M., Kalogirou, S. Theodorou, R., Markoussi, D., & Motti-Stefanid, F. (2009). Acculturation and school adjustment of immigrant adolescents. *Psychology: The Journal of the Hellenic Psychological Society, 16,* 400–421.

Philogène, G. (2004). Introduction: Race as a defining feature of American culture. In G. Philogène (Ed.), *Racial identity in context: The legacy of Kenneth B. Clark* (pp. 3–11). Washington, DC: American Psychological Association.

Phinney, J. S. (1989). Stages of ethnic identity in minority group adolescence. *The Journal of Early Adolescence, 9,* 34–49. doi:10.1177/0272431689091004

Phinney, J. S. (1990). Ethnic identity in American adolescents and adults: Review of research. *Psychological Bulletin, 108,* 499–514. doi:10.1037/0033-2909.108.3.499

Phinney, J. S. (1992). The Multigroup Ethnic Identity Measure: A new scale for use with diverse groups. *Journal of Adolescent Research, 7,* 56–176. doi:10.1177/074355489272003

Phinney, J. S. (1996). When we talk about American ethnic groups, what do we mean? *American Psychologist, 51,* 918–927. doi:10.1037//0003-066X.51.9.918

Phinney, J. S., DuPont, S.,Espinosa, C.,Revill, J., & Sanders, K. (1994). Ethnic identity and American identification among ethnic minority youths. In A. Bouvy, F. J. R. van de Vijer, P. Boski, & P. Schmitz (Eds.), *Journeys into cross-cultural psychology* (pp. 167–183). Berwyn, PA: Swets & Zeitlinger.

Phinney, J. S., & Ong, A. D. (2007). Conceptualization and measurement of ethnic identity: Current status and future directions. *Journal of Counseling Psychology, 54,* 271–281. doi:10.1037/0022-0167.54.3.271

Piaget, J. (1962). The stages of intellectual development of the child. *Bulletin of the Menninger Clinic, 26,* 120–128.

Plummer, D. L. (1996). Black racial identity attitudes and stages of the life span: An exploratory investigation. *Journal of Black Psychology, 22,* 169–181. doi:10.1177/00957984960222003

Psaltis, C. (2012). Culture and social representations: A continuing dialogue in search for heterogeneity in social developmental psychology. *Culture & Psychology, 18,* 375–390. doi:10.1177/1354067X12446233

Puchner, L., Szabo, Z., & Roseboro, D. L. (2012). The short-term effect of a race-related course on racial identity of White students. *Teaching in Higher Education, 17,* 399–410. doi:10.1080/13562517.2011.641003

Quintana, S. M. (2007). Racial and ethnic identity: Developmental perspectives and research. *Journal of Counseling Psychology, 54,* 259–270. doi:10.1037/0022-0167.54.3.259

Quijada, P. D. (2008). Culture. In N. J. Salkind & K. Rasmussen (Eds.), *Encyclopedia of educational psychology* (Vol. 1, pp. 223–228). Los Angeles, CA: Sage.

Reber, A. S. (1985). *The Penguin dictionary of psychology.* New York, NY: Penguin.

Rivas-Drake, D., Hughes, D., & Way, N. (2009). A preliminary analysis of associations among ethnic-racial socialization, ethnic discrimination, and ethnic identity among urban sixth graders. *Journal of Research on Adolescence, 19,* 558–584. doi:10.1111/j.1532-7795.2009.00607.x

Roberts, R. E., Phinney, J. S., Masse, L. C., Chen, Y. R., Roberts, C. R., & Romero, A. (1999). The structure of ethnic identity of young adolescents from diverse ethnocultural groups. *The Journal of Early Adolescence, 19,* 301–322. doi:10.1177/0272431699019003001

Rockquemore, K. A., & Brunsma, D. L. (2002). *Beyond Black: Biracial identity in America.* Thousand Oaks, CA: Sage.

Scottham, K. M., & Dias, R. H. (2010). Acculturative strategies and the psychological adaptation of Brazilian migrants to Japan. *Identity: An International Journal of Theory and Research, 10,* 284–303. doi:10.1080/15283488.2010.523587

Scottham, K. M., Sellers, R. M., & Nugyên, H. X. (2008). A measure of racial identity in African American adolescents: The development of the Multidimensional Inventory of Black Identity—Teen. *Cultural Diversity and Ethnic Minority Psychology, 14,* 297–306. doi:10.1037/1099-9809.14.4.297

Sellers, R. M., Rowley, S. A. J., Chavous, T. M., Shelton, J. N., & Smith, M. A. (1997). Multidimensional Inventory of

Black Identity: A preliminary investigation of reliability and construct validity. *Journal of Personality and Social Psychology, 73*, 805–815. doi:10.1037/0022-3514.73.4.805

Sellers, R. M., Shelton, J. N., Cooke, D. Y., Chavous, T. M., Rowley, S. A., & Smith, M. A. (1998). A multidimensional model of racial identity: Assumptions findings, and future directions. In R. L. Jones (Ed.), *African American identity development* (pp. 275–302). Hampton, VA: Cobb & Henry Publishers.

Sellers, R. M., Smith, M. A., Shelton, J. N, Rowley, S. A., & Chavous, T. M. (1998). Multidimensional model of racial identity: A reconceptualization of African-American racial identity. *Personality and Social Psychology Review, 2*, 18–39. doi:10.1207/s15327957pspr0201_2

Shernock, S., & Russell, B. (2012). Gender and racial/ethnic differences in criminal justice decision making in intimate partner violence cases. *Partner Abuse 3*, 501–530. doi:10.1891/1946-6560.3.4.501

Simmons, D. D. (1970). Development of an objective measure of identity achievement status. *Journal of Projective Techniques and Personality Assessment, 34*, 241–244. doi:10.1080/0091651X.1970.10380242

Shih, M., Pittinsky, T. L., & Ambady, N. (1999). Stereotype susceptibility: Identity salience and shifts in quantitative performance. *Psychological Science, 10*, 80–83. doi:10.1111/1467–9280.00371

Smith, R. C. (2003). *Encyclopedia of African-American politics*. New York, NY: Facts on File.

Spencer, M. S., Icard, L. D., Harachi, T. W., Catalano, R. F., & Oxford, M. (2000). Ethnic identity among monoracial and multiracial early adolescents. *The Journal of Early Adolescence, 20*, 365–387. doi:10.1177/0272431600020004001

Steele, C. M. (1997). A threat in the air: How stereotypes shape intellectual identity and performance. *American Psychologist 52*, 613–629. doi:10.1037/0003-066X.52.6.613

Steele, C. M. (2010). *Whistling Vivaldi and other clues to how stereotypes affect us*. New York, NY: Norton.

Steele, C. M., & Aronson, J. (1995). Stereotype threat and the intellectual test performance of African Americans. *Journal of Personality and Social Psychology 69*, 797–811. doi:10.1037/0022-3514.69.5.797

Stone, J., Lynch, C. I., Sjomeling, M., & Darley, J. M. (1999). Stereotype threat effects on Black and White athletic performance. *Journal of Personality and Social Psychology, 77*, 1213–1227.

Street, J. C., Taha, F., Jones, A. D., Jones, K. A., Carr, E., Woods, A.,... Kaslow, N. J. (2012). Racial identity and reasons for living in African American female suicide attempters. *Cultural Diversity and Ethnic Minority Psychology, 18*, 416–423. doi:10.1037/a0029594

Tatum, B. D. (1997). *"Why are all the Black kids sitting together in the cafeteria" And other conversations about race*. New York, NY: Basic Books.

Telesford, J., Mendoza-Denton, R., & Worrell, F. C. (2013). Clusters of CRIS scores and psychological adjustment. *Cultural Diversity and Ethnic Minority Psychology, 19*, 86–91. doi:10.10.37/a0031254

Teo, T. (2009). Psychology without Caucasians. *Canadian Psychology, 50*, 91–97. doi:10.1037/a0014393

Thompson, C. E. (2008). Race. In F. T. L. Leong, M. G. Constantine, & R. L. Worthington (Eds.), *Encyclopedia of counseling* (Vol. 3, pp. 1279–1284). Los Angeles, CA: Sage.

Thompson, T. L., & Kiang, L. (2010). The model minority stereotype: Adolescent experiences and links with adjustment. *Asian American Journal of Psychology, 1*, 119–128. doi:10.1037/a0019966

Tran, A. G. T. T., & Lee, R. M. (2008). Ethnic identity. In F. T. L. Leong, M. G. Constantine, & R. L. Worthington (Eds.), *Encyclopedia of counseling* (Vol. 3, pp. 1135–1137). Los Angeles, CA: Sage.

Triandis, H. C. (1994). *Culture and social behavior*. New York, NY: McGraw-Hill.

US National Center for Health Statistics. Table 313. Homicide victims by race and sex: 1980 tp 2007. *Deaths: Final Data for 2007, 58*(19). Retrieved from http://www.census.gov/compendia/statab/2012/tables/12s0313.pdf

Valsiner, J., & Connolly, K. J. (2003). The nature of development: The continuing dialogue of processes and outcomes. In J. Valsiner & K. J. Connolly (Eds.), *Handbook of developmental psychology* (pp. ix–xviii). Thousand Oaks, CA: Sage.

VandenBos, G. R. (Ed.). (2007a). Culture. In *APA dictionary of psychology* (p. 250). Washington, DC: American Psychological Association.

VandenBos, G. R. (Ed.). (2007b). Ethnicity. In *APA dictionary of psychology* (p. 345). Washington, DC: American Psychological Association.

VandenBos, G. R. (Ed.). (2007c). Race. In *APA dictionary of psychology* (p. 765). Washington, DC: American Psychological Association.

VandenBos, G. R. (Ed.). (2007d). Racial identity. In *APA dictionary of psychology* (p. 765). Washington, DC: American Psychological Association.

Vandiver, B. J., Cross, W. E., Jr., Fhagen-Smith, P. E., Worrell, F. C., Swim, J. K., & Caldwell, L. D. (2000). *The Cross Racial Identity Scale*. State College, PA: Author.

Watson, J. C. (2009). Native American racial identity development and college adjustment at two-year institutions. *Journal of College Counseling, 12*, 125–136. doi:10.1002/j.2161-1882.2009.tb00110.x

Whittaker, V. A., & Neville, H. A. (2010). Examining the relation between racial identity attitude clusters and psychological health outcomes in African American college students. *Journal of Black Psychology, 36*, 383–409. doi:10.1177/0095798409353757

Wijeyesinghe, C. L. (2001). Racial identity in multiracial people: An alternative paradigm. In C. L. Wijeyesinghe, & B. W. Jackson, III (Eds.), *New perspectives on racial identity development: A theoretical and practical anthology* (pp. 129–152). New York, NY: New York University Press.

Worrell, F. C. (2000). A validity study of scores on the Multigroup Ethnic Identity Measure based on a sample of academically talented adolescents. *Educational and Psychological Measurement, 60*, 439–447. doi:10.1177/00131640021970646

Worrell, F. C. (2005). Cultural variation within American families of African descent. In C. L. Frisby & C. R. Reynolds (Eds.), *Comprehensive handbook of multicultural school psychology* (pp. 137–172). Hoboken, NJ: Wiley.

Worrell, F. C. (2008a). Cross, William E., Jr. In F. T. L. Leong (Series Ed.) & M. G. Constantine & R. L. Worthington (Vol. Eds.), *Encyclopedia of counseling. Volume 3: Cross-cultural counseling* (pp. 1078–1080). Thousand Oaks, CA: Sage Publications.

Worrell, F. C. (2008b). Nigrescence attitudes in adolescence, emerging adulthood, and adulthood. *Journal of Black Psychology, 34*, 156–178. doi:10.1177/0095798408315118

Worrell, F. C. (2011, February). *Are cultural identities developmental? Perspectives on racial and ethnic identity*. Paper presented at the Institute for Human Development, University of California, Berkeley, CA.

Worrell, F. C. (2012). Forty years of Cross' nigrescence theory: From stages to profiles, from African Americans to all Americans. In J. M. Sullivan & A. M. Esmail (Eds.), *African American identity: Racial and cultural dimensions of the Black experience* (pp. 3–28) Lanham, MD: Lexington Books.

Worrell, F. C., Conyers, L. M., Mpofu, E., & Vandiver, B. J. (2006). Multigroup Ethnic Identity Measure (MEIM) scores in a sample of adolescents from Zimbabwe. *Identity: An International Journal of Theory and Research, 6*, 35–59. doi:10.1207/s1532706xid0601_4

Worrell, F. C., Cross, W. E., Jr., & Vandiver, B. J. (2001). Nigrescence theory: Current status and challenges for the future. *Journal of Multicultural Counseling and Development, 29*, 201–213. doi:10.1002/j.2161-1912.2001.tb00517.x

Worrell, F. C., & Gardner-Kitt, D. L. (2006). The relationship between racial and ethnic identity in Black adolescents: The Cross Racial Identity Scale (CRIS) and the Multigroup Ethnic Identity Measure (MEIM). *Identity: An International Journal of Theory and Research, 6*, 293–315. doi:10.1207/s1532706xid0604_1

Worrell, F. C., Mendoza-Denton, R., Telesford, J., Simmons, C., & Martin, J. F. (2011). Cross Racial Identity Scale (CRIS) scores: Stability and relationships with psychological adjustment. *Journal of Personality Assessment, 93*, 637–648. doi:10.1080/00223891.2011.608762

Worrell, F. C., Vandiver, B. J., & Cross, W. E., Jr. (2004). *The Cross Racial Identity Scale: Technical manual – 2nd edition.* Berkeley, CA: Author.

Worrell, F. C., Vandiver, B. J., Schaefer, B. A., Cross, W. E., Jr., & Fhagen-Smith, P. E. (2006). Generalizing nigrescence profiles: A cluster analysis of Cross Racial Identity Scale (CRIS) scores in three independent samples. *The Counseling Psychologist, 34*, 519–547. doi:10.1177/0011000005278281

Worrell, F. C., White, L. H., & Andretta, J. R. (2010, October). *Cultural identities and academic achievement at Berkeley High School.* Paper presented at the Berkeley Unified School District Educational Research Symposium, Berkeley, CA.

Yancey, A. K., Aneshensel, C. S., & Driscoll, A. K. (2001). The assessment of ethnic identity in a diverse urban youth population. *Journal of Black Psychology, 27*, 190–208. doi:10.1177/0095798401027002003

Yip, T., Seaton, E. K., & Sellers, R. M. (2006). African American racial identity across the lifespan: Identity status, identity content, and depressive symptoms. *Child Development, 77*, 1504–1517. doi:10.1111/j.1467-8624.2006.00950.x

Zack, N. (2001). Philosophical aspects of the 'AAA statement on "race." *Anthropological Theory, 1*, 445–465. doi:10.1177/14634990122228836

CHAPTER 17

"[T]hey Say Black Men Won't Make It, But I Know I'm Gonna Make It": Ethnic and Racial Identity Development in the Context of Cultural Stereotypes

Niobe Way *and* Onnie Rogers

Abstract

For more than a century, scholars have defined the self as a social phenomenon dependent on relationships and embedded within a sociohistorical context. Yet a review of the empirical study of identity over the past forty years reveals significant divergence from this individual-in-context perspective. This chapter returns to the sociocultural roots of identity development study, reviewing our own research and the works of others that focus on how cultural stereotypes intersect to form the context within which individuals construct, experience, and interpret their ethnic and racial identities. This review makes evident that identity is simultaneously personal and social and that stereotypes about social categories are the link that binds them. The chapter concludes with a discussion of the implications of these findings for research and theory on identity development and for the field of psychology more broadly.

Key Words: identity, culture, stereotypes, intersectionality

For more than a century, scholars have defined the self as a social phenomenon dependent on relationships and embedded within a sociohistorical context (James, 1890; Cooley, 1902; Mead, 1934). Erik Erikson, a seminal theorist of identity development said that identity is "'located' *in the core of the individual* and yet also *in the core of his communal culture*" (Erikson, 1968, p. 22; emphasis in original). Yet a review of the empirical study of identity development over the past forty years reveals a significant divergence from this individual-in-context perspective. Identity has been, for the most part, extracted from its relational and sociohistorical roots and is typically conceptualized either as an individual-level process (i.e., personal identity) or as a social process (i.e., social identity) that can be separated from the contexts and cultures in which it exists. This representation does not acknowledge the contextually embedded nature of identity and the ways in which identities are, as Erikson indicated, a reflection of both the individual and of his or her "communal culture."

In this chapter, we return to the sociocultural roots of identity. Our own contextually embedded research and the works of others reveal the ways in which stereotypes about race, gender, sexuality, social class, and nationality serve as context within which individuals construct, experience, and interpret their identities. Thus, they are an integral part of identity development, including ethnic and racial identity development (Brown & Gilligan, 1992; Chu, 2004; Cunningham, 1999; Lei, 2003; Nasir, 2011; Robinson & Ward, 1991; Rogers, 2013; Spencer, Dupree, & Hartmann, 1997; Way, 2011; Way, Hernandez, Rogers, & Hughes, 2013; Way, Santos, Niwa, & Kim-Gervy, 2008). The data make evident that identity is simultaneously personal and social and that the stereotypes about social categories that exist in American culture (and elsewhere) are the link that binds them. In this chapter, we discuss the implications of these findings for research and theory on identity development, as well as for the field of psychology more broadly. The data we present from our own studies comes from four of our longitudinal and mixed method studies[1] that we have conducted with students attending six middle schools and three high schools located in two cities in the United States. Our samples include White, Black, Dominican, Chinese, and Puerto Rican adolescents and attend schools in which the majority of the students qualified for free/reduced lunch.

Identity Development

Erikson (1968) defined identity as "a subjective sense of invigorating sameness and continuity" (p. 19), referring to the integration of personal experiences, social roles and expectations, and desires and ideals into a coherent sense of self. This foundational definition has given rise to two broad, and largely distinct, perspectives toward the study of identity: (a) "personal identity," which emphasizes an individual's life story, experiences, and choices; and (b) "social identity," which is oriented toward understanding one's experience as a function of social group membership. Both orientations focus on the extent to which one has explored an identity, with the implicit assumption that the meaning of identity (or the way it has been or is being defined by the individual) is rooted in how much one likes or is attached to the identity, how much one has thought about or engaged in activities related to one's identities, and/or considered future roles related to one's identity. The emphasis in both of these approaches, particularly in the study of social identities, has been on asking "how much" rather than more qualitative questions such as: how does the social context shape racial and ethnic identity development, or why are particular identities maintained or why are other identities rejected?

The study of personal identity focuses on identity as "an anchor in the sea of possibilities" or a lever that enables one to control his or her life direction (Schwartz, 2005, p. 294). This line of research is most often linked to an Eriksonian perspective, in part due to James Marcia's (1966) identity status paradigm (see Crocetti & Meeus, this volume; Kroger, this volume). Marcia was first to operationalize Erikson's theory using the concepts of *exploration* and *commitment*. According to Marcia's model, the ideal identity, *identity achievement*, is the product of high levels of exploration—learning about the self and considering options for who one wants to be—followed by a strong, stable commitment or clear view of one's self and purpose. En route to an achieved identity, individuals may pass through or fixate in less optimal statuses: a *foreclosed identity*, defined by strong convictions and attitudes (high commitment) that are established in the absence of exploration; a state of *moratorium*, with high levels of exploration but little conviction or commitment to any particular self story; or the *diffused* identity in which self-discovery is halted (or perhaps yet to be initiated), demonstrated by low levels of exploration and commitment. The assumption is that individuals need to explore their options and make steadfast commitments in order for development to proceed optimally. Early studies found the combination of high exploration and commitment to be associated with positive indicators of adolescent adjustment, such as high self-esteem and positive and productive social behaviors and relationships (Marcia, 1966; Orlofsky, Marcia, & Lesser, 1973). More recent work on personal identity development investigates the construction of one's life story or life choices, such as chosen career paths (e.g., Cote & Schwartz, 2002 McAdams, 1990; 2001).

In essence, research on personal identities focuses on how individuals grapple with the "sameness and continuity" of the self through time and space (e.g., Cote & Schwartz, 2002; McAdams, 1990; 2001). Collectively, these findings indicate that exploration and the opportunity for introspection are essential for formulating a coherent identity and that such exploration is ongoing throughout adolescence and adulthood (e.g., McAdams, 2001; Syed & Azmitia, 2009). What this work rarely tells us, however, is how social categories, such as gender, race and ethnicity, and sexuality, shape the pathway of personal identification or how micro- and macrocontexts shape the construction of the self or personal identity (Azmitia, Syed, & Radmacher, 2008; Hammack & Cohler, 2011).

If personal identity is concerned with an individual's sense of "me-ness," then social identity is attuned to the sense of "we-ness" that one develops as a result of membership in social categories, such as race/ethnicity or gender (Azmitia et al.,

2008). Tajfel (1981) defined social identity as "that part of an individual's self-concept which derives from his knowledge of his membership of a social group together with the value and emotional significance attached to that membership" (p. 63). This framing recognizes that the self is relational, extending the concept of identity beyond the individual. Although a full review of social identity theory (Tajfel & Turner, 1986) and its measurement frameworks is beyond the scope of this chapter (see Hammack, this volume), this literature, in sum, highlights the individual variability in social group identifications (See Ashmore, Deaux, & McLaughlin-Volpe, 2004, for a review.) Individuals of the same racial or ethnic group, for example, vary in the degree to which they identify with their race or ethnicity (e.g., centrality/importance), how they feel about being a member of the racial or ethnic group (e.g., evaluation/regard), and the racial or ethnic group beliefs or ideologies that they endorse (Ashmore et al., 2004; Sellers, Smith, Shelton, Rowley, & Chavous, 1998). As with the personal identity literature, studies on social identity indicate that a strong sense of social group membership (i.e., high levels of engagement and pride) is an essential aspect of healthy development, with significant links to self-esteem and academic achievement (e.g., Chavous et al., 2003; Phinney, 1990; Quintana, 2007; Seaton, Scottham, & Sellers, 2006).

The research on both personal and social identities has significantly extended our understanding of identity development and its psychological, social and academic correlates. Yet the division of identity into "personal" and "social" has ironically reduced its conceptualization to an individual-level construct or to a process that occurs *within* the individual rather than *within* a relationship, a context, and a culture (see Korobov, this volume). Even though scholarship acknowledges that the self is shaped by social forces and occasionally examines the cultural context (e.g., the dimension of public regard found in Sellers' Multidimensional Model of Racial Identity), the focus is typically on the self. For example, in the study of personal identity, career pathways are examined as a process of individual choice, with little consideration of how social and cultural expectations inform—and constrain—the choices that one perceives possible. Even the few personal identity researchers who have examined the cultural context (e.g., McAdams, 2013) do not examine the macrocontext of beliefs and expectations about social categories (e.g., race, gender, class) and how this macrocontext shapes personal identities.

A similar focus on the self is evident in social identity research. Current empirical work examines the extent to which an individual identifies with or is attached to his or her gender or race, for example, rather than how a culturally perpetuated set of stereotypes shape and infuse the meaning of liking or not liking one's gender or racial group. Although early studies of ethnic and racial identity focused on how individuals spoke about and experienced their racial and ethnic groups in context (e.g., Cross, 1991; Phinney, 1992) and laid the foundation for the measures of ethnic and racial identity (Phinney, 1992; Sellers et al., 1998), later studies, with a few exceptions (e.g., Umaña-Taylor, 2004; Syed & Azmitia, 2008; 2010), have downplayed the context and focused instead on individual differences in "stages" or "levels" of identity development. These studies have provided us with insight into the ways in which different levels of engagement and affect toward one's social group, for example, is associated with adjustment, but not into how these levels develop or exist within a relational or cultural context.

Another limitation of the social identity research is its tendency to treat race, ethnicity, gender, and other social categories as "natural" and static rather than as socially constructed and dynamic. Whereas race, for example, is defined as a set of phenotypic characteristics that are shared by a group of individuals (Hirschfeld, 1996; Paabo, 2001), and ethnicity is defined as the geographical location or language that is shared by a group of people (e.g., Quintana, 2007; Slaughter-Defoe, 2012), one's racial and ethnic identity is bound to the culturally derived meaning and significance of race and ethnicity within a set of geographical, social, and political realities rather than simply by a biological reality (Hirschfeld, 1996; Paabo, 2001; Segall, 1999). Racial identity, in other words, is not merely reflective of one's membership in the racial category of, for example, Black, but also by the social meaning of being Black within a particular context of, for example, the United States.

A similar case can be made for gender. Investigating, for example, when a child categorizes herself as a girl or how good she feels about being a girl or the extent to which she is attached to being a girl are important questions. Yet they only mark a part of gender identity and do not offer information regarding how gender identity is shaped by the cultural constructs of girlhood, feminity, or masculinity within a particular context. In the development of social identity, ethnic, racial, and gender labels, for example, are plugged into and activated by culturally and contextually charged meanings of those ethnic, racial, and gender labels. According to theory and research, Chinese American girls, for example, do not simply have an experience of being Chinese American girls; they experience being Chinese American girls within a larger culture and context that regularly communicates to them what it means to be a Chinese American girl. To investigate ethnic, racial, and gender identities without examining the social nature of social identities, in other words, is to downplay the social in social identities.

There are, however, a few scholars who have indeed examined racial identity as a process embedded in a larger cultural narrative about race and ethnicity in American culture (e.g., Cunningham, 1999; Nasir, 2011; Nasir & Shah, 2011; Spencer et al., 1997; Spencer, Fegley, Harpalani, & Seaton, 2004; Stevenson, 1997). Spencer and colleagues (1997) use their *phenomenological variant of ecological systems theory* (P-VEST) that positions the child as an active agent, interpreting and responding to a cultural context. These responses are referred to as "coping strategies" and may be *reactive* and counterproductive or *proactive*, positively challenging cultural expectations and ideals that are harmful.

Identity, according to Spencer and her colleagues, is the result of one's ongoing response patterns and the strategies that youth select—and thus the identities that emerge—are based on the risks and opportunities presented to them. For example, a young Black male in low-income, violent neighborhood may embrace a hypermasculine identity of toughness and anger to shield himself from the physical and emotional vulnerabilities of his environment (Cunningham, 1999; Spencer et al., 2004). In other words, Black males who don the image of the "cool pose"—stoic, quick to anger, and aggressive—are not merely accepting a "negative identity" but creating a protective shield as they actively negotiate a set of environmental stressors and risk factors that expose their vulnerability and threaten their livelihood. Similarly, the Black youth who constructs a "raceless" identity to achieve in school (Fordham, 1988) does so in response to a racist context that questions his intelligence and thus necessitates such a strategy (see Cooper et al., this volume). The few studies of the cultural context of identities have been, however, limited to Black youth and thus we know little about how the identities of Asian, Latino, and White youth are also intimately shaped by culture and context (Steele, 2011).

Apart from these exceptions, the empirical response to Erikson's (1968) cultural, historical, and contextual theory of identity has been to ignore the "psychosocial relativity" of identity and the dynamic "interplay between the psychological, the social, the developmental, and the historical" (Erikson, 1968, p. 23). It has been a response that takes identity development, as well as race, ethnicity, and other social categories, out of context. A return to Erikson's (1968) seminal text, *Identity: Youth and Crisis*, places identity, as well as race, ethnicity, and other social categories, firmly in culture and in context.

Erikson defined identity development as a "process of simultaneous reflection and observation…by which the individual judges himself in light of what he perceives to be the way in which others judge him" (p. 22). Erikson argued that the self derives its meaning from the other and that, during this peak of identity construction, adolescents are "preoccupied with what they appear to be in the eyes of others" (p. 128). The social "other" more broadly represents society. Spencer and colleagues (1997) contend: "the self is constructed in response to stereotypes and biases" (p. 819). Similarly, Suárez-Orozco (2004) argues that cultural expectations and stereotypes function as "social mirrors" reflecting to youth who society expects them to be. Drawing on Vygotskian theory, Nasir and Shah (2011) construct stereotypes as "cultural artifacts" or tools that youth use to make sense of their identities. Thus, it is the interplay of the self and other, the self reflected "in the eyes of others," that constitutes identity. Identity development, in other words, is socially constructed, relational, and inextricable linked to society and its members.

Erikson (1968) also underscores that identity formation involves the *avoidance* of the negative identity that is projected onto the self about the self. Thus, identity is not only about "becoming" (i.e., achievement) but also about "*not* becoming" (i.e., avoidance) (Way et al., 2008). Erikson explains: "The human being, in fact, is warned *not* to become what he often had no intention of becoming so that he can learn to anticipate what he must avoid" (p. 303). Articulating a similar idea, Oyserman, Grant, and Ager (1995) argue that youth possess both an *ideal self* that they desire and a *feared self* that they want to avoid. Although Oyserman et al. (1995) do not specify what constitutes the feared self, an Eriksonian interpretation suggests that it is comprised of cultural stereotypes—those negative images, messages, and expectations that "haunt us at night" (Erikson, 1968, p. 22). Conceptualizing identity as relational and as responsive to stereotypes shifts the conversation from what identities look like—the status or stage of identity or the level of group belonging—to an investigation of who adolescents *do* and *do not* want to be and how ideal and feared selves inform their identity formation.

Our research with adolescents (Rogers, 2013; Way, 2011; Way et al., 2008; 2013) reveals the nested relationships that give rise to identity development. The semistructured interviews of the hundreds of adolescents in our studies underscore the ways that cultural stereotypes about race, ethnicity, nationality, gender, sexuality, and social class actively shape and give meaning to adolescents' identities and relationships. Our data, as well as the works of others (Brown & Gilligan, 1992; Cunningham, 1999; Lei, 2003; Robinson & Ward, 1991; Nasir & Shah, 2011; Spencer et al., 2004; Stevenson, 1997; Ward, 1996; Waters, 1996), bring to light three interrelated patterns: (a) the prevalence of stereotypes in adolescents' constructions of their identities, (b) the intersecting nature of different types of stereotypes (e.g., gender and race stereotypes) in the construction of identities, and (c) the ways that adolescents' identities are grounded in not only the desire to *become* a particular type of person but also the desire to avoid, reject, or resist stereotypes (Way et al., 2008; 2013). In the remainder of this chapter, we illustrate these patterns using data from our research and others' and discuss the implications of these findings for research and theory in the study of identity development.

Stereotypes and Identity Development

Stereotypes are widely held cultural beliefs and expectations, generalized attitudes, or evaluations about individuals who share a social group, such as ethnicity, race, gender, social class, or nationality (Stagnor & Schaller, 1996). More than mental representations, however, stereotypes are "shared storylines" that are lived and experienced in relationship (Nasir, 2011). Stereotypes transform individuals who possess unique characteristics into caricatures without nuance or variation, such that all individuals within an ethnic or racial group, for example, are homogenized. For example, common stereotypes about African-American youth in the United States are that they have rhythm and are athletic, lazy, dumb, loud, and angry (Fordham, 1993; Ghavami & Peplau, 2013; hooks, 2004; Stevenson, 1997). Latino youth are similarly stereotyped as lazy and dumb, as well as gang members and drug lords (e.g., López, 2003). Asian-American youth, in contrast, are typically stereotyped as the "model minorities"—smart, quiet, shy, and obedient (Lee, 1994). At the same time, as members of an immigrant group, Asian American immigrant youth are also viewed as dirty, poor, weak, girly, and gay (Chua & Fujino, 2008; Lei, 2003; Shek, 2006). Stereotypes are not restricted to ethnic, racial, or sexual minorities. Whiteness in the United States is often stereotyped as being wealthy, successful, physically weak, and gay (Ghavami & Peplau, 2013; Pascoe, 2007; Perry, 2001).

Research, furthermore, suggests that stereotypes both shape and infuse identities through codes based on social categories, which are constructed in relationship to each other. For example, studies show that academic achievement is coded as "White," and students of color who excel in school (except for Asians) are deemed "acting White" (Carter, 2006; Cooper et al., this volume; Fordham & Ogbu, 1986). In contrast, "acting Black" means the opposite of "acting White" and refers to speaking in urban slang, dressing in urban style, and listening to hip hop music (Carter, 2006; Delpit, 1995). Nguyen (personal communication, August 3, 2009) described a phenomenon among Asian youth who call themselves "pencils," referencing their Asian-ness on the outside (i.e., their "yellow" skin tone) and Blackness on the inside because they ditch school, listen to hip hop, and get in fights. Nasir and Shah (2011) describe these racial and ethnic contrasts in this way:

> As with "Asians are good at math," the notion that "White men can't jump" exemplifies how racialized narratives tend to be inherently relational in character. The inability of White men to jump is only visible because of the (presumed) certainty that non-White men (usually African American men) *can* jump (p. 30).

Such ethnic and racial coding of characteristics, behaviors, and abilities illustrates how cultural stereotypes are relational and infuse self-perceptions and developing identities.

Ethnic and racial stereotypes also operate alongside other social stereotypes, a concept referred to as *intersectionality* (Ghavami & Peplau, 2013; Shields, 2008). Intersectionality theory argues that the stereotypes that define social categories intersect with each other to create unique identity constellations (Collins, 2000; Shields, 2008). In other words, neither a "genderless race" nor a "raceless gender" exists; instead, stereotypes are simultaneously "raced" and "gendered" (as well as "classed" and "sexualized"). The stereotypes that characterize Black girls and women are unique and distinct from the stereotypes about Black boys and men. Likewise, White boys and men are stereotyped differently from Asian boys and men. Thus, embedding the study of identity development in cultural and historical context not only requires attention to stereotypes, but also to the intersectionality of these stereotypes within a particular context.

Although the idea of intersectionality is widely accepted on a theoretical level, it is rarely investigated empirically. One exception is the study by Ghavami and Peplau (2013) who investigated whether the content of cultural stereotypes was different for the general social category (e.g., race or gender) compared to a specific social group (e.g., Black women). They asked more than 600 college students to list ten cultural stereotypes for either a gender group (men or women), an ethnic group (Black, White, Latino, Asian, or Middle Eastern), or a gender-by-ethnic group (e.g., Black women, Black men, White women, White men, etc.). Analyzing more than 7,000 cultural stereotypes gathered from their sample, Ghavami and Peplau found that each gender-by-ethnic group elicited distinct stereotypes from the general ethnic group as well as the general gender group. For example, Black women were stereotyped as "promiscuous" and "overweight," whereas Black men were uniquely stereotyped as "rappers" and "quick to anger"; none of these stereotypes was listed as stereotypes about Black people, men, or women in general. This pattern was consistent across the ethnic groups in their study. White women, for example, were stereotyped as "ditsy" but Whites, in general, were characterized as intelligent. Asian men were stereotyped as "short" and "effeminate," whereas their female peers were defined as "studious," none of which was used to stereotype Asian people as a whole. In other words, Ghavami and Peplau's (2013) data illustrate that stereotypes about "race, class, and gender...overlap, intersect, and fuse with each other in countless ways" (Omi & Winant, 1994, p. 68) and the necessity of investigating identity with consideration of these interrelationships.

Our data also consistently show that when adolescents speak about their racial and ethnic identities they rely on an intersecting web of stereotypes to guide them (Rogers, 2013; Way et al., 2013). For example, when Roger, a Black male in one of our longitudinal studies of identity development, was asked about what he likes about being Black, he explains:

> I don't know. I just like being a Black person...A lot of rappers are Black, a lot of basketball and football players are Black. It's like Michael Jordan was Black. He was like the best man in the NBA and he was Black also. It's like he's good and then he's Black also. Like somebody sees you and they see you playing basketball or football or listening to rap music, like they'll respect you for it.

Although Roger may be correct that "a lot of rappers are Black" and many play sports, his response suggests that his identity as a Black person is constrained by the stereotypes of Black men. Roger's response also reveals the ways in which stereotypes intersect across social categories, with gender stereotypes (basketball player, rapper) being the lens through which Roger's race is experienced and negotiated.

Marcus, another boy in one of our studies, explains how his identity as a young Black male is directly shaped by society's stereotypes:

> [Be]cause society has its boxes for everybody and they don't like it when you like jump outside of it...
> Q: What kind of boxes are you in, or do you think society wants to put you in?
> A: Like, the, well you're-never-going-to-be-anything 'cause you're in the Black box and I don't think you can do this cause you're Black...Like Black kids are always doing the drugs.... and they're always doing sports, or always the one that's just trying to shoot somebody up, they're always the violent ones.... You're not supposed to be a bookworm, be feminine, be gay. Oh yeah, you're Black, you're not supposed to be gay, you're supposed to have like fifty women and get a lot of people pregnant and then leave them all.

In this conversation about what it is like to be a Black male, Marcus articulates how his "expected" identity is based on a set of intersecting stereotypes about race, social class, gender, and sexuality that "box" him in.

The literature on Black masculinity (e.g., Cunningham, 1999; Davis, 2001; hooks, 2004; Stevenson, 1997) provides additional evidence of the "box" that Marcus speaks about, a set of rigid expectations that define the Black male identity as a stoic image of strength, independence, and hypersexuality referred to as the "cool pose" (Majors & Billson, 1992). Davis (2001) finds, based on his observational research of Black boys in elementary school, that: "Black boys who do not meet the standards of an acceptable masculinity are treated as masculine mistakes," they are teased by their peers, called "gays" and "sissies," and relegated to socialize with girls (p. 147). Thus, in American culture, adhering to the Black male stereotype becomes essential to gaining and maintaining membership in the Black male social group.

Josh, a White American boy in one of our studies, also acknowledges the ways in which his Black male peers get boxed in and intersects social class and racial stereotypes in his description of what he likes about being White:

> There are certainly advantages to being White... Well if I were to walk into a store, no storekeeper would like be on us, but if a kid walked in with a doo-rag and like that and maybe some storekeeper would be on his alert.... Just because people have these images in their heads of what certain groups of people are, which I find is messed up and stuff because—Like when I first came to my building on Washington Street I was like... "Oh those [Black] guys are going to beat me up after school". But after being friends with [Black people] [that] has really changed a lot.

The meaning of whiteness for Josh is based on perceived advantages and disadvantages that hinge on intersecting stereotypes ("of what certain groups are") of race, social class, and gender, referring not simply to Black people but Black males from low-income families who are stereotyped to wear "doo-rags" and are followed by "storekeepers."

Lori, a Dominican-American student, also reveals the intersections of stereotypes in her ethnic identity and the relational nature of identity formation as she describes why she would want to be "White":

> [I would like to be White because] people don't criticize them a lot... like a lot [of] people they don't really say like "you're White" and all that, criticize you like they do to Dominicans. They say good things about White people, like they're rich and they like have [a] good education.

Lori suggests that it is not being White, per se, that she desires, it is the privilege and wealth that she perceives White people to have—the stereotypes about Whiteness in American culture—that makes being White desirable and distinct from her own ethnicity.

Michael, a Chinese-American boy, describes the "types" of Chinese students at his school and in the process illustrates how stereotypes about ethnicity and immigrant status delineate and inform his identity:

> [The Chinese who are not born here] they're different by how they act.... They spit on the ground. Even though it was [in] the school. We don't care if you spit like outside in the street, but like in the school and the hallway, ya know, people gonna slip, like step on it. What's gonna happen? It starts fights and stuff. And then like, they dress differently, like, ya know, they really dress like *so* bright. We don't really like dress bright, and like shorts, even guys, like shorts up to like here... And like they have clothes different from us. Like their brands, stuff like that. And their hairstyle all spiked up, and I'm like, uh.
>
> Q: What group do you think you're in?
> A: The Chinese kids that are like born here....
> Mostly I hang out with them.

The youth in our studies in our studies often made such distinctions between the American-born and immigrant students, divisions that were grounded in intersecting stereotypes about social class, ethnicity, and sexuality, and they based their identities on these stereotypes (Way et al., 2013).

Mary Waters's (1996) research on ethnic and racial identity among Caribbean immigrant youth revealed a similar pattern. A Trinidadian-American female in her research says:

> My feelings are more like blacks [in the United States]... I am lazy. I am really lazy and my parents are always making comments and things about how I am lazy. They are always like in Trinidad you could not be this lazy. In Trinidad you would have to go on working.
>
> (Waters, 1996, p. 72)

Weaving together stereotypes about race and nationality, this young woman constructs her racial and ethnic identity in response to such stereotypes.

Stereotypes of the intersection of race and sexuality were also evident in our studies. When asked what race he would like to be, a White boy in one of our studies explains: "Black [because] you get to wear a lot more things that an average White person couldn't wear...you get to wear pink without looking fruity or anything." In other words, being Black offers an opportunity to maintain a heterosexual image while, at the same time, having more flexibility in one's appearance. For young White males who are often stereotyped as "soft" or "weak," it is a way that stereotypes about race and sexuality intersect and is the reason that being Black is so attractive (Ghavami & Peplau, 2013; Pascoe, 2007). Carter's (2006) research on the "acting White" phenomenon and Waters's research on identity among immigrant youth also unearthed gendered patterns whereby, for boys, "acting White" was equivalent to "talking soft" or "acting gay." Such research, as well as our own, illustrate how identities are entangled in a web of intersecting stereotypes.

Looking from the outside, stereotypes can be seen as an impetus for identity development—a macrocontextual factor that drives the content and process of identity formation. At the same time, youth draw on and use stereotypes to make sense of their identities; thus, stereotypes are integral to and cannot be separated from the development of identities. In researching racial identity, Nasir and Shah (2011) find that stereotypes are more like cultural narratives than "mental representations." They state: "Narratives are not static—they are continually taken up, reproduced, and resisted in multiple ways in daily life" (p. 26). Similarly, we find that stereotypes are both cultural phenomena and proximal "tools" that youth use as they formulate their identities. Youth, then, are not simply influenced by stereotypes in the construction of their identities, they react to them by resisting or accommodating to stereotypes (Anyon, 1984; Hammack, 2008; Spencer et al., 1997; Way, 2011: Way & Rogers, in progress; Way et al., In Press).

Our research with adolescents has also revealed that youth define their ethnic and racial identities as "not being" an ethnic or racial stereotype (Rogers, 2013; Way et al., 2008; 2013). Black adolescents in our studies speak about not wanting to be perceived as lazy or dumb; Chinese American students speak about not wanting to be seen as nerds or victims of peer harassment and discrimination. Adolescents, we find, often speak more about who they *do not want to be* than who they want to be, and their ideal identities—who they aspire to become—are reflections of the stereotypes they most wish to avoid (Way et al., 2008; 2013).

For example, Monique, an African-American girl in one of our studies, responds to a question about what being African American means to her:

I'm trying to make a point of myself. I don't want to become—not another gangster, I don't want to become another thug in the street selling drugs being a hustler and I don't want to be another rapper, I don't want to be another hip-hopper. I want to be myself. That's thinking smart. Thinking dumb means that like all Black people are supposed to become rappers, that's the stereotype. I'm not going to become no rapper. I'm going to become a singer maybe. I want to become a lawyer, I want to become a doctor, I want to become a veterinarian.

A Chinese-American boy, Lee, responds similarly. When asked why being Chinese American is important for him, Lee says:

To be smart. I don't really try in school and I actually know the stuff.... Like strangers like always [think I am] a nerd...so, then [someone called me] a nerd and I'm like, "Oh, I'm not a nerd." And I stood up for myself...I started, you know, stepping up to him. And he was [like] chill out.... Because not every Chinese person has to be a nerd.... Like I'm not a good kid...I'm not a nerd or any of that.

Viewing themselves through the lens of society's stereotypes, Monique and Lee illustrate how the adolescents in our studies explicitly define who they are and want to be by delineating who they do *not* want to be—a direct response to ethnic and racial stereotypes.

John, an African-American boy in one of our studies, also describes his self definition as in opposition to racial stereotypes:

Well, I don't like basketball. Where I grew up, basketball, everybody, every Black person wants to be Michael Jordan. Um, um, most of us, like guys who wear their pants like to their thighs or their knees, Doo-rag, purple bandana or whatever, care more about getting Air Jordans than an "A" or get like a "C-" and don't care about grades or that stuff. African Americans [are] like the lowest percentage at graduation. They are only 48 Percent at graduation.... I'm not, I'm not like the average African American; like I'm different. I know that some of them, most of them probably like don't study or care about school, and I'm not like that. My backpack has a lot of books and you won't find a lot of African Americans reading Harry Potter.

Wen, a fourteen-year-old Chinese-American boy, responds similarly to a question about his ethnicity:

Q: What kind of things did you learn growing up about what it means to be Chinese?

A: You have to stand up for yourself or everybody's gonna pick on you if they think you're Chinese.

Q: Mm. How did you learn that?

A: Cause people try to pick on me and I didn't let them pick on me. So, now they don't mess with me anymore.

Q: Who tried to pick on you?

A: Black kids and, Hispanic kids, like in 6th grade. Like when they first met me and everything. They thought I was just another regular Chinese kid, like a nerdy one and they tried to pick on me and stuff. So, I don't let them pick on me, so now they don't pick on me.

Like John, who identified himself as "not the average African American," Wen's ethnic identity is defined by not being a "regular Chinese kid." In essence, who they are is grounded principally in who they are *not*. Deon, a Black male in one of our studies, explains how he would describe himself to someone new:

I'm [a] tall, Black, handsome young man.... I love God. I'm a positive man.

Q: So what do you mean by positive man?

A: Um, not like the other men on the street that would, um, go and sell drugs, get high. And do the all the ordinary stuff like uh, like another Black man would: leave out on his wife or kids when she is about to have a kid or somethin'. I don't care if I have twenty kids, I'm gonna be there for every last one of 'em. Because I wouldn't want to end up like my father. I wouldn't want my kids to cry every night tryin' to see where they're father at or nothin like that.

Deon draws a clear contrast between his ideal self as a "positive man" and feared self as a Black male stereotype (a drug user and absent father), revealing how identity is tied to that which he wishes to avoid.

Similarly, Jaire, describes what he likes most about himself:

I love the fact that different people um, think of me to be um a more complex individual and a more intelligent individual. Because there's no 14-year-old—let's be real, a young African American 14-year-old, you know, that can use different words in different situations and give his opinion about Barack Obama or the state the economy is in, the Iraq war, and different situations or the lesbian movement or whatever.

Like many of his peers, Jaire positions himself outside of the stereotyped category, defining himself in opposition to the cultural stereotypes. Implicitly, however, this strategy perpetuates the stereotypes by suggesting that they will become exceptions rather than questioning the truth of the stereotypes themselves. Robinson and Ward (1991; Ward, 1996) call this response pattern "resistance for survival"—a response to stereotypes that is oriented toward "quick fixes" that, over the long term, advance neither individual nor group goals (Ward, 1996, p. 95). The alternative response—or challenging the stereotypes themselves—is called is "resistance for liberation", which is a critical consciousness that disrupts the cultural narrative, replacing "negative critique with positive recognition" of the self and others (Ward, 1996, p. 95). The tension of who to be and not to be is rooted in cultural stereotypes and produces, as Robinson and Ward note, either strategies for survival or for liberation.

The centrality of avoiding stereotypes also surfaces in the adolescent's motive to prove the stereotypes wrong (Suárez-Orozco, 2004). Imelda, a Dominican girl, explains why it is important for her to be Dominican (vs. Dominican-American):

It's important for me to be Dominican because I guess I get to prove to everyone else that Dominicans can do something with their lives... First of all I am proving it to myself and second of all I'm proving to like school, teachers, and I guess that's why I've kept up with all these grades... I was the very first person in my family to ever do private school [in elementary school], so it's sort of a good feeling to know that I can say I got into a good school because I earned it.

Ahmad, a Black male, answers the question about why being Black is important: "Well [being

Black] is important 'cause, like, you don't want to live up to the, like the Caucasian people type of reputation they think you have...I think that's just important for every Black male to prove 'em wrong."

Devin explains why he likes being Black:

> I'm just glad to be Black you know, even though there's like a lot of stereotypes.... Like, Black men really don't like to grow up, either they're like drug dealers or gang bangers, or end up dead or something like that, or end up in jail. No, since I'm Black I feel like I gotta, you know, achieve somethin' other than that, you know? I've got goals to do.
>
> Q: Do you like that?
>
> A: Yeah! It keeps me focused.... Like they say Black men probably won't make it, but I know I'm going to make it and even if I don't make it I'll still try to do something. I just can't—it's not me, I just can't be nothing. I've got to do something.... I look in the mirror and wonder if you'll be a powerful Black man like Obama. Who knows I might be president!

This process of avoiding stereotypes is not just part of identity development, it is essential to it. Stereotypes fuel adolescents' self-perceptions and the identities they strive to construct or the "possible selves" they envision (Oyserman et al., 1995).

Marcus, a Black male, explains:

> Well I guess some people are so used to seeing the gang bangers and the gangsters and stuff like that on the outside, so they think that every Black male is like that. But that's actually a stereotype.... So um, we just trying to change their minds about Black men in general, being the best that we can be and getting our educations and proving them wrong.
>
> Q: So how do you feel about that when you think about the stereotypes and that people think all Black males are gang bangers?
>
> A: [sigh] I actually get kind of mad but I try to keep that anger under wraps cause you don't want that anger coming out in the wrong way. So um, I try to focus it in, do my schoolwork, so I can like prove, like break the stereotype. And like, I'd like to get out into the community and like tell people that you know this is not how we act. So I guess you could say, that I'm kind of inspired but then again I'm kind of like pissed off. That's kind of how I feel about it.

For Michael, proving stereotypes wrong is how he defines being a Black male:

> Q: Is being Black important to you?
>
> A: Yeah, it is. I want to say because, um, there are very few African American males that graduate from college and succeed in life and I know that I'm gonna be one to succeed in life because of how my mother and father have been pushin' me through all my, um, years of getting my education. So, I just wanna prove the statistics wrong and help other people prove the statistics wrong that a Black man can graduate from college and be successful.

The hope of being something other than a stereotype resonates with what Waters (1996) found among her immigrant Black youth who aspired to be more than "just" a Black American stereotype (p. 73).

The motive to avoid stereotypes operates for "positive" stereotypes as well. Lee (1994) coined the term "model minority myth" to describe stereotypes of Asian immigrants as smart, well-behaved, hardworking, and destined for success. Yet, as Lee's (1994) research revealed, this seemingly positive cultural narrative not only perpetuates negative stereotypes about immigrants from other countries but also puts inordinately high pressure on Asian immigrant youth and thus undermines their psychological and social well-being. For example, Andy, a Chinese-American boy, describes how hard it is for him to receive math tutoring:

> That's the only thing I hate about school. And sometimes I'm trying to like concentrate. Sometimes I get bothered. Sometimes I don't get like one-on-one tutoring help. And I need it for math cause math is my worst subject.
>
> Q: Okay. So, tell me why would you like one on-one-tutoring help?
>
> A: Why I would want tutoring help is that I can understand more better...And sometimes I'm kind of a little bit timid cause when people are around me and I'll say something like "I don't get it" and then like I told the teacher to like, "Can you explain it?" And then some people were like, "Why do you need all that? Explain it again? Don't you get it?" And they look at me and then like, and then they're like, um, "You're supposed to know." Like that. But, I'm not good at math. So, what?

Meiling articulates the explicit stereotype that Andy refers to in his response:

> Like there is a stereotype that a lot of Asian people are smart and people think that's the case and then sometimes they feel like that you're not and then they look down on you?...Like if I fail a test they'll say um why didn't you pass and stuff like

that. Mm it kind of makes me feel a little bad, then it makes me want to improve the stereotype or to prove it's wrong. Well not that it's wrong, but that you shouldn't judge somebody by the stereotype.

Pam, a White American girl, gives a similar response when she explains what she doesn't like about being White:

Something that I feel uncomfortable about is that people expect more of you because you're White. Like if I was [an] African-American young man they would probably not expect me to smart or well educated. But, you know, because I am White they expect you know "Oh you must know this and you must know that." But, I don't know what the heck they're talking about.

Regardless of the valence of the stereotype, the adolescents in our studies communicate that "you shouldn't judge somebody by a stereotype." Their narratives reveal that stereotypes about race, ethnicity, sexuality, gender, social class, and/or nationality intersect to form a core context within which identities are explored, constructed, and understood. These data offer a new perspective in which identity is concurrently a personal and social process and is considered part and parcel of a culture and a context.

Implications for Identity Research

The work we have reviewed in this chapter underscores the important role of stereotypes in the identity development of ethnic and racial minority and majority youth and the extent to which the desire to avoid such stereotypes forms a crucial part of the process. The research, furthermore, suggests that cultural stereotypes are not only a context of identity development, but also a core feature of identity. In addition, the research suggests that a desire for a particular career, or what is typically considered a component of "personal identity," is just as "social" in its construction as a feeling of connectedness with one's ethnic or racial group, a typical indicator of social identity. Both choices and feelings appear to be constructed in response to those around them and the expectations and stereotypes of the peers and adults in their lives. As Erikson indicated, identity development—at the personal and collective level—is inherently social, reflective of the cultural, historical, and economic context.

For the remainder of the chapter, we discuss the implications of the patterns evident in our own research and the research of others (e.g., Nasir, 2011; Robinson & Ward, 1991; Spencer et al., 1997; Stevenson, 1997). Such research underscores the importance of investigating: (1) the macrocontext or the larger system of cultural beliefs, expectations, and stereotypes that exist within contexts (e.g., the United States); (2) the relational nature of both personal and social identities; (3) the intersectionality of social categories and identities; (4) understanding identity development as a process of not becoming as well as becoming and (5) using methods that allow for more qualitative investigations in the study of racial and ethnic identity development.

The Importance of the Macrocontext

In its early years, the field of psychology distinguished itself from other social sciences by focusing on individual processes, such as mental functioning and cognition. The implicit assumption of much of the early work in psychology, with a few exceptions (e.g., Sullivan, 1956; Erikson, 1968; Lewin, 1951), was that such processes were, by and large, intrapersonal and universal or independent of culture. The introduction of the ecological model of human development marked a significant theoretical shift in psychology (Bronfenbrenner, 1977; Bronfenbrenner & Morris, 2006). Bronfenbrenner (1977) conceptualized the developing child as nested within a set of contexts ranging from the microcontexts of family, schools, and peers to macrocontexts of cultural beliefs and governmental laws and argued that the ongoing, reciprocal interactions within these contexts facilitated and shaped developmental pathways. Following Bronfenbrenner's lead, alternative ecological models emerged that focused specifically on the macro- and microecologies of ethnic and racial minority youth (García-Coll et al., 1996; Spencer, 1995). For example, García-Coll and colleagues (1996) placed "social position variables" such as race and ethnicity in their model to emphasize how position on the social hierarchy has direct implications for developmental pathways. Similarly, Spencer (1995) revealed how children's experiences of stereotypes and discrimination serve as filters through which they engage with the social world around them. With the guidance of these ecological maps, psychologists began to acknowledge the ways that both the micro- and macrocontext shape human development (Bronfenbrenner, 1977; García-Coll et al., 1996; Spencer, 1995).

The study of identity development, however, with a few exceptions (e.g., Cunningham, 1999;

Hammack, 2008; Nasir, 2011; Stevenson 1997; Spencer et al., 2004; Umaña-Taylor, 2004), has either treated identity as an individual-level variable or as a process that is shaped by the microcontexts of family and peers but not by macro-level cultural beliefs and practices. Microcontexts, however, such as parents' goals for their children have been shown to be directly influenced by larger cultural goals and ideologies (Tamis-LeMonda et al., 2007; Yoshikawa, Way, & Chen, 2013).

Moreover, culture in the field of psychology is still often conceptualized, especially in the U.S., as the beliefs and practices of specific ethnic or racial groups within the U.S. rather than as the beliefs and practices of the U.S. Studies tend to focus on, for example, "Black culture" or "Chinese culture," but rarely examine how the macrocontext of American culture shapes the identities of ethnic and racial minority youth. Exceptions to this pattern include the investigation of immigrants and their families (e.g., Suárez-Orozco & Suárez-Orozco, 2001), which suggests that American culture is only relevant when one is not or is only newly American. Given that the beliefs, expectations, stereotypes, and practices evident in American culture is part of the macrocontext for those living in (and out of) the United States, examining the influence of American culture on identity development is important regardless of ethnic, racial or immigrant status (Hammack, 2008; Steele, 2011). Furthermore, as the research suggests, stereotypes in American culture, in particular, are important to examine in studies of identity development.

The Relational Nature of Personal and Social Identity

The findings presented in this chapter point to the centrality of relationships and the social nature of both personal and social identity development. In a recent review of research on the self, neuroscientist Michael Bond reported: "[T]here is now a growing recognition that our sense of self may be a *consequence* of our relationships with others" (Bond, 2013, p. 41; emphasis added). In other words, rather than considering identity as the basis for building relationships with others, the data are pointing to the idea that relationships actually allow for a grounded sense of self (Gilligan, 1982). Our data also align with this shifting perspective, indicating how relationships between individuals and culture give rise to identities.

Our findings are consistent with a larger shift that is happening in the sciences of which David Brooks, an editorial writer at the *New York Times*, refers to as the "New Humanism" in the sciences. Research from the neurosciences and developmental psychology to evolutionary anthropology is underscoring our social and emotional human nature (de Waal, 2006; Hrdy, 2009; Tomasello, 1999). Our research and that of many others suggest a need for an expansion of what we mean by and how we investigate identity processes and identity development to account for the relational or social nature of human beings. Without such an expansion, we are left with a constrained understanding of what it means to have an identity or for these identities to develop over time.

The Intersectionality of Social Categories

Scholars have long pointed out the intersecting nature of social categories and stereotypes (Collins, 2000; Omi & Winant, 1994), but psychology, in particular, has been slow to integrate intersectionality perspectives into empirical research (Shields, 2008). Sociologist Paul Willis (1977) embedded the academic identities of urban Black males with the intersections of race, gender, and social class, and MacLeod's (1995) groundbreaking research on social class identity among working-class White males underscored the links between gender, masculinity, and social class. Similarly, Ladner's (1971) in-depth study of working-class Black females illustrated how the restrictions of social class, gender, and race shaped how Black females in her study constructed and experienced their identities as women.

Only recently have psychologists conducted empirical studies of identity intersectionality (e.g., Azmitia et al., 2008; Rogers, 2013; Settles, 2006; Spencer et al., 2004) and found that social categories do, in fact, intersect. Each of these studies, and the data presented in this chapter, suggest, furthermore, that stereotypes play a key role in forging the connections among social categories. Ghavami and Peplau's (2013) study reviewed earlier in the chapter, in fact, demonstrates how stereotypes about ethnicity and gender overlap in the cultural construction of social groups. Thus, it is not simply that race and gender as social categories are related but that the *stereotypes* about these categories intersect to form unique identity constellations. In this way, integrating stereotypes into identity theory may indeed provide a tangible method for translating intersectional theory into empirical study.

From a developmental perspective, it is also of interest to consider whether and how intersectionality of social categories changes over time. Existing studies of intersectionality do not explicitly address the developmental nature of intersectionality; thus, it remains unclear whether or how the link between stereotypes in identity formation changes across time and social contexts, perhaps being more salient at different developmental periods, among certain social groups, or in more ethnically or racially diverse social settings. Azmitia and colleagues' (2008) data with college-aged students suggest a development trend whereby, as adolescents transitioned through college, they became increasingly aware of, and perhaps able to articulate, the ways multiple social group expectations shaped their identities and career choices. It remains unclear, however, the age at which an awareness of intersectionality might emerge. For example, do children understand cultural stereotypes about White girls to be distinct from stereotypes about White men and White people in general? How does such awareness shape their own identity development? We know that generally children are aware of gender before they are aware of race (Ruble et al., 2004), but, from the perspective of intersectionality, it is also of interest when they begin to view gender through a *racial lens* and vice versa. Such questions will push the scientific study of identity to explore the more dynamic nature of identity embedded.

Becoming and Not Becoming

We find in our research that adolescents both become as well as avoid becoming stereotypes and that these processes spur identity choices and affiliations. In other words, adolescents both resist and accommodate to images projected onto them by others in their distal and proximal contexts in the construction of their own identities (Anyon, 1984; Brown & Gilligan, 1992; Robinson & Ward, 1991; Spencer et al., 1997).

The theme of resisting stereotypes has been found in other studies as well (Brown & Gilligan, 1992; Rogers, 2013; Ward, 1996; Way, 2011; Way et al., 2013). Such studies suggest that youth actively resist cultural messages that are bad for them (Brown, 1999; Brown & Gilligan, 1992; Cvencek, Nasir, O'Connor, Wischnia, & Meltzoff, In Press; Rogers, 2012; Rogers & Way, In Press; Thorne & McLean, 2003; Way, 2011; Way et al., 2013; Way et al., In Press). This resistance has, furthermore, been found to be linked to psychological and social well-being (Gupta et al., 2013; Santos, 2010; Way & Rogers, in progress). For example, Santos (2010) measured boys' resistance to masculine norms and stereotypes and found that boys who reported higher levels of resistance in their friendships, in particular, reported higher levels of psychological adjustment over time. In a separate study, he found a positive link between boys' resistance to masculine norms and greater levels of engagement in school (Santos, Galligan, Pahlke, & Fabes, 2013). Examining how adolescents resist and accommodate to cultural stereotypes in the construction of their ethnic and racial identities seems like an important direction for future studies.

Expanding the Methodology in the Study of Identity

Scholars have long argued that open-ended and narrative methods are necessary to provide meaning to the identity literature (McAdams, 2013; Syed & Azmitia, 2008, 2010; Way et al., 2008). Indeed, our findings underscore the need to diversify our methodological toolkit. Although survey methods provide critical insight into the correlates associated with various levels of ethnic or racial identity (e.g., Ashmore et al., 2004; Sellers et al., 1998) and address the questions of "how much," they do not address the ways the macrocontext influences the development and meaning of identity development. In our studies, we have found that it is often in the language that young people use to describe their ethnic and racial identities that we hear and see the micro- and macrocontext of identity (Rogers & Way, In Press; Way, 2011). The finding that youth "avoid" stereotypes and define themselves in opposition to them, for example, is evident in the language of adolescents. Identity research must pay greater attention to the ways in which the culture and context is revealed in the language of adolescents and the ways that this language provides insight into the process of identity development.

Conclusion

The data presented in this chapter illustrate that identity is a cultural, contextual, and relational process. To more thoroughly understand how identities develop, what they mean, and how they matter, we need more research that conceptualizes the personal and the social as social. Research on identities, in other words, needs to return to its theoretical roots and explore how cultures and contexts give identities their meanings. The data over the past few decades suggest that identities and the macrocontext are bound tightly together, with the macrocontext shaping the identities constructed and the identities shaping the meaning and understanding of the macrocontext. Understanding ethnic and racial identity within the micro and macro-contexts in which they exist allows for a more theoretically rich understanding of identity development.

Note

1. The four main studies we draw data from for this chapter are: The Connections Project, Project RAP, The RAP Project, and The Identity Project. The Connections study and Project RAP, funded by the National Science Foundation and The William T. Grant Foundation, were longitudinal, mixed-method research projects conducted by Niobe Way in co-educational high schools in the northeast. The RAP project was another mixed-method, longitudinal project conducted by Diane Hughes and Niobe Way at the Center for Research on Child Development and Education at New York University and was funded by the National Science Foundation. This project was a six-year, mixed method, longitudinal project that included six middle schools that took place from sixth to eleventh grade. The Identity Project, supported by the Spencer Foundation, was a two-year dissertation study conducted by Onnie Rogers at a single-sex high school in a midwestern urban city. This study examined racial and gender identity development as boys transitioned from co-ed middle schools and into an all-male high school.

References

Anyon, J. (1984). Intersections of gender and class: Accommodation and resistance by working-class and affluent females to contradictory sex role ideologies. *Journal of Education, Boston, 166*, 25–48.

Ashmore, R. D., Deaux, K., & McLaughlin-Volpe, T. (2004). An organizing framework for collective identity: Articulation and significance of multidimensionality. *Psychological Bulletin, 130*, 80–114.

Azmitia, M., Syed, M., & Radmacher, K. (2008). *The intersections of personal and social identities*. San Francisco: Jossey-Bass.

Bond, M. (2013, Feb. 28). The self: Why are you like you are? *New Scientist Magazine, The Great Illusion of the Self* (pp. 41–43).

Bronfenbrenner, U. (1977). Toward an experimental ecology of human development. *American Psychologist, 32*, 513–531.

Bronfenbrenner, U., & Morris, P. A. (2006). The bioecological model of human development. In R. M. Lerner and W. Damon (Eds.) *Handbook of child psychology (6th ed.). Theoretical models of human development* (pp. 793–828). Hoboken, NJ: John Wiley & Sons.

Brown, L. M. (1999). *Raising their voices: The politics of girls' anger*. Cambridge, MA: Harvard University Press.

Brown, L. M., & Gilligan, C. (1992). *Meeting at the crossroads: Women's psychology and girls' development*. Cambridge, MA: Harvard University Press.

Carter, P. L. (2006). Straddling boundaries: Identity, culture, and school. *Sociology of Education, 79*, 304–328.

Chavous, T. M., Bernat, D. H., Schmeelk-Cone, K., Caldwell, C. H., Kohn-Wood, L., & Zimmerman, M. A. (2003). Racial identity and academic attainment among African American adolescents. *Child Development, 74*, 1076–1090.

Chu, J. Y. (2004). A relational perspective on adolescent boys' identity development. In N. Way, & J. Y. Chu (Eds.), *Adolescent boys: Exploring diverse cultures of boyhood.* (pp. 78–104). New York: New York University Press.

Chua, P., & Fujino, D. C. (2008). Negotiating new Asian-American masculinities: Attitudes and gender expectations. *Journal of Men's Studies, 7*, 391–413.

Cole, M. (1998). *Cultural psychology: A once and future discipline*. Cambridge, MA: Harvard University Press.

Collins, P. H. (2000). *Black feminist thought: Knowledge, consciousness, and the politics of empowerment*. New York: Routledge.

Cooley, C. H. (1902). *Human nature and the social order*. New York: Scribner.

Cote, J. E., & Schwartz, S. J. (2002). Comparing psychological and sociological approaches to identity: Identity status, identity capital, and the individualization process. *Journal of Adolescence, 25*, 571–586.

Cross, W. (1991). *Shades of Black: Diversity in African American identity*. Philadelphia: Temple University Press.

Cunningham, M. (1999). African-American adolescent males' perceptions of their community resources and constraints: A longitudinal analysis. *Journal of Community Psychology, 27*, 569–588.

Cvencek, D. Nasir, N. S., O'Connor, K., Wischnia, S. A., & Meltzoff, A. N. (In Press). "They say Chinese people are the best at math": Elementary- and middle-school students' explicit and implicit math–race stereotypes. *Journal of Adolescent Research*.

Davis, J. E. (2001). Transgressing the masculine: African American boys and the failure of schools. In W. Martino, & B. Meyenn (Eds.), *What about the boys?: Issues of masculinity in schools* (pp. 140–153). Maidenhead, UK: Open University Press.

de Waal, F. (2006). *Primates and philosophers: How morality evolved*. Princeton, NJ: Princeton University Press.

Delpit, L. D (1995). *Other people's children: Cultural conflict in the classroom*. New York: New Press.

Erikson, E. H. (1968). *Identity, youth, and crisis*. New York: W. W. Norton.

Fordham, S. (1988). Racelessness as a factor in black students' school success: Pragmatic strategy or pyrrhic victory? *Harvard Educational Review, 58*, 54–84.

Fordham, S. (1993). "Those loud Black girls": (Black) women, silence, gender "passing" in the academy. *Anthropology and Education Quarterly, 24*, 3–32.

Fordham, S., & Ogbu, J. (1986). Black students' school success: Coping with the burden of "acting white." *Urban Review, 18*, 1–31.

García-Coll, C., Lamberty, G., Jenkins, R., Pipes McAdoo, H., Crnic, K., Wasik, B. H., & et al. (1996). An integrative model for the study of developmental competencies in minority children. *Child Development, 67*, 1891–1914.

Gilligan, C. (1982). *In a different voice: Psychological theory and women's development.* Cambridge, MA: Harvard University Press.

Ghavami, N., & Peplau, L. A. (2013). An intersectional analysis of gender and ethnic stereotypes: Testing three hypotheses. *Psychology of Women Quarterly, 37*, 113–127.

Gupta, T., Way, N., McGill, R., Hughes, D., Santos, C., Jia, Y., Yoshikawa, H., Chen, X., & Deng, H. (2013). Gender-typed behaviors in friendships and well-being: A cross-cultural study of Chinese and American boys. *Journal of Research on Adolescence, Special Issue: Adolescents in the Majority World, 23*, 57–68.

Hammack, P. L. (2008). Narrative and the cultural psychology of identity. *Personality and Social Psychology Review, 12*, 222–247.

Hammack, P. L., & Cohler, B. J. (2011). Narrative, identity, and the politics of exclusion: Social change and the gay and lesbian life course. *Sexuality Research and Social Policy, 8*(3), 162–182.

Hirschfeld, L. A. (1996). *Race in the making: Cognition, culture, and the child's construction of human kinds.* Cambridge, MA: MIT Press.

hooks, b. (2004). *We real cool: Black men and masculinity.* New York: Routledge.

Hrdy, S. B. (2009). *Mothers and others: The evolutionary origins of mutual understanding.* Cambridge, MA: Harvard University Press.

James, W. (1890). *The principles of psychology* (vol. I). New York: Henry Holt and Co.

Ladner, J. A. (1971). *Tomorrow's tomorrow: The black woman.* Garden City, NY: Doubleday.

Lee, S. J. (1994). Behind the model-minority stereotype: Voices of high-and low-achieving Asian American students. *Anthropology & Education Quarterly, 25*, 413–429.

Lei, J. L. (2003). (Un)Necessary toughness? Those "loud Black girls" and those "quiet Asian boys." *Anthropology and Education Quarterly, 34*, 158–181.

Lewin, K. (1951). *Field theory in social science.* New York: Harper

López, N. (2003). *Hopeful girls, troubled boys: Race and gender disparity in urban education.* New York: Routledge.

MacLeod, J. (1995). *Ain't no makin' it: Aspirations and attainment in a low-income neighborhood.* Boulder, CO: Westview Press.

Majors, R., & Billson, J. M. (1992). *Cool pose: The dilemmas of Black manhood in America.* New York: Lexington Books.

Marcia, J. E. (1966). Development and validation of ego-identity status. *Journal of personality and social psychology, 3*, 551–558.

McAdams, D. P. (1990). Unity and purpose in human lives: The emergence of identity as a life story. In A. I. Rabin, R. A. Zucker, R. A. Emmons, & S. Frank (Eds.), *Studying persons and lives* (pp. 148–200). New York: Springer.

McAdams, D. P. (2001). The psychology of life stories. *Review of General Psychology, 5*, 100–122.

McAdams, D. P. (2013). *The redemptive self: Stories Americans live by.* New York, NY: Oxford University Press.

McIntosh, P. (1988). White privilege: Unpacking the invisible knapsack. *Race, Class, and Gender in the United States: An Integrated Study, 4*, 165–169.

Mead, G. H. (1934). *Mind, self, and society.* Chicago: University of Chicago Press.

Nasir, N. S. (2011). *Racialized identities: Race and achievement among African American youth.* Stanford, CA: Stanford University Press.

Nasir, N., & Shah, N. (2011). On defense: African American males making sense of racialized narratives in mathematics education. *Journal of African American Males in Education*, 23–45.

Orlofsky, J. L., Marcia, J. E., & Lesser, I. M. (1973). Ego identity status and the intimacy versus isolation crisis of young adulthood. *Journal of Personality and Social Psychology, 27*, 211–219.

Omi, M., & Winant, H. (1994). *Racial formation in the United States: From the 1960s to the 1990s.* New York: Routledge.

Oyserman, D., Grant, L., & Ager, J. (1995). A socially contextualized model of African American identity: Possible selves and school persistence. *Journal of Personality and Social Psychology, 69*, 1216–1232.

Paabo, S. (2001). The human genome and our view of ourselves. *Science, 291*, 1219–1220.

Pascoe, C. J. (2007). *Dude, you're a fag: Masculinity and sexuality in high school.* Los Angeles: University of California Press.

Perry, P. (2001). White means never having to say you're ethnic/racial: White youth and the construction of "cultureless" identity. *Journal of Contemporary Ethnography, 30*, 56–91.

Phinney, J. S. (1990). Ethnic identity in adolescents and adults: Review of research. *Psychological Bulletin, 108*, 499–514.

Phinney, J. S. (1992). The multigroup ethnic identity measure: A new scale for use with diverse groups. *Journal of Adolescent Research, 7*, 156–176.

Quintana, S. M. (2007). Racial and ethnic identity: Developmental perspectives and research. *Journal of Counseling Psychology. Special Issue: Racial and Ethnic Identity Theory, Measurement, and Research in Counseling Psychology: Present Status and Future Directions, 54*, 259–270.

Robinson, T., & Ward, J. V. (1991). "A belief in self far greater than anyone's disbelief": Cultivating resistance among African American female adolescents. *Women & Therapy. Special Issue: Women, Girls & Psychotherapy: Reframing Resistance, 11*, 87–103.

Rogers, O. (2012). Young, Black, and male: Exploring the intersections of racial and gender identity in an all-Black, all-male high school. Available from ProQuest Dissertation Abstracts (UMI No. 10197).

Rogers, O. (2013). Black males narrating identities and stereotypes in an all-Black male high school. In S. Sirin (Chair), *Negotiating cultural identities among youth.* Paper presented at biennial meeting for Society for Research on Child Development. Seattle, WA.

Rogers, O. & Way, N. (In Press). Using semi-structured interviews to examine adolescent racial-ethnic identity. Invited chapter in C. Santos & A. J. Umaña-Taylor (Eds.) *Studying ethnic identity: Methodological advances and consideration for the future.* APA.

Rogers, O., Zosuls, K., Halim, M. L., Ruble, D., Hughes, D, & Fuligni, A. (2012). Meaning making in middle childhood: An exploration of the meaning of ethnic identity. *Cultural Diversity and Ethnic Minority Psychology, 18*, 99–108.

Rogoff, B. (2003). *The cultural nature of human development.* New York: Oxford University Press.

Ruble, D. N., Alvarez, J., Bachman, M., Cameron, J., Fuligni, A., Coll, C. G., & Rhee, E. (2004). The development of a sense of "we": The emergence and implications of children's collective identity. In M. Bennett, & F. Sani (Eds.), *The development of the social self* (pp. 29–76). New York: Psychology Press.

Santos, C. E. (2010). The missing story: Resistance to norms of masculinity in the friendships of adolescent boys. Available from ProQuest Dissertations and Theses database. (UMI No. 3426967).

Santos, C. E., Galligan, K., Pahlke, E., & Fabes, R. (2013). Gender-typed behaviors, achievement, and adjustment among racially and ethnically diverse boys during early adolescence. *American Journal of Orthopsychiatry 83*, 252–264.

Schwartz, S. J. (2005). New identity for identity research: Recommendations for expanding and refocusing the identity literature. *Journal of Adolescent Research, 20*, 293–308.

Seaton, E. K., Scottham, K. M., & Sellers, R. M. (2006). The status model of racial identity development in African American adolescents: Evidence of structure, trajectories, and well-being. *Child Development, 77*, 1416–1426.

Segall, M. H. (1999). Why is there still racism if there not such thing as "race"? In W. J. Lonner, D. L. Dinnel, D. K. Forgays, & S. A. Hayes (Eds.), *Merging past, present, and future in cross-cultural psychology*. Lisse: Swets & Zeitlinger.

Sellers, R. M., Smith, M. A., Shelton, J. N., Rowley, S. A. J., & Chavous, T. M. (1998). Multidimensional model of racial identity: A reconceptualization of African American racial identity. *Personality and Social Psychology Review, 2*, 18–39.

Settles, I. H. (2006). Use of an intersectional framework to understand Black women's racial and gender identities. *Sex Roles, 54*, 589–601.

Shek, Y. L. (2006). Asian American Masculinity: A Review of the Literature. *Journal of Men's Studies, 14*, 379–391.

Shields, S. A. (2008). Gender: An intersectionality perspective. *Sex Roles, 59*, 301–311.

Slaughter-Defoe, D. T. (2012). Introduction in D. T. Slaughter-DeFoe (Ed.) Racial stereotyping and child development. *Psychotherapy and Psychosomatics, 81*(4), 199–264. Basal, Switzerland: Karger.

Spencer, M. B. (1995). Old and new theorizing about African-American youth: A phenomenological variant of ecological systems theory. In R. L. Taylor (Ed.), *Black youth: Perspectives on their status in the United States* (pp. 37–69). Westport, CT: Praeger.

Spencer, M. B., Dupree, D., & Hartmann, T. (1997). A phenomenological variant of ecological systems theory (PVEST): A self-organization perspective in context. *Development and Psychopathology, 9*, 817–833.

Spencer, M. B., Fegley, S., Harpalani, V., & Seaton, G. (2004). Understanding hypermasculinity in context: A theory-driven analysis of urban adolescent males' coping responses. *Research in Human Development, 1*, 229–257.

Stagnor, C., & Schaller, M. (1996). Stereotypes as individual and collective representations. In C. N. Macrae, C. Stagnor, & M. Hewstone (Eds.), *Stereotypes and stereotyping* (pp. 3–37). New York: Guilford Press.

Steele, C. M. (2011). *Whistling Vivaldi: How stereotypes affect us and what we can do*. New York: W. W. Norton & Company.

Stevenson, H. C. (1997). "Missed, dissed, and pissed": Making meaning of neighborhood risk, fear and anger management in urban Black youth. *Cultural Diversity and Mental Health, 3*, 37–52.

Suárez-Orozco, C. (2004). Formulating identity in a globalized world. In M. M. Suárez-Orozco, & D. B. Qin-Hilliard (Eds.), *Globalization: Culture and education in the new millennium*. (pp. 173–202). Berkeley, CA: University of California Press.

Suárez-Orozco, C., & Suárez-Orozco, M. (2001). *Children of Immigration*. Cambridge, MA: Harvard University Press.

Syed, M., & Azmitia, M. (2008). A narrative approach to ethnic identity in emerging adulthood: Bringing life to the identity status model. *Developmental Psychology, 44*, 1012–1027.

Syed, M., & Azmitia, M. (2009). Longitudinal trajectories of ethnic identity during the college years. *Journal of Research on Adolescence, 19*, 601–624.

Syed, M., & Azmitia, M. (2010). Narrative and ethnic identity exploration: A longitudinal account of emerging adults' ethnicity-related experiences. *Developmental Psychology, 46*, 208–219.

Tajfel, H. (1981). *Human groups and social categories: Studies in social psychology*. Cambridge, UK: University of Cambridge Press

Tajfel, H., & Turner, J. C. (1986). The social identity theory of intergroup behavior. In S. Worchel, & W. Austin (Eds.), *Psychology of inter-group relations* (pp. 7–24). Chicago: Nelson Hall.

Tamis-LeMonda, C. S., Way, N., Hughes, D., Yoshikawa, H., Kalman, R. K., & Niwa, E. Y. (2007). Parents' goals for children: The dynamic coexistence of individualism and collectivism in cultures and individuals. *Social Development, 17*, 183–209.

Thorne, A., & McLean, K. C. (2003). Telling traumatic events in adolescence: A study of master narrative positioning. In R. Fivush and C. A. Haden (Eds.) *Autobiographical memory and the construction of a narrative self: Developmental and cultural perspectives* (pp. 169–185).

Tomasello, M. (1999). *The cultural origins of human cognition*. Cambridge, MA: Harvard University Press.

Umaña-Taylor, A. J. (2004). Ethnic identity and self-esteem: Examining the role of social context. *Journal of Adolescence, 27*, 139–146.

Ward, J. V. (1996). Raising resisters: The role of truth telling in the psychological development of African American girls. In B. J. R. Leadbeater, & N. Way (Eds.), *Urban girls: Resisting stereotypes, creating identities* (pp. 85–99). NY: New York University Press.

Waters, M. C. (1996). The intersection of gender, race, and ethnicity in identity development of Caribbean American teens. In B. J. R. Leadbeater, & N. Way (Eds.), *Urban girls: Resisting stereotypes, creating identities* (pp. 65–81). NY: New York University Press.

Way, N. (2011). *Deep secrets: Boys' friendships and the crisis for connection*. Cambridge, MA: Harvard University Press.

Way, N., Cressen, J., Bodian, S., Presten, J., Nelson, J., & Hughes, D. (In Press). "It might be nice to be a girl…then you wouldn't have to be emotionless:" Boys' resistance to norms of masculinity during adolescence. In Press at *Psychology of Men and Masculinities*.

Way, N., Hernandez, M. G., Rogers, O., & Hughes, D. (2013). "I'm not going to become no rapper": Stereotypes as a context of ethnic and racial identity development." *Journal of Adolescent Research, 28*, 407–430.

Way, N. & Rogers, O. (in progress). Resistance as a developmental process. In preparation for submission to *Human Development*.

Way, N., Santos, C., Niwa, E. Y., & Kim-Gervey, C. (2008). To be or not to be: An exploration of ethnic/racial identity development in context. In M. Azmitia, M. Syed, & K. Radmacher (Eds.), *The intersections of personal and social identities: New directions for child and adolescent development* (pp. 61–78). San Francisco: Jossey-Bass.

Willis, P. (1977). *Learning to labor: How working class kids get working class jobs*. New York: Columbia University Press.

Yoshikawa, H., Way, N., & Chen (2013). Large-scale economic change and youth development: The case of urban China. *New Directions of Youth Development, 135*, 39–55.

CHAPTER 18

Reflections on the Cultural Lenses of Identity Development

Margarita Azmitia

Abstract

In this chapter, the author reflects on Worrell's and Way and Rogers's chapters on culture and identity development. First, a brief overview is provided of their key contributions and theoretical frameworks. The author suggests that the concept of narratives, and in particular master narratives, may provide one way for addressing the tensions between personal and social identities. Second, the author reflects on Worrell's proposal that racial and ethnic identities and culture are equivalent and that encounters with prejudice and discrimination motivate identity development. Third, the chapter discusses Way and Rogers's proposal that identity is best conceptualized as the intersections of gender, ethnicity, social class, and immigration in youth's everyday lives. The chapter concludes with suggestions for future directions for theory and research.

Key Words: adolescents, emerging adults, identity, personal identity, social identity, intersectionality, development, gender, ethnicity/race, social class

Culture embodies meanings, practices, and shared narratives about ancestral and historical experiences, symbols, and worldviews that are passed down through enculturation and change over time as children, adolescents, and adults develop personal relationships and adapt to their changing environments. Since Whiting's (1976) seminal piece on "unpacking" culture, social scientists have theorized about and researched the cultural context of children, adolescents, and adult lives. In this volume, Way and Rogers operationalize the cultural context of identity development as the intersections of gender, ethnicity/race, social class, and immigration in adolescents' everyday lives. Worrell, in contrast, equates culture to ethnicity and race, focusing particularly on how African Americans negotiate their ethnic identity in the context of racism and discrimination. Despite their differences, both sets of authors share the views that discrimination, prejudice, and stigma contour identity development, that context matters in the salience and meanings of identity, and that within-group heterogeneity in identity development has been understudied relative to between-group contrasts.

My reflections on Worrell's and Way and Rogers's chapters are organized as follows: first, I present a brief overview of their key contributions. Second, I build on their discussion of personal and social identity development and address the tension between developmental and social psychological approaches to identity, and in particular, their conceptualization of personal and social identities. I suggest that narratives, particularly master narratives, may provide a way for reducing the tension and providing a more contextual, dynamic approach to identity development (see also Thorne, 2004). Third, I expand on the importance of viewing identity through a cultural lens as I reflect on Worrell's views that racial and ethnic identities and culture are equivalent and that encounters with prejudice and discrimination motivate identity development (cf., Cross, 1995). Fourth, I discuss Way and Rogers's proposal that identity is best conceptualized as the intersections of gender, ethnicity, social class, and immigration in youth's everyday lives. I conclude with suggestions for future directions for theory and research, and in particular, I propose that the disciplinary distinction between personal and social identity may be impeding progress in the field and that we need new methodologies that allow us to study and test hypotheses about the complex intersectionalities of identities and their development.

Identity Development Viewed Through a Cultural Lens

Applying a cultural lens to identity development helps us understand how and why communities, institutions, parents, and other potential mentors guide adolescents and young adults toward particular ideologies about work, relationships, and values. As Erikson (1968), and more recently Chandler (2013) and Schachter and Ventura (2008), proposed, these cultural agents help adolescents become psychologically healthy, productive members of society.

Although theory and research has increasingly conceptualized identity development through a cultural lens, developmental psychologists have tended to focus on between-group differences in how adolescents and emerging adults draw on culture to negotiate their identities. Therefore, Way and Rogers's and Worrell's focus on heterogeneity in identity pathways is a welcome and much needed contribution.

Within developmental psychology, Marcia's *identity status framework*, which builds on Erikson's emphasis on exploration and commitment, has been a fruitful area for exploring heterogeneity, and in particular, individual differences, in identity pathways. Social psychologists have addressed this issue by demonstrating the role of context in the salience of social identities. The salience and centrality of individuals' social identities may depend, at least in part, on whether they view themselves as prototypical group members and on whether they feel accepted by the group (Smith & Leaper, 2006). Worrell suggests that these feelings arise as adolescents and emerging adults reflect on their identities. They may ask themselves such questions as "Am I Black enough?" "Am I woman enough?" and so on. Their answers to these questions depend on their autobiographical narratives—their personal identities—and their coordination of their group memberships—their social identities.

The Development of Personal and Social Identities: The Legacies of Erikson and Tajfel

In this section, I provide an overview of the primary theories that frame Way and Rogers and Worrell's chapters. I then suggest that the concept of master narrative may help build on Worrell's and Way and Rogers's proposals about the politics of ethnic identity development and Way and Rogers's view that positive identity development may be especially difficult for African-American male adolescents.

Erikson proposed that identities are constructed in sociocultural, historical contexts. He primarily focused on how adolescents explore and commit to particular identities in the domains of work, love and relationships, and values. For Erikson, the continuity of self or identity over contexts and time is crucial for well-being. Without self-continuity, people lose their sense of purpose and cannot anticipate how their past and present actions will impact their future (Chandler, Lalonde, Sokol, & Hallett, & Marcia, 2003). Erikson illustrated the importance of self-continuity with his work with war veterans who, upon returning home, could not integrate their current, war-changed self should be selves with their prior lives. More recently, Chandler et al. (2003) showed that Canadian Indigenous adolescents who are not socialized into their cultural traditions and practices and also feel disconnected from mainstream Canadian culture are at risk for depression and suicide.

Social (e.g., Deaux and Perkins, 2001; Hurtado & Silva, 2008) and educational psychologists (e.g., Worrell, this volume) have argued that Erikson did not consider how discrimination and prejudice affect identity processes and resolutions. However, in his seminal work, *Identity, Youth and Crisis* (1968), Erikson wrote about the challenges African Americans face in constructing a positive identity, thereby anticipating Tajfel's proposal that oppressed groups have to engage in *psychological work* to view their group positively and protect their self-esteem.

Social identities only exist when groups differ from each other in characteristics, power, and status. Intergroup conflicts can arise as groups strive to retain or increase their resources, power, and status. To protect their self-esteem in the face of prejudice and discrimination, members of groups with low status, such as women, ethnic minorities, and the poor construe the "other" as having negative traits and values, attribute discrimination to historical and not personal circumstances, or try to "pass" as a member of a more powerful group by adopting its values and behaviors (Goffman, 1963; Tajfel & Turner, 1986). Worrell's discussion of McWhorter's (2000) ideas about black self-sabotage provides an excellent example of how, at least in theory, *victimology*, *separatism*, and *anti-intellectualism* help explain African Americans' academic difficulties (see also Fordham & Ogbu, 1986; Warikoo & Carter, 2009).

Victimology, separatism, and anti-intellectualisms are cultural frames of reference (cf., Ogbu, 1994) that are transmitted across generations and help African Americans survive in an oppressive, unfair society. These frames of reference, which are akin to *master narratives*—the shared cultural stories that organize people's lives and guide their meaning-making of their experiences—may provide a mechanism for reconciling Erikson's proposals about self-continuity with social psychologists' proposal about contextual dynamics of identity. Adolescents and emerging adults draw on master narratives as they construct and share their personal narratives with others and select the self-defining narratives that will anchor their life stories—that is, their identities (McLean, 2005). Although master narratives are fairly resistant to change (Hammack, 2008), over time, individuals can reinterpret their experiences in ways that shift their adherence to cultural master narratives or alter the content of these narratives. This change in narratives and perspectives is essential for reducing intergroup conflicts (Tajfel, 1981; Hammack, 2008).

Regardless of whether one conceptualizes them as personal identities, social identities, or master narratives, identity "boxes" or categories—especially those that structure social interactions and opportunities for exploration in all societies, such as gender, ethnicity/race, and social class—provide a starting point for learning the values, roles, symbols, discourse, and more generally, the behaviors that cultural communities expect of their members. As I elaborate, Worrell's proposal that we use social identity profiles and not categories to study the development and meaning of social identities provides a way to describe and explain heterogeneity and avoid the monolithic, "boxes" approach to identity (cf., Gjerde, 2004).

Identity profiles were also the focus of Marcia's (1966) operationalization of Erikson's theory; following Erikson, Marcia theorized that the profiles represent adolescents' degree of exploration and commitment to identities in the domains of love, work, and values. The concept of identity profiles has also been used productively in discussions about how youth coordinate potentially conflicting identities, such as Schachter's (2004) study of how Israeli youth reconcile conflicts in their religious and sexual identities. In contrast to Worrell and other social identity theorists, however, Marcia and Schachter did not consider how prejudice limits adolescents' opportunities for exploration; that is, the opportunity structure of identity development (cf., Cooper, 2011; Phinney, 1989).

Discrimination, Stigma, and Identity Development

Worrell and Way and Rogers build on the large literature that has documented the emotional toll of social identity development for low-status groups; as noted by Hammack (2011), social identities and their master narratives are inherently political because they inform their members about their status in their cultural communities. When members of low-status groups become aware of their position in society, they react with anger and, at times, hatred toward members of higher status groups, that is, the "other." They also pressure group members to not assimilate into the mainstream, such as when ethnic minorities pressure their peers to not "act white" (see Cooper et al., this volume). It is only as they work through the stages of social identity development that individuals learn to manage these negative emotions, protect their self-esteem, and, eventually, view members of higher status groups positively (Cross, 1995; Worrell, this volume). As they become aware of their privileged positions, members of higher status groups also experience negative emotions such as "white guilt" and manage this emotion and its accompanying anxiety, shame, and ambivalence by denying the significance of race, gender, social class, or any other source of privilege in their lives, justifying their privileged position, or working to improve the lives of lower status groups (Dottolo & Stewart, 2008; Iyer, Leach, & Crosby, 2003; Powell, Branscombe, & Schmitt, 2005).

Its attention to the affective dimension of identity is a strength of social identity theory. Although the moratorium stage also embodies anxiety and other negative emotions that motivate individuals to move to another stage of identity development (Erikson, 1968), the focus on exploration has often led researchers to view moratorium positively. This is unfortunate because, as Strayer (2002) proposed, emotions organize and motivate identity negotiation across the lifespan and can help explain individual differences in identity pathways and why some individuals revisit and recycle through the identity statuses. Developmental measures that include items assessing belonging and affirmation (e.g., Phinney [1990] and Umaña-Taylor, Yazedjian, & Bámaca-Gómez [2004]) contributed to our understanding of the role of affect in identity exploration and ethnic identity. However, as shown by Syed and Azmitia (2008), collecting and analyzing adolescent and emerging adults' narratives of their everyday positive and negative identity experiences will provide a deeper, more nuanced picture of the emotional dynamics of these negotiations.

Identity Development: A Lifespan Developmental Task?

One enduring debate is whether identity development is linked to particular periods of the lifespan (McAdams & Zapata-Gietl, this volume). Erikson located identity development in adolescence and young adulthood, and most developmental psychologists, including Way and Rogers, this volume represent the "yes" side of the debate, noting that although identity development occurs across the lifespan, it takes center stage during adolescence and emerging adulthood (Kroger, 2000). Although they do not deny that self-understanding emerges in early childhood, following Erikson, developmental psychologists propose that the cognitive, perspective-taking skills that are needed to construct an identity narrative that integrates the past, present, and future do not emerge until adolescence (Arnett, this volume; Erikson, 1968; Habermas & Bluck, 2000; Kroger, 2000; McAdams & Zapata-Gietl, this volume). Identity also takes center stage during this period because communities provide opportunities and mentoring for adolescents to explore adult roles (Erikson, 1968).

In contrast, Worrell and social identity theorists represent the "no" side of the debate, noting that social identities can develop at any point of the lifespan because encounters (cf., Cross, 1995) and not age, prompt social identity development. Cross (1978) defined encounters as "a shocking personal or social event that temporarily dislodges the person from his old world view, making the person receptive (and vulnerable) to a new interpretation of his identity and his condition" (p. 17). The encounter, or a succession of encounters, sets the stage for the person to develop a new frame of reference about his or her position in society, be it one of privilege or one of disadvantage. There is considerable empirical evidence that negative encounters prompt social identity development; however, positive encounters, such as exposure to the practices and values of one's social group, can also motivate social identity development (Syed & Azmitia, 2008; 2010).

The debate about whether identity development is located at a specific period of the lifespan endures because there is empirical support for both sides of the debate. By elementary school, children have constructed gender and ethnic/racial identities and already show the predicted ingroup favoritism. However, they do not show outgroup derogation (Pfeifer et al., 2007), a finding that suggests that these identities may not be as nuanced and complex as those of adolescents and emerging adults. Possibly, age-related changes also occur in individuals' ability to integrate their personal and social identities and articulate the intersections between their various social identities.

To date, there is a scarcity of research on developmental changes in adolescents and emerging adults' understanding and articulation of the intersectionalities among their multiple identities. In our own research, we have found significant changes from the sophomore to the senior year of college in emerging adults' perception of and ability to explain the intersection among their gender, ethnic, and social class identities (Azmitia, Syed, & Radmacher, 2008). Creating and testing a developmental model of identity intersectionalities is a key direction for future research. Ideally, this interdisciplinary developmental model will integrate theory and research on personal and social identities in a way that specifies a role for age and context, be it the local contexts of home, peers, and school or the more global contexts of culture and historical time. As illustrated by Way and Rogers, this volume, for example, ethnicity/race and gender are intimately linked in African-American boys' identity narratives about school and relationships. Following Worrell's and Way and Roger's emphasis on within-group heterogeneity, this developmental model should also investigate variability in adolescents' and emerging adults' intersectionality profiles and configurations

Culture, Race, and Ethnicity

Worrell's chapter nicely illustrates how heterogeneity in identity development occurs both within and between cultures. Cultures are not monolithic entities that can be defined independently of their members; rather, cultures and cultural stories are created and changed by people through discourse and power (Gjerde, 2004), and these cultural narratives can unite social groups as well as be the source of conflicts, wars, and revolutions (Hammack, 2008; Maalouf, 2001). Race and ethnicity have often been privileged in cultural analyses of identity development, and, more generally, in discussions of how cultural communities socialize children, adolescents, and young adults (cf., Cross, 1981; Gjerde, 2004; Quintana & Mckown, 2008). As Worrell suggests, "it is through identity that culture as race and ethnicity is manifested" (this volume). In equating racial and ethnic identity with culture, Worrell builds on Fordham and Ogbu's (1986) seminal work on how race and ethnicity provide an attitudinal and motivational lens through which minorities interpret their experiences. Because these attitudes and attributions—cultural frames of reference—allow individuals to process experiences in their everyday worlds, these attitudinal lenses, and not age, fuel identity development; that is, "neither racial nor ethnic identity is developmental" (Worrell, this volume).

Worrell's overview of theories, debates, and measures of ethnic and racial identity are ably intertwined with his thoughts about what it means to be Black in America, brought poignantly into relief by Trayvon Martin's shooting in February 2012 and research on how African-American parents socialize their children to anticipate negative stereotyping in school and society at large (Hughes et al., 2009). Historically, no ethnic group in the United States has been stereotyped as negatively as African Americans, so much so that African-heritage Caribbean immigrants accentuate their accent and dress in ways that convey that they are not US born (Waters, 1996). In constructing their identities, US-born African Americans must challenge stereotypes and find a way to succeed in an unjust, prejudicial society. Although some adolescents and young adults react to prejudice and discrimination by constructing oppositional or negative identities that reject mainstream cultural values and practices, others challenge the negative stereotypes and work to attain mainstream markers of success, such as college educations and professional occupations, to prove racists and classists wrong (Cooper, 2011; Way & Rogers, this volume).

Worrell's research focuses primarily on African Americans, but he and others (e.g., Ogbu, 1994) view their theories and findings as applicable to other minority groups such as Latinos and Native Americans that have historically been discriminated against in the United States and to other countries with racial/ethnic stratification. A growing body of research has revealed commonalities in minority groups' experiences of discrimination, ranging from ethnic/racial teasing and discrimination at school to unemployment and incarceration. Yet, just as ethnic minority groups are stereotyped, so are members of ethnic majorities. For example, low-income white college students are often stereotyped as middle or upper class (Azmitia et al., 2008). Some ethnic minority individuals also assume that all majority group members are racist or stereotype and derogate majority group members (Fine, Wise, Addleston, & Marusza, 1997).

Worrell, this volume, shows how viewing ethnic/racial identities as attitudes, frames of reference, or worldviews—and not as stereotypes—is the first step against essentialist, monolithic views of identity and culture. His approach draws heavily on Cross's expanded *nigrescence model* (Vandiver, Fhagen-Smith, Cokley, Cross, & Worrell, 2001; Worrell, Cross, & Vandiver, 2001; Worrell, Vandiver, Cross & Fhagen-Smith, 2004), which specifies and assesses six attitudes toward developing an ethnic/racial identity in a majority world: assimilation, miseducation, self-hatred, anti-white, Afrocentricity, and multiculturalist. Individuals' scores on scales that measure these attitudes can be used to create profiles that predict a variety of positive and negative outcomes. Within-group variations in these profiles can be used to index heterogeneities in the ethnic and racial identities. Worrell's profile approach has promise. Although his work, and more broadly, Cross's framework, has not addressed ethnic/racial socialization and identity development in childhood, research has shown that racial stereotypes influence preschool and elementary school children's behavior and attitudes (Ambady, Shih, Kim, & Pittinsky, 2001; McKown & Weinstein, 2003). Thus, it would be especially useful to study age-related changes in children's ethnic awareness and responses to prejudice and discrimination and link them to ethnic identity profiles in adolescence and emerging adulthood. A longitudinal approach will be especially important for bridging personal and social identities and uncovering the association between individuals' cognitive and social competencies, lived experiences, and their profiles of ethnic/racial identity development. To date, ethnic/racial, gender, and social class development are primarily inferred from cross-sectional studies and thus represent age-related—but not developmental—identity pathways.

Social identity theorists, and social psychologists in general, have underscored the importance of context in the development and performance of identity. Goodnow (2011) reminds us, however, that how we define context has theoretical, empirical, and practical implications. Worrell's definition of context includes cultural models or frames of reference that mark social groups and specify the heterogeneity of identity pathways. He also discusses how the salience and meaning of social identities changes across contexts. Worrell's focus on ethnicity and race, however, deflects attention from other hierarchies that create boundaries between societal groups, such as social class, that are often conflated with ethnicity and race.

The lack of attention paid to social class identities is surprising given that class figures prominently in the American Dream, which embodies the idea that through hard work, people can move up the class ladder. In contrast to ethnicity/race and other social identities such as gender and religion, however, in contemporary society it is more difficult to take pride in being poor or working class, and it is more acceptable to be openly derogatory of the poor and accuse them of being lazy, unmotivated, unsophisticated, and dirty and refer to them as rednecks, white trash, or crackers (Jarosz & Lawson, 2002). The closest we have come to painting the poor in a positive light is the recent Occupy Movement, which had as its slogan "we are the 99 percent," that referenced the idea that, in the United States, wealth is concentrated in the top 1 percent. The Occupy Movement brought together a broad cross-section of people working for class equality and social change.

Class is also at the center of Bourdieu's (1989) *social capital theory*, which specifies how the upper classes maintain their resources and privileges; thus, class reproduction is more common than class mobility. Social capital and its associated informational, relational, and financial resources have long been at the core of theory and research on variations in adolescents' academic and identity pathways. Much like ethnic minorities, working class students often construe academic success as a betrayal of their social group, with peers playing a particularly important role in maintaining class boundaries (Eckert, 1989; Willis, 1977).

Although class is undoubtedly an important structural hierarchy in all cultures and has been at the heart of the political discourse of democracy, socialism, and Marxism, it is more difficult for US adolescents and emerging adults to construct their class identities because discourses about class have been less prominent than discourses about ethnicity/race and gender (hooks, 2000). In our longitudinal study of the transition to and through college, poor and working class students typically referred to class as financial resources and struggled to articulate values and practices related to class identity. Possibly, the fact that class is seen as more fluid than other identities because individuals can move up or down the class ladder also contributes to adolescents' and young adults' difficulties in constructing and articulating a class identity. Finally, because class and race/ethnicity are often associated, it may be difficult for adolescents and young adults to view class as separable from other sources of stigma such as race and ethnicity.

Identity Intersectionalities, Stereotypes, and Desired and Feared Selves

Way and Rogers incorporate class and gender in their intersectional approach to how ethnic/racial minority adolescents negotiate their identities in ways that challenges societal prejudices and stereotypes and intertwine personal and social identities. Their work also addresses other stereotypes that contour identity development in US high schools, such as nationality and immigration and sexuality. Unlike Worrell, this volume, who uses ethnic/racial identity profiles to characterize the heterogeneity of African-American adolescents' ethnic/racial identity development, Way and Rogers include African-American, white, Chinese, Dominican, and Puerto Rican adolescents' narratives of their daily lives in low-income neighborhoods and schools. However, both sets of authors underscore the difficulties of male ethnic minority adolescents in forming nonstereotypic, positive identities.

Way and Rogers propose that the focus on the person (Erikson and neo-Eriksonians) or the group (social identity theorists) has resulted in a lack of theory and research on the role of relationships in identity development. This criticism seems unwarranted, given an extensive body of research that has highlighted how parent–child relationships foster the acquisition of the cognitive and social competencies needed for identity development (e.g., Grotevant & Cooper, 2006; Fivush & Zaman, this volume; McLean & Jennings, 2012; Reis & Youniss, 2004). Research has also illustrated how peers influence adolescents' academic and career identities (Azmitia & Cooper, 2002; Eckert, 1989; MacLeod, 1987; Willis, 1977). Way and Rogers are correct, however, in noting that theory and research on identity intersectionalities has not considered the role of relationships in the development of intersectionality. The intersectionalities of boys'/men's identities have also been understudied.

From its inception, theory and research on intersectionality focused on the experiences of girls and women because they have less power than men in most societies (see also Fivush & Zaman, this volume). In this light, Way and Rogers's focus on adolescent boys is a welcome contribution to the field. Ethnic minority males, particularly African-American and Latino males, experience the most negative stereotyping in US society. This stereotyping leads to them being treated negatively by police, teachers, store owners, and peers (Aronson, 2004; Greene, Way, & Pahl, 2006; Solorzano, Ceja, & Yosso, 2000) and contributes to the high levels of school drop-out, unemployment, and incarceration of African-American and Latino male adolescents. Through their participants' narratives, Way and Rogers illustrate how these boys distance themselves from the stereotypes as they try to build positive identities (cf., Cooper, 2011). These acts of resistance contribute to these adolescents' resilience and survival in an unjust society, a point Worrell also makes in his chapter. Like Worrell, Way and Rogers also highlight the negative stereotypes that apply to white boys (e.g., not very good athletes) or to adolescents from minority groups with greater status (e.g., Asian males as weak or gay). It may seem that being portrayed as nonathletes, weak, or gay is not as serious as being portrayed as dangerous thugs, but in the world of boys, where strength and athletic prowess are valued, these stereotypes can be devastating to identity and self-esteem and, as illustrated by Mathew Shepard, a gay college student who was beaten to death in Montana by two homophobic men and whose widely-publicized case contributed to the hate bias act approved by the U.S. Congress in 2009, can result in violence and death.

Nationality and immigration are another source of stereotypes and heterogeneity in adolescents' identity development. Way and Rogers illustrate how the Chinese adolescents they interviewed distanced themselves from recent Chinese immigrants who they saw as dirty and unsophisticated, and similar attitudes toward recent immigrants have been reported for second- and third-generation Latinos (Stephan, Ybarra, & Bachman, 1999). Negative stereotypes of immigrants are also reflected in national debates about immigration in the United States and other nations. These debates contribute to the tensions in schools and communities about who belongs and deserves resources and a chance at the American Dream. Yet, as Waters (1996) has shown, being an immigrant can be advantageous because it allows adolescents to distance themselves from the negative stereotypes of native-born youth.

What all of these identity negotiations and performances have in common is that they allow adolescents to position themselves as exceptions to stereotypic portrayals and pursue identity and developmental pathways that mark them as role models with the potential to infiltrate powerful groups in society and better their lives and communities. As noted by participants in Way and Rogers's research, resisting stereotypes allows these adolescent boys to dream about becoming the next Black president, going to college, and helping their families escape poverty.

Identities, Intersectionalities, and Future Directions for Theory and Research

Differentiating between personal and social identities may reflect more of a disciplinary difference than a meaningful distinction that can be tested empirically; Worrell's and Way and Rogers's chapters illustrate the advantages of attending to both dimensions of identity for theory and research. Deaux and Perkins (2001) made a similar point in their discussion of the difficulties of determining where personal identity ends and social identities begin. *Optimal distinctiveness theory* (Brewer, 1991) may be a way to integrate personal and social identities and create a productive interdisciplinary approach to studying the cultural, historical, and local contexts of identity development. Brewer argued that people are motivated to attain a balance between inclusiveness and distinctiveness within and between their social groups and situations. When the balance is disrupted (e.g., people feel isolated and too different from the group or the group feels too homogeneous and anonymous), they engage in strategies and behaviors to restore the optimal balance between distinctiveness and group belonging. Brewer also proposed that people will choose social identities that are optimally distinct— neither too assimilated nor too different. Brewer's argument resonates with Erikson's ideas about individuation, the process through which adolescents and young adults learn to balance individuality and connectedness (for an extensive discussion of individuation, see Grotevant & Cooper, 2006. Possibly, studying how adolescents and young adults balance their need to belong with their need to be independent and unique will help create a mutually beneficial dialogue between developmental and social psychology and other social scientists. This dialogue should address the issue that adolescents and emerging adults belong to multiple places and worlds, which adds complexity to their identity configurations, and should challenge us to research not only the development of intersecting identities, but address the likely possibility that these intersections change over time.

I end my reflections on culture and identity development by addressing a topic that receives very little attention in Worrell's and Way and Rogers's chapters and yet is a key issue for theory, research, and practice: how adolescents and young adults negotiate hybrid identities, and, in particular, mixed-race identities. When the 2000 US census allowed people to identify as multiracial, 9 million chose to do so, and the numbers have been growing dramatically since then, making it one of the fastest growing demographics (Sumabat-Estrada, 2013). Despite much theorizing about how mixed-race people construct their identities, empirical research has yielded inconsistent results, perhaps because there is heterogeneity in how adolescents and young adults construct these identities (Rockquemore, Brunsma, & Delgado, 2009; Root, 1992; 1996; Sánchez, Reyes, & Sinh, 2006).

Globalization and immigration will increase mixed-race and other forms of hybrid identities (Arnett, 2002; this volume), and our theories and research will have to address these more complex identities and identity narratives. Way and Rogers propose that narrative methods are ideal for capturing how adolescents experience identities in their everyday lives. Since Erikson, narrative and other qualitative approaches have contributed significantly to our understanding of identity development. Yet, because mainstream psychology privileges quantitative methods, it will be important to incorporate these methodologies into theory and research on the intersectionalities of adolescents' and young adults' identities (see also Arnett, this volume; Josselson & Flum, this volume). Supplementing Worrell's quantitative identity profiles with narratives that bring them to life might provide insights about the many meanings of culture, ethnicity, and race and how these narratives change over time.

Claiming that one takes a "mixed methods" approach to a research problem, such as explicating the relation between culture and identity, has become commonplace. Yet, there remains an uneasy tension between quantitative and qualitative approaches, particularly when there is a discrepancy in the findings. In our own research, for example, we have found that qualitative interviews can often reveal nuances that are not captured by surveys. Possibly, these differences may be due to our interviews tapping adolescents' memories for specific events or experiences—episodic memories, so to speak—and surveys measuring more global experiences—generalized narratives or semantic memories. Clearly, much work is still needed to find optimal combinations of qualitative and quantitative methods in ways that bring out the strengths of each approach.

Intersectionality is another concept that has challenged extant dichotomies that essentialize groups. Despite its popularity, intersectionality can conjure an endless list of potential identity intersections (Cole, 2009), and the term has been so vaguely defined that it has been difficult to assess whether people conceptualize their identities as intersecting or as relatively independent domains (Azmitia & Thomas, in press; Davis, 2008). The popularity of the concept is due, at least to an extent, to its powerful metaphor of intersecting selves, which resonates with researchers from a variety of disciplines and popular discourse. It would be interesting to investigate cultural variations in the salience and intersection of multiple identities and whether multiple intersecting identities are more common in societies where there are multiple identity pathways and individuals' agency has a prominent role in identity development.

More information is also needed on how adolescents and young adults manage identity development in a globalized, technological world. Globalization and immigration have promoted the development of a variety of identities that help youth learn and accept their roles and craft identities that help them become productive members of their groups and cultures. A contextual, intersectional, developmental model that brings together personal and social identities will help us understand variations in how youth carry out the important task of identity development. In our own research, for example, we have been studying how college-going emerging adults who are the first in their families to go to college coordinate their "home" and "university" identities in the context of close relationships and their gender, ethnic, and social class identities. We are interested in whether these identity coordinations or profiles change over the course of their college careers and whether these changes are linked to educational and career identities. Their surveys and interviews often reveal the challenges of feeling different and marginalized at home and school and how, over time, academically successful emerging adults create cohesive identity narratives that provide meaning and a sense of purpose to their lives.

In conclusion, Way and Rogers's and Worrell's chapters build on and extend Erikson's and Tajfel and Turner's foundational approaches to identity development and provide ample evidence of how situating identity development in its cultural context informs theory, research, and practice. As they actively engage with their multiple worlds, adolescents and emerging adults filter identity values, beliefs, practices, and goals through the intersectional lenses of their identities. At times, their identity pathways require that they resolve contradictions among cultural messages, roles, and goals and manage tensions between their own and their families' and peers' expectations. Their identity stories illustrate the rich complexity of growing up in this globalized world.

References

Ambady, N., Shih, M., Kim, A., & Pittinsky, T. L. (2001). Stereotype susceptibility in children: Effects of identity activation on quantitative performance. *Psychological Science*, 12(5), 385–390.

Arnett, J. J. (2002). The psychology of globalization. *American Psychologist*, 57(10), 774.

Aronson, J. (2004). The threat of stereotype. *Educational Leadership*, 62, 14–20.

Azmitia, M., & Cooper, C. R. (2002). Good or bad? Peer influences on Latino and European American adolescents' pathways through school. *Journal of Education for Students Placed at Risk*, 6(1–2), 45–71.

Azmitia, M., Syed, M., & Radmacher, K. (2008). On the intersection of personal and social identities: Introduction and evidence from a longitudinal study of emerging adults. *New Directions for Child and Adolescent Development*, 120, 1–16.

Azmitia, M., & Thomas, V. D. (in press). Intersectionality and the development of self and identity. In R. Scott, S. Kosslyn, & N. Pinkerton (Eds.), *Emerging trends in the social and behavioral sciences*. New York: Wiley.

Bourdieu, P. (1989). Social space and symbolic power. *Sociological Theory*, 7(1), 14–25.

Brewer, M. B. (1991). The social self: On being the same and different at the same time. *Personality and Social Psychology Bulletin*, 17(5), 475–482.

Chandler, M. J. (2013). On being indigenous: An essay on the hermeneutics of cultural identity. *Human Development*, 56(2), 83–97.

Chandler, M. J., Lalonde, C. E., Sokol, B. W., Hallett, D., & Marcia, J. E. (2003). Personal persistence, identity development, and suicide: A study of Native and non-native North American adolescents. *Monographs of the Society for Research in Child Development*, i–138.

Cole, E. R. (2009). Intersectionality and research in psychology. *American Psychologist*, 64(3), 170–180.

Cooper, C. R. (2011). *Bridging multiple worlds: Cultures, identities, and pathways to college*. New York: Oxford University Press.

Cross, W. E. (1978). The Thomas and Cross models of psychological nigrescence: A review. *Journal of Black Psychology*, 5(1), 13–31.

Cross, W. E. (1995). The psychology of nigrescence: Revising the Cross Model. In J. G. Ponderotto, M. J. Casas, L. A. Suzuki, & C. M. Alexander (Eds.), *Handbook of multicultural counseling* (pp. 93–122). Thousand Oaks, CA: Sage.

Davis, K. (2008). Intersectionality as buzzword: A sociology of science perspective on what makes a feminist theory successful. *Feminist Theory*, 9(1), 67–85.

Deaux, K., & Perkins, T. S. (2001). The kaleidoscopic self. In C. Sedikides & M. B. Brewer (Eds.), *Individual self, relational self, collective self.* (pp. 299–313). New York: Psychology Press.

Dottolo, A. L., & Stewart, A. J. (2008). "Don't ever forget now, you're a black man in America": Intersections of race, class and gender in encounters with the police. *Sex Roles*, 59(5–6), 350–364.

Eckert, P. (1989). *Jocks and burnouts: Social categories and identity in the high school*. New York: Teachers College Press.

Erikson, E. (1968). *Identity, youth, and crisis*. New York: Basic Books.

Fine, M., Weis, L., Addleston, J., & Marusza, J. (1997). In-secure times: Constructing white, working class masculinities in the 20th century. *Gender and Society* 11(1), 52–68.

Fordham, S., & Ogbu, J. U. (1986). Black students' school success: Coping with the "burden of 'acting white.'" *Urban Review*, 18(3), 176–206.

Gjerde, P. F. (2004). Culture, power, and experience: Toward a person-centered cultural psychology. *Human Development*, 47(3), 138–157.

Goffman, E. (1963). *Stigma: Notes on the management of spoiled identity*. New York: Simon & Schuster.

Goodnow, J. J. (2011). Merging cultural and psychological accounts of family contexts. *Bridging cultural and developmental psychology: New syntheses in theory, research and policy*, 73–91.

Greene, M. L., Way, N., & Pahl, K. (2006). Trajectories of perceived adult and peer discrimination among Black, Latino, and Asian American adolescents: Patterns and psychological correlates. *Developmental Psychology*, 42(2), 218–236.

Grotevant, H. D., & Cooper, C. R. (2006). Individuality and connectedness in adolescent development. In E. Skoe & A. von der Lippe (Eds.), *Personality development in adolescence: A cross national and lifespan perspective*. New York: Routledge.

Habermas, T., & Bluck, S. (2000). Getting a life: The emergence of the life story in adolescence. *Psychological Bulletin*, 126(5), 748.

Hammack, P. L. (2008). Narrative and the cultural psychology of identity. *Personality and Social Psychology Review*, 12(3), 222–247.

Hammack, P. L. (2011). Narrative and the politics of meaning. *Narrative Inquiry*, 21(2), 311–318.

hooks, b. (2000). *Where we stand: Class matters*. New York: Routledge.

Hughes, D., Witherspoon, D., Rivas-Drake, D., & West-Bey, N. (2009). Received ethnic–racial socialization messages and youths' academic and behavioral outcomes: Examining the mediating role of ethnic identity and self-esteem. *Cultural Diversity and Ethnic Minority Psychology*, 15(2), 112.

Hurtado, A., & Silva, J. M. (2008). Creating new social identities in children through critical multicultural media: The case of Little Bill. *New Directions for Child and Adolescent Development*, 2008(120), 17–30.

Iyer, A., Leach, C. W., & Crosby, F. J. (2003). White guilt and racial compensation: The benefits and limits of self-focus. *Personality and Social Psychology Bulletin*, 29(1), 117–129.

Jarosz, L., & Lawson, V. (2002). "Sophisticated people versus rednecks": Economic restructuring and class difference in America's West. *Antipode*, 34(1), 8–27.

Kroger, J. (2000). Ego identity status research in the new millennium. *International Journal of Behavioral Development*, 24(2), 145–148.

Maalouf, A. (2001). *In the name of identity: Violence and the need to belong*. New York: Arcade Publishing.

MacLeod, J. (1987). *Ain't no makin' it: Leveled aspirations in a low-income neighborhood*. Boulder, CO: Westview Press.

Marcia, J. E. (1966). Development and validation of ego-identity status. *Journal of Personality and Social Psychology*, 3(5), 551.

McKown, C., & Weinstein, R. S. (2003). The development and consequences of stereotype consciousness in middle childhood. *Child Development*, 74(2), 498–515.

McLean, K. C. (2005). Late adolescent identity development: Narrative meaning making and memory telling. *Developmental Psychology*, 41(4), 683–691.

McLean, K. C., & Jennings, L. E. (2012). Teens telling tales: How maternal and peer audiences support narrative identity development. *Journal of Adolescence*, 35(6), 1455–1469.

McWhorter, J. H. (2000). *Losing the race: Self-sabotage in Black America*. New York: Simon & Schuster.

Ogbu, John U. (1994). From cultural differences to differences in cultural frame of reference. In P. M. Greenfield & R. Cocking (Eds.), *Cross-cultural roots of minority child development* (pp. 365–391). Hillsdale, NJ: Lawrence Erlbaum Associates.

Pfeifer, J. H., Ruble, D. N., Bachman, M. A., Alvarez, J. M., Cameron, J. A., & Fuligni, A. J. (2007). Social identities and intergroup bias in immigrant and nonimmigrant children. *Developmental Psychology*, 43(2), 496.

Phinney, J. S. (1989). Stages of ethnic identity development in minority group adolescents. *Journal of Early Adolescence*, 9(1–2), 34–49.

Phinney, J. S. (1990). Ethnic identity in adolescents and adults: Review of research. *Psychological Bulletin*, 108(3), 499–514.

Powell, A. A., Branscombe, N. R., & Schmitt, M. T. (2005). Inequality as ingroup privilege or outgroup disadvantage: The impact of group focus on collective guilt and interracial attitudes. *Personality and Social Psychology Bulletin*, 31(4), 508–521.

Reis, O., & Youniss, J. (2004). Patterns in identity change and development in relationships with mothers and friends. *Journal of Adolescent Research*, 19(1), 31–44.

Rockquemore, K. A., Brunsma, D. L., & Delgado, D. J. (2009). Racing to theory or retheorizing race? Understanding the struggle to build a multiracial identity theory. *Journal of Social Issues*, 65(1), 13–34.

Root, M. P. (1992). *Back to the drawing board: Methodological issues in research on multiracial people*. Sage Publications.

Root, M. P. P. (Ed.) (1996). *The multiracial experience: Racial borders as the new frontier*. Thousand Oaks, CA: Sage Publications.

Quintana, S. M., & McKown, C. (Eds.). (2008). *Handbook of race, racism, and the developing child*. New York: Wiley.

Sánchez, B., Reyes, O., & Singh, J. (2006). Makin' it in college: The value of significant individuals in the lives of Mexican American adolescents. *Journal of Hispanic Higher Education*, 5(1), 48–67.

Schachter, E. P. (2004). Identity configurations: A new perspective on identity formation in contemporary society. *Journal of Personality*, 72(1), 167–200.

Schachter, E. P., & Ventura, J. J. (2008). Identity agents: Parents as active and reflective participants in their children's identity formation. *Journal of Research on Adolescence*, 18(3), 449–476.

Smith, T. E., & Leaper, C. (2006). Self-perceived gender typicality and the peer context during adolescence. *Journal of Research on Adolescence*, 16(1), 91–104.

Solorzano, D., Ceja, M., & Yosso, T. (2000). Critical race theory, racial microaggressions, and campus racial climate: The experiences of African American college students. *The Journal of Negro Education*, 7, 60–73.

Stephan, W. G., Ybarra, O., & Bachman, G. (1999). Prejudice toward immigrants. *Journal of Applied Social Psychology*, 29(11), 2221–2237.

Strayer, J. (2002). The dynamics of emotions and life cycle identity. *Identity: An International Journal of Theory and Research*, 2(1), 47–79.

Sumabat-Estrada, G. (2013, April). *As time goes by: A longitudinal study of ethnic identity development in monoethnic and biethnic emerging adults*. Poster presented at the biennial meeting of the Society for Research in Child Development, Seattle, WA.

Syed, M., & Azmitia, M. (2008). A narrative approach to ethnic identity in emerging adulthood: bringing life to the identity status model. *Developmental psychology*, 44(4), 1012.

Syed, M., & Azmitia, M. (2010). Narrative and ethnic identity exploration: A longitudinal account of emerging adults' ethnicity-related experiences. *Developmental Psychology*, 46(1), 208.

Tajfel, H. (1981). *Human groups and social categories: Studies in social psychology*. New York: Cambridge University Press.

Tajfel, H., & Turner, J. C. (1986). The social identity theory of intergroup behavior. In S. Worchel & W. G. Austin (Eds.), *The psychology of intergroup relations* (pp. 7–24). Chicago: Nelson-Hall Publishers.

Thorne, A. (2004). Putting the person into social identity. *Human Development*, 47(6), 361–365.

Umaña-Taylor, A. J., Yazedjian, A., & Bámaca-Gómez, M. (2004). Developing the ethnic identity scale using Eriksonian and social identity perspectives. *Identity: An International Journal of Theory and Research*, 4(1), 9–38.

Vandiver, B. J., Fhagen-Smith, P. E., Cokley, K. O., Cross, W. E., & Worrell, F. C. (2001). Cross's nigrescence model: From theory to scale to theory. *Journal of Multicultural Counseling and Development*, 29(3), 174–200.

Warikoo, N., & Carter, P. (2009). Cultural explanations for racial and ethnic stratification in academic achievement: A call for a new and improved theory. *Review of Educational Research*, 79(1), 366–394.

Waters, M. C. (1996). The intersection of gender, race, and ethnicity in identity development of Caribbean American teens. *Urban girls: Resisting stereotypes, creating identities* (pp. 65–81). New York: New York University Press.

Willis, P. E. (1977). *Learning to labour: How working class kids get working class jobs*. New York: Columbia University Press.

Whiting, B. B. (1976). Unpackaging variables. In K. F. Riegel & J. A. Meacham (Eds) *The developing individual in a changing world* (Vol. 1, pp. 303–309). Chicago: Aldine.

Worrell, F. C., Cross, W. E., & Vandiver, B. J. (2001). Nigrescence theory: Current status and challenges for the future. *Journal of Multicultural Counseling and Development*, 29(3), 201–213.

Worrell, F. C., Vandiver, B. J., Cross, W. E., & Fhagen-Smith, P. E. (2004). Reliability and structural validity of cross racial identity scale scores in a sample of African American adults. *Journal of Black Psychology*, 30(4), 489–505.

PART 6

Applied Issues in Identity Development

CHAPTER 19

Identities, Cultures, and Schooling: How Students Navigate Racial-Ethnic, Indigenous, Immigrant, Social Class, and Gender Identities on Their Pathways Through School

Catherine R. Cooper, Elizabeth Gonzalez, *and* Antoinette R. Wilson

Abstract

How can racial-ethnic minority, immigrant, Indigenous, and low-income youth navigate pathways through school without losing their cultural identities? In this chapter, we draw on writings of Erikson and Tajfel on the development of personal and social group identities across contexts to consider roots and remedies for the *academic pipeline problem*, a global issue of identities and schooling in multicultural societies. We extend these analyses with early interdisciplinary models and recent advances in understanding how *social capital*, *alienation*, and *challenge* shape students' capacities to integrate academic and racial-ethnic identities on their pathways through school. We focus on variation within racial-ethnic groups in the meanings and impact of intragroup discrimination for identities and schooling, highlighting experiences of African American and Indigenous Mexican immigrant youth. Finally, we consider how aligning multilevel theories and tools can support integrating students' academic and racial-ethnic identities; opening academic pipelines; and advancing cycles of research, practice, and policies.

Key Words: schooling, race-ethnicity, Indigenous, immigration, social class, gender, policy, Erikson, social capital, alienation/belonging

---

The developmental pathways of youth through school can be seen as moving through *academic pipelines* from early childhood to their adult career, family, cultural, and civic identities (Cooper, 2011; Gándara, Larson, Mehan, & Rumberger, 1998; Swail, Cabrera, Lee, & Williams, 2005). Many nations hold ideals that their children will have equal access to schooling and advance through their merits. In reality, for each cohort of children that starts school, the numbers of racial-ethnic minority, immigrant, Indigenous, and low-income youth who graduate from high school, enroll in college, transfer from community college to universities, and complete undergraduate and graduate degrees shrink at each of these transitions—leading to their label as "underrepresented minorities" (URM) (Bowen, Chingos, & McPherson, 2009; Cooper, 2011). For example, in 2010, 88 percent of European Americans had graduated from high school and 30 percent had graduated from college, compared to 63 percent and 14 percent for Latinos, 77 percent and 13 percent for Native Americans, 84 percent and 20 percent for African Americans, and 89 percent and 52 percent for Asian Americans, respectively (US Census Bureau, 2012). Gender gaps also appear; for example, among European Americans, 47 percent and 53 percent of undergraduates under age 24 are males and females, respectively, compared to 42 percent and 58 percent for Latinos, and 41 percent and 59 percent for African Americans (American Council on Education, 2010). This *academic pipeline problem* makes college enrollments and college-based professions unrepresentative of their broader communities, and its significance is intensifying worldwide as low-income, immigrant, racial-ethnic minority, and Indigenous youth make up growing segments of primary school enrollments.

Of course, a college education is not the only definition of success, and schooling extends only to primary schools in some regions and to universities in others. But in each cultural group and region worldwide, education is strongly linked to lifelong opportunities. Those alienated from education are at higher risk for marginalized life pathways that are costly for them and their communities. The academic pipeline problem is motivating researchers, educators, and policymakers to consider new approaches to its roots and remedies. Increasingly, these approaches center on the interplay among academic, racial-ethnic, and institutional identities.

Academic and Racial-Ethnic Identities and the Academic Pipeline Problem

Throughout the history of the United States, the price of school success for racial-ethnic minority, immigrant, and Indigenous youth has been for them to "become American" and relinquish their cultures and languages. Parallel dilemmas occur worldwide. In the United States and Canada, now-discredited policies sent Indigenous and immigrant children away from their families to boarding schools that allowed only English to be spoken, consistent with widespread views that schools should assimilate these children (Dewey, 1916). However, in recent years, educators, researchers, and policymakers, along with students, families, and community leaders, have asked how ethnically diverse students can integrate their *academic identities*—seen in making good grades, aspiring to attend college, and pursuing college-based careers—with their *social identities* or sense of belonging to their racial-ethnic, immigrant, Indigenous, gender, and social class groups (Phinney & Alipuria, 1996; Sellers, Smith, Shelton, Rowley, & Chavous, 1998).

The language and definitions of race, ethnicity, immigration, and culture have been evolving over the history of the United States, along with persisting issues of racism, exclusion, and moral superiority of higher status racial, ethnic, immigrant, and social class groups. Rumbaut (2009) has recounted Benjamin Franklin's writing with alarm in 1751 about the impossibility of "alien" German newcomers ever integrating with British-descent citizens of Pennsylvania. The enduring complexities of these issues to the present day can be heard when Black, Native American, Latino, and Asian American youth with strong academic identities are teased for being an "Oreo" (chocolate cookie with white filling), apple, coconut, or "Twinkie" (yellow cake with white filling), respectively. In this chapter, we examine how and in what contexts students' identities intersect—and for some, become integrated—on their pathways through school.

Chapter Overview

We set the foundation of our chapter in writings about personal and social identities in context by Erikson (1950, 1968a) and Tajfel (1982; Tajfel & Turner, 1986). To extend our understanding of the developmental contexts of identity development, we then consider early models and recent advances about how three forces—*social capital, alienation*, and *challenge*—shape students' academic and racial-ethnic identities on their pathways through school (Cooper, 2011). First, in his theory of *social capital*, French sociologist Bourdieu (Bourdieu & Passeron, 1986) pointed to the continuity or *cultural reproduction* in social class hierarchies across family generations; recent work has asked how low-income and ethnic minority families and students can disrupt such cultural reproduction by helping children "move up" to a better life. Second, in his pioneering writings on alienation and schooling, educational anthropologist Ogbu, an immigrant from Nigeria to the United States, traced how low-income, ethnic minority, and immigrant parents often hold high aspirations for their children's education but that discrimination and poor schools dim these hopes and lead children to develop *oppositional identities* and disengage from school (Fordham & Ogbu, 1986; Ogbu & Simons, 1988). We consider recent research on the roles of discrimination and stereotyping in the academic and racial-ethnic identities of African American and Indigenous Mexican immigrant youth. Third, early writings on identity and resiliency marked the paradoxical interplay of challenges and resources (Erikson, 1968; Werner, 1993); we consider recent work asking when discrimination, poverty, and other challenges can foster identity development and motivate youth to succeed on behalf of their families and communities (Cooper, 2011; Kumar, Seay, & Warnke, 2012; Phelan, Davidson, & Yu, 1998). Here, we also examine how institutional identities of schools and universities can support students' academic and racial-ethnic identities and open academic pipelines. Finally, we look ahead to next steps and close with an invitation.

In this chapter, we hope to make four distinctive contributions. First, we seek to align concepts of identities, cultures, and schooling with Erikson's and Tajfel's theories, as well as with new and converging theoretical work across the social sciences, to advance research, practice, and policies on the academic pipeline problem (Syed & Mitchell, 2013). Second, because we view racial-ethnic, Indigenous, social class, immigrant, gender, and other identities as comprising youth's multifaceted cultural identities, we examine how, as social actors, youth construct intersecting and sometimes integrated meanings of these identities from demographic labels and stereotypes and from continuities and changes in the values and practices across their cultural worlds (Cooper, 2011; Phelan et al., 1998; Way & Rogers, this volume). We ground our approach in the individual, social, and historical nature of concepts of race and ethnicity, the longstanding racialization of ethnicity (Rumbaut, 2009), and in how children and adults intertwine racial, ethnic, gender, and other identity labels and their meanings. Third, we highlight variations in meanings of identities and schooling within groups and both similarities and differences across groups (Sue & Sue, 1987); this approach contrasts with more common between-group or "race-comparative" designs that can foster deficit thinking about ethnic minority youth (Cooper, Garcia Coll, Thorne, & Orellana, 2005; McLoyd, 2005). Finally, we foreground the importance of cultural contexts in identity development across domains, including families, peers, communities, school, and work. Taken together, we hope these perspectives will spark productive debate on the issues encompassed by this volume.

Erikson's Theory of Identity Development: "Identity Won in Action"

For Erik H. Erikson (born Erik Salomonson), a German immigrant to the United States, a complex family history led to identity becoming both a personal and professional focus. His mother was a Danish-born Jew and his biological father, also Danish. Although renamed Erik Homburger after his adoption by his mother's second husband, perhaps because of teasing from public school peers for being Jewish and from Jewish religious school peers for his Nordic appearance, he later named himself Erik H. Erikson. Erikson conceptualized identity development as a lifelong intergenerational project that reaches across the histories of individuals, families, cultural communities, and societies (1950, 1968a; see also Cooper, Behrens, & Trinh, 2009).

For Erikson and those who built on his work, identity reflects both personal and group-level domains that are valued in cultural communities, such as education, careers, religion, politics, gender roles, and family and peer relations (Adams, 2010; Grotevant & Cooper, 1981, 1998; Marcia, 1966, 2013). According to Erikson, as we actively construct our identities, we have the potential for a growing sense of personal and historical integration across our past, present, and future.

Erikson proposed that identity develops as a series of challenges or crises: their resolutions can lead infants to experience themselves as distinctive persons and to trust their caregivers; young children to feel both autonomy and connections with caregivers; and school-aged children to value or doubt their skills—especially those in school—through the eyes of their families, peers, and teachers. Adolescents' cognitive growth offers them skills to consider their future education, careers, and relationships, and middle adulthood offers the capacity to "give back" or pass on wisdom to younger generations. Mature identity is attained if adults can see their lives with a sense of personal and cultural integration.

In his analyses of personal agency and cultural communities in identity development, Erikson wrote eloquently about constraints and opportunities that stem from poverty, racism, and political and economic forces, including schooling (1950, 1968a, b). He highlighted these in studies of African American youth confronting racism, privileged youth working in the civil rights movement, and Native American youth from Dakota Sioux and California Yurok communities struggling with assimilation (see stories by Kurtz [2009, 2010] of how a Yurok girl attends the university and returns to her community as a teacher of the Yurok language). Although many researchers assume youth have unrestricted opportunities for identity exploration, this chapter reinstates Erikson's focus on both resources and challenges for identity development in individual, social, community, and institutional contexts (Cooper, 2011; Syed, 2012).

Tajfel and Social Identity Theory: A Sense of Group Belonging

Henri Tajfel (born Hersz Mordche), a Polish Jew who immigrated to France and ultimately to Great Britain, became interested in prejudice and intergroup relations from his experiences during World War II as a French prisoner of war, from losing his family during the Nazi Holocaust, and from his postwar work with Jewish refugee children. Tajfel defined social group identities in terms of the interplay of group affiliations and intergroup conflicts that shape self-esteem as well as intergroup prejudice (1982; Tajfel & Turner, 1986). Further studies by social and developmental psychologists have supported the importance of social identities, showing how children and adults categorize and recategorize their social identities to maintain their self-esteem (Ruble et al., 2004). Our motivation to claim and express particular social identities depends on needs for both uniqueness and inclusion. In turn, such expressions lead to intergroup conflict, prejudice, and discrimination, as well as to cooperation.

Children's early social identities reflect gender and race (marked by socially recognized features) compared to later emerging identities based on social class, religion, or immigrant status. With increasing age, children choose more social identity labels for themselves (Cooper et al., 2009; Ruble et al., 2004). Evidence of adolescents recategorizing their social identities can be seen when immigrant youth shift from using national labels such as *Vietnamese* or *Mexican* to describing themselves with more inclusive pan-ethnic labels such as *Asian* or *Latino* (Rumbaut, 2005). Along their developmental pathways, youth learn what settings are safe or risky for revealing their complex or potentially stigmatized social identities, such as being an undocumented immigrant or being a "schoolboy" when among gang-identified peers.

Some developmental and social psychologists have worked to align the viewpoints of Erikson and Tajfel in their measures of cognitive, behavioral, and emotional dimensions of identity development. For example, the Multigroup Ethnic Identity Measure (MEIM-R; Phinney & Ong, 2007) taps Erikson's focus on *personal identity exploration* with items such as, "I have spent time trying to find out more about my ethnic group, such as its history, traditions, and customs," and Tajfel's focus on *group belonging and pride*, with items such as, "I have a strong sense of belonging to my ethnic group." Similarly, the Ethnic Identity Scale (Umaña-Taylor, Yazedjian, & Bámaca-Gómez, 2004) assesses ethnic identity *exploration, resolution* (called *commitment* by Phinney & Ong, 2007), and *affirmation*. Scholars continue to draw on the writings of Erikson and Tajfel in refining definitions and measures of identities (Cross, 1991; Syed & Mitchell, 2013) while also drawing from across the social sciences in mapping the role of social and institutional contexts in identity development.

New Views of Social Capital: Children from Low-Income Families and Communities of Color "Moving Up"

In their early writings on social capital theory, sociologists Bourdieu and Passeron (1986) defined social capital in terms of families' social class, often measured by families' education, occupation, and income, and by their social ties and everyday practices or *habitus*, through which families connect with one another and build such ties. Current research documents how, worldwide, children of college-educated parents are most likely to develop college-based career identities or, as commonly stated, "the rich stay rich and the poor stay poor" (Mehan, 2012). This pattern has too often led to defining low-income families and families of color as holding low aspirations for their children's education (Valencia & Black, 2002) and designing interventions to raise their aspirations.

In recent years, however, scholars have asked how cultural reproduction can be disrupted so that children from low-income and ethnic minority families can "move up" to college and college-based careers. To address this question, Yosso (2005) proposed the Community Cultural Wealth framework to map the assets used by communities of color in the United States, including African Americans, Native Americans, Asian Americans/Pacific Islanders, and Latinos, to support students' school pathways in ways that may not be evident when social capital is defined solely by parents' formal education and job status (Kao & Rutherford, 2007). Yosso (2005) proposed six resources for upward mobility. *Social capital* is defined by networks of social and community resources. *Familial capital* refers to cultural knowledge nurtured among families that carries a sense of community, history, memory, and cultural intuition. *Linguistic capital* includes intellectual and social skills gained by communicating in more than one language or style. *Navigational capital* includes skills in maneuvering among social institutions. *Resistant capital* refers to knowledge and skills that challenge inequality and resist subordination, and *aspirational capital* refers to the ability to maintain dreams for the future despite real or perceived barriers.

In a longitudinal study of fifteen Chicana PhD students in education in California, Burciaga investigated how these students used community cultural wealth strategies to persist from preschool through graduate school and how cultural values of *educación*—respect, integrity, and communal responsibility—related to their strategies (Burciaga,

2008, cited in Cooper & Burciaga, 2011; see also Burciaga & Erbstein, 2012). Burciaga used *testimonio*, a narrative interview approach developed in Latin America that draws on political, social, and cultural histories that shape personal life experiences. She asked students about their aspirations from childhood to beyond the doctorate, classes they had taken in school, their families' schooling, and people who influenced their lives and persistence through school.

All fifteen students linked their aspirations beyond the PhD to how their career identities could "give back" resources to families and communities. Many sought to address problems of schools tracking underrepresented students away from college-prep classes; all had experiences or observations of tracking. Vitoria described being one of few students of color or low-income students in her high school honors courses "where the White kids were.... Kids with houses took honors classes and kids in apartments didn't. That's the way it broke down at our school." Vitoria was pursuing a PhD in education because she felt there were too few people in positions of power who advocated for students, "not...to be a superintendent or use it as a stepping stone but because I really want to enact reform and make it better for kids and for futures."

With few exceptions, all six community cultural wealth strategies were evident in each student's interview. Here we highlight examples of aspirational, familial, and social capital. Soledad described aspirational capital when she recalled that, as a child, "I didn't know exactly what [college] was and neither did my parents, but I knew it was a place I was going." Despite her immigrant parents not knowing the path to higher education in the United States, they supported her aspirations to go to college. Familial capital was most often evident in families' stories of hardships and perseverance fueling students' desires to persist to the PhD. Cristina recounted her grandfather's emotionally wrenching stories about immigrating to the United States. He and her grandmother found a home near the packing plant where he worked that was close to a school, so his children could have more opportunities than they had in Mexico. With regard to social capital, students reported developing strongest ties with teachers, professors, and program staff or *institutional agents* (Stanton-Salazar, 2004) who shared their cultural values of respect, integrity, and communal responsibility and helped bridge families and school.

Thus, students' strategies for persisting through school defined their families as resources who motivated their aspirations and integration of their academic, career, and cultural identities. Such agency, illustrating Erikson's "identity won in action," is a resource that can be overlooked when social capital is measured only by formal education or job status.

Future Directions

Recent research has revealed how cultural reproduction takes place but also how the actions of students, families, teachers, and others can foster upward social mobility, transmit community cultural wealth and thus create social capital to support students' aspirations and identities and community values of mutual support (Mehan, 2012; Rios-Aguilar, Kiyama, Gravitt, & Moll, 2011). We have much more to learn about how community cultural wealth is transmitted and expanded, particularly across generations. An important example involves the revival of Indigenous languages and cultural practices that support students' schooling. In one case, Hare (2012) found that Indigenous children in Canada who were learning about their Aboriginal culture and language were teaching it to their parents. Many parents had been removed from their homes as children and sent to residential schools as part of Canada's now-discredited policy of cultural assimilation of Indigenous children. Likewise, among Native Hawaiian children, heritage-language instruction, conducted with families as part of reviving the Hawaiian language, has been shown to enhance students' personal and collective esteem and their academic pathways (Yamauchi, Lau-Smith, & Luning, 2008).

New Views of Alienation and Belonging: Within-Group Discrimination and Students' Ethnic and Academic Identities

Early research on alienation and schooling focused on how intergroup discrimination and stereotyping can derail minority families' and students' academic aspirations as well as shape their ethnic and academic identities (Fisher, Wallace, & Fenton, 2000; Fordham & Ogbu, 1986; Phinney, Madden, & Santos, 2008; Tajfel, 1982). However, new evidence suggests within-group conflict among ethnic peers can also lead to alienation and shape racial-ethnic and academic identities (Carter, 2006; Rosenbloom & Way, 2004). In this section, we continue our focus on variation within cultural groups by examining the role of discrimination and stereotyping among African American and Indigenous Mexican immigrant youth in their sense of alienation/belonging and the intersections of their racial-ethnic, academic, and gender identities (Gonzalez, 2013; Wilson, 2013).

"Acting White": Racial-Ethnic and Academic Identities Among African American Youth

As they defend against experiences of discrimination, both across and within racial-ethnic groups, youth may disengage from school to affirm their racial-ethnic identities (Fordham & Ogbu, 1986; Mehan, 2012; Portes & Fernández-Kelly, 2008; Solórzano, 1998; Vigil, 2004). As one African American high school girl explained:

> They basically ask me, 'Why aren't you true to your color?' And I'm like, 'Well, how am I not true?' I'm sorry if I'm smart, you know. I'm not going to sit there and hold myself back just so you can have this feeling that I am being black. I'm being black whether I'm smart, dumb, stupid, or whatever.
> *(Bergin & Cooks, 2002, p. 121)*

For ethnic minority youth, one of their most salient social identities involves their race-ethnicity. However, pressure from ethnic peers to affirm their racial-ethnic identity may mean internalizing and conforming to racial-ethnic stereotypes. Indeed, as Way and Rogers discuss in this volume, youth often use (or resist) common racial-ethnic stereotypes as a basis for their own racial and ethnic identity development. Students who do not conform to these stereotypes and cultural scripts of what it means to be African American may be accused of "acting white."

There has been much debate on "acting white," particularly concerning its role in academic achievement (Bergin & Cooks, 2002; Tyson, Darity, & Castellino, 2005). We begin by tracing its historical basis and its role in black boys and girls' school achievement and then consider current debates and evidence about this hypothesis.

What Does It Mean to "Act White?"

Accusations of "acting white" in the African American community can be traced back to the times of slavery—what Ogbu (2004) called "involuntary immigration"—when African slaves were forced to give up their cultural traditions and adopt white customs, culture, behaviors, and speech. In response to this forced assimilation, they created their own cultural traditions and English dialect, remnants of which persist in present-day African American culture. After their emancipation from slavery, when African Americans began to have opportunities for upward mobility, adopting the behaviors and speech of white culture was required for educational success and acceptance by the white people who acted as gatekeepers for such mobility.

Although "acting white" could lead to opportunities for success in white society, people who displayed such behaviors were seen by black peers as denouncing their black identity. Historically, "acting white" included "being more inhibited, more formal, or lacking soul" (McArdle & Young, 1970, cited in Bergin & Cooks, 2002, p. 113). Fordham and Ogbu (1986) found that among African American high school students, "acting white" included "speaking Standard English, listening to white music, working hard to get good grades in school, getting good grades in school" (p. 186). In recent years, reports of these indicators have remained remarkably consistent, with African American high school students including using "proper" speech, listening to classical music, dressing "preppy," getting good grades, and having white friends (Bergin & Cooks, 2002; Carter, 2006; Worrell, this volume).

Across studies, many features of "acting white," including speaking Standard English and getting good grades, are also seen as important for success in US schools and mainstream society. This link holds implications for understanding how students' resisting behaviors considered "acting white" can translate to poor academic performance. Still, despite consensus about what defines "acting white," findings diverge on its effects on youth, especially in school.

Evolving Debates on "Acting White" (or Resisting "Acting White") and Schooling

Numerous studies have sought to identify the roots of achievement gaps between ethnic minority and majority youth. One early explanation that gained widespread recognition is Fordham and Ogbu's (1986) hypothesis that black students fear being accused that their academic success marks them "acting white" and thus disloyal to their black identity. According to this hypothesis, black students adopt different strategies for "coping with the burden of acting White," including complete assimilation by adopting the behaviors and speech styles of white Americans (what Fordham and Ogbu call *cultural and linguistic assimilation*); code switching between black and white cultural behaviors depending on the context (*accommodation without assimilation*; see also Carter, 2006, 2012; Gibson & Bejinez, 2002); and knowing the benefits of adopting white cultural behaviors for school and work success but not believing this will increase social mobility because students are still black (*ambivalence*). The strategy drawing the most attention is *resistance* or *opposition*. According to Fordham and Ogbu, because school achievement is seen as a stereotypical identity domain for white students, black students may adopt an *oppositional cultural frame of reference* by avoiding behaviors that promote school success.

What factors contribute to variation among African American students in their adopting these strategies? Recent studies reveal intersections of gender and racial-ethnic stereotypes, so that ethnic minority boys who succeed in school face more ridicule from peers than ethnic minority girls who do so (see Saenz, 2009, for parallel analyses of Latino males). For this reason, feelings of belonging to their racial-ethnic group may hold more importance for academic success for racial-ethnic minority boys than girls (Oyserman, Bybee, & Terry, 2003).

Scholars have mapped how skin tone appears to play a particularly important role in ethnic minority boys' experiences with these issues (Harvey, LaBeach, Pridgen, & Gocial, 2005). Oyserman, Brickman, Bybee, and Celious (2006) studied relations among skin tone, academic self-efficacy, and school engagement of Latino and African American high school boys. They predicted that African American boys who lacked typical physical markers of their racial group—"markers of belonging"—would seek to prove their ingroup status in ways that could undermine their school success, such as with aggression and disengaging from school (Cousins, 1999). Consistent with these predictions, African American high school boys with lighter skin tones felt less accepted by their ethnic peers than those with darker or medium skin tones. Lighter-skinned boys also reported lower academic self-efficacy than did medium-skinned boys. In this sample, darker skin tones seemed to serve as a protective factor because boys with darker skin did not fear being teased by peers if they were academically successful. In contrast, the lighter-skinned boys felt they should prove their ethnic identity, even at the cost of academic success. This study illustrates Fordham and Ogbu's *resistance* or *opposition* coping, as well as individual variation in susceptibility to disengaging from school.

Although Fordham and Ogbu reported a variety of ways that African American youth cope with accusations of "acting white," current debates focus on the *oppositional cultural frame of reference*, although doing so implies that black culture is homogeneous. Scholars continue to report variation in African American students' views and that many African American students and parents place high value on school success (Bergin & Cooks, 2002; Ogbu, 2003; Sohn, 2011). Still, because racial achievement gaps persist, scholars examine under what conditions fears of "acting white" may or may not undermine school performance.

Such conditions include schools' racial-ethnic composition and cultural practices. Fordham and Ogbu conducted their original work in a predominately African American high school in Washington, DC. However, just as black students' identities are heterogeneous, so too are the racial composition and cultural values and practices of schools and hence the experiences of black students with being accused of "acting white." To compare racially integrated and racially homogenous schools, Bergin and Cooks (2002) investigated links between "acting white" and school performance among African American and Mexican American high-achieving high school students in the Midwest. Students of color at predominantly black schools were more likely to be accused of "acting white" for their speech styles, music preferences, peer groups, or dress, but not necessarily for achieving academically. This parallels Carter's (2006) finding that high achieving African American students at predominately African American schools in New York were considered cool and popular.

Bergin and Cooks also found that students of color at predominantly white schools were less likely to be accused of "acting white" because there were so few students of color, although they might be teased in their neighborhoods. Bergin and Cooks proposed that white students might not notice "acting white" among ethnic minority youth because they might see "white" behaviors as the norm. Finally, students of color in racially balanced schools were more likely to be accused of "acting white" if they were taking advanced classes with many white peers. These black students were more likely to have white friends and were accused of denouncing their ethnic identity by their black peers, although they denied such accusations.

These findings are valuable in showing that the costs of "acting white" for academic achievement depend on the school context. Students in one school may face ridicule for taking advanced classes and having only white peers, but students taking the same classes in a different school might feel support for their academic success. Discrimination among African Americans may be more likely in predominantly black schools, where within-group contrasts are more salient. However, where African American youth are in the minority, comparisons with white students may be more salient than within-group differences, and within-group bonds are strengthened.

Thus, in designing programs or interventions addressing intragroup discrimination, it appears important to differentiate racially homogenous from racially heterogeneous school settings. Interventions at racially homogenous schools should address within-group discrimination, which is more likely to occur in these settings. Racially heterogeneous schools should focus on intergroup contact and cooperation (Tajfel & Turner, 1986), as well as on creating inclusive and accepting climates for all students.

Future Directions

Most research about the effects of "acting white" or resisting "acting white" on academic achievement involves high school students. Further research is needed to understand earlier and later developmental pathways, including the college years (Wyche-Hall, 2011). Adolescence may appear to be an optimal time to study how youth develop racial and academic identities, but children as young as six know about ethnic and gender stereotypes about their group and often endorse these stereotypes (Bigler & Liben, 2007). For example, children whose behavior and appearance conform to gender stereotypes are more likely to hold strict stereotypes of acceptable gender role behavior in others (Martin, Ruble, & Szkrybalo, 2002). Future research should explore whether a similar relationship between conforming to racial-ethnic stereotypes and expectations for racial-ethnic behavior in others occurs among racial-ethnic minority children. This would provide opportunities to intervene before adolescence, when students' academic self-efficacy may already have been constrained by such alienating experiences.

Because children and adolescents draw on stereotypes of their racial-ethnic and gender groups, among other sources, in developing their own identities (Way, Hernandez, Rogers, & Hughes, 2013), students' developing awareness of these stereotypes about academic pathways is an important topic for further investigation. In a study conducted in a university–community partnership with Mexican American middle and high school students (Wilson & Cooper, 2011), we asked students to offer their own explanations for the gaps in college attendance between ethnic minorities and European Americans, as well as between Latina/o girls and boys. Students were more likely to give external reasons for ethnic differences (such as access to resources or encouragement) and internal reasons for gender differences (such as intelligence or motivation). One seventh-grader wrote: "I think because girls are smarter than boys. More girls want to go to college and fewer boys don't. The girls look ahead and the boys just think about [being] cool and not a nerd." Essentialist explanations of gender differences (based on innate factors) are common because of salient biological features of men and women (Heyman & Giles, 2006). Such thinking is common among young children, but ethnic minority children and adolescents also understand the social constructions of race and ethnic differences (Quintana, 1998). In the activities of our university–community partnership, students discussed racial-ethnic gaps in college going but had not discussed gender gaps. This may help explain the students attributing racial-ethnic differences but not gender differences to external factors.

In sum, racial, ethnic, and gender patterns in schooling do not go unnoticed by children and adolescents. To progress in opening academic pipelines among ethnic minority boys and girls, we need to address how youth make their meanings of racial-ethnic, gender, and other stereotypes as they seek to integrate their multiple cultural identities along successful pathways through school to adulthood.

Discrimination, Intersecting Identities, and School Engagement Among Indigenous Mexican Immigrant Youth

Similar patterns of within-group discrimination and stereotyping as reported among African American students have also been found among Mexican immigrants (Castillo, Conoley, Brossart, & Quiros, 2007; Mendez, Bauman, & Guillory, 2012; Rosenbloom & Way, 2004). Although tensions among African American youth about their racial-ethnic and academic identities often involve issues of "acting white," those among Mexican adolescents center on immigration, assimilation, language, and indigeneity (Córdova & Cervantes, 2010; Mendez et al., 2012). For example, interviews with high school students attending a predominantly Latino public school in the state of Washington revealed that Mexican American students born in the United States, because they spoke

English better and had legal status, felt superior to recently immigrated and undocumented Mexican immigrant students (Mendez et al., 2012).

The growing numbers of Indigenous Mexican immigrants in the United States have drawn attention to ethnic heterogeneity among Mexican immigrants and cultural tensions between *mestizo* (those from both Spanish and Indigenous heritage who speak Spanish only) and Indigenous Mexicans. Indigenous Mexican migrants engage in cultural practices such as *tequios* (community work projects), *guezas* (mutual assistance), and languages that predate Spanish colonization. These cultural practices, interpreted with stereotypes about what it means to be Indigenous, can mark Indigenous people as primitive, stupid, short, and dirty (Barillas-Chón, 2010; Fox & Rivera-Salgado, 2004; Stephen, 2007). Next, we examine how Indigenous Mexican youth construct their ethnic and academic identities in the context of within-group discrimination and stereotypes about Indigenous people. We also examine how gender roles in Indigenous families that define women as vulnerable and at risk of single motherhood and men as strong and capable of self-protection can shape engagement in school and community settings. We offer suggestions on what schools, communities, and universities can do to address these challenges.

Indigenous Mexican Migrants

The racial hierarchy that dominates Mexico relegates Indigenous people to its lowest rungs (Menchaca, 1993). Although the Mexican government traditionally based Indigenous status on language, Indigenous organizations persuaded the officials designing the 2000 Census to include a question on ethnic self-identification independent of language use; this revealed an Indigenous population of 12.7 million or 13 percent of the Mexican population. In 2010, 6 million people (6.7 percent) spoke one of the eighty-five identified Indigenous languages (Instituto Nacional de Estadística Geografica de Informática of Mexico [INEG], 2010). More than half of the Indigenous population lives in poverty, compared to 21 percent of the general population (INEG, 2010). Compared to *mestizo* peers, Indigenous Mexican youth score lower on high school entrance exams and are more likely to attend teacher training colleges and technical institutions than universities (Florez-Crespo, 2007). The state of Oaxaca, where 35 percent speak an Indigenous language, has one of the largest Indigenous populations (INEG, 2010). The stereotype that being from Oaxaca is synonymous with being dark-skinned, of short stature, and *indio/a* is reflected in the use of the derogatory racial term *Oaxaquita* (Barillas-Chón, 2010; Batalla, 1996; Fox & Rivera-Salgado, 2004; Stephen, 2007).

Most Mexican immigrants to the United States have been *mestizos* from the states of Guanajuato, Jalisco, and Michoacán, but since the 1980s, poverty, sociopolitical marginalization, and discrimination by the *mestizo* population have contributed to growing numbers of Indigenous people emigrating, particularly from the states of Oaxaca, Puebla, and Chiapas (Fox & Rivera-Salgado, 2004). Attracted by jobs in agriculture, California has been a primary receiving state; an estimated 165,000 Indigenous Mexican adults and their children live in rural California (Marcelli & Cornelius, 2001; Mines, Nichols, & Runsten, 2010).

Agricultural areas in California, such as Greenfield on the central coast, have become sites of culture clashes between Indigenous and *mestizo* Mexican immigrants (Esquivel, 2012). Local newspapers reported growing hostility toward Zapoteco and Mixteco migrants from Oaxaca and Guerrero (Wozniacka, 2011). *Mestizo* immigrants and long-term Mexican-American residents have blamed Indigenous migrants for growing crime in their communities and marginalized them because of their cultural practices and language. These tensions provide evidence that the racial hierarchy that relegates Indigenous people to the lowest level in Mexico is being reproduced in Mexican immigrant communities in the United States.

Discrimination and Indigenous Identity

Although the research literature is small, scholars have begun to examine both discrimination against Indigenous Mexican youth and possible resources for their pathways through school. Barillas-Chón (2010) observed and interviewed four Oaxaqueño immigrant high school students living in California, three of whom spoke an Indigenous language. He examined what he called "unwelcoming" and "welcoming" school practices that either constrained or facilitated students' school adjustment. The most salient unwelcoming practice was discrimination from Spanish-speaking Mexican-American students and second-generation Latino students. Oaxaqueño students described being called *Oaxaquito/a* and ridiculed by both Spanish- and English-speaking students for speaking their Indigenous language, with many assuming that they did not speak Spanish well or did not speak it at all.

Such discrimination can lead Indigenous youth to reject or conceal their identity. In studies of Indigenous Mexican high school students in the central coast region of California (Ruiz & Barajas, 2012) and San Diego (Kovats, 2010), youth reported denying they were Indigenous and refusing to speak their Indigenous language for fear of discrimination. One student explained:

> So at school they would make fun of us because we didn't speak Spanish well. I remember I used to say *la mapa* [the map] and they would say, 'It's not *la mapa*, it's *el mapa*.' So they gave me the nickname of *la mapa*. So in that moment you feel ashamed for being, I don't know, because you are Mixteco, because you speak Mixteco you don't learn the other language well. So you get embarrassed and you say, well, 'No, we aren't Mixtecos.'
>
> (Kovats, 2010, p. 50)

These accounts are consistent with tenets of social identity theory (Tajfel, 1982; Tajfel & Turner, 1986) that individuals who experience discrimination try to maintain their self-esteem and group membership by separating from their marginalized group and/or emphasizing positive aspects of their group. Although less common, embracing one's marginalized identity and emphasizing its positive aspects have been found among politically active Indigenous youth. Ramos Arco (2012) interviewed twelve first- and second-generation young adults who were active in the Binational Front of Indigenous Organizations, based in California and Oaxaca. Political and ethnic socialization from organization members and from elders in the Indigenous community contributed to young adults' involvement in the organization and embracing their Indigenous heritage. There appear to be gender differences in the level of involvement in these organizations. For example, research with Oaxaqueño young adults in Fresno, California revealed that parents allowed young men more freedom to participate in these activities while frowning on young women's participation, although young women still asserted their participation in community organizing (Mendoza, Martínez, & Mendoza, 2013). We also need to learn how and in what settings such affirmation occurs among youth who are not politically active.

Discrimination and Academic Integration

In addition to influencing their racial-ethnic identities, discrimination, stereotypes, and gender role expectations challenge Indigenous students' social integration when their schools are primarily comprised of *mestizo* students. Barillas-Chon (2010) found that three Oaxaqueño/a students whom he interviewed spent most of their in- and out-of-class time in the newcomers' classroom (for immigrant students) with Spanish-speaking peers and teachers.

The most salient welcoming practices, provided by their teachers and other Spanish-speaking staff, gave them access to the Migrant Education Program office, the library, and the newcomers' classroom during lunch or after school. In these "safe spaces," students felt comfortable talking with peers and teachers in Spanish and found peers with whom they could belong and identify. However, the same "safe spaces" that helped Oaxaqueño students feel welcome could also isolate them from bilingual and English-only-speaking students.

Gibson and Hidalgo (2009) documented similar welcoming practices in their four-year ethnographic study of 160 migrant students at a public high school in California. Migrant youth, who move between Mexico and the United States as their parents follow agricultural labor opportunities, are at high risk of dropping out of high school. The US Department of Education's Office of Migrant Education estimated that 45–50 percent of migrant youth graduate from high school. The students in this study received academic support and medical assistance from the federal Migrant Education Program at their high school. These migrant students saw their migrant program teachers, many from migrant families themselves, as mentors, counselors, and role models who connected them with resources and networks that helped them navigate successfully through high school. In 2002, 80 percent of migrant youth graduated from this high school.

Indigenous students' social integration at school also reflects gender role expectations in their Indigenous communities (Fox, 2013). Indigenous parents allow girls more freedom in school than in community activities. Parents worry about their daughters' physical safety and their becoming single mothers, so girls have more freedom with chaperones, in "safe places" such as school, and when monitored by frequent phone calls. Such gender role expectations help explain why girls participate in school club activities more than boys (Mendoza et al., 2013).

Speaking an Indigenous language presents migrants with institutional barriers in US schools (Kovats, 2010; Ruiz & Barajas, 2012). US schools often do not have staff to translate or give instruction in the native language of Indigenous Mexican children and their parents who want to learn

Spanish and English while also keeping their cultural and linguistic identities (Machado-Casas, 2009; Ruiz & Barajas, 2012). Although immigrant students, including Indigenous youth, may encounter welcoming spaces and teachers who link them to institutional resources and networks, school staff and teachers must also serve as *institutional agents* (Stanton-Salazar, 2004) or *cultural brokers* (Cooper, 2011) to connect these youth with both English-only and bilingual students and adults to ensure their full integration. Barillas-Chon (2010) cautioned against a "presently-absent" immigrant student body, in which students are physically present at school but not represented in school clubs and cultural events such as Cinco de Mayo celebrations. More needs to be learned about how the integration of immigrant students —and Indigenous students in particular—proceeds as students interact with mainstream peers in and beyond "safe spaces."

Future Directions

As we have noted throughout this chapter, identity development begins in childhood, extends beyond adolescence, and can be retriggered during college. In a longitudinal study of 100 ethnically diverse students who were the first in their families to attend college (Azmitia & Sumabat-Estrada, 2013; Azmitia, Syed, & Radmacher, 2008; Syed & Azmitia, 2009), both challenges and resources prompted students to redefine and integrate their identities. In their first year at the university, many saw their academic identities (college major and career goals) and ethnic identities as disconnected, but by their senior year, racism and discrimination, consciousness-raising classes, and extracurricular activities had provoked changes and integration of their academic identities and their racial-ethnic, social class, and gender identities. These important findings merit further investigation.

Most research on Indigenous immigrant youth has involved adolescents, but young Indigenous adults redefine their identities as they get older and enter new settings. A young Oaxaqueña attending college in San Diego described this *positive identity shift*:

> I started meeting other people that were nicer and then college…I think that when I was like really proud to be from Oaxaca. I don't know, it's like, I have an identity and I can say that I'm from here and I'm proud to say it. I remember how ashamed I was. How foolish could I have been to be ashamed of the place that I was born? It makes me feel mad in a way that I was ashamed but then again, I guess, I was forced to be.
> *(Kovats, 2010, p. 61)*

This student attributed her reidentifying with her Indigenous culture and language to support from her university professors and classmates. For the first time, her Indigenous culture was valued, and the experiences that had made her feel shame for being Indigenous were explained in her social science classes. The cultural awareness and respect for Mexico's Indigenous cultures seem to be in part a result of a multicultural college curriculum. As one University of California (UCLA) graduate described:

> My indigenous identity was definitely as a result of my politicization and educational experience in college […] I majored in Sociology and Labor Studies so I took many Latino study courses that focused on inequality, the history of minorities in the U.S. and other Latin American Studies courses which made me aware of my history as an indigenous woman.
> *(Nicolás, 2011, p. 105)*

We need to learn more about how multicultural curricula—in college and earlier—can help students critically re-examine, renegotiate, and redefine their ethnic and academic identities (Patton, 2010). But what happens to youth who do not attend college? When and where do they experience positive identity shifts? Are there community contexts where they can connect with their cultures and learn about the conditions that made them reject or conceal their ethnic identities and find or create settings that can affirm their claiming their identities? We need further research to address these questions, especially about how community organizations can prompt positive identity shifts for young adults who are not in college. In one such case, the Pan Valley Institute in Fresno, California has provided resources for Indigenous Oaxaqueño youth to make video narratives of their pathways of racial-ethnic, Indigenous, academic, and gender identity development (https://afsc.org/office/fresno-ca).

Public schools also have the power to address discrimination experienced by Indigenous youth and thereby foster positive identity shifts. One example comes from the Oxnard Unified School District in California. In early 2012, the Mixteco/Indigena Community Organizing Project (MICOP) led the *No Me Llames Oaxaquita/Don't Call Me Oaxaquita* campaign in Oxnard (Esquivel,

2012). The campaign proposed a resolution asking the school district to prohibit the use of "Oaxaquita" and "indio". In May 2012, the district unanimously approved the resolution and agreed to create an antibullying committee and prohibit the use of these derogatory terms on school grounds. Although it is too early to detect changes in youth identity, MICOP continues to help the district educate students and teachers about Indigenous Mexican culture and history.

These reports provide important examples of how community organizations and schools can create programs and partnerships that address issues faced by their students. More broadly, it is critical for researchers to work in ethnically heterogeneous communities to address issues identified by youth, school and community leaders, and researchers.

New Views of Challenges and Resources on Pathways Through School: "The Good Burden"

Building on early writings on the challenges of immigration, poverty, and discrimination for identity development and resiliency (Erikson, 1968b; Werner, 1993), recent research has clarified Erikson's concept of "identity won in action." As a young Somali immigrant woman attending college in Australia wrote, "The challenges I face put me down sometimes but most of the time I overcome them and I always look (for) something to push myself.... Overall, those challenges are what keep me going all the time" (Booker & Lawrence, 2013, p. 108).

New research asks how students access both personal resources and those across their cultural worlds, so that their challenges can motivate them to succeed in school and careers on behalf of their families, peers, and cultural communities, particularly those who may not have had these opportunities (Cooper, 2011; LaFromboise, Hoyt, Oliver, & Whitbeck, 2006; Syed, 2010, 2012; Syed & Mitchell, 2013). This sense of purpose, grounded in feelings of cultural belonging, can be heard as an African American female engineering student explained: "Money is important, but it is not the issue. We have a burden—and it's a good burden—of helping our people" (Cooper, Jackson, Azmitia, Lopez, & Dunbar, 1995, p. 11).

Bridging Multiple Worlds: Navigating Resources and Challenges on Pathways to College

Bridging Multiple Worlds theory draws on writings of Erikson (1950, 1968a, b), of Phelan et al., (1998), and on related work to trace how youth build pathways to their identities in college, career, and cultural domains as they navigate challenges and resources across their cultural worlds (Cooper, 2011; Cooper, Cooper, Trinh, Wilson, & Gonzalez, 2013a; Syed, Azmitia, & Cooper, 2011). As illustrated in Figure 19.1, this multilevel theory maps the interplay of five dimensions over time: *demographics* of culturally diverse families and youth on their pathways through school; youth *aspirations and identities* in college, career, and cultural domains; their math and language *academic pathways* through

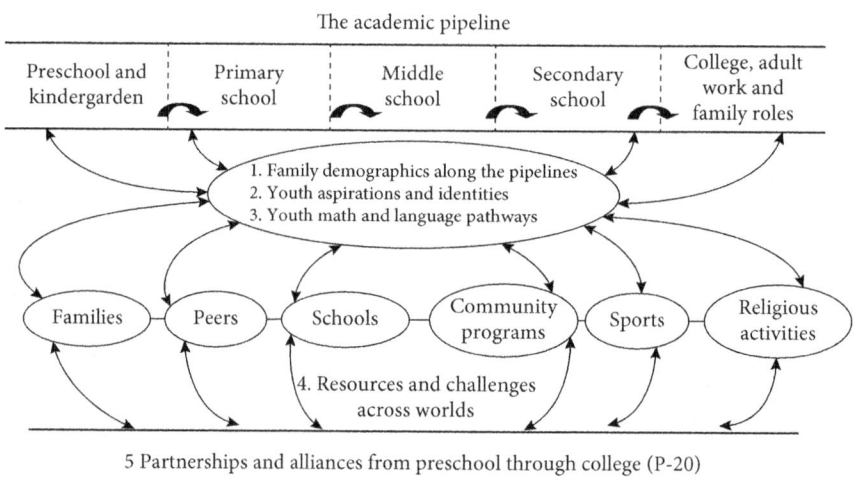

Fig. 19.1 The Bridging Multiple Worlds model. From Cooper, C. R. (2011). *Bridging multiple worlds: Cultures, identities, and pathways to college*. With permission of Oxford University Press.

school; *challenges and resources* across their cultural worlds of families, peers, schools, and communities; and *university–community partnerships* from preschool through college (known as P–20 partnerships) that boost resources youth can draw from their worlds and open academic pipelines. Studies of this theory have been conducted with children, youth, and families from Native American, Latino, African American, Japanese, Asian American, Native Hawaiian, and working-class European American communities, as well as with multiethnic youth (Cooper, 2011).

To illustrate key findings with this theory, we draw on studies with Mexican immigrant youth and their families, the largest immigrant group in the United States. Recent studies with Latino youth (e.g., Phinney & Baldelomar, 2011) call into question earlier descriptions of their identity development as foreclosed—making commitments without exploration—because of deference to cultural expectations to obey parents (Abraham, 1986). Scholars also question assumptions that all youth have opportunities for identity exploration, particularly when ethnic minority, low-income, and rural students attend underresourced schools that constrain such opportunities (Grotevant & Cooper, 1988; Yoder, 2000).

One line of research addressing these issues has been conducted in a long-term university–community partnership with a precollege program in California. The program serves more than 500 students, with scholarships and support for youth from low-income, mostly Mexican immigrant families (both *mestizo* and Indigenous) from sixth grade to college (Cooper, 2011; Cooper, Gonzalez, & Wilson, 2013b). The partnership collects responses to surveys and open-ended questions, school transcripts, and program observations, from program entry at age twelve through follow-up of program alumni. We now highlight key findings aligned with the five dimensions of the theory.

With respect to *demographics* of students in the program, their parents' formal education, usually in rural Mexico, was typically less than high school and, for many, elementary level or less. Most parents worked picking strawberries, mushrooms, or lettuce; on cannery or factory assembly lines; or cleaning houses and hotels, and sometimes more than one of these jobs.

Regarding students' *educational and career aspirations and identities,* on their program application essays, most students described their aspirations for college and college-based careers. Each year, at the program's annual summer institute, students were asked, "What is your #1, #2, and #3 job goal?" From the start to the close of the institute and over the course of two years, students' first career choices were remarkably stable (90 percent), such as to become a doctor or firefighter. In contrast, their second choices reflected more identity exploration (with 79 percent changing), such as from doctor to police officer or from mechanic to chef. These shifts may have been sparked by summer institute classes, in which students explored careers in public health, public safety, and culinary arts and the "career ladders" in each field that require progressively greater levels of education (Cooper et al., 2013b).

Students' *academic pathways* diverged early: Compared to students with lower grades, sixth-graders with higher math grades more often passed algebra 1 in ninth grade and later entered universities directly from high school. Still, some alumni who completed algebra 1 in later grades had also graduated from universities by age twenty-five, showing there is more than one pathway to college. Students' early aspirations were not always matched by their mastering the academic skills required to reach these dreams, but some moved up "career ladders" by taking jobs in their chosen field requiring less education while earning credentials toward higher-level careers. In our current research, we are tracing *second chances* pathways of youth who left school because of early parenthood, prison, military service, or to earn money to support their families and then returned to school. Thus, some skills may take more time to develop; however, once mastered, they can still lead to college and careers so that, despite initial failures, students can build viable pathways.

When we asked students in the program about their challenges and resources ("What do your families/ friends/teachers do that cause you difficulties/help you?"), students consistently reported experiencing both challenges and resources from each of their worlds (Cooper et al., 2013b). For example, about their families, students described challenges: "Not letting you go away (to college)," and resources: "They say to not do drugs and to study hard to graduate from college." About peers, students wrote, "They tell me they are not going to go to college. That makes me want to blend in with them," but also "Some friends encourage me to not listen to my bad friends. They help me reach my goal because they have the same goals as me." And about teachers, students wrote, "They are racist sometimes. They don't treat everyone the same," but also "They encourage me to follow my dreams and go to college."

From childhood into young adulthood, students reported that their immigrant parents remained central to their staying on track through college, not in spite of their modest educations but because of them. Students became *cultural and college brokers* themselves by guiding siblings, cousins, friends, and even parents toward college. Over time, students reported growth and differentiation in resources within each world: 61 percent reported larger school networks, from listing only teachers helping them go to college to listing both teachers and counselors, and 44 percent reported larger program networks, from listing only the director to listing both the director and program tutors. Alumni participated as tutors, mentors, and even donors to the program.

Finally, this *university–community partnership* strengthened the program with institutional changes that open the academic pipeline. Each fall, students participate as researchers to review the previous summer's findings, suggest program improvements, and ask new questions. After students learned that more girls than boys and more younger than older students attended the summer institute, they made suggestions that have engaged more boys and high school students (Yonezawa & Jones, 2011). And in longitudinal case studies from sixth grade through college developed in collaboration with the program director and university students, some students' pathways reflected cultural reproduction of social capital by reproducing parents' educational levels; others reflected alienation by disengaging from school to claim gang identities and underground occupations; and others reflected challenge and resiliency by interpreting obstacles as motivation to succeed on behalf of families, peers, and communities and "prove the gatekeeper wrong" (Cooper, 2011). These findings point to converging roles of capital, alienation, and challenge in identity development. As one university student researcher said, "I used to be on the alienation pathway, but now I'm on the challenge pathway."

Bridging Multiple Worlds Alliance: A Common Language for Research, Practice, and Policy

Studies of Bridging Multiple Worlds theory, conducted in long-term university–community partnerships, have illuminated multiple pathways of ethnically diverse youth through school while forging connections across research, practice, and policy (Cooper, 2011). The Bridging Multiple Worlds Alliance (BMWA; www.bridgingworlds.org) is a growing network of US and international partners that offers tools to build a common language by aligning concepts and evidence about cultures, identities, and pathways through school, with qualitative and quantitative measures, activities for schools and programs, and templates for graphing trajectories and longitudinal case studies. Materials about college in nineteen languages support youth and families in integrating cultural, college, and career identities.

In one partnership, BMWA members worked in a team of scholars from education, sociology, anthropology, law, and psychology from the ten campuses of the University of California to identify critical conditions for education partners to foster equity in students' access to college (Oakes, 2003). These "college-going conditions" include creating a *college-going school culture*, increasing *academic rigor*, cultivating *qualified teachers*, providing *intensive academic and social supports*, providing opportunities for students to develop *multicultural college-going identities*, and building *family-neighborhood-school connections*.

To measure progress in fostering college-going conditions, educators developed and use the School Self-Assessment Rubric (SSAR; California GEAR UP, 2012). Partners can assess providing opportunities for students to develop multicultural college-going identities when:

> Students see college going as integral to their identities; have confidence and skills to negotiate college without sacrificing their own identities and connections with their home communities. They recognize college is a pathway to careers that are valued in their families, peer groups, and local communities.
>
> *(California GEAR UP, 2012, p. 1)*

To assess one aspect of this dimension, first-generation students' college preparation, partners rate their school at phase 1 when "there is no cultural support to deal with first generation and historically low college attendance issues and few students from underrepresented populations are enrolled in classes leading to college preparatory classes in high school"; phases 2, 3, or 4 when such support and enrollment can be seen among some, most, or all staff and students, respectively; or phase 5 when "this is a strength we can share with other sites and organizations."

BMWA members have used the SSAR with school district partners in setting priorities for improving and sustaining the college-going conditions. In one partnership, five school district teams used the SSAR to map priorities and develop plans for sustaining their college-going cultures as a federal grant to their districts to launch college-going cultures was ending.

Future Directions: Aligning Resources to Support Individual and Institutional Identities

In a second example of aligning concepts to open the academic pipeline, BMWA researchers are aligning students' academic and racial-ethnic identities with institutional identities to help one university become a Hispanic-Serving Institution, as part of the Minority-Serving Institutions initiative of the US Department of Education (Benitez & DeAro, 2004; Contreras, Malcom, & Bensimon, 2008; Hurtado & Ruiz, 2012; Santiago, 2008). Student researchers worked with the BMWA to interview Latino/a second-year students in biology, economics, and psychology about their racial-ethnic and academic identities and their challenges and resources building a sense of belonging to their campus and cultural communities, entering their majors, and graduating (Cooper, Bandera, & Macias, 2014). Most had doubted their abilities in mathematics, and many failed their first college math class, yet underutilized class and campus resources. Still, those who took action with these challenges, showing agency and educational resilience (Cabrera & Padilla, 2004), entered their majors and drew resources within and beyond their racial-ethnic groups (reflecting Erikson's "identities won in action"). Latino students with a lower sense of belonging to the campus were more likely to leave during their first two years. University staff, faculty, and students are working to strengthen and unify resources for students facing these challenges (Engstrom & Tinto, 2008; Pérez, Cortés, Ramos, & Coronado, 2010; Yeado, 2013).

More generally, scholars and educators have begun to map ethnically diverse college students' realities involving capital, alienation/belonging, and challenge across their worlds, including classes, extracurricular activities, cultural centers, and ethnic student organizations, as well as families and home-town peers (Kuh, Kinzie, Buckley, Bridges, & Hayek, 2006; Patton, 2010). These findings point to how successful college pathways are fostered by students' educational resilience, academic self-efficacy, and skills navigating cultural worlds that help integrate their racial-ethnic, social class, and gender identities with a sense of belonging (Azmitia & Sumabat-Estrada, 2013; Nasir, 2012). Such progress will help researchers, practitioners, and policy investors understand students' realities and how institutions can support them and their identity development (Laird, Bridges, Morelon-Quainoo, Williams, & Holmes, 2007).

Next Steps and an Invitation

In this chapter, we have considered evidence that opening academic pipelines rests on integrating multiple identities—not only students' academic and racial-ethnic identities across their cultural worlds of families, peers, teachers, and community members, but also institutional identities of schools and universities in supporting pathways from childhood through college.

Looking ahead, we need further progress in three key areas. The first lies in greater interdisciplinary understanding of intersections and gaps across individual, relationship, and institutional identities, including their ongoing constraints and opportunities and how issues of cultures, economics, and histories thread through them all (Dietrich, Parker, & Salmela-Aro, 2012; Mehan, 2012). This alignment will build a much-needed common language for research, practice, and policies (Ignatowski, 2013). Private and public leaders are linking short-term interventions into sustainable alliances among educational systems, community organizations, families, and youth from preschool through graduate school. Aligning measures of individual and institutional identities with students' learning, retention, and graduation is helping to advance this work (Hurtado, Cuellar, & Guillermo-Wann, 2011; University of California, 2008).

Our next steps will also be increasingly international and transnational. Scholars with interests in identities and schooling are working to advance research, practice, and policies in multicultural nations worldwide with histories of inequities in access to schooling; they are mapping variations within nations and both parallels and differences across them (Cooper, 2011; Crul, Schneider, & Lelie, 2012; Seginer, 2009). In South Africa and the United States, Carter (2012) found that educational inequities continue despite policies to promote racial inclusiveness, but that students who could cross cultural boundaries in their academic and extracurricular activities were more likely to thrive in their academic and racial-ethnic identities and their schoolwork. In Europe and the United States, policy investments in "second chances" programs for re-entering school through community colleges are important options for immigrant youth and young adults (Crul et al., 2012). Thus, students' academic and racial-ethnic identities and institutional identities reflect social capital, alienation/belonging, and challenge, with striking parallels across cultural communities (Florez-Gonzales, 2002; Fuligni, Witkow, & Garcia, 2005; Waters, 1996).

Finally, our next steps will be increasingly intergenerational. In this chapter, we have seen how identities and schooling develop in partnerships in which youth experience safety and respect as students, research participants, and researchers, and how students also serve as cultural brokers through their tutoring and mentoring younger students, peers, and adults, including their parents. We have more to learn about how bridging cultural identities among college faculty, staff, and students can foster climates in which underrepresented students graduate and become productive members of multicultural societies (Hurtado & Ruiz, 2012; Reid, 2013).

In closing, we invite readers to contribute to advancing research, practice, and policy that engage racial-ethnic minority, immigrant, Indigenous, and low-income youth and adults in opening the educational systems of their nations. Building on work from many cultural communities will foster greater understanding of identities, cultures, and schooling in the multicultural societies of which we are all a part.

References

Abraham, K. G. (1986). Ego-identity differences among Anglo-American and Mexican-American adolescents. *Journal of Adolescence, 9,* 151–166.

Adams, G. R. (2010). *Ego-identity formation in adolescence and early adulthood: Theory and measurement.* https://www.createspace.com/3426973

American Council on Education. (2010). *Gender equity in higher education: 2010.* Washington, DC: American Council on Education.

Azmitia, M., & Sumabat-Estrada, G. (2013). *Relationships, identities, and belonging: First-generation college students' college journeys.* Paper presented at meetings of the Society for Research in Identity Formation, Minneapolis, MN.

Azmitia, M., Syed, M., & Radmacher, K. (2008). On the intersection of personal and social identities: Introduction and evidence from a longitudinal study of emerging adults. In M. Azmitia, M. Syed, & K. Radmacher (Eds.), *The intersections of personal and social identities. New directions for child and adolescent development, 120,* 1–16.

Barillas-Chón, D. W. (2010). Oaxaqueño/a students' (un)welcoming high school experiences, *Journal of Latinos and Education,* 9, 303–320. doi: 10.1080/15348431.2010.491043

Batalla, G. B. (1996). *Mexico profundo: Reclaiming a civilization.* Austin: University of Texas Press.

Benitez, M., & DeAro, J. (2004). Realizing student success at Hispanic-Serving Institutions. *New Directions for Community Colleges, 127,* 35–48.

Bergin, D. A., & Cooks, H. C. (2002). High school students of color talk about accusations of "acting White." *Urban Review, 34,* 113–134.

Bigler, R. S., & Liben, L. S. (2007). Developmental intergroup theory: Explaining and reducing children's social stereotyping and prejudice. *Current Directions in Psychological Science, 16,* 162–171.

Booker, A., & Lawrence, J. A. (2013). Challenges for refugee young people moving into Australian culture and education. In K. De Gioia & P. Whiteman (Eds.), *Children and childhoods. Vol. 3: Immigrant and refugee families* (pp. 91–110). Newcastle upon Tyne, UK: Cambridge Scholars Publishing.

Bourdieu, P., & Passeron, C. (1986). *Reproduction in education, society, and culture.* London: Sage.

Bowen, W. G., Chingos, M. M., & McPherson, M. S. (2009). *Crossing the finish line: Completing college at America's public universities.* Princeton, NJ: Princeton University Press.

Burciaga, R., & Erbstein, N. (2012). Latina/o dropouts: Challenging stereotypes and highlighting agency through community cultural wealth. *Association of Mexican American Educators Journal, 6,* 24–33.

Cabrera, N. L., & Padilla, A. M. (2004). Entering and succeeding in the "culture of college": The story of two Mexican heritage students. *Hispanic Journal of Behavioral Sciences, 26,* 152–170.

California GEAR UP. (2012). *School Self-Assessment Rubric (SSAR).* Sacramento, CA: California GEAR UP. Retrieved from http://www.castategearup.org/tools/for-schools/ssar

Carter, P. (2006). Straddling boundaries: Identity, culture, and school. *Sociology of Education. 79,* 304–328.

Carter, P. (2012). *Stubborn roots: Race, culture, and inequality in U.S. and South African schools.* New York: Oxford University Press.

Castillo, L. G., Conoley, C. W., Brossart, D. F., & Quiros, A. E. (2007). Construction and validation of the Intragroup Marginalization Inventory. *Cultural Diversity and Ethnic Minority Psychology, 13,* 232–240. doi: 10.1037/1099-9809.13.3.232

Contreras, F. E., Malcom, L. E., & Bensimon, E. M. (2008). Hispanic-Serving Institutions: Closeted identity and the production of equitable outcomes for Latino/a students. In M. Gasman, B. Baez, & C. S. V. Turner (Eds.), *Understanding Minority-Serving Institutions* (pp. 71–90). Albany, NY: SUNY Press.

Cooper, C. R. (2011). *Bridging multiple worlds: Cultures, identities, and pathways to college.* New York: Oxford University Press.

Cooper, C. R., Bandera, M., & Macias, C. (2014). Bridging worlds of research, practice, and policy: An emerging Hispanic-Serving Institution partners with P-20 alliances. Paper presented at meetings of the American Educational Research Association, Philadelphia, PA.

Cooper, C. R., Behrens, R., & Trinh, N. (2009). Identity. In R. A. Shweder (Ed.), *The Chicago companion to the child* (pp. 474–477). Chicago: University of Chicago Press.

Cooper, C. R., & Burciaga, R. (2011). Pathways to college, to the professoriate, and to a green card: Linking research, policy, and practice on immigrant Latino youth. In T. N. Maloney & K. Korinek (Eds.), *Migration in the 21st century: Rights, outcomes, and policy.* (pp. 177–191). London: Routledge Kegan Paul.

Cooper, C. R., Cooper, R. G., Trinh, N. T., Wilson, A., & Gonzalez, E. (2013a). Bridging multiple worlds: Helping immigrant youth from Africa, Asia, and Latin America on their pathways to college identities. In E. Grigorenko (Ed.), *Handbook of U.S. immigration and education* (pp. 301–322). New York: Springer.

Cooper, C. R., García Coll, C., Thorne, B., & Orellana, M. F. (2005). Beyond demographic categories: How immigration, ethnicity, and "race" matter for children's emerging identities at school in C. R. Cooper, C. García Coll, W. T. Bartko, H. M. Davis, & C. M. Chatman (Eds.), *Developmental pathways through middle childhood: Rethinking contexts and diversity as resources.* (pp. 235–61). Mahwah, NJ: Erlbaum.

Cooper, C. R., Gonzalez, E., & Wilson, A. (2013b). Committed while exploring: How Mexican immigrant youth build identity pathways to college and careers. Paper presented at meetings of the Society for Research in Identity Formation, Minneapolis, MN.

Cooper, C. R., Jackson, J. F., Azmitia, M., Lopez, E. M., & Dunbar, N. (1995). Bridging students' multiple worlds: African American and Latino youth in academic outreach programs. In R. F. Macias & R. G. García-Ramos (Eds.), *Changing schools for changing students: An anthology of research on language minorities* (pp. 211–234). Santa Barbara: University of California Linguistic Minority Research Institute.

Córdova, D., & Cervantes, R. C. (2010). Intergroup and within-group perceived discrimination among US-born and foreign-born Latino youth. *Hispanic Journal of Behavioral Sciences, 32,* 259–274.

Cousins, L. H. (1999). Playing between classes: America's troubles with class, race, and gender in a Black high school and community. *Anthropology and Education Quarterly, 30,* 294–316.

Cross, W. (1991). *Shades of black: Diversity in African American identity.* Philadelphia: Temple University Press.

Crul, M., Schneider, J., & Lelie, F. (Eds.). (2012). *The European second generation compared: Does the integration context matter?* Amsterdam: Amsterdam University Press.

Dewey, J. (1916). *Democracy and education: An introduction to the philosophy of education.* New York: Macmillan.

Dietrich, J., Parker, P., & Salmela-Aro, K. (2012). Phase-adequate engagement at the post-school transition. *Developmental Psychology, 48,* 1575–1593. doi: 10.1037/a0030188

Engstrom, C. M., & Tinto, V. (2008). Learning better together: The impact of learning communities on the persistence of low-income students. *Opportunity Matters, 1,* 5–21.

Erikson, E. H. (1950). Childhood in two American Indian tribes: Hunters across the prairie and fishermen along a salmon river. In E. H. Erikson, *Childhood and society* (pp. 109–186). Oxford, UK: Norton.

Erikson, E. H. (1968a). *Identity: Youth and crisis.* New York: Norton.

Erikson, E. H. (1968b). Race and the wider identity. In E. H. Erikson, *Identity: Youth and crisis* (pp. 295–320). New York: Norton.

Esquivel, P. (2012, May 28). Epithet that divides Mexicans is banned by Oxnard school district. *Los Angeles Times.* Retrieved from http://www.losangelestimes.com

Fisher, C. B., Wallace, S. A., & Fenton, R. E. (2000). Discrimination distress during adolescence. *Journal of Youth and Adolescence, 29,* 679–695.

Florez-Crespo, P. (2007). Ethnicity, identity and educational achievement in Mexico. *International Journal of Educational Development, 27,* 331–339.

Flores-Gonzalez, N. (2002). *School kids/street kids: Identity development in Latino students.* New York: Teachers College Press.

Fordham, S., & Ogbu, J. U. (1986). Black students' school success: Coping with the "burden of acting white." *Urban Review, 18,* 176–206.

Fox, J. (2013). Introduction: Indigenous Oaxacan Immigrants and Youth-led Organizing in California. In Oaxacalifornian Reporting Team, *Voices of Indigenous Oaxacan youth in the Central Valley: Creating our sense of belonging in California,* UC Center for Collaborative Research for an Equitable California, Research Report No. 1.

Fox, J., & Rivera-Salgado, G. (2004). Building civil society among Indigenous migrants. In J. Fox & G. Rivera-Salgado (Eds.), *Indigenous Mexican migrants in the United States* (pp. 1–65). La Jolla, CA: Center for U.S.-Mexican Studies and the Center for Comparative Immigration Studies.

Fuligni, A. J., Witkow, M., & Garcia, C. (2005). Ethnic identity and the academic adjustment of adolescents from Mexican, Chinese, and European backgrounds. *Developmental Psychology, 41,* 799–811.

Gándara, P., Larson, K., Mehan, H., & Rumberger, R. (1998). Capturing Latino students in the academic pipeline. *Chicano/Latino Policy Project (CLPP) Report, 1,* 1, ERIC Document ED427094.

Gibson, M. A. (1988). *Accommodation without assimilation: Sikh immigrants in an American high school.* Ithaca, NY: Cornell University Press.

Gibson, M. A., & Bejinez, L. F. (2002). Dropout prevention: How migrant education supports Mexican youth. *Journal of Latinos and Education, 1*(3), 155–175.

Gibson, M. A., & Hidalgo, N. D. (2009). Bridges to success in high school for migrant youth. *Teachers College Record, 111,* 683–711.

Gonzalez, E. (2013). Coraje sin vergüenza: *Discrimination, emotions, and ethnic identity development of Indigenous Mexican youth.* Santa Cruz: University of California Press.

Grotevant, H. D., & Cooper, C. R. (1981). Assessing adolescent identity in the areas of occupation, religion, politics, friendship, dating, and sex roles: Manual for administration and coding of the interview. *JSAS Catalog of Selected Documents in Psychology, 11,* 52.

Grotevant, H. D., & Cooper, C. R. (1998). Individuality and connectedness in adolescent development: Review and prospects for research on identity, relationships, and context. In E. Skoe & A. Von der Lippe (Eds.), *Personality development in adolescence: A cross national and life span perspective* (pp. 3–37). London: Routledge.

Hare, J. (2012). Children teaching parents about Aboriginal culture. Paper presented at the meetings of the American Educational Research Association, Vancouver, BC, Canada.

Harvey, R. D., LaBeach, N., Pridgen, E., & Gocial, T. M. (2005). The intragroup stigmatization of skin tone among Black Americans. *Journal of Black Psychology, 31,* 237–253.

Heyman, G. D., & Giles, J. W. (2006). Gender and psychological essentialism. *Enfance, 58,* 293–310.

Hurtado, S., Cuellar, M., & Guillermo-Wann, C. (2011). Quantitative measures of students' sense of validation: Advancing the study of diverse learning environments.

Enrollment Management Journal: Student Access, Finance, and Success in Higher Education, 5, 53–71.

Hurtado, S., & Ruiz, A. (2012). *Realizing the potential of Hispanic-Serving Institutions: Multiple dimensions of institutional diversity for advancing Hispanic higher education.* White paper prepared for the Hispanic Association of Colleges and Universities. Los Angeles: University of California, Los Angeles.

Ignatowski, C. A. (2013). Commentary: Special issue on adolescents in the majority world. *Journal of Research on Adolescence, 23,* 193–194.

Instituto Nacional de Estadística Geografica de Informática of Mexico. (2010). *Perfil sociodemográfico de la poblacíon que habla lengua indígena [Sociodemographic profile of the population that speaks an indigenous language].* Retrieved from http://www.inegi.org.mx/prod_serv/contenidos/espanol/bvinegi/productos/censos/poblacion/poblacion_indigena/leng_indi/PHLI.pdf

Kao, G., & Rutherford, L. T. (2007). Does social capital still matter? Immigrant minority disadvantage in school-specific social capital and its effects on academic achievement, *Sociological Perspectives, 50,* 27–52.

Kovats, A. G. (2010). *Invisible students and marginalized identities: The articulation of identity among Mixteco youth in San Diego, California.* Master's thesis, San Diego State University. Retrieved from http://sdsu-dspace.calstate.edu/xmlui/handle/10211.10/520?show=full

Kuh, G. D., Kinzie, J., Buckley, J. A., Bridges, B. K., & Hayek, J. C. (2006). *What matters for student success: A review of the literature. Commissioned Report for the National Symposium on Postsecondary Student Success: Spearheading a Dialog on Student Success.* Washington, DC: National Postsecondary Education Cooperative.

Kumar, R., Seay, N., & Warnke, J. H. (2012). Risk and resilience in adolescents' transnational school transitions: Academic motivation and psychological well-being. *Advances in Motivation and Achievement, 17,* 147–176.

Kurtz, V. (2009). *Tasha goes to university.* Long Beach: California Academic Partnership Program. Retrieved from http://www.calstate.edu/capp/publications/docs/TashaGoesToUniversity-acc.pdf

Kurtz, V. (2010). *Tasha comes home.* Long Beach: California Academic Partnership Program. Retrieved from http://calstate.edu/capp/publications/docs/TashaComesHome-acc.pdf

LaFromboise, T. D., Hoyt, D. R., Oliver, L., & Whitbeck, L. B. (2006). Family, community, and school influences on resilience among American Indian adolescents in the upper Midwest. *Journal of Community Psychology, 34,* 193–209.

Laird, T. F. N., Bridges, B. K., Morelon-Ouainoo, C. L., Williams, J. M., & Holmes, M. S. (2007). African American and Hispanic student engagement at minority-serving and predominantly white institutions. *Journal of College Student Development, 48,* 39–56.

Machado-Casas, M. (2009). The politics of organic phylogeny: The art of parenting and surviving as transnational multilingual Latino indigenous immigrants in the U. S. *High School Journal, 92,* 82–99.

Marcelli, E. A., & Cornelius, W. A. (2001). The changing profile of Mexican migrants to the United States: New evidence from California and Mexico. *Latino American Research Review, 36,* 105–131.

Marcia, J. E. (1966). Development and validation of ego-identity status. *Journal of Personality and Social Psychology, 3,* 551–558.

Marcia, J. E. (2013). Integrity: The final identity challenge. Paper presented at meetings of the Society for Research in Identity Formation, Minneapolis, MN.

Martin, C. L., Ruble, D. N., & Szkrybalo, J. (2002). Cognitive theories of early gender development. *Psychological Bulletin, 128,* 903–933.

McArdle, C. G., & Young, N. F. (1970). Classroom discussion of racial identity or how can we make it without "acting white?". *American Journal of Orthopsychiatry, 40,* 135–141.

McLoyd, V. C. (2005). Pathways to academic achievement among immigrant children: A commentary. In C. R. Cooper, C. García Coll, T. Bartko, H. Davis, & C. Chatman (Eds.), *Developmental pathways through middle childhood: Rethinking contexts and diversity as resources* (pp. 283–293). Mahwah, NJ: Erlbaum.

Menchaca, M. (1993). Chicano Indianism: A historical account of racial repression in the United States. *American Ethnologist, 20,* 583–603.

Mehan, H. (2012). *In the front door: Creating a college-going culture of learning.* Boulder, CO: Paradigm.

Mendez, J. J., Bauman, S., & Guillory, R. M. (2012). Bullying of Mexican immigrant students by Mexican American students: An examination of intracultural bullying. *Hispanic Journal of Behavioral Sciences, 34,* 279–304. doi: 10.1177/0739986311435970

Mendoza, A., Martínez, S., & Mendoza, M. (2013). Gender roles and their influence on civic participation. In Equipode Croistas Oaxacalifornianos (ECO) (Eds.), *Voices of Indigenous Oaxacan youth in the Central Valley: Creating our sense of belonging in California* (pp. 89–92). Santa Cruz: UC Center for Collaborative Research for an Equitable California.

Mines, R., Nichols, S., & Runsten, D. (2010). *California's indigenous farmworkers. Final Report of Indigenous Farmworker Study (IFS).* Retrieved from http://indigenousfarmworkers.org/IFS%20Full%20Report%20_Jan2010.pdf

Nasir, N. S. (2012). *Racialized identities: Race and achievement among African American youth.* Stanford, CA: Stanford University Press.

Nicolás, B. (2011). *Reclamando lo que es nuestro: Identity formation among Zapoteco youth in Oaxaca and Los Angeles.* Master's thesis. University of California, San Diego.

Oakes, J. (2003). *Critical conditions for equity and diversity in college access: Informing policy and monitoring results.* Los Angeles: University of California All Campus Consortium on Research for Diversity (UC/ACCORD). Retrieved from http://ucaccord.gseis.ucla.edu/research/indicators/pdfs/criticalconditions.pdf

Ogbu, J. U. (2004). Collective identity and the burden of "acting White" in black history, community, and education. *Urban Review, 36,* 1–35.

Ogbu, J. U. (2003). *Black American students in an affluent suburb: A study of academic disengagement.* Mahwah, NJ: Erlbaum.

Ogbu, J. U., & Simons, H. D. (1988). Voluntary and involuntary minorities: A cultural-ecological theory of school performnce, with some implications for education. *Anthropology of Education Quarterly, 29,* 1–24.

Oyserman, D., Brickman, D., Bybee, D., & Celious, A. (2006). Fitting in matters: Markers of in-group belonging and academic outcomes. *Psychological Science, 17,* 854–861.

Oyserman, D., Bybee, D., & Terry, K. (2003). Gendered racial identity and involvement with school. *Self and Identity, 2,* 307–324.

Patton, L. D. (Ed.). (2010). *Culture centers in higher education: Perspectives on identity, theory, and practice*. Sterling, VA: Stylus.

Pérez, W., Cortés, R. D., Ramos, K., & Coronado, H. (2010). "Cursed and blessed": Examining the socioemotional and academic experiences of undocumented Latina and Latino college students. *New Directions for Student Services, 131*, 35–51. doi: 10.1002/ss366.

Phelan, P., Davidson, A. L., & Yu, H. C. (1998). *Adolescents' worlds: Negotiating family, peer, and school*. New York: Teachers College Press.

Phinney, J. S., & Alipuria, L. L. (1996). At the interface of cultures: Multiethnic/multiracial high school and college students. *Journal of Social Psychology, 136*, 139–158.

Phinney, J. S., & Baldelomar, O. A. (2011). Identity development in multiple cultural contexts. In L. A. Jensen (Ed.), *Bridging cultural and developmental approaches to psychology: New syntheses in theory, research, and policy* (pp. 161–186). New York: Oxford University Press.

Phinney, J. S., Madden, T., & Santos, L. J. (1998). Psychological variables as predictors of perceived ethnic discrimination among minority and immigrant adolescents. *Journal of Applied Social Psychology, 28*, 937–953.

Phinney, J. S., & Ong, A. D. (2007). Conceptualization and measurement of ethnic identity: Current status and future directions. *Journal of Counseling Psychology, 54*, 271–281.

Portes, A., & Fernández-Kelly, P. (2008). No margin for error: Educational and occupational achievement among disadvantaged children of immigrants. *Annals of the American Academy of Political and Social Science, 620*, 12–36.

Quintana, S. M. (1998). Children's developmental understanding of ethnicity and race. *Applied & Preventative Psychology, 7*, 27–45.

Ramos Arco, H. (2012). *Socialización y participación política de jóvenes de origen indígena en California: El caso del FIOB*. Master's thesis, El Colegio de la Frontera Norte, Tijuana, BC, Mexico.

Reid, K. W. (2013). Understanding the relationships among racial identity, self-efficacy, institutional integration, and academic achievement of Black males attending research universities. *Journal of Negro Education, 82*, 75–93.

Rosenbloom, S. R., & Way, N. (2004). Experiences of discrimination among African American, Asian American, and Latino adolescents in an urban high school. *Youth and Society, 35*, 420–451.

Rios-Aguilar, C., Kiyama, J. M., Gravitt, M., & Moll, L. C. (2011). Funds of knowledge for the poor and forms of capital for the rich? A capital approach to examining funds of knowledge. *Theory and Research in Education, 9*, 163–184.

Ruble, D. N., Alvarez, J., Bachman, M., Cameron, J., Fuligni, A., García Coll, C., & Rhee, E. (2004). The development of a sense of "we": The emergence and implications of children's collective identity. In M. Bennett & F. Sani (Eds.), *The development of the social self* (pp. 29–74.) New York: Psychology Press.

Ruiz, N. T., & Barajas, M. (2012). Multiple perspectives on the schooling of Mexican Indigenous students in the U.S.: Issues for future research. *Bilingual Research Journal: The Journal of the National Association for Bilingual Education, 35*, 125–144. doi: 10.1080/15235882.2012.703639

Rumbaut, R. G. (2005). Sites of belonging: Acculturation, discrimination, and ethnic identity among children of immigrants. In T. S. Weisner (Ed.), *Discovering successful pathways in children's development: New methods in the study of childhood and family life* (pp. 111–163). Chicago: University of Chicago Press.

Rumbaut, R. G. (2009). Pigments of our imagination: On the racialization and racial identities of "Hispanics" and "Latinos." In J. A. Cobas, J. Duany, & J. R. Feagin (Eds.), *How the U.S. racializes Latinos: White hegemony and its consequences* (pp. 15–36). Boulder, CO: Paradigm.

Saenz, V. B. (2009). The vanishing Latino male in higher education. *Journal of Hispanic Higher Education, 8*, 54–89.

Santiago, D. A. (2008). *Modeling Hispanic-Serving Institutions (HSIs): Campus practices that work for Latino students*. Washington, DC: Excelencia in Education.

Seginer, R. (2009). *Future orientation: Developmental and ecological perspectives*. New York: Springer.

Sellers, R. M., Smith, M. A., Shelton, J. N., Rowley, S. A. J., & Chavous, T. M. (1998). Multidimensional model of racial identity: A reconceptualization of African American racial identity. *Personality and Social Psychology Review, 2*, 18–39.

Sohn, K. (2011). Acting white: A critical review. *Urban Review, 43*, 217–234.

Solórzano, D. G. (1998). Critical race theory, race and gender microaggressions, and the experience of Chicana and Chicano scholars. *Qualitative Studies in Education, 11*, 121–136.

Stanton-Salazar, R. D. (2004). Social capital among working-class minority students: Prospects for applying a new concept to peer influences on achievement. In M. Gibson, P. Gándara, & J. Koyama (Eds.), *School connections: U.S. Mexican youth, peers and academic achievement* (pp. 18–38). New York: Teachers College Press.

Stephen, L. (2007). *Transborder lives: Indigenous Oaxacans in Mexico, California, and Oregon*. Durham, NC: Duke University Press.

Sue, D., & Sue, S. (1987). *Cultural factors in the clinical assessment of Asian Americans. Journal of Consulting and Clinical Psychology, 55*, 479–487.

Swail, W. S., Cabrera, A. F., Lee, C., & Williams, A. (2005). *Latino students and the educational pipeline. III. Pathways to the bachelor's degree for Latino students*. Stafford, VA: Educational Policy Institute.

Syed, M. (2010). Memorable everyday events in college: Narratives of the intersection of ethnicity and academia. *Journal of Diversity in Higher Education, 3*, 56–69.

Syed, M. (2012). The past, present and future of Eriksonian research: Introduction to the special issue. *Identity: An International Journal of Theory and Research, 12*, 1–7.

Syed, M., & Azmitia, M. (2009). Longitudinal trajectories of ethnic identity during college years. *Journal of Research on Adolescence, 19*, 601–624.

Syed, M., Azmitia, M., & Cooper, C. R. (2011). Identity and academic success among under-represented ethnic minorities: An interdisciplinary review and integration. *Journal of Social Issues, 67*, 442–468.

Syed, M., & Mitchell, L. L. (2013). Race, ethnicity, and emerging adulthood: Retrospect and prospects. *Emerging Adulthood, 1*, 83–95.

Tajfel, H. (1982). Social psychology of intergroup relations. *Annual Review of Psychology, 33*, 1–39.

Tajfel, H., & Turner, J. C. (1986). The social identity theory of intergroup behavior. In S. Worchel, & W. Austin (Eds.), *Psychology of inter-group relations* (pp. 7–24). Chicago: Nelson Hall.

Tyson, K., Darity, W., & Castellino, D. R. (2005). It's not "a black thing": Understanding the burden of acting white and other dilemmas of high achievement. *American Sociological Review, 70*, 582–605.

Umaña-Taylor, A. J., Yazedjian, A., & Bámaca-Gómez, M. Y. (2004). Developing the Ethnic Identity Scale using Eriksonian and social identity perspectives. *Identity: An International Journal of Theory and Research, 4*, 9–38.

University of California. (2008). *University of California Undergraduate Experiences Survey (UCUES)*. Oakland: UC Office of the President. Retrieved from http://studentsurvey.universityofcalifornia.edu/pdf/UCUES_2008_Survey_Instrument.pdf

US Census Bureau. (2012). *Population projections*. Retrieved from http://www.census.gov

Valencia, R. R., & Black, M. S. (2002). "Mexican Americans don't value education!": On the basis of the myth, myth-making, and debunking. *Journal of Latinos and Education, 1*, 81–103.

Vigil, J. D. (2004). Gangs, streets, and schooling: Peer dynamics. In M. A. Gibson, P. Gándara, & J. Koyama (Eds.), *School connections: U.S. Mexican youth, peers, and school achievement* (pp. 87–106). New York: Teachers College Press.

Waters, M. C. (1996). The intersection of gender, race, and ethnicity in identity development of Caribbean American teens. In B. J. R. Leadbeater & N. Way (Eds.), *Urban girls: Resisting stereotypes, creating identities* (pp. 65–81). New York: New York University Press.

Way, N., Hernandez, M. G., Rogers, L. O., & Hughes, D. (2013). "I'm not going to become no rapper": Stereotypes as a context of ethnic and racial identity development. *Journal of Adolescent Research, 28*, 407–430.

Werner, E. E. (1993). Risk, resilience, and recovery: Perspectives from the Kauai Longitudinal Study. *Development & Psychopathology, 5*, 503–515.

Wilson, A. R. (2013). *You're not really one of us: How do media perpetuate stereotypes relating to intra-racial discrimination and racial identity among African American youth?* Unpublished paper, University of California Santa Cruz.

Wilson, A. R., & Cooper, C. R. (2011). *Knowledge is power: Latino adolescents' understanding of racial discrepancies in college attendance*. Poster presented at the Society for Research in Child Development, Montreal, Canada.

Wozniacka, G. (2011, August 12). Latino-Indigenous Mexican divide stirs Greenfield. *KSBW The Central Coast*. Retrieved from http://www.ksbw.com

Wyche-Hall, M. (2011). *Demystifying the lens of color: Examining the relationship between academic achievement and racial identity*. Unpublished doctoral dissertation, University of New Mexico.

Yamauchi, L., Lau-Smith, J., & Luning, R. J. (2008). Family involvement in a Hawaiian language immersion program. *School Community Journal, 18*, 39–60.

Yeado, J. (2013). *Intentionally successful: Improving minority student college graduation rates*. Washington, DC: The Education Trust. Retrieved from http://www.edtrust.org/sites/edtrust.org/files/Intentionally_Successful.pdf

Yoder, A. E. (2000). Barriers to ego identity status formation: A contextual qualification of Marcia's identity status paradigm. *Journal of Adolescence, 23*, 95–106.

Yonezawa, S., & Jones, M. (2011). Shaping youth's identity through student-driven research. In C. M. Hands & L. Hubbard (Eds.), *Including families and communities in urban education*. (pp. 213–232). Charlotte, NC: Information Age Publishing.

Yosso, T. J. (2005). Whose culture has capital? A critical race theory discussion of community cultural wealth. *Race, Ethnicity and Education, 8*, 69–91.

CHAPTER 20

Transformation, Erosion, or Disparity in Work Identity?: Challenges During the Contemporary Transition to Adulthood

Jeylan T. Mortimer, Jack Lam, *and* Shi-Rong Lee

Abstract

Work identity is a multidimensional construct attached to job, occupation, workplace, or organization. This chapter highlights the precarious labor market that contemporary young workers confront worldwide and how the shifting economic terrain may be changing the ways younger workers understand their work and the formation of their work identities. Employment has become more transitory, insecure, and nonstandard, rendering young workers' school-to-work transition increasingly prolonged and difficult; the authors propose that work identities may also become more individualized and destandardized. Stryker's identity theory and Rosenberg's theory of self-concept formation offer important insights regarding the mechanisms through which more insecure and less rewarding jobs for young workers may diminish work's position in the hierarchy of role identities. Work identities may also become more flexible as workers adjust themselves to their changing employment circumstances. Given increasing inequalities in work conditions, growing disparities in the formation and character of work identities are expected.

Key Words: work identity, young adults, transition to adulthood, precarious employment, identity formation

---

Labor market entry is important to young adults because it plays a decisive role in the transition to adulthood. Although scholars debate the relative importance of various role markers and other criteria for acquiring an identity as an adult (Arnett, 2000; Shanahan, Porfeli, Mortimer, & Erickson, 2005), making a successful transition from school to work has become a near-universal consideration as young people, regardless of gender, expect to work in adulthood (Johnson & Mortimer, 2000). Young adults seek stable work that enables financial independence from the family of origin; once secured, such work facilitates other major transitions defining entry to adulthood, such as leaving the parental home, establishing an independent residence, marriage, and parenthood. The lengthening transition to adulthood, coupled with the increasing difficulty young adults have in acquiring paid work, have altered the timing and character of work identity formation. This chapter examines recent changes in the contexts of work and the transition from school to work, the implications of these changes for the work identities of young people, and probable shifts in the meanings and identities attached to work in the future. First, however, we consider the definition of work identity, the objects to which it is attached, and prominent theoretical frameworks that elucidate the process of work identity formation.

The Meanings and Development of Work Identity

In this chapter, the term "identity" is used broadly to reflect various "subparts of self" or "internalized expectations" of the self (Serpe & Stryker, 2011, p. 232). The general concept of role identity is based on the assumption that people typically do not enact their role obligations without changes in their self-conceptions. Anticipating, learning, and carrying out behaviors oriented toward the fulfillment of role expectations are usually accompanied by shifts in identity, such that one's very conception of self becomes linked to a role. Identities may also reference character traits that are linked to role-related behaviors, such as conceptions of oneself as honest, nurturant, or productive.

Work identities are multifaceted phenomena, attached to a multitude of work-related circumstances—occupational roles, jobs, organizations, and the like. Skorikov and Vondracek (2011, p. 693) use the term "occupational identity" to refer to "the conscious awareness of oneself as a worker"; it "represents a complex structure of meanings in which the individual links his or her motivation and competencies with acceptable career roles" (p. 694). As such, occupational identities may be attached to the full range of occupations (e.g., teacher, social worker, personnel manager, electrician, etc.). Work identity also encompasses the conception of self as part of a particular employing organization, for example, an employee of General Mills or a work team or group within an organization, such as the Human Relations Department (Haslam & Ellemers, 2011). Work identities may also reference a particular job (e.g., as substitute teacher at Mayflower Elementary School). Skorikov and Vondracek (2011, p. 696) distinguish between "job" and "career" identities, with the former signifying a "lack of long-term perspective and a sense of uniqueness, along with passive adoption of an ascribed identity." In contrast, the "career" occupational identity "is marked by an active construction of occupational identity and focus on long-term career prospects and occupational success." In addition, work identities may refer to a constellation of work-related character traits, to "one's perception of occupational interests, abilities, goals and values" (Skorikov & Vondracek, 2011, p. 694); for example, the conception of self as responsible, trustworthy, cooperative and calm in the face of work stressors and difficulties, loyal to the employer, and as having a strong work ethic. Such general character traits are applicable to a wide variety of occupational roles.

Acquiring these various work identities may be considered a key aspect of vocational socialization. Often, identity shifts begin to occur well before incumbency of an occupation. For example, during graduate and professional school, students gradually take on an identity as physicist (Hermanowicz, 2009), sociologist (Wright, 1967), or physician (Becker, Geer, Hughes, & Strauss, 1961). Through processes of socialization, the person's evaluation of self becomes tied to expressing work-related character traits in role performances. For example, one may come to think of oneself as a good, competent, dedicated teacher; an expert and caring nurse; or an honest broker, and evaluate one's behavior on the basis of how well one lives up to these standards. Such character traits may take innumerable forms, depending on individual values and prior experiences, occupational goals, or organizational missions. Thus, one lawyer will take pride in her ability to help others or serve society through her work, tying altruistic values and impulses to her work identity. Another worker, in the very same occupation and organization, might focus on her competitiveness and ambition, which fosters acquisition of partnership status in a law firm.

Recognizing that individuals play multiple roles simultaneously, and therefore have several, often many, potential roles to identify with in multiple domains of life (e.g., as worker, parent, member of a voluntary organization, citizen of a community, etc.), social psychologists have asked what determines the salience of a particular role identity. Why are some identities more important to the person than others? According to Stryker (Serpe & Stryker, 2011; Stryker & Statham, 1985), the individual's many role identities are placed in a hierarchy of importance, such that some are more psychologically salient and likely to be invoked, subjectively and behaviorally, in more situations than others. Furthermore, according to this theory, identities are placed higher in the hierarchy as more social relationships are linked to, dependent on, and built on them. That is, "social network relationships are proximate structures impacting on the organization and content of the self" (Serpe & Stryker, 2011, p. 231). As a result, work identities may typically be stronger than other identities (e.g., identity as friend or volunteer) since so many interpersonal relationships are linked directly to the work role, both in the workplace itself (including supervisors, co-workers, customers, and clients) and outside the workplace (because friends and acquaintances in the community may be current, or past, work associates). Much interaction in the family is also oriented to work, as couples go over the events of the day, discussing work-related events, issues, and problems, and parents share their work lives with their children. Even the most casual meeting of strangers provides the occasion for inquiries—"what do you do?"

As others recognize and relate to a person in a given work role, the identity is affirmed and its position in the hierarchy of identities is strengthened. Commitment to roles is conceptualized "as interactional and affective ties to others in social network" (Serpe & Stryker, 2011, pp. 233–234). Role identities that are supported by greater commitment rise in the hierarchy of identities. They have greater "identity salience," which increases the likelihood that they will be expressed and enacted in multiple situations. Individuals will spend more time playing a role when it is more highly salient. Thus, as commitment increases, identify salience is enhanced, and behavioral choices increasingly privilege role-related enactments.

But not all work roles involve satisfying social relationships, positive reflected appraisals, or convey the same benefits for the individual. Rosenberg (1979) points out that the more rewarding roles become more central to the person and that people will emphasize those roles and activities that help them to maintain positive self-evaluations (self-esteem and self-efficacy). In this regard, it is important to note that work has the potential to offer, or to withhold, many different kinds of rewards. Scholars have found it useful to distinguish between those that are inherent in the work itself from those that are extrinsic, or obtained for performing a job (Johnson, Mortimer, Lee, & Stern, 2007; Skorikov & Vondracek, 2011). Thus, one may be intrinsically rewarded at work if allowed to express individual interests and abilities, to be creative, to be self-directed, and to take responsibility. Extrinsic rewards take the form of earnings, health and retirement benefits, sick and parental leave, vacation time, social status or prestige, control over one's work schedule, and other good working conditions. A primary extrinsic reward is security, the degree of certainty that one's work role is safe, that one is not likely to lose one's job.

Vocational psychologists and occupational sociologists often assume that work identities, because so much is dependent on them, are, in fact, central in individual lives. Skorikov and Vondracek (2011, p. 694) comment, "occupational identity has frequently been conceptualized as a major component of one's overall sense of identity." As such, "it represents a core, integrative element of identity, serving not only as a determinant of occupational choice and attainment, but also as a major factor in the emergence of meaning and structure in individuals' lives." But in light of Stryker and Rosenberg's theorizing about the hierarchy of identities, one might ask how work identity is likely to be changing as a result of shifting work conditions and economic transformation. If work roles are becoming less stable and less satisfying, they may be relegated to lower positions in the hierarchy of identities in recent cohorts of young people, those who are completing their education and moving into the workforce in precarious economic times. We might expect that as work becomes more insecure and less rewarding, current generations of young adults are likely to acquire work identities that are weaker, less salient than those of their parents and grandparents.

In a prior era, through at least the mid-twentieth century and beyond, vocational development and work identity formation were seen as major developmental tasks occurring during adolescence (Erikson, 1968; Mortimer, Vuolo, & Staff, forthcoming). Individuals moved from school to "adult-like" full-time jobs shortly after completing high school or, for a minority of the population, after attending or graduating from a two- or four-year college. As a result, teenagers were expected to be actively engaged in thinking about their future work roles. As the knowledge and skill demands of the labor force increased, postsecondary education was increasingly seen as a requirement for the acquisition of good jobs and a middle-class lifestyle, and college enrollments grew. With more youth attending colleges, multiple markers of the transition to adulthood were postponed, including economic independence from the family, entry into marriage, parenthood, and full-time work (Shanahan, 2000; Swartz, 2009). Although most teens held "survival jobs" (Huiras, Uggen, & McMorris, 2000) during high school (Mortimer, 2003) and college, securing a "real job" became an increasingly distant phenomenon. Teenagers focused their attention on getting into college, rather than embarking on a serious process of vocational exploration. According to Schneider and Stevenson (1999), youth had become "motivated," but at the same time, "directionless."

In accord with these trends, social scientists interested in the process of vocational development and work identity formation shifted their own scholarly focus away from the adolescent years. Whereas mid-twentieth century sociologists and psychologists emphasized the period of adolescence in their theories of occupational status attainment and vocational development, those interested in much the same phenomena several decades later turned their attention to the period of transition to adulthood and beyond.

In studying the graduating class of 1957, sociologists in the prominent Wisconsin School (Featherman, 1980; Kerckhoff, 1995; 2003; Sewell & Hauser, 1975; Spenner & Featherman, 1978; Warren, Sheridan, & Hauser, 2002) emphasized the importance of parents, teachers, and peers in encouraging adolescents to have high educational and occupational aspirations, which, in turn, fostered educational attainment and high status jobs. Mid-twentieth century vocational psychologists (Ginzberg, Ginsburg, Axelrad, & Herma, 1951; Super, 1963) similarly saw adolescence as a critical period for work identity formation. For them, the process of vocational development involved searching for and finding a good "fit" between individual values, needs, and abilities and the experiences and rewards to be found in particular occupations (Fouad, 2007). Vocational exploration occurred in the family, as adolescents observed and discussed work with their parents; in school, as they studied particular subjects; and in early jobs, enabling the teenager to "try out" various work-related tasks and consider their congruency with developing interests and abilities. Through these experiences and successive trials, work identities would be formed, work values crystallized, and vocational preferences established. Crystallized vocational interests and goals would provide the impetus for the acquisition of educational credentials and work experiences that act as "stepping stones," fostering the development of skills and contacts that would equip young people for their desired future occupations (Zimmer-Gembeck & Mortimer, 2006).

The classic vocational psychologists also believed that individuals who could find good "matches" between their preferences and the conditions of their work would be more satisfied and committed to work and have more stable work careers. Highlighting the importance of the adolescent period for success in the adult work domain, Jordaan and Super (1974) linked adolescent planfulness, responsibility, and future orientation to occupational attainment at age twenty-five. Similarly, the sociologist John Clausen (1991) identified a constellation of traits in children who grew up during the Great Depression that he called "planful competence," including productivity, interest in school, ambition, and dependability. "Planfully competent" children actively explored their interests and sought opportunities to express them. They sought out information and new experiences relevant to their goals and were sensitive to the "fit" of these experiences with their developing abilities. Interviews with the same persons later in life (Clausen, 1993) showed that planful orientations and activities paid off in more successful adult work careers.

These classic theories of status attainment, vocational development, and competent action, developed in the mid-twentieth century, thus provided general theoretical frameworks for subsequent scholars who increasingly recognized that career development extends well beyond adolescence, with continuing potential for change in occupational identities. For example, in their longitudinal study of earlier occupational reward values and later occupational outcomes, Johnson and Mortimer (2011) focused attention on work values in the early twenties, not values expressed by the same teenagers during high school, as predictors of the quality of work approximately a decade later. In fact, Vondracek's (Skorikov & Vondracek, 1997; Vondracek, 1990; Vondracek, Lerner, & Schulenberg, 1986) developmental contextual theory extends the process of career development throughout the lifespan, highlighting the interdependence of individual change and shifting environmental contexts. Vocational identities are seen as fluid and changing in adulthood. They are formed and crystallized as actors seek and find environments that confirm their identities. Otherwise, actors modify their identities when confronted with new information and reactions from others, an important factor to consider given the changing nature of employment (Hackett & Lent, 1992; Holland, 1985; Lent, Brown, & Hackett, 1994; Super, 1990; Swanson & Gore, 2000).

The remaining sections of this chapter consider likely shifts in the several components of work identity, now and in the future, particularly among young adults who are newly entering the labor force, given numerous changes in societal contexts and opportunities. We first consider change in context of work itself and then in the process of transition from school to work, which has become more uncertain, individualized, and prolonged. We then examine the consequences of these economic and social trends for work identity formation in light of the prominent theoretical formulations discussed in this section. We give special attention to gender, social class, and cross-national differences in work identity. We conclude with some speculations regarding the transformation, erosion, or disparity in work identity in the future.

Changing Contexts of Work and Transition from School to Work

Previous generations of young (primarily male) workers in the United States could anticipate long-term occupational careers, often acquired shortly after leaving secondary school. The corporate logic was to build employee loyalty and keep employees for long periods of time. Employees were offered benefits and incentives to stay with a company, including opportunities for internal mobility within a firm (Cappelli, 1999; Kalleberg, 2009; Osterman, 2000; Uchitelle, 2007). Young men built a strong sense of identity around their paid employment and employer as they sought to climb the corporate ladder and become an "organization man" (Whyte, 1956).

In recent decades, this employment relationship has undergone dramatic changes. Increasing global competition, rapid technological advances, and the rise of nonstandard employment have made paid work much more precarious. In the face of global competition, the corporate logic has shifted such that companies now see their primary responsibility as promoting the interests and ensuring the loyalty of shareholders, not workers (Ho, 2009; Kalleberg, 2009). Jobs are increasingly "nonstandard," set apart from traditional standard (full-time, full year) employment by their temporary nature, often for a predetermined duration, with workers hired for specific time-limited tasks (Kalleberg, Reskin, & Hudson, 2000). Such contractors or temporary workers are often hired through an intermediary "temp agency," which facilitates the logistic and legal paperwork for the hiring company and the workers. In comparison to standard workers, nonstandard workers typically make less pay; are not considered qualified for retirement, health insurance coverage, and other benefits; and are excluded from the social life of the firm (Smith, 1998; Smith & Neuwirth, 2008). Importantly, they are also left out of company mobility ladders, which offer standard workers chances for promotion and opportunities to make attractive lateral moves within the firm. The trend toward nonstandard work has occurred not only in the United States but also in other postindustrial societies. The rise of part-time and agency/contract work is clearly apparent in European countries (Burchell, Fagan, O'Brien, & Smith, 2007).

Increasing insecurity, turbulence, and technological change make the transition from school to work more difficult and prolonged as youth are increasingly faced with transient employment and nonstandard contracts, recurrent job losses and spells of unemployment, and shifts in career lines as they attempt to adapt to the changing labor market. Diminishing opportunities likely make it more difficult to engage in the focused vocational exploration envisioned by classic scholars in vocational psychology (Ginzberg, Super, Holland, etc.) or to express planful competence (Clausen, Elder, etc.), which moved previous generations of youth toward a good fit between their interests and values, on the one hand, and their work experiences and rewards, on the other. Greater uncertainty and difficulty appear to be reflected in young workers' attitudes, suggesting declining investment in work. A declining percentage of young workers wants more responsibility on the job and longer hours of work (Families and Work Institute, 2012). In 1992, 75 percent of young workers wanted more responsibility and longer hours; by 2002, only 57 percent did so. Moreover, the MacArthur Network on the Transition to Adulthood found that, in 1980, three-quarters of young adults reported work as central to their lives; in 2004, just 60 percent viewed work as central (Settersten & Ray, 2010).

In the "new economy," young and old alike are told that they must carve out their own careers rather than climb well-established career ladders (Heinz, 2003). They must become self-employed entrepreneurs, freelancers, and consultants, generating their own "start-ups" and clienteles. A recent article in the *New York Times* (Rampell, 2012) noted that personal trainers had become one of the fastest growing occupations. Employment is quite unstable as young people try their luck with various entrepreneurial pursuits. Many youth work without pay, volunteering or in unpaid internships, as they aim to build valuable employment networks or gain the kinds of work-related experiences that employers seek. Others return to school, hoping to establish the skills and acquire the knowledge needed in rapidly expanding occupational sectors. But with continuing job displacement and change, the value of any particular educational credentials in the labor market may be increasingly short-lived.

Occupational change renders anticipatory socialization to work more challenging. Adolescents, as they look to the future, might even wonder whether the kinds of jobs they observe around them will be present when they complete their educations and become adults. Will any given job still be available, or might it be moved overseas, eliminated by new technologies, or disappear as a result of shifting consumer demand? A young respondent in the Youth Development Study, a longitudinal study of adolescents in St. Paul, Minnesota,, told an interviewer that whatever work he would likely do in the future "probably hasn't been invented yet." He felt that it was important for him to develop general skills, especially those involving computers. While this could be a beneficial strategy, such uncertainty about the future could disrupt long-term anticipatory socialization to work and early development of work identities, which were more likely to occur in more stable times.

As the timing of vocational development and the acquisition of work identities have been postponed, the character of the transition from school to work has also changed. In a previous era, teenage employment was a near-universal experience in the United States; almost all adolescents held part-time jobs while school was in session, at least for some time during high school (Mortimer, 2003), and teens were even more likely to be employed during the summers. Through this experience, they could begin to develop an identity as a worker, learn about the importance and value of work, and begin to develop occupational values and preferences. The workplace offered teenagers many opportunities for vocational exploration and anticipatory socialization (Zimmer-Gembeck & Mortimer, 2006). This context of anticipatory socialization to work, however, has now been lost due to the virtual collapse of the teenage labor market during the past few decades (Fogg & Harrington, 2011). Opportunities for teen work have declined as a result of displacement by adult workers and change in the distribution of occupations and industries, as with the disappearance of the "paper boy" (or girl), the loss of full-service gas stations, and increasing self-service in retail and other sectors.

Whereas the movement from school to work used to be a clearer, more distinct singular event, this transition has become increasingly individualized and destandardized as contemporary youth, in transition to adulthood, combine postsecondary schooling and employment for long periods of time, move from school to full-time work and back to school as they discover the need for additional educational credentials, and spend periods of time doing neither (Staff & Mortimer, 2007). Although some young people continue to move into "career-like" occupational positions shortly after completing vocational school programs, associates' degrees, or four-year college degrees, others "flounder" with unrelated, short-term jobs, often punctuated by spells of unemployment (Vuolo, Staff, & Mortimer, 2012).

Young adults in many Western nations are finding it more difficult to secure "good jobs" (Kalleberg, 2011). The shift away from standard employment relations perhaps affects young people the most, given their shorter time in the labor force and relative lack of work experience. Young workers are especially vulnerable to precarious employment because they have relatively few resources, such as work experience, job skills, and social networks that might enhance their bargaining position in the labor market. Indeed, young workers, as labor market entrants, are most at risk of nonstandard work contracts (Blossfeld, Buchholz, Bukodi, & Kurz, 2008) and "bad" jobs (Kalleberg, 2011; Kalleberg et al., 2000). Not surprisingly, young adults also make up a higher percentage of the unemployed and underemployed than workers in other age groups.

This plight of young workers throughout North America and most of Europe is gaining much attention during the aftermath of the recent Great Recession, since youth unemployment remains especially high. According to Eurostat (2012), while the unemployment rate in the European Union (EU-27) was 7.1 percent for all workers, it was 15 percent for younger workers, age fifteen to twenty-four in 2008; youth unemployment increased to about 22.5 percent by the beginning of 2012. Importantly, many youth no longer are seeking employment and therefore are not counted among the unemployed. In Spain, 23.7 percent of those between fifteen and twenty-nine have simply given up looking for work, while in France, 16.7 percent, and in Italy 20.5 percent have done so (Mascherini, Salvatore, Meierkord, & Jungblut, 2012). Youth exclusion from employment has stimulated research on how unemployment and nonstandard forms of early employment influence young workers' later careers (Blossfeld et al., 2008; Kahn, 2010).

Consequences of Changing Contexts for Work Identities

Let us now focus our attention on the implications of these structural shifts in the labor force and in the transition from school to work for work identity formation and change.

With increasingly transitory, insecure, and nonstandard employment and an increasingly prolonged and difficult school-to-work transition, how might work identities be affected? Stryker's and Rosenberg's theories of identity formation would suggest a weakening of identity salience and identity enactment in relation to particular roles when individuals are no longer recognized by others in those roles and when rewards from role enactment are less forthcoming. If an individual's work roles are changing or intermittent, punctuated by frequent spells of unemployment, interactions with work role partners will be less stable and enduring. Moreover, it will become less likely that others outside the workplace will recognize an individual as a representative of a particular occupation, work organization, or work team. Thus, work role commitment, indexed by the extent to which social relationships are dependent on the work role, will decline, lessening work role salience.

Consistent with Stryker's and Rosenberg's theoretical formulations, Skorikov and Vondracek (2011, p. 697) recognize the critical importance of the period of transition from school to work for occupational identity formation: "During that period, successful employment strengthens the sense of occupational identity and its salience within the overall identity structure, whereas failure to find adequate employment increases the subjective importance of relational identity, which may then replace occupational identity as a main source of meaning and psychological well-being" (p. 697). Individuals who cannot enact preferred occupational identities are subject to "identity loss" (p. 701).

Evidence from a Dutch study supports the expectation that disruptions in employment during the transition from school to work are particularly damaging to fragile emergent work identities. No differences in psychological well-being and work identity were found between young workers and school-leavers who were not yet employed; however, the unemployed youth with prior work experience had significantly lower psychological well-being and less strong work identity than the young workers (Meeus, Deković, & Iedema, 1997).

Moreover, expectations and values attached to work are found to be responsive to the rewards one is able to actually obtain. Most occupational values decline during the early occupational career as individuals confront difficulties in the labor market and learn that their earlier values cannot be realized (Johnson, 2001). In the Youth Development Study panel, job security was the most highly evaluated work condition from ages twenty-one to thirty-five. Departing from the general work value trend, interest in job security actually increased slightly after the start of the recent recession (Johnson, Sage, & Mortimer, 2012). Whereas this aggregate trend indicates continued concern with the stability of work through the transition to adulthood, at the individual level, turbulence in the early work career (as indicated by deteriorating pay, perceptions of job instability, low levels of intrinsic rewards, and jobs that were unrelated to career goals) erodes work values in general. That is, extrinsic values declined with decreases in earnings, job security, advancement opportunity, and intrinsic rewards. Intrinsic values were lower when the respondent lacked intrinsic rewards at work, held a job that was not considered to be a career, and when there was little job opportunity. It is reasonable to suppose that as deteriorating work conditions diminish the occupational reward values that support and sustain commitment and psychological engagement in work, work identities may also be eroded.

An occupational role identity that includes expectation of a long-term "career" may become a thing of the past as young people move from one occupation to another, interspersed with periods of unemployment and job search. Indeed, any given occupational role may be increasingly thought of not as a long-term identity or "career" but instead as a much more transitory endeavor. And, although in difficult economic times education with vocational relevance is highly sought after (putting college liberal arts programs on the defensive), the person whose skills are highly specialized may be less able to move flexibly from one type of occupation to another, an increasing necessity in a rapidly changing economy.

As attachment to particular jobs, and even to the labor force in general, becomes ever more unstable, unpredictable, and precarious, young adults may move away from work as an occupational, character, or organizational identity. In accord with identity theory, one might expect that work identities would recede in importance as the social relationships attached to them become more transitory. Among younger cohorts, it may be more important for new acquaintances to learn about who a person is—one's distinct interests, political commitments, hobbies, or family relationships—rather than one's present or anticipated occupational role.

Similarly, the character traits associated with work may fluctuate as workers move from one occupational position to another. As occupations become less secure, the character identities attached to work may shift accordingly. For example, workers in a more stable economy may come to think of themselves as conscientious, loyal to the occupational community or employing organization, and take pride in being a good economic provider. But in "the new economy," other work-related character identities may come to the fore. Workers may increasingly pride themselves on being able to take risks in the economic arena and on their flexibility, enabling them to swiftly respond to new entrepreneurial opportunities. Young people may be less likely to see themselves as embodiments of occupational roles, specializing and developing competencies relevant to particular occupational tasks, but instead as a "jack of all trades," able to move between positions that express quite different character traits.

The component of the work identity referencing organizational affiliation may be the most vulnerable of all. Haslam and Ellemers (2011) argue that "the capacity for organizations to furnish their members with a sense of social identity (and for them to project this identity to the world at large) is commonly considered to be one of their defining features" (p. 718). They refer to "people's desire for organizational identities that are positive, distinct, and enduring" (p. 719). Strong organizational identity would appear to be most likely when employment within an organization is long-term and secure. In fact, Haslam and Ellemers (2011) refer to the loss or devaluation of organizational identity in the event of organizational change, such as merger, acquisition, and restructuring. After many such changes or moves between firms, it may no longer seem realistic to attach very much salience to one's position as an employee of a particular organization. Just as musicians describe their "gigs," workers in a wide range of occupations may come to see their incumbency in jobs in particular organizations as temporary.

Studies also find that workers in recent years have become more inured to employment uncertainty (Kelan, 2008; Lane, 2011). Brushes with unemployment could very well affect workers' expectations for future job security (Kelan, 2008; Smith, 2002). In a study of unemployed workers in a job search club, Smith (2002) finds that individuals who become unemployed shift their orientation away from the employment relationship after such experiences.

And, if all these forms of work identity recede in importance in the hierarchy of identities, in reaction to turbulence, uncertainty, and lack of opportunity in the labor force, work may become less important generally as a source of self-esteem and sense of efficacy. Continuing to place high importance on work when it does not even provide basic sustenance, much less intrinsic and extrinsic rewards, would only foster strain, cognitive dissonance, and low self-evaluations (Rosenberg, 1979). It is plausible to assume, then, that young people will increasingly focus and find meaning and identity in other more stable and seemingly controllable spheres of life, including their intimate relationships or other relationships in their immediate and extended families. Sports and other recreational activities, religion, aesthetic forms of self-expression, and other activities may offer alternative forms of fulfillment and assume high salience in the identity structure. Work may increasingly be considered as simply a means of sustaining one's livelihood, not as a central source of identity or self-expression.

We now turn to the universality of work identity processes. Do work-related identities differ by social class, gender, or cultural tradition? Might alterations in work identities occur among young people across the board or might there be distinctive reactions to changing labor market conditions and the increasingly problematic transition from school to work, depending on the person's social location?

Differences in Work Identity by Social Location
Social Class

Given Stryker's theory of the hierarchy of identities and Rosenberg's notions about identity centrality, one would expect that work identities would be stratified along class lines. The more prestigious occupations receive widespread esteem; at the highest levels, most, if not all, of a person's relationships will involve recognition of his or her occupational position. At the extreme, consider ministers—highly respected by all in their congregations; doctors—accorded high rank and prestige by their patients and throughout the community; and political and corporate leaders, who likewise receive widespread recognition. Thus, work commitment and work identity salience, key elements of Stryker's identity theory, are likely to be strong. Moreover, such occupational roles are all-consuming in terms of time and energy, likely to affect all other aspects of life, and highly rewarding. High levels of rewards foster self-esteem, self-efficacy, and role centrality, consistent with Rosenberg's approach. Whereas these most prestigious examples of occupational roles likely foster the strongest work identities, workers in occupations of higher socioeconomic status in general have occupational experiences and social relationships connected to work that are both more satisfying and affirming of personal worth than those of workers in lower ranked occupational positions. They receive greater extrinsic rewards of money, social status, advancement opportunities, and security; they also have more intrinsically rewarding experiences—occupational tasks that are more interesting, more self-expressive of abilities, that involve more opportunities to be creative, and greater self-direction. Self-direction or work autonomy is found to be especially promotive of job satisfaction and commitment (Lorence & Mortimer, 1985). Moreover, along with occupational status comes greater authority, responsibility, and recognition. All of these features would lead one to expect that the occupational role identity would assume a more central place in the hierarchy of identities as one ascends the socioeconomic hierarchy. Moreover, long periods of formal socialization in higher educational programs promote the acquisition of strong occupational identities among professionals and managers.

Lamont's (1992) study of professional and managerial men living in the suburbs of New York City identified distinctive class-related perspectives on work identity and work-related values. Not surprisingly, given their own advantaged social location, they were prone to judge others, as well as themselves, by their achieved occupational roles and their status and authority in the workplace, signifying their socioeconomic success. They looked to work not so much as providing validation for their ability to be steady providers for their families but for their own self-actualization. Kohn and Schooler (1969; 1983) similarly found that higher status workers valued self-directed character traits, those attributes that enabled them to be effective in dealing with the complex realities and choices they faced in their occupational positions.

The lesser occupational rank and rewards obtained by those with lower status might lead them to hold less central occupational identities while instead identifying more strongly with the general status of worker. Lamont's (2000) interviews with working men, mainly blue-collar and lower status white-collar workers in the New York metropolitan area, yielded rich narratives demonstrating the strength of their identities as workers, but not their occupational identities. They prided themselves on being stable, full-time workers, which differentiated them from what they conceived as lower level part-time and temporary workers, as well as the poor. They stressed that they were "hard-working" and that this attribute enabled them to support themselves and their families. Instead of succumbing to frivolous temptations, they emphasized their disciplined behavioral routines. As a result, they described themselves as steadfast in fulfilling their work role obligations despite their lack of rewards and satisfactions in the workplace and their multiple hardships and challenges. Indeed, they took pride in their persistence, their capacity to keep going, "not giving up" no matter what the obstacles. These highly salient character traits set them apart, in their own minds, from those who lacked the ability to maintain gainful work—the poor and homeless.

In Lamont's study, blue-collar workers were able to maintain a sense of personal dignity, a positive self-evaluation, although they lacked the accoutrements of status—occupational prestige and higher educational attainment. Their self-images were protected by their emphasis on their morality, integrity, honesty, practicality, and productivity. They stressed their capacity to make it by dint of hard work and perseverance, despite their lack of privilege and little help from others. As Lamont points out (2000, p. 129), "by stressing morality over socioeconomic success, workers affirm their own value and dignity and reject the notion that one's station in life defines one's worth." Kohn and Schooler (1969; 1983) found that workers' occupational values reflected the traits that enabled them to be successful in their predominant lines of work. As a result, workers of lower socioeconomic status, whose occupations involved closer supervision, more repetitive tasks, and most important, lower levels of substantive complexity, evaluated more highly those traits signifying conformity (e.g., the ability to follow rules and directives set by others) for themselves as well as for their children.

Gender

Beginning in the mid-twentieth century, writers like Betty Friedan (1963) challenged traditional assumptions surrounding the gendered division of labor in paid employment and unpaid domestic work. In the period of the postwar economic boom, employers were able to provide white-collar and unionized blue-collar men in the United States with a large enough salary to support a single-earner breadwinner household, giving (primarily middle-class) families the opportunity to arrange their lives such that women focused their energy and attention on the domestic sphere and men on the public sphere of paid work. As such, men's work identity was ascendant because men were the "breadwinners" of the family, while women's identity was primarily that of a "housewife," a mother, a homemaker, and a caretaker of husband and children.

These traditional gendered arrangements and assumptions about paid work and care work have been challenged by the movement of women into the workforce, the increase in dual-earner couples, and the decline of the "living wage," prompting a reexamination of gendered work identities. Women, at all class levels, moved into the labor force to increase their families' standards of living, as well as to enhance their own self-actualization (Aronson & Mortimer, forthcoming). As women are becoming accountants, managers, doctors, lawyers, and other professionals (in addition to being partners, spouses, and caretakers), are their work identities as salient as those of men in the same occupations and professions? In Stryker's language, do career women consider work as salient as men in their hierarchy of identities, do they have a more balanced recognition of work and family, or do they still prioritize family over other life domains? At the same time, as men come to devote more time to household chores and caregiving tasks (Bianchi, 2011), might they deprioritize the salience of work and develop a stronger family identity? Would these two simultaneous trends promote similarity in men's and women's work identities as they devote themselves more equally to work and family?

Extant research would suggest that it may be some time before we see this happening. Although great strides have been made in women's labor force participation and advancement and the enactment of policies to promote equal treatment of employed women and men, work organizations remain highly gendered (Acker, 1990; Britton, 2000). The Ideal Worker Norm (Williams, 2000), assuming high levels of commitment to work and accommodation to the employer, is still more applicable to men than to women, who, despite their high rates of employment, still do the bulk of housework and conform, through their caretaking activities, to gendered cultural expectations for parenthood (Cooper, 2000; Hays, 1998). Even in dual-earner households, women who have full-time jobs take on a "second shift" in the household (Hochschild, 1997). Acknowledging this reality, women may select themselves out of certain occupations in the first place to fulfill cultural expectations and to express their identities, choosing jobs that provide them with the ability to easily enact their work and home responsibilities and to keep these roles from influencing one another (Graham, Sorell, & Montgomery, 2004). In addition, some women, but very few men, opt out of employment once they have children, leaving the workforce altogether (Stone, 2007). Thus, contemporary organizational arrangements and cultural expectations lead many women to be marginalized or excluded from the realm of paid work while encouraging them to be more involved in care work, with implications for their work identities.

How are recent trends in the transition to adulthood influencing the gendered character of work and work identities? As educational preparation for adult work takes longer, young adults postpone intimate partnership and marriage, as well as childbearing, as they seek to establish their careers first before starting a family (Settersten & Ray, 2010). This strategy may enable young men and women to balance work and family, thus developing similar work identities, in contrast to earlier generations that privileged men's work identities over those of women. The phrase "to have it all" has ignited intense debates about women's equal participation at home and in the workplace. Whereas women seek satisfaction from involvement in both spheres, they experience great difficulties in doing so, especially if both partners are in highly demanding jobs. Workplaces are making greater demands on professional and managerial workers. Aided by technology, they work longer hours than their predecessors, putting in time in the evenings and on the weekends (Jacobs & Gerson, 2004). The increasing precariousness of work may even exacerbate professional and managerial workers' single-minded devotion to their jobs. At the same time, lower level workers may have to hold two or more jobs just to make ends meet.

Taken together, cultural shifts toward greater equality for women and women's increasing educational attainment, now exceeding that of men in the United States, make it likely that men's and women's work identities will eventually move toward greater convergence. Both men and women encounter strains resulting from the increasingly competitive and insecure character of work, making it more difficult to enact traditionally gendered work and family arrangements. But, given the trends in work and family just described, it seems safe to say that among young adults work identity will continue to be stronger for men than for women in the near future.

Much popular rhetoric as well as scientific analysis surrounding work identity in the upper classes point to the potential for work to become all-encompassing and entirely consuming when such high levels of reward are at stake, so much so that other values and satisfactions, especially those related to one's nuclear family and relations with extended kin, are crowded out. Lamont's (2000) blue-collar men stressed that the professionals and managerial workers "above" them lacked the strong family ties and friendships that they themselves experienced. They saw these men as prioritizing occupational success above all; their competitiveness and driven pursuit of status and wealth undermined the family and what these blue-collar workers considered more human values and traits.

Conflict between valued identities has been a major theme in the literature on work and family at least since the 1970s, when scholarly interest in this topic became prominent. Kanter (1977a; 1977b) pointed out that men in corporate management had strong incentive to devote their energies single-mindedly to work, given their capacity to obtain high levels of reward by climbing internal job ladders. In contrast, those at lower levels, and the women in the corporation she studied, were not poised to climb those ladders (they were mostly secretaries and other low-level white-collar workers) and obtain the same rewards. Whereas job tasks performed by lower level workers may be put aside at the end of the work day, professionals and managers were expected to be fully, even exclusively, committed to their jobs, as if their families did not exist. Blair-Loy (2001) refers to this ethic as the "work devotion schema." Such dedication to work and the firm on the part of high-level managers and executives was well integrated with the single provider family form because full-time homemakers attended to the family work, parenting, and home maintenance that expressed and enabled middle-class life styles (Blair-Loy's "family devotion schema"). However, both the rising cost of living and the feminist movement have eroded this traditional family form, fostering rapid movement of women into the labor force. Relatively few contemporary upper middle-class families can afford, nor do they desire, this traditional arrangement. In contrast, having a wife "at home," caring for children, husband, and maintaining the household, was considered the ideal although usually unattained, among Lamont's (2000) blue-collar interviewees.

The oppositional character of "work devotion" and "family devotion" and the work-based and family-based identities thereby implied come to a head for women in highly demanding professional and managerial occupations. Blair-Loy (2001) shows how successful female financiers in the most recent cohort she studied (who completed college between 1974 and 1980) attempted to resolve this conflict by becoming mothers "at a distance," entrusting the care of their children to hired caretakers or to their own mothers. One mother described her ambivalence resulting from this adaptation: "It was an internal battle between wanting to perceive myself as a perfect mother but knowing I couldn't fit into it" (p. 705). Shifts in cultural schemas, promoting women's rights in the labor force along with a more egalitarian family, enabled these women to combine work and family, particularly motherhood, whereas those in earlier cohorts either relinquished these roles or failed to sustain stable families. Still, Blair-Loy reminds us that the "work devotion" and "family devotion" schemas remained relatively intact because the financial executives in her youngest cohort did not challenge the importance, even necessity, to their firms of long working hours, frequent travel, and full commitment to work. They remained responsible for the management of their hired family surrogates and for attending to the relatively few tasks that such hired helpers couldn't fulfill.

These are the likely circumstances facing the parents of today's young women and men, the role models that provide live illustration of the joys and dilemmas of combining work and family roles. It may be that observing the struggles and difficulties in their parents' generation, as well as the satisfactions and rewards in more egalitarian dual-worker arrangements, will influence young people's commitment to work as a locus of identity.

Both Lamont's studies of blue-collar and upper middle-class men and Blair-Loy's study of women financiers were conducted from the late 1980s to the mid-1990s. As noted, since that time, women have made significant inroads into high-level professional and managerial occupations; in the United States, women now surpass men in educational attainment. These advances and the continuing growth of egalitarian ideologies surrounding work and family roles raise the question as to whether the traditional and class-based work identities revealed in these earlier studies continue to hold sway among young men and women today.

According to Kathleen Gerson (2009), "changing lives are colliding with resistant institutions" (p. 735) since, despite the decline of the traditional, homemaker–breadwinner family, employers still reward "ideal workers who provide uninterrupted full-time—often overtime—commitment" (p. 736). Her more recent interviews with 120 young adults, aged 18–32 and from varied socioeconomic backgrounds, revealed widespread skepticism about the "career mystique" (Moen & Roehling, 2004) that promised intraorganizational mobility via internal career ladders to male executives and managers in prior cohorts who gave their utmost loyalty and devotion to the firm. Gerson argues that traditional gendered devotions to work and family have been supplanted by women's interest in economic self-reliance, whereas contemporary young men prefer a "neo-traditional" arrangement in which they are the primary breadwinners and their wives the primary caretakers. Still, her male interviewees wished to balance their work and family lives in ways that their fathers did not, devoting more of their time to childcare and transcending work and family boundaries. Contrary to earlier gender role definitions, both men and women are now expecting to play "juggling acts." It thus remains to be seen whether contemporary young men and women will be able to enact their preferences and whether the highly gendered and class-based work identities of the past will continue to prevail. Whereas these young adults projected future work identities or "possible selves" that would enable both men and women to more successfully balance work and family roles, the growing occupational inequality and continuing erosion of the middle class in the United States proffers a somewhat different scenario.

If, as Gerson says, employers continue to most strongly reward those who conform, whether male or female, to a single-minded devotion to work, we might expect that workers at the highest levels will continue to privilege work identities over those linked to family. Moreover, as the stable middle class shrinks and increasing proportions of workers find themselves in precarious, lower level white-collar and service occupations, we might see increasing bifurcation of work identities. That is, those in higher level professional, technical, and managerial occupational levels will be strongly identifying with their occupational roles, and self-actualization in the workplace will be an important part of their identities. In contrast, those at lower levels will be attempting to protect fragile self-concepts and to maintain their dignity by emphasizing their identities as workers, including their capacity to work "hard," "hold on," and hang in there despite all odds. Still, changing cultural contexts responsive to structural changes in the labor market may be eroding a previous imperative to define oneself by work. If this is the case, blue-collar workers of the future may consider it less necessary to define themselves in work-related terms.

Cross-Cultural Variation in Work Identity

Culturally specific meanings of work pervade individuals' work identities across societies; the hierarchy of role identities is constructed, expressed and reinforced by dominant values and taken-for-granted institutional practices. For example, the German "dual system" of coordinated job training and work-related education in vocational schools, accompanied by apprenticeship in a firm, supports the development of strong occupationally specific work identities. Companies pay the apprentices while also training and evaluating students' performance. Once certified in an occupation, the individual has a monopoly on work in that field (because those without certification are excluded) and the right to particular pay rates (Mortimer & Krueger, 2006). This vocational qualification is highly recognized and valued in the German labor market. This system also protects young people from unemployment because many apprentices find jobs with the same employers that trained them as apprentices. If they do not, they still enter the labor market with valuable skills and work experience that enable them to compete with older job seekers. These circumstances are quite different from those facing young people in the United States who lack such institutional bridges from school to work and typically flounder from job to job, with spells of unemployment, before they secure what might be called a "career" or stable job (Vuolo, Staff, & Mortimer, Forthcoming). Many youth still have not found a job that might constitute a more-or-less stable career even by the age of thirty. These circumstances foster more transient work identities focused on particular jobs, when they are secured, or on employers rather than occupations per se.

Further illustration of cross-cultural variation derives from a recent study of the meaning of "hard work" among more than 100 male professionals in the United States, France, and Norway. Questions about their motivations for working hard in a demanding workplace revealed that American male professionals were more inclined to emphasize career success, attributing their devotion to hard work to the extrinsic rewards thereby gained. They considered their capacity to work hard as flowing from their inherent personalities, leading them to limit or closely regulate their leisure time. By contrast, French and Norwegian male professionals emphasized the challenging and enriching features of the job. Among the younger respondents, the American professionals showed more concern about a successful career and extrinsic rewards, whereas young European professionals viewed hard work as stimulating a learning process that could enhance their personal development and social capabilities. The author argues that the distinctive work ethics of American and European male professionals are due to "societally specific cultural configurations" (Schulz, 2012). As Rosenberg (1979) would suggest, the socially recognized rewards of work are important for self-evaluations, but these tend to be different depending on cultural contexts.

Work identity in this cross-national study is framed as "job identity" or perhaps "occupational identity." As noted earlier, work identity may also be attached to particular work organizations or employers. In many so-called collectivist cultures, emotions and actions are considered primarily interdependent rather than independent (Markus & Kitayama, 1991). As a result, work identities are group-oriented and collective, with the employing organization as the focal referent. For example, scholars have pointed out that when Japanese employees are asked about their occupations, they seldom respond in terms of their own job features but instead talk about their affiliation with a company. The typical goal of Japanese workers in large and medium-sized corporations is to become "a company person." Thus, Japanese employees' work identities focus on their employing organizations instead of their jobs (Ishikawa, 2007).

This phenomenon can be understood by considering the collectivist nature of organizational institutions and routines. Japanese corporations tend to recruit new graduates directly after they complete their degrees. The new workers lack prior work experience and usually stay in the same company for a long time or for their entire careers. Employees are expected to have absolute commitment and loyalty to their companies, and the companies, in turn, provide them with education, training, and promotion opportunities. These institutional practices have led young workers and new entrants to the labor market to focus more on the reputation, size, or future of a company instead of an occupation or job features, which might change over the course of the career (Ishikawa, 2007). As we have seen, this orientation is quite different from the expectations and attitudes of contemporary young workers in Western countries.

It should be noted, however, that the tradition of life-long employment in Japan has been eroded by the same global economic pressures that have produced nonstandard employment in other countries. As opportunities for such regular or standard employment have declined, the importance of work in the hierarchy of role identities may also have declined among recent cohorts in Japan. Indeed, work identity in the younger generation in Japan is diverging from that of older generations. There are more "fleeters" or "floating" young people, who drift from one job to another and have no intention, or hope, of being integrated into the old system (Ishikawa, 2007).

Studies of cross-cultural differences in work ethics and identities deliver a complex and heterogeneous picture of work identity formation and the importance of broad cultural understandings that define the nature of work, the norms governing work, and the place of work in the hierarchy of role identities. Individuals use these scripts to understand and interpret their work and their own place within the workplace. The East Asian case also offers the insight that work identity does not necessarily reside in a job or in an occupation, and in an organization only by default when these other referents are unsatisfying and unattractive. Work identity may instead be lodged primarily in the organization or employer or in the social relationships within a firm. However, it must also be remembered that because the work environment has undergone dramatic change worldwide during the past decades, young adults may deviate from such traditional meanings of work identity.

Outlook for the Future

Since the mid-twentieth century, the proportion of the US population that is employed has declined. In fact, the male employment-to-population ratio has been declining since at least the 1950s—from more than four-fifths to about two-thirds. During the same period, women moved into the labor force in large numbers. As of September 2012, the employment-to-population ratio was 58.7 percent—just over half the population age sixteen and over was employed, with men employed at rates just slightly higher than those of women. Unemployment stood at 7.8 percent. Several trends account for the long-term reduction in employment, which, in addition to the trends we have discussed, has the potential to erode work identities. First, fewer young people are working than in the past. We have already commented on the collapse of the teenage labor market, declining since the mid-1980s; arguably, teens are less likely to hold jobs now than ever before in US history. With fewer adolescents able to find paid work, some seek to obtain work experience by volunteering or holding unpaid internships. With declining opportunities for paid work during adolescence and the lengthening of formal education, the development of work identities has been postponed. Moreover, with the lengthening period of education and delayed transition to adulthood has come a tendency to enter the full-time labor force at later ages.

With the growing institutionalization of retirement through the postwar period, older people have also decreased their labor force participation (except for a small uptick very recently in response to the reduction in retirement investment value and other economic hardships associated with the Great Recession). As the large Baby Boom cohort moves into retirement and lives to older ages than their predecessors, the employment-to-population ratio will likely decline even further.

Although it is possible for young people not yet in the labor force to develop anticipatory work identities, it may be more difficult for unemployed workers to retain the identities attached to their prior jobs, occupations, and employing organizations, and for older people to hold on to their past work identities. It therefore seems fair to say that when fewer people are at work, work identity will be less central overall. These population trends may render work as a less significant source of identity even for those who are working, as it becomes less expected and normative that adults will work. And, as discussed earlier, nonstandard work is now becoming so common that it may increasingly be considered the norm, the new "standard" for employment. Scholars associate nonstandard work with low quality and low pay (Kalleberg, 2011); however, many individuals "voluntarily" work part-time in order to gain more time to be with their children, to care for elderly parents and other relatives, or to pursue non–work-oriented life styles (Casey & Alach, 2004).

The "Occupy" movement has made inequality increasingly visible in the United States, focusing attention on the top 1 percent of the population, which controls more than a third of the nation's wealth. But while the public debate focuses on the inequitable distribution of income and wealth, there has also been growing occupational inequality. Several developments in the labor force have fueled this trend, for example, the increasing demand for highly skilled professional and managerial workers; the decline of "middle-class" occupations, especially in the once vibrant manufacturing sector that has largely moved overseas; and the expansion of low-level service sector employment. Exacerbating these trends in occupational inequality, job growth following the most recent Great Recession has been mostly limited to low-wage jobs in food services, retail trade, and in the temporary employment services industry. With these developments, the intrinsic and extrinsic occupational rewards that sustain positive work identities and commitment to work likewise have become distributed more unequally, as high-ranking professional and managerial workers' occupations and employment conditions promote strong work identity and commitment. Workers at lower levels, facing growing job insecurity and transient employment, may be increasingly less likely to locate their identities in their jobs, occupations, or employing organizations. As Marks (1977) noted decades ago, those who have much to gain from work effort and commitment will attach ever great importance to work whereas their less advantaged counterparts will be under-invested in this domain. With the erosion of work identity more generally, we may see greater disparity in work identity among various segments of the population.

Some evidence from Europe suggests an emerging cultural shift in expectations in the new regime of uncertain and precarious youth unemployment. Whereas full-time work, with full benefits and permanent contracts, have been thought of as the ideal form of employment, increasing proportions of the young adult population may no longer view such jobs as feasible for them. Under these conditions, part-time, nonstandard work may not necessarily be regarded as a "bad job" among those young workers who have been socialized in increasingly insecure conditions. Apparently, some European young people embrace, even welcome, the new opportunities and lifestyles that may accompany the decline in standard employment and job security. Some young workers are as inclined to accept an "independent and flexible employment relationship" which offers them some degree of security and protection, as they are to accept a normal permanent job (Paparella, 2002). A survey of 1,000 young Italian workers (aged 18–36) found that 46 percent considered work as a means of acquiring security and only 5 percent regarded the job as a professional environment in which they could develop their identity (Paparella, 2002). More broadly, the Eurostat Labour Force Survey reported that two-thirds of female part-timers and one-third of male part-timers did not want full-time jobs in 1999 (Fagan, 2003). Some scholars suggest that female part-time workers do not want full-time jobs because of childcare or other domestic needs (Eszter, 2011). Despite the prevalent notion that people who work part-time are doing so involuntarily, the data suggest that such work may be embraced as more individuals orient their lives outside of workplaces.

However, the declining salience of work is only one adaptation to the growing insecurity of work. There are signs of an emerging, dynamic process of identity formation that allows individuals to adapt to changing circumstances of work by constructing more flexible work identities that are less dependent on traditional organizational and institutional work contexts but still centrally important in the hierarchy of identity domains. Some workers, in fact, prefer nonstandard work arrangements, allowing part-time involvement in a still centrally important life sphere while meaningfully investing in other life spheres. Others may relish the variety and challenge in constructing their own entrepreneurial job sequences, as opportunities to acquire long-term careers in corporate settings diminish. As Skorikov and Vondracek note, "adjustment to the nature of careers in modern economies progressively depends on establishing and maintaining a strong sense of proactive, dynamic, and highly individualized occupational identity" (2011, p. 706). In today's world, workers may be becoming more flexible in their work identities as compared to the "organization man" of yesteryear. Many of the new progressive organizations have policies that may promote just such adaptation, including Google, Apple, and other ICT firms, with increasingly flexible work schedules and entrepreneurial opportunities. Although such new work identities could be the province of a small and highly advantaged segment of workers, these highly visible employers could serve as models outside high-tech industries, extending their reach throughout the labor force. As workers realize that success and fulfillment in the world of work increasingly depend on their own agency and actions, strong work identities could emerge that are perhaps more individualized, malleable, and responsive to new circumstances than the work identities of the past. These new orientations toward work and the self could become increasingly prevalent in the twenty-first century.

References

Acker, J. (1990). Hierarchies, jobs, bodies: A theory of gendered organizations. *Gender & Society*, 4(2), 139–158. doi: 10.1177/089124390004002002

Aronson, P., & Mortimer, J. T. (forthcoming). Subjective preferences vs. objective realities: Voices of full—and part-time employed mothers. *Contemporary Perspectives in Family Research*.

Arnett, J. J. (2000). Emerging adulthood: A theory of development from the late teens through the twenties. *American Psychologist*, 55(5), 469–480. doi: 10.1037/0003-066X.55.5.469

Becker, H. S., Geer, B., Hughes, E. C., & Strauss, A. L. (1961). *Boys in white: Student culture in medical school*. Chicago: University of Chicago Press.

Bianchi, S. M. (2011). Family change and time allocation in American families. *The ANNALS of the American Academy of Political and Social Science*, 638(1), 21–44. doi: 10.1177/0002716211413731

Blair-Loy, M. (2001). Cultural constructions of family schemas: The case of women finance executives. *Gender & Society*, 15(5), 687–709. doi: 10.1177/089124301015005004

Blossfeld, H.-P., Buchholz, S., Bukodi, E., & Kurz, K. (Eds.). (2008). *Young workers, globalization and the labor market: Comparing early working life in eleven countries*. Cheltenham: Edward Elgar Publishing.

Britton, D. M. (2000). The epistemology of the gendered organization. *Gender and Society*, 14(3), 418–434. doi: 10.2307/190136

Burchell, B., Fagan, C., O'Brien, C., & Smith, M. (2007). *Working conditions in the European Union: The gender perspective*. Eurofound. Retrieved from http://www.eurofound.europa.eu/publications/htmlfiles/ef07108.htm

Cappelli, P. (1999). *The new deal at work: Managing the market-driven workforce*. Cambridge: Harvard Business Review Press.

Casey, C., & Alach, P. (2004). "Just a temp?" Women, temporary employment and lifestyle. *Work, Employment & Society*, 18(3), 459–480. doi: 10.1177/0950017004045546

Clausen, J. A. (1991). Adolescent competence and the shaping of the life course. *American Journal of Sociology*, 96(4), 805–842. doi: 10.2307/2780732

Clausen, J. A. (1993). *American lives: Looking back at the children of the Great Depression*. Berkeley, CA: University of California Press.

Cooper, M. (2000). Being the "go-to guy": Fatherhood, masculinity, and the organization of work in Silicon Valley. *Qualitative Sociology*, 23(4), 379–405.

Erikson, E. H. (1968). *Identity: Youth and crisis* (1st ed.). New York: Norton.

Eszter, S. (2011). *Part-time work in Europe*. Eurofound. Retrieved from http://www.eurofound.europa.eu/publications/htmlfiles/ef1086.htm

Eurostat. (2012). Retrieved from http://epp.eurostat.ec.europa.eu/statistics_explained/index.php/Unemployment_and_underemployment_statistics

Fagan, C. (2003). *Working-time preferences and work-life balance in the EU: Some policy considerations for enhancing the quality of life*. Eurofound. Retrieved from http://www.eurofound.europa.eu/publications/htmlfiles/ef0342.htm

Families and Work Institute. (2012). *Generation and gender in the workplace*. The American Business Collaboration. Retrieved from http://familiesandwork.org/site/research/reports/genandgender.pdf

Featherman, D. L. (1980). Schooling and occupational careers: Constancy and change in worldly success. In O. G. Brim & J. Kagan (Eds.), *Constancy and change in human development* (pp. 675–739). Cambridge: Harvard University Press.

Fogg, N. P., & Harrington, P. E. (2011). Rising mal-employment and the Great Recession: The growing disconnection between recent college graduates and the college labor market. *Continuing Higher Education Review*, 75, 51–65.

Fouad, N. A. (2007). Work and vocational psychology: Theory, research, and applications. *Annual Review of Psychology*, 58, 543–564. doi: 10.1146/annurev.psych.58.110405.085713

Friedan, B. (1963). *The feminine mystique.* New York: W. W. Norton & Company.

Gerson, K. (2009). Changing lives, resistant institutions: A new generation negotiates gender, work, and family change. *Sociological Forum,* 24(4), 735–753. doi: 10.1111/j.1573-7861.2009.01134.x

Ginzberg, E., Ginsburg, S. W., Axelrad, S., & Herma, J. L. (1951). *Occupational choice, an approach to a general theory.* New York: Columbia University Press.

Graham, C. W., Sorell, G. T., & Montgomery, M. J. (2004). Role-related identity structure in adult women. *Identity: An International Journal of Theory and Research,* 4(3), 251–271. doi: 10.1207/s1532706xid0403_3

Hackett, G., & Lent, R. W. (1992). Theoretical advances and current inquiry in career psychology. In S. D. Brown & R. W. Lent (Eds.), *Handbook of counseling psychology* (2nd ed., pp. 419–451). Oxford, UK: John Wiley & Sons.

Haslam, S. A., & Ellemers, N. (2011). Identity Processes in Organizations. In S. J. Schwartz, K. Luyckx, & V. L. Vignoles (Eds.), *Handbook of identity theory and research* (pp. 691–715). New York: Springer Science+Business Media.

Hays, S. (1998). *The cultural contradictions of motherhood.* New Haven/London: Yale University Press.

Heinz, W. R. (2003). From work trajectories to negotiated careers: The contingent work life course. In J. T. Mortimer & M. J. Shanahan (Eds.), *Handbook of the life course* (1st ed., pp. 185–204). New York: Springer.

Hermanowicz, J. C. (2009). *Lives in science: How institutions affect academic careers.* Chicago: University of Chicago Press.

Ho, K. (2009). *Liquidated: An ethnography of wall street.* Durham, NC: Duke University Press Books.

Hochschild, A. R. (1997). *The time bind: When work becomes home and home becomes work.* New York: Metropolitan Books.

Holland, J. L. (1985). *Making vocational choices: A theory of vocational personalities and work environments.* Englewood Cliffs, NJ: Prentice-Hall.

Huiras, J., Uggen, C., & McMorris, B. (2000). Career jobs, survival jobs, and employee deviance: A social investment model of workplace misconduct. *Sociological Quarterly,* 41(2), 245–263. doi: 10.1111/j.1533-8525.2000.tb00094.x

Ishikawa, A. (2007). Work identity in the Japanese context: Stereotype and reality. In A. Brown, S. Kirpal, & F. Rauner (Eds.), *Identities at work* (pp. 315–336). Dordrecht, Netherlands: Springer Netherlands.

Jacobs, J. A., & Gerson, K. (2004). Understanding changes in American working time: A synthesis. In C. F. Epstein & A. L. Kalleberg (Eds.), *Fighting for time: Shifting boundaries of work and social life* (pp. 25–45). New York: Russell Sage Foundation.

Johnson, M. K. (2001). Change in job values during the transition to adulthood. *Work and Occupations,* 28(3), 315–345. doi: 10.1177/0730888401028003004

Johnson, M. K., & Mortimer, J. T. (2000). Work-family orientations and attainments in the early life course. In T. L. Parcel & D. B. Cornfield (Eds.), *Work and family: Research informing policy* (1st ed., pp. 215–248). Thousand Oaks, CA: Sage Publications.

Johnson, M. K., & Mortimer, J. T. (2011). Origins and outcomes of judgments about work. *Social Forces,* 89(4), 1239–1260. doi: 10.1353/sof.2011.0056

Johnson, M. K., Mortimer, J. T., Lee, J. C., & Stern, M. J. (2007). Judgments about work dimensionality revisited. *Work and Occupations,* 34(3), 290–317. doi: 10.1177/0730888407303182

Johnson, M. K., Sage, R. A., & Mortimer, J. T. (2012). Work values, early career difficulties, and the U.S. economic recession. *Social Psychology Quarterly,* 75(3), 242–267. doi: 10.1177/0190272512451754

Jordaan, J. P., & Super, D. E. (1974). The prediction of early adult vocational behavior. In M. Ricks, D. F. Ricks, & M. Pollack (Eds.), *Life history research in psychopathology* (pp. 108–130). University of Minnesota Press.

Kahn, L. B. (2010). The long-term labor market consequences of graduating from college in a bad economy. *Labour Economics,* 17(2), 303–316.

Kalleberg, A. L. (2009). Precarious work, insecure workers: Employment relations in transition. *American Sociological Review,* 74(1), 1–22. doi: 10.1177/000312240907400101

Kalleberg, A. L. (2011). *Good jobs, bad jobs: The rise of polarized and precarious employment systems in the United States, 1970s–2000s.* New York: Russell Sage Foundation.

Kalleberg, A. L., Reskin, B. F., & Hudson, K. (2000). Bad jobs in America: Standard and nonstandard employment relations and job quality in the United States. *American Sociological Review,* 65(2), 256–278. doi: 10.2307/2657440

Kanter, R. M. (1977a). *Men and women of the corporation.* New York: Basic Books.

Kanter, R. M. (1977b). *Work and family in the United States: A critical review and agenda for research and policy.* New York: Russell Sage Foundation.

Kelan, E. (2008). Gender, risk and employment insecurity: The masculine breadwinner subtext. *Human Relations,* 61(9), 1171–1202.

Kerckhoff, A. C. (1995). Social stratification and mobility processes: The interaction between individuals and social structures. In K. S. Cook, G. A. Fine, & J. S. House (Eds.), *Sociological perspectives on social psychology* (pp. 476–496). Boston: Allyn & Bacon.

Kerckhoff, A. C. (2003). From student to worker. In J. T. Mortimer & M. J. Shanahan (Eds.), *Handbook of the life course* (pp. 251–267). New York: Kluwer Academic/Plenum Publishers.

Kohn, M., & Schooler, C. (1969). Class and conformity: A study in values. Homewood, IL: Dorsey Press.

Kohn, M., & Schooler, C. (1983). *Work and Personality.* New York: Ablex Publishing.

Lamont, M. (1992). *Money, morals, and manners: The culture of the French and the American upper-middle class.* Chicago: University of Chicago Press.

Lamont, M. (2000). *The dignity of working men: Morality and the boundaries of race, class, and immigration.* Cambridge: Harvard University Press.

Lane, C. M. (2011). *A company of one: Insecurity, independence, and the new world of white-collar unemployment.* Ithaca, NY: Cornell University Press.

Lent, R. W., Brown, S. D., & Hackett, G. (1994). Toward a unifying social cognitive theory of career and academic interest, choice, and performance. *Journal of Vocational Behavior,* 45(1), 79–122. doi: 10.1006/jvbe.1994.1027

Lorence, J., & Mortimer, J. T. (1985). Job involvement through the life course: A panel study of three age groups. *American Sociological Review,* 50(5), 618–638. doi: 10.2307/2095378

Marks, S. R. (1977). Multiple roles and role strain: Some notes on human energy, time and commitment. *American Sociological Review,* 42(6), 921–936. doi: 10.2307/2094577

Markus, H., & Kitayama, S. (1991). Culture and the self: Implications for cognition, emotion, and motivation. *Psychological Review*, 98(2), 224–253. doi: 10.1037/0033-295X.98.2.224

Mascherini, M., Salvatore, L., Meierkord, A., & Jungblut, J. -M. (2012). *NEETs—Young people not in employment, education or training: Characteristics, costs and policy responses in Europe*. Eurofound. Retrieved from http://www.eurofound.europa.eu/publications/htmlfiles/ef1254.htm

Meeus, W., Deković, M., & Iedema, J. (1997). Unemployment and identity in adolescence: A social comparison perspective. *Career Development Quarterly*, 45(4), 369–380. doi: 10.1002/j.2161-0045.1997.tb00540.x

Moen, P., & Roehling, P. (2004). *The career mystique: Cracks in the American dream*. Lanham, MD: Rowman & Littlefield Publishers.

Mortimer, J. T. (2003). *Working and growing up in America*. Cambridge, MA: Harvard University Press.

Mortimer, J. T., & Krueger, H. (2006). Transition from school to work in the United States and Germany: Formal pathways matter. In Maureen T. Hallinan (Ed.), *Handbook of the sociology of education* (1st ed., pp. 475–497). New York: Springer.

Mortimer, J. T., Vuolo, M., & Staff, J. (forthcoming). Agentic pathways toward fulfillment in work. In M. M. Bergman, A. C. Keller, R. Samuel, & N. K. Semmer (Eds.), *Success and well-being in education and employment*. New York: Springer.

Osterman, P. (2000). *Securing prosperity: The American labor market: How it has changed and what to do about it*. Princeton, NJ: Princeton University Press.

Paparella, D. (2002). *Report examines relationship between young people and work* (Article). Eurofound. Retrieved from http://www.eurofound.europa.eu/eiro/2001/12/feature/it0112151f.htm

Rampell, C. (2012, June 30). For personal trainers, a boom fueled by a belt-tightening age. *The New York Times*. Retrieved from http://www.nytimes.com/2012/07/01/business/for-personal-trainers-a-boom-fueled-by-a-belt-tightening-age.html

Rosenberg, M. (1979). *Conceiving the self*. New York: Basic Books.

Schneider, B., & Stevenson, D. (1999). *The ambitious generation: America's teenagers, motivated but directionless* (1st ed.). New Haven, CT: Yale University Press.

Schulz, J. (2012). Talk of work: Transatlantic divergences in justifications for hard work among French, Norwegian, and American professionals. *Theory and Society*. doi: 10.1007/s11186-012-9179-3

Serpe, R. T., & Stryker, S. (2011). The symbolic interactionist perspective and identity theory. In S. J. Schwartz, K. Luyckx, & V. L. Vignoles (Eds.), *Handbook of identity theory and research* (pp. 225–248). New York: Springer Science+Business Media.

Settersten, R., & Ray, B. E. (2010). *Not quite adults: Why 20-somethings are choosing a slower path to adulthood, and why it's good for everyone*. New York: Bantam.

Sewell, W. H., & Hauser, R. M. (1975). *Education, occupation and earnings: Achievement in the early career*. New York: Academic Press.

Shanahan, M. J. (2000). Pathways to adulthood in changing societies: Variability and mechanisms in life course perspective. *Annual Review of Sociology*, 26(1), 667–692. doi: 10.1146/annurev.soc.26.1.667

Shanahan, M. J., Porfeli, E. J., Mortimer, J. T., & Erickson, L. D. (2005). Subjective age identity and the transition to adulthood: When do adolescents become adults? In R. A. Settersten, Jr., F. F. Furstenberg, Jr., & R. G. Rumbaut (Eds.), *On the frontier of adulthood: Theory, research, and public policy* (pp. 225–255). Chicago: University of Chicago Press.

Skorikov, V. B., & Vondracek, F. W. (1997). Longitudinal relationships between part-time work and career development in adolescents. *Career Development Quarterly*, 45(3), 221–235. doi: 10.1002/j.2161-0045.1997.tb00466.x

Skorikov, V. B., & Vondracek, F. W. (2011). Occupational identity. In S. J. Schwartz, K. Luyckx, & V. L. Vignoles (Eds.), *Handbook of identity theory and research* (pp. 671–93). New York: Springer Science+Business Media.

Smith, V. (2002). *Crossing the great divide: Worker risk and opportunity in the new economy*. Ithaca, NY: Cornell University Press.

Smith, V. (1998). The fractured world of the temporary worker: Power, participation, and fragmentation in the contemporary workplace. *Social Problems*, 45(4), 411–430. doi: 10.2307/3097205

Smith, V., & Neuwirth, E. B. (2008). *The good temp*. Ithaca, NY: Cornell University Press.

Spenner, K. I., & Featherman, D. L. (1978). Achievement ambitions. *Annual Review of Sociology*, 4(1), 373–420. doi: 10.1146/annurev.so.04.080178.002105

Staff, J., & Mortimer, J. T. (2007). Educational and work strategies from adolescence to early adulthood: Consequences for educational attainment. *Social Forces*, 85(3), 1169–1194.

Stone, P. (2007). *Opting out?: Why women really quit careers and head home* (1st ed.). Berkeley, CA: University of California Press.

Stryker, S., & Statham, A. (1985). Symbolic interaction and role theory. In G. Lindzey & E. Aronson (Eds.), *Handbook of social psychology: Theory and method* (pp. 311–377). New York: Random House.

Super, D. E., Starishevsky, R., Matlin, N., Jordaan, J. P. (1963). *Career development; Self-concept theory*. New York: College Entrance Examination Board.

Super, D. E. (1990). A life-span, life-space approach to career development. In D. Brown & L. Brooks (Eds.), *Career choice and development: Applying contemporary theories to practice* (2nd ed., pp. 197–261). San Francisco: Jossey-Bass.

Swanson, J. L., & Gore, P. A. (2000). Advances in vocational psychology theory and research. In S. D. Brown & R. W. Lent (Eds.), *Handbook of counseling psychology* (3rd ed., pp. 233–269). New York: Wiley.

Swartz, T. T. (2009). Intergenerational family relations in adulthood: Patterns, variations, and implications in the contemporary United States. *Annual Review of Sociology*, 35(1), 191–212. doi: 10.1146/annurev.soc.34.040507.134615

Uchitelle, L. (2007). *The disposable American: Layoffs and their consequences*. New York: Vintage.

Vondracek, F. W. (1990). A developmental-contextual approach to career development research. In W. A. Borgen & R. A. Young (Eds.), *Methodological approaches to the study of career*. New York: Praeger.

Vondracek, F. W., Lerner, R. M., & Schulenberg, J. E. (1986). *Career development: A life-span developmental approach*. Hillsdale, NJ: Erlbaum.

Vuolo, M., Staff, J., & Mortimer, J. T. (2012). Weathering the Great Recession: Psychological and behavioral trajectories in the transition from school to work. *Developmental psychology*, 48(6), 1759–1773. doi: 10.1037/a0026047

Vuolo, M., Staff, J., & Mortimer, J. T. (forthcoming). Adolescent precursors of pathways from school to work. *Journal of Research on Adolescence*. doi: 10.1111/jora.12038

Warren, J. R., Sheridan, J. T., & Hauser, R. M. (2002). Occupational stratification across the life course: Evidence from the Wisconsin longitudinal study. *American Sociological Review*, 67(3), 432–455. doi: 10.2307/3088965

Whyte, W. H. (1956). *The organization man*. Garden City, NY: Doubleday.

Williams, J. (2000). *Unbending gender: Why family and work conflict and what to do about it*. New York: Oxford University Press.

Wright, C. R. (1967). Changes in the occupational commitment of graduate sociology students: A research note. *Sociological Inquiry*, 37(1), 55–62. doi: 10.1111/j.1475-682X.1967.tb00638.x

Zimmer-Gembeck, M. J., & Mortimer, J. T. (2006). Adolescent work, vocational development, and education. *Review of Educational Research*, 76(4), 537–566. doi: 10.2307/4124414

CHAPTER 21

Identity and Positive Youth Development: Advances in Developmental Intervention Science

Kyle Eichas, Alan Meca, Marilyn J. Montgomery, *and* William M. Kurtines

Abstract

This chapter provides an overview of advances in developmental intervention science that have contributed to an emerging literature on identity-focused positive youth development interventions. Rooted in the tradition of applied developmental science, developmental intervention science aims to advance the evolution of sustainable developmental intervention strategies targeting positive developmental outcomes. These developmental intervention strategies are intended to complement the wide array of well-established treatment and prevention intervention strategies targeting risky and problem behaviors. Within this framework, positive identity interventions seek to create empowering intervention contexts that promote the development of an increasingly integrated—and therefore an increasingly complex, coherent, and cohesive—self-constructed self-structure. By linking applied developmental science with treatment and prevention intervention science, developmental intervention science appears to have significant potential for facilitating the evolution of evidence-based positive development strategies for promoting positive life course change.

Key Words: positive youth development, positive identity, developmental intervention science, identity interventions

How do we support young people in the task of identity development? How do we empower them to enhance and expand those aspects of their lives that are meaningful to them? One answer to these questions is provided by applied developmental scientists who focus on promoting *positive youth development* (PYD) as a key outcome of developmental intervention efforts. This chapter reviews advances in developmental intervention science specifically as they apply to promoting positive identity development.

Positive identity refers to the sense of coherence, integration, and direction that individuals construct through their life choices. The challenge of forming a positive identity first confronts young people when the biological, cognitive, and social changes of adolescence create the possibility of systematically and seriously addressing the question "Who am I?" (Erikson, 1968). Young people take on the difficult challenge and responsibility of forming a positive identity by choosing the goals, roles, and beliefs about the world that give life direction and purpose, as well as coherence and integration (Montgomery et al., 2008*b*). The self-structure that emerges as a young person begins to make life choices is the person's sense of identity. *Positive identity development* therefore refers to the consolidation of an integrated self-structure that becomes increasingly complex, coherent, and cohesive as the person creates a path through life. This self-structure begins to emerge during adolescence, continues to develop into adulthood, and functions as an individual's "steering mechanism" throughout the life course (Elder & Shanahan, 2006; Kurtines et al., 2008*d*).

Erikson (1963) described adolescence as the time when individuals are most focused on questions about who they are and what they want out of life. More recently, Arnett (2000) has suggested that sociohistorical changes over the past four decades have, for many young people, extended the time available for forming an identity and deciding on a life path. Although the first tentative steps toward forming a sense of identity still occur during adolescence, the most intensive identity exploration now takes place during emerging adulthood, the transitional period between adolescence and adulthood that occurs during the third decade of life (Arnett, 2007; see also Arnett, this volume). During emerging adulthood, young people move beyond the childhood structure imposed by family and school. These life changes bring greater freedom and a sense of the world as being "wide open" to new possibilities, especially in the domains of love, work, and worldviews (Arnett, 2004). The possibility of new life directions presents emerging adults with the challenge of making identity choices that will shape their life course. During this time, positive and negative life trajectories begin to separate from one another, and identity often plays a critical role in determining which path a person will follow (Arnett, 2000).

Opportunities to support young people's positive identity development present themselves throughout the transition to adulthood, from adolescence through emerging adulthood. As discussed herein, a developmental intervention science approach to promoting positive identity draws on the strengths of applied developmental science, prevention intervention science, and treatment intervention science to target the developmental period from adolescence through emerging adulthood. This approach appears to have significant potential for facilitating the evolution of sustainable evidence-based positive development intervention strategies for promoting positive life course change.

An Applied Developmental Science Perspective

Applied developmental science fuses developmental science research with policies and programs to promote positive human development across the lifespan (Lerner, Fisher, & Weinberg, 2000). The emergence of applied developmental science coupled with a rapidly growing research literature on promoting PYD has opened up new directions for extending the range and scope of the contributions of developmental science to intervention science.

Among the most important contributions that applied developmental science has made to intervention science has been to shift the field from a deficit view of youth toward the view of youth as resources to be developed (Roth & Brooks-Gunn, 2003), with direct practice, service, and public health implications (Catalano, Berglund, Ryan, Lonczak, & Hawkins, 2004; Kurtines et al., 2008a; Lerner, 2005; McCall & Groark, 2000). Positive youth development views youth, including those from the most disadvantaged backgrounds, as able and eager to "explore the world, gain competence, and acquire the capacity to contribute importantly to the world" (Damon, 2004, p. 15). This shift has fostered the development of PYD programs that engage young people in growth-promoting productive activities rather than treat them for maladaptive tendencies (Damon, 2004).

The emergence of applied developmental science and PYD has been framed by a relational developmental systems theoretical model that depicts human development as a property of systematic change in the multiple and integrated levels of organization that comprise human life and its ecology, rather than a property of the individual or of the environment (Lerner & Overton, 2008; Lerner, Wertleib, & Jacobs, 2005; Overton, 2010). Relational developmental systems theory rejects false dichotomies (e.g., nature vs. nurture, qualitative vs. quantitative, etc.), including the dichotomy of person versus context. Instead, it conceptualizes the unit of development as the embodied *person-in-context* and the unit of analysis as the bidirectional relation between person and context (person ↔ context). This perspective shifts the focus from the attributes of the individual to the attributes of the dynamic developmental system. For example, a relational developmental systems perspective on resilience does not consider resilience to be an attribute of the individual. It instead considers resilience to be an attribute of the developmental system that describes the fit between individual characteristics and features of the ecology in the face of changing environmental challenges (Lerner et al., 2013).

Relational developmental systems theory provides a framework for PYD. From this perspective, PYD is the development of mutually adaptive relations between individuals and the settings in which they live (Lerner, 2005; Lerner & Overton, 2008; Spencer, 2006). Positive youth development programs (e.g., 4-H Clubs, Boy/Girl Scouts, Big Brothers/Big Sisters, Outward Bound, etc.) promote health-supportive alignments between youth and their contexts in order to foster contextually and culturally meaningful positive change (Benson, Scales, Hamilton, & Sesma, 2006). Positive youth development research asks, "What contextual resources, for what youth, at what points in their adolescence, result in what features of PYD?" (Lerner & Overton, 2008, p. 248). However, formal theory construction and model testing of specific, direct PYD strategies has only recently emerged in the literature.

Promoting Identity in Positive Youth Development Programs

A wide range of PYD programs have targeted positive identity development during adolescence (Benson, Mannes, Pittman, & Ferber, 2004; Catalano, Berglund, Ryan, Lonczak, & Hawkins, 1999; 2004; Lerner, 2005; Montgomery et al., 2008b). These programs have drawn largely on Erikson's (1963; 1968) description of the identity crisis as the central developmental challenge of adolescence. Adolescents must integrate the roles, skills, and identifications learned in childhood with the expectations of the adult world into an inner sense of continuity and self-sameness matched by a sense of social continuity and self-sameness. The tension between identity synthesis and identity confusion represents a time of increased vulnerability and potential for developmental change (Erikson, 1968; 1985).

Erikson (1963; 1968) suggested that a sense of identity provides individuals with a foundation for what would now be described as PYD: feeling satisfaction with oneself (self-esteem), meaning and direction (purpose in life), and agency (internal locus of control). Today, identity synthesis is widely seen as a desirable outcome of PYD programs. In a major review of the empirical literature on PYD programs, Catalano and colleagues (Catalano et al., 1999) determined that eleven of twenty-five well-evaluated (i.e., using either experimental or quasi-experimental designs) PYD programs targeted positive change in concepts and constructs broadly related to identity formation (e.g., self-esteem, self-efficacy, autonomy, empowerment, etc.). The programs used a variety of strategies (e.g., mentoring, tutoring, skills training, classroom psychoeducation, volunteer work, etc.) and measured identity-related concepts and constructs from a diverse array of theoretical orientations. Catalano and colleagues found that despite their differing theoretical orientations, these programs "sought to develop healthy identity formation and achievement in youth, including positive identification with a social or cultural sub-group that supports their healthy development of sense of self" (Catalano et al., 1999, p. 17).

The idea of intervening to promote identity development has also been an important theme in the identity literature. As Ferrer-Wreder and colleagues (Ferrer-Wreder, Montgomery, & Lorente, 2003) point out, Erikson and Erikson (1957) described the importance of intervening with troubled adolescents to promote productive styles of living and to prevent a young person's commitment to, and society's confirmation of, a socially marginalized identity. Over the past twenty-five years, the identity literature has provided extensive examination of the theoretical rationale and practical utility of identity interventions for youth (Archer, 1989; 1994; 2008; Kerpelman, Pittman, & Adler-Baeder, 2008; Kurtines et al., 2008d; Marcia, 1989; Montgomery, Hernandez, & Ferrer-Wreder, 2008a; Waterman, 1989). This literature suggests that assessing identity processes (identity exploration), orientations (identity style), and outcomes (identity distress, identity cohesion, turning points) in intervention contexts would advance knowledge about for whom interventions work and why they work, thereby facilitating the evolution of more effective and potent youth interventions (Montgomery et al., 2008a).

Despite twenty-five years of research highlighting the potential for identity interventions, it is only recently that a literature on identity interventions has emerged to systematically incorporate identity theory into models of intervention outcome. In a recent review of the literature on identity interventions, Ferrer-Wreder and colleagues (Ferrer-Wreder, Montgomery, Lorente, & Habibi, in press) found that researchers have begun to examine identity development both as a targeted intervention outcome and, in the effort to explain why interventions work and for whom they work, as a theory-based mediator or moderator of intervention change. Some programs have targeted ethnic identity as a focal intervention outcome for minority youth. For instance, Sisters of Nia (Belgrave et al., 2004) targeted ethnic identity by focusing on African-American girls' knowledge of Afrocentric culture, customs, and values. The program also sought to increase girls' self-concept, androgynous gender role orientation, and positive peer relations. Similarly, YES! (Thomas, Davidson, & McAdoo, 2008) targeted ethnic identity exploration by focusing on adolescent African-American girls' knowledge and awareness of cultural values, history, and racism. Other programs included an ethnic identity component in a larger culturally grounded intervention program. For example, the Seventh Generation Program (Moran & Bussey, 2007) used American Indian cultural values (harmony, respect, generosity, courage, wisdom, humility, and honesty) as an organizing framework while also targeting cognitive and social skills.

Other identity-focused interventions have conceptualized identity processes (e.g., self-construction and self-discovery processes, discussed later) as mediators of intervention effects on problem outcomes (e.g., Eichas et al., 2010) or moderators of intervention effects on relationship outcomes (e.g., Kerpelman et al., 2008). Kerpelman and colleagues found that, in the context of a school-based curricular intervention, the cognitive processing style adolescents use to make identity-related decisions (i.e., identity style) moderated change in perceived ability to handle conflict and perceived ability to stand up for oneself in a troubled relationship. Eichas and colleagues (Eichas et al., 2010) found that the use of an information-seeking identity style and the degree to which an adolescent's goal pursuit resonates with his or her sense of self and identity (i.e., generates feelings of personal expressiveness) mediated changes in internalizing and externalizing problems (see the later section on the Changing Lives Program).

When taken together, the emergence of positive identity as a core concept in the PYD literature and the model-building process described in the identity intervention literature suggests significant convergence between the two literatures. This convergence also points to the potential for a systematic integration of PYD and intervention science.

Treatment, Prevention, and Developmental Interventions: The Need for Integrated Intervention Models

Interest in building positive identity interventions illustrates a growing recognition of the need to integrate the PYD approach with treatment and prevention intervention approaches (Catalano, Hawkins, Berglund, Pollard, & Arthur, 2002; Guerra & Bradshaw, 2008; Haegerich & Tolan, 2008; Lerner et al., 2000). In contrast to PYD programs that seek to promote positive functioning in core developmental domains, treatment interventions seek to ameliorate dysfunction once it occurs, and prevention interventions seek to reduce the likelihood that a dysfunction will occur in the future. Despite targeting different outcomes, PYD and prevention approaches have a shared emphasis on developmental regulation and the interplay between individuals and the contexts in which they function (e.g., relationships with family, peers, and schools). This shared emphasis provides a conceptual foundation for developing integrated intervention models (Catalano & Hawkins, 1996; Guerra & Bradshaw, 2008; Kurtines et al., 2008a; Masten, 2006; Schwartz, Pantin, Coatsworth, & Szapocznik, 2007). A similar trend toward integration has emerged in the treatment intervention literature. Weisz and colleagues (Weisz, Sandler, Durlak, & Anton, 2005), for example, proposed an integrated model for promoting and protecting youth mental health through evidence-based prevention and treatment interventions.

This chapter seeks to extend the integrative process just described by reviewing the literature on the emergence of developmental intervention science (Kurtines et al., 2008a) and the critical role that the concept of positive identity has played in its emergence. As Figure 21.1 illustrates, the developmental intervention science literature draws directly on the tradition of applied developmental science and relational developmental systems theory. Figure 21.1 further illustrates that developmental intervention science also draws on and extends models from treatment and prevention intervention science. By developing links between advances in applied developmental science and advances in treatment and prevention science, developmental intervention science has begun to generate theory-informed, empirically supported developmental intervention strategies specifically targeting positive developmental outcomes.

Positive identity has emerged as a key developmental intervention outcome that, rooted in the PYD and identity literatures, rejects the dichotomy of person versus context. Because a person's sense of identity develops at the interface between self and society (Kurtines, Berman, Ittel, & Williamson, 1995), identity development is relational change that cannot be coherently divided into self and social components (Bosma & Kunnen, 2001; Josselson, 1994). Instead of splitting person from context, a person's sense of identity reflects the embodied person-in-context and provides a psychosocially integrated target for developmental interventions.

A Developmental Intervention Science Approach to Positive Identity Development

Drawing on relational developmental systems theory (Lerner, 2002; Lerner & Overton, 2008;

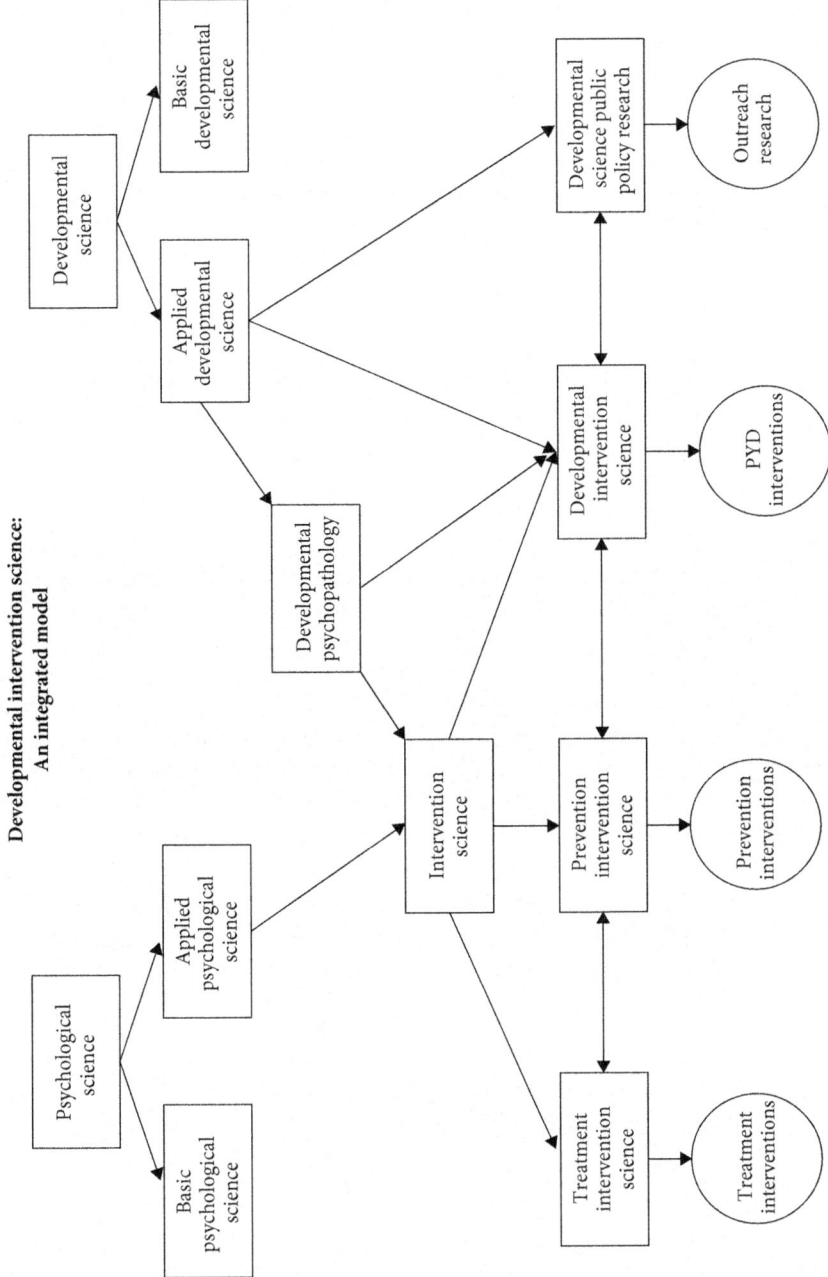

Fig. 21.1 Developmental intervention science: An integrated model.

Overton, 2010), developmental intervention science conceptualizes positive development as progressive change. Developmental change in the most general sense has two basic characteristics—it is systematic and successive. That is, it is systematic change rather than random, chaotic, disorganized, or dispersive change. In addition, it may also be characterized as successive change when change that occurs at a later point in time is influenced by change that occurs earlier in time. The concept of development thus implies systematic and successive change in the hierarchy, structure, or organization of the ordered systems that make up a specific developmental system. Progressive change occurs when systematic, successive change in the structural organization of a developmental system serves an adaptive function (Ford & Lerner, 1992; Nisbet, 1980). Werner and Kaplan (1956) proposed that progressive change only occurs in a particular sequence, when a system changes from being organized in a very general and global way (with few, if any, differentiated parts) to having differentiated parts that are organized into an integrated hierarchy (developmental change as differentiated change; Lerner, 2002).

Progressive change in the structural organization of the developmental system emerges as the result of the dynamic process of individuals acting on their contexts and contexts acting on individuals, in a process called *developmental regulation* (Brandtstädter, 2006). The individual contributes to developmental regulation through *self-regulation* (Gestsdóttir & Lerner, 2008). Self-regulation has been used in diverse theoretical models to describe the organism's ability to adapt to its environment. Self-regulation is "the ability to flexibly activate, monitor, inhibit, persevere and/or adapt one's behavior, attention, emotions and cognitive strategies in response to direction from internal cues, environmental stimuli and feedback from others, in an attempt to attain personally-relevant goals" (Moilanen, 2007, p. 835). Although some self-regulations are primarily physiological, other intentional self-regulations are goal-directed actions that can be actively selected and controlled by the person to transform situations in accordance with desired future states (Gestsdóttir & Lerner, 2007). For example, an adolescent who adopts a different style of dress in order to fit in because it is not possible to change what his or her peer group thinks is socially acceptable has used intentional self-regulation (Lerner, Freund, De Stefanis, & Habermas, 2001). Thus, intentional self-regulations are "contextualized actions that are actively aimed toward harmonizing demand and resources in the context with personal goals to attain better functioning and to enhance self-development" (Gestsdóttir & Lerner, 2008, p. 204).

A Focus on Developmental ↔ Intervention Processes

A basic premise of developmental intervention science is that interventions can promote progressive change in the structural organization of a human developmental system because contextual contributions to developmental regulation of the person ↔ context relationship may also be intentionally directed. From a developmental intervention science perspective, an intervention process is a specific type of person ↔ context (structural-interactive) exchange intended to have an effect on a specific outcome process. In an identity-focused developmental intervention, the contextual contribution to this person ↔ context exchange is directed toward promoting a specific type of progressive change: the consolidation of a self-constructed self-structure. Identity-focused developmental interventions have, for example, supported adolescents in discovering their unique potentials, talents, skills, and capabilities and encouraged them to use what they have discovered to construct long-term life goals, thereby helping them incorporate self-knowledge into a plan for the future.

Although progressive structural organizational change could be operationalized as a contextual "effect" on a specified individual- (person-) level "outcome" process, this change does not follow explicit instructions from the environment. Instead, an intervention is a contextual individual- (person-) level *resource* for structural organizational change as it emerges through the developmental system's active exchange of matter, energy, and information with the environment (the reciprocal co-action of an open system and its environment; Overton, 2010). For instance, if an adolescent participant in an identity-focused developmental intervention begins to incorporate knowledge of his or her unique potentials, talents, skills, and capabilities into his or her life goals, it is not because the intervention *caused* this change. Instead, the intervention provided resources that the adolescent used to envision a new direction in life.

Because all behavioral changes, positive and problematic, emerge out of the activity of the developmental system (Overton, 2010), progressive structural organizational change that emerges out of a developmental ↔ intervention process may manifest as multidirectional positive change across domains of development, including the problem domains targeted by treatment and prevention interventions (Eichas et al., 2010). For instance, an adolescent who commits to pursuing a particular life goal has probably experienced a change in self-structure—that is, a change in how his or her drives, abilities, beliefs, and personal history, as well as plans for the future, are organized. The adolescent is likely to also exhibit behavioral change in multiple domains. The adolescent might study more to get better grades (a positive domain), drink less alcohol (a problem domain), and report increased psychological well-being (a positive domain). The emergence of a more integrated self-structure (a structural organizational change in the developmental system) may in this way produce variational changes (increases/decreases) across domains of development (e.g., academic achievement, drinking, and well-being).

Developmental Intervention Timing: Developmental Transitions

Interventions are most likely to contribute to progressive structural organizational change when intervention strategies target the transformations that occur during normative developmental transitions (Granic & Patterson, 2006). Adolescence, for example, is characterized by complex biological, cognitive, and social transformations. Emerging adulthood is also characterized by complex psychosocial transformations. Developmental transitions such as these are periods of flux, when an open (i.e., nonisolated) system becomes unstable through exchange of matter, energy, and information with the environment (Overton, 2010). Lewis (2000) suggests that emotion-laden events during periods of flux such as adolescence and early adulthood can trigger a structural reorganization of personality and identity.

During developmental transitions, fluctuation in a lower level of the system may spread to the macroscopic level through positive and negative feedback mechanisms in a process called amplification (Overton, 2010). In the context of an identity-focused developmental intervention, for example, an adolescent might try a novel behavior such as taking on a leadership role in a counseling group. By exploring this new role, the adolescent might discover that he or she is capable of and enjoys being a leader. The mastery experience (Bandura, 1997) associated with using this newly discovered ability might then amplify to a higher level of the system by becoming part of an emerging sense of identity. Amplification of local fluctuations to the macroscopic level may result in a transformation: the emergence of a more complex structural organization with novel properties (Overton, 2010). In this case, when an adolescent incorporates a newly discovered ability into his or her sense of identity, the result may be the emergence of a *self-transformation*: a new, more complex structural organization of the self.

Developmental Intervention Targets: Self-Transformative Processes

During adolescence, newly emergent cognitive and communicative competencies transform the individual's intentional self-regulation, in part because their emergence also brings the challenge and responsibility of forming a coherent sense of identity (Kurtines et al., 1995; 2008*d*). As Gestsdóttir and colleagues (Gestsdóttir, Lewin-Bizan, von Eye, Lerner, & Lerner, 2009) point out, a child's self-regulations are primarily observed in terms of attention and inhibition, whereas an adolescent's self-regulations involve increased intentions to promote his or her own development in a manner consistent with his or her identity. During adolescence, newly emergent cognitive and communicative competencies create the potential for a self-constructed self-structure that will provide direction for individuals' intentional self-regulations as they become active producers of, or contributors to, their own development (Brandtstädter & Lerner, 1999). Two processes of self-transformation are *self-construction* and *self-discovery*.

SELF-CONSTRUCTION

Identity alternatives afforded by the individual's context provide opportunities for the individual to proactively construct the self through identity-related choices made from among these alternatives (Berzonsky, 1986; Schwartz, 2002). Because the self-construction process involves the individual's evaluation of presently available alternatives, it requires the use of a complex set of cognitive and communicative competencies acquired during the developmental process, including the capacity for critical thinking and critical discussion (Berman, Schwartz, Kurtines, & Berman, 2001; Kurtines et al., 1995). As individuals form and test hypotheses about identity-related choices, they create a self-theory about "who they think they are and what they think they want" (Berzonsky, 2011, p. 57), a conceptual structure that helps them make sense of their experience (Berzonsky, 1993). A proactive information-seeking approach to self-construction is associated with indices of positive adjustment, such as openness to ideas and experience, problem-focused coping, and decreased problem behaviors (Adams et al., 2001; Berzonsky, 1992; Berzonsky & Sullivan, 1992).

SELF-DISCOVERY

Identity alternatives afforded by the individual's context also provide opportunities for the individual to discover and actualize his or her set of unique potentials, talents, skills, and capabilities (Waterman, 1984). Because the self-discovery process involves an individual's feeling or intuition that an activity or choice resonates with his or her true self, it is primarily emotion-focused. Self-discovery theories have described the importance of self-actualization (Maslow, 1968), flow (Csikszentmihalyi, 1990), and feelings of personal expressiveness (Waterman, 1990). The most integrated level of emotion-focused processing is self-actualization, which refers to fulfilling one's potentials and living up to one's ideals on a consistent basis (Maslow, 1968). Flow, the least integrated level of emotion-focused processing, is an affective state characterized by a balance between the challenge at hand and the skills one brings to it (Csikszentmihalyi, 1990). Feelings of personal expressiveness are similar to, but less integrated than, self-actualization because they specifically describe the subjective experience of identity-related activities (Schwartz, 2006; Schwartz, Montgomery, & Kurtines, 2005; Waterman, 1990). By pursuing personally expressive activities, individuals integrate their unique potentials, talents, skills, and capabilities into their sense of self and identity. Engaging in personally expressive activities predicts higher levels of intrinsic motivation to accomplish life tasks, perceived competence, self-determination, optimism, and subjective well-being (Coatsworth, Palen, Sharp, & Ferrer-Wreder, 2006; Waterman, 2005; Waterman et al., 2003).

Identity-focused developmental interventions create opportunities for self-discovery and self-construction. Figure 21.2 depicts a self-transformative model proposed by Albrecht (2007) for conceptualizing pathways of change in a developmental intervention. As shown in Figure 21.2, the individual's historical, social, and personal context provides opportunities for and constraints on self-discovery (path a) and self-construction (path b). Self-discovery and self-construction, in turn, promote positive development of an individual's sense of self (paths d and e, respectively). Historical, social, and personal contexts are likely to also influence the development of an individual's sense of self via other pathways (path c). According to this model, a developmental intervention is a person-level contextual resource for self-transformation because it provides opportunities for self-construction and self-discovery.

Developmental Intervention Strategy: Providing Resources for Self-Transformation

Schwartz and colleagues (Schwartz, 2000; Schwartz et al., 2005) were among the first to design and evaluate developmental intervention strategies

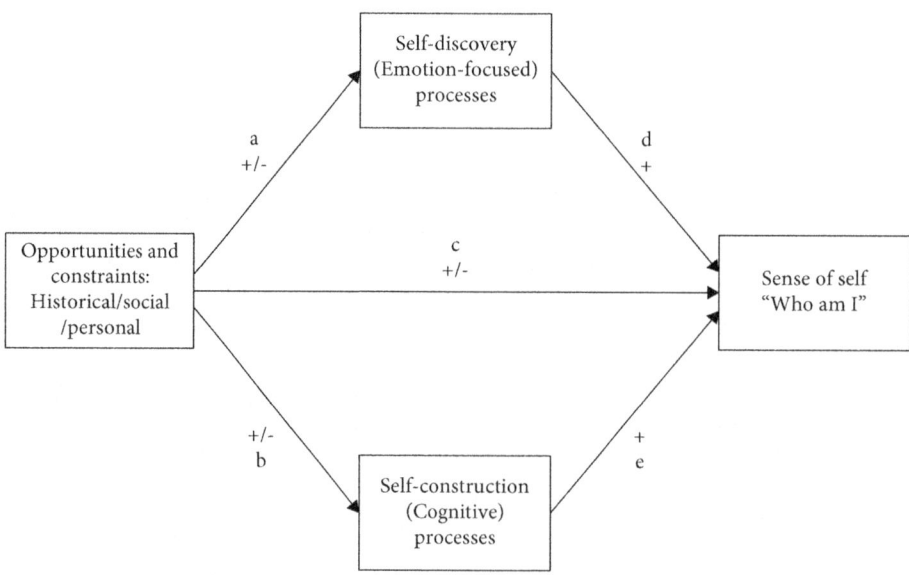

Fig. 21.2 Promoting positive identity: A self-transformative model.

for promoting self-construction and self-discovery. Working with a university-based sample of emerging adults, the researchers used a group-based empowerment approach to implement these strategies. An intervention team drew on Freire's (1970/1983) transformative pedagogy to help the participants identify life challenges and co-construct solutions to these challenges. Rather than transferring expert knowledge to the students through a structured, content-oriented didactic approach, the intervention team participated as co-learners in dialogue with the students. This empowerment approach assumed an equality of basic competence between teachers and learners (Freire, 1970/1983). Specific self-construction and self-discovery strategies used by the intervention team are described next.

SELF-CONSTRUCTION STRATEGY

Schwartz and colleagues (Schwartz, 2000; Schwartz et al., 2005) used cognitive intervention strategies to target self-construction processes. Group work in a self-construction intervention condition consisted of self-transformative activities to identify and evaluate solutions to life dilemmas. Specifically, each participant shared an identity-related life choice or dilemma that he or she faced. The group then collaborated to identify sources of information useful in addressing the dilemma, possible alternative solutions, and pros and cons for each alternative, as well as a critical evaluation of the different alternatives.

Schwartz (2000) described two examples of dilemmas presented by participants. One participant faced the choice of getting married or delaying marriage and starting graduate school. Another participant had no idea what to do with his life and wanted a serious romantic relationship but did not know how to achieve it. The group helped the participants identify new alternatives, and each participant found a solution that worked. Schwartz reported that, in the first case, the participant decided to delay marriage for a year and start preparing for graduate school. In the second case, the participant decided to pursue internship experience in his field of study.

SELF-DISCOVERY STRATEGY

Schwartz and colleagues (Schwartz, 2000; Schwartz et al., 2005) used emotion-focused intervention strategies to target self-discovery processes. Group work in a self-discovery intervention condition consisted of self-transformative activities to identify relations between flow-producing activities (Csikszentmihalyi, 1990) and short-term life goals. Specifically, each participant shared three short-term life goals. The group collaborated to break each goal down into component activities, and the participant identified his or her feelings associated with each activity. Then, the participant identified activities associated with feelings of flow, and the group worked together to construct goals based on these flow-producing activities and integrate them into the participant's existing short-term goals.

Schwartz (2000) described two examples of short-term life goals presented by participants. One participant wanted to please her boyfriend, maintain a harmonious relationship with him, and improve their communication. Another participant wanted to identify a career path for herself and have a more fulfilling relationship with her parents. The group helped the participants explore and uncover feelings associated with their goals, and each participant made progress toward accomplishing her goals. Schwartz (2000) reported that, in the first case, the participant afterward felt more able to talk with her boyfriend about their relationship. In the second case, the participant committed to a specific plan for graduate school.

Both quantitative outcome findings and narrative accounts provided by the participants indicated that cognitive intervention strategies were associated with increases in self-construction processes, whereas emotion-focused intervention strategies were associated with increases in self-discovery processes (see Schwartz et al., 2005). Schwartz and colleagues thus provided an initial examination of developmental intervention strategies for promoting self-construction and self-discovery. Similar co-participatory and transformative intervention approaches have been used in positive development programs for troubled adolescents and college-going emerging adults and adults. These programs are discussed in the next section.

Positive Development Programs

This section describes three positive development programs that target positive identity development. Each program illustrates developmental intervention science: each targets self-transformative processes during a developmental transition with the goal of promoting long-term positive development. The three programs are also closely related because the first program, the Miami Youth Development Project, developed many of the strategies used in the other two programs. However, the programs were designed for different samples and settings, including troubled adolescents in alternative high schools and emerging adults and adults in college.

Positive Youth Development with an Identity Focus

THE MIAMI YOUTH DEVELOPMENT PROJECT

The Miami Youth Development Project (Kurtines et al., 2008b) provides community-supported PYD services for troubled youth growing up in disempowering urban contexts. For nearly two decades, the Youth Development Project implemented the Changing Lives Program as a selected/indicated PYD intervention for the culturally diverse multiproblem youth attending the alternative high schools of the Miami Dade County Public Schools (Kurtines et al., 2008b). These students came from neighborhood contexts characterized by pervasive violence, crime, abuse, and limited access to resources. They came to the alternative schools on negative life course pathways and at risk for multiple negative developmental outcomes and/or engaged in multiple problem behaviors. Many of them displayed histories of attendance, behavior, or motivational problems in the regular high schools.

Intervention strategy. The Changing Lives Program's primary intervention goal was to create intervention contexts that empowered troubled youth to change their lives in positive directions and, in the process, form rather than neglect their sense of self and identity (Montgomery et al., 2008b). Like the university-based intervention piloted by Schwartz et al. (2005), the Changing Lives Program used a participatory transformative group counseling approach informed by Freire's (1970/1983) transformative pedagogy and multicultural counseling theory (Sue & Sue, 2003). However, because the intervention was located in a community setting, program implementation was designed to be flexible and adaptable to diverse populations and problems, goals, and school settings. Program implementation involved three phases designed to be flexible and adaptable: (1) engagement, (2) participatory co-learning, and (3) transformative activities. Group members co-participated in identifying the life challenges they wanted to work on, and they co-constructed solutions to these challenges. They worked at changing their lives for the better by engaging in transformative activities to address their life challenges, and they obtained support from group members while doing so.

The Changing Lives Program developed the Life Course Journal to provide a focal point for the participatory transformative group process. Consistent with a narrative conception of identity as an evolving story that individuals begin to work on during adolescence (McAdams, 2011; McAdams & Zapata-Gietl, this volume), the Life Course Journal facilitated participants' construction of a narrative story line about "who I am" and "what I want to do with my life." The journal included exercises that were interwoven into the implementation phases. During the engagement phase, two exercises oriented the participants toward the concept of life change while also addressing the issues of counseling change goals and life history experiences. In the first exercise, participants identified their most important life course events and turning points. They began to co-construct their life stories by taking turns sharing with the group where they came from, where they were now, and where they were going in their lives. The second exercise built on the emerging narrative frame by focusing on the relation between participants' most important life goals and their personal strengths. Participants collaborated with the group to identify their most important life goal, to break the life goal into activities essential for achieving the goal, and to explore their emotional reactions to engaging in the activities. This exercise targeted self-discovery processes (Figure 21.2, path a).

During the participatory co-learning phase, two additional journal exercises encouraged participants to identify a challenge that they wanted to work on and to create a life *change* goal. Life change goals reflect the parts of their lives youth want to change most in order to achieve their life goals. In the third exercise, group members conceptualized their life change goals and shared them with the group so they could envision how the group would be different if members accomplished their life change goals. The fourth exercise targeted self-construction processes (Figure 21.2, path b). Group members created a path toward their life change goals by co-constructing with the group potential alternatives for accomplishing the life change goal. With help from the group, they critically evaluated these alternatives. Selected solutions that emerged from this process represented potential transformative activities.

The engagement and participatory co-learning phases provided the foundation for self-directed transformative activities, hypothesized to be a key change-producing behavioral intervention strategy for facilitating empowerment and positive identity development (Kurtines et al., 2008d). Because these transformative activities are self-directed and aimed at solving self-selected problems, they help youth learn "to see a closer correspondence between their goals and a sense of how to achieve them, gain greater access to and control over resources and gain mastery over their lives" (Zimmerman, 1995, p. 583). That is, whereas transformative activities may create change that solves participants' current problems, they also create opportunities for mastery experiences (Bandura, 1997). Mastery experiences that provide resources for self-construction and self-discovery help youth transform the way they understand and feel about themselves and their current life course (Kurtines et al., 2008*d*).

Outcome results. Results from evaluation of the Changing Lives Program have shown intervention-related benefits on indicators of self-construction and self-discovery in samples of primarily Hispanic and African American adolescents (fourteen to eighteen years old). In a study of change from pre- to posttest (measured immediately following the program), Ferrer-Wreder and colleagues (2002) found that intervention participants increased in self-construction processing, including increased problem-solving competence and sense of control and responsibility for life choices, relative to participants in a comparison group. Participants with low initial levels of engagement in the identity process also increased in information-seeking behavior. In a second study of change from pre- to posttest (measured immediately following the program), Eichas and colleagues (2010) found that intervention participation was associated with changes in both self-construction and self-discovery processing. Specifically, participants increased more in information-seeking behavior and decreased less in feelings of personal expressiveness than did participants in a comparison group. The pattern of results further suggested that targeting self-construction and self-discovery promotes change that "spills over" to impact problem behavior outcomes not specifically targeted by the intervention. Intervention participation was directly or indirectly related to decreases in both externalizing and internalizing problem behaviors, findings that are consistent with the premise that promoting positive identity fosters multidirectional positive change across domains of development (Eichas et al., 2010).

Positive Emerging Adult Development with an Identity Focus
THE MIAMI ADULT DEVELOPMENT PROJECT

The Youth Development Project developed the Changing Lives Program for community-based work with marginalized adolescents (Ferrer-Wreder et al., 2002; Montgomery et al., 2008*b*). The program's participatory transformative intervention approach to promoting positive identity has been adapted and extended by the Miami Adult Development Project for university-based work with emerging adults. As noted, the challenge of forming a sense of identity often intensifies during emerging adulthood as young people experience greater freedom as a result of moving beyond the childhood structure imposed by family and school (Arnett, 2007). However, many emerging adults in university settings have life course pathways that are already positive, at least relative to the troubled youth whose negative life course pathways bring them to the alternative high schools. Therefore, the Adult Development Project works with emerging adults to refine current life pathways (rather than to change negative life pathways into positive ones) by providing opportunities for participants to optimize their unique potentials through in-depth exploration of their current sense of self, identity commitments, and long-term life goals.

Intervention strategy. The Adult Development Project draws on the Changing Lives Program's participatory transformative intervention framework to promote self-guided, self-directed, and self-facilitated change, but its intervention strategy differs in ways that reflect the developmental level of the participants (i.e., nineteen- to twenty-nine-year-old emerging adults rather than adolescents). First, the intervention is implemented at an urban university as part of a psychology course on emerging adulthood. The course instructor uses traditional classroom techniques (i.e., lecture, weekly readings, class discussion, etc.) to teach students about identity theory and research, with a focus on issues central to emerging adulthood and research methodology. During the last six weeks of the semester, formal instruction is replaced for one class per week by the Adult Development Project intervention group sessions.

Second, Adult Development Project intervention group sessions are guided not by faculty or staff but by peer facilitators. At the beginning of the semester, the course instructor selects volunteers to receive training on group work and peer facilitation. Prior to each group session, volunteers meet with the instructor or a teaching assistant for supervision and general discussion about the group process. Group work involves the same phases as in the Changing Lives Program (i.e., engagement, participatory co-learning, and transformative activities), as well as the same core set of group exercises. Thus, students participate in a series of self-transformative activities designed to engage them in critical problem solving and cognitive exploration of solutions to self-selected life-change goals (Figure 21.2, path b) while also exploring the fit between their current long-term life goals and their sense of self and identity (Figure 21.2, path a).

Outcome results. The Adult Development Project is a recent extension of the Changing Lives Program, and outcome evaluation is currently ongoing. However, initial outcome findings (Meca et al., in press) indicate that intervention participants had significantly greater reductions in identity-related distress than did participants in a comparison group. Initial results further suggest that reductions in identity distress were associated with indices of identity development and psychosocial adjustment. Specifically, intervention-related decreases in identity distress predicted increases in identity consolidation (as indicated by measures of identity commitment and identity synthesis). Identity consolidation, in turn, predicted increases in subjective well-being. This pattern of results is consistent with the premise that promoting positive identity fosters multidirectional positive change across domains of development (Eichas et al., 2010).

Positive Adult Development with an Identity Focus

THE DAYTONA ADULT IDENTITY DEVELOPMENT PROGRAM

The Changing Lives Program's participatory transformative intervention approach has also been adapted and extended by the Daytona Adult Identity Development Program for university-based work with adult students (Berman, Kennerly, & Kennerly, 2008). Berman et al. (2008) point out that identity work is not limited to adolescence or even to emerging adulthood (see also Kroger, this volume; Lilgendahl, this volume). Rather, adults continue to construct and reconstruct their identities throughout their lives. Renewed identity work may be prompted by life course transitions such as entering college, becoming a parent, or retiring, as well as by sociohistorical factors such as an economic downturn that leads to financial pressure or job loss (Berman et al., 2008). For its work with adults, the Adult Identity Development Program uses participatory and transformative strategies to expand self-understanding and insight through identity exploration, teach critical thinking and problem-solving skills, and foster a disposition for taking control and accepting responsibility for life decisions (Berman et al., 2008).

Intervention strategy. The Adult Identity Development Program is implemented as part of an elective personal growth psychology course for juniors and seniors at a public university. Participants include individuals from across the adult lifespan (Berman et al., 2008). Students enrolled in the course are assigned to small groups of seven to ten members. Group facilitators are interns in a clinical psychology masters' program at the university, supervised by faculty. The students complete weekly readings on identity issues (e.g., careers, relationships, gender, sexuality, values) and homework tasks promoting self-examination, such as self-tests and journaling. After group rapport is established, the facilitators introduce transformative activities in which group members assist each other in focusing on a specific identity-related issue. Critical thinking about life choices is explicitly targeted by the group facilitators (Figure 21.2, path b), who assist group members in framing issues in terms of personal control and responsibility (Berman et al., 2008).

Outcome results. Findings suggest that the Adult Identity Development Program has a positive impact (unmoderated by age) on positive identity markers. Results from an outcome study of the intervention (Berman et al., 2008) indicated that participants experienced a significant increase in identity exploration and significant decrease in identity distress. The study also evaluated outcomes using Marcia's (1994) identity status classification system. According to Marcia's formulation, individuals who have explored possible life directions and made a commitment to a particular life path are classified as identity achieved, whereas those who have not explored or committed are classified as identity diffused. Individuals who have explored but have not yet committed to a particular path are in a moratorium, whereas those who have committed without exploring have a foreclosed status. Outcome results indicated that the number of participants classified as having a foreclosed identity status decreased, whereas the number of participants classified as having an achieved identity status increased (Berman et al., 2008). If replicated, this pattern of results will support the use of participatory and transformative strategies for promoting positive identity development among adults.

The pattern of findings across the three programs just described suggests that it is possible to promote positive identity development throughout the transition from childhood to adulthood, and as well as during life course transitions that occur in adulthood. The pattern of findings also suggests that, consistent with Figure 21.2, engaging participants in self-construction and self-discovery promotes these processes. Taken as a whole, these findings provide support for identity-focused positive development.

Future Directions

Despite promising findings that provide support for positive development programs targeting positive identity, key questions remain and should be targeted by future work. Three of these questions are discussed here.

How do we capture the richness of subjective identity experiences? Erikson's (1963) description of the identity crisis and the challenge of forming a mature and coherent sense of identity provides a rich conceptualization of identity development. He described the process in terms of *qualitative* change in the structural organization of self and identity; that is, a process involving more than quantitative change in either positive or problem outcomes. Identity development involves the consolidation of an integrated self-structure that becomes increasingly complex, coherent, and cohesive as young people construct and reconstruct the meaning of identity-related life course experiences, a conceptualization that echoes much of the narrative identity literature (e.g., McLean, 2005). Thus, an important challenge for positive development programs that target identity development is to use methods capable of capturing the content, structure, and organization of self and identity and its subjective meaning and significance—that is, to richly reflect rather than reduce the life course experiences of the young people participating in these programs (Kurtines et al., 2008a).

An important part of the solution appears to be the integrated use of quantitative and qualitative methods (see Kurtines et al., 2008c; 2008d; Rinaldi et al., 2012). Within the Changing Lives Program, recent investigation of self-selected long-term life goals in a sample of 238 African-American and Latino adolescents illustrates how quantitative and qualitative methods can be integrated to detect properties that indicate theoretically meaningful differences in structural organizations of self and identity. From a developmental perspective, self-selected life goals are an expression of the future-oriented component of self and identity and the means by which youth begin to give direction to their lives as active producers of their own development (Brandtstädter & Lerner, 1999). Researchers elicited participants' descriptions of their most important life goals and their meaning and significance by adding a free response component to an established quantitative identity measure (Rinaldi et al., 2012). Examination of participants' life goal descriptions, as well as those of a comparison group suggested that, consistent with developmental expectations for youth at the earliest stages of the identity process, the majority (75 percent) of participants' life goals at pretest were self-satisfying and focused on personal gain. For example, one participant's life goal was to "Travel a lot. Explore the world. Having freedom. Free my mind and be like an eagle." The percentage of self-satisfying life goals did not vary significantly across age, gender, ethnicity, or intervention condition.

On the other hand, the study identified a small percentage (8 percent) of participants whose most important life goals indicated a more consolidated and complex structural organization of self and identity. Specifically, the life goals of these participants indicated a special fit between elements of the life goal and the youth's unique interests, talents, and potentials (i.e., feelings of personal expressiveness). For example, one participant's life goal was to be a nurse: "Being a Nurse means a lot to me because I always have liked helping others. I have always known I would be good at taking care of others." Another's life goal was to help people: "I grew up in a family where if someone gets hurt my father would take care of that. I want to help people, I inherited it and I am meant to do it." These participants appeared to have begun to integrate an emerging sense of identity into their most important life goals for their future.

How do we document significant "qualitative" intervention change in the meaning and significance of the subjective experience of the content, structure, and organization of self? A strictly quantitative approach cannot capture changes in the meaning and significance of critical experiential components of self and identity, not only because the changes are subjective in nature, but also because they are nonlinear, discontinuous, and not easily quantifiable (i.e., they constitute structural organizational change). One approach to documenting intervention change in structural organizations of self and identity and their meaning and significance is to build *quantitative* models of intervention outcome to evaluate the probability of the emergence of properties identified through *qualitative* analysis of adolescents' subjective experiences of self and identity as indicative of a more complex, coherent, and cohesive self-structure.

Results from the study described earlier indicated that participating in the Changing Lives Program was associated with positive qualitative change in youth's most important life goals and their meaning and significance. Specifically, among participants who described self-satisfying life goals at pretest, those participating in the intervention condition were significantly more likely than those participating in a comparison condition to describe a personally expressive life goal at posttest (measured immediately after intervention). This finding provided initial empirical support for positive intervention-related structural organizational change in participants' sense of self and identity within the Changing Lives Program.

The study further examined how positive qualitative change in life goals occurred and whether it spilled over to impact other outcomes by evaluating potential mediators, moderators, and effects of life goal change. A number of interesting findings emerged. Consistent with the program's focus on self-discovery processes, positive life goal change was predicted by intervention-related increases in the degree to which participants' life goal pursuit generated feelings of personal expressiveness. Positive life goal change was also predicted by intervention-related decreases in identity resolution, an indicator of engaging in the identity crisis. Positive life goal change from pre- to posttest had additional benefits for intervention participants at four-month follow-up. Specifically, positive life goal change predicted significant reductions in internalizing problem behaviors four months later, an outcome not specifically targeted by the intervention. Although tentative, these findings suggest that the integrated use of qualitative and quantitative methods may provide an important tool for modeling mediators, moderators, and the cascading effects of qualitative change in the content, structure, and organization of self and identity and its meaning and significance. Cascading effects may include reducing the incidence rate of risky and problem behaviors.

How do we tailor positive identity developmental intervention strategies to the developmental moment? Opportunities for supporting positive identity development present themselves throughout the transition to adulthood, from adolescence through emerging adulthood. However, the transformations that occur during adolescence and those that occur during emerging adulthood create different opportunities for promoting positive identity. Adolescence brings biological, cognitive, and social changes that create the possibility of systematically and seriously addressing for the first time the question "Who am I?" (Erikson, 1968). Emerging adulthood brings greater freedom and new possibilities for exploring answers to this question as young people move beyond the childhood structure imposed by family and school. Although adolescence and emerging adulthood together constitute the transition to adulthood, they represent qualitatively different developmental moments that likely require different types of support for identity development. Because adolescents are at the earliest stages of the identity process, a primary challenge for identity-focused intervention work with adolescents is to promote engagement in the identity process. Emerging adults, on the other hand, may already be more fully engaged in the identity process. Therefore, a primary challenge for identity-focused intervention work with emerging adults may be to support individuals as they refine and optimize their current positive life course pathways. For emerging adults on negative pathways, the challenge is to provide opportunities for directional change onto a more positive life course pathway. If emerging adulthood is indeed an "age of possibilities" (Arnett, 2004), then self-transformative activities may be especially beneficial during this time.

Identity-focused developmental interventions have primarily targeted the transition from childhood to adulthood. However, renewed identity work can occur later in adulthood (Anthis & LaVoie, 2006; Cramer, 2004; Strayer, 2002). This renewed identity work may be prompted by predictable life course transitions, such as becoming a parent or retiring (Berman et al., 2008). It may also occur when less predictable macrolevel events shape life course transitions, such as when an economic downturn leads to financial pressure or job loss and a return to formal education to pursue a different career (Clausen, 1998). Although university-based identity interventions have included individuals from across the adult lifespan (e.g., Berman et al., 2008), little is known about how to systematically target the life course transitions associated with adulthood. This may be a fruitful area for future developmental intervention research.

Conclusion

Advances in developmental intervention science are part of the broader movement within the fields of behavioral and mental health in the direction of a more fully integrated intervention science (Weisz et al., 2005). They represent a natural progression and extension of treatment and prevention science toward an intersection with the emergence of applied developmental science. At this intersection, developmental intervention science seeks to develop links among treatment, prevention, and developmental intervention models and approaches that will help build a more fully integrated intervention science. An integrated intervention science will include a complete set of intervention tools for treating dysfunction when it occurs, reducing risk for future dysfunction, and promoting positive development.

In this context, future advances in evaluating theoretical claims about intervention outcome will require the development of sustainable, theory-driven empirically informed positive development intervention strategies. The emerging developmental intervention science literature has focused on refining intervention strategies for promoting positive identity development during the transition from childhood to adulthood. For troubled adolescents on a negative life course trajectory, developmental interventions have aimed at empowering youth to change their lives in positive directions. For emerging adults exploring the possibilities afforded by higher education, developmental interventions have aimed at helping young people optimize a current life course. Although initial outcome findings have been promising, the developmental intervention approach is still in its infancy. Future advances in developmental intervention science appear to have significant potential for facilitating the evolution of sustainable evidence-based positive development intervention strategies for promoting positive life course change.

References

Adams, G. R., Munro, B., Doherty-Poirer, M., Munro, G., Petersen, A. R., & Edwards, J. (2001). Diffuse-avoidant, normative, and informational identity styles: Using identity theory to predict maladjustment. *Identity*, *1*(4), 307–320.

Albrecht, R. E. (2007). *A model of self-transformative identity development in troubled adolescent youth*. Unpublished doctoral dissertation. Florida International University, Miami.

Anthis, K., & LaVoie, J. C. (2006). Readiness to change: A longitudinal study of changes in adult identity. *Journal of Research in Personality*, *40*(2), 209–219.

Archer, S. L. (1989). The status of identity: Reflections on the need for intervention. *Journal of Adolescence*, *12*(4), 345–359.

Archer, S. L. (1994). *Interventions for Adolescent Identity Development*. Thousand Oaks, CA: Sage.

Archer, S. L. (2008). Identity and interventions: An introduction. *Identity: An International Journal of Theory and Research*, *8*(2), 89–94

Arnett, J. J. (2000). Emerging adulthood: A theory of development from the late teens through the twenties. *American Psychologist*, *55*(5), 469–480.

Arnett, J. J. (2004). *Emerging adulthood: The winding road from the late teens through the twenties*. New York: Oxford University Press.

Arnett, J. J. (2007). Emerging adulthood: What is it, and what is it good for? *Child Development Perspectives*, *1*(2), 68–73.

Bandura, A. (1997). *Self-efficacy: The exercise of control*. New York: Freeman.

Belgrave, F. Z., Reed, M. C., Plybon, L. E., Butler, D. S., Allison, K. W., & Davis, T. (2004). An evaluation of Sisters of Nia: A cultural program for African American girls. *Journal of Black Psychology*, *30*, 329–343.

Benson, P. L., Mannes, M., Pittman, K., & Ferber, T. (2004). Youth development, developmental assets, and public policy. In R. M. Lerner & L. Steinberg (Eds.), *Handbook of adolescent psychology* (2nd ed., pp. 781–814). New York: John Wiley.

Benson, P. L., Scales, P. C., Hamilton, S. F., & Sesma, A. Jr. (2006). Positive youth development: Theory, research, and application. In W. Damon & R. M. Lerner (Eds.), *Handbook of child psychology. Vol. 1: Theoretical models of human development*. New York: John Wiley.

Berman, S. L., Kennerley, R. J., & Kennerley, M. A. (2008). Promoting adult identity development: A feasibility study of a university-based identity intervention program. *Identity: An International Journal of Theory and Research*, *8*(2), 139–150.

Berman, A. M., Schwartz, S. J., Kurtines, W. M., & Berman, S. L. (2001). The process of exploration in identity formation. The role of style and competence. *Journal of Adolescence*, *24*, 513–528.

Berzonsky, M. D. (1986). Discovery versus constructivist interpretations of identity formation: Considerations of additional implications. *Journal of Early Adolescence*, *6*(2), 111–117.

Berzonsky, M. D. (1992). Identity style and coping strategies. *Journal of Personality*, *60*(4), 771–788.

Berzonsky, M. D. (1993). Identity style, gender, and social-cognitive reasoning. *Journal of Adolescent Research*, *8*, 289–296.

Berzonsky, M. D. (2011). A social-cognitive perspective on identity construction. In S. J. Schwartz, Luyckx, K., & Vignoles, V. L (Eds.), *Handbook of identity theory and research* (pp. 55–76). New York: Springer.

Berzonsky, M. D., & Sullivan, C. (1992). Social-cognitive aspects of identity style: Need for cognition, experiential openness, and introspection. *Journal of Adolescent Research*, *7*, 140–155.

Bosma, H. A., & Kunnen, E. S. (2001). Determinants and mechanisms in ego identity development: A review and synthesis. *Developmental Review*, *21*, 39–66.

Brandtstädter, J. (2006). Action perspectives on human development. In W. Damon & R. M. Lerner (Eds.), *Handbook of child psychology. Vol. 1: Theoretical models of human development* (6th ed., pp. 516–568). Hoboken, NJ: Wiley.

Brandtstädter, J., & Lerner, R. M. (1999). *Action and self-development: Theory and research through the life span*. Thousand Oaks, CA: Sage.

Catalano, R. F., Berglund, M. L., Ryan, J. A. M., Lonczak, H. S., & Hawkins, J. D. (1999). *Positive youth development in the United States: Research findings on evaluations of positive youth development programs*. Washington, DC: U.S. Department of Health and Human Services.

Catalano, R. F., Berglund, M. L., Ryan, J. A. M., Lonczak, H. S., & Hawkins, J. D. (2004). Positive youth development in the United States: Research findings on evaluations of positive youth development programs. *Annals of the American Academy of Political and Social Science, 591*, 98–124.

Catalano, R. F., & Hawkins, J. D. (1996). The social development model: A theory of antisocial behavior. In J. D. Hawkins (Ed.), *Delinquency and crime: Current theories* (pp. 149–197). New York: Cambridge University Press.

Catalano, R. F., Hawkins, J. D., Berglund, M. L., Pollard, J. A., & Arthur, M. W. (2002). Prevention science and positive youth development: Competitive or cooperative frameworks? *Journal of Adolescent Health, 31*(6S), 230–239.

Clausen, J. (1998). Life reviews and life stories. In J. Z. Giele & G. H. Elder (Eds.), *Methods of life course research: Qualitative and quantitative approaches* (pp. 189–212). Thousand Oaks, CA: Sage.

Coatsworth, J. D., Palen, L. A., Sharp, E. H., & Ferrer-Wreder, L. (2006). Self-defining activities, expressive identity, and adolescent wellness. *Applied Developmental Science, 10*(3), 157–170.

Cramer, P. (2004). Identity change in adulthood: The contribution of defense mechanisms and life experiences. *Journal of Research in Personality, 38*(3), 280–316.

Csikszentmihalyi, M. (1990). *Flow: The psychology of optimal experience*. New York: Basic Books.

Damon, W. (2004). What is positive youth development? *Annals of the American Academy of Political & Social Science. Special Positive Development: Realizing the Potential of Youth, 591*, 13–24.

Eichas, K., Albrecht, R. E., Garcia, A. J., Ritchie, R. A., Varela, A., Garcia, A., Rinaldi, R., Montgomery, M. J., Silverman, W. K., Jaccard, J., & Kurtines, W. M. (2010). Mediators of positive youth development intervention change: Promoting change in positive and problem outcomes? *Child and Youth Care Forum, 39*(4), 211–237.

Elder, G. H., Jr., & Shanahan, M. J. (2006). The life course and human development. In W. Damon & R. M. Lerner (Eds.), *Handbook of child psychology. Vol. 1: Theoretical models of human development* (6th ed., pp. 665–715). New York: Wiley.

Erikson, E. H. (1963). *Childhood and society*. New York: Norton.

Erikson, E. H. (1968). *Identity: Youth and crisis*. New York: Norton.

Erikson, E. H. (1985). *The life cycle completed*. New York: Norton.

Erikson, E. H., & Erikson, K. T. (1957). The confirmation of the delinquent. *Chicago Review, 10*(4), 15–23.

Ferrer-Wreder, L., Lorente, C. C., Kurtines, W., Briones, E., Bussell, J., Berman, S., & Arrufat, O. (2002). Promoting identity development in marginalized youth. *Journal of Adolescent Research, 17*, 168–187.

Ferrer-Wreder, L., Montgomery, M. J., & Lorente, C. C. (2003). Identity promotion, adolescence. In T. Gullotta & M. Bloom (Series Ed.) & G. R. Adams (Vol. Ed.), *The encyclopedia of primary prevention and health promotion: Adolescent Volume* (600–607). New York: Kluwer Academic/Plenum.

Ferrer-Wreder, L., Montgomery, M. J., Lorente, C. C., & Habibi, M. (in press). Promoting optimal identity development in adolescents. In Gullotta, T. P., & Bloom, M. (Eds.), *Encyclopedia for primary prevention interventions for adolescents*.

Ford, D. H., & Lerner, R. M. (1992). *Developmental systems theory: An integrative approach*. Newbury Park, CA: Sage.

Freire, P. (1970/1983). *Pedagogy of the oppressed*. New York: Herder & Herder.

Gestsdóttir, S., & Lerner, R. M. (2007). Intentional self-regulation and positive youth development in early adolescence: Findings from the 4-H study of positive youth development. *Developmental Psychology, 43*(2), 508–521.

Gestsdóttir, S., & Lerner, R. M. (2008). Positive development in adolescence: The development and role of intentional self-regulation. *Human Development, 51*, 202–224.

Gestsdóttir, S., Lewin-Bizan, S., von Eye, A., Lerner, J. V., & Lerner, R. M. (2009). The structure and function of selection, optimization, and compensation in middle adolescence: Theoretical and applied implications. *Journal of Applied Developmental Psychology, 30*, 585–600.

Guerra, N. G., & Bradshaw, C. P. (2008). Linking the prevention of problem behaviors and positive youth development: Core competencies for positive youth development and risk prevention. In N. G. Guerra & C. P. Bradshaw (Eds.), *Core competencies to prevent problem behaviors and promote positive youth development. New Directions for Child and Adolescent Development, 122*, 1–17.

Granic, I., & Patterson, G. R. (2006). Toward a comprehensive model of antisocial development: A dynamic systems approach. *Psychological Review, 113*(1), 101–131.

Haegerich, T. M., & Tolan, P. H. (2008). Core competencies and the prevention of adolescent substance use. In N. G. Guerra & C. P. Bradshaw (Eds.), *Core competencies to prevent problem behaviors and promote positive youth development. New Directions for Child and Adolescent Development, 122*, 47–60.

Josselson, R. (1994). Identity and Relatedness in the Life Cycle. In H. A. Bosma, D. J. DeLevita, T. L. G. Graafsma, & H. D. Grotevant (Eds.), *Identity and development: An interdisciplinary approach* (pp. 81–102). Newbury Park, CA: Sage Publications.

Kerpelman, J. L., Pittman, J. F., & Adler-Baeder, F. (2008). Identity as a moderator of intervention-related change: Identity style and adolescents' responses to relationships education. *Identity: An International Journal of Theory and Research, 8*, 151–171.

Kurtines, W. M., Berman, S. L., Ittel, A., & Williamson, S. (1995). Moral development: A co-constructivist perspective. In W. M. Kurtines & J. L. Gewirtz (Eds.), *Moral development: An introduction* (pp. 337–376). New York: Wiley.

Kurtines, W. M., Ferrer-Wreder, L., Berman, S. L., Lorente, C. C., Silverman, W. K., & Montgomery, M. J. (2008a). Promoting positive youth development: New directions in developmental theory, methods, and research. *Journal of Adolescent Research, 23*(3), 233–244.

Kurtines, W. M., Ferrer-Wreder, L., Berman, S. L., Lorente, C. C., Briones, E., Montgomery, M. J., Albrecht, R., Garcia, A. J., & Arrufat, O. (2008b). Promoting positive youth development: The Miami Youth Development Project (YDP). *Journal of Adolescent Research, 23*(3), 256–267.

Kurtines, W. M., Montgomery, M. J., Arango, L. L., Kortsch, G., Albrecht, R., Garcia, A., Ritchie, R., & Eichas, K. (2008c). Promoting positive youth development: Relational data analysis (RDA). *Journal of Adolescent Research, 23*(3), 291–309.

Kurtines, W. M., Montgomery, M. J., Eichas, K, Ritchie, R., Garcia, A., Albrecht, R., Berman, S., Ferrer-Wreder, L., & Lorente, C. C. (2008d). Promoting positive development in troubled youth: A developmental intervention science outreach research approach. *Identity: An International Journal of Theory and Research, 8*, 125–138.

Lerner, R. M. (2002). *Concepts and theories of human development* (3rd ed.). Mahwah, NJ: Lawrence Erlbaum.

Lerner, R. M. (2005). *Promoting positive youth development: Theoretical and empirical bases*. White paper: Workshop on the Science of Adolescent Health & Development, NRC/Institute of Medicine. Washington, DC: National Academies of Science.

Lerner, R. M., Agans, J. P., Arbeit, M. R., Chase, P. A., Weiner, M. B., Schmid, K. L., & Warren, A. E. A. (2013). Resilience and positive youth development: A relational developmental systems model. In S. Goldstein & R. B. Brooks (Eds.), *Handbook of resilience in children* (pp. 293–308). New York: Springer.

Lerner, R. M., Fisher, C. B., & Weinberg, R. A. (2000). Toward a science for and of the people: Promoting civil society through the application of developmental science. *Child Development, 71*(1), 11–20.

Lerner, R. M., Freund, A. M., De Stefanis, I., & Habermas, T. (2001). Understanding developmental regulation in adolescence: The use of the selection, optimization, and compensation model. *Human Development, 44*(1), 29–50.

Lerner, R. M., & Overton, W. F. (2008). Exemplifying the integrations of the relational developmental system: Synthesizing theory, research, and application to promote positive development and social justice. *Journal of Adolescent Research, 23*(3), 245–255.

Lerner, R. M., Wertleib, D., & Jacobs, F. (2005). Historical and theoretical bases of applied developmental sciences. In R. M. Lerner, D. Wertlieb, & F. Jacobs (Eds.), *Applied developmental science: An advanced textbook* (pp. 3–29). Thousand Oaks, CA: Sage.

Lewis, M. D. (2000). The promise of dynamic systems approaches for an integrated account of human development. *Child Development, 71*(1), 36–43.

Marcia, J. E. (1989). Identity and intervention. *Journal of Adolescence, 12*(4), 401–410.

Marcia, J. E. (1994). The empirical study of ego identity. In H. A. Bosma, T. L. G. Graafsma, H. D. Grotevant, & D. J. de Levita (Eds.), *Identity and development: An interdisciplinary approach* (pp. 67–80). Newbury Park, CA: Sage Publications.

Maslow, A. (1968). *The farther reaches of human nature*. New York: Penguin.

Masten, A. S. (2006). Developmental psychopathology: Pathways to the future. *International Journal of Behavior Development, 30*(1), 47–54.

McAdams, D. P. (2011). Narrative identity. In S. J. Schwartz, Luyckx, K., & Vignoles, V. L (Eds.), *Handbook of identity theory and research* (pp. 99–115). New York: Springer.

McCall, R. B., & Groark, C. J. (2000). The future of applied child development research and public policy. *Child Development, 71*(1), 197–204.

McLean, K. C. (2005). Late adolescent identity development: Narrative meaning making and memory telling. *Developmental Psychology, 41*(4), 683–691.

Meca, A., Eichas, K., Quintana, S., Maximin, B. M., Ritchie, R. A., Madrazo, V. L., Harari, G. M., & Kurtines, W. M. (in press). Reducing identity distress: Results of an identity intervention for emerging adults. *Identity: An International Journal of Theory and Research*.

Moilanen, K. L. (2007). The adolescent self-regulatory inventory: The development and validation of a questionnaire of short-term and long-term self-regulation. *Journal of Youth and Adolescence, 36*, 835–848.

Montgomery, M. J., Hernandez, L., & Ferrer-Wreder, L. (2008a). Identity development and intervention studies: The right time for a marriage? *Identity: An International Journal of Theory and Research, 8*, 173–182.

Montgomery, M. J., Kurtines, W. M., Ferrer-Wreder, L., Berman, S. L., Lorente, C. C., Briones, E., Silverman, W., Ritchie, R., & Eichas, K. (2008b). A developmental intervention science (DIS) outreach research approach to promoting youth development: Theoretical, methodological, and meta-theoretical challenges. *Journal of Adolescent Research, 23*(3), 268–290.

Moran, J. R., & Bussey, M. (2007). Results of an alcohol prevention program with urban American Indian youth. *Child and Adolescent Social Work Journal, 24*(1), 1–24.

Nisbet, R. A. (1980). *History of the idea of progress*. New York: Basic Books.

Overton, W. F. (2010). Life-span development: Concepts and Issues. In R. M Lerner (Ed.), *The handbook of lifespan development*. Hoboken, NJ: Wiley.

Rinaldi, R. L., Meca, A., Eichas, K., Kurtines, W. M., Albrecht, R. E., & Goodletty, S. (2012). The development of a qualitative extension for the Personally Expressive Activities Questionnaire (PEAQ-QE): A construct validation study. *Identity: An International Journal of Theory and Research, 12*(4), 320–344.

Roth, J. L., & Brooks-Gunn, J. (2003). Youth development programs: Risk, prevention, and policy. *Journal of Adolescent Health, 32*, 170–182.

Schwartz, S. J. (2000). *The Exploration Enhancement Workshop: An exploration-based approach to facilitating identity formation in young adults*. Unpublished doctoral dissertation. Florida International University, Miami.

Schwartz, S. J. (2002). In search of mechanisms of change in identity development: Integrating the constructivist and discovery perspectives in identity. *Identity: An International Journal of Theory and Research, 2*(4), 317–339.

Schwartz, S. J. (2006). Predicting identity consolidation from self-construction, eudaimonistic self-discovery, and agentic personality. *Journal of Adolescence, 29*, 277–293.

Schwartz, S. J., Montgomery, M. J., & Kurtines, W. K. (2005). A comparison of two approaches for facilitating identity exploration processes in emerging adults. *Journal of Adolescent Research, 20*, 309–345.

Schwartz, S. J. Pantin, H., Coatsworth, J. D., & Szapocznik, J. (2007). Addressing the challenges and opportunities for today's youth: Toward an integrative model and its implications for research and intervention. *Journal of Primary Prevention, 28*, 117–144.

Spencer, M. B. (2006). Phenomenology and ecological systems theory: Development of diverse groups. In W. Damon & R. Lerner (Eds.), *Handbook of child psychology. Vol. 1: Theoretical models of human development* (pp. 829–893). New York: John Wiley.

Strayer, J. (2002). The dynamics of emotions and life cycle identity. *Identity: An International Journal of Theory and Research, 2*(1), 47–79.

Sue, D. W., & Sue, D. (2003). *Counseling the Culturally Diverse: Theory and Practice*. New York: Wiley & Sons.

Thomas, O., Davidson, W., & McAdoo, H. (2008). An evaluation study of the Young Empowered Sisters (YES!) Program: Promoting cultural assets among African American adolescent girls through a culturally relevant school-based intervention. *Journal of Black Psychology, 34*, 281–308.

Waterman, A. S. (1984). Discovery or creation? *Journal of Early Adolescence, 4*(4), 329–341.

Waterman, A. S. (1989). Curricula interventions for identity change: Substantive and ethical considerations. *Journal of Adolescence, 12*(4), 389–400.

Waterman, A. S. (1990). Personal expressiveness: Philosophical and psychological foundations. *Journal of Mind and Behavior, 11*, 47–74.

Waterman, A. (2005). When effort is enjoyed: Two studies of intrinsic motivation for personally salient activities. *Motivation and Emotion, 29*(3), 165–188.

Waterman, S., Schwartz, S., Goldbacher, E., Green, H., Miller, C., & Philip, S. (2003). Predicting the subjective experience of intrinsic motivation: The roles of self-determination, the balance of challenges and skills, and self-realization values. *Personality and Social Psychology Bulletin, 29*, 10, 1–12.

Weisz, J. R., Sandler, I. N., Durlak, J. A., & Anton, B. S. (2005). Promoting and Protecting Youth Mental Health through Evidence-Based Prevention and Treatment, *American Psychologist, 60*(6), 628–648.

Werner, H., & Kaplan, B. (1956). The developmental approach to cognition: Its relevance to the psychological interpretation of anthropological and ethnolinguistic data. *American Anthropologist, 58*, 866–880.

Zimmerman, M. A. (1995). Psychological Empowerment: Issues and illustrations. *American Journal of Community Psychology, 23*(5), 581–599.

CHAPTER 22

A Translational Research Approach to Narrative Identity in Psychotherapy

Jefferson A. Singer *and* Adam M. Kasmark

Abstract

Questions of meaning and purpose in life, as they relate to one's sense of identity, continue to be prominent concerns in psychotherapy. As the field of clinical science develops translational research models that focus on microprocesses as targets of study linking basic research and therapeutic intervention, operationalization of identity constructs is increasingly important. Narrative identity, based in self-defining memories, narrative scripts, and life stories, offers a framework for empirical investigation in both the laboratory and the clinic. Translational research on each of these identity variables is reviewed, and a case study illustrates their potential for intervention in psychotherapy. Recommendations for future translational research on narrative identity and psychotherapy are provided.

Key Words: narrative identity, translational research, self-defining memories, scripts, life stories, psychotherapy

Any working therapist who has a more general practice in psychotherapy will tell you that some clients do not present with a specified psychological disorder. Although they may display symptoms of anxiety and depression, their initial presenting complaint is both much larger and yet far more specific in its content. "I don't know who I am. I can no longer figure out where my life is heading. I look at what I've done and what I am doing, and try to think about where I want to be, and none of it seems to hang together."

There are no criteria in the *Diagnostic and Statistical Manual of Mental Disorders* (DSM-5) to encompass this statement, but it clearly reflects a crisis of identity. As Erikson (1963) conceptualized it, identity is the thread that allows one to achieve a sense of continuity and stability among the various dimensions and across the various periods of one's life. Yet it is also fundamentally social—not only does it provide individuals with a sense of internal unity and coherence, it positions them within their community and culture. "Identity attainment enables the individual, with all of his or her own biological givens, psychological interests, aptitudes, needs, and defenses, to find satisfying vocational, ideological, and relational roles within a particular social setting during a particular historical epoch" (Kroger, 2004, p. 61).

As we strive to develop a clinical science grounded in evidence-based treatment (Kazdin, 2011) and a translational research paradigm (National Advisory Mental Health Council Behavioral Science Workgroup, 2000), how might we still make room for a therapy that focuses on questions of identity disturbance and problems of finding meaning and purpose in one's life? We do not see this question as an academic exercise but as a practical problem, given that clinical psychology training programs, health systems, and reimbursement practices are increasingly limiting their resources to approaches that have validated treatment protocols that specify delineated problems, operationalized interventions, and measurable outcomes.

One immediate challenge in envisioning a rigorous evidence-based identity therapy is that, as James Marcia, one of the pioneers in the scientific study of identity, has emphasized, "There is no Eriksonian 'school' of psychotherapy " (Marcia, 2004, p. 43). In recounting his many decades of conducting Eriksonian-informed psychotherapy, he views identity theory as providing a developmental context that informs the use of various therapeutic techniques in the interest of promoting psychological growth and health. However, our immediate concern is that if we do not provide translational constructs to therapists that link basic identity concerns to measurable processes in psychotherapy, more familiar and already manualized treatment perspectives will neglect or simply place out of bounds clients' underlying identity struggles, such as their concern about ethical action, their ability to find meaning in their work and relationships, and their connection to an overarching sense of spirituality or life purpose.

In this chapter, we offer some ideas about how we might propose a translational research approach to an identity-based psychotherapy. We first give a brief overview of the criteria of translational research in clinical science. We then outline a contemporary scientific perspective on identity theory, arguing that one promising extension of Erikson's framework is McAdams's (1985) conceptualization of identity as a life story, an approach that has evolved into the emerging field of narrative identity (McAdams, 2011; McLean, 2008; Singer, Blagov, Berry, & Oost, 2013). Within a model of narrative identity, certain specific components—self-defining memories (SDMs), narrative scripts, and life story themes of redemption and contamination, as well individuals' capacity for narrative coherence—can be operationalized and assessed within psychotherapy and may serve as targets of intervention for addressing problems of identity and meaning. Although we acknowledge the great importance of narrative therapy (Parry & Doan, 1994; White & Epston, 1990) in articulating how cultural forces interact with internal psychological processes of identity, these theorists and practitioners have been less inclined to develop operationalized models of their approach that lend themselves to empirical translation (see Freedman & Combs, 2008, for an explicit acknowledgment of this stance). Nevertheless, narrative therapy, as well as multicultural counseling perspectives, point to some emerging possibilities for assessment and integration of these cultural factors into treatment research on identity. However, as a starting point for a translational research approach to identity, we focus specifically on narrative identity constructs and end the chapter with a case study that highlights these constructs in the course of treatment.

Translational Research

Perhaps driven by the demand of the public for greater accountability in how federal research dollars are spent, as well as recognition that many of our medical and psychological interventions have shown only limited efficacy in addressing major ongoing health crises such as cancer, Alzheimer's disease, addiction, and depression, the past decade has spawned a powerful movement toward *translational research*. Translational research emphasizes the identification of specific links between basic research and treatment variables. Investigations in both laboratory and clinic are more focused on dysfunctional processes that are identifiable in both settings rather than traditional diagnostic categories; it is believed that zeroing in on these processes is a more efficient way to develop targeted interventions.

As Heyman and Slep (2009, p. 284) put it, translational research relies on basic research to look for "pathways or causes that have explicit applications in preventing or treating a disorder or problems" and similarly identifies "research-informed efficacious interventions" that might be shown to have wider implications on basic behavioral and personality change processes. In recent examples, Shoda et al. (2013) and Strauman et al. (2013) have highlighted how clinical science is shifting away from an emphasis on larger psychological disorders to the identification of "microprocesses" in models of cognition, affect, and behavior that can be isolated in both basic research and clinical practice. The linkage of these processes from "bench" to "clinic" allows for identification of mechanisms in controlled settings and subsequent interventions in clinical practice. Differential treatment outcomes can then be traced to specific actions taken on these precise microprocesses.

For example, Strauman et al. (2013) conducted basic laboratory research to define specific regulatory coping strategies involving promotion (approach-oriented thoughts and behaviors) or prevention (avoidance-oriented thoughts and behaviors) in response to an experimental stressor. Further research established that the tendency toward these particular regulatory strategies helps to differentiate individuals with chronic depression from those with chronic anxiety. Moving from the laboratory to the clinic, these researchers then demonstrated that providing individuals suffering from depression or anxiety with alternative regulatory strategies broke their particular repetitive cycles and helped decrease levels of these mood conditions.

Given the burgeoning emphasis on translational research in fields as diverse as family violence, cognitive-behavioral therapy, and neuroscience, how might this perspective find its way into an identity-based therapy? Our proposal is that the best route for achieving this synthesis of basic research on identity and current clinical practice is through application of narrative identity theory.

Narrative Identity

The first significant operationalization of Erikson's psychosocial stage theory of identity across the life cycle was Marcia's (1966) development of the identity status framework. By creating a matrix of exploration and commitment, he developed an ego identity status interview that captured four constellations of identity formation (identity achieved, foreclosed, moratorium, and identity diffusion) (see Crocetti & Meeus, this volume). Marcia's original conceptualization and additional elaboration of statuses in intimacy, generativity, and integrity, along with the work of Adams (Adams, Shea, & Fitch, 1979), Kroger (2004), and Waterman (1993), among others, within this same identity paradigm have generated more than 500 published studies and 1,000 dissertations (Marcia, 2004). As this research has evolved, it has provided much information about the personality and behavioral correlates of different identity statuses; it has also helped to track the preconditions and struggles that individuals face in coming to terms with the demands of identity consolidation at different phases of the life cycle. However, as strong as it has been in articulating identity processes and the concomitant psychological variables associated with particular statuses (see Kunnen & Metz, this volume), this line of research has been largely silent on what the nature of an internalized sense of identity might be for a given individual—in other words, the product of identity formation (McAdams, 2011 p. 101). If identity integrates one's experience of past, present, and hoped-for future, how does this unified sense of self materialize within one's consciousness? Put simply, how do we know who we are?

McAdams (1985; 1996; 2011) has proposed that contemporary individuals understand who they are through the construction of an evolving and developmentally sensitive life story. If in prior historical periods individuals were able to claim identity from inherited traditions of family, vocation, religion, class, and geographical locale, contemporary individuals are challenged by social mobility and cultural upheaval to forge their own paths that lead to a balance of autonomy and relationship. They are pressed to write their own stories, drawing on the raw material of their lived experiences to fashion a coherent narrative that gives meaning and purpose to their lives (see also Habermas & Köber, this volume). McAdams calls this process of life story creation, *narrative identity* and defines it as

> an internalized and evolving story of the self that provides a person's life with some semblance of unity, purpose, and meaning. [It] combines a person's reconstruction of his or her personal past with an imagined future in order to provide a subjective historical account of one's own development, an instrumental explanation of a person's most important commitments in the realms of work and love, and a moral justification of who a person was, is, and will be.
> *(McAdams, 2011, p. 100)*

There have been many efforts to operationalize and code various dimensions of narrative identity in developmental (Habermas & Bluck, 2000; McLean, 2008; McLean & Pasupathi, 2011), personality (Bauer & McAdams, 2004; Lilgendahl & McAdams, 2011; McAdams, 1985; 1996), and clinical psychology (Adler, 2013; Blagov & Singer, 2004; Singer & Bonalume, 2010). Recently, in an effort to create a more integrated and tightly operationalized model of narrative identity, Singer et al. (2013) proposed a hierarchical model of narrative identity that specified cognitive building blocks that comprise the internal generation of narrative identity. As outlined in Figure 22.1, narrative identity begins with a dual memory system that blends an imagistic rendering of immediate experience (the episodic memory system) with prior memories and conceptual knowledge (the long-term self) to generate *autobiographical memories* (Conway, Singer, & Tagini, 2004).

Autobiographical memories are the raw material that precipitates over and over again from both our sensory engagement with the world and our running interior dialogue with our stream-of-conscious thought (e.g., thoughts, fantasies, older memories).

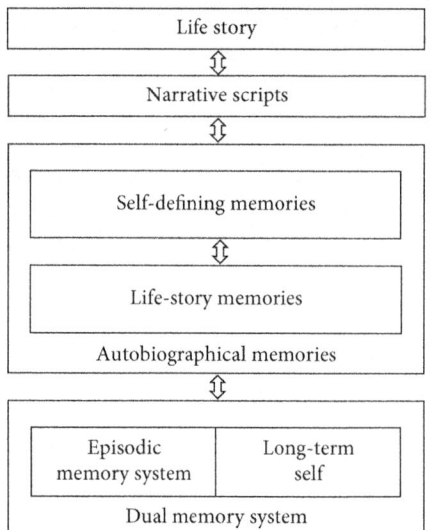

Fig. 22.1 Model of narrative identity. Reproduced with permission from Singer, J. A., Blagov, P., Berry, M., & Oost, K. M. (2013). Self-defining memories, scripts, and the life story: Narrative identity in personality and psychotherapy. *Journal of Personality, 81*(6), 569–582.

Out of this raw material only a certain infinitesimal portion of memories are retained in long-term storage and afforded some temporary significance to our current life goals during a particular period of our life. These *life story memories* are additionally culled over time, depending on their relevance to our most enduring long-term goals and/or unresolved conflicts (Thomsen, Olesen, Schnieber, Jensen, & Tønnesvang, 2012). This rarefied subset of memories, by nature of their thematic significance, emotional intensity, vividness of recollection, repetitive revival, and linkage to networks of other important memories take on the form of *self-defining memories* (Blagov & Singer, 2004; Singer & Salovey, 1993; Sutin & Robins, 2005).

Self-defining memories, through their relationship to critical goals and themes within the individual personality, are likely to include peak and nadir experiences, turning points, and emblematic memories of continuity and stability that span the emotional spectrum of an individual's internalized life narrative. In their encapsulation of central recurring experiences within individuals' lives, they offer templates for *narrative scripts* that schematize repetitive action–outcome–emotional response sequences (Demorest, 2013; Tomkins, 1979; 1987). These scripts become defining schemas within narrative identity that both organize past experience and become a projective filter for shaping new experiences into a preexisting framework of interactional dynamics and outcomes.

These various units of memories and knowledge structures contribute to and coalesce into an overall *life story* narrative that encompasses the long view of the individual's life (McAdams, 2001; 2008). The life story draws on memories and scripts to generate an overall setting, key characters, prominent life story episodes, thematic lines of agency versus communion, and a degree of narrative complexity in the story's plotline and telling. As the life story develops over the life course, it shares a reciprocal relationship with the memories and scripts that come to comprise it. Just as these memories and schemas influence its shape and manner of unfolding, the life story becomes a channeling force for bringing emphasis and structure to the memories that continue to constitute its chapters. In making this point, and true to Erikson's commitment, one cannot overemphasize the role of cultural influence on the particular form the life story takes. Individuals craft their life stories from a "cultural menu"; "A person constructs a narrative identity by appropriating stories from culture. Self and culture come to terms with each other through narrative" (McAdams & Pals, 2006, p. 212).

Hammack (2010*a*) has identified cultural "master narratives" that can be both internalized or problematized as individuals work to construct their own coherent narrative identity. He has looked at the role that competing and changing cultural narratives have played in individuals' efforts to construct meaningful life story narratives in the face of social oppression; these studies have included life stories of Palestinian youth, gay men, and even President Obama's own life story (Cohler & Hammack, 2006; Hammack, 2010*a*; 2010*b*). As Hammack (2010*a*, p. 178) writes, "Narrative identity provides a document of person-culture co-constitution...in its ability to reflect a process of discursive engagement and internalization of various circulating master narratives."

Within the history and ongoing cultural traditions of the United States, McAdams (2006) has identified the master narrative of redemption that influences the overarching shape and tone of many Americans' life stories. In favoring redemptive life stories, stemming all the way back to the Pilgrims' journey to the New World and moving through the Horatio Alger stories of "rags-to-riches" right up to our present fascination with "tell-all memoirs" of celebrities who chronicle their rise, fall, and recovery, our culture has placed a premium on narratives that depict talented or virtuous individuals who endure obstacles or hardships only to triumph and find moral and/or material vindication in the end. Although redemption stories and psychological well-being have evinced strong relationships over several studies (Adler & Poulin, 2009; McAdams, Reynolds, Lewis, Patten, & Bowman, 2001; McLean & Breen, 2009), McAdams and other researchers (Adler & Poulin, 2009; McAdams, 2006; Singer et al., 2013) have also been able to demonstrate that *contamination stories* or narratives that begin on a positive note and end badly are associated with greater psychological distress and poorer physical and mental health outcomes.

Given that this current model of narrative identity has detailed specific units that have been studied in both laboratory and clinical settings, we have the beginnings of a translational research paradigm for narrative identity and psychotherapy. In the next section, we take a selection of these narrative identity components—SDMs, narrative scripts, and life stories—and look at first steps to identify microprocesses that might link basic and clinical research.

Self-Defining Memories

Research on SDMs has recently been collected on a website devoted to published articles and chapters that report SDM and related autobiographical memory findings (www.self-definingmemories.com). These studies generally can be categorized as looking at one or more of four dimensions—affect, content, specificity, and meaning-making—and their correlates with personality and psychological disorder. As a recent example, Lardi Robyn, Ghisletta, and Van der Linden (2012) examined the affective quality, specificity, content, and meaning-making for the SDMs of individuals with higher levels of hypomania on the Mood Disorder Questionnaire. They collected and coded three SDMs from a mixed sample of community and undergraduate participants (m age = 23.29 years) for content, using the Thorne and McLean (2001) coding manual, as well as specificity and meaning-making, applying the Singer and Blagov (2002) coding procedures. Participants rated their affective responses to each memory. These researchers found that greater hypomania was associated with more relationship-themed memories and fewer achievement-oriented themes. Individuals higher in hypomania also reported more tension-themed memories and also showed more evidence of meaning-making efforts with regard to these memories compared to memories that expressed less conflict. This finding replicated earlier work by McLean and Thorne (2003), which found greater meaning-making in conflict-based memories. Compared to individuals lower in hypomania, the hypomanic individuals' tension memories were also significantly less specific. This finding also replicates earlier research that has shown an overgeneral memory effect, especially for negative events, in individuals with bipolar disorder (Mansell & Lam, 2004; Tzemou & Birchwood, 2007).

Studies similar to this one have found relationships between the four dimensions of SDMs and other psychological disorders, including autism, depression, borderline personality disorder, complicated grief, posttraumatic stress disorder, and schizophrenia (e.g., Berna et al., 2011; Blagov & Singer, 2004; Crane, Goddard, & Pring, 2010; Maccullum & Bryant, 2008; Raffard et al., 2009; Singer et al., 2013; Sutherland & Bryant, 2005). In our own recent work (Singer, Blagov, Berry, & Oost, 2013) we found links among proneness to depression, lower numbers of specific positive memories, and greater number of contamination sequences in SDMs. In addition, higher levels of meaning-making in SDMs were related to a capacity for impulse control and greater receptivity to positive emotion, as measured respectively by the Weinberger Adjustment Inventory–Short Form (Weinberger, 1997) and the Schedule of Nonadaptive and Adaptive Personality (SNAP, Clark, 1993). Other researchers have found similar links between psychological disorder and decreased meaning-making in SDMs (e.g., Berna et al., 2011; Crane et al., 2010), However, Singer et al. (2013) have clarified that effective meaning-making must be coherent, flexible, and accurate (Singer et al., 2013), whereas McLean and Mansfield (2010) have identified instances in which meaning-making may overcomplicate positive experiences or undermine more adaptive repressive coping.

Singer and Bonalume (2010) set out to translate basic research findings on SDMs into an assessment method within psychotherapy. Working from the transcript of an intensive evaluation of a nineteen-old-year old female undergraduate at an outpatient clinic, they extracted twenty-four autobiographical memory narrative units through the application of their Coding System for Autobiographical Memory Narratives in Psychotherapy (CS-AMNP). Applying the Singer and Blagov (2002) Classification and Scoring System for Self-defining Autobiographical Memory, Singer and Bonalume coded specificity and meaning-making in the client's memories. Scoring revealed an unusually high number of summary memories (45.8 percent) compared to nonclinical sample percentages of 15–20 percent. Higher numbers of summary memories have been associated both with depressed mood (Williams et al., 2007) and greater levels of defensiveness (Blagov & Singer, 2004; Singer & Salovey, 1993). The client also showed a diminished capacity to extract meaning or lessons from her memory narratives. She generated only 12.5 percent meaning-making memories, whereas nonclinical samples of similar age to the client have shown a range of 20–40 percent (Blagov & Singer, 2004; Thorne, McLean, & Lawrence, 2004).

To examine the clinical assessment and intervention potential of these narrative identity analyses, the authors made predictions about the course of psychotherapy, emphasizing the client's likelihood to engage in defensive behaviors and to display relatively little insight into some of her more troubling self-destructive behavior. These predictions were matched against the actual therapist's depiction of the client's year-long treatment. Despite being generated without the benefit of contact with the client, these memory-based predictions displayed strong overlap with the therapist's account of treatment. Although this was a preliminary and qualitative test, it shows a promising direction for how psychotherapy could incorporate the assessment of narrative identity memory process and content for diagnostic and treatment planning purposes.

Specifically, we would advocate for the use of a life-story interview during assessment that would probe for potential SDMs from across the lifespan of the client. Collection of these memories would enable the clinician to assess defensive tendencies (by evaluating a specificity percentage across the collected memories), potential level of adjustment (by evaluating quantity and quality of meaning-making in the memories), and underlying narrative identity concerns (by looking for narrative scripts and life story themes that emerge from the memories, as described in the next two sections).

Narrative Scripts

In addition to coding the client's autobiographical memories, Singer and Bonalume evaluated the memories for repetitive action–outcome–emotional response sequences—narrative scripts. The client displayed a narrative script that emerged in twelve of the twenty-four memories. This script took the form of a main protagonist (either the client or her mother) undergoing an actual or imagined social rejection. In response, the memory protagonist would withdraw from social interaction and take up a solitary and protective behavior (e.g., television-viewing, daydreaming, substance use). Once again, the authors were able to use this narrative script to generate predictions about the course of therapy and, in particular, propose how the dynamic of the therapeutic relationship would evolve. They correctly predicted that the client would begin with an idealized picture of the therapist, but that typical limit-setting and minor misunderstandings would gradually cause the client to experience a negative transference, resulting in cancellations and acting-out behaviors. These predictions were also borne out, as the client initially attended regularly but over time increasingly cancelled, refused to answer follow-up phone calls, and acted out with substance abuse.

Demorest and her colleagues (Demorest, 1995; 2008; Demorest & Alexander, 1992; Demorest, Popovska, & Dabova, 2012; Siegel & Demorest, 2010) have made great advances in meshing laboratory research on narrative scripts with identification of script microprocesses in therapy. They have also been able to document a relationship between script transformation and therapeutic outcome. In a laboratory study, Demorest, Popovska, and Dabova (2012) initially collected ten memories of emotional importance from forty-seven college students. They coded event–outcome sequences across the memories and identified the most repeated sequences as the students' unique scripts. One month later, students completed a reaction-time task in response to emotion prompts that invoked a mix of action–outcome sequences that both reflected and did not reflect participants' previous personal scripts. Participants were unaware that they were being timed. Participants not only responded more quickly to prompts connected to their personal scripts, but were able to identify the similar emotion that they associated with this script a month earlier 78 percent of the time.

Extending this study of narrative scripts to the clinic, Siegel and Demorest (2010) applied a coding system called FRAMES (Fundamental Repetitive and Maladaptive Emotion Structure; Dahl & Teller, 1994; Hoelzer & Dahl, 1996; Siegel, Sammons, & Dahl, 2002) to narrative sequences from archived transcripts of a long-term psychotherapy. The FRAMES system consists of standardized categories of interpersonal exchanges that delineate wishes and states of satisfaction/dissatisfaction of these wishes, as well as an active/passive dimension. For example, a positive active wish—to get close to someone, or a negative active wish—to hurt someone, could lead respectively to the positive passive state of warmth or the negative passive state of sadness. These sequences of interpersonal exchanges can be coded from the client's self-report of experiences outside treatment or from the interchanges between the client and therapist. In Siegel and Demorest's case study, they identified five maladaptive scripts that repeatedly surfaced from several hundred sequences in the client's narratives and interactions with the therapist. Dividing the therapy into beginning, middle, and ending phases, they were then able to show a significant decline in the frequency of these maladaptive scripts and an increase in healthier and more positive narrative sequences. This shift toward more adaptive narrative scripts was corroborated by other empirical measures that reflected a positive therapeutic outcome in this treatment (Jones & Windholz, 1990).

Once therapists learn to see linkages across narrative memories that are also reflected in client–therapist interactions, they have a potent tool to reflect back to the client key identity themes in their lives. Working with their therapist, clients are then able to apply a variety of therapeutic tools, including cognitive restructuring, role-playing, and behavioral activation to break the hold of a particular script within the client's narrative identity. We next turn to a consideration of translational approaches to the life story within treatment.

The Life Story

As one example of a translational linkage between the life story and psychotherapy, Adler (2012; 2013; Adler & Hershfield, 2012) has developed an extensive research program to look at how individuals incorporate the narratives of their psychotherapies into their larger life story. Although focusing on the treatment narrative is only a small piece of individuals' overall life stories, Adler's work provides an excellent example of more empirically based translational research that could eventually be applicable to the larger life story. For example, Adler has found that individuals who tell narratives of their treatment that describe enhanced agency (e.g., a sense of increasing competence and independence) over the course of therapy are much more likely to show higher levels of psychological well-being and ego development (Adler, Skalina, & McAdams, 2008).

In a sophisticated longitudinal study, Adler (2012) assessed clients' ongoing narratives of their psychotherapies before the first session and then between each subsequent session over the course of twelve sessions. Simultaneously with collecting each client narrative, Adler also had the client fill out scales of psychological well-being and, paralleling his earlier research (Adler et al., 2008), coded the therapy narratives for agency. Using growth curve analysis, he was able to map the gradual increase of the client's sense of agency and well-being over the twelve sessions. Most interestingly, he was able to show that increases in agency preceded reports of increased psychological well-being, suggesting that the development of an agentic narrative (or, in other words, an internalized life story of greater competence and autonomy) may be a precursor to one's sense of psychological health and adjustment.

Adler (2013) reports additional research that looks at another dimension of the life story critical to narrative identity—the ability of the story to unite past, present, and future into a coherent whole. To examine narrative coherence of his clients' psychotherapy narratives, Adler drew on the work of Habermas and Bluck (2000) to identify four different forms of narrative coherence. Narrative coherence can include temporal sequences, causal connections, thematic repetitions, and cultural touchstones that reflect societal norms within a typical life story. In his analysis of the psychotherapy narratives collected in Adler (2012), he was able to demonstrate that improved narrative coherence in therapy narratives immediately preceded junctures in therapy when substantial improvement in psychological well-being was reported.

These findings illustrate once again the progress that researchers are making in translating the constructs of narrative identity into microprocesses that can be isolated and examined for outcome implications in ongoing psychotherapy treatment. Adler's work highlights that therapists may evaluate the initial life stories that clients bring to treatment for overall levels of agentic themes and narrative coherence; these markers of healthy narrative identity are likely to be strong predictors of psychological growth and enhanced well-being over the course of treatment.

To illustrate the assessment and therapeutic application of each of these narrative identity variables—SDMs, narrative scripts, and the life story—we present a case study that takes identity and meaning as its central therapeutic concerns.

A Case Study of Narrative Identity in Psychotherapy

Andrew was a fifty-two-year-old Caucasian unmarried male temporarily living in a friend's condominium in a beach community (name and identifying details changed to protect the client's anonymity and confidentiality). This was not Andrew's first time in treatment with me (JAS); he had met with me for a year and a half during a series of relational and career crises and had stopped approximately twelve months earlier due to financial reasons and extensive travel out of state. We had resumed treatment after he had called in despair about his virtually homeless and penurious condition. Andrew's LinkedIn profile displayed a ruggedly handsome tanned face with shoulder length blonde hair and shining white teeth. The profile described his activities as a writer, television producer, and CEO of a company called SureWord (there was no clear indication of what this company's products or services were). I had to smile at the typically glamorous impression that Andrew exuded. When Andrew would visit his ailing mother in the hospital in his leather jacket, hand-tooled boots, and aviator shades, the nurses called him "Fabio" after the Italian male model with his trademark open shirt fronts and ample blond locks.

The Andrew sitting with me in my office, unshaven and in extreme anxiety, seemed worlds away from his internet image. When Andrew first began to see me in therapy, his presenting complaints were in the two major domains of adult identity: "love and work." At the time, he was heading up a nonprofit foundation that focused on human rights and exploitation of children. He was also living with a woman twenty years younger, who assisted him in his work and was herself a survivor of exploitative conditions. In the early months of therapy, it was not unusual for Andrew to recap his foundation-related television interviews, attendance at celebrity functions, and his interactions with high-level public officials here and abroad.

Yet despite this high-charged and "hold my calls" appearance, Andrew faced major difficulties with his foundation. He was the only full-time employee and, despite the ambitious activities presented on the website, between trying to raise money and publicize its causes, he had little or no time to enact its proposed interventions. Barely able to pay the rent on a small house and meet his monthly bills, he had no additional funds to pay employees or implement programs. The harder he had to work to raise money, the less time he had to make the foundation something more than his public appearances and fundraising appeals.

There were eerie parallels in his intimate life as well. Having met his younger girlfriend at a fund-raising event, they had shared their passion for helping children. She began to volunteer to support his activities and gradually they developed a romantic relationship. However, over time, they had fallen into a pattern that seemed to avoid rather than build intimacy. Despite living together, they increasingly engaged in parallel activities, and Andrew often felt that she found ways to distance herself from interaction with him. Even so, he continued to cover all of her living expenses and even help some of her relatives and friends. Trapped by the escalating demands and uncertain future of his foundation, Andrew felt a similar sense of both pressure and fragility in his intimate life.

Much of the early therapy centered on weekly crises and upsets with either the foundation or his girlfriend. Even so, I still gathered important details about his family of origin and his previous work before the foundation. Andrew was considerably younger than his two older siblings, and they were both out of the house by the time he was thirteen. His thirteenth year was a critical time for him because it was the year that his father walked out on his mother for another woman. This desertion was the culmination of an affair that had lasted over a couple of years and brought extreme conflict and distress to the household. One of Andrew's SDMs is of his mother sobbing in his arms as she explained that his father had packed his bags and was not coming back. Andrew strongly associated two ideas with this memory; he needed to do everything possible to save his mother, and he would never be the deceptive and heartless person his father seemed to be. He remained the only one at home with his mother for the rest of high school, and later, as an adult, was the only one of her children to live nearby and care for her as she grew older.

Despite his closeness to his mother, he described her as tending to be critical of him and placing a strong premium on propriety. She was part of a group of upper middle class "society" women and was exacting in her expectations about appearances and social niceties. As the youngest and most sensitive of her children, he often felt himself falling short in meeting her standards. His most powerful early SDM from age five or six, and one that he repeated a number of times to me in the course of treatment, was of an incident in which he interrupted her bridge game with the "ladies" to ask for a snack. He was severely rebuked and told, "We do not engage in this kind of behavior in this house." He slumped away with the distinct feeling of terror that if he continued to behave in this way, he would have to leave his home and no longer be with his family any more. Andrew recalled other memories, not quite as distinct, but connected to this same theme of disappointing his mother—of wanting to make her happy or proud of him but somehow falling short and not living up to appearances.

A third pivotal SDM for Andrew occurred during his high school years. Once his father was gone from the home, he would make periodic attempts to see Andrew, but Andrew hated these visits and continued to resent him for how he had betrayed his mother. Although Andrew's mother remarried and ultimately resumed a secure and reasonably prosperous life, his father worked in low-level sales positions and was never very successful, despite trying to present himself as otherwise.

The specific SDM focused on a particular time when his father tried to pick up Andrew at school, and the office called Andrew's class to say that his father was waiting for him. Andrew actually began to panic and ran out of the school, past the front office and the profile of his father within. Seeing his father's image only spurred his flight. He ran from the school filled with anger and fear and finally made his way to the town hall and a pay phone. He called his mother and told her that he never wanted to see his father again and that he wanted to come home rather than return to school.

Andrew majored in journalism in college and went into public relations work after graduation. His public relations positions led him to contracts with evangelical organizations, and he soon found a niche in this work, including writing for megachurches and celebrity pastors. He himself had turned increasingly to religion and had grown heavily involved with a local church, participating in all facets of the congregation, including leading the Sunday alternative service and giving his own homilies.

As he experienced success as a publicist, a narrative script in his life was starting to coalesce. A number of the churches that he worked for highlighted mission work and human rights concerns. Connecting back to his own experience as a vulnerable youngest child in a conflicted family, but also to his role as his mother's lone protector in the face of his father's absence, Andrew felt a powerful calling to work against the exploitation of children. He began to highlight these social concerns in his church writings and even ended up self-publishing a book on this topic. In Hammack's terms, Andrew had tapped into a master narrative within our society of public activists with a strong religious affiliation who organize their lives and livelihood around the protection of a vulnerable population (modeled for him by the successful pastors who employed him).

At the same time that this narrative theme of protecting and saving the vulnerable was crystallizing as an organizing focus in his work and personal identity, he was playing out a parallel pattern in his intimate relationships. In a series of relationships lasting approximately two to three years, he would step in as a "savior" for women in emotional difficulties or crises. Over time, they would become more difficult to please, and he would feel increasingly inadequate. In at least one case, he recalled a relationship that ended when he made it clear that he was unwilling to take on the responsibility of having children. After these relationships had devolved into antagonistic or avoidant endings, Andrew would find himself devastated by the break-ups, often falling into depressions and self-lacerating periods of shame and loneliness.

There is one other critical thread that was woven into this central script of Andrew's narrative identity. The powerful pastors who were his models of altruistic commitment lived lavish lifestyles that seemed rather at odds with the messages of humility and Christ-like devotion that they expressed to their congregants. His writing supported their churches' quests for donations, but the allocation of resources and the personal behavior of the church leaders raised many doubts in his mind. At some level, not yet fully conscious for him, he knew that he had run from his father's hypocrisy and deception—that he had most desperately wanted not to become his father—but here he was working with and supporting men for whom he felt mounting distrust.

Eventually, he broke away from his work for these churches despite the substantial financial windfalls for him and started up his own foundation that would directly address his concern for exploited children. Yet within three years of this venture, he was going into debt, overwhelmed, and unable to meet all of the foundation's commitments. Underneath his own celebrity aura, he felt increasingly hollow, and his loosening bond with his younger girlfriend only reinforced this sense of emptiness.

Soon his worst fears were realized when vicious blogs challenged his foundation's authenticity and a state official opened up an inquiry. He fell into a deep depression, and we worked intensively together during this period to help him stabilize.

He eventually improved, but then started a new relationship that did not last. He also began another self-published book on exploited children. He had been humbled by his crash, but as he rebuilt his life, he seemed to reassemble it with many of the same problematic components. His money woes continued and as he pursued new ventures (e.g., a reality show about exploited children based overseas), he slowly drifted away from therapy. A year passed, and we had very little contact. Finally, despairing emotionally and financially, he contacted me to resume therapy, but there was a very different flavor this time. Rather than moving from crisis to crisis and simply trying to help him manage his anxiety and depression, we focused the therapy on the most fundamental questions of identity—the meaning and purpose of his life. To do so, I encouraged him to work with me in looking at the key components of his narrative identity—his most important SDMs, his narrative scripts, and the themes and motifs of his overarching life story. With his background in writing, Andrew embraced this task of looking for and uncovering the connections that linked his memories and larger life story.

The translational work of narrative identity therapy, as we have constructed it, is to locate the microprocesses isolated in basic research and reconstitute them in psychotherapy practice. Andrew's case presents us with these processes. In working with him, we extracted these key SDMs: (1) memory of his mother's sobbing at her abandonment and his wish to save her from his deceptive father; (2) memory of his propriety-oriented mother criticizing him during her bridge game; (3) memory of running in panic from his father's profile; (4) memory of a relationship breaking down when he confessed his unwillingness to assume responsibility for raising a child.

In combination with similarly themed life events, these memories coalesced into the following narrative script that contained a powerful contamination sequence:

Andrew, putting great stock in appearance and presentation, conveys the air of someone who can step in and save others.

↓

Over time Andrew experiences a sense of disappointment in these efforts and fears his own inadequacy.

↓

Questioning his own motives and worrying that he is "becoming his father" (e.g., deceptive and irresponsible), he panics and runs from commitment.

↓

The result is an overarching sense of emptiness and despairing confusion about who he is and how to be authentic and self-sustaining.

Andrew's life story fell short of fundamental commitments in both arenas of agency and communion. Regarding agency, he had often relied on his writing ability and media savvy, not to mention his movie star looks, to create the illusion of success but found more substantial follow-through and genuine integrity in his undertakings more problematic. In reality, his lobbying efforts and public speaking had done much to bring awareness to issues involving exploited children, but his own missteps and blindness to how his high profile could alienate others had undermined his effectiveness. Regarding communion, his similar concern with the powerful first impressions he could make as a "savior" and accommodating lover had undermined his ability to build depth and longevity in his relationships.

In our new work together, we discussed at length the meaning of commitment in identity—commitment to vocation, to relationship, to spiritual beliefs. Andrew felt that his life story had been one of running—running away from the day-in and day-out solidity of a career and running away from the responsibility and vulnerability of being a partner and parent; he had even repeatedly distanced himself from any trusting faith in God after all the years of seeing the hypocrisy of the many ministers he had served. For so long he had determined with fierce resolve not to become his father and, despite running in the opposite direction, had found himself circling back to him with an uncanny similarity in fundamental ways. Ironically, the one certain commitment that he had kept all of these years was to his mother. As she had aged and begun to develop symptoms of Alzheimer's disease, he had been the one sibling to take care of her on a daily basis, bringing her groceries and driving her to her many medical appointments.

As Andrew explored his memories with me and we traced the narrative script and life story that emerged from these signal events, we felt as if we had scraped away layers of artifice and were now slowly finding his authentic and tentative sense of self. He soon made a decision to move back to the community in which he had been living when I had first met him and was immediately comforted by a sense of taking root in a familiar place. He resumed attending church, but in a small congregation with a down-to-earth pastor with no ambition beyond meeting the needs of his immediate parishioners.

He took on some small public relations writing jobs, but with a careful eye on how his material would be used and with a determination to feel no contradiction between his words and deeds. He removed the hyperbole from his onscreen profile and turned down some seemingly glamorous, but long-shot, media ventures. If the theme of his life story was running away, he was determined to counteract that message by staying put.

In the midst of this reassessment of his basic life commitments and his tentative efforts to build more authentic ones, Andrew described a recent incident that had shaken him and that he felt connected powerfully to the identity struggles we had been exploring. With his mother's dementia worsening, the family had finally moved her to the memory unit of a nursing home. One day, Andrew had gone to visit her and, as he approached the unit, had heard another woman on her floor screaming out in misery. Stopped in his tracks, he could not bring himself to turn the corner to find his mother. Frozen with the thought that he could not save her and that he could not stand to see her suffer, he literally turned and ran out of the home.

Bringing this story to the therapy, we were able to use all the devices of our narrative identity work to interpret the meaning of his panic. We were able to return to his SDMs and apply a "meaning-making" lens to see the connection to his fear of loss and powerlessness. He could now see how his life story continually cast him in the role of "the frustrated savior." He was able to go back to his mother the next day with a more realistic acceptance of what he could and could not do. Reframing his narrative, he worked to forgive himself for the fact that he might not be able to save her (or anyone else) from all distress that life brings but that he could still be good enough (as son, as social reformer, as lover).

Interestingly, at the same time that we were conducting this narrative identity work in treatment, Andrew learned that earlier advocacy work he had done had finally resulted in a legislative ban on some particularly egregious child-oriented internet websites. The positive threads of his work had always been there, and now he could connect them in a healthier and more substantive way. He could see the *narrative of his psychotherapy* (in contrast to his earlier effort at treatment with me) as helping him to find more agentic themes in his life story. As the pieces of his memories, scripts, and life story tied together around these central themes, he also felt an emerging sense of narrative coherence—what had often seemed fragmented in his life could now be shaped into a more unified and meaningful linkage of past, present, and future.

Corresponding to Adler's findings on the psychological value of an internalized agentic therapy narrative within the larger life story, Andrew also experienced a steady increase in his spirits and sense of well-being. Yet, even as his life stabilized, he was certain that it was too soon for him to explore the development of a new intimate relationship. He felt that his work in identity reconstruction and commitment to an authentic self was so new and tentative that any romantic entanglement might undermine this fledging structure. Even this decision conveyed a seriousness of purpose that I had not fully seen in Andrew over the prior three years.

Thrown to his existential knees by a self-defeating flight from the task of identity formation in love and work, Andrew had worked with me in a therapy based in memories, scripts, and life story to explore and then commit to a new and more congruent narrative identity. Our work together offers an evocative case example of how narrative identity microprocesses identifiable in both basic research and clinical practice can become tools of insight and intervention for positive therapeutic outcome. Focus on these processes demonstrates that one can conduct an identity-oriented therapy without straying from research-based and laboratory-tested constructs.

Conclusion

Psychotherapy is clearly in a transition period. With the powerful advent of psychopharmacological treatments and the increasing emphasis on brain science, the media are fond of highlighting the shrinking market for "talk therapy" (Gottlieb, 2012). As Kazdin (2011) has argued, the therapies that are likely to carry the day and remain viable options in the long run are those that are scientifically validated and backed by evidence of efficacy. As clinical psychologists with a commitment to the roles of personality and identity in human functioning, we feel strongly that identity processes—questions about one's larger purpose and meaning in life and within one's society—must still retain a foothold in the emerging clinical science and its shifting paradigm of psychotherapy.

With this goal in mind, we have proposed that identity concerns raised by clients who are seeking psychotherapy can be operationalized within a theoretical model of narrative identity and that this model provides a concrete path to translational research that connects laboratory and clinic.

As elaborated in Singer et al. (2013), the narrative identity model includes microprocesses of SDMs, narrative scripts, and life stories that can be isolated, measured, and translated into identifiable processes within psychotherapy treatment. Drawing on a recent case study, we illustrated how a client's identity reconstruction work in treatment in pursuit of meaning and redefined purpose in his life could be broken down into these units of narrative identity. Successful intervention for this client made explicit use of his ability to identify key SDMs, a dominant narrative script, and troubling patterns and themes in his overarching life story. His improved well-being and enhanced agency grew out of his fledgling efforts to fashion a revised life story that felt more authentic and of greater solidity than his previous narrative.

We recognize the extremely preliminary nature of our translational model of narrative identity in psychotherapy. A single case study is no replacement for carefully controlled intervention studies that will ground the narrative identity approach in a quantitative and replicable research base. However, this chapter does offer a reasonable direction for embarking on exactly this kind of research, building on stable findings from several years of basic research in autobiographical memory, scripts, and life stories.

One area that begs for new methods of translational research is how to connect the work of Hammack and others (e.g., White & Epston, 1990) on cultural co-construction of narrative identity to a measurable analysis of psychotherapy treatment and outcome. In this brief chapter, we did not have the space to delve more deeply into the role of master narratives in Andrew's original, misaligned narrative identity, but there is no question that many of his struggles could be traced to powerful cultural messages about appearance, celebrity, and status. As Andrew often unconsciously ran from laying down a deep structure of identity, he was consistently reinforced in multiple ways for his ability to succeed through a surface presentation—through his physical attractiveness, facility with press releases and publicity, skill with social media and websites, and his knack for social networking with celebrities and public officials. If we are to develop a rigorous translational research paradigm for narrative identity, we are going to have to find a way to document the role of internalized "toxic" narratives (as White and Epston [1990] might term them) and how successful treatment helps clients to "externalize" them and dissociate their identity from these influences.

Similarly, the work of social developmental personality researchers, such as that by McLean and Pasupathi (McLean & Pasupathi, 2006; McLean, Pasupathi, & Pals, 2007), on how narratives are co-constructed and contextualized within interpersonal dyads cannot be ignored. As the work of translational research moves forward, we will need methods for documenting the dynamic process of co-constructing narrative identity that inevitably takes place between client and therapist.

In conclusion, we urge identity researchers and clinical scientists with a commitment to identity processes to take up the collaborative challenge of defining a role for narrative identity within the translational research paradigm, which is already becoming the future of scientifically based psychotherapy. How unfortunate it would be for us as psychotherapists, not to mention for our clients, if questions of an individual's sense of personal meaning and purpose ceased to hold a respected place in the list of concerns that treatment might address!

References

Adams, G. R., Shea, J., & Fitch, S. A. (1979). Toward the development of an objective assessment of ego-identity status. *Journal of Youth and Adolescence, 8*, 223–237.

Adler, J. M. (2012). Living into the story: Agency and coherence in a longitudinal study of narrative identity development and mental health over the course of psychotherapy. *Journal of Personality and Social Psychology, 102*(2), 367–389.

Adler, J. M. (2013). Clients' and therapists' stories about psychotherapy. *Journal of Personality, 81*(6), 595–605.

Adler, J. M., & Hershfield, H. E. (2012). Mixed emotional experience is associated with and precedes improvements in psychological well-being. *PLoS ONE, 7*(4), 1–10.

Adler, J. M., & Poulin, M. J. (2009). The political is personal: Narrating 9/11 and psychological well-being. *Journal of Personality, 77*(4), 903–932.

Adler, J., Skalina, L., & McAdams, D. P. (2008). The narrative reconstruction of psychotherapy and psychological health. *Psychotherapy Research, 18*, 719–734.

Bauer, J. J., & McAdams, D. P. (2004). Personal growth in adults' stories of life transitions. *Journal of Personality, 72*(3), 573–602.

Berna, F., Bennouna-Greene, M., Potheegadoo, J., Verry, P., Conway, M. A., & Danion, J. (2011). Self-defining memories related to illness and their integration into the self in patients with schizophrenia. *Psychiatry Research, 189*(1), 49–54.

Blagov, P. S., & Singer, J. A. (2004). Four dimensions of self-defining memories (specificity, meaning, content, and affect) and their relationships to self-restraint, distress, and repressive defensiveness. *Journal of Personality, 72*(3), 481–511.

Cohler, B. J., & Hammack, P. L. (2006). Making a gay identity: Life story and the construction of a coherent self. In D. P. McAdams, R. Josselson, & A. Lieblich (Eds.), *Idnetity and story: Creating self in narrative* (pp. 151–172). Washington, DC: American Psychological Association.

Conway, M. A., Singer, J. A., & Tagini, A. (2004). The self and autobiographical: Correspondence and coherence. *Social Cognition, 22*(5), 491–529.

Clark, L. A. (1993). *The Schedule for Nonadaptive and Adaptive Personality* (SNAP). Minneapolis: University of Minnesota Press.

Crane, L., Goddard, L., & Pring, L. (2010). Brief report: Self-defining and everyday autobiographical memories in adults with autism spectrum disorders. *Journal of Autism and Developmental Disorders, 40*(3), 383–391.

Dahl, H., & Teller, V. (1994). The characteristics, identification, and applications of FRAMES. *Psychotherapy Research, 4*(3–4), 253–276.

Demorest, A. P. (1995). The personal script as a unit of analysis for the study of personality. *Journal of Personality, 63*(3), 569–592.

Demorest, A. P. (2008). A taxonomy for scenes. *Journal of Research in Personality, 42*(1), 239–246.

Demorest, A. P. (2013). The role of scripts in psychological maladjustment and psychotherapy, *Journal of Personality, 81*(6), 583–594.

Demorest, A. P., & Alexander, I. E. (1992). Affective scripts as organizers of personal experience. *Journal of Personality, 60*(3), 645–663.

Demorest, A., Popovska, A., & Dabova, M. (2012). The role of scripts in personal consistency and individual differences. *Journal of Personality, 80*(1), 187–218.

Erikson, E. H. (1963). *Childhood and society*. New York: W. W. Norton & Co.

Freedman, J., & Combs, G. (2008). Narrative couple therapy. In A. S. Gurman (Ed.), *Clinical handbook of couple therapy* (4th ed., pp. 229–258). New York, NY: Guilford Press.

Habermas, T., & Bluck, S. (2000). Getting a life: The emergence of the life story in adolescence. *Psychological Bulletin, 126*(5), 748–769.

Hammack, P. L. (2010a). Identity as burden of benefit? Youth, historical narrative, and the legacy of political conflict. *Human Development, 53*, 173–201.

Hammack, P. L. (2010b). The political psychology of personal narrative: The case of Barack Obama. *Society for the Psychological Study of Social Issues, 10*(1), 182–206.

Heyman, R. E., & Slep, A. M. (2009). A translational research orientation to family violence. *Violence and Victims, 24*, 283–301.

Hoelzer, M., & Dahl, H. (1996). How to find FRAMES. *Psychotherapy Research, 6*(3), 177–197.

Gottlieb, L. (2012, Nov. 23). What brand is your therapist? *The New York Times* Retrieved from:http://www.nytimes.com/2012/11/25/magazine/psychotherapys-imageproblem-pushes-some-therapists-to-become-brands.html?hpw.

Jones, E., & Windholz, M. (1990). The psychoanalytic case study: Toward a method for systematic inquiry. *Journal of the American Psychoanalytic Association, 38*(4), 985–1015.

Kazdin, A. E. (2011). Evidence-based treatment research: Advances, limitations, and next steps. *American Psychologist, 66*, 685–698.

Kroger J. (2004). Identity in formation. In K. Hoover (Ed.), *Future of identity* (pp. 61–76). New York: Lexington Books.

Lardi Robyn, C., Ghisletta, P., & Van der Linden, M. (2012). Self-defining memories and self—defining future projections in hypomania prone individuals. *Consciousness and Cognition, 21* (2), 764–774.

Lilgendahl, J. P., & McAdams, D. P. (2011). Constructing stories of self-growth: How individual differences in patterns of autobiographical reasoning relate to well-being in midlife. *Journal of Personality, 79*(2), 391–428.

Maccallum, F., & Bryant, R. A. (2008). Self-defining memories in complicated grief. *Behaviour Research and Therapy, 46*(12), 1311–1315.

Mansell, W., & Lam, D. (2004). A preliminary study of autobiographical memory in remitted bipolar and unipolar depression and the role of imagery in the specificity of memory. *Memory, 12*(4), 437–446.

Marcia J. E. (1966). Development and validation of ego development status. *Journal of Personality and Social Psychology, 3*, 551–558.

Marcia J. (2004). Why Erickson? In K. Hoover (Ed.), *Future of identity* (pp. 43–60). New York: Lexington Books.

McAdams, D. P. (1985). *Power, intimacy, and the life story: Personological inquiries into identity*. New York: Guilford.

McAdams, D. P. (1996). Personality, modernity, and the storied self: A contemporary framework for studying persons. *Psychological Inquiry, 7*(4), 295–321.

McAdams, D. P. (2001). Psychology of life stories. *Review of General Psychology, 5*(2) 100–122.

McAdams, D. P. (2006). *The redemptive self: Stories Americans live by*. New York: Oxford University Press.

McAdams, D. P. (2008). Personal narratives and the life story. In O. John, R. Robins, & L. Pervin (Eds.), *Handbook of personality: Theory and research* (3rd ed., pp. 242–262). New York: Guilford Press.

McAdams, D. P. (2011). Narrative identity. In S. J. Schwartz et al. (Eds.), *Handbook of identity theory and research* (pp. 99–115). New York, NY: Springer Science + Business Media.

McAdams, D. P., & Pals, J. L. (2006). A new big five: Fundamental principles for an integrative science of personality. *American Psychologist, 61*(3), 204–217.

McAdams, D. P., Reynolds, J., Lewis, M., Patten, A. H., & Bowman, P. J. (2001). When bad things turn good and good things turn bad: Sequences of redemption and contamination in life narrative and their relation to psychosocial adaptation in midlife adults and in students. *Personality and Social Psychology Bulletin, 27*(4), 474–485.

McLean, K. C. (2008). The emergence of narrative identity. *Social and Personality Psychology Compass, 2*, 1685–1702.

McLean, K. C., & Breen, A. V. (2009). Processes and content of narrative identity development in adolescence: Gender and well-being. *Developmental Psychology, 45*(3), 702–710.

McLean, K. C., & Mansfield, C. D. (2010). To reason or not to reason: Is autobiographical reasoning always beneficial? *New Directions for Child and Adolescent Development, 131*, 85–97.

McLean, K. C., & Pasupathi, M. (2006). Collaborative narration of the past and extraversion. *Journal of Research in Personality, 40*(6), 1219–1231.

McLean, K. C., & Pasupathi, M. (2011). Old, new, borrowed, blue? The emergence and retention of personal meaning in autobiographical storytelling. *Journal of Personality, 79*(1), 135–163.

McLean, K. C., Pasupathi, M., & Pals, J. L. (2007). Selves creating stories creating selves: A process model of self-development. *Personality and Social Psychology Review, 11*(3), 262–278.

McLean, K. C., & Thorne, A. (2003). Late adolescents' self-defining memories about relationships. *Developmental Psychology, 39*, 635–645.

National Advisory Mental Health Council Behavioral Science Workgroup. (2000). *Translating behavioral science into action*. (No. NIH 00–4699). Bethesda, MD: National Institute of Mental Health.

Parry, A., & Doan, R. E. (1994). *Story re-visions: Narrative therapy in the post-modern world*. New York: Guilford Press.

Raffard, S., D'Argembeau, A., Lardi, C., Bayard, S., Boulenger, J., & Van Der Linden, M. (2009). Exploring self-defining memories in schizophrenia. *Memory, 17*(1), 26–38.

Shoda, Y., Wilson, N. L., Chen, J., Gilmore, A. K., & Smith, R. E. (2013). Cognitive-affective processing system analysis of intra-individual dynamics in collaborative therapeutic assessment: Translating basic theory and research into clinical applications. *Journal of Personality, 81*(6), 554–568.

Siegel, P., & Demorest, A. (2010). Affective scripts: A systematic case study of change in psychotherapy. *Psychotherapy Research, 20*(4), 369–387.

Siegel, P. F., Sammons, M., & Dahl, H. (2002). FRAMES: The method in action and the assessment of its reliability. *Psychotherapy Research, 12*(1), 59–77.

Singer, J. A. (2013). Lost in translation? Find the person in the emerging paradigm of clinical science: Introduction to a special issue on personality and psychotherapy. *Journal of Personality, 81*(6), 511–514.

Singer, J. A., & Blagov, P. S. (2002). *Classification system and scoring manual for self-defining autobiographical memories*. Department of Psychology, Connecticut College, New London, CT.

Singer, J. A., Blagov, P., Berry, M., & Oost, K. M. (2013). Self-defining memories, scripts, and the life story: Narrative identity in personality and psychotherapy. *Journal of Personality, 81*(6), 569–582.

Singer, J. A., & Bonalume, L. (2010). Autobiographical memory narratives in psychotherapy: A coding system applied to the case of Cynthia. *Pragmatic Case Studies in Psychotherapy, 6*(3), 134–188 [Target Article for Issue].

Singer, J. A., & Salovey, P. (1993). *The remembered self: Emotion, memory, and personality*. New York: Free Press.

Strauman, T. J., Goetz, E. L., Detloff, A. M., MacDuffie, K. E., Zaunmüller, L., & Lutz, W. (2013). Self-Regulation and mechanisms of action in psychotherapy: A theory-based translational perspective, *Journal of Personality, 81*(6), 542–553.

Sutherland, K., & Bryant, R. A. (2005). Self-defining memories in post-traumatic stress disorder. *British Journal of Clinical Psychology, 44*(4), 591–598.

Sutin, A. R., & Robins, R. W. (2005). Continuity and correlates of emotions and motives in self-defining memories. *Journal of Personality, 73*(3), 793–824.

Thomsen, D. K., Olesen, M. H., Schnieber, A., Jensen, T., & Tønnesvang, J. (2012). What characterizes life story memories? A diary study of freshmen's first term. *Consciousness and Cognition. 21*, 366–382.

Thorne, A., & McLean, K. (2001). *Manual for coding events in self-defining memories*. University of California, Santa Cruz.

Thorne, A., McLean, K. C., & Lawrence, A. M. (2004). When remembering is not enough: Reflecting on self-defining memories in late adolescence. *Journal of Personality, 72*(3), 513–541.

Tomkins, S. S. (1979). Script theory: Differential magnification of affects. *Nebraska Symposium on Motivation, 26*, 201–236.

Tomkins, S. S. (1987). Script theory. In J. Aronoff, A. I. Rabin, & R. A. Zucker (Eds.), *The emergence of personality* (pp. 147–216). New York: Springer.

Tzemou, E., & Birchwood, M. (2007). A prospective study of dysfunctional thinking and the regulation of negative intrusive memories in bipolar 1 disorder: Implications for affect regulation theory. *Psychological Medicine, 37*, 689–698.

Waterman, A. S. (1993). Developmental perspectives on identity formation from adolescence to adulthood. In J. E. Marcia, A. S. Waterman, D. R. Matteson, S. L. Archer, & J. L. Orlofsky (Eds.), *Ego identity: A handbook for psychosocial research* (pp. 42–68). New York: Springer-Verlag.

White, M., & Epston, D. (1990). *Narrative means to therapeutic ends*. New York: W. W. Norton.

Weinberger, D. A. (1997). Distress and self-restraint as measures of adjustment across the life span: Conformity factor analysis in clinical and nonclinical samples. *Psychological Assessment, 9*(2), 132–135.

Williams, J. G., Barnhofer, T., Crane, C., Herman, D., Raes, F., Watkins, E., & Dalgleish, T. (2007). Autobiographical memory specificity and emotional disorder. *Psychological Bulletin, 133*(1), 122–148.

CHAPTER 23

Youths' Constructions of Meanings About Experiences with Political Conflict: Implications for Processes of Identity Development

Cecilia Wainryb *and* Holly Recchia

Abstract

This chapter outlines distinct ways in which political conflict may become associated with identity construction. In the context of politically framed events involving violence and injustice, youth must grapple with the meanings of these experiences while protecting themselves from some of their devastating implications. Their varied attempts at meaning-making can thus be viewed as understandable responses to the threats associated with these experiences and as being adaptive in light of the unique circumstances afforded by specific sociopolitical features. Also important, youths' ways of grappling with war experiences implicate identity work, with unique consequences for their enduring understandings of themselves. The authors' analysis suggests that, in grappling with these experiences, youths may initiate identity pathways that, while protective in the short-term, can undermine identity development in the long run. Thus, thinking about identity processes in relation to how youths make sense of their war experiences can illuminate the developmental sequelae of political conflict.

Key Words: identity development, political conflict, war, narrative, risk and resilience

For many youth growing up in the midst of war or political conflict, experiences with violence and injustice are an everyday reality. Hundreds of thousands of adolescents around the world witness acts of violence and discrimination and endure the threat of violence against members of their communities and their families; others may themselves participate in various forms of violence and armed struggle. Understandably, given the danger and fear implicated in war and violence exposure, research to date has primarily been based on a trauma model that has focused on the negative psychosocial impact of such events, whereas less attention has been devoted to investigating other developmental sequelae of such experiences. In general, this body of research has identified connections between adolescents' exposure to political violence and a variety of psychological outcomes characteristic of post-traumatic stress disorder (PTSD) symptomatology including feelings of distress, anxiety, and arousal, as well as avoidance and numbing (for comprehensive reviews, see Barber & Schluterman, 2009; Barenbaum, Ruchkin, & Schwab-Stone, 2004; Betancourt & Khan, 2008).

Nevertheless, research has also demonstrated that the negative psychosocial impact of political conflict is not inevitable. Indeed, although some researchers have posited a "dose–response" relation between exposure to political violence and psychological maladjustment (e.g., Jones & Kafetsios, 2005), many studies have failed to reveal such a pattern of association (Barber & Schluterman, 2009). For this reason, considerable effort has been devoted to identifying the factors accounting for variability in youths' responses; this effort, in turn, led to the critical recognition that the psychological impact of war-related events is significantly moderated by the subjective meanings that individuals attach

369

to those experiences (e.g., Ozer, Best, Lipsey, & Weiss, 2003). Moreover, and especially germane to identity-relevant processes, many researchers have moved away from conceptions of youth as passive victims of war-related events, instead acknowledging youths' active role as agents who strive to make sense of their experiences. As a consequence, youths' own understandings of their experiences with political conflict have been increasingly considered in studies examining the impact of war-related events—a shift in focus that opened the door to examining the relations between political conflict and identity development.

Within the trauma literature, researchers have noted that experiences of violence and injustice not only have the potential to be highly distressing, but can also lead individuals to question their fundamental assumptions about themselves and their place in the world (e.g., Janoff-Bulman, 1992; Ozer & Weiss, 2004). In this respect, the threat invoked by trauma often leads to preoccupation with questions surrounding how and why the events occurred: "Why are they doing this? Why is this happening to us?" More broadly, research has shown that negative emotional experiences that violate expectations are especially likely to initiate an active search for meaning (McLean & Pasupathi, 2012). All of this implies that exposure to political violence and injustice may exert prospective effects on youths' understandings of themselves and identity development.

As has been amply illustrated in a number of chapters in this volume, as well as in previous discussions (e.g., Hammack, 2008; 2010; McLean & Pasupathi, 2012), the study of identity has been characterized by epistemological and methodological diversity. To date, the most common framework for examining identity development in the context of war and political conflict has focused on the construction of polarized collective identities emerging out of oppositional group processes. This research, which has proceeded from social-identity theory (Tajfel & Turner, 1979) and taken a group processes perspective (e.g., Bar-Tal, 2007; Rouhana & Bar-Tal, 1998), has effectively demonstrated that political conflict can significantly shape identity processes while also pointing to the complex mixture of risks and benefits associated with this particular form of identity. However, as we explain later, polarized collective identities appear to be especially likely to arise in the context of intractable conflicts that are historically based and rooted in a competition for territorial control or political recognition (Bar-Tal, 2007). But political conflicts around the world vary widely in their defining features, presenting different types of threats and distinct affordances. Importantly, also, there is evidence suggesting that adolescents' subjective responses to war depend on the unique features of the political conflict within which they are embedded, as well as on youths' specific positioning within that conflict (e.g., Muldoon, Cassidy, & McCullough, 2009; Straker, Mendelsohn, Moosa, & Tudin, 1996). Research has also shown that youth make sense of their experiences with political conflicts in widely different ways (Barber, 2009; Wainryb & Pasupathi, 2010).

Inasmuch as grappling with everyday experiences can be seen as having implications for identity formation, it is likely that youths' different forms of meaning-making initiate distinct pathways for identity construction. We thus propose that understanding the effects of political violence on identity development may require a broader framework, one that goes beyond the notion of collective identities and examines the multiplicity of forms of identity construction that arise in the midst of different types of conflicts. In this chapter, we take a developmental perspective (e.g., McLean & Pasupathi, 2012) and focus on youths' individual engagement with their social and political environment and the varied identity-relevant meanings they construct about these experiences. In the following sections, we outline some of the distinct ways in which political conflict may become associated with identity construction and discuss how each may be understandable and even adaptive in light of the circumstances in which they are formed but that, in the longer term, may nevertheless pose developmental risks.

Us Versus Them: The Construction of Polarized Collective Identities

Individuals typically see themselves as defined in multiple ways by their social commitments and group memberships; each of these various social identities can be personally significant and provide a framework for making sense of experiences, depending on the context (Sen, 2006). However, in the context of war, collective identities that distinguish between groups in conflict (e.g., Palestinians and Israelis; Catholics and Protestants) tend to become unusually self-definitional, partly because they are institutionalized and actively propagated as societies engage in special efforts to maintain them (Bar-Tal, 2007; Sen, 2006). Tajfel and Turner's

(1979) social identity theory has provided a framework for understanding how the salience of such social identities can contribute to the development of ingroup bias. Specifically, they theorized that once group memberships are formed, the very act of categorizing oneself as a member of a group is linked to efforts to achieve positive ingroup distinctiveness. Thus, especially under some circumstances (i.e., when individuals strongly identify with an ingroup and the context provides opportunities for group comparison), group members tend to discriminate in favor of the ingroup and develop relatively positive ingroup perceptions.

In line with this theory, but more specific to the context of political conflict, Bar-Tal (2000) has outlined a set of societal beliefs that tend to be particularly characteristic of groups that are locked in intractable conflict and that ultimately lead to polarized collective identities. These include a belief in the justness of one's ingroup goals along with a simultaneous negation or delegitimization of the outgroup's perspective, as well as a positive collective self-image (e.g., as courageous, fair, and humane) that is juxtaposed against a negative view of the outgroup. As group-based identities become increasingly salient as a result of these processes, a sense of patriotism and unity with one's ingroup also contribute to social cohesiveness. Bar-Tal (2007) also emphasized that this ethos of conflict and the ensuing polarized patterns of identity development may be particularly likely to emerge in the context of historically grounded intractable conflicts. Although acknowledging that each conflict has its unique context, contents, and characteristics, Bar-Tal suggested that intractable historical conflicts share some common dynamics inasmuch as they are not only protracted but are often perceived by all parties as irresolvable and as central to their existence. Historically intractable conflicts also tend to reach beyond the political sphere and touch on many aspects of public and cultural life, coloring the construction of history, art, and other forms of public and ideological discourse. Such conditions support the construction and maintenance of polarized collective identities, which in turn serve as a coherent means for coping with and giving meaning to the unique challenges posed by this type of conflict.

Although this framework was originally posited to operate at the level of the group, researchers (e.g., Daiute, 2010; Hammack, 2011) have recognized that youth do not passively reproduce the ethos of conflict propagated in their cultures, but rather engage with and selectively appropriate aspects of the polarized societal discourse as they strive to make sense of events in which they and members of their families and communities become the targets of violence and injustice. It is noteworthy, however, that in spite of youths' capacity to contest and question their societies' perspectives on conflict, their interpretations of their own experiences tend to replicate, to a considerable extent, the predominant polarized societal discourse, thus underscoring the degree to which the realities of political violence place constraints on agency.

To illustrate, consider the following two excerpts from interviews of Jewish-Israeli and Palestinian youth (respectively), conducted in the context of their participation in an intergroup contact program (from Hammack, 2011):

> I think the first thing, they should stop the terrorist attacks against us. The whole thing started because of the terrorist acts against us.... They actually started it. They fired first. They were the first to use suicide bombers.... Of course, I think that I'm right—that my country's right. Everybody thinks that his country's right. Let's start from the first thing [Palestinian youth participating in the program] say, when they say, "I am from Palestine." I mean, there is no such country named Palestine. You can check the UN. There is no country written in the UN notebook called Palestine! There is such country called Israel. So he can say, "I'm a Palestinian from Israel." But when you say, "Hi. I'm from Palestine," "Jerusalem, Palestine," or something, it hurts the people that are from Israel and are from Jerusalem.... This is the problem: they don't have a country, and they feel like they have it. And they're speaking like there is no Israel! (pp. 135–136)

> We don't have anything. We don't have zoos, parks, nothing.... And it's a terrible life. It's like a jail. You can't do anything. Even in jail, people don't worry about their food. But us, we're worried about our food, how we're going to drink water. The Israelis control everything in our lives.... And now, the new, what's called the new separation wall, makes a big difference. Smaller jail. Every time, smaller and smaller. They're trying to cage us in. Until we just disappear.... [On discussing his motivations to participate in intergroup contact] I want to show all the people that Palestinians are suffering. The Israelis occupied our land. They don't have any rights, no human rights. They use all the ways to torture us. Plus, freedom fighters are not terrorists because they are fighting for the country, and we don't have

an army. I [want] to show all the people, Israelis, Americans, Jews, any nationality, I want to show them all what Palestinians are actually going through, how much we suffer.... I feel that I'm going to explode... I don't know, it makes me angry... would kill any Israeli, I don't care. Being Palestinian, and living the Palestinian life, going through hundreds of checkpoints, getting beaten by soldiers. (pp. 190–192, 195)

Both of these examples illustrate the ways in which youth may draw on societal discourses about war to make sense of their own experiences of political conflict and thus inform their understandings of themselves and others. Both narratives reflect many of the societal beliefs that Bar-Tal describes as characteristic of intractable conflict. In the case of the Jewish-Israeli youth, his emotional and cognitive experiences in the context of the intergroup contact program are colored by his beliefs that Israel has a unique legal and political status that Palestine does not. In turn, the Palestinian adolescent interprets the actions of Israelis as maliciously aimed at "[caging] us in" and "[torturing] us," evoking powerful reactions of anger and indignation. When considered in juxtaposition to each other, the mutual exclusivity of these two viewpoints on the Israeli–Palestinian conflict is apparent. In each case, we see the delegitimization of outgroup members' goals and perspectives that serve to highlight the unique validity of the ingroup position, as well as negative stereotyping of the outgroup.

Such group-based ideological commitments may serve psychologically protective functions for youth who are faced with the grim realities of armed conflict. Indeed, past research has revealed that youth who are exposed to armed conflict may experience less distress when they are able to construct coherent meanings about political violence through the lens of their cultural belief systems. For example, Punamaki (1996) demonstrated that, among Jewish-Israeli youth, patriotism and ideological commitment (i.e., a belief in the justifiability of war and a readiness to participate in it) attenuated the association between war experiences and adolescents' anxiety and depression. She argued that teens' ability to find meaning in war-related events and incorporate them into their life experiences served to mitigate the negative consequences of this exposure. Kostelny and Garbarino (1994) also revealed similar findings for Palestinian youth and noted that the buffering effects of ideological commitments appeared to be uniquely operative during adolescence (rather than earlier in childhood), when identity-relevant processes become increasingly salient to youths' understandings of their experiences.

In addition to serving psychologically protective functions for individuals, the construction of an ethos of conflict that uniquely legitimizes the aims of one's ingroup serves important functions for societies at war by justifying their conflict actions and promoting ingroup solidarity and patriotism (Bar-Tal, 2007). Related to this, Hammack (2010; 2011) has argued that the construction of polarized identities can undergird efforts to protect collective rights in the face of injustices. For example, the salience of Palestinian identities may serve as a tool to support the struggle for independence. From this standpoint, political conflict is not viewed as a wholly negative phenomenon but rather as a means whereby oppressed or marginalized groups can achieve social change. Indeed, the *identity politics* movement is premised on the importance of salient minority identities (e.g., as women, ethnic minorities) in supporting efforts to achieve equality with dominant groups (Taylor, 1994).

In his analysis of the narratives of Palestinian youth, Barber (2009) provided an illustration of the constructive processes underlying these patterns by demonstrating the ways in which Palestinian adolescents tie their experiences of conflict to identity-relevant meaning systems and, indeed, derive a sense of competence and growth from their involvement in these events. In this way, his work highlights how the construction of polarized identities can undergird efforts to protect one's collective rights in the face of perceived injustices (Hammack, 2011). Consider the following example from an adolescent Palestinian boy, reporting on his experiences during the first intifada (Barber, 2009):

> My emotions took me. Where? I didn't know. I just wanted to fight and help end our suffering. We wanted this occupation to end. I can't describe, believe me, I just can't describe what a wonderful feeling it was to share with my people in the struggle against the occupation. (p. 299)

This narrative makes evident that, for this youth, his experiences of political conflict are tightly tied to his sense of collective identity and his desire to address perceived injustices against his people. Barber and Olsen (2009) revealed that activism was uniquely related to political engagement, volunteerism, and social initiative for Palestinian boys. In this sense, deriving a sense of meaning from experiences of political conflict may protect youth against the feelings of powerlessness and lack of control that may occur as a result of *failing* to find meaning in war. Indeed, for Palestinian (but not Israeli) youth, Slone (2009) found that greater exposure to violence was associated with *less* distress. Hammack (2010) speculated that identity-relevant processes may partially account for this pattern inasmuch as resistance-based meaning systems may act as a buffer, particularly for Palestinian adolescents.

Despite these individual- and societal-level benefits of youths' tendency to draw personally significant meanings from their experiences of political conflict, other research suggests that the construction of these meanings may also confer various forms of risk. Specifically, it has been noted that adaptive processes of identity development imply a certain fluidity that allows youth to maintain multifaceted and flexible self-views that can accommodate changing circumstances and experiences; in the long term, such flexible patterns of self-understanding are linked to both well-being and maturity (McAdams, 1993; Pals, 2006). For this reason, the construction of rigid collective identities that are bound up with experiences of political conflict may also pose risks for individual development. Bar-Tal's (2007) work highlights that these identities emerge as a consequence of societal beliefs that help to meet the individual and collective challenges posed by political conflict. However, to the extent that these identities become reified, they might eventually become straightjackets that outlive their usefulness (Appiah, 1994). For example, although the identity-relevant meaning systems that characterize the experience of some Palestinian youth may serve an important function by supporting struggle aimed at achieving political goals and providing a buffer against psychological distress, it is possible that they may also interfere with the development of broader and more flexible notions of self that are not so fundamentally bound up with the negatively interdependent collective identities characteristic of intractable conflict.

In addition to these individual-level psychological risks, it is widely recognized that the construction of polarized identities in the context of armed conflicts can serve as important barriers to peacemaking and may serve to perpetuate cycles of violence. Specifically, once constructed, polarized identities tend to maintain, reproduce, and even exacerbate the ethos of conflict that led to them in the first place (Bar-Tal, 2007). It is not difficult to see why; in all of the narratives in this section, when youth speculate about the perspectives of outgroup members, they tend to be described as malicious, senseless, or misinformed. It is worth noting that these biases may also be manifested in more subtle ways. Specifically, Wainryb and Pasupathi (2010) have called attention to the stark imbalance in the extent to which youth exposed to violence represent the psychological experiences of ingroup and outgroup members. Specifically, in youths' accounts, the actions of ingroup members are made comprehensible via references to their legitimate goals, understandings, and emotions, whereas the perspectives of outgroup members are rarely elaborated. Although these patterns do not reflect blatant forms of dehumanization (i.e., depicting the other as subhuman or animalistic; Bandura, 2002), the tendency to overlook or invalidate outgroup members' internal experience nevertheless suggests a lack of empathy that may facilitate moral exclusion and the perpetration of violence against others, thereby perpetuating cycles of conflict (Wainryb & Pasupathi, 2010; see also Moshman, 2007).

Taken as a whole, a substantial body of research makes clear that the group-based ideological commitments that are constructed out of youths' experiences of armed conflict may serve as both benefits and burdens to societies (Hammack, 2010) and also constitute sources of both individual resilience and risk. Specifically, whereas polarized collective identities may undergird resistance and liberation for groups that feel oppressed and serve to protect youth against the distress associated with exposure to violence and injustice, they may also lead to Manichean processes that serve to justify violence against others and perpetuate conflict, in addition to constraining individual identity-related possibilities for youth.

In considering these associations between political conflict and identity development, researchers have typically focused on distinctions between the construction of collective ideologies that lead to polarized identities and, alternatively, the *absence* of such meanings. Yet we contend that there are at least two distinctive ways in which youth can neglect to draw meaning from their experiences of war: whereas some youth may engage in avoidant strategies that disrupt their ability to draw self-relevant meanings from their experiences, other adolescents may actively search for meaning in their experiences, but nevertheless fail to find it. Whereas the first strategy may be more psychologically protective in the short term, we suggest that each of these patterns may be linked to distinctive problematic developmental outcomes in the longer term. In the following sections, we discuss each in turn.

Diffused Identities: Political Violence and the Disruption of Youths' Meaning-Making Capacities

In the immediate aftermath of trauma, feelings of numbness and disconnection are a common psychological response to the extreme stress and terror that may accompany these events. In conjunction with these feelings, many victims of trauma also report engaging in other forms of avoidance, such as concrete behavioral strategies aimed at avoiding physical or psychological reminders of traumatic experiences or reliance on drugs or alcohol to cope with emotional reactions (e.g., Kerig, Bennett, Thompson, & Becker, 2012). Research has shown that such avoidant reactions and other symptoms of PTSD are relatively common among youth exposed to high levels of political violence, especially when youth struggle to make sense of political conflict or experience particularly distressing events, such as family disruptions or direct witnessing of injuries or deaths (Jones & Kafetsios, 2005; Qouta, Punamaki, & El Sarraj, 2008). Psychological avoidance may also be a relatively common coping strategy among youth combatants who have themselves perpetrated violence against others (Wainryb, 2011).

In the short-term, some of these forms of psychological avoidance may be adaptive as a mechanism for coping with the overwhelming emotions implicated by experiences with armed conflict (Jones, 2002; Punamaki, Muhammed, & Abdulrahman, 2004) and perhaps especially in circumstances in which youth themselves have engaged in actions that cause irreparable harm to another person (Betancourt et al., 2010; Klasen et al., 2010) and thus pose threats to their positive understandings of themselves (Wainryb, 2011). Indeed, the therapeutic literature makes clear that, particularly as long as youth continue to face threats to their security (e.g., refugee claimants whose cases have not yet been resolved; adolescents who continue to live under unstable conditions), youth may not feel an adequate sense of safety and trust to feel prepared to acknowledge and grapple with these aspects of their experiences (e.g., Rousseau, 2011; Rousseau & Measham, 2007).

However, psychological avoidance and numbing may be linked to problematic developmental consequences when these symptoms persist over time, manifest themselves in extreme ways (e.g., dissociation), or become generalized into an overall interpersonal style. More specifically, inasmuch as these tendencies may result in the blunting of normative emotional responses to events, when taken to the extreme, they may result in acquired (or "secondary") psychopathic characteristics, such as a lack of empathy and remorse (Kerig et al., 2012). In turn, this emotional detachment has been linked to problematic outcomes, such as increased risk-taking, aggression, and juvenile delinquency (Allwood, Bell, & Horan, 2011; Kerig & Becker, 2010; Punamaki, 2009).

Arguably, if such processes of psychological avoidance and numbing in response to war-related traumas become enduring and generalized, they may also result in profound disruptions in youths' identity development that may partially account for the problematic outcomes associated with these patterns. Under normal circumstances, as youth construct understandings of their experiences, their narrative accounts are rich in references to their motivations, cognitions, and emotions that imbue experiences with personally relevant meaning (Pasupathi & Wainryb, 2010); by the adolescent years, youth also show evidence of drawing connections between important events in their lives and their broader understandings of themselves and their relationships with others (McLean, Breen, & Fournier, 2010). Thus, youths' narrative accounts of their experiences are crucial contexts for the development of identity, inasmuch as they provide opportunities for reflecting on the psychological worlds of self and other and making sense of personally experienced events.

Importantly, it is these very processes that may be disrupted by patterns of emotional numbing and avoidance that occur in the aftermath of trauma. For example, consider the following two narratives. The first is told by a former Colombian child soldier who was asked to describe an experience in which his actions caused harm to another person (Wainryb, 2011; see also Recchia & Wainryb, 2011); the second is told by a Sudanese adolescent describing his experience in a refugee camp (Lustig, Weine, Saxe, & Beardslee, 2004):

> So that, so that day, well, when they ordered me to kill someone and so—we went, we left like, like three and—we got there and, and, we killed a cop and, then we left, well, the guerrilla told me to kill someone, so then they ordered me, then we got there and, and we killed a cop and then we returned to—returned to our camp. (p. 62)

This is about life in Kakuma [Refugee Camp], up until now. Also if you went outside and hung around, sometimes you'd get problems there. They would stalk you and kill you, and beat you, or take your things. Like this guy, the tall guy [referring to a current housemate], was coming from the Ethiopian market. He tried to cross a certain place. They stopped him and asked what he had in his pocket. He said, "I don't have anything." They beat him here [pointing to his head] with a gun, and then he ran away, but they left him because he didn't have anything. He was very small then. So all these things happened in Kakuma. There was insecurity. (p. 38)

What is most remarkable about these accounts is what is *absent*; both narratives are almost devoid of references to goals, emotions, and cognitions. In the first account, the narrator does not describe why he was ordered to kill the cop, why he obeyed, or how he felt about doing so. Similarly, in the second account, the motivations of all actors are sparsely described, and, despite the horrifying nature of these events, the emotional experience of the victim is utterly absent. More broadly, both narratives lack the coherence and self-relevant meanings that generally typify adolescents' accounts of personally significant events.

It is not clear the extent to which this numbing of agency results from a passive blunting of psychological experience or from youths' more active attempts to avoid exploring the psychological implications of their actions. Regardless, when generalized across events and persisting over time, this numbing of agency may become a source of serious concern with respect to identity development because it implies that these young people are unable to draw links between their own behavior and their sense of who they are. Consequently, these youth may also fail to draw clear connections between their past and present selves, as well as to project themselves into the future. Furthermore, even when these patterns of psychological and emotional numbing are circumscribed to youths' understandings of their war-related experiences, they may nevertheless obstruct in significant ways youths' abilities to reconcile such events with their broader understandings of themselves and thus interfere with the process of recovery. In these respects, such disruptions of a process fundamental to meaning-making and identity development may partially explain why emotional and psychological numbing are ultimately linked to dysregulated, aggressive behavior and poor psychosocial adjustment (Fonagy, 2003; Wainryb, Komolova, & Florsheim, 2010).

Taken together, these findings suggest that, for some youth, exposure to war-related violence may result in identity diffusion due to the ways in which trauma may interfere with the very processes undergirding the narrative construction of meaning. In the following section, we explore the implications for identity development when youth *do* engage in active attempts to make sense of their experiences in light of their self-understandings, but ultimately fail to do so.

Powerlessness in the Face of the Incomprehensibility of Political Conflict: Searching for but Failing to Find Meaning in War

When discussing meaning-making in the context of therapeutic trauma work, Rousseau and Measham (2007) stressed the importance of considering the absurdity that is often a central aspect of traumatic experiences: "reestablishing fragments of meaning must be anchored to a recognition of the radical doubt that these people have experienced when faced with a universe without any purpose" (p. 284). Indeed, by definition, traumatic events are those that shake the foundations of our belief systems about ourselves and our worlds (Janoff-Bulman, 1992; see also Bonanno, 2013). However, the extent to which experiences of armed conflict result in trauma depends on how youth interpret events in the context of their own goals, histories, and ideological commitments. As noted earlier, past research has revealed that when youth search for but fail to find personally significant meaning in their experiences of armed conflict, they are at particular risk for experiencing distress (Barber, 2009; Jones, 2002). This distress can be partially accounted for by the fact that, under these conditions, youth may experience war-related violence as frightening, jarring, and dissonant with the ways in which they perceive themselves. To illustrate, consider the following two examples of Bosnian youth describing their experiences of conflict (from Barber, 2009, and Weine, Klebic, Celik, & Bicic, 2009, respectively):

> I couldn't understand the situation the way it was. It was without any meaning. My parents didn't know and they didn't know what to tell me, why this was happening, what is going to become of us, are we going to be alive. (p. 296)

When the war started we were too young to understand what was going on and why, but not too young to feel pain, to be scared and hopeless. Maybe we were not too young to understand but we did not have anyone to teach us more about our neighbors, about history, about who we are. My Serbian classmates, kids that I grew up with, were carrying weapons. In one day they became complete strangers. In some ways I became a stranger to myself, too. My life and the lives of my family members were in danger because of our names and religion. I never knew those things mattered, which means that I did not know many things about myself, too. (p. 269)

It is worth noting that the relative prevalence of such failures to find meaning in conflict might depend on the specific sociopolitical realities faced by youth in the context of particular conflicts. For example, in a comparative analysis, Barber (2009) demonstrated that, in contrast to Palestinian youth, it may be difficult for Bosnian youth to make sense of their conflict experiences in light of historical explanations or political commitments. Furthermore, Jones (2002) provided converging evidence of the psychological risks associated with youths' attempts to make sense of the Bosnian conflict. Her data revealed that youths' engagement with the conflict (i.e., attempting to understand why it took place, what it was about) was linked to lower psychological well-being among both Bosnian and Serbian youth. In interpreting these findings, she noted that both groups of youth felt alienated from politics and had few opportunities for meaningful participation in the conflict (e.g., via political activism); the families of both Serbian and Bosnian youth expressed a sense of powerlessness and insignificance in the face of conflict. Under these circumstances then, engagement with the conflict appears to be linked to a sense of threat and lack of control that results from attempting to come to grips with the apparent senseless and absurdity of their war-related experiences of violence and injustice; youth are engaged in questioning their previous assumptions about themselves and their worlds, but are arriving at few satisfying answers.

Both Barber (2009) and Jones (2002) underscored that perception of one's own helplessness may be a characteristic feature of this pattern of meaning-making. In her analysis of the narrative accounts of child soldiers, Wainryb (2011) observed a pattern among some youth combatants that seemed to reflect a similar sense of constrained agency. The following example is drawn from an interview with a sixteen-year-old boy (Wainryb, 2011):

> Well—once the comandante he ordered, he ordered me and another guy—to go kill a man in a plantation—because he had cows, all of that, he had cattle. So he ordered us to kill him because he didn't, he didn't give away any of the cows he had—so he ordered us to kill him. And we killed him. And we had to take him, we took him and buried him. We tied him up and we—and we killed him over there where all our compañeros were. [Interviewer: What else do you remember?] The comandante like—he ordered me to kill him and I was afraid and—he said to me that if I didn't kill him that—that they will kill me and so I had to do it—so I was all—all scared—thinking that they would kill me too. [Interviewer: And how old were you when that happened?] I was—I was about 9 years old. (p. 286)

Although this narrator does not elaborate fully on his own psychological experience, he nevertheless conveys a clear sense of coercion, fear, and diminished control. In contrast to the earlier examples, this pattern is particularly striking in that this adolescent was asked to describe an instance in which *he himself* engaged in a hurtful behavior.

We argue that the powerlessness that emerges from youths' failed attempts to make sense of their conflict experiences in light of their self-understandings and sense of agency may have important implications for identity development that are distinct from those described in relation to the avoidance of meaning making. To reiterate, earlier, we described a process whereby youths' experiences with violence can result in the disruption of narrative processes of identity development, in that youth did not consider the identity implications of their conflict experiences for their understandings of themselves. In contrast, the pattern described in the present section is such that youth *are* actively considering connections between their self-understandings and their conflict experiences, but failing to identify such connections. Consequently, this perceived disconnect may result in youths' experiences being characterized by a sense of passive victimhood and diminished control.

This pattern is likely to be particularly problematic when it is generalized into an overall interpretive style dominated by a sense of incomprehensibility, fear, and helplessness. In other words, although it may emerge from youths' experiences of political violence, for some adolescents it may become the lens through which they make sense of their everyday experiences. An example of this type of generalization is hinted at in the following account of a peer conflict, as narrated by a Bosnian adolescent (from Daiute, 2010):

> [A] boy from another class put a firecracker in my rucksack which was on my back. I didn't even notice that until other students started to laugh and move away from me. Then I realized that my books were burning, so I threw the rucksack onto the ground, and ran away because I was scared. I was very angry and scared because I didn't find it to be funny, but rather dangerous. The worst thing was that the other students either ran away or laughed; none of them defended me, nobody said anything to that boy. (p. 64)

If youth internalize a prevailing sense of themselves as victims of uncontrollable circumstances or the senseless aggressive or unjust actions of others, in the long-term, we argue that this interpretive style may interfere with an experiential ownership of their own choices and actions. For example, in the following account, an internally displaced Colombian adolescent describes an experience in which he harmed a peer (Wainryb & Pasupathi, 2010). Colombia has been disrupted by violent wars for more than fifty years, with guerrilla and paramilitary groups fighting against the government and against each other. As a result of the widespread and often random violence, approximately 2 million children have been forcibly displaced from their homes, relocating to slums on the outskirts of large cities that are themselves plagued by instability, violence, and poverty. Thus, despite substantial differences between the Bosnian and Colombian conflicts, the latter context may also be characterized by the sort of unpredictable and incomprehensible violence and injustice that resists the construction of coherent ideological meanings (from Wainryb & Pasupathi, 2008; see also Wainryb & Pasupathi, 2010):

> I remember a time when we were in the classroom and the teacher left. Then I tried to hurt one of my best friends with a rope that was hanging from the roof. I put it around his neck and started pulling. I don't know why I did it. Everybody saw that, and they called the principal... and she began to scold me and she told me that she might expel me from school. And then she told me that I was useless, and after that everybody avoided me and they made me feel like I don't belong in there. And so I felt really bad, I cried. (p. 178)

What is particularly salient in this account is the narrator's apparent conflation of victim and perpetrator roles. Although he describes (but is unable to explain) his own harmful actions against his friend, his account focuses on his own pain and humiliation at becoming the target of others' disapproval. When this relatively elaborated understanding of his own victimization is considered alongside the apparent incomprehensibility of his hurtful behavior, this narrative seems to suggest a uniquely impoverished understanding of his own capacity for choice and action. In the long term, then, it is possible that this sense of constraint may ultimately interfere with a sense of self-directedness and future orientation, underscoring a narrow self-focus and the selective blaming of others for conflict or its consequences. Partially in line with these speculations, McCouch (2009) found that, among Bosnian youth, a negative sense of the future explained the association between exposure to violence and later criminal activity. Nevertheless, it is important to note that, to date, almost no studies have delved into these particular questions; thus, more research is needed to test these claims.

In sum, when adolescents experience themselves as victims of incomprehensible acts of political violence and injustice, this may be associated with both short- and long-term psychological risks, including the potential for disrupted trajectories of identity development. Yet simultaneously, it may also be the case that this pattern of *failing* to make sense of experiences of political conflict may have the consequence of circumventing some of the problematic implications for identity development that may result when youth do draw connections between their conflict experiences and their understandings of themselves.

In the following section, we introduce an alternative pathway that may characterize the experiences of youth who observe or become victims of systematic and deliberate violence that comes from *within* their own society (e.g., by their own government). We propose that, under these circumstances, rather than disrupting the construction of meaning from their experiences, political violence may challenge youths' understandings of their societies in ways that serve to degrade their collective ideological commitments.

Systemic Violence from Within: Political Conflict and the Abandonment of Collective Identities

In this section, we wish to raise the possibility that, under some circumstances, rather than increasing the salience of collective identities, war-related violence and injustice may result in a sense of social fragmentation and disillusionment that is essentially the opposite of the processes articulated earlier. This may be particularly likely to occur when governments and societal institutions are viewed as turning against their own citizens, as in the instances of state-sponsored terrorism, abductions, and torture that characterized the conflicts in 1970s Argentina and Pinochet-era Chile, as well as other Latin American countries. Although in these sociopolitical contexts, various groups of citizens (e.g., left wing activists) may potentially develop collective identities in opposition to repressive forces in their societies, youths' experiences of organized and calculated terror and violence at the hands of their own governments may also challenge their previously constructed meanings about their own societies. Although no research has directly examined this issue, Latin American scholars writing in the aftermath of these conflicts describe sociological and psychological trends that are suggestive of such a pattern (e.g., Barrero-Cuellar, 2011; Berezin, 1998).

We can only speculate about how this disintegration of solidarity and collective meanings may influence patterns of identity development. It may result in a sort of fatalism whereby youth conclude that nothing can be trusted and that meaningful action is not possible; in this respect, this type of violence may result in a process similar to that described earlier for youth who search for and fail to find meaning in their war-related experiences. Alternatively, it might lead to a form of "everyone for himself" detachment that works against a sense of ingroup solidarity. Indeed, similar theoretical propositions have been made with respect to children and adolescents exposed to community violence (Arsenio & Gold, 2006) and war-related violence (Punamaki, 2009). Specifically, these authors have suggested that exposure to violence and injustice may lead youth to view social relationships as characterized by a lack of caring and by coercion, to perceive that opportunities are limited by systemic inequalities, and to suspect that others are not willing or capable of protecting them from such harm or unfairness. Under these circumstances, youth are likely to cease thinking of social cohesion and justice-oriented action as organizing features of their daily interactions, but rather view power and domination as more central concerns for understanding and functioning in their world (Wainryb & Recchia, 2013). As a consequence, then, it seems possible that a generalized sense of mistrust in social systems and institutions may be constructed out of such experiences. For this reason, it is also plausible that these processes may result in behaviors reflecting a disregard for laws and institutions, including bribery and revenge-based actions (e.g., "taking the law into your own hands").

Again, we reiterate that these propositions are all speculative and remain to be tested empirically. Nevertheless, these possibilities suggest that youth may draw connections between their war-related experiences and understandings of self that are not premised on polarized distinctions between ingroups and outgroups. In the following section, we discuss another way political conflict may impact youths' understandings of themselves. Specifically, we suggest that youths' self-understandings may become encapsulated by their experiences in war, such that these experiences become self-definitional and preclude alternative identity-related possibilities.

Essentialized Identities: Becoming Defined by Experiences of War

As noted earlier, youth who become involved in political conflict as combatants are faced with particularly salient challenges to their views of themselves (see also Wainryb & Kerig, 2013). Certainly, being victimized by another person or group of people can lead adolescents to question their basic sense of trust in their own worthiness (Janoff-Bulman, 1992). However, adolescents who have engaged in violent or unjust acts against others are faced with the unique difficulty of reconciling their own hurtful behavior with their understandings of themselves as people who are capable of doing good as well as harm. When these acts result in harms that are largely irreparable, such as the death or serious injury of another person, these psychological conflicts may be particularly devastating. Under these circumstances, some youth may engage in avoidant strategies, such as emotional and psychological numbing, that protect them from considering the implications of their actions for their understandings of themselves. However, inasmuch as youth *do* engage in efforts to reconcile their actions with their self-understandings, this process may have especially profound implications for adolescents' understandings of themselves. Consider the following example of a narrative told by a former youth combatant in Colombia (from Wainryb, 2011):

> So the day that I hurt a person was the day that they killed my cousins. We were fighting the Autodefensas

Campesinas, and in the battle three of my cousins died. That day we captured—we killed 25 paracos [members of the paramilitary], we captured 10, and the comandante's order was to dismember them and to send the pieces to each of their families. And that day was when—from the rage of having seen my cousins killed by those same people we had caught—I was so enraged that I started out by removing the fingers off a person with a power-saw, I cut the fingers off both hands, then an arm, I cut off the arm all around until I got to the shoulders, then I started out with the feet, I removed everything until I cut off his head, I took off his tongue, and I cut off the eyes, and I sent it all to his mom. That day I will never forget and I always carry this burden. Being here I remember it and sometimes I feel like crying for having done this to a person. And a few days later I thought about it and said to myself—how will be my death, will it be like that or how. (p. 289)

In this account, this youth describes a horrifying experience that is clearly linked to an ongoing sense of guilt and pain. Unlike the earlier example that reflected processes of psychological and emotional numbing, this boy is clearly engaged in trying to make sense of his previous behavior; his overwhelming rage at the death of his cousins is central to his explanation of his actions. In this respect, there is little that is self-protective about this account; he has come face to face with a dark and angry part of himself. Equally salient in his account is his inability to reconcile these actions with some alternative current and future self. He appears to be haunted by his actions in a way that suggests that they are inescapable, and even that they have some enduring and causal meaning in relation to his future self.

This account implies that this youth's interpretations of his experiences of conflict are linked to a highly negative view of himself. However, not all experiences of war may be construed in such negative ways. To the extent that youth develop crystallized understandings of themselves as defined by their conflict experiences, even positive essentialized self-views have the potential to interfere with adolescents' capacity to move beyond conflict and consider alternative future selves. These issues are articulated clearly by a former youth combatant in South Africa, in the period following the election of a democratic government in 1994 (from Langa & Eagle, 2008):

When we were fighting they [the community] used to respect us. They used to respect, he carries guns and he protects us [so] we can sleep well. You walk in the street they [the community] ask you: are you hungry? They will give you food. Are you okay? They will give you money, because they know you are protecting them. You see. Then after the violence each and every individual started to look at their own lives which are normal. I can understand but now we tend to be a laughter, we tend to be a joke. When you are passing by they say: "look at him—you know—look at him, he doesn't even have shoes." Shoes are torn up and whatsoever. He was running up and down and protecting; now you are a laughing thing, now when you pass by... you become what? You become an enemy of your own community, which you were protecting. (p. 167)

In some ways, this account is distinct from the instance presented earlier, in that this youth does not focus on being psychologically troubled by his conflict experiences and associates his former role as a combatant with a sense of masculinity and prestige. Indeed, it has been noted that such participatory combatant roles may provide marginalized youth with a potent source of self-efficacy and competence that they cannot easily hope to obtain via more usual routes in their communities (Perez-Sales, 2010; Langa & Eagle, 2008). Similar to Palestinian youth, "young lions" in South Africa were able to draw on politically relevant meaning systems (i.e., the need to act as agents of political change by struggling and defending their community against repressive security forces) to give meaning to their experiences. Nevertheless, in the postconflict period, the identities developed by these South African youth in the context of political conflict appeared to interfere with the development of alternative positive self-conceptions that are less bound up with experiences of war.

These problems are also compounded by the fact that many such youth have not developed the skills and qualifications that are crucial for success in the postwar period. For example, due to their military involvement, many leave school at an early age. Thus, they tend to lack access to the opportunities that could provide a route to meaningful roles and alternative self-understandings. In the case of South African youth, given high rates of unemployment, marginalization, and a sense of emasculation, some former combatants have experienced tumultuous and sometimes violent family relationships. Some youth also resorted to violent crime, explaining such involvement as a legitimate response to marginalization and exclusion (Gear, 2002; Langa & Eagle, 2008). Kostelny and Garbarino (1994) noted similar challenges among some Irish Republican Army (IRA) members in Northern Ireland, whose identities constructed in the context of conflict continued to contribute to the perpetuation of violence even in the postwar period. In both Northern Ireland and South Africa (as well as elsewhere), these problems have been exacerbated by the stigmatization of former combatants as deviant and dangerous individuals, which further limits their opportunities for meaningful participation in their communities (Gear, 2002; Harland, Barclay, & McNamee, 2006). Consider the following extract from an interview with a former Colombian youth combatant, in which he clearly conveys these impediments to developing more positive, alternative self-conceptions (from Perez-Sales, 2010):

> My profession is killing people. The only thing I know how to do is kill. Now, I am tired of that, I want a job. My family is happy that I've changed, but there is unemployment. My life has been horrible. I've had to kill and dismember...I want a quiet life now....I have children, but there is hunger, brother. There is no chance for those who want to reinsert themselves in the system here. Everyone wants to kill you...Marihuana is my only friend (laughing). (p. 409)

As noted earlier, past research reveals that adaptive processes of identity development are characterized by a flexibility that stands in contrast to the rigidified nature of these self-understandings. Thus, inasmuch as youths' identities become shackled to their war-related experiences, this may serve to limit growth, leading to lower well-being and maturity (McAdams, 1993; Pals, 2006).

Taken together, the examples in this section emphasize the psychological risks associated with youths' essentialized understandings of themselves in relation to their war-related experiences. In many circumstances, these identities are highly negative and are linked to a substantial degree of psychological distress. Nevertheless, even when these encapsulated identities are more positive, youth are faced with both psychological and practical barriers to the development of alternative self-conceptions, as well as their ability to flexibly project themselves into the future. In this respect, these identities may also be linked to the continuation of violence and delinquent behavior in the postwar period.

In the following section, we discuss one final way in which experiences of political conflict may impact processes of identity development, when youth exposed to conflict relocate to new societies as immigrants or refugees. Although the challenges facing these adolescents may overlap to some extent with the processes outlined in this section (in that discrimination against these youth may threaten their positive self-views and pose constraints to their self-development), their pathways are also unique, inasmuch as it becomes necessary for them to negotiate the tension between their extant identities and their efforts to adapt to a new culture.

Facing an Identity Dilemma: Negotiating Competing Collective Identities in the Aftermath of War

Similar to many war-affected youth who remain in their home countries, youth who relocate to a new society in response to persecution and threat may develop salient collective identities. This may in part be because a group's history of intimidation and discrimination may imbue that group's identity with a unique value that renders membership precious—thus, refugee groups may have a marked desire to retain parts of their cultural identifications in diaspora (Pasupathi & Wainryb, 2008). But, to a large extent, too, the salience of the collective identity is a result of external forces that are uniquely associated with refugee status because youths and families seeking refugee status are repeatedly required to conceive of and present themselves in terms of a single group identity in order to be protected and helped toward safety (Dummett, 2001). Therefore, to some extent, this collective identity may be forced on individuals who might not otherwise see it as central to them, inasmuch as they require legal protection.

At the same time, successful adaptation to the new country requires refugee youth to adopt new habits, attitudes, and alliances—some of which may conflict with the remnants of their former culture. To make things worse, in the midst of their efforts to negotiate between multiple collective identities, refugee youth often experience discrimination—not necessarily the type of discrimination addressed by legal institutions, but rather the more ambiguous interpersonal encounters, termed "racial microaggressions," that highlight a person's sense of him- or herself as a member of a particular group, often in negative ways (e.g., Sue, Capodilupo, Torino, Bucceri, Holder, Nadal, & Esquilin, 2007). These encounters, which may be more prevalent and insidious than legal discrimination in their impact on individuals, may push refugee youths into a denigrated and devalued group identity. Consider the following two examples of events described by Bosnian refugee youth, after immigrating to the United States (from Pasupathi & Wainryb, 2008):

> Well yeah. I mean, I remember one time, it was...there were these girls in class and I was like,

oh you know, they were saying like, "oh that's weird, because, you know, she's from a different country. She doesn't... and our American culture"... how um, how I–I can't like communicate with them and, how, you know, my parents don't drive, you know, a nice car...

I actually I have one more thing that happened at the college. With uh, but it was after the uh Trolley Square shooting [a mass shooting that occurred at a local mall and was deemed the responsibility of a youth from the refugee community]. I had class next morning and this girl that was sitting in front of me.... somebody was talking about the Trolley shooting and then um she said "well, yeah that's what will happen when you let the immigrants coming to this country." So that kinda, you know, I mean.... everybody is the same but she said "yeah, I don't care where he is from. That will happen when you let immigrants coming to this country."

Differential treatment on the basis of group membership is always intrinsically reductive inasmuch as in being discriminated against as a member of a particular group people are denied the complexity of their individual identities and are treated as simply "an X." The reductiveness and potential dangers of everyday discrimination may, however, be exaggerated for youths who are negotiating multiple identities. The contents of the experiences recounted in the narratives here pose a complex dilemma to refugee youth who are being told that they are incompetent at fitting in and a threat to society. In a group of people who might be expected to want to retain a sense of themselves as Bosnian but also construct a sense of themselves as American, these experiences make that duality problematic. They render that Bosnian identity a devalued one and also implicitly juxtapose it with the impossible, unattainable American identity. It is worth noting, too, that although these incidents may look like typical schoolchild unkindness, the explicit group-based devaluing may evoke greater distress for refugee youth who have a history of group-based discrimination and persecution (Pasupathi & Wainryb, 2008).

Research suggests that the well-being of refugee youth is most clearly promoted when they can hold and integrate multiple group affiliations (Berry, Phinney, Sam, & Vedder, 2006; Cameron, Rutland, Brown, & Douch, 2006). Such a process is often fraught with difficulties because youth must inevitably face conflicts between the set of identities related to their countries and cultures of origin and the new possibilities in the receiving country. Experiences of everyday discrimination may interfere further with the adaptive development of multiple collective identities, since the way refugee youth construct the meaning of such experiences may have implications for their ability to think of themselves in positive, multifaceted ways. Ultimately, the way youth resolve these issues may be important not only for their own individual well-being (Mahalingam, 2006; Scott & Scott, 1989), but also for dynamics between immigrant groups and other groups within society (Dummett, 2001).

Conclusion

The variety of meaning-making strategies described in this chapter draws attention to and illustrates the vast heterogeneity of youth experiences growing up in the midst of political conflict. We have argued that polarized collective identities are most likely to be constructed when youth are able to draw on personally relevant meaning systems to make sense of their experiences of violence and injustice; intractable conflicts may be particularly likely to provide the conditions that are conducive to developing such identities. In contrast, for youth who experience extreme stress and terror or who perpetrate violence themselves, especially when they fail to make sense of the conflict, we have proposed that processes of identity development may become diffused as a consequence of adolescents' reliance on psychological avoidance and numbing as a coping strategy. In turn, other youth who search for but fail to find personally relevant meaning from political violence may experience a sense of helplessness and lack of control; this pathway may be particularly likely in contexts when conflicts are more difficult to connect to historical or political meaning systems and perhaps also when youth lack access to meaningful ways of participating in conflict. Next, we speculated that when systemic violence comes from within youths' own societies and is directed by governments at their own citizens, for some youth, collective identities may be abandoned, resulting in a sense of social fragmentation and disillusionment. Subsequently, we argued that when youth combatants engage in efforts to reconcile their perpetration of irreparable harm with their self-understandings, this may result in the construction of essentialized identities that are bound up with youths' war-related experiences; this process may be compounded by a lack of meaningful opportunities for youth to develop more positive self-conceptions in the postwar period. Finally, we underscored the unique identity challenges faced by refugee youth as they attempt to adapt to life in a new society where they often become the victims of discrimination.

In the context of politically framed events involving diverse instantiations of hostility, aggression, and discrimination, youth arguably have the need to grapple with the meanings of these experiences while at the same time protecting themselves from some of the devastating implications of the violence and injustice they suffered and the violence that they may have themselves perpetrated. Each of the forms of meaning-making presented in this chapter can thus be thought of as an understandable response to the threats associated with these experiences and the complex needs they give rise to; each of them can be understood as being adaptive in light of the unique circumstances afforded by the specific sociopolitical features and also as posing unique developmental risks.

Importantly, also, each of these ways of grappling with experiences of political conflict (including those attempts at sidestepping or avoiding certain meanings) implicates identity work. In other words, each of the ways in which youths make sense of their experiences with political conflict is likely to have unique consequences for their enduring understandings of themselves. Indeed, it is often thought (e.g., Fivush, Habermas, Waters, & Zaman, 2011; McAdams, 1993) that identity creation relies on stories of an autobiographical nature—the kind of "life stories" that implicate active reflection on self-defining events from one's personal past and the drawing of explicit connections between one's past and current and future self. However, the propositions outlined in this chapter are premised on the assumption (see also Bamberg, 2007; McLean & Pasupathi, 2012) that youths also engage in identity exploration and construction via narration about less deep and momentous, more mundane, events. This is because the very act of grappling with what everyday events mean tends to shape the conclusions that youths draw about themselves and the kind of world they inhabit. Therefore, even if an account of being insulted by girls at school may not end up becoming the sort of self-defining episode that these youths might ultimately choose to include in their autobiographical life stories, such narration may nevertheless become integrally connected with their sense of who they are. So when an adolescent makes sense of disparate events in her everyday life by resorting to explanations or metaphors that invoke, as an example, a view of a righteous and self-sacrificing ingroup and a selfish and uncompromising outgroup, she is implicitly engaged in creating a certain type of identity, even if she isn't drawing explicit autobiographical connections (see also Pasupathi, this volume).

Also relevant to our proposition about the significant identity implications of meaning-making in this context is the broad understanding that grappling with the meaning of an experience is not something that happens at a single point in time. Rather, the storying of an experience can be—and often is—done over and over again and its meaning continues to be reframed within the context of a person's ongoing life. Youth are thus likely to revisit and rethink the meanings and implications of any one event at different times (see also Dekel & Bonanno, 2013; Pasupathi, 2013). And although, in general, the ways in which people initially narrate an event shape and constrain how they will remember and understand that event and what they will come to believe about themselves in relation to it, the retelling of experiences can also become an avenue for change (McAdams, 1993; Pasupathi, 2001).

In this respect, the extent to which each of these specific forms of meaning-making is problematic will depend in a large measure on their stability and generality. Stability refers to the extent to which any one way of making sense of experiences with political conflict or violence persists relatively unchanged over time or gives way to other ways of constructing themselves in the world. Thus we might worry less if, for example, avoidant or polarized forms of identity constructed in the context of ongoing conflict give way to more elaborated or balanced strategies once the political conflict has subsided than if they persist relatively unchanged over time. A related and equally important question refers to the extent to which the unique ways in which youths make sense of their experiences are circumscribed to their thinking about themselves (and others) around experiences of political violence or become more generalized to grappling with diverse and disparate experiences. It is plausible, for example, that some youth might be able to find ways of accommodating different views of themselves and might thus move relatively freely or flexibly between, for example, polarized or helpless and victimized constructions of themselves vis-à-vis conflicts of a political nature and more balanced or agentic ways of thinking of themselves in relation to conflicts of an interpersonal nature. For others, the ways in which they have constructed themselves in relation to situations of political violence may occlude or preclude other possible views of themselves both concurrently and over time—a problem that may be most marked for essentialized constructions of identity that become encapsulated within a narrow swath of experience.

In reference to victims of trauma, Rousseau and Measham (2007) have argued that the process of recovery tends to be characterized by the reestablishment of oscillation between different strategies for grappling and coping with traumatic events, whereas a continued and exclusive reliance on one strategy is seen as more problematic: "Gaining even the slightest ability to move back and forth between two opposing strategies is seen as a key moment in which an individual or group begins to emerge from a predominantly inward-looking state of stupor or disconnection or begins to contain a process previously characterized by being overwhelmed by uncontainable traumatic experiences" (p. 281; see also Bonanno, 2013). We suggest that this point also extends to the implications of these problematic forms of narrative construction for youths' identity development. Thus it may be crucial to support youths' ability to establish more balanced and less rigid understandings of themselves and to envision future selves that are connected to the personal past but are not unduly constrained by their own previous actions (see Perez-Sales, 2010; Wainryb, 2011).

In this respect, the narrative accounts that youth produce about their own experiences of political conflict may be not only a key to understanding their identity-relevant struggles, but also a context for putting things right again, precisely because it is in the process of constructing and reconstructing accounts of their experiences that a newer, perhaps more elaborated, balanced, or complex sense of identity may emerge. This process might ideally be accomplished via the creation of narrative accounts in conjunction with others, especially parents and other supportive adults, because it is through such joint narration that young people, especially, can garner new perspectives on actions and events, create different meanings, and change their initial understandings. But in contexts of ongoing political conflict and violence, and the often resulting processes of dislocation and displacement, adults are less likely to be available for eliciting or listening to their accounts or offering much perspective or containment. Furthermore, even when available, adults are quite likely to experience the conflict through a lens similar to that of their children (e.g., Rousseau & Jamil, 2010). Thus, the assistance these youths will require to successfully navigate this task may need to come as part of broader psychosocial interventions provided to them in the aftermath of conflict (see also Wainryb, 2011).

In general, the therapeutic literature (e.g., Blaustein & Kinniburgh, 2010; Briere & Lanktree, 2012) suggests that encouraging youths to recount their own experiences in ways that help them reconstruct the events and elaborate on their own emotions, goals, intentions, and thoughts might work against numbing and diffusion, provided that these explorations are conducted in a supportive context characterized by safety and trust. Similarly, strategies that encourage youth to remain open to reinterpreting the meaning of past experiences over time might be generally helpful for youth for whom certain experiences precipitated rigidified constructions of self. This might include encouraging youth to retell their stories in a way that helps them consider distortions and unexamined beliefs formed during a traumatic event not necessarily as wrong but as understandable reactions to overwhelming circumstances, and ultimately helps them to appreciate the complexity of events, to question negative assumptions about themselves, and to work toward accepting themselves as complex human beings. And, finally, in the context of encouraging youth to retell their stories in an effort to promote development, it may also be important to recognize the limits of redemptive storytelling (Breen & McLean, 2013; McAdams, 2006; Pals & McAdams, 2004). Indeed, encouraging youths to recount their experiences in ways that result in more elaborated, balanced, and growth-promoting identity forms should not necessarily entail encouraging them to transform their gruesome and deeply hurtful experiences into positive or redeeming ones because some events may never get completely "resolved." Therefore a more appropriate goal may be to help youths retell their stories in ways that release them from the grip of these events and allow them to integrate their past experiences with some broader possibilities for future action.

And yet, even as the distinct ways in which youth construct identity in the context of experiences with political conflict suggest somewhat distinct strategies for scaffolding growth, it is also important to consider that even very deliberate outside efforts at intervention specifically designed for addressing the identity-related consequences of youths' exposure to political conflict may be met with unique difficulties and challenges. At the very least, we emphasize that much more research is needed before we can fully understand the specific features that may be required of potential interventions geared at addressing the distinct identity-laden implications of exposure to political conflict. Indeed, the little extant research suggests that interventions with a decided intuitive appeal may not work as desired and may in fact produce undesirable results. For example, in his research on American intervention programs for Israeli and Palestinian youth that aim to transcend mutually polarized identities and promote, instead, the construction of a shared cosmopolitan identity, Hammack (2011) revealed that, for a substantial proportion of youth, participation in such programs was ultimately associated with an *accentuation* of polarized identities. In other words, despite their best efforts, his analysis implied that some interventions may actually result in identity change that is the opposite of that which is desired and anticipated. Similarly, ongoing research in our lab (Twali, Wainryb, & Pasupathi, in progress) suggests that, under specific conditions, encouraging youths who have been hurt by another to broaden their own view of themselves as victims (e.g., by considering the perspective of the person who hurt them) tends to actually reinforce the narrow self-view as victim, increase anger, and give rise to more negative views of the other and the relationship. Accordingly, in the absence of further research, and given the imperative to avoid doing harm, we urge extreme caution in translating this set of propositions into actual interventions.

In sum, in this chapter, we have proposed that thinking about identity processes conceived in relation to how youths variously make sense of their war-related experiences can help us better understand the developmental sequelae of political conflict. In many respects, the propositions we have outlined are consistent with recent scholarship that challenges the one-sided view of war-affected youths as helpless victims, replacing it with a view of young people as continuously engaged in making sense of the sociopolitical realities in which they participate (e.g., Barber, 2009; Boothby, Strang, & Wessells, 2006; Daiute, 2010; Franks, 2011; Hammack, 2011; Wessells, 2006). Critically, we also underscore that youths' capacity to make sense of their own experiences is not necessarily associated, exclusively and in an uncomplicated fashion, with optimal identity growth (Recchia & Wainryb, 2011; Wainryb, 2010; 2011). Rather, the analyses outlined in this chapter suggest that, in grappling with their war-related experiences, youths may initiate identity pathways that, although protective in the short term, can ultimately constrain and even undermine development in the long run (see also Hammack, 2011; Wainryb & Pasupathi, 2010).

References

Allwood, M., Bell, D., & Horan, J. (2011). Posttrauma numbing of fear, detachment, and arousal predict delinquent behaviors in early adolescence. *Journal of Clinical Child and Adolescent Psychology*, 40, 659–667.

Appiah, K. A. (1994). Identity, authenticity, survival: Multicultural societies and social reproduction. In A. Gutmann (Ed.), *Multiculturalism* (pp. 149–164). Princeton, NJ: Princeton University Press.

Arsenio, W. F., & Gold, J. (2006). The effects of social injustice and inequality on children's moral judgments and behavior: Towards a theoretical model. *Cognitive Development*, 21, 388–400.

Bamberg, M. (2007). Stories: Big or small. Why do we care? In M. Bamberg (Ed.), *Narrative: State of the art* (pp. 165–174). Amsterdam: John Benjamins.

Bandura, A. (2002). Selective disengagement in the exercise of moral agency. *Journal of Moral Education*, 31, 101–119.

Barber, B. K. (2009). Making sense and no sense of war: Issues of identity and meaning in adolescents' experience with political conflict. In B. K. Barber (Ed.), *Adolescents and war: How youth deal with political violence* (pp. 281–311). New York: Oxford University Press.

Barber, B. K., & Olsen, J. A. (2009). Positive and negative psychosocial functioning after political conflict: Examining adolescents of the first Palestinian Intifada. In B. K. Barber (Ed.), *Adolescents and war: How youth deal with political violence*. New York: Oxford University Press.

Barber, B. K., & Schluterman, J. M. (2009). Adolescents and political violence: A review of the empirical literature. In B. K. Barber (Ed.), *Adolescents and war: How youth deal with political violence*. New York: Oxford University Press.

Barrero-Cuellar, E. (2011). *Estética de lo atroz: Psicohistoria de la violencia política en Colombia*. Bogotá-Colombia: Ediciones Cátedra Libre.

Bar-Tal, D. (2000). *Shared beliefs in a society: Social psychological analysis*. Thousand Oaks, CA: Sage.

Bar-Tal, D. (2007). Sociopsychological foundations of intractable conflicts. *American Behavioral Scientist*, 50, 1430–1453.

Barenbaum, J., Ruchkin, V., & Schwab-Stone, M. (2004). The psychosocial aspects of children exposed to war: Practice and policy initiatives. *Journal of Child Psychology and Psychiatry*, 45, 41–62.

Berezin, A. (1998). *La oscuridad en los ojos: Ensayo psicoanalítico sobre la crueldad*. Rosario, Argentina: Homo Sapiens Ediciones.

Berry, J. W., Phinney, J. S., Sam, D. L., & Vedder, P. (2006). Immigrant youth: Acculturation, identity, and adaptation. *Applied Psychology: An International Review*, 55, 303–332.

Betancourt, T. S., Borisova, I. I., Williams, T. P., Brennan, R. T., Whitfield, T. H., de la Soudiere, M., Williamson, J., & Gilman, S. E. (2010). Sierra Leone's former child soldiers: A follow-up study of psychosocial adjustment and community reintegration, *Child Development*, 81, 1077–1095.

Betancourt, T. S., & Khan, K. T. (2008). The mental health of children affected by armed conflict: Protective processes and pathways to resilience. *International Review of Psychiatry*, 20(3), 317–328.

Blaustein, M., & Kinniburgh, K. (2010). *Treating traumatic stress in children and adolescents: How to foster resilience through attachment, self-regulation, and competency*. New York: Guilford.

Bonanno, G. A. (2013). Meaning making, adversity, and regulatory flexibility. *Memory*, 21, 150–156.

Boothby, N., Strang, A., & Wessells, M. (Eds.). (2006). *A world turned upside down: Social ecological approaches to children in war zones.* Bloomfield, CT: Kumarian Press.

Breen, A. V., & McLean, K. C. (2013). The intersection of personal and master narratives: Is redemption for everyone? Unpublished manuscript, University of Guelph.

Briere, J., & Lanktree, C. (2012). *Treating complex trauma in adolescents and young adults.* New York: Sage.

Cameron, L., Rutland, A., Brown, R., & Douch, R. (2006). Changing children's intergroup attitudes toward refugees: Testing different models of extended contact. *Child Development*, 77, 1208–1219.

Daiute, C. (2010). *Human development and political violence.* New York: Cambridge University Press.

Dekel, S., & Bonanno, G. A. (2013). Changes in trauma memory and patterns of posttraumatic stress. *Psychological Trauma: Theory, Research, Practice, and Policy*, 5, 26–34.

Dummett, M. (2001). *On immigration and refugees.* New York: Routledge.

Fivush, R., Habermas, T., Waters, T., & Zaman, W. (2011). The making of autobiographical memory: Intersections of culture, narratives and identity. *International Journal of Psychology*, 46, 321–345.

Fonagy, P. (2003). The developmental roots of violence in the failure of mentalization. In F. Pfafflin (Ed.), *Matter of security: The application of attachment theory to forensic psychiatry and psychotherapy* (pp. 13–56). Philadelphia: Jessica Kingsley.

Franks, B. (2011). Moving targets: A developmental framework for understanding children's changes following disasters. *Journal of Applied Developmental Psychology*, 32, 58–69.

Gear, S. (2002). *Wishing us away: Challenges facing ex-combatants in the 'new' South Africa.* Centre for the Study of Violence and Reconciliation, Violence and Transition Series, Vol. 8. Braamfontein, South Africa.

Hammack, P. L. (2008). Narrative and the cultural psychology of identity. *Personality and Social Psychology Review*, 12, 222–247.

Hammack, P. L. (2010). Identity as burden or benefit? Youth, historical narrative, and the legacy of political conflict. *Human Development*, 53, 173–201.

Hammack, P. L. (2011). *Narrative and the politics of identity: The cultural psychology of Israeli and Palestinian youth.* New York: Oxford University Press.

Harland, K., Barclay, L., & McNamee, D. (2006). RU right in the head? The development and dissemination of educational resources addressing positive mental and emotional health issues for adolescent males in Northern Ireland. *Journal of Men's Health and Gender*, 3, 204–209.

Janoff-Bulman, R. (1992). *Shattered assumptions: Towards a new psychology of trauma.* New York: Free Press.

Jones, L. (2002). Adolescent understandings of political violence and psychological wellbeing: A qualitative study from Boznia-Herzegovina. *Social Science and Medicine*, 55, 1351–1371.

Jones, L., & Kafetsios, K. (2005). Exposure to political violence and psychological well-being in Bosnian adolescents: A mixed method approach. *Clinical Child Psychology and Psychiatry* 10, 157–176.

Kerig, P. K., & Becker, S. P. (2010). From internalizing to externalizing: Theoretical models of the processes linking PTSD to juvenile delinquency. In S. J. Egan (Ed.), *Post-traumatic stress disorder: Causes, symptoms, and treatment* (pp. 33–78). Hauppauge, NY: Nova Science Publishers.

Kerig, P. K., Bennett, D. C., Thompson, M., & Becker, S. P. (2012). "Nothing really matters:" Emotional numbing as a link between trauma exposure and callousness in delinquent youth. *Journal of Traumatic Stress*, 25, 272–279.

Klasen, F., Oettingen, G., Daniels, J., Post, M., Hoyer, C., & Adam, H. (2010). Posttraumatic resilience in former Ugandan child soldiers. *Child Development*, 81, 1096–1113.

Kostelny, K., & Garbarino, J. (1994). Coping with the consequences of living in danger: The case of Palestinian children and youth. *International Journal of Behavioral Development* 17, 595–611.

Langa, M., & Eagle, G. (2008). The intractability of militarized masculinity: A case study of former Self-Defense Unit members in the Kathorus area, South Africa. *South African Journal of Psychology*, 38, 152–175.

Lustig, S., Weine, S., Saxe, G., & Beardslee, W. (2004). Testimonial psychotherapy for adolescent refugees: A case series. *Transcultural Psychiatry*, 41, 31–45.

Mahalingam, R. (2006). *Cultural psychology of immigrants.* Hillsdale, NJ: Lawrence Erlbaum.

McAdams, D. (1993). *The stories we live by: Personal myths and the making of the self.* New York: Guilford Press.

McAdams, D. (2006). *The redemptive self: Stories Americans live by.* New York: Oxford University Press.

McCouch, R. J. (2009). The effects of wartime violence on young Bosnians' postwar behaviors: Policy contours for the reconstruction period. In B. K. Barber (Ed.), *Adolescents and war: How youth deal with political violence* (pp. 177–204). New York: Oxford University Press.

McLean, K. C., Breen, A., & Fournier, M. (2010). Constructing the self in early, middle, and late adolescent boys: Narrative identity, individuation, and well-being. *Journal of Research on Adolescence*, 20, 166–187.

McLean, K. C., & Pasupathi, M. (2012). Processes of identity development: Where I am and how I got there. *Identity: An International Journal of Theory and Research*, 12, 8–28.

Moshman, D. (2007). Us and them: Identity and genocide. *Identity: An International Journal of Theory and Research*, 7, 115–135.

Muldoon, O. Cassidy, C., & McCullough, N. (2009). Young people's perceptions of political violence: The case of Northern Ireland. In B. K. Barber (Ed.), *Adolescents and war: How youth deal with political violence* (pp. 125–144). New York: Oxford University Press.

Ozer, E. J., Best, S. R., Lipsey, T. L., & Weiss, D. S. (2003). Predictors of posttraumatic stress disorder and symptoms in adults: A meta-analysis. *Psychological Bulletin*, 129, 52–73.

Ozer, E. J., & Weiss, D. S. (2004). Who develops posttraumatic stress disorder? *Current Directions in Psychological Science*, 13, 169–172.

Pals, J. (2006). Constructing the "springboard effect": Causal connections, self-making, and growth within the life story. In D. McAdams, R. Josselson, & A. Lieblich (Eds.), *Identity and story: Creating self in narrative* (pp. 175–199). Washington, DC: American Psychological Association.

Pals, J., & McAdams, D. (2004). The transformed self: A narrative understanding of posttraumatic growth. *Psychological Inquiry*, 15, 65–69.

Pasupathi, M. (2001). The social construction of the personal past and its implications for adult development. *Psychological Bulletin*, 127, 651–672.

Pasupathi, M. (2013). Making meaning for the good life. *Memory*, 21, 143–149.

Pasupathi, M., & Wainryb, C. (2008). *Collective identity and everyday discrimination among Bosnian refugee youth*. Paper delivered at the IPIA conference on "Migration, Rights and Identities." University of Utah.

Pasupathi, M., & Wainryb, C. (2010). On telling the whole story: Facts and interpretations in autobiographical memory narratives from childhood through mid-adolescence. *Developmental Psychology, 46*, 735–746.

Perez-Sales, P. (2010). Identity and trauma in adolescents within the context of political violence: A psychosocial and communitarian view. *Clinical Social Work Journal, 38*, 408–417.

Punamaki, R. L. (1996). Can ideological commitment protect children's psychosocial wellbeing in situations of political violence? *Child Development, 67*, 55–69.

Punamaki, R. L. (2009). War, military violence, and aggressive development: Child, family, and social preconditions. In B. K. Barber (Ed.), *Adolescents and war: How youth deal with political violence* (pp. 62–80). New York: Oxford University Press.

Punamaki, R. L., Muhammed, A., & Abdulrahman, H. (2004). Impact of traumatic events on coping strategies and their effectiveness among Kurdish children. *International Journal of Developmental Behavior, 28*, 59–70.

Qouta, S., Punamaki, R. L., & El Sarraj, E. (2008). Child development and family mental health in war and military violence: The Palestinian experience. *International Journal of Behavioral Development, 32*, 310–321.

Recchia, H., & Wainryb, C. (2011). Youths making sense of political conflict: Considering protective and maladaptive possibilities. *Human Development, 54*, 49–59.

Rouhana, N. N., & Bar-Tal, D. (1998). Psychological dynamics of intractable ethnonational conflicts: The Israeli-Palestinian case. *American Psychologist, 53*, 761–770.

Rousseau, C. (2011, March). *Trauma in children*. Paper presented at the Continuing Education Seminar for Mental Health Professionals, McGill University Division of Child Psychiatry, Montreal, QC, Canada.

Rousseau C., & Jamil, U. (2010). Muslim families understanding and reacting to "The War on Terror". *American Journal of Orthopsychiatry, 80*, 601–609.

Rousseau, C., & Measham, T. (2007). Posttraumatic suffering as a source of transformation: A clinical perspective. In L. Kirmayer, R. Lemelson, & M. Barad (Eds.), *Understanding trauma: Integrating biological, clinical, and cultural perspectives* (pp. 275–293). Cambridge: Cambridge University Press.

Scott, W. A., & Scott, R. (1989). *Adaptation of immigrants: Individual differences and determinants*. New York: Pergamon.

Sen, A. (2006). *Identity and violence: The illusion of destiny*. New York: Norton.

Slone, M. (2009). Growing up in Israel: Lessons on understanding the effects of political violence on children. In B. K. Barber (Ed.), *Adolescents and war: How youth deal with political violence* (pp. 81–104). New York: Oxford University Press.

Straker, G., Mendelson, M., Moosa, F., & Tudin, P. (1996). Violent political contexts and the emotional concerns of township youth. *Child Development, 67*, 46–54.

Sue, D., Capodilupo, C., Torino, G., Bucceri, J., Holder, A., Nadal, K., & Esquilin, M. (2007). Racial microaggressions in everyday life: Implications for clinical practice. *American Psychologist, 62*, 271–286.

Tajfel, H., & Turner, J. C. (1979). An integrative theory of intergroup conflict. In W. G. Austin & S. Worchel (Eds.), *The social psychology of intergroup relations* (pp. 33–47). Monterey, CA: Brooks-Cole.

Taylor, C. (1994). The politics of recognition. In A. Gutmann (Ed.), *Multiculturalism* (pp. 25–74). Princeton, NJ: Princeton University Press.

Twali, M., Wainryb, C., & Pasupathi, M. (in progress). *Implications of different ways of narrating harm*. Unpublished manuscript. University of Utah.

Wainryb, C. (2010). Resilience and risk: How teens experience their violent world, and what they learn—and lose—in the process. *Journal of Applied Developmental Psychology, 31*, 410–412.

Wainryb, C. (2011). "And so they ordered me to kill a person": Conceptualizing the impacts of child soldiering on the development of moral agency. *Human Development, 54*, 273–300.

Wainryb, C., & Kerig, P. K. (2013). The person and the social context: Future directions for research on the traumatic effects of child soldiering around the world. *Journal of Aggression, Maltreatment, Trauma, 22*, 1–9.

Wainryb, C., Komolova, M., & Florsheim, P. (2010). How violent youth offenders and typically-developing adolescents construct moral agency in narratives about doing harm. In K. C. McLean & M. Pasupathi (Eds.), *Narrative development in adolescence: Creating the storied self* (pp. 185–206). New York: Springer.

Wainryb, C., & Pasupathi, M. (2008). Developing moral agency in the midst of violence: Children, political conflict, and values. In I. A. Karawan, W. McCormack, & S. E. Reynolds (Eds.), *Values and violence: Intangible aspects of terrorism* (pp. 169–188). New York: Springer.

Wainryb, C., & Pasupathi, M. (2010). Political violence and disruptions in the development of moral agency. *Child Development Perspectives, 4*, 48–54.

Wainryb, C., & Recchia, H. (2013). Moral lives across cultures: Heterogeneity and conflict. In M. Killen & J. G. Smetana (Eds.), *Handbook of moral development* (2nd ed.) (pp. 259-278). New York: Taylor & Francis.

Weine, S., Klebic, A., Celik, A., & Bicic, M. (2009). Tasting the world: Life after wartime for Bosnian teens in Chicago. In B. K. Barber (Ed.), *Adolescents and war: How youth deal with political violence* (pp. 225–280). New York: Oxford University Press.

Wessells, M. (2006). *Child soldiers: From violence to protection*. London: Harvard University Press.

PART 7

Extensions

CHAPTER 24

Puberty, Identity, and Context: A Biopsychosocial Perspective on Internalizing Psychopathology in Early Adolescent Girls

Misaki N. Natsuaki, Danielle Samuels, *and* Leslie D. Leve

Abstract

Early pubertal maturation is a risk factor for girls' internalizing psychopathology. Little is known, however, regarding the mechanisms that link early pubertal maturation and internalizing psychopathology. The authors propose that gender role identity, which is overlooked in the puberty literature, would provide a key to this query. The authors provide an integrative model of pubertal timing, gender role identity, and context to explain the heightened vulnerability to internalizing psychopathology in early maturing girls. Three hypotheses are formulated: (1) early maturation and feminine gender role identity act in concert to increase the likelihood of internalizing psychopathology; (2) puberty-related changes in neuroendocrine systems heighten the risks for internalizing psychopathology when girls are in stressful contexts; and (3) early pubertal timing elicits and accentuates contextual risks, which contribute to the development of internalizing psychopathology. These factors are expected to operate simultaneously and synergistically to contribute to increased emotional problems in early maturing girls.

Key Words: puberty, gender role identity, early maturation, internalizing psychopathology, female, context

Puberty is a normative biological event that happens universally to healthy humans and animals. Interestingly, however, this expected biological transformation has been implicated in the development of internalizing psychopathology during adolescence (Mendle, Turkheimer, & Emery, 2007; Rudolph, in press). Substantial research evidence has shown that early pubertal maturation constitutes a significant risk factor for internalizing psychopathology for both males and females (for review of the literature on males, see Mendle & Ferrero, 2012). Yet its effect is particularly pronounced for females: girls who undergo pubertal maturation earlier than their same-age female peers are more likely to experience a wide range of internalizing symptoms, including emotional distress, depressive symptoms, anxiety symptoms, major depressive disorders, and anxiety disorders (for reviews, see Mendle et al., 2007; Negriff & Susman, 2011; Rendron, Leen-Feldner, & Hayward, 2009; Rudolph, in press). Although researchers have reached a general consensus that early puberty is linked to internalizing problems in females, the mechanisms underlying these associations are poorly understood.

The overarching aim of this chapter is to answer the following "why" questions: Why is early maturation associated with elevated risks for depression and anxiety among girls? Why do some early maturing girls develop internalizing psychopathology, yet others do not? Our theoretical orientation is that the effects of puberty on psychopathology are best understood by taking an integrative approach in which biological, psychological, and contextual factors are all considered. For this chapter, we argue that consideration of gender role identity (defined as culturally shared expectations of how females [or males] should behave; Galambos, 2004), which has been neglected in the puberty literature, would significantly enhance our ability to elucidate the mechanisms underlying the relations between puberty and internalizing psychopathology. We speculate that along with gender-specific morphological changes in puberty come changes in how youths think of what is sex-appropriate behavior and how much to identify with it. Appearing physically more mature before anyone from her cohort, an early maturing girl faces unique challenges related to a feeling of "being different" while feeling external pressure to act "adult-like" in accordance with her more adult-like morphology. Thus, emerging female-specific morphological transformations (e.g., breast development, arrival of menarche, attainment of a curvier body) may influence her identification with a socially prescribed gender role as a sexually mature female. At the same time, however, the endorsement of a female-typed gender role *before* attaining effective cognitive and emotional coping skills may put girls at risk of developing gender role-linked maladaptive coping strategies (e.g., ruminative coping, silencing), which could, in turn, lead to emotional maladjustment in the face of stressful events. Three hypotheses are put forth in this chapter. Specifically, we propose that early puberty is associated with internalizing psychopathology in girls (especially in Western cultures) because (1) most pertinent to this chapter, early maturation and feminine gender role identity act in concert to increase the likelihood of internalizing psychopathology; (2) puberty-related neuroendocrine systems heighten the risks for anxiety and depression when girls are in stressful contexts; and (3) early puberty elicits and accentuates contextual risks. These three hypothesized paths are considered to operate in a synergistic manner to contribute to the development of internalizing psychopathology among early maturing girls.

This chapter is organized into four major sections. First, we define puberty. Second, we propose a theoretical model to explain the associations between puberty and internalizing psychopathology. Third, we provide a specific example whereby puberty, gender role identity, and context jointly result in the development of internalizing psychopathology. Finally, we discuss the implications of puberty research for prevention and intervention efforts.

The foci of this chapter are further specified in several ways. First, we focus on the effects of *pubertal timing*, rather than pubertal status or tempo (the distinction is discussed later). Although pubertal timing has been linked to various types of psychopathologies (for comprehensive reviews, see Mendle et al., 2007; Rudolph, in press), this chapter focuses on *internalizing* psychopathology. Furthermore, although research on boys and puberty is accumulating (for reviews, see Huddleston & Ge, 2003; Mendle & Ferrero, 2012), this report places particular emphasis on adolescent girls because girls are known to be at higher risk of developing internalizing psychopathology than boys during the transition from childhood to adolescence (Ge, Lorenz, Conger, Elder, & Simons, 1994; Ge, Natsuaki, & Conger, 2006; Hankin et al., 1998; Wichstrom, 1999). In addition, our review primarily concentrates on pubertal timing and internalizing psychopathology in early adolescence. It should be noted, however, that the long-lasting effects of pubertal timing have been examined in previous studies (e.g., Graber, Seeley, Brooks-Gunn, & Lewinsohn, 2004). Finally, although an increasing body of research exists on the biological (including genetic) and contextual factors predicting individual differences in pubertal maturation (e.g., Belsky, Steinberg, & Draper, 1991; Ellis, 2004; Ellis & Garber, 2000; Ge, Natsuaki, Neiderhiser, & Reiss, 2007; Mendle et al., 2006; Rowe, 2002), these factors are not discussed thoroughly given the limited focus of this chapter.

Defining Puberty
The Biological Definition of Puberty

Puberty is inherently a biological experience. Although puberty is often misconstrued as an abrupt, discrete event that occurs between childhood and adolescence, puberty is in fact a gradual process that takes several years to complete (Dorn & Biro, 2011). It involves a series of complex alterations at neuroendocrine levels over an extended period that result in changes in morphology, including the maturation of primary and secondary sex characteristics and, ultimately, the acquisition of reproductive maturity (Dorn & Biro, 2011).

Two components of puberty, *adrenarche* and *gonadarche*, are relevant in understanding the link between puberty and psychopathology. Adrenarche, which typically occurs between ages six and nine, refers to the maturation of the hypothalamic-pituitary-adrenal (HPA) axis, during which the levels of adrenal androgens (e.g., dehydroepiandrosterone [DHEA] and its sulfate [DHEAS]) begin to increase. Adrenal androgens contribute to the growth of pubic and axillary hair. On the other hand, gonadarche, which begins at approximately ages nine to eleven, involves the reactivation of the hypothalamic-pituitary-gonadal (HPG) axis (for a review, see Sisk & Foster, 2004). The process begins in the brain as gonadotropin-releasing hormone (GnRH) is secreted from the hypothalamus. The activation of GnRH is not unique to the pubertal transition; GnRH is also active during pre- and perinatal periods of development but undergoes a quiescent period during the first year of postnatal life until it reawakens during the pubertal transition. GnRH stimulates the pituitary gland to secrete luteinizing hormone (LH) and follicle-stimulating hormones (FSH), which then stimulate the ovary and testes to secrete estradiol and testosterone. The rise of these gonadal steroid hormones to adult levels is primarily responsible for breast and genital development in girls. The consequence of these complex changes in HPA and HPG axes at the neuroendocrine level is a coordinated series of overt, signature morphological changes in body parts. In girls, these changes include the appearance of breast budding, the growth of public and axillary hair, a growth spurt, changes in skin tone (e.g., acne) and body odor, the accumulation of body fat, and the arrival of the first period (i.e., menarche).

The Social and Psychological Meaning of Puberty

Whereas the term "puberty" refers to biological changes in the body, the concept of puberty cannot be simply broken down into its biological constituents. Because the physical changes associated with pubertal maturation are often overt and semiprivate, they connote psychological and social valence (Graber, Nichols, & Brooks-Gunn, 2010; Rudolph, in press). For instance, in the United States, menstruation is acknowledged as a normal biological event, yet at the same time is often accompanied by feelings of shame and the need to conceal it from others, particularly males (Stubbs, 2008). As a result, the arrival of a girl's first menstrual cycle is often accompanied by embarrassment and ambivalence (Brooks-Gunn, Newman, Holderness, & Warren, 1994; Moore, 1995; Tang, Yeung, & Lee, 2003), as well as by negative feelings (Rembeck, Moller, & Gunnarsson, 2006), including anxiety, surprise, dismay, panic, and confusion (Brooks-Gunn & Ruble, 1982; Ruble & Brooks-Gunn, 1982).

In some non-Western societies, a girl's pubertal maturation, most often signaled by menarche, is clearly a social event. Many cultures celebrate the arrival of a girl's first menstruation through rites of passage (Weisfeld, 1997). Although the forms of and activities involved in puberty rites may differ by culture, a general function of these rites is to incorporate girls into adult society and redefine their roles in that society by training and preparing them for their upcoming adult roles as wives and mothers (Alsaker, 1995; Weisfeld, 1997). The major theme underlying these ceremonies is reproductive success and fecundity. Thus, it is not surprising that puberty rites typically occur immediately after menarche; the time at which menarche occurs is considered the time at which the value associated with a girl's fertility is at its peak. From an evolutionary perspective, her value as a mate is consequently maximal at this point of life because the girl is now reproductively mature but cannot have been already pregnant with someone else's baby (Weisfeld, 1997). Soon after the menarche rites, the parents of a girl may start negotiating the daughter's marriage and publicizing her reproductive maturity and readiness as an adult female. As such, although the experience of puberty-related transformation at neuroendocrine levels is a private and personal matter, the experience of puberty as a whole is partially social because the pubertal transition unfolds in context. Thus, the meaning and impact of pubertal maturation are qualified by values, norms, and cultures.

Pubertal Status, Timing, and Tempo

In considering the link between puberty and psychopathology, it is useful to distinguish three distinct yet interrelated ways to conceptualize individual differences in pubertal maturation. *Pubertal status* refers to how mature adolescents have become in the continuum of pubertal maturation. For instance, if an eleven-year-old adolescent girl has just had menarche, she is considered to have acquired an advanced stage of physical maturity because menarche is the last event that occurs in the process of the female pubertal transition. Pubertal status is inherently confounded with age because older adolescents are more likely to have attained advanced pubertal status.

Pubertal timing, on the other hand, refers to how mature an adolescent is compared to his or her same-sex peers who are at the same age. Therefore, the girl who experiences menarche at age eleven may be considered as an earlier maturer in the United States because her menarcheal timing is earlier than the national average of menarcheal age in the United States (the average age at menarche = 12.4 years in the recent cohort of girls who were born between 1980 and 1984; McDowell, Brody, & Hughes, 2007). Only 10 percent of girls in the United States are estimated to have experienced menarche before 11.11 years of age (Chumlea et al., 2003), suggesting that the girl in our example would be considered as an early maturer. Unlike pubertal status, pubertal timing is not confounded by age because, by definition, pubertal timing is inherently standardized within same-sex, same-age peers.

As noted earlier, puberty is a gradual process in which a series of physiological and morphological changes unfold over time. *Pubertal tempo* refers to how quickly one completes these sets of pubertal changes. Although the concept of pubertal tempo is not a recent innovation (Eveleth & Tanner, 1990; Marshall & Tanner, 1969), it has been gaining more research attention recently with the rise of sophisticated longitudinal methodology and the availability of intensive longitudinal data on pubertal maturation (e.g., Ge et al., 2003; Marceau, Ram, Houts, Grimm, & Susman, 2011; Mendle, Harden, Brooks-Gunn, & Graber, 2010). Although the three concepts of pubertal status, timing, and tempo are all relevant for internalizing psychopathology, we focus here on *pubertal timing*. Pubertal timing has been found to be a more potent predictor of girls' internalizing psychopathology than pubertal tempo (Ge et al., 2003; Mendle et al., 2010) and is more consistently associated with internalizing symptoms than is pubertal status (Ge, Conger, & Elder, 2001). Research has shown that the effect of pubertal status is equally salient as pubertal timing, but its effect is captured only when pubertal status is assessed in early adolescence—the time at which the differences among early, on-time, and late maturers is presumably most conspicuous in youths' eyes (Ge, Conger, et al., 2001), which makes the concepts of pubertal timing and status overlap. Therefore, going through rites of passage *earlier* than peers appears to connote special meaning for girls' emotional lives and is something that cannot be explained by how much a girl has completed the transition or how quickly she navigates it.

A Biopsychosocial Model of Pubertal Timing and Internalizing Psychopathology

As noted earlier, pubertal timing, and early maturation in particular, is a risk factor for the development of internalizing psychopathology in adolescent girls—but not in all girls. Two important questions remain: Why are early maturing girls more depressive and anxious compared to their on-time and later-maturing counterparts? Why do some early maturing girls develop internalizing problems whereas other early maturing girls do not? In this chapter, we propose three answers to these "why" and "for whom" questions. We hypothesize that (1) early maturation and feminine gender role identity act in concert to increase the likelihood of internalizing psychopathology; (2) puberty-related changes in neuroendocrine systems heighten the risks for anxiety and depression, particularly when girls are in stressful interpersonal contexts; and (3) early pubertal timing elicits and accentuates contextual risks, which together contribute to the development of internalizing psychopathology. Figure 24.1 presents our proposed model. The model illustrates the probabilistic associations among biological, psychological, and contextual risk factors for early maturing girls' vulnerability to internalizing psychopathology. In the following section, we discuss each hypothesis.

Hypothesis 1: Early Maturation and Feminine Gender Role Identity Act in Concert to Increase the Likelihood of Internalizing Psychopathology

An early maturing girl encounters a cacophony of unique pressures, discourses, and beliefs that she may not be socially, emotionally, or cognitively prepared to navigate (Ge & Natsuaki, 2009). Her precocious adult morphology often elicits an onslaught of identity-related cultural messages imbued with adult norms and expectations. She must navigate these while engaging in her own process of self-reflection and attributing meaning to her body's observable (and unobservable) changes (Paikoff & Brooks-Gunn, 1990). Because most girls mature at earlier ages than boys, the early maturing girl is ahead of her peers regarding her physical development at a time in life when she is keenly aware of herself in relation to others. Such comparisons are an inherent part of identity development, particularly during early adolescence, when social acceptance and "fitting in" is of paramount importance and exclusion by peers is something to be avoided at all costs. Research on adult reflections from experiences of early maturation underscores the negative emotional impact of this pervasive feeling of "being out of step" with peers (feeling different or inferior) and the persistence of these feelings of deviance even after peers have caught up in physical development (Liao, Missenden, Hallam, & Conway, 2005).

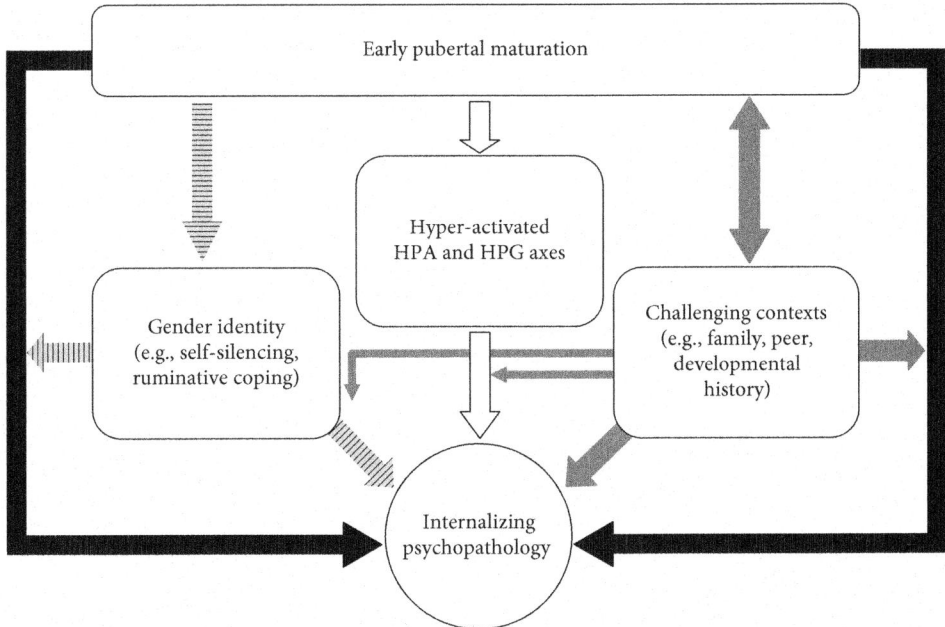

Fig. 24.1 The biopsychosocial model of pubertal timing and internalizing psychopathology. Dotted arrows, hypothesis 1; white arrows, hypothesis 2; gray arrows, hypothesis 3.

Thus, it appears that the early maturing girl is confronted with a unique developmental task in negotiating her identity and integrating these inner and outer changes, which may lead to maladaptive outcomes if not navigated smoothly. Despite their relevance, pubertal timing and identity have been rarely examined empirically in relation to internalizing psychopathology. In one of the few studies that exists on pubertal timing and identity development, Berzonsky and Lombardo (1983) found that girls who experienced a personal, self-examining identity crisis (in the Eriksonian sense) reported earlier pubertal onset than their non-crisis experiencing peers. The puberty-identity crisis relation varied with sex; boys who experienced an identity crisis reported later pubertal onset than their non-crisis peers. The authors suggested that the driver behind the identity crises among both early maturing girls and late maturing boys was the experience of feeling physically different or inferior to one's same-sex peers.

As such, the effect of puberty, or at least some aspects of it, is inherently gender-specific. It is not surprising to see that conceptions of oneself around the time of pubertal transition are increasingly divided along the lines of gender and the norms and expectations associated with the concept of gender (Barrett & White, 2002; Hill & Lynch, 1983). To further illuminate the link between pubertal timing and internalizing psychopathology among adolescent girls, gender role identity is a useful concept to explore. Here, *gender role identity* (often referred to as *gender role orientation* or *gender identity*) is defined as the extent to which individuals identify with *gender roles* or shared cultural expectations on sex-appropriate behavior (Galambos, 2004; Spence & Helmreich, 1978). Gender role identity is further conceptualized into several domains, such as masculinity and femininity. Traditionally, masculinity is associated with instrumental traits of independence, assertiveness, and leadership, whereas femininity is associated with expressive traits of interdependence, compassion, and sensitivity (Holt & Ellis, 1998; Horwitz & White, 1987).

The *gender intensification hypothesis* set forth by Hill and Lynch (1983) proposes the onset of puberty as the harbinger of increasingly gender-differentiated behaviors and attitudes whereby girls' and boys' diverging physical appearances cue increased pressures from peers and adults in their social environment to conform to prescribed gender roles, which are then internalized and manifested. Thus, driven by gender-specific physical changes associated with puberty, conformity to particular gender role identities is thought to be salient during early adolescence (Kroger, 2007), at which time boys and girls are especially vigilant to ensure gender role conformity in their peers (Steinberg & Morris, 2001). However, the nature and intensity of gender identification may depend on contextual factors, such as parents' views toward gender role (Crouter, Manke, & McHale, 1995; Crouter, Whiteman, McHale, & Osgood, 2007). For example, Crouter et al. (2007) found that although girls tended to adopt more traditional gender roles during early adolescence and become increasingly flexible over time, this pattern varied depending on their age, birth order, siblings' gender, and parents' traditional gender role attitudes.

Whereas puberty, which occurs universally to all healthy girls, may operate as the harbinger of gender-typed identification for all girls, going through puberty *early* seems to exert a unique impact on conformity to a prescribed gender role. The time at which early maturing girls go through the biological transformation coincides with the developmental stage during which youths hold cognitively inflexible gender-typed roles. Early adolescence has been considered as the time of more rigidly gendered behaviors, roles, and identities, although this sharp gender-segregated delineation tends to wane over time (Barrett & White, 2002). Some researchers note that later cognitive shifts, such as older adolescents' increasingly flexible sense of self, imply a corresponding flexibility in gender role identity with age (Bartini, 2006). Thus, when contexualizing the association between puberty and gender identification in a developmental framework, it becomes plausible that early maturing girls' precocity probabilistically leads to uniquely stricter conformity to a prescribed female-typed gender role. Indeed, identification with a prescribed gender role may be adaptive and even helpful in guiding and socializing early maturing girls to behave in socially acceptable ways; after all, they have little guidance or precedents to help them navigate this confusing transition, have truncated time to adjust to new mature body, and thus are in an active state of self-exploration and identification. There are, however, unintended consequences of a strong identification with a feminine gender role identity. That is, the endorsement of certain coping behaviors ascribed to femininity (e.g., ruminative coping styles and silencing behaviors, as discussed later) is a risk factor for internalizing psychopathology when combined with life stress (Nolen-Hoeksema & Girgus, 1994).

Collectively, it does not appear to be mere coincidence that the early arrival of puberty, the increased salience of gender role identity, and the emergence of internalizing psychopathology occur simultaneously during early adolescence. Borrowing ideas from the gender intensification hypothesis, we propose that intensified pressure to conform to feminine gender role identity, which is often facilitative of maladaptive coping behaviors (e.g., ruminative coping styles and self-silencing behaviors, as discussed later), may explain the salience and consistency of the finding that rates of depressive symptoms diverge along gendered lines beginning in adolescence, especially in early maturing girls (Crick & Zahn-Waxler, 2003; Ge et al., 1994; 2006; Hankin et al., 1998; Wichstrom, 1999).

It has been shown that the relationship between gender role identity and mental health strengthens in adolescence (Horwitz & White, 1987). Depressive symptoms are negatively associated with masculinity (Barrett & White, 2002; Hart & Thompson, 1996; Priess, Lindberg, & Hyde, 2009) and positively correlated with femininity, particularly in early adolescence (Aube, Fichman, Saltaris, & Koestner, 2000; Broderick & Korteland, 2002; Marcotte, Alain, & Gosselin, 1999; Tolman, Impett, Tracy, & Michael, 2006; Wichstrom, 1999). A similar association has also been seen in anxiety: masculinity is negatively related to anxiety symptoms, and femininity is positively associated with anxiety symptoms during this time (Muris, Meesters, & Knoops, 2005).

If, in accordance with the gender intensification hypothesis, an early-maturing girl adopts a more inflexible feminine identity earlier than her on-time and late maturing peers and is therefore potentially at a higher risk for depression and anxiety, by what mechanism might this occur? Here, we must bear in mind the previous discussion regarding the unique challenges and feelings of difference that early maturing girls must navigate in combination with a consideration of two theorized maladaptive coping mechanisms associated with the feminine gender role or with gender socialization processes: self-silencing behavior and ruminative response styles.

The development of gender role identity and associated gender-typed behaviors are theorized to be facilitated by socialization processes in childhood, and socialization processes tend to limit the range of opportunities for females (Block, 1973; Block & Robins, 1993). One example of female-prone passive behavior is self-silencing. The theoretical model behind self-silencing (Jack & Dill, 1992) or false-self behavior (Harter, Waters, & Whitesell, 1997) is an outgrowth of Gilligan's (1982) and Jordan's (Jordan, Kaplan, Miller, Stiver, & Surrey, 1991) work on "loss of voice" among adolescent girls. Based on an image of the female self as interconnected (Fivush &

Zaman, this volume), theorists set forth the idea that, as girls enter adolescence, the societal pressures they encounter to adopt more feminine attitudes and behaviors simultaneously cause a loss of voice by encouraging them to suppress certain aspects of their personality in an effort to preserve interpersonal relationships. Although there is scant empirical research on femininity and loss of voice in early adolescence, evidence has shown that among high school students, more feminine girls reported lower levels of voice projection, which was correlated with lower self-worth (Harter, Waters, Whitesell, & Kastelic, 1998). Relatedly, false-self behaviors, often manifest as not explicating what one thinks and not expressing one's true opinions (Harter et al., 1997), are associated with depression. For example, Harter and colleagues (1996) found that adolescents who identify high levels of false-self behavior report a host of poor affective symptoms, such as depressed affect, hopelessness, and low self-esteem. As discussed later in this chapter, self-silencing behavior or false-self behavior within the context of a romantic relationship has been found to predict depressive symptomatology among adolescent girls (Hart & Thompson, 1996; Jack & Dill, 1992) and among both sexes (Duarte & Thompson, 1999; Harper & Welsh, 2007).

Ruminative response style (Nolen-Hoeksema, 1987; Nolen-Hoeksema & Girgus, 1994), which is a maladaptive coping strategy linked to the feminine gender role, is a proclivity to focus on depressive cognitions and symptoms and to scrutinize the possible causes and effects of those symptoms in response to depressed moods. Consistent with this theoretical framework, Hart and Thompson (1996) found that adolescent girls endorsed more ruminative coping than boys, and although ruminating was related to higher depressive symptoms among both girls and boys, only among girls was it positively associated with duration of depressive symptoms. Although there has not been, to our knowledge, research conducted on pubertal timing and ruminative response styles among adolescent girls, it seems that there is reason to infer a theoretical link. Specifically, it is theorized that the underlying risk factors for depression (such as a ruminative coping style) are the same for both boys and girls, yet, even prior to adolescence, girls are more likely to possess these characteristics by way of gender-typed socialization that encourages passive behaviors in girls and instrumental behaviors in boys (Nolen-Hoeksema, 1987). When these characteristics interact with certain challenges associated with maturing early (e.g., feeling "deviated" and "different," feeling pressure to act maturely, being aware of own sexuality, and being a target of peers' curiosity and harassment), to the extent that early maturation bears on the intensification of gender-typed attitudes and associated maladaptive coping behaviors, early maturing girls would be at heightened risk of ongoing depression.

It is noteworthy that an emerging body of literature also contends that variability in levels of masculinity, irrespective of femininity, can predict and explain internalizing psychopathology in adolescents. In a longitudinal study covering ages corresponding to grades five through nine, Priess et al. (2009) found that masculinity rather than femininity predicted fewer depressive symptoms in both boys and girls. Carter, Silverman, and Jaccard (2011) confirmed this association in their study of clinic-referred anxious youth and found that levels of masculinity explained anxiety levels among both girls and boys. Levels of femininity did not account for the variance in internalizing psychopathology more than masculinity and pubertal development.

Although depressogenic features of the feminine gender role identity may intensify during the pubertal transition, particularly when the transition occurs early, it is important to keep in mind that not all girls experience depression and/or anxiety in early adolescence. In fact, many girls, even early maturing girls, traverse this phase of life without manifesting internalizing symptoms. Could this heterogeneity in girls' emotional outcomes be explained by variability in their gender role identity? Indeed, not all girls are bound to depressogenic aspects of the feminine gender role. Girls who endorse gender role flexibility; that is, those with a more flexible attitude toward gender roles (Katz & Ksansnak, 1994), and girls (and boys) who identify with higher initial levels of masculinity (Barrett & White, 2002) fare better psychologically than their female peers favoring a more gender-differentiated outlook. Thus, early maturing girls who endorse a highly flexible attitude toward how females should behave are expected to show lower levels of internalizing psychopathology than their early maturing counterparts who hold more traditional gender role beliefs.

It is also important to note that femininity per se is not a direct threat to girls' emotional lives; rather, it is the cultural meaning of femininity and masculinity *as experienced and expressed* by developing adolescents in our society that more directly influences girls' well-being. As pointed out by Barrett and White (2002), there is a pervasive aspect of social reinforcement that underlies these divergent developmental trajectories, for in a culture that values individual achievement and ambition, those adolescents who endorse traditionally masculine/instrumental traits at the outset are more highly rewarded (and subsequently reinforced) than those with initially low levels of masculinity. The relative lack of social approval and felt reinforcement among these adolescents may lead to a reduced sense of self-worth and corresponding decreases in masculine traits such as assertiveness and confidence over time.

A complex relationship emerges here between pubertal timing, gender role identity, and the development of internalizing psychopathology among adolescent girls, whereby early maturation and gender role identity act in concert to increase (or decrease) the likelihood of internalizing psychopathology. In one sense, it appears that early maturation may intensify the processes of gender role development or the endorsement of feminine identity (in accordance with the gender intensification hypothesis). This, in turn, can increase or intensify gender-typed maladaptive coping styles at a time when girls are navigating the unique developmental challenges associated with early maturation, such as feelings of difference associated with secondary sex characteristics. Alternatively, the risk of early maturation is moderated by the degree to which an individual is influenced by feminine gender-typed socialization and corresponding rigidity or flexibility in her gender role identity. Both of these hypothesized pathways are complementary rather than competing in explaining the link between pubertal timing and internalizing psychopathology.

Hypothesis 2: Puberty-Related Neuroendocrine Systems Heighten the Risks for Internalizing Psychopathology

We now shift to focus on a biological mechanism that might explain why some early maturing girls develop internalizing psychopathology and others do not. Given the biological nature of puberty, the fact that pubertal development coincides with increasing trajectories of internalizing psychopathology (Ge et al., 1994; 2006; Hankin et al., 1998; Wichstrom, 1999) makes a hormonal explanation intuitive. Although some evidence suggests that increases in puberty-related hormones (particularly sex steroids, including testosterone and estradiol) are implicated in girls' depression (Angold, Costello, Erkanli, & Worthman, 1999), the associations between puberty-related hormones and internalizing psychopathology are likely complex, and the empirical support for direct hormonal effects is rather fragmented. The hormones known to increase during the pubertal transition are only weakly or inconsistently associated with girls' internalizing psychopathology (Alsaker, 1996; for more details see Buchanan, Eccles, & Becker, 1992).

The mechanisms through which hormones affect psychopathology are undoubtedly highly complex, and elucidation of the pathways is still underway. One potential mechanism through which puberty-related hormones influence depression and anxiety is that pubertal hormones alter stress sensitivity, making adolescent girls particularly sensitive to exogenous stressors. Recent studies using salivary cortisol as an index of stress regulation have documented heightened stress reactivity and delayed post-stress recovery in pubescent adolescents (Gunnar, Wewerka, Frenn, Long, & Griggs, 2009; Schreiber et al., 2006; Stroud, Papandonatos, Williamson, & Dahl, 2004; Walker, Sabuwalla, & Huot, 2004). Cortisol is a steroid hormone released by the HPA axis, and disruption to this axis has been implicated in the development of symptoms of depression and anxiety (e.g., Gold & Chrousos, 2002; Guerry & Hastings, 2011; Sapolsky, 2000). In fact, cortisol secretion is closely intertwined with age, puberty, and sex, which together appear to contribute to adolescent girls' vulnerability to external stressors (Walker et al., 2004; Young & Altemus, 2004).

Although much research is needed to understand the impact of sex steroids (e.g., estradiol) on the HPA axis during the pubertal transition (Rubinow & Schmidt, 1999), the dramatic alterations in sex steroid production that occur during puberty are thought to play a potential modulatory role on the HPA axis, possibly contributing to vulnerability toward depression in adolescent girls via heightened stress reactivity (Stroud et al., 2004; Young & Altemus, 2004). Animal studies have confirmed this idea by showing that high doses of estrogen amplify the stress response, which may in turn increase susceptibility to stress-related disorders such as anxiety and depression (Shansky et al., 2004), thus bolstering the hypothesis on why girls (compared to boys) are sensitive to life stressors after the onset of puberty. An alternative hypothesis is that the activation of estradiol secretion at puberty may modulate serotonergic pathways in the brain, which places pubescent girls at risk for internalizing psychopathology (Martel, Klump, Nigg, Breedlove, & Sisk, 2009).

The aforementioned description of puberty-related neuroendocrine systems and heightened stress reactivity provides a good explanation of why pubertal status may be related to internalizing psychopathology. After all, hormonal alterations occur whenever puberty happens, irrespective of the timing of puberty. Could this framework be useful in explaining the effect of pubertal timing? Our knowledge remains limited, but it has been hypothesized that the timing of puberty-related hormone secretion is implicated in how susceptible one is to the adverse effects of hormones, how reactive one is to exogenous stressors, and how much one produces hormones (Ge & Natsuaki, 2009). For instance, evidence from an animal experiment has demonstrated that testosterone treatments administered to castrated male hamsters were most effective in organizing mating behaviors when treatments were given earlier during the pubertal transition (Schultz, Molenda-Figueria, & Sisk, 2009). Although suggestive, this finding leads to an interesting hypothesis that hormones that are secreted earlier may exert greater influences on behavioral organization than hormones that are secreted later, making early maturing girls particularly susceptible to the depressogenic and/or anxiety-enhancing effects of hormones. Furthermore, early maturation is also linked to enlarged volume of the pituitary gland. A recent neuroimaging study in humans has shown that the volume of the pituitary gland in early maturing adolescents (both boys and girls) tends to be larger than those of their peers, which in turn influences depressive symptoms positively and prospectively (Whittle et al., 2012). Note that the pituitary gland is an integral part of both the HPA (stress reactivity) and HPG (gonadarche) systems. Whittle et al. (2012) speculate that activation of the HPG axis and the resulting secretion of sex steroids leads to increased pituitary size, which hyperactivates the hormonal stress response in the HPA axis. Early maturing girls' heightened sensitivity to stressors, particularly interpersonal ones, has also been noted in recent studies involving cortisol (Natsuaki, Klimes-Dougan, et al., 2009). Therefore, perhaps early secretion of sex steroids may hyperactivate the stress reactivity system, leading early maturing girls to be more susceptible to environmental stressors (Whittle et al., 2012). This biological dysregulation in the stress response systems seems ill-timed for early maturing girls because the dysregulation is happening prior to the development of alternative coping strategies, such as cognitive and executive skills, that assist individuals in successfully managing stress (Sontag-Padilla et al., 2012). Furthermore, early maturers not only begin secreting puberty-related hormones early, but also produce more of the hormones beginning from the early stages of puberty and most notably during mid to late stages of the pubertal transition (Ibanez, Street, Potau, Carrascosa, & Zampolli, 1997), which could lead to an amplification of the effects of these hormones on internalizing psychopathology. The testing of these hypotheses remains at a very early stage, and more work is required to elucidate the neurobiological mechanisms underlying the associations between pubertal timing and girls' internalizing psychopathology.

Hypothesis 3: Early Maturation Elicits and Accentuates Contextual Risks

Puberty is a semiprivate matter because biological changes at puberty, particularly the development of secondary sex characteristics, are external and visible to others. It has "social stimulus value" (Petersen & Taylor, 1980, p. 137) because it triggers reactions from other people. Referred to as *the puberty-initiated mediation hypothesis* (Ge, Natsuaki, Jin, & Biehl, 2011), it is expected that girls' early physical maturation could evoke certain reactions—often awkward, stressful, and confusing ones—from surrounding social contexts, which in turn exacerbate girls' emotional well-being. Note again that early maturing girls are the first group in their cohort to experience these overt changes in their body. Given that observing someone undergoing sexual maturation is also a novel experience for peers and parents of early maturers, the reactions to early maturing girls' maturation can be uncertain, surprised, amused, curious, confused, and potentially harsh. This evocative process wherein biology elicits socialization has been well acknowledged in behavioral genetics (Plomin, DeFries, & Loehlin, 1977; Scarr & McCartney, 1983); however, to our surprise, empirical application of this idea to puberty research remains scant.

Existing research suggests that physical changes in their daughters' bodies do elicit social reactions from parents that can be challenging and confusing for maturing daughters. For instance, daughters' sexual maturation often elicits confusion, discomfort, and awkwardness in parents (Paikoff & Brooks-Gunn, 1991). An illustrative study using a design similar to the Thematic Appreciation Test has shown that, according to girls' perceptions, their fathers were likely to show negative (e.g., embarrassed, disappointed, insensitive) and ambivalent (e.g., surprised, confused, uncertain, and amused) feelings when they discovered that their daughters had just bought their first bras (Brooks-Gunn et al., 1994). Girls perceived that about two-thirds of mothers were comfortable and positive about their daughters' puberty (still, one-third of them were negative and/or ambivalent), but more than half of fathers were perceived as generally or very uncomfortable about their daughter's sexual maturation. This discomfort in discussing puberty is considered to peak in early adolescence, the period during which early maturing girls go through the pubertal transition. Because puberty is yet to be a topic of high relevance for the majority of youths, pubertal discussions are less frequent and often neither open nor encouraged at this point of time (Brooks-Gunn et al., 1994; Brooks-Gunn & Ruble, 1983). Such negative, ambivalent, and somewhat hesitant reactions could plausibly contribute to the risk for internalizing problems because it creates confusion and insecurity in daughters' feelings and identity, especially for early maturing daughters who are already facing unique challenges of being "different" from the rest of their cohort. Still, it is noteworthy that a recent study focusing on hormones did not find estradiol or testosterone to prospectively predict family problems in girls (Marceau, Dorn, & Susman, 2012). The inconsistency between this study and the aforementioned studies of reactions to puberty may suggest that the evocative effects of puberty cannot be simply attributed to hormones. The "social stimulus value" of puberty may be most conspicuous when the assessment of puberty includes external (or visible) features of puberty (e.g., breast development, acne, and fat accumulation).

Peers also react to girls' early pubertal maturation, which often constitutes risks for internalizing psychopathology. In a classic study, Stattin and Magnusson (1990) found that early maturing girls tended to associate with older peers and have established relations with boys. Their adult-like physical appearance opens the door to a social group of older male peers, which in turn may increase early maturing girls' engagement in adult-like behavior that may be risky for young adolescent girls (Magnusson, Stattin, & Allen, 1985). Early maturing girls are also at heightened risk of becoming victims of physical and nonphysical aggression, including peer sexual harassment (McMaster, Connolly, Pepler, & Craig, 2002) and violent victimization (Haynie & Piquero, 2006). Moreover, early maturing girls are more likely to be the victims of rumors and to experience more peer-related stressful life events, which in turn leads to increased internalizing psychopathology (Conley, Rudolph, & Bryant, 2012).

Based on the aforementioned studies, early maturation in girls tends to evoke negative and ambivalent reactions from others, at least in Western cultures. This awkwardness, discomfort, and negativity in the responses of others, in turn, appears to contribute to the risk for internalizing psychopathology in early maturing girls by creating stressful social contexts. This mechanism has implications for prevention and intervention; if social attitudes toward girls' precocious puberty and sexual maturation are improved, then adverse outcomes associated with early pubertal maturation may be prevented. Also, as discussed later in this chapter, a focus on providing girls with the skills to cope with negative peer/family attention or behaviors may also be a fruitful intervention approach.

Developmental contexts not only mediate the associations between pubertal timing and internalizing psychopathology, but also moderate it. Researchers subscribing to *the contextual amplification hypothesis* maintain that contexts can either facilitate or impede the effects of early puberty through opportunities, norms, expectations, and implicit reward and punishment structures (Ge & Natsuaki, 2009; Ge et al., 2011; Rudolph, in press). Adaptation is particularly difficult for children who negotiate an early pubertal transition in a stressful social environment because new challenges at the entry to puberty and a widening array of social stressors may overtax their relatively undeveloped coping resources. Thus, according to this hypothesis, early maturing girls living in challenging environments are at an elevated risk for developing internalizing psychopathology. The hypothesis also suggests that supportive, nurturing environments can offset the adverse effects of early maturation.

The contextual amplification hypothesis has been applied to a wide range of psychopathologies (e.g., externalizing problems and substance use); herein, we focus on recent findings on internalizing psychopathology. Interested readers are referred to more comprehensive reviews elsewhere on this hypothesis (Ge & Natsuaki, 2009; Ge et al., 2011; Rudolph, in press). In general, empirical research has shown that early maturing girls are at heightened risk for experiencing depressive and anxiety symptoms when they are confronted with developmentally challenging contexts, including child maltreatment (Natsuaki, Leve, & Mendle, 2011), peer stress (Blumenthal, Leen-Feldner, Trainor, Babson, & Bunaciu, 2009; Conley & Rudolph, 2009; Sontag-Padilla, Graber, & Clemans, 2011; Teunissen et al., 2011), romantic relationships (Natsuaki, Biehl, & Ge, 2009), family adversity (Ge, Conger, & Elder, 1996; Rudolph & Troop-Gordon, 2010), stressful life events (Ge, Conger, et al., 2001), and neighborhood characteristics such as lack of diversity (White, Deardoff, & Gonzales, 2012).

Emerging from the above-mentioned empirical evidence is the possibility that early maturing girls are particularly vulnerable to interpersonally challenging contexts (Natsuaki, Klimes-Dougan, et al., 2009). Theorists who study the effect of gender differences on internalizing problems have long known that the strong interpersonal orientation observed in females may be a liability to their emotional well-being (Cyranowski, Frank, Young, & Shear, 2000; Rose & Rudolph, 2006; Rudolph, 2002; Zahn-Waxler, Shirtcliff, & Marceau, 2008). The investment that girls put into attachment, relational closeness, social approval, and acceptance could lead to magnified interpersonal sensitivity, which in turn could tax girls' emotional adjustment when their valued relationships do not fare well (Rudolph, 2002). As noted earlier, girls view interpersonal relationships as an essential ingredient to their identity (Fivush & Zaman, this volume); therefore, conflict and stress within relationships threaten girls in a salient fashion (Rudolph, 2002). Compared to their female peers, early maturing girls may be particularly sensitive to interpersonal acceptance and loyalty because, by default, their physical precocity marks them as a deviation from the norm, and they may be overtly motivated to "fit in" socially to overcome the deviation. In fact, one study has shown that the associations between early maturation and depressive symptoms in girls are partially mediated by heightened stress (cortisol) reactivity to interpersonal challenges (Natsuaki, Klimes-Dougan, et al., 2009).

Thus far, we have conceptualized "context" as an actual physical place or experience. However, the conceptualization of context does not have to be constrained as such; it could also refer to a girl's developmental history or prepubertal condition, which provides an enriched meaning ("context") to her pubertal maturation. According to the *accentuation hypothesis,* early maturation accentuates preexisting vulnerabilities (Caspi & Moffitt, 1991; Ge et al., 1996; Rudolph, in press; Rudolph & Troop-Gordon, 2010). Therefore, "(t)he reticent become withdrawn, the irritable become aggressive, and the capable take charge" (Caspi & Moffitt, 1993, p. 256). Empirical evidence supports this notion, showing that girls with a history of emotional distress display signs of internalizing psychopathology when they undergo the pubertal transition earlier than their peers (Rudolph & Troop-Gordon, 2010).

Summary

Early pubertal maturation is a risk factor for girls' development of internalizing psychopathology. However, the mechanisms underlying this association are likely complex and require a multilevel approach that incorporates biological, psychological, and contextual correlates of early maturation. Adopting a biopsychosocial model of puberty and internalizing psychopathology, we propose three hypotheses (Figure 24.1). We hypothesize that (1) early maturation may accentuate a facet of gender role identity that is depressogenic; (2) biological changes associated with puberty, including hormones and stress reactivity, place early maturing girls at risk for internalizing psychopathology; and (3) early maturation elicits challenging reactions from others and accentuates preexisting vulnerabilities and adversity in girls' lives. In addition, the biological, psychological, and contextual factors do not operate in isolation but rather in interaction with one another such that a risk in one factor can be offset (or enhanced) by a strength in another factor (e.g., a negative developmental history could increase the association between gender identity and internalizing psychopathology, whereas a supportive context could buffer the negative effects of HPA axis reactivity on internalizing problems).

An Integrative Approach: A Case of Early Maturing Girls in Romantic Relationships

Our three hypotheses are not independent; we assume that all pieces in the theoretical model presented in Figure 24.1 operate jointly and simultaneously, creating a complex link between early pubertal maturation and internalizing psychopathology in girls. To cement the three hypotheses more cohesively, we provide the following illustrative example of early maturing girls in romantic relationships.

Romantic relationships, which emerge rapidly in early adolescence, provide a unique developmental context that promotes growth and maladjustment simultaneously. Romantic relationships serve as a challenging event because girls and boys (in heterosexual relationships) now need to act out a relatively unfamiliar situation in comparison to their largely gender-segregated childhood (Maccoby, 1990), and therefore romantic relationships are a known risk factor for adolescents' emotional well-being (Joyner & Udry, 2000). However, these experiences are pivotal to an adolescent's development of intimacy, emotional expression, and identity (Brown, 1999), and adolescents correspondingly report that many of their strongest experiences of emotion arise from real or fantasized romantic relationships (Larson & Asmussen, 1991). For some, Kegan (1982) suggests, these relationships may represent their entire world, perhaps their sole identity. Thus, romantic relationships in early adolescence are somewhat stressful—and important—by nature.

Interestingly, the increased incidence of romantic involvement corresponds to increased rates of depression (Joyner & Udry, 2000), more so in girls than in boys (Nolen-Hoeksema & Girgus, 1994) and even more in early maturing girls than in on-time and late maturing girls (Ge et al., 1996; Ge, Conger, et al., 2001). Research has shown that early maturing girls are doubly disadvantaged; they are not only more likely than on-time or late-maturing girls to be involved in romantic relationships (Smolak, Levine, & Gralen, 1993), but are also particularly vulnerable to the adverse effect of early romantic relationships, responding with higher levels of depressive mood (Natsuaki, Biehl, et al., 2009). Here, the question arises: by what mechanisms are early maturing girls who are involved in romantic relationships at higher risk for becoming depressed? The three hypothesized pathways (Figure 24.1) can provide a roadmap in guiding us to potential answers. In particular, precocious physical development in early maturing girls propels them into the world of dating, and the girls' endorsement of the feminine gender role and its associated maladaptive coping styles and cognitive schemas, compounded with their hyperactive stress reactivity system, may serve to increase their risk of depression in the face of challenging dating contexts that unfold in the midst of a dramatic biological transformation that occurs off time.

As noted earlier, early childhood socialization and some female biological characteristics are thought to foster adolescent girls' emphasis on the importance of relationships as a core of their identity at this phase of life, which may increase their vulnerability to internalizing psychopathology (Cyranowski et al., 2000; Rose & Rudolph, 2006; Rudolph, 2002; Zahn-Waxler et al., 2008). Specifically, adolescent girls' status and identity is often somewhat dependent on their success in relationships; however, romantic relationships are typically short-lived and less stable during early adolescence (Joyner & Udry, 2000), making it difficult for them to sustain a stable, happy emotional life. To maintain romantic interpersonal relationships, adolescent girls, particularly those whose identities are bound more tightly to traditional gender roles, may engage in behaviors designed to preserve their relationships at all costs, particularly self-silencing. Self-silencing behavior is predictive of depressive symptomatology, particularly among girls (Duarte & Thompson, 1999; Harper & Welsh, 2007; Hart & Thompson, 1996). Furthermore, the integration of the gender intensification hypothesis and the puberty-initiated mediation hypothesis suggests a possible pathway whereby dating partner's reactions to a girl's early sexual maturation could intensify conformity to her feminine gender role. Thus, the combination of stress and high expectations entailed in adolescent girls' experiences and in conceptions of their romantic relationships, especially among those early maturing girls who endorse a more feminine gender role, may make them more susceptible to disturbances within these relationships. Coupled with the fact that early maturing girls are more likely to elicit romantic and sexual attention from boys (Compian, Gowen, & Hayward, 2004) and be biologically reactive to external (perhaps interpersonal) stressors (Natsuaki, Klimes-Dougan, et al., 2009; Whittle et al., 2012), the risk for developing depression and anxiety is exacerbated for early maturing girls.

Compounding this risk is the salience of physical attractiveness that adolescent girls attach to romantic relationships. Puberty is accompanied by the acquisition of fuller, curvier body contours—an inevitable change in female anatomy during puberty. Early maturing girls are known to have more disturbances related to body image, feeling that they are obese, not svelte enough (Ge, Elder, Regnerus, & Cox, 2001; Stice, 2003), or less physically attractive (Ackard & Peterson, 2001; Duncan, Ritter, Dornbusch, Gross, & Carlsmith, 1985) than their on-time and late maturing peers. Research has shown that such disturbed body image associated with pubertal timing is predictive of later depressive pathology (Rierdan, Koff, & Stubbs, 1989; Stice, Hayward, Cameron, Killen, & Taylor, 2000). Given that adolescents in today's industrialized countries are led to believe that being thin is important to having successful romantic relationships (Paxton, Schutz, Wertheim, & Muir, 1999) and that girls' concerns often center on the importance of the relationship and their own physical attractiveness (Clemans, DeRose, Graber, & Brooks-Gunn, 2010), the presence of a romantic partner, or even as subtle a factor as the acknowledgment of romantic interest, may impose additional pressure on early maturing girls whose body satisfaction is already low due to puberty-associated fat accumulation. In response to such heightened vulnerability, early maturing girls, who are highly sensitive to interpersonal stress, may intensify depressogenic cognitive and behavioral strategies such as engaging in self-silencing behavior in an effort to maintain their relationships, which leads to depressive symptomatology.

Future Directions and Implications

Combined with the extant literature on pubertal timing and internalizing psychopathology, the theoretical model and hypotheses put forth in this chapter provide a roadmap for future research on puberty, identity, and context. For example, extending the puberty-initiated mediation hypothesis, sibling studies might provide insights into the extent to which the novelty of puberty and the reactions of parents affect associations between pubertal timing and internalizing psychopathology. It would be expected that there would be greater novelty and reaction to puberty in a first-born daughter (as compared to later-born daughters). However, what if the later-born daughter experienced early pubertal timing and the first-born did not? How would the parents react to each daughter's pubertal maturation? How do differences in parental reaction affect daughters' gender role identities? Examination of the associations between pubertal timing and internalizing psychopathology across sibling dyads and comparing siblings' experiences within the family could provide an opportunity to test whether family context is a crucial mechanism linking pubertal timing and internalizing problems. Furthermore, we have just begun to understand the importance of peers and romantic relationships in adolescent girls' lives and the salience of these nonfamilial interpersonal contexts for early maturing girls. How does the endorsement of prescribed gender roles assist (or impede) early maturing girls' coping strategies to peer stress? How does gender role conformity assist (or hinder) early maturing girls to navigate the confusing world of adolescent romance? The field awaits answers to these important questions. In addition, the investigation of pubertal timing and internalizing psychopathology in non-Western cultures could further help provide a window into the extent to which societal values and norms around puberty and gender role identity influence the association between pubertal timing and psychopathology.

We also need to begin developing and testing targeted preventive interventions that might improve the well-being for girls who are at risk for developing internalizing psychopathology; that is, those who experience early pubertal maturation. The research reviewed in this chapter indicates several potential avenues for intervention. First, following hypothesis 1, a logical place to intervene would be around gender role identity issues. Interventions that teach action-oriented coping styles and enhance direct communication skills might interrupt the pathway from early pubertal maturation to the development of internalizing symptoms by way of more effective coping strategies and modified gender identities. Alternatively, as noted in hypothesis 3, the peer and family contexts play a strong role in mediating associations between early pubertal timing and internalizing symptoms. Family interventions could be delivered to teach girls and their parents about the normative nature of pubertal timing and to provide family members opportunities to learn effective skills to maintain strong, supportive family relationships. Last, early prevention strategies might be employed for girls who have experienced more extreme contextual challenges, such as childhood maltreatment, in their developmental histories. Research evidence has shown that this population, especially girls with sexual abuse, is highly vulnerable to early puberty and internalizing psychopathology (Natsuaki et al., 2011). Service provision to this population during childhood, prior to the onset of puberty, might help them to develop the social skills and flexible gender role identity to better weather the social consequences of early puberty.

In summary, the present chapter posits a theoretical model that explains the closely knit connections between pubertal timing, gender identity, biological processes, and contextual processes, all of which contribute jointly to the development of internalizing psychopathology. Although there is preliminary evidence to support the different components of this theoretical model, additional research is needed to fill in key knowledge gaps. However, the puberty field is progressed to a point at which it is also time to draw from the evidence base to date and develop and test interventions aimed at helping offset the harmful effects of early puberty on girls' internalizing symptomatology.

References

Ackard, D. M., & Peterson, C. B. (2001). Association between puberty and disordered eating, body image, and other psychological variables. [collected-PDF]. *International Journal of Eating Disorders, 29*, 187–194.

Alsaker, F. D. (1995). Timing of puberty and reactions to pubertal changes. In M. Rutter (Ed.), *Psychosocial disturbances in young people* (pp. 37–82). Cambridge, UK: Cambridge University Press.

Alsaker, F. D. (1996). Annotation: The impact of puberty. *Journal of Child Psychology and Psychiatry and Allied Disciplines, 37*, 249–258.

Angold, A., Costello, E. J., Erkanli, A., & Worthman, C. M. (1999). Pubertal changes in hormone levels and depression in girls. *Psychological Medicine, 29*, 1043–1053.

Aube, J., Fichman, L., Saltaris, C., & Koestner, R. (2000). Gender differences in adolescent depressive symptomatology: Toward an integrated social-developmental model. *Journal of Social and Clinical Psychology, 19*, 297–313.

Barrett, A., & White, H. (2002). Trajectories of gender role orientation in adolescence and early adulthood: A prospective study of the mental health effects of masculinity and femininity. *Journal of Health and Social Behavior, 43*, 451–468.

Bartini, M. (2006). Gender role flexibility in early adolescence: Developmental change in attitudes, self-perceptions, and behaviors. *Sex Roles, 55*, 233–245.

Belsky, J., Steinberg, L., & Draper, P. (1991). Childhood experience, interpersonal development, and reproductive strategy: An evolutionary theory of socialization. *Child Development, 62*, 647–670.

Berzonsky, M. D., & Lombardo, J. P. (1983). Pubertal timing and identity crisis: A preliminary investigation. *The Journal of Early Adolescence, 3*, 239–246.

Block, J. (1973). Conceptions of sex-roles: Some cross-cultural and longitudinal perspectives. *American Psychologist, 28*, 512–526.

Block, J., & Robins, R. W. (1993). A longitudinal study of consistency and chance in self-esteem from early adolescence to early adulthood. *Child Development, 64*, 909–923.

Blumenthal, H., Leen-Feldner, E. W., Trainor, C. D., Babson, K. A., & Bunaciu, L. (2009). Interactive roles of pubertal timing and peer relations in predicting social anxiety symptoms among youth. *Journal of Adolescent Health 44*, 401–403.

Broderick, P. C., & Korteland, C. (2002). Coping style and depression in early adolescence: Relationships to gender, gender role, and implicit beliefs. *Sex Roles, 46*, 201–213.

Brooks-Gunn, J., Newman, D. L., Holderness, C., & Warren, M. P. (1994). The experience of breast development and girls' stories about the purchase of a bra. *Journal of Youth and Adolescence, 23*, 539–565.

Brooks-Gunn, J., & Ruble, D. N. (1982). The development of menstrual-related beliefs about behaviors during early adolescence. *Child Development, 53*, 1567–1577.

Brooks-Gunn, J., & Ruble, D. N. (1983). The experience of menarche from a developmental perspective. In J. Brooks-Gunn & A. C. Petersen (Eds.), *Girls at puberty. Biological and Psychosocial perspectives* (pp. 155–178). New York: Plenum Press.

Brown, B. B. (1999). "You're going out with who?": Peer group influences on adolescent romantic relationships. In W. Furman, B. B. Brown, & C. Fering (Eds.), *The development of adolescent romantic relationships in adolescence* (pp. 291–329). New York: Cambridge University Press.

Buchanan, C. M., Eccles, J. S., & Becker, J. B. (1992). Are adolescents the victims of raging hormones: Evidence for activational effects of hormones on moods and behavior at adolescence. *Psychological Bulletin, 111*, 62–107.

Carter, R., Silverman, W. K., & Jaccard, J. (2011). Sex variations in youth anxiety symptoms: Effects of pubertal development and gender role orientation. *Journal of Clinical Child and Adolescent Psychology, 40*, 730–741.

Caspi, A., & Moffitt, T. E. (1991). Individual differences are accentuated during periods of social change: The sample case of girls at puberty. *Journal of Personality and Social Psychology, 61*, 157–168.

Caspi, A., & Moffitt, T. E. (1993). When do individual differences matter? A paradoxical theory of personality coherence. *Psychological Inquiry, 4*, 247–271.

Chumlea, W. C., Schubert, C. M., Roche, A. F., Kulin, H. E., Lee, P. A., Himes, J. H., & Sun, S. S. (2003). Age at menarche and racial comparisons in US girls. *Pediatrics, 111*, 110–113.

Clemans, K. H., DeRose, L. M., Graber, J. A., & Brooks-Gunn, J. (2010). Gender in adolescence: Applying a person-in-context approach to gender identity and roles. In J. C. Chrisler & D. R. McCreary (Eds.), *Handbook of gender research in psychology* (pp. 527–557). New York: Springer.

Compian, L., Gowen, L. K., & Hayward, C. (2004). Peripubertal girls' romantic and platonic involvement with boys: Associations with body image and depression symptoms. *Journal of Research on Adolescence, 14*, 23–47.

Conley, C. S., & Rudolph, K. D. (2009). The emerging sex difference in adolescent depression: Interacting contributions of puberty and peer stress. *Development and Psychopathology, 21*, 593–620.

Conley, C. S., Rudolph, K. D., & Bryant, F. B. (2012). Explaining the longitudinal associations between puberty and depression: Sex differences in the mediating effects of peer stress. *Development and Psychopathology, 24*, 691–701.

Crick, N. R., & Zahn-Waxler, C. (2003). The development of psychopathology in females and males: Current progress and future challenges. *Development and Psychopathology, 15*, 719–742.

Crouter, A. C., Manke, B. A., & McHale, S. M. (1995). The family context of gender intensification in early adolescence. *Child Development, 66*, 317–329.

Crouter, A. C., Whiteman, S. D., McHale, S. M., & Osgood, D. W. (2007). Development of gender attitude traditionality across middle childhood and adolescence. *Child Development, 78*, 911–926.

Cyranowski, J. M., Frank, E., Young, E., & Shear, K. (2000). Adolescent onset of the gender difference in lifetime rates of major depression. *Archives of General Psychiatry, 57*, 21–27.

Dorn, L. D., & Biro, F. M. (2011). Puberty and its measurement: A decade in review. *Journal of Research on Adolescence, 21*, 180–195.

Duarte, L. M., & Thompson, J. M. (1999). Sex differences in self-silencing. *Psychological Reports, 85*, 145–161.

Duncan, P. D., Ritter, P. L., Dornbusch, S. M., Gross, R. T., & Carlsmith, J. M. (1985). The effects of pubertal timing on body-image, school behavior, and deviance. *Journal of Youth and Adolescence, 14*, 227–235.

Ellis, B. J. (2004). Timing of pubertal maturation in girls: An integrated life history approach. *Psychological Bulletin, 130*, 920–958.

Ellis, B. J., & Garber, J. (2000). Psychosocial antecedents of variation in girls' pubertal timing: Maternal depression, stepfather presence, and marital and family stress. *Child Development, 71*, 485–501.

Eveleth, P., & Tanner, J. M. (1990). Worldwide variation in human growth *Worldwide variation in human growth* (2nd edition ed.). New York: Cambridge University Press.

Fivush, R., & Zaman, W. (in press). Gendered narrative voices: Sociocultural and feminist approaches to emerging identity in childhood and adolescence. In K. McLean & M. Syed (Eds.), *Oxford handbook of identity development*. Oxford University Press.

Galambos, N. L. (2004). Gender and gender role development in adolescence. In R. M. Lerner & L. Steinberg (Eds.), *Handbook of adolescent psychology* (2nd ed., pp. 233–262). New York: Wiley.

Ge, X., Conger, R. D., & Elder, G. H. (1996). Coming of age too early: Pubertal influences on girls' vulnerability to psychological distress. *Child Development, 67*, 3386–3400.

Ge, X., Conger, R. D., & Elder, G. H. (2001). Pubertal transition, stressful life events, and the emergence of gender differences in adolescent depressive symptoms. *Developmental Psychology, 37*, 404–417.

Ge, X., Elder, G. H., Regnerus, M., & Cox, C. (2001). Pubertal transitions, perceptions of being overweight, and adolescents' psychological maladjustment: Gender and ethnic differences. *Social Psychology Quarterly, 64*, 363–375.

Ge, X., Kim, I. J., Brody, G. H., Conger, R. D., Simons, R. L., Gibbons, F. X., & Cutrona, C. E. (2003). It's about timing and change: Pubertal transition effects on symptoms of major depression among African American youths. *Developmental Psychology, 39*, 430–439.

Ge, X., Lorenz, F. O., Conger, R. D., Elder, G. H., & Simons, R. L. (1994). Trajectories of stressful life events and depressive symptoms during adolescence. *Developmental Psychology, 30*, 467–483.

Ge, X., & Natsuaki, M. N. (2009). In search of explanations for early pubertal timing effects on developmental psychopathology. *Current Directions in Psychological Science, 18*, 327–331.

Ge, X., Natsuaki, M. N., & Conger, R. D. (2006). Trajectories of depressive symptoms and stressful life events among male and female adolescents in divorced and nondivorced families. *Development and Psychopathology, 18*, 1–21.

Ge, X., Natsuaki, M. N., Jin, R., & Biehl, M. C. (2011). *A contextual amplification hypothesis: Pubertal timing and girls' emotional and behavioral problems*. London: Wiley.

Ge, X., Natsuaki, M. N., Neiderhiser, J. M., & Reiss, D. (2007). Genetic and environmental influences on pubertal timing: Results from two national sibling studies. *Journal of Research on Adolescence, 17*, 767–788.

Gilligan, C. (1982). *In a difference voice: Psychological theory and women's development*. Cambridge, MA: Harvard University Press.

Gold, P. W., & Chrousos, G. P. (2002). Organization of the stress system and its dysregulation in melancholic and atypical depression high vs. low CRH/NE states. *Molecular Psychiatry, 7*, 254–275.

Graber, J. A., Nichols, T. R., & Brooks-Gunn, J. (2010). Putting pubertal timing in developmental context: Implications for prevention. *Developmental Psychobiology, 52*, 254–262.

Graber, J. A., Seeley, J. R., Brooks-Gunn, J., & Lewinsohn, P. M. (2004). Is pubertal timing associated with psychopathology in young adulthood? *Journal of the American Academy of Child and Adolescent Psychiatry, 43*, 718–726.

Guerry, J. D., & Hastings, P. D. (2011). In search of HPA axis dysregulation in child and adolescent depression. *Clinical Child and Family Psychology Review, 14*, 135–160.

Gunnar, M. R., Wewerka, S., Frenn, K., Long, J. D., & Griggs, C. (2009). Developmental changes in hypothalamus-pituitary-adrenal activity over the transition to adolescence: Normative changes and associations with puberty. *Development and Psychopathology, 21*, 69–85.

Hankin, B. L., Abramson, L. Y., Moffitt, T. E., Silva, P. A., McGee, R., & Angell, K. E. (1998). Development of depression from preadolescence to young adulthood: Emerging gender differences in a 10-year longitudinal study. *Journal of Abnormal Psychology, 107*, 128–140.

Harper, M. S., & Welsh, D. P. (2007). Keeping quiet: Self-silencing and its association with relational and individual functioning among adolescent romantic couples. *Journal of Social and Personal Relationships, 24*, 99–116.

Hart, B. I., & Thompson, J. M. (1996). Gender role characteristics and depressive symptomatology among adolescents. *Journal of Early Adolescence, 16*, 407–426.

Harter, S., Marold, D. B., Whitesell, N. R., & Cobbs, G. (1996). A model of the effects of perceived parent and peer support on adolescent false-self behavior. *Child Development, 67*, 360–374.

Harter, S., Waters, P. L., & Whitesell, N. R. (1997). Lack of voice as a manifestation of false-self behavior among adolescents: The school setting as a stage upon which the drama of authenticity is enacted. *Educational Psychologist, 32*, 153–173.

Harter, S., Waters, P. L., Whitesell, N. R., & Kastelic, D. (1998). Level of voice among female and male high school students: Relational context, support, and gender orientation. *Developmental Psychology, 34*, 892–901.

Haynie, D. L., & Piquero, A. R. (2006). Pubertal development and physical victimization in adolescence. *Journal of Research in Crime and Delinquency, 43*, 3–35.

Hill, J. P., & Lynch, M. E. (1983). The intensification of gender-related role expectations during early adolescence. In J. Brooks-Gunn & A. C. Petersen (Eds.), *Girls at puberty: Biological and psychosocial perspectives* (pp. 201–228). New York: Plenum Press.

Holt, C. L., & Ellis, B. J. (1998). Assessing the current validity of the Bem sex-role inventory. *Sex Roles, 39*, 929–941.

Horwitz, A., & White, H. (1987). Gender role orientations and styles of pathology among adolescents. *Journal of Health and Social Behavior, 28*, 158–170.

Huddleston, J., & Ge, X. (2003). Boys at puberty: Psychosocial implications. In C. Hayward (Ed.), *Gender differences at puberty*. (pp. 113–134). Cambridge, UK: Cambridge University Press.

Ibanez, L., Street, M. E., Potau, N., Carrascosa, A., & Zampolli, M. (1997). Girls diagnosed with premature pubarche show an exaggerated ovarian androgen synthesis from the early stages of puberty: Evidence from gonadotropin-releasing hormone agonist testing. *Fertility and Sterility, 67*, 849–855.

Jack, D. C., & Dill, D. (1992). The silencing the self scale: Schemas of intimacy associated with depression in women. *Psychology of Women Quarterly, 16*, 97–106.

Jordan, J. V., Kaplan, A. G., Miller, J. B., Stiver, I. P., & Surrey, J. L. (1991). *Women's growth in connection: Writings from the Stone Center*. New York: Guilford Press.

Joyner, K., & Udry, J. R. (2000). You don't bring me anything but down: Adolescent romance and depression. *Journal of Health and Social Behavior, 41*, 369–391.

Katz, P. A., & Ksansnak, K. R. (1994). Developmental aspects of gender role flexibility and traditionality in middle childhood and adolescence. *Developmental Psychology, 30*, 272–282.

Kegan, R. (1982). *The Evolving Self: Problem and Process in Human Development*. Cambridge, MA: Harvard University.

Kroger, J. (2007). *Identity Development: Adolescence Through Adulthood*. Thousand Oaks, CA: Sage Publications.

Larson, R., & Asmussen, L. (1991). Anger, worry, and hurt in early adolescence: An enlarging world of negative emotions.

In M. E. Colten & S. Gore (Eds.), *Adolescent stress: Causes and consequences* (pp. 21–41). New York: Adeline de Gruyter.

Liao, L. M., Missenden, K., Hallam, R. S., Conway, C. S. (2005). Experience of early pubertal development: A preliminary analysis. *Journal of Reproductive and Infant Psychology, 23*, 219–233.

Maccoby, E. E. (1990). Gender and relationships: A developmental account. *American Psychologist, 45*, 513–520.

Magnusson, D., Stattin, H., & Allen, V. L. (1985). Biological maturation and social development: A longitudinal study of some adjustment processes from mid-adolescence to adulthood. *Journal of Youth and Adolescence, 14*, 267–283.

Marceau, K., Dorn, L. D., & Susman, E. J. (2012). Stress and puberty-related hormone reactivity, negative emotionality, and parent-adolescent relationships. *Psychoneuroendocrinology, 37*, 1286–1298.

Marceau, K., Ram, N., Houts, R. M., Grimm, K., & Susman, E. J. (2011). Individual differences in boys' and girls' timing and tempo of puberty: Modeling development with nonlinear growth models. *Developmental Psychology, 47*, 1389–1409.

Marcotte, D., Alain, M., & Gosselin, M. J. (1999). Gender differences in adolescent depression: Gender-typed characteristics or problem-solving skills deficits? *Sex Roles, 41*, 31–48.

Marshall, W. A., & Tanner, J. M. (1969). Variations in pattern of pubertal changes in girls. *Archives of Disease in Childhood, 44*, 291–303.

Martel, M. M., Klump, K., Nigg, J. T., Breedlove, S. M., & Sisk, C. L. (2009). Potential hormonal mechanisms of attention-deficit/hyperactivity disorder and major depressive disorder: A new perspective. *Hormones and Behavior, 55*, 465–479.

McDowell, M. A., Brody, D. J., Hughes, J. P. (2007). Has age at menarche changed? Results from the National Health and Nutrition Examination Survey (NHANES) 1999-2004. *Journal of Adolescent Health, 40*, 227–231.

McMaster, L. E., Connolly, J., Pepler, D., & Craig, W. M. (2002). Peer to peer sexual harassment in early adolescence: A developmental perspective. *Development and Psychopathology, 14*, 91–105.

Mendle, J., & Ferrero, J. (2012). Detrimental psychological outcomes associated with pubertal timing in adolescent boys. *Developmental Review, 32*, 49–66.

Mendle, J., Harden, K. P., Brooks-Gunn, J., & Graber, J. A. (2010). Development's tortoise and hare: Pubertal timing, pubertal tempo, and depressive symptoms in boys and girls. *Developmental Psychology, 46*, 1341–1353.

Mendle, J., Turkheimer, E., D'Onofrio, B. M., Lynch, S. K., Emery, R. E., Slutske, W. S., & Martin, N. G. (2006). Family structure and age at menarche: A children-of-twins approach. *Developmental Psychology, 42*, 533–542.

Mendle, J., Turkheimer, E., & Emery, R. E. (2007). Detrimental psychological outcomes associated with early pubertal timing in adolescent girls. *Developmental Review, 27*, 151–171.

Moore, S. M. (1995). Girls' understanding and social constructions of menarche. *Journal of Adolescence, 18*, 87–104.

Muris, P., Meesters, C., & Knoops, M. (2005). The relation between gender role orientation and fear and anxiety in nonclinic-referred children. *Journal of Clinical Child and Adolescent Psychology, 34*, 326–332.

Natsuaki, M. N., Biehl, M. C., & Ge, X. (2009). Trajectories of depressed mood from early adolescence to young adulthood: The effects of pubertal timing and adolescent dating. *Journal of Research on Adolescence, 19*, 47–74.

Natsuaki, M. N., Klimes-Dougan, B., Ge, X., Shirtcliff, E. A., Hastings, P. D., & Zahn-Waxler, C. (2009). Early pubertal maturation and internalizing problems in adolescence: Sex differences in the role of cortisol reactivity to interpersonal stress. *Journal of Clinical Child and Adolescent Psychology, 38*, 513–524.

Natsuaki, M. N., Leve, L. D., & Mendle, J. (2011). Going through the rites of passage: Timing and transition of menarche, childhood sexual abuse, and anxiety symptoms in girls. *Journal of Youth and Adolescence 40*, 1357–1370.

Negriff, S., & Susman, E. J. (2011). Pubertal timing, depression, and externalizing problems: A framework, review, and examination of gender differences. *Journal of Research on Adolescence, 21*, 717–746.

Nolen-Hoeksema, S. (1987). Sex differences in unipolar depression: Evidence and theory. *Psychological Bulletin, 101*, 259–282.

Nolen-Hoeksema, S., & Girgus, J. S. (1994). The emergence of gender differences in depression in adolescence. *Psychological Bulletin, 115*, 424–443.

Paikoff, R. L., & Brooks-Gunn, J. (1990). Physiological processes: What role do they play during the transition to adolescence? In R. M. Montemayor, G. R. Adams & T. P. Gullotta (Eds.), *From childhood to adolescence: A transitional period?* (pp. 33–56). Newbury Park: Sage Publications.

Paikoff, R. L., & Brooks-Gunn, J. (1991). Do parent-child relationships change during puberty. *Psychological Bulletin, 110*, 47–66.

Paxton, S. J., Schutz, H. K., Wertheim, E. H., & Muir, S. L. (1999). Friendship clique and peer influences on body image concerns, dietary restraint, extreme weight-loss behaviors, and binge eating in adolescent girls. *Journal of Abnormal Psychology, 108*, 255–266.

Petersen, A. C., & Taylor, B. (1980). The biological approach to adolescence. In J. Adelson (Ed.), *Handbook of adolescent psychology* (pp. 117–155). New York: Wiley.

Plomin, R., DeFries, J. C., & Loehlin, J. C. (1977). Genotype-environment interaction and correlation in the analysis of human behavior. *Psychological Bulletin, 84*, 309–322.

Priess, H., Lindberg, S., & Hyde, J. (2009). Adolescent gender-role identity and mental health: Gender intensification revisited. *Child Development, 80*, 1531–1544.

Rembeck, G. I., Moller, M., & Gunnarsson, R. K. (2006). Attitudes and feelings towards menstruation and womanhood in girls at menarche. *Acta Pediatrica, 95*, 707–714.

Rendron, L. E., Leen-Feldner, E. W., & Hayward, C. (2009). A critical review of the empirical literature on the relation between anxiety and puberty. *Clinical Psychology Review, 29*, 1–23.

Rierdan, J., Koff, E., & Stubbs, M. L. (1989). A longitudinal analysis of body image as a predictor of the onset and persistence of adolescent depression. *Journal of Early Adolescence, 9*, 454–466.

Rose, A. J., & Rudolph, K. D. (2006). A review of sex differences in peer relationship processes: Potential trade-offs for the emotional and behavioral development of girls and boys. *Psychological Bulletin, 132*, 98–131.

Rowe, D. C. (2002). On genetic variation in menarche and age at first sexual intercourse—A critique of the Belsky-Draper hypothesis. *Evolution and Human Behavior, 23*, 365–372.

Rubinow, D. R., & Schmidt, P. J. (1999). The neurobiology of menstrual cycle-related mood disorders. In D. S. Chamey,

E. J. Nestler & B. S. Bunney (Eds.), *Neurobiology of mental illness* (pp. 907–914). New York: Oxford University Press.

Ruble, D. N., & Brooks-Gunn, J. (1982). The experience of menarche. *Child Development, 53,* 1557–1566.

Rudolph, K. D. (2002). Gender differences in emotional responses to interpersonal stress during adolescence. *Journal of Adolescent Health, 30,* 3–13.

Rudolph, K. D. (in press). Puberty as a developmental context of risk for psychopathology. In M. Lewis & K. D. Rudolph (Eds.), *Handbook of developmental psychopathology.* New York: Plenum.

Rudolph, K. D., & Troop-Gordon, W. (2010). Personal-accentuation and contextual amplification models of pubertal timing: Predicting youth depression. *Development and Psychopathology, 22,* 433–451.

Sapolsky, R. M. (2000). Glucocorticoids and hippocampal atrophy in neuropsychiatric disorders. *Archives of General Psychiatry, 57,* 925–935.

Scarr, S., & McCartney, K. (1983). How people make their own environments: A theory of genotype—> environment effects. *Child Development, 54,* 424–435.

Schreiber, J. E., Shirtcliff, E. A., van Hulle, C., Lemery-Chlfant, K., Klein, M. H., Kalin, N. H.,...Goldsmith, H. H. (2006). Environmental influences on family similarity in afternoon cortisol levels: Twin and parent-offspring designs. *Psychoneuroendocrinology, 31,* 1131–1137.

Schultz, K. M., Molenda-Figueria, H. A., & Sisk, S. L. (2009). Back to the future: The organizational-activational hypothesis adapted to puberty and adolescence. *Hormones and Behavior, 55,* 597–604.

Shansky, R. M., Glavis-Bloom, C., Lerman, D., McRae, D., Benson, C., Miller, K.,...Arnsten, A. F. T. (2004). Estrogen mediates sex differences in stress-induced prefrontal cortex dysfunction. *Molecular Psychiatry, 9,* 531–538.

Sisk, C. L., & Foster, D. L. (2004). The neural basis of puberty and adolescence. *Nature Neuroscience, 7,* 1040–1047.

Smolak, L., Levine, M. P., & Gralen, S. (1993). The impact of puberty and dating on eating problems among middle school girls. *Journal of Youth and Adolescence, 22,* 355–368.

Sontag-Padilla, L. M., Dorn, L. D., Tissot, A., Susman, E. J., Beers, S. R., & Rose, S. R. (2012). Executive functioning, cortisol reactivity, and symptoms of psychopathology in girls with premature adrenarche. *Development and Psychopathology, 24,* 211–223.

Sontag-Padilla, L. M., Graber, J. A., & Clemans, K. H. (2011). The role of peer stress and pubertal timing on symptoms of psychopathology during early adolescence. *Journal of Youth and Adolescence, 40,* 1371–1382.

Spence, J. T., & Helmreich, R. L. (1978). *Masculinity and femininity: Their psychological dimensions, correlates, and antecedents.* Austin: University of Texas Press.

Stattin, H., & Magnusson, D. (1990). *Pubertal maturation in female development.* Hillsdale, NJ: Erlbaum

Steinberg, L., & Morris, A. S. (2001). Adolescent development. *Annual Reviews of Psychology, 52,* 83–110.

Stice, E. (2003). Puberty and body image. In C. Hayward (Ed.), *Gender differences at puberty.* (pp. 61–76). Cambridge, UK: Cambridge University Press.

Stice, E., Hayward, C., Cameron, R. P., Killen, J. D., & Taylor, C. B. (2000). Body image and eating disturbances predict onset of depression among adolescent females: A longitudinal study. *Journal of Abnormal Child Psychology, 109,* 438–444.

Stroud, L. R., Papandonatos, G. D., Williamson, D. E., & Dahl, R. E. (2004). Sex differences in the effects of pubertal development on responses to a corticotropin-releasing hormone challenge *Annals of the New York Academy of Sciences, 1021,* 348–351.

Stubbs, M. L. (2008). Cultural perceptions and practices around menarche and adolescent menstruation in the United States. *Annals of New York Academy of Sciences, 1135,* 58–66.

Tang, C. S., Yeung, D. Y., & Lee, A. M. (2003). Psychosocial correlates of emotional responses to menarche among Chinese adolescent girls. *Journal of Adolescent Health, 33,* 193–201.

Teunissen, H. A., Adelman, C. B., Prinstein, M. J., Spijkerman, R., Poelen, E. A. P., Engels, R. C. M. E., & Scholtes, R. H. J. (2011). The interaction between pubertal timing and peer popularity for boys and girls: An integration of biological and interpersonal perspectives on adolescent depression. *Journal of Abnormal Child Psychology, 39,* 413–423.

Tolman, D. L., Impett, E. A., Tracy, A. J., Michael, A. (2006). Looking good, sounding good: Femininity ideology and adolescent girls' mental health. *Psychology of Women Quarterly, 30,* 85–95.

Walker, E. F., Sabuwalla, Z., & Huot, R. (2004). Pubertal neuromaturation, stress sensitivity, and psychopathology. *Development and Psychopathology, 16,* 807–824.

Weisfeld, G. (1997). Puberty rites as clues to the nature of human adolescence. *Cross-Cultural Research, 31,* 27–54.

White, R. M. B., Deardoff, J., & Gonzales, N. A. (2012). Contextual amplification or attenuation of pubertal timing effects on depressive symptoms among Mexican girls. *Journal of Adolescent Heath 50,* 565–571.

Whittle, S., Yucel, M., Lorenzetti, V., Byrne, M. L., Simmons, J. G., Wood, S. J.,...Allen, N. B. (2012). Pituitary volume mediates the relationship between pubertal timing and depressive symptoms during adolescence. *Psychoneuroendocrinology, 37,* 881–891.

Wichstrom, L. (1999). The emergence of gender difference in depressed mood during adolescence: The role of intensified gender socialization. *Developmental Psychology, 35,* 232–245.

Young, E. A., & Altemus, M. (2004). Puberty, ovarian steroids, and stress. *Annals of the New York Academy of Science, 1021,* 124–133.

Zahn-Waxler, C., Shirtcliff, E. A., & Marceau, K. (2008). Disorders of childhood and adolescence: Gender and psychopathology. *Annual Review of Clinical Psychology, 4,* 275–303.

CHAPTER 25

Body Image and Identity: A Call for New Research

Elizabeth A. Daniels *and* Meghan M. Gillen

Abstract

Despite the central importance of satisfaction with one's physical appearance to overall psychological well-being, very little research has investigated how body image is related to identity construction, a key developmental task for young people. This chapter discusses theories on body image that the authors believe have utility in studying the relation between body image and identity because they encompass both sociocultural norms about appearance and one's self-perceptions and self-evaluations about the body. The authors then outline several factors that may be relevant to body image and identity formation including gender, biological factors, social group factors, and sociocultural factors. In the conclusion, the authors briefly highlight main points and offer some ideas for future research on this important and emerging area of inquiry.

Key Words: body image, identity, theory, objectification, gender, muscularity, thin ideal, media, careers

Satisfaction with one's physical appearance plays a pivotal role in overall psychological adjustment because it is an important predictor of global self-esteem among both males and females (Harter, 2012; Mendelson, Mendelson, & Andrews, 2000). Body image concerns and eating pathologies have historically been considered problems affecting primarily European-American girls and women. Presently, it is clear that these issues impact females from many ethnic/racial backgrounds, as well as boys and men (e.g., Grabe & Hyde, 2006; Ricciardelli, McCabe, Williams, & Thompson, 2007). Dissatisfaction with one's body is so prevalent among girls and women in many Western contexts it is considered a normative perception (e.g., Murnen, 2011). Over the past approximately ten years, it has become increasingly apparent that boys and men in many Western contexts are also dissatisfied with their bodies (e.g., McCreary, 2011).

The US National Eating Disorders Association (NEDA) identifies four components that comprise body image: (1) how you see yourself when you look in the mirror or picture yourself in your mind; (2) what you believe about your own appearance, including your memories, assumptions, and generalizations; (3) how you feel about your body, including your height, shape, and weight; and (4) how you sense and control your body as you move, which includes how you feel in your body, not just your thoughts about your body (NEDA, 2005). NEDA characterizes a positive body image as having an accurate perception of and appreciating one's shape, as well as feeling proud of and comfortable in one's body. Individuals with a positive body image also understand that physical appearance does not dictate one's value as a person, and these individuals refuse to spend excessive time worrying about food and weight. In contrast, a negative body image is characterized as having a distorted perception of one's shape; feeling ashamed, self-conscious, and anxious about one's body; viewing one's body as a personal failure; and feeling uncomfortable and awkward in one's body.

Markey (2010) recently issued a call to developmental psychologists to prioritize research on body image, given their ability to consider a range of intrapersonal (e.g., pubertal development) and interpersonal (e.g., family relationships) factors related to body image from a lifespan perspective. Indeed, developmental psychologists are well-positioned to consider how body image impacts self-concept and identity, both of which transform during adolescence (Erikson, 1968; Harter, 2012). *Self-concept* is how individuals view and evaluate themselves; a component of self-concept is *self-esteem*, which refers to one's sense of worth (Harter, 2012). Self-perceptions are global (e.g., overall sense of worth) and domain-specific (e.g., appearance esteem). Identity is a related construct but refers to one's sense of who one is and how one fits into the world (Erikson, 1968).

When considering the relationship between body image and identity, we propose that Erikson's (1950; 1968) seminal theoretical work on identity, as well as subsequent research paradigms based on Eriksonian theory (e.g., Marcia, 1966), are especially relevant. Erikson proposed that identity formation involves considering one's traits, abilities, and interests; trying out life choices available in one's culture (termed exploration); and committing to specific choices. Erikson identified identity construction in love, work, and ideology (i.e., beliefs and values) as a central task of adolescence, but noted that identity work begins before and continues after adolescence (see Fivush & Zaman, this volume; Kroger, this volume). Contemporary theorists have proposed additional domains for identity development and have suggested that significant identity work occurs in emerging adulthood, a period from late adolescence through the mid-twenties (Arnett, this volume; Arnett & Tanner, 2006). Accordingly, the present chapter focuses primarily on research using adolescent and emerging adult samples.

A key aspect of Eriksonian theory we identify as particularly relevant to understanding the relationship between body image and identity is the emphasis on the sociocultural environment within which individuals are embedded. Specifically, Erikson stated that identity is a "process 'located' *in the core of the individual* and yet also *in the core of his* [sic] *communal culture*" (1968, p. 22). At the time of Erikson's original writing, women's roles in US society were seriously constrained for the majority of middle-class and wealthy women (Douglas & Michaels, 2004; Friedan, 1963). Opportunities for paid work were limited, and the primary social goals for women were finding a husband and raising a family. During this period, the body and physical attractiveness were important concerns among adolescent girls and young women as a means to attract male attention (Brumberg, 1997). Indeed, the practice of displaying female bodies for the sake of others can be traced back to the 1920s, when both the film and fashion industries "encouraged a massive 'unveiling' of the female body" (Brumberg, 1997, p. 98) such that "modern femininity required some degree of exhibitionism or, at least, a willingness to display oneself as a decorative object" (p. 107). Thus, since the early twentieth century, prioritizing and emphasizing the aesthetics of the body has been a cultural mandate for girls and women in US society. We propose that, given the limitations of women's roles in society until the second wave of the women's movement in the 1960s and the cultural emphasis on women's physical appearance since the beginning of the twentieth century, the body has been a primary site for female identity for several generations of women.

Even today, when women occupy central roles in public life, including the workforce and education, the body remains an important means through which girls and women judge themselves and are judged by others (Strelan & Hargreaves, 2005). Accordingly, body image likely plays an important role in identity, especially for girls and women. The importance of the body for psychological well-being for boys and men is becoming increasingly clear in psychological research on male body image. However, the salience and centrality of the body for boys and men is likely not the same as for girls and women. Historically, boys and men have dominated the public sphere; accordingly, they have had many avenues other than their looks to define themselves.

A fairly large body of research has investigated the relationship between body image and self-concept, specifically self-esteem (e.g., Gillen & Lefkowitz, 2011; Jones & Newman, 2009). Unfortunately, very little research has investigated how body image is related to identity. The research that does exist on body image and identity has primarily focused on associations between ethnic/racial identity (e.g., Sabik, Cole, & Ward, 2010) or sexual identity (e.g., Wagenbach, 2003) and body image. We located just one study examining the relationship between body image and general identity development as originally conceptualized by Erikson. In a large sample of Swedish late adolescents, Wängqvist and Frisén

(2013) examined identity formation in relation to body esteem and body ideal internalization. In investigating identity formation, the authors studied both ideological (e.g., religion, politics) and interpersonal (e.g., friendships, romantic partnerships) explorations and commitments. They found that for young women interpersonal identity commitment and exploration were related to more positive thoughts about how others evaluate their appearance, and exploration only was related to more internalization of societal body ideals. For young men, stronger interpersonal identity commitment was related to more positive self-evaluations about their appearance. Overall, young women explored identity issues more, had poorer body esteem, and internalized societal body ideals more than did young men. These findings provide some initial insights into how body image and identity are related and the gendered nature of those relationships.

We believe there is much work to be done in considering how body image is related to identity. Given the central role body image plays in overall psychological adjustment, it is highly likely that body image is an important aspect of identity. For example, there is evidence that heightened self-objectification—that is, the tendency to view the body as an object—negatively impacts math performance (Fredrickson, Roberts, Noll, Quinn, & Twenge, 1998) and the availability of cognitive resources (Gay & Castano, 2010) in women; however, no research as of yet has investigated whether increased self-objectification impacts females' occupational choices, for example, avoidance of science, technology, engineering, and math (STEM) fields. There is a clear need for this type of research because females continue to be underrepresented in STEM fields (National Science Foundation, 2011). In general, much more research is necessary to understand the relationship between body image and identity across a range of domains.

We begin this chapter by discussing those theories on body image that we believe could be useful in studying body image and identity. We then articulate several factors that may be relevant to body image and identity formation including gender, biological factors, social group factors, and sociocultural factors. In the conclusion, we briefly highlight key points and offer some ideas for future work in this emerging area of research.

Body Image Theories

A number of theoretical frameworks typically guide research on body image. We describe several general theories that are commonly applied to body image research, including a specific model that fits within one of these larger frameworks. All of these perspectives involve an emphasis on perceptions of the self within a sociocultural context, which Erikson observed is crucial to identity construction and are therefore relevant to the construction of body image and identity.

One of the more general theories seen in the body image literature is *social comparison theory* (Festinger, 1954). According to this perspective, individuals are motivated to evaluate themselves by means of comparison to others. This theory is frequently utilized in body image research because appearance is one dimension on which individuals may compare themselves to others. Given the widespread, intense focus on looks in Western cultures and the objectification of both men and women in the media (McCreary, 2011; Murnen, 2011), appearance comparisons may be quite common. Individuals who engage in more appearance-based social comparisons tend to have higher body dissatisfaction, with relations being stronger for women than for men (Myers & Crowther, 2009; Tantleff-Dunn & Gokee, 2002). Also, women who have more body image concerns are more likely to participate in "fat talk," a style of conversation in which one person states she is fat and others insist she is not fat; this association is stronger for women who have a greater tendency to engage in social comparison (Corning & Gondoli, 2012; Nichter, 2000).

Another general theory commonly used in body image research is *self-discrepancy theory* (Higgins, 1987). This theory predicts that individuals perceive multiple aspects of the self, including actual, ideal, and ought selves. Discrepancies between the actual self and these latter selves are associated with negative psychological outcomes. This theory has a natural connection to body image in that appearance is one domain in which individuals may perceive or envision various selves (e.g., what do I actually look like? what do I ideally want to look like?). Pictorial measures of body image have been frequently used to capture perceptions of these various selves and therefore map nicely into this theory (e.g., Gillen & Lefkowitz, 2011). On these measures, individuals must select from a series of bodily figures those that represent various aspects of the self (e.g., the figure that best matches their own, the figure they would ideally like to resemble). The discrepancy between actual and ideal figures has been frequently used as a measure of body dissatisfaction, although some have questioned this approach (Gardner & Brown, 2010; Polivy & Herman, 2002).

A third theoretical framework often used in body image research is the sociocultural perspective. In general, this perspective postulates that culture influences people's attitudes, behaviors, and values (see Jackson, 2002; Thompson, Heinberg, Altabe, & Tantleff-Dunn, 1999). What is deemed physically attractive in Western cultures, including thinness for girls and women (the "thin ideal") and muscularity for boys and men (Murnen, 2011; McCreary, 2011), influences individuals' attitudes and behaviors with regard to their own bodies. For example, in an effort to achieve a thinner body, women may diet or get cosmetic surgery, whereas men may lift weights or take steroids to gain muscle. A specific model that fits within this larger sociocultural framework is the *tripartite model* (Thompson et al., 1999). In this model, media, parents, and peers are the primary sources of sociocultural influence on body dissatisfaction. Appearance-based comparisons and internalization of the thin ideal mediate the influence of these sources on body dissatisfaction. Furthermore, body dissatisfaction is related to eating disturbances, which are in turn related to psychological well-being. This model, including modified versions of it, has received empirical support in multiple samples, including adolescents (Keery, van den Berg, & Thompson, 2004; Papp, Urban, Czegledi, Babusa, & Tury, 2013), college students (Menzel et al., 2011; Tylka, 2011), and gay men (Tylka & Andorka, 2012). Although this model generally fits both boys/men and girls/women, these studies indicate that it may operate differently for each gender (e.g., strength of associations, variables added).

A fourth theoretical framework is *objectification theory*. Objectification theory was developed specifically to explain the experiences of girls and women in Western contexts who are embedded within a culture that routinely sexually objectifies the female body (Fredrickson & Roberts, 1997; McKinley & Hyde, 1996). The theory proposes that women's bodies are scrutinized as objects for the pleasure and evaluation of others, specifically men (and boys). This objectification can occur within interpersonal and social encounters, as well as through individuals' experiences with visual media. Moreover, there is substantial evidence documenting the widespread objectification of women in mainstream media and the negative effects of this objectification on female viewers (see American Psychological Association [APA], 2007, for a review; Grabe, Ward, & Hyde, 2008). When looking at magazines directed especially toward men, such as *Maxim,* a focus on women's sexual attractiveness is especially prominent (Krassas, Blauwkamp, & Wesselink, 2003). As a result, engagement with virtually any type of media is likely to involve objectified portrayals of women that send the message to viewers that women are sexual objects. Thus, the sociocultural environment that girls and women in many Western contexts experience prioritizes their physical and sexual attractiveness.

Because of this cultural pressure, there is a tendency among girls and women to view themselves from an outsider's perspective as an object to be evaluated. This self-objectified view of one's body can lead to an objectified body consciousness, which involves perceiving and describing one's body according to externally observable traits (i.e., how I appear) instead of internal traits (i.e., what I can do) (McKinley & Hyde, 1996). An objectified body consciousness is characterized by constant monitoring of one's appearance (body surveillance), body shame, and the belief that, given enough effort, one can control one's appearance to comply with societal standards of beauty. These practices and feelings can be considered the effects of living in a culture that objectifies the female body.

Self-objectification has implications for girls' and women's mental health, including a heightened risk for disordered eating, negative body esteem, and decreased psychological well-being (APA, 2007; Fredrickson et al., 1998; Lindberg, Hyde, & McKinley, 2006; McKinley, 1999; Tiggemann & Lynch, 2001; Zurbriggen & Roberts, 2013). Compared to college men, college women infer more negative emotions in a woman who self-objectifies, suggesting women are aware of the negative consequences of self-objectification on women's psychological well-being (Newheiser, LaFrance, & Dovidio, 2010). In addition, as mentioned earlier, self-objectification negatively impacts math performance (Fredrickson et al., 1998) and the availability of cognitive resources (Gay & Castano, 2010) in women. In short, a range of serious negative consequences, which women may be aware of, are associated with self-objectification in girls and women (for in-depth reviews, see APA, 2007; Moradi & Huang, 2008).

Whereas objectification theory was developed to explain the experiences of girls and women specifically, it has since been tested among boys and men. In general, it appears that self-objectification and its components are more common among women and girls than men and boys (Frederick, Forbes, Grigorian, & Jarcho, 2007; Hebl, King, & Lin, 2004; Oehlof, Musher-Eizenman, Neufeld, & Hauser, 2009; Slater & Tiggemann, 2010). However, when college men are put in a situation that induces self-objectification (e.g., wearing a Speedo swimsuit), like women, they too report increased body shame, lower self-esteem (marginal effect), and their math performance is impaired (Hebl et al., 2004). Thus, it appears that objectification theory has utility in understanding body image among both girls/women and boys/men.

To summarize, we believe the theories discussed here are highly relevant to the study of body image and identity because they explicitly connect self-evaluations and self-perceptions about the body to the sociocultural context, which in many Western contexts objectifies the female body. Next, we turn to a discussion of how body image is gendered.

Gender and Body Image

In considering the relevance of body image to identity, it is necessary to reflect on cultural ideals of attractiveness, which differ by gender.

Girls and Women

Thinness has been a key component of female beauty since roughly the 1970s among European-American groups (Murnen, 2011). The 1960s saw the rise of the first super-models, including Jean Shrimpton and Twiggy, both of whom were very slender (Quick, 1997). These models stood in contrast to the full-figured body type preferred in the 1950s (e.g., Marilyn Monroe) and sparked a cultural preference for thinness that has intensified over time. In terms of adolescent development, a study of girls' diaries from 1830 to the 1990s found a clear shift from an emphasis on "good works" in the nineteenth century to "good looks" in the twentieth century (Brumberg, 1997). Whereas in the 1800s girls' moral character was considered more important than their beauty, today girls' appearance and the shape of their bodies are paramount.

In addition to thinness, sexiness has become a cultural mandate for girls and (especially young) women (Levin & Kilbourne, 2008; Roberts & Zurbriggen, 2013; Smolak & Murnen, 2011); indeed, the contemporary beauty ideal for females is thin and sexy (Murnen, 2011). The socialization of sexiness is apparent in consumer products aimed at even the youngest of girls, including sexualized dolls such as Bratz, which are marketed toward six- to twelve-year-old girls; thongs and lingerie sold at "tween" retail stores like the *Limited Too,* which markets to children aged seven through teenagers; and mock high-heeled shoes for newborn to six-month-old babies (e.g., heelarious, her first high heels; see APA, 2007 for a full review; heelarious.com). A content analysis of websites for fifteen popular clothing stores for children in the United States found that 29 percent of clothing had at least some sexualizing characteristics; furthermore, stores aimed at "tweens," such as *Abercrombie Kids,* had the highest proportion of sexualized clothing out of the fifteen stores studied (Goodin, Van Denburg, Murnen, & Smolak, 2011). In addition, reality TV contributes to this phenomenon with shows like *Toddlers and Tiaras,* which began airing in 2009 and features young girls as beauty contestants. Young girls on this show are made up to resemble adult women with make-up, false eyelashes, spray tans, fake hair, and elaborate costumes.

Even young girls appear to know that sexiness is preferred. Starr and Ferguson (2012) found that six- to nine-year-old girls chose a sexualized doll rather than a nonsexualized doll as their ideal self and as popular. The preference for sexualized portrayals of females appears to be especially likely among grade-school girls who are aware of and have internalized the thin beauty ideal for women (Murnen, Smolak, Mills, & Good, 2003). These girls are more likely to like how sexualized women look, to want to look like them, to think it is important to look like them, and to believe that it is easy to look like them.

In summary, the contemporary beauty standard for European-American girls and women in the United States is a thin, sexy body. Even young girls are aware of this ideal. Accordingly, as girls begin the process of identity development in adolescence, they are immersed in a sociocultural environment that prioritizes their physical and sexual attractiveness.

Boys and Men

Muscularity is a key component of male attractiveness in Western cultures. Despite its importance, researchers only identified this appearance concern in males within approximately the past decade (McCreary, 2011). Accordingly, there is far less research on the muscular ideal and body image in males as compared to the thin ideal and body image in females. Pope, Phillips, and Olivardia (2000) detailed a number of different body image concerns that afflict boys and men, such as body and muscle dysmorphia, eating disorders, and steroid abuse, which they attribute, in part, to society's emphasis on a muscular ideal for men.

Typically, males report higher levels of body and weight satisfaction compared to females even when they are overweight, and males tend to be less likely to suffer from eating disorders as compared to females (McCreary, 2011). However, large numbers of boys and men report dissatisfaction with their bodies (e.g., Cohane & Pope, 2001; McCabe & Ricciardelli, 2004a). No recent research using nationally representative samples has been conducted on the prevalence of body dissatisfaction in the population (Frederick, Jafary, Gruys, & Daniels, 2012); however, findings from the Growing Up Today Study, an ongoing longitudinal study of close to 17,000 youth in the United States, show body dissatisfaction increases for both girls and boys from preadolescence to late adolescence (Calzo et al., 2012). At ages eleven to twelve, 20 percent of girls and 15 percent of boys report body dissatisfaction, whereas at ages seventeen to eighteen, 35 percent of girls and 18 percent of boys do. In contrast to females who typically prefer a thinner body size, ideal body size tends to vary among males. For example, 59–72 percent of female college students want to be thinner whereas only 6–8 percent want to be larger (Gillen & Lefkowitz, 2006; Yates, Edman, & Aruguete, 2004). Among their male counterparts, however, 38–41 percent want to be thinner and 24–31 percent want to be larger (Gillen & Lefkowitz, 2006).

Evidence suggests that discontent with muscularity is widespread among college men in the United States (Frederick, Buchanan, Sadehgi-Azar, Peplau, Haselton, & Lipinski, 2007). Men may desire a more muscular body for aesthetic reasons (exposure to widespread cultural images of muscular men presented as "ideal") or for performance purposes (to improve athletic skills). In one study of college men, men chose an ideal body size with a mean of approximately 25 pounds more muscle than their own actual level of muscularity and about 8 pounds less body fat than their own actual levels of fat, suggesting a preference for quite a bit more muscularity (Olivardia, Pope, Borowiecki, & Cohane, 2004). This preference, in fact, outpaces the level of muscularity that women prefer in men (Olivardia et al., 2004). Increased drive for muscularity is related to decreased self-esteem and increased depression in adolescent boys (McCreary & Sasse, 2000). In college men, body dissatisfaction (including degree of muscularity and body fat) is related to depression, lower self-esteem, eating pathology, and the use of performance-enhancing substances such as creatine and steroids (Olivardia et al., 2004).

In pursuit of muscularity, males may consume supplements, such as creatine, and illicit substances, such as steroids. Even though little is known about the effects of long-term use, creatine is one of the most popular dietary supplements worldwide because it is thought to improve skeletal muscle function and increase body mass (Bahrke, 2007). Between 1 and 5 percent of male secondary school students in the United States use anabolic steroids to improve athletic performance, increase strength and muscle mass, and improve appearance (Goldberg & Elliot, 2007; Johnston, O'Malley, Bachman, & Schulenberg, 2012; Morbidity and Mortality Weekly Report, 2012). Steroid use is linked with a number of serious physical (e.g., heart attack) and mental health (e.g., mood changes) consequences (Goldberg & Elliot, 2007). Although the vast majority of youth do not use steroids, thousands do risk their health in pursuit of muscularity.

Cultural pressures toward increased muscularity in males are reflected in consumer products, such as children's toys and media. Action figures marketed to boys, such as GI Joe dolls, became increasingly muscular from the 1960s to the 1990s; many modern figures resemble elite bodybuilders, and some outpace what a human male could ever physically attain (Pope, Olivardia, Gruber, & Borowiecki, 1999). Furthermore, male bodies in magazines marketed toward men (e.g., *Men's Health*) are more muscular than male bodies in magazines marketed toward women (e.g., *Cosmopolitan*) suggesting that men's engagement with this type of media is especially likely to result in unrealistic body ideals (Frederick, Fessler, & Haselton, 2005).

In summary, muscularity is a central feature of male attractiveness in Western contexts. Accordingly, as boys begin the process of identity development in adolescence, they are immersed in a sociocultural environment that prioritizes a fit and muscular body, even through their exposure to children's toys. Some boys and men may attempt to alter their bodies through taking supplements (e.g., creatine) or steroids in order to achieve the aesthetic muscular ideal and/or to improve their athletic performance. As with girls, the specific role of cultural standards for attractiveness on boys' developing identities is an empirical question.

Biological Factors
Pubertal Timing and Body Image

On average, girls enter puberty twelve to sixteen months before boys (Nottelmann, Inoff-Germain, Susman, & Chrousos, 1990). During puberty, body fat increases for both girls and boys, but more so for girls. By adulthood, females have twice as much body fat as males and males have 1.5 times more lean body mass and skeletal mass than females (Fechner, 2003). These changes require adolescents to adjust to bodies that are quite different from those they had in childhood. At the same time, cognitive advances enable adolescents to engage in social comparisons about their bodies with their peers and media images (Jones, 2001).

The timing of maturation (early, on-time, late) can be especially important for boys' and girls' body perceptions, eating practices, and overall psychological well-being (Mendle & Ferrero, 2012; Mendle, Turkheimer, & Emery, 2007; Natsuaki, Samuels, & Leve, this volume). Early maturing girls are more likely than their peers to report body dissatisfaction, poor self-esteem, dieting behaviors, disordered eating, depression, and anxiety (Mendle et al., 2007; Natsuaki et al., this volume; cf., Stice & Whitenton, 2002). Furthermore, some of these problems persist for early maturing girls even after their peers have caught up to them in development. Girls who mature early tend to have higher body mass index (BMI) levels relative to their peers (Striegel-Moore et al., 2001), which is inconsistent with Western cultures' value on thinness in females (Thompson et al., 1999). In contrast, late-maturing girls tend to be thinner than earlier-maturing girls or on-time girls; they also report less body dissatisfaction and drive for thinness than their peers (Striegel-Moore et al., 2001). Thus, among girls, early development appears to be a risk factor for body image disturbances, whereas late development may be a protective factor. However, it is important to note that the contribution of pubertal timing to a range of psychosocial outcomes including body perceptions tends to be modest (Mendle et al., 2007).

Very little research has investigated the role of pubertal timing in adolescent boys' body image, perhaps due to difficulty in assessing pubertal development in boys for whom there is no clear biological marker signifying pubertal onset (Ricciardelli & McCabe, 2007). Early maturation may confer positives and negatives in terms of boys' body image. Some evidence has demonstrated that early developing boys are more satisfied with their bodies than on-time and late maturing boys (McCabe & Ricciardelli, 2004b). However, early puberty in boys is also associated with engagement in strategies to increase muscle, use of food supplements, dependence on exercise, bulimic behaviors (also found in late-maturing boys), dietary restraint, body shape concerns, and weight concerns (Kaltiala-Heino, Rimpela, Rissanen, & Rantanen, 2001; McCabe & Ricciardelli, 2004b; Zehr, Culbert, Sisk, & Klump, 2007).

Pubertal development may be relevant to identity development via social comparison. For early developers, looking different from one's peers may lead to an increased focus on appearance, including strategies for managing one's appearance, and a reduced focus on other domains, such as academic performance. In addition, older peers may approach early developers and encourage engagement in an older peer network. Thus, physical appearance may have implications for identity within interpersonal relationships by shaping one's access to particular peer environments, including access to romantic partners.

Body Mass Index and Body Image

Body mass index is another factor relevant to the development of body image and identity. In Western cultures, there is a widespread preference for thinness, even in young children. In one study, for example, preschool aged children made more positive attributions (e.g., nice, smart) to thin figures than chubby figures and made more negative attributions (e.g., ugly, has no friends) to chubbier figures than thin figures (Holub, 2008). A larger body size may be a risk factor for body dissatisfaction because of its distance from sociocultural beauty ideals. Indeed, there is a growing body of research documenting the negative effects of weight stigma on physical and psychological health for women in particular (Major, Eliezer, & Rieck, 2012).

Studies have demonstrated that, among children, both boys and girls who have a higher BMI want to be thinner, are more likely to experience feelings and thoughts about losing weight, and are more likely to engage in weight loss behaviors as compared to children with lower BMIs (McCabe & Ricciardelli, 2003a; Rolland, Farnill, & Griffiths, 1996). Prospective research from a five-year longitudinal study with adolescent girls and boys found that BMI was a strong and consistent predictor of increased body dissatisfaction across time (Paxton, Eisenberg, & Neumark-Sztainer, 2006). A similar pattern has been found with college students, such that higher BMI is associated with greater body dissatisfaction (Yates et al., 2004).

Given the intense stigma associated with being overweight in the United States, BMI likely has implications for identity for girls and women specifically. Overweight girls and women face weight-based discrimination in educational and occupational settings, which in turn limits their economic opportunities (Fikkan & Rothblum, 2012). They also report fewer opportunities to date and less involvement in romantic relationships relative to their thinner peers (Fikkan & Rothblum, 2012). Thus, biased social attitudes about weight can seriously restrict romantic and occupational identity opportunities among females. Overweight boys and men are subject to weight bias as well, but the negative effects are not as severe compared to girls and women (Fikkan & Rothblum, 2012).

Social Group Factors

Social groups are important for body image because perceptions of beauty may differ by group. Here, we discuss how ethnicity/race and sexual orientation are related to body image because these two social identities may be especially important for body image concerns. In addition, we encourage body image researchers to consider multiple social groups (e.g., gender and ethnicity/race) in study designs on body perceptions because beauty norms may vary by the combination of identities (Way & Rogers, this volume). This recommendation mirrors the broader call for adopting an intersectional lens in social scientific research (Baca Zinn & Dill, 1994; Cole, 2009; Collins, 1991).

Ethnicity/Race and Body Image

Females and males across many ethnic/racial groups experience body image concerns. Indeed, a meta-analysis found few ethnic/racial differences in body dissatisfaction among white, Asian-American, Hispanic, and black samples of females ranging in age from elementary school age through adulthood (Grabe & Hyde, 2006). One significant comparison, however, demonstrated a small difference indicating that white women are more dissatisfied with their bodies than are black women (see Roberts, Cash, Feingold, & Johnson, 2006, for similar findings); the few remaining group differences were smaller in magnitude and several were close to zero. The difference between white and black females in body dissatisfaction was largest in adolescence and early adulthood. Overall, Grabe and Hyde's (2006) research demonstrates that body dissatisfaction is a broad social issue impacting most girls and women and not one that is restricted to a particular racial/ethnic group.

Possible explanations as to why black females are more satisfied with their bodies than are white females include differing cultural definitions of beauty. Whereas white definitions of beauty for females emphasize thinness, black beauty standards are more accepting of larger body sizes and prioritize other qualities, such as personal style, over thinness (see Grabe & Hyde, 2006; Sabik et al., 2010). Sabik and colleagues found that black college students reported higher mean scores on appearance esteem, lower drive for thinness, and weight-based contingency of self-worth compared to their Asian-American and white peers. However, they found that black women who reported low appearance esteem and higher levels of orientation toward other ethnic groups (or higher weight-based contingency of self-worth) had higher drive for thinness. The interaction between ethnic identity, which is distinct from other-group orientation, and appearance esteem was also examined and did not significantly predict drive for thinness. These findings suggest that the relationship between ethnicity/race and body image is more complex than simple group membership; interactions with and attitudes toward ethnic groups different from one's own may be relevant to how some women feel about their bodies. Indeed, black women in predominantly white contexts might be vulnerable to body image concerns typically found among white women.

There is a growing body of research on body image among boys and men from different ethnic/racial groups; Ricciardelli and colleagues (2007) provided a systematic review of 104 existing studies. Mirroring findings for females, black males report higher body satisfaction than do white males, and there were few differences between Hispanic and white males. Findings for Asian males were inconsistent across studies.

It is important to note that existing meta-analytic findings (Grabe & Hyde, 2006; Roberts et al., 2006) have not captured specific appearance concerns that vary by ethnic/racial group membership (e.g., skin tone, hair texture, eyelid shape; Gillen, 2013; Kawamura, 2011; Patton, 2006). These specific concerns may prompt a range of behaviors including skin bleaching, chemically straightening hair, and cosmetic surgery, all of which carry health risks. In addition, ethnic/racial group membership may interact with a range of individual difference factors associated with body satisfaction, such as media consumption (Rivadeneyra, Ward, & Gordon, 2007), acculturation (Schooler, 2008), and pubertal timing (see Siegel, Yancy, Aneshensel, & Schuler, 1999). Identification with one's ethnic group may also be a protective factor against global body dissatisfaction for girls and women of color (Sabik et al., 2010; Schooler & Daniels, 2013). For example, in a quasi-experimental study with Latina adolescents, Schooler and Daniels (2013) found that ethnic identity buffered girls from the negative effects of viewing sexualized, thin-ideal white media images. Specifically, among girls who viewed these images, spontaneously using an ethnic label to describe the self was related to more positive descriptions of one's own body and appearance compared to girls who did not offer an ethnic label. Thus, ethnic identity has implications for body image among females. Similar research on the role of ethnicity/race in body image is necessary among males.

Sexual Orientation and Body Image

Much of the research on sexual orientation and body image has examined the relationship between membership in a sexual orientation group and body image, rather than investigating the relationship between sexual identity and body image. More research is clearly necessary to determine whether group membership or sexual identity is more relevant to body image. Looking at group membership, homosexual men tend to report somewhat more body dissatisfaction than do heterosexual men, and homosexual and heterosexual women do not differ from each other in body satisfaction (Morrison & McCutcheon, 2011; Peplau et al., 2009). Somewhat similar patterns were observed in a large adolescent sample (French, Story, Remafedi, Resnick, & Blum, 1996). In this study, homosexual boys were more likely to report poor body image and problematic eating behaviors than were heterosexual boys. Homosexual girls were more likely than heterosexual girls to report positive body image; however, they were not less likely to report problematic eating behaviors. These patterns suggest body image concerns and disordered eating practices start at younger ages for homosexual males and remain problematic over time. For homosexual females, there may be a somewhat later onset of negative self-perceptions about the body.

We located only two studies that investigated sexual identity and body image, both of which were conducted with adults. Wagenbach (2003) found that the degree to which women identified as lesbian did not influence their body satisfaction or eating problems. However, lesbians were less invested in their appearance, less involved in maintaining their appearance, less concerned with dieting, and less concerned with thinness compared to heterosexual women and homosexual men. In a study with homosexual men, Udall-Weiner (2009) found that stage of homosexual identity development significantly, but weakly, predicted body and appearance satisfaction among white men but not men of color. Taken together, these findings suggest that sexual identity is related to components of body image for homosexual adults. Future research should investigate the relationship between sexual identity and body image among sexual-minority adolescents who may be more actively engaged in sexual identity development as compared to adults. In addition, future research should also investigate body image and sexual identity among sexual-minority subgroups, for example, "femme" versus "butch" lesbians (Morrison & McCutcheon, 2011), as well as bisexual individuals (Chmielewski & Yost, 2013). Like ethnicity/race, membership in a particular sexual orientation group or holding a particular sexual identity may exacerbate or be protective in body image concerns; more research is necessary to understand the role of membership versus identity. Identifying these patterns is important for tailoring interventions to address relevant concerns about the body. In addition, bringing attention to body image concerns related to social groups allows for the opportunity to deconstruct and critique group norms related to the body.

Sociocultural Factors
Parents and Body Image

Parental attitudes and behaviors are important to youths' body perceptions and weight-control behaviors. Both direct (e.g., verbal commentary about the body or appearance, including encouraging children to diet) and indirect (e.g., modeling dieting behaviors and weight concerns) influences have been examined (e.g., Fulkerson et al., 2002; Wertheim, Mee, & Paxton, 1999). This research has primarily focused on mothers (exceptions include Field et al., 2001; McCabe & Ricciardelli, 2003*b*), with less research on fathers or on male-typed body concerns, such as drive for muscularity or steroid use. In general, direct parental behaviors seem to be more strongly related to children's body-related beliefs and behaviors than indirect behaviors (Paxton et al., 2006; Wertheim et al., 1999; Wertheim, Martin, Prior, Sanson, & Smart, 2002).

More than 90 percent of college students report receiving direct feedback on physical appearance from mothers and fathers (Schwartz, Phares, Tantleff-Dunn, & Thompson, 1999), and approximately one-third of mothers report that they encourage their adolescent children to diet

(Fulkerson et al., 2002). Females perceive more appearance-related comments from parents than do males (Schwartz et al., 1999). Direct comments from parents about weight or dieting are generally associated with their children's body image, weight control behaviors, and/or psychological functioning (Fulkerson et al., 2002; Schwartz et al., 1999; Smolak, Levine, & Schermer, 1999). These impacts may be greater for daughters (Schwartz et al., 1999; Smolak et al., 1999), and mothers may be more influential than fathers (Smolak et al., 1999). However, when examining strategies to increase muscle tone, feedback from fathers is more influential than feedback from mothers among boys (McCabe & Ricciardelli, 2003b).

There is also evidence that parents' indirect influences are associated with their children's body image and weight control behaviors. However, adolescents' *perceptions* of their mothers' dieting behaviors are associated with adolescent girls' and boys' weight-related concerns and behaviors, whereas maternal self-reports of dieting are not related (Fulkerson et al., 2002; Keery, Eisenberg, Boutelle, Neumark-Sztainer, & Story, 2006). Measuring youths' perceptions of parental attitudes and behaviors may be a more sensitive method of investigating modeling influences as compared to relying on parents' self-reported behaviors. For example, girls (but not boys) who report that it is important to either parent that they are thin were twice as likely as their peers to become highly concerned with weight over time (Field et al., 2001). This finding suggests a transmission of values about weight from parents to children.

Through making comments about their children's weight or by modeling weight control behaviors, parents may shape their children's identity. For example, if parents tell a child that he or she is overweight, that child might wish to avoid activities in which his or her weight is more visible (e.g., swimming in the pool, playing sports in tight-fitting uniforms). Consequently, children may never develop an interest in these sorts of physical activities and, paradoxically, may actually gain more weight from avoiding them. Parents who model appearance and weight concerns might (perhaps inadvertently) encourage their children to pursue hobbies or extracurricular activities that focus on these areas, such as beauty pageants or cheerleading. By focusing on appearance-related pursuits, children may begin to self-objectify and may fail to develop identities that focus more on skills rather than appearance.

Peers and Body Image

Reflecting the more general tendency for friends to be similar across a range of demographic and behavioral characteristics among adolescents, body image concerns and behaviors appear to be similar in friendship groups (Paxton, Schutz, Wertheim, & Muir, 1999). Peer appearance culture impacts adolescent boys as well as girls (Jones & Crawford, 2006; Jones, Vigfusdottir, & Lee, 2004). However, adolescent girls engage in more appearance conversations with friends than do adolescent boys; this pattern holds for girls across BMI categories (Jones & Crawford, 2006). "Fat talk," a particular style of appearance conversation, is common among girls (Nichter, 2000). According to Nichter (2000), by engaging in fat talk, girls ask for support from and disclose vulnerability to other girls; thus, it serves a social cohesiveness function. Girls report pressure to engage in fat talk to demonstrate that they do not feel superior to their peers and do not seem "stuck up."

Peer discourse pertaining to appearance or the body is linked to body image concerns and weight control behaviors. Specifically, peer appearance criticism is associated with greater body dissatisfaction, and perceived pressure to lose weight from friends and family is associated with greater body dissatisfaction and more negative eating attitudes and behaviors (Ata, Ludden, & Lally, 2007; Jones, 2004). The tendency to make social comparisons based on appearance (girls only; Jones, 2004), as well as the extent to which adolescents internalize body ideals seen in the media (Jones et al., 2004) are important mediators in the relationship between appearance conversations and body dissatisfaction.

Receiving negative feedback from peers on appearance might alter young people's activity choices and hence restrict their opportunity for identity exploration in various domains, particularly within a school setting (e.g., dance team). Negative comments from peers might also hinder the development of relational identities—what it means and feels like to be in a healthy friendship or romantic relationship. Having peers who repeatedly criticize appearance may begin to feel normative, which might lead to foreclosing on similar negative relationships without exploring potentially positive ones.

Media and Body Image

A large body of psychological research has focused on the impact of mass media on female viewers (e.g., Levine & Murnen, 2009; Lopez-Guimera, Levine, Sanchez-Carracedo, &

Fauquet, 2010). In general, these studies have found that engagement with mass media negatively impacts female viewers' body-related self-perceptions and eating behaviors (with small to moderate effect sizes in most studies). A number of moderators (such as age, ethnicity, and type of media) and mediators (such as internalization of the thin beauty ideal and social comparison processes) have been identified (Lopez-Guimera et al., 2010).

Far less research has examined the impact of media on males as compared to females. However, one meta-analysis of experimental and correlational studies demonstrated that, similar to women, men feel worse about their bodies in response to idealized mass media images (Barlett, Vowels, & Saucier, 2008). Results indicated associations between pressure from mass media and lower body satisfaction, body esteem, and self-esteem, as well as increased depression and behavioral outcomes (e.g., excessive exercising). In addition, the overall effect size estimate for experimental studies measuring the impact of the muscular ideal on male viewers was comparable to the overall effect size estimate in Groesz, Levine, and Murnen's (2002) meta-analysis assessing the impact of the thin ideal on female viewers. Thus, both males' and females' self-perceptions are negatively impacted to a similar degree by viewing idealized media images.

Much of the existing research on body image and media has relied on traditional media (e.g., magazines), with less work on the impact of new media, such as social networking sites and other websites. For example, girls may seek out online content that encourages eating disorders, such as pro-anorexia or pro-bulimia websites, or other websites that provide information about losing weight. Social networking sites might even serve as information hubs for advice or tips on particular body-related practices among groups of peers (Norris, Boydell, Pinhas, & Katzman, 2006) and may reinforce in-person appearance conversations and teasing. Tiggemann and Miller's (2010) work supports the contention that body-related content on internet websites can be problematic in girls' pursuit of thinness.

More research investigating the effects of nonidealized media imagery on viewers is urgently needed. Daniels (2009) found that teenage girls and college women who viewed images of female athletes performing a sport were more likely to make self-descriptions about their own physical abilities as compared to girls and women shown sexualized images of female athletes who, in contrast, tended to make more self-descriptions about their own physical appearance. Furthermore, teen girl, teen boy, and college female viewers focused on the athletes' physical skill and athleticism only in response to the performance-focused images; sexualized athlete images yielded a focus on the athletes' physical appearance (Daniels, 2012; Daniels & Wartena, 2011). Taken together, these patterns indicate that media images of female athletes portrayed as athletes may positively impact female viewers and prompt instrumental rather than appearance evaluations of women in both male and female viewers. These images may be a counterweight to dominant media images of women that objectify female bodies and prompt self-objectification in female viewers (Aubrey, 2006; Harper & Tiggemann, 2008).

We believe the unrealistic, sexually objectified images young people view in the media can have a significant influence on their identity formation, particularly for girls and women. These images suggest to girls and women that appearance is an integral part of their identity and one on which they will certainly be judged. For example, reality make-over shows such as *I Want a Famous Face* or *The Swan* suggest that by getting cosmetic surgery, one's life, identity, and relationships will be dramatically improved. The media also suggest which appearance-related activities are appropriate for each gender. For example, observing girls and women in reality shows on beauty pageants (e.g., *Toddlers and Tiaras*) and boys and men in commercials for exercise equipment might encourage individuals to pursue these gender-specific activities, contributing to their identities as "beauty queens" or athletes. Future research should examine how exposure to media ideals shapes identity choices.

Careers and Body Image

There is little empirical work on the association between careers and body image—how body image may affect perceptions of certain careers or career choices or how entering particular fields may shape body image. The few studies that have been conducted on this topic are quite diverse in their samples and methodology. In an experimental study with four- to seven-year old girls, Sherman and Zurbriggen (under review) investigated girls' career aspirations after they played with either Barbie™, a thin and sexualized doll, or Mrs. Potato Head™, a doll that is not thin or sexualized. They found that girls who played with Barbie reported that boys could do more jobs than they themselves could do as compared to girls who played with Mrs. Potato

Head who reported no difference in the number of jobs that they could do compared to the number boys could do. Studies on college women suggest connections between job status, career type, and the body. In one study, college women who had high status aspirations reported higher ineffectiveness and body dissatisfaction after exposure to thin, successful career women as compared to women with low-status aspirations (Smith, Li, & Joiner, 2011). In qualitative work on ethnic minority female physics students (Ong, 2005), women described their challenges fitting in to the physics community due to not embodying the stereotypical physical traits of a physicist and the strategies they use to overcome them, such as "passing" and purposeful manipulation of stereotypes. Not only might perceptions of the body relate to experiences within work- or career-related contexts, but also the experience of leaving these contexts. For example, Stephan and Bilard (2003) compared active athletes and those transitioning away from their athletic careers after the Sydney Olympic games. Results showed that the transitioning group reported perceived decreases in their social value, somatic issues, and lower body satisfaction than the active group five months later. Taken together, these studies suggest that there may be a significant connection between body image, identity, and careers, and these associations might start early in life for girls. The context of the work environment (e.g., characteristics of co-workers) may matter for body image and identity; in addition, leaving a physical vocation from which people derive a strong sense of identity or social status may also be important.

As articulated in the previous sections, parents, peers, and media can have a significant influence on body image. We propose that these processes may have important implications for individuals' career choices. Parents may, for example, express or model concerns about their children's or their own bodies, which may in turn limit their children's exploration of particular vocational pursuits in which their bodies might be highly visible (e.g., careers that involve public speaking). Complying with the social norms or demands of peer groups regarding appearance may also impact career choices. For example, Nichter (2000) argued that fat talk may result in self-silencing, in which girls downplay their achievements and positive attributes (including appearance) to comply with group modesty norms. Girls high in self-silencing may, as a result, avoid particular fields of study that require self-assertion and/or self-promotion (e.g., debate, law, business). In the media, famous women tend to be clustered in appearance-focused jobs (e.g., actresses), whereas famous men can be found in a wider array of skill-oriented domains (e.g., sports, business; Smolak & Murnen, 2001). Observing few female role models in higher level, skill-oriented positions, such as CEOs of large companies or professional athletes, may discourage girls and women from exploring these careers (Riger, 2000). Perhaps the increasing objectification of men in the media (McCreary, 2011) will encourage boys and men to explore career opportunities where appearance is important as well (e.g., modeling, fashion). As no research to our knowledge has yet investigated these possibilities, we strongly encourage researchers to do so in future studies.

Conclusion

Body image concerns and problematic weight control behaviors are common among females and males across many social groups. These concerns are gendered in nature, with different beauty ideals for males and females. A number of biological, social group, and sociocultural factors are relevant to body perceptions, and these are, in turn, relevant to overall feelings of self-worth. In addition, body perceptions likely have implications for identity development yet, to date, little research has focused on this issue. Perceiving negative messages from various sociocultural sources about the body may restrict young people's opportunities for healthy relationships and limit their educational, extracurricular, and career choices. These restrictions may have important implications for identity development.

As we have articulated throughout this chapter, research on body image and identity is scarce and needs significant development. More research on relationships between intersecting social identities (e.g., sexual and ethnic identities) and body image is warranted, especially with adolescent samples. Furthermore, Wängqvist and Frisén's (2013) study on body image and identity should be a jumping off point for future work examining body image and general identity development as articulated by Erikson. Researchers should continue to investigate associations between identity statuses (e.g., exploration, commitment) and body image, including possible moderators (e.g., gender, age) and mediators (e.g., social comparison, internalization of media ideals). It is important that theory be tied into this work. Processes such as self-objectification (Fredrickson & Roberts, 1997) and social comparison (Festinger, 1954) may restrict individuals from making healthy identity choices. For example, a girl/woman who frequently self-objectifies may be more likely to pursue appearance-focused activities or careers (e.g., cheerleading, fashion design), rather than less appearance-focused areas (e.g., engineering, sports) in which she may be equally or even more adept. It is also important to uncover the direction of associations between body image and identity. That is, does body image lead to changes in identity or vice versa? Longitudinal studies may help answer this question. Finally, we suggest that future studies on body image and identity use mixed-methods approaches, combining quantitative and qualitative techniques. Qualitative techniques may be useful for exploring basic yet potentially rich questions about body image and identity in smaller samples (e.g., how has your body image affected your life choices, including academic classes, extracurricular activities, and career options?), whereas validated survey measures may be used to assess correlational associations between body image and identity in large-scale studies. Both types of data may be fruitful for investigating the interplay between these essential aspects of the self.

References

American Psychological Association (APA), Task Force on the Sexualization of Girls. (2007). *Report of the APA Task Force on the Sexualization of Girls*. Washington, DC: American Psychological Association. Retrieved from www.apa.org/pi/wpo/sexualization.html.

Arnett, J. J. (this volume). Identity development from adolescence to emerging adulthood: what we know and (especially) don't know. In K. C. McLean & M. Syed (Eds.), *The Oxford handbook of identity development*. New York: Oxford University Press.

Arnett, J. J., & Tanner, J. L. (2006). *Emerging adults in America: Coming of age in the 21st century*. Washington, DC: American Psychological Association. doi: 10.1037/11381-000

Ata, R. N., Ludden, A. B., & Lally, M. M. (2007). The effects of gender and family, friend, and media influences on eating behaviors and body image during adolescence. *Journal of Youth and Adolescence, 36*, 1024–1037. doi: 10.1007/s10964-006-9159-x

Aubrey, J. S. (2006). Effects of sexually objectifying media on self-objectification and body surveillance in undergraduates: Results of a 2-year panel study. *Journal of Communication, 56*, 366–386. doi: 10.1111/j.1460-2466.2006.00024.x

Baca Zinn, M., & Dill, B. T. (1994). *Women of color in U.S. society*. Philadelphia: Temple University Press.

Bahrke, M. S. (2007). Muscle enhancement substances and strategies. In J. K. Thompson & G. Cafri (Eds.), *The muscular ideal: Psychological, social, and medical perspectives* (pp. 141–159). Washington, DC: American Psychological Association.

Barlett, C. P., Vowels, C. L., & Saucier, D. A. (2008). Meta-analyses of the effects of media images on men's body-image concerns. *Journal of Social and Clinical Psychology, 27*, 279–310. doi: 10.1521/jscp.2008.27.3.279

Brumberg, J. J. (1997). *The body project: An intimate history of American girls*. New York: Vintage Books.

Calzo, J. P., Sonneville, K. R., Haines, J., Blood, E. A., Field, A. E., & Austin, S. B. (2012). The development of associations among body mass index, body dissatisfaction, and weight and shape concern in adolescent boys and girls. *Journal of Adolescent Health, 51*, 517–523. doi: 10.1016/j.jadohealth.2012.02.021

Chmielewski, J. F., & Yost, M. R. (2013). Psychosocial influences on bisexual women's body image: Negotiating gender and sexuality. *Psychology of Women Quarterly, 37*, 224–241. doi: 10.1177/0361684311426126

Cohane, G. H., & Pope, H. G. (2001). Body image in boys: A review of the literature. *International Journal of Eating Disorders, 29*, 373–379. doi: 10.1002/eat.1033

Cole, E. R. (2009). Intersectionality and research in psychology. *American Psychologist, 64*, 170–180. doi: 10.1037/a0014564

Collins, P. H. (1991). *Black feminist thought: Knowledge, consciousness, and the politics of empowerment*. New York: Routledge.

Corning, A. F., & Gondoli, D. M. (2012). Who is most likely to fat talk? A social comparison perspective. *Body Image, 9*, 528–531. doi: 10.1016/j.bbr.2011.03.031

Daniels, E. A. (2009). Sex objects, athletes, and sexy athletes: How media representations of women athletes can impact adolescent girls and young women. *Journal of Research on Adolescence, 24*, 399–422. doi: 10.1177/0743558409336748

Daniels, E. A. (2012). Sexy versus strong: What girls and women think of female athletes. *Journal of Applied Developmental Psychology, 33*, 79–90. doi: 10.1016/j.appdev.2011.12.002

Daniels, E. A., & Wartena, H. (2011). Athlete or sex symbol: What boys think of media representations of female athletes. *Sex Roles, 65*, 566–579. doi: 10.1007/s11199-011-9959-7

Douglas, S. J., & Michaels, M. W. (2004). *The idealization of motherhood and how it has undermined all women: The mommy myth*. New York: Free Press.

Erikson, E. H. (1950). *Childhood and society*. New York: W. W. Norton & Company.

Erikson, E. H. (1968). *Identity: Youth and crisis*. New York: W. W. Norton & Company.

Fechner, P. Y. (2003). The biology of puberty: New developments in sex differences. In C. Haywood (Ed.), *Gender differences at puberty* (pp. 17–28). Cambridge, UK: Cambridge University Press.

Festinger, L. (1954). A theory of social comparison processes. *Human Relations, 7*, 117–140. doi: 10.1177/001872675400700202

Field, A. E., Camargo, C. A., Taylor, C. B., Berkey, C. S., Roberts, S. B., & Colditz, G. C. (2001). Peer, parent, and media influences on the development of weight concerns and frequent dieting among preadolescent and adolescent girls and boys. *Pediatrics, 107*, 54–60. doi: 10.1542/peds.107.1.54

Fikkan, J. L., & Rothblum, E. D. (2012). Is fat a feminist issue? Exploring the gendered nature of weight bias. *Sex Roles, 66*, 575–592. doi: 10.1007/s11199-011-0022-5

Fivush, R., & Zaman, W. (this volume). Gendered narrative voices: Sociocultural and feminist approaches to emerging identity in childhood and adolescence. In K. C. McLean & M. Syed (Eds.), *The Oxford handbook of identity development*. New York: Oxford University Press.

Frederick, D. A., Buchanan, G. M., Sadeghi-Azar, L., Peplau, L. A., Haselton, M. G., Berezovskaya, A., & Lipinski, R. E. (2007). Desiring the muscular ideal: Men's body satisfaction in the United States, Ukraine, and Ghana. *Psychology of Men & Masculinity, 8*, 103–117. doi: 10.1037/1524-9220.8.2.103

Frederick, D. A., Fessler, D. M. T., & Haselton, M. G. (2005). Do representations of male muscularity differ in men's and women's magazines? *Body Image, 2*, 81–86. doi: 10.1016/j.bodyim.2004.12.002

Frederick, D. A., Forbes, G. B., & Grigorian, K. E., & Jarcho, J. M. (2007). The UCLA Body Project I: Gender and ethnic differences in self-objectification and body satisfaction among 2,206 undergraduates. *Sex Roles, 57*, 317–327. doi: 10.1007/s11199-007-9251-z

Frederick, D. A., Jafary, A. M., Gruys, K., & Daniels, E. A. (2012). Surveys and the epidemiology of body image dissatisfaction. In T. F. Cash (Ed.), *Encyclopedia of body image and human appearance* (pp. 766–773). San Diego: Academic Press.

Fredrickson, B. L., & Roberts, T. (1997). Objectification theory: Toward understanding women's lived experiences and mental health risks. *Psychology of Women Quarterly, 21*, 173–206. doi: 10.1111/j.1471-6402.1997.tb00108.x

Fredrickson, B. L., Roberts, T., Noll, S. M., Quinn, D. M., & Twenge, J. M. (1998). That swimsuit becomes you: Sex differences in self-objectification, restrained eating, and math performance. *Journal of Personality and Social Psychology, 75*, 269–284. doi: 10.1037/0022-3514.75.1.269

French, S. A., Story, M., Remafedi, G., Resnick, M. D., & Blum, R. W. (1996). Sexual orientation and prevalence of body dissatisfaction and eating disordered behaviors: A population-based study of adolescents. *International Journal of Eating Disorders, 19*, 119–126. doi: 10.1002/(SICI)1098-108X(199603)19:2<119::AID-EAT2>3.0.CO;2-Q

Friedan, B. (1963). *The feminine mystique*. New York: W. W. Norton and Company.

Fulkerson, J. A., McGuire, M. T., Neumark-Sztainer, D., Story, M., French, S. A., & Perry, C. L. (2002). Weight-related attitudes and behaviors of adolescent boys and girls who are encouraged to diet by their mothers. *International Journal of Obesity, 26*, 1579–1587. doi: 10.1038/sj.ijo.0802157

Gardner, R. M., & Brown, D. L. (2010). Body image assessment: A review of figural drawing scales. *Personality and Individual Differences, 48*, 107–111. doi: 10.1016/j.paid.2009.08.017

Gay, R. K., & Castano, E. (2010). My body or my mind: The impact of state and trait objectification on women's cognitive resources. *European Journal of Social Psychology, 40*, 695–703.

Gillen, M. M. (2013). An examination of multiple aspects of body image in racially/ethnically diverse emerging adults. *North American Journal of Psychology, 15*, 71–88.

Gillen, M. M., & Lefkowitz, E. S. (2006). Gender role development and body image among male and female first year college students. *Sex Roles, 55*, 25–37. doi: 10.1007/s11199-006-9057-4

Gillen, M. M., & Lefkowitz, E. S. (2011). Body size perceptions in racially/ethnically diverse men and women: Implications for body image and self-esteem. *North American Journal of Psychology, 13*, 447–468.

Goldberg, L., & Elliot, D. L. (2007). The prevention of anabolic steroid use among adolescents. In J. K. Thompson & G. Cafri (Eds.), *The muscular ideal: Psychological, social, and medical perspectives* (pp. 161–180). Washington, DC: American Psychological Association.

Goodin, S. M., Van Denburg, A., Murnen, S. K., & Smolak, L. (2011). "Putting on" sexiness: A content analysis of the presence of sexualizing characteristics in girls' clothing. *Sex Roles, 65*, 1–12. doi: 10.1007/s11199-011-9966-8

Grabe, S., & Hyde, J. S. (2006). Ethnicity and body dissatisfaction among women in the United States: A meta-analysis. *Psychological Bulletin, 132*, 622–640. doi: 10.1037/0033-2909.132.4.622

Grabe, S., Ward, L. M., & Hyde, J. S. (2008). The role of the media in body image concerns among women: A meta-analysis of experimental and correlational studies. *Psychological Bulletin, 134*, 460–476. doi: 10.1037/0033-2909.134.3.460

Groesz, L. M., Levine, M. P., & Murnen, S. K. (2002). The effect of experimental presentation of thin media images on body satisfaction: A meta-analytic review. *International Journal of Eating Disorders, 31*, 1–16. doi: 10.1002/eat.10005

Harper, B., & Tiggemann, M. (2008). The effect of thin ideal media images on women's self-objectification, mood, and body image. *Sex Roles, 58*, 649–657. doi: 10.1007/s11199-007-9379-x

Harter, S. (2012). *The construction of the self* (2nd ed.). New York: Guilford Press.

Hebl, M. R., King, E. B., & Lin, J. (2004). The swimsuit becomes us all: Ethnicity, gender, and vulnerability to self-objectification. *Personality and Social Psychology Bulletin, 30*, 1322–1331. doi: 10.1177/0146167204264052

Heelarious [product description]. (n. d.). Retrieved October 26, 2012, from http://www.heelarious.com

Higgins, E. T. (1987). Self-discrepancy: A theory relating self and affect. *Psychological Review, 94*, 319–340. doi: 10.1037/0033-295X.94.3.319

Holub, S. C. (2008). Individual differences in the anti-fat attitudes of preschool-children: The importance of perceived body size. *Body Image, 5*, 317–321. doi: 10.1016/j.bodyim.2008.03.003

Jackson, L. A. (2002). Physical attractiveness: A sociocultural perspective. In T. F. Cash & T. Pruzinsky (Eds.), *Body image: A handbook of research, theory, and clinical practice* (pp. 13–21). New York: Guilford Press.

Johnston, L. D., O'Malley, P. M., Bachman, J. G., & Schulenberg, J. E. (2012). *Monitoring the Future national results on adolescent drug use: Overview of key findings, 2011*. Ann Arbor: Institute for Social Research, The University of Michigan.

Jones, D. C. (2001). Social comparison and body image: Attractiveness comparisons to models and peers among adolescent girls and boys. *Sex Roles, 45*, 645–664. doi: 10.1023/A:1014815725852

Jones, D. C. (2004). Body image among adolescent girls and boys: A longitudinal study. *Developmental Psychology, 40*, 823–835. doi: 10.1037/0012-1649.40.5.823

Jones, D. C., & Crawford, J. K. (2006). The peer appearance culture during adolescence: Gender and body mass variations. *Journal of Youth and Adolescence, 35*, 257–269. doi: 10.1007/s10964-005-9006-5

Jones, D. C., & Newman, J. B. (2009). Early adolescent adjustment and critical evaluations by self and other: The prospective impact of body image dissatisfaction and peer appearance teasing on global self-esteem. *European Journal of Developmental Science, 3*, 17–26.

Jones, D. C., Vigfusdottir, T. H., & Lee, Y. (2004). Body image and the appearance culture among adolescent girls and boys: An examination of friend conversations, peer criticism, appearance magazines, and the internalization of appearance ideals. *Journal of Adolescent Research, 19*, 323–339. doi: 10.1177/0743558403258847

Kaltiala-Heino, R., Rimpela, M., Rissanen, A., & Rantanen, P. (2001). Early puberty and early sexual activity are associated with bulimic-type eating pathology in middle adolescence. *Journal of Adolescent Health, 28*, 346–352. doi: 10.1016/S1054-139X(01)00195-1

Kawamura, K. Y. (2011). Asian American body images. In T. F. Cash & L. Smolak (Eds.), *Body image: A handbook of science, practice, and prevention* (2nd ed., pp. 229–236). New York: Guilford Press.

Keery, H., van den Berg, P., & Thompson, J. K. (2004). An evaluation of the tripartite influence model of body dissatisfaction and eating disturbance with adolescent girls. *Body Image, 1*, 237–251. doi: 10.1016/j.bodyim.2004.03.001

Keery, H., Eisenberg, M. E., Boutelle, K., Neumark-Sztainer, D., & Story, M. (2006). Relationships between maternal and adolescent weight-related behaviors and concerns: The role of perception. *Journal of Psychosomatic Research, 61*, 105–111. doi: 10.1016/j.jpsychores.2006.01.011

Krassas, N. R., & Blauwkamp, J. M., & Wesselink, P. (2003). "Master your Johnson": Sexual rhetoric in Maxim and Stuff magazines. *Sexuality & Culture, 7*, 98–119. doi: 10.1007/s12119-003-1005-7

Kroger, J. (this volume). Identity development through adulthood: The move toward "wholeness." In K. C. McLean & M. Syed (Eds.), *The Oxford handbook of identity development*. New York: Oxford University Press.

Levin, D. E., & Kilbourne, J. (2008). *So sexy so soon: The new sexualized childhood and what parents can do to protect their kids*. New York: Ballantine Books.

Levine, M. P., & Murnen, S. K. (2009). "Everybody knows that mass media are/are not [pick one] a cause of eating disorders": A critical review of evidence for a causal link between media, negative body image, and disordered eating in females. *Journal of Social and Clinical Psychology, 28*, 9–42. doi: 10.1521/jscp.2009.28.1.9

Lindberg, S. M., Hyde, J. S., & McKinley, N. M. (2006). A measure of objectified body consciousness for preadolescent and adolescent youth. *Psychology of Women Quarterly, 30*, 65–76. doi: 10.1111/j.1471-6402.2006.00263.x.

Lopez-Guimera, G., Levine, M. P., Sanchez-Carracedo, D., & Fauquet, J. (2010). Influence of mass media on body image and eating disordered attitudes and behaviors in females: A review of effects and processes. *Media Psychology, 13*, 387–416. doi: 10.1080/15213269.2010.525737

Major, B., Eliezer, D., & Rieck, H. (2012). The psychological weight of weight stigma. *Social Psychological and Personality Science, 3*, 651–658. doi: 10.1177/1948550611434400

Marcia, J. (1966). Development and validation of ego identity status. *Journal of Personality and Social Psychology, 3*, 551–558.

Markey, C. N. (2010). Invited commentary: Why body image is important to adolescent development. *Journal of Youth and Adolescence, 39*, 1387–1391. doi: 10.1007/s10964-010-9510-0

McCabe, M. P., & Ricciardelli, L. A. (2003a). Body image and strategies to lose weight and increase muscle among boys and girls. *Health Psychology, 22*, 39–46. doi: 10.1037/0278-6133.22.1.39

McCabe, M. P., & Ricciardelli, L. A. (2003b). Sociocultural influences on body image and body changes among adolescent boys and girls. *Journal of Social Psychology, 143*, 5–26. doi: 10.1080/00224540309598428

McCabe, M. P., & Ricciardelli, L. A. (2004a). Body image dissatisfaction among males across the lifespan: A review of past literature. *Journal of Psychosomatic Research, 56*, 675–685. doi: 10.1016/S0022-3999(03)00129-6

McCabe, M. P., & Ricciardelli, L. A. (2004b). A longitudinal study of pubertal timing and extreme body change behaviors among adolescent boys and girls. *Adolescence, 39*, 145–166.

McCreary, D. R. (2011). Body image and muscularity. In T. F. Cash & L. Smolak (Eds.), *Body image: A handbook of science, practice, and prevention* (2nd ed., pp. 198–205). New York: Guilford Press.

McCreary, D. R., & Sasse, D. K. (2000). An exploration of the drive for muscularity in adolescent boys and girls. *Journal of American College Health, 48*, 297–304. doi: 10.1080/07448480009596271

McKinley, N. M. (1999). Women and objectified body consciousness: Mothers' and daughters' body experience in cultural, developmental, and familial context. *Developmental Psychology, 35*, 760–769. doi: 10.1037/0012-1649.35.3.760

McKinley, N. M., Hyde, J. S. (1996). The Objectified Body Consciousness Scale: Development and validation. *Psychology of Women Quarterly, 20*, 181–215. doi: 10.1111/j.1471-6402.1996.tb00467.x

Mendelson, M. J., Mendelson, B. K., & Andrews, J. (2000). Self-esteem, body esteem, and body-mass in late adolescence: Is a competence x importance model needed? *Journal of Applied Developmental Psychology, 21*, 249–266. doi: 10.1016/S0193-3973(99)00035-0

Mendle, J., & Ferrero, J. (2012). Detrimental psychological outcomes associated with pubertal timing in adolescent boys. *Developmental Review, 32*, 49–66. doi: 10.1016/j.dr.2011.11.001

Mendle, J., Turkheimer, E., & Emery, R. E. (2007). Detrimental psychological outcomes associated with early pubertal timing in adolescent girls. *Developmental Review, 27*, 151–171. doi: 10.1016/j.dr.2006.11.001

Menzel, J. E., Sperry, S. L., Small, B., Thompson, J. K., Sarwer, D. B., & Cash, T. F. (2011). Internalization of appearance ideals and cosmetic surgery attitudes: A test of the tripartite influence model of body image. *Sex Roles, 65*, 469–477. doi: 10.1007/s11199-011-9983-7

Moradi, B., & Huang, Y. (2008). Objectification theory and psychology of women: A decade of advances and future directions. *Psychology of Women Quarterly, 32*, 377–398. doi: 10.1111/j.1471-6402.2008.00452.x

Morbidity and Mortality Weekly Report. (2012, June 8). *Surveillance summaries: Youth Risk Behavior Surveillance—United States 2011*. Retrieved October 28, 2012, from http://www.cdc.gov/mmwr/pdf/ss/ss6104.pdf.

Morrison, T. G., & McCutcheon, J. M. (2011). Gay and lesbian body images. In T. F. Cash & L. Smolak (Eds.), *Body image: A handbook of science, practice, and prevention* (2nd ed., pp. 214–220). New York: Guilford Press.

Murnen, S. K. (2011). Gender and body images. In T. F. Cash & L. Smolak (Eds.), *Body image: A handbook of science, practice, and prevention* (2nd ed., pp. 173–179). New York: Guilford Press.

Murnen, S. K., Smolak, L., Mills, J. A., & Good, L. (2003). Thin, sexy women and strong, muscular men: Grade-school children's responses to objectified images of women and men. *Sex Roles, 49*, 427–437. doi: 10.1023/A:1025868320206

Myers, T. A., & Crowther, J. H. (2009). Social comparison as a predictor of body dissatisfaction: A meta-analytic review. *Journal of Abnormal Psychology, 118*, 683–698. doi: 10.1037/a0016763683

National Eating Disorders Association [NEDA]. (2005). *Body image*. New York: Author. Retrieved from http://www.natio

naleatingdisorders.org/nedaDir/files/documents/handouts/BodyImag.pdf

National Science Foundation. (2011). *Women, minorities, and persons with disabilities in science and engineering: 2011.* Retrieved November 12, 2012 from http://www.nsf.gov/statistics/wmpd/pdf/nsf11309.pdf

Natsuaki, M. N., Samuels, D., & Leve, L. D. (this volume). Puberty, identity, and context: A biopsychosocial perspective on internalizing psychopathology in early adolescent girls. In McLean, K. C., & Syed, M. (Eds.), *The Oxford handbook of identity development.* New York: Oxford University Press.

Nichter, M. (2000). *Fat talk: What girls and their parents say about dieting.* Cambridge, MA: Harvard University Press.

Newheiser, A., LaFrance, M., & Dovidio, J. F. (2010). Others as objects: How women and men perceive the consequences of self-objectification. *Sex Roles, 63,* 657–671. doi: 10.1007/s11199-010-9879-y

Norris, M. L., Boydell, K. M., Pinhas, L., & Katzman, D. K. (2006). Ana and the Internet: A review of pro-anorexia websites. *International Journal of Eating Disorders, 39,* 443–447. doi: 10.1002/eat.20305

Nottelmann, E. D., Inoff-Germain, G., Susman, E. J., & Chrousos, G. P. (1990). Hormones and behavior at puberty. In J. Bancroft & J. M. Reinisch (Eds.), *Adolescence and puberty* (pp. 88–123). New York: Oxford University Press.

Oehlof, M. E. W., Musher-Eizenman, D. R., Neufeld, J. M., & Hauser, J. C. (2009). Self- objectification and ideal body shape for men and women. *Body Image, 6,* 308–310. doi: 10.1016/j.bodyim.2009.05.002

Olivardia, R., Pope, H. G., Borowiecki, J. J., & Cohane, G. H. (2004). Biceps and body image: The relationship between muscularity and self-esteem, depression, and eating disorder symptoms. *Psychology of Men & Masculinity, 5,* 112–120. doi: 10.1037/1524-9220.5.2.112

Ong, M. (2005). Body projects of young women of color in physics: Intersections of gender, race, and science. *Social Problems, 52,* 593–617. doi: 10.1525/sp.2005.52.4.593

Papp, I., Urban, R., Czegledi, E., Babusa, B., & Tury, F. (2013). Testing the tripartite influence model of body image and eating disturbance among Hungarian adolescents. *Body Image, 10,* 232–242. doi: 10.1016/j.bodyim.2012.12.006

Patton, T. O. (2006). Hey girl, am I more than my hair?: African American women and their struggles with beauty, body image, and hair. *Feminist Formations, 18,* 24–51.

Paxton, S. J., Eisenberg, M. E., & Neumark-Sztainer, D. (2006). Prospective predictors of body dissatisfaction in adolescent girls and boys: A five-year longitudinal study. *Developmental Psychology, 42,* 888–899. doi: 10.1037/0012-1649.42.5.888

Paxton, S. J., Schutz, H. K., Wertheim, E. H., & Muir, S. L. (1999). Friendship clique and peer influences on body image concerns, dietary restraint, extreme weight-loss behaviors, and binge eating in adolescent girls. *Journal of Abnormal Psychology, 108,* 255–266. doi: 10.1037/0021-843X.108.2.255

Peplau, L. A., Frederick, D. A., Yee, C., Maisel, N., Lever, J., & Ghavami, N. (2009). Body image satisfaction in heterosexual, gay, and lesbian adults. *Archives of Sexual Behavior, 38,* 713–725. doi: 10.1007/s10508-008-9378-1

Polivy, J., & Herman, C. P. (2002). Causes of eating disorders. *Annual Review of Psychology, 53,* 187–213. doi: 10.1146/annurev.psych.53.100901.135103

Pope, H. G., Olivardia, R., Gruber, A., & Borowiecki, J. (1999). Evolving ideals of male body image as seen through action toys. *International Journal of Eating Disorders, 26,* 65–72. doi: 10.1002/(SICI)1098-108X(199907)26:1<65::AID-EAT8>3.0.CO;2-D

Pope, H. G., Phillips, K. A., & Olivardia, R. (2000). *The Adonis complex: The secret crisis of male body obsession.* New York: The Free Press.

Quick, H. (1997). *Catwalking: A history of the fashion model.* London: Hamlyn.

Ricciardelli, L. A., & McCabe, M. P. (2007). Pursuit of muscularity among adolescents. In J. K. Thompson & G. Cafri (Eds.), *The muscular ideal: Psychological, social, and medical perspectives* (pp. 199–216). Washington, DC: American Psychological Association.

Ricciardelli, L. A., McCabe, M. P., Williams, R. J., & Thompson, J. K. (2007). The role of ethnicity and culture in body image and disordered eating among males. *Clinical Psychology Review, 27,* 582–606. doi: 10.1016/j.cpr.2007.01.016

Riger, S. (2000). *Transforming psychology: Gender in theory and practice* (pp. 119–123). New York: Oxford University Press.

Rivadeneyra, R., Ward, L. M., & Gordon, M. (2007). Distorted reflections: Media exposure and Latino adolescents' conceptions of self. *Media Psychology, 9,* 261–290. doi: 10.1080/15213260701285926

Roberts, A., Cash, T. F., Feingold, A., & Johnson, B. T. (2006). Are black-white differences in females' body dissatisfaction decreasing? A meta-analytic review. *Journal of Consulting and Clinical Psychology, 74,* 1121–1131. doi: 10.1037/0022-006X.74.6.1121

Roberts, T., & Zurbriggen, E. L. (2013). The problem on sexualization: What is it and how does it happen? In E. L. Zurbriggen & T. Roberts (Eds.), *The sexualization of girls and girlhood: Causes, consequences, and resistance* (pp. 3–21). New York: Oxford University Press.

Rolland, K., Farnill, D., & Griffiths, R. A. (1996). Children's perceptions of their current and ideal body sizes and body mass index. *Perceptual and Motor Skills, 82,* 651–656. doi: 10.2466/pms.1996.82.2.651

Sabik, N. J., Cole, E. R., & Ward, L. M. (2010). Are all minority women equally buffered from negative body image? Intra-ethnic moderators of the buffering hypothesis. *Psychology of Women Quarterly, 34,* 139–151. doi: 10.1111/j.1471-6402.2010.01557.x

Schooler, D. (2008). Real women have curves: A longitudinal investigation of TV and the body image development of Latina adolescents. *Journal of Adolescent Research, 23,* 132–153. doi: 10.1177/0743558407310712

Schooler, D., & Daniels, E. A. (2013). "I am not a skinny toothpick and proud of it." Latina adolescents' ethnic identity and responses to mainstream media images. *Body Image*, Advanced online publication. 10.1016/j.bodyim.2013.09.001

Schooler, D., & Daniels, E. A. (2014). "I am not a skinny toothpick and proud of it:" Latina adolescents' ethnic identity and responses to mainstream media images. *Body Image, 11,* 11–18. doi: 10.1016/j.bodyim.2013.09.001

Schwartz, D. J., Phares, V., Tantleff-Dunn, S., & Thompson, J. K. (1999). Body image, psychological functioning, and parental feedback regarding physical appearance. *International Journal of Eating Disorders, 25,* 339–343. doi: 10.1002/(SICI)1098-108X(199904)25:3

Sherman, A. M., & Zurbriggen, E. L. (under review). "Boys can be anything": Effect of Barbie play on girls' career cognitions.

Sherman, A. M., & Zurbriggen, E. L. (2014). "Boys can be anything": Effect of Barbie play on girls' career cognitions. *Sex Roles, 70,* 195–208. doi: 10.1007/s11199-014-0347-y

Siegel, J. M., Yancey, A. K., Aneshensel, C. S., & Schuler, R. (1999). Body image, perceived pubertal timing, and adolescent mental health. *Journal of Adolescent Health, 25,* 155-165. doi: 10.1016/S1054-139X(98)00160-8

Slater, A., & Tiggemann, M. (2010). Body image and disordered eating in adolescent girls and boys: A test of objectification theory. *Sex Roles, 63,* 42–49. doi: 10.1007/s11199-010-9794-2

Smith, A. R., Li, N., & Joiner, T. E. (2011). The pursuit of success: Can status aspirations negatively affect body satisfaction? *Journal of Social and Clinical Psychology, 30,* 531–547. doi: 10.1521/jscp.2011.30.5.531

Smolak, L., Levine, M. P., & Schermer, F. (1999). Parental input and weight concerns among elementary school children. *International Journal of Eating Disorders, 25,* 263–271. doi: 10.1002/(SICI)1098-108X(199904)25:3<263::AID-EAT3>3.0.CO;2-V

Smolak, L., & Murnen, S. K. (2001). Gender and eating problems. In R. H. Striegel-Moore & L. Smolak (Eds.), *Eating disorders: Innovative directions in research and practice* (pp. 91–110). Washington, DC: American Psychological Association.

Smolak, L., & Murnen, S. K. (2011). The sexualization of girls and women as a primary antecedent of self-objectification. In R. M. Calogero, S. Tantleff-Dunn, & J. K. Thompson (Eds.), *Self-objectification in women: Causes, consequences, and counteractions* (pp. 53–75). Washington, DC: American Psychological Association. doi: 10.1037/12304-003

Starr, C. R., & Ferguson, G. M. (2012). Sexy dolls, sexy grade-schoolers? Media & maternal influences on young girls' self-sexualization. *Sex Roles, 67,* 463–476. doi: 10.1007/s11199-012-0183-x

Stephan, Y., & Bilard, J. (2003). Repercussions of transition out of elite sport on body image. *Perceptual and Motor Skills, 96,* 95–104. doi: 10.2466/PMS.96.1.95-104

Stice, E., & Whitenton, K. (2002). Risk factors for body dissatisfaction in adolescent girls: A longitudinal investigation. *Developmental Psychology, 38,* 669–678. doi: 10.1037/0012-1649.38.5.669

Strelan, P., & Hargreaves, D. (2005). Women who objectify other women: The vicious circle of objectification? *Sex Roles, 52,* 707–712. doi: 10.1007/s11199-005-3737-3

Striegel-Moore, R. H., McMahon, R. P., Biro, F. M., Schreiber, G., Crawford, P. B., & Voorhees, C. (2001). Exploring the relationship between timing of menarche and eating disorder symptoms in black and white adolescent girls. *International Journal of Eating Disorders, 30,* 421–433. doi: 10.1002/eat.1103

Tantleff-Dunn, S., & Gokee, J. L. (2002). Interpersonal influences on body image development. In T. F. Cash & T. Pruzinsky (Eds.), *Body image: A handbook of research, theory, and clinical practice* (pp. 108–116). New York: Guilford Press.

Thompson, J. K., Heinberg, L. J., Altabe, M., & Tantleff-Dunn, S. (1999). *Exacting beauty: Theory, assessment, and treatment of body image disturbance.* Washington, DC: American Psychological Association. doi: 10.1037/10312-000

Tiggemann, M., & Lynch, J. E. (2001). Body image across the lifespan in adult women: The role of self-objectification. *Developmental Psychology, 37,* 243–253. doi: 10.1037/0012-1649.37.2.243

Tiggemann, M., & Miller, J. (2010). The Internet and adolescent girls' weight satisfaction and drive for thinness. *Sex Roles, 63,* 79–90. doi: 10.1007/s11199-010-9789-z

Tylka, T. L. (2011). Refinement of the tripartite influence model for men: Dual body image pathways to body change behaviors. *Body Image, 8,* 199–207. doi: 10.1016/j.bodyim.2011.04.008

Tylka, T. L., & Andorka, M. J. (2012). Support for an expanded tripartite influence model with gay men. *Body Image, 9,* 57–67. doi: 10.1016/j.bodyim.2011.09.006

Udall-Weiner, D. (2009). Sexual identity development and self-esteem as predictors of body image in a racially diverse sample of gay men. *Journal of Homosexuality, 56,* 1011–1029. doi: 10.1080/00918360903275419

van den Berg, P., Thompson, J. K., Obremski-Brandon, K., & Coovert, M. (2002). The tripartite influence model of body image and eating disturbance: A covariance structure modeling investigation testing the mediational role of appearance comparison. *Journal of Psychosomatic Research, 53,* 1007–1020. doi: 10.1016/S0022-3999(02)00499-3

Wagenbach, P. (2003). Lesbian body image and eating issues. *Journal of Psychology & Human Sexuality, 15,* 205–227. doi: 10.1300/J056v15n04_04

Wängqvist, M., & Frisén, A. (2013). Swedish 18-year-olds' identity formation: Associations with feelings about appearance and internalization of body ideals. *Journal of Adolescence, 36,* 485–493. doi: 10.1016/j.adolescence.2013.02.002

Way, N., & Rogers, O. (this volume). "[T]hey say Black men won't make it, but I know I'm gonna make it": Ethnic and racial identity development in the context of American culture. In K. C. McLean & M. Syed (Eds.), *The Oxford handbook of identity development.* New York: Oxford University Press.

Wertheim, E. H., Mee, J., & Paxton, S. J. (1999). Relationships among adolescent girls' eating behaviors and their parents' weight-related attitudes and behaviors. *Sex Roles, 41,* 169–187. doi: 10.1023/A:1018850111450

Wertheim, E. H., Martin, G., Prior, M., Sanson, A., & Smart, D. (2002). Parent influences in the transmission of eating and weight related values and behaviors. *Eating Disorders: The Journal of Treatment & Prevention, 10,* 321–334. doi: 10.1080/10640260214507

Yates, A., Edman, J., & Aruguete, M. (2004). Ethnic differences in BMI and body/self-dissatisfaction among Whites, Asian subgroups, Pacific Islanders, and African-Americans. *Journal of Adolescent Health, 34,* 300–307. doi: 10.1016/j.jadohealth.2003.07.014

Zehr, J. L., Culbert, K. M., Sisk, C. L., & Klump, K. L. (2007). An association of early puberty with disordered eating and anxiety in a population of undergraduate women and men. *Hormones and Behavior, 52,* 427–435. doi: 10.1016/j.yhbeh.2007.06.005

Zurbriggen, E. L., & Roberts, T. (Eds.). (2013). *The sexualization of girls and girlhood: Causes, consequences, and resistance.* New York: Oxford University Press.

CHAPTER 26
Cultural Neuroscience of Identity Development

Alissa J. Mrazek, Tokiko Harada, *and* Joan Y. Chiao

Abstract

Identity development is conceptualized as a series of distinct stages in the developmental pathway, including acquisition of self-knowledge, establishment of independence and personal continuity, and acquisition of a sense of affiliation. For those negotiating more than one cultural/racial/ethnic identity, a unique set of stages may be undertaken in the development of identity, particularly during the transition from adolescence to adulthood. Although the sociocultural factors that shape identity development are relatively well-conceptualized, much less well understood are the biological mechanisms that facilitate identity development throughout the lifespan for both majority and minority group members. This chapter discusses sociocultural and biological pathways of identity development through the lens of cultural neuroscience, elucidating how dynamic culture-biology interactions shape the development of social identity in majority and minority group members and the etiology underlying adaptive social development in people living in monocultural and diverse multicultural communities.

Key Words: cultural neuroscience, identity development, social and affective neuroscience, developmental neuroscience, diversity, race and ethnicity, self-construal style

Cultural Neuroscience Framework

Research in cultural neuroscience bridges theories from distinct fields, including anthropology, cultural psychology, neuroscience/neurogenetics, and population genetics (Chiao & Ambady, 2007; Chiao, Cheon, Pornpattananangkul, Mrazek, & Blizinsky, 2013). We posit that cultural neuroscience is an important way to approach studying identity development because conceptualizations of the self vary dramatically across the globe from early childhood, although little is known about neural representations of self and identity across development. Unfortunately, most of the empirical evidence on the self, as is the case across many psychological topics, comes from limited population samples. For example, approximately 95 percent of psychological studies come from nations that compose only 12 percent of the world's population (Arnett, 2008). Likewise, about 90 percent of neuroimaging studies examine people from Western, industrialized, rich, educated, democratic (WEIRD) populations (Chiao, 2009; Chiao & Cheon, 2010; Henrich, Heine, & Norenzayan, 2010). To better understand the interaction of cultural and biological factors that give rise to social, cognitive, and affective behavior, cultural neuroscience has begun to examine how brain function, behavior, and cognition vary as a function of cultural and genetic diversity (Chiao et al., 2013). In particular, we have recently proposed a causal cultural neuroscience model of human behavior to examine how environmental factors lead to genetic and cultural influences on mind, brain, and behavior (Chiao et al., 2013; Chiao & Blizinsky, 2013; Chiao & Immordino-Yang, 2013; Figure 26.1). This model indicates a pathway for explaining human behavior as product of environmental factors that

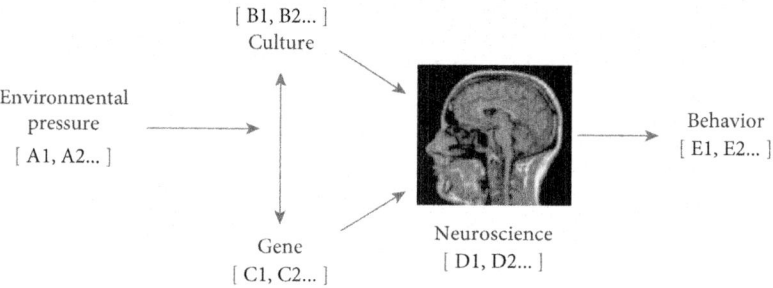

Fig. 26.1 Cultural neuroscience model of human behavior. Each factor in the cultural neuroscience model may be composed of a set of variables of each type (e.g., A1, A2 refer to environmental pressures; B1, B2 refer to cultural traits).
From Chiao & Immordino-Yang, 2013

bidirectionally influence culture–gene interactions that regulate the human mind and brain.

Much of the cultural neuroscience research on the self builds off self-construal theory, whereby one's identity is formed through specific perceptions of the self that vary across cultures. Self-construal theory asserts that independent individuals think of themselves as autonomous from others, whereas interdependent individuals think of themselves as interdependent or connected with others (Markus & Kitayama, 1991). More specifically, those who focus on the importance of differing from others and asserting themselves tend to be more independent, while those who attend to fitting in with others harmoniously tend to be more interdependent. We posit that these individual differences in cultural values play a fundamental role in developing an identity, as well as in developing social relationships throughout development. For decades, scholars have believed that such construals can actually *determine* the nature of individual experiences through shaping much of cognition, emotion, and motivation (Markus & Kitayama, 1991; Shweder & LeVine, 1984; Triandis, 1989). Two forms of self-construal are often referred to in the domain of individualism-collectivism: individualists value independence and stable personality traits (e.g., I am honest), whereas collectivists value interconnectedness and situation-specific attributes (e.g., When talking to my mother, I am honest; Chiao et al, 2009; Markus & Kitayama, 1991; Oyserman, Coon, & Kemmelmeier 2002; Triandis, 1995). The research on self-construal style lays the foundation for much of our discussion on the cultural neuroscience of identity development. Cultural learning begins during infancy (Meltzoff & Moore, 1977) and may play a formative role in the development of self-identity. We suggest that the development of self-identity is shaped by both cultural learning, such as imitation of caregiver and peer thinking styles and behavior, as well as by culture–gene coevolutionary factors.

Advances in cultural neuroscience research indicate that the development of individualistic and collectivistic identities is influenced by an interaction of cultural, genetic, and environmental factors. Consistent with these empirical findings, culture–gene coevolutionary theory indicates that the human mind and brain have been shaped by both cultural and genetic selection. For example, recent evidence indicates that nations with increased prevalence of the short allele of the serotonin transporter gene (*5-HTTLPR*) show increased prevalence of collectivistic or interdependent identities (Chiao & Blizinsky, 2010). People likely demonstrate increased collectivism within these regions as a response to the presence of pathogens or infectious diseases in the environment. By emphasizing social norms of harmony and ingroup conformity rather than social norms of expression and autonomy, collectivistic cultures may reduce the probability of social contact with outgroup members that may lead to the increased prevalence of infectious disease or pathogen prevalence. Hence, collectivistic cultural identities likely serve an adaptive function, particularly in geographic regions with prevalence of pathogens. This cultural and genetic selection of individualistic or collectivistic identities then leads to a developmental cascade of social cognitive and affective neural and behavioral repertoires that vary across geography.

In addition to the cultural influence of individualism-collectivism on the human mind and brain, cross-cultural and cultural psychologists have identified key cultural dimensions, including power distance, masculinity-femininity, uncertainty avoidance, and long-term/short-term orientation (Hofstede, 2001), that may shape different facets of identity development throughout the lifespan. In this chapter, we focus on the cultural dimensions of individualism-collectivism, power distance, and racial identification and the primary role that they play in shaping the neural architecture of social cognition and identity. Because our world is intrinsically social, many of the factors that shape a developing self-concept are influenced by social processes such as mentalizing, perspective taking, and empathizing. In addition to examining how these social processes shape the self-concept, we also discuss much of the recent cultural neuroscience research that has advanced the understanding of various forms of social perception.

Another important factor to the study of identity development is aging. The theoretical paradigm of *developmental biocultural co-constructivism* states that biology and culture are continuously interacting in an interdependent dynamical system that works across multiple time scales (Baltes, Reuter-Lorenz, & Rösler, 2006; Li, 2003). This reciprocal link occurs at all stages throughout the lifespan and emphasizes the significance of plasticity across development due to interactions of culture and neurobiology. By gaining a richer understanding of how social perception and empathy-related skills develop across the lifespan at both the behavioral and neural levels, we can start to examine the complex interactions between culture and biology in the development of one's identity across the lifespan, from infancy to late adulthood.

In this chapter, we aim to cover three objectives: (1) review the extant literature in cultural neuroscience on social cognition and the specific influence of cultural identity on neural bases of social cognition, (2) examine the benefits of integrating the science of identity development into cultural neuroscience particularly during early developmental periods, and (3) suggest the benefits of incorporating a cultural neuroscience approach to the field of identity development across multiple developmental periods.

Examining the Role of Social Cognition in Identity Formation via Extant Cultural Neuroscience Research

Due to the importance of social cognition in forming and maintaining a social identity, we will review three types of social cognition in the following sections: self-processing, empathy, and social perception. Recent research in cultural neuroscience has helped shed light on the neural underpinnings of these processes that are critical for fluid social interaction and identity development, particularly in young adults. Although focusing the discussion on evidence for the neural bases of these three types of social cognition in young adults, we also review a growing literature on the social neuroscience of self in children and adolescents across racial and cultural groups. In the fourth subsection, we also present research examining how culture plays a role in the neural development within older populations.

Cultural Neuroscience of Self-Processing

Knowledge about the self is a key component for conceptualizations of the self and identity formation. Is knowledge about the self uniquely represented in the brain? Scientists have been intrigued for decades about whether the functional activity during self-processing differs from other forms of semantic processing and social representation. In an early attempt, Rogers and colleagues (1977) first demonstrated a memory advantage for self-related information. For example, when asked to remember the trait adjective presented in questions framed as relevant to the self (e.g., Does the word "honest" describe you?), adjectives were recalled better than the adjectives in questions framed as irrelevant to the self (e.g., Does the word "honest" mean the same as "trustworthy"?; Rogers et al., 1977). Based on these memory differences, scientists across disciplines became motivated to understand whether introspection and self-referential processing are in some ways special at both cognitive and neural levels.

One avenue of pursuing this question is through studying self-referential processing with functional magnetic resonance imaging (fMRI). Self-referential processing often involves stimuli that are implicitly and subjectively experienced as strongly related to one's own person (Northoff et al., 2006). Stimuli in self-referential studies can target any domain or sensory modality but are categorized by the strength of their relation to the self. For instance, Kelley and colleagues (2002) studied self-referential processing in a memory task by having participants judge each trait adjective (e.g., dependable, polite, daring) in one of three ways: whether the adjective describes the self, the adjective describes the current US president (George Bush at that time), or whether the adjective is presented in uppercase letters. Trait adjectives judged in a self-relevant manner were remembered best and elicited greater recruitment of the medial prefrontal cortex (MPFC) compared to non–self-relevant trait adjectives (Kelley et al., 2002).

Similar to this study, a vast array of research over the past 15 years has begun to elucidate which brain regions are involved during self-referential tasks. Although subtle aspects of self-referential processing

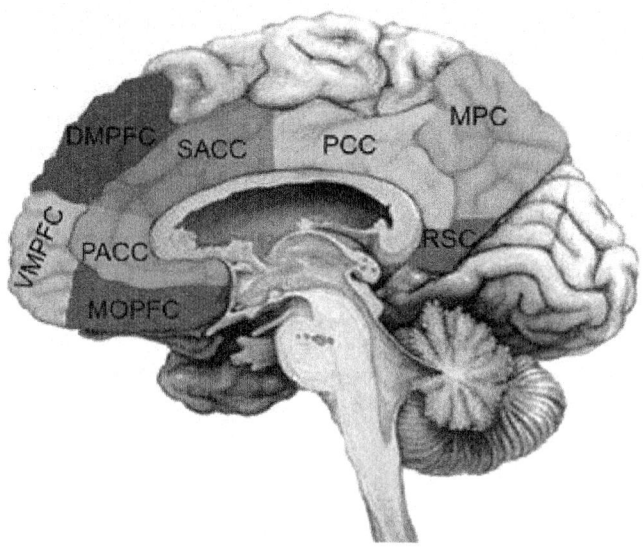

Fig. 26.2 Schematic illustration of cortical midline structures (Northoff et al., 2006).

differ in their recruitment of neural activity, several core regions are frequently involved in most self-related tasks. Primarily, neuroimaging studies report involvement of cortical midline structures such as the medial orbital prefrontal cortex (MOFC), the ventromedial prefrontal cortex (VMPFC), the sub/pre- and supragenual anterior cingulate cortex (PACC, SACC), the dorsomedial prefrontal cortex (DMPFC), the medial parietal cortex (MPC), the posterior cingulate cortex (PCC), and the retrosplenial cortex (RSC) during self-related tasks (Gillihan & Farah, 2005; Northoff et al., 2006; Figure 26.2). Meta-analytic evidence indicates that this cortical midline network of brain regions are simultaneously activated during self-processing tasks, often regardless of the design paradigm (Amodio & Frith, 2006; Northoff et al., 2006). For example, there are similar patterns of activation in self-referential processing across the domains of verbal, spatial, memory, emotion, facial, and social processing (Northoff et al., 2006). This evidence of a consistent pattern of additionally recruited neural regions during self-processing tasks supports the claim that the functional representation of the self, a critical component of identity, is unique from other types of neural processing.

One crucial component that highly shapes conceptualization of self is the relationship between self and others; that is, how people define themselves and their relation to other individuals in their environment. As mentioned earlier, an important cultural dimension of defining the self is through self-construal style, which refers to the degree that one categorizes the self as separate from others. Markus and Kitayama (1991) first recognized that Western cultures view the self as separate from social context whereas Eastern cultures tend to construe the self as part of a larger social framework. Thus, these two types of perceptions lead to either an independent or interdependent self.

More recently, through the lens of cultural neuroscience, we are beginning to see that cultural influences such as self-construal style have been shown to modulate neural response while people think about themselves and others in specific social contexts. For example, several cultural neuroimaging studies have suggested cultural modulation in neural response during self-processing tasks, specifically within the cortical midline structures such as MPFC (Chiao et al., 2009; 2010a; Zhu, Zhang, Fan, & Han, 2007) and posterior cingulate cortex (PCC; Chiao et al., 2010a), which are brain regions that have been suggested to play an important role in processing self-related information (Amodio & Frith, 2006; Northoff & Bermpohl, 2004; Northoff et al., 2006). In an early neuroimaging study by Zhu and colleagues (2007), Chinese and Westerners living in China were asked to judge whether a given trait adjective described either (a) themselves, (b) a close other (i.e., their mother), or (c) a famous politician (Bill Clinton in the Western version and Zhu Rongju in the Chinese version). The results from their study indicated that both Chinese and Western participants showed greater neural activity within the MPFC for judgments of self and mother compared to the famous politician.

However, Western participants showed less neural response within MPFC for mother compared to self-judgments, whereas Chinese participants showed no significant difference in neural response within MPFC between self and mother judgments. These results are accounted for in terms of independent and interdependent self-construals; people with independent or individualistic self-construals (e.g., people from Western countries such as the United States) think of people as independent from each other, whereas people with interdependent or collectivistic self-construals (e.g., people from East Asian countries such as China) think of people as highly interconnected to one another.

Chiao and colleagues (2009) provided further neuroimaging evidence for the cultural modulation in shaping the neural basis of self-representation (Chiao et al., 2009; 2010b). For example, native Japanese participants living in Japan and Caucasian-American participants living in the United States performed a self-judgment task in which they viewed both contextual (e.g., "when talking to my mother, I am caring") and general (e.g., "I am caring") self statements and indicated whether or not they agreed with the statements (Chiao et al., 2009). Results indicated greater neural activity within MPFC in the conditions corresponding to the participants' individualistic or collectivistic tendencies, with a robust association between degree of neural activity within MPFC and the individuals' degree of individualistic or collectivistic orientation, regardless of nationality. Interestingly, participants' individualistic or collectivistic tendencies did not necessarily reflect group-based affiliations (i.e., their nationality or race). For example, Japanese and Caucasian-American individuals who reported a relatively high collectivistic orientation showed greater MPFC activation during the contextual condition compared to the general condition (Chiao et al., 2009). This result is consistent with a notion that cross-cultural differences in individualism and collectivism are not static (Oyserman & Lee, 2008) and might be dynamic, evolving across macro- (e.g., generations, lifespan; Chiao & Ambady, 2007; Li, 2003; Mesoudi, Whiten, & Laland, 2006) and microlevel (e.g., situations) time scales (Gardner, Gabriel, & Lee, 1999; Oyserman & Lee, 2008). Critically, this neuroimaging evidence demonstrates the importance of self-identity and an individual's belief or endorsement of cultural values as a primary modulator of neural response during self-processing.

Cultural Priming, Self, and Identity

People living in multicultural environments tend to readily switch between different cultural schemas depending on their immediate sociocultural contexts (Hong et al., 2000). However, the neurobiological mechanisms underlying cultural identity and frame-switching remain relatively less well understood. Recently, Chiao and colleagues (2010) primed bicultural Asian-American participants with either individualistic or collectivistic values. Participants performed a self-judgment task in context-dependent and -independent conditions, and participants showed greater neural activity within MPFC and PCC during the condition that was consistent with their cultural prime. Chiao and colleagues (2010) suggested that modulation of MPFC and PCC activity by cultural beliefs reflected enhanced evaluation and integration of a culturally congruent self-representation. In other words, individualists described themselves in a general context rather than in a situation-specific context, whereas collectivists described themselves in a situation-specific context rather than in a general context.

Even processing of autobiographical memories is susceptible to cultural influences at the neurobiological level of analysis. Harada and colleagues (2010) primed bicultural Asian Americans with either an individualistic or collectivistic prime via a pronoun circling task and then measured neural response while showing them autobiographical information about themselves, their father, or an unfamiliar person. Participants viewing the autobiographical or social information made simple judgments about whether the information was presented on the left- or right-hand of the screen. Results showed that neural response within the dorsal, but not ventral, portion of MPFC showed differential activation to the autobiographical information compared to father judgments for participants who were primed with individualism only. These findings indicate that cultural values of individualism and collectivism dynamically shape neural response during the evaluation rather than the detection of self-relevant information. Taken together, these studies provide evidence that cultural beliefs can modulate the neural underpinning of individuals' perceptions of themselves and their relation to others in young adulthood.

Culture, Self, and Identity Development

How does culture shape psychological and neural mechanisms of self and identity during the course of development? Developmental research on the self and identity has long suggested that identity is primarily formed during the transition from adolescence to adulthood through socialization and the amalgamation of self-definitions that we attach to ourselves (Harter, 1999; Mead, 1934); however, several important changes occur during childhood prior to ages 7–9 with regard to self-knowledge processing. For instance, young children described themselves with trait words in momentary situations that reflected current states rather than stable attributes (Harter, 1999). Additionally, the evaluative content of self-appraisal tended to be more black and white (e.g., "I am all bad") than that of adults (Harter, 1999; Saltz & Medow, 1971). An important question based on this developmental research is how neural function during self-reflection changes from childhood to adulthood.

Neuroimaging research is beginning to answer this question. Previous work suggests that important components of forming an identity, such as self-concept and self-evaluation, emerge at different times during development and rely on different parts of the prefrontal cortex. For example, researchers speculate that the time during development when toddlers of 18 months to 2 years of age begin to recognize the self (Amsterdam, 1972; Gallup, 1970) may be a crucial period when the ventral premotor region begins to develop as well (Sadato, Morita, & Itakura, 2008). Similarly, the middle frontal gyrus, which is important for self-related, higher level processing, likely begins to develop around the age of 3, when children are beginning to evaluate the self and recall autobiographical memories (Sadato et al., 2008).

In addition to self-concept and self-evaluation, older children begin to show neural patterns that are more similar to adults but maintain significant differences. For example, in a study by Pfeifer and colleagues (2007), adults and children around the age of 10 years participated in a self-knowledge/social knowledge retrieval task. Participants responded as to whether specific academic and social attributes described (a) themselves or (b) a fictional, highly familiar other, Harry Potter. Results indicated that both children and adults recruited MPFC and MPPC activity during the self-knowledge retrieval tasks, but children demonstrated significantly greater activation in the MPFC compared to adults. These results indicated that adults and children do in fact rely on similar cortical midline structures during self-knowledge retrieval but that MPFC activity in children is recruited to a much stronger magnitude, perhaps due to this retrieval task requiring greater neural resources in task-central regions for children (Pfeifer et al., 2007).

After the neural changes relevant to self-processing in childhood, adolescence begins a stage of life when the sense of "self" changes dramatically (Sebastian, Burnett, & Blakemore, 2008). Neuroimaging studies have demonstrated that the dorsal MPFC, one of the most important regions for self-processing, undergoes substantial structural development during adolescence and is one of the last neural regions to finish developing (Shaw et al., 2008). In the MPFC and the superior temporal sulcus (STS), adolescents undergo synaptic reorganization during development of the "social brain," particularly social perception and understanding of others (Blakemore, 2008). In addition to cortical midline regions, we posit that lateral and limbic brain regions, such as the STS, amygdala, and temporoparietal junction (TPJ), which are important in understanding others, are also crucial to a richer theory of identity development because of the complexities of social relationships that catalyze important aspects of self-concept, such as self-awareness and self-consciousness (Steinberg & Morris, 2001). Additionally, during adolescence, individuals become more sociable, form relationships based on social hierarchies, and develop a keen sensitivity to social inclusion (Brown, 2004; Steinberg & Morris, 2001), which researchers suggest may be due to changing brain structure (Blakemore, 2008).

Identity development and a concept of self are central to human experience and occur during the transition from adolescence to adulthood. The capacity to have an awareness of one's identity and knowledge that self-concept is comprised of one's sense of identity—including a feeling of belonging and commitment, values, and attitudes that are shared by one's self and others in a social group (Phinney, 1990)—is supported by neurobiological mechanisms within cortical midline structures, such as the prefrontal cortex and cingulate cortex (Mathur, Harada, & Chiao, 2012). Neuroplasticity within prefrontal cortex during early childhood and adolescence facilitates psychological development of identity and self-concept. Cultural values, practice, and beliefs may shape the neural development of prefrontal cortex as identity and self-concept emerge; similarly, neuroplasticity within prefrontal cortex plays a key role in the maintenance and transmission of cultural variation in identity and self.

Cultural Neuroscience of Empathy

Identity development is formed in part by an understanding of the shared and distinct aspects of one's self from others. Empathy, or the social ability to understand and share the feelings of others, is closely associated with another important facet of identity development—affiliation—because of the important role of empathy in acquiring a sense of affiliation, including belonging and commitment, between self and others, such as those in an ethnic social group. Building off our previous discussion of self-processing as a product of social relationships, empathic neural response may also vary as a function of social overlap or distance between self and other. For instance, racial identification refers to closeness of self to others of the same racial heritage, which can often serve as a protection against psychological and physical stressors associated with prejudice or discriminatory behaviors toward minorities in multicultural communities (Phinney, 1990). Social dominance orientation, or preference for social hierarchy (Pratto et al., 1994; Sidanius & Pratto, 2001), which reflects social norms that encourage social distance (i.e., hierarchical preference) or closeness (i.e., egalitarian preference) between self and others, also may produce variation in empathy and social cognitive capacities due to the need to create and maintain social and cognitive capacities that are culturally competent or that facilitate cultural niche construction.

When comparing empathic neural response within African Americans and Caucasian Americans living in the United States, Mathur and colleagues (2010) found that both African Americans and Caucasian Americans show increased MPFC response when empathizing with same-race compared to other-race others, which predicts altruistic motivation or intention to give time or money to help another minority. Importantly, racial identification, or the degree to which people identify with their racial heritage, predicts neural response within cortical midline structures including MPFC, ACC, and PCC toward ingroup compared to outgroup members during empathic processing (Mathur et al., 2012). The cortical midline structures have been associated with utilization of introspection, perceived personal significance, and evoked emotion (Andrews-Hanna, Reidler, Sepulcre, Poulin, & Bucker, 2010), as well as with self-referential and social cognitive processing (Mitchell, Banaji, & MacRae, 2005; Ochsner et al., 2004). When empathizing with members of their own racial group, African Americans who typically show increased racial identification show greater neural response within cortical midline structures (MPFC, ACC, PCC), whereas Caucasian Americans who typically display racial identification to a lesser extent show greater neural response within medial temporal lobe (MTL) regions (Mathur et al., 2012) that have been related to memory-based scene construction (Andrews-Hanna et al., 2010). Taken together, these findings demonstrate that racial identity predicts distinct empathic neural pathways.

Cultural values of preference for social hierarchy affect empathic neural response to ingroup and outgroup members (Cheon et al., 2011). In a recent cross-cultural neuroimaging study, Cheon and colleagues (2011) discovered that for hierarchical cultures (as in Korea), people are more likely to show increased empathic response to group members due in part to neural response within left TPJ (L-TPJ); by contrast, in egalitarian cultures as defined by Hofstede's Power Distance Index (Hofstede, 2001), such as the United States, people are more likely to show no difference within the L-TPJ in empathic response across group members. These results indicate that members of hierarchical cultures may think more about what their group members are thinking or feeling when in pain compared to members of egalitarian cultures who may expect their group members to express what they are thinking or feeling, rather than to infer these expectations or needs automatically.

Another cultural dimension that modulates empathic neural response for group members is "other-focusedness." Cheon and colleagues (2013) recently found that empathic neural response within the ACC for group members is correlated with degree of "other-focusedness" or how much another person is attuned to the feelings of others in Koreans, but not in Americans. Additionally, empathic neural response for group members within right anterior insula (r-AI) is correlated with "other-focusedness" for both Koreans and Americans. Notably, there were no cultural differences in the degree to which Koreans and Americans reported attunement or sensitivity toward the feelings of others; however, the neural mechanisms associated with cultural values of "other-focusedness" vary for Koreans and Americans. These findings demonstrate the importance of understanding culture and the neurobiological level of analysis and suggest that neural development within ACC and r-AI may vary as a function of culture.

Importantly, even across the formative years of childhood, brain regions important in a conceptual understanding of others, such as the TPJ, show developmental changes. We speculate that these changes in neural activity may affect how and why cultural values (such as preference for social hierarchy) are transmitted and acquired during development. Specifically, younger children (ages 6–8) recruited the bilateral TPJ for many tasks, such as inferring mental states of narrative characters and interpreting biological motion. However, older children (ages 9-11) only recruited the bilateral TPJ during theory of mind tasks, such as inferring mental states (Saxe, Whitfield-Gabrieli, Scholz, & Pelphrey, 2009). These findings suggest that skills critical for social development are becoming fine-tuned at the neural level through these formative years. Based on previous research examining culture differences and theory of mind, we speculate that cultural identities, such as preference for social hierarchy, may be acquired during developmental transitions and that neural changes within the bilateral TPJ likely facilitate cultural changes in identity formation.

By adulthood, cultural and ethnic identity affect how people respond to the feelings of others. However, little is known about the developmental psychological and neural processes that contribute to the formation of identity with and empathy for one's ethnic or cultural group. Future research may examine the developmental changes within a network of brain regions, including MPFC, ACC, PCC, r-AI, TPJ, and MTL, that contribute to empathic response to social group members and the role of acquisition or transmission of cultural values in neural development of empathic brain networks.

Cultural Neuroscience in Perception of Social Cues

Culture has been shown to affect several types of social perceptions, some of which are relatively primitive perceptions of social cues, such as the faces and facial expressions of one's own cultural group members. Cultural modulation of social perception might cause cultural variation on identity formation across different cultures. For instance, African Americans and Caucasian Americans show increased fusiform and MTL response when encoding faces of the same race compared to faces of the other race (Golby, Gabrieli, Chiao, & Eberhardt, 2001). These findings are likely the result of perceptual tuning within perceptual regions of the brain that leads to increased response within the visual and medial temporal cortices toward faces of one's own cultural or racial group, similar to the perceptual tuning that occurs for language.

Evolutionarily ancient limbic circuitry, such as the human amygdala, also shows increased response toward fear faces of one's own cultural group compared to fear faces of another's cultural group (Chiao et al., 2008). These findings likely reflect increased processing of fear expressed by members of one's own group either due to enhanced vigilance to or attention toward social signals of group members. When danger is present in the environment, it may be adaptive for people to interpret the social signals of group members as conveying information important to their survival to a greater extent compared to the social signals of outgroup members who may not necessarily share the same cultural beliefs about what kinds of circumstances in the world are dangerous or threatening. These findings demonstrate the flexibility in amygdala response to the social communication cues of ingroup and outgroup members, given recent demonstrations of increased amygdala response for outgroup rather than ingroup members due to the role that the amygdala plays in heightened vigilance for novel or ambiguous others (Cunningham et al. 2004; Hart et al., 2000; Phelps et al., 2003).

The capacity to infer the mental states of others from the eye region—not only emotional expressions but also subtler social cues such as compassion and empathy—is necessary for social survival. Brain regions important in the ability to infer the mental states of others from minimal perceptual cues, such as the STS, show increased response to the eye region of own cultural group compared to other cultural group members (Adams et al., 2009). Specifically, Japanese and Caucasian Americans show increased STS response toward the eye region of the face of own-group compared to other-group members. These findings indicate that neural regions important to social perception show increased response when inferring the mental states of members of one's own cultural group.

Heightened processing for the mental states of cultural group members likely reflects either perceptual experience with interpreting the communicative signals of people who are perceptually similar to one's self (i.e., perceptual distance—sharing similar physiognomic or physical appearance features) or top-down conceptual processing of social signals that are thought to convey communicative information that is of greater relevance due to cultural similarity to one's self (i.e., cultural distance—sharing conceptual or social beliefs).

An important question in cultural neuroscience research is when developmental changes in neural processing facilitate cultural changes in social perception ability. Prior cultural neuroscience research in young adults has shown that fusiform and MTL responses vary across group members (Golby et al.,

2001). One possibility of a developmental neural mechanism for social knowledge is that during childhood perceptual experience with group members facilitates neural pruning of face representations toward faces of members within one's own cultural or racial group. For instance, children show increased distribution of fusiform response during face processing compared to adults, possibly reflecting increased neural space dedicated to representations of distinct faces that, in adulthood, becomes specially recruited for faces of one's own racial or cultural group.

Heightened amygdala response to fear faces of one's own cultural group in adulthood may result from developmental neural changes in adolescence. Specifically, adolescents have shown increased amygdala, OFC, and ACC response to fearful faces compared to adults (Monk et al., 2003). Enhanced perceptual experience with or vigilance toward emotions expressed by members of one's own cultural group during adolescence may lead to subsequent cultural variation in amygdala response to fear faces in adulthood. Telzer and colleagues (2013) recently showed that amygdala sensitivity to race emerges during adolescence, not childhood, and is predicted by peer diversity in African-American adolescents. Adolescents who have friends of different races are more likely to show reduced amygdala to African-American compared to Caucasian-American faces, suggesting the importance of diversity in social experience on neural response to other people (Telzer et al., 2013).

From infancy, the human brain is attuned to social cues, such as faces, that are within the infant's immediate physical environment (e.g., caregivers, family members; Slater et al., 2010). Neuroplasticity of the visual system during infancy leads to differences in perceptual tuning within brain regions associated with face perception for distinct kinds of social cues, such as faces of different species (Scott & Monesson, 2010) and races (Vogel, Monesson, & Scott, 2012). During adolescence, social experience with peers from diverse racial and ethnic backgrounds predicts amygdala response to faces of minority groups, such as African Americans in Africa. By adulthood, a network of brain regions implicated in social perception, including the amygdala, superior temporal gyrus, fusiform gyrus, and MTL regions, shows sensitivity to faces of one's own social group. Neural tuning within perceptual and learning neural regions is associated with behavioral advantages for processing of social cues from one's own social group, such as heightened memory for group members. Heightened psychological and neural representation of social group members may facilitate identity development by providing the individual with knowledge of others who are perceptually or culturally close to the self.

Cultural Neuroscience in Late Development

The cognitive neuroscience of development has made great progress in highlighting exciting, converging evidence between the mind and brain in both children and adults alike. However, most of the research across the lifespan has been conducted in Western populations, which raises doubts about how these findings can be extrapolated to people in other parts of the world. To further the progress of this developmental approach, cultural neuroscience has begun examining the relationship between aging and culture at the neural level in late adulthood, comparing elderly and younger adults (Park & Gutchess, 2002).

The objective of this neuroscientific work is not only to identify age-related functional and structural neural differences that exist across cultures, but also to examine neural changes that are influenced by culture-specific experience. Culture serves an important role later in life as a compensatory mechanism for the decline in cognitive abilities due to neural changes in cellular and structural organization of the brain (Park & Gutchess, 2002). Although much evidence within cultural psychology highlights cultural variation in how people think during young adulthood (Nisbett et al., 2001), brain changes in structural and functional organization due to aging may result in even greater cultural variation in how people think in older age (Park & Gutchess, 2002). The goal of investigating aging from a cultural neuroscience perspective is to facilitate an understanding of both environmental influences and biological constraints on cognitive functioning in late adulthood (Park & Gutchess, 2002).

Neuroimaging data reveal that, compared to the brains of young adults, the brains of older adults are constantly striving to adapt to their diminished efficiency in the domains of speed, working memory capacity, and long-term memory (Reuter-Lorenz & Lustig, 2005). Detecting general similarities across brains of older adults points in the direction of biological aging, whereas vast neural differences in older brains suggest that cultural influences play a role in shaping neural circuitry. Cultural differences may be heightened in old age due to differences in acquired cultural learning; conversely, cultural differences may be more robust in young adulthood before capacity limitations begin to constrain flexibility (Park et al., 1999). Although both factors—culture and age—continually influence cognition, certain types of thinking may depend on these factors to different extents.

As far as we know, no research in cultural neuroscience has yet addressed the topics of self-processing or identity in older populations. Due to this gap in the literature, we believe examining identity changes in older populations would be a fruitful future direction for cultural neuroscience, especially in light of our earlier discussion of self-construal style. Perhaps cultural learning diminishes with age as a result of decreased cognitive and neural efficiency, leading people's identities to depend less on cultural factors as one becomes elderly. Conversely, independent and interdependent self-processing may become strengthened over the lifespan, leading parents and older community members to teach or transmit these cultural aspects of social identity to the younger generations. More cultural neuroscience research is needed to answer complicated questions such as this. In the upcoming two sections, we discuss how an integration between cultural neuroscience and the study of identity development would be beneficial.

Integrating the Science of Identity Development into Cultural Neuroscience

Abundant progress has been made in understanding identity development in the social, personality, and developmental literatures. As interdisciplinary scientists who aspire to represent the mind, the brain, and behavior in dynamic states across populations, we appreciate themes of fluidity, such as change and variability across time, that are keeping research on identity development on the cutting edge. The majority of cultural neuroscience research has thus far been conducted on young adults, which is a limiting factor when seeking to represent human kind as thoroughly as possible.

Functional magnetic resonance imaging has been one of the primary tools utilized in investigating how culture might modulate the neural mechanisms of a wide range of cognitive processes and behaviors. It would be useful to understand neural activity at all ages across the lifespan, including infancy, to elucidate some of the crucial components of early-developing psychological processes. However, there are two major limitations to applying fMRI methodologies to infants. There is the risk of collecting blurred images due to the participants' head movements, as well as the second limitation of infants' inability to provide behavioral responses that allow researchers to determine relations between psychological states and neural states.

Functional near-infrared spectroscopy (FNIRS) is one promising approach in examining neural activity in infants; FNIRS allows for a noninvasive and naturalistic experimental condition due to the portable nature of the methodology. A recent neuroimaging study with FNIRS suggested that infants selectively process and attend to communicative signals (e.g., eye contact, calling a person's name) directed at them (Grossmann, Parise, & Friederici, 2010). Another FNIRS study by Naoi and colleagues (2012) examined cerebral hemodynamic responses of infants during speech perception by their own mothers versus unfamiliar mothers. This task yielded greater activation observed in the frontal area when infants listened to infant-directed speech by their own mothers.

Although it is still unknown whether or how culture may affect such infants' behaviors, as well as what the neural underpinning at this early stage during development are, social behaviors such as kin perception observed during the early stage of development play an important role in identity development. For instance, frontal brain regions associated with social cognition may develop preferentially in response to specific cultural cues of social identity, such as auditory or visual cues of kinship. This preferential neural response may in turn provide the psychological foundation for social identity development during childhood and adolescence, when these brain regions undergo neural maturation. Hence, the integration of identity development research into the recently developed cultural neuroscientific methodology of FNIRS will allow us to better understand how culture modulates human social behavior and the neural mechanisms underlying identity development even from the early stages of development.

During childhood and adolescence, cultural identity plays a key role in shaping neural responses to kin perception, as well as how reward is evaluated as a function of kin relations. In particular, the family may be an important kind of cultural identity that shapes immunological and neural responses to social information, particularly for families from Latin America and Asia (Fuligni & Telzer, 2013). For instance, teens who spend more time helping their family demonstrate increased biological burden in immunological response, specifically increased levels of interleukin 6 receptor (sIL-6r) and C-reactive protein (CRP), which are considered downstream biomarkers of high levels of the proinflammatory cytokine IL-6 (Fuligni et al., 2009). However, Telzer and colleagues (2013) recently showed that Mexican adolescents' neural response was greater within the ventral striatum during costly donation rather than financial reward. Furthermore, individual differences in Mexican adolescents' neural activity within ventral striatum were predicted by family values such as obligation and family assistance fulfillment (Telzer, Fuligni, Lieberman, & Galvan, 2013; Telzer, Masten, Berkman, Lieberman, & Fuligni, 2010). Despite the immunological cost of family obligation, fulfilling family duties or assisting family members elicits greater reward neural response for Mexican adolescents. Understanding such empirical differences requires not only a neuroscientific basis, but also a general comprehension for how culture and familial relations shape our sense of self and duty.

Integrating Cultural Neuroscience Research into the Field of Identity Development

We believe that the integration of cultural neuroscience theory and methodology has the potential to broaden the scope of the extant research on identity development. One major advancement would be to begin conducting cultural neuroscience research on the topic of identity development. Such an endeavor is now possible through the development of novel cross-cultural imaging and electrophysiological methods (Chiao et al., 2010b) that allow for the comparison of neural response during social cognitive and affective response across cultures using event-related potentials (ERP) and neuroimaging (fMRI) techniques. To date, very little research has been conducted integrating these multiple approaches, and we posit that there is much to be learned from the science of identity development while integrating cross-cultural neuroimaging. Discovery of cultural influences on neural representations of self and identity have led to further conceptual development within cultural neuroscience and, in particular, the introduction of the concept of "looping effects." This concept demonstrates the notion that culture is a dynamic system of bidirectional influences within individuals, including psychological and biological processes that facilitate social interaction (Vogeley & Roepstorff, 2009). Given that culture mutually influences individual processes such as mind, brain, and behavior, important questions in cultural neuroscience include culture mapping (i.e., what kinds of cognitive processes vary across cultures at the neural level) and source analysis (i.e., from where cultural universals and differences emerge; Ambady & Bharucha, 2009).

These questions would be particularly relevant for the science of identity development to understand how identities are manifested differently across the globe. In geographic regions with distinct environmental or ecological pressures, development of social brain regions may occur in response to these ecological pressures and result in global variation of cultural identities by adulthood. For instance, in geographic regions with a high prevalence of pathogens or infectious diseases, as in the developing world, frontal brain regions early in infancy may preferentially respond to social identity cues that facilitate development of collectivistic cultural identity due to the adaptive function of collectivism in protecting against infectious disease (Chiao & Blizinsky, 2010; Fincher et al., 2008). Furthermore, in geographic regions with high prevalence of distal ecological pressures, such as high population density and territorial conflict, frontal brain regions early in development may also tune to social cues of norm abidance and deviance that facilitate development of tight or loose cultural identity, which may protect people from such ecological pressures (Gelfand et al., 2011; 2012; Mrazek, Chiao, Blizinsky, Lun, & Gelfand, 2013). Future research in cultural neuroscience may examine the extent to which cultural, genetic, and environmental factors shape the psychological and neural processes that shape identity across development (Chiao et al., 2010b; Chiao et al., 2013).

Conclusion

This chapter reviewed relevant cultural psychology, cognitive neuroscience, and cultural neuroscience research to highlight the interdisciplinary progress that is being made in the study of identity development, primarily through the study of self-referential processing. Primarily, we demonstrate that (a) views of the self are shaped by cultural differences in self-construal style in the mind and brain, (b) developmental neuroimaging research in toddlers and children demonstrates that neural activity of the self is shaped by cultural learning and neural plasticity, and (c) cultural neuroscience studies of identity development and aging are beginning to shed light on how culture affects neural plasticity of the self. We suggest that the field of cultural neuroscience can be further strengthened by studying populations across the lifespan and that the field of identity development can benefit from future cultural neuroscience work, especially examining the influence of other prominent cultural dimensions beyond individualism-collectivism. Learning from the strengths of each area may provide effective ways to expand the breadth and sophistication of theory and evidence within cultural neuroscience research, as well as identity development research in the future.

References

Adams, R. B. Jr., Rule, N. O., Franklin, R. G. Jr., Wang, E., Stevenson, M. T., Yoshikawa, S.,...Ambady, N. (2009). Cross-cultural reading the mind in the eyes: An fMRI Investigation. *Journal of Cognitive Neuroscience, 22*(1), 97–108.

Andrews-Hanna, J. R., Reidler, J. S., Sepulcre, J., Poulin, R., & Bucker, R. L. (2010). Functional-anatomic fractionation of the Brain's Default Network. *Neuron, 65*, 550–562.

Ambady, N., & Bharucha, J. (2009). Culture and the brain. *Current Directions in Psychological Science, 18*(6), 342–344.

Amodio, D. M., & Frith, C. D. (2006). Meeting of minds: The medial frontal cortex and social cognition. *Nature Reviews Neuroscience, 7*, 268–277.

Amsterdam, B. (1972). Mirror self-image reaction before age two. *Developmental Psychobiology, 5*, 297–305.

Arnett, J. J. (2008) The neglected 95%: Why American psychology needs to become less American. *American Psychologist, 63*(7), 602–614.

Baltes, P. B., Reuter-Lorenz, P. A., & Rösler, F. (2006). *Lifespan development and the brain: The perspective of biocultural co-constructivism.* West Nyack, NY: Cambridge University Press.

Blakemore, S. J. (2008). The social brain in adolescence. *Nature Reviews Neuroscience, 9*, 267–277.

Brown, B. B. (2004). Adolescents' relationships with peers. In R. M. Lerner & L. Steinberg (Eds.), *Handbook of adolescent psychology* (2nd ed., pp. 363–394). Hoboken, NJ: Wiley.

Cheon, B. K., Im, D., Harada, T., Kim, J., Mathur, V. A., Scimeca, J. M.,...Chiao, J. Y. (2011). Cultural influences on neural basis of intergroup empathy. *Neuroimage, 57*(2), 642–650.

Cheon, B. K., Im, D. M., Harada, T., Kim, J. S., Mathur, VA., Scimeca, J. M.,...Chiao, J. Y. (2013). Cultural modulation of the neural correlates of empathy: The role of other-focusedness. *Neuropsychologia, 51*(7), 1177–1186.

Chiao, J. Y. (2009). *Cultural neuroscience: Cultural influences on brain function. Progress in Brain Research,* New York: Elsevier Press.

Chiao, J. Y., & Ambady, N. (2007). Cultural neuroscience: Parsing universality and diversity across levels of analysis. In S. Kitayama & D. Cohen (Eds.), *Handbook of cultural psychology* (pp. 237–254). New York: Guilford.

Chiao, J. Y., & Blizinsky, K. D. (2010). Culture-gene coevolution of individualism-collectivism and the serotonin transporter gene (5-HTTLPR). *Proceedings of the Royal Society B: Biological Sciences, 277*(1681), 529–537.

Chiao, J. Y., & Blizinsky K. D. (2013). Population disparities in mental health: Insights from cultural neuroscience. *American Journal of Public Health, 103*(S1), S122–S132.

Chiao, J. Y., & Cheon, B. K. (2010). The weirdest brains in the world. *Brain and Behavioral Sciences, 33*, 88–90.

Chiao, J. Y., Cheon, B. K., Pornpattananangkul, N., Mrazek, A. J., Blizinsky, K. D. (2013). Cultural neuroscience: Progress and promise. *Psychological Inquiry, 24*(1), 1–19.

Chiao, J. Y., Harada, T., Komeda, H., Li, Z., Mano, Y., Saito, D. N.,...Iidaka, T. (2010a). Dynamic cultural influences on neural representations of the self. *Journal of Cognitive Neuroscience. 22*(1), 1–11.

Chiao, J. Y., Harada, T., Komeda, H., Li, Z., Mano, Y., Saito, D. N.,...Iidaka, T. (2009). Neural basis of individualistic and collectivistic views of self. *Human Brain Mapping, 30*(9), 2813–2820.

Chiao, J. Y., Hariri, A. R., Harada, T., Mano, Y., Sadato, N., Parrish, T. B., & Iidaka, T. (2010b). Theory and methods in cultural neuroscience. *Social Cognitive and Affective Neuroscience, 5*(2–3), 356–361.

Chiao, J. Y., Iidaka, T., Gordon, H. L., Nogawa, J., Bar, M., Aminoff, E.,...Ambady, N. (2008). Cultural specificity in amygdala response to fear faces. *Journal of Cognitive Neuroscience, 20*(12), 2167–2174.

Chiao, J. Y., & Immordino-Yang, M. H. (2013). Modularity and the cultural mind: Contributions of cultural neuroscience to cognitive theory. *Perspectives on Psychological Science, 8*(1), 56–61.

Cunningham, W. A., Johnson, M. K., Raye, C. L., Gatenby, J. C., Gore, J. C., & Banaji, M. R. (2004). Separable neural components in the processing of black and white faces. *Psychological Science, 15*, 806–813.

Fincher, C. L., Thornhill, R., Murray, D. R., & Schaller, M. (2008). Pathogen prevalence predicts human cross-cultural variability in individualism/collectivism. *Proceedings of the Royal Society, 275*(1640), 1279–1285.

Fuligni, A. J., & Telzer, E. H. (2013). Another way the family can get in the head and under the skin: The neurobiology of family assistance. *Perspectives in Child Development, 7*, 138–142.

Fuligni, A. J., Telzer, E. H., Bower, J., Irwin, M. R., Kiang, L., & Cole, S. R. (2009). Daily family assistance and inflammation among adolescents from Latin American and European backgrounds. *Brain, Behavior and Immunity, 23*, 803–809.

Gallup, G. G. Jr. (1970). Chimpanzees: Self recognition. *Science, 167*, 86–87.

Gardner, W. L., Gabriel, S., & Lee, A. Y. (1999). "I" value freedom but "we" value relationships: Self construal priming mirrors cultural differences in judgment. *Psychological Science, 10*, 321–326.

Gelfand, M. J., Raver, J. L., Nishii, L., Leslie, L. M., Lun, J., Lim, B. C.,...Yamaguchi S. (2011). Differences between tight and loose cultures: A 33-nation study. *Science, 332*(6033), 1100–1104.

Gelfand, M., Shteynberg, G., Lee, T., Lun, J., Lyons, S., Bell, C.,...Soomro N. (2012). The cultural contagion of conflict. *Philosophical Transactions of the Royal Society of London, B Biological Science, 367*(1589), 692–703.

Gillihan, S. J., & Farah, M. J. (2005). Is self special? A critical review of evidence from experimental psychology and cognitive neuroscience. *Psychological Bulletin, 131*(1), 76–97.

Golby, A. J., Gabrieli, J. D. E., Chiao, J. Y., & Eberhardt, J. L. (2001). Differential fusiform responses to same- and other-race faces. *Nature Neuroscience, 4*(8), 845–850.

Grossmann, T., Parise, E., & Friederici, A. D. (2010). The detection of communicative signals directed at the self in infant prefrontal cortex. *Frontiers in Human Neuroscience, 4*(201), 1–5.

Harada, T., Li, Z., & Chiao, J. Y. (2010). Differential dorsal and ventral medial prefrontal representations of the implicit self modulated by individualism and collectivism: An fMRI study. *Social Neuroscience, 22*, 1–15.

Hart, A. J., Whalen, P. J., Shin, L. M., McInerney, S. C., Fischer, H., & Rauch, S. L. (2000). Differential response in the human amygdala to racial outgroup vs. ingroup face stimuli. *NeuroReport, 11*, 2351–2355.

Harter, S. (1999). *The construction of the self: A developmental perspective*. New York: Guilford.

Henrich, J., Heine, S., & Norenzayan, A. (2010). The weirdest people in the world? *Behavioral and Brain Science, 33*(2–3), 61–83.

Hofstede, G. (2001). *Culture's consequences: Comparing values, behaviors, institutions and organizations across nations*. Thousand Oaks, CA: Sage.

Hong, Y., Morris, M. W., Chiu, C., & Benet-Martinez, V. (2000). Multicultural minds: A dynamic constructivist approach to culture and cognition. *American Psychologist, 55*, 709–720.

Kelley, W. M., Macrae, C. N., Wyland, C. L., Caglar, S., Inati, S., & Heatherton, T. F. (2002). Finding the self? An event related fMRI study. *Journal of Cognitive Neuroscience, 14*(5), 785–794.

Li, S. C. (2003). Biocultural orchestration of developmental plasticity across levels: The interplay of biology and culture in shaping the mind and behavior across the life span. *Psychological Bulletin, 129*(2), 171–194.

Markus, H. R., & Kitayama, S. (1991). Culture and the self: Implications for cognition, emotion, and motivation. *Psychological Review, 98*, 224–253.

Mathur, V. A., Harada, T., & Chiao, J. Y. (2012). Racial identification modulates default network activity for same- and other-races. *Human Brain Mapping, 33*(8), 1883–1893.

Mathur, V. A., Harada, T., Lipke, T., & Chiao, J. Y. (2010). Neural basis of extraordinary empathy and altruistic motivation. *Neuroimage, 51*(4), 1468–1475.

Mead, G. H. (1934). *Mind, self and society from the standpoint of a social behaviorist*. Chicago: University of Chicago Press.

Meltzoff, A. N., & Moore, M. K. (1977). Imitation of Facial and Manual Gestures by Human Neonates. *Science, 198*, 75–78.

Mesoudi, A., Whiten, A., & Laland, K. N. (2006). Toward a unified science of cultural evolution. *Behavioral and Brain Science, 29*, 329–383.

Mitchell, J. P., Banaji, M. R., & MacRae, C. N. (2005). The link between social cognition and self-referential thought in the medial prefrontal cortex. *Journal of Cognitive Neuroscience, 17*, 1306–1315.

Monk, C. S., McClure, E. B., Nelson, E. E., Zarahn, E., Bilder, R. M., Leibenluft, E.,…Pine, D. S. (2003). Adolescent immaturity in attention-related brain engagement to emotional facial expressions. *Neuroimage, 20*(1), 420–428.

Mrazek, A. J., Chiao, J. Y., Blizinsky, K. D., Lun, J., & Gelfand, M. J. (2013). Culture-gene coevolution of tightness-looseness and allelic variation of the serotonin transporter gene: The dual influence on morality. *Culture and Brain*. doi: 10.1007/s40167-013-0009-x

Naoi, N., Minagawa-Kawai, Y., Kobayashi, A., Takeuchi, K., Nakamura, K., Yamamoto, J., & Kojima, S. (2012). Cerebral responses to infant-directed speech and the effect of talker familiarity. *Neuroimage, 59*, 1735–1744.

Northoff, G., & Bermpohl, F. (2004). Cortical midline structures and the self. *Trend in Cognitive Sciences, 8*(3), 102–107.

Northoff, G., Heinzel, A., Greck, M., Bermpohl, F., Dobrowolny, H., & Panksepp, J. (2006). Self-referential processing in our brain-a meta-analysis of imaging studies on the self. *Neuroimage, 31*, 440–457.

Nisbett, R. E., Peng, K., Choi, I., & Norenzayan, A. (2001). Culture and systems of thought. *Psychological Review, 108*(2), 291–310.

Ochsner, K. N., Knierim, K., Ludlow, D. H., Ramachandran, T., Glover, G., & Mackey, S. C. (2004). Reflecting upon feelings: An fMRI study of neural systems supporting the attribution of emotion to self and other. *Journal of Cognitive Neuroscience, 16*, 1746–1772.

Oyserman, D., Coon, H. M., & Kemmelmeier, M. (2002): Rethinking individualism and collectivism: Evaluation of theoretical assumptions and meta-analyses. *Psychological Bulletin, 128*(1), 3–72.

Oyserman, D., & Lee. S. W. (2008). Priming "culture": Culture as situated cognition. In S. Kitayama & D. Cohen (Eds.), *Handbook of cultural psychology* (pp. 255–276). New York: Guilford.

Park, D. C., & Gutchess, A. H. (2002). Aging, cognition and culture: A neuroscientific perspective. *Neuroscience and Biobehavioral Reviews, 26*(7), 859–867.

Park, D. C., Nisbett, R., & Hedden, T. (1999). Aging, culture, and cognition. *Journal of Gerontology, Psychological sciences*, 54B, 75–84.

Pfeifer, J. H., Lieberman, M. D., & Dapretto, M. (2007). "I know you are but what am I?!": Neural bases of self- and social knowledge retrieval in children and adults. *Journal of Cognitive Neuroscience, 19*(8), 1323–1337.

Phelps, E. A., Cannistraci, C. J., & Cunningham, W. A. (2003). Intact performance on an indirect measure of race bias following amygdala damage. *Neuropsychologia, 41*, 203–208.

Phinney, J. S. (1990). Ethnic identity in adolescents and adults: Review of research. *Psychological Bulletin, 108*(3), 499–514.

Pratto, F., Sidanius, J., Stallworth, L., & Malle, B. F. (1994). Social dominance orientation: A personality variable predicting social and political attitudes. *Journal of Personality and Social Psychology, 67*(4): 741–63.

Reuter-Lorenz, P. A. & Lustig C. (2005). Brain aging: Reorganizing discoveries about the aging mind. *Current Opinion in Neurobiology*, 15, 245–251.

Rogers, T. B., Kuiper, N. A., & Kirker, W. S. (1977). Self-reference and the encoding of personal information. *Journal of Personality and Social Psychology, 35*, 677–688.

Sadato, N., Morita, T., & Itakura, S. (2008). The roles of neuroimaging in developmental social psychology. *Brain Imaging and Behavior, 2*, 335–342.

Saltz, E., & Medow, M. L. (1971). Concept conservation in children: The dependence of belief systems on semantic representation. *Child Development, 42*, 1533–1542.

Saxe, R. R., Whitfield-Gabrieli, S., Scholz, J., & Pelphrey, K. A. (2009). Brain regions for perceiving and reasoning about other people in school-aged children. *Child Development, 80*(4), 1197–1209.

Scott, L. S., & Monesson, A. (2010). Experience-dependent neural specialization during infancy. *Neuropsychologia, 48*(6), 1857–1861.

Sebastian, C., Burnett, S., & Blakemore, S. J. (2008). Development of the self-concept during adolescence. *Trends in Cognitive Sciences, 12*(11), 441–446.

Shaw, P., Kabani, N. J., Lerch, J. P., Eckstrand, K., Lenroot, R., Gogtay, N., et al. (2008). Neurodevelopmental trajectories of the human cerebral cortex. *Journal of Neuroscience, 28*, 3586–3594.

Sidanius, J. & Pratto, F. (2001). *Social Dominance: An Intergroup Theory of Social Hierarchy and Oppression.* Cambridge: Cambridge University Press.

Steinberg, L., & Morris, A. S. (2001). Adolescent development. *Annual Review in Psychology, 52*, 83–110.

Shweder, R. A., & LeVine, R. A. (Eds.). (1984). *Culture theory: Essays on mind, self, and emotion.* Cambridge: Cambridge University Press.

Slater, A., Quinn, P. C., Kelly, D. J., Lee, K., Longmore, C. A., McDonald, P. R., & Pascalis, O. (2010). The shaping of the face space in early infancy: Becoming a native face processor. *Child Development Perspectives, 4*(3), 205–211.

Telzer, E. H., Fuligni, A. J., Lieberman, M. D., Galván, A. (2013). Meaningful family relationships: Neurocognitive buffers of adolescent risk taking. *Journal of Cognitive Neuroscience, 25*(3), 374–387.

Telzer, E. H., Humphreys, K., Shapiro, M., & Tottenham, N. L. (2013). Amygdala sensitivity to race is not present in childhood but emerges in adolescence. *Journal of Cognitive Neuroscience, 25*, 234–244.

Telzer, E. H., Masten, C. L., Berkman, E. T., Lieberman, M. D., & Fuligni, A. J. (2010). Gaining while giving: An fMRI study of the rewards of family assistance among white and Latino youth. *Social Neuroscience, 5*, 508–518.

Triandis, H. C. (1989). The self and social behavior in differing cultural contexts. *Psychological Review, 96*, 506–520.

Triandis, H. C. (1995). *Individualism and Collectivism.* Boulder, CO: Westview Press.

Vogel, M., Monesson, A., & Scott, L. S. (2012). Building biases in infancy: The influence of race on face and voice emotion matching. *Developmental Science, 15*(3), 359–372.

Vogeley, K., & Roepstorff, A. (2009). Contextualising culture and social cognition. *Trends in Cognitive Science, 13*(12), 511–516.

Zhu, Y., Zhang, L., Fan, J., & Han, S. (2007). Neural basis of cultural influences on self-representation. *Neuroimage, 34*(3), 1310–1316.

CHAPTER 27

Parenting, Adolescent–Parent Relationships, and Social Domain Theory: Implications for Identity Development

Wendy M. Rote *and* Judith G. Smetana

Abstract

This chapter explores connections among parenting, children's construction of the personal domain as defined within social domain theory, and adolescents' identity development. It begins by describing the framework of social domain theory and its potential links with identity development. It highlights differences among social-cognitive domains (moral, conventional, and personal) in the ways they relate to identity processes and emphasizes the importance of the personal domain, which encompasses matters of personal choice and preference, for adolescent identity processes. Next, the authors focus on parents' and children's views of the personal domain and their interactions, drawing special attention to the way parents' control of the personal domain potentially impacts adolescents' adjustment and identity. The chapter concludes by focusing on ways social domain theory research, and specifically parenting and domain distinctions, can illuminate research on identity development.

Key Words: parenting, parent–child relationships, social domain theory, identity, autonomy

Identity development consists of establishing a set of unique personal values and roles and developing a coherent and continuous sense of self across situations and time (Erikson, 1968; Kroger, 2003). This is central for defining and maintaining a direction and sense of purpose in life. It also sets the stage for successful completion of later life tasks, such as maintaining intimate relationships and feeling generative and satisfied with one's life (Erikson, 1968). Identity development is a particularly salient task during adolescence because teenagers' maturing social and cognitive understandings allow them to construct more coherent and elaborate conceptions of themselves across situations and time (Erikson, 1968; Harter, 2008). However, precursors to a mature understanding of identity develop during childhood. This includes the formation and elaboration of a self-concept, including an understanding of agency and the unique qualities of the self (Damon & Hart, 1988). Adolescents' later conceptions of identity then build on these earlier, nascent understandings of the self (Damon & Hart, 1988; Erikson, 1968; Harter, 2008; McAdams, 2003). As we consider the role of parents and parent–youth interactions in the development of identity, we discuss parental contributions to both precursors of identity (in younger children) and mature identity (in adolescents).

Identity development is often considered to be an internal, psychological process, but it also takes place within the context of social relationships. These relationships help to shape adolescents' eventual values, goals, and self-concept, as well as their ability to subjectively understand and provide continuity to their experiences. Indeed, research has shown that many aspects of adolescents' developing identity, including identity exploration, commitment, and narrative identity development, depend on social interactions (Fivush, Bohanek, & Marin, 2010; Kroger, 2003; Luyckx, Schwartz, Goossens, Beyers, & Missotten, 2011; Weeks & Pasupathi, 2010).

The parent–child relationship and, in turn, parents' parenting behaviors, are of particular importance for adolescents' developing sense of identity (Luyckx et al., 2011). Children begin to co-construct precursors to identity with parents during childhood, often by identifying with parents and adopting aspects of their values and behaviors or by jointly constructing autobiographical narratives with them (Weeks & Pasupathi, 2010). Parents also consciously attempt to shape children's identity by teaching them about their history and background and helping them understand themselves in context (Schachter & Ventura, 2008), again at times through narrative processes. These positive relationships and early conceptualizations of the self provide continuity to behaviors and beliefs over time, which adolescents draw on when developing a coherent sense of identity at later ages. Parents also encourage identity formation through their general provision of structure, guidance, and support. During childhood, these parenting behaviors encourage positive parent–child relationships and identification processes helpful for developing a consistent set of values and behaviors (Kochanska, 1997). During adolescence, they provide the scaffolding and security necessary for adolescents to question, explore, and identify which values, behaviors, and talents are fundamental to their sense of self. Indeed, these parenting behaviors, either alone or together in the form of authoritative parenting, have been associated with more positive identity styles (Berzonsky, 2004) and more identity exploration and achievement, including greater depth and breadth of both (Adams, 1985; Beyers & Goossens, 2008; Grotevant & Cooper, 1985; Sartor & Youniss, 2002).

In this chapter, we draw connections among parenting, parent–child relationships, and identity development. Although we do not study identity directly in our program of research, we are interested in two processes relevant to identity formation and processes. Specifically, our research on parents' and children's interactions around the boundaries of parents' legitimate authority and the development of adolescents' autonomy, as it relates to domain distinctions specified within social-cognitive domain theory (such as differences between conventional and personal issues; Smetana, 2006), has important implications for adolescent identity development. We speculate on these connections here. In the first sections of the chapter, we describe the theoretical framework of our research and elaborate on potential links between social-cognitive domains and identity processes. Next, we focus on the personal domain, considering adolescents' and parents' conceptions of it and how the intersection of their views and consequent communication processes potentially impact the development of identity. Then, we describe associations between parental control of the personal domain and adolescents' adjustment and developing identity. Finally, we conclude by reviewing how the study of identity development can benefit from considering domain-differentiated parenting, and we outline possible directions for future research.

Identity in Childhood Versus Adolescence

Parenting begins to impact identity development when children are still quite young. However, parenting interacts differently with children's identity development depending on the child's age and the ways in which he or she conceptualizes identity-relevant constructs. Thus, to understand the associations between parenting and identity development, one must first understand age-related changes in how children understand identity.

A mature understanding of identity requires being able to connect and find patterns in one's actions and beliefs across time and situations, actively associating with these underlying traits, and viewing the self as purposefully creating such continuity in behavior (Damon & Hart, 1988; Erikson, 1968; Kroger, 2003). Given the complex nature of these cognitions, identity development disproportionately takes place during adolescence. However, children begin to form conceptions of the self and agency much earlier in life, and these serve as precursors to identity. When asked to describe themselves, young children focus primarily on observable features of their body, behavior, and group membership, and children in middle and late childhood highlight their capabilities and emotional states (Damon & Hart, 1988). Children also begin to form narratives of personal experiences that include subjective components (Fivush & Zamanm, this volume; McAdams, 2003). Although many features that children cite when describing themselves or narrating life events are relatively stable across time and situation, children typically do not focus on such stability as an important or integrating aspect of their self-understanding. As such, their conceptions of the self are nascent and lack the continuity and conceptual complexity traditionally considered to define identity (Kroger, 2003; Weeks & Pasupathi, 2010).

With the social and cognitive advances of adolescence, youth begin to focus on their behavior and thoughts in more abstract terms, identifying and defining the continuities, beliefs, and agentic decisions that underlie their unique patterns of functioning (Harter, 2008; Weeks & Pasupathi, 2010). It is only at this point that true identity development can be said to occur. This process builds on earlier conceptions of the self and patterns of reasoning about past behaviors evident in childhood, but it includes more reflective, evaluative, and integrative components necessary for conceptualizing a psychological self underlying one's behavior across time and situations (Damon & Hart, 1988; Erikson, 1968). Thus, prior to adolescence, children do not develop a true identity; rather it is the *precursors* of identity, such as self-concept and agency, which become solidified and elaborated, often with parental aid.

Social Domain Theory

Our approach to parenting and adolescents' identity development is based on *social domain theory* (Smetana, 2006; Turiel, 1983), which focuses on how individuals across the lifespan identify, coordinate, and apply different types of social knowledge in social situations. The domain model posits that, through their interactions with others, children construct three conceptually and developmentally distinct domains of social knowledge. The *moral* domain pertains to individuals' prescriptive judgments about how to treat others and concerns issues of justice, rights, and others' welfare. Examples of moral behaviors are acts of violence or physical harm to others, psychological harm (e.g., teasing or verbal abuse), vandalism, and distribution of goods (e.g., theft). Moral behaviors are considered right or wrong due to their intrinsic effects on others; their (un)acceptability is therefore nonalterable and generalizable across contexts (Smetana, 2006; 2013; Turiel, 1983). In contrast, the *societal* domain concerns issues of social convention, social organization, and group identity. Examples of conventional violations (at least in mainstream North American culture) are wearing pyjamas or a bathing suit to school, eating food with fingers rather than a fork, talking in class without raising one's hand, and calling teachers by their first rather than last name. Although conventional acts are often considered right or wrong and legitimately regulated by others, their acceptability is based on social consensus or authority dictates, and thus conventional issues are considered alterable and relative to particular contexts rather than broadly generalizable (Smetana, 2006; Turiel, 1983).

Finally, the *psychological* domain concerns psychological processes, including motivations, emotions, intentions, and attributions for one's own and others' behaviors, as well as understanding of self and identity. Personal issues are related to the latter concerns and are an aspect of the psychological domain that has received a great deal of research attention. Personal issues are not right or wrong, but rather pertain to personal preferences or choices, privacy, and control over one's body. Thus, they are not legitimately regulated by others. Examples of personal issues (again, at least within North American culture) include appearance (style of clothes, choice of hairstyle), choice of friends, what one talks about with friends, how one spends his or her own money, and leisure time activities (Nucci, 1981; Smetana, 2011). Children's understanding of personal issues is based on their underlying conceptions of the self and psychological integrity (Nucci & Lee, 1993). Although personal issues are only one aspect of the psychological domain, they are often referred to as the *personal* domain, as we do here.

The Moral Domain and Identity Development

Research on the moral domain typically examines children's and adolescents' prescriptive judgments about the "correct" or "moral" action to take in a situation, why they believe this to be true, and how such judgments translate into actual behavior (Smetana, 2006; 2013). From a social domain theory perspective, individuals' actions involve a coordination of multiple concerns, only some of which are moral. Actions also may involve personal, conventional, or even pragmatic components (Smetana, 2006; 2013). Although much research focuses on *how* individuals coordinate these concerns (e.g., Killen, Lee-Kim, McGlothlin, & Stangor, 2002), other research focuses more on the outcome of these coordinations and on predicting which individuals will ultimately perform behaviors consistent with their moral values (e.g. Blasi, 1983; Reynolds & Ceranic, 2007). It is this second line of research that is most closely linked with identity—specifically, moral identity.

Moral identity is the degree to which being a moral person is important to an individual's identity or sense of self (Hardy & Carlo, 2011). Researchers have asserted that the need to maintain self-consistency provides the motivation to act in a moral manner and thus that the link between moral judgments and moral actions depends on the extent to which individuals view moral behavior as central to their self-concept (Blasi, 1983). The development of moral identity appears to involve learning to access morally relevant schemas across various situations and to integrate morality and the self-system (or agency and communion motivations) such that personal interests and fulfillment are accomplished by promoting the needs of others (Hardy & Carlo, 2011).

Although most of the research on moral identity focuses on adults, family relationships appear to impact the development of moral identity. Indeed, interviews with adolescent moral exemplars show that parental influences are more salient for these adolescents than for their age mates (Reimer & Wade-Stein, 2004). Likewise, adolescents who are more involved in joint activities with their parents, such as watching movies, playing sports, going shopping or out to dinner, and working on schoolwork together, are more likely to do voluntary community service, which can serve as an indirect indicator of moral identity (Hart, Atkins, & Ford, 1999). In particular, authoritative parenting appears to be a key feature impacting the development of moral identity. Adolescents who rate their parents higher in responsiveness and demandingness endorse moral traits as more central to their sense of self, and adolescents with parents higher in responsiveness, demandingness, and autonomy granting are more involved in activities that demonstrate moral ideals and caring (Hardy, Bhattacharjee, Reed, & Aquino, 2010). Likewise, late adolescents with authoritative parents show more congruence between their own moral values and those they believe their parents want them to hold (Pratt, Hunsberger, Pancer, & Alisat, 2003).

Although people may vary in which behaviors they prioritize in moral functioning and thus in the content of their moral identity (as articulated by moral foundations theory; Graham et al., 2011), many of the behaviors considered to be moral (or immoral), such as promotion of justice and care, are by definition generalizable across individuals and contexts (Smetana, 2006; 2013). It is therefore not surprising that research on the development of moral identity mainly focuses on individual differences in the *extent* rather than *content* of moral identity. Indeed, most of the research on parenting and moral identity mirrors socialization research, where the goal is the internalization of parental values rather than independent exploration and commitment to various identities. For instance, parental responsiveness is theorized to lead to greater moral identity by encouraging more accurate perception and acceptance of parental moral values (Knafo & Schwartz, 2003). Likewise, parental demandingness is believed to highlight the importance of moral principles and the consequences of violating them (Grolnick & Pomerantz, 2009) but only functions as such to the extent that parents endorse a given moral principle in the home. Thus, although there is individual variation in the extent to which moral values are integrated into the self, the values themselves often appear predefined and the process conceptualized as occurring from the "top down" rather than involving much individual exploration or reasoning.

Recent work on narrative identity, however, indicates that there are individual differences in the extent to which individuals view themselves as agentic when describing past moral transgressions (Pasupathi & Wainryb, 2010). Consistent with more traditional work on moral identity, parents may be one source of these differences as they scaffold the development of adolescents' narrative processes (McLean & Mansfield, 2012). However, many other situational and adolescent-driven processes, such as severe hardship or experience with violence, also may contribute (Wainryb, 2011; Wainryb, Komolova, & Florsheim, 2010; Wainryb & Recchia, this volume). Although these issues are still relatively unexplored, they draw attention to the importance of considering "bottom-up" processes such as exploration and agency when conceptualizing moral identity development. However, moral identity, or the salience of moral concerns in one's self-description and moral agency, or the experience of one's morally relevant behavior as rooted in personal beliefs and decisions, are interrelated but not identical constructs (Pasupathi & Wainryb, 2010). Thus, research aiming to fully understand identity development within the moral domain, as well as parental contributions to it, must consider the distinction between moral identity and moral agency and the way these two constructs interact.

The Societal Domain and Identity Development

In contrast to the moral domain, little research has examined identity as it specifically relates to social conventions. However, it would seem that conventions have an important role to play in defining identity. Indeed, Berzonsky (1989) identified a "normative" identity style, in which adolescents' identities are largely based on the expectations of significant others, like parents, and their behavior closely adheres to social conventions. However, even for adolescents who do not display such a normative identity style, social conventions are likely to be important. For instance, research on crowd membership during adolescence indicates that these reference groups, which are based mainly on conventional stereotypes and shared reputations, help adolescents locate themselves and others within a social hierarchy and serve as a basis for testing out various identities (Collins & Steinberg, 2006). Likewise, questioning (and often rejecting) the importance of societal rules and standards is a normative part of adolescence (Moffitt, 1993; Nucci, 2001), and adolescents' ultimate stance on such conventions may help to define their adult identity. Furthermore, the patterning of issues viewed as more and less valued or central to one's identity may be particularly relevant for conventional behaviors. For instance, a high school "jock" may view the masculine convention of "being strong" as very central to his identity but have little concern for whether he adheres to the convention of referring to his teachers by their last name. In contrast, a "brain" may find it very important maintain the academic hierarchy and show respect by referring to teachers by their last name but may care little about whether his actions are consistent with a masculine "strength" stereotype.

As this example indicates, many of the values and behaviors we commonly think of as part of our self-concept appear to relate to the societal domain. Nevertheless, there is little research on the role of parenting in conventional identity development. We do know that both authoritative and authoritarian parenting appear to contribute to a normative identity style, although in potentially different ways (Berzonsky, 2004). For instance, adolescents with authoritative parents may develop values similar to their parents and choose to maintain these beliefs due to a close parent–adolescent relationship. Indeed, late adolescents with authoritative parents report more congruence between their own values and the values they believe their parents want them to have for social-conventional issues like being polite and courteous (Pratt et al., 2003). In contrast, adolescents with authoritarian parents may have their options limited and feel constrained to have similar values as their parents. Such a dual pathway to valuing social and parental conventions is consistent with findings that adolescents with a normative identity style are more likely to have either a foreclosed or an achieved identity status (Berzonsky, 1989). Additionally, specific parenting behaviors, such as an emphasis on achievement, monitoring, and joint decision making, have been shown to indirectly influence adolescents' crowd affiliations in high school by impacting adolescents' behavior (e.g., academic performance, drug use, and self-reliance; Brown Mounts, Lamborn, & Steinberg, 1993). If crowd membership is taken as a proxy for adolescents' conventional values and behaviors, such research implies that specific parenting behaviors may lead to different patterns of conventional identity for adolescents.

The Personal Domain and Identity Development

Whereas moral identity involves integrating the moral domain and the self-system, and identity within the societal domain involves selecting among (or being classified into) preexisting conventional standards, identity as it involves the personal domain mainly involves feelings of choice and agency. By its very definition, the personal domain defines the bounds of individual authority and consists of a set of issues over which a person can have control. Although autonomy and identity are distinct constructs, they are also interdependent. Identity concerns individuals' specific values and roles and the underlying self that unites them across time (Kroger, 2003), whereas autonomy concerns individuals' agency and freedom from external coercion to enact those personal values and roles (Zimmer-Gembeck & Collins, 2003). Thus, people may act autonomously—or in line with their own personal desires—without understanding how those actions may be concordant with a broader self-concept. Likewise, people may have a relatively well-formed identity—understanding who they are and what they value—but due to external constraints be unable to act in accordance with those beliefs. However, more often than not, identity and autonomy are intertwined, especially in reference to the development and expansion of the personal domain.

Establishing a personal domain also delineates boundaries between the self and others and allows individuals to feel a sense of ownership over their actions. This subjective sense of ownership is what James (1981/1890) refers to as the "I" aspect of self-understanding. Thus, the establishment, maintenance, and expansion of the personal domain allows individuals to understand that they are autonomous agents with a "self" directing and providing continuity to their actions. Indeed, children's and adolescents' understanding of why it is important to be able to act autonomously regarding personal issues shows the same pattern of development as changes in their conceptions of the self (Nucci & Lee, 1993). For instance, in mid-adolescence, teens come to view control over the personal domain as essential for coordinating their actions with their inner essence. This mirrors middle adolescents' understanding of the self as a coordinator of multiple beliefs and behaviors and their focus on uncovering an inner self and resolving apparent discrepancies. Similarly, late adolescents and early adults view control over their personal domains as necessary to shape their selves in ways that are consistent with internally chosen values. At the same time, teens come to view the self as an internally driven, flexible, and evolving product of their decisions (Damon & Hart, 1988; Nucci & Lee, 1993). Thus, controlling personal issues allows adolescents to feel agentic in discovering and maintaining a self that is consistent with their chosen identity.

Finally, establishing and maintaining a personal domain also provides opportunities for individuals to construct a sense of the "self as object", or what James (1981/1890) refers to as the "Me." The specific choices individuals make within the personal domain define the elements of thought and behavior that are unique to each individual. Indeed, although the extent of valuing moral precepts (moral identity) can be seen as part of the moral domain, and the ways in which an individuals' patterning of choices conforms to existing social norms might be considered conventional identity, the individual decisions (and ability to make them) comprising these patterns of values and behavior are, by and large, choices about personal issues. That is, even though behaviors involving fairness and harm are moral issues, beliefs and values regarding such behaviors actually contain a large component of personal choice (e.g., "I endorse/do not endorse affirmative action"). Likewise, wearing black clothes and eye makeup, listening to gothic rock music, being interested in the macabre, and hanging out with others who do the same may lead to a self- and other-described identity as "goth," but the ability to choose one's dress, physical appearance, music, interests, and friends are all squarely within the personal domain. Thus, by being able to assert preferences and act on choices within the personal domain, even if the decisions also relate to moral or conventional concepts, individuals can discover and define how they differ from others. The personal domain is therefore more relevant for identity processes than is any other domain. Being able to direct and choose one's own behavior and interests not only allows adolescents to identify unique behavioral and value patterns, but also provides the feelings of agency necessary for adolescents to understand and contribute to a coherent sense of self. We therefore devote the rest of the chapter to exploring the ways in which the personal domain and its associations with identity development are related to parenting and the parent–adolescent relationship.

Parenting and Youths' Construction of the Personal Domain

The personal domain primarily relates to parenting in terms of its differentiation from other domains of social knowledge and its expansion during adolescence. Parents help children identify personal behaviors through their provision of choice and lack of censure. They also set limits on the issues that children and adolescents can control and work to guide age-appropriate expansion of the personal domain. This second aspect of parents' behavior has received the most attention and is most likely related to adolescents' identity processes. That is, by guiding children and adolescents' expansion of the personal domain, parents provide youth with the scaffolding and autonomy support necessary for identifying agentic and consistent aspects of their behavior and understanding how these components relate to their sense of self and continuity. Like identity development itself, however, youths' construction of the personal domain throughout development is based on both internally driven processes and their interaction with parenting behaviors.

Children's Perspectives on the Personal Domain

Beginning in early childhood, children identify certain issues as under their personal control and distinguish them from moral or conventional behaviors. Preschool children state that they are less obligated to comply with parental wishes, that parents have less authority, and that they (children) should have the final say for personal behaviors, such as their choice of shirt color and the types of play they engage in, compared to moral or conventional behaviors, such as hitting, stealing, standing during dinner, or saying please (Nucci & Weber, 1995). These distinctions emerge whether children are interviewed directly or observed and are consistent across various cultures and ethnicities (Smetana, 2006; 2011). They also become more well-defined with age (Nucci, 1981). For instance, over the primary school years, children become more accepting of divergent personal preferences (e.g., whether an individual views chocolate ice cream as tasting yucky or yummy) but uniformly reject the notion that there can be more than one right belief about moral or factual matters (Wainryb, Shaw, Langley, Cottam, & Lewis, 2004).

Children develop these domain conceptions and distinctions by observing regularities in their social interactions with others (Smetana, 2006; Turiel, 1983). Specifically, whereas moral and conventional (mis)behaviors typically result in reprimands from peers or adults, and in the case of moral issues, observable distress to the victim, personal choices typically elicit no negative reactions and are often encouraged by others. Moral and conventional (mis)behaviors are also subject to rules and treated as wrong in some contexts (for conventional issues) or all contexts (for moral issues), but personal behaviors are neither right nor wrong and are usually left up to the child to decide (Smetana, 1984). Parents further scaffold children's understanding of domains through their different reactions to personal, moral, and conventional behaviors (Smetana, 2006). They primarily focus on harm to others for moral events, social organization for conventional events, and personal choice and preference for personal issues (Nucci & Weber, 1995). Children therefore may infer that issues should be personal and up to them to decide both because they do not appear to cause harmful effects for others and because parents relax their control and identify the issues as matters of choice.

The personal domain does not consist simply of what is left unregulated by parents, however. Children often claim personal control (stating a preference, claiming personal prerogative, or insisting that the matter is private) even when parents do not encourage or allow it (Nucci & Weber, 1995; Smetana & Asquith, 1994). These disagreements appear to occur because children recognize the importance of personal control for their sense of self, beginning quite early in development. Lagattuta, Nucci, and Bosacki (2010) examined four- to seven-year-old children's emotional and behavioral reactions to personal and moral restrictions when events were described as either essential or peripheral to the child's self-concept. They found that children generally judged that characters would comply with rules and feel good or transgress and feel bad for moral behaviors, but they did so less often for personal issues, especially those described as essential to children's self-concept. Children of all ages likewise used identity-relevant explanations to justify their judgments about personal issues but moral-evaluative explanations to justify judgments about moral behaviors. These distinctions, especially between personal behaviors varying in their salience to the self, also became more pronounced with age. Thus, the personal domain appears to hold identity-relevant meaning even for very young children, but such understanding increases with age.

Indeed, children view an increasing number of issues as within their personal domain and assert their right to more fully control these behaviors with age (Smetana, 2011). For instance, Tisak (1986) found that the majority of six- to ten-year-old American children believe that it is not acceptable for parents to make rules regulating children's friendship choices, but more ten- than six- or eight-year-old children believe that they are not obligated to report violations of such rules to parents and justify their judgments by referencing personal choice. This expansion of the personal domain becomes particularly notable during adolescence as children focus on the dual developmental tasks of autonomy and identity development (Collins & Steinberg, 2006; Erikson, 1968). In a study of American fifth- through twelfth-graders and their parents, Smetana (1988) found that mothers, fathers, and adolescents were less likely to judge personal and multifaceted events as legitimately subject to parental authority (and thus not up to the child to decide) than were parents and their preadolescent children. In turn, parents and their late adolescent offspring treated multifaceted issues as less legitimately subject to parental authority than did parents and their middle adolescents. Although these reductions in perceived legitimate control were found among all family members as adolescents grew older, adolescents in particular showed developmental change in their understanding of a need for personal control. When asked to justify why parents did not have legitimate authority over personal and multifaceted issues, adolescents' (but not parents') reasoning increasingly focused on the importance of personal prerogatives and preferences from preadolescence through late adolescence. Similar developmental changes in perceptions of legitimate parental authority have been found when examining friendship issues (which are also multifaceted; Smetana & Asquith, 1994) and when studying parental authority beliefs longitudinally and across a range of ethnicities, countries, and cultures (Smetana, 2011). The consistency and universality of youth's increasing desire for personal control during adolescence, as well as the justifications adolescents' provide for desiring personal jurisdiction, highlight the particular relevance of this domain for youths' developing sense of identity.

Parents' Perspectives on the Personal Domain

As suggested by their provision of choice and personal prerogative during interactions with young children, parents recognize that children both have and need a personal domain. Indeed, parents may understand reasons for personal control before children themselves do—mothers of young children across multiple cultures and ethnicities believe that children's individuality and identity develops primarily through children's choices and experiences (Smetana, 2002). In interviews, mothers have reported that control over the personal domain encourages children's sense of agency, autonomy, self-esteem, and competence (Nucci & Smetana, 1996; Nucci & Weber, 1995), with references to autonomy promotion particularly common from Asian and Brazilian mothers and references to agency promotion most common from European-American mothers (Smetana, 2002). Not surprisingly, therefore, mothers of children around the world believe that their offspring should be able to make decisions and have choices about certain types of issues—particularly clothing, play activities, food preferences, and friendships. They overwhelmingly treat these issues as up to the child to decide and justify such provision of choice on personal bases, as children do (Nucci & Smetana, 1996; Nucci & Weber, 1995; Smetana, 2002).

Like their children, parents also believe that children should gain more control over personal matters as they grow older. Compared to parents of sixth- and eighth-graders, parents of tenth-grade European-American teens judge personal issues as less legitimately under parental authority (Smetana & Asquith, 1994). Likewise, parents of African-American adolescents judge that personal issues should be more up children to decide over time (Smetana, Campione-Barr, & Daddis, 2004). Similar to findings for other ethnic minority youth, however, African-American parents tend to treat a more restricted range of issues as personal than do their European-American counterparts (Smetana, 2000). Nevertheless, African-American parents, like all parents, perceive that children should have personal control over a range of issues and that such control should expand with age. Indeed, African-American mothers' and adolescents' timetables for decision-making autonomy show that they have very similar conceptions of which items are personal. For older children, this includes choices regarding reading material, clothing, friendship, TV, and the appearance of the bedroom (Daddis & Smetana, 2005).

The Intersection of Parents' and Children's Views

Thus, in the abstract, mothers and children agree that children need to have control over personal issues in order to develop their autonomy and identity and that children's personal domains should expand with age. But they do not agree about the particular situations in which this should occur. For instance, even though mothers of five- to seven-year-olds note that certain activities (like children's recreational activities, food, clothing, and playmate choices) should be up to the child to decide, they also indicate that they sometimes set limits on these same behaviors (Nucci & Smetana, 1996). Likewise, parents are more likely than their adolescents to describe personal issues as under parental jurisdiction and less likely to view them as up to the child to decide (or decide alone; Smetana & Asquith, 1994; Smetana et al., 2004). Thus, although parents provide adolescents more control over personal issues than over prudential, conventional, or moral behaviors, they lag behind their adolescents in just how much control they are willing to concede (Smetana & Asquith, 1994; Smetana et al., 2004).

During adolescence, these differences are particularly pronounced for multifaceted issues (which contain both personal and prudential or conventional components), such as not cleaning one's room, spending time with a friend parents do not like, or getting a piercing or a tattoo (Nucci & Smetana, 1996; Smetana & Asquith, 1994). Almost all of these situations involve personal aspects that parents identify as being up to the child to control (i.e., state of the bedroom, friendship choice, personal appearance), but they involve other concerns as well. Thus, multifaceted issues can be seen as defining the boundaries of adolescents' personal control and highlighting the intersection of parents' and adolescents' views of the personal.

Generally, parents limit adolescents' control of personal and multifaceted behaviors because they view the act as being unhealthy or posing danger to the child (e.g., prudential concerns) or because they view the teen as not sufficiently competent or responsible to make an informed decision (Nucci & Smetana, 1996). However, adolescents often do not agree with these perceptions, leading to parent–adolescent conflict (Nucci & Smetana, 1996). This is particularly true for multifaceted issues because parents and teens actively reject each others' interpretation of the issue (Smetana, 2011). Indeed, conflict over multifaceted issues is quite frequent, especially in early adolescence (Collins & Steinberg, 2006; Smetana, 1996; 2011), but it also can contribute to autonomy and identity development, as we now discuss.

Parent–Adolescent Conflict, Communication, and Identity Development

Although parent–adolescent conflict can be distressing, especially for parents, it is usually temporary and a necessary part of the renegotiation of the parent–adolescent relationship. And it is functional in that, at least under some circumstances (e.g., if the conflict is not too intense), it can contribute to children's development of independence and a unique identity (Laursen & Collins, 2009). Indeed, analyses of data from several studies (Smetana, 1996) showed that most families with early to middle adolescents experienced frequent, low-intensity conflict (referred to as frequent squabbler families) or infrequent, moderate-intensity conflict (referred to as placid families); far fewer families experienced frequent, high-intensity conflict (referred to as tumultuous families). In turn, it is only such high-intensity, frequent conflict that appears to have negative consequences for autonomy and identity development. Adolescents from tumultuous families show the poorest academic outcomes, most extreme peer orientation, and least advanced social cognition (Smetana, 1996), and only adolescents who are not able to effectively communicate autonomy desires during conflicts with parents show increased hostile conflict with parents over time (Allen, Hauser, O'Connor, Bell, & Eickholt, 1996). Further connecting these findings to identity development, adolescents with an information-oriented identity (considered most advanced) show less overall conflict with mothers and more positive forms of problem solving during conflicts, whereas adolescents with a diffuse-avoidant identity (considered least adaptive) show the reverse patterns of associations (Missotten, Luyckx, Branje, Vanhalst, & Goossens, 2011).

Thus, in well-functioning parent–adolescent relationships, in which identity development is most successful, conflict and positive styles of interaction generally coexist (Smetana, 1995a). This is because successful individuation requires maintaining relational bonds with parents while increasing personal control (Laursen & Collins, 2009). Thus, parent–adolescent conflict stemming from adolescents' expansion of the personal domain appears not only developmentally normative, but adaptive, to the extent that it contributes to greater mutuality and feelings of adolescent efficacy within the relationship. Indeed, adolescents higher in identity exploration and commitment generally report better communication with parents and perceive the parent–adolescent relationship as more affectionate and trusting (Meeus, Oosterwegel, & Vollebergh, 2002; Weinmann & Newcombe, 1990). In turn, adolescents who are not able to maintain connectedness with parents while acquiring more autonomy show poorer identity exploration (Grotevant & Cooper, 1985).

Findings regarding adolescents' disclosure and secrecy further support the importance of open parent–child communication for individuation and identity processes. Adolescents typically report that they keep information secret from parents because they are afraid parents will not approve (for prudential and multifaceted issues) or they view information as private (for personal and multifaceted issues; Smetana, Villalobos, Tasopoulos-Chan, Gettman, & Campione-Barr, 2009). Although such nondisclosure has been posited as an alternative route to autonomy for some adolescents (Finkenauer, Kubacka, Engels, & Kerkhof, 2009), research shows that secrecy is almost always problematic and that disclosure is almost always beneficial for adolescent adjustment, regardless of the issue considered (Laird & Marrero, 2010; Smetana et al., 2009). In large part, this may be because nondisclosure of disagreement is associated with poorer parent–adolescent relationships (Darling, Cumsille, Caldwell, & Dowdy, 2006), which in turn provide less opportunities for adolescents to explore and express their identity. Indeed, adolescents who have better communication with parents or who experience more parental solicitation have more normative and informational identity styles, respectively. In contrast, adolescents who disclose less information to parents are more likely to express a diffuse avoidance identity style (Berzonsky, Branje, & Meeus, 2007). Likewise, adolescents whose identity scores decline relative to peers during high school increase least in their communication with mothers during this time (Reis & Youniss, 2004). Thus, establishing broader boundaries of the personal domain and exerting control over these behaviors does not require that adolescents keep personal behaviors secret. Rather, the evidence suggests that, at least for American and Dutch children, it is healthier to establish autonomy and develop personal identity through open parent–adolescent communication.

Parental Control, Adolescent Psychosocial Adjustment, and Identity

Adaptive Patterns of Parental Control and Adolescent Outcomes

As just discussed, identity development progresses best when adolescents bring up behaviors over which they desire more personal control and negotiate for greater autonomy from parents. However, parents must also listen and negotiate with their children, granting adolescents greater autonomy gradually and at different levels depending on the domain of the behavior. When these two processes occur in tandem, a normative progression occurs in which adolescents gradually gain autonomy while parents relinquish control. Typically, early adolescents have sole decision-making control over many personal and some multifaceted issues in their lives, with the majority of other decisions made jointly with parents, and rarely, by parents alone. By late adolescence, many of the issues decided jointly with parents in early adolescence have become solely youth decisions, and a small percentage of personal and multifaceted issues remain joint decisions (Dornbusch, Ritter, Mont-Reynaud, & Chen, 1990; Smetana et al., 2004).

Consistent with these normative patterns, adolescents have the most adaptive outcomes when parents provide personal control slowly over time and when parents and adolescents collaborate in deciding about personal and multifaceted behaviors (Dornbusch et al., 1990; Smetana et al., 2004). Throughout adolescence, parent–adolescent joint decision making about adolescents' personal and multifaceted behaviors is associated with more advanced psychosocial development (Dornbusch et al., 1990; Lamborn, Dornbusch, & Steinberg, 1996). Likewise, regardless of how much initial decision-making control adolescents have over personal issues, increases over time, particularly between middle and late adolescence, in decision-making autonomy about personal and multifaceted issues are associated with higher levels of self-worth in late adolescence (Smetana et al., 2004). The "goodness of fit" between adolescents' and parents' expectations for adolescents' behavioral autonomy also influences teens' psychosocial adjustment. Juang, Lerner, McKinney, and von Eye (1999) found that the correspondence between Asian Americans' desired and actual autonomy better predicted their adjustment (including identity-relevant constructs such as self-esteem, depression, and willingness to work for what they want) than the specific age at which they experienced control over personal, multifaceted, and prudential behaviors.

Research has not directly assessed associations between family decision-making control and adolescent identity. However, the impact of decision-making control on identity-relevant constructs implies that high levels of joint decision making and gradual increases in adolescent control would benefit its development. Indeed, autonomy-supportive parenting is associated with more adolescent identity exploration and commitment during late adolescence (Beyers & Goossens, 2008), in part due to increased feelings of adolescent self-determination (Soenens & Vansteenkiste, 2005). Additionally, the successful outcomes associated with joint decision-making and gradual acquisition of personal control likely occur both because adolescents have developmentally appropriate levels of control over personal issues and because such patterns are associated with positive parent–child relationships (Juang et al., 1999; Smetana, 2011; Smetana, Crean, & Daddis, 2002). As we have discussed, positive parent–child relationships provide the support and communication necessary to help adolescents explore and commit to personal identities (Grotevant & Cooper, 1985; Laursen & Collins, 2009).

Adaptive parental control also requires that parents exert different amounts of control depending on the domain of the issue and provide domain-specific explanations for their parenting. Parents generally distinguish between personal and other issues in terms of their rationales, explanations, and beliefs about parental authority (Smetana, Crean, & Campione-Barr, 2005). However, not all parents make clear distinctions between the different types of issues in their thinking and behavior. Smetana (1995b) examined the association between parenting style and parents' distinctions of moral, conventional, personal, and multifaceted issues using classic domain criteria (whether parents ought to have legitimate authority, whether authority is dependent on the existence of rules, whether parents are obligated to make rules, etc.; Smetana, 2006). Smetana found that only authoritative parents consistently distinguished among the domains in their judgments and justifications. Authoritarian parents moralized conventional and multifaceted issues, whereas permissive parents treated moral issues as conventional and treated multifaceted issues as personal. Thus, by defining these boundaries appropriately, only authoritative parents effectively negotiate the boundaries of the personal domain with their adolescents and adjust these boundaries over time to their teens' changing developmental abilities and needs. This, in turn, may underlie the commonly observed links between authoritative parenting and positive identity formation, such as the increased likelihood of an informational identity style (involving active consideration of identity alternatives; Berzonsky, 2004).

Maladaptive Forms of Parental Control and Adolescent Outcomes

Not all parent–adolescent relationships progress smoothly toward adolescents' ownership of decision making for personal issues or differentiate appropriately between personal, multifaceted, and other types of issues. Indeed, sometimes parents retain too much or too little control over adolescents' personal domains, in which case adolescents' identity development and broader adjustment are negatively impacted.

PARENTAL OVERCONTROL

Parent unilateral decision making about adolescents' personal domain is consistent with an authoritarian style of parenting in which parents are highly demanding and not responsive to children's feelings (Baumrind, 1991; Lamborn et al., 1996). As such, this style of decision making is associated with greater deviance and poorer psychosocial development, including more depression and emotional detachment (Holmbeck & O'Donnell, 1991), less self-esteem and pride in one's accomplishments (Lamborn et al., 1996), poorer family relationships (Fuligni & Eccles, 1993), and diffuse-avoidant and normative identity styles, which are relatively less advanced (Berzonsky, 2004). Such autonomy-restrictive parenting becomes particularly problematic as adolescents grow older and the lack of personal control interferes with their ability to identify unique values and coordinate them with their behavior. For instance, in a group of African-American youth studied over the course of five years, Smetana et al. (2004) found that adolescents who did not acquire more decision-making autonomy over personal and multifaceted issues over time reported lower self-worth in late adolescence, regardless of initial levels of parental decision-making control. Although self-worth is not a measure of identity development, it does reflect negative conceptions of the self and identity and therefore supports the proposition that personal control is integral to healthy identity development (Nucci & Lee, 1993). Indeed, Quintana and Lapsley (1987) found that late adolescents' perceptions of high levels of parental control were associated with lower levels of ego identity achievement.

Relatedly, adolescents view parental overcontrol of personal issues as psychologically controlling (Kakihara & Tilton-Weaver, 2009; Smetana & Daddis, 2002), which has direct implications for identity processes. Psychological control refers to behaviors that impinge on individuals' sense of self and their ability to develop personal identity (Barber, Stolz, & Olsen, 2005) and is associated with less identity achievement (Beyers & Goossens, 2008; Luyckx, Soenens, Vansteenkiste, Goossens, & Berzonsky, 2007) as well as with more internalizing and externalizing problems (Barber et al., 2005). Smetana and Daddis (2002) examined longitudinal associations among African-American early adolescents' beliefs about legitimate parental authority, actual levels of parental control (both rule setting and decision making), and ratings of parental psychological control. They found that adolescents who believed that their parents had less legitimate authority to regulate ambiguously personal (personal, multifaceted, and peer) issues or had parents who were more restrictive over these issues also perceived their mothers as more psychologically controlling, both concurrently and two years later. Kakihara and Tilton-Weaver (2009) confirmed and extended these findings. Using hypothetical scenarios, they showed that adolescents interpreted both behavioral and psychological control over personal issues as indicating that they were less competent and mattered less to parents than did similar levels of control over prudential issues. As feelings of competence and mattering are integral to a healthy sense of identity and self (Harter, 2008), and psychological control is integrally related to identity development (Luyckx et al., 2011), these associations provide strong support for links between parental overcontrol of the personal domain and problems in adolescent identity formation.

Finally, parental overcontrol of the personal domain appears problematic for adolescents' identity development because it encourages overreliance on and conformity to peers. Fuligni and Eccles

(1993) examined the association between early adolescents' decision-making opportunities over a year and two forms of peer orientation: peer advice seeking, in which adolescents talk with peers rather than parents about their educational plans and personal problems, and extreme peer orientation, in which adolescents sacrifice their own achievements, commitments, and personality in order to gain peer approval. They found that adolescents who initially felt less involved in making decisions about their own lives were higher in both forms of peer orientation and that decreases in decision-making opportunities over time were associated with further increases in these maladaptive peer orientations. Although it is normative for youth to become more involved with peers and more distant from parents during early adolescence, optimal development entails a renegotiation of the parent–adolescent relationship toward more mutuality and transformations in the forms rather than absolute levels of closeness (Collins & Steinberg, 2006). Indeed, parents remain an important source of guidance and support for children throughout adolescence, with late adolescents reporting more purpose and less identity diffusion when they have secure attachments with and less attitudinal independence from parents (Downing & Nauta, 2010; Schultheiss & Blustein, 1994). Thus, too great an orientation toward peers is often detrimental for adolescents' psychosocial adjustment, likely including their identity development.

PARENTAL UNDERCONTROL

Adolescents also show negative identity-relevant outcomes when they are given too much personal control at too young an age. Throughout adolescence, teens who report more youth-alone decision making about personal and multifaceted issues relative to same-age peers show increased deviant behavior, poorer school engagement and grades, and less psychosocial development, including lower self-esteem, self-reliance, and pride in successful completion of tasks (Dornbusch et al., 1990; Lamborn et al., 1996). Similar effects have been found in early and middle adolescence for high levels (not relative to peers) of adolescent control over personal, multifaceted, and prudential issues (Smetana et al., 2004). As mentioned previously, such psychosocial measures are not direct indicators of identity development; however, problems in these areas imply negative conceptions of agency and identity (Nucci & Lee, 1993).

Additionally, adolescents who judge more issues (including multifaceted and friendship issues) to be personal report more frequent and intense conflict with parents (Smetana, 1996) and greater emotional autonomy from parents (Smetana, 1995b). As previously discussed, high and frequent levels of conflict with parents are associated with less adaptive identity styles (Missotten et al., 2011) Likewise, despite some debate, standard measures of emotional autonomy appear to function more like emotional detachment than positive autonomy development (Beyers & Goossens, 1999) and thus may interfere with adolescents' development of a positive sense of self, perceived competence, and identity. In summary, adolescents' identity development suffers when they experience either too little or too much control over their personal domain. This is because it is not merely having personal control, but the process of negotiating for such control and the scaffolding parents provide as they slowly relinquish control over personal and multifaceted issues that appears to provide the combination of structure and autonomy support necessary for optimal identity development.

Conclusion

Moral, conventional, and personal issues all have relevance for adolescents' identity development and are influenced by parenting processes. Whereas moral and conventional identities are more related to the adoption and transmission of values, however, identity in the personal domain is particularly focused on choice, agency, and internal consistency. Due to this difference, children's and adolescents' construction and control of a personal domain may be more broadly relevant for identity processes, including identity understanding as well as exploration and commitment, and may contribute to the formation of identity in the other two domains.

Parents are integral to adolescents' understanding of the personal domain in a variety of ways. When children are young, parents help them construct a personal domain by relaxing control, negotiating, and providing choice over certain issues, and by actively identifying behaviors subject to the child's personal prerogative. As youth grow older and expect more autonomy, parent's guidance and negotiation facilitates the expansion of children's personal domain and sense of efficacy and self-worth. Furthermore, this is not a passive process; children and adolescents actively advocate for greater personal control. Parents must find a balance between acquiescing to their adolescents' demands (providing adolescents with too much control over issues that could have serious consequences for their health, safety, or social standing) and retaining too much control (so that adolescents do not feel able to test out and align their behavior with internal beliefs and desires).

Generally, this balance hinges on maintaining a positive and supportive parent–adolescent relationship. Parenting and adolescent identity development is a transactional process, with both aspects contributing to and being influenced by the parent–adolescent relationship. When relationships are supportive and open, adolescents feel comfortable bringing up desires for greater personal control, and parents are receptive to adolescents' needs. Under these conditions, parents and adolescents have the relational base necessary to allow for experimentation and the gradual expansion of teens' personal domain. This allows adolescents to individuate while maintaining the parental support and guidance necessary to maintain healthy views of the self and solidify personal beliefs—both crucial for identity formation. In turn, adolescents who feel supported and are given age-appropriate amounts of personal control are better adjusted and exhibit more advanced identity styles, which help to maintain positive and open parent–adolescent relationships that support identity development. Without positive relationships and developmentally sensitive parenting, adolescents may be less competent to explore their choices within the personal domain, and the outcomes of their exploration may result in less adaptive identity-processing styles and a poorer overall sense of themselves and their values.

Future Directions

Although considerable connections have been made between parenting and identity development, little research has explored these issues from a social domain perspective. As we have discussed in this chapter, however, the social-cognitive domains identified by social domain theory (and their related parenting processes) have specific and differing theoretical links with identity development. Consequently, we conclude with some suggestions for new ways to integrate social domain theory into future research on identity development.

The links we have drawn here among social domains, parenting, and identity remain speculative and need to be explicitly examined in further research. Thus far, there is no research exploring connections between family-level differences in domain-differentiated control and adolescent identity formation. Future research needs to examine whether associations between parenting (and in particular parental control) and identity development depend on the domain considered. As we have discussed in this chapter, research has clearly shown that children and adolescents view parental control of the personal domain as psychologically controlling but view parental control of other issues as appropriate. Additionally, the processes influencing identity formation may function differently depending on domain because moral and conventional identity involve value acquisition processes, whereas identity in the personal domain focuses on feelings of agency and personal continuity. Thus, it may be that high levels of parent-unilateral control in the moral (and potentially conventional) domain aid in value acquisition and moral identity formation (and perhaps a more normative identity style), but similar levels of parent control in the personal domain undermine adolescents' sense of agency, the adoption of an information identity style, and eventual identity achievement. These domain differences in parental control may also interact with adolescent age when predicting optimal identity development. For instance, it is possible that relaxation of parental control is necessary for complete identity commitment in all domains but that moral identity and agency development require more parental scaffolding for a longer period of time than does development of identity regarding many personal issues (McLean & Mansfield, 2012).

Future research also needs to examine interactions among identity development in the various domains. Social-cognitive domain theory posits that children's and adolescents' conceptual understanding of issues in different domains is interdependent—for instance, children's understanding of the personal is theorized to be central to their development and understanding of morality (Nucci & Lee, 1993). Such interdependencies and coordinations may have particular implications for diverse identity processes. For instance, adolescents experiencing overcontrol of the personal domain may be more likely to develop a normative identity style and identify highly with conventional and moral standards, but may do so in a way that involves identity foreclosure rather than identity achievement. Likewise, identity development in the personal domain may be more relevant for the development of moral agency than moral identity, as each is commonly defined (Pasupathi & Wainryb, 2010). Although such connections and differentiations have theoretical support, they have not been explicitly examined.

Relatedly, research should examine how the breadth and content of adolescents' personal domains impacts the extent to which adolescents feel able to explore and commit to various identities, including conventional ones. The personal domain expands greatly throughout adolescence, and its content is more culturally and individually variable than the other domains. It is therefore likely that adolescents' ability to distinguish and coordinate aspects of their behavior and identity corresponds directly with their desire for and actual control over specific personal behaviors. Thus, an adolescent who views maintaining friendships and procuring high social status as integral components of her identity may likewise come to view her friends' identities, where she goes with them, and how late she stays out as inherently personal issues. However, this expansion of personal authority and identity development regarding social issues may not affect her beliefs regarding the need for control over her choice of school classes (a different multifaceted issue). In turn, these beliefs may impact the way she interacts with her parents regarding those decisions. Lagattuta and colleagues (2010) provided preliminary support for such a process when examining associations between young children's compliance and the relevance of personal issues to their self-concepts, but similar research involving adolescents and their more mature conceptions of identity has not been undertaken.

It is also possible that adolescents' specific choices and patterning of decisions over personal, conventional, and moral issues have important implications for understanding their identity. Such research would need to be more person-centered and microlevel than is often seen in current research on domain differences, parenting, or identity. Indeed, instead of focusing on general processes and outcomes such as exploration, commitment, and identity status, or what and how much adolescents versus parents control, this research would need to focus on the decisions adolescents make within various domains—for instance, whether they wear the blue or the black shirt and whether they view that choice as important to their identity. Researchers could then examine the way parents discuss and help their children weigh different options in different domains (especially as it relates to joint decision making) and how those behaviors impact the decisions children make and the extent to which they are viewed as central or peripheral to the adolescents' identity. We believe that this patterning of decisions and decision making within various domains is an important and relatively unexplored line of future research in parenting and identity development.

Other areas of identity development, such as ethnic identity, might similarly be well served by integrating connections with children's control of the personal, their conventional understanding, and parenting. Considerable research has examined ethnic variations in parenting and children's control of the personal domain, and certain differences have been found. For instance, some ethnic minority youth have later expectations for autonomy than majority youth (Fuligni, 1998), and African-American mothers are more restrictive of their children's personal domains than are majority mothers, possibly due to the risks in the environment that American minority children may face in exercising their personal choices (Smetana, 2000). We do not know whether such variations contribute to children's development and understanding of their own ethnic identity, however. Such research would be especially interesting because ethnic variability in autonomy expectations and personal control becomes less strong as individuals acculturate (Fuligni, 1998).

Finally, little research has examined the impact of parental identity on adolescent identity formation. However, parents who have stronger identity systems may be better able to distinguish between what is best for them and what would be best for their children. In this way, they may better support their children's expansion of the personal domain while maintaining relatedness with their children, which, in turn, aids adolescent identity formation. In contrast, parents with less developed identities may display much more self-interested parenting, inhibiting their children's autonomy development through excessive personal and psychological control (Koepke & Denissen, 2012). Indeed, Adams (1985) found that parents with more mature identities were likely to have young adult daughters with a similarly mature identity. Intriguingly however, Wiley and Berman (2012) found evidence for the opposite pattern of effects; parents higher in identity commitment had adolescents higher in identity distress. However, these adolescents were all diagnosed with psychological disorders, and, as the authors note, many of their parents were in identity foreclosure rather than identity achievement. As such, these parents may have been relatively controlling, stifling their adolescents' attempts at identity exploration and leading adolescents to feel pressured to commit to goals, roles, or values before they were ready. Thus, rather than parents' identity status per se (as might be expected from a social learning perspective), it is likely that the ways in which parental identity manifests in parent–adolescent interactions has the stronger impact on adolescent identity formation. Future research should therefore examine how parental identity impacts parenting behaviors across various domains, especially in terms of its association with adolescent individuation processes, value commitments, and adolescent identity formation.

Adolescents' differentiation, understanding, and control of behaviors in the moral, conventional, and personal domains and their links with parenting and identity development are an unexplored but potentially fruitful area for future study. In particular, control of the personal domain is theoretically crucial for individuals' ability to develop and understand their own identities. In this chapter, we explicated some of these connections to provide insight into the ways that parenting, social-cognitive domains, and identity development can be understood as integrated and interdependent parts of a broader developmental whole.

References

Adams, G. R. (1985). Family correlates of female adolescents' ego-identity development. *Journal of Adolescence, 8*, 69–82. doi: 10.1016/S0140-1971(85)80008-7

Allen, J. P., Hauser, S. T., O'Connor, T. G., Bell, K. L., & Eickholt, C. (1996). The connection of observed hostile family conflict to adolescents' developing autonomy and relatedness with parents. *Development and Psychopathology, 8*, 425–442. doi: 10.1017/S0954579400007173

Barber, B. K., Stolz, H. E., & Olsen, J. A. (2005). Parental support, psychological control, and behavioral control: Assessing relevance across time, culture, and method. In W. F. Overton (Series Ed.), *Vol. 70: Monographs of the society for research in child development.* Hoboken, NJ: Wiley-Blackwell.

Baumrind, D. (1991). Parenting styles and adolescent development. In J. Brooks-Gunn, R. Lerner, & A. C. Petersen (Eds.), *The encyclopedia of adolescence* (pp. 746–758). New York: Garland.

Berzonsky, M. D. (1989). Identity style: Conceptualization and measurement. *Journal of Adolescent Research, 4*, 268–282. doi: 10.1177/074355488943002

Berzonsky, M. D. (2004). Identity style, parental authority, and identity commitment. *Journal of Youth and Adolescence, 33*, 213–220. doi: 10.1023/B:JOYO.0000025320.89778.29

Berzonsky, M. D., Branje, S. J., & Meeus, W. (2007). Identity-processing style, psychosocial resources, and adolescents' perceptions of parent-adolescent relations. *The Journal of Early Adolescence, 27*, 324–345. doi: 10.1177/0272431607302006

Beyers, W., & Goossens, L. (1999). Emotional autonomy, psychosocial adjustment and parenting: Interactions, moderating and mediating effects. *Journal of Adolescence, 22*, 753–769. doi: 10.1006/jado.1999.0268

Beyers, W., & Goossens, L. (2008). Dynamics of perceived parenting and identity formation in late adolescence. *Journal of Adolescence, 31*, 165–184. doi: 10.1016/j.adolescence.2007.04.003

Blasi, A. (1983). Moral cognition and moral action: A theoretical perspective. *Developmental Review, 3*, 178–210.

Brown, B., Mounts, N., Lamborn, S. D., & Steinberg, L. (1993). Parenting practices and peer group affiliation in adolescence. *Child Development, 64*, 467–482.

Collins, W., & Steinberg, L. (2006). Adolescent development in interpersonal context. In N. Eisenberg (Ed.), *Handbook of child psychology. Vol. 3: Social, emotional, and personality development* (6th ed., pp. 1003–1067). Hoboken, NJ: John Wiley & Sons.

Daddis, C., & Smetana, J. (2005). Middle-class African American families' expectations for adolescents' behavioral autonomy. *International Journal of Behavioral Development, 29*, 371–381. doi: 10.1080/01650250500167053

Damon, W., & Hart, D. (1988). *Self-understanding in childhood and adolescence.* Cambridge: Cambridge University Press.

Darling, N., Cumsille, P., Caldwell, L. L., & Dowdy, B. (2006). Predictors of adolescents' disclosure to parents and percieved parental knowledge: Between- and within-person differences. *Journal of Youth and Adolescence, 35*, 667–678. doi: 10.1007/s10964-006-9058-1

Dornbusch, S. M., Ritter, P. L., Mont-Reynaud, R., & Chen, Z. (1990). Family decision making and academic performance in a diverse high school population. *Journal of Adolescent Research, 5*, 143–160. doi: 10.1177/074355489052003

Downing, H. M., & Nauta, M. M. (2010). Separation-individuation, exploration, and identity diffusion as mediators of the relationship between attachment and career indecision. *Journal of Career Development, 36*, 207–227.

Erikson, E. H. (1968). *Identity, youth, and crisis.* New York: Norton.

Finkenauer, C., Kubacka, K. E., Engels, R. C. M., & Kerkhof, P. (2009). Secrecy in close relationships: Investigating its intrapersonal and interpersonal effects. In T. D. Afifi & W. A. Afifi (Eds.), *Uncertainty, information managment, and disclosure decisions: Theories and applications.* (pp. 300–319). New York: Routledge.

Fivush, R., Bohanek, J., G, & Marin, K. (2010). Patterns of family narrative co-construction in relation to adolescent identity and well-being. In K. C. Mclean & M. Pasupathi (Eds.), *Narrative development in adolescence* (pp. 45–63). New York: Springer.

Fuligni, A. J. (1998). Authority, autonomy, and parent-adolescent conflict and cohesion: A study of adolescents from Mexican, Chinese, Filipino, and European backgrounds. *Developmental Psychology, 34*, 782–792. doi: 10.1037/0012-1649.34.4.782

Fuligni, A. J., & Eccles, J. S. (1993). Perceived parent-child relationships and early adolescents' orientation toward peers. *Developmental Psychology, 29*, 622–632. doi: 10.1037/0012-1649.29.4.622

Graham, J., Nosek, B. A., Haidt, J., Iyer, R., Koleva, S., & Ditto, P. H. (2011). Mapping the moral domain. *Journal of Personality and Social Psychology, 101*, 366–385.

Grolnick, W. S., & Pomerantz, E. M. (2009). Issues and challenges in studying parental control: Toward a new conceptualization. *Child Development Perspectives, 3*, 165–170. doi: 10.1111/j.1750-8606.2009.00099.x

Grotevant, H. D., & Cooper, C. R. (1985). Patterns of interaction in family relationships and the development of identity exploration in adolescence. *Child Development, 56*, 415–428. doi: 10.1111/j.1467-8624.1985.tb00116.x

Hardy, S. A., Bhattacharjee, A., Reed, A., II, & Aquino, K. (2010). Moral identity and psychological distance: The case of adolescent parental socialization. *Journal of Adolescence, 33*, 111–123. doi: 10.1016/j.adolescence.2009.04.008

Hardy, S. A., & Carlo, G. (2011). Moral identity. In S. J. Schwartz, K. Luyckx, & V. L. Vignoles (Eds.), *Handbook of identity theory and research* (pp. 495–513). New York: Springer.

Hart, D., Atkins, R., & Ford, D. (1999). Family influences on the formation of moral identity in adolescence: Longitudinal analyses. *Journal of Moral Education, 28*, 375–386.

Harter, S. (2008). The developing self. In W. Damon & R. L. Lerner (Eds.), *Child and adolescent development: An advanced course.* (pp. 216–262). Hoboken, NJ: Wiley.

Holmbeck, G. N., & O'Donnell, K. (1991). Discrepancies between perceptions of decision making and behavioral autonomy. *New Directions for Child Development, 51*, 51–69. doi: 10.1002/cd.23219915105

James, W. (1981/1890). *The principles of psychology*. Cambridge, MA: Harvard University Press.

Juang, L. P., Lerner, J. V., McKinney, J. P., & von Eye, A. (1999). The goodness of fit in autonomy timetable expectations between Asian-American late adolescents and their parents. *International Journal of Behavioral Development, 23*, 1023–1048. doi: 10.1080/016502599383658

Kakihara, F., & Tilton-Weaver, L. (2009). Adolescents' interpretations of parental control: Differentiated by domain and types of control. *Child Development, 80*, 1722–1738. doi: 10.1111/j.1467-8624.2009.01364.x

Killen, M., Lee-Kim, J., McGlothlin, H., & Stangor, C. (2002). How children and adolescents evaluate gender and racial exclusion. *Monographs of the Society for Research in Child Development, 67*. doi: 10.1111/1540-5834.00218

Knafo, A., & Schwartz, S. H. (2003). Parenting and adolescents' accuracy in perceiving parental values. *Child Development, 74*, 595–611.

Kochanska, G. (1997). Mutually responsive orientation between mothers and their young children: Implications for early socialization. *Child Development, 68*, 94–112. doi: 10.1111/j.1467–8624.1997.tb01928.

Koepke, S., & Denissen, J. J. (2012). Dynamics of identity development and separation-individuation in parent-child relationships during adolescence and emerging adulthood—A conceptual integration. *Developmental Review, 32*, 67–88.

Kroger, J. (2003). Identity development during adolescence. In G. R. Adams & M. D. Berzonsky (Eds.), *Blackwell handbook of adolescence* (pp. 205–226). Malden, NJ: Blackwell Publishing.

Lagattuta, K. H., Nucci, L., & Bosacki, S. L. (2010). Bridging theory of mind and the personal domain: Children's reasoning about resistance to parental control. *Child Development, 81*, 616–635. doi: 10.1111/j.1467-8624.2009.01419.x

Laird, R. D., & Marrero, M. D. (2010). Information management and behavior problems: Is concealing misbehavior necessarily a sign of trouble? *Journal of Adolescence, 33*, 297–308. doi: 10.1016/j.adolescence.2009.05.018

Lamborn, S. D., Dornbusch, S. M., & Steinberg, L. (1996). Ethnicity and community context as moderators of the relations between family decision making and adolescent adjustment. *Child Development, 67*, 283–301. doi: 10.1111/j.1467-8624.1996.tb01734.x

Laursen, B., & Collins, W. A. (2009). Parent-child relationships during adolescence. In R. M. Lerner & L. Steinberg (Eds.), *Handbook of adolescent psychology. Vol 2: Contextual influences on adolescent development* (3rd ed., pp. 1–42). New York: Wiley-Blackwell.

Luyckx, K., Schwartz, S. J., Goossens, L., Beyers, W., & Missotten, L. (2011). Processes of personal identity formation and evaluation. In S. J. Schwartz, K. Luyckx, & V. L. Vignoles (Eds.), *Handbook of identity theory and research* (vol. *1*, pp. 77–98). New York: Springer.

Luyckx, K., Soenens, B., Vansteenkiste, M., Goossens, L., & Berzonsky, M. D. (2007). Parental psychological control and dimensions of identity formation in emerging adulthood. *Journal of Family Psychology, 21*, 546–550. doi: 10.1037/0893-3200.21.3.546

McAdams, D. P. (2003). Identity and the life story. In R. Fivush & C. A. Haden (Eds.), *Autobiographical memory and the construction of a narrative self: Developmental and cultural perspectives* (pp. 187–207). Mahwah, NJ: Lawrence Erlbaum.

McLean, K. C., & Mansfield, C. D. (2012). The co-construction of adolescent narrative identity: Narrative processing as a function of adolescent age, gender, and maternal scaffolding. *Developmental Psychology, 48*, 436–447.

Meeus, W., Oosterwegel, A., & Vollebergh, W. (2002). Parental and peer attachment and identity development in adolescence. *Journal of Adolescence, 25*, 93–106. doi: 10.1006/jado.2001.0451

Missotten, L. C., Luyckx, K., Branje, S., Vanhalst, J., & Goossens, L. (2011). Identity styles and conflict resolution styles: Associations in mother-adolescent dyads. *Journal of Youth and Adolescence, 40*, 972–982.

Moffitt, T. E. (1993). Adolescence-limited and life-course-persistent antisocial behavior: A developmental taxonomy. *Psychological Review, 100*, 674–701.

Nucci, L. (1981). Conceptions of personal issues: A domain distinct from moral or societal concepts. *Child Development, 52*, 114–121. doi: 10.1111/j.1467–8624.1981.tb03022.x

Nucci, L. (2001). *Education in the moral domain*. Port Chester, NY: Cambridge University Press.

Nucci, L., & Lee, J. (1993). Morality and personal autonomy. In G. G. Noam, T. E. Wren, G. Nunner-Winkler, & W. Edelstein (Eds.), *The moral self: Building a better paradigm* (pp. 123–148). Cambridge, MA: MIT Press.

Nucci, L., & Smetana, J. G. (1996). Mothers' concept of young children's areas of personal freedom. *Child Development, 67*, 1870–1886. doi: 10.2307/1131737

Nucci, L., & Weber, E. K. (1995). Social interactions in the home and the development of young children's conceptions of the personal. *Child Development, 66*, 1438–1452. doi: 10.1111/j.1467–8624.1995.tb00944.x

Pasupathi, M., & Wainryb, C. (2010). Developing moral agency through narrative. *Human Development, 53*, 55–80. doi: 10.1159/000288208

Pratt, M. W., Hunsberger, B., Pancer, S., & Alisat, S. (2003). A longitudinal analysis of personal values socialization: Correlates of a moral self-ideal in late adolescence. *Social Development, 12*, 563–585. doi: 10.1111/1467–9507.00249

Quintana, S. M., & Lapsley, D. K. (1987). Adolescent attachment and ego identity: A structural equations approach to the continuity of adaptation. *Journal of Adolescent Research, 2*, 393–409. doi: 10.1177/074355488724007

Reimer, K., & Wade-Stein, D. (2004). Moral identity in adolescence: Self and other in semantic space. *Identity: An International Journal of Theory and Research, 4*, 229–249. doi: 10.1207/s1532706xid0403_2

Reis, O., & Youniss, J. (2004). Patterns in identity change and development in relationships with mothers and friends.

Reynolds, S. J., & Ceranic, T. L. (2007). The effects of moral judgment and moral identity on moral behavior: An empirical examination of the moral individual. *Journal of Applied Psychology, 92*, 1610–1624. doi: 10.1037/0021-9010.92.6.1610

Sartor, C. E., & Youniss, J. (2002). The relationship between positive parental involvement and identity achievement during adolescence. *Adolescence, 37*, 221–234.

Schachter, E. P., & Ventura, J. J. (2008). Identity agents: Parents as active and reflective participants in their children's identity formation. *Journal of Research on Adolescence, 18*, 449–476. doi: 10.1111/j.1532-7795.2008.00567.x

Schultheiss, D. E., & Blustein, D. L. (1994). Role of adolescent-parent relationships in college student development and adjustment. *Journal of Counseling Psychology, 41*, 248–255.

Smetana, J., Crean, H. F., & Campione-Barr, N. (2005). Adolescents' and parents' changing conceptions of parental authority. In W. Damon (Series Ed.), *New directions for child and adolescent development. Vol. 108: Changing boundaries of parental authority during adolescence* (pp. 31–46). San Francisco: Jossey-Bass.

Smetana, J. G. (1984). Toddlers' social interactions regarding moral and conventional transgressions. *Child Development, 55*, 1767–1776.

Smetana, J. G. (1988). Adolescents' and parents' conceptions of parental authority. *Child Development, 59*, 321–335. doi: 10.2307/1130313

Smetana, J. G. (1995a). Conflict and coordination in adolescent-parent relationships. In S. Schulman (Ed.), *Close relationships and socioemotional development* (pp. 155–184). Norwood, NJ: Ablex Publishing.

Smetana, J. G. (1995b). Parenting styles and conceptions of parental authority during adolescence. *Child Development, 66*, 299–316. doi: 10.2307/1131579

Smetana, J. G. (1996). Adolescent-parent conflict: Implications for adaptive and maladaptive development. In D. Cicchetti & S. L. Toth (Eds.), *Adolescence: Opportunities and challenges* (pp. 1–46). Rochester, NY: University of Rochester Press.

Smetana, J. G. (2000). Middle-class African American adolescents' and parents' conceptions of parental authority and parenting practices: A longitudinal investigation. *Child Development, 71*, 1672–1688. doi: 10.1111/1467-8624.00257

Smetana, J. G. (2002). Culture, autonomy, and personal jurisdiction in adolescent-parent relationships. In R. Kail & H. W. Reese (Eds.), *Advances in child development and behavior* (vol. *29*, pp. 51–87). San Diego: Academic Press.

Smetana, J. G. (2006). Social-cognitive domain theory: Consistencies and variations in children's moral and social judgments. In M. Killen, & J. G. Smetana (Ed.), *Handbook of moral development* (pp. 19–154). Mahwah, NJ: Lawrence Erlbaum.

Smetana, J. G. (2011). *Adolescents, families, and social development: How teens construct their worlds.* Malden, MA: Wiley-Blackwell.

Smetana, J. G. (2013). Moral development: The social domain theory view. In P. D. Zelazo (Ed.), *Oxford handbook of developmental psychology* (vol. *1*, pp. 823–866). New York: Oxford University Press.

Smetana, J. G., & Asquith, P. (1994). Adolescents' and parents' conceptions of parental authority and personal autonomy. *Child Development, 65*, 1147–1162. doi: 10.2307/1131311

Smetana, J. G., Campione-Barr, N., & Daddis, C. (2004). Longitudinal development of family decision making: Defining healthy behavioral autonomy for middle-class African American adolescents. *Child Development, 75*, 1418–1434. doi: 10.1111/j.1467-8624.2004.00749.x

Smetana, J. G., Crean, H. F., & Daddis, C. (2002). Family processes and problem behaviors in middle-class African American adolescents. *Journal of Research on Adolescence, 12*, 275–304. doi: 10.1111/1532-7795.00034

Smetana, J. G., & Daddis, C. (2002). Domain-specific antecedents of parental psychological control and monitoring: The role of parenting beliefs and practices. *Child Development, 73*, 563–580. doi: 10.1111/1467-8624.00424

Smetana, J. G., Villalobos, M., Tasopoulos-Chan, M., Gettman, D. C., & Campione-Barr, N. (2009). Early and middle adolescents' disclosure to parents about activities in different domains. *Journal of Adolescence, 32*, 693–713. doi: 10.1016/j.adolescence.2008.06.010

Soenens, B., & Vansteenkiste, M. (2005). Antecedents and outcomes of self-determination in 3 life domains: The role of parents' and teachers' autonomy support. *Journal of Youth and Adolescence, 34*, 589–604.

Tisak, M. S. (1986). Children's conceptions of parental authority. *Child Development, 57*, 166–176. doi: 10.1111/j.1467-8624.1986.tb00017.x

Turiel, E. (1983). *The development of social knowledge: Morality and convention.* New York: Cambridge University Press.

Wainryb, C. (2011). "And so they ordered me to kill a person": Conceptualizing the impacts of child soldiering on the development of moral agency. *Human Development, 54*, 273–300. doi: 10.1159/000331482

Wainryb, C., Komolova, M., & Florsheim, P. (2010). How violent youth offenders and typically developing adolescents construct moral agency in narratives about doing harm. In K. C. Mclean & M. Pasupathi (Eds.), *Narrative development in adolescence: Advancing responsible adolescent development.* New York: Springer Science & Business Media.

Wainryb, C., Shaw, L. A., Langley, M., Cottam, K., & Lewis, R. (2004). Children's thinking about diversity of belief in the early school years: Judgments of relativism, tolerance, and disagreeing persons. *Child Development, 75*, 687–703. doi: 10.1111/j.1467-8624.2004.00701.x

Weeks, T. L., & Pasupathi, M. (2010). Autonomy, identity, and narrative construction with parents and friends. In K. C. McLean & M. Pasupathi (Eds.), *Narrative development in adolescence: Creating the storied self* (pp. 65–91). New York: Springer Science & Business Media.

Weinmann, L. L., & Newcombe, N. (1990). Relational aspects of identity: Late adolescents' perceptions of their relationships with parents. *Journal of Experimental Child Psychology, 50*, 357–369. doi: 10.1016/0022-0965(90)90075-J

Wiley, R. E., & Berman, S. L. (2012). The relationships among caregiver and adolescent identity status, identity distress and psychological adjustment. *Journal of Adolescence, 35*, 1203–1213.

Zimmer-Gembeck, M. J., & Collins, W. A. (2003). Autonomy development during adolescence. In G. R. Adams, & M. D. Berzonsky (Ed.), *Blackwell handbook of adolescence* (pp. 175–204). Malden, MA: Blackwell Publishing.

CHAPTER 28

Who Am I If We're Not Us? Divorce and Identity Across the Lifespan

Jeffrey T. Cookston *and* Luke N. Remy

Abstract

If marriage involves integrating separate individuals into a single pair, divorce explicitly involves a return to separate entities; thus, it is a threat to individual identity. Informed by Erikson's perspective on identity and the symbolic interactionist perspective, this chapter explores a number of important identity themes presented by divorce. The chapter reviews how divorce threatens identity coherence during separation, with unique attention paid to the individual who decides to leave versus the one who may seek to maintain the relationship. We consider how separation threatens parenting identity and the differences between parents who spend more time with their children after divorce versus noncustodial parents who see their children less often. We also explore how divorce threatens intimacy processes post-divorce. Because the overwhelming majority of research on divorce has focused on its impact on children, the limited research of divorce's impact on child identity development is reviewed. Finally, we consider limitations of past research at the intersection of identity and divorce, focusing on suggestions for future investigation.

Key Words: divorce, identity, adult development, adjustment, marital dissolution, Erikson

---

> I am emotionally devastated. I am trying my best to cope daily but it has been extremely difficult.
> *– A man's response to the question, "How has your divorce affected you?"*

In terms of the most stressful life events experienced by adults, only the death of a spouse is more distressing than divorce (Holmes & Rahe, 1967; Scully, Tosi, & Banning, 2000). Compared to married couples, after divorce both women and men report more anxiety, depression, and substance abuse (Amato & Hohmann-Marriott, 2007; Bierman, Fazio, & Milkie, 2006; Waite, Luo, & Lewin, 2009). Immediately after divorce, men begin to report worse health than men who stay married (Williams & Umberson, 2004), and although divorced women don't report worse health right after the separation, by 10 years after the divorce, women appear to be less healthy than their married counterparts (Lorenz, Wickrama, Conger, & Elder, 2006). A meta-analysis of 104 studies and more than 600 million persons concluded that marital dissolution is associated with increased risk for death, especially for men, even when age and other covariates are explained (Shor, Roelfs, Bugyi, & Schwartz, 2012). Interestingly, the negative impact of divorce on physical health appears to have increased since the 1970s, despite slight declines in the divorce rate since the 1990s (Liu & Umberson, 2008). Furthermore, a substantial literature has amassed implicating the risks of divorce for children who experience the divorce of their parents—increased psychological distress, greater relationship instability, and disrupted relations with parents (see Amato & Keith, 1991a, and Amato, 2001, for meta-analytic reviews). Although some have posited that parents could cooperate post-divorce, thus creating a "good divorce" (Ahrons, 1998), only modest evidence suggests such cooperation is better for children than parallel or autonomous parenting (Amato, Kane, & James, 2011).

Because compelling evidence demonstrates that divorce is linked to negative long-term public health outcomes, in this chapter we review the literature on divorce and relationship dissolution at the intersection of identity. Furthermore, we have chosen to focus on those conceptions of the self that change prior to, during, and following divorce because such perceptions may lend themselves to intervention and could possibly reduce the public health burden of divorce. Our review of the intersection of identity processes and the divorce literature focuses on three themes for divorcing adults. First, divorce challenges identity coherence by necessitating a change in how the self is viewed through the lens of a romantic relationship. We will consider this change from the viewpoint of the person who wishes to end the relationship, as well as from the person who is reacting to the dissolution. Second, for parents who separate, divorce can be threatening to the generative parenting identity of adults who are negotiating a transition from parenting as part of a team to single parenting. Because women tend to be awarded greater physical custody than men following divorce, we focus our review of changes in parenting identity following divorce literature as they are experienced by custodial parents (traditionally mothers) and noncustodial parents (more likely a father). Third, although this literature is more limited, we address the challenges for subsequent intimacy among adults who experience a divorce, with a focus on changes in schemas about the self, attitudes about relationships, and the integration of parenting and romantic identities. Finally, because a review of the effects of divorce on identity would be incomplete if we overlooked the impacts on the children who experience their parents' divorce, we review the literature on links between divorce and identity across a number of developmental periods.

Two important themes merit early attention. First, we recognize there is a growing trend of couples delaying marriage (Furstenberg, 2010), choosing to cohabit instead of marry (Smock & Manning, 2004), and having children born outside of marriage (Demo & Fine, 2010). Due to this growing diversity in family formation and dissolution, when we refer to divorce, we believe these themes apply to both married couples who undergo the dissolution of their marriage contract as well as cohabiting couples who decide to dissolve their relationship. Although married relationships tend to last longer before they dissolve than cohabiting relationships (Osborne, Manning, & Smock, 2007), similar threats to identity are likely present regardless of marital status, yet few studies have explored dissolution experiences among cohabitating couples. Second, existing knowledge about divorce is largely based on evidence from samples of families who are predominately European American (Amato, 2000; Wolchik et al., 2009). As a result, theory about how divorce impacts development over time has been extrapolated from one cultural group (i.e., European Americans) to fit all groups, despite emerging evidence that divorce may impact cultural family values in addition to traditional family processes (Zeiders, Roosa, & Tien, 2011). A number of cultural and ecological considerations are faced by individuals from ethnic minority groups (e.g., increased likelihood to live with family, exposure to stigma; Gonzales, Germán, & Fabrett, 2012). Furthermore, culturally linked resources are available to them that may promote adaptive coping (e.g., familism, bicultural competence, ethnic identity). Because identity researchers have been pioneers in the study of ethnicity, it is likely that culturally inclusive research on identity threats during marital dissolution would add a great deal to the existing literature; however, we do not explore these themes in this chapter given their absence in the larger family literature. Finally, because same-sex marriage is a more recent phenomenon and researchers have studied the topic less than policy-makers (Dodge, 2006; Herman, 2012), our chapter reviews evidence on divorce among heterosexual couples.

Identity Theory and the Relationship with the Former Spouse: Going From Us to Me

Multiple theoretical frameworks highlight the immediate and direct challenge to the otherwise stable identity and sense of self that is common among adults (Kroger, 2007; Kroger, this volume). As Erikson (1963) noted, identity during adulthood is characterized by themes of intimacy, generativity, and integrity, and, as we review in this chapter, all are threatened by divorce. Early and middle adulthood (compared to adolescence and emerging adulthood) are characterized by stability in emotional functioning (Robins, Tracy, & Trzesniewski, 2008), financial status (George, 1992), and generativity in the workplace (Ehlman & Ligon, 2012; McAdams & de St. Aubin, 1992). However, divorce and marital dissolution represent significant threats to the certainty of life circumstances, especially in terms of living arrangements and the sense of self informed by a committed intimate relationship with a romantic partner.

Alternatively, in comparison to Erikson's perspective, we argue that the symbolic interactionist perspective tends to explain identity processes among divorcing adults with greater accuracy. According to the symbolic interactionist perspective, identity is hierarchically organized within the self, such that separate identities form a coherent system (Stryker, 1987). Identities, thus, are informed by internalized concepts about role expectations that operate uniquely for the combinations of social relationships that exist in the lives of individuals. Furthermore, because internalized concepts emerge as a result of direct involvement in a role, we can expect that individuals have a unique understanding of their identities (LaRossa & Reitzes, 1993). Two concepts that are core to the symbolic interaction perspective on identity and play a special role for families are the *salience* and *centrality* of a role. A role is salient not simply because it is performed often but because the schema for the expression of that role is readily accessible to the individual (Stryker & Serpe, 1994). A role is, thus, salient when there is a high probability it will be evoked in a situation. Comparatively, a role is central to an identity when it is ascribed importance in an individual's life. A man who is in a committed romantic relationship expresses his role centrality by thinking about his partner throughout the day (Marazziti & Canale, 2004). The unique roles and responsibilities of social life offer opportunities for both pleasure and frustration, yet it is the meaning drawn from the experiences that appears to matter for well-being (Fiese, 2006; Kroska, 2003). The more stress experienced by working mothers, the greater the psychological distress they report except when the parenting role is central to the parental identity, in which case role-related stress is not linked to psychological distress (Luchetta, 1995). Whereas individuals tend to be aware of the centrality of their life roles and can organize them hierarchically, there is less conscious awareness of the salience of respective roles, and, thus, individuals may not be aware when they are performing (or not performing) behaviors that are salient to the role (Stryker & Serpe, 1994).

Pair-bonding and marriage offer opportunities for both conscious and implicit changes in both role salience and centrality (Kelman, 2006; Wamboldt & Reiss, 1989). In the early months and years of a relationship, role salience emerges as couple' routines and responsibilities are delegated to one partner or shared between partners. Routines for meal planning and preparation, cleaning, shared intimacy, time spent together, and responsibilities for housework and finances all provide opportunities for the expression of role salience. Although the salience of a couple's identity can be expressed behaviorally, the centrality of the couple identity emerges within each partner as a social cognitive interpretation. Thus, centrality is akin to the commitment component of Sternberg's (1986) three-part model of love because the decision to remain in a committed relationship is typically a strong indicator of its importance. However, as wondrous and grounding as falling in love can be for an individual's sense of self, falling out of love and divorcing is associated with symptoms of depression and anxiety, as well as with hostility toward the partner (Amato & Keith, 1991b; Hackney & Ribordy, 1980). When couples separate and divorce, the salience of the couple identity is interrupted as partners spend less time together, new routines emerge, and responsibilities are no longer delegated or shared but are assumed autonomously. However, despite no longer being together, the couple identity may retain its importance and centrality to identity for many years (DeGarmo & Kitson, 1996). Because these themes of centrality and salience play a strong role in the decision to divorce and the experiences post-divorce, our review focuses separately on the experiences of the partner who seeks the divorce and the partner who reacts to the divorce. Although an imperfect distinction, we believe these two groups offer a valuable perspective on how divorce and identity intersect because a large majority of divorced individuals can identify the member in the couple who *initiated* the divorce as compared to the one who *responded* to the divorce request (Hopper, 1993).

Identity and the Partner Who Seeks the Divorce

The decision to seek a divorce is one that tends to take place over a long period of time and is accompanied by disruptions in the salience and centrality of the marriage relationship (from the symbolic interaction perspective), as well as emphasizing Erikson's view that individuals will move away from intimacy with the partner toward isolation. Demographic evidence, conversely, is compelling that women are more likely to file for divorce than men, and this has been true since the Colonial era in the United States (Phillips, 1991) and continues to be true today (Amato & Irving, 2006). Even divorced men and women agree that women are more likely to leave a failing relationship (Amato & Previti, 2003). And when men file for divorce, at least some appear to be motivated by a perception that taking the initiative in the divorce proceedings would favor them at the time of child custody arrangements (Dixon & Weitzman, 1982). However, because men are more likely than women to be substance abusers (Rodrigues, Hall, & Fincham, 2006), violent (Felson, 2002), and emotionally cruel (Rogers & Follingstad, 2011), women are more likely to leave an unhealthy relationship because of character flaws in men. Furthermore, in one study of marital dissolution, identity exploration on behalf of divorcing women appeared to be more important than qualities of the marriage (Young, Stewart, & Miner-Rubino, 2001). In other words, in divorce, there tends to be an exploration of identity prior to, during, and following the divorce. Women tend to think about divorce more than men and, prior to separation, engage in more planning for life post-divorce (Crane, Soderquist, & Gardner, 1995). Women also provide longer and more detailed explanations of why they divorced than do men (Kitson, 1992). Importantly, however, although women are more likely to leave, there do not appear to be differences between men and women on the organized hierarchies of their identities because both men and women (married and divorced) place a strong emphasis on parenting and relationship identities (Thoits, 1992).

A number of explanations for why relationships deteriorate and dissolve have implications for identity (Huston & Houts, 1998). One interpretation suggests that some couples have *perpetual problems* that include intra- and interpersonal incompatibilities that exist during courtship and persist over time until the relationship erodes to the point of being unsalvageable. In the divorce literature, such problems suggest a *selection effect of divorce*— that divorced adults have personality traits and communication skills that place them at risk for more interpersonal conflict and, subsequently, divorce (Cherlin, Furstenberg, Chase-Landsale, & Kiernan, 1991). From this perpetual problems perspective, it is possible that the consistency in personality traits that places marriages at risk may be linked to earlier identity development and may place limits on the possibility of meaningful change in identity post-divorce.

However, other evidence suggests that behavioral patterns within couples, rather than personality problems, may be more likely to explain divorce. In one sample of unhappily married individuals, more than 50 percent had doubts about the marriage at some point in the first year of the marriage (Kayser & Rao, 2006). Amato and Hohmann-Marriott (2007) used waves 1 and 2 from the National Survey of Families and Households and identified the 11 percent (N = 509) who had divorced in the 5 years between interviews. For these 509 pairs, a cluster analysis estimated two groups based on wave 1 life happiness, marital quality (e.g., happiness, conflict, perceived chance of divorce), and perceptions about marriage (e.g., alternatives to marriage, barriers to divorce, rewards and costs of marriage). Of the two groups that appeared at wave 1, one included high-distress couples, and the other was comprised of low-distress couples. Compared to the 3,951 continuously married couples and the low-distress couples, at wave 1, the high-distress couples were less happy, interacted less, fought more, and perceived a greater likelihood of divorce. However, both divorced groups had married younger, had children, and held more positive attitudes about divorce than did the continuously married couples. The low-distress divorces were more likely than the high-distress divorces to have a child, report alcohol problems, and view life after the divorce more positively. After the divorce, those in high-conflict divorces reported increased happiness compared to those from low-conflict divorces, who tended to report less happiness. Asking similar questions about preexisting factors that place couples at risk for divorce, Lavner and Bradbury (2012) followed a sample of 136 couples who reported high relationship satisfaction at the time of marriage, and they explored the differences between those who had divorced in the first 10 years of marriage and those who stayed together. Although couples tended to be equally satisfied initially and showed similar levels of positive behaviors, the divorcing couples used more negative communication behaviors and were more likely to express negative emotions. Although behavior patterns tend to be ongoing, behavioral patterns may be more amenable to intervention than personality problems, thus offering opportunities for intervention.

Another perspective on why couples separate suggests that *disillusionment* emerges in relationships over time, and whether members of the couple are able to resolve the problems determines the longevity of the relationship. From this perspective, an individual in an intimate relationship experiences disillusion and, over time, views the couple identity as less central to the organization of the self. Typically, when disillusionment begins, thoughts of divorce become more common (Demo & Fine,

2010), and, thus, we believe the marriage identity becomes less central. However, as individuals experience disillusionment, many continue to perform the shared roles of the couple identity through shared routines and responsibilities, even as the internal importance ascribed to the centrality of the role declines.

Although population-level evidence suggests marital satisfaction normatively declines in the first decade of marriage (Glenn, 1998), there appears to be great variability in responses. Some couples start high in satisfaction and remain high, others couples begin with less initial satisfaction and show minimal declines, and another group of couples marries with low satisfaction that declines more quickly (Lavner & Bradbury, 2010). However, it appears to be the initial differences in couples on stress, personality, and interpersonal interactions that best explain marital deterioration, rather than change over time in marital satisfaction (Lavner & Bradbury, 2010), and this link may be especially strong if the man experiences low initial satisfaction (Hirschberger, Srivastava, Marsh, Cowan, & Cowan, 2009).

The language of divorce motives described in Hopper's (1993) ethnographic study of 30 divorcing individuals provides insights into the links between identity and divorce. When asked about their marriages, three common themes emerged. First, all divorcing individuals knew their marriages were in trouble and thought about divorce over a long period of time. Second, individuals were able to identify a number of complaints about their marriages. Third, although the decision to divorce was met with ambivalence and hesitancy, the motive for divorce substantially differed between the initiator of the divorce and the respondent to the divorce. Interestingly, regardless of the discontent that either partner experienced prior to the divorce or the reasons why one member of the couple might leave the other, there appears to be a symbolic status in relationships afforded to the partner who seizes the decision to leave. As the person who makes the decision to leave, the initiators likely had reconstructed their views of themselves prior to requesting the separation and, once the decision to leave was made, tended to emphasize individualism over connection. Prior to separation, relationship-relevant cues are opportunities to look for confirmatory evidence that the relationship is at risk and seek information to justify separation. Synthesizing the Eriksonian and symbolic interaction perspectives, the initiator has entered a period of psychological moratorium in which the salience of the couple relationship continues while the centrality of the role loses importance. This moratorium period offers time to process and react to the divorce and plan for life after the separation, and, as such, much of the difficult work of shifting one's identity from pair to individual occurs while the couple is still together. However, from the perspective of the individual who responds to the divorce, a similar moratorium stage is not available, and the lack of that transition has implications over time.

Identity and the Partner Who Responds to the Divorce

In the previous section, we reviewed ethnographic evidence for the motives of individuals who had initiated the divorce and the conclusion that initiators tend to conclude that divorce is inevitable (Hopper, 1993). Although the narratives of individuals who respond to divorce also include a recognition that the relationship was at risk, that they had thought about divorce themselves, and that they had specific complaints about the relationship, by declaring the relationship over, the initiator seizes control of the separation and leaves the respondent in the position of arguing for the continuation of the relationship while negotiating feelings of loss and abandonment. When individuals are less accepting of the divorce, they tend to report worse psychological adjustment than those who were more accepting of the divorce (Mason, Sbarra, Bryan, & Lee, 2012).

ATTACHMENTS DURING AND AFTER DIVORCE

Throughout history, marriage has protected property rights and inheritance, but, over time, in Western society, that economic and political motive abated and was replaced by an emotional connection between spouses (Coontz, 2006). As a perspective on how couples bond, maintain their relationship, and manage loss, attachment theory offers an important framework for understanding couple processes, including divorce (Mikulincer & Shaver, 2007; Saini, 2012). Traditional marriage offers a number of opportunities to promote attachment, namely, shared proximity, a strong emotional connection, and a means of making meaning from common experiences. Similar to the parent–child attachment, the adult attachment relationship provides a secure base for emotional expression and informs a cognitive script for the self about how to approach situations (Mikulincer & Shaver, 2007). Unlike parent–child attachment, which demands parents be more responsive to their child's attachment needs than vice versa, adult partners typically share responsibilities for providing care for one another and offering emotional support (Fraley & Shaver, 2000).

When couples divorce, the attachment system responds as it would in the case of bereavement by coping with feelings of loss and abandonment and a desire to promote contact (Feeney & Monin, 2008). Eighty-five percent of adults who are going through a divorce show qualities of attachment to their ex-spouses, and this attachment is strongest at the time of separation and for the partner responding to the divorce (Kitson, 1982). From an identity perspective, divorce leads to a disruption in attachment and reorganization of identity that leads to the inevitable question, "Who am I if we are not us?" Attachments to former spouses persevere following separation as divorced couples maintain contact well after the divorce decree, especially when children are involved (Masheter, 1991; Metts & Cupach, 1995). In the first months after divorce, regardless of whether they have a child, couples tend to maintain high levels of contact, with 68 percent of coparent couples and 69 percent of nonparental couples reporting frequent in-person contact (Metts & Cupach, 1995). Up to 2 years following divorce, half of all divorced couples are in contact at least once a month, and a quarter of couples report weekly contact (Masheter, 1991). However, contact with former spouses over time appears to depend on whether the couple has a child. For couples with children, contact with the ex-spouse following divorce is more likely, with 86 percent of couples reporting seeing each other occasionally (Masheter, 1991).

In a sample of individuals divorced more than 6 years, 83 percent of nonparental couples reported seeing their ex-spouse less than once a year, whereas 44 percent of coparents reported monthly contact (Ambert, 1989). Divorced couples with children also appear to be at higher risk for continued interpersonal conflict following divorce as nonparent divorced couples have significantly fewer quarrels than do divorced couples with children (Masheter, 1991). The conflict that parents experience following divorce is strongly related to the amount of time since the divorce event, with only between 8 and 12 percent of couples remaining in high conflict 3 years following divorce, as compared to the higher percentage of couples in high conflict at the time of divorce (King & Heard, 1999; Maccoby & Mnookin, 1992).

Although conflict typically decreases eventually, when the attachment to the ex is strong, psychological functioning tends to be worse, even when all of the other changes associated with divorce are explained. Based on a sample of custodial mothers, Madden-Derdich and Arditti (1999) predicted attachment after divorce from interpersonal processes such as conflict, coparenting, support, and interaction, as well as from contextual variables such as custody status, who requested the divorce, and financial support. Their results showed that coparental support and length of marriage explained stronger attachment, suggesting that (at least for mothers) when children are involved, attachment to the former spouse may be necessary to share parenting responsibilities (Madden-Derdich & Arditti, 1999). Furthermore, the attachment bond appears to continue long after love and affection disappear (Weiss, 1991). Because attachment informs emotional responses and because divorce results in complicated and conflicting emotions (Johnston, Roseby, & Keunhle, 2009), individuals who are experiencing divorce, especially those who respond to the divorce, may be at increased risk for psychological distress.

Prior to divorce, conflict is common within 25 percent of marriages (Hetherington & Kelly, 2002), but only 10 percent of couples remain in high conflict following the divorce, and the high-conflict couples increase the pressure on family courts and children (Kelly, 2000). For the individual reacting to a request for a divorce, high levels of conflict have been proposed to be a response to a maladapted adult attachment (Saini, 2012). Individuals in couples do not appear to be aware that many of their conflict behaviors and interaction patterns with their former partners are informed by attachment patterns that were present prior to the separation (Ahrons, 2004). Saini offers the conceptual metaphor of an emotional iceberg in which observed behaviors appear at the top of the iceberg, above the water level, with other visible surface emotions informing those behaviors but explained by deeper, hidden primary emotions informed by the attachment fears of loss and abandonment. From an attachment perspective, divorce challenges the integrated identity of individuals because decision making is no longer shared and because individuals are faced with novel and challenging new environments (e.g., dating, moving to a new home). The individual who responds to the divorce must juggle feelings of loss and abandonment while simultaneously reorganizing the self-schema to be more autonomous.

Parenting Identity and Divorce: The Transition from "Our Kids" to "My Kids"

When cohabitating and married couples have children, family roles and responsibilities shift to accommodate raising a child. For both parents, common concerns include worries about responding to the child's needs and anxiety about trying to be good romantic partners while also assuming the responsibilities of parenthood (Cowan & Cowan, 2012). Most couples worldwide report a decline in marital satisfaction following the transition to parenthood (as compared to childless couples) (Stanca, 2012), but the decline tends to be temporary and is followed by a reorganized family unit that functions largely as it did prior to the introduction of the child to the system (Keizer & Schenk, 2012). Many of the declines in marital satisfaction following the arrival of a new child can be accounted for by the reduced time with their partners, as well as by a perceived increase in housework following the arrival of the child (Dew & Wilcox, 2011), although one study found that declines were rare (Galatzer-Levy, Murzursky, Mancini, & Bonanno, 2011). However, as we described in the previous section, divorce up-ends the stability of the family and creates a period of physical and psychological reorganization. Because divorced families are more likely than married ones to experience residential relocations (Ford, 1997) and divorced parents tend to spend more time alone with their children than before the divorce (Greif, 1995), these parents must reorganize their parenting identity following the separation.

Parent role identity refers to the salience and centrality of the parenting role in the lives of adults with children (Pleck, 1997; Rane & McBride, 2000). When the parenting identity is more salient, involvement increases for parents; however, divorce is a direct threat to involvement. In this section, we review the literature on parenting identity following divorce for two groups of parents who face unique challenges: custodial and noncustodial parents. Although rates of joint legal custody have been on the rise for years (Greene, Sullivan, & Anderson, 2008), in the majority of divorced families, children spend more of their time with one parent, typically the mother. Although men are more involved in their children's lives than at any time in history (Lamb, 2010), mothers still spend more time with their children prior to the divorce and, thus, are usually awarded more physical custodial rights than fathers (Amato & Dorius, 2010). In efforts to maintain consistency from the time prior to the divorce to the period following the divorce, this *approximation rule* has guided child custody decision making more than assumptions about what is "best for the child" (Warshak, 2007). Whether a family chooses joint custody (vs. primary custody for one parent) is explained by shared responsibilities during the marriage; briefly, more shared responsibilities during the marriage have been linked to a greater likelihood of joint custody (Juby, Le Bourdais, & Macil-Gratton, 2005). Because custodial parenting status and gender tend to be confounded in the majority of divorces, for the purposes of our review, we focus on custodial parenting for mothers and noncustodial parenting for fathers, with limited attention paid to situations in which men and women switch these traditional arrangements.

Custodial Parent Identity Post-Divorce

Compared to divorced childless women, divorced mothers report more negative emotional aftermath following the separation (Williams & Dunne-Bryant, 2006). However, for the parent who is awarded more custody, parent identity post-divorce is fostered by increased time with children and the familiarity of this primary role, although these parents still must balance work, new romantic relationships, and the relationship with the former spouse. As the parent responsible for the majority of the parenting duties, the custodial parent's effectiveness as a parent tends to decline after divorce as warmth can be replaced by rejection and as the consistency of discipline declines (Sandler et al., 2012). Fortunately, preventive interventions for custodial mothers have proven effective in helping parents to maintain high-quality parenting despite a divorce transition (Sigal, Sandler, Wolchik, & Braver, 2011).

Because time with the child tends to be greater for custodial parents (as compared to noncustodial parents), parenting identity for custodial parents involves slight alterations to identity. Most women offer a similar definition to describe a "good mother," even if their own circumstances and views about mothering differ from that general script (Miller, 2007). Briefly, most women will argue that optimal mothering will occur when there are two parents available, both parents are involved in child rearing, and the family has adequate financial resources to support the family. Divorce is a direct threat to this definition as shared parenting is replaced by single parenting, parents are less aware of how the former spouse is involved with the child, and economic resources are fewer. As a result, custodial mothers post-divorce are faced with altering their definitions of good mothering in favor of their understanding of their unique situation and abilities to respond. Because the interpersonal script of mothering has been more clearly articulated within the narrative of the lives of women than those of men (Parke, 2002; Tamis-Lemonda & Cabrera, 1999), it is possible for women to adapt their conceptions of good parenting to accommodate single parenthood.

It is common for new mothers to perceive an inequity in the amount of childcare performed by themselves and their partners, with a general theme for fathers to be less impacted than mothers (Sevón, 2012). Likewise, one challenge for custodial parents concerns the amount of time that the noncustodial parent is involved. When noncustodial parents are involved, offering financial support, and helpful with the child, custodial mothers report less stress over time; however, when noncustodial fathers want to be involved without providing financial support, then mothers tend to report more stress over time (Fung & Cookston, 2011). Thus, it appears that, following divorce, the link between custodial and noncustodial parents continues to be influential for both partners.

Noncustodial Parent Identity Post-Divorce

There are a number of myths about noncustodial parenting (and fathering) post-divorce that have the potential to interfere with a smooth transition from a married parent identity to a single parent role (Braver & O'Connell, 1998). First, since Furstenburg and Nord (1985) reported that 40 percent of noncustodial parents are no longer involved with their children 2 years after divorce, noncustodial parents have been viewed as being at high risk to abandon their children. Although more recent evidence (and better controlled analyses) now demonstrate that whereas father involvement after divorce does decrease (Arendell, 1995), most remain as highly involved as custody plans allow (Amato & Dorius, 2010), and high levels of father involvement following divorce promote positive adjustment for children (Fabricius, Braver, Diaz, & Velez, 2010). Second, there is a perception that, after divorce, men are better off than women despite compelling evidence that noncustodial parents consistently report more anxiety, depression, and loneliness than custodial parents (Arditti, 1995). In this section, we review evidence for how noncustodial parents, specifically men, navigate the transition to single parenthood.

Baum (2003) found that men—and likely noncustodial parents more generally—appear to experience divorce differently than women. Men are more likely to respond to a divorce rather than initiate it and, thus, tend to experience the divorce later than women who, as described earlier, may experience disillusionment and begin planning for life after divorce while still in the marriage. Furthermore, whereas more women report the loss of the intimate relationship as a challenge in divorce, men are less likely to focus on the loss of their wives versus the loss of their homes and children (Baum, 2003). Both of these differences have implications for how men (and female noncustodial parents) navigate the complicated transition to divorce.

Just as the involvement of noncustodial fathers impacts custodial mother stress, it appears that mothers play a role in parenting identity for men. In married couples with young children, mothers' beliefs about father involvement alter the trajectory from his desire to be involved to his actual involvement (McBride et al., 2005). When fathers perceive involvement as important and share a child with a mother who also values father involvement, his involvement increases. However, when fathers perceive themselves as less involved, no level of mother expectation for father involvement can increase his time with a child. For divorcing parents and noncustodial parents, it is essential to separate the identities of spouse and parent. Baum (2003) offered case studies of noncustodial fathers that highlight the challenges for noncustodial parents who suddenly find themselves parenting their children alone and without the spouse to support parenting. Baum observed three patterns among noncustodial parents. One pattern involved consistently high levels of parent involvement despite the challenges of noncustodial parenting with minimal interference from the former spouse. A second pattern emerged for noncustodial parents who maintain high levels of involvement with their children despite high levels of conflict with the former spouse. Finally, there is a pattern of noncustodial parents who become disengaged from their children and their former spouses. For these fathers, it is likely that the challenge of being involved with the child but not the former spouse proves too difficult to integrate into the schema of the self. In fact, even after divorce, it appears that father involvement is reduced when mothers have preferences for less father involvement or when mothers are less emotionally stable (Ihinger-Tallman, Pasley, & Beuhler, 1993). Although mothering pre- and post-divorce appears to be linked to father involvement after the separation, the parenting identity of noncustodial fathers appears to be influenced by a number of psychological phenomena.

One study followed a sample of divorced fathers over 18 months and explored links among custody, parenting identity, and father involvement (DeGarmo, 2010). Although the fathers in the three groups (i.e., full custody, shared custody, no custody) differed in terms of the *quantity* of time the fathers spent with their children, the groups did not differ on *quality* of involvement. Additionally, the longitudinal design allowed for an assessment of the role saliency perspective on father involvement. According to parenting role saliency predictions, more involved fathers (i.e., those who assume the role more often) acquire more meaning about the fathering role through social interaction (Burke, 1991; Burke & Reitzes, 1991) and, thus, should report a more salient identity than those who report less involvement. In DeGarmo's study, this was supported as the fathers with a more coherent parenting identity at the time of divorce tended to see their children more often, had more overnight visits, and engaged in more activities with their children. Furthermore, there was evidence that father involvement remained consistent over time (although fathers tended to differ from one another in whether their rates remained consistent, increased, or declined). Importantly, in their longitudinal design, it appeared to be the concurrent predictors of father involvement that did a better job of explaining adjustment than baseline measures. In other words, predicting a father's level of involvement post-divorce from the salience and centrality of his parenting identity at the time of divorce did a worse job of explaining involvement than did his parenting identity at each wave of the study.

Parenting Identity for Noncustodial Moms and Custodial Dads

Whether children live with their mothers or fathers after the divorce appears to be unrelated to changes in self-esteem for children (Van Houtte & Jacobs, 2004), and children are at no increased risk for problem behavior when parental supervision levels are high (Cookston, 1999). However, although the psychological adjustment of children may be unaffected, there are implications to being in a nontraditional parenting role post-divorce.

Because fathers are more likely to be noncustodial parents, women who are not custodial parents or are absent altogether are perceived to be unbecoming mothers (Gustafson, 2005). Additionally, noncustodial mothers perceive more stigmatization and experience a high degree of identity threat (Babcock, 1997). Although demographically the number of noncustodial mothers is increasing, the associated stigma tends to place these mothers at risk for depression and social isolation, affecting their ability to construct their new parenting identity (Arditti & Madden-Derdich, 1993). Because the Western definition of motherhood is closely tied with taking care of family, noncustodial mothers suffer from a lack of role definition and are at increased risk for clinical treatment (Greif, 1997). Most noncustodial mothers report changing their mothering-related role behaviors to better account for their new situation, integrating their previous expectations about motherhood with their experiences as a noncustodial mother, whereas some mothers actually redefine their idea of motherhood to account for their new identity (Babcock, 1997).

The circumstances and implications of custodial fathers appear to be different from those of custodial mothers (Bronte-Tinkew, Scott, & Lilja, 2010). Using data from the National Longitudinal Study of Youth, Bronte-Tinkew and colleagues found that custodial fathers tend to be more educated than single mothers, had higher incomes than single mothers (but less than married couples), and were more likely to have an uninvolved former spouse than children in single-mother homes are to have an uninvolved father. Fathers in the custodial parent role experience many of the advantages of custodial parenting that appeared for women; namely, a salience of the parenting role and the comfort provided by time with children. Also, like mothers, custodial fathers must juggle work, negotiating the relationship with the child's other parent, and reestablishing an autonomous social life. Unique for custodial fathers after divorce, however, is whether the child is living with the father by choice versus some other circumstance, such as the child having a poor relationship with the mother, the incarceration of the mother, or because the child's problem behaviors have resulted in the child living with the father (Greif, 1995). In such cases where fathers do not choose to be a custodial parent, the transition to custodial parenthood is more stressful.

Future Intimacy for Divorced Adults: I've Just Gotten Used to Me, Do I Really Want More Us?

Second marriages are more likely to end in divorce than first marriages (Bramlett & Mosher, 2002) because life course patterns are more complex following divorce (Teachman, 2008) and because of pervasive personality problems that make individuals incompatible with the requirements of a marriage (Cherlin et al., 1991). Supporting Erikson's perspective, a lack of trust appears to be the primary factor that prevents second marriages from being successful, and trust is compromised by the past relationship and by behaviors during dating and after remarriage (Brimhall, Wampler, & Kimball, 2008). Clinicians, therefore, have argued that partners in second marriages should participate in assessment and intervention earlier than later to stem the rising tide of hostility that may build in a relationship (McCarthy & Ginsberg, 2007).

Divorced coparents, on the other hand, are faced with the equally daunting challenge of creating an independent identity for themselves outside of their former marriage while maintaining a functional relationship with the former spouse. Although it is common for formerly married partners to transition to a more friendly relationship post-divorce, this period of so-called separate togetherness (Masheter & Harris, 1986) tends to be temporary because 50 percent of divorced parents had dated other people prior to a final divorce decree, and 80 percent of divorced individuals report they are in a romantic relationship within a year of the divorce (Anderson et al., 2004). The transition to a new romantic relationship can threaten the coparental relationship unless former spouses develop informal privacy rules about which information to share about romantic relationships and how the information is shared (Miller, 2009). Such rules will allow for the evaluation of motives, situations, and implications of shared information and should reduce coparental conflict.

In one longitudinal study of how custodial mothers negotiate the transition from single parent to dating single parent, Anderson and Greene (2011) found that the orientation of custodial mothers to repartner exists on a continuum from more child-focused to more adult-focused. When mothers adopt a child focus to repartnering, over time, they are more likely to respond to their children's concerns about the new relationship than are mothers who offer a more adult focus. The adult-focused mothers tended to be older, were married longer, were more likely to be employed, tended to be less close to their children, and spent less time with their children. It appears, thus, that the parenting identity and sensitivity to the needs of the child play an important role in decision making about repartnering.

Divorcing parents evoke different strategies for sharing information with their children about dating practices (Greene et al., 2004). Thirteen percent of divorced custodial mothers encapsulate the dating relationship by not making the child aware of the relationship, 47 percent gradually expose the child to the relationship, and 40 percent are completely transparent from the first date forward. Likely, these different strategies are responses to parent assessments of the maturity of the child, the parents' goals for themselves, and potential threats to the relationship with the former spouse. In terms of children accepting the new partners, when mothers are divorced for a longer period of time, children struggle more to establish a healthy stepfather–child relationship, and cohabitation with the stepfather prior to remarriage appear to be protective for children's subsequent social competence, possibly because poor-quality stepfather–child relationships don't result in marriage (Montgomery, Anderson, Hetherington, & Clingempeel, 1992).

Additionally, whereas first marriages tend to be characterized by adherence to gender role norms, individuals who have divorced view remarriage as an opportunity to "regender" their roles, and less traditional patterns emerge (Walzer, 2008). Although divorce offers an opportunity for a fresh start, and many remarriages are healthier than the first marriages of divorced individuals (Hetherington, 2003), divorce also creates threats to intimacy identity. From this perspective, divorce offers opportunities for adults to experience a renewed commitment and definition of intimacy following divorce.

Identity Implications for Children of Divorce: My Parents Got Divorced. Will I?

In the majority of this chapter thus far, we have focused on identity processes for adults who divorce; however, when parents divorce, the dissolution has implications for the identity development of the approximately 1 million children per year who experience the divorce of their parents (Krieder & Ellis, 2011). Up until the 1990s, the prevailing sentiment was that children of divorce were "doomed" to suffer from a wave of negative outcomes (e.g., Dornbusch et al., 1985; Wallerstein, 1987). The prevailing perspective is that exposure to changes in family processes, especially marital conflict, explain child adjustment rather than solely implicating family structure changes (Kelly, 2000). Clearly, child adjustment following divorce is multiply determined and includes environmental influences (Robbers et al., 2012), child effects (Whitton, Rhoades, Stanley, & Markman, 2008), and selection effects (Cherlin et al., 1991). Furthermore, the differences between children of divorce and children of intact families may be smaller than previously thought, suggesting that we still have much to learn about the links between parental divorce and the development of self-concept (Amato, 1994; Amato & Keith, 1991a). For children, family dissolution means exposure to marital conflict (Kelly, 2000), changes in residence (Braver, Ellman, & Fabricius, 2003), and challenges in school (Sun & Li, 2008), and it has implications for attitudes about marriage and divorce in adulthood (Whitton et al., 2008). However, because divorcing spouses may separate shortly after marriage or after several decades of partnership, references to "children of divorce" include fetuses and middle-aged adults. In this section, we examine at different stages of lifespan development the identity themes of how children of divorce view basic trust, how they approach vocational identity in their educational and vocational attainment, and how they engage developmentally salient aspects of intimacy.

Early Childhood

Only a few studies have examined the effect of divorce on very young children. Although identity development is widely associated with adolescence and young adulthood, Erikson asserts that normative psychosocial development of young children, which includes establishing trust, autonomy, initiative, and industry, is necessary for healthy identity development later in the lifespan. In addition, when these childhood "crises" are not successfully resolved, an individual may struggle to develop a sense of identity later in life. However, Erikson argues that it is never too late to achieve or re-evaluate earlier crises, optimistically suggesting that even young children who experience negative psychosocial adjustment as a result of parental divorce can potentially achieve a secure identity later in life (Erikson, 1963).

One study has shown that children of divorce younger than 3 years old demonstrate worse attachment security, worse cognitive and social abilities, worse behavior with mother, and more problem behavior in general as compared to children of two parent families, which may stem from difficulty in establishing basic trust in their parents and a lack of development of autonomy from their parents (Clarke-Stewart, Vandell, McCartney, Owen, & Booth, 2000). Furthermore, when children experience parental divorce at a very young age, they may believe the divorce is their fault and have difficulty expressing those feelings or coping with those thoughts (Portes, Lehman, & Brown, 1999) and may develop problems with trust, manifested in fears of abandonment (Cohen & Ronan, 1999).

For preschool aged children who believe the divorce is their fault, it may be difficult to successfully establish a sense of initiative, in that they may struggle to develop a strong identification with whichever parent loses primary custody. Subsequently, children of divorce may struggle to achieve the sense of industry that Erikson describes as the main developmental challenge that children face prior to adolescence because they may experience feelings of inadequacy and inferiority as a result of their parents' divorce.

In contrast, it is possible that younger children may have greater mental flexibility to accept the family process changes that accompany divorce, which should lead to better adjustment and later identity development. In support of this idea, when children experience divorce at a young age, they retain few negative memories of the separation process and virtually no positive memories of a happy, intact family (Cohen & Ronan, 1999; Portes et al., 1999). Given that a sense of self and identity for young children post-divorce has been studied less, we now turn our attention to the experience of parental divorce for adolescents.

Adolescence

Adolescence seems to be an especially risky time for children to experience parental divorce, as youth negotiate the normative identity exploration and formation of this age accompanied by the unique stressors experienced by children of divorce. As before, we note some key findings on psychosocial adjustment for adolescents of divorce, but focus on the effects of divorce on identity.

Wallerstein (1987) proposed the "overburdened child syndrome" as an explanation for the negative outcomes commonly reported by children of divorce, arguing that parents begin to rely on their children for emotional support (rather than their ex-spouse) and that the child is forced to take on more parental responsibilities. Because researchers have traditionally focused on the negative outcomes associated with divorce, a number of studies report adverse identity-related outcomes for adolescents who experience parental divorce (e.g., Barber & Eccles, 1992). For example, adolescents experiencing parental divorce are more likely to receive less parental supervision and exhibit more delinquent behavior (Dornbusch et al., 1985), give in to peer pressure to commit deviant acts (Steinberg, 1987), report lower academic self-concept (Smith, 1990), report lower overall self-concept (Parish & Dostal, 1980), and have negative attitudes regarding marriage itself (Kinnaird & Gerrard, 1986).

From an Eriksonian perspective, adolescence appears to be a particularly risky time to experience the divorce of one's parents because the normative transition from identity achievement to intimacy exploration may be informed by an expectation that divorce may be more likely. In fact, experiencing a parental divorce is linked to a greater likelihood of getting divorced as an adult (Amato & Keith, 1991b). Evidence suggests, in fact, that exposure to parental divorce creates a weaker commitment to marriage (Glenn & Kramer, 1987) and more positive attitudes about divorce (Cui & Fincham, 2010). Because identity formation during adolescence involves conceptualizing adult romantic relationship, experiencing the divorce of one's parents during this time can compromise the capacity to engage in intimacy.

Emerging Adulthood

As important as adolescence is, the age range of 18 to 25 years old, commonly referred to as *emerging adulthood* (Arnett, 2000; this volume), may represent an even more critical time for identity development, including the important identity tasks of leaving the parental home, completing education, beginning a career, marriage, and parenthood. Erikson argued that younger emerging adults are completing the identity crisis of ego identity versus identity diffusion, as demonstrated by the gradual occupational and ideological commitment seen in individuals of this age. Their identity statuses should be a reflection of their style of coping with the psychosocial demands of forming an identity (Marcia, 1966), and emerging adults experiencing parental divorce are more likely to experience unique psychosocial demands, compared to those individuals whose parents do not separate.

In an effort to build on the identity statuses proposed by Erikson and Marcia, Benson and Elder (2011) have proposed that young adults base their identities on the dimensions of subjective age (i.e., their perceived age, relative to their same-age peers) and psychosocial maturity, which is comprised of feelings of independence, confidence, and responsibility. Young adults from a variety of family structures, including two biological parent families, stepparent families, adoptive families, single biological mother families, single biological father families, and all other family types, gave responses on identity-related constructs, and the following four identity profiles emerged: *late adults* (low subjective age and low psychosocial maturation), *pseudo-adults* (low subjective age and high psychosocial maturation), *anticipatory adults* (high subjective age and low psychosocial maturation), and *early adults* (high subjective age and high psychosocial maturation).

Regarding the link between parental divorce and identity profiles, late adults were more likely to come from intact, two-parent families, have close relationships with their parents, have a lower self-esteem, and have a lower level of adult-like responsibilities; anticipatory adults were more likely to be male, come from intact, two-parent families, have close parental relationships, have clear generational boundaries with their parents, and have high self-esteem; pseudo-adults were more likely to be female, come from nonintact families, and report a lack of coping resources, low self-esteem, a lack of close parental relationships, and peer-like communication with their parents; and, last, early adults were more likely to come from any family type other than that with two biological parents and to report high self-esteem and adult-like responsibilities. Overall, these findings suggest that children in single-parent or stepparent families are more likely to not only report feeling older than their peers as compared to children from either adoptive or biological two-parent families, but to also report a higher level of psychosocial maturity (Benson & Johnson, 2009).

Adding to these findings, emerging adults are more likely to self-identify as adults if they have undergone parental divorce, and individuals living in an intact family with either two biological parents or two adoptive parents were less likely to report identifying as an adult than in any other family type. Family resources and processes, including parental control and parent–child relationship quality, mediated these results (Benson & Johnson, 2009). The authors argue that the family process of parental monitoring is a crucial factor in this relationship, in that single-parent families typically provide less monitoring than do two-parent families. This finding that children of divorce are more likely to consider themselves adults as compared to children of intact families warrants further examination, especially considering the unique role that parental monitoring may play in identity development. Furthermore, this finding reinforces that family processes are more important in predicting identity development (and overall adjustment) than is family structure (e.g., Kelly, 2000), a consistent theme in the divorce literature.

Improving Our Understanding of the Effects of Divorce on Identity Processes

Typically, research on children of divorce involves cross-sectional or longitudinal studies, with each design having unique advantages. In quasi-experimental designs, researchers tend to use child reports or retrospective reports of adults who experienced a divorce as a child and compare them to children or adults from two-parent families. These designs are economical but can be plagued by design issues that include the lack of validity in retrospective accounts, poor attention to preexisting differences between groups, and the bias to expect worse outcomes for individuals who have experienced a divorce as compared to those who were raised by two parents. In longitudinal designs, by comparison, it is possible to track children over time to explore how disruptions in family life are linked to adjustment over time. However, such longitudinal designs can be expensive to carry out, may be plagued by attrition, and are complicated when parents divorce within the comparison married sample. Because divorce has been implicated as a risk factor for children, the wealth of varied research designs on the topic is impressive; however, much of the work has focused on mental health and occupational outcomes, with comparatively less emphasis placed on the self-schemas traditionally explored in the identity literature. Important next steps in the identity literature could be offered by additional emphasis in both cross-sectional and longitudinal designs on the meaning and interpretations provided by individuals as they experience a divorce to understand how meaning translates into adjustment.

As we have noted, families structure themselves in increasingly complicated ways. Traditionally, there were married families and divorced families. The differences between these groups are apparent. Married families live together and share resources and responsibilities. Comparatively, divorced families have separate residences and have full responsibility for children at some times and none at other times. More recently, the demographics of family structure have added a number of complications to the polar opposites of married and divorced. For example, status as a single-parent family may be transitional before a divorced parent meets another partner or may be more-or-less permanent in the case of a never-married single-parent family. Included in this mix are the experiences of being in a family with a stepparent and even of children in adoptive families. Complex family structures such as these vary in terms of the co-residence of both parents, the timing of a child's entry into the family, and the degree of stigma the child may perceive from being from a divorced family. All of these varied structures present challenges for systematic research because they may be infrequent or may change quickly.

Another complication in conducting and interpreting research of the effects of divorce on children is the confounding impact of preexisting marital conflict, which often occurs for several years leading up to the actual separation. To highlight this fact, one study found that children from high-conflict homes reported higher levels of well-being as young adults if their parents divorced as compared to those whose parents stayed together, but the opposite was true for children of low-conflict homes, who fared better if their parents stayed together (Amato, Loomis, & Booth, 1995).

Although we have shown that it is no longer believed that children of divorce are "doomed," this is not to suggest that they are not still at risk. Furthermore, the risk inherent to children of divorce does not necessarily end with their generation. A study examining the effects of divorce across three generations found that, independent of the effects that their own parents' divorce had on them, grandchildren of divorce are more likely to experience less educational attainment, marital discord, divorce, poorer relations with mother, poorer relations with father, and poorer psychological well-being (Amato & Cheadle, 2005). In a somewhat chilling statement, the authors caution "divorce has consequences for subsequent generations, including individuals who were not yet born at the time of the original divorce" (Amato & Cheadle, 2005, p. 191).

Suggestions for Future Research and Conclusion
Identity in Divorce Research

Research on the effects of divorce often focuses on specific outcomes that are clearly linked with identity development, such as psychological adjustment, social relations, educational attainment, and occupational quality, to name a few (e.g., Amato & Keith, 1991*a*). However, there is a relative lack of divorce-related findings that use scales derived from the identity literature itself, such as those based on Erikson's and Marcia's identity statuses. For us to make definitive statements on the impact of divorce on later identity development, there is a need for more research that integrates findings from the past 20 years of divorce research (e.g., measuring marital conflict as a predictor for later outcomes rather than the separation of divorce itself) with identity-specific measures such as the Erikson Psychosocial Stage Inventory and the Identity Style Inventory and others.

Furthermore, as the identity literature has developed, so have the approaches used in defining and studying identity itself. Josselson (1982) applied Marcia's identity statuses to the identity development of women and observed fewer differences between categories than had been found among men. Possibly, a similar view is relevant for divorced individuals, such that divorce should not be implicated in changing identities but, rather, that identity is the cause of the change and not the implication of the divorce. Schwartz (2005) argues for a lesser focus on Marcia's concepts of exploration and commitment as they relate to identity statuses and for a return to Erikson's broader conceptualization of identity, which includes personal and social aspects of self as well as a focus on applied identity research.

Using a lens of identity to explore the implications of divorce for children and adults offers a perspective to understand the constantly reorganizing self-schemas present within families. With the exception of the noncustodial father literature, the majority of research on identity and divorce has been circumstantial because this topic has been understudied; however, in this chapter, we've offered perspectives on how the literatures intersect with the extant identity literature to create opportunities for future research. Because families will continue to divorce, and those who are proximal to those divorces will continue to be impacted by them, it is essential to include support for the reorganization of identity in services offered to those affected by divorce.

References

Ahrons, C. (1998). *The good divorce: Keeping your family together when your marriage comes apart*. New York: HarperCollins.

Ahrons, C. R. (2004). *We're still family: What grown children have to say about their parents' divorce*. New York: Harper Collins.

Amato, P. R. (1994). Life-span adjustment of children to their parents' divorce. *The Future of Children, 4*(1), 143–164. doi:10.2307/1602482

Amato, P. R. (2000). The consequences of divorce for adults and children. *Journal of Marriage and Family, 62*, 1269–1287.

Amato, P. R. (2001). Children of divorce in the 1990s: An update of the Amato and Keith (1991) meta-analysis. *Journal of Family Psychology, 15*(3), 355–370. doi:10.1037/0893-3200.15.3.355

Amato, P. R., & Cheadle, J. (2005). The long reach of divorce: Divorce and child well-being across three generations. *Journal of Marriage and Family, 67*(1), 191–206. doi:10.1111/j.0022-2445.2005.00014.x

Amato, P. R., & Dorius, C. (2010). Fathers, children, and divorce. In M. E. Lamb (Ed.), *The role of the father in child development* (5th ed., pp. 177–200). Hoboken, NJ: John Wiley & Sons.

Amato, P. R., & Hohmann-Marriott, B. (2007). A comparison of high- and low-distress marriages that end in divorce. *Journal of Marriage and Family, 69*(3), 621–638. doi: 10.1111/j.1741-3737.2007.00396.x

Amato, P. R., & Irving, S. (2006). Historical trends in divorce and dissolution in the United States. In M. A. Fine & J. H. Harvey (Eds.), *Handbook of divorce and relationship dissolution* (pp. 41–57)., Mahwah, NJ: Lawrence Erlbaum.

Amato, P. R., Kane, J. B., & James, S. (2011). Reconsidering the "good divorce." *Family Relations: An Interdisciplinary Journal of Applied Family Studies, 60*(5), 511–524. doi:10.1111/j.1741-3729.2011.00666.x

Amato, P. R., & Keith, B. (1991*a*). Parental divorce and the well-being of children: A meta-analysis. *Psychological Bulletin, 110*(1), 26–46. doi:10.1037/0033-2909.110.1.26

Amato, P. R., & Keith, B. (1991b). Parental divorce and adult well-being: A meta-analysis. *Journal of Marriage and Family, 53*(1), 43–58. doi:10.2307/353132

Amato, P. R., Loomis, L., & Booth, A. (1995). Parental divorce, marital conflict, and offspring well-being during early adulthood. *Social Forces, 73*(3), 895–915. doi:10.2307/2580551

Amato, P. R., & Previti, D. (2003). People's reasons for divorcing: Gender, social class, the life course, and adjustment. *Journal of Family Issues, 24*(5), 602–626. doi:10.1177/0192513X03024005002

Ambert, A.-M. (1989). *Ex-spouses and new spouses: A study of relationships*. Greenwich, CT: JAI Press.

Anderson, E. R., & Greene, S. M. (2011). "My child and I are a package deal": Balancing adult and child concerns in repartnering after divorce. *Journal of Family Psychology, 25*(5), 741–750. doi:10.1037/a0024620

Anderson, E. R., Greene, S. M., Walker, L., Malerba, C. A., Forgatch, M. S., & DeGarmo, D. S. (2004). Ready to take a chance again: Transitions into dating among divorced parents. *Journal of Divorce and Remarriage, 40*, 61–75.

Arditti, J. (1995). Noncustodial parents: Emergent issues of diversity and process. *Marriage & Family Review 20*, 283–304.

Arditti, J. A., & Madden-Derdich, D. A. (1993). Noncustodial mothers: Developing strategies of support. *Family Relations: An Interdisciplinary Journal of Applied Family Studies, 42*(3), 305–314. doi:10.2307/585560

Arendell, T. (1995). *Fathers and divorce*. Newbury Park, CA: Sage Publications.

Arnett, J. (2000). Emerging adulthood: A theory of development from the late teens through the twenties. *American Psychologist, 55*(5), 469–480. doi:10.1037/0003-066X.55.5.469

Babcock, G. M. (1997). Stigma, identity dissonance, and the nonresidential mother. *Journal of Divorce & Remarriage, 28*(1–2), 139–156. doi:10.1300/J087v28n01_10

Barber, B. L., & Eccles, J. S. (1992). Long-term influence of divorce and single parenting on adolescent family- and work-related values, behaviors, and aspirations. *Psychological Bulletin, 111*(1), 108–126. doi:10.1037/0033-2909.111.1.108

Baum, N. (2003). The male way of mourning divorce: When, what, and how. *Clinical Social Work Journal, 31*(1), 37–50. doi:10.1023/A:1021462517875

Benson, J. E., & Elder, G. R. (2011). Young adult identities and their pathways: A developmental and life course model. *Developmental Psychology, 47*(6), 1646–1657. doi:10.1037/a0023833

Benson, J. E., & Johnson, M. (2009). Adolescent family context and adult identity formation. *Journal of Family Issues, 30*(9), 1265–1286. doi:10.1177/0192513X09332967

Bierman, A., Fazio, E. M., & Milkie, M. A. (2006). A multifaceted approach to the mental health advantage of the married: Assessing how explanations vary by outcome measure and unmarried group. *Journal of Family Issues*, 27(4), 554–582. doi:10.1177/0192513X05284111

Bramlett, M., & Mosher, W. (2002). Cohabitation, marriage, divorce, and remarriage in the United States. *Vital Health Statistics*, Series 23, No. 22. Hyattsville, MD: National Center for Health Statistics.

Braver, S. L., Ellman, I. M., & Fabricius, W. V. (2003). Relocation of children after divorce and children's best interests: New evidence and legal considerations. *Journal of Family Psychology*, 17(2), 206–219. doi:10.1037/0893-3200.17.2.206

Braver, S. L., & O'Connell, E. (1998). *Divorced dads: Shattering the myths*. New York: Tarcher/Putnam.

Brimhall, A., Wampler, K., & Kimball, T. (2008). Learning from the past, altering the future: A tentative theory of the effect of past relationships on couples who remarry. *Family Process*, 47(3), 373–387. doi:10.1111/j.1545-5300.2008.00259.x

Bronte-Tinkew, J., Scott, M. E., & Lilja, E. (2010). Single custodial fathers' involvement and parenting: Implications for outcomes in emerging adulthood. *Journal of Marriage and Family*, 72(5), 1107–1127. doi:10.1111/j.1741-3737.2010.00753.x

Burke, P. J. (1991). Identity processes and social stress. *American Sociological Review*, 56, 836–849.

Burke, P. J., & Reitzes, D. C. (1991). An identity theory approach to commitment. *Social Psychology Quarterly*, 54, 239–251.

Cherlin, A. J., Furstenberg, F. F., Chase-Lansdale, P., & Kiernan, K. E. (1991). Longitudinal studies of effects of divorce on children in Great Britain and the United States. *Science*, 252(5011), 1386–1389. doi:10.1126/science.2047851

Clarke-Stewart, K., Vandell, D. L., McCartney, K., Owen, M. T., & Booth, C. (2000). Effects of parental separation and divorce on very young children. *Journal of Family Psychology*, 14(2), 304–326. doi:10.1037/0893-3200.14.2.304

Cohen, O., & Ronen, T. (1999). Young children's adjustment to their parents' divorce as reflected in their drawings. *Journal of Divorce and Remarriage*, 30, 47–70.

Cookston, J. T. (1999). Parental supervision and family structure: Effects on adolescent problem behavior. *Journal of Divorce & Remarriage*, 32(1/2), 107–122.

Coontz, S. (2006). *Marriage, a history: How love conquered marriage*. New York: Penguin.

Cowan, P. A., & Cowan, C. (2012). Normative family transitions, couple relationship quality, and healthy child development. In F. Walsh (Ed.), *Normal family processes: Growing diversity and complexity* (4th ed., pp. 428–451). New York: Guilford Press.

Crane, D., Soderquist, J. N., & Gardner, M. D. (1995). Gender differences in cognitive and behavioral steps toward divorce. *American Journal of Family Therapy*, 23(2), 99–105. doi:10.1080/01926189508251341

Cui, M., & Fincham, F. D. (2010). The differential effects of parental divorce and marital conflict on young adult romantic relationships. *Personal Relationships*, 17(3), 331–343. doi:10.1111/j.1475-6811.2010.01279

DeGarmo, D. S. (2010). A time varying evaluation of identity theory and father involvement for full custody, shared custody, and no custody divorced fathers. *Fathering*, 8(2), 181–202. doi:10.3149/fth.1802.181

DeGarmo, D. S., & Kitson, G. C. (1996). Identity relevance and disruption as predictors of psychological distress for widowed and divorced women. *Journal of Marriage and Family*, 58(4), 983–997. doi:10.2307/353985

Demo, D. H., & Fine, M. A. (2010). *Beyond the average divorce*. Thousand Oaks, CA: Sage.

Dew, J., & Wilcox, W. (2011). If momma ain't happy: Explaining declines in marital satisfaction among new mothers. *Journal of Marriage and Family*, 73(1), 1–12. doi:10.1111/j.1741-3737.2010.00782.x

Dixon, R. B., & Weitzman, L. J. (1982). When husbands file for divorce. *Journal of Marriage and Family*, 44(1), 103–115. doi:10.2307/351266

Dodge, J. A. (2006). Same-sex marriage and divorce: A proposal for child custody mediation. *Family Court Review*, 44(1), 87–103. doi:10.1111/j.1744-1617.2006.00069.x

Dornbusch, S. M., Carlsmith, J. M., Bushwall, S. J., Ritter, P. L., Leiderman, H., Hastork, A. H., & Gross, R. T. (1985). Single parents, extended households, and the control of adolescents. *Child Development*, 56(2), 326–341. doi:10.2307/1129723

Ehlman, K., & Ligon, M. (2012). The application of a generativity model for older adults. *International Journal of Aging & Human Development*, 74(4), 331–344.

Erikson, E. H. (1963). *Childhood and society* (2nd edition). New York, Norton.

Fabricius, W. V., Braver, S. L., Diaz, P., & Velez, C. E. (2010). Custody and parenting time: Links to family relationships and well-being after divorce. In M. E. Lamb (Ed.), *The role of the father in child development* (5th ed., pp. 201–240). Hoboken, NJ: John Wiley & Sons.

Feeney, B. C., & Monin, J. K. (2008). An attachment-theoretical perspective on divorce. In J. Cassidy, P. R. Shaver (Eds.), *Handbook of attachment: Theory, research, and clinical applications* (2nd ed., pp. 934–957). New York: Guilford Press.

Felson R. (2002) Comparing frequencies. *Violence and gender reexamined*. Washington, DC US: American Psychological Association.

Fiese, B. H. (2006). *Family routines and rituals*. New Haven, CT: Yale University Press.

Ford, C. (1997). Untying the relocation knot: Recent developments and a model for change. *Columbia Journal of Gender and Law*, 7, 1–53.

Fraley, R. C., & Shaver, P. R. (2000). Adult romantic attachment: Theoretical developments, emerging controversies, and unanswered questions. *Review of General Psychology*, 4(2), 132–154.

Fung, W. W., & Cookston, J. T. (2011, March). *The influence of father support on maternal parenting stress among adolescent mothers*. Poster session presented at the biannual meeting of the Society for Research on Child Development, Montreal, Canada.

Furstenberg, F. R. (2010). On a new schedule: Transitions to adulthood and family change. *The Future Of Children*, 20(1), 67–87. doi:10.1353/foc.0.0038

Fursternberg, F. F., Jr., & Nord, C. W. (1985). Parenting apart: Patterns of childrearing after marital dissolution. *Journal of Marriage and Family*, 47, 893–904.

Galatzer-Levy, I., Murzursky, H., Mancini, A. D., & Bonanno, G. A. (2011). What we don't expect when expecting: Evidence for heterogeneity in subjective well-being in response to parenthood. *Journal of Family Psychology*, 25, 384–392.

George, L. K. (1992). Economic status and subjective well-being: A review of literature and an agenda for future research. In N. E. Cutler, D. W. Gregg, & M. P. Lawton

(Eds.), *Aging, money, and life satisfaction: Aspects of financial gerontology* (pp. 69–99). New York: Springer.

Glenn, N. D. (1998). The course of marital success and failure in five American 10-year marriage cohorts. *Journal of Marriage and Family, 60*(3), 569–576.

Glenn, N. D., & Kramer, K. B. (1987). The marriages and divorces of the children of divorce. *Journal of Marriage and Family, 49*(4), 811–825. doi:10.2307/351974

Gonzales, N. A., Germán, M., & Fabrett, F. C. (2012). US Latino youth. In E. C. Chang, C. A. Downey (Eds.), *Handbook of race and development in mental health* (pp. 259–278). New York: Springer Science + Business Media. doi:10.1007/978-1-4614-0424-8_15

Greene, S. M., Sullivan, K., & Anderson, E. R. (2008). Divorce and custody. In M. Hersen, A. M. Gross (Eds.), *Handbook of clinical psychology, 2: Children and adolescents* (pp. 833–855). Hoboken, NJ: John Wiley & Sons.

Greif, G. L. (1995). Single fathers with custody following separation and divorce. *Marriage & Family Review, 20*(1–2), 213–231. doi:10.1300/J002v20n01_10

Greif, G. L. (1997). Working with noncustodial mothers. *Families in Society, 78*(1), 46–51.

Gustafson, D. L. (2005). The social construction of maternal absence. In D. L. Gustafson (Ed.), *Unbecoming mothers: The social production of maternal absence* (pp. 23–50). Binghamton, NY: Haworth Clinical Practice Press.

Hackney, G. R., & Ribordy, S. C. (1980). An empirical investigation of emotional reactions to divorce. *Journal of Clinical Psychology, 36*(1), 105–110. doi:10.1002/1097-4679(198001)36:1<105::AID-JCLP2270360107>3.0.CO;2-C

Herman, G. (2012). Legal effects of same-sex marriage and divorce. *American Journal of Family Law, 26*(1), 5–6.

Hetherington, E. (2003). Intimate pathways: Changing patterns in close personal relationships across time. *Family Relations: An Interdisciplinary Journal of Applied Family Studies, 52*(4), 318–331. doi:10.1111/j.1741-3729.2003.00318.x

Hetherington, E. M., & Kelly, H. (2002). *For better or for worse: Divorce reconsidered.* New York: W. W. Norton.

Hirschberger, G., Srivastava, S., Marsh, P., Cowan, C., & Cowan, P. A. (2009). Attachment, marital satisfaction, and divorce during the first fifteen years of parenthood. *Personal Relationships, 16*(3), 401–420. doi:10.1111/j.1475-6811.2009.01230.x

Holmes, T. H., & Rahe, R. H. (1967). The social readjustment rating scale. *Journal of Psychosomatic Research, 11*(2), 213–218. doi:10.1016/0022-3999(67)90010-4

Hopper, J. (1993). The rhetoric of motives in divorce. *Journal of Marriage and Family, 55*, 801–813.

Huston, T. L., & Houts, R. (1998). The psychological infrastructure of courtship and marriage: The role of personality and compatibility in the evolution of romantic relationships. In T. Bradbury (Ed.), *The developmental course of marital dysfunction* (pp. 114–151). New York: Cambridge University Press.

Ihinger-Tallman, M., Pasley, K., & Beuhler, C. (1993). Developing a middle range theory of father involvement postdivorce. *Journal of Family Issues, 14*, 550–571.

Johnston, J., Roseby, E., & Keunhle, K. (2009). *In the name of the child: A developmental approach to understanding and helping children of conflicted and violent divorce* (2nd ed.). New York: Springer.

Josselson, R. (1982). Personality structure and identity status in women as viewed through early memories. *Journal of Youth and Adolescence, 11*(4), 293–299. doi:10.1007/BF01537171

Juby, H., Le Bourdais, C., & Marcil-Gratton, N. (2005). Sharing roles, sharing custody? Couples' characteristics and children's living arrangements at separation. *Journal of Marriage and Family, 67*(1), 157–172. doi:10.1111/j.0022-2445.2005.00012.x

Kayser, K., & Rao, S. S. (2006). Process of disaffection in relationship breakdown. In M. Fine & J. Harvey (Eds). *Handbook of Divorce and Relationship Dissolution.* New Jersey: Lawrence Erlbaum Associates.

Keizer, R., & Schenk, N. (2012). Becoming a parent and relationship satisfaction: A longitudinal dyadic perspective. *Journal of Marriage and Family, 74*(4), 759–773.

Kelly, J. B. (2000). Children's adjustment in conflicted marriage and divorce: A decade review of research. *Journal of the American Academy of Child and Adolescent Psychiatry, 39*(8), 963–973. doi:10.1097/00004583-200008000-00007

Kelman, H. C. (2006). Interests, relationships, identities: Three central issues for individuals and groups in negotiating their social environment. *Annual Review of Psychology, 57*, 1–26. doi:10.1146/annurev.psych.57.102904.190156

Kinnaird, K. L., & Gerrard, M. (1986). Premarital sexual behavior and attitudes toward marriage and divorce among young women as a function of their mothers' marital status. *Journal of Marriage and Family, 48*(4), 757–765. doi:10.2307/352568

King, V., & Heard, H. E. (1999). Nonresident father visitation, parental conflict, and mother's satisfaction: What's best for child well-being? *Journal of Marriage and Family, 61*, 385–396.

Kitson, G. C. (1982). Attachment to the spouse in divorce: A scale and its application. *Journal of Marriage and Family, 44*(2), 379–393. doi:10.2307/351547

Kitson, G. C. (1992). *Portrait of divorce: Adjustment to marital breakdown.* New York: Guilford.

Krieder, R., & Ellis, R. (2011). *Living arrangements of children: 2009. Current population reports, P70–126.* Washington DC: Census Bureau.

Kroger, J. (2007). *Identity development: adolescence through adulthood* (2nd ed.). Thousand Oaks, CA: Sage.

Kroska, A. (2003). Investigating gender differences in the meaning of household chores and child care. *Journal of Marriage and Family, 65*(2), 456–473. doi:10.1111/j.1741-3737.2003.00456.x

Lamb, M. E. (2010). How do fathers influence children's development? Let me count the ways. In M. E. Lamb (Ed.), *The role of the father in child development* (5th ed., pp. 1–26). Hoboken, NJ: John Wiley & Sons.

LaRossa, R., & Reitzes, D. C. (1993). Symbolic interactionism and family studies. In P. G. Boss, W. J. Doherty, R. LaRossa, W. R. Schumm, & S. K. Steinmetz (Eds.), *Sourcebook of family theories and methods: A contextual approach* (pp. 135–166). New York: Plenum Press. doi:10.1007/978-0-387-85764-0_6

Lavner, J. A., & Bradbury, T. N. (2010). Patterns of change in marital satisfaction over the newlywed years. *Journal of Marriage and Family, 72*(5), 1171–1187. doi:10.1111/j.1741-3737.2010.00757.x

Lavner, J. A., & Bradbury, T. N. (2012). Why do even satisfied newlyweds eventually go on to divorce? *Journal of Family Psychology, 26*(1), 1–10.

Liu, H., & Umberson, D. J. (2008). The times they are a-changin': Marital status and health differentials from 1972 to 2003. *Journal of Health and Social Behavior, 49*(3), 239–253. doi:10.1177/002214650804900301

Lorenz, F. O., Wickrama, K. S., Conger, R. D., & Elder, G. R. (2006). The short-term and decade-long effects of divorce on women's midlife health. *Journal of Health and Social Behavior, 47*(2), 111–125. doi:10.1177/002214650604700202

Luchetta, T. (1995). Parental and work role salience, everyday problems, and distress: A prospective analysis of specific vulnerability among multiple-role women. *Women and Health, 22,* 21–50.

Maccoby, E. E., & Mnookin, R. (1992). *Dividing the child.* Cambridge, MA: Harvard University Press.

Madden-Derdich, D. A., & Arditti, J. A. (1999). The ties that bind: Attachment between former spouses. *Family Relations: An Interdisciplinary Journal of Applied Family Studies, 48*(3), 243–249. doi:10.2307/585633

Marazziti, D., & Canale, D. (2004). Hormonal changes when falling in love. *Psychoneuroendocrinology, 29*(7), 931–936.

Marcia, J. E. (1966). Development and validation of ego-identity status. *Journal of Personality and Social Psychology, 3*(5), 551–558. doi:10.1037/h0023281

Masheter, C. (1991). Postdivorce relations between ex-spouses: The roles of attachment and interpersonal conflict. *Journal of Marriage and Family, 53,* 103–110.

Masheter, C., & Harris, L. M. (1986). From divorce to friendship: A study of dialectic relationship development. *Journal of Social and Personal Relationships, 3,* 177–189.

Mason, A. E., Sbarra, D. A., Bryan, A. B., & Lee, L. A. (2012). Staying connected when coming apart: The psychological correlates of contact and sex an ex-partner. *Journal of Social and Clinical Psychology, 31*(5), 408–507. doi:10.1521/jscp.2012.31.5.488

McAdams, D. P., & de St. Aubin, E. (1992). A theory of generativity and its assessment through self-report, behavioral acts, and narrative themes in autobiography. *Journal of Personality and Social Psychology, 62*(6), 1003–1015. doi: 10.1037/0022-3514.62.6.1003

McBride, B. A., Brown, G. L., Bost, K. K., Shin, N., Vaughn, B., & Korth, B. (2005). Paternal Identity, Maternal Gatekeeping, and Father Involvement. *Family Relations: An Interdisciplinary Journal of Applied Family Studies, 54*(3), 360–372. doi:10.1111/j.1741-3729.2005.00323.x

McCarthy, B. W., & Ginsberg, R. L. (2007). Second marriages: Challenges and risks. *The Family Journal, 15*(2), 119–123. doi:10.1177/10664807062978467

Metts, S., & Cupach, W. R. (1995). Postdivorce relations. In M. A. Fitzpatrick & A. L. Vangelisti (Eds.), *Explaining family interactions* (pp. 232–251). London: Sage.

Mikulincer, M., & Shaver, P. R. (2007). *Attachment in adulthood: Structure, dynamics and change.* New York: Guilford

Miller, A. E. (2009). Revealing and concealing postmarital dating information: Divorced coparents' privacy rule development and boundary coordination processes. *Journal of Family Communication, 9*(3), 135–149. doi:10.1080/15267430902773287

Miller, T. (2007). 'Is this what motherhood is all about?' Weaving experiences and discourse through transition of first-time motherhood. *Gender & Society, 21*(3), 337–358.

Montgomery, M. J., Anderson, E. R., Hetherington, E., & Clingempeel, W. (1992). Patterns of courtship for remarriage: Implications for child adjustment and parent–child relationships. *Journal of Marriage and Family, 54*(3), 686–698. doi:10.2307/353254

Osborne, C., Manning, W. D., & Smock, P. J. (2007). Married and cohabiting parents' relationship stability: A focus on race and ethnicity. *Journal of Marriage and Family, 69*(5), 1345–1366. doi:10.1111/j.1741-3737.2007.00451.x

Parish, T. S., & Dostal, J. W. (1980). Evaluations of self and parent figures by children from intact, divorced, and reconstituted families. *Journal of Youth and Adolescence, 9*(4), 347–351. doi:10.1007/BF02087986

Parke, R. D. (2002). Fathers and families. In M. Bornstein (Ed.), *Handbook of parenting*: Vol. 3. *Being and becoming a parent* (2nd ed., pp. 27–73). Hillsdale, NJ: Erlbaum.

Phillips, R. (1991). *Untying the Knot: A Short History of Divorce.* New York: Cambridge University Press.

Pleck, J. H. (1997). Paternal involvement: Levels, sources, and consequences. In M. E. Lamb (Ed.), *The role of fathers in child development* (3rd. ed., pp. 66–103). New York: Wiley.

Portes, P. R., Lehman, A. J., & Brown, J. H. (1999). The Child Adjustment Inventory: Assessing transition in child divorce adjustment. *Journal of Divorce and Remarriage, 30*(1–2), 37–45. doi:10.1300/J087v30n01_03

Rane, T. R., & McBride, B. A. (2000). Identity theory as a guide to understanding fathers' involvement with their children. *Journal of Family Issues, 21*(3), 347–366. doi:10.1177/019251300021003004

Robbers, S., van Oort, F., Huizink, A., Verhulst, F., van Beijsterveldt, C., Boomsma, D., & Bartels, M. (2012). Childhood problem behavior and parental divorce: Evidence for gene-environment interaction. *Social Psychiatry and Psychiatric Epidemiology, 47*(10), 1539–1548. doi:10.1007/s00127-011-0470-9

Robins, R. W., Tracy, J. L., & Trzesniewski, K. H. (2008). Naturalizing the self. In O. P. John, R. W. Robins, & L. A. Pervin (Eds.), *Handbook of personality: Theory and research* (3rd ed., pp. 421–447). New York: Guilford Press.

Rodrigues, A. E., Hall, J. E., & Fincham, F. D. (2006). What predicts divorce and relationship dissolution? In M. A. Fine & J. H. Harvey (Eds.), *Handbook of divorce and relationship dissolution* (pp. 85–112). Mahwah, NJ: Lawrence Erlbaum.

Rogers, M., & Follingstad, D. (2011). Gender differences in reporting psychological abuse in a national sample. *Journal of Aggression, Maltreatment & Trauma, 20*(5), 471–502. doi:10.1080/10926771.2011.586573

Saini, M. (2012). Reconceptualizing high-conflict divorce as a maladaptive adult attachment response. *Families in Society, 93*(3), 173–180.

Sandler, I., Wolchik, S., Winslow, E. B., Mahrer, N. E., Moran, J. A., & Weinstock, D. (2012). Quality of maternal and paternal parenting following separation and divorce. In K. Kuehnle, L. Drozd (Eds.), *Parenting plan evaluations: Applied research for the family court* (pp. 85–122). New York: Oxford University Press.

Sevón, E. (2012). 'My life has changed, but his life hasn't': Making sense of the gendering of parenthood during the transition to motherhood. *Feminism & Psychology, 22*(1), 60–80. doi:10.1177/0959353511415076

Schwartz, S. J. (2005). A new identity for identity research: Recommendations for expanding and refocusing the identity literature. *Journal of Adolescent Research, 20*(3), 293–308. doi:10.1177/0743558405274890

Scully, J. A., Tosi, H., & Banning, K. (2000). Life event checklists: Revisiting the Social Readjustment Rating Scale after

30 years. *Educational and Psychological Measurement, 60*(6), 864–876. doi:10.1177/00131640021970952

Shor, E., Roelfs, D. J., Bugyi, P., & Schwartz, J. E. (2012). Meta-analysis of marital dissolution and morality: Reevaluating the intersection of gender and age. *Social Science & Medicine, 75*(1), 46–59.

Sigal, A., Sandler, I., Wolchik, S., & Braver, S. (2011). Do parent education programs promote healthy postdivorce parenting? Critical distinctions and a review of the evidence. (1), 120–139. doi:10.1111/j.1744-1617.2010.01357.x

Smith, T. E. (1990). Parental separation and the academic self-concepts of adolescents: An effort to solve the puzzle of separation effects. *Journal of Marriage and Family, 52*(1), 107–118. doi:10.2307/352843

Smock, P. J., & Manning, W. D. (2004). Living together unmarried in the United States: Demographic perspectives and implications for family policy. *Law & Policy, 26*(1), 87–117.

Stanca, L. (2012). Suffer the little children: Measuring the effects of parenthood on well-being worldwide. *Journal of Economic Behavior & Organization, 81*(3), 742–750. doi:10.1016/j.jebo.2010.12.019

Steinberg, L. (1987). Single parents, stepparents, and the susceptibility of adolescents to antisocial peer pressure. *Child Development, 58*(1), 269–275. doi:10.2307/1130307

Sternberg, R. J. (1986). A triangular theory of love. *Psychological Review, 93*(2).

Stryker, S. (1987). Identity theory: Developments and extensions. In K. Yardley & T. Honess (Eds.), *Self and identity: Psychosocial perspectives* (pp. 89–103). Oxford: John Wiley & Sons.

Stryker, S., & Serpe, R. T. (1994). Identity salience and psychological centrality: Equivalent, overlapping, or complementary concepts?. *Social Psychology Quarterly, 57*(1), 16–35. doi:10.2307/2786972

Sun, Y., & Li, Y. (2008). Parents' marital disruption and its uneven effect on children's academic performance—A simulation model. *Social Science Research, 37*(2), 449–460. doi:10.1016/j.ssresearch.2007.03.005

Tamis-LeMonda, C. S., & Cabrera, N. (1999). Perspectives on father involvement: Research and policy. *Social Policy Report: Society for Research in Child Development, 13*(1), 1–32.

Teachman, J. (2008). Complex life course patterns and the risk of divorce in second marriages. *Journal of Marriage and Family, 70*(2), 294–305. doi:10.1111/j.1741-3737.2008.00482.x

Thoits, P. A. (1992). Identity structures and psychological well-being: Gender and marital status comparisons. *Social Psychology Quarterly, 55*(3), 236–256. doi:10.2307/2786794

Van Houtte, M., & Jacobs, A. (2004). Consequences of the sex of the custodial parent on three indicators of adolescents' well-being: Evidence from Belgian data. *Journal of Divorce & Remarriage, 41*(3–4), 143–163. doi:10.1300/J087v41n03_08

Waite, L. J., Luo, Y., & Lewin, A. C. (2009). Marital happiness and marital stability: Consequences for psychological well-being. *Social Science Research, 38*(1), 201–212. doi:10.1016/j.ssresearch.2008.07.001

Wallerstein, J. S. (1987). Children of divorce: Report of a ten-year follow-up of early latency-age children. *American Journal of Orthopsychiatry, 57*(2), 199–211.

Walzer, S. (2008). Redoing gender through divorce. *Journal of Social and Personal Relationships, 25*(1), 5–21. doi:10.1177/0265407507086803

Wamboldt, F. S., & Reiss, D. (1989). Defining a family heritage and a new relationship identity: Two central tasks in the making of a marriage. *Family Process, 28*(3), 317–335. doi:10.1111/j.1545-5300.1989.00317.x

Warshak, R. A. (2007). The approximation rule, child development research, and children's best interests after divorce. *Child Development Perspectives, 1*(2), 119–125. doi:10.1111/j.1750-8606.2007.00026.x

Weiss, R. S. (1991). The attachment bond in childhood and adulthood. In C. M. Parkes, J. Stevenson-Hinde, & P. Marris (Eds.), *Attachment across the lifecycle* (pp. 66–76). New York: Routledge.

Whitton, S. W., Rhoades, G. K., Stanley, S. M., & Markman, H. J. (2008). Effects of parental divorce on marital commitment and confidence. *Journal of Family Psychology, 22*(5), 789–793. doi:10.1037/a0012800

Williams, K., & Dunne-Bryant, A. (2006). Divorce and adult psychological well-being: Clarifying the role of gender and child age. *Journal of Marriage and Family, 68*(5), 1178–1196. doi:10.1111/j.1741-3737.2006.00322.x

Williams, K., & Umberson, D. (2004). Marital status, marital transitions, and health: A gendered life course perspective. *Journal of Health and Social Behavior, 45*(1), 81–98. doi:10.1177/002214650404500106

Wolchik, S. A., Sandler, I., Jones, S., Gonzales, N., Doyle, K., Winslow, E., et al. (2009). The new beginnings program for divorcing and separating families: Moving from efficacy to effectiveness. *Family Court Review, 47*(3), 416–435.

Young, A. M., Stewart, A. J., & Miner-Rubino, K. (2001). Women's understandings of their own divorces: A developmental perspective. In D. P. McAdams, R. Josselson, & A. Lieblich (Eds.), *Turns in the road: Narrative studies of lives in transition* (pp. 203–226). Washington, DC: American Psychological Association. doi:10.1037/10410-008

Zeiders, K. H., Roosa, M. W., & Tein, J. (2011). Family structure and family processes in Mexican–American families. *Family Process, 50*(1), 77–91. doi:10.1111/j.1545-5300.2010.01347.x

CHAPTER 29

Identity Development in the Context of the Risk and Resilience Framework

Frosso Motti-Stefanidi

Abstract

Individual differences in identity development are examined through the lenses of the risk and resilience framework. Identity development is considered a core developmental task in adolescence and emerging adulthood that influences the subsequent quality of adaptation with respect to other developmental tasks, psychological well-being, and mental health. This chapter defines positive identity development, identifies contextual- and individual-level risks and resources that can account for positive identity development, and examines whether and how positive identity outcomes predict future adaptation and mental health. The identity development literature contributes to the risk and resilience framework by offering a basis on which to define positive identity outcomes, processes, and trajectories and by providing a detailed description of identity trajectories. The risk and resilience literature allows a developmental, contextualized, process-oriented, and dynamic approach to describing and explaining positive identity trajectories, thus complementing identity development literature and providing a more complete description and explanation of interindividual differences in intraindividual identity development.

Key Words: identity development, risk, resilience, protective factors, status approach, narrative approach

The interest of researchers in the phenomenon of resilience spans almost half a century and was triggered by the observation that many young people who were believed to be "at risk" for developmental and mental health problems managed to overcome adversities and do well in life (Masten & Tellegen, 2012). Resilience research emerged from studies of children of mentally ill parents, who were at elevated risk of developing mental disorders. Initially, researchers sought to understand early influences and pathways to psychopathology. Soon, they realized that there is significant variation in the life course development and outcomes of these individuals and found evidence of positive functioning in spite of adversity. Thus, pioneers in resilience research, such as Garmezy (1974), Rutter (1987), and Werner (1993), began to search for those factors that could explain why some young people beat the odds and do well in the context of disadvantage.

The study of the phenomenon of resilience is considered to be an integral part of the field of developmental psychopathology (Cicchetti & Rogosch, 2002). Developmental psychopathologists are interested in the interface between normal and abnormal, which they consider mutually informative. They focus on the full range of individual functioning when exposed to conditions of adversity and are committed to discovering which youth at risk for problems are following pathways toward mental health and/or positive adjustment; which, in contrast, are following pathways toward psychological problems and/or adaptation difficulties; and why (Cicchetti & Toth, 2009).

Resilience work focuses precisely on positive patterns of adaptation or development in the context of adversity and searches for positive factors and processes that can account for this outcome (Masten & Tellegen, 2012). An important contribution of resilience researchers is the development of criteria for judging positive adaptation. The criteria used to make the decision that a person is doing well in spite of adversity sometimes are based on the absence of psychopathology but more often rely on the presence of successful adaptation with respect to age-salient developmental tasks (Masten, 2013).

However, the resilience framework also closely followed the *zeitgeist*, generally expressed by the positive youth development perspective (see Lerner, Phelps, Forman, & Bowers, 2009; see also Eichas, Meca, Montgomery, & Kurtines, this volume), that wanted the focus dominating developmental science at the time to shift from a deficit view of youth focusing on symptoms and disorders toward a strengths-based view focusing on competence and resilience. These positive approaches to human development have their basis in key principles of developmental science; namely, they examine individual strengths in developmental context and stress the importance of continual bidirectional interactions between the individual and his or her unfolding environments in explaining the diverse pathways toward and away from positive adaptation and mental health, as well as the plasticity of human development (Lerner, 2006).

The purpose of this chapter is to examine individual differences in identity development through the lenses of the risk and resilience framework, which allows a developmental, contextualized, process-oriented, and dynamic approach to the issue (Masten, 2013). Identity formation is considered a core developmental task of the period of adolescence (Erikson, 1968; McCormick, Kuo, & Masten, 2011; Sroufe, Egeland, Carlson, & Collins, 2005) and emerging adulthood (Arnett, 2000). It involves answering the question: "Who am I?" The formation of a secure, coherent, and integrated identity that offers the individual a sense of continuity and sameness is the optimal outcome and a sign of positive adaptation.

The focus in the chapter, situated in Eriksonian theory (Erikson, 1968), is mainly on personal identity, which refers to aspects of self-definition with respect to roles, values, beliefs, standards for behavior, decision making, and lifestyles, that mark a person's individuality (Vignoles, Schwartz, & Luyckx, 2011). However, examples from the ethnic identity literature are used to illustrate some of the arguments along the way. *Ethnic identity* refers to a self-constructed internalization of a person's group membership based on that person's attitudes and feelings toward his or her cultural background, ethnic heritage, and racial phenotype. It shares similarities with personal identity in the way it develops, but is considered to be a component of social identity, which refers to a person's self-definition with respect to group belongingness (Phinney, 2006).

Even though identity formation is a normative process, because the majority of adolescents deal with this issue, significant group and individual differences have been observed, with young people differing in how well they are able to negotiate this task. Some manage, after a period of exploration, to achieve an integrated and coherent sense of identity; others accept an assigned identity; and still others struggle to find their way and may end up in identity confusion. To explain such differences in identity formation, Erikson (1968) had already stressed, in addition to the role of "an inner agency," the role of the context in which adolescents' lives are embedded and emphasized that identity development during adolescence is a process of person–context interactions.

Currently, two predominant research traditions have focused on addressing the issue of individual differences in identity development, namely, the identity status approach (Marcia, 1980) and the narrative approach (McAdams, 2001). These two approaches have had mostly parallel lives, even though they seem to provide complementary information regarding individual differences in identity formation (McLean & Pasupathi, 2012). The status approach focuses on individual-level intrapsychic processes, such as exploration and commitment, and stresses the role of active exploration and commitments in guiding the person from the present to the future (Marcia, 1980). The narrative approach focuses on the construction of the self via the reconstruction of one's past, emphasizing the sorting through of past experiences in order to make sense of one's present state (McAdams, 2001; McAdams & McLean, 2013). According to this perspective, individuals' stories tie together their pasts with the present and guide them into the future. There is significant individual variation in the processes of exploration, commitment, and telling stories, which may account for individual differences in identity development. Both of these approaches mainly stress the agentic role of the individual, neglecting to some degree that identity formation is a socially embedded process (Yoder, 2000). Thus, the need to integrate more contextual parameters into the psychological study of identity has been called for (Côté, 2009).

In this chapter, individual differences in identity formation are examined in developmental context. Ideas and extant evidence stemming mostly from the status and narrative approaches, and to a lesser extent from the self-development (Harter, 2006) and lifespan development literatures (Nurmi, 2004; Salmela-Aro, 2009; Shulman & Nurmi, 2010), will be organized based on the risk and resilience framework, first, to examine how to define positive identity development; second, to identify contextual- and individual-level risks and resources that, independently and/or in interaction with each other, can account, concurrently and over time, for positive identity development; and third, to examine whether and how positive identity outcomes predict individuals' future adaptation and mental health.

The chapter is organized accordingly into four sections. The first section examines core concepts and principles of the risk and resilience framework. The second section draws on conceptual arguments from the identity development literature and related empirical findings to define what constitutes a positive identity outcome and a successful identity trajectory. The third section focuses on explaining individual and group differences in identity formation trajectories. The fourth section considers positive identity development itself as a resource for youth's successful adaptation with respect to later developmental tasks.

Core Constructs and Principles of the Resilience Framework

Resilience refers to pathways and patterns of positive adaptation during or following significant risk or adversity (Masten, 2011; Masten & Tellegen, 2012). It is not an attribute of the individual but is instead a phenomenon that is inferred based on two fundamental judgments: first, the person must be, or have been, exposed to significant risk or adversity, and second, he or she must be "doing ok" despite stress exposure.

Positive adaptation in young people is defined based on how well they are doing with respect to age-salient developmental tasks (Masten, 2011; Masten & Motti-Stefanidi, 2009; McCormick et al., 2011; Sroufe et al., 2005). These tasks reflect the expectations and standards for behavior and achievement that parents, teachers, and society set for them and that they themselves usually come to share. Developmental tasks can be organized into broad domains: individual development; relationships with parents, teachers, and peers; and functioning in the proximal environment and in the broader social world (Sroufe et al., 2005). Success in meeting these developmental expectations and standards for behavior and achievement does not imply that children should exhibit "ideal" or "superb" effectiveness, but rather that they should be doing "adequately well" with respect to developmental tasks (Masten, Burt, & Coatsworth, 2006).

Some theorists focus on external behavior to judge the quality of adaptation with respect to developmental tasks (Masten et al., 2006). For example, positive adaptation in the adolescent years might be judged based on success in school, having close friends, and knowing and obeying the laws of society. Other theorists include criteria for internal adaptation (Sroufe et al., 2005). For example, adolescents are expected to develop more advanced self-control and to establish a cohesive, integrated, and multifaceted sense of identity. Yet others adopt psychological well-being (vs. distress) as an additional criterion for judging positive adaptation (Luthar, 2006). Resilience researchers often examine these indexes of adaptation separately (Luthar, 2006; McCormick et al., 2011). However, they are interrelated concurrently and over time in complex and dynamic ways, such as in developmental cascades shown to link adaptation with respect to developmental tasks and psychological well-being (Masten et al., 2006). In this chapter, identity formation is considered a developmental task pertinent to self-development (McCormick et al., 2011; Sroufe et al., 2005). It is examined in developmental context as an outcome, as well as a possible influence on adolescents' subsequent quality of adaptation with respect to other developmental tasks. However, the first task in the next section is to attempt, based on the extant literature, a definition of positive identity development.

To identify the phenomenon of resilience, evidence is also required that there has been threat, trauma, or negative life experiences in the life of the individual. Such risks predict higher rates of a negative and undesirable outcome (Obradović, Shaffer, & Masten, 2012). Without the presence of risk in the life of the individual, positive adaptation is not considered an expression of resilience but of competence (Masten & Tellegen, 2012). The resilience literature includes different types of risks, such as high-risk status variables (e.g., low socioeconomic status [SES], immigrant status, single-parent family), exposure to traumatic and stressful experiences (e.g., maltreatment, community violence, war, natural disasters), or biological markers of risk (e.g., low birth weight, physical illness). Interaction effects (such as gene-by-environment interactions) between risk factors have also been studied. For example, a significant interaction effect on several indices of adaptation was found between "biological sensitivity to context" and different environmental exposures (e.g., Boyce & Ellis, 2005). The extant evidence regarding the effect of individual, societal-level (e.g., socioeconomic and minority status) and proximal context-level risks (e.g., child abuse) on positive identity development will be examined later in the chapter.

The goal of resilience research is not only to identify who is well-adapted in spite of adversity, but also to explain why. To account for group and individual differences in adaptation in the context of risk, potential predictors of positive adaptation are examined at multiple context levels and levels of analysis (Luthar, 2006; Masten, 2011). Two broad types of factors that ameliorate, or prevent, the effect of risk exposure on adaptation and development have been described (Masten & Tellegen, 2012). The first type, *promotive factors*, involves main effects on adaptation. Promotive factors are sometimes also referred to as assets, resources, compensatory or social or human capital. They promote positive adaptation independently of the presence or absence of adversity in the individual's life and under both low and high adversity. The second type, *protective factors*, refers to moderators of risk. The expected positive relationship between the protective factor and adaptation is more pronounced in the high-risk group, revealing a special role for this factor under high-risk conditions. In this chapter, evidence is presented regarding the potential promotive and/or protective role, both concurrently and over time, of individual- (e.g., personal agency) and contextual-level (e.g., quality of parent–adolescent relationship) resources on identity formation. Furthermore, the potentially promotive and/or protective role of positive identity development for future adaptation will also be examined.

Core principles of the field of developmental psychopathology guide the study of resilience (Cicchetti & Toth, 2009). Three principles of particular relevance for this treatise follow. First, individual development is coherent, and adaptive functioning shows continuity over time (Sroufe et al., 2005). The coherence of individual development is reflected in the observation developmental tasks are not passed or failed. Rather the way developmental tasks of an earlier stage are negotiated sets the stage for the way developmental tasks of later stages will be negotiated. Positive resolution of earlier stage developmental tasks increases the probability of subsequent successful adaptation. Thus, continuity in adaptive functioning is expected. However, it is not expected to be homotypic, but rather heterotypic (Cicchetti & Toth, 2009; McCormick et al., 2011; Sroufe et al., 2005). This implies that continuity is not sought at the level of particular behaviors because their meaning changes with development. Instead, it is sought in the way behavior, affect, and cognition are organized over time with respect to developmental tasks, suggesting that the same underlying organization may become manifested through different behaviors in different developmental periods.

The argument that adaptive functioning shows continuity over time does not preclude the possibility for change. According to the second principle, called the *multifinality principle*, individuals with a similar quality of adaptive functioning at one point may follow different developmental pathways (Cicchetti & Rogosch, 2002). In addition to the quality of prior developmental organization, the current interplay between risks and resources (Sroufe et al., 2005) and their dynamic balance over the course of development (Cicchetti & Rogosch, 2002), contribute to individual differences in the quality of youth's adaptation trajectories. Both risks and resources for positive adaptation and development stem from factors situated within individuals (genetic and hormonal systems, personality, and cognition), as well as in the proximal (e.g., family, school) and distal contexts (societal, cultural, and institutional-level) in which their lives are embedded (Bronfenbrenner & Morris, 2006). Finally, the third principle emphasizes the role of children in this process, seeing them as active processors, not passive receivers, of experience (Cicchetti & Rogosch, 2002) and positing that they exert human agency (and thus influence the course of their own development) within the opportunities and constraints of historical and social circumstances (Bronfenbrenner & Morris, 2006).

Positive Identity Trajectories and Outcomes

Identity development is a lifelong process, but it takes center stage during the period of adolescence (Erikson, 1968) and emerging adulthood (Arnett, 2000). Three questions regarding identity be addressed in this section. First, a positive identity outcome will be [defined], the processes that the status and [approa]ches emphasize to explain how a [positive] outcome is achieved will be examined. [Finally], what constitutes a potentially optimal identity trajectory toward the achievement of a positive identity outcome will be critically discussed.

The main developmental task of young people is to solve the conflict between identity synthesis and identity confusion (Erikson, 1968). Identity synthesis involves the synchronic and diachronic integration of the young person's seemingly disparate aspects of the self, including their different and at times conflicting roles, relationships, values, beliefs, and the like. This integration provides him or her with the sense that he or she is one and the same unified and continuous individual in spite of inevitable and often dramatic personal change. The integrated self-concept has been likened to a self-theory (Epstein, 1973). This identity work guides young people into making provisional commitments to future plans. Thus, the formation of an integrated and coherent identity, one that offers the individual a sense of continuity and sameness, is the optimal outcome of identity development. The achievement of this developmental goal, as is the case in general with the achievement of developmental goals, is a positive sign that development is proceeding well (McCormick et al., 2011).

How is this developmental goal achieved? The identity status and narrative approaches stress different processes in identity development. Identity status theorists initially described two processes to account for identity development (Kroger & Marcia, 2011; Marcia, 1980). The first is exploration, which refers to the active questioning and weighing of alternative roles, beliefs, values, and life plans before deciding which to adopt and pursue. Exploration is often treated as the sine qua non of positive identity formation (e.g., Grotevant, 1987; Marcia, 1980). The second is commitment, which involves personal investment in particular alternatives and the adoption of a course of action that will lead to the implementation of these choices. The crossing of the two dimensions of exploration and commitment results in Marcia's (1980) widely researched identity statuses: achievement (exploration leading to commitment), foreclosure (commitment without much exploration), moratorium (high exploration, low commitment), and diffusion (low systematic exploration, low commitment).

This model has been extended in recent years. The processes of exploration and commitment have been further unpacked, and dual-cycle models of identity formation have been proposed. These models reflect better the observation that identity formation is a recurrent theme throughout the lifespan, neither starting nor ending in adolescence (see Kroger, this volume). For example, Meeus and colleagues (e.g., Crocetti, Rubini, & Meeus, 2008; also see Meeus, 2011; Crocetti & Meeus, this volume) proposed three identity processes: commitment, in-depth exploration, and reconsideration of commitment. They argue that young people enter adolescence with a set of more or less strong commitments mostly internalized from their parents. They construct and revise their identity, in a first cycle, by exploring these initial commitments in depth and deciding which to keep and which to change because they do not fit their needs and potentials. In a second cycle, if their initial commitments are not satisfying, alternative commitments are explored and present commitments may be changed. The interplay among these three processes captures the dynamic by which identity is continuously developed and revised.

Narrative theorists argue that people create their identity through constructing and telling stories about their lives (McAdams & McLean, 2013). They reflect or talk about episodes and periods in their past and about what those experiences mean to them, actively trying to link past elements of their life and of the self with their current selves, a process called *autobiographical reasoning* (Habermas & Bluck, 2000). Stories about the self are constantly changed as new experiences are incorporated through the addition of new episodes and the reworking of old ones. Thus, individuals construct and internalize an evolving and integrative life story, called *narrative identity* (McAdams & McLean, 2013). McAdams (2001) argued that identity is an internalized life story. This internalized and evolving story of the self helps the person integrate synchronically often conflicting self-elements (roles, relationships, etc.) and to bridge diachronic personal discontinuities, bringing them meaningfully together into a temporally organized coherent whole. Through constructing a life story, young people address Erikson's three key identity questions: Who am I? How did I get here? Where is my life going from here?

Individuals' life stories differ on a number of formal aspects, such as their coherence, the richness and complexity of narrative elaboration, or vagueness in discourse. This variation in people's narratives reflects significant individual differences in various identity aspects (e.g., see Hauser & Allen,

2007; Pals, 2006). For example, adults whose narratives of difficult life experiences were characterized by a rich and complex elaboration were more likely to actively engage in an in-depth exploration of the experience, trying to understand its role in their life story (Pals, 2006). In another example, young adults who exhibited in their narratives of turning point events in their lives more elaborate processing of the experience, connecting the turning point to some aspect of understanding of the self, tended to score higher on an overall index of identity maturity (McLean & Pratt, 2006).

The ability to construct a life story emerges in adolescence, to a large extend because individuals have the cognitive tools to represent the self in more abstract ways, to deal with the contradictions of life experiences and self-attributes (Harter, 2006), and to form a coherent life story (Habermas & Bluck, 2000). Chandler and colleagues (see Chandler, Lalonde, Sokol, & Hallett, 2003) proposed a developmental sequence of five qualitatively different and progressively more adequate arguments people make to explain how they remain one and the same continuous person in spite of often dramatic personal change. Individuals using less advanced arguments rely on the identification of some aspect of the self that is more enduring ("my name is the same," "my DNA is the same"), thus minimizing the significance of personal change. It is not until adolescence that individuals who have achieved the Piagetian stage of formal operations are able to use the more advanced of these arguments. They base their claims of personal continuity on autobiographical reasoning, which helps them to reinterpret their past in light of the present (see also Habermas & Köber, this volume).

The status and narrative approaches to identity development provide complementary information regarding individual differences in identity formation (McLean & Pasupathi, 2012). The processes of exploration and commitment are closely connected to the process of telling stories. For example, Syed and Azmitia (2008) found that individuals in the achieved ethnic identity status were more likely to tell stories about prejudice and about feeling connected to their ethnic group when asked to provide a written narrative about a time when they became particularly aware of their ethnicity. The authors argued that identity status membership may provide different "ethnic lenses" through which ethnicity-related experiences are filtered and interpreted. Furthermore, narratives may also be the means through which the processes of exploration and commitment are carried out (McLean & Pasupathi, 2012). For example, Syed and Azmitia (2010) found that individuals who increased in ethnic identity exploration over time were more likely to change their narrative theme than were participants who decreased or remained stable in exploration. This finding suggests that the construction of different ethnicity-related narratives may be used as a way to explore various identity alternatives.

The question that arises concerns the way these processes are optimally related over time. What constitutes a positive identity trajectory? According to the narrative approach, identity develops slowly as young people tell stories about their experiences and what they mean to them. Over time, stories help young people construct an identity that, as it gets broader and more integrative, helps them process and reinterpret old stories under a new light, and, thus, identities in their turn influence the stories they tell about their lives (McAdams & McLean, 2013). However, there have been few systematic, large-scale longitudinal studies of narrative development. In contrast, the status perspective on identity formation captures better the developmental shifts and nuances in the interplay of identity processes over time (McLean & Pasupathi, 2012).

Even though Marcia's four identity statuses can be seen as outcomes of the identity formation process, they have also been treated as substages of the identity stage (Côté & Levine, 1988), arguably reflecting different levels of developmental maturity (see Bosma & Kunnen, 2001). Diffusion is considered to be the lowest status with respect to maturity and achievement the highest. The other two hold an intermediary position. It has been argued that the transition from either the diffusion or the foreclosed statuses to the moratorium and the movement out of the moratorium into achievement status defines the optimal developmental progression and reflects developmental maturity (see Côté & Levine, 1988). However, a recent meta-analysis of longitudinal data collected using Marcia's Identity Status Interview found that a significant proportion of adolescents did not change identity status, although, among those who did, most showed a developmental progression (most frequently from moratorium to achievement) rather than a developmental regression (Kroger, Martinussen, & Marcia, 2010).

Another recent review of longitudinal studies that include, in addition to adolescent and emerging adult samples, older adult samples, and are based on these new models of identity development, also reports significant variation in identity trajectories, as well as a trend toward greater identity maturation (Meeus, 2011). However, this maturation often takes different forms than previously suggested. For example, during adolescence, decreases in diffusion and moratorium statuses along with increases in foreclosure and achievement statuses are observed. Similarly, over the adult years, decreases in identity diffusion and increases in identity foreclosure and achievement are reported (Cramer, 2004). Based on Meeus's (2011) review, the identity status continuum has the order D → M → F → A, in contrast to the theorizing that proposes moratorium always precedes identity achievement because it expresses the identity crisis without which identity achievement cannot be reached (see Côté & Levine, 1988). Finally, both achievement and foreclosure identity trajectories seem to constitute successful outcomes of the identity process, as evidenced by the finding that they are both related to psychological well-being, as well as to other indices of positive functioning, and to low levels of self-compromising behaviors (e.g., Luyckx, Schwartz, Berzonsky, et al., 2008; Meeus, Iedema, Helsen, & Vollebergh, 1999; Schwartz et al., 2011).

In line with these findings is the observation that a significant proportion of the population does not seem to reach the identity achievement status. As Côté (2009) reported, by the end of adolescence, about half of adolescents are still in the diffusion and foreclosure statuses, and only about 30 to 40 percent of college seniors can be classified as identity achievers, whereas an equal proportion of the adult population are foreclosures. Based on these figures and on the findings from the recent longitudinal studies, the deeply held belief that the only optimal identity trajectory leads, at the end of emerging adulthood, to identity achievement may be put into question, and foreclosure may be argued to be another possible positive identity trajectory. In accordance, it has been argued that successful identity development should not be framed in terms of identity statuses but in terms of changes in the quality and strength of the individual's commitments (see Bosma & Kunnen, 2001; Luyckx, Schwartz, Berzonsky, et al., 2008; Kunnen & Metz, this volume). Some individuals may make self-chosen commitments, whereas others may adopt assigned commitments.

A further caveat to the argument that identity achievement is the only desired goal of the identity process is that cultures may vary in this respect. Cultures differ in terms of two important and interrelated dimensions: individualism–collectivism, and dependence–independence, which affect the way they construe the self (e.g., Markus & Kitayama, 1991). In this vein, Kağıtçıbaşı (2007) distinguished cultures on the basis of the degree to which they value and promote the related or the separate self. Erikson's theory and Marcia's empirical test of this theory, as well as all the extensions and expansions that followed, were realized mostly in North American and Northern European countries, which are more individualistic societies and are placed on the independence or separateness side of the continuum. These cultures construe the self in terms of internal attributes such as traits, abilities, values, and preferences. The person is expected to act in an independent and autonomous manner. "Others" and social contexts are important but are used as sources of reflected appraisal or to verify and affirm the inner core of the self. Thus, the goal during adolescence is to increasingly separate one's self from others, to be decreasingly influenced by them (Markus & Kitayama, 1991), and thus to experience one's self as being unique and differentiated, the same over time and across contexts.

In sharp contrast, a significant part of the world, including Asian, African, Latin-American, and many Southern-European countries, consists of more collectivistic societies that construe the self in terms of the person's relationships with others (Oyserman, Gant, & Ager, 1995). According to this view, the person is not seen as separate from, but interdependent with, the social context (Kağıtçıbaşı, 2007). Personal views, values, and desires become subordinated to a complex system of duties and obligations that the person has toward significant others. In these cultural contexts, young people learn to align their own goals with those of their group and also learn how to "fit in," and not be distinctive (see Markus & Kitayama, 1991).

It follows that in the context of an individualistic society a successful identity pathway involves the active exploration between different alternatives, free choice among them, and the firm commitment to these choices, whereas in a collectivistic society the successful identity process may be more conformity-driven, based on imitation and identification (see also Schwartz, Montgomery, & Briones, 2006), and result in a foreclosure type of identity.

However, as Erikson (1968) suggested, people, independently of the type of culture they live in, should be able to develop a good sense of their ego identity—whether based on free choice or conformity—as long as their community supports them in their roles and presents unambiguous messages regarding expectations. One could argue then that the meaning of the identity types and dimensions may vary depending on the cultural context in which the individual lives (also see Côté, 2009). Having a foreclosed identity in a country that promotes free choice may have a different meaning and consequences for the individual than having such an identity in a society that promotes embeddedness and conformity.

In sum, the optimal endpoint of identity development may be "to have an identity," meaning that it is important that the person arrives to some firm commitments, independently of how they achieve this. Following Erikson's (1968) postulation that the identity crisis may be resolved as identity consolidation or identity confusion, the diffusion and moratorium statuses would be considered as less mature, reflecting identity confusion, and the achievement and foreclosure statuses as more mature, reflecting identity consolidation (see Côté, 2009). The adoption of this perspective results in about 60–80 percent of the adult population "having an identity" because they have made firm commitments, whether self-chosen or assigned. This is a more reasonable estimate of the percentage of people in a population that successfully resolve the identity crisis than taking into account only the 30–40 percent of identity achievers.

Identity Trajectories in Developmental Context

Recent longitudinal studies based on the identity status perspective have provided detailed maps of the different identity trajectories that young people may follow during their adolescent and emerging adulthood years (e.g., Klimstra, Hale, Raaijmakers, Branje, & Meeus, 2010; Luyckx, Goosens, & Soenens, 2006; Luyckx, Schwartz, Berzonsky, et al., 2008; Meeus, van de Schoot, Keijsers, Schwartz, & Branje, 2010). However, this work is often more descriptive than explanatory. Less emphasis has been placed on identifying who follows positive identity formation trajectories, who follows less optimal ones, and, more importantly, in accounting for such group and individual differences. The need to move more vigorously from the description of the developmental course of identity formation to explanation has been recently stressed in the literature (e.g., Syed & Seiffge-Krenke, 2012; Syed, 2010).

To understand who follows a positive developmental path and why, identity formation needs to be examined in developmental context (Bronfenbrenner & Morris, 2006; Cicchetti & Rogosch, 2002; Masten, 2011). Youth's adaptive history, the characteristics of their proximal and distal contexts, as well as their own personal characteristics are expected to contribute, both independently and in interaction with each other, to group and individual differences in identity formation trajectories. In this section, evidence and hypotheses stemming from the risk and resilience developmental framework regarding these influences on identity formation will be examined and discussed. This section, in addition to examining the role of adolescents' adaptive history, revolves around two main issues, one focusing on risks and the other on resources for positive identity development.

ADAPTIVE HISTORY

A basic premise in this treatise is that individual development is coherent, and adaptive functioning shows continuity over time (Sroufe et al., 2005). As expected based on the principle of heterotypic continuity, the quality of organization of thought, affect, and behavior in the face of prior developmental challenges, and thus the efficiency of dealing with these challenges, significantly contributes to individual differences in adaptation with respect to developmental tasks during the period of adolescence (Cicchetti & Rogosch, 2002; Masten & Tellegen, 2012; Sroufe et al., 2005) and would therefore also be expected to contribute to individual differences with respect to identity formation.

Young people who enter adolescence having competently addressed the challenges of earlier developmental periods would be expected to have the internal resources and organization that will allow them to successfully navigate between and explore the vast array of possible alternative choices that the Western world offers them in a self-directed, flexible, and integrated manner. Thus, based on the principle of heterotypic continuity, coherence in individual development is expected (Cicchetti & Toth, 2009), such that these adolescents, compared with adolescents with a more compromised earlier organization, will be more likely to follow a developmental trajectory toward positive identity development.

Another possible route connecting early adaptive success to positive identity development during the period of adolescence is via self-esteem. Self-esteem refers to the overall evaluation of one's worth or value as a person (Harter, 2006). Adaptive success with respect to developmental challenges has been argued to have an effect on self-development and more particularly on self-esteem (Sroufe et al., 2005). For example, success or failure with respect to school achievement and peer relations, both core developmental goals (Masten et al., 2006), is expected to influence children's perception of the self and, relatedly, self-esteem (Harter, 2006). Self-esteem, which is for the majority (about 60 percent) of young people stable over time, functioning in a trait-like fashion (Harter, 2006), and which actually seems to be also stable across generations of youth (Trzesniewski & Donnellan, 2010), contributes to positive identity formation. High self-esteem enhances the motivation to engage with the world, to take risks, and consider among different alternatives, and thus promotes identity exploration (Grotevant, 1987). In that line, it was found in a two-wave three-year longitudinal study of ethnic identity that self-esteem at time 1 predicted ethnic identity development at time 2, although the reverse was also true, suggesting that high self-esteem may promote exploration of ethnic issues, such as the questioning of stereotypes or the search for positive role models (Phinney & Chavira, 1992).

RISKS

The quality of resolution of earlier developmental challenges is likely then to influence how the adolescent will approach and deal with the new developmental challenges, including identity formation issues. However, even though the likelihood of continuity between earlier and later forms of adaptation is significant, the effect of early experience is not inevitable (Cicchetti & Toth, 2009; Masten & Tellegen, 2012; Sroufe et al., 2005).

Based on the multifinality principle, it is expected that the dynamic interplay, concurrently and over time, of risks and resources in interaction with the individual adaptive history will contribute to group and individual differences in identity formation. Both risks and resources may stem from any of the two levels of young people's social ecology, societal- and proximal-context levels, as well as from their own individual characteristics (Masten & Tellegen, 2012).

Risks may negatively affect identity contents and their organization, as well as identity processes. For example, risks may place barriers in adolescents' integration of their different and sometimes contradictory self-attributes and multiple selves across roles and contexts (Harter, 1998), or they may contribute to the formation of a negative or oppositional identity (Cooper et al., this volume; Ogbu, 1993; Yoder, 2000), both of which may have deleterious consequences, both in the short and the long term, for the individual and society's well-being. Furthermore, risks may thwart young people's attempts at and opportunities for exploration of identity alternatives, and/or they may place barriers to their commitment with respect to, for example, certain goals for the future (Nurmi, 2004). Sometimes risks may keep young people in a continuously diffused state, neither exploring much nor committing themselves to a future path. Risks may also affect different aspects of the stories adolescents tell about their lives, such as the content of the stories told and the quality of resolution of negative life events (e.g., McAdams & McLean, 2013).

Thus, to explain group and individual differences in identity trajectories (and outcomes), potential risks for positive identity development need to be identified. In this section, first, the way status and narrative theorists describe the experiences that trigger identity work in individuals will be discussed in light of the risk and resilience framework, and, second, risks that are out of the control of the individual (Yoder, 2000) will be presented. However, the list of risks considered is not meant to be exhaustive. Instead, the focus will be on factors that have been implicated in the literature as problematic for identity formation.

According to status theorists, identity work during the period of adolescence is triggered by a crisis, which is the result of pressures from rapid physical development (puberty and physical growth toward adult stature), as well as from parental and generally societal expectations that young people start making commitments with respect to issues of education, work, and love (e.g., Côté & Levine, 1988). However, they argue that this crisis is a normative phenomenon and does not have to be (and is usually not) severe for identity development to take place (Côté, 2009). In contrast, narrative theorists focus on difficult life challenges and on threats (e.g., parents' divorce, psychiatric hospitalization of the adolescent) as triggering identity work and presenting opportunities for learning about the self (e.g., McLean & Pasupathi, 2012).

Through the lens of the risk and resilience framework, the pressure for change exerted on individuals during transitions between developmental periods (such as the transition to adolescence) may render them particularly vulnerable for certain risks (although developmental transitions may also function as a window of opportunity for changing one's life course toward a more positive direction) (Masten et al., 2004; Obradović et al., 2012). Furthermore, the type of challenging life events on which narrative theorists focus may be considered risk factors because they place the individual at higher risk for adaptation difficulties and/or mental health problems. Thus, the identity trajectory that the individual who is exposed to a normative crisis or to a difficult life event will follow largely depends on the personal and contextual resources that he or she has available. Some individuals will follow a positive trajectory toward identity synthesis, and others will have difficulty embarking on the exploration of and effective navigation between alternative identity options and/or deciding on some initial commitments and end up in identity confusion.

Among risks for identity formation that are out of the control of the individual (Yoder, 2000), and taking a top-down approach, social and minority/immigrant status are two societal-level variables that contribute significantly to group differences in different aspects of identity formation (see Motti-Stefanidi, Berry, Chryssochoou, Sam, & Phinney, 2012; Nurmi, 2004). Societal-level variables may have an impact on youth's adaptation by filtering through the contexts of their proximal environment (e.g., Boyce et al., 1998).

Low socioeconomic and/or minority/immigrant status present significant barriers for adolescents' identity formation (Yoder, 2000). Low SES and minority adolescents are more likely to be exposed to chronic and high levels of stress and negative life events, as well as to experience prejudice and discrimination (Wong, Eccles, & Sameroff, 2003). They may face disparaging and derogatory information and feedback at school regarding the self (Phillips & Pittman, 2003) and lower achievement expectations from teachers (Eccles & Roeser, 2009). As a result, they are at greater risk than their counterparts for developing a negative identity, which will include fewer and mostly self-deprecatory representations of self (Phillips & Pittman, 2003).

Thus, Ogbu (1993) argued that some minority youth, such as African Americans who are involuntary immigrants, when faced with discrimination are at greater risk of developing an oppositional identity that will include beliefs, values, and attitudes defined in opposition to those adopted by the dominant majority culture. In this process, they devalue and disidentify with school, which is the predominant institution representing the dominant culture. However, in sharp contrast, Wong, Eccles, and Sameroff (2003) found that African-American adolescents who anticipated future discrimination in the labor market, contrary to Ogbu's theorizing, valued and identified more with their school and were motivated to equip themselves to deal with future discrimination. These adolescents did not seem to have developed an oppositional identity.

Furthermore, recently, an "immigrant paradox" has been described, whereby first-generation immigrant students are doing better in school and have fewer conduct problems and higher psychological well-being than second-generation immigrants or nonimmigrants (Garcia Coll & Marks, 2012; Masten, Liebkind, & Hernandez, 2012). Such results do not hint at the development of an oppositional identity either. However, the immigrant paradox does not hold for all ethnic groups or all host countries (Motti-Stefanidi et al., 2012).

Poor and minority youth also face other significant long-term barriers that may affect their identity work (Nurmi, 2004; Phillips & Pittman, 2003; Yoder, 2000). They often have a limited opportunity structure with fewer life choices than their counterparts, little choice but to make subsistence decisions and start working after finishing high school, and adult models in their proximal context with limited lives who often serve as standards for themselves. These experiences often render identity exploration a luxury that these young people cannot afford (Yoder, 2000). Thus, after a short period of exploration, many may prematurely commit themselves to goals, others may adopt an assigned identity, and still others may fall into the diffuse identity status, neither exploring nor committing to any goals.

In a society that values free choice and self-determination, early foreclosure may be considered a negative outcome. However, two considerations may be important in evaluating this outcome. First, it should be examined whether the commitments made are consonant with the young person's unique potential and, second, what effect this identity trajectory has on a youth's well-being. The second point is in line with findings, mentioned earlier, showing that both the achievement and foreclosure identity statuses are related to psychological well-being, as well as to other indices of positive functioning (e.g., Luyckx, Schwartz, Berzonsky, et al., 2008; Meeus et al., 1999).

At the proximal level, experiences in the family are a significant influence on adolescents' identity formation (e.g., Grotevant, 1987; Koepke & Denissen, 2012). Some traumatic experiences at home may have a lastingly detrimental effect on children. Child maltreatment by primary caregivers is one of the most pernicious risk factors for adolescents' identity formation (Cicchetti & Valentino,

2006; Harter, 1998). It reflects a serious dysfunction in the family system, which fails to provide the child with opportunities essential for normal development. Maltreated children often suffer more than one form of abuse including sexual, physical, and/or psychological abuse and/or neglect. This traumatic experience has deleterious short- and long-term effects on many domains of adaptation and mental health.

To protect themselves from trauma, abused children often use dissociative defensive reactions that help them eliminate the event from consciousness and shield them from the pain. In contrast to the normative affective splitting or dissociation of childhood, which is related to the limited cognitive capacity of school-aged children to integrate their different self-attributes (Harter, 2006), this mechanism is seriously pathological. During adolescence, abused adolescents, instead of working toward integrating their various selves into a coherent whole, further fragment them. In the case of extreme abuse, they are at risk of developing dissociative identity disorders, formerly called multiple personality disorder (Cicchetti & Valentino, 2006). This disorder involves a failure to integrate one's different selves, memory, and consciousness. The person experiences different personality states, each having a distinct personal history, self-image, and identity. These identities take control in sequence and may not have knowledge of one another. Thus, child abuse in the family, even if it occurred in early childhood, compromises severely the young person's ability to develop an integrated identity (Harter, 1998).

Similarly, experiences of peer rejection, bullying, victimization, and humiliation in the school context would also be expected to have a negative effect on students' identities. For example, being labeled by classmates as a "nerd" or "brainiac," which connotes that one is a social outcast although perceived as intelligent, had a significant and distressing impact on junior high school adolescents' identities (Kinney, 1993). However, this situation was reversed when these adolescents entered senior high school. During this educational transition, they became involved in new school activities and friendship groups in which they felt accepted. As a result, they gradually developed more positive self-evaluations and higher self-confidence. As Kinney (1993) states "nerds came to view themselves as normals." This interesting study highlights both the power of context for identity formation and that of developmental "turning points" (see Masten et al., 2004), which may provide a window of opportunity for change in a more positive direction.

In another study conducted in the tradition of the identity status perspective, the mediating role of identity between degrading and disparaging school experiences and negative mental health outcomes was shown, such that adolescents' peer victimization in the school context predicted difficulty in integrating their school, home, and leisure time identities into one coherent whole, which in turn predicted a higher level of depressive symptoms (van Hoof, Raaijmakers, van Beek, Hale, Aleva, 2008).

Finally, an extreme proximal context that would be expected to have a significant impact on adolescents' identity development is institutionalization. A group of incarcerated delinquent adolescents in middle adolescence was compared with a group of clinically referred adolescents institutionalized due to serious internalizing problems and with a normative sample of adolescents living at home (Klimstra et al., 2011). It was found that the delinquent adolescents, compared to both the referred and the normative control groups, were significantly more often classified into the diffuse identity status. It was argued that, because neither the delinquent nor the clinically referred adolescents had many opportunities to explore identity alternatives and to find a satisfying commitment, the former's diffuse identity state cannot be attributed solely to, but could instead be the cause of, their incarceration. In that respect, the differentiation in a future study between adolescents with life course-persistent antisocial behavior, which begins in childhood and is often exacerbated by a high risk social environment, and those with adolescence-limited antisocial behavior, which emerges in adolescence, desists in young adulthood and has been linked to a "maturity gap", may help shed light on this cause–effect relationship (Moffitt, 2006). The former adolescents may be at higher risk than the latter for presenting a diffuse identity status because their adaptation difficulties have a long history dating back in early childhood, which may have affected identity formation and contributed to their incarceration.

RESOURCES

As discussed previously, based on the multifinality principle (e.g., Cicchetti & Toth, 2009), significant individual variation is expected in identity trajectories within high-risk groups, with some young people who are at high risk for following problematic trajectories toward identity formation beating the odds and instead following more positive pathways. This diversity in outcomes suggests that certain resources contribute to youth's positive adaptation despite the adversity in their lives (Cicchetti & Rogosch, 2002; Masten & Tellegen, 2012). The role of two key resources that have been shown to predict individual differences in identity formation will be examined and discussed through the lens of the risk and resilience framework. These are the quality of parent–adolescent relationships and personal agency.

The family has been extensively studied as a context for identity development (e.g., Grotevant, 1987; Koepke & Denissen, 2012). Parents who allow their adolescent children to express their individuality within the context of a warm and caring relationship, thus addressing their children's needs both for individuality and belongingness, support their ability to successfully negotiate the challenges of identity formation (Grotevant, 1987). For example, parents who provide structure and follow their late adolescent children's daily activities while at the same time providing emotional support had children higher on identity achievement (vs. identity confusion) (Sartor & Youniss, 2002).

As Côté (2009) argued, authoritarian parenting, characterized by attempts to overcontrol the adolescent, and permissive parenting, characterized by a tendency to undercontrol and/or neglect the adolescent, do not provide the foundation to practice exploration of identity alternatives and learn how to self-regulate behavior. Instead, authoritative parenting, characterized by a moderate degree of connectedness with parents and reflecting a shared affection and respect for the young person's individuality, provides the secure ground from which adolescents can work through identity issues.

Parents also play a critical role in the development of narrative skills in their children (Reese, Jack, & While, 2010). Early conversations between parents and their children about the latter's everyday personal events are the foundation for learning how to make meaning of these events and how to go beyond the plot of the story to explore what the story reveals about the self.

Koepke and Denissen (2012) conceptualized parents and children as two interrelated identity systems. They argued that for parents to be able to leave room for their adolescent children to express their individuality while at the same time providing acceptance and warmth (both necessary for positive identity development) requires that they themselves are satisfied with the opportunities they had in life and with the choices they made.

The connection between autonomy-supportive parenting and identity processes may be mediated by adolescents' personal agency (Soenens & Vansteenkiste, 2005). Personal agency is an individual-level attribute that has been consistently linked with individual differences in identity formation (e.g., Schwartz, Côté, & Arnett, 2005). It refers to the sense that individuals are responsible for their decisions, their actions, and their life course, as well as for their outcomes. As such, it is a central component of individualized identity development.

This concept has been variously operationalized. For example, Schwartz et al. (2005) operationalized it as self-esteem, purpose in life, ego strength, and internal locus of control. Such a composite measure of agency they found to be positively related to exploration, flexible commitment, and deliberate choice making and negatively to avoidance and aimlessness. Both agentic and less agentic individuals explored various life alternatives. However, they differed in the quality of their exploration. The former explored in a coherently organized and systematic way, whereas the latter explored in an unguided and aimless way that led them to further identity confusion. These results held equally across three American ethnic groups studied (non-Hispanic whites, non-Hispanic blacks, and Hispanics).

Similarly, agentic characteristics are central to exploring an event in depth and to deciding what it signifies for the life story (McAdams & McLean, 2013). Thus, individuals who exhibit higher identity maturity tend to provide narratives of challenging life events that (a) reflect agency (focus on accomplishment and on the ability to control one's fate) and self-reflection (evidence of increasing awareness of their thoughts and feelings); (b) reveal an active and engaged effort to explore, reflect on, or analyze the difficult experience; and (c) conclude with a positive resolution and closure (McAdams & McLean, 2013, see also Syed & Azmitia, 2010; Pals, 2006).

The presentation and discussion of potential risks and resources for positive identity development reveals that, even though the different parts of the puzzle that will allow researchers to examine identity development through the lens of a risk and resilience framework exist, there is scant evidence regarding their interrelationship, both concurrently and across time. Thus, an attempt at a definition of positive identity formation, although value-laden, was possible, and some key factors that may positively or negatively independently contribute to group and individual differences in identity trajectories were identified.

It is not clear whether these resources function as promotive (main effect on identity outcome) or protective (interaction between risk and resource differentially predicts identity outcome) factors (Masten, 2013) for identity formation when the individual lives under adversity. Furthermore, there is a paucity of studies regarding the dynamic covariation, for example, between risks and identity outcomes (Obradović et al., 2012). Such studies are important because most risks are not static but dynamic processes that change over time. Thus, they would allow us to answer questions such as "How does initial level of, and change in, risk relate to initial level and change in identity outcomes"? Another example would be studies focusing on the dynamic interplay over time between adaptation with respect to other developmental tasks (e.g. academic achievement) or between individual resources (e.g. personal agency) and identity processes in high risk versus low risk groups that are critical for understanding whether the direction of influence is similar in such groups. These studies would require longitudinal designs with repeated measures not only of identity processes and outcomes but also of risks and resources (Masten, 2013; Obradović et al., 2012).

Identity as a Resource for Future Adaptation

Identity formation was treated in the previous section as a developmental task, and different contextual and individual-level influences that may account for group and individual differences in the negotiation of this task were examined. However, the quality of resolution of this age-salient developmental task is expected in turn to influence the way future developmental tasks are negotiated (Bronfenbrenner & Morris, 2006; Cicchetti & Rogosch, 2002; Masten, 2012). Thus, positive identity formation may itself serve as a resource for future adaptation with respect to other, related, core developmental tasks.

Addressing the identity question "Who am I?," which requires connecting one's reconstructed past with one's current self, guides young people to imagine their future; that is, to set goals for the future. According to the lifespan model of motivation, personal goals, which are part of the identity formation process, function as motivational forces guiding adolescents' planning, strategy construction, behavior, and identification of opportunities aimed at reaching their attainment (e.g., Nurmi, 2004; Salmela-Aro, 2009; Shulman & Nurmi, 2010). Therefore they are important, particularly during the transition from adolescence to emerging adulthood, in the way young people make choices and select different directions for their future lives. They actually serve as a compass that helps chart their lifespan and directs the way they spend their time and invest their energy.

Longitudinal studies have shown that personal goals for the future predict actual adaptation at later stages and are related to educational, occupational, and family-related trajectories (e.g., Nurmi, 2004). For example, Nurmi, Salmela-Aro, and Koivisto (2002) found that young people who appraised their education-related goals in vocational school as important were less likely to be unemployed after graduation. Similarly, Salmela-Aro and Nurmi (1997) found that emerging adults' family-related goals predicted their subsequent decision to marry or live in cohabitation relationships. In contrast, self-focused, existential type goals predicted subsequent negative life events, such as the breaking up of an intimate relationship.

A number of longitudinal studies conducted from the narrative identity perspective have examined the effect of different aspects of identity, expressed through narratives of negative life events, on their participants' quality of future adaptation and psychological well-being. The formal characteristics of the narratives (e.g., coherence of narrative), the content of the narratives concerning the past event, the exploration of its meaning for the self and its connection with the current self, and the personal characteristics of the narrator (e.g., agency) that are reflected in his or her narratives were all shown to be important predictors of individual differences in future adaptation.

Hauser and Allen (2007) followed adolescents who, between the ages of thirteen and sixteen years, were committed to a psychiatric hospital for a period of two to twelve months, into their young adult years. These adolescents had been diagnosed as having disruptive behavior disorders, mood disorders, and personality disorders. They also included a sample of volunteers from a freshman class of a local high school. Using a profile definition based on the clinical and normative samples' level of ego development, attachment coherence, close relationships, and social competence, they identified nine resilient young adults who were now functioning in the upper fiftieth percentile of all former patients and same-age nonclinical adolescents. They examined patients' narratives, which were embedded in interviews taken between the ages of fourteen to seventeen years, to look for clues in how they made sense of their path and their stay in the psychiatric hospital. They found that the narratives of the nine resilient adolescents reflected a higher sense of agency, self-reflection, and ability to recruit and retain relationships, especially with mentors, than did the narratives of the less well-adapted adolescents and were characterized by increasing coherence and diminished passive discourse over time.

In a long-term longitudinal study, Pals (2006) examined the narratives of difficult life experiences provided by women at age fifty-two. They found that adults who at age twenty-one and fifty-two engaged in an open (vs. defensive) style of coping were more likely to actively explore the meaning and impact of a difficult identity-challenging experience in terms of its potential to enrich and transform the self and to provide a coherent positive resolution, which in turn predicted higher identity maturity (defined as the level of awareness and cognitive complexity one brings to self-understanding and affective experience) and higher subjective well-being (defined as the sense of feeling good about oneself and one's life) at age sixty-two.

Ball and Chandler (1989), in a cross-sectional study, compared the way institutionalized adolescents at varying degrees of risk to suicide and a normative sample of adolescents drawn from public schools reasoned about their own personal continuity over time. They found that the vast majority of highly suicidal adolescents were completely unable to understand how they could change over time in important ways and still continue to be themselves. In contrast, nonsuicidal institutionalized adolescents presented more adequate, but still relatively immature, arguments in favor of self-continuity in spite of change, and the normal controls presented more mature arguments, mostly resting on the assumption that one's past, present, and future lives are all linked together. The authors argued, based on strong theoretical grounds, that having developed a sense that one's self is persistent in time is foundational to any conception of self worth having (Chandler et al., 2003). However, the results do not warrant the firm conclusion that identity continuity problems are the cause of self-destructive behaviors because it is conceivable that suicidal tendencies actually function as a risk factor for identity development.

Finally, the contents of adolescent identity have also been linked to future adaptation. For example, Barber, Eccles, and Stone (2001), in an ingenious study, asked late adolescents to indicate which of five characters (the Princess, the Jock, the Brain, the Basket Case, or the Criminal) of the movie The Breakfast Club were most like them. They found that these adolescents' social identity choices predicted both levels and longitudinal patterns in substance use, education and work outcomes, and psychological adjustment during the emerging adulthood years. In general, adolescents who chose the Jock or the Brain identity were better adjusted, and those who chose the Criminal identity worst.

The findings in this section reveal that different aspects of identity formation predict individual differences in future adaptation with respect to core developmental tasks. However, to examine whether identity functions as a promotive or protective factor for adaptation in the context of adversity, in addition to testing for main effects of the resource (here identity) on adaptation, the effect of the interplay between risks and identity on future adaptation needs also to be examined.

For example, results from Project Competence, a longitudinal study of resilience spanning more than twenty years (see Masten & Tellegen, 2012), revealed that a small number of individuals who grew up with chronic adversity showed dramatic improvements in competence over the transition to adulthood. Planfulness, future motivation, and autonomy, attributes related to identity formation, were among the resources that predicted their change from maladaptive to resilient status (Masten et al., 2004). The young people who between emerging and early adulthood showed resilience differed significantly on these attributes from their peers who were already competent by emerging adulthood and also from their peers who remained maladaptive. Thus, these attributes played a protective role for these adolescents' adaptation.

Another longitudinal study that also tested for the protective role of the resource (ethnic identification) on adaptation (academic achievement) under conditions of risk (perceived discrimination) found that as ethnic identification increased, greater perceived discrimination was related to smaller decreases in academic achievement (Wong et al., 2003).

Following this line of thought, a very interesting argument that has been advanced by identity researchers regarding the adaptation under adverse conditions of individuals with achieved versus foreclosed identity status can be examined from a risk and resilience point of view (e.g., Schwartz et al., 2011). As mentioned earlier, both statuses are related to psychological well-being, as well as to other indices of positive functioning (e.g., Luyckx,

Schwartz, Berzonsky, et al., 2008; Meeus et al., 1999). However, it is argued that individuals with an achieved identity, in contrast to individuals with a foreclosed identity, have the personal internal resources (a sense of purpose, self-direction, autonomy, inner agency) that will allow them to better and more flexibly adapt if life's conditions change abruptly (e.g., Schwartz et al., 2011). In risk and resilience terms, achieved versus foreclosed identity would moderate the relationship between risk (the stressful, negative life condition) and adaptation. It would be expected, if this hypothesis is true, that under low-risk conditions individuals with achieved and foreclosed identities would not differ in their adaptation but that under high-risk conditions achieved individuals would be better adapted than foreclosed individuals or else that achieved identity would have a special role for adaptation under high-risk conditions.

Conclusion

This chapter examined identity development through the lens of the risk and resilience framework. Identity development was considered to be a core developmental task of the adolescent (Erikson, 1968) and emerging adulthood years (Arnett, 2000), pertinent to self-development (McCormick et al., 2011; Sroufe et al., 2005). It was examined from both the identity status and narrative identity perspectives in developmental context as an outcome, as well as a possible influence on adolescents' subsequent quality of adaptation with respect to other developmental tasks, psychological well-being, and mental health.

The identity development literature mainly contributes to the risk and resilience framework, first, by offering a basis on which to define positive identity outcomes, processes, and trajectories, and, second, by providing a detailed description of identity trajectories.

The formation of a secure, coherent, and integrated identity that offers a sense of sameness and continuity is a positive identity outcome. Status theorists argue that this result is achieved through active exploration, which leads the person to make some firm commitments. The sine qua non status of active exploration for positive identity development was critically discussed, and it was argued that the optimal endpoint may be to "have an identity," independently of whether this is achieved through free choice or conformity. Narrative theorists, conversely, focus on the stories people tell about their lives. Individuals construct and internalize an evolving and integrative life story. They consider identity to be such an internalized life story.

Significant individual variation in the processes of exploration, commitment, and telling stories, and their longitudinal interrelationship, may account for individual differences in identity development. The status perspective currently captures more fully than the narrative perspective the developmental shifts and nuances in the interplay over time of exploration and commitment. However, even though the identity status literature has provided detailed maps of the different identity formation trajectories, less emphasis has been placed on identifying who follows positive identity trajectories and who follows less optimal ones and, more importantly, in accounting for such group and individual differences.

The risk and resilience perspective also contributes to the identity development literature because it provides a developmental conceptual framework that allows a contextualized, process-oriented, and dynamic approach to explaining group and individual differences in identity trajectories. According to this developmental framework, the formation of an integrated and coherent identity is considered to be both a developmental goal during the periods of adolescence and emerging adulthood and a predictor of future adaptation with respect to other developmental goals. When individual differences in identity development are examined through the lens of the risk and resilience developmental model, one can address currently rarely addressed key questions, such as "who follows a positive identity trajectory and why?"

Even though both the status and narrative perspectives have examined different types of risks, as well as potential personal and contextual resources, for identity development, there is a dearth of studies focusing on the effect of the interplay between risks and resources on identity formation, both concurrently and over time, which is critical for understanding individual differences in developmental trajectories. The concepts and principles of the risk and resilience perspective offer the tools that allow researchers to frame such questions. Finally, this framework brings into the forefront the important role of individuals' adaptive history in understanding the identity trajectory they take. Thus, the identity development and the risk and resilience literatures complement each other, and their integration provides a more complete description and explanation of interindividual differences in intraindividual identity development.

References

Arnett, J. J. (2000). Emerging Adulthood: A theory of development from the late teens through the twenties. *American Psychologist, 55,* 469–480.

Ball, L., & Chandler, M. J. (1989). Identity formation in suicidal and non-suicidal youth: The role of self-continuity. *Development and Psychopathology, 1*(3), 257–275.

Barber, B. L., Eccles, J. S., & Stone, M. R. (2001). Whatever happened to the Jock, the Brain, and the Princess? Young adult pathways linked to adolescent activity involvement and social identity. *Journal of Adolescent Research, 16* (5), 429–455.

Bosma, H. A., & Kunnen, E. S. (2001). Determinants and mechanisms in ego identity development: A review and synthesis. *Developmental Research, 21,* 39–66.

Boyce, W. T., & Ellis, B. J. (2005). Biological sensitivity to context: An evolutionary- developmental theory of the origins and functions of stress reactivity. *Development and Psychopathology, 17,* 271–301.

Boyce, W. T., Frank, E., Jensen, P. S., Kessler, R. C., Nelson, C. A., & Steinberg, L. (1998). Social context in developmental psychopathology: Recommendation for future research from MacArthur network on psychopathology and development. *Development and Psychopathology, 10* (2), 143–164.

Bronfenbrenner, U., & Morris, P. A. (2006). The bioecological model of human development. In R. M. Lerner (Ed.), *Handbook of child psychology. Vol. 1: Theoretical models of human development* (pp. 793–828). New Jersey: John Wiley & Sons.

Chandler, M. J., Lalonde, C. E., Sokol, B. W., & Hallett, D. (2003). Personal persistence, identity, and suicide: A study of Native and non-Native North American adolescents. *Monographs for the Society for Research in Child Development, serial No. 273, Vol. 68* (2), i–138.

Cicchetti, D., & Rogosch, F. A. (2002). A developmental psychopathology perspective on adolescence. *Journal of Consulting and Clinical Psychology, 70* (1), 6–20.

Cicchetti, D., & Toth, S. L. (2009). The past achievements and future promises of developmental psychopathology: The coming of age of a discipline. *Journal of Child Psychology and Psychiatry, 50* (1–2), 16–25.

Cicchetti, D., & Valentino, K. (2006). An ecological- transactional perspective on child maltreatment: Failure of the average expectable environment and its influence on child development. In D. Cicchetti, & D. J. Cohen (Eds.), *Developmental psychopathology. Vol. 3: Risk, disorder, and adaptation* (pp. 129–201). New Jersey: John Wiley & Sons.

Côté, J. E. (2009). Identity formation and self- development in adolescence. In R. M. Lerner, & L. Steinberg (Eds.), *Handbook of adolescent psychology. Vol. 1: Individual bases of adolescent development* (pp. 266–304). New Jersey: John Wiley & Sons.

Côté, J. E., & Levine, C. (1988). A critical examination of the ego identity status paradigm. *Developmental Review, 8,* 147–184.

Cramer, P. (2004). Identity change in adulthood: The contribution of defense mechanisms and life experiences. *Journal of Research in Personality, 38,* 280–316.

Crocetti, E., Rubini, M., & Meeus, W. (2008). Capturing the dynamics of identity formation in various ethnic groups: Development and validation of a three-dimensional model. *Journal of Adolescence, 31,* 207–222.

Eccles, J. S., & Roeser, R. W. (2009). Schools, academic motivation, and stage-environment fit. In R. M. Lerner, & L. Steinberg (Eds.), *Handbook of adolescent psychology. Vol. 1: Individual bases of adolescent development* (pp. 404–434). New Jersey: John Wiley & Sons.

Epstein, S. (1973). The self- concept revisited. Or a theory of a theory. *American Psychologist, 28* (5), 404–416.

Erikson, E. (1968). *Identity: Youth, and crisis.* New York: Norton.

Garcia-Coll, C., & Marks, A. K. (2012). *The immigrant paradox in children and adolescents: Is becoming American a developmental risk?* Washington, DC: American Psychological Association.

Garmezy, N. (1974). The study of competence in children at risk for severe psychopathology. In E. J. Anthony & C. Koupernik (Eds.), *The child in his family. Vol. 3: Children at psychiatric risk* (pp. 77–97). New York: Wiley.

Grotevant, H. D. (1987). Toward a process model of identity formation. *Journal of Adolescent Research, 2,* 203–222.

Habermas, T., & Bluck, S. (2000). Getting a life: The development of the life story in adolescence. *Psychological Bulletin, 126,* 748–769.

Harter, S. (1998). The effects of child abuse on the self- system. *Journal of Aggression, Maltreatment and Trauma, 2* (1), 147–169.

Harter, S. (2006). The self. In N. Eisenberg (Ed.), *Handbook of child psychology. Vol. 3: Social, emotional, and personality development* (pp. 505–570). Hoboken, New Jersey: John Wiley & Sons.

Hauser, S. T., & Allen, J. P. (2007). Overcoming adversity in adolescence: Narratives of resilience. *Psychoanalytic Inquiry: A Topical Journal for Mental Health Professionals, 26*(4), 549–576.

Kağitçibaşi, C. (2007). *Family, self, and human development across cultures. Theory and applications.* Mahwah, New Jersey: Lawrence Erlbaum Associates.

Kinney, D. A. (1993). From nerds to normals: The recovery of identity among adolescents from middle school to high school. *Sociology of Education, 66,* 21–40.

Klimstra, T. A., Crocetti, E., Hale, W. W., Kolman, A. I., Fortanier, E., & Meeus, W. H. (2011). Identity formation in juvenile delinquents and clinically referred youth. *Revue Europeenne de Psychologie Appliquee, 61,* 123–130.

Klimstra, T. A., Hale, W. W., Raaijmakers, Q. A., Branje, S. J., & Meeus, W. (2010). Identity formation in adolescence: Change or stability? *Journal of Youth and Adolescence, 39,* 150–162.

Koepke, S., & Denissen, J. A. J. (2012). Dynamics of identity development and separation–individuation in parent–child relationships during adolescence and emerging adulthood—A conceptual integration, *Developmental Review, 32, 1,* 67–88.

Kroger, J., & Marcia, J. E. (2011). The identity statuses: Origins, meanings, and interpretations. In S. J. Schwartz, K. Luyckx, & V. L. Vignoles (Eds.), *Handbook of identity theory and research. Vol. 1: Structures and Processes* (pp. 31–53). New York: Springer.

Kroger, J., Martinussen, M., & Marcia, J. E. (2010). Identity status change during adolescence and young adulthood: A meta-analysis. *Journal of Adolescence, 33*(5), 683–698.

Lerner, J. V., Phelps, E., Forman, Y., & Bowers, E. P. (2009). Positive youth development. In R. M. Lerner, & L. Steinberg (Eds.), *Handbook of adolescent psychology. Vol. 1: Individual bases of adolescent development* (pp. 404–434). Hoboken, New Jersey: John Wiley & Sons.

Lerner, R. M. (2006). Developmental science, developmental systems, and contemporary theories. In R. M. Lerner (Ed.), *Handbook of child psychology. Vol. 1: Theoretical models of human development* (pp. 1–17). Hoboken, NJ: Wiley.

Luthar, S. S. (2006). Resilience in development: A synthesis of research across five decades. In D. Cicchetti, & D. J. Cohen (Eds.), *Developmental psychopathology* (2nd ed., vol. *3*, pp. 739–795). Hoboken, NJ: Wiley.

Luyckx, K., Goossens, L., & Soenens, B. (2006). A developmental contextual perspective on identity construction in emerging adulthood: Change dynamics in commitment formation and commitment evaluation. *Developmental Psychology, 42*, 366–380.

Luyckx, K., Schwartz, S. J., Berzonsky, M. D., Soenens, B., Vansteenkiste, M., Smits, I., et al. (2008). Capturing ruminative exploration: Extending the four- dimensional model of identity formation in late adolescence. *Journal of Research in Personality, 42*, 58–82.

Luyckx, K., Seiffge-Krenke, I., Schwartz, S. J., Goossens, L., Weets, I., Hendrieckx, C., et al. (2008). Identity development, coping, and adjustment in emerging adults with a chronic illness: The sample case of type 1 diabetes. *Journal of Adolescent Health, 43*, 451–458.

Marcia, J. E. (1980). Identity in adolescence. In J. Adelson (Ed.), *Handbook of adolescent psychology* (pp. 159–187). New York: John Wiley & Sons.

Markus, H. R., & Kitayama, S. (1991). Culture and the self: Implications for cognition, emotion, and motivation. *Psychological Review, 98*, 224—253.

Masten, A. (2013). Risk and resilience in development. In P. D. Zelazo (Ed.), *Oxford handbook of developmental psychology*. New York: Oxford University Press.

Masten, A. S. (2011). Resilience in children threatened by extreme adversity: Frameworks for research, practice, and translational synergy. *Development and Psychopathology, 23*, 493–506.

Masten, A. S., Burt, K. B., & Coatsworth, J. D. (2006). Competence and psychopathology in development. In D. Cicchetti, & D. J. Cohen (Eds.), *Developmental psychopathology* (2 ed., vol. *3*, pp. 696–738). New York: Wiley.

Masten, A. S., Burt, K., Roisman, G. I., Obradović, J., Long, J. D., & Tellegen, A. (2004). Resources and resilience in the transition to adulthood: Continuity and change. *Development and Psychopathology, 16*, 1071–1094.

Masten, A. S., Liebkind, K., & Hernandez, D. J. (2012). *Realizing the potential of immigrant youth*. Cambridge: Cambridge University Press.

Masten, A. S., & Motti-Stefanidi, F. (2009). Understanding and promoting resilience in children: Promotive and protective processes in schools. In T. Gutkin & C. Reynolds (Eds.), *The handbook of school psychology* (4th ed., pp. 721–738). Hoboken, NJ: Wiley.

Masten, A. S., & Tellegen, A. (2012). Resilience in developmental psychopathology: Contributions of the project competence longitudinal study. *Development and Psychopathology, 24*, 345–361.

McAdams, D. P. (2001). The psychology of life stories. *Review of General Psychology, 5*, 100–122.

McAdams, D. P., & McLean, K. C. (2013). Narrative identity. *Current Directions in Psychological Science, 22*(3), 233–238. doi: 10.1177/0963721413475622

McCormick, C. M., Kuo, S. L., & Masten, A. S. (2011). Developmental tasks across the lifespan. In K. L. Fingerman, C. Berg, J. Smith, & T. C. Antonucci (Eds.), *The handbook of lifespan development* (pp. 117–140). New York: Springer.

McLean, K. C., & Pasupathi, M. (2012). Processes of identity development: Where am I and how I got there. *Identity: An International Journal of Theory and Research. 12*(1), 8–28.

McLean, K. C., & Pratt, M. W. (2006). Life's little (and big) lessons: Identity status and meaning-making in the turning point narratives of emerging adults. *Developmental Psychology, 42*, 714–722.

Meeus, W. (2011). The study of adolescent identity formation 2000–2010: A review of longitudinal research. *Journal of Research on Adolescence, 21* (1), 75–94.

Meeus, W., Iedema, J., Helsen, M., & Vollebergh, W. (1999). Patterns of adolescent identity development: Review of literature and longitudinal analysis. *Developmental Review, 19*, 419–461.

Meeus, W., van de Schoot, R., Keijsers, L., Schwartz, S. J., & Branje, S. (2010). On the progression and stability of adolescent identity formation. A five-wave longitudinal study in early-to-middle and middle-to-late adolescence. *Child Development, 81*, 1565–1581.

Moffitt, T. E. (2006). Life-course persistent versus adolescence-limited antisocial behavior. In D. Cicchetti, & D. J. Cohen (Eds.), *Developmental psychopathology (2nd ed.). Vol. 3, Risk, disorder, and adaptation* (pp. 570–598). Hoboken, New Jersey: John Wiley & Sons.

Motti-Stefanidi, F., Berry, J., Chryssochoou, X., Sam, D. L., & Phinney, J. (2012). Positive immigrant youth adaptation in context: Developmental, acculturation, and social psychological perspectives. In A. S. Masten, K. Liebkind, & D. J. Hernandez (Eds.), *Realizing the potential of immigrant youth*. Cambridge: Cambridge University Press.

Nurmi, J. -E. (2004). Socialization and self- development. Channeling, selection, adjustment, and reflection. In R. M. Lerner, & L. Steinberg (Eds.), *Handbook of adolescent psychology* (2nd ed., pp. 85–124). New Jersey: John Wiley & Sons.

Nurmi, J. -E., Salmela-Aro, K, & Koivisto, P. (2002). Goal importance, related achievement-beliefs and emotions during the transition from vocational school to work: Antecedents and consequences. *Journal of Vocational Behavior, 60*, 241–261.

Obradović, J., Shaffer, A., & Masten, A. (2012). Risk and adversity in developmental psychopathology: Progress and future directions. In L. C. Mayes, & M. Lewis (Eds.), *The Cambridge handbook of environment in human development*. (pp. 35–57). New York: Cambridge University Press.

Ogbu, J. U. (1993). Differences in cultural frame of reference. *International Journal of Behavioral Development, 16* (3), 483–506.

Oyserman, D., Gant, L., & Ager, J. (1995). A socially contextualized model of African American identity: Possible selves and school persistence. *Journal of Personality and Social Psychology, 69*, 1216–1232.

Pals, J. L. (2006). Narrative identity processing of difficult life experiences: Pathways of personality development and positive self-transformation in adulthood. *Journal of Personality, 74*(4), 1079–1109.

Phillips, T. M., & Pittman, J. F. (2003). Identity processes in poor adolescents: Exploring the linkages between economic disadvantage and the primary task of adolescence. *Identity: An International Journal of Theory and Research, 3*(2), 115–129.

Phinney, J. (2006). Ethnic identity exploration in emerging adulthood. In J. Arnett & J. Tanner (Eds.), *Emerging adults in American* (pp. 117–134). Washington, DC: American Psychological Association.

Phinney, J. S., & Chavira, V. (1992). Ethnic identity and self-esteem: An exploratory longitudinal study. *Journal of Adolescence, 15,* 271–281.

Reese, E., Jack, F., & White, N. (2010). Origins of adolescents' autobiographical memories. *Child Development, 25,* 352–367.

Rutter, M. (1987). Psychosocial resilience and protective mechanisms. *American Journal of Orthopsychiatry, 57,* 316–331.

Salmela-Aro, K. (2009). Personal goals and well-being during critical life transitions: The 4 C's —channeling, choice, co-agency and compensation. *Advances in Life Course Research. 14,* 63–73.

Salmela-Aro, K., & Nurmi, J-E. (1997). Goal contents, well-being, and life context during transition to university: A longitudinal study. *International Journal of Behavioral Development, 20, 3,* 471–491.

Sartor, C. E., & Younnis, J. (2002). The relationship between positive parental involvement and identity achievement in adolescence. *Adolescence, 37,* 221–234.

Schwartz, S. J., Beyers, W., Luyckx, K., Soenens, B., Zamboanga, B. L., Forthun, L. F., et al. (2011). Examining the light and dark sides of emerging adults' identity: A study of identity status differences in positive and negative psychosocial functioning. *Journal of Youth and adolescence, 40,* 839–859.

Schwartz, S. J., Côté, J. E., & Arnett, J. J. (2005). Identity and agency in emerging adulthood: Two developmental routes in the individualization process. *Youth and Society, 37,* 201–229.

Schwartz, S. J., Montgomery, M. J., & Briones, E. (2006). The role of identity in acculturation among immigrant people: Theoretical propositions, empirical questions, and applied recommendations. *Human Development, 49,* 1–30.

Soenens, B., & Vansteenkiste, M. (2005). Antecedents and outcomes of self-determination in three life-domains: The role of parents' and teachers' autonomy support. *Journal of Youth and Adolescence, 34,* 589–604.

Shulman, S., & Nurmi, J. E. (2010). Understanding emerging adulthood from a goal-setting perspective. In S. Shulman & J.-E. Nurmi (Eds.), *The role of goals in navigating individual lives during emerging adulthood. New Directions for Child and Adolescent Development, 130,* 1–11.

Sroufe, A. L., Egeland, B., Carlson, E. A., & Collins, A. (2005). *The development of the person. The Minnesota study risk and adaptation from birth to adulthood.* New York: The Guilford Press.

Syed, M. (2010). Developing an integrated self: Academic and ethnic identities among ethnically diverse college students. *Developmental Psychology, 46* (6), 1590–1604.

Syed, M., & Azmitia, M. (2008). A narrative approach to ethnic identity in emerging adulthood: Bringing life to the identity status model. *Developmental Psychology, 44,* 1012–1027.

Syed, M., & Azmitia, M. (2010). Narrative and ethnic identity exploration: A longitudinal account of emerging adults' ethnically-related experiences. *Developmental Psychology, 46,* 208–219.

Syed, M., & Seiffge-Krenke, I. (2012). Personality development from adolescence to emerging adulthood: Linking trajectories of ego development to the family context and identity formation. *Journal of Personality and Social Psychology,* doi: 10.1037/a0030070, 1–14.

Trzesniewski, K. H., & Donnellan, M. B. (2010). Rethinking "Generation Me": A Study of Cohort Effects From 1976–2006. *Perspectives on Psychological Science, 5*(1), 58–75.

Van Hoof, A. Raaijmakers, Q. A. W., van Beek, Y., Hale, W. W., & Aleva, L. (2008). A multi-mediation model on the relations of bullying, victimization, identity, and family with adolescent depressive symptoms. *Journal of Youth Adolescence, 37,* 772–782.

Vignoles, V. L., Schwartz, S. J., & Luyckx, K. (2011). Introduction: Toward an integrative view of identity. In S. J. Schwartz, K. Luyckx, & V. L. Vignoles (Eds.), *Handbook of identity theory and research. Vol. 1: Structures and processes* (pp. 1–27). New York: Springer.

Werner, E. E. (1993). Risk, resilience, and recovery: Perspectives from the Kauai longitudinal study. *Development and Psychopathology, 5,* 503–515.

Wong, C. A., Eccles, J. S., & Sameroff, A. J. (2003). The influence of ethnic discrimination and ethnic identification on African-Americans adolescents' school and socioemotional adjustment. *Journal of Personality, 71,* 1197–1232.

Yoder A. E. (2000). Barriers to ego identity status formation: A contextual qualification of Marcia's identity status paradigm. *Journal of Adolescence, 23,* 95–106.

CHAPTER
30
The Dynamic Role of Identity Processes in Personality Development: Theories, Patterns, and New Directions

Jennifer Pals Lilgendahl

Abstract

This chapter examines the role of identity processes (exploration, commitment, meaning-making) in personality functioning and development throughout adulthood. The chapter first addresses theoretical perspectives on personality and their implications for identity, with an emphasis on the view that identity processes are integrative and dynamic mechanisms of personality continuity and change over time. Next, empirical evidence is examined for the roles of identity processes in two distinct trajectories of personality development: adjustment and maturity. Whereas meaning-making about positive self-defining events is critical for the formation of identity commitments and development of a well-adjusted personality in emerging adulthood, negative events and their potential for transformative self-growth are critical for the development of maturity during midlife. The chapter then addresses new directions for research on identity and personality, focusing on how personality traits may moderate the optimal path of identity development and how intersections among identity domains are essential to an understanding of the whole person.

Key Words: identity processes, personality development, positive and negative events, emerging adulthood, midlife, adjustment, maturity, traits as moderators, identity intersections, culture

Although identity development is a universal developmental task, there are pronounced individual differences in how people go about this process and in the outcomes that result. These individual differences are intimately tied to personality functioning. Indeed, no complete accounting of personality or personality development can proceed without a consideration of identity, nor can the study of identity development afford to ignore connections with personality differences. In this chapter, my goal is to examine closely these connections between personality and identity, with the specific aim of articulating how identity, as a collection of ongoing and interrelated psychological processes, operates as a dynamic and integrative force in how personality develops over time (Helson & Srivastava, 2001; Roberts & Caspi, 2003).

The term "identity" has been used in a variety of ways. The definition employed in this chapter is the neo-Eriksonian conceptualization of identity as an enduring theory or set of meanings that one constructs about oneself and that provides a sense of continuity, integration, and purposeful connection to the adult world (e.g., McAdams, 2001). Although the specific processes involved in these identity functions are most certainly quite diverse and varied, I focus here on those drawn from two well-known developmental theories, the *identity status* approach (e.g., Grotevant, 1987; Luyckx, Goossens, Soenens, & Beyers, 2006; Marcia, 1966; Meeus, 2011) and the *narrative identity* approach (McAdams, 2001; McLean, 2008a; Singer, 2004), and how the specific processes identified in these two approaches may be dynamically related to one another in personality development (McLean & Pasupathi, 2012).

This chapter is divided into three sections. The first section addresses the question of what, exactly, we mean by the term "personality" and the implications of our definitions and theories for how we conceptualize the personality–identity relationship. The second section offers a selective review of the literature on the role of identity processes in personality development in both emerging adulthood and midlife, with a specific focus on the importance of both positive and negative life experiences in this relationship. In the third section, I identify some questions pertaining to the dynamic connection between identity and personality that beg for more in-depth, systematic examination. Specifically, I address the question of how personality traits may moderate processes of identity development, such that what is optimal and effective may differ in important ways across people, and the question of how processes in different content domains of identity interact with one another to affect personality development.

What Do We Mean When We Say "Personality"? Definitions, Theories, and Their Implications for Identity

Personality is a notoriously broad, complex, and difficult to define construct, which makes it no surprise that how we go about defining and measuring it has been an enduring preoccupation in the field (Barenbaum & Winter, 2008). In this section, I draw from the recent integrative model presented by McAdams and Pals (2006), in which personality is conceptualized as a dynamic and developing system that is both biologically and culturally shaped and incorporates three distinct levels of functioning—dispositional traits, characteristic adaptations, and narrative identity. Here, I briefly consider each level and its implications for how we understand the personality–identity relationship.

Level 1: Personality as Traits

In its narrowest definition, which is also the most dominant usage of the term in the literature, personality refers to basic traits or stable dispositional differences in patterns of thought, feeling, and behavior. Indeed, for many researchers, the term "personality" has come to be used as shorthand to refer to the traits of the five-factor model or the "Big Five," which are extraversion, agreeableness, conscientiousness, neuroticism, and openness to experience (John & Srivastava, 1999; McCrae & Costa, 1999). Trait approaches have traditionally emphasized the biological basis of personality and the stability of personality over change. The most extreme contemporary example of this perspective is McCrae and Costa's (1999) *five-factor theory* (FFT). According to FFT, the five core traits are basic biological tendencies that may affect the development and expression of identity-relevant constructs such as self-concept, attitudes, and goals. However, in this theory, traits are not themselves affected by any dynamic factors (e.g., development, context, etc.) outside of their biological roots. Thus, when personality is conceptualized in this manner, identity is simply one of many possible manifestations of stable traits. For example, one manifestation of the trait of openness to experience may be identity exploration (Tesch & Cameron, 1987), in that adults who are higher on openness are, as a function of this disposition, more likely than those low on openness to explore many identity possibilities.

Although it is most certainly the case that stable traits have a shaping influence on processes of identity development, the shortcoming of FFT is that it does not adequately capture the more dynamic and contextualized view of traits and their development that has emerged across many longitudinal studies of adulthood in recent years (e.g., Helson & Srivastava, 2001; Neyer & Asendorpf, 2001; Pals, 1999; Roberts, Caspi, & Moffitt, 2003). This perspective is best represented theoretically by the cumulative continuity model of personality development (Roberts & Caspi, 2003). In this model, Roberts and Caspi (2003) maintain the central importance of traits for how we define personality, but they also acknowledge that trait stability and trait change are the result of dynamic interactions with the environment that are actively mediated by processes of identity development. In terms of the continuity of traits, as adults begin to form an identity and structure their lives around that identity, the social environment serves to stabilize the very personality traits that brought them there (e.g., Roberts et al., 2003). For example, a young adult who is quite introverted may consider many identity options and decide on accounting as a good career path for her; once she becomes an accountant, her career identity will actively reinforce her introverted personality. In this way, the presence of stable identity structures may help to explain the increase in the relative stability of traits in adulthood (Caspi, Roberts, & Shiner, 2005). Identity processes also promote personality continuity over time by mediating the impact of traits on important life outcomes (e.g., Helson & Srivastava, 2001; Pals, 2006a).

Roberts and Caspi's (2003) theoretical perspective further asserts that, just as identity processes promote the continuity of traits, they can also cause change in personality traits. Indeed, not only do traits change, they do so in some more than others and in different ways for different people, depending on their life experiences and the implications of these life experiences for identity development. Going back to the woman in the example, it may also be the case that the responsibilities of her new job will require more discipline and organization than was required earlier in her life, thus providing an opportunity in which behavioral change reflecting increases in the trait of conscientiousness will be rewarded. In other words, the very same identity-defining role commitment that promoted the continuity of introversion may also operate as a mechanism of change on a different trait. Indeed, increases in the trait of conscientiousness have been found to be normative in adulthood, along with decreasing neuroticism and increasing agreeableness, which is an overall pattern of increasing adjustment that is likely to be facilitated by investing identity in adult social roles, including career, relationships, and parenthood (Roberts, Wood, & Smith, 2005).

In sum, when we define personality in terms of basic traits, identity is reciprocally related to personality, in terms of being shaped by traits and in terms of playing an active role in promoting both personality stability and change over time. However, there is much more to personality than traits. The next two levels of McAdams and Pals's (2006) model—characteristic adaptations and narrative identity—serve to fill in the dynamic and contextualized details of personality and, in doing so, make identity and the specific kinds of processes involved in its development part of the definition of personality itself.

Level 2: Personality as Contextualized and Dynamic Characteristic Adaptations

Cantor (1990) argued that whereas traits constitute the "having" side of personality, there is also a "doing" side of personality, which is well-captured by the level of personality functioning McAdams and Pals (2006) call characteristic adaptations. At this level, personality includes "motives, goals, plans, strategies, values, virtues, schemas, self-images, mental representations of significant others, developmental tasks, and many other aspects of human individuality that speak to motivational, social-cognitive, and developmental concerns" (McAdams & Pals, 2006; p. 208). Thus, personality as defined at this level of analysis is more changeable, process-oriented, and contextualized than at the trait level, and it contains several types of characteristics (e.g., values, goals, self-images) that are expected to be an integral part of one's identity. Here, I consider the implications of this definition of personality for identity, from the perspective of identity as a developmental task and as a contextualized construct.

At this "doing" level of personality, a big part of what we do as humans involves active engagement with significant, age-graded development tasks, one of the most important of which is forming an identity (Erikson, 1963; Marcia, 1966; McAdams, 2001). Thus, the task of identity formation, which rises to prominence in adolescence and is critical for the transition into emerging adulthood (Arnett, this volume) becomes the central force in personality development at this stage of life. As originally conceived by Marcia (1966), healthy identity development at this stage requires two processes—exploration of various identity-defining alternatives and commitment to identity-defining choices (see Kunnen & Metz, this volume). These processes and their associated identity statuses of achievement (exploration and commitment), moratorium (exploration without commitment), foreclosure (commitment without exploration), and diffusion (neither exploration nor commitment) have been studied extensively over the past several decades (see Meeus, 2011; Crocetti & Meeus, this volume) in the context of specific identity domains (e.g., occupation, politics, relationships), as well as in overall identity. Identity achievement, in which people have explored options and formed meaningful and lasting identity commitments, is considered to be the optimal outcome, and this is supported empirically (Luyckx, Schwartz, Goossens, Soenens, & Beyers, 2008).

In general support of the identity status model, research has shown a normative progression toward increasing identity achievement with age from adolescence through the thirties (Pulkkinen & Kokko, 2000). More importantly with respect to personality, however, there are pronounced individual differences in how these processes play out for different people during this stage of life, and these differences relate to broader patterns of personality development (e.g., Luyckx, Soenens, & Goossens, 2006; Pals, 1999). Additionally, it is important to note that although it is assumed that identity formation is at its most intense during adolescence and emerging adulthood, the processes of exploration and commitment have been linked to both enduring patterns of stability (e.g., Helson & Srivastava, 2001) and dynamic processes of change in response to life events and transitions (e.g., Anthis & LaVoie, 2006; Kroger, this volume) throughout adulthood.

In contrast to basic traits, which are intentionally conceived as transcendent of specific contexts, personality at the second level of analysis is explicitly manifested within specific roles, contexts, and domains (e.g., work, parenthood, religion, etc.) in which identity becomes invested through the processes of exploration and commitment. This has important implications for thinking about identity in relation to basic traits. On the one hand, the investment of identity in contextualized adult roles has been shown to be a mechanism of trait change in adulthood, as described earlier. When traits change, they often do so through identity-mediated changes within specific role-related contexts. On the other hand, it is important to note that, from the perspective articulated by McAdams and Pals (2006), contextualized identities may become autonomous, causal units within the personality system that provide explanatory value for thinking, feeling, and behaving beyond basic traits. For example, if a woman views her role as a mother as central to her identity, this identity will have strong implications for her values, goals, and daily behaviors and will be an organizing force within her personality regardless of her basic traits.

Level 3: Personality as Story—Narrative Identity

In the third, most contextualized level of McAdams and Pals's (2006) model, personality and identity fully merge in the lifelong task of narrating a coherent and meaningful self-defining life story (McAdams, 2001; McLean, 2008a; Singer, 2004). A critical process in this theoretical approach to identity is autobiographical reasoning, which involves forming meaningful connections between past events and the present self through narration (Habermas & Bluck, 2000; Habermas & Köber, this volume). The resulting "self-event connections" carry significant themes of self-defining meaning that serve to transform and reinforce identity over time (Pasupathi, Mansour, & Brubaker, 2007). As with the identity status approach, research in this approach to identity shows normative gains in identity development with age, with increases in the amount and sophistication of patterns of autobiographical reasoning about past experiences during both adolescence (Habermas & Paha, 2001) and adulthood (Pasupathi & Mansour, 2006).

In addition to normative patterns, pronounced identity-related individual differences have been found in how adolescents and adults narrate significant events in their lives. The specific kinds of qualities that have been coded from a variety of different kinds of memory-based personal narratives include event type (e.g., Blagov & Singer, 2004); thematic content, such as the themes of agency and communion (e.g., McAdams et al., 2004); affective qualities, including resolution (Pals, 2006a) and redemption and contamination sequences (McAdams, Reynolds, Lewis, Patten, & Bowman, 2001); structural properties, including coherence (e.g., Baerger & McAdams, 1999) and complexity (McAdams et al., 2004); process-oriented qualities, such as accommodation (King, Scollon, Ramsey, & Williams, 2000) and exploratory processing (Pals, 2006a); and interpretative outcomes, such as meaning-making (McLean, 2005; Blagov & Singer, 2004), growth (Bauer, McAdams, & Sakaeda, 2005; Lilgendahl & McAdams, 2011; Pals, 2006a), and connections of self-change versus self-stability (e.g., McLean, 2008b). Research has shown that Level 1 and Level 2 characteristics relate to these narrative qualities in meaningful ways, establishing narrative identity as an integrative part of a coherent system of personality (Lilgendahl, Helson, & John, 2013; Lilgendahl, McLean, & Mansfield, 2013; McAdams et al., 2004; Moffitt & Singer, 1994).

Individual differences in narrative identity patterns have also been shown to relate to important outcomes (e.g., well-being, maturity) even after controlling for the effects of other aspects of personality, such as basic traits (e.g., Lilgendahl & McAdams, 2011). Such findings suggest that narrative identity is a distinct level of personality that cannot simply be explained or accounted for by other aspects of personality. Thus, theory and research have begun to grapple with and demonstrate a dynamic and possibly even causal role for narrative identity processes with the personality system. Sophisticated, process-oriented theories of narrative identity have emerged that focus on how our self-defining stories develop and change in social contexts (McLean, Pasupathi, & Pals, 2007) and how identity narratives, as enduring cognitive representations of self, may actively motivate goal-directed behavior (e.g., Singer & Blagov, 2004) and cause enduring identity-related changes in personality (Sutin & Robins, 2005).

In support of these theoretical advancements in narrative identity, several new short-term longitudinal studies provide vivid examples of how the narration of various kinds of significant, transformative life experiences—for example, quitting drinking or going through therapy—may facilitate patterns of behavior and personality change (Adler, 2012; Cox & McAdams, 2012; Dunlop & Tracy, 2013). For example, Cox and McAdams (2012) examined American college students' narratives of a spring break volunteer trip and found that the presence of self-transformation in the narratives was associated with an increase in volunteer behavior from before the trip extending to three months after the trip. In other words, a life experience resulted in major behavioral change (and possibly enduring personality change) through the integration of a self-transformative experience into narrative identity (see also McLean & Pasupathi, 2012). Far from being the final product of developmental processes that have already occurred, narrative identity is an active, dynamic, ever-changing causal mechanism of personality development.

In sum, McAdams and Pals's (2006) model of personality offers an inclusive definition of the distinct but also interactive levels of functioning within the personality system, the second and third of which fully integrate identity into what we mean when we say "personality." Furthermore, McAdams and Pals (2006) allow for fully reciprocal pathways of relational causality across the different levels, therefore acknowledging that whereas Level 1 traits will undoubtedly affect the identity processes at Levels 2 and 3, as suggested by FFT, it is also the case that these same identity processes have the power to shape personality through their various influences on all three levels of personality functioning, including traits. In this respect, the cumulative continuity model of Roberts and Caspi (2003) provides a very useful complement to McAdams and Pals (2006) by providing a framework for conceptualizing *how* identity processes—most notably identity exploration, identity commitment, and narrative identity processing—may actively shape personality stability and change over time. Figure 30.1 provides a visual summary of this dynamic process perspective on the identity and personality relationship, incorporating specific elements that will become relevant as specific empirical issues are addressed in the next two sections.

Tracking the Connection Between Identity Processes and Optimal Personality Development from Adolescence Through Midlife: The Role of Positive and Negative Experiences

Optimal personality development in adulthood has been conceptualized as involving two distinct trajectories: the *adjustment* trajectory, which emphasizes well-adjusted functioning in society, competence, emotional stability, and well-being, and the *maturity* trajectory, which emphasizes cognitive complexity, personal growth, emotional awareness, and wisdom (Staudinger & Kunzmann, 2005; Helson & Wink, 1987; Labouvie-Vief & Medler, 2002). The adjustment trajectory has been shown to follow a clear normative increase in adult samples and is demonstrated by average increases in the traits of conscientiousness and emotional stability between the ages of twenty and forty (Roberts & Mroczek, 2008). The most commonly used tool to assess the maturity trajectory is Loevinger's (1976; Hy & Loevinger, 1996) sentence completion test of ego development, which assesses the level of complexity with which one understands the world and self in relation to others. Although it had been assumed that ego-level change is very individual in adulthood, with no clear normative changes occurring after adolescence (Cohn, 1998), more recent data suggest that midlife may be an especially fertile time for increases in ego development (Lilgendahl, Helson, & John, 2013).

What are the roles of identity processes in these two trajectories of personality development? In other words, how do individual differences in the formation of identity relate to individual differences in the extent to which optimal personality outcomes (i.e., adjustment and maturity) are achieved? I address these questions with a specific focus on the role of positive and negative life experiences in identity development.

Identity and the Adjustment Trajectory of Personality Development in Emerging Adulthood: Building a Positive Foundation

Emerging adulthood may be broadly defined as the period between the ages of eighteen and thirty, particularly in the United States and similarly individualistic and industrialized countries. Indeed, Arnett (2000) created this unique stage of development in response to the increasingly lengthy time during which it was deemed acceptable in the United States to continue to explore possibilities prior to entering into serious adult commitments. This stage of life has significant implications for both identity development and the adjustment trajectory of personality. On the one hand, identity exploration is considered to be necessary for healthy identity development, so it would seem to be beneficial that identity exploration would be sanctioned and supported by society. On the other hand, however, research has shown that the identity

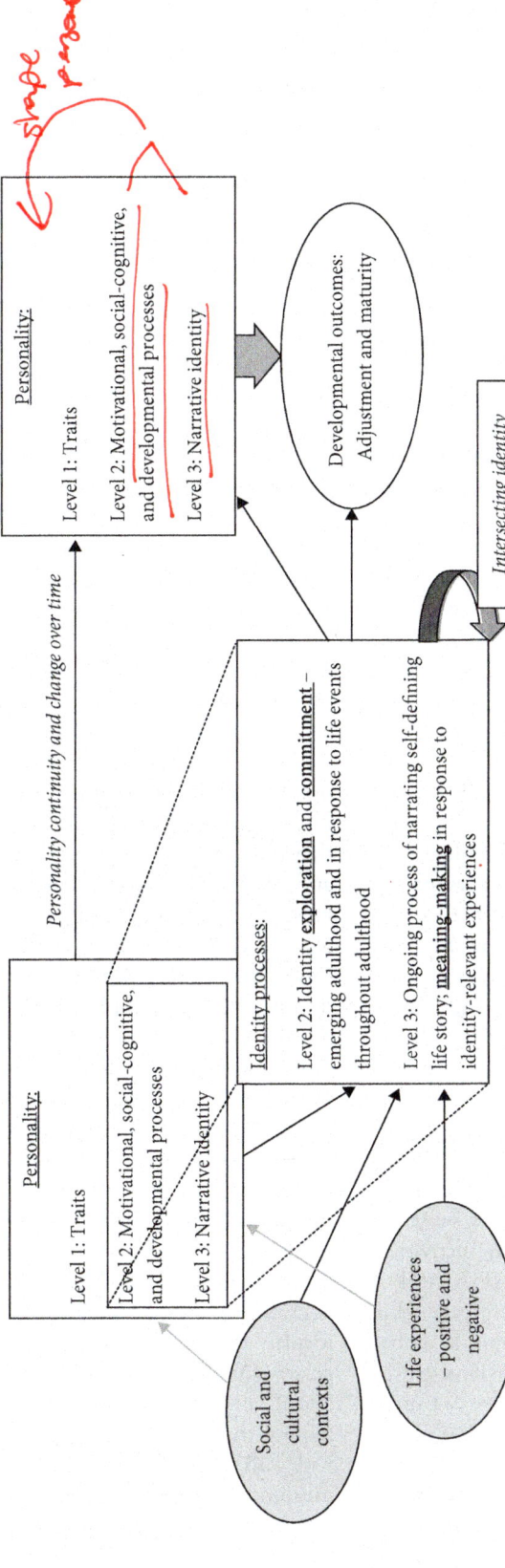

Fig. 30.1 Process model of role of identity processes in personality development over time; integrates elements of Grotevant (1987), McAdams and Pals (2006), and Roberts and Caspi (2003). Bold arrows going into and out of identity processes are the focus of this chapter. According to this model, identity processes are simultaneously part of personality (Level 2 and Level 3) and actively shape personality continuity and change over time. Social and cultural contexts and life experiences shape personality development, the effects of which are at least partly mediated through identity processes. Personality development is also assumed to be shaped by how identity processes within specific identity domains dynamically intersect with one another over time.

status of moratorium—active exploration without commitment—can be highly anxiety-provoking (Marcia, 1967; Schwartz et al., 2011), perhaps because prolonged identity questioning and the absence of clear commitments to guide one's actions and choices can create a great deal of uncertainty about oneself and one's future. Given this view of emerging adulthood, it is not surprising that personality adjustment would be relatively poor during this turbulent, transitional period. Indeed, scores on the trait of neuroticism (i.e., emotional instability, anxiety, depressive feelings, self-doubt) are (a) generally at their highest levels in late adolescence (e.g., Caspi et al., 2005), and (b) tend to decrease over the next several years, as a function of gains in identity development. For example, Luyckx, Soenens, and Goossens (2006) showed that, among college students, increases over time in two aspects of identity commitment—commitment making and identification with commitments—were associated with corresponding decreases in the trait of neuroticism. In contrast, those who showed decreases in these commitment processes along with an increase in exploration in breadth (i.e., wide consideration of identity alternatives) increased in neuroticism over time.

These findings demonstrate how individual differences in the adjustment trajectory of personality development corresponded closely with the extent to which emerging adults progress toward versus away from a committed sense of identity. The presence of solid identity-defining commitments, whether in the form of abstract goals for the future or connected to concrete roles and daily behaviors (Roberts & Caspi, 2003), provide an emotionally stabilizing structure to one's life. Indeed, identity is emotionally stabilizing because it serves to guide decisions and actions, it fuels one's sense of self-worth in the world, and it provides a sense of meaningful connection between daily activities and long-term goals and broad values (Pals, 1999; Roberts & Caspi, 2003). However, as critical as the formation of identity commitments appear to be for optimal personality development, we have yet to develop a nuanced understanding of the exact processes by which identity exploration transitions into identity commitment. One way we may be able to make deeper sense of the mechanisms involved in this transition is to integrate recent findings from the narrative identity approach.

In the narrative identity approach, identity development proceeds through a process of forming meaningful connections between past events and present self as one narrates a life story (Habermas & Köber, this volume). During emerging adulthood, when identity is first forming, one is likely to have many life experiences that inform the identity process, some of which will be self-defining and become integrated into one's developing story and others that will not. In their argument for the integration of the identity status and narrative identity approaches, McLean and Pasupathi (2012) suggested that meaning-making about new life experiences may facilitate identity exploration and also that the resulting self–event connections that are formed through meaning-making may serve to help solidify and reinforce identity commitments over time. In support of this perspective, identity maturity (exploration and commitment) in twenty-three-year-olds was found to be positively associated with meaning-making in turning point narratives (McLean & Pratt, 2006).

An important observation regarding McLean and Pratt's (2006) study, which was the first to examine links between narrative identity and identity status, is that although they differentiated between more and less sophisticated or elaborated meaning-making (with more elaborated meaning-making associated with identity maturity), they did not differentiate explicitly between positive and negative meaning-making. This distinction may be very important (see, e.g., Lilgendahl, McLean, & Mansfield, 2013) because it is certainly possible to form self-defining meaning that reflects negatively on the self. For example, consider the hypothetical case in which an emerging adult completes a narrative about a difficult break-up in the following way: "This relationship made me lose faith in the idea of love and leads me to believe that I am probably destined to be alone." This is meaning-making, but it is unlikely to contribute to a healthy foundation for long-term identity commitments.

Building on this idea, I propose that the distinction between positive and negative meaning-making is critical for understanding the process by which identity commitments solidify and a well-adjusted personality develops during emerging adulthood. Specifically, whereas identity exploration may require that a person be open to the impact of a wide variety of life experiences and the self-defining meanings they could generate, positive or negative, *the shift toward identity commitment during emerging adulthood will require the narration process to involve connecting the self to events in ways that generate positive self-defining meaning*. Narrative processes that result in meaning characterized by, for example, pride in one's abilities and accomplishments, excitement and enthusiasm about new goals and plans, a sense of positive self-transformation or growth, or loving connection to important others all may serve to lay the positive emotional foundation that begins to crystallize commitment making. Indeed, when such positive emotions are embedded in meaning-making, a person may be propelled forward by them and continue to build on and grow from that experience (Fredrickson, 2001). The challenge is that, in order to discover what generates positive self-defining meanings, one must be in a heightened "meaning-making mode" and may therefore be vulnerable to generating negative meanings as well.

Although much research needs to be done to test the value of distinguishing between positive and negative meaning-making, a close examination of narrative identity research during emerging adulthood provides some preliminary support. For example, McLean and Lilgendahl (2008) examined the reminiscence functions of highly positive and negative memories (i.e., high points and low points) in emerging and older adults. Endorsement of the identity function (i.e., seeing the memory as clarifying one's identity) was found to be highest for the high-point memories of emerging adults. Additionally, it was found that among emerging adults (but not older adults), viewing high points as identity-defining was associated with higher levels of positive psychological well-being, especially feeling a sense of purpose in life. These findings provide support for the idea that associating self-defining meaning with positive events during emerging adulthood is critically important for healthy identity development.

Whereas positive experiences may provide an unambiguous source of positive self-defining meaning, the question of what emerging adults do with negative experiences is also critically important in the progression toward healthy identity commitments. With respect to low points, McLean and Lilgendahl (2008) found that, for emerging adults only, (a) low points were viewed as identity-defining only if they ended positively, and (b) positive endings to low points were associated with well-being. These findings suggest that, during emerging adulthood, the positive resolution of negative events, either in the service of generating positive self-defining meaning or minimizing negative self-defining meaning, is important for healthy identity development. Consistent with this idea, Dumas, Lawford, Tieu, and Pratt (2009) showed that identity achievement mediated the relationship between positive resolution in low-point narratives and optimal emotional adjustment in a sample of twenty-six-year olds. In other words, for emerging adults, being able to positively resolve a negative experience may benefit well-being through its positive and perhaps protective impact on the formation of identity commitments.

What about evidence linking positive meaning-meaning to actual personality change over time? Although there is little evidence yet at this point explicitly linking meaning-making in connection with specific life events to personality change, several longitudinal studies using narrative methods provide indirect evidence. For example, Sutin and Robins (2005) examined how academic self-defining memories related to patterns of personality change in a longitudinal study of college students. They found that whereas positive affect and the theme of achievement in the memories were associated with increases in conscientiousness, agreeableness, and emotional stability (i.e., decrease in neuroticism), negative affect was associated with increases in neuroticism over time. To the extent that academic self-defining memories are likely to be closely connected to one's developing sense of career identity, such findings point to the critical importance of having academic experiences that generate positive self-defining meaning during the college years as a foundation for the work-related experiences during the twenties that will continue to play a critical role in personality development (Roberts et al., 2003).

As emerging adulthood progresses through the twenties, another domain of great identity importance for many is the pursuit of and commitment to a life partner. Although research has shown that committing to a serious relationship in itself may play a stabilizing role in that it relates to decreasing neuroticism in emerging adulthood (Neyer & Asendorpf, 2001), other studies suggest that *how* a relationship commitment is interpreted as affecting identity may also be very important for identity and personality development. For example, in a longitudinal study following women from age twenty-one to age twenty-seven, Pals (1999) coded open-ended interview responses about marriage for four different prototypes for how a woman perceived the ongoing impact of marriage on her identity (i.e., role-related meaning-making). Those prototypes that reflected negative meaning-making (identity restricted by marriage and identity confused by marriage) each were negatively predictive of overall identity consolidation at age twenty-seven, and low identity consolidation, in turn, was associated with decreases in the trait of ego-resiliency from age twenty-one to age twenty-seven. In other words, negative meaning-making in marriage was part of a broader dynamic of struggling with identity development and decreases in healthy personality functioning.

Finally, in addition to these domain-specific findings, evidence for healthy personality development during emerging adulthood has also been found in the context of patterns of narration assessed at a broader, integrative level of identity. Lodi-Smith et al. (2009) examined students' narratives of how their personalities had changed over four years of college and found that those whose stories of self-development were positive also decreased in neuroticism over time. Additionally, Bauer and McAdams (2010) examined college students' narrative of future life goals and found that an emphasis on positive personal growth was associated with increases in emotional well-being over the next three years. In sum, becoming better adjusted during emerging adulthood involves developing a positive story of self-development, both looking back and looking forward.

To summarize this section on emerging adulthood, I have argued that during this time of extended identity exploration, a critical source of individual differences in the development of a well-adjusted personality is the extent to which an individual is able to form identity-defining commitments that are built on experiences that provide positive self-defining meanings and feelings. Such experiences may be self-affirming or self-transformative, but the critical factor is to form connections between experiences and self that are fundamentally positive. To test this proposition more thoroughly, it would be informative to conduct longitudinal studies following individuals all the way through and out of emerging adulthood, collecting narratives of significant life experiences within specific identity-defining domains, as well as measures of identity exploration and commitment and personality traits. By coding narratives for positive and negative self-defining meaning over time, we could test whether changes toward positive meaning-making precede positive changes in personality, as mediated by shifts from identity exploration to identity commitment.

Identity Processes and Personality Development in Midlife: Transforming the Self in Response to Negative Events

As adults transition into midlife, negative events become increasingly important for a full understanding of how identity processes relate to personality development. As time progresses, it becomes increasingly likely that life does not go exactly according to plan and that negative events are going to be encountered (Pals, 2006a; 2006b). Furthermore, in contrast to emerging adulthood, when identity is not yet fully formed, the negative events of midlife often threaten the positive elements of identity on which one has long relied for stability and meaning (Pals, 2006a; 2006b). Indeed, the challenges that are typical of those faced by midlife—divorce, job loss, health challenges, struggles with children—often destabilize the roles and assumptions that served as the positive foundation for identity during the earlier years of adulthood. Thus, whereas an emerging adult may be more likely to easily move on from a negative event by shifting identity commitments elsewhere (e.g., a student fails out of college and decides to start a business as a house painter), a middle-aged adult may have to engage in a much more involved process of identity revision in order to rebuild herself in the wake of more deeply self-challenging negative events.

Research suggests that the unique role of negative events in identity processes during midlife has important implications for both the adjustment and maturity trajectories of personality development. First, in terms of the adjustment trajectory, the most well-adjusted midlife adults do not minimize but rather fully acknowledge negative events in their lives and incorporate them into narrative identity in positive and growth-oriented ways. In a recent study of midlife adults' life stories, Dan McAdams and I (Lilgendahl & McAdams, 2011) analyzed causal connections—that is, each time that the narrator described a past experience, positive or negative—as having a significant causal impact on self-growth. We found that interpreting negative events as causing a variety of different forms of positive self-growth was associated with well-being, but the same pattern was not found for positive events. Thus, adults who fully acknowledged negative life experiences and integrated them into identity in a way that provided a richly differentiated story of self-growth were better adjusted than those who did not.

Interpreting a negative event as causing positive self-growth is beneficial at least in part because it is one way to provide a positive conclusion for the event. However, the potential value for personality development of narrating negative events as growth-promoting does not only come from the resulting positive endings. In my research (Pals, 2006a; 2006b), I have argued that individual differences in how midlife adults respond to the challenge that negative events pose for identity can be understood in terms of two separate but interactive narrative processes: exploratory-accommodative processing and positive resolution. Specifically, narratives of difficult events have been shown to differ in terms of (a) how open and exploratory versus closed and minimizing they are with respect to the potential transformative impact of the event on the self and (b) the extent to which they conclude with a positive ending that emphasizes emotional resolution or a negative ending that emphasizes a lack of resolution and ongoing difficulties. Although narratives may involve any combination of these two dimensions (see Pals, 2006b), the combination of high exploratory/accommodative processing and positive resolution—a narrative pattern I have referred to as "transformational processing" (Pals, 2006b)—has been shown to be optimal for identity development in that it produces the greatest sense of positive self-growth as a narrative outcome.

The key idea captured by this model of transformational processing is that if a person first acknowledges the full emotional impact of a negative event and explores its meaning in depth, then positive emotional resolution can be created by building on that reflective process and creating a positive ending through seeing the self as positively transformed (Pals, 2006b). Thus, the kind of growth produced by transformational processing is expected to be more central to identity and richly developed than other kinds of statements of positive self-growth in narratives because of the level of exploratory processing also evidenced in the narrative. For example, a person may conclude a narrative about a difficult experience by saying, "it made me a stronger person." Although this is clearly a positive growth-oriented statement, it is not equivalent in an identity-transformative sense to a woman saying: "Thus, the responsibility, guilt, anger, pain, fear, led me into deep evaluation of my life circumstances, and the setting of goals in the most conscious way yet" (as quoted in Lilgendahl et al., 2013). In the latter example, the woman is clearly engaged in a profound, growth-oriented identity transformation in response to first actively exploring the impact of a very painful and life-altering event.

Several recent studies lend support to the idea that responding to the difficult, identity-challenging events of middle adulthood with an exploratory-accommodative approach, regardless of whether a positive resolution is also achieved, may relate to the maturity trajectory of personality development through facilitating increases in ego development (King & Raspin, 2004; King et al., 2000; Lilgendahl et al., 2013). Most recently, my colleagues and I (Lilgendahl et al., 2013) examined how exploratory-accommodative processing of difficult life events related to patterns of change in ego development from early midlife (age forty-three) to late midlife (age sixty-one) in the Mills Longitudinal Study of Women (see Helson & Strivastava, 2001; Lilgendahl et al., 2013). These women also provided a narrative of a very difficult life experience from adulthood at age fifty-two, which was positioned between the two assessments of ego level. Consistent with our hypotheses, we found that there was a normative increase in ego level from age forty-three to age sixty-one, which supports the idea of a normative developmental tendency to become more complex and appreciative of a diversity of perspectives—in other words, more mature—during midlife. More importantly, however, we also found that this increase in ego level was not displayed by everyone and was most pronounced among those women whose narratives displayed high levels of exploratory-accommodative processing about difficult events that had occurred after age forty-three (i.e., during midlife). In other words, increased personality maturity during midlife was unique to those women who grappled deeply with the identity challenges posed by negative events.

In sum, we have examined the connection between identity processes and personality development across two distinct stages of adulthood—emerging adulthood and midlife. During emerging adulthood, positive experiences and the generation of positive self-defining meaning were emphasized as critical for the development of enduring identity commitments and a well-adjusted personality profile that includes emotional stability. In contrast, midlife was characterized as a time when negative experiences that pose fundamental challenges to identity become increasingly likely and come to matter more for personality development, specifically ego development. Research suggests that engaging in transformational processing of negative events in midlife—that is, exploring their impact and then resolving them positively in order to form a story of self-growth—is an integrative narrative identity process that relates to both adjustment and ego development, two distinct and optimal outcomes of personality development in adulthood that, when integrated, have been referred to as "the good life" (King, 2001). Thus, the broad developmental picture painted here for identity development is that it is important to form a life story that integrates both positive and negative life experiences and infuses them with growth-oriented self-defining meaning (see also Labouvie-Vief & Medler, 2002).

More Questions About Personality and Identity: New Directions for Examining the Variations in and Complexities of Identity Processes

As much as we have discovered about the dynamic relationship between identity and personality, there is still much more to be understood. For example, how might the basic traits that individuals take with them into identity formation moderate the way the process plays out, with implications for what is most effective or optimal for each individual? Additionally, how do adults negotiate the intersections of identity processes occurring in distinct identity domains? As I explore in this final section, these questions have significant implications for the relationship between identity and personality.

Not the Same for Everyone? How Traits May Moderate the Optimal Path of Identity Development

In large part, our understanding of what constitutes an optimal path to a healthy sense of identity is assumed to be essentially the same for everyone. However, does it really make sense to conceptualize the process of identity development in such a "one size fits all" fashion? From the perspective of the integrative model of personality shown in Figure 30.1, one might expect that biologically based traits that are already well-established by late adolescence might shape how people may most effectively engage in the process of identity formation.

Here, I focus on two traits—openness to experience and extraversion—because they may have significant implications for how people engage with the world and go about exploring identity possibilities. DeYoung (2010) has argued that the common variance shared by openness and extraversion creates a higher order "meta-trait," labeled plasticity, which is defined as "an exploratory tendency, whereby the individual is actively engaged with the possibilities of the environment, both generating and attending to novel aspects of the experience" (p. 27). The extent to which a person exhibits a high level of dispositional plasticity is likely to have important implications for core identity processes in a variety of contexts, both individual and interpersonal.

OPENNESS TO EXPERIENCE

Highly open individuals are comfortable with ambiguity and emotional complexity and are interested in a wide variety of ideas, perspectives, and possibilities in life. In contrast, those who are less open appreciate familiarity, predictability, and a greater reliance on social norms, traditions, and conventions in their approach to life (McCrae & Costa, 1980). Not surprisingly, the trait of openness has been shown to correlate positively with identity exploration (Tesch & Whitbourne, 1987), identity flexibility (Whitbourne, 1986) and an information-oriented identity style (Dollinger, 1995). Given that identity exploration has been described as necessary for healthy identity development (Marcia, 1966; Grotevant, 1987), such findings suggest that more open individuals have an advantage in identity development and that less open individuals may be at risk for identity foreclosure and an overly rigid adult identity.

Yet, identity exploration is a very broad concept and could play out in a variety of different ways and through a variety of different kinds of experiences. Thus, it is important to look beyond this basic, bivariate correlation between openness and identity exploration to consider how the process of identity exploration may be optimally approached by people on both the higher and lower end of the openness spectrum. Very useful in this regard is the recent distinction made by Luyckx, Goossens, et al. (2006) between exploration in breadth and exploration in depth. Exploration in breadth refers to the wide consideration of identity alternatives and corresponds most closely to the original conception of identity exploration proposed by Marcia (1966). In contrast, exploration in depth involves the more focused, reflective, and evaluative exploration of identity, such as in the case of the ongoing evaluation of a new identity commitment (e.g., possible career choice). It may be the case that exploration in breadth—for example, taking a variety of different college courses, studying abroad, making friends from a wide variety of backgrounds, putting oneself in unfamiliar situations of various kinds for the sake of learning from those experiences—may be a style of identity exploration that is a more comfortable fit for those higher in openness to experience. In contrast, those who are lower in openness to experience may prefer to forego exploration in breadth, sticking to a more familiar path and set of identity options, but may still be able to navigate a successful path for identity development by engaging in exploration in depth.

In support of this idea, Luyckx, Schwartz, Goossens, et al. (2008) conducted a person-level cluster analysis to identify distinct identity trajectories and their relation to patterns of adjustment. In addition to categories that map onto the traditional identity statuses, they also found a new category, labeled "consolidators." Consolidators scored high on identity commitment and exploration in depth but low on exploration in breadth, and they also displayed a very positive adjustment trajectory. This group was characterized as confident in their identity commitments, not interested in considering a variety of alternatives, but also reasonably flexible, reflective, and potentially open to identity revisions as needed over time, in response to context-specific challenges. Although it requires future research, it seems plausible that such a path, with its reliance on exploration in depth as opposed to exploration in breadth, may be the optimal identity pathway for those who are low on openness.

On the opposite end of the spectrum, it is also important to consider carefully not only the obvious benefits but also the potential costs of high levels of openness for healthy identity development. Indeed, although highly open people may find the period of emerging adulthood, which has come to allow and even support extended and broad identity exploration (Arnett, 2000), to be an exciting and stimulating time that provides a natural outlet for their openness, there are potential dangers as well. For example, although high openness leads to increasing levels of exploration in breadth over time during emerging adulthood (Luyckx, Soenens, & Goossens, 2006), this same study also showed that increases in exploration in breadth were associated with increases in neuroticism. This pattern exposes a danger of the identity development process for very open people. Specifically, they may be so open to the exploration of alternatives that they get stuck in this openness and struggle with making commitments. This danger has been well-captured by the recent addition of the concept of *ruminative exploration*, a maladaptive form of exploration that involves getting stalled in the more anxious and worried side of identity questioning (Luyckx, Schwartz, Berzonsky, Soenens, Vansteenkiste, Smith, & Goossens, 2008). Similarly, recent work has distinguished between more and less healthy forms of exploration in the context of ethnic identity development (Syed et al., 2013).

Finally, it is worth noting that exploration in breadth may not inevitably result in ruminative, confused exploration. This may be especially true for highly open individuals who, given their highly "plastic" nature (DeYoung, 2010), find novelty, variety, and the consideration of alternatives, including various possible alternatives for self-definition, inherently enjoyable and rewarding. From this perspective, the challenge for highly open people who enjoy identity exploration for its own s[ake is to be] able to let go of many different exciting [options] for the future self (see Dunkel, 200[0]) [to] form a lasting commitment to one vers[ion of the] current and future self.

EXTRAVERSION VERSUS INTROVERSION

The "how" of identity development from the narrative identity perspective involves forming self-defining meaning through the narration of life experiences. As argued by McLean, Pasupathi, and Pals (2007), narratives do not get formed in a vacuum but rather develop within situated contexts, often through social interactions with others. Several recent studies provide support for this perspective by demonstrating an association between various aspects of memory telling and the meaning of a memory in relation to the self (Lilgendahl, McLean, & Mansfield, 2013; McLean, 2005; McLean & Pasupathi, 2011; Pasupathi & Rich, 2005). Although most of this research has been correlational, it suggests that an important part of narrative identity development may be to talk about significant life experiences with others in order to affirm, develop, or transform their self-defining meanings and integrate them into narrative identity (McLean & Pasupathi, 2011).

However, research is also beginning to suggest that the trait of extraversion may moderate the role of memory telling in the process of narrative identity construction. Specifically, extraverts have been found to engage in and enjoy "collaborative narration" more so than introverts, both in terms of sharing self-defining memories and in terms everyday mutual reminiscing with others (McLean & Pasupathi, 2006). Furthermore, a series of conversation-based studies by Thorne and colleagues (Nelson, Thorne, & Shapiro, 2011; Thorne, Korobov, & Morgan, 2007) demonstrate qualitative differences in how extraverts and introverts interact and share stories in dyads. For example, Thorne et al. (2007) compared extraverted friendship pairs with introverted friendship pairs in terms of how they engaged in conversational storytelling. Extraverts' stories involved greater co-construction on the part of the listener (invited and offered) than those told in the introverts' conversations, even for stories about unshared events.

These findings suggest that extraverts may be more attuned and responsive to the influence of listeners as they engage in the process of forming self-defining meaning about past experiences. Indeed, given the proposed connection between xtraversion and greater plasticity (DeYoung, 2010), extraverts' social interactions may be more inherently exploratory and involve the greater incorporation of listeners' novel ideas and reactions into the ongoing consideration of identity possibilities. Extraverts may also be more likely to seek out affirmation of their identity choices and commitments. In contrast, for introverts, these identity processes may play out more internally and privately, the outcomes of which may be less contingent on the nature of responses from others. Thus, although the differences in reliance on narrative co-construction have been established, future research should explore the extent to which optimal identity outcomes, assessed over substantial periods of time, are more contingent on the constructive input of listeners for extraverts than for introverts.

In sum, it has long been assumed that successful personality development requires a good fit or match between the person and his or her environment (e.g., Roberts & Robins, 2004). The preceding discussion took this principle a step further by asserting that successful identity development may require a good fit between the person's basic traits and the processes or strategies employed to achieve that identity.

How Do Domain-Specific Identity Processes Interact? When It Comes to the Whole Person, Identity Is More than the Sum of Its Parts

Given that personality is explicitly concerned with the functioning of the whole person, the question of how distinct content domains of identity interact with one another and come together to form a coherent whole should be of great interest to personality psychologists. However, despite the fact that Grotevant (1987) highlighted the importance of this issue in his process model of identity formation more than twenty-five years ago, very little research (see Archer, 1985, for an early noteworthy exception) has addressed it explicitly. This is starting to change. In recent years, a small but growing number of researchers have taken on the questions of how identity processes within different identity domains interact and how individuals navigate these intersecting processes (e.g., Hammack, 2010; Schachter, 2004; Schuck & Liddle, 2001; Syed, 2010). In this section, I highlight some important points that can be drawn from these exciting and innovative studies, with the goal of moving toward a more comprehensive model of how identity intersections relate to the broader processes of identity and personality development.

First, from a methodological standpoint, studies have convincingly demonstrated that if we do not ask participants directly about intersections among identity domains, we may miss a critical psychological space in which important identity processing take place. For example, Archer (1985) used the traditional domain-specific questions of the identity status interview (Marcia, 1966) to assess career identity exploration and commitment in adolescent boys and girls. When focusing on career only, boys and girls showed equal levels of identity exploration. However, when Archer (1985) added questions that explicitly targeted how participants intended to combine their career plans with having a family, conflicts and unanswered questions were exposed among the girls but not the boys. Not surprisingly, girls scored higher than boys on identity exploration when assessed in the context of how career and family—two distinct and potentially important aspects of identity—would be prioritized and integrated. Thus, focusing on career identity by itself was not adequate to fully understand career identity development, particularly for adolescent girls. Rather, for the girls only, the intersection between career and family identities was an important location of intense identity work.

Despite Archer's (1985) early lead, we saw a long period of identity research in which the focus was either on specific, isolated identity domains or on overall identity (typically assessed as a simple average of scores on exploration and commitment across several domains). What was missing was attention to the dynamic interplay between these two levels of analysis. However, we are finally starting to see more interview and narrative studies in which the explicit focus is on the intersection of identities. Several such studies have taken Archer's basic approach of developing questions designed to target specific types of identity intersections (e.g., Schachter, 2004; Schuck & Liddle, 2001; Syed, 2010). Taking a broader narrative approach, McLean, Syed, Yoder, and Greenhoot (under review) coded self-defining memories for the presence of themes related to different identity contents. They found that self-defining memories were more likely to contain meaning-making (i.e., evidence for active identity processes) if two or more identity contents were present within the same memory (e.g., religion and career). Consistent with Archer (1985), McLean et al.'s study supports the idea that where identity domains intersect, added layers of identity exploration and meaning-making are likely to be found.

Second, studies have shown that identity intersections take different forms and arise out of different circumstances. One of the most obvious and researched ways that identities intersect is identity conflict, or the perceived incompatibility between two identities. Identity conflict is likely to be important for identity development because it is an aversive state that works against the broader goal of a well-integrated, cohesive identity and may therefore stimulate meaning-making and exploration in order to achieve resolution (McLean et al., under review). Examples include career–family conflict (Archer, 1985), bicultural identity conflict (Benet-Martinez & Haritatos, 2005), conflicts between religion and sexuality (Schachter, 2004; Schuck & Liddle, 2001) and conflicts between woman and scientist identities (Settles, 2004). In contrast to identity conflict, Syed's (2010) innovative research on choice of college major and ethnicity demonstrates that, through the process of identity development, students may form a meaningful connection between two seemingly disparate identities. As noted by Syed (2010), those students for whom ethnicity was highly important were more likely to have their choice of a major informed by ethnic identity. Thus, it may be the case that the most central or important identities become a sort of anchor for identity formation and, in the process, shape the development of and become meaningfully connected to several specific identities. For example, Konik and Stewart (2004) showed that lesbian-gay-bisexual (LGB)-identified college students scored higher than straight-identified college students on identity achievement in several domains that are distinct from sexuality, including religion and politics. Consistent with the identity anchoring idea, Konik and Stewart (2004) argued that the press for intensive sexual identity exploration in LGB individuals may "spill over" into and enhance exploration in other identity domains, particularly those that may be meaningfully connected, such as religion and politics (Konik & Stewart, 2004).

Third, these examples—career–family priorities for young women, bicultural identity, ethnicity and college major, etc.—vividly highlight how important cultural and social context are in determining whether and how identity intersections become meaningful to individuals. Reflecting our increasingly diverse culture in the United States, developmental perspectives on identity have begun to conceptualize "personal" (e.g., career choice, personal value orientation) and "social" identities (i.e., those identities that designate one's membership in a group, such as ethnicity, sexual orientation, gender, etc.) as interconnected and mutually influencing, as opposed to separate levels of identity functioning (Azmitia, Syed, & Radmacher, 2008). Additionally, in the narrative identity literature, the influence of culture on identity has been conceptualized in terms of "master narratives" or culturally shared scripts for how a life—within a given context, for a particular type of person, at a particular point in time—is supposed to go (McLean, 2008a). Master narratives are critical for identity development because they can shape how individuals engage in meaning-making in response to their own life experiences. For example, Archer's (1985) research on career and family vividly demonstrates how young women deal with a different master narrative than do young men with respect to the balancing of these two identities. Identity intersections may become especially complicated and difficult when master narratives associated with distinct identities come into conflict with one another, as in the case of bicultural identity or the case of being gay and Christian. For example, a young woman who identifies as South Asian and American may find the culturally conflicting narratives of marriage (arranged vs. personally chosen) challenging to reconcile. Indeed, bicultural identity integration (Benet-Martinez & Haritatos, 2005), which is defined as the harmonious blending of two cultural identifications, is viewed as an optimal identity outcome for bicultural individuals but may be a difficult ideal to achieve if there is no clear master narrative for what it means to have a blended cultural identity that uniquely fuses elements of two distinct cultural traditions.

Fourth, and most important for the current focus on personality development, there are pronounced individual differences in the extent to which and how identity intersections come into play in identity development (Schacter, 2004; Schuck & Liddle, 2001; Syed, 2010). For example, in his study of how orthodox Jews dealt with the conflicting identity domains of religion and sexuality, Schacter (2004) identified four distinct "identity configurations," which he described as choice and suppression (choosing one and eliminating the other), synthesis (embracing both in a way that resolves conflict), "confederacy of identifications" (embracing both with ongoing conflict), and "thrill of dissonance" (the excitement of embracing seemingly incompatible identities). Likewise, Syed

(2010) identified several different identity configurations for how students viewed the relationship (or lack thereof) between their college major choice and ethnic identity. Some students did not identify with their ethnicity, thus making the intersection a nonfactor for identity, some compartmentalized the two and saw no connection, whereas others integrated the two, either through choosing a major to reflect the growing importance of ethnic identity or the opposite—becoming more aware of ethnicity in response to topics covered in the major. Together, these studies show that identity configurations may take a variety of different forms, challenging the traditional notion that coherent synthesis is the desired identity outcome (Schachter, 2004). They also show that there are pronounced differences in the extent to which individuals grapple with and consciously acknowledge identity intersections as part of the process of identity development.

Moving forward, this growing focus on identity intersections should be formalized and integrated with personality psychology in order to better understand the whole person as a uniquely constituted individual developing within situated social and cultural contexts. To this end, I promote three specific goals. First, we need to develop more standardized interview- and narrative-based procedures that allow for identity intersections of various kinds to emerge authentically in how people reflect on identity issues and narrate identity-defining experiences. Researchers have been successful at targeting specific types of identity intersections, but these kinds of methods should be broadened and formalized to apply to anyone, regardless of the specific identities he or she claims. Indeed, Schachter's (2004) call to examine "identity configurations" requires an approach that can capture any person's particular configuration and the self-defining meaning that emerges from it.

Second, we need to understand both the individual and contextual factors that give rise to the pronounced individual differences in how identity intersections are processed and integrated into one's broader sense of identity. One factor likely to be of great importance is the trait level of personality. For example, neuroticism is associated with higher levels of bicultural identity conflict among bicultural individuals (e.g., Chinese Americans) (Benet-Martinez & Haritatos, 2005). It may be the case that neuroticism increases the likelihood of viewing identities as in conflict and of having trouble with resolving that conflict. Openness to experience, a trait that involves creative thought, tolerance of ambiguity, and interest in new ideas, may facilitate creative or contradictory ways of working through identity intersections, such as finding meaningful connections between seemingly disparate identities, being comfortable with contradictory or conflicting identities (e.g., "thrill of dissonance" configuration identified by Schachter [2004]), or finding ways to blend identities in new and creative ways (e.g., Benet & Haritatos, 2005).

In addition to traits, social and cultural contexts are likely to be important factors in whether and how particular identity intersections become important and the identity configurations that ultimately result. For example, for Palestinians living in Israel, the conflict generated by that particular bicultural identity, given the history of the region, is likely to be very different from the bicultural conflict experienced by someone who is Mexican American. In the former group, research suggests that choosing one identity over the other is more likely and possibly more adaptive than a harmonious blending (Hammack, 2010). In another example, it might be that African-American youths growing up during the Obama presidency conceptualize the connection between their racial and political identities differently than African Americans who grew up during the Bush presidency. In myriad ways, social, historical, and cultural factors shape identity development, perhaps especially in terms of the ways that intersections among identities are understood.

Finally, we need to examine the impact of identity intersections and the individual differences they engender for the adjustment and maturity trajectories of personality development. Interestingly, although the ideal of having a coherent, well-integrated identity has been a standard assumption of identity theorizing, Schachter's (2004) work showed that synthesis, the identity configuration that best captures coherent integration, was only one of several possible outcomes. Longitudinal research should examine the long-term implications of synthesized versus dissonant identities for personality adjustment, particularly when situational and cultural factors dictate that synthesis may not be optimal or even possible. With respect to intense identity conflicts, it would be very interesting to examine the importance of transformational processing (i.e., exploration and resolution) for both adjustment and maturity. Consider a new mother experiencing an intense conflict between career and family identities, both very important to her. On the one hand, the identity conflict could fester in an unresolved fashion (i.e., always going back and forth in one's mind about what is best, ruminating and questioning one's choices), potentially resulting in increasing neuroticism over time. On the other hand, the conflict could stimulate an intensive period of self-reflection and identity exploration in which a positive sense of self-growth and a personally satisfying identity resolution could be the outcome, resulting in both increased adjustment and a more mature, complex perspective on life.

In conclusion, this chapter has approached the personality–identity relationship from the perspective of broad theories and definitions, the role of identity processes in the adjustment and maturity trajectories of personality development, and the need to better understand how traits moderate optimal identity processes and how identity processes within distinct domains interact. Despite its wide-ranging scope, the take-home message of this chapter should be clear: identity and personality are powerfully intertwined, and the interactive and interrelated processes of identity exploration, identity commitment, and identity narration are crucial to our understanding of how personality—conceived of as the whole person embedded in social and cultural contexts—functions and develops throughout adulthood.

References

Adler, J. M. (2012). Living into the story: Agency and coherence in a longitudinal study of narrative identity development and mental health over the course of psychotherapy. *Journal of Personality and Social Psychology, 102,* 367–389.

Anthis, K., & LaVoie, J. C. (2006). Readiness to change: A longitudinal study of changes in adult identity. *Journal of Research in Personality, 40,* 209–219.

Archer, S. L. (1985). Career and/or family: The identity process for adolescent girls. *Youth & Society, 16,* 289–314.

Arnett, J. J. (2000). Emerging adulthood: A theory of development from the late teens through the twenties. *American Psychologist, 55,* 469–480.

Arnett, J. J. (this volume). Identity development from adolescence to emerging adulthood: What we know and (especially) don't know. In K. McLean & M. Syed (Eds.), *The Oxford Handbook of Identity Development.* New York: Oxford University Press.

Azmitia, M., Syed, M., & Radmacher, K. (2008). On the intersection of personal and social identities: Introduction and evidence from a longitudinal study of emerging adults. In M. Azmitia, M. Syed, & K. Radmacher (Eds.), *The intersections of personal and social identities: New directions for child and adolescent development* (Issue 120, pp. 1–16). San Francisco: Jossey-Bass.

Baerger, D. R., & McAdams, D. P. (1999). Life story coherence and its relation to psychological well-being. *Narrative Inquiry, 9,* 69–96.

Barenbaum, N. B., & Winter, D. G. (2008). History of modern personality theory and research. In O. P. John, R. W. Robins, & L. A. Pervin (Eds.), *Handbook of personality: Theory and research* (3rd ed., pp. 3–28). New York: Guilford Press.

Bauer, J. J., & McAdams, D. P. (2010). Eudaimonic growth: Narrative growth goals predict increases in ego development and subjective well-being three years later. *Developmental Psychology, 46,* 761–772.

Bauer, J. J., McAdams, D. P., & Sakaeda, A. R. (2005). Interpreting the good life: Growth memories in the lives of mature, happy people. *Journal of Personality and Social Psychology, 88,* 203–217.

Benet-Martínez, V., & Haritatos, J. (2005). Bicultural identity integration (BII): Components and psychosocial antecedents. *Journal of Personality, 73,* 1015–1050.

Blagov, P. S., & Singer, J. A. (2004). Four dimensions of self-defining memories (specificity, meaning, content, and affect) and their relationships to self-restraint, distress, and repressive defensiveness. *Journal of Personality, 72,* 481–511.

Cantor, N. (1990). From thought to behavior:" Having" and "doing" in the study of personality and cognition. *American Psychologist, 45,* 735–750.

Caspi A., Roberts B. W., & Shiner, R. L. (2005). Personality development: Stability and change. *Annual Review of Psychology, 56,* 453–484.

Cohn, L. D. (1998). Age trends in personality development: A quantitative review. In Westenberg, P. M., Blasi, A., & Cohn, L. D. (Eds.), *Personality development: Theoretical, empirical, and clinical investigations of Loevinger's conception of ego development* (pp. 133–143). Mahwah, NJ: Lawrence Erlbaum Associates.

Cox, K., & McAdams, D. P. (2012). The transforming self: Service narratives and identity change in emerging adulthood. *Journal of Adolescent Research, 27,* 18–43.

Crocetti E., & Meeus, W. (this volume). The identity statuses: Strengths of a person-centered approach. In K. McLean & M. Syed (Eds.), *The Oxford Handbook of Identity Development.* New York: Oxford University Press.

DeYoung, C. G. (2010). Toward a theory of the Big Five. *Psychological Inquiry, 21,* 26–33.

Dollinger, S. M. C. (1995). Identity styles and the five-factor model of personality. *Journal of Research in Personality, 29,* 475–479.

Dumas, T. M., Lawford, H., Tieu, T. T., & Pratt, M. W. (2009). Positive parenting in adolescence and its relation to low point narration and identity status in emerging adulthood: A longitudinal analysis. *Developmental Psychology, 45,* 1531–1544.

Dunkel, C. S. (2000). Possible selves as a mechanism for identity exploration. *Journal of Adolescence, 23,* 519–529.

Dunlop, W. L., & Tracy, J. L. (2013). Sobering stories: Narratives of self-redemption predict behavioral change and improved health among recovering alcoholics. *Journal of Personality and Social Psychology, 104,* 576–590.

Erikson, E. H. (1963). *Childhood and society* (rev. ed.) New York: Norton.

Fredrickson, B. L. (2001). The role of positive emotions in positive psychology: The broaden-and-build theory of positive emotions. *American Psychologist, 56,* 218–226.

Grotevant, H. D. (1987). Toward a process model of identity formation. *Journal of Adolescent Research, 2,* 203–222.

Habermas, T., & Bluck, S. (2000). Getting a life: The emergence of the life story in adolescence. *Psychological Bulletin, 126,* 748–769.

Habermas, T., & Köber, C. (this volume). Autobiographical reasoning is constitutive for narrative identity: The role of the life story for personal continuity. In K. McLean & M. Syed (Eds.), *The Oxford Handbook of Identity Development.* New York: Oxford University Press.

Habermas, T., & Paha, C. (2001). The development of coherence in adolescents' life narratives. *Narrative Inquiry, 11*, 35–54.

Hammack, P. L. (2010). Narrating hyphenated selves: Intergroup contact and configurations of identity among young Palestinian citizens of Israel. *International Journal of Intercultural Relations, 34*, 368–385.

Helson, R., & Srivastava, S. (2001). Three paths of adult development: Conservers, seekers, and achievers. *Journal of Personality and Social Psychology, 80*, 995–1010.

Helson, R., & Wink, P. (1987). Two conceptions of maturity examined in the findings of a longitudinal study. *Journal of Personality and Social Psychology, 53*, 531–541.

Hy, L. X., & Loevinger, J. (1996). *Measuring ego development* (2nd ed.). Mahwah, NJ: Lawrence Erlbaum.

John, O. P., & Srivastava, S. (1999). The Big Five trait taxonomy: History, measurement, and theoretical perspectives. In L. A. Pervin & O. P. John (Eds.), *Handbook of personality: Theory and research* (2nd ed., pp. 102–138). New York: Guilford Press.

King, L. A. (2001). The hard road to the good life: The happy, mature person. *Journal of Humanistic Psychology, 41*, 51–72.

King, L. A., & Raspin, C. (2004). Lost and found possible selves, subjective well-being, and ego development in divorced women. *Journal of Personality, 72*, 603–632.

King, L. A., Scollon, C. K., Ramsey, C., & Williams, T. (2000). Stories of life transition: Subjective well-being and ego development in parents of children with Down syndrome. *Journal of Research in Personality, 34*, 509–536.

Konik, J., & Stewart, A. (2004). Sexual identity development in the context of compulsory heterosexuality. *Journal of Personality, 72*, 815–844.

Kroger, J. (this volume). Identity development through adulthood: The move toward "wholeness." In K. McLean & M. Syed (Eds.), *The Oxford Handbook of Identity Development*. New York: Oxford University Press.

Kunnen, E. S. & Metz, M. (this volume). Commitment and exploration: the need for a developmental approach. In K. McLean & M. Syed (Eds.), *The Oxford Handbook of Identity Development*. New York: Oxford University Press.

Labouvie-Vief, G., & Medler, M. (2002). Affect optimization and affect complexity: Modes and styles of regulation in adulthood. *Psychology and Aging, 17*, 571–587.

Lilgendahl, J. P., Helson, R., & John, O. P. (2013). Does ego development increase during midlife? The effects of openness and accommodative processing of difficult events. *Journal of Personality, 81*, 403–416.

Lilgendahl, J. P., & McAdams, D. P. (2011). Constructing stories of self-growth: How individual differences in patterns of autobiographical reasoning relate to well-being in midlife. *Journal of Personality, 79*, 391–428.

Lilgendahl, J. P., McLean, K. C., & Mansfield, C. D. (2013). When is meaning making unhealthy for the self? The roles of neuroticism, implicit theories, and memory telling in trauma and transgression memories. *Memory, 21*, 79–96.

Lodi-Smith, J., Geise, A. C., Roberts, B. W., & Robins, R. W. (2009). Narrating personality change. *Journal of Personality and Social Psychology, 96*, 679–689.

Loevinger, J. (1976). *Ego development: Conceptions and theories*. San Francisco, CA: Jossey-Bass.

Luyckx, K., Goossens, L., Soenens, B., & Beyers, W. (2006). Unpacking commitment and exploration: Preliminary validation of an integrative model of late adolescent identity formation. *Journal of Adolescence, 29*, 361–378.

Luyckx, K., Schwartz, S. J., Berzonsky, M. D., Soenens, B., Vansteenkiste, M., Smits, I., & Goossens, L. (2008). Capturing ruminative exploration: Extending the four-dimensional model of identity formation in late adolescence. *Journal of Research in Personality, 42*, 58–82.

Luyckx, K., Schwartz, S. J., Goossens, L., Soenens, B., & Beyers, W. (2008). Developmental typologies of identity formation and adjustment in female emerging adults: A latent class growth analysis approach. *Journal of Research on Adolescence, 18*, 595–619.

Luyckx, K., Soenens, B., & Goossens, L. (2006). The personality-identity interplay in emerging adult women: Convergent findings from complementary analyses. *European Journal of Personality, 20*, 195–215.

Marcia, J. E. (1966). Development and validation of ego-identity status. *Journal of Personality and Social Psychology, 3*, 551–558.

Marcia, J. E. (1967). Ego identity status: Relationship to change in self-esteem, "general maladjustment," and authoritarianism. *Journal of Personality, 35*, 118–133.

McAdams, D. P. (2001). The psychology of life stories. *Review of General Psychology, 5*, 100–122.

McAdams, D. P., Anyidoho, N. A., Brown, C., Huang, Y. T., Kaplan, B., & Machado, M. A. (2004). Traits and stories: Links between dispositional and narrative features of personality. *Journal of Personality, 72*, 761–784.

McAdams, D. P., & Pals, J. L. (2006). A new Big Five: Fundamental principles for an integrative science of personality. *American Psychologist, 61*, 204–217.

McAdams, D. P., Reynolds, J., Lewis, M., Patten, A. H., & Bowman, P. J. (2001). When bad things turn good and good things turn bad: Sequences of redemption and contamination in life narrative and their relation to psychosocial adaptation in midlife adults and in students. *Personality and Social Psychology Bulletin, 27*, 474–485.

McCrae, R. R., & Costa, P. T. (1980). Openness to experience and ego level in Loevinger's Sentence Completion Test: Dispositional contributions to developmental models of personality. *Journal of Personality and Social Psychology, 39*, 1179–1190.

McCrae, R. R., & Costa, P. T. Jr. (1999). A five-factor theory of personality. In L. A. Pervin & O. P. John (Eds.), *Handbook of personality: Theory and research* (2nd ed., pp. 139–153). New York: Guilford Press.

McLean, K. C. (2005). Late adolescent identity development: Narrative meaning making and memory telling. *Developmental Psychology, 41*, 683–691.

McLean, K. C. (2008a). The emergence of narrative identity. *Social and Personality Psychology Compass, 2*, 1685–1702.

McLean, K. C. (2008b). Stories of the young and the old: Personal continuity and narrative identity. *Developmental Psychology, 44*, 254–264.

McLean, K. C., & Lilgendahl, J. P. (2008). Why recall our highs and lows: Relations between memory functions, age, and well-being. *Memory, 16*, 751–762.

McLean, K. C., & Pasupathi, M. (2006). Collaborative narration of the past and extraversion. *Journal of Research in Personality, 40*, 1219–1231.

McLean, K. C., & Pasupathi, M. (2011). Old, new, borrowed, blue? The emergence and retention of personal meaning in autobiographical storytelling. *Journal of Personality, 79*, 135–164.

McLean, K. C., & Pasupathi, M. (2012). Processes of identity development: Where I am and how I got there. *Identity, 12*, 8–28.

McLean, K. C., Pasupathi, M., & Pals, J. L. (2007). Selves creating stories creating selves: A process model of self-development. *Personality and Social Psychology Review, 11*, 262–278.

McLean, K. C., & Pratt, M. W. (2006). Life's little (and big) lessons: Identity statuses and meaning-making in the turning point narratives of emerging adults. *Developmental Psychology, 42*, 714–722.

McLean, K. C., Syed, M., Yoder, A., & Greenhoot, A. F. (under review). Identity integration: The importance of domain content in linking narrative and status approaches to emerging adult identity development.

Meeus, W. (2011). The study of adolescent identity formation 2000–2010: A review of longitudinal research. *Journal of Research on Adolescence, 21*, 75–94.

Moffitt, K. H., & Singer, J. A. (1994). Continuity in the life story: Self-defining memories, affect, and approach/avoidance personal strivings. *Journal of Personality, 62*, 21–43.

Nelson, P. A., Thorne, A., & Shapiro, L. A. (2011). I'm outgoing and she's reserved: The reciprocal dynamics of personality in close friendships in young adulthood. *Journal of Personality, 79*, 1113–1148.

Neyer, F. J., & Asendorpf, J. B. (2001). Personality–relationship transaction in young adulthood. *Journal of Personality and Social Psychology, 81*, 1190–1204.

Pals, J. L. (1999). Identity consolidation in early adulthood: Relations with ego-resiliency, the context of marriage, and personality change. *Journal of Personality, 67*, 295–329.

Pals, J. L. (2006a). Narrative identity processing of difficult life experiences: Pathways of personality development and positive self-transformation in adulthood. *Journal of Personality, 74*, 1079–1110.

Pals, J. L. (2006b). Authoring a second chance in life: Emotion and transformational processing within narrative identity. *Research in Human Development, 3*, 101–120.

Pasupathi, M., & Mansour, E. (2006). Adult age differences in autobiographical reasoning in narratives. *Developmental Psychology, 42*, 798–808.

Pasupathi, M., Mansour, E., & Brubaker, J. (2007). Developing a life story: Constructing relations between self and experience in autobiographical narratives. *Human Development, 50*, 85–110.

Pasupathi, M., & Rich, B. (2005). Inattentive listening undermines self-verification in personal storytelling. *Journal of Personality, 73*, 1051–1086.

Pulkkinen, L., & Kokko, K. (2000). Identity development in adulthood: A longitudinal study. *Journal of Research in Personality, 34*, 445–470.

Roberts, B. W., & Caspi, A. (2003). The cumulative continuity model of personality development: Striking a balance between continuity and change in personality traits across the life course. In U. M. Staudinger & U. Lindenberger (Eds.), *Understanding Human Development: Dialogues with Lifespan Psychology* (pp.183–214). New York: Kluwer.

Roberts, B. W., Caspi, A., & Moffitt, T. E. (2003). Work experiences and personality development in young adulthood. *Journal of Personality and Social Psychology, 84*, 582–593.

Roberts, B. W., & Mroczek, D. (2008). Personality trait change in adulthood. *Current Directions in Psychological Science, 17*, 31–35.

Roberts, B. W., & Robins, R. W. (2004). Person-environment fit and its implications for personality development: A longitudinal study. *Journal of Personality, 72*, 89–110.

Roberts, B. W., Wood, D., & Smith, J. L. (2005). Evaluating five factor theory and social investment perspectives on personality trait development. *Journal of Research in Personality, 39*, 166–184.

Schachter, E. P. (2004). Identity configurations: A new perspective on identity formation in contemporary society. *Journal of Personality, 72*, 167–199.

Schuck, K. D., & Liddle, B. J. (2001). Religious conflicts experienced by lesbian, gay, and bisexual individuals. *Journal of Gay & Lesbian Psychotherapy, 5*, 63–82.

Schwartz, S. J., Beyers, W., Luyckx, K., Soenens, B., Zamboanga, B. L., Forthun, L. F.,…, & Waterman, A. S. (2011). Examining the light and dark sides of emerging adults' identity: A study of identity status differences in positive and negative psychosocial functioning. *Journal of Youth and Adolescence, 40*, 839–859.

Settles, I. H. (2004). When multiple identities interfere: The role of identity centrality. *Personality and Social Psychology Bulletin, 30*, 487–500.

Singer, J. A. (2004). Narrative identity and meaning making across the adult lifespan: An introduction. *Journal of Personality, 72*, 437–460.

Singer, J. A., & Blagov, P. (2004). The integrative function of narrative processing: Autobiographical memory, self-defining memories, and the life story of identity. In D. R. Bieke & J. R. Lampinen, et al. (Eds.), *The self and memory, studies in self and identity* (pp. 117–138). New York: The Psychology Press.

Staudinger, U. M., & Kunzmann, U. (2005). Positive adult personality development. *European Psychologist, 10*, 320–329.

Sutin, A. R., & Robins, R. W. (2005). Continuity and correlates of emotions and motives in self-defining memories. *Journal of Personality, 73*, 793–824.

Syed, M. (2010). Developing an integrated self: Academic and ethnic identities among ethnically-diverse college students. *Developmental Psychology, 46*, 1590–1604.

Syed, M., Walker, L. H. M., Lee, R. M., Umaña-Taylor, A. J., Zamboanga, B. L., Schwartz, S. J., Armenta, B. E., & Huynh, Q.-L. (2013). A two-factor model of ethnic identity exploration: Implications for identity coherence and well-being. *Cultural Diversity and Ethnic Minority Psychology, 19*, 143–154.

Tesch, S. A., & Cameron, K. A. (1987). Openness to experience and development of adult identity. *Journal of Personality, 55*, 615–630.

Thorne, A., Korobov, N., & Morgan, E. M. (2007). Channeling identity: A study of storytelling in conversations between introverted and extraverted friends. *Journal of Research in Personality, 41*, 1008–1031.

Whitbourne, S. K. (1986). Openness to experience, identity flexibility, and life change in adults. *Journal of Personality and Social Psychology, 50*, 163–168.

CHAPTER 31

Identity Development in the Digital Age: The Case of Social Networking Sites

Adriana M. Manago

Abstract

Youth are growing up amid profound sociocultural change driven by the worldwide spread of the Internet and social media that position the individual at the center of expansive social networks unrestricted by physical propinquity. Personal self-expression and the concept of *customized sociality* are key to understanding how young people manage these large networks. This chapter reviews literature on the use of social networking sites among adolescents and emerging adults in Western societies and stakes out potential implications for identity development, arguing that social networking sites usher in new practices and meanings for interpersonal relatedness and personal autonomy that adolescents and emerging adults must negotiate during the process of exploration and commitment in identity formation. Customized sociality and self-expression are cultural practices that manifest an emphasis on autonomy during identity development; however, ironically, evidence suggests that social networking sites may also foster a reliance on others to validate one's identity claims and self-worth.

Key Words: social networking sites, friendship, autonomy, relatedness, sociocultural change, identity development

The digital age is a time of profound sociocultural change driven by technologies that facilitate the transmission of information faster and more efficiently than ever before in human history. Since Marshall McLuhan's notion of the "global village" (1962), many have speculated that the convenience and efficiency of digital communication technologies would bring individuals around the world closer together. However, as we move further into the twenty-first century, human interdependence and individual independence are both paradoxically amplified in the panorama of social changes. For example, on the macrolevel, the Internet promotes the interdependence and homogeneity of globalization on the one hand and the atomization and heterogeneity of "glocalization" on the other (Meyrowitz, 2005). That is, Internet technologies accelerate the spread of dominant, often Western, paradigms around the world, but local interpretations can also be easily articulated on the web, creating a plurality of differentiated perspectives on a global stage. This paradox of social change penetrates the interpersonal level. The Internet and mobile devices offer "perpetual" human contact (Katz & Aakhus, 2002), yet ironically, the conveniences of these technologies are also conducive to independent mobility, fleeting social connections, and self-promotion (Turkle, 2011).

Adolescents are coming of age in the throes of these paradoxical sociocultural shifts. The Internet is a portal to a barrage of multimedia instilling young people all over the world with a global youth culture largely dominated by commercialism and values of consumption (Schlegel, 2000); however, the Internet, especially social media, also allows them to assert their unique voice in the cultural landscape as they co-construct their own media environments (Mazzarella, 2005; Subrahmanyam, Smahel, & Greenfield, 2006). Indeed, the decentralization of media production and distribution that characterizes social media represents an important source of increasing personal agency and self-expression around the world (Benkler, 2006). Some even suggest that social media, such as social networking sites, promote a hyper preoccupation with the self by providing tools to broadcast personal information such as thoughts, feelings, preferences, needs, and life events (Gentile, Twenge, Freeman, & Campbell, 2012; Malikhao & Servaes, 2011; Turkle, 2011). At the same time, social networking sites promote a heightened focus on peer relationships (Subrahmanyam & Smahel, 2011). In short, media in the digital age are now "social media," and as their popularity spreads, they may usher in new practices, values, and meanings for interpersonal relatedness and personal autonomy that adolescents and emerging adults must negotiate in forming a sense of self.

Social Networking Sites in the Landscape of Social Media

Social media are defined as websites that facilitate the creation and exchange of user-generated content, and thus the term encapsulates a vast and diverse swath of online activities (Kaplan & Haenlein, 2010). Social media include collaborative projects such as Wikipedia, social bookmarking websites such as Delicious, blogs and microblogs such as Twitter and Tumblr, content communities such as YouTube and Flickr, virtual game worlds such as World of Warcraft, virtual social worlds such as Second Life, and, of course, social networking sites such as Facebook. To understand the influence of social media on development, we must consider how young people make use of their various affordances (Ito et al., 2010; Valkenburg & Peter, 2011). Using Tumblr for entertainment and using Facebook to interact with school friends likely have differing implications for development. For example, Blais and colleagues (2008) found that adolescents using the Internet more often for gaming or general entertainment had lower quality relationships with best friends and romantic partners, whereas using the Internet for instant messaging had a positive association with intimate relationship quality. These online contexts for friendship have a unique and perhaps powerful impact on identity development.

To precisely capture the social affordances of adolescents' and emerging adults' Internet use, I limit this review to social networking sites, which have been the most thoroughly researched of all the social media domains. I adopt boyd and Ellison's (2008) definition of social networking sites as "web-based services that allow individuals to (1) construct a public or semi-public profile within a bounded system, (2) articulate a list of other users with whom they share a connection, and (3) view and traverse their list of connections and those made by others within the system" (p. 211). Social networking sites beg for more research in the field of identity development because, unlike other social media, websites such as Facebook are "nonymous" virtual spaces (Zhao, Grasmuck, & Martin, 2008); that is, they are used to socialize with, and maintain a reputation to, friends and acquaintances known in the offline world. In this way, social networking sites infiltrate one of the most important contexts for identity development during adolescence and the transition to adulthood, the peer group. In essence, social networking sites have transformed electronic screens from places where youth consume commercial entertainment media to settings for peer interaction that are mediated by youth's production of their own multimedia content.

A focus on social networking sites is also warranted by their remarkable pervasiveness among young people, not only in Western countries, but also in many other parts of the world. Their popularity tells us something about the mass appeal of communication technologies in human relationships. Of the 95 percent of US adolescents on the Internet, 80 percent of them use a social networking site (Lenhart, 2012); of the 94 percent of eighteen- to twenty-nine-year-olds in the United States on the Internet, 87 percent of them use a social networking site (Zickuhr & Smith, 2012). Similar rates exist in Europe: for example, in the United Kingdom, 91 percent of Internet users aged sixteen to twenty-four use a social networking site (Office of National Statistics, 2011). The growing popularity of social networking sites has also been documented in China (Jackson & Wang, 2013), Japan (Barker & Ota, 2011), Korea (Bae, 2010), Qatar (Leage & Chalmers, 2010), and Jordan (Al Omoush, Yaseen, & Alma'aitah, 2012). The most visited social networking site in the world is Facebook, with 1.19 billion monthly active users worldwide (Facebook, 2013). There are also social networking sites that are dominant in particular countries such as Cyworld in Korea, Mixi in Japan, and Orkut in India and Brazil. However, because the majority of the research on social networking sites has been conducted with youth, often college students, in the West, I provide an overview of Western adolescents' and emerging adults' behaviors on these websites.

A Historical and Sociocultural Approach to Identity Development

The aim of this review is to consider cultural changes in relatedness and autonomy that are crystallized in the use of social networking sites and the potential implications for identity development. I define identity from Erikson's (1968) perspective of the *ego identity*, a unique, coherent, and stable sense of self that is continuous over time. Understanding the nature of relatedness and autonomy afforded by social networking sites is significant for identity development because a balance between social connection and self-determination constitutes the fulcrum on which a coherent identity is consolidated during the transition to adulthood (Kroger, 2004). Indeed, the field of identity development is built on the basic idea that the primary task of adolescence and emerging adulthood is to individuate and find a sense of personal volition while maintaining a secure sense of attachment to parents and peers (e.g., Allen, Hauser, Bell, O'Connor, 1994; Arnett, 2004; Grotevant & Cooper, 1985). The way in which autonomy and relatedness is balanced in the process of establishing an identity in the transition from childhood to adulthood varies across cultures and historical time.

A historical and sociocultural perspective provides a reference point for recognizing current practices, meanings, and values for relatedness and autonomy and how they impact identity formation (see Cote & LeVine, 2002). In his presentation of historical evidence of changes in conceptions of the self across time, Baumeister (1987) cogently argues how the self has increasingly become a "problem" since the medieval period. That is, as the notion of a self separate from others has increased over the course of history, personal meaning-making and personal fulfillment have become emphasized, which has made defining the self and one's place in society a more onerous developmental task. In essence, navigating a complex process of exploration and then commitment has become central to identity formation. This is in contrast to premodern societies, where an emphasis on the self as related to others channeled adolescent identity formation through a process of apprenticeship, adherence to hierarchy, and fulfillment of social obligations (see also Arnett, this volume). Youth learned traditional knowledge to acquire ascribed social roles within enduring, interdependent networks of kin. This process would be categorized as "foreclosure" and maladaptive in the West (Phinney & Baldelomar, 2011); however, it is adaptive to sociodemographic conditions where possibilities for adult roles are limited and where functional interdependence facilitates survival. Moreover, identity exploration is irrelevant in premodern environments, which generally have high levels of social consensus based on tradition (Lerner, 1958; Manago, 2012). Social consensus means collective validation of an ascribed social identity, such that experimentation and reconciliation of diverse possibilities is unnecessary.

In this chapter, I consider how social networking sites are extending trends in the modern era toward increasing emphasis on autonomy in identity development. In reviewing the literature with this historical lens of analysis, I hope to avoid what others have pointed to as a tendency to view the social significance of the Internet in either optimistic or pessimistic terms (Hogan & Wellman, 2012; McKenna & Bargh, 2000). The goal here is to explore the complex aspects of sociocultural changes via social media and consider the ways in which adolescents are enacting new forms of relatedness and autonomy to adapt to increasingly digital social worlds. In doing so, I aim to highlight that there are tradeoffs in the sociocultural changes for identity development, some potentially positive and some potentially negative, depending on one's perspective and values.

Relatedness, Autonomy, and Networked Individualism on Social Networking Sites

New forms of relatedness on social networking sites must be understood in terms of the enhanced capacities for individual agency engendered by these technologies. Social networking sites facilitate the creation of egocentric networks—webs of close and distant associations all relative to the individual (Donath, 2008). In other words, they provide the individual with efficient and convenient tools for maintaining contact with potential social resources based on personal needs and interests, rather than based on superordinate needs of a community. As such, social networking sites epitomize the kind of relatedness that sociologist Barry Wellman (2002) calls "networked individualism." He suggests that the Internet reflects and further amplifies social and technological changes that have promoted individual mobility and independence in developed nations across the twentieth century, all of which have shifted the nature of social relations from tightly knit, homogenous face-to-face social groups based on common goals and shared geography to "personal communities that supply the essentials of community separately to each individual.... The person, rather than the household or group, is the primary unit of connectivity" (Wellman, Boase, & Chen, 2002; p. 160). Networked individualism provides a useful framework for conceptualizing the way in which human needs for relatedness persist in the digital age, but in a way that prioritizes the autonomy of the individual operating as an independent agent among multiple social circles.

Indeed, there is little evidence of a psychological sense of community among young people using MySpace and Facebook (Reich, 2010). Adolescents and college students tend not to express feelings of group membership or common goals with their social network site community; rather, they describe their experiences as nodes of individuals operating within personalized webs of connections. Although youth do sometimes use Facebook to form groups based on common interests (which is associated with civic engagement; Valenzuela, Park, & Kee, 2009), much of the behavior on social networking sites has been described as *social grooming*, defined as the cultivation of social ties (Tufekci, 2008b; Donath, 2008). With social grooming on social networking sites, the individual independently traverses through the announcements and photos broadcast by people in their personalized networks. This involves observing others' activities for entertainment or information, posting announcements or offering commentaries in response to others' broadcasted activities, and generally maintaining a reputation to friends by way of the self-expressions posted on these network excursions.

Social grooming suggests that social practices in a culture of networked individualism revolve around consuming and producing personal self-expressions, a hallmark of increased individual agency that is engendered by social media. In a clever experiment, Schwammlein and Wodzicki (2012) showed that the design and structure of social networking sites evoke communications referencing the self, in contrast to communications addressing a superordinate group's goals and interests, which are more common in online content communities such as Wikipedia. In fact, the marketing taglines on the two most popular social networking sites in the world, Facebook and Twitter (Alexa, 2012), emphasize that achieving a sense of belonging comes from engaging in the ongoing real-time flow of digital self-expressions: "*Connect with friends and the world around you*" by reading and posting to the Facebook newsfeed, and "*Find out what's happening, right now, with the people and organizations you care about*" via 140-character tweets on Twitter. If personhood in premodern societies was about being embedded in tight-knit, interdependent communities of social obligations, personhood in the digital age, at least on the Internet, seems about being embedded in streams of human expression that offer information and entertainment, as well as an audience for one's own personal broadcasts. Under these conditions, heightened levels of exploration with larger networks of peers become possible, as well as an increasing expectation to create, and consolidate, an image of the self that is appropriately packaged for an audience.

Self-expression on social networking sites is distinctive from self-expression on other social media in that it is directed to large numbers of contacts anchored in offline relationships. Study after study finds that adolescents' and college students' primary motivation for using social networking sites is to stay in touch with their offline peers, rather than to meet new people or connect with strangers (Ellison et al., 2007; Pempek, Yermolayeva, & Calvert, 2009; Reich, Subrahmanyam, & Espinoza, 2012; Subrahmanyam, Reich, Waechter, & Espinoza, 2008; Steinfield, Ellison, & Lampe, 2008). However, friendship networks on social networking sites are larger than youths' offline networks of friends (Acar, 2008), numbering in the hundreds and reaching 1,000 at the extreme ends (Manago, Taylor, & Greenfield, 2012; Reich et al., 2012; Steinfield et al., 2008). Adolescents report that they interact "frequently" in face-to-face settings with about 77% of the friends listed on their social network site profile (Reich et al., 2012), and it is estimated that about 21% of undergraduates' Facebook networks are comprised of close friends, whereas 51% are acquaintances (Manago et al., 2012). Because maintaining connections on social networking sites is so convenient, the technology provides an effective way to materialize a "latent" or potential social tie deriving from a fleeting offline encounter into something more permanent (Haythornthwaite, 2005). As such, social networking sites allow users to sustain large numbers of acquaintances and thus gain more diversity and breadth in social relationships that transcend offline–online dichotomies (Donath, 2008; Donath & boyd, 2004).

In sum, networked individualism is a useful starting point for understanding new forms of relatedness and autonomy on social networking sites, where relatedness assumes and prioritizes the autonomy of the individual. The dominant mode by which individuals connect on Facebook or Twitter is not through privately shared experiences or mutually sustained obligations, but by independently navigating and contributing to streams of publicly broadcast personal self-expressions. In the following sections, I describe new forms of relatedness and autonomy evidenced in studies of adolescents' and emerging adults' use of social networking sites and their impacts on exploration and commitment.

First, I suggest that new forms of relatedness can be understood as *customized sociality,* a term that reflects the way in which social networking sites support the individual's pursuit of social resources that meet her or his needs. Second, I examine the nature of self-expression on social networking sites as a heightened form of personal agency and autonomy in the digital age. Both of these practices reflect increasing opportunities for exploration. I propose that customized sociality and self-expression must be understood in terms of the need to sustain connections with others in a loosely connected world. That is, in contrast to preindustrial and even modern societies, where relationships were rather stable, based on kinship and physical communities, social relations in a postmodern networked individualistic world are considerably more impermanent. Although social networking sites make it easy to digitally preserve a social tie in the list of "friends," the association must still be nurtured to some extent for the relationship to yield social resources. I suggest that youth in the digital age are learning to nurture and tend their relationships through a one-to-many style of interaction that emphasizes individual expressions. As they broadcast self-expressions on social networking sites, they are experiencing themselves as a public brand or image that is appropriate for, and appealing to, large online networks. In describing each of these trends—customized sociality and public self-expression—I summarize both potential costs and potential benefits for identity formation during adolescence and the transition to adulthood.

Relatedness on Social Networking Sites: Customized Sociality

In the early days of the Internet, much of the research was framed by the "displacement hypothesis," which posited that adolescents' online interactions with relative strangers would replace more stable, permanent, and high-quality in-person relationships, leading to isolation and loneliness (e.g., Kraut et al., 1998; Sanders, Field, Diego, & Kaplan, 2000). Although the developmental consequences of supplanting face-to-face interactions with screen time, especially among children, begs for further investigation (e.g., Pea et al., 2012), studies with adolescents, emerging adults, and adults reveal that using the Internet specifically to augment, rather than replace, offline relationships is associated with a variety of positive outcomes, including higher levels of social support and less loneliness (Blais et al., 2008; Desjarlais & Willoughby, 2010; Valkenburg & Peter, 2011). Hogan and Wellman (2012) argue that, in fact, this is largely how the Internet is being used in networked individualistic societies—technologically mediated interactions are intertwined with offline connections such that it makes little sense to treat them as discrete processes. Online and offline communication modalities aid, extend, and supplement one another. As these technologies become more widespread and embedded into the social fabric, the poignant questions will revolve around how the Internet penetrates our everyday social lives. I suggest that social networking sites constitute part of the digital age infrastructure that enables adolescents and emerging adults to manage their everyday relationships, and further, to explore larger social networks outside the family and customize their social worlds to suit their needs.

Social networking sites enable the customization of social worlds because they make connecting to friends easy and convenient. During adolescence, peers emerge as a primary source of social support (e.g., Furman & Buhrmester, 1992), yet those relationships are subject to restrictions such as curfews, lack of transportation, and limited access to unsupervised social spaces. Social networking sites (along with cell phones, Instant Messenger, and other social media) provide adolescents with increased control over their social environments and make peers accessible 24/7 at the wave of a computer mouse or press of a touch screen (Clark, 2005; Valkenburg & Peter, 2011). As boyd (2008) nicely articulated in her ethnographic account of youth and social networking sites, Friendster, MySpace, and then Facebook have given adolescents a place to interact in unregulated public spaces while living in regulated physical environments. Social networking sites equip adolescents with enhanced mastery over their social lives, allowing them to circumvent physical constraints and restrictions imposed by parents and other authority figures to sustain ongoing contact with peers.

For emerging adults, social networking sites offer sociality customized for instability. Youth in this period of life are often trying out a number of different jobs, relationships, and living arrangements, and embracing opportunities to move to a new city or backpack through Europe before settling down into adult commitments and responsibilities (Arnett, 2004). Facebook is useful for this kind of hypermobile, unsettled existence because it can be used to integrate into new social milieus while maintaining attachment to past communities (Ellison et al., 2007; Stephenson-Abetz & Holman, 2012). Correlational studies show that intensity of Facebook use predicts increased involvement in college life and, at the same time, increased connection to hometown friends and resources (Ellison et al., 2007; Ellison, Steinfield, Lampe, 2010; Kalpidou, Costin, & Morris, 2011; Lou, Yan, Nickerson, & McMorris, 2012). Emerging adults in the digital age can have their cake and eat it too; they can pursue new adventures at college, while preserving a safe home base by keeping track of hometown friends on Facebook and posting status updates to them.

Conveniently, college students can find something to post home about by using social networking sites as a lubricant for social engagement in their new social settings. In an ethnographic exploration of the role of Facebook in college life, Barkhuus and Tashiro (2010) found that Facebook facilitates social gatherings with new acquaintances because it provides a noninvasive way to extend invitations. They also describe how Facebook facilitates ad hoc meet-ups. In one example, a student posts a status update, "who wants to go to taco Tuesday?" to summon companions from the network; in another example, a student posts, "I need caffeine" evoking a response from someone in the network, "let's go." Thus, Facebook can be an efficient platform for mobilizing face-to-face interactions when you want it, how you want it.

A central reason why social networking sites are optimized for integration into new social circles is that they provide quick and easy access to social information. "Social supernets" comprised of large numbers of "weak ties" (Granovetter, 1973) on social networking sites expand users' informational resources (Donath, 2008). Normative Facebook activities, such as creating a profile and exchanging public commentary, reveal a number of data points about users and their relationships, which means one can find out a lot about people whom one does not know very well (Brandtzæg et al., 2010; Ellison et al., 2010; Livingstone, 2008; Tufekci, 2008b). Indeed, young people do use Facebook to seek social information from their "social supernets" (Brandtzæg, Luders, & Skjetne, 2010; Courtois, Anissa, & Vanwynsberghe, 2012; Raacke & Bonds-Raacke, 2008; Tufekci, 2008b; Valenzuela et al., 2009). One daily diary study showed that college students spend more time observing content on Facebook than posting information themselves (Pempek et al., 2009). Youth today can mobilize elaborate social knowledge more than ever before, which enhances their independence, exploration, and mobility between social groups.

Benefits of Customized Sociality for Identity Development

A benefit of customized sociality is the potential to effectively mobilize social support. Social networking sites function as a foundation for maintaining and seeking relationships, and also as a sounding board for self-reflection. As outlined earlier, social networking sites offer a way to fortify a home base, which can embolden the pursuit of new experiences, such that exploration serves as a central process in identity achievement. College students do indeed report that they value Facebook because it provides them with a sense of security, knowing that past associations will not be lost as they seek new adventures (Stephenson-Abetz & Holman, 2012). In addition, online social networks are a source of feedback for adolescents' identity experimentations (Valkenburg & Peter, 2011). Adolescents can try out versions of themselves and gauge responses from their network. Status updates are also frequently used to convey one's current emotional state to the network, and the more people college students estimate to be observing their status updates, the more they perceive that Facebook is a useful tool for garnering social support (Manago et al., 2012). College students who are substantially invested in Facebook report that when others respond to their feelings and needs broadcasted via status updates, it signals to them that someone out there cares about them and how they are doing (Vitak & Ellison, 2012).

As cursory as virtual feedback to status updates may be, it can be psychologically significant. Evidence for this comes from a study with a sample of college students who felt socially rejected, anxious, and depressed (Szwedo, Mikami, & Allen, 2012). A year later, they showed a decline in anxious-depressive symptoms that was related to the volume of comments they received on their Facebook profile pages over that period of time. Valkenburg, Peter, and Schouten (2006) also showed in a self-report survey study with adolescents that positive feedback in response to status updates predicted higher levels of self-esteem. Another study demonstrated that college students who disclosed more about their emotional needs on Facebook were more likely to receive social support on Facebook, which then predicted higher subjective well-being (Kim & Lee, 2011). However, studies also suggest that emotional disclosures may be conducive to well-being only within more intimate social networks. For example, those with smaller, tight-knit Facebook networks are more likely to emotionally disclose via status updates and report higher levels of emotional social support from Facebook than those with larger networks (Kim & Lee, 2011; Stutzman, Vitak, Ellison, Gray, & Lampe, 2012). Yang and Brown (2012) found an association between the frequency with which college students post status updates and poor psychosocial adjustment, but only among those who reported using Facebook to meet new people and thus had less intimate networks.

However, large networks can be beneficial in that they offer a window into the lives of peers who are outside one's immediate social circles, thus providing a more expansive consciousness for identity explorations. Adolescents can gather information about various cliques and crowds at school, which then leads to increased understanding of acquaintances' points of view (Antheunis, Valkenburg, & Peter, 2010; Courtois et al., 2012). This may be especially useful for shy or socially anxious youth. As one fifteen-year-old explains, "Facebook makes it easier to talk to people at school that you may not see a lot or know very well" (from Ito et al., 2010; p. 89). However, very little research has empirically examined whether social networking sites in fact foster exposure to alternative perspectives or whether they are used to locate similar others. Compelling evidence for the former comes from a longitudinal study with 2,000 people in Norway, aged fifteen to seventy-five (Brandtzæg, 2012). The study found that social networking site users, compared to nonusers, reported having more people in their network of friends who were different from them (i.e., endorsed another political view, came from a different cultural background). Evidence for the latter comes from a study that asked college students to think about a person on their Facebook network with whom they frequently interact online but not offline (Craig & Wright, 2012). Perceived similarity to the self predicted more social attraction, more depth of conversation, and more closeness. Taken together, the studies suggest that, although social networking sites are conducive to amassing large networks of diverse others, young people are more likely to be engaged with people in those large networks who represent the familiar. Customized sociality on social networking sites means a potpourri of diverse others from which to choose but also a vehicle to find people with similar views and values.

Youth from sexual, ethnic, or other minority groups may especially benefit from this new tool for gaining social information about others (Antheunis et al., 2010; Ito et al., 2010). Minority youth may feel marginalized in their hometown communities but may be able to find peers more similar to them on social networking sites, peers with sympathetic perspectives who can support a better understanding of themselves. Gray (2009) notes that lesbian-gay-bisexual-transsexual (LGBT) youth in rural America use social networking sites and other social media to find other LGBT individuals, alleviate feelings of isolation, and help legitimize their queer sexual identities. Tynes and colleagues (2010) have found that some ethnic minority adolescents use Facebook to find others who are engaging in sophisticated discussions on race relations, thereby providing opportunities to explore their ethnic identities more elaborately. These examples illustrate how social networking sites empower the individual by opening up access to a broader range of possibilities for customizing a social world accommodated to one's particular circumstances and interests. An important caveat here is that shy and socially awkward youth who prefer online communication to expand their social networks are at a higher risk for Internet addiction (Smahel, Brown, & Blinka, 2012). Social networking sites may be most beneficial to identity development when online resources translate to the offline social world.

Finally, this access to a broad purview of social information can also be conducive to acquiring *bridging social capital* or instrumental social resources in the process of identity development. Bridging capital has been defined as the sense that one is linked to and can effectively derive resources from an all-encompassing, heterogeneous community of humanity (Ellison et al., 2007). Bridging social capital is associated with a specific kind of Facebook use among college students, *social searching*, perusing Facebook profiles and public exchanges to learn more about acquaintances in the network (Brandtzæg et al., 2010; Ellison et al., 2010). In effect, having more bridging social capital endows young people with many practically useful contacts that can be exploited to enrich their identity explorations, such as connections to a new job, volunteer opportunities, internships, or involvement in social organizations. Others have found that simply the frequency of Facebook use and the centrality of the site to one's social life predicts college students' beliefs that human beings are good and can be trusted (Valenzuela et al., 2009). These studies suggest that using social networking sites to access social information outside of one's immediate social circles may increase young people's faith that "everyone is connected" and thus feel a sense of belonging to a far-reaching community of diverse others. However, it is important to keep in mind that these studies are correlational. It is therefore possible that those who are already skilled and socially competent in the first place may be drawn to Facebook, although longitudinal studies also support the idea that Facebook use over time promotes bridging capital (Steinfield et al., 2008).

Costs of Customized Sociality for Identity Development

The costs involved with customized sociality begin with the way digital communication technologies foster perpetual contact with peers, perhaps detracting from quality time with parents and family. One correlational study with a nationally representative sample of US adolescents found that time spent online with peers was associated with less time spent with parents (Lee, 2008). Other studies have found correlations between the time adolescents spend online and lower levels of perceived closeness with parents (Mesch, 2003; Willoughby, 2008). Although peer relationships offer valuable opportunities for identity work, the importance of parental support and closeness persists during adolescence (Youniss & Smollar, 1985). Adolescents face unrelenting peer presentation contexts with digital communication technologies such that they have fewer opportunities to let down their guard and experience unconditional love and support from their families (Clark, 2005). This lack of distance from peers is particularly troubling given the rise of cyberbullying, when negative experiences with peers follow adolescents home from school and are thereby intensified (Tokunaga, 2010).

Another potential drawback of convenient access to peers involves the ease by which friends can be accumulated on social networking sites, which may draw young people's attention to the superficiality of popularity as a goal during identity development. In a survey study with undergraduates, the need for popularity was the most potent predictor of Facebook use, over and above the need for social stimulation, need for belonging, and desire to learn about what friends are doing (Utz, Tanis, & Vermeulen, 2012). Others find that some youth use Facebook to increase their popularity and self-esteem (Zywica & Danowski, 2008), but that, in fact, accumulating friends rather indiscriminately is associated with low self-esteem, especially among those with higher levels of concern about how others view them (Lee, Moore, Park, & Park, 2012). An emphasis on popularity could devalue the importance of close, intimate relationships as contexts for identity development in young people's lives. Instead of seeking belonging within smaller, intimate groups, young people may increasingly seek acceptance within large, shallow networks, which demands promoting a socially desirable self, an issue discussed in the next section on self-expression.

Moreover, collecting large numbers of friends, many of whom one does not interact with regularly in face-to-face contexts, may be detrimental to identity development because of tendencies for social comparison. Qualitative studies with adolescents and college students (Livingstone, 2008; Manago, Graham, Greenfield, & Salimkhan, 2008), as well as a large-scale international survey of more than 1,000 Facebook users of various ages (McAndrew & Jeong, 2012), suggest that a substantial amount of social comparison occurs on social networking sites. This is problematic because users are likely to be exposed to a disproportionate amount of positive information about others on Facebook, given that social networking sites provide tools for selective self-presentation and self-promotion. When observing acquaintances, youth do not have an accurate picture of their lives because they are not interacting with acquaintances regularly offline. One study finds that the more time college students spend on Facebook and the more casual acquaintances on their Facebook friend lists, the more likely they are to believe that other people have better lives than they do (Chou & Edge, 2012). Another experimental study manipulated whether undergraduate participants looked at a physically attractive or unattractive Facebook profile; those who looked at the attractive profiles reported lower body image and less positive emotions (Haferkamp & Kramer, 2011). Exposure to attractive peer presentations online could have a more powerful effect than exposure to beautiful celebrities because the former represent more relevant standards for self-evaluation.

The cognitive demands of filtering all this readily accessible social information could also derail adolescents' attempts to organize and integrate information about experiences and relationships to consolidate a sense of self. In their sample of emerging adults, Misra and Stokols (2012) concluded that cyber-based information overload, when cognitive demands exceed an individual's ability to process content, was predictive of higher levels of perceived stress, which interferes with concentration and self-reflection. Social networking sites create unrelenting demands to manage social information and needs, perhaps overwhelming younger teens before they have established a coherent and stable sense of self capable of selectively regulating the bombardment of stimuli. The storehouses of information provided by social networking sites may be convenient and efficient for socializing but may also interrupt in-depth contemplations during sensitive periods for identity development.

In sum, the pernicious effects of social networking sites often are difficult to observe because the websites are socially sanctioned and have become widely popular across social strata. Thus, although many studies show that young people often report positive feelings about social networking sites, they may not be fully cognizant of the ways Facebook and other social media could subtly and adversely affect their happiness and well-being.

Autonomy on Social Networking Sites: Self-Expression

To exist on a social networking site is to "write oneself into being" (boyd, 2008) by expressing who one is to one's network of friends. Expressing who one is begins with constructing a profile, selecting a representative photo, articulating defining characteristics, likes and preferences, and adding friends. "Writing oneself into being" continues as the user broadcasts status updates to the network, uploads photos, shares links and news stories, and "likes" or comments on someone's newsfeed post. These communications are asynchronous, meaning that they are nonspontaneous, allowing users to edit and reflect on the kinds of messages they want to project and thereby giving them increased control over their self-expressions (Valkenburg & Peter, 2007; 2011). Increased control means more responsibility for crafting a self-image for audience consumption. It also translates into opportunities to promote idealized aspects of the self to one's friends (Manago et al., 2008; Livingstone, 2008; Salimkhan, Manago, & Greenfield, 2010; Zhao et al., 2008). Idealized selves on social networking sites are not artificial selves, largely because these websites are "nonymous" (Zhao et al., 2008), thus users are motivated to present accurate identity statements to people they know in the offline world. In fact, a number of personality researchers have found high correspondence between offline and online personality traits on Facebook (Wilson, Gosling, & Graham, 2012).

Notwithstanding this tendency for accuracy, portraying oneself in a flattering light is an important motivating factor in young people's social networking site use (Kramer & Winter, 2008; Mehdizadeh, 2010; Zhao et al., 2008). Computer-mediated communication allows people to employ strategic self-presentations to optimize their most attractive features because it affords time to craft ideal messages and highlight positive attributes (Ellison, Heino, & Gibbs, 2006; Walther, 2007). Emerging adult users of social networking sites utilize various applications such as self-descriptions and selection of flattering photos that are conducive to boasting and putting forth a worthwhile persona (Kramer & Winter, 2008; Salimkhan et al., 2010). Thus, self-expression can be thought of as self-conscious self-presentations, virtual refractions of hoped-for or possible selves that are perceived to be socially desirable in one's community (Manago et al., 2008; Zhao et al., 2008).

The use of photos is especially popular among young people in these digital worlds (Livingstone, 2008; Pempek et al., 2009; Siibak, 2010; Tufekci, 2008a; Zhao et al., 2008). Photos highlight how important it is for both young men (Hirdman, 2010; Manago, 2013; Siibak, 2010) and young women (Ringrose, 2010; Manago et al., 2008; Magnuson & Dundes, 2008) to reproduce themselves online as physically attractive. Photos are considered a premier strategy for establishing the validity of one's attractive persona because they "show rather than tell" (Zhao et al., 2008). Yet, photos can also be used to creatively stretch the truth or promote a certain positive aspect of the self by distributing only photos that reflect how one wants to be seen, in just the right light, involved in exciting or other valued activities, and socially situated within certain peer groups to demonstrate that one is popular and well-liked (Manago et al., 2008; Zhao et al., 2008). In addition, young people can embellish who they are online by incorporating multimedia such as music, videos, or brands from pop culture into their self-presentations and thus define themselves through popularly valued aesthetics and trends (Livingstone, 2008; Pempek et al., 2009; Salimkhan et al., 2010; Zhao et al., 2008).

The imagery and strategies for self-presentation that appear in advertising and mass media entertainment emerge within youths' own self-portrayals of beauty and sexual appeal on social networking sites (Hall, West, & McIntyre, 2012; Manago, 2013; Ringrose, 2010; Siibak, 2010).

However, juxtaposed to the increased power to control and craft the self, social networking site users are also at the mercy of others to authorize their self-presentations. The lack of physical cues online means that social endorsements from the network are critical to the legitimacy of self-presentations (Donath, 2008; Donath & boyd, 2004; Livingstone, 2008, Manago et al., 2008). In fact, research on impression formation with college students has found reliable support for the "warranting principle," which suggests that other-generated information is regarded as more truthful on social networking sites because it is perceived to be unsanctioned by a profile owner (Walther, Van Der Heide, Hamel, & Shulman, 2009). Experiments find that when drawing conclusions about a profile owner's likeability and attractiveness, evaluators prioritize peer commentaries over self-statements on the profile (Hong, Tandoc, Kim, Kim, & Wise, 2012; Walther et al., 2009). This phenomenon may be particularly strong with regards to claims to physical attractiveness, which can be deceptive online (Walther, Van der Heide, Kim, Westerman, & Tong, 2009).

Moreover, social networking site users articulate their social connections in order to promote a particular self-image. Having more contacts in one's Facebook friend list and appearing with friends in photos strengthens evaluators' perceptions that a target is socially connected, although having an excessive amount of friends weakens judgments about the target's "real" level of social connectedness (Tong, Van Der Heide, Langwell, & Walther, 2008; Zwier, Araujo, Boukes, & Willemsen, 2011). The list of contacts can also serve as indicators of identity markers such as social status, political beliefs, and artistic tastes because evaluators assume Facebook users have things in common with the people on their friend list (Donath & boyd, 2004; Ellison et al., 2010; Tong et al., 2008; Zwier et al., 2011). College students judge how good-looking Facebook targets are by how attractive their friends are (Walther et al., 2008) and how friendly Facebook targets are by how extraverted their friends appear in their photos (Utz, 2010). Indeed, undergraduate MySpace users reported that they enjoyed exchanging messages with friends publicly on the site because it demonstrated their social competency and offered statements about who they are through the people with whom they are affiliated (Manago et al., 2008; Salimkhan et al., 2010).

Along this vein, boyd and Heer (2006) suggest that constructing the self on social networking sites is not a solitary endeavor, but rather is constituted through public conversations. Qualitative analyses of youth interactions on social networking sites highlight the way friends use language to validate, shore up, and also add meanings to an individual's self-expressions. In a study of a group of Dutch emerging adults on MySpace, Van Doorn (2010) describes how men and women exchanged sexually charged flirtations with same and other sex friends and, in doing so, established their queer sexual identities in their networks. Another qualitative study demonstrated how adolescent girls collaborate by sharing sexually explicit messages on each other's walls to construct self-confident, sexually knowledgeable selves (Garcia-Gomez, 2011). Other examples come from research on the behaviors of romantic partners on social networking sites (Manago, 2013; Mod, 2010; Salimkhan et al., 2010; Utz & Beukeboom, 2011). These studies illustrate how adolescents and college students engage in public displays of affection online, reciprocating comments on each other's profiles such as "*I love you billy buns*" to socially construct their identities as loving and worthy of devotion and affection. Thus, ironically, although social networking sites afford increased opportunities for agency through self-expression, and customized sociality involves heightened autonomy in interpersonal relatedness, communication on social networking sites also involves dependence on others to verify and shore up identity claims in virtual spaces.

Benefits of Self-Expression for Identity Development

The ability to express oneself to audiences of friends can be beneficial in that larger numbers of people in one's network can validate self-conceptions and help the individual shape and manifest desired selves. Valkenburg and Peter (2011) suggest that social networking sites create enhanced opportunities for adolescents to gauge the desirability of their self-presentations through feedback from friends, adjust accordingly, and thus feel better about themselves. In one study, the frequency of social networking site use among a sample of Dutch adolescents predicted higher levels of feedback from friends, and the more feedback adolescents received, the more likely that feedback was positive, which in turn predicted higher levels of self-esteem (Valkenburg et al., 2006). Negative feedback decreased adolescents' self-esteem, although negative feedback was rare. On the other hand, feedback on social networking sites could also reinforce deviant behavior as part of youths' self-image. One study showed that college students who posted pictures of alcohol use on their social networking site profiles were more likely to have alcohol-related problems a year later (Szwedo et al., 2012).

Yet, even without the feedback, simply seeing oneself projected to an audience may heighten the awareness of one's self-image and, if it is crafted in a flattering way that realizes a desired self, increase self-esteem. Evidence for this comes from a study with three experimental conditions; college students completed a task either next to a mirror, next to a computer screen with their Facebook profile open, or in an empty cubicle (Gonzales & Hancock, 2011). Those with their Facebook profiles open reported the highest levels of self-esteem after the manipulation, whereas those next to the mirror reported the lowest levels of self-esteem. The authors concluded that awareness of a self that has been enhanced on Facebook might remind young people of their ideal selves, leading to the boost in self-esteem. Supporting this view is another study that asked college students to either edit and write about their Facebook profiles or use and write about Google Maps: those assigned to the Facebook condition subsequently scored higher on self-esteem than those assigned to the Google Maps condition (Gentile et al., 2012). Kim and Lee (2011) found that, among college students, there is a direct association between using Facebook to present oneself favorably (i.e., "I only show the happy side of me") and feeling good about oneself and one's life.

In addition, because social networking sites require users to create a profile and thus commit to a particular construction of the self in a public or semipublic space, these sites could promote identity consolidation. One study provides evidence that young people integrate qualities they display online into their identity (Gonzales & Hancock, 2008). College student participants were randomly assigned to either behave in extraverted or introverted ways by answering questions about their lives either in a private Word document or in a public online blog. Those who answered questions as if they were extraverted in the public blog subsequently rated themselves as more extraverted compared to those who were assigned to behave as if they were introverted, but no difference was found in the private condition. In this way, the increasing normativity of self-expression on social networking sites in the digital age could provide enhanced opportunities for self-concept clarity.

Certainly, the experience of the self is heightened on social networking sites; young people are drawn into managing their reputations to large online networks, and some studies suggest that this translates to higher levels of self-regard and self-worth. So could the proliferation of social media contribute to an exaggerated sense of self-worth and self-importance among the millennial generation? On the one hand, social networking sites provide forums for self-promotion, vanity, and attention-getting, and nonclinical narcissists do collect larger number of friends and are more likely to engage in self-promotional behaviors on these websites (Carpenter, 2012; McKinney, Kelly, & Duran, 2012; Mehdizadeh, 2010). An intergenerational study of MySpace showed that adolescents (thirteen to nineteen years old) are more likely than older users (more than sixty years old) to collect more friends and more likely to use more self-references when describing themselves (Pfeil, Arjan, & Saphiris, 2009). It is unclear whether this finding is due to maturation or due to sociocultural and psychological shifts in self-involvement across generations.

On the other hand, perhaps we are witnessing a new form of sociality and personhood in the digital age that is simply perceived as narcissism among "digital immigrants" but normative among "digital natives" (Prensky, 2001). Recent studies find that narcissism is not related to general Facebook use, partly because use of the site is so normative (Bergman, Fearrington, Davenport, & Bergman, 2011; Gentile et al., 2012). Broadcasting information about the self on Facebook is also increasingly common. A study using Facebook servers to collect data among a 140,000-person sample of new users across a variety of ages (Burke, Marlow, & Lento, 2009) and another with a sample of college students (Christofides, Muise, & Desmarais, 2009) showed that people begin to disclose more about themselves the more that their contacts are doing so. In other words, to acculturate to Facebook is to engage in public self-expression at the expense of a certain amount of intimacy and privacy in social interactions. Thus, youth growing up with social media are acculturating to a social world permeated by an Internet media spotlight.

Indeed, a number of researchers have noted intergenerational changes related to social networking sites and the meaning of privacy (Christofides, Muise, & Desmarais, 2012; Livingstone, 2008; Tufekci, 2008b). It seems that millennial youth are concerned about privacy, but they prioritize other benefits such as publicity, attention, and customized sociality. In fact, one study provided evidence to show that it is not narcissism, but rather openness to sharing information about oneself (i.e., "I like letting people know a lot about me," "I let a wide circle of friends know a lot about me") that predicts posting self-focused updates and photos to Facebook (McKinney et al., 2012). This is the sociality of networked individualism, a way of connecting to others that emphasizes the appropriateness and value of self-expression to wide circles of known others. Self-expression may be more valued because it is necessary for forming and sustaining connections in a digital mediated social world of loose relations. That is to say, with increasing autonomy in the relatedness of customized sociality comes increased opportunities to choose among a wide selection of potential affiliations. Thus, individuals must prove their desirability, value, and worthiness in the marketplace of potential connections. In this way, young people may be under increased pressure in their identity formation to create selves that are easily attractive to a broad range of others, thus dependent on shallow relations for validation and worth.

Costs of Self-Expression for Identity Development

Some studies illustrate how this pressure to be popular could play out on social networking sites. The finding that college students associate social support on Facebook with higher numbers of people paying attention to their status updates (Manago et al., 2012) suggests that attention to the self is becoming an important social resource in the digital age (see also Donath, 2008). Might young people become dependent on attention from audiences to feel good about themselves? One study examined this possibility. University students who reported public-based contingencies of self-worth (deriving good feelings about themselves from appearance and social approval), especially those who ranked higher in appearance contingency of self-worth, were more likely to engage in photo sharing on Facebook (Stefanone, Lackaff, & Rosen, 2011). Those who had higher levels of private-based contingencies (i.e., virtue and family) were less likely to spend as much time on social networking sites. Of course, peer social acceptance has long been an important component of feeling a sense of security in one's identity, yet what happens when youth seek this belonging in very large, shallow social networks? More work is needed to understand the social developmental impacts of seeking attention from expansive online audiences.

Moreover, because status updates on social networking sites require a "one-to-many style of interaction" (Pempek et al., 2009), multiple identities may be constrained when adolescents communicate to a flat, one-dimensional audience (boyd, 2008; Brandtzæg et al., 2010; Tufekci, 2008a). This issue has been termed "context collapse" (Marwick & boyd, 2010). Tufekci (2008a) suggests that this phenomenon represents a return to village life, one in which everyone "knows your business." However, networks on social networking sites are not homogenous; they represent multiple, independent groups of people with differing beliefs and agendas. This presents youth with a challenging landscape to navigate. Maintaining multiple identities is necessary when one holds multiple group memberships in a society of networked individualism, yet the culture of social networking sites seems to encourage young people to create an identity that is appropriately packaged for and desirable to a homogenous singular audience.

Take, for example, a qualitative study that illustrated how first-year college students struggled to present themselves on Facebook in ways that would be appropriate for both hometown and college communities (Stephenson-Abetz & Holman, 2012). The task they faced was to maintain a connection with past selves while cultivating an updated sense of self in their new social milieus, all in one social context. These youth desired to express their uniqueness and individuality, but had to yield to a certain amount of conformity in their self-presentations so as not to offend differing social groups. Marwick and boyd (2010) found similar themes among adult and emerging adult users of Twitter, which is becoming increasingly popular with teens. Twitter users wanted to amass large audiences for their tweets but also wanted to be unique and authentic. In reconciling these needs, they talked about "audience management" and "personal branding," in essence, commodifying themselves with strategic hooks that are palatable to a mass audience. How will young people negotiate a desire for attention from an audience with a desire to be authentic and unique? Does creating the self as a personal brand offer a new vehicle for consolidating a sense of self, a chance to be our "real" selves regardless of our interaction partners? Or does it flatten the complexity and flexibility of self-constructions that are attuned to various social situations?

Conclusion

Shifts in the organization of sociality from premodern, to modern, and now digital societies represents a movement away from tight-knit close communities to increasingly large, diverse, and geographically distant networks of connections revolving around the autonomy and agency of the individual. As we move further into the twenty-first century, the Internet and social networking sites position young people at the command center of their social lives, endowing them with the capacity to create personalized networks of contacts that can be explored and accommodated to their needs. Deriving the potential benefits of social networking sites requires transmitting signals to effectively transform online resources into offline realities, and, to do so, one must engage in public self-expression. In some sense, these self-expressions represent efforts to socially construct attractive selves that will be evaluated positively in the marketplace of the newly customized social world. Digitally manufactured representations of the self for audience consumption is becoming increasingly normative, and we are only beginning to understand implications of these shifting social practices on identity development.

References

Acar, A. (2008). Antecedents and consequences of online social networking site behavior: The case of Facebook. *Journal of Website Promotion, 5,* 3, 62–83.

Alexa. (2012). Alexa top 500 global sites. Retrieved from http://www.alexa.com/topsites/global

Al Omoush, K., Yaseen, S. G., & Alma'aitah, M. A. (2012). The impact of Arab cultural values on online social networking: The case of Facebook. *Computers in Human Behavior, 28,* 2387–2399.

Allen, J. P., Hauser, S. T., Bell, K. L., & O'Connor, T. G. (1994). Longitudinal assessment of autonomy and relatedness in adolescent-family interactions as predictors of adolescent ego development and self-esteem. *Child Development, 65,* 179–194.

Antheunis, M. L., Valkenburg, P. M., & Peter, J. (2010). Getting acquainted through social network sites: Testing a model of uncertainty reduction and social attraction. *Computers in Human Behavior, 26,* 100–109.

Arnett, J. J. (2004). *Emerging adulthood: The winding road from the late teens through the twenties.* New York: Oxford University Press.

Bae, M. S. (2010). Go Cyworld!: Korean diasporic girls producing new Korean femininity. In S. R. Mazzarella (Ed.), *Girl wide web 2.0: Revisiting girls, the Internet and the negotiation of identity* (pp. 91–116). New York: Peter Lang.

Barker, V., & Ota, H. (2011). Mixi diary versus Facebook photos: Social networking site use among Japanese and Caucasian American females. *Journal of Intercultural Communication research, 40,* 39–63.

Barkhuus, L., & Tashiro, J. (2010). Student socialization in the age of Facebook. In *Proceedings of the Conference on Human Factors and Computing Systems* (pp. 133–142). New York: ACM Press.

Baumeister, R. F. (1987). How the self became a problem. A psychological review of historical research. *Journal of Personality and Social Psychology, 52,* 163–176.

Bergman, S. M., Fearrington, M. E., Davenport, S. W., & Bergman, J. Z. (2011). Millennials, narcissism, and social networking: What narcissists do on social networking sites and why. *Personality and Individual Differences, 50,* 706–711.

Benkler, Y. (2006). *The wealth of networks.* New Haven, CT: Yale University Press.

Blais, J. J., Craig, W. M., Pepler, D., & Connolly, J. (2008). Adolescents online: The importance of Internet activity choices to salient relationships. *Journal of Youth & Adolescence, 37,* 522–536.

boyd, d. m. (2008). Why youth heart social network sites: The role of networked publics in teenage social life. In D. Buckingham (Ed.), *Youth, identity, and digital media* (pp. 119–142). Cambridge, MA: MIT Press.

boyd, d. m., & Ellison, N. B. (2008). Social network sites: Definition, history, and scholarship. *Journal of Computer-Mediated Communication, 13,* 210–230.

boyd, d. m., & Heer, J. (2006). Profiles as Conversation: Networked Identity Performance on Friendster. *Proceedings of the Hawai'i International Conference on System Sciences* (HICSS-39). Kauai, HI: IEEE Computer Society.

Brandtzæg, P. B. (2012). Social networking implications: A longitudinal study. *Journal of Computer-Mediated Communication, 17,* 467–488.

Brandtzæg, P. B., Luders, M., & Skjetne, J. H. (2010). Too many Facebook "friends"? Content sharing and sociability versus the need for privacy in social network sites. *International Journal of Human-Computer Interaction, 26,* 123–138.

Burke, M., Marlow, C., & Lento, T. (2009). Feed me: Motivating newcomer contribution in social networking sites. In *Proceedings of the 27th International Conference on Human Factors in Computing Systems* (pp. 945–954). New York, NY: ACM.

Carpenter, C. (2012). Narcissism on Facebook: Self-promotional and anti-social behavior. *Personality and Individual Differences, 52,* 482–486.

Chou, H., & Edge, N. (2012). They are happier and having better lives than I am: The impact of using Facebook on perceptions of others' lives. *Cyberpsychology, Behavior, and Social Networking, 15,* 117–121.

Christofides, E., Muise, A., & Desmarais, S. (2009). Information control and disclosure on Facebook: Are they two sides of the same coin or two different processes? *Cyberpsychology and Behavior, 12,* 1–5.

Christofides, E., Muise, A., & Desmarais, S. (2012). Hey mom, what's on your facebook? Comparing facebook disclosure and privacy in adolescents and adults. *Social Psychological and Personality Science, 3,* 48–54.

Clark, L. S. (2005). The constant contact generation: Exploring teen friendship networks online. In S. R. Mazzarella (Ed.), *Girl wide web: Girls, the Internet and the negotiation of identity* (pp. 203–222). New York: Peter Lang.

Cote, J. E., & LeVine, C. G. (2002). *Identity formation, agency, and culture: A social psychological synthesis.* Mahwah, NJ: Lawrence Erlbaum Associates.

Courtois, C., Anissa, A., & Vanwynsberghe, H. (2012). Social network profiles as information sources for adolescents' offline relations. *Cyberpsychology, Behavior, and Social Networking, 15*, 290–295.

Craig, E., & Wright, K. B. (2012). Computer-mediated relational development and maintenance on Facebook. *Communication Research Reports, 29*, 119–129.

Desjarlais, M., & Willoughby, T. (2010). A longitudinal study of the relation between adolescent boys and girls' computer use with friends and friendship quality: Support for the social compensation or the rich-get-richer hypothesis? *Computers in Human Behavior, 26*, 896–905

Donath, J. (2008). Signals in social supernets. *Journal of Computer-Mediated Communication, 13*, 231–251.

Donath, J., & boyd, d. m. (2004). Public displays of connection. *BT Technology Journal, 22*, 71–82.

Ellison, N., Heino, R., & Gibbs, J. (2006). Managing impressions online: Self-presentation processes in online dating environment. *Journal of Computer-Mediated Communication, 11*, 415–441.

Ellison, N., Steinfield, C., & Lampe, C. (2007). The benefits of Facebook "friends": Social capital and college students' use of online social network sites. *Journal of Computer-Mediated Communication, 12*, 1143–1168.

Ellison, N. B., Steinfield, C., & Lampe, C. (2010). Connection strategies: Social capital implications of Facebook-enabled communication practices. *New Media & Society, 13*, 873–892.

Erikson, E. (1968). *Identity: Youth and crisis*. New York: W. W. Norton.

Facebook (2013). *Statistics*. Palo Alto, CA: Facebook. Retrieved from http://newsroom.fb.com/Key-Facts

Furman, W., & Buhrmester, D. (1992). Age and sex differences in perceptions of networks of personal relationships. *Child Development, 63*, 103–115.

Garcia-Gomez, A. (2011). Regulating girlhood: Evaluative Language, discourses of gender socialization and relational aggression. *European Journal of Women's studies, 18*, 243–264.

Gentile, B., Twenge, J. M., Freeman, E. C., & Campbell, W. K. (2012). The effect of social networking websites on positive self-views: An experimental investigation. *Computers in Human Behavior, 28*, 1929–1933.

Gonzales, A. L., & Hancock, J. T. (2008). Identity shift in computer-mediated environments. *Media Psychology, 11*, 167–185.

Gonzales, A. L., & Hancock, J. T. (2011). Mirror, mirror on my Facebook wall: Effects of exposure to Facebook on self-esteem. *Cyberpsychology, Behavior, and Social Networking, 14*, 79–83.

Granovetter, M. (1973). The strength of weak ties. *American Journal of Sociology, 78*, 1360–1380.

Gray, M. L. (2009). *Out in the country: Youth, media, and queer visibility in rural America*. New York University Press.

Grotevant, H. D., & Cooper, C. R. (1985). Patterns of interaction in family relationships and the development of identity exploration in adolescence. *Child Development, 56*, 415–428.

Haferkamp, N., & Kramer, N. (2011). Social comparison 2.0: Examining the effects of online profiles on social networking sites. *Cyberpsychology, Behavior, and Social Networking, 14*, 309–314.

Hall, P. C., West, J. H., & McIntyre, E. (2012). Female self-sexualization in MySpace.com personal profile photographs. *Sexuality & Culture, 16*, 1–16.

Hirdman, A. (2010). Vision and intimacy: Gendered communication online. *Nordicom Review, 31*, 3–13.

Haythornthwaite, C. (2005). Social networks and Internet connectivity effects. *Information, Communication & Society, 8*, 125–147.

Hogan, B., & Wellman, B. (2012). The immanent Internet redux. In P. H. Cheong, P. Fischer-Nielsen, S. Gelfgren, & C. Ess (Eds.), *Digital religion, social media and culture: Perspectives, practices and futures* (pp 43–62). New York: Peter Lang.

Hong, S., Tandoc E. Jr., Kim, E. A., Kim, B., Wise, K. (2012). The real you? The role of visual cues and comment congruence in perceptions of social attractiveness from Facebook profiles. *Cyberpsychology, Behavior, and Social Networking, 15*, 339–344.

Ito, M., Baumer, S., Bittanti, M., boyd, d. m., Cody, R., Stephenson-Herr, B., Horst, H. A., Lange, P. G., Mahendran, D., Martinez, K., Pascoe, C. J., Perkel, D., Robinson, L., Sims, C., & Tripp, L. (2010). *Hanging out, messing around, and geeking out. Kids living and learning with new media*. Cambridge, MA: MIT Press.

Jackson, L., & Wang, J. L. (2013). Cultural differences in social networking site use: A comparative study of China and the United States. *Computers in Human Behavior, 29*, 910–921.

Kalpidou, M., Costin, D., & Morris, J. (2011). The relationship between Facebook and the well-being of undergraduate college students. *Cyberpsychology, Behavior, and Social Networking, 14*, 183–189.

Kaplan, A. M., & Haenlein, M. (2010). Users of the world, unite! The challenges and opportunities of social media. *Business Horizons, 53*, 59–68.

Katz, J. E., & Aakhus, M. A. (2002). Introduction: Framing the issues. In J. Katz & M. Aakhus (Eds.), *Perpetual contact: Mobile communication, private talk, public performance* (pp 1–14). Cambridge, UK: Cambridge University Press.

Kim, J., & Lee, J. E. (2011). The Facebook paths to happiness: Effects of the number of Facebook friends and self-presentation on subjective well-being. *Cyberpsychology, Behavior and Social Networking, 6*, 359–364.

Kraut, R. E., Patterson, M., Lundmark, V., Kiesler, S., Mukhopadhyay, T., & Scherlis, W. (1998). Internet paradox: A social technology that reduces social involvement and psychological well-being? *American Psychologist, 53*, 1017–1032.

Kramer, N. C., & Winter, S. (2008). Impression Management 2.0. The relationship of self-esteem, extraversion, self-efficacy, and self-presentation within social networking sites. *Journal of Media Psychology, 20*, 106–116.

Kroger, J. (2004). *Identity in adolescence: The balance between self and other*. New York: Routledge.

Leage, R., & Chalmers, I. (2010). Degrees of caution: Arab girls unveil on Facebook. In S. R. Mazzarella (Ed.), *Girl wide web 2.0: Revisiting girls, the Internet and the negotiation of identity* (pp. 27–44). New York: Peter Lang.

Lee, S. K. (2008). Online communication and adolescent social ties: Who benefits more from Internet use? *Journal of Computer-Mediated Communication, 14*, 509–531.

Lee, J. R., Moore, D. C., Park, E., & Park, S. G. (2012). Who wants to be "friend-rich"? Social compensatory friending on Facebook and the moderating role of public self-consciousness. *Computers in Human Behavior, 28*, 1036–1043.

Lenhart, A. (2012). Teens and online video. *Reports from the Pew Research Center's Internet & American Life Project*.

Retrieved from http://pewinternet.org/Reports/2012/Teens-and-online-video.aspx

Lerner, D. (1958). *The passing of traditional society: Modernizing the Middle East.* New York: Free Press.

Livingstone, S. (2008). Taking risky opportunities in youthful content creation: Teenagers' use of social networking sites for intimacy, privacy, and self-expression. *New Media Society, 10,* 393–411.

Lou, L. L., Yan, Z., Nickerson, A., & McMorris, R. (2012). An examination of the reciprocal relationship of loneliness and Facebook use among first-year college students. *Journal of Educational Computing Research, 46,* 105–117.

Magnuson, M. J., & Dundes, L. (2008). Gender differences in "social portraits" reflected in MySpace profiles. *CyberPsychology and Behavior, 11,* 239–241.

Manago, A. M. (2012). The new emerging adult in Chiapas, Mexico: Perceptions of traditional values and value change among first generation Maya university students. *Journal of Adolescent Research, 27,* 663–713.

Manago, A. M. (2013). Negotiating a sexy masculinity on MySpace. *Feminism & Psychology, 23,* 478–497.

Manago, A. M., Graham, M. B., Greenfield, P. M., & Salimkhan, G. (2008). Self-Presentation and gender on MySpace. *Journal of Applied Developmental Psychology, 29,* 446–458.

Manago, A. M., Taylor, T., & Greenfield, P. M. (2012). Me and My 400 Friends: The anatomy of college students' Facebook networks, their communication patterns, and well-being. *Developmental Psychology, 48,* 369–380.

Marwick, A. E., & boyd, d. m. (2010). I tweet honestly, I tweet passionately: Twitter users, context collapse, and the imagined audience. *New Media & Society, 13,* 114–133.

Mazzarella, S. R. (2005). Claiming a space: The cultural economy of teen girl fandom on the web. In S. R. Mazzarella (Ed.), *Girl wide web: Girls, the Internet, and the negotiation of identity* (pp. 141–160). New York: Peter Lang.

Malikhao, P., & Servaes, J. (2011). The media use of American youngsters in the age of narcissism: Surviving in a 24/7 media shock and awe- distracted by everything. *Telematics and Informatics, 28,* 66–76.

McAndrew, F. T., & Jeong, H. S. (2012). Who does what on Facebook? Age, sex, and relationship status as predictors of Facebook use. *Computers in Human Behavior, 28,* 2359–2365.

McKinney, B. C., Kelly, L., & Duran, R. L. (2012). Narcissism or openness?: College students' use of Facebook and Twitter. *Communication Research Reports, 29,* 108–118.

McLuhan, M. (1962). *The Gutenberg galaxy: The making of typographic man.* Toronto: University of Toronto Press.

Mehdizadeh, S. (2010). Self-presentation 2.0: Narcissism and self-esteem on Facebook. *Cyberpsychology, Behavior, and Social Networking, 13,* 357–364.

Mesch, G. S. (2003). The family and the Internet: The Israel case. *Social Science Quarterly, 84,* 1038–1050.

Meyrowitz, J. (2005). The rise of glocality: New senses of place and identity in the global village. In N. Kristof (Ed.), *A sense of place, the global and the local in mobile communication* (pp. 21–30). Vienna: Passagen Verlag.

McKenna, K. Y. A., & Bargh, J. A. (2000). Plan 9 from cyberspace: Implications of the Internet for personality and social psychology. *Personality and Social Psychology Review, 4,* 57–75.

Misra, S., & Stokols, D. (2012). Psychological and health outcomes of perceived information overload. *Environment and Behavior, 44,* 737–759.

Mod, G. (2010). Reading romance: The impact Facebook rituals can have on a romantic relationship. *Journal of Comparative Research in Anthropology and Sociology, 1,* 61–77.

Office of National Statistics, UK (2011). *Internet access: Households and individuals.* Retrieved from http://www.ons.gov.uk/ons/dcp171778_227158.pdf

Pea, R., Nass, C., Meheula, L., Rance, M., Kumar, A., Bamford, H., Nass, M., Simha, A., Stillerman, B., Yang, S., & Zhou, M. (2012). Media use, face-to-face communication, media multitasking, and social well-being among 8- to 12-year-old girls. *Developmental Psychology, 48,* 327–336.

Pfeil, U., Arjan, R., & Zaphiris, P. (2009). Age differences in online social networking: A study of user profiles and the social capital divide among teenagers and older users in MySpace. *Computers in Human Behavior, 25,* 643–654.

Phinney, J. S., & Baldelomar, O. A. (2011). Identity development in multiple cultural contexts. In L. Arnett-Jensen (Ed.), *Bridging cultural and developmental approaches to psychology: New syntheses in theory, research, and policy* (pp. 161–186). New York: Oxford University Press.

Prensky, M. (2001). Digital natives, digital immigrants. *On the Horizon, 9,* 1–6.

Raacke, J., & Bonds-Raacke, J. (2008). MySpace and Facebook: Applying the uses and gratification theory to exploring friend networking sites. *Cyberpsychology and Behavior, 11,* 169–174.

Reich, S. M. (2010). Adolescents' sense of community on MySpace and Facebook: A mixed-methods approach. *Journal of Community Psychology, 38,* 688–705.

Reich, S. M., Subrahmanyam, K., & Espinoza, G. (2012). Friending, IMing, and hanging out face-to-face: Overlap in adolescents' online and offline social networks. *Developmental Psychology, 48,* 356–368.

Ringrose, J. (2010). Are you sexy, flirty, or a slut? Exploring 'sexualization' and how teen girls perform/ negotiate digital sexual identity on social networking sites. In R.Gill & C.Scharff (Eds.), *New femininities, post-feminism, neoliberalism and identity* (pp. 99–116). London: Palgrave.

Sanders, C. E., Field, T. M., Diego, M., & Kaplan, M. (2000). The relationship of Internet use to depression and social isolation among adolescents. *Adolescence, 35,* 237–242.

Salimkhan, G., Manago, A. M., & Greenfield, P. M. (2010). The construction of the virtual self on MySpace. *CyberPsychology: Journal of Psychosocial Research on Cyberspace, 4,* article 1.

Schlegel, A (2000). The global spread of adolescent culture. In L. J.Crockett & R. K.Silbereisen (Eds.), *Negotiating adolescence in times of social change* (pp. 71–88). New York: Cambridge University Press.

Schwammlein, E., & Wodzicki, K. (2012). What to tell about me? Self-presentation in online communities. *Journal of Computer-Mediated Communication, 17,* 387–407.

Siibak, A. (2010). Constructing masculinity on a social network site. *Young: Nordic Journal of Youth Research, 18,* 403–425.

Smahel, D., Brown, B., & Blinka, L. (2012). Associations between online friendship and Internet addiction among adolescents and emerging adults. *Developmental Psychology, 48,* 381–388.

Stutzman, F., Vitak, J., Ellison, N. B., Gray, R., & Lampe, C. (2012). Privacy in interaction: Exploring disclosure and social capital in Facebook. *Proceedings of the Sixth International AAAI Conference on Weblogs and Social Media.* Dublin, Ireland.

Subrahmanyam, K., Reich, S. M., Waechter, N., & Espinoza, G. (2008). Online and offline social networks: Use of social networking sites by emerging adults. *Journal of Applied Developmental Psychology, 29*, 420–433.

Subrahmanyam, K., & Smahel, D. (2011). *Digital youth: The role of media in development.* New York: Springer.

Subrahmanyam, K., Smahel, D., & Greenfield, P. M. (2006). Connecting developmental constructions to the Internet: Identity presentation and sexual exploration in online teen chat rooms. *Developmental Psychology, 42*, 395–406.

Stefanone, M. A., Lackaff, D., & Rosen, D. (2011). Contingencies of self-worth and social networking site behavior. *Cyberpsychology, Behavior, and Social Networking, 14*, 41–49.

Steinfield, C., Ellison, N. B., & Lampe, C. (2008). Social capital, self-esteem, and use of online social network sites: A longitudinal analysis. *Journal of Applied Developmental Psychology, 29*, 434–445.

Stephenson-Abetz, J., & Holman, A. (2012). Home is where the heart is: Facebook and the negotiation of "old" and "new" during the transition to college. *Western Journal of Communication, 76*, 175–193.

Szwedo, D. E., Mikami, A. Y., & Allen, J. P. (2012). Social networking site use predicts changes in young adults' psychological adjustment. *Journal of Research on Adolescence, 22*, 453–466.

Tokunaga, R. (2010). Following you home from school: A critical review and synthesis of research on cyberbullying victimization. *Computers in Human Behavior, 26*, 277–287.

Tong, S. T., Van Der Heide, B., Langwell, L., & Walther, J. B. (2008). Too much of a good thing? The relationship between number of friends and interpersonal impressions on Facebook. *Journal of Computer-Mediated Communication, 13*, 531–549.

Tufekci, Z. (2008a). Can you see me now? Audience and disclosure regulation in online social network sites. *Bulletin of Science, Technology & Society, 28*, 20–36.

Tufekci, Z. (2008b). Grooming, gossip, Facebook and Myspace. *Information, Communication and Society, 11*, 544–564.

Turkle, S. (2011). *Alone Together: Why we expect more from technology and less from each other.* New York: Basic Books.

Tynes, B., Garcia, E., Giang, M., & Coleman, N. (2010). The racial landscape of social network sites: Forging identity, community, and civic engagement. *I/S: A Journal of Law and Policy for the Information Society, 7*, 1–30.

Utz, S. (2010). Show me your friends and I will tell you what type of person you are: How one's profile, number of friends, and type of friends influence impression formation on social network sites. *Journal of Computer-Mediated Communication, 15*, 314–335.

Utz, S., & Beukeboom, C. J. (2011). The role of social network sites in romantic relationships: Effects on jealousy and relationship happiness. *Journal of Computer-Mediated Communication, 16*, 511–527.

Utz, S., Tanis, M., & Vermeulen, I. (2012). It is all about being popular: The effects of need for popularity on social network site use. *Cyberpsychology, Behavior, and Social Networking, 15*, 37–42.

Van Doorn, N. (2010). The ties that bind: The networked performance of gender, sexuality and friendship on MySpace. *New Media Society, 12*, 583–602.

Valenzuela, S., Park, N., & Kee, K. F. (2009). Is there social capital in a social network site? Facebook use and college students' life satisfaction, trust, and participation. *Journal of Computer-Mediated Communication, 14*, 875–901.

Valkenburg, P. M., & Peter, J. (2007). Preadolescents' and adolescents' online communication and their closeness to friends. *Developmental Psychology, 43*, 267–277.

Valkenburg, P. M., & Peter, J. (2011). Online communication among adolescents: An integrated model of its attraction, opportunities, and risks. *Journal of Adolescent Health, 48*, 121–127.

Valkenburg, P. M., Peter, J., & Schouten, A. P. (2006). Friend networking sites and their relationship to adolescents' well-being and social self-esteem. *CyberPsychology & Behavior, 9*, 584–590.

Vitak, J., & Ellison, N. B. (2012). 'There's a network out there you might as well tap': Exploring the benefits of and barriers to exchanging information and support-based resources on Facebook. *New Media Society, 15*, 243–259.

Walther, J. B. (2007). Selective self-presentation in computer mediated communication: Hyperpersonal dimensions of technology, language, and cognition. *Computers in Human Behavior, 23*, 2538—2557.

Walther, J. B., Van der Heide, B., Hamel, L. M., & Shulman, H. C. (2009). Self-generated versus other-generated statements and impressions in computer-mediated communication: A test of warranting theory using Facebook. *Communication Research, 36*, 229–253.

Walther, J. B., Van der Heide, B., Kim, S., Westerman, D., & Tong, S. (2008). The role of friends' appearance and behavior on evaluations of individuals on Facebook: Are we known by the company we keep? *Human Communication Research, 34*, 28–49.

Wellman, B. (2002). Little boxes, glocalization, and networked individualism. In M. Tanabe, P. van den Besselaar, & T. Ishida (Eds.), *Digital cities II: Computational and sociological approaches* (pp. 10–25). Berlin: Springer.

Wellman, B., Boase, J., Chen, W. (2002). The networked nature of community: Online and offline. *IT & Society, 1*, 151–165.

Willoughby, T. (2008). A short-term longitudinal study of Internet and computer game use by adolescent boys and girls: Prevalence, frequency of use, and psychosocial predictors. *Developmental Psychology, 44*, 195–204.

Wilson, R. E., Gosling, S. D., & Graham, L. T. (2012). A review of Facebook research in the social sciences. *Perspectives on Psychological Science, 7*, 203–220.

Pempek, T., Yermolayeva, Y. A., & Calvert, S. (2009). College students' social networking experiences on Facebook. *Journal of Applied Developmental Psychology, 30*, 227–238.

Yang, C., & Brown, B. (2012). Motives for using Facebook, patterns of Facebook activities and late adolescents' social adjustment to college. *Journal of Youth and Adolescence, 42*, 403–416.

Youniss, J., & Smollar, J. (1985). *Adolescent relations with mothers, fathers, and friends.* Chicago: University of Chicago Press.

Zhao, S., Grasmuck, S., & Martin, J. (2008). Identity construction on Facebook: Digital empowerment in anchored relationships. *Computers in Human Behavior, 24*, 1816–1836.

Zickuhr, K., & Smith, A. (2012). Digital Differences. *Reports from the Pew Research Center's Internet & American Life Project.*

Retrieved from http://pewinternet.org/Reports/2012/Digital-differences.aspx

Zwier, S., Araujo, T., Boukes, M., & Willemsen, L. (2011). Boundaries to the articulation of possible selves through social networking sites: The case of Facebook profilers' social connectedness. *Cyberpsychology, Behavior, and Social Networking, 14*, 571–576.

Zywica, J., & Danowski, J. (2008). The faces of Facebookers: Investigating social enhancement and social compensation hypotheses, predicting Facebook and offline popularity from sociability and self-esteem, and mapping the meanings of popularity with semantic networks. *Journal of Computer-Mediated Communication, 14*, 1–3.

PART 8

Reflections, Conclusions, and the Future

CHAPTER
32

Identity Formation Research from a Critical Perspective: Is a Social Science Developing?

James E. Côté

Abstract

This chapter examines the contributions in this handbook and the field as a whole from a critical, catholic point of view. This broad and discerning perspective sees the field of identity studies as including various social sciences and the concept of identity as multidimensional, varying by level of analysis, manifestation, and interacting with other phenomena. Although a number of chapters in this volume also recognize this broad nature of the field and that no one perspective "owns" the identity concept, some chapters take a more parochial view of "identity." Given that the social scientific study of identity is past the half-century mark, the author argues that the time has come when such parochial perspectives are no longer sustainable. If the identity studies field is to grow beyond its current state of terminological and conceptual confusion, empirical and theoretical rapprochements are necessary among the various disciplines studying the diverse subject matter of this promising field.

Key Words: Identity formation, identity maintenance, taxonomy, perspectives, bias, epistemological divide, development vs. socialization

Over the course of my thirty-five-year publishing career in the field of identity studies, I have had occasion to comment on the state of the field (Côté, 1996a; 1996b; 2006a; 2009a; 2009b; Côté & Levine, 1987; 1988; 2002). I welcome the present opportunity to extend those commentaries, particularly the 2006 publication of my presidential address to the Society for Research on Identity Formation (SRIF). My charge from the editors in writing this chapter was, in light of my previous observations, "to write a closing chapter on 'identity development from a critical perspective'" (Syed, email communication, March 13, 2012), making particular note of signs of progress in the field, with specific reference to the entries in this handbook.

The chapters in this handbook cover much ground from wide-ranging perspectives. My reading of some chapters encourages me that the field is making progress, but, at the same time, I am disappointed in the limited contribution of others. In this commentary, however, I do not identify those particular chapters with which I am disappointed. Instead, I point out how researchers in general can fail to contribute to the growth of the field, and I identify some of the reasons for this failure. Indeed, many of the limitations noted in my previous commentaries on the field can be found in these chapters. At the same time, in order to encourage further advancement, I do identify those chapters that appear most promising in advancing the field.

Before commenting on the contribution of this handbook to the field, it is first useful to clarify my understandings of two of the terms in this charge, namely, "critical" and "development." Like the word "identity," both terms have several usages. I find it necessary to point out these usages because of problems in several chapters in this handbook.

Defining the Terms "Critical" and "Development"
Critical

From the outset, it is important to distinguish "critical analyses" from "critical theories." A critical analysis of the chapters in this handbook would evaluate them in terms of the strengths and weaknesses of their contribution to the field of identity formation. At the same time, a high-quality critical analysis rises above biases and takes account of *all* the available information that can provide for a balanced analysis. In contrast, a second usage of the concept "critical" is found in the term "critical theories," which can be understood in contrast with "status quo theories." Critical theories have a long history in the more macro-oriented social sciences (e.g., Burrell & Morgan, 1979; and as Schachter notes in this volume). These theories take the analysis deeper than do other types of theories, probing the root causes of phenomena, rather than their surface manifestations.

It is vital to distinguish these two usages of the term "critical" for a variety of reasons, but especially because the second usage has political implications not found in the first usage. The remainder of this section focuses on the first usage, with a critical perspective referring to the use of critical thinking.

A high-quality critical analysis that is social scientific in scope—meaning that it recognizes the intersections among the various social sciences in studying similar topics—has several important qualities that make it more useful than a simple description of empirical results or a literature review. First, a critical analysis examines the merits—strengths and weaknesses—of perspectives in developing a comprehensive understanding of a phenomenon at hand. The objective is to create a balanced evaluation that provides a more defensible judgment than would be the case in a one-sided or less well-informed analysis. Thus, by "critical" we are not dealing with only negative judgments, or with political ones, but rather with balanced and informed analyses that take into account multiple points of view in understanding, and multiple levels of manifestations of, a given phenomenon.

The following analogy is helpful in understanding these distinctions. A good movie review informs its readers about the strengths and weakness of a movie so that readers/audiences can have a basis for judging whether to watch it themselves. A poor movie review would inform audiences more about the critic's biases and opinions than about the movie's qualities. Just like a good movie critic, a good academic critic should leave readers with a better understanding of the issues at hand and not merely impressions of the critic's biases, opinions, or limited understanding of an issue or field. To accomplish this, an academic critic needs to meet certain standards of scholarship that include comprehensiveness in representing the extant academic work on the topic, accuracy in the depiction of other academics, precision in the use of concepts, and balance in the portrayal of plausible conclusions of the arguments and evidence.

In specific reference to a multidimensional concept like "identity," a good critical analysis of the now-massive body of interdisciplinary work would specify ways in which specific works (or chapters, in this case) succeed or fail to advance the field. Works that fail to advance the field of identity studies as a social science often use one or more of the following shortcuts:

• Adopting a conceptualization that fails to recognize the multiple uses of the term "identity" by different social scientists, thereby ignoring the fact that it is a multidimensional concept with different meanings at different levels of analysis (e.g., the psychological, interactional, and societal levels, with variations and nuances at each of these levels of analysis)

• Using a single perspective to examine one aspect of identity in an imperialistic manner, dismissing other approaches in identity studies for not taking this single perspective or using a single method. This shortcut may be taken because of questionable expertise or a limited grasp of the field as a whole.

• Applying a boilerplate analysis to an issue at hand; that is, employing unexamined disciplinary or perspectival preconceptions in ways that predetermine outcomes of research (i.e., findings), thereby exhibiting the confirmation bias (Nickerson, 1998; Oswald & Grosjean, 2004):

• Related to the boilerplate approach, using "scare words" and various other rhetorical devices designed to encourage readers to suspend their critical-analytical skills and accept a particular position on its face out of fear of being "politically incorrect" or insensitive to some new trend (e.g., terms like "suspicious of" or "interrogate" in reference to imputed qualities of other theories)

• Engaging in bandwagoning, following a current popular trend in research while at the same time disparaging other approaches, often making unjustified claims (e.g., dismissing one

methodology in favor of another without providing sufficient justification)
- Cherry-picking from or caricaturing other perspectives to create straw arguments that artificially make one's approach sound more convincing

Development

With this understanding of critical thinking applied to identity studies in mind, we can now turn to another ambiguous concept—identity development. This is a handbook of identity *development*, or *formation*, terms that are usually understood as synonymous. However, the field of identity studies involves more manifestations of human identity than the *development* of specific social identities or general "identity statuses." Another manifestation of identity that is conceptually and methodologically distinct from identity development is identity *maintenance* (Côté & Levine, 2002). However, because of a tendency to use the term "identity" as if it had just one meaning and application, numerous misunderstandings have plagued the literature. Reflecting this shortcoming in the general literature, several chapters in this handbook do not make it clear that they are dealing with just one aspect of "identity" among many.

The study of identity *maintenance* has been a major undertaking in sociology for some time, especially by symbolic interactionists, most notably Erving Goffman (1959; 1963). The preferred method involves observational techniques in monitoring the self-presentations of individuals. This literature reveals that, for the individual, identity maintenance is only possible after a particular personal or social identity has been formed. Once formed, people engage in various types of impression management and the negotiation of images/roles/identities in the presentation of self during face-to-face interactions. Accordingly, the attempts of individuals to maintain a given personal or social identity may lead to change in that identity, but their intention is often to sustain that identity. Thus, for taxonomic purposes, studies of such behaviors and interactions should not be counted as investigations of identity *development*. This form of symbolic interactionism is subjectivist in nature, based on G. H. Mead's work. Another interpretation of Mead's work is more objectivist and focuses on aspects like identity salience and hierarchies and role-playing (e.g., Stryker, 1987). A useful text summarizing the field of identity *maintenance* from a symbolic interactionist perspective can be found in Hewitt (2003).

Besides, simple psychological or behavioral change cannot necessarily be considered a form of "development." In the case of identity development, something must be added to some aspect of the person's identity(ies) beyond simple change, whether progressive or regressive; if a set of experiences does not have predictable value-added consequences other than amorphous change over time, it would not be considered developmental by most developmental psychologists (cf. Lerner, 2002). In this context, readers may feel challenged in finding theory and research on identity *development* in some chapters in this handbook, and rightly so, because of their differing conceptions of identity or a focus on factors tangential to identity formation (e.g., the Korobov and Smetana chapters).

Finally, psychologists often define developmental stages as involving qualitative reorientations in a person's operational capacities, and usually thresholds are identified that mark stage transitions (e.g., Muuss, 1996; Snarey, Kohlberg, & Noam, 1983). Other social scientists, notably sociologists, view human development as involving more incremental and linear changes, whereby people tend to "absorb" elements of their culture through socialization processes. These changes can be accelerated or redirected by contextual thresholds, as when the person moves to a new social milieu or institution (e.g., from high school to university). But these changes are usually taken for granted by sociologists and rarely studied in terms of individual differences in the mental processes producing or resulting from these changes. For example, the existence of ethnic identities is usually taken as a given by symbolic interactionists and others, with their research examining variations in how salient various ethnic identities are for people, or how people manage multiple ethnic identities. Studies then typically go on to examine how this salience is maintained in the face of challenges. However, sociologists are not as interested as psychologists in how the person developed a level of salience in the first place (i.e., how a child born without a sense of ethnicity eventually develops one as an adolescent or adult). This unrecognized disciplinary hiatus between the concepts of "development" and "socialization" is an example of how the field suffers from a lack of collaboration among researchers ostensibly studying the same things, especially when there is a failure to clearly define and distinguish basic concepts like identity formation and identity maintenance as well as development and socialization. This applies both between sociology and psychology and, within psychology, between social and developmental psychology.

The Field of Identity Studies: Past Concerns

The identity studies field is now clearly an interdisciplinary social science, with economics being a recent discipline to discover the utility of the concept through the work of Akerlof, the winner of the 2001 Nobel Prize in Economics (Akerlof & Kranton, 2010). To the task at hand within this broad context, it is necessary to find ways to best characterize the subfield of *identity-development studies*. My own interest in this field has focused more on identity development than identity maintenance, but my perspective has been interdisciplinary from the outset. My degrees span psychology and sociology, and my career focus in identity studies can be characterized as a "developmental social psychology," with some work following Erikson's call for "a social psychology that is psychoanalytically sophisticated" (Erikson, 1968, p. 24; Côté, 1993). In some publications with my colleague Charles Levine, this work has emphasized the multidimensionality of the identity concept and offered suggestions for a taxonomy to match this dimensionality in terms of levels of analysis and historical/cultural settings, taking into account disciplinary differences (Côté, 1996a, 1996b; Côté & Levine, 2002; Côté & Schwartz, 2002).

From this broader interdisciplinary perspective, we criticized the dominant psychological (identity status) paradigm as "too psychological and ignor[ing] the sociological, social psychological, and historical factors that Erikson contends must be attended to if one is to reach a full understanding of ego identity formation" (Côté & Levine, 1987, p. 312). We argued that the psychological emphasis of this approach has been useful in documenting the roles of explorations and commitments, but has ignored other aspects of identity formation that Erikson theorized to be important, including the identity crisis (in its various manifestations, which range from minor and ritualized to major and anomic depending on sociohistorical factors), the institutionalized moratoria (e.g., based on technological and humanistic values, but their bases vary historically), and the value orientation stages (which could be considered forms of moral-identity development) (Côté & Levine, 1987; 1988). Our conclusion from this appraisal of the attempts to empirically investigate Erikson's work on identity was that:

> A more valid approach is one that complements the psychological perspective with theory and measures that are sensitive to those social psychological, sociological, and historical perspectives utilized by Erikson. We believe that such an interdisciplinary effort enables one to appreciate more fully the formation of identity within the context of Erikson's overall developmental model.
>
> *(Côté & Levine, 1987, p. 320)*

Of course, it is extremely difficult to undertake such comprehensive empirical research, especially measuring or assessing all the relevant factors in one study or even a series of studies. Still, without interdisciplinary theoretical frameworks to guide researchers, it is unlikely that studies will stray from disciplinary orthodoxies, and that appears to have been the case with psychological research, especially until recently, as we see in this handbook with the expansion of the narrative approach.

I revisited these concerns in my presidential address to SRIF (Côté, 2006a), arguing that the situation appeared to have worsened as more researchers from other disciplines have entered the identity studies field without adopting a common taxonomy. More researchers appear to have entered the "identity field," but it is unclear how their definitions of identity matches previous ones. Consequently, a social scientific Tower of Babel appears to be growing, especially as some newer perspectives have attempted to dominate the field by imperialistically asserting ownership of the identity concept and, in the process, overextending their own highly specific usage of the concept while dismissing other usages. Researchers adopting subjectivist epistemologies appear most prone to this, especially those who engage in a disciplinary struggle to dominate the field. I noted this tendency in the postmodernist approach, which emphasizes the "multiplicity, fluidity, and context-dependent operation" (Rattansi & Phoenix, 1997/2005, p. 121) of identities, especially among the youth population. It is important for these postmodernists to see identity as "decentered" and "de-essentialized" in contemporary contexts, meaning that "identity" is not primarily a property of persons, but rather of interactional processes, which are now inherently unstable (Côté, 2006a, p. 13).

Referring to my earlier cautions about the failure of some researchers to acknowledge the multidimensionality of the identity concept, especially distinguishing between "development" and "maintenance," the limitations of these postmodernist claims are obvious, particularly because their boilerplate assumptions regarding identity (multiple, decentered, nonessentialist) have never been empirically tested (cf. Bennett, 2011).

An illustration of the unfortunate proliferation of imperialistic approaches in identity studies can be found in some publications that have recently come out of the United Kingdom, where there is a tradition of qualitative approaches buttressing nominalist ontologies that is largely set apart from a weaker tradition of quantitative methods based on realist ontologies. In such an environment, a rift can form among academics that can be described as an "epistemological divide." For example, recently, in introducing the results of a research program on "social identity" undertaken in the United Kingdom, Wetherell (2009; Wetherell & Mohanty, 2010) claimed that the general field of identity studies has moved away from the modernist (read: realist) conceptions of identity, such as those proposed by Erikson. She argued that: "Scholars are now *suspicious of* stasis and fixed traits and determining and unchanging essences, which were so crucial to the past history and etymology of 'identity'" (2009, p. 2, emphasis added).

Although Wetherell does not self-identify as a postmodernist, she employs much of the postmodernist boilerplate in her characterizations of the "old" and "new" approaches. As we see in the present handbook and in the field in general, her claim of the moribund status of "old" Eriksonian approaches is premature, and her pronouncement of the acceptance of new approaches is an exaggeration. Furthermore, her portrayal of the "old" approach is a caricature because Erikson did not view "identity" as a fixed trait or as an "essence"; neither do neo-Eriksonians, as we see in this handbook and as is evident in the literature as a whole. And her use of the word "suspicious" is a "tell" of the antirealist nominalism in her characterization of the field, as if the "old" approach has done something wrong on the basis of ulterior motives.

The epistemological divide Wetherell and others are perpetuating is readily evident when one compares two recently published handbooks of identity: *The Sage Handbook of Identities* (Wetherell & Mohanty, 2010) and *Handbook of Identity Theory and Research* (Schwartz, Luyckx & Vignoles, 2011). The former is premised on a rejection of the so-called old approaches, whereas the latter attempts to embrace all approaches regardless of age ("old/new"), ontology, or methodology. The editors of the latter handbook framed their approach as follows:

> We believe that the identity literature is in need of an integrative perspective that brings together the strengths of these seemingly contrasting theoretical and methodological approaches without losing sight of the unique contributions that each of these approaches can make. Such integrative perspectives have been advanced within a number of identity literatures ... but broader integration across the broader field of identity studies remains lacking. (p. 12)

These editors are critical of the former handbook because it does not attempt this integrative task. In this light, it is unlikely that the former handbook will influence many non-postmodernists or that many postmodernists will read the latter handbook.

Even an open discussion of the relevant issues in a special issue of *Identity* (Côté, 2005) does not appear to have helped develop any rapprochements (e.g., see Phoenix & Rattansi, 2005). Regrettably, in spite of the congenial nature of this exchange in *Identity*, little has been accomplished in bridging the epistemological divide with respect to identity studies since then. Instead, the epistemological divide appears to be even wider, at least from the stated views of some prominent postmodernists in the identity studies field (e.g., Phoenix, 2010; Wetherell & Mohanty, 2010).

Current Contributions

My (2006) presidential address to SRIF also provided a typology with which to classify the various perspectives that have been brought to bear on "identity." The typology thus constitutes an attempt to map the subject matter of the interdisciplinary field of identity studies in terms of the specific perspectives that focus on various aspects of that subject matter. Eight perspectives were identified based on a cross-tabulation of three dimensions: epistemology (subjectivist and objectivist), focus (individual and social), and political assumptions (status quo and critical). Of those eight perspectives, only two have produced a critical mass of publications concerning identity development, with the remainder focused more with identity maintenance and other aspects of identity. The two perspectives focused on identity development involve individual, status quo approaches, with one favoring an objectivist epistemology (especially the identity status paradigm) and the other an subjectivist epistemology (including life history and narrative approaches). The objectivist approach to identity development has been far more popular than the subjectivist approach, but the present handbook provides a useful corrective to that imbalance.

As also noted in the 2006 presidential address, the study of identity has an unfortunately low status in many disciplines, especially psychology. The identity field does not fit the mold of other fields that can more easily be put into textbooks because of their less ambiguous terminology, because there is a high degree of consensus about theories and methods for various manifestations of the subject matter, and because there is sense that the field is advancing based on common assumptions and unambiguous findings. At the same time, some social scientists from other fields find that the concepts of self, self-concept, and self-esteem suffice to give us an understanding of the subjective attempts of humans to engage in self-reflection. As McAdams and Zapata-Gietl (this volume) note, many researchers find it easier to break the identity concept down to its components and study them separately. McAdams and Zapata-Gietl note that "researchers in personality and social psychology have extensively examined this developmental process through such constructs as life goals, life tasks, life longings, personal strivings, personal projects, and the development of human values." Similarly, the study of the sense of purpose has promise as a global construct that captures much of what identity formation researchers study, as Damon's (2009) recent popular book shows.

In other words, when Occam's razor is used, ways can be found to cut through the elaborate theories and jargon of the identity field. Unfortunately, when this done, the conceptual and ethical richness that drew people to the identity field in the first place (largely through Erikson's writings) is lost. Still, in light of these observations, it may well be better to assign much of what now counts as identity studies to the humanities rather than to the social sciences (of course, making distinctions between the two can lead to endless debates). However, this might only exacerbate the epistemological divide if it were also part of an academic status competition.

Nevertheless, the research output continues among those who adopt an objectivist epistemology and take an individual focus in studying normative development. Recently, there have been more advances in this paradigm, especially in Europe, that appear to be increasing its precision (Kunnen & Metz, this volume). In the developmental psychology literature, the identity status paradigm has drawn some respect and consensus from its parent discipline, possibly because of the simplicity of the operationalization and the hiatus between its conceptual structure and Erikson's sometimes ambiguous theorizing (cf. McAdams & Zapata-Gietl, this volume).

Narrative approaches hold promise for helping us understand many facets of identity development and maintenance that are beyond the reach of questionnaires and semistructured interviews, but these can draw even more skepticism from hardcore empiricists in disciplines like psychology. In the past, hard-nosed empiricists have raised the basic issue of cause and effect, the self-serving nature of recall and the unreliability of memory, and the possibility that narratives are mere epiphenomena (a favorite claim of behaviorists with respect to mental activity since the early days of psychology).

From the entries in this handbook, the narrative approach has been strongly endorsed by several authors, sometimes with the implication that it will save the day for the field (e.g., Arnett, this volume; see also the Wainryb and Pals Lilgendahl entries for strong endorsements). This enthusiasm should be tempered, however, by the recognition that the narrative approach represents only the subjectivist epistemology and, for the most part, has taken an individual focus that is status quo in its approach. At the same time, in this volume, the individually focused, objectivist, status quo perspective has been advanced by authors like Kroger, Kunnen and Metz, Mortimer, and Eichas et al.

I am encouraged by the number of authors who recognize the multidimensional nature of the identity construct and the need to accept that "every complex object of analysis, such as identity, requires to be examined from different angles and through different lenses. Therefore, to grasp somehow identity complexity and multidimensionality it is mandatory to adopt multiple approaches and multiple methods of data collection" (Crocetti & Meeus, this volume). Waterman's chapter nicely fleshes out these issues as well, as does Hammack's.

Readers will also detect numerous examples in which the author of one chapter makes a claim that is contradicted by the author of another chapter (e.g., compare Arnett's understanding of Erikson's work with that in chapters by Hammack, Kroger, and Crocetti & Meeus). This shows just how difficult the identity field can be to grasp, and it highlights the fact that authors should do their homework before claiming things that can be shown to factually incorrect or at least contradicted by empirical evidence of which they were apparently unaware.

Is a Rapprochement Possible?

For a social science (and humanities?) of identity studies to advance, researchers from various disciplines and perspectives will need to recognize that a larger project is necessary, one beyond "proving" the validity of their own approaches, which are inevitably based on specific assumptions (epistemological, disciplinary, and political, as per the typology offered in Côté, 2006a; see also Côté, 2010). The challenge is to identify superordinate goals that help researchers see the utility in bridging their work across epistemological, disciplinary, and political divides. And, to recognize how these bridges can be built, researchers need to recognize that other perspectives have valid concerns in matching their assumptions with the various dimensions of identity development and identity maintenance.

For example, based on the exchange in *Identity* representing Eriksonian and postmodernist perspectives (Côté, 2005), it appears that a postmodernist perspective is best applied to studying youth subjectivities because young people encounter fragmented microcontexts in their transition to adulthood, in which they can creatively engage contexts associated with managing personal and social identities. At the same time, an Eriksonian perspective best highlights the importance of mental processes undergirding personal agency, such as ego identity processes enabling the proactive assumption of societal roles and commitments in contemporary Western societies (the Eriksonian perspective also allows for a study of the problems in identity formation, especially those related to forms of personal agency that do not match current societal contexts). The common ground of these two perspectives is the recognition that both subjectivity and agency are important features of identity: the Eriksonian perspective is strongest in explaining forms of identity development, whereas the postmodernist perspective helps to understand identity maintenance in problematic societal contexts. Neither focus is incompatible with the other on logical, theoretical, or methodological grounds but are only made so by the preconceptions of the researcher.

If we are to follow the map laid out in the typology of epistemology, individual/social focus, and politics (Côté, 2006a) and take the catholic view that each of the eight perspectives has valid claims in terms of its particular subject matter, it logically follows that each perspective is to be respected in its own terms, even as collegial critiques are undertaken (a model for collegial critique can be found within SRIF and *Identity*, which provide the space for respectful dialogue). This all-embracing position makes it incumbent on each identity theorist to understand all of the perspectives on identity because only then will researchers fully appreciate the multidimensional nature of identity and the various ways in which this multidimensionality can be approached.

One way to visualize the map suggested by this typology is to imagine the field as a jigsaw puzzle in which pieces can fit together. With this model, the task for social scientists is to cooperate in identifying the various pieces of the puzzle and communicate in order to determine how they fit together, perhaps following the example of the human genome project or by engaging in "wiki" projects of open-source, online collaboration. Some pieces fit into one cell of the typology by merit of their subject matter, whereas other pieces fit into other cells. However, to get to this point of massive cooperation unfettered by academic politics, the identity studies community must pose questions like "why are we doing this research," and "what do we want to know/achieve"? All researchers should engage is this type of self-reflection, asking themselves what their value priorities are. For example, if their research agenda were followed, would the effect on the young people they study be one of "prediction and control," or would it be more humanistic, helping people to reach their human potentials?

Identity researchers should also make frank assessments of what their subject matter is in terms of studying manifestations of identity and thus how they might contribute to solving the jigsaw puzzle of human identity. Table 32.1 provides a version of the typology presented in Côté (2006a) that focuses specifically on identity development (and not other manifestation of identity, such as identity maintenance).

In Table 32.1, it is proposed that the subject matter of identity development research varies by three sets of assumption. For example, some researchers study developmental processes whereas others examine developmental experiences (represented by the two rows). Many process-oriented researchers—especially psychologists—are interested in individual/subjective, normative manifestations, whereas others are interested in non-normative manifestations (with "normative" defined as the dominant mode of resolution undertaken by those without financial, social, or psychological obstacles to the resolution of their identity stage, especially goals that they have targeted after a period of self-reflection or urging from others, such as their parents or faith).

Table 32.1 The subject matter of identity development research, based on underlying assumptions

	Individual/subjective focus		Social/interactional focus	
	Normative	Non-normative	Normative	Non-normative
(Developmental) Processes leading to…	Variations in psychosocial resolutions leading to integration, opportunity, fulfillment	Alternative psychosocial resolutions or barriers to normative resolutions	Contexts conducive to various adaptive identity configurations and social integrations	Contexts hindering normative resolutions, requiring alternative resolutions
(Developmental) Experiences leading to…	Events leading to a personal sense of integration, opportunity, fulfillment	Events producing or reinforcing a personal sense of marginalization, discrimination, alienation	Events producing a shared sense of integration, opportunity, fulfillment	Events producing or reinforcing a shared sense of marginalization, discrimination, alienation

Other process-oriented researchers prefer social and/or interactional approaches, especially sociologists and social psychologists, in the study of normative and non-normative development (represented in the top two cells to the right). As we see below, the study of youth identities by sociologists has favored an approach based on the concept of "individualization," which bears a resemblance to the range of identity statuses (the diffusion-achievement range). The focus of these sociologists is on the individualization process in late modernity. According to this theory, late-modern social contexts are often anomic, leaving young people to engage in choice making in the absence of normative guidance. For example, the virtual disappearance of social markers for adulthood for young people in secular segments of these societies makes the transition to adulthood more complex and uncertain.

The work of Beck (e.g., 1992; 2002) exemplifies the European approach to late modernity, and the work of Furlong and Cartmel (2007) applies it to the transition to adulthood. However, it must be stressed that the individualization process and certain identities continue to be circumscribed by class, gender, and ethnicity/race to the extent that certain norms prevail to sustain these social attributes as restrictive areas of functioning. Thus, although the boundaries of certain social statuses are more permeable and obscure than in early modernity, the access to certain social roles and statuses still depends on the specific circumstances found in the countries and culture in question, with some cultures providing more opportunities than others, with the class/gender/ethnicity "identity" of the incumbent and prospective member still influencing access to those statuses (cf. Furlong & Cartmel's, 2007, concept of the epistemological fallacy).

Similarly, some researchers are more interested in the social and interactional contexts of identity development, and Table 32.1 shows four possible ways of doing so, the products of which can highlight different developmental possibilities. Studying identity in these contexts would be appropriately accomplished using qualitative techniques, such as narrative methods when the focus is on the individual and ethnographies when the focus is on the social.

The chief lesson to be taken from this exercise in mapping the subject matter of various researchers is just that—different researchers are studying different manifestations of identity development, and they are doing so because their assumptions have pointed them in that direction. Hence, each of the eight perspectives has valid concerns. For example, some identity development is normative, whereas other identity development is non-normative, but the existence of non-normative development does not negate the validity of normative development or the approaches used to study it.

My own research based on the identity capital model looks at normative development for ways of understanding how to help those in non-normative situations, both individual and social, to improve their life chances and human potentials. The social focus involves identifying the characteristics of late-modern societies, such as the "individualization process." The individual focus examines the range of strategies people can take in response to the societal requirement to individualize, which have been identified as ranging from the "default" to the "developmental." On the one hand, the results of investigations of this model highlight the importance of personal agency in dealing with (i.e., penetrating) institutional structures so the person can go from non-normative to normative contexts if he or she has the desire and wherewithal (e.g., becoming upwardly mobile from the working class to the middle class through higher educational settings). At the same time, the individualization contradiction is postulated to characterize the situations in which "people are expected to be the architects of their own destinies, but for many the avenues do not exist to turn this expectation into a reality" (Côté & Allahar, 2006, p. 115). Some of the blockages to aspirations may be social/institutional obstacles that are not surmountable for a person with a particular social identity, but it is also possible that the person does not have the developmental requisites to handle roles that require higher levels of functioning. This model thus links the four cells in Table 32.1 representing the developmental processes.

In empirical examinations of the identity capital model, several attempts have been made to demonstrate the links between the social and psychological through the individualization concept. For example, Côté and Schwartz (2002) argue that psychologists and sociologists have been studying similar identity processes with differing terminologies, the former with Eriksonian theory and the latter with individualization theory. That is, identity confusion (or the "diffusion" status) and identity synthesis (or the identity "achievement" status) were hypothesized to represent forms of default and developmental individualization, respectively. Not coincidentally, I would add, these two identity statuses are also closest to Erikson's original postulate of a continuum between identity diffusion and identity synthesis. Thus, the link between these two disciplinary approaches is that the individualization processes can be operationalized in terms of differing levels of agency in identity formation. Proactive approaches to identity synthesis constitute developmental forms of individualization characterized by planful and purposeful strategic approaches to personal growth and a life project, which can lead to finding a niche in an adult community. In contrast, diffuse or inactive approaches to identity formation exemplify default individualization, characterized by following paths of least resistance and effort, where people "allow" decisions to be made for them as a result of their inaction; in turn, this lack of effort can lead to a deferred or passive formation of an adult identity and adult community commitments.

In another study, Schwartz, Côté, and Arnett (2005) followed this postulated homology between the diffused/achieved identity statuses and default/developmental individualization. This study replicated the relationship between a measure of personal agency with proactive identity formation (agency correlates positively with exploration and flexible commitment). Cluster analysis found that the sample could be split about evenly between developmental and default forms of individualization, confirming that the two types of individualization can be empirically identified categorically and that they are related to clear variations in the use of identity-based agentic capacities. Finally, Côté (2002; 2006b) provides longitudinal results showing the importance of identity-based agency in a variety of outcomes for a sample followed from their late teens to late twenties.

This identity capital research is discussed in such detail because it shows how a sociological approach can be reconciled with a psychological approach while adopting assumptions compatible with the postmodernist approach without "otherizing" different approaches to the same topic and rejecting them offhandedly on the basis of dogmatic epistemological preconceptions (i.e., an anti-realist nominalism). Readers are referred to Syed (2012) and Schwartz et al. (2011) for examples of other integrative models.

Conclusion

My aim in this chapter, as it has been in my previous commentaries on the identity studies literature, is to appeal to researchers to adopt broader, more catholic approaches to help them recognize the various barriers that divide identity researchers. Table 32.1 shows how the field can be seen as having a varied subject matter; studying that subject matter thus requires different approaches, including different methodologies. This way of viewing the field invites theorists and researchers to become less judgmental of each other's perspective as "right or wrong" and instead to evaluate them along dimensions such as usefulness and appropriateness for the subject matter at hand. Taking this project seriously requires that identity researchers be more open to each other's work and methods and to thus gain a better appreciation of the complexities of contemporary identity formation. Critiques of each other's position would then be more constructive and less political, based on the issues at hand rather than often-unstated epistemological and disciplinary assumptions. As it stands, many critiques form barriers to mutual understandings. As a result of this intransigence, unconstructive critiques become impediments to the field as a whole. If the field is to mature, members of the identity studies community will need to examine, admit, and overcome their prejudices so they can engage in cooperative, multidimensional projects. Many of the authors in this handbook and in the wider community understand this, whereas others apparently do not.

Future Directions

• The identity studies community needs to learn how to cooperate in order to cover all of the subject matter representing identity development and maintenance at all levels of analysis (e.g., intrapsychic, interpersonal, social), other manifestations of this multidimensional construct at each level (e.g., national identities, sexual identities), variations in the basis of identity in different types of societies (e.g., premodern vs. late-modern societies with their differences in ascription and achievement), and in combination with other factors (e.g., intergroup relations, identity and violence, identity and genocide, identity politics, etc.).

• The "Identity Tower of Babel" needs to recognized and corrected through the development of a common taxonomy.

• The field needs to see the end of singular, overextended perspectives that imperialistically claim that other perspectives are invalid. This might help eliminate the epistemological divide.

• Models for planning and executing cooperative research projects covering multiple aspects of identity with multiple methods need to be developed. This might be accomplished by creating divisions or research committees in SRIF similar to those found in larger societies. Alternatively, a new society could be founded that is dedicated to studying all levels and dimensions of identity (perhaps using something like Table 32.1 as a map). A name like the International Society of Interdisciplinary Identity Studies (ISIIS) seems appropriate. With or without these more formal efforts, an informal identity wiki could be set up to allow for the unfettered compilation of ideas, debates, theories, and research findings.

• Some of the neglected areas need attention. In particular, the psychological implications of macrosocial variations need to be better understood through theory development and innovative research methods. For example, a variety of social theories from mainstream sociology could be brought to bear on understanding macrocontexts. It is cliché in psychology that Bronfenbrenner's (1977) ecological model is the gold standard for understanding "the environment." Although Bronfenbrenner's model provides a useful and logical framework, it treats all types of societies as the same and that is clearly not the case. Besides, his argument that culture permeates all aspects of life is axiomatic in disciplines like sociology that have been investigating the nature of these cultural penetrations for over a century, producing a rich set of social theories that provide clues as to which variables might be useful in identity research applied in particular societies.

Taking a simple variable approach based only on concepts like meso-, exo-, and macrosystems not only puts the (empty) cart before the horse, but it is like doing research blindfolded (pardon the mixed metaphor). We saw earlier that by employing late-modern theory, researchers were alerted to the importance of social anomie in the decline of social markers and the rise of the individualization process in the transition to adulthood. Simply treating the "environment" as a black box into which a series of variables can be inserted without taking account of societal conditions is to rely on researchers' intuition, which invites all sorts of bias, some of which were discussed earlier. And it misses what are perhaps the key features facilitating or hindering identity formation in the society under study.

• Bringing sociology into play alongside psychology could yield numerous insights. For example, the notion of alienated identity has received little attention in the identity studies community (alienation, for sociologists, refers to a lack of control over one's environment; see Wexler, 1983, and Côté & Allahar, 1996; 2006, for accounts of the exploitative nature of identity moratorium contexts in capitalist societies). A radical critique of identity formation in current late-modern societies would begin with the assumption that the relationships between the young person and formal influences like schools, the workplace, and corporations is currently heavily influenced by rightwing, neoliberal government policies. If this is the case, then what development psychologist call "identity achievement" for many people may simply be a socialization outcome in which the person accepts conformity to alienated relationships. In other words, by advocating explorations/commitments to the neoliberal status quo as the gold standard of identity formation, identity researchers may be inadvertently contributing to the exploitation of the masses to alienated conditions in their personal and work lives. If this scenario sounds far-fetched, it should be pointed out that the identity status paradigm would have counted some of the most ardent Nazis as "identity achieved" in Nazi Germany. This is because that paradigm is only able to detect functional resolutions of the identity stage, not epigenetic ones (e.g., Côté & Levine, 1987; 2002). The "moral neutrality" of the identity status paradigm is an illusion.

In light of these concerns, current and future identity researchers would do well to pay heed to the rich tradition of theory provided by parent disciplines but also by key figures like Erikson, and I dare say would benefit from reading other figures like Fromm (1955) and Marx (e.g., Marx & Engels, 1969). Not only would some factual issues be cleared up (e.g., some of the misconceptions about what Erikson wrote about the nature of the identity crisis that we see in the present volume), but the field could also develop a moral compass that has been lacking, a compass that might help answer the questions posed earlier: "why are we doing this research," and "what do we want to know/achieve"?

References

Akerlof, G. A., & Kranton, R, E. (2010). *Identity economics: How our identities shape our work, wages, and well-being*. Princeton, NJ: Princeton University Press.

Beck, U. (1992). *Risk society: Towards a new modernity*. London: Sage.

Beck, U. (2002). *Individualization: Individualized individualism and its social and political consequences*. Thousand Oaks, CA: Sage.

Bennett, A. (2011). The post–subcultural turn: Some reflections 10 years on. *Journal of Youth Studies, 14*, 493–506.

Bronfenbrenner, U. (1977). Toward an experimental ecology of human development. *American Psychologist, 32*, 513–31.

Burrell, G., & Morgan, G. (1979). *Sociological paradigms and organisational analysis*. London: Heinemann.

Côté, J. E. (1993). Foundations of a psychoanalytic social psychology: Neo-Eriksonian propositions regarding the relationship between psychic structure and cultural institutions. *Developmental Review, 13*, 31–53.

Côté, J. E. (1996a). Identity: A multidimensional analysis. In G. Adams, R. Montemayor, & T. Gullotta (Eds.), *Psychosocial development in adolescence. Vol. 8: Advances in adolescent development*. Beverley Hills, CA: Sage.

Côté, J. E. (1996b). Sociological perspectives on identity formation: The culture–identity link and identity capital. *Journal of Adolescence, 19*, 417–28.

Côté, J. E. (2002). The role of identity capital in the transition to adulthood: The individualization thesis examined. *Journal of Youth Studies, 5*(2), 117–34.

Côté, J. E. (Ed.). (2005). The postmodern critique of developmental perspectives [Special issue]. *Identity: An International Journal of Theory and Research, 5*(2), 95–225.

Côté, J. E. (2006a). Identity studies: How close are we to developing a social science of identity? – An appraisal of the field. *Identity: An International Journal of Theory and Research, 6*, 3–25.

Côté, J. E. (2006b). Emerging adulthood as an institutionalized moratorium: Risks and benefits to identity formation. In J. J. Arnett & J. Tanner (Eds.), *Emerging adults in America: Coming of age in the 21st century* (pp. 85–116). Washington, DC: American Psychological Association.

Côté, J. E. (2009a). Identity and self development. In R. M. Lerner & L. Steinberg (Eds.), *Handbook of adolescent psychology (3rd ed.). Vol. 1: Individual bases of adolescent development* (pp. 266–304). Hoboken, NJ: Wiley.

Côté, J. E. (2009b). Youth identity studies: History, controversies, and future directions. In A. Furlong (Ed.), *International handbook of youth and young adulthood* (pp. 375–83). London: Routledge International Handbook Series.

Côté, J. E. (2010). Adolescent psychology and the sociology of youth: Toward a rapprochement. In R. Zukauskiene (Ed.), *The 12th Biennial Conferences of the European Association for Research on Adolescence* (pp. 93–9). Bologna, Italy: Medimond.

Côté, J. E., & Allahar, A. (1996). *Generation on hold: Coming of age in the late twentieth century*. New York: New York University Press.

Côté, J. E., & Allahar, A. (2006). *Critical youth studies: A Canadian focus*. Toronto: Pearson Education.

Côté, J. E., & Levine, C. G. (1987). A formulation of Erikson's theory of ego identity formation. *Developmental Review, 7*, 273–325.

Côté, J. E., & Levine, C. G. (1988). A critical examination of the ego identity status paradigm. *Developmental Review, 8*, 147–84.

Côté, J. E., & Levine, C. G. (2002). *Identity formation, agency, and culture: A social psychological synthesis*. Mahwah, NJ: Erlbaum.

Côté, J. E., & Schwartz, S. (2002). Comparing psychological and sociological approaches to identity: Identity status, identity capital, and the individualization process. *Journal of Adolescence, 25*, 571–86.

Damon, W. (2009). *The path to purpose: How young people find their calling in life*. New York: Free Press.

Erikson, E. H. (1968). *Identity: Youth and crisis*. New York: Norton.

Fromm, E. (1955). *The sane society*. Greenwich, CT: Fawcett Publications.

Furlong, A., & Cartmel, F. (2007). *Young people and social change: New perspectives* (2nd ed.). Buckingham, UK: Open University Press.

Goffman, E. (1959). *The presentation of self in everyday life*. Garden City, NY: Doubleday.

Goffman, E. (1963). *Stigma: Notes on the management of spoiled identity*. Englewood Cliffs, NJ: Prentice-Hall.

Hewitt, J. P. (2003). *Self and society: A symbolic interactionist social psychology* (9th ed.). Boston: Allyn and Bacon.

Lerner, R. M. (2002). *Concepts and theories of human development* (3rd ed.). Mahwah, NJ: Lawrence Erlbaum.

Marx, K., & Engels, F. (1969). *The German ideology*. New York: International Publishers.

Muuss, R. (1996). *Theories of adolescence* (6th ed.). New York: McGraw Hill.

Nickerson, R. S. (1998). Confirmation bias: A ubiquitous phenomenon in many guises. *Review of General Psychology, 2,* 175–220.

Oswald, M. E., & Grosjean, S. (2004). Confirmation bias. In R. F. Pohl (Ed.), *Cognitive illusions: A handbook on fallacies and biases in thinking, judgment and memory* (pp. 79–96). Hove, UK: Psychology Press.

Phoenix, A. (2010). Ethnicities. In M. Wetherell & C. T. Mohanty (Eds.), *The Sage handbook of identities* (pp. 297–320). Los Angeles: Sage.

Phoenix, A., & Rattansi, A. (2005). Proliferating theories: Self and identity in post–Eriksonian context: A rejoinder to Berzonsky, Kroger, Levine, Phinney, Schachter, and Weigert and Gecas. *Identity: An International Journal of Theory and Research, 5,* 205–25.

Rattansi, A., & Phoenix, A. (1997/2005). Rethinking youth identities: Modernist and postmodernist frameworks. *Identity: An International Journal of Theory and Research, 5,* 97–123. [Reprinted from Bynner, J., Chisholm, L., & Furlong, A. (Eds.). (1997). *Youth, citizenship and social change in a European context.* Aldershot, UK: Ashgate.]

Schwartz, S. J., Côté, J. E., & Arnett, J. J. (2005). Identity and agency in emerging adulthood: Two developmental routes in the individualization process. *Youth and Society, 37,* 201–29.

Schwartz, S. J., Luyckx, K., & Vignoles, V. L. (Eds.). (2011). *Handbook of identity theory and research.* New York: Springer.

Snarey, J., Kohlberg, L., & Noam, G. (1983). Ego development in perspective: Structural stage, functional phase, and cultural age–period models. *Developmental Review, 3,* 303–38.

Syed, M. (2012). The past, present, and future of Eriksonian identity research: Introduction to the special issue. *Identity: An International Journal of Theory and Research, 12,* 1–7.

Stryker, S. (1987). Identity theory: Developments and extensions. In K. Yardley and T. Honess (Eds.), *Self and identity: Psychosocial perspectives* (pp. 89–105). New York: Wiley.

Wetherell, M. (Ed.). (2009). *Theorizing identities and social action.* Houndmills, UK: Palgrave MacMillan.

Wetherell, M., & Mohanty, C. T. (Eds.). (2010). *The Sage handbook of identities.* Los Angeles: Sage.

Wexler, P. (1983). *Critical social psychology.* London: Routledge & Kegan Paul.

CHAPTER 33

What Have We Learned Since Schwartz (2001)?: A Reappraisal of the Field of Identity Development

Seth J. Schwartz, Koen Luyckx, *and* Elisabetta Crocetti

Abstract

This chapter reviews the neo-Eriksonian personal identity literature, focusing on advances that have occurred since 2001. The majority of the chapter is dedicated to the development of new identity status models, continuing research on existing status-based models, and the continued emergence and expansion of narrative identity models and studies. The chapter also reviews measurement issues and domain specificity in neo-Eriksonian identity literature, focusing on the need to consider identity domains separately rather than summing across them. The chapter concludes with a summary of major correlates of identity and of intersectionality between and among different identity domains and processes. Recommendations for future neo-Eriksonian identity theory and research are provided.

Key Words: narrative identity, cultural identity, identity status, neo-Eriksonian, developmental, domains, well-being, internalizing symptoms, externalizing symptoms, health risk behaviors

---

The introductory part of this chapter is written in first person by the senior author (SJS), because he was the author of the 2001 article to which the present chapter serves as an update. Setting the context for the publication of that article may help readers to understand why it is important to assess the progress of the field since that specific point in time. The 2001 article came at a critical juncture in the evolution of neo-Eriksonian identity theory and research: leaders in the field had been calling for fundamental changes in the ways in which identity was being studied, but the precise nature of these changes was not yet clear.

When I first published my review of the neo-Eriksonian identity literature (Schwartz, 2001), I saw a field ripe for change. The identity status model had been in use for thirty-five years (Berzonsky & Adams, 1999), but the model had pretty much run its course. We knew how personality, adjustment, logical reasoning, and attitudinal variables differed among the statuses, but what we did not know was something much more fundamental—were the statuses really the best way to represent identity? This question had been posed in a critical way on a number of occasions (e.g., Côté & Levine, 1988; van Hoof, 1999), but, to that point, there did not seem to be a viable solution.

When I published the 2001 article, I was torn regarding the future of our field. On one hand, there seemed to be an almost unlimited set of correlates that we could examine across the statuses—but on the other hand, the information that we would gain from such investigations seemed to be quite limited. Knowing that achieved individuals manifested the most balanced perspective taking, for example (e.g., Boyes & Chandler, 1992), was interesting, but what practical value did this kind of research have for understanding how to promote perspective taking among young people? What did these findings tell us about the developmental adequacy of the identity status model? Were the statuses even developmental at all? In short, the work being conducted on identity development was of some theoretical import, but it did not address the key questions that needed to be answered to effectively advance the field of neo-Eriksonian identity theory and research.

One of the first major issues, then, was whether we needed to throw the baby out with the bath water, or whether there might be a way to extend and expand the identity status model so as to increase its relevance for understanding human development, promoting adaptive developmental outcomes, and preventing undesirable behaviors and outcomes. A number of theorists, including Berzonsky (1989), Waterman (1990), Grotevant (1987; see also Kerpelman, Pittman, & Lamke, 1997), Kurtines (Kurtines, Berman, Ittel, & Williamson, 1995), Côté (1996), Adams (Adams & Marshall, 1996; see also Bosma & Kunnen, 2001), and Meeus (1996), had already begun to propose new models that drew, to varying extents, on identity status. These models linked the identity statuses with decision-making styles and competencies, with intrinsic motivation and self-actualization, and with the functions of identity vis-à-vis negotiating for societal resources (e.g., jobs, relationships). These models also highlighted the role of agency in identity development (Côté & Levine, 2002), revisited the assumption within the identity status literature (see Marcia, 1993) that foreclosure represented a less desirable resolution to the identity development process than achievement did (Bosma & Kunnen, 2001; Meeus, Iedema, Helsen, & Vollebergh, 1999), and began to reframe both commitment and exploration as processes—rather than conceptualizing commitment simply as an outcome of the exploration process (Kerpelman et al., 1997).

Much of what I called for in my 2001 article was a return to Erikson. Several writers (Côté & Levine, 1988; van Hoof & Raiijmakers, 2002; Waterman, 1988; see also Arnett, this volume) have highlighted differences between the identity status model and the Eriksonian lifespan theory from which it emerged. A major emphasis of my argument was that classifying participants into static categories did not adequately represent the person–context interplay that underlay Erikson's work. One of my recommendations was to move away from comparing status categories and toward a dynamic process approach based on identifying predictors, correlates, and antecedents of identity exploration and commitment. Such a dynamic perspective was more consistent with Erikson's work than were the identity statuses. Furthermore, the largely intrapersonal focus of the identity status model implied that individual differences among individuals in terms of their identity status categories were somehow reflective of "choices" made by young people themselves. Labeling foreclosure as a choice, for example, allowed some writers (e.g., Kroger & Marcia, 2011) to adopt a pejorative view of foreclosure as a form of taking the easy way out rather than enduring the rigors and discomfort involved with exploration. Similarly, diffused individuals were labeled as maladjusted, with the assumption that the person had somehow *decided* not to explore identity alternatives or to enact commitments. The roles of family relationships, cultural contexts, peer groups, and socioeconomic opportunities were generally not considered within the identity status perspective.

A number of advances have occurred within the field of neo-Eriksonian identity theory and research since my 2001 article was published. The majority of these advances can be grouped into two primary strands: further progress on the models I reviewed in that article and the emergence of new models and methods. These two strands of advances in identity development research are reviewed in the two sections that immediately follow this introductory section.

Before proceeding, however, it is essential to note that, in a chapter on identity development, one must be clear regarding what is meant by the terms "identity" and "development." For the purposes of this chapter, identity refers to the "organization of self-understandings that define one's place in the world" (Schwartz, Montgomery, & Briones, 2006, p. 5). For example, at the personal level, identity denotes a set of goals, values, and beliefs that guide one's decisions. At the group level, such as when one is considering one's role in one's ethnic or cultural group, identity denotes the subjective meaning that one assigns to the group membership, as well as one's degree of solidarity with the group (Spears, 2011).

The term "development" also has a number of potential meanings, most of which refer to some sort of change over time. The issues at hand often address questions about what is seen as developing, the time span over which development is assumed to occur, and the permanence of the developmental process (Lichtwarck-Aschoff, van Geert, Bosma, & Kunnen, 2009). For the purpose of this chapter, development is regarded as a process that takes place on time scales ranging from day-to-day micro-level changes to macro-level changes occurring over months or years. Identity processes have been found to be reversible (regressive) in some cases, but most changes in indices of identity have been found to be progressive (cf. al-Owidha, Green, & Kroger, 2009).

Models Reviewed in Schwartz (2001): Research Update

In the 2001 article, Schwartz reviewed six models that had been developed to complement and move beyond the identity status approach. Some of these approaches were solidly grounded in identity status and were labeled as "extensions," whereas others moved considerably beyond identity status and were labeled as "expansions." The extension models were identity style (Berzonsky, 1989), eudaimonic identity theory (Waterman, 1990), and the exploration-as-process approach proposed by Grotevant (1987) and revised by Kerpelman, Pittman, and Lamke (1997). The expansion models were identity capital (Côté, 1996), the co-constructivist approach (Kurtines et al., 1995), and the functions of identity (Adams & Marshall, 1996).

These models have been pursued to varying degrees in the years since the 2001 article was published. The largest research literatures have developed around identity style, eudaimonic identity theory, and identity capital—and those are reviewed briefly here. *Identity style* (Berzonsky, 1989), which posits three primary ways of approaching life decisions, has been the most heavily researched of the six extension and expansion models included in my 2001 review. The three identity styles are informational (seeking information, open-mindedness and flexible commitment), normative (rigid conformity to authority figures), and diffuse-avoidant (procrastination, hesitation, and efforts to delay or avoid making life decisions) (see Berzonsky, 2011, for a recent review). Research has examined the motivational correlates of the three styles (Smits, Soenens, Vansteenkiste, Luyckx, & Goossens, 2010; Soenens, Berzonsky, Vansteenkiste, Beyers, & Goossens, 2005), the links between perceived parenting and identity style (Berzonsky, 2003; Smits, Soenens, Luyckx, Duriez, Berzonsky, & Goossens, 2008), and associations between identity style and well-being (Vleioras & Bosma, 2005). Identity style research has been conducted in a number of countries, including the United States (Berzonsky & Ferrari, 2009), Canada (Wheeler, Adams, & Keating, 2001), Italy (Crocetti, Rubini, Berzonsky, & Meeus, 2009), Belgium (Smits et al., 2010), the Netherlands (Berzonsky, Branje, & Meeus, 2007), Greece (Vleioras, 2007; Vleioras & Bosma, 2005), Poland (Berzonsky, Cieciuch, Duriez, & Soenens, 2011), Switzerland (Zimmermann, Mahaim, Mantzouranis, Genoud, & Crocetti, 2012), and Iran (Crocetti & Shokri, 2010).

Broadly speaking, the majority of identity style studies have found that the informational style is associated with openness and flexibility, with a willingness to explore and examine new ideas, and with firm commitments that can be revised when and if necessary. The normative style is often associated with rigidly held commitments and with an unwillingness or inability to consider other options. The diffuse-avoidant style is generally associated with the poorest outcomes, including low well-being, high neuroticism, and distant social relationships (see Berzonsky, 2011, for an in-depth review of the correlates of the three styles). Generally speaking, the informational and normative styles may both be linked with well-being, given that both of them lead to enactment of commitments (Vleioras & Bosma, 2005). The diffuse-avoidant style appears to represent a strategy aimed to intentionally and strategically avoid making life choices and assuming responsibility for the consequences of those choices (Berzonsky & Ferrari, 2009). Although the identity styles are similar to, and overlap considerably with, the identity statuses (Berzonsky, 2011), the styles were developed to tap into the decision-making processes that underlie the statuses. For example, an informational style, reflecting an open-minded and flexible approach, is closely associated with achievement and moratorium; the normative style, reflecting a rigid and conformity-based approach, is closely related to foreclosure; and the diffuse/avoidant style, reflecting a procrastinatory approach, is closely related to diffusion. The process-oriented nature of the styles was assumed to move beyond the identity statuses, which represent categorical placements based on the extent to which the person has explored alternatives and has enacted commitments.

Eudaimonic identity theory (Waterman, 2011) has also received a considerable amount of research attention. This theory is centered around two primary constructs—intrinsic motivation and eudaimonic well-being. Intrinsic motivation operates at the level of the activity, and eudaimonic well-being operates at the level of the person. Both of these constructs, however, focus on a sense of fit between the person and the activities or goals that he or she maintains, an orientation toward a life that presents considerable challenges and requires the expenditure of effort, and discovering who one "really is." Both in terms of the activities in which one engages (in the case of intrinsic motivation) and in terms of personal traits, eudaimonic identity theory attends to the extent to which one is oriented toward pursuing a fulfilling life characterized by self-realization.

Several postulates of the theory have been empirically supported (see Waterman & Schwartz, 2013, for a more extensive review). First, interest, flow experiences (becoming absorbed in an activity and forgetting about worries and stressors; Csikszentmihalyi, 1990), and personal expressiveness (a sense of fit between the person and the activity) map onto a latent construct that can be labeled as intrinsic motivation—and this latent construct is predicted by self-determination, the balance between the challenges posed by an activity and the skills brought to it, and the extent to which an activity offers opportunities for self-realization (Schwartz & Waterman, 2006; Waterman, Schwartz, & Conti, 2008; Waterman et al., 2003). Second, activities experienced as personally expressive and that give rise to flow experiences are generally those on which the person expends a great deal of effort (Waterman, 2005). Third, eudaimonic well-being explains the association of identity commitments with well-being and with low levels of internalizing symptoms (Waterman et al., 2013). So, in essence, self-discovery is a function of an activity or goal being self-selected, presenting an optimal amount of challenge, and providing opportunities to realize one's highest potentials—and discovering one's "true self" explains the association between identity commitments and well-being. Eudaimonic identity theory adopts a self-discovery perspective on identity development, one in which self-discovery represents identifying and living in accordance with one's true self (Waterman & Schwartz, 2013). This self-discovery approach stands somewhat in contrast to the constructivist approach adopted by many identity perspectives, in which the person is assumed to create a sense of identity "from the ground up" (Vignoles, Schwartz, & Luyckx, 2011).

The *identity capital model* (Côté, 1996) posits that intangible identity assets—skills, knowledge, belief in oneself, personal accountability, and a sense of purpose—are likely to help young people to thrive and to "get ahead" in the Western world. Research has supported this postulate. For example, Burrow and Hill (2011) found that commitment to a sense of life purpose was strongly predictive of well-being. Luyckx, Duriez, Klimstra, and De Witte (2010) found that perceiving oneself to have reached adulthood offset the effects of perceived life instability (e.g., confusion, inability to settle down into a permanent lifestyle) on self-esteem and depressive symptoms. Schwartz (2006) found that perceived adulthood and the belief that one had found a community in which to settle explained the associations of eudaimonic well-being and the informational identity style with identity synthesis. In other words, using an agentic and exploratory approach to identity issues and living in accordance with one's highest potentials appears to permit the person to view her- or himself as an adult and to settle into a validating community—and, in turn, perceiving oneself as an adult and as a member of a supportive community is closely related to having developed a synthesized sense of personal identity (where personal identity refers to a set of goals, values, and beliefs).

Identity capital is important because it represents what identity "does"—that is, it explains how a clear and coherent sense of identity can facilitate success in interpersonal relationships, career preparation and job performance, and other areas of one's life. That is, identity capital refers to the "value" of identity in the postmodern world. Employers, for example, are often searching for employees who are reliable and who know where they are looking to take their lives (Kalleberg, 2009).

New Models and Methods

Although some of the models reviewed in the Schwartz (2001) article continued to flourish, new neo-Eriksonian models were also developed, based in part on the propositions and suggestions that Schwartz put forth. Some of these models have been based in the identity status model, whereas others have been grounded in Erikson's work but have emerged outside of the identity status model. Most prominent among the identity status–based models are the dual-cycle commitment formation and evaluation model (Luyckx, Goossens, Soenens, & Beyers, 2006a) and the three-factor identity model (Crocetti, Rubini, & Meeus, 2008b). The primary models that have emerged outside of identity status have been based in the narrative identity literature (see McAdams, 2011; Singer, 2004, for reviews). Narrative identity research was alive and well before the Schwartz (2001) review was published, but it has become much more integrated with other neo-Eriksonian perspectives. Models focusing on storytelling—both in terms of recounting past events (Pasupathi, 2001) and in terms of making sense of key points in one's life story (McLean, 2005; McLean & Pratt, 2006)—have, in many cases, drawn on Erikson's work to connect narrative principles with the neo-Eriksonian identity tradition (and in some cases directly with the identity statuses). We review both new identity status models and neo-Eriksonian narrative identity models in this section.

New Identity Status Based Models

Both the dual-cycle and three-process models (see Crocetti & Meeus, this volume) have expanded the number of dimensions considered within the identity status approach. More specifically, both of these models have unpacked commitment and/or exploration into a larger set of processes. Luyckx et al. have delineated two types of exploration—exploration in breadth (Marcia's original dimension) and exploration in depth (thinking and talking with others about commitments that one has already enacted; cf. Meeus, 1996). They have also delineated commitment into commitment making (Marcia's original dimension) and identification with commitment (incorporating commitments into one's sense of self; cf. Bosma, 1985). Luyckx, Goossens, and Soenens (2006b) have provided evidence for the developmental ordering of these four processes, in which exploration in breadth and commitment making represent the mechanism through which identity commitments are *formed*, and in which exploration in depth and identification with commitment represent the mechanism through which identity commitments are *evaluated*.

Luyckx, Schwartz, et al. (2008) later introduced a fifth identity process, ruminative exploration, to represent maladaptive, unproductive perfectionism and hesitation during the identity development process. Broadly, ruminative exploration involves becoming "stuck" and being unwilling or unable to move forward in the process of developing a sense of self (Luyckx, Soenens, Goossens, Beckx, & Wouters, 2008). Like other counterproductive identity processes, ruminative exploration can conceivably occur because the person is genuinely afraid, confused, or overly perfectionistic.

Crocetti et al. (2008b) have identified three core identity processes—commitment, exploration in depth, and reconsideration of commitment. Exploration in depth carries the same meaning in this model as it does in Meeus's (1996) earlier writings and in the Luyckx et al. (2006a) model. Commitment and reconsideration represent a polarity between certainty and uncertainty, respectively. Reconsideration appears to occur largely in response to dissatisfaction with one's current set of commitments and with the sense of self that results from the amalgamation of these commitments (Schwartz, Klimstra, Luyckx, Hale, & Meeus, 2012). Reconsideration can be employed either as a way of revising one's identity or, like ruminative exploration, as a way of continually avoiding the task of making life choices (Crocetti et al., 2009). Nonetheless, reconsideration represents the loosening of commitments in preparation for exploration and for settling on a revised set of commitments. As such, reconsideration likely represents an essential component of the identity development and evaluation process, despite the discomfort associated with feeling uncertain about where one's life is headed.

A further contribution made by the Luyckx and Crocetti/Meeus models was to validate the connection between the underlying identity processes and the identity status categories. Using empirically based, cluster-analytic methodology, these authors were able to demonstrate that all of Marcia's identity statuses—plus some additional statuses not proposed by Marcia—could be extracted from the exploration and commitment processes postulated within each of the new models (Crocetti, Rubini, Luyckx, & Meeus, 2008a; Crocetti, Schwartz, Fermani, Klimstra, & Meeus, 2012; Luyckx, Goossens, Soenens, Beyers, & Vansteenkiste, 2005; Luyckx, Schwartz, Berzonsky, et al., 2008). The new statuses extracted had been hypothesized, to some extent, by earlier identity theorists and researchers. The undifferentiated status found by Luyckx et al. (2005; 2008) was characterized by scores on all five identity processes that were close to their sample means, similar to the low profile moratorium status that Bennion and Adams (1986) used to classify participants who could not be safely placed into one of the other statuses. The two variants of diffusion—troubled diffusion and carefree diffusion—that Luyckx et al. (2005; 2008) identified are consistent with Marcia (1989), who proposed a differentiation between aimless and "playboy" diffusion. The demarcation between classical and searching moratorium (i.e., a moratorium status that does not require relinquishing one's existing commitments; Crocetti et al., 2008a) draws on Côté and Schwartz (2002), who noted that the personality traits associated with moratorium and with achievement are so diametrically opposed that a "massive personality reconfiguration" would be required to support the transition from moratorium to achievement. Indeed, Meeus, van de Schoot, Keijsers, Schwartz, and Branje (2010) found that early adolescents in the classical moratorium status were only 22 percent likely to transition to achievement within four years, compared to 32 percent of adolescents in the searching moratorium status.

These cluster-analytic studies, particularly longitudinal studies in which the status solution was extracted using multiple time points (e.g., Luyckx, Klimstra, Schwartz, & Duriez, 2013; Meeus et al., 2010), have served as somewhat of a response to criticisms of the identity status model's internal validity. The finding that most young people remain in the same status over a span of several years (e.g., Meeus et al., 2010) suggests that the status model, including the new statuses reported by Luyckx, Meeus, Crocetti, and their colleagues, possesses adequate internal validity and internal consistency. Specifically, contrary to Marcia's (1966) original formulation, identity statuses represent more than a snapshot of identity development in late adolescence and emerging adulthood. Rather, the statuses may be viewed as somewhat stable personality configurations and as characteristic ways of addressing important life decisions across time.

Neo-Eriksonian Narrative Identity Approaches

A number of narrative identity principles have been introduced into the neo-Eriksonian literature during the twenty-first century. The various approaches to narrative identity use similar methodologies—generally open-ended interviews (oral or written) that are then coded for specific themes or insights (McAdams, 2011; McLean, Pasupathi, & Pals, 2007). The various narrative identity approaches differ in terms of the specific skills or insights around which these coding systems center—such as the ability to extract meaning from life events, the ability to connect one's current sense of self to events from one's past, or the ability to articulate what one's life story is about (e.g., forgiving others, overcoming rejection, helping those in need).

Most narrative identity approaches draw, to varying extents, on Bruner's (1987; 1991) and McAdams's (2011; Bauer & McAdams, 2010) pioneering qualitative approaches to studying people's life stories. These approaches maintain that identity emerges out of a person's reflective consideration of her or his life story, ability to integrate that life story into a coherent account, and ability to extract wisdom from both positive and negative life events. For example, McAdams (2013) examines the life story of Barack Obama and, quoting from Obama's own writings, observes that Obama developed a sense of himself as a black American, as a man without a father, and as an agent of change through reflecting on his experiences in college and on his early experiences in community work. A key difference between identity status and narrative approaches is that, whereas the identity is claimed almost exclusively by the person her- or himself in identity status theory, narrative approaches adopt a co-constructivist viewpoint (Pasupathi, 2001; Korobov, this volume; Pasupathi, this volume) in which the identity is extracted both by the storyteller and by those who are listening to or interpreting the story. In this sense, narrative approaches parallel the principles proposed by Cooley (1908), Mead (1934), and James (1890), in which an identity must be negotiated within social and interpersonal space in order to be recognized by others (Hammack, this volume).

Most neo-Eriksonian narrative identity models share in common the tenet that meaning-making, or the ability to derive a set of themes from one's life story, represents an indicator of identity maturity. For example, McLean (2008) indexes meaning-making in terms of recognizing connections between events and the self (e.g., one has come to regard oneself as trustworthy because one has been trusted by others), as well as in terms of recognizing connections between events and other events. For example, someone who has had a series of unsatisfying or abusive relationships might recognize that she has repeatedly made choices that led to her entering these relationships. McAdams and colleagues (e.g., Lilgendahl & McAdams, 2011; McAdams, Reynolds, Lewis, Patten, & Bowman, 2001) measure meaning-making in terms of the construction of an overall life story—in other words, "What has my life been about?" Pasupathi, Mansour, and Brubaker (2007) have found that meaning-making results from connections between/among life events and from subsequently integrating these connections into one's sense of self. A common thread among these perspectives is that a person with a mature sense of self is able to find a deeper and more overarching meaning across the various events that have occurred in her or his life and that the coherence among the various meanings extracted from one's life narratives serve as an index of identity maturity.

This principle of meaning-making, which has sometimes been referred to as *autobiographical reasoning* (Habermas & Bluck, 2000; Habermas & Köber, this volume), is akin to the principle of agency within the identity capital model (Côté & Levine, 2002) and other neo-Eriksonian perspectives. That is, the person recognizes how his decisions and actions have contributed to his current life situation. Supporting this contention, McLean and Pratt (2006) found that emerging adults classified into the diffused and foreclosed statuses (which tend to be low on agency; Schwartz, Côté, & Arnett, 2005) engaged in less meaning-making relative to their counterparts in moratorium and achievement.

A key theme in narrative identity research has been meaning-making regarding negative life events. Creating an integrated life story involves understanding the ways in which negative events may have helped the individual to experience growth in ways that would not likely have been possible without these events. Lilgendahl and McAdams (2011) found that, in a sample of midlife adults, framing negative past events as positive precursors for growth was associated with life satisfaction and with general well-being. McAdams et al. (2001) found that not only could negative events be recast positively (e.g., as life lessons), but also that positive events could be recast negatively (e.g., wishing that one had not entered a satisfying romantic relationship because the partner had died). McAdams et al. found that the valence with which the event was described and recounted, more than the valence with which it was initially experienced, predicted the person's satisfaction with her or his current life. These narrative studies and concepts illustrate that one's sense of self—as the sum total of the themes and meanings (or lack thereof) that the person extracts from her or his life experiences—serves as a strong predictor of one's mental health.

Summing Up New Models

To summarize, the newer identity models introduced or refined since Schwartz (2001) have served to better clarify what identity is, how it develops, and how it can be used to help the person acquire important social resources. Although the newer identity status models and the narrative identity approaches evolved largely separately from one another, some connections can be drawn between them, as well as between these models and some of the models reviewed by Schwartz (2001). For example, although narrative identity perspectives appear to imply the *construction* of a sense of identity through extracting meaning from life events (as opposed to *discovering* oneself as per eudaimonic identity theory), narrative approaches have been used to study eudaimonic well-being as well (Bauer, McAdams, & Pals, 2006). The definition provided by Waterman (2008), in terms of having discovered one's true self, enjoying challenging activities, and preferring to engage in self-chosen versus assigned activities, can be found in the life stories of many of the participants whom Bauer, McAdams, and their colleagues have identified as displaying eudaimonic well-being. Such individuals have overcome many difficult life events, seek opportunities for growth, and relish life challenges as opportunities to learn and grow. Such findings echo Waterman (2005), who found that activities giving rise to eudaimonic well-being generally require a great deal of effort and personal investment.

As another example of parallels between narrative and status-based perspectives that have evolved over the past decade, the various forms of exploration and commitment proposed by Luyckx et al. (2008) and by Crocetti, Rubini, and Meeus (2008b) may be intertwined with growth in meaning-making and autobiographical reasoning. For instance, people identifying with commitments that they have made may be likely to reflect back on their lives and derive a sense of self consistent with the commitments that have been internalized. A person who is reconsidering her commitments might have looked back at recent events and decided that something needed to be changed or that she was not happy with how her life was unfolding. Someone in a state of carefree diffusion might show little interest in creating a coherent life narrative, preferring to "live for the moment." Further exploring such connections might help us to understand the specific processes that prompt identity exploration in breadth, underlie the exploration process, and predict when exploration will stop. Narrative identity principles might also help to explain the connections between status-based processes and psychosocial and health outcomes. We return to these issues later in the chapter.

Measurement Issues and Domain Specificity in Identity Research

We discuss measurement concerns and domain specificity together here because these issues are strongly interconnected (see also Crocetti & Meeus, this volume; Josselson, this volume). For example, measurement instruments assess identity processes within a specific set of content areas, and the content areas chosen for inclusion in a given measure will shape the identity profile that is provided for each respondent. It is possible for identity instruments to assess a person's "overall" sense of self without referring to specific content domains, but only a small number of identity measures—not connected to the identity status model—have adopted such an approach (e.g., the Erikson Psychosocial Stage Inventory; Rosenthal, Gurney, & Moore, 1981). The relative merits of generality versus domain-specificity in measuring identity are discussed further here.

The earliest identity measures were structured interviews. The Identity Status Interview (originally used in Marcia, 1966; revised by Marcia & Archer, 1993) was a semistructured protocol in which participants were asked about their identity work (exploration in breadth and commitment making) in domains that Erikson had proposed—career, religion, and politics. Based on the person's responses to the various prompts, she or he would be placed into one of the four identity statuses within each of the three content domains assessed. In many cases, a global identity status classification was also assigned.

Although the interview provided a great deal of in-depth information about young people's identity development, the interview was somewhat cumbersome, and much of the qualitative information was not used (see Arnett, this volume; Josselson, this volume). Aside from informing an identity status placement for the participant, the in-depth answers were generally discarded. In the 1980s, Adams and colleagues (Bennion & Adams, 1986; Grotevant & Adams, 1984) developed a series of self-report identity status instruments, and many researchers began using these instruments to collect data from large samples with long instrument batteries. Conversely, Marcia's original Identity Status Interview, as well as subsequent adaptations, continued to be used (e.g., Grotevant, Thorbecke, & Meyer, 1982; Kroger & Haslett, 1988). Some lines of research, such as work on adoptive identity, rely almost exclusively on narrative methods (using specific interview measures developed for these research programs; Grotevant & Von Korff, 2011). In essence, the methodological split between paper-and-pencil and interview measures of identity status paved the way for separate literatures on status-related processes and narrative identity.

Although Marcia's (1966) original Identity Status Interview only assessed the three domains proposed by Erikson, later versions of the Identity Status Interview (Grotevant et al., 1982; Marcia & Archer, 1993) and paper-and-pencil measures (Bennion & Adams, 1986) expanded the range of topics under examination to include interpersonal domains as well. These domains included friendships, dating relationships, gender roles, family, and recreational preferences. Although such an expanded set of content domains increased the breadth of identity research, this expansion also introduced complications—namely, the problem of aggregating across a wide range of domains to derive a measure of "overall" identity.

Largely because of the heterogeneity of content domains that they surveyed, early paper-and-pencil identity measures, such as the Ego Identity Process Questionnaire (Balistreri, Busch-Rossnagel, & Geisinger, 1995) and the Extended Objective Measure of Ego Identity Status (Bennion & Adams, 1986), were characterized by questionable psychometric properties. To reduce participant burden, only a small number of items were used within each of several domains—a strategy that did not permit analyses within specific domains. Subsequent research (Goossens, 2001; Pastorino, Dunham, Kidwell, Bacho, & Lamborn, 1997) indicated that participants were often assigned to different identity statuses across domains, and that exploration in breadth was generally confined to a small number of domains at any given point in time. Such research suggested that the idea of an "overall," non–domain-specific identity was likely a misnomer.

Indeed, the domain-specificity of identity was borne out in the low internal consistency estimates often obtained for identity status instruments. The Ego Identity Process Questionnaire, for example, derives total scores for exploration and for commitment by summing across items referring to political preference, religious beliefs, career choices, personal values, friendships, dating relationships, gender roles, and family relationships (Balistreri et al., 1995). Not surprisingly, the internal consistency reliability estimates for these total scores are somewhat low (Schwartz, Côté, & Arnett, 2005, report Cronbach α's below .71). Although one can also derive separate scores for "ideological" and "interpersonal" domain clusters, internal consistency estimates for these scores are also low. However, it would take a number of years before measures were introduced and widely used to address this problem. Indeed, for much of the history of neo-Eriksonian identity research, methodological advances lagged considerably behind theoretical developments.

Studies using identity status interviews (e.g., Kroger, 1988) have also provided evidence against aggregating across identity domains. Specifically, in Kroger's study, no individual identity domain agreed with the overall identity status assignment more than 66 percent of the time. Perhaps for this reason, many narrative identity studies either are restricted to a specific set of domains (e.g., Bauer & McAdams, 2004; Bohanek, Marin, & Fivush, 2008; Syed & Azmitia, 2008) or focus on a theme, such as reframing negative events as growth opportunities (McAdams et al., 2001) or making connections between life events and one's sense of self (McLean, 2005, 2008) that are not explicitly connected to content domains.

The measures created by the Luyckx et al. and Meeus–Crocetti research teams—the Dimensions of Identity Development Scale (DIDS; Luyckx, Schwartz, Berzonsky, et al., 2008) and the Utrecht-Management of Commitments Scale (U-MICS; Crocetti et al., 2008b) provided significant improvements in the quantitative measurement of identity by focusing on specific domains (see also Crocetti & Meeus, this volume). The DIDS assesses identity processes with reference to future plans[1] (although other versions of the measure have been introduced to assess various domains), and the U-MICS assesses identity processes in the domains of education and friendships (as with the DIDS, the U-MICS items can be adapted to assess additional domains).

The domain-specificity of identity, which was often not recognized or attended to in earlier identity instruments, has become a prominent issue in the field (Schwartz, Zamboanga, Luyckx, Meca, & Ritchie, 2013). Indeed, there are a number of literatures on domain-specific identity processes that are only somewhat connected to the identity status model—such as career development (Porfeli, Lee, Vondracek, & Weingold, 2011), sexuality (Savin-Williams & Ream, 2007), morality (Hardy & Carlo, 2005), and ethnicity (Phinney & Ong, 2007). In some cases, these literatures began as "offshoots" of identity status (e.g., Phinney, 1990; Vondracek, Schulenberg, Skorikov, Gillespie, & Wahlheim, 1995), but many of these domain-specific literatures have become more separated from the neo-Eriksonian identity literature. Recent work has attempted to reintegrate some of these domain-specific literatures with "mainstream" neo-Eriksonian identity research (e.g., Luyckx et al., 2010; Syed et al., 2013).

The issue of domain-specificity has been less widely addressed in the narrative identity literature. Some narrative studies ask participants to describe experiences within specific domains (e.g., Bauer & McAdams, 2004, instructed respondents to talk about goals and growth experiences in the areas of career and religiosity), whereas others have not specified the domains in which stories are to be told (e.g., McLean, 2008, asked participants to describe self-defining memories but did not restrict these memories to specific content areas). Like identity status studies, narrative studies use similar methodologies (e.g., looking for coherence within the story or for connections between the events and the person's sense of self) regardless of the domains in which the story is told. Because domain-specificity is not a focus within the narrative identity literature, attempts to aggregate data across domains are generally not made. However, narrative methods have been used to explore people's experiences within specific domains. For example, Syed and Azmitia (2008) asked ethnic minority emerging adults to recount the first time they became aware of their ethnicity. The narrative responses were used to explore the content and valence of participants' identities. For another example, Kiesling, Sorell, Montgomery, and Colwell (2006) used narrative methods to gain a deeper understanding of the structure and content of spiritual identity in religiously devout individuals.

One issue that has been sparsely addressed within the neo-Eriksonian identity literature is the relative importance that each individual places on various identity domains (see Frisén & Wängqvist, 2011, for an example of a study that did attend to the relative importance of identity domains). Within early identity status instruments, responses to items measuring the same process or status were summed across several content domains, with the assumption that each domain was equally salient for the respondent. However, it stands to reason that some content areas may be more important than others for some individuals. For example, the domain of religion may be of utmost importance to many individuals who claim a specific religious affiliation and attend a house of worship regularly, but religion may be quite unimportant to many other people. The importance of a given content area to a specific individual would be expected to moderate the impact of identity work in that domain on psychosocial and health outcomes for that individual. For example, Brittian et al. (2013) found that, among Hispanic and Asian American college students, the centrality (relative importance) of ethnicity moderated the links between ethnic identity commitment and internalizing symptoms. Specifically, ethnic identity commitment was most strongly related to symptoms of anxiety and depression among those individuals for whom ethnicity was a central identity concern.

Are "General" Identity Measures Appropriate?

So we return to the issue of whether general "domain-free" identity measures are appropriate. An overall sense of identity may exist in the sense of "feeling mixed up" or "having it all together," but such an overall identity refers to a *general impression of oneself*, rather than *summing across content domains*. A person may be able to indicate whether she feels as though she has a coherent sense of self, and this sense of coherence is likely related to specific content domains such as ethnicity (Syed et al., 2013) and future plans (Schwartz, Beyers, et al., 2011). However, aggregating responses across content domains—as was done in many earlier paper-and-pencil and interview identity status measures—should be discouraged. The lower than desired internal consistency estimates on measures such as the Ego Identity Process Questionnaire, and the fairly low correspondence between domain-specific and overall identity status assignments on interview measures, provide ample evidence for this recommendation.

Where specific domains are referenced within identity measures, it is important that these domains are culturally and developmentally syntonic with the population being studied. For instance, regarding culture, Frisén and Wängqvist (2011) found that Swedish emerging adults do not consider dating and religion to be important to them—and, as a result, these domains should not be included in measures administered to this population. Developmentally speaking, issues of career, politics, and values may not be salient for individuals in their early teens, but important identity activity may be occurring in domains such as physical appearance, academic performance, and popularity with peers (Bouchey & Harter, 2005). Attention to such measurement issues, which were not often considered in neo-Eriksonian identity research prior to the Schwartz (2001) review, has helped to advance the identity literature considerably in the years since.

Correlates of Identity Development

As discussed earlier, it is important to talk about not only what identity *is*, but also what it *does*. That is, what functions does identity serve vis-à-vis various domains of psychosocial functioning? Understanding how identity relates to psychosocial functioning can guide the development and delivery of interventions to promote adaptive identity development and, by extension, to facilitate adaptive psychosocial outcomes in young people.

A number of variables have been found to be associated with the identity development process. These variables can be subdivided into at least five major groups: family functioning, well-being, internalizing, externalizing/antisocial behavior, and health risks (see Schwartz, Zamboanga, Luyckx, Meca, & Ritchie, 2013, for a more in-depth review). This list is certainly not exhaustive: for example, identity has also been examined in relation to other constructs such as the Big Five personality traits (Luyckx, Soenens, & Goossens, 2006c), to the extent to which one's choices are viewed as self-determined (Soenens et al., 2005), and to social responsibility and civic engagement (Crocetti, Jahromi, & Meeus, 2012). When considering potential correlates of identity processes, the reader should bear in mind the domain-specificity of identity, such that, for example, a person's identity may be less well developed in the area of politics but better consolidated in the area of personal goals. Domain-specific identity findings are reviewed here where available.

Concerning *family relationships*, relationships with parents must often be renegotiated on an ongoing basis during adolescence and emerging adulthood (Aquilino, 2006; Steinberg & Silk, 2002). As individuals prepare for adulthood, they will begin to claim more and more autonomy for themselves, although the ways in which this process occurs may vary from one cultural context to another (e.g., Pan, Gauvain, & Schwartz, 2013; Soenens, Vansteenkiste, & Sierens, 2009). This renegotiation of parent–child relationships provides "room" for young people to develop a sense of identity for themselves (Grotevant & Cooper, 1985; Soenens & Vansteenkiste, 2011). However, unconditional parental love and support is still needed to facilitate the personal autonomy and self-directed decision making that facilitates adaptive identity choices (Luyckx, Soenens, Vansteenkiste, Goossens, & Berzonsky, 2007; Soenens & Vansteenkiste, 2010).

Family relationships are generally characterized more favorably by individuals with more integrated and consolidated identities than by those whose identities are more fragmented or underdeveloped. Such findings have emerged within the identity status model (Crocetti et al., 2008a; Crocetti et al., 2012; Luyckx et al., 2007), within the identity style model (Berzonsky, 2003), and within narrative and life-story approaches to identity (e.g., Bohanek et al., 2008). Foreclosed individuals—those who have internalized their sense of themselves from others—tend to report idealized images of their parents (Kroger & Marcia, 2011). On the other hand, individuals who have undergone a period of doubting and questioning their commitments and who have arrived at a mature and flexible life story and set of commitments are most likely to characterize their parents as people with both strengths and weaknesses (Grotevant & Von Korff, 2011). Of course, in heavily collectivist cultural contexts, criticizing one's family of origin—or even appearing to do so—may be strongly disapproved, such that idealized, foreclosed images of parents and other family members may be quite common.

Well-being refers to a number of dimensions of positive psychological functioning, including self-esteem, life satisfaction, competence and mastery, and a sense of meaning or purpose (Waterman, 2008). Broadly, subjective well-being refers to self-esteem and satisfaction with life (Diener, 2006), psychological well-being refers to a sense of competence and mastery regarding one's life tasks (Ryff & Singer, 2008), and eudaimonic well-being (also referenced within eudaimonic identity theory) refers to a sense of meaning (Steger, Kashdan, Sullivan, & Lorentz, 2008) and of living in accordance with one's highest potentials (Waterman & Schwartz, 2013). These general dimensions of well-being—particularly subjective and psychological well-being—are among the most commonly researched correlates of identity (e.g., Berzonsky, 2003; Park, 2004; Yip & Fuligni, 2002). Generally, identity status studies have found positive correlations between identity commitments (especially those established through a process of exploration in breadth) and all three forms of well-being (Waterman, 2004; Waterman et al., 2013). Narrative identity studies have found that young people whose life stories are well integrated, who extract lessons from negative events, and who understand the "turning points" in their life narratives are most likely to experience the highest levels of well-being (e.g., Bauer & McAdams, 2004; Lilgendahl & McAdams, 2011). It can be surmised, therefore, that individuals who have enacted commitments and who understand the connections among the events in their lives are likely to report the most favorable degrees of happiness, satisfaction, competence, and fulfillment.

Internalizing symptoms refer primarily to anxiety and depression, as well as to the various subtypes of each of these symptom clusters (e.g., social anxiety, dysthymia). For the most part, from a psychosocial perspective, internalizing symptoms refer to a perception that one's life is not going well and that the negative events in one's life are out of one's control (Muris, 2002). Within the achieved and foreclosed statuses, in which the presence of commitments provides a great deal of certainty, symptoms of anxiety and depression tend to be low (Crocetti et al., 2008a; Crocetti, Schwartz, et al., 2012; Schwartz, Beyers, et al., 2011). Troubled diffusion tends to be linked with high levels of anxiety and depressive symptoms because the person is attempting to develop identity commitments but is unable to sustain exploration in breadth long enough to identify a suitable set of commitments. Links between carefree diffusion and internalizing symptoms have been inconsistent in prior research: Luyckx, Goossens, Soenens, Beyers, and Vansteenkiste (2005), in their Belgian college sample, found that carefree-diffused individuals scored low on depressive symptoms, whereas Schwartz, Beyers et al. (2011), in their American college sample, found that carefree diffusion was associated with high scores on symptoms of depression, general anxiety, and social anxiety. Given the small number of studies in which the link between carefree diffusion and internalizing symptoms has been examined, it is not known whether the inconsistency between the Luyckx et al. and Schwartz et al. findings represents a cross-cultural difference or a result of some other methodological variation.

Narrative identity research supports the conclusion that internalizing symptoms are associated with dissatisfaction with one's present sense of self or with lack of understanding of the rootedness of one's current self within one's life story. Tavernier and Willoughby (2012) found that the inability to extract meaning from "turning point" life events may be associated with diminished well-being (e.g., low self-esteem and unhappiness with one's current life circumstances). McAdams et al. (2001) found that individuals who see their life story as turning from positive to negative (e.g., regretting entering into a romantic relationship) tend to report elevated levels of depressive symptoms. Dissatisfaction with any part of oneself—where one's current commitments and past experiences represent parts of who one is (McAdams, 2011)—is linked with internalizing problems. Similar to the conclusions for well-being, the making of commitments, understanding the themes and messages underlying one's life story, and framing of these themes in a constructive way appear to protect against symptoms of anxiety and depression.

Externalizing and health risk behaviors refer to conduct problems, delinquency, substance use, unsafe sexual activity, and impaired driving. These outcomes have been investigated in relation to personal identity less extensively than have other types of outcomes discussed here (there is more research on specific domains of identity, which we discuss later).

Using measures of identity coherence and confusion, Schwartz and colleagues (Schwartz, Mason,

Pantin, & Szapocznik, 2009; Schwartz, Pantin, Prado, Sullivan, & Szapocznik, 2005) found that, among Hispanic adolescents, identity confusion was predictive of delinquent behavior, cigarette smoking, alcohol use, early sex initiation, and unprotected sex. Crocetti, Rubini, and Meeus (2008b) found that reconsideration of commitments was related to delinquent behavior. Crocetti, Klimstra, Hale, Koot, and Meeus (2013) found that adolescents (especially girls) at high risk for externalizing problems in early adolescence are likely to report elevated reconsideration scores later in adolescence—suggesting a potential reciprocal effect between reconsideration and externalizing symptoms. Using a narrative approach, Dunlop and Tracy (2013) found that recovering alcoholics who provided narratives of redemption (i.e., bouncing back from a setback) were more likely to maintain sobriety over time compared to those recovering alcoholics who did not include redemptive themes in their narratives.

These results suggest that risky behavior may be reflective of a maladaptive identity structure, but that some mild forms of risk taking may represent a type of exploration. For example, some young people may experiment with negative behaviors, drugs and alcohol, and different forms of sexual activity as part of exploring their identities and "trying out" adult roles (Arnett, 2007; Ravert, 2009). Research has identified a fairly clear demarcation between individuals who experiment with problematic behavior and those whose levels of engagement are likely to persist into adulthood (Moffitt, 2006; Walton & Roberts, 2004). The risky behavior associated with moratorium, then, may be quite different from the risky behavior associated with diffusion. Specifically, it is possible that individuals in moratorium use risky behaviors as a form of experimentation, whereas those in diffusion may use risky behaviors as a form of thrill seeking (carefree diffusion) or self-medication (troubled diffusion). Furthermore, among those individuals who do experience problems with risky behavior, resilience and redemption— reflective of a positive identity structure—are associated with returning to an adaptive life path.

Specific dimensions of identity that appear to protect against risky behaviors include identity synthesis, commitment making, and a sense of consistency across time and place (i.e., that one is the "same person" in various situations; Schwartz et al., 2010). These dimensions of identity consolidation appear to be most protective against using hard drugs, inhalants, and prescription drugs without authorization from a doctor; against having sex with strangers or casual acquaintances; and against riding with a drunk driver. Similarly, Skorikov and Vondracek (2007) found that identity development through work and positive attitudes toward schooling were protective against minor delinquency, alcohol use, and drug use in middle and high school students. What these sets of findings suggest is that holding commitments, possessing a synthesized and internally consistent sense of self, and being invested in one's future create a long-term perspective that protects against engagement in behaviors that may be pleasurable in the short run but that may compromise one's future.

Some specific identity domains have been strongly associated with risk-taking behavior. Among heterosexual—but not sexual minority—adolescents and emerging adults, spirituality and religiosity appear to be protective against drug and alcohol use (Hardy & Raffaelli, 2003) and against sexual risk taking (Rew & Wong, 2006). In terms of sexuality, Mustanski, Garofalo, Herrick, and Donenberg (2007) found that young gay and bisexual men are more likely than their heterosexual counterparts to engage in hard drug use, to binge drink and smoke marijuana at least once per week, and to engage in unprotected sexual activity with multiple partners. For members of ethnic minority groups, evidence regarding the links between ethnic identity and risk-taking behavior is mixed. For example, some studies (e.g., Marsiglia, Kulis, Hecht, & Sills, 2004) have found ethnic identity to be protective against substance use, whereas other studies (e.g., Schwartz, Weisskirch, et al., 2011; Zamboanga, Raffaelli, & Horton, 2006; Zamboanga, Schwartz, Jarvis, & Van Tyne, 2009) have identified ethnic identity as a risk for substance use. Further research, with nuanced measures of ethnic identity, is needed to clarify these inconsistencies in the literature.

Connections Among Identity Models

One of the primary themes in Schwartz (2001) was facilitating connections among various identity models. At the time that review was written, several neo-Eriksonian models, based to varying degrees on identity status, had been proposed, but little work had been conducted to explore links between or among them. Schwartz (2001) recommended proposing theoretical integrations and conducting integrative studies to connect components of these models together. Such studies, if conducted thoughtfully and in a way that respects all of the perspectives being integrated, would help to further our understanding of identity at a broader level. We must be careful when integrating models based on incompatible assumptions—and it is important to work through the potential incompatibilities before proposing an integrative perspective.

An example of such incompatibilities can be found in the series of empirical studies and theoretical formulations aimed toward resolving the seeming philosophical incompatibility between identity style theory and eudaimonic identity theory. Identity style theory was introduced as an explicitly constructivist perspective (Berzonsky, 2011), one in which, by use of the informational, normative, and diffuse-avoidant identity styles, the person is assumed to construct a self that did not previously exist. By contrast, eudaimonic identity theory was based on the assumption that people would be most self-realized when they were engaging in activities and setting goals that were most consistent with their highest talents and potentials (Waterman & Schwartz, 2013). Eudaimonic identity theory is grounded in eudaimonist philosophy, in which the person is assumed to possess a "daimon," or true self, and where living in accordance with that true self represents a primary goal to be pursued (Aristotle, 1985; Norton, 1976). Identity style theory and eudaimonic identity theory are therefore based on incompatible philosophical assumptions—how can a self be constructed when an underlying true self already exists, and why would there be a need to discover and actualize a self that has already been constructed (Berzonsky, 1986; Waterman, 1984)?

Schwartz and colleagues have addressed this incompatibility both theoretically and empirically (Schwartz, 2002; Schwartz, Mullis, Waterman, & Dunham, 2000). Theoretically speaking, the identity styles may represent constructing a "path" (more or less successfully, depending on the specific identity styles used) toward self-realization. That is, through the process of sorting through multiple identity alternatives, or possibly through identifying with the expectations put forth by significant others, one may move closer to actualizing one's potentials and talents. Empirically speaking, personal expressiveness and the informational identity style are closely associated with one another (Schwartz et al., 2000), and interventions to promote self-constructive and self-realization processes both led to improvements in one's general sense of identity (Schwartz, Kurtines, & Montgomery, 2005). Furthermore, using a self-determination theory perspective, in which people are assumed to possess a basic need for autonomy (i.e., self-directed actions), Smits, Soenens, Vansteenkiste, Luyckx, and Goossens (2010) found that either the informational or normative styles can be used for intrinsic (out of choice) or extrinsic (based on other people's expectations) reasons, where intrinsic reasons may be more likely to lead to one's true self (Soenens & Vansteenkiste, 2011).

A second integrative model centers on the concept of identity consolidation (Schwartz, 2007), which refers to a developing a "solid" sense of identity that would be most effective in guiding decision making and goal formation. Identity consolidation is indexed by making commitments, endorsing characteristics consistent with the achieved status, possessing a synthesized sense of identity, and having indices of identity capital (perceiving oneself as an adult and viewing oneself as a member of a validating community). Schwartz (2007) found that a latent variable representing identity consolidation was very strongly positively linked to well-being, negatively related to internalizing symptoms, and negatively associated with impulsivity and deviant attitudes. A further study by Schwartz et al. (2010) indicated that identity consolidation was protective against hazardous drinking, illicit drug use, unsafe sexual behavior, and drunk driving.

In another integrative effort, Crocetti, Sica, Schwartz, Serafini, and Meeus (2013) connected the basic "functions" of identity as proposed by Adams and Marshall (1996) with identity status and identity style. The five proposed functions—or benefits—of a healthy sense of identity include a structure through which to interpret self-relevant information, a sense of harmony or coherence among one's various commitments, an anticipated future, a set of life goals and aspirations, and a sense of personal control over one's life. In a sample of Italian adolescents, Crocetti et al. found that identity commitments, especially in the educational domain, were significantly associated with all five of these functions and that all of the functions were lowest in the classical moratorium status. These patterns are consistent with the premise that identity commitments anchor the person within specific social roles (Stryker, 2003) and that, because classical moratorium involves suspending or discarding these commitments, the individual may feel somewhat lost or disequilibrated.

Larger Integrative Work in Identity

Whereas the integrative efforts just described focused on connecting various neo-Eriksonian perspectives, more recent theoretical efforts (summarized in Schwartz, Luyckx, & Vignoles, 2011) have focused on connecting identity perspectives across disciplinary boundaries. The fundamental problem to be addressed in this regard involves the existence of no fewer than twenty different streams of identity theory and research, most of which do not reference or acknowledge one another (see Côté, this volume). This "Tower of Babel" issue has created a great deal of fragmentation in the larger identity literature, such that a search using the term "identity" within PsycInfo, Sociological Abstracts, Google Scholar, Scopus, or similar databases produces a large set of records that have little in common with one another. Côté (2006) issued a challenge for the identity research community to lend some degree of integration to the larger field of identity studies (see also Côté, this volume). Indeed, five separate handbooks have been published in the identity studies field since 2000 (Elliott, 2011; Fishman, 2001; Leary & Tangney, 2002; Schwartz, Luyckx, & Vignoles, 2011; Wetherell & Mohanty, 2010), with minimal overlap among the content of these volumes. Although many of the perspectives proposed within the discipline of identity studies and covered in these handbooks are not explicitly developmental and are therefore beyond the scope of this chapter, there may be important insights from some of these perspectives that can be used to inform the study of identity development.

For one example, the concept of "commitment" carries different, but complementary, meanings within neo-Eriksonian models and within symbolic interactionism. Within symbolic interactionist models, commitments refer to social roles that people occupy—such as husband, father, and physician (Serpe & Stryker, 2011). In many cases, commitments enacted at the personal level, either through purposeful choice or through identifications with significant others, serve to place the person into one or more social roles. For example, the commitment enacted during the process of marrying one's romantic partner places one into the role of spouse, and the decision (intentional or otherwise) to have children places one into the role of parent. So the neo-Eriksonian and symbolic interactionist operationalizations of commitment appear to be closely connected.

For a second example, developmental conceptions of identity often assume that one's sense of identity is at least somewhat stable—that is, a set of commitments enacted at a given point in time are likely to remain in place for some time. However, just as looking inside a solid, stationary object with a powerful microscope would reveal many small particles moving very quickly, seemingly stable commitments may appear quite different when examined on a "micro" time scale. The strengths of personal identity commitments have been found to fluctuate from one day to the next (Klimstra et al., 2010), and a commitment that appears to be stable over time may in fact require a great deal of effort to maintain. For example, maintaining a college major requires attending class regularly, completing projects, and performing other tasks. The fact that a specific student retains the same major across her college career does not mean that "nothing is happening"—rather, she is doing quite a lot to maintain that major. However, she may experience doubts about the major that she has chosen, any of which might lead her to switch majors. So short-term processes have a lot to tell us about how longer term identity mechanisms work, and Eriksonian and neo-Eriksonian identity theory is beginning to benefit from the insights provided by short-term, social-psychological identity processes (see Crocetti, Avanzi, Hawk, Fraccarolli, & Meeus, in press, for an empirical example).

Intersectionality: Interface Between Personal and Cultural Identity

Intersectionality is a concept that has received attention in the wider identity studies literature but has only recently entered the neo-Eriksonian identity field[2] (Way & Rogers, this volume). Intersectionality refers to the principle whereby individuals possess different identities (or different aspects of their identity; the question of whether people have a single identity or multiple identities is largely an issue of semantics; Vignoles et al., 2011). For example, Azmitia, Syed, and Radmacher (2008) have examined intersectionality in terms of overlap between personal and social identities—such as identities based in personal goals and values, as well as in gender, ethnicity, and social class. Schachter (2004) has looked at ways in which young people create coherent identities from among conflicting elements, such as sexuality and strict adherence to traditional religious principles.

Intersectionality is a core principle in connecting the neo-Eriksonian identity literature with the wider field of identity studies. One of the key implications of intersectionality is that the "overall" identity being developed is greater than the sum of its parts. For example, being a black woman represents more than simply the sum total of black and female identities (Bowleg, 2008). Similar principles likely apply across other domains commonly used in neo-Eriksonian identity theory and research. For instance, for homosexual immigrants, gay identities intersect with immigrant identities in which the valence of the identity being developed depends on the attitudes of the society and community of settlement toward gays and toward immigrants (Berg & Millbank, 2009). Indeed, in a society where both homosexuality and immigration are viewed negatively, gay immigrants may experience even more persecution than what would be expected given the sum of anti-gay and anti-immigrant prejudice (Heller, 2009). The intersectionality principle, in which different aspects or roles that one maintains interact to define who one is at a more global level, is one key reason why the concept of an "overall" identity, summed across content domains, may not make sense.

One example of intersectionality that is especially salient in today's world is the convergence between personal and cultural dimensions of identity (see Schwartz, Zamboanga, & Weisskirch, 2008, for a more extensive review). The United States, Canada, Western Europe, and Oceania are experiencing unprecedented levels of international migration, primarily from developing countries (Steiner, 2009). Young first-generation (born outside the society of settlement) and second-generation (born in the society of settlement but raised by foreign-born parents) immigrants often must develop a sense of themselves both (a) in terms of personal goals and values and (b) in terms of reconciling the values and behaviors from the society of settlement with those from the heritage country or region. Sometimes these tasks conflict with one another—for example, individuals from some traditional cultural backgrounds may not be permitted to marry whomever they wish, may be discouraged from pursing certain careers, and may receive pressure to maintain their heritage religious and cultural behaviors, values, and identities (e.g., Ketner, Buitelaar, & Bosma, 2004). Furthermore, cultural or religious restrictions may proscribe against certain modes of identity exploration, such as reckless behavior, substance use, and casual sex.

Phinney (1990) and Cross (1991) have proposed culture and ethnicity as an additional domain of identity work that is most salient for those individuals who belong to ethnic minority groups. Social-psychological research (e.g., Devos, Gavin, & Quintana, 2010; Devos & Heng, 2009) suggests that people who are phenotypically different (and likely lower in status) from the dominant cultural group in a given society are often regarded as inferior to the dominant group and, in some cases, may be perceived as "foreigners" even if they were born and raised in the country in question. Examples of such groups include Hispanics and Asians in the United States and Africans, Middle Easterners, and South Asians in Western Europe. In cases such as these, a sense of ethnic identity—connection to one's ethnic or cultural group—helps to buffer against and reframe the effects of exclusion from the majority group (Quintana, 2007). For members of visible-minority groups, or of groups whose beliefs and customs are markedly different from those of the dominant group in a given society, ethnicity represents a domain of identity in which exploration and commitment are likely to occur (Pahl & Way, 2006; Syed & Azmitia, 2009).

For members of the dominant ethnic or cultural group in a given society, ethnicity and culture are often "taken for granted" and are not considered important components of one's identity. For example, in the United States, compared to other ethnic groups, whites are more likely to consider themselves American and less likely to report thinking about their ethnicity (Rodriguez, Schwartz, & Whitbourne, 2010). Similar trends are evident in the European Union (Licata, Sanchez-Mazas, & Green, 2011). Ethnicity and culture are therefore largely optional domains of identity for dominant-group members, largely because the "master narratives" (underlying cultural scripts) of the dominant group are consonant with those of the larger society in general (see Hammack, 2008, for further discussion).

Although the personal and ethnic/cultural identity literatures were generally unconnected until recently, theoretical and empirical work has suggested strongly that these areas of identity develop in concert and may interact with one another. Schwartz, Montgomery, and Briones (2006) suggested that, among international migrants, a set of personal values and goals would serve to anchor the person during a time of cultural adaptation and change. Schwartz, Kim, et al. (2013) found that, across ethnic groups, first- and second-generation immigrants in the achieved personal identity status had considered heritage and US practices, values, and identifications to the greatest extent and that those in the carefree-diffused status had considered these cultural identity issues to the least extent. Usborne and Taylor (2010) found that self-concept clarity mediated the link between cultural identity clarity (clear and confident beliefs about one's cultural group and about one's membership in that group) and self-esteem. In a longitudinal study using a multiethnic college sample, Syed and Azmitia (2009) found that, over time, Eriksonian identity synthesis mediated the association of ethnic identity commitments with self-esteem. Syed et al. (2013) empirically delineated two forms of ethnic identity exploration—participation (engagement in activities characteristic of one's ethnic group) and search (thinking about the meaning of one's ethnic group membership). Syed et al. found that personal identity confusion mediated the link between ethnic identity search and well-being, whereas personal identity synthesis mediated the link between ethnic identity participation and well-being.

Taken together, these results suggest a number of conclusions. First, personal identity and cultural identity are closely related, and this relationship appears to generalize across ethnic groups (including whites). Second, personal identity appears to explain the effects of ethnic and cultural identity variables on indices of well-being. Third, these patterns emerge over time as well as cross-sectionally, suggesting that they may be especially robust. Taken together, these conclusions appear to support our contention that ethnic and cultural identity may represent a *component* of personal identity. For example, the values espoused by one's ethnic or cultural group may become internalized as personal values, and goals that are important to one's group (such as reducing inequalities) may be internalized as personal goals.

Further highlighting the role of intersectionality in identity development, identity status-based models have been developed within domain-specific literatures on sexuality (Dillon, Worthington, & Moradi, 2011), spirituality (MacDonald, 2011; Roehlkepartain, Benson, & Scales, 2011), and career development (Porfeli et al., 2011). Some research has been conducted on the interfaces among these content areas—for example, Schachter (2004) has found that some groups of domains—such as religion and sexuality—intersect more strongly than others. Many organized faiths impose prescriptions and proscriptions on sexual expression, such that some sexual relationships and behaviors are considered appropriate and others are not.

Although intersectionality has been explored largely in terms of overlap among identity domains, Syed and colleagues (e.g., Azmitia et al., 2008; Syed, 2010) have suggested that intersectionality may also apply to overlap among identity processes. For example, the situational and largely unconscious processes that underlie many social-psychological approaches to identity may serve as building blocks for more "macro" developmental identity processes such as exploration in breadth and in depth. For example, short-term threats to the self—such as negative feedback from important others—may, over time, lead to a process through which such feedback prompts reconsideration of one's ideas about oneself (see Josselson, 2009; Vignoles et al., 2011, for further discussion). For instance, Pasupathi and Hoyt (2009) found that the process of telling identity-related stories to close friends is compromised when the friend appears not to be listening or not to care about what one is saying. Because identity is developed through interactions with important others (Chen, Boucher, & Tapias, 2006), perceived inattentiveness or rejection from others can compromise the identity that one develops.

Within both the personal and ethnic identity literatures, daily fluctuations in identity commitments and in the extent to which one's sense of self is experienced as clear and positive may result from situational threats to the self—and empirical evidence suggests that these daily fluctuations are predictive of longer term changes in the strength of one's commitments and in one's sense of identity (Schwartz, Klimstra, et al., 2011; Yip, 2005). The concept of intersectionality, when applied broadly and across the various literatures that comprise the field of identity studies, may be extremely important in understanding how identity develops.

Conclusion

A great deal of progress has been made in identity theory and research since the Schwartz (2001) review was published. Within the neo-Eriksonian tradition, new theoretical models—both status-based and narrative—have been developed to explicate the process of identity development in more nuanced ways than would have been possible using the original identity status model—and new and more psychometrically sound measurement instruments have been introduced to assess the identity processes proposed within these models. The practice of summing across identity domains has been somewhat de-emphasized as domain-specific, and general measures have been introduced—and this trend dovetails with the increased amount of work within domain-specific identity literatures. Identity work is unlikely to proceed at the same pace across areas as diverse as career, values and morality, spirituality and religion, ethnicity and culture, and sexuality (Pastorino et al., 1997). Studies focusing on intersectionality (e.g., Azmitia et al., 2008; Schachter, 2004; Syed, 2010) have provided valuable information regarding how identity work overlaps and interacts across content areas and about how people develop an overall sense of self from the individual content areas that define their everyday lives.

Work on other neo-Eriksonian models, such as eudaimonic identity theory, identity style, and identity capital, has progressed considerably since the Schwartz (2001) review was published. All of these models have been examined across time and across cultural contexts, and the theoretical propositions furthered by each of these models have been supported cross-sectionally, longitudinally, and cross-culturally. The interrelationships of processes proposed by these models with one another and with identity status have permitted us to map the structure and functions of identity more closely (e.g., Berman, Schwartz, Kurtines, & Berman, 2001; Côté & Schwartz, 2002; Crocetti et al., 2013; Schwartz et al., 2000). Studies linking narrative and status-based models (e.g., McLean & Pratt, 2006) have also linked the processes by which people interpret their experiences with the identity structure that these people develop. Such studies are important both for advancing the study of identity and for designing interventions to promote adaptive identity development.

Perhaps the most expansive direction in which neo-Eriksonian identity theory and research has begun to move involves intersectionality and integration with other streams of identity work. The complementarity of the commitment constructs between the identity status and symbolic interactionist—in which commitments enacted at the personal level lead the person to be committed to specific roles at the social-structural level—represents an example of integration across different streams of identity literature. The intersectionality between microlevel social-psychological threat and defense processes and macrolevel developmental processes represents a different kind of potential integration—one in which understanding the "building blocks" of identity development could facilitate the design of intervention programs that operate at both the micro- and macrolevels.

In the same way that the Schwartz (2001) review article appeared to serve as somewhat of a launching point for more expansive and transformative work in the field of identity development, we hope that this chapter will inspire another generation of transformative scholarship in identity. Intervention is likely the next frontier for the neo-Eriksonian identity tradition (see Eichas et al., this volume). In particular, despite repeated calls for intervention programs based on neo-Eriksonian identity theory and research, few interventions have been evaluated in any type of rigorous research program. It is time for the field to move beyond promising pilot studies and conduct efficacy and effectiveness research on interventions that can promote adaptive identity development in young people. Given the importance of identity in differentiating successful from unsuccessful life paths (Côté, 2002; Schwartz, Côté, & Arnett, 2005; Luyckx et al., 2013), it is time to use this knowledge to better the lives of adolescents and emerging adults. Just as the Schwartz (2001) review article, written largely in response to criticisms of the current state of the identity literature at that time, helped to launch more than a decade of work that transformed the field, we hope that this chapter will launch a similar wave of advances into the applied realm.

Acknowledgments

Seth J. Schwartz's work on this chapter was supported by United States National Institute of Health awards DA025694 and AA021888. Elisabetta Crocetti's work on this chapter was supported by a Marie Curie fellowship (FP7-PEOPLE-2010-IEF).

This chapter is dedicated to the memory of my mother, Eileen, who died on the day I (SJS) completed a first draft.

Notes

1. Although future plans are not necessarily an identity domain in and of itself, the DIDS does not mention any other content areas and thus may avoid the priming issues that may come into play when specific domains (e.g., politics, religion, dating) are mentioned.
2. Note that, although the concept of intersectionality was developed to refer to ways in which individuals managed membership in multiple minority groups (e.g., groups based on ethnicity, gender, and social class), here we extend the term "intersectionality" to refer to any overlap between different domains of identity.

References

Adams, G. R., & Marshall, S. K. (1996). A developmental social psychology of identity: Understanding the person-in-context. *Journal of Adolescence, 19*, 429–442.

al-Owidha, A., Green, K. E., & Kroger, J. (2009). On the question of an identity status category order: Rasch model step and scale statistics used to identify category order. *International Journal of Behavioral Development, 33*, 88–96.

Aristotle. (1985). *Nicomachean ethics* (T. Irwin, Trans.). Indianapolis, IN: Hackett.

Arnett, J. J. (2007). Emerging adulthood: What is it, and what is it good for? *Child Development Perspectives, 1*, 68–73.

Aquilino, W. (2006). Family relationships and support systems in emerging adulthood. In J. J. Arnett & J. L. Tanner (Eds.), *Emerging adults in America: Coming of age in the 21st century* (pp. 193–217). Washington, DC: American Psychological Association.

Azmitia, M., Syed, M., & Radmacher, K. (2008). On the intersection of personal and social identities: Introduction and evidence from a longitudinal study of emerging adults. In M. Azmitia, M. Syed, & K. Radmacher (Eds.), *The intersections of personal and social identities: New directions for child and adolescent development* (pp. 1–16). New York: Wiley.

Balistreri, E., Busch-Rossnagel, N. A., & Geisinger, K. F. (1995). Development and preliminary validation of the Ego Identity Process Questionnaire. *Journal of Adolescence, 18*, 179–190.

Bauer, J. J., & McAdams, D. P. (2004). Personal growth in adults' stories of life transitions. *Journal of Personality, 72*, 573–602.

Bauer, J. J., & McAdams, D. P. (2010). Eudaimonic growth: Narrative growth goals predict increases in ego development and subjective well-being 3 years later. *Developmental Psychology, 46*, 761–772.

Bauer, J. J., McAdams, D. P., & Pals, J. L. (2006). Narrative identity and eudaimonic well-being. *Journal of Happiness Studies, 9*, 81–104.

Bennion, L. D., & Adams, G. R. (1986). A revision of the extended version of the Objective Measure of Ego Identity Status: An identity instrument for use with late adolescents. *Journal of Adolescent Research, 1*, 183–198.

Berg, L., & Millbank, J. (2009). Constructing the personal narratives of lesbian, gay and bisexual asylum claimants. *Journal of Refugee Studies, 22*(2), 195–223.

Berman, A. M., Schwartz, S. J., Kurtines, W. M., & Berman, S. L. (2001). The process of exploration in identity formation: The role of style and competence. *Journal of Adolescence, 24*, 513–528.

Berzonsky, M. D. (1986). Discovery versus constructivist interpretations of identity formation: Consideration of additional implications. *Journal of Early Adolescence, 6*, 111–117.

Berzonsky, M. D. (1989). Identity style: Conceptualization and measurement. *Journal of Adolescent Research, 4*, 267–281.

Berzonsky, M. D. (2003). Identity style and well-being: Does commitment matter? *Identity: An International Journal of Theory and Research, 3*, 131–142.

Berzonsky, M. D. (2011). A social-cognitive perspective on identity construction. In S. J. Schwartz, K. Luyckx, & V. L. Vignoles (Eds.), *Handbook of identity theory and research* (pp. 55–76). New York: Springer.

Berzonsky, M. D., & Adams, G. R. (1999). Reevaluating the identity status paradigm: Still useful after 35 years. *Developmental Review, 19*, 557–590.

Berzonsky, M. D., Branje, S. J. T., Meeus, W. (2007). Identity processing style, psychosocial resources, and adolescents' perceptions of parent-adolescent relations. *Journal of Early Adolescence, 27*, 324–345.

Berzonsky, M. D., Cieciuch, J., Duriez, B., & Soenens, B. (2011). The how and what of identity formation: Associations between identity styles and value orientations. *Personality and Individual Differences, 50*, 295–299.

Berzonsky, M. D., & Ferrari, J. R. (2009). A diffuse-avoidant identity processing style: Strategic avoidance or self-confusion? *Identity: An International Journal of Theory and Research, 9*, 145–158.

Bohanek, J. G., Marin, K. A., & Fivush, R. (2008). Family narratives, self, and gender in early adolescence. *Journal of Early Adolescence, 28*, 153–176.

Bosma, H. A. (1985). *Identity development in adolescence: Coping with commitments*. Groningen, The Netherlands: University of Groningen Press.

Bosma, H. A., & Kunnen, E. S. (2001). Determinants and mechanisms in ego identity development: A review and synthesis. *Developmental Review, 21*, 39–66.

Bowleg, L. (2008). When black + lesbian + woman ≠ black lesbian woman: The methodological challenges of qualitative and quantitative intersectionality research. *Sex Roles, 59*, 312–325.

Bouchey, H., & Harter, S. (2005). Reflected appraisals, academic self-perceptions, and math/science performance during early adolescence. *Journal of Educational Psychology, 97*, 673–686.

Boyes, M. C., & Chandler, M. J. (1992). Cognitive development, epistemic doubt, and identity formation in adolescence. *Journal of Youth and Adolescence, 21*, 277–304.

Brittian, A. S., Umaña-Taylor, A. J., Lee, R. M., Zamboanga, B. L., Kim, S. Y., Weisskirch, R. S., … Caraway, S. J. (2013). The moderating role of centrality on associations between ethnic identity affirmation and ethnic minority college students' mental health. *Journal of American College Health, 61*, 133–140.

Bruner, J. (1987). Life as narrative. *Social Research, 54*, 11–32.

Bruner, J. (1991). The narrative construction of reality. *Critical Inquiry, 18*, 1–21.

Burrow, A. L., & Hill, P. L. (2011). Purpose as a form of identity capital for positive youth adjustment. *Developmental Psychology, 47*, 1196–1206.

Chen, S., Boucher, H. C., & Tapias, M. P. (2006). The relational self revealed: Integrative conceptualization of the implications and interpersonal life. *Psychological Bulletin, 132*, 151–179.

Cooley, C. H. (1908). *Human nature and the social order*. New York: Scribner.

Côté, J. E. (1996). Sociological perspectives on identity formation: The culture-identity link and identity capital. *Journal of Adolescence, 19*, 419–430.

Côté, J. E. (2002). The role of identity capital in the transition to adulthood: The individualization thesis examined. *Journal of Youth Studies, 5*(2), 117–134.

Côté, J. E. (2006). Identity studies: How close are we to developing a social science of identity? An appraisal of the field. *Identity: An International Journal of Theory and Research, 6*, 3–26.

Côté, J. E., & Levine, C. (1988). A critical examination of the ego identity status paradigm. *Developmental Review, 8*, 147–184.

Côté, J. E., & Levine, C. G. (2002). *Identity formation, agency, and culture: A social psychological synthesis*. Mahwah, NJ: Erlbaum.

Côté, J. E., & Schwartz, S. J. (2002). Comparing psychological and sociological approaches to identity: Identity status, identity capital, and the individualization process. *Journal of Adolescence, 25*, 571–586.

Crocetti, E., Avanzi, L., Hawk, S. T., Fraccarolli, F., & Meeus, W. (in press). Personal and social facets of job identity: A person-centered approach. *Journal of Business Psychology*.

Crocetti, E., Jahromi, P., & Meeus, W. (2012). Identity and civic engagement in adolescence. *Journal of Adolescence, 35*, 521–532.

Crocetti, E., Klimstra, T. A., Hale, W. W., III, Koot, H. M., & Meeus, W. (2013). Impact of early adolescent externalizing problem behaviors on identity development in middle to late adolescence: A prospective 7-year longitudinal study. *Journal of Youth and Adolescence, 42*, 1745-1758.

Crocetti, E., Rubini, M., Berzonsky, M. D., & Meeus, W. (2009). The Identity Style Inventory: Validation in Italian adolescents and college students. *Journal of Adolescence, 32*, 425–433.

Crocetti, E., Rubini, M., Luyckx, K., & Meeus, W. (2008a). Identity formation in early and middle adolescents from various ethnic groups: From three dimensions to five statuses. *Journal of Youth and Adolescence, 37*, 983–996.

Crocetti, E., Rubini, M., & Meeus, W. (2008b). Capturing the dynamics of identity formation in various ethnic groups: Development and validation of a three-dimensional model. *Journal of Adolescence, 31*, 207–222.

Crocetti, E., Schwartz, S. J., Fermani, A., Klimstra, T. A., & Meeus, W. (2012). A cross-national study of identity statuses in Dutch and Italian adolescents: Status distributions and correlates. *European Psychologist, 17*(3), 171–181.

Crocetti, E., & Shokri, O. (2010). Iranian validation of the Identity Style Inventory. *International Journal of Testing, 10*, 185–199.

Crocetti, E., Sica, L. S., Schwartz, S. J., Serafini, T., & Meeus, W. (2013). Identity styles, processes, statuses, and functions: Making connections among identity dimensions. *European Review of Applied Psychology, 63*, 1–13.

Cross, W. E., Jr. (1991). *Shades of black: Diversity in African-American identity*. Philadelphia, PA: Temple University Press.

Csikszentmihalyi, M. (1990). *Flow: The psychology of optimal experience*. New York: Harper and Row.

Devos, T., Gavin, K., & Quintana, F. J. (2010). Say "adios" to the American dream? The interplay between ethnic and national identity among Latino and Caucasian Americans. *Cultural Diversity and Ethnic Minority Psychology, 16*, 37–49.

Devos, T., & Heng, L. (2009). Whites are granted the American identity more swiftly than Asians: Disentangling the role of automatic and controlled processes. *Social Psychology, 40*, 192–201.

Diener, E. (2006). Guidelines for national indicators of subjective well-being and ill-being. *Applied Research in Quality of Life, 1*, 151–157.

Dillon, F. R., Worthington, R. L., & Moradi, B. (2011). Sexual identity as a universal process. In S. J. Schwartz, K. Luyckx, & V. L. Vignoles (Eds.), *Handbook of identity theory and research* (pp. 649–670). New York: Springer.

Dunlop, W. L., & Tracy, J. L. (2013). Sobering stories: Narratives of self-redemption predict behavioral change and improved health among recovering alcoholics. *Journal of Personality and Social Psychology, 104*, 576–590.

Elliot, A. (2011). *Routledge handbook of identity studies*. New York: Routledge.

Fishman, J. (2001). *Handbook of language and ethnic identity*. Oxford, UK: Oxford University Press.

Frisén, A., & Wängqvist, M. (2011). Emerging adults in Sweden: Identity formation in the light of love, work, and family. *Journal of Adolescent Research, 26*, 200–211.

Goossens, L. (2001). Global versus domain-specific statuses in identity research: A comparison of two self-report measures. *Journal of Adolescence, 24*, 681–699.

Grotevant, H. D. (1987). Toward a process model of identity formation. *Journal of Adolescent Research, 2*, 203–222.

Grotevant, H. D., & Adams, G. R. (1984). Development of an objective measure to assess ego identity in adolescence: Validation and replication. *Journal of Youth and Adolescence, 13*, 419–438.

Grotevant, H. D., & Cooper, C. R. (1985). Patterns of interaction in family relationships and the development of identity exploration in adolescence. *Child Development, 56*, 415–428.

Grotevant, H. D., Thorbecke, W., & Meyer, M. L. (1982). An extension of Marcia's identity status interview into the interpersonal domain. *Journal of Youth and Adolescence, 11*, 33–47.

Grotevant, H. D., & Von Korff, L. (2011). Adoptive identity. In S. J. Schwartz, K. Luyckx, & V. L. Vignoles (Eds.), *Handbook of identity theory and research* (pp. 585–601). New York: Springer.

Habermas, T., & Bluck, S. (2000). Getting a life: The development of the life story in adolescence. *Psychological Bulletin, 126*, 748–769.

Hammack, P. L. (2008). Narrative and the cultural psychology of identity. *Personality and Social Psychology Review, 12*, 222–247.

Hardy, S. A., & Carlo, G. (2005). Identity as a source of moral motivation. *Human Development, 48*, 232–256.

Hardy, S. A., & Raffaelli, M. (2003). Adolescent religiosity and sexuality: An investigation of reciprocal influences. *Journal of Adolescence, 26*, 731–739.

Heller, P. (2009). Challenges facing LGBT asylum-seekers: The role of social work in correcting oppressive immigration processes. *Journal of Gay and Lesbian Social Services, 21*, 294–308.

James, W. (1890). *The principles of psychology*. Cambridge, MA: Harvard University Press.

Josselson, R. (2009). The present of the past: Dialogues with memory over time. *Journal of Personality, 77*, 647–668.

Kalleberg, A. L. (2009). Precarious work, insecure workers: Employment relations in transition. *American Sociological Review, 74*, 1–22.

Kerpelman, J. L., Pittman, J. F., & Lamke, L. K. (1997). Toward a microprocess perspective on adolescent identity development: An identity control theory approach. *Journal of Adolescent Research, 12*, 325–346.

Ketner, S. L., Buitelaar, M. W., & Bosma, H. A. (2004). Identity strategies among adolescents of Moroccan descent in the Netherlands. *Identity: An International Journal of Theory and Research, 4*, 145–169.

Kiesling, C., Sorell, G. T., Montgomery, M. J., & Colwell, R. K. (2006). Identity and spirituality: A psychosocial exploration of the sense of spiritual self. *Developmental Psychology, 42*, 1269–1277.

Klimstra, T. A., Luyckx, K., Hale, W. W., Frijns, T., van Lier, P. A. C., & Meeus, W. H. J. (2010). Short-term fluctuations in identity: Introducing a micro-level approach to identity formation. *Journal of Personality and Social Psychology, 99*, 191–202.

Kroger, J. (1988). A longitudinal study of identity status interview domains. *Journal of Adolescence, 11*, 49–64.

Kroger, J., & Haslett, S. J. (1988). Separation-individuation and ego identity status in late adolescence: A two-year longitudinal study. *Journal of Youth and Adolescence, 17*, 59–79.

Kroger, J., & Marcia, J. E. (2011). The identity statuses: Origins, meanings, and interpretations. In S. J. Schwartz, K. Luyckx, & V. L. Vignoles (Eds.). *Handbook of identity theory and research* (pp. 31–54). New York: Springer.

Kurtines, W. M., Berman, S. L., Ittel, A., & Williamson, S. (1995). Moral development: A co-constructivist perspective. In W. M. Kurtines & J. L. Gewirtz (Eds.), *Moral development: An introduction* (pp. 337–376). New York: Wiley.

Leary, M. R., & Tangney, J. P. (2002). *Handbook of self and identity*. New York: Guilford.

Licata, L., Sanchez-Mazas, M., & Green, E. G. T. (2011). Identity, immigration, and prejudice in Europe: A recognition approach. In S. J. Schwartz, K. Luyckx, & V. L. Vignoles (Eds.), *Handbook of identity theory and research* (pp. 895–916). New York: Springer.

Lichtwarck-Aschoff, A., van Geert, P. L. C., Bosma, H. A., & Kunnen, E. S. (2008). Time and identity: A framework for research and theory formation. *Developmental Review, 28*, 370–400.

Lilgendahl, J. P., & McAdams, D. P. (2011). Constructing stories of self-growth: How individual differences in patterns of autobiographical reasoning relate to well-being in midlife. *Journal of Personality, 79*, 391–428.

Luyckx, K., Duriez, B., Klimstra, T. A., & De Witte, H. (2010). Identity statuses in young adult employees: Prospective relations with work engagement and burnout. *Journal of Vocational Behavior, 77*, 339–349.

Luyckx, K., Goossens, L., Soenens, B., & Beyers, W. (2006a). Unpacking commitment and exploration: Validation of an integrative model of adolescent identity formation. *Journal of Adolescence, 29*, 361–378.

Luyckx, K., Goossens, L., & Soenens, B. (2006b). A developmental contextual perspective on identity construction in emerging adulthood: Change dynamics in commitment formation and commitment evaluation. *Developmental Psychology, 42*, 366–380.

Luyckx, K., Goossens, L., Soenens, B., Beyers, W., & Vansteenkiste, M. (2005). Identity statuses based upon four rather than two identity dimensions: Extending and refining Marcia's paradigm. *Journal of Youth and Adolescence, 34*, 605–618.

Luyckx, K., Klimstra, T. A., Schwartz, S. J., & Duriez, B. (2013). Personal identity in college and the work context: Developmental trajectories and psychosocial functioning. *European Journal of Personality, 27*, 222–237.

Luyckx, K., Schwartz, S. J., Berzonsky, M. D., Soenens, B., Vansteenkiste, M., Smits, I., & Goossens, L. (2008). Capturing ruminative exploration: Extending the four-dimensional model of identity formation in late adolescence. *Journal of Research in Personality, 42*, 58–82.

Luyckx, K., Soenens, B., & Goossens, L. (2006c). The personality-identity interplay in emerging adult women: Convergent findings from complementary analyses. *European Journal of Personality, 20*, 195–215.

Luyckx, K., Soenens, B., Goossens, L., Beckx, K., Wouters, S. (2008). Identity exploration and commitment in late adolescence: Correlates of perfectionism and mediating mechanisms on the pathway to well-being. *Journal of Social and Clinical Psychology, 27*, 333–361.

Luyckx, K., Soenens, B., Vansteenkiste, M., Goossens, L., & Berzonsky, M. D. (2007). Parental psychological control and dimensions of identity formation in emerging adulthood. *Journal of Family Psychology, 21*, 546-550.

MacDonald, D. A. (2011). Spiritual identity: Individual perspectives. In S. J. Schwartz, K. Luyckx, & V. L. Vignoles (Eds.), *Handbook of identity theory and research* (pp. 531–543). New York: Springer.

Marcia, J. E. (1966). Development and validation of ego identity status. *Journal of Personality and Social Psychology, 5*, 551–558.

Marcia, J. E. (1989). Identity and intervention. *Journal of Adolescence, 12*, 401–410.

Marcia, J. E. (1993). The ego identity status approach to ego identity. In J. E. Marcia, A. S. Waterman, D. R. Matteson, S. L. Archer, & J. L. Orlofsky (Eds.), *Ego identity: A handbook for psychosocial research* (pp. 1–21). New York: Springer-Verlag.

Marcia, J. E., & Archer, S. L. (1993). The Identity Status Interview, Late Adolescent College Form. In J. E. Marcia, A. S. Waterman, D. R. Matteson, S. L. Archer, & J. L. Orlofsky (Eds.), *Ego identity: A handbook for psychosocial research* (pp. 205–240). New York: Springer-Verlag.

Marsiglia, F. F., Kulis, S., Hecht, M. L., & Sills, S. (2004). Ethnicity and ethnic identity as predictors of drug norms and drug use among preadolescents in the U. S. Southwest. *Substance Use and Misuse, 39*, 1061–1094.

McAdams, D. P. (2011). Narrative identity. In S. J. Schwartz, K. Luyckx, & V. L. Vignoles (Eds.), *Handbook of identity theory and research* (pp. 99–116). New York: Springer.

McAdams, D. P. (2013). Life authorship: A psychological challenge for emerging adulthood, as illustrated in two notable case studies. *Emerging Adulthood, 1*, 151–158.

McAdams, D. P., Reynolds, J., Lewis, M., Patten, A. H., & Bowman, P. J. (2001). When bad things turn good and good things turn bad: Sequences of redemption and contamination in life narrative and their relation to psychosocial adaptation in midlife adults and in students. *Personality and Social Psychology Bulletin, 27*, 474–485.

McLean, K. C. (2005). Late adolescent identity development: Narrative meaning making and memory telling. *Developmental Psychology, 42*, 714–722.

McLean, K. C. (2008). Stories of the young and old: Personal continuity and narrative identity. *Developmental Psychology, 44*, 254–264.

McLean, K. C., Pasupathi, M., & Pals, J. L. (2007). Selves creating stories creating selves: A process model of narrative self-development in adolescence and adulthood. *Personality and Social Psychology Review, 11*, 262–278.

McLean, K. C., & Pratt, M. W. (2006). Life's little (and big) lessons: Identity statuses and meaning-making in the turning-point narratives of emerging adults. *Developmental Psychology, 42*, 714–722.

Mead, G. H. (1934). *Mind, self and society*. Chicago: University of Chicago Press.

Meeus, W. (1996). Studies on identity development in adolescence: An overview of research and some new data. *Journal of Youth and Adolescence, 25*, 569–598.

Meeus, W., Iedema, J., Helsen, M., & Vollebergh, W. (1999). Patterns of adolescent identity development: Review of literature and longitudinal analysis. *Developmental Review, 19*, 419–461.

Meeus, W., van de Schoot, R., Keijsers, L., Schwartz, S. J., & Branje, S. (2010). On the progression and stability of adolescent identity formation: A five-wave longitudinal study in early-to-middle and middle-to-late adolescence. *Child Development, 81*, 1565–1581.

Moffitt, T. E. (2006). *Life-course persistent versus adolescence-limited antisocial behavior: Research review*. New York: Wiley.

Muris, P. (2002). Relationships between self-efficacy and symptoms of anxiety disorders and depression in a normal adolescent sample. *Personality and Individual Differences, 32,* 337–348.

Mustanski, B., Garofalo, R., Herrick, A., & Donenberg, G. (2007). Psychosocial health problems increase risk for HIV among urban young men who have sex with men: Preliminary evidence of a syndemic in need of attention. *Annals of Behavioral Medicine, 34,* 37–45.

Norton, D. L. (1976). *Personal destinies.* Princeton, NJ: Princeton University Press.

Pahl, K., & Way N. (2006). Longitudinal trajectories of ethnic identity among urban Black and Latino adolescents. *Child Development, 77,* 1403–1415.

Pan, Y., Gauvain, M., & Schwartz, S. J. (2013). Do parents' collectivistic tendency and attitudes toward filial piety facilitate autonomous motivation among young Chinese adolescents? *Motivation and Emotion, 37,* 701-711.

Park, N. (2004). The role of subjective well-being in positive youth development. *Annals of the American Academy of Political and Social Science, 591,* 25–39.

Pastorino, E., Dunham, R. M., Kidwell, J., Bacho, R., & Lamborn, S. D. (1997). Domain-specific gender comparisons in identity development among college youth: Ideology and relationships. *Adolescence, 32,* 559–577.

Pasupathi, M. (2001). The construction of the personal past and its implications for adult development. *Psychological Bulletin, 127,* 651–672.

Pasupathi, M., & Hoyt, T. (2009). The development of narrative identity in late adolescence and emergent adulthood: The continued importance of listeners. *Developmental Psychology, 45,* 558–574.

Pasupathi, M., Mansour, E., & Brubaker, J. R. (2007). Developing a life story: Constructing relations between self and experience in autobiographical narratives. *Human Development, 50,* 85–110.

Phinney, J. S. (1990). Ethnic identity in adolescents and adults: A review of research. *Psychological Bulletin, 108,* 499–514.

Phinney, J. S., & Ong, A. D. (2007). Conceptualization and measurement of ethnic identity: Current status and future directions. *Journal of Counseling Psychology, 54,* 271–281.

Porfeli, E. J., Lee, B., Vondracek, F. W., & Weigold, I. K. (2011). A multi-dimensional measure of vocational identity status. *Journal of Adolescence, 34,* 853–871.

Quintana, S. M. (2007). Racial and ethnic identity: Developmental perspectives and research. *Journal of Counseling Psychology, 54,* 259–270.

Ravert, R. D. (2009). "You're only young once": Things college students report doing now before it is too late. *Journal of Adolescent Research, 24,* 376–396.

Rew, L., & Wong, Y. J. (2006). A systematic review of associations among religiosity/spirituality and adolescent health attitudes and behaviors. *Journal of Adolescent Health, 38,* 433–442.

Rodriguez, L., Schwartz, S. J., & Whitbourne, S. K. (2010). American identity revisited: The relation between national, ethnic, and personal identity in a multiethnic sample of emerging adults. *Journal of Adolescent Research, 25,* 324–349.

Roehlkepartain, E. C., Benson, P. L., & Scales, P. C. (2011). Spiritual identity: Contextual perspectives. In S. J. Schwartz, K. Luyckx, & V. L. Vignoles (Eds.), *Handbook of identity theory and research* (pp. 545–562). New York: Springer.

Rosenthal, D. A., Gurney, R. M., & Moore, S. M. (1981). From trust to intimacy: A new inventory for examining Erikson's stages of psychosocial development. *Journal of Youth and Adolescence, 10,* 525–537.

Ryff, C. D., & Singer, B. (2008). Know thyself and become what you are: A eudaimonic approach to psychological well-being. *Journal of Happiness Studies, 9,* 13–39.

Savin-Williams, R. C., & Ream, G. L. (2007). Prevalence and stability of sexual orientation components during adolescence and young adulthood. *Archives of Sexual Behavior, 36,* 385–394.

Schachter, E. P. (2004). Identity configurations: A new perspective on identity formation in contemporary society. *Journal of Personality 72,* 167–200.

Schwartz, S. J. (2001). The evolution of Eriksonian and neo-Eriksonian identity theory and research: A review and integration. *Identity: An International Journal of Theory and Research, 1,* 7–58.

Schwartz, S. J. (2002). Convergent validity in objective measures of identity status: Implications for identity status theory. *Adolescence, 37,* 609–626.

Schwartz, S. J. (2006). Predicting identity consolidation from self-construction, eudaimonistic self-discovery, and agentic personality. *Journal of Adolescence, 29,* 777–793.

Schwartz, S. J. (2007). The structure of identity consolidation: Multiple correlated constructs or one superordinate construct? *Identity: An International Journal of Theory and Research, 7,* 27–49.

Schwartz, S. J., Beyers, W., Luyckx, K., Soenens, B., Zamboanga, B. L., Forthun, L. F., Hardy, S. A., Vazsonyi, A. T., Ham, L. S., Kim, S. Y., Whitbourne, S. K., & Waterman, A. S. (2011). Examining the light and dark sides of emerging adults' identity: A study of identity status differences in positive and negative psychosocial functioning. *Journal of Youth and Adolescence, 40,* 839–859.

Schwartz, S. J., Côté, J. E., & Arnett, J. J. (2005). Identity and agency in emerging adulthood: Two developmental routes in the individualization process. *Youth and Society, 37,* 201–229.

Schwartz, S. J., Forthun, L. F., Ravert, R. D., Zamboanga, B. L., Rodriguez, L., Umaña-Taylor, A. J., … Hudson, M. (2010). The protective role of identity consolidation against health risk behaviors in college-attending emerging adults. *American Journal of Health Behavior, 34,* 214–224.

Schwartz, S. J., Kim, S. Y., Whitbourne, S. K., Zamboanga, B. L., Weisskirch, R. S., Forthun, L. F., … Luyckx, K. (2013). Converging identities: Dimensions of acculturation and personal identity status among immigrant college students. *Cultural Diversity and Ethnic Minority Psychology, 19,* 155–165.

Schwartz, S. J., Klimstra, T. A., Luyckx, K., Hale, W. W., III, Frijns, T., Oosterwegel, A., van Lier, P. A. C., Koot, H. M., & Meeus, W. H. J. (2011). Daily dynamics of personal identity and self-concept clarity. *European Journal of Personality, 25,* 373–385.

Schwartz, S. J., Klimstra, T. A., Luyckx, K., Hale, W. W., III, & Meeus, W. H. J. (2012). Characterizing the self-system over time in adolescence: Internal structure and associations with internalizing symptoms. *Journal of Youth and Adolescence, 41,* 1226–1239.

Schwartz, S. J., Kurtines, W. M., & Montgomery, M. J. (2005). A comparison of two strategies for facilitating identity formation processes in emerging adults: An exploratory study. *Journal of Adolescent Research 20,* 309–345.

Schwartz, S. J., Luyckx, K., & Vignoles, V. L. (Eds.). (2011). *Handbook of identity theory and research.* New York: Springer.

Schwartz, S. J., Mason, C. A., Pantin, H., & Szapocznik, J. (2009). Longitudinal relationships between family functioning and identity development in Hispanic immigrant adolescents: Continuity and change. *Journal of Early Adolescence, 29*, 177–211.

Schwartz, S. J., Montgomery, M. J., & Briones, E. (2006). The role of identity in acculturation among immigrant people: Theoretical propositions, empirical questions, and applied recommendations. *Human Development, 49*, 1–30.

Schwartz, S. J., Mullis, R. L., Waterman, A. S., & Dunham, R. M. (2000). Ego identity status, identity style, and personal expressiveness: An empirical investigation of three convergent constructs. *Journal of Adolescent Research, 15*, 504–521.

Schwartz, S. J., Pantin, H., Prado, G., Sullivan, S., & Szapocznik, J. (2005). Family functioning, identity, and problem behavior in Hispanic immigrant early adolescents. *Journal of Early Adolescence, 25*, 392–420.

Schwartz, S. J., & Waterman, A. S. (2006). Predicting the subjective experience of intrinsic motivation: A longitudinal study. *Journal of Research in Personality, 40*, 1119–1136.

Schwartz, S. J., Weisskirch, R. S., Zamboanga, B. L., Castillo, L. G., Ham, L. S., & Huynh, Q.-L., … Cano, M. A. (2011). Dimensions of acculturation: Associations with health risk behaviors among college students from immigrant families. *Journal of Counseling Psychology, 58*, 27–41.

Schwartz, S. J., Zamboanga, B. L., Luyckx, K., Meca, A., & Ritchie, R. A. (2013). Identity in emerging adulthood: Reviewing the field and looking forward. *Emerging Adulthood, 1*, 96–113.

Schwartz, S. J., Zamboanga, B. L., & Weisskirch, R. S. (2008). Broadening the study of the self: Integrating the study of personal identity and cultural identity. *Social and Personality Psychology Compass, 2*, 635–651.

Schwartz, S. J., Zamboanga, B. L., Weisskirch, R. S., & Rodriguez, L. (2009). The relationships of personal and ethnic identity exploration to indices of adaptive and maladaptive psychosocial functioning. *International Journal of Behavioral Development, 33*, 131–144.

Serpe, R. T., & Stryker, S. (2011). The symbolic interactionist perspective and identity theory. In S. J. Schwartz, K. Luyckx, & V. L. Vignoles (Eds.), *Handbook of identity theory and research* (pp. 225–247). New York: Springer.

Singer, J. A. (2004). Narrative identity and meaning making across the adult lifespan: An introduction. *Journal of Personality, 72*, 437–459.

Skorikov, V. B., & Vondracek, F. W. (2007). Positive career orientation as an inhibitor of adolescent problem behavior. *Journal of Adolescence, 30*, 131–146.

Smits, I., Soenens, B., Luyckx, K., Duriez, B., Berzonsky, M. D., & Goossens, L. (2008). Perceived parenting dimensions and identity styles: Exploring the socialization of adolescents' processing of identity-relevant information. *Journal of Adolescence, 31*, 151–164.

Smits, I., Soenens, B., Vansteenkiste, M., Luyckx, K., & Goossens, L. (2010). Why do adolescents gather information or stick to parental norms? Examining autonomous and controlled motives behind adolescents' identity style. *Journal of Youth and Adolescence, 39*, 1343–1356.

Soenens, B., Berzonsky, M. D., Vansteenkiste, M., Beyers, W., & Goossens, L. (2005). Identity styles and causality orientations: In search of the motivational underpinnings of the identity exploration process. *European Journal of Personality, 19*, 427–442.

Soenens, B., & Vansteenkiste, M. (2010). A theoretical upgrade of the concept of parental psychological control: Proposing new insights on the basis of self-determination theory. *Developmental Review, 30*, 74–99.

Soenens, B., & Vansteenkiste, M. (2011). When is identity congruent with the self? A self-determination theory perspective. In S. J. Schwartz, K. Luyckx, & V. L. Vignoles (Eds.), *Handbook of identity theory and research* (pp. 381–402). New York: Springer.

Soenens, B., Vansteenkiste, M., & Sierens, E. (2009). How are parental psychological control and autonomy-support related? A cluster-analytic approach. *Journal of Marriage and Family*, 187–202.

Spears, R. (2011). Group identities: A social identity approach. In S. J. Schwartz, K. Luyckx, & V. L. Vignoles (Eds.), *Handbook of identity theory and research* (pp. 201–224). New York: Springer.

Steger, M. F., Kashdan, T. B., Sullivan, B. A., & Lorentz, D. (2008). Understanding the search for meaning in life: Personality, cognitive style, and the dynamic between seeking and experiencing meaning. *Journal of Personality, 76*, 199–228.

Steinberg, L., & Silk, J. S. (2002). Parenting adolescents. In M. H. Bornstein (Ed.), *Handbook of parenting* (vol. *1*, pp. 103–133). Mahwah, NJ: Erlbaum.

Steiner, N. (2009). *International migration and citizenship today*. New York: Routledge.

Stryker, S. (2003). Whither symbolic interactionism? Reflections on a personal odyssey. *Symbolic Interaction, 26*, 95–109.

Syed, M. (2010). Developing an integrated self: Academic and ethnic identities among ethnically diverse college students. *Developmental Psychology, 46*, 1590–1604.

Syed, M., & Azmitia, M. (2008). A narrative approach to ethnic identity in emerging adulthood: Bringing life to the identity status model. *Developmental Psychology, 44*, 1012–1027.

Syed, M., & Azmitia, M. (2009). Longitudinal trajectories of ethnic identity during the college years. *Journal of Research on Adolescence, 19*, 601–624.

Syed, M., Walker, L. H. M., Lee, R. M., Umaña-Taylor, A. J., Zamboanga, B. L., Schwartz, S. J., Armenta, B. E., & Huynh, Q.-L. (2013). A two-factor model of ethnic identity exploration: Implications for identity coherence and well-being. *Cultural Diversity and Ethnic Minority Psychology, 19*, 143–154.

Tavernier, R., & Willoughby, T. (2012). Adolescent turning points: The association between meaning-making and psychological well-being. *Developmental Psychology, 48*, 1058–1068.

Usborne, E., & Taylor, D. M. (2010). The role of cultural identity clarity for self-concept clarity, self-esteem and subjective well-being. *Personality and Social Psychology Bulletin, 36*, 883–897.

van Hoof, A. (1999). The identity status field re-reviewed: An update of unresolved and neglected issues with a view on some alternative approaches. *Developmental Review, 19*, 497–556.

van Hoof, A., & Raaijmakers, Q. A. W. (2002). The spatial integration of adolescent identity: Its relation to age, gender, and subjective well-being. *Scandinavian Journal of Psychology, 43*, 201–212.

Vignoles, V. L., Schwartz, S. J., & Luyckx, K. (2011). Introduction: Toward an integrative view of identity. In S. J. Schwartz, K. Luyckx, & V. L. Vignoles (Eds.), *Handbook of identity theory and research* (pp. 1–28). New York: Springer.

Vleioras, G. (2007). Not all identity style items refer to identity: Does it matter? *Identity, 7*, 255–262.

Vleioras, G., & Bosma, H. A. (2005). Are identity styles important for psychological well-being? *Journal of Adolescence, 28,* 397–409.

Vondracek, F. W., Schulenberg, J., Skorikov, V., Gillespie, L. K., & Wahlheim, C. (1995). The relationship of identity status to career indecision during adolescence. *Journal of Adolescence, 18,* 17–29.

Walton, K. E., & Roberts, B. W. (2004). On the relationship between substance use and personality traits: Abstainers are not maladjusted. *Journal of Research in Personality, 38,* 515–535.

Waterman, A. S. (1984). Identity formation: Discovery or creation? *Journal of Early Adolescence, 4,* 329–341.

Waterman, A. S. (1988). Identity status theory and Erikson's theory: Commonalties and differences. *Developmental Review, 8,* 185–208.

Waterman, A. S. (1990). Personal expressiveness: Philosophical and psychological foundations. *Journal of Mind and Behavior, 11,* 47–74.

Waterman, A. S. (2004). Finding someone to be: Studies on the role of intrinsic motivation in identity formation. *Identity: An International Journal of Theory and Research, 4,* 209–228.

Waterman, A. S. (2005). When effort is enjoyed: Two studies of intrinsic motivation for personally salient activities. *Motivation and Emotion, 29,* 165–188.

Waterman, A. S. (2008). Reconsidering happiness: A eudaimonist's perspective. *Journal of Positive Psychology, 3,* 234–252.

Waterman, A. S. (2011). Eudaimonic identity theory. In S. J. Schwartz, K. Luyckx, & V. L. Vignoles (Eds.), *Handbook of identity theory and research* (pp. 357–379). New York: Springer.

Waterman, A. S., & Schwartz, S. J. (2013). Eudaimonic identity theory. In A. S. Waterman (Eds.), *The best within us: Positive psychology perspectives on eudaimonia* (pp. 99–118). Washington, DC: American Psychological Association.

Waterman, A. S., Schwartz, S. J., & Conti, R. (2008). The implications of two conceptions of happiness (hedonic enjoyment and eudaimonia) for the understanding of intrinsic motivation. *Journal of Happiness Studies, 9,* 41–79.

Waterman, A. S., Schwartz, S. J., Goldbacher, E., Green, H., Miller, C., & Philip, S. (2003). Self-determination, flow, and self-realization values as predictors of intrinsic motivation. *Personality and Social Psychology Bulletin, 29,* 1447–1458.

Waterman, A. S., Schwartz, S. J., Hardy, S. A., Kim, S. Y., Lee, R. M., Armenta, B. E., … Agocha, V. B. (2013). Good choices, poor choices: Relationship between the quality of identity commitments and psychosocial functioning. *Emerging Adulthood, 1,* 163–174.

Wetherell, M., & Mohanty, C. T. (2010). *The SAGE handbook of identities.* Thousand Oaks: CA.

Wheeler, H. A., Adams, G. R., & Keating, L. (2001). Binge eating as a means for evading identity issues: The association between an avoidance identity style and bulimic behavior. *Identity: An International Journal of Theory and Research, 1,* 161–178.

Yip, T. (2005). Sources of situational variation in ethnic identity and psychological well-being: A Palm Pilot study of Chinese American students. *Personality and Social Psychology Bulletin, 31,* 1603–1616.

Yip, T., & Fuligni, A. J. (2002). Daily variation in ethnic identity, ethnic behaviors, and psychological well-being among American adolescents of Chinese descent. *Child Development, 73,* 1557–1572.

Zamboanga, B. L., Raffaelli, M., & Horton, N. J. (2006). Acculturation status and heavy alcohol use among Mexican American college students: An investigation of the moderating role of gender. *Addictive Behaviors, 31,* 2188–2198.

Zamboanga, B. L., Schwartz, S. J., Jarvis, L. H., & Van Tyne, K. (2009). Acculturation and substance use among Hispanic early adolescents: Investigating the mediating roles of acculturative stress and self-esteem. *Journal of Primary Prevention, 30,* 315–333.

Zimmermann, G., Mahaim, E. B., Mantzouranis, G., Genoud, P. A., & Crocetti, E. (2012). Brief report: The identity style inventory (ISI-3) and the Utrecht Management of Identity Commitments Scale (U-MICS): Factor structure, reliability, and convergent validity in French-speaking university students. *Journal of Adolescence, 35,* 461–465.

CHAPTER 34

The Future of Identity Development Research: Reflections, Tensions, and Challenges

Moin Syed *and* Kate C. McLean

Abstract

This chapter reviews the contents of the Handbook and discusses important future directions for research on identity development. First, the authors reflect on the three major sections of the book: debates, applications, and extensions, highlighting why the sections are important and what has been learned. Second, they discuss tensions in the study of identity development that were identified as the Handbook was edited. These tensions include the aspect of identity being studied, how culture is defined, and the strong emphasis on individual agency over context and opportunity. Finally, the authors discuss two major challenges to the field of identity development: conceptualizing exactly what is developing in identity development and bridging the divide between identity process and identity content. Taken together, this chapter, like the Handbook more broadly, is meant to serve as a catalyst and inspiration for future identity development in the coming decades.

Key Words: identity development, identity process, identity content, culture

When we agreed to edit this *Handbook*, we were determined to do something different. Handbooks serve an important function within a field. They contain authoritative reviews by leading scholars, providing a snapshot of the state of the art of an area of inquiry. We wanted to honor this tradition of the handbook format while at the same time pushing our thinking about what a handbook *can be*. In particular, rather than only looking backward by reviewing an area, we sought to create a resource that looked forward. Additionally, we were committed to bringing together researchers from different perspectives on identity development to facilitate cultural exchange. We felt that this approach would be best suited to getting researchers' creative juices flowing and push the field into new, important territory. We enlisted an incredible team of authors and invited them to share our vision, encouraging them to be provocative in their writings. The contributors enthusiastically accepted our invitations, and we could not be happier about the rigor and thoughtfulness that they brought to the task.

This concluding chapter contains three broad sections that are consistent with our general approach of looking backward to where we have been, but emphasizing a forward-looking orientation toward where we are headed. First, we reflect on the content of the Handbook. In particular, we evaluate the effectiveness of the three major sections of the book—debates, application, and extensions—and discuss areas for further development within each. In the second section, we highlight a few of the tensions in the field that we feel are still unresolved. Finally, in the third section we discuss challenges to the future of identity development research.

How Did We Do? Reflecting on the Success of the Editorial Vision

Ultimately, it is up to the readers of this handbook to gauge its success. The true impact of a product is best assessed through its generativity—the degree to which it leads to more and/or different research—which cannot be known for some time. However, now that we have completed the project, we thought we would reflect on the degree to which the final product fits our vision. Our review here largely focuses on the sections and chapters as a whole, rather than reviewing each individual chapter, although we do draw on specific chapters to illustrate our points.

Debates

The debate section of the book is the first that we developed. As soon as we began discussing ideas for the handbook, we began honing in on the debates in the field, how to best represent them, and how to include them in the book. As we discussed in our opening chapter (McLean & Syed, this volume), there was some initial resistance among authors to the use of the word "debate." Some felt there was not really a debate at all, but rather a matter of preference among researchers. Others felt we had miscast the "sides" of the debate altogether. Still others grappled with what exactly it was we were asking them to do. We made it clear that what we were looking for was conversations, which we felt were lacking in the literature on these topics. We likened this approach to the Swedish cultural practice of *fika*, in which people take time out of their day for coffee, treats, and conversation. Furthermore, although the topics included in the debates section may not be *active* debates in which scholars are trading barbs, we view them as *implicit* debates, with authors making choices about one approach over another.

To be clear, it was not at all our intention to declare a winner of these debates. We were explicit about this fact to the authors whom we asked to write the commentaries. Furthermore, we wanted the chapters to both stand alone and fit together, and therefore the authors were not charged with "responding" to one another. The end product was a cluster of three to four chapters on the same topic written from different perspectives. Although they are not debates in the traditional sense, they bring these differing perspectives in alignment with one another, which represents an advance in how these topics are currently treated.

When taking the five debates together, one of the most striking features we see is the detail and clarity about *why* the authors use the approaches that they do. In the course of editing the debate chapters, we pushed the authors—hard—for such clarity. In our view, too much in the identity literature is taken for granted, and we wanted to see the origins of thinking among these prominent scholars. The debate cluster on internal, external, and interactional approaches to identity is an excellent example. Both of the debate chapter authors (Waterman and Korobov) and the commentary author (Schachter) detailed the philosophical backgrounds to their thinking, clearly linking these origins to their research practice and theorizing. This type of treatment is not typical of the identity development literature. However, including it can help readers better understand the perspective at play, whether or not they agree with it and whether or not they want to adopt it in their own work.

We hope to see more of this kind of conversation in the written pages of journals and books, as well as in conferences and other venues designed to encourage interaction among scholars. There is already evidence that this approach is valued among researchers. The journals *Human Development* and *Developmental Review* have long included critical commentaries on target articles. The signature event of the Conference on Emerging Adulthood is a debate between two scholars on a pressing issue in the field. More recently, the Society for Research in Child Development (SRCD) and the Society for Research on Adolescence (SRA) have included "Views by Two" sessions, which are essentially debates between two scholars with differing views. We wholeheartedly support this movement and hope to see even more of it in the future.

Applications

Why does identity matter? Any researchers worth their salt could readily supply answers to this question. When considering the identity literature as a whole, however, there is relatively little attention paid to practical applications of identity development. The purpose of this section was to make some of these applications more apparent. Identity sounds like (and is) a highly abstract construct, one that does not have immediately evident connections to the important and pressing issues with which people around the world are wrestling. However, when you stop to think about it, identity lies at the core of some of the major problems of human society. Much of the conflict around the world can be traced to issues of identity, whether they are disagreements over national identity or religious identity (e.g., Hammack, 2011). Although modern research on posttraumatic stress disorder (PTSD) is largely disconnected from identity, the roots of PTSD go back to Erikson's (1950) work with combat veterans returning from World War II, struggling to reconcile the stark contrast between their pre-war and post-war selves. Chandler and colleagues have linked identity problems with suicidality among indigenous youth in Canada (Chandler, Lalonde, Sokol, & Hallett, 2003). Few problems in this world are as distressing and compelling as suicide. Thus, it is clear that the problem of identity is not simply an academic exercise, but one that has real meaning for people around the world. This section provides a view of those real meanings.

The first two chapters in the applications section focus on the positive aspects of development, how we can support individuals to thrive via a healthy sense of identity. Both Eichas et al. (this volume) and Singer and Kasmark (this volume) discuss interventions to promote identity, but in different ways: Eichas et al. seek to develop large-scale interventions that are relatively easy and affordable to implement. In contrast, Singer and Kasmark are concerned with individually focused interventions through one-on-one therapy. Despite these differences, both approaches are deeply rooted in identity theory and involve direct translation of theoretical ideas into points of action. In general, interventions have not been a substantial focus within the identity literature. However, those who have advanced identity interventions have demonstrated their effectiveness to support positive development (Kurtines et al., 2008).

In contrast to the intervention approach of Eichas et al. and Singer and Kasmark, the other three chapters in the applications sections draw attention to the role and relevance of identity development for adolescents and adults in their "natural" contexts, specifically school (Cooper et al., this volume), work (Mortimer et al., this volume), and political conflict (Wainryb & Recchia, this volume). That is, rather than seeking primarily to intervene in the process of identity development, these researchers describe how these contexts of development can be fundamentally seen as vehicles for identity development. Understanding first that these are contexts of identity development then allows for a more tailored approach to interventions.

Taken together, these chapters make a clear and direct case for the real-world importance of identity. In particular, they highlight how identity underlies institutions and contexts that are foundational to modern human existence: school, work, political systems, and living a psychologically healthy life. We urge our colleagues in the field to think deeply about the significance of identity, beyond the issues of general psychological distress and well-being that are typically examined and into the life decisions and experiences that have a profound influence on how we live our lives.

Extensions

In many ways, the extensions section is the most exciting aspect of the book. With all due respect to the authors of chapters in the other sections, we believe that the extensions authors had the most difficult assignment. Our view is that identity is one of the major developmental tasks of the lifespan and, as such, must be inextricably linked to other major aspects of development. However, the field of identity development has been rather narrow in its view of identity within the broader context of development. In an attempt to correct this trend, we asked non–identity researchers to author chapters for this section. We posed a two-part reciprocal question for them to consider: what can research in their area of expertise offer to the study of identity development, and what can the study of identity development offer to the study of their area of research? Given the relative lack of research they had to work with, these authors are to be commended for learning new literatures, masterfully synthesizing these new ideas with their existing ways of thinking, and offering creative and provocative speculations. Indeed, these chapters provide some of the most fertile ground for new directions because of the relative lack of attention paid to how identity relates to other aspects of development. The results, we think, are better than we ever could have imagined. Here, we highlight a few of the innovations that have come about through the chapters in this section.

It became clear in examining the chapters on the body and biology that there is a near total lack of attention paid to the body in identity development research (Daniels & Gillen, this volume; Matsuaki, et al. this volume; see Wängqvist & Frisén, 2013, for a recent exception). This is despite the fact that Erikson (1968) wrote that one of the key features of mature identity is "a feeling of being at home in one's body" (p. 165). Of course, there are many features of Erikson's theory that have not been taken up by researchers, but this omission is somewhat ironic given that the transformations that the body undergoes during adolescence are some of the most obvious "discontinuities" in self that must be reconciled. The chapters in this book will help to forge this new and important path for identity (and body) research.

Two of the chapters in the extensions section move the study of family and identity to new territory. Working within social domain theory, Rote and Smetana (this volume) provide a more nuanced perspective on how parenting might be related to identity, moving beyond the broad notion that authoritative parenting styles support identity exploration whereas authoritarian parenting restricts it. Cookston and Remy (this volume) bring attention to the potential importance of divorce—both for the parents and for the children. The title of their chapter includes the question, "Who am I if we are not us?" That question gets at the heart of identity and how disruptions throughout the lifespan can require individuals to reconsider and possibly reconfigure their identities.

Finally, Lilgendahl's (this volume) chapter takes on a perennial question: what is the relation between identity and personality? Numerous empirical studies over the years have examined the relations between identity status classifications and personality traits (e.g., extraversion, openness; see Klimstra, 2012). These studies, however, have not led to a very sophisticated understanding of the similarities and differences between these two constructs. Lilgendahl's chapter takes us into that territory, in part by going beyond equating personality with personality traits. She adopts McAdams's (2013; McAdams & Pals, 2006) tri-level model of personality, in which traits are but one of the three levels. The other two levels, characteristic adaptations and life stories, capture the more dynamic aspects of personality. She moves beyond this three-level approach, however, to consider how various aspects of personality interact in predicting pathways of identity development. Focusing on these aspects of personality—in addition to traits—as well as their interaction provides an excellent way to conceptualize the complexities that we know exist in the individual differences in how identities develop.

The "extensions" section of the *Handbook* highlights potential directions for the next generation of identity development research. A hallmark of developmental psychology is viewing domains of development as interconnected and reciprocally related (Baltes, 1987; Lerner, 1996). Thus, if identity development is a major task of adolescence and emerging adulthood (as well as other phases of the lifespan), it *must* be related to other major aspects of development, such as family, personality, and biological changes. The question is not one of "if" but rather "how." The chapters in this section help get those kinds of conversations going.

In sum, we are very pleased with the degree to which the final product fit with our vision for the *Handbook*. We aimed to assemble a collection of chapters that adequately took stock of what we know about identity development, while at the same time generating ideas for new directions in research. That is not to say that all extant issues in the literature were "settled" through this handbook. Indeed, there are many remaining questions and, of course, plenty of research still to do. In the remainder of this chapter, we discuss some of these unresolved issues. First, we examine some tensions that we believe underlie the chapters when taken together as a set. These tensions have to do with different approaches, perspectives, or assumptions that are not often explicitly addressed. Second, we discuss some challenges to the future of identity development research. These challenges are what we see as major issues in the field that researchers should play close attention to in their work.

Tensions in the *Handbook* and Lurking in the Field

As we worked through editing this handbook, we became acutely aware of several areas of tension that were running through the contributions. By tensions, we mean potential conflicts in points of view that are rarely surfaced in written works. Some of these tensions were already known to us, which laid the foundation for the debates section. Others, however, came into greater relief over time. In this section, we discuss of few of those tensions, providing the basic background and some possible solutions for how to diffuse these tensions and move the field forward. In particular, we discuss three tensions: levels of analysis, definitions of culture, and agency versus opportunity. We end this section by suggesting that consideration of *master narratives* may be one route to resolving all of these tensions.

First, we asked ourselves the question of what this handbook would look like if it were done by different editors. We think the strength of our co-editorship is in the breadth of perspective that we bring. Although we both obviously share an expertise in identity development, Moin has focused more on issues of ethnic identity as it intersects with other domains, along with connections to academic experiences, and has done more work to connect status and narrative perspectives (see Syed, in press-*b*). Kate, in contrast, has focused more exclusively on narrative identity development and issues relating to personality and well-being (see McLean, 2008). Both of us have an appreciation for, and have focused on, "external" and

...roaches to identity, and we were both ...graduate program that provided a rich ...phasis on the sociocultural nature of ...pment. Thus, in our co-editorship we ...highlight a full representation of contemporary approaches to identity development.

In our aim for a full representation of the literature, we return to the tension between narrative and status approaches to identity. We intentionally included a strong representation of narrative research because we both wholeheartedly feel that these two approaches should be viewed as equally viable. Yet, we also see that many current researchers still privilege the status approach and that, for those outside the field, the status approach is viewed as the dominant way of defining identity in developmental psychology (e.g., Schwartz, Zamboanga, Luyckx, Meca, & Ritchie, 2013). This can be seen in the ways that those less familiar with identity defined the construct in their contributions to the volume, as well as in the broader developmental literature. Although we could have included a debate section on narrative and status approaches (and perhaps we should have), instead we proceeded with the volume as though they were equally viable. We do not argue here that one is better or worse, but we do hope that researchers consider both these approaches in their endeavors to understand identity and are intentional in explaining their use of one approach over the other. Moreover, we do not believe that these are the only two ways to examine identity development, and we must all remain open-minded enough to accommodate new and different models.

As we discussed in the introductory chapter (McLean & Syed, this volume), our read of Erikson and the existing literature suggests an alignment between the narrative approach and *ego identity* and the status approach and *personal identity* (see also McLean et al., under review). Not only are these two aspects of identity seldom brought together, but the third level of Eriksonian identity, *social identity*, is rarely integrated with either of the other two (Way & Rogers, this volume). In fact, research on links between Erikson's three levels—ego, personal, and social—would be a lovely way to target the intersection of various aspects of identity development. As we all know but seldom investigate in our work, ego identity does not develop separately from personal identity, which does not develop separately from social identity (Schwartz, Zamboanga, & Weisskirch, 2008). What happens when one's personal story does not match the cultural narrative of one's group or the values to which one has committed? Despite the excellent work that does exist on culture and identity processes and content, culture is a comparatively less well-developed component of identity development than are other components.

Although most identity researchers acknowledge the importance of culture in their theoretical approaches, the specification of how culture relates to particular identity processes and contents is relatively lacking. Within the study of identity development, most of the work linking identity and culture has focused on ethnic identity (Umaña-Taylor et al., 2014) or the degree to which individuals identify with their ethnic group (Phinney, 1992). However, as with any aspect of identity, there are multiple approaches to culture, which can create diffusion or confusion in how to approach the question of culture and identity development (Cooper & Denner, 1998). The contents of this handbook reflect these various approaches. Arnett (this volume) and Manago (this volume) both wrestle with the impact of globalization on identity, linking cultural and historical changes of industrialization to expanded notions of what it is possible to be. Both Way and Rogers (this volume) and Cooper et al. (this volume) take a much more local approach, examining how conditions within schools and neighborhoods shape the interrelations of identity process and content. Indeed, these chapters may come closest to integrating Erikson's three levels of identity because they focus on how youth adopt specific roles, how multiple roles are interrelated, and how youth conceptualize their futures, all within a cultural and social context. These authors, along with the chapters by Worrell (this volume) and Azmitia (this volume), push identity researchers to think about culture in terms of its complexity and urge them to embrace rather than shun the complexity.

The chapters on culture, along with other chapters that draw heavily from sociological perspectives (Côté, this volume; Hammack, this volume; Mortimer et al., this volume), highlight another major tension in the identity development literature: the tension of agency and resources. On the whole, regardless of the approach one takes to identity development, most people view it as an agentic process. One *chooses* to explore or not, to commit or not, to reflect on the past or not. But there are a variety of resources, outside of one's control, which likely play into the ability to engage in this developmental task. What are the domains available to choose from—what kinds of occupations, religions, dating partners? What are the developmental assets that one holds on entry into adolescence? An inquiring personality style that is comfortable with uncertainty? A history of supportive scaffolding from parents? Finances to travel or go to college? In short, adolescents and emerging adults have a developmental history that can support or impinge on identity development. They have traits and geography and relationships that can constrain and support them. Thus, as researchers, it is important to remember that identities always develop in context and can be thought of as a collaboration between parties near (e.g., parents), far (e.g., political systems), and everything in between.

So how to approach and resolve these tensions? We are both taken with the idea of using *master narratives* as a way to examine how culture intersects with personal and ego identity development. Master narratives represent culturally agreed upon stories or structures for how to interpret experiences. McAdams (2006) has written about redemption as a narrative form to which Americans respond especially well. This does not mean that Americans are more redemptive in their stories (they could be, we don't know yet), but that in storying the difficult parts of their pasts, this is a structure available for use, and in many ways it is a structure that is expected from one's audiences. That is, if one does not story the self in a redemptive fashion, this creates a dissonance that needs to be explained.

Phil Hammack (2011) has linked the master narrative approach to Israeli and Palestinian youth defining themselves in the context of larger narratives about what it means to be Israeli in reference to Palestinians and vice-versa. We have both also touched on master narratives in terms of gender roles (Thorne & McLean, 2003), sexuality (Weststrate & McLean, 2010), and in reference to an understanding of the meaning of emerging adulthood (Syed, in press-*a*) and of one's ethnic group (Syed, 2012). Taking this approach, we can begin to see how the different levels that Erikson proposed were critical to identity development might come together. One's personal experiences (ego identity) are examined in relation to the roles one takes (personal identity), which are in reference to the larger culture in which one is defining the self (social identity). Despite the emphasis on master *narrative*, this approach does not negate the status approach because processes of exploration and commitment are likely closely related to these intersections. For example, if one has explored and committed to a role that is contrary to cultural expectations, the intersection of levels will likely function differently, and be storied differently, than if one has explored and committed to a role within the master narrative. The point here is that it is in the *intersections* that we are likely to see a full representation, a fidelity, to Erikson's theory.

Challenges to the Future of Identity Development Research

Taking the contents of the *Handbook* and putting them in the context of the field, we have identified two key areas of progress and future development: (1) understanding what it is that is developing within identity development, and (2) the importance of examining identity content in addition to identity process. As we discussed in the introduction to this volume (McLean & Syed, this volume), these two issues are major themes in contemporary identity development research and should be key foci of future research. In each section, we highlight what we have learned and areas in which work still needs to be done.

What Is Development?

Despite the decades of research on identity development, it is still reasonable to ask a number of questions about how identity actually develops. There remains plenty of work to be done to address fundamental questions such as *when* identity develops, *what* develops, and *how* it develops. To be sure, there is plenty of existing research focused on identity development. For example, Kroger, Martinussen, and Marcia's (2010) meta-analysis of longitudinal identity status studies supported the hypothesized move from the moratorium to achieved status across adolescence and emerging adulthood. From a narrative perspective, Habermas and de Silveira (2008) demonstrated that coherence in autobiographical memories, a key indicator of narrative identity, increases across adolescence. Despite these and many other efforts to address development, different perspectives and approaches in the field have not been integrated into a clear portrait of the developmental processes of identity. Part of the impetus for this handbook was to bring together researchers wrestling with questions of development in order to take stock of what we know and provide directions for where we should head. As always, the outcome of the collective effort was to produce many more new questions rather than satisfactory answers. In this section, we provide a summative view of the topic of development, drawing on the chapters in the *Handbook* and the broader literature.

The first question that likely arises for most researchers is the question of *when* identity develops. At first glance, it would seem that this question has some reasonably clear answers. Most identity researchers will readily cite Erikson (1968) for identifying adolescence as the period of the lifespan in which identity issues take center stage. Although this is accurate, it is not entirely clear what Erikson meant by "adolescence." Seen through a contemporary lens, most researchers interpret Erikson's adolescence to be approximately ages 10–18. However, adolescence was not so rigidly defined in Erikson's day, and when reading his original works it becomes clear that the 10–18 age range had little meaning to him. Indeed, the struggles of the search for love, work, and a guiding ideology that he described involve decidedly adult themes. Looking at the empirical research that followed, particularly within the identity status model, shows that the foundational researchers understood this because a great deal of the research was conducted with college-aged youth (see Kroger, 2013, for a series of meta-analyses). In developing his theory of emerging adulthood, Arnett (2004) took the theoretical stance that identity development is primarily centered in emerging adulthood—roughly ages 18–29—and not adolescence. Contemporary identity researchers would likely agree that identity development is centered in adolescence and emerging adulthood, which is essentially what Erikson outlined in the first place. So what's the problem?

One limitation of arguing for adolescence and emerging adulthood is that it privileges the role of age for identity development. Developmentalists, practically by definition, seek to understand age-graded changes among individuals, so privileging age should not be a surprise. However, a fundamental truth for developmentalists is that *age is not the explanation* (Baltes, 1987). That is, age, in and of itself, does not have a causal influence on developmental processes. Rather, age acts as a proxy for underlying and co-occurring processes. For example, several major identity theorists cite the beginning of adolescence as the beginning of identity development in earnest (Erikson, 1968; Habermas & Bluck, 2000; Harter, 1999; McAdams, 2013). This is not because there is anything special about age 10 or age 12, per se. It is because the dawn of adolescence is associated with qualitative shifts in individuals' cognitive abilities, allowing for the abstract thinking necessary to reflect on who one is and to develop a sense of identity that is extended in time, as well as a greatly expanded social sphere. In this way, age is similar to other demographic markers that are similarly void of explanatory power, such as race (Helms, Jernigan, & Mascher, 2005), gender (Egan & Perry, 2001), and immigrant generational status (Cooper, García Coll, Thorne, & Orellana, 2005). Indeed, there is very little mention of specific age markers for identity development in this handbook.

So, if age is not singularly useful for thinking about development, what is? There is certainly no clear answer to this question, but taking together the contents of this handbook provides some initial clues. As we discussed in the introductory chapter, Erikson's original writings point to the importance of coherence, synthesis, or integration of one's identity through time and space. This focus fits with Erikson's view of identity as optimally providing a sense of continuity to one's life. Thinking of identity development as fundamentally about integration allows for a true lifespan conceptualization of identity. The need for integration of the self can be seen in the first few months of life, as infants are working to coordinate their thoughts and actions through circular reactions (Piaget, 1954). The need for integration continues across the first three decades of life, as children increasingly coordinate an integration between self and other (Decety & Sommerville, 2003; Ruble et al., 2004); adolescents integrate the cognitive, behavioral, and affective dimensions of a given identity domain (Phinney, 1993); and emerging adults work to integrate the multiple identity domains that are important to their lives (Azmitia, Syed, & Radmacher, 2008). The need for integration continues throughout adulthood as identity enters a relative maintenance phase, needing to integrate both the non–age-graded (e.g., birth of a child, career advancement) and non-normative (e.g., death of a loved one, divorce) life events that occur (Cookston & Remy, this volume; Kroger, this volume). Thus, integration is not an end-point to be reached but rather an optimal state of balance to be maintained throughout life.

Surprisingly, however, there is relatively little discussion of integration of identities in the chapters in this book. So, have contemporary researchers moved away from the idea that integration is the critical task for identity? Not quite. Throughout the chapters, there is a strong theme of the importance of *challenge* or *conflict* for identity development. These are most often discussed, explicitly or implicitly, as challenges to continuity. Thus, it seems that rather than focusing on how people integrate their identities successfully, researchers have tended to train their gaze on potential barriers to integration. To put it another way, rather than focus on integration per se, researchers examine the challenges that individuals face that necessitate integration. In this way, integration and challenge are intimately linked, with challenges being situations that prompt the need for integration and thus identity development (Bruner, 1990; Cross & Cross, 2008; Grotevant & Cooper, 1985). In this way, one could argue that integration is the *what* of identity development, whereas challenges are the *how* of identity development.

Interestingly, the focus on challenge is one commonality among narrative and status researchers, although the challenges seem to play a larger role in process-oriented status studies versus categorical status studies (see, e.g., Kunnen & Metz, this volume vs. Crocetti & Meeus, this volume). A common approach to conceptualizing challenges to identity can be traced back to Piaget's distinction between the cognitive processes of assimilation and accommodation in contributing to adaptation. Generically, assimilation is the ability to integrate new experiences into existing cognitive structures, whereas accommodation occurs when new experiences necessitate the creation of new structures or modifications of existing ones. Periods of rapid change involve a greater need for accommodation over assimilation, whereas periods of stability involve more assimilation relative to accommodation. Successful adaptation involves reaching a state of equilibration, when individuals can mostly assimilate but also easily accommodate when necessary without serious disruption to functioning.

When surveying the identity literature, Piaget's ideas on adaptation are much more prevalent than one might think at first glance because Piaget is not typically associated with the field of identity. However, Piagetian adaptation seems to pop up in a number of places, both explicitly and implicitly. Within the narrative identity literature, there is a history of thinking of identity in terms of adaptation to challenge, in part due to Bruner's (1990) thesis that conflict lies at the heart of storytelling (c.f., Labov & Waletsky, 1967). However, it can also be seen within some of the identity status research as well. Saskia Kunnen, in particular, has examined the processes of exploration and commitment in the context of identity conflicts (Kunnen, 2006; Kunnen & Metz, this volume). In her chapter on identity in adulthood, Kroger discusses Whitbourne's *identity processing theory* approach to adult identity (Whitbourne, Sneed, & Skultety, 2002), which is a direct application of Piaget's assimilation and accommodation to understand how adults maintain balance in their identities.

Other work that focuses on role-based also tends to emphasize disruptions ity to successfully maintain those rol occupation (Mortimer et al., this volume, spouse (Cookston & Remy, this volume). The focus on adaptation also nicely interfaces with related work in personality psychology, both old and new. Block's (2002) classic constructs of ego-resiliency and ego-control map onto accommodation and assimilation, respectively, as do DeYoung's (2010) recent higher order trait model of plasticity (shared variance of extraversion and openness) and stability (shared variance of agreeableness, conscientiousness, and low neuroticism). The purpose of the preceding laundry list is to bring attention to the fact that there is a large collection of similar ideas on how individuals adapt to their environments that are being discussed in various niches of identity and personality—niches that do not often dialogue with one another. As a field, we need greater awareness of points of similarities in what we are up to because doing so can lead to deeper and farther-reaching theorizing on the nature and consequences of identity development.

What Is the Content of the Identity?

One of the limitations of being able to understand identity development has been the overemphasis placed on the *processes* of identity development at the expense of examining the *content* of identity. That is, there has been a historical privileging of examining and understanding how individuals arrived at their identities (process), with little regard for what those identities actually are (content). This can be seen in both the identity status and narrative identity perspectives, but in different ways.

Research within the identity status model has either focused on the four statuses or on their two component processes of exploration and commitment. Recent work has extended this model considerably (Crocetti & Meeus, this volume), but the major extensions have been increased differentiation, leading to a greater number of statuses based on more nuanced aspects of exploration and commitment. There are two ways in which identity content has been overlooked within this literature. First, the precise identity domains in which exploration and commitment are assessed do not figure prominently in the interpretation of the findings. From the very first identity status study to the present day, exploration and commitment have been sampled across several identity domains and then aggregated into an overall identity status classification (e.g., Crocetti, Rubini, & Meeus, 2008; Marcia, 1966). In the early 1980s, there was some attention given to the importance of domain content because this was when the interpersonal identity domains of friendships, family, and sex roles were added to the standard assessments of identity processes (Grotevant, Thorbecke, & Meyer, 1982). Yet, overall, the implied message attached to this approach is that identity domain content is not particularly crucial for understanding identity processes; any domain will do. This is a hard position to defend, however, because research has demonstrated that different domains develop at different rates (Meeus, Iedema, Helsen, & Vollebergh, 1999), thus casting doubt on the meaningfulness of an overall status classification.

Some areas of identity research that operate within the identity status model have focused on a single domain. Phinney's (1990) model of ethnic identity is one of the most prominent examples, along with some aspects of research on occupational identity (Porfeli, Lee, Vondracek, & Weigold, 2011). These domain-specific investigations, however, have largely operated in isolation. That is, there has been little comparative work done to examine how ethnic identity develops in relation to other identity domains.

Although there have been some investigations into identity domain content, there has been very little work looking into the content of the identity itself. For example, within the occupational domain, identity achievement is considered a positive developmental state, but does it matter what occupations the individuals have settled on? If they choose stock broker or pro surfer, does that matter? Is this important for understanding identity development? There are few answers to these questions because they have hardly ever been asked.

In contrast to the identity status approach clearly privileging process over content, the narrative identity approach has been largely disengaged from thinking about identity in this way at all. That is, the language of process and content will be familiar to most status researchers, but perhaps not as much for narrative researchers. However, looking at the practices in the field, the distinction clearly applies. Take, for example, McAdams's (2008) life story interview. The interview protocol comprises requests for several key scenes from an individual's life: high point, low point, turning point, self-defining memory, earliest memory, and so on. The interview requests different types of memories, but these memories are not tied to specific identity domains. Moreover, those aspects of the narratives that are typically coded correspond to identity processes, namely, various forms of autobiographical reasoning (e.g., meaning-making, personal growth, self-event connections) or story construction (e.g., complexity, coherence), and are then aggregated across memories (McAdams et al., 2006). The closest thing to content that is studied is the emotional tone of the narrative, either in terms of overall tone or the sequencing of emotion from the beginning to the end of the story (e.g., redemption, contamination), but it is not entirely clear whether emotional tone is process or content (or both!). What the story *is actually about* seldom factors into the analysis. Some narrative studies will code for event type (e.g., achievement, relationship, mortality), but doing so is largely for descriptive purposes, and the event types rarely figure into the primary analysis (e.g., McLean, 2005; Thorne, McLean, & Lawrence, 2004). Other studies focus in on one identity domain, but do not examine content variations within that domain (e.g., McLean & Thorne, 2003).

The importance of identity content and how exactly to study it remain unresolved questions. Interestingly, some of the chapters in this handbook take on this issue without directly acknowledging it. Numerous chapters in this volume invoke William James's distinction between the "I" and the "me" (Waterman, this volume; Motti-Stefandi, this volume; Habermas & Köber, this volume; McAdams & Zapata-Gietl, this volume). The "I" is the self as the subject, the agent who creates, manages, and synthesizes the self. In contrast, the "me" is the self as the object, the description of who one is. In reviewing these chapters, we became aware of how the "I" maps onto identity process and the "me" maps onto identity content. Although the I and the me were discussed in numerous chapters, the nature of their interaction was not consensual.

In his chapter on interactional identities and storytelling, Korobov (this volume) indirectly theorizes on the role of process and content. Korobov argues that social categories and identities are synced up through positioning in conversation. Thus, the practice of storytelling is the glue that binds different parts of the self. In terms of identity process and content, this is a fairly traditional view, in which process (the I) is privileged and seen as the main "action" through which identities are managed. This perspective is similar to the one expressed by McLean and Pasupathi (2012), who suggested that storytelling promotes consolidation—or commitment—to identities. In contrast, in their chapter on autobiographical reasoning, Habermas and Köber (this volume) describe the me as being the anchor for self-continuity, allowing the I to do its work. To put it another way, having a sense of self as an object—what one is—facilitates the ability for the higher order synthesis of the self across time and context. Thus, in this formulation, identity content is privileged over identity process.

So, which is more important for identity development, the I or the me? The process or the content? When one of us (Syed) began conducting narrative studies of ethnicity-related experiences, the primary interest was in examining narrative processes, such as meaning-making, resolution, and coherence. After getting into the stories, however, the research team was struck by the variety of types of stories that people told. We felt as if we first had to understand what people were telling stories about before we endeavored to understand how they were telling them. In other words, we were captivated by the content of the identities. We maintained this focus on narrative content for some time because we found that the content of the stories was linked to ethnic identity processes assessed using survey measures (Syed & Azmitia, 2008, 2010). In short, focusing on the content of ethnic identities allowed us to better understand the process of ethnic identity development.

One of the challenges of studying identity content is that it does not have a clear taxonomy. Content can include attitudes, beliefs, values, behaviors, and lived experiences (see Syed & Azmitia, 2010), which constitutes a vast and diffuse set of constructs for investigation. How can we even begin to wrangle these constructs into a meaningful set that can be studied with consistency? In our view, this question represents a major challenge to the future of identity development research. Sadly, the fact that we are discussing identity content at all already reflects some progress in the field. But we will take whatever progress we can get.

Conclusion

As we edited this book, we had constant conversations with each other about our process. Reading and commenting on the chapters made us think deeply about what we were trying to accomplish with this project, but also about the field more broadly. We view the different approaches to identity development research as akin to different cultures, each with its own beliefs (e.g., theories), practices (e.g., methods), and language (e.g., terms).

Looking back, what we were really trying to do was build a new, common culture through cross-cultural exchange. This prompted us to think about who goes about the business of initiating cross-cultural interaction. Generally, the burden falls on the minority view to reach out to the majority about the value of its perspectives. This is the process in society at large (i.e., ethnicity, gender), but also within the niche-happy fields of psychology. As we noted in the introductory chapter (McLean & Syed, this volume), all of the studies examining the interface of status and narrative approaches to identity have been initiated by narrative researchers, which constitute the minority view in the field. However, we feel that this minority view is slowly emerging into the mainstream, and this has led to initiations from the other side. This type of interaction is critical for both cultures because it will doubtlessly lead to new ways of thinking about a construct as complex as identity.

But how do we truly facilitate cultural exchange? An important theme throughout this handbook is that of researchers being explicit about their approach to identity development. Why do you emphasize adolescence versus other ages? Process over content? Reasoning versus experience? Focused self-examination allows us to see what possible narratives are being silenced due to maintenance of the status quo. Outsiders looking in can be particularly helpful in this regard because they view a field with fresh eyes and little investment in one approach over another. We need to engage in conversations, debates, and *fika* to push our thinking and rethink our assumptions. This is the only way through which we can truly understand how and why we become the way we are.

Acknowledgments

Thanks to Cade Mansfield, Lauren Mitchell, Sarah Morrison-Cohen, and Monisha Pasupathi for feedback on earlier drafts of this chapter.

References

Arnett, J. J. (2004). *Emerging adulthood: The winding road from late teens through the twenties*. New York: Oxford University Press.

Azmitia, M., Syed, M., & Radmacher, K. (2008). On the intersection of personal and social identities: Introduction and evidence from a longitudinal study of emerging adults. In M. Azmitia, M. Syed, & K. Radmacher (Eds.), *The intersections of personal and social identities. New directions for child and adolescent development* (120, 1–16). San Francisco: Jossey-Bass.

Baltes, P. B. (1987). Theoretical propositions of life-span developmental psychology: On the dynamics between growth and decline. *Developmental Psychology, 23*(5), 611.

Block. J. (2002). *Personality as an affect-processing system: Toward an integrative theory.* Mahwah, NJ: Erlbaum.

Bruner, J. S. (1990). *Acts of meaning.* Cambridge, MA: Harvard University Press.

Chandler, M. J., Lalonde, C. E., Sokol, B. W., & Hallett, D. (2003). Personal persistence, identity development, and suicide: A study of Native and Non-native North American adolescents. *Monographs of the Society for Research in Child Development, 138.*

Cooper, C. R., & Denner, J. (1998). Theories linking culture and psychology: Universal and community-specific processes. *Annual Review of Psychology, 49*(1), 559–584.

Cooper, C. R., & Denner, J. (1998). Theories linking culture and psychology: Universal and community-specific processes. *Annual Review of Psychology, 49*(1), 559–584.

Cooper, C. R., García Coll, C. T., Thorne, B., & Orellana, M. F. (2005). Beyond demographic categories: How immigration, ethnicity, and "race" matter for children's identities and pathways through school. In C. R. Cooper, C. Garcia Coll, T. Bartko, H. Davis, & C. Chatman (Eds.), *Developmental pathways through middle childhood: Rethinking contexts and diversity as resources* (pp. 181–206). Mahwah, NJ: Erlbaum

Crocetti, E., Rubini, M., & Meeus, W. (2008). Capturing the dynamics of identity formation in various ethnic groups: Development and validation of a three-dimensional model. *Journal of Adolescence, 31*(2), 207–222.

Cross, W. E., & Cross, T. B. (2008). Theory, research, and models. In S. M. Quintana & C. McKown (Eds.), *Handbook of race, racism, and the developing child* (pp. 154–181). Hoboken, NJ: Wiley.

Decety, J., & Sommerville, J. A. (2003). Shared representations between self and other: A social cognitive neuroscience view. *Trends in Cognitive Sciences, 7*(12), 527–533.

DeYoung, C. G. (2010). Toward a theory of the Big Five. *Psychological Inquiry, 21*(1), 26–33.

Egan, S. K., & Perry, D. G. (2001). Gender identity: A multidimensional analysis with implications for psychosocial adjustment. *Developmental Psychology, 37*(4), 451.

Erikson, E. H. (1950). *Childhood and society.* New York: W. W. Norton & Co.

Erikson, E. H. (1968). *Identity: Youth and crisis.* New York: Norton.

Grotevant, H. D., & Cooper, C. R. (1985). Patterns of interaction in family relationships and the development of identity exploration in adolescence. *Child Development, 56*(2), 415–428.

Grotevant, H. D., Thorbecke, W., & Meyer, M. L. (1982). An extension of Marcia's identity status interview into the interpersonal domain. *Journal of Youth and Adolescence, 11*(1), 33–47.

Habermas, T., & Bluck, S. (2000). Getting a life: The emergence of the life story in adolescence. *Psychological Bulletin, 126,* 248–269.

Habermas, T., & de Silveira, C. (2008). The development of global coherence in life narratives across adolescence: Temporal, causal, and thematic aspects. *Developmental Psychology, 44*(3), 707.

Hammack, P. L. (2011). *Narrative and the politics of identity: The cultural psychology of Israeli and Palestinian youth.* New York: Oxford University Press.

Harter, S. (1999). *The construction of the self: A developmental perspective.* New York: Guilford Press.

Helms, J. E., Jernigan, M., & Mascher, J. (2005). The meaning of race in psychology and how to change it: A methodological perspective. *American Psychologist, 60*(1), 27.

Klimstra, T. A. (2012). The dynamics of personality and identity in adolescence. *European Journal of Developmental Psychology, 9*(4), 472–484.

Kroger, J. (Ed.). (2013). Special Issue: Meta-analytic studies of identity and personality. *Identity, 13*(3).

Kroger, J., Martinussen, M., & Marcia, J. E. (2010). Identity status change during adolescence and young adulthood: A meta-analysis. *Journal of Adolescence, 33*(5), 683–698.

Kunnen, E. S. (2006). Are conflicts the motor in identity change? *Identity, 6*(2), 169–186.

Kurtines, W. M., Ferrer-Wreder, L., Berman, S. L., Lorente, C. C., Silverman, W. K., & Montgomery, M. J. (2008). Promoting positive youth development. New directions in developmental theory, methods, and research. *Journal of Adolescent Research, 23*(3), 233–244.

Labov, W., & Waletsky, J. (1967). Narrative analysis: Oral version of personal experience. In J. Helm (Ed.), *Essays on the verbal and visual arts: Proceedings of the 1966 annual spring meeting of the American Ethnological Society* (pp. 12–44). Seattle: University of Washington Press.

Lerner, R. M. (1996). Relative plasticity, integration, temporality, and diversity in human development: A developmental contextual perspective about theory, process, and method. *Developmental Psychology, 32*(4), 781.

Marcia, J. E. (1966). Development and validation of ego identity status. *Journal of Personality and Social Psychology, 3,* 551–558.

McAdams, D. P. (2006). *The redemptive self: Stories Americans live by.* New York: Oxford University Press.

McAdams, D. P. (2008). *The life story interview.* Unpublished manuscript.

McAdams, D. P. (2013). The psychological self as actor, agent, and author. *Perspectives on Psychological Science, 8*(3), 272–295.

McAdams, D. P., Bauer, J. J., Sakaeda, A. R., Anyidoho, N. A., Machado, M. A., Magrino-Failla, K., … & Pals, J. L. (2006). Continuity and change in the life story: A longitudinal study of autobiographical memories in emerging adulthood. *Journal of Personality, 74*(5), 1371–1400.

McAdams, D. P., & Pals, J. L. (2006). A new Big Five: Fundamental principles for an integrative science of personality. *American Psychologist, 61*(3), 204.

McLean, K. C. (2005). Late adolescent identity development: Narrative meaning-making and memory telling. *Developmental Psychology, 41,* 683–691.

McLean, K. C. (2008). The emergence of narrative identity. *Social and Personality Psychology Compass, 2*(4), 1685–1702.

McLean, K. C., & Pasupathi, M. (2012). Processes of identity development: Where I am and how I got there. *Identity, 12*(1), 8–28.

McLean, K. C., & Thorne, A. (2003). Late adolescents' self-defining memories about relationships. *Developmental Psychology, 39*(4), 635.

Meeus, W., Iedema, J., Helsen, M., & Vollebergh, W. (1999). Patterns of adolescent identity development: Review of literature and longitudinal analysis. *Developmental Review, 19*(4), 419–461.

Phinney, J. S. (1990). Ethnic identity in adolescents and adults: A review of research. *Psychological Bulletin, 108,* 499–514.

Phinney, J. S. (1992). The multigroup ethnic identity measure: A new scale for use with diverse groups. *Journal of Adolescent Research, 7*(2), 156–176.

Phinney, J. S. (1993). A three-stage model of ethnic identity in adolescence. In M. E. Bernal & G. P. Knight (Eds.), *Ethnic identity: Formation and transmission among Hispanics and other minorities* (pp. 61–79). Hillsdale, NJ: Erlbaum.

Piaget, J. (1954). *The construction of reality in the child.* New York: Basic Books.

Porfeli, E. J., Lee, B., Vondracek, F. W., & Weigold, I. K. (2011). A multi-dimensional measure of vocational identity status. *Journal of Adolescence, 34*(5), 853–871.

Ruble, D. N., Alvarez, J., Bachman, M., Cameron, J., Fuligni, A., Garcia Coll, C., & Rhee, E. (2004). The development of a sense of "we": The emergence and implications of children's collective identity. In M. Bennett and F. Sani (Eds.), *The development of the social self (pp. 29–76)* East Sussex, England: Psychology Press.

Schwartz, S. J., Zamboanga, B. L., & Weisskirch, R. S. (2008). Broadening the study of the self: Integrating the study of personal identity and cultural identity. *Social and Personality Psychology Compass, 2*(2), 635–651

Schwartz, S. J., Zamboanga, B. L., Luyckx, K., Meca, A., & Ritchie, R. A. (2013). Identity in emerging adulthood: Reviewing the field and looking forward. *Emerging Adulthood, 1*(2), 96–113.

Schwartz, S. J., Zamboanga, B. L., & Weisskirch, R. S. (2008). Broadening the study of the self: Integrating the study of personal identity and cultural identity. *Social and Personality Psychology Compass, 2*(2), 635–651.

Syed, M. (in press-*a*). Emerging adulthood: Theory, developmental stage, or nonsense? In J. J. Arnett (Ed.), *The Oxford handbook of emerging adulthood.* New York: Oxford University Press.

Syed, M. (in press-*b*). Theoretical and methodological contributions of narrative psychology to ethnic identity research. In C. Santos & A. J. Umaña-Taylor (Eds.), *Studying ethnic identity: Methodological advances and considerations for future research.* Washington, DC: American Psychological Association.

Syed, M. (2012). College students' storytelling of ethnicity-related events in the academic domain. *Journal of Adolescent Research, 27*(2), 203–230.

Syed, M., & Azmitia, M. (2008). A narrative approach to ethnic identity in emerging adulthood: Bringing life to the identity status model. *Developmental Psychology, 44*(4), 1012–1027.

Syed, M., & Azmitia, M. (2010). Narrative and ethnic identity exploration: A longitudinal account of emerging adults' ethnicity-related experiences. *Developmental Psychology, 46*(1), 208–219.

Thorne, A., & McLean, K. C. (2003). Telling traumatic events in adolescence: A study of master narrative positioning. In R. Fivush & C. Haden (Eds.), *Autobiographical memory and the construction of a narrative self: Developmental and cultural perspectives* (pp. 169–185). Mahwah, NJ: Erlbaum.

Thorne, A., McLean, K. C., & Lawrence, A. M. (2004). When remembering is not enough: Reflecting on self, defining memories in late adolescence. *Journal of Personality, 72*(3), 513–542.

Umaña-Taylor, A. J., Quintana, S. M., Lee, R. M., Cross, W. E., Rivas-Drake, D., Schwartz, S. J., Syed, M., Yip, T., Seaton, E., & Ethnic/Racial Identity Study Group. (2014). Ethnic and racial identity revisited: An integrated conceptualization. *Child Development, 85*(1), 21–39.

Wängqvist, M., & Frisén, A. (2013). Swedish 18-year-olds' identity formation: Associations with feelings about appearance and internalization of body ideals. *Journal of Adolescence, 36*(3), 485–493.

Weststrate, N. M., & McLean, K. C. (2010). The rise and fall of gay: A cultural-historical approach to gay identity development. *Memory, 18*(2), 225–240.

Whitbourne, S. K., Sneed, J. R., & Skultety, K. M. (2002). Identity processes in adulthood: Theoretical and methodological challenges. *Identity: An International Journal of Theory and Research, 2*(1), 29–45.

INDEX

Academic pipeline, 299–300, 310f, 311
Achievement
  adaptive resources, 486
  adolescents, 56, 60, 61
  adulthood, 68, 69, 71, 72, 75
  alienated achievement, 137
  characteristics, definitions, 18, 56, 61, 68, 133, 200, 201, 250, 270, 476, 477, 492
  classification, 100–102, 100t, 117
  cultural differences, 478
  developmental changes meta analyses, 60, 61, 108
  dynamic systems theory, 139
  ethnic/racial identity, 20, 261
  gendered narrative identity, 45
  identity maturation, 477–78
  identity trajectories, 142
  integrative identity model, 104
  internalizing symptoms, 549
  lifespan identity development, 82, 87
  normative identity style, 441
  psychometric studies, 138
  well-being, 481
"Acting White" phenomenon, 273, 276, 288
Adair, V., 73–74
Adams, G. R., 211, 357, 450, 543, 551
Addis, D. R., 152, 155
Adelson, J., 141–42
Adler, A., 2
Adler, J. M., 361, 365
Adolescence/emerging adulthood
  age range definitions, 61
  autobiographical reasoning, 150–51, 155–56, 160, 162, 167, 170, 184–85
  biculturalism, 59–60
  causal/thematic coherence, 62
  as center of identity formation, 567–68
  courtship, dating, marriage, sexuality, 55–58
  cultural influences, 54–60, 63
  cultural neuroscience, 427–28, 431
  cultural stereotypes, 273–81, 287–91
  developing vs. developed countries, 57–59, 63
  developmental intervention science, 338–40, 342–43, 346–50
  developmental trajectories, 109–10
  divorce, 464–65
  elaborative reminiscing, 43, 44–45t, 46–49, 47t
  emotional reminiscing, 43, 44–45t, 46–49, 47t
  externalizing, health risk behaviors, 549–50
  false-self behaviors, 395
  gendered narrative identity, 43–48, 44–47t (see also gendered narrative identity)
  gendered personal narratives emergence, 41–43
  globalization in identity development, 58–60, 293, 566
  hybrid identity, 59–60, 293–94
  identity crisis, 17–18, 53–54, 56, 58, 61–62, 100–101, 100t, 116–17, 301, 339, 393, 476, 480
  identity development universality, 53–54, 56–58
  identity domains, 56–57, 62–63
  identity status (see identity status model)
  identity vs. identity confusion, 100
  ideological diversity, 55–58
  individuation, 292–93
  intergenerational narratives, 45–49, 46–47t
  internal state language, 43, 46–47, 46t
  life story emergence, 41
  moratorium, 17–18, 56, 60, 61
  multiple worlds, 8
  narrative method, 62–63
  parenting authority vs. autonomy, 8, 438, 440–50
  personality development, 492, 494–97, 499, 501
  phylogenetic history, 54–56
  political conflict, 370–81
  positioning in narratives, 171
  self-concept, 40, 48–49, 59
  self-esteem, 41–43, 56–57, 60
  social conventions, 439–41
  storm and stress period, 18
  validation of identity claims, 233
  values, assimilation of, 59, 569
Adulthood
  accommodative challenge, 73, 74
  achievement, 68, 69, 71, 72, 75
  autobiographical memory, 72
  cohort effect, 74
  cultural effects, 67, 77
  diffuse-avoidant processing style, 69
  diffusion, 68, 69, 71, 72, 75
  disequilibration, 68
  ego identity, 3–4, 14–15, 17, 66, 82, 100, 510, 566
  epigenetic principle, 67, 75–78
  Erikson, 66–68, 70–72
  fidelity, 66
  foreclosure, 68, 69–72, 74, 75
  generativity vs. stagnation, 67, 68, 76
  identity accommodation, 69
  identity assimilation, 69
  identity development generally, 67, 70–72, 77–78
  identity processing model, 69
  identity regression, 68
  identity roles, 65
  identity vs. role confusion, 3, 66–68, 72, 75–77
  informational processing style, 69
  integrity vs. despair, 67, 68, 76–77
  intimacy vs. isolation, 67, 68, 75–76
  Marcia's theories, 67, 68, 70–71
  McAdams' theories, 69–70
  meta-analyses, 71, 74
  moratorium, 68, 69, 71, 72, 75
  moratorium-achievement moratorium-achievement (MAMA cycles), 68, 129
  narrative identity model, 69–70, 72 (see also narrative identity model)
  normative-avoidant processing style, 69
  progressive identity status, 71–74, 77–78
  revision, maintenance processes, 73–74
  social-cognitive theories, 69
  stability, 73–74
Affonso, D., 76
African Americans
  black cultural learning styles model, 257
  black culture, 255–57
  black identity as stage model, 258–59
  black self-sabotage, 256

African Americans (*Cont.*)
  cultural stereotypes, 272–78, 281, 288, 292
  culture as ethnicity, 253, 257, 290
  developmental intervention science, 339–40, 347, 349
  parenting, 444, 447, 450
  racial/ethnic identity development, 20, 26n1
  school, schooling, 299–302, 304–6
Agency
  autobiographical reasoning, 162, 177, 204, 544–45
  lifespan identity development, 89, 145n2
  narrative identity model, 361, 364
  parenting, 437, 440, 444, 483
  personality development, 493
  political conflict, 374–76, 440
  risk, resilience, 473, 483, 485
Ager, J., 273
Akerlof, G. A., 530
Albrecht, R. E., 344
Allen, J. P., 486
Allen, V. L., 99
Allport, G. W., 16, 140
Al-Owidha, A., 108
Althusser, L., 215
Amato, P. R., 457
Ambady, N., 257
Antaki, C., 216
Anthis, K. S., 73
Appiah, K. A., 24
Applications section, 563–64
Archer, S. L., 199, 502, 503
Arco, R., 308
Arditti, J. A., 459
Aristotle, 202
Arnett, J. J., 6, 82–83, 87, 92, 338, 494, 535, 566, 568
Asian Americans
  cultural stereotypes, 273–74
  culture as ethnicity, 253, 257
  lifespan identity development, 89
  school, schooling, 299, 300, 302
Asquith, P., 443
Assimilation, 59, 69, 300, 304, 569
Autobiographical reasoning. *see also* meaning-making
  adolescence/emerging adulthood, 150–51, 155–56, 160, 162, 167, 170, 184–85
  agency, 162, 177, 204, 544–45
  autobiographical arguments, 150, 155–59
  big stories, 182–83, 185, 186, 203–4, 238–40
  biographical ruptures, 150, 155–56, 159–60
  body-as-if loop, 172–76, 189
  body-right-now map, 172–76, 189

body-there-and-then map, 172–76, 189
coherence, unity, 151, 156–60, 171–72, 177, 204
concepts, definitions, 149–50, 167–68, 183, 184, 189–90
context of narration, 174, 177–78, 185, 188
coping mechanisms, 159–62, 170
culture, gender issues, 176–77
developmental status, 157
diachronics, 183, 184, 187
discontinuity, 153–54, 159–60, 162, 171, 177, 185
ego resiliency, 161, 476
embodied narration, 172–76, 189
environmental stability, 153–55, 157, 168–70
episodics, 183, 184
essentialism, 156, 159, 198, 202–3, 306
events causing personality change, 157
exemplification, 157
formative influences, 157, 168–69
goals for narration, 175
identity resolution, 168–69, 171, 186–87
I/me distinction, 187, 204, 570–71
life narratives, 7–8, 150, 154, 157–61
lifespan identity development, 90–91, 190
life story schema, 149, 154–59, 162, 166, 167, 183–86, 476–77, 545
life transitions, 159–60
memory, 152–55, 170, 172–76, 184
narrative identity, 167–69, 184–89, 476
narrativist arguments, 156, 159
over-general memory, 175
personality, explanations of actions by, 157, 160
personality development, 493
physiological states, 175–76
positioning in narratives, 171–72
redemption sequence, 91, 161, 358–59
relational positioning, 170–72, 188–89
rumination, 103, 104, 118, 135, 161, 395, 501, 543
self-construction, 162
self-continuity, 150–62, 167, 184–89
situated identity performances, 154
small stories, 182–83, 185, 186, 203–4, 238–40
social relations, 153–55, 157, 168–70
subjective outlook changes, 158, 160
synchronics, 187
tacit themes, 169–70, 188
victimization themes, 170, 177
well-being, 159–62, 185
Autonomy

autonomy *vs.* authority in parenting, 8, 438, 440–50
gendered narrative identity, 45
identity development as process, 124
racial/ethnic identity development, 20
Azmitia, M., 7, 281, 289, 477, 552, 554

Bakhtin, M. M., 212
Balistreri, E., 102
Ball, L., 485
Bamberg, M., 22, 154, 171, 184, 186, 215, 242
Banks. M. V., 161
Barber, B. K., 372, 376
Barber, B. L., 485
Barillas-Chón, D. W., 307, 309
Barkhuus, L., 513
Bar-Tal, D., 371–73
Bauer, J. J., 498, 545
Baum, N., 461
Baumeister, R. F., 510
Beaumont, S. L., 75–76
Beck, U., 534
Bell, N. J., 205
Belonging, group affiliation
  difference and sameness, 16
  identity status, 139
  political conflict, 371–73
  racial/ethnic identity development, 20
  school, schooling, 300, 302–6
  social networking sites, 511, 515, 516, 518
Bennion, L. D., 543
Benson, J. E., 465
Bergin, D. A., 305
Berman, S. L., 450
Bernal, M. E., 260
Berntsen, D., 162
Berry, J., 261–62
Berzonsky, M. D., 19, 69, 76, 119, 122, 135, 143, 393, 440
Beyers, W., 110, 549
Big stories, 182–83, 185, 186, 203–4, 238–40
Bilard, J., 417
Binational Front of Indigenous Organizations, 308
Blagov, P. S., 359
Blair-Loy, M., 329
Blais, J. J., 509
Block, J., 99, 121, 569
Bluck, S., 7, 156, 361
Bodily states mapping, 172–74, 189
Body-as-if loop, 172–76, 189
Body image. *see also* puberty
  body mass index, 412–13
  careers, 408, 416–17
  components, 406–7
  depression, 411

early maturation, 389–90, 392–99, 393f, 412
eating disturbances, 409, 415–16
ethnicity/race, 413–14
explorations, commitments, 407–8
femininity, 407
gender roles, 407, 410–11, 416–17
identity formation, 407–8, 416–17
media, 415–16
objectification, 408, 416, 417
objectification theory, 409–10
parental attitudes, behaviors, 414–15, 417
peer pressure, 415, 417
psychosocial theory, 407
pubertal timing, 8, 17, 390–92, 396, 397, 400, 401, 411–12
puberty, 397–98
self-concept, 407
self-discrepancy theory, 408–9
self-esteem, 407, 411, 416
self-silencing, 394–95, 400–401, 417
sexualization, 410–11, 416
sexual orientation, 414
social comparison theory, 408
social groups, 413, 417
sociocultural theory, 409
steroids, 411
thin ideal, 409, 410
tripartite model, 409
well-being, 409
Body-right-now map, 172–76, 189
Bonalume, L., 359, 360
Bond, M., 280
Borderline personality, 142
Bosacki, S. L., 443
Bosma, H. A., 103, 121, 122, 126
Bosman, K., 129
Bosnian youth, 375–77, 381
Bourdieu, P., 291, 300, 302
Bourne, E., 19
boyd, d. m., 509, 512, 517, 519
Bradbury, T. N., 457
Bradley, C. L., 76
Branje, S. J. T., 107, 109, 543
Breen, A. V., 160
Brewer, M. B., 292
Bridging Multiple Worlds Alliance, 310–13, 310f
Briones, E., 553
Brittian, A. S., 547
Bronfenbrenner, U., 279, 536
Bronte-Tinkew, J., 462
Brooks, D., 280
Brown, B., 514
Brubaker, J. R., 157, 544
Bruner, J. S., 35, 569
Burciaga, R., 302–3
Burkitt, I., 13
Burrow, A. L., 542

Campbell, C. G., 124
Cantor, N., 492
Carter, P. L., 276, 305, 313
Carter, R., 395
Cartmel, F., 534
Caspi, A., 491–92, 494, 495f
Catalano, R. F., 339
Chandler, M. J., 150, 156, 287, 485, 564
Chang, L., 59
Chavez-Korell, S., 260
Chen, Y., 160
Cheon, B. K., 429
Chiao, J. Y., 8, 427
Childhood and Society (Erikson), 53, 54, 81
Chinese-Americans, 275, 276–78
Chodorow, N., 82
Christiansen, S. L., 76
Clausen, J., 322
Cohler, B. J., 21, 22
Coleman, B. R., 262
Coleman, M. N., 253
Colombia, 377–80
Colwell, R. K., 547
Commitment
  body image, 407–8
  concepts, definitions, 552
  development of, 120
  identity development as process, 116–20
  identity status, 98, 133–38
  identity status model, 100, 100t, 102, 103, 117, 200, 201, 250, 270, 476
  integrative identity model (Luyckx), 103, 104, 118, 119, 126
  personality development, 492–97, 495f, 499
  reconsideration of, 104–6, 109, 118, 120, 143, 476, 543, 545
Community Cultural Wealth framework, 302
Conceptual self (tacit themes of narratives), 153
Connerly, Ward, 255
Consolidation of identity, 550, 551
Context
  closed contexts, 74
  cultural stereotypes, 279–80, 290–91
  dynamic systems theory, 125
  identity development as process, 120
  identity status, 135, 138–40
  I/me distinction, 197, 204
  integrative identity model (Schachter), 238–40
  lifespan identity development, 87
  microinteractional, 211
  of narration, 174, 177–78, 185, 188
  open contexts, 74
  personality development, 493, 504
  puberty, 393–94, 397–99

risk, resilience, 473, 478–79, 482
work identity, 322–26
Contextual amplification hypothesis, 398–99
Conway, M. A., 91, 153
Cooks, H. C., 305
Cookston, J., 8
Cooley, C. H., 13
Cooper, C. R., 210–11
Cooper, K., 8
Copeland, B., 255
Coping strategies
  autobiographical reasoning, 159–62, 170
  cultural stereotypes, 272–79
  divorce, 455
  identity development as process, 119–20
  political conflict, 373–75, 378–80, 382–84
  puberty, 394–95, 397, 401
  risk, resilience, 484–85
  school, schooling, 302–6, 310–12
Costa, P. T., 491
Cota, M. K., 260
Côté, J. E., 3, 9, 19, 211, 230, 241, 478, 483, 530, 531, 535, 543, 552
Cox, K., 494
Crocetti, E., 6, 104, 107, 108, 110, 133–37, 139, 143, 543, 545, 547, 550, 551
Cross, W. E., Jr., 20, 258, 259–60, 289, 553
Cross Racial Identity Scale (CRIS), 259, 262–63
Crouter, A. C., 394
Cultural neuroscience
  adolescence to adulthood transition, 427–28, 431
  affiliation, 428–30
  aging, 425, 431–32
  amygdala, 428, 430, 431
  anterior cingulate cortex (ACC), 429–31
  brain regions, 425–26, 426f, 429, 430
  culture–gene coevolutionary theory, 424
  developmental biocultural co-constructivism, 425
  developmental neuroscience, 427–28
  empathy, 428–30
  event-related potentials (ERP), 433
  family values, 433
  fMRI studies, 425, 432, 433
  functional near-infrared spectroscopy (FNIRS), 432
  fusiform gyrus, 430–31
  identity development, 424–25, 427–28
  individualism-collectivism, 424, 427
  interleukin 6 receptor (sIL-6r), 432–33

Cultural neuroscience (*Cont.*)
  medial prefrontal cortex (MPFC), 426–30, 426f
  medial temporal lobe (MTL), 429–31
  mental state inference, 430
  middle frontal gyrus, 428
  MPPC, 428
  neuroimaging studies, 425–28, 426f
  neuroplasticity, 425, 428, 431
  orbital prefrontal cortex (OFC), 431
  posterior cingulate cortex (PCC), 426, 426f, 427, 429, 430
  race and ethnicity, 429, 431
  self-construal theory, 424
  self-processing, 425–27, 426f
  self-reflection, 427–28
  serotonin transporter gene (*5-HTTLPR*), 424
  social cognition, 425–27, 426f
  social cue perception, 430–31, 433
  superior temporal gyrus, 431
  superior temporal sulcus (STS), 428, 430
  temporoparietal junction (TPJ), 428–30
  ventral premotor region, 428
  ventral striatum, 433
Cultural stereotypes
  "acting White" phenomenon, 273, 276, 288
  adolescence/emerging adulthood, 273–81, 287–91
  African Americans, 272–78, 281, 288, 292
  Asian Americans, 273–74
  avoidance, 272–73, 276–78
  Chinese-Americans, 275, 276–78
  class identities, 291
  context, 279–80, 290–91
  coping strategies, 272–79
  cultural artifacts, 272
  gender differences, 273–74
  gender identification, 271–74
  group identification, 271
  hybrid identity, 59–60, 293–94
  identity status model, 270
  immigrants, 273, 275, 276, 290, 292
  intersectionality, 274–76, 280–81, 289, 291–94, 553–54
  Latinos, 273–74, 290, 292
  mixed-race identity, 293–94
  model minority myth, 278
  narratives, 276, 278, 287, 288, 293
  optimal distinctiveness theory, 292–93
  Pacific Islanders, 275, 277, 290
  personal identity, 270, 279, 280, 287–88, 566
  phenomenological variant of ecological systems theory (P-VEST), 272
  privilege, 288, 291
  psychosocial theory, 270, 272, 287–88
  self-concept, 271–72, 276–77, 292
  social capital theory, 291, 300, 302–3
  social expectations, 274–75, 281
  social identity, 270–72, 279, 280, 287–89
  stereotypes in identity formation, 273–79
  whites, 273–76, 278–79, 290
Culture as ethnicity
  acculturation model, 261–62
  African Americans, 253, 257, 290
  anti-intellectualism, 256, 288
  Asian Americans, 253, 257
  authenticity, 255–56, 287
  black cultural learning styles model, 257
  black culture, 255–57
  black identity as stage model, 258–59
  black self-sabotage, 256
  concepts, definitions, 251–54, 252t, 262
  consistency, validation of measures, 262–63
  Cross Racial Identity Scale (CRIS), 259, 262–63
  discrimination/stigma, 251, 253, 288–92
  ethnic identity, 254–55, 290
  ethnic identity model (Phinney), 261
  ethnic identity models, 260–62
  ethnic identity profiles, 261–62, 288, 293–94
  ethnicity, 252–54, 252t
  group identity, 255–56
  identity status model, 261
  immigrants, 253
  lifespan identity development, 85, 289
  master narratives, 63, 91, 288, 358, 363, 366, 503, 567
  multidimensional model of racial identity (MMRI), 20, 258
  Multigroup Ethnic Identity Measure (MEIM), 254, 261
  Native Americans, 253, 290
  nigrescence theory, 258–60, 290
  personal/ego identity, 250
  psychosocial theory, 250–51
  racial/ethnic groups, 252–54, 252t
  racial identity, 254–55
  Racial Identity Attitude Scale (RIAS), 259
  racial identity models, 257–60
  racial identity profiles, 259–60, 288, 293–94
  racial socialization, 253, 260–61, 290
  rejection sensitivity, 260
  role-identity theory, 15
  self-determination, 255–56
  separatism, 256, 288
  social identity, 250–51
  stereotype threat, 257
  structural symbolic interactionism, 15–16
  victimology, 256, 288
  world views, 249
Culture–gene coevolutionary theory, 424
Cumulative continuity model, 491–92, 494

Dabova, M., 360
Daddis, C., 447
Damasio, A., 172, 173, 189
Daniels, E. A., 8, 416
Darley, J. M., 257
Davies, B., 154
Deaux, K., 34, 292
Debate format, 6, 563
DeGarmo, D. S., 462
Dellas Identity Status Inventory-Occupation (DISI-O), 102, 106
Demorest, A., 360–61
Denissen, J. A. J., 483
De Roover, K., 128
Descartes, R., 13
Developmental intervention science
  adolescence/emerging adulthood, 338–40, 342–43, 346–50
  African-Americans, 339–40, 347, 349
  cognitive intervention strategies, 345
  developmental processes, 342–43
  developmental regulation, 342
  developmental transitions, 343
  ethnic identity exploration, 339–40
  identity formation, 337–38, 349
  identity interventions, 339–40, 349–50
  identity styles, 340
  Latinos, 347, 349
  life goals, 345, 346, 349–50
  Native Americans, 340
  personal expressiveness, 344
  person-in-context principle, 338, 340
  positive identity, 337
  positive identity development, 337, 340–45, 349–50
  positive youth development, 337–39
  positive youth development programs, 339–40, 345–49
  prevention, 340
  principles, applications, 338–39, 342–43
  progressive change, 340–43

self-actualization, 344
self-construction, 340, 343–45, 344f, 347
self-discovery, 340, 344, 344f, 345, 347, 350
self-regulation, 342
self-structure change, 342–43
self-transformative model, 343–45, 344f, 350
De Waal, F., 280
De Witte, H., 542
DeYoung, C. G., 500, 569
Dialogistic theories, 204–5
Diaries, 127, 143
Difference and sameness
  belonging, group affiliation, 16
  identity as tool, 11–12
  role-identity theory, 15
  self as social construct, 13–14
  self-concept, 4, 12
  self in social interaction, 14, 85
  social identity theory, 4, 15, 16–17, 566
  stigma theory, 14–15
  structural symbolic interactionism, 15–16
  symbolic interactionism, 14
  terminology, 12
Diffusion
  adolescents, 56–57, 60, 61
  adulthood, 68, 69, 71, 72, 75
  characteristics, definitions, 18, 56–57, 61, 68, 117, 134, 200, 201, 250, 270, 476, 477, 492
  classification, 100–102, 100t
  developmental changes meta analyses, 60, 61
  dynamic systems theory, 139
  ethnic identity, 261
  externalizing, health risk behaviors, 549–50
  identity development as process, 117
  identity maturation, 477–78
  identity trajectories, 142–43, 145n4
  integrative identity model, 104
  internalizing symptoms, 549
  lifespan identity development, 82, 87
  modern concepts of, 540, 545
  psychometric studies, 138
  racial/ethnic identity development, 20
  systonic pole of identity diffusion, 116–17
DiLorenzo, M. L., 262
Dilthey, W., 13, 151, 189
Dimensions of Identity Development Scale (DIDS), 104, 547, 555n1

Discontinuity
  autobiographical reasoning, 153–54, 159–60, 162, 171, 177, 185
  lifespan identity development, 85
Discrimination, 14–15, 251, 253, 288–92, 302–10
Discursive positioning, 212, 214–15, 222–25, 230–34
Divorce
  adjustment, 457, 462–65
  adolescence/emerging adulthood, 464–65
  attachments, 455, 458–59, 464
  behavioral patterns, 457
  child custody, 460
  cohabitation, 455
  conflict, 459, 466
  coping strategies, 455
  custodial parent, 460–62
  disillusionment, 457–58, 461
  early childhood impacts, 464
  ethnic identity, 455
  family structure, 466
  identity coherence, 455
  identity profiles, 465
  interactionism, 456
  intimacy effects, 455, 458–59, 462–65
  moratorium, 458
  non-custodial parent, 461–62
  nontraditional parenting roles, 462
  overburdened child syndrome, 464
  parenting (see parenting)
  parenting identity, 455, 459–62
  privacy, 463
  psychosocial theory, 456
  repartnering, remarriage, 462–63
  role salience, centrality, 456, 460, 462
  selection effect, 457
  self-concept, 455–56, 464
  separate togetherness, 463
  trust issues, 3, 462–63
Domino, G., 76, 77
Donenberg, G., 550
Du Bois, W. E. B., 26n1, 85
Dumas, T. M., 497
Dunlop, W. L., 550
DuPont, S., 254
Duriez, B., 542
Dynamic systems theory
  applications, 124
  context, 125
  developmental time scale, 122–23
  feedback loops, 123–24
  iterativity, 123, 123f
  principles, 122–24, 123f, 126
  real-time interactions, 123, 123f
  top-down processes, 123

Ebbinghaus, H., 152
Eccles, J. S., 447–48, 481, 485
Edwards, D., 215
Ego identity, 3–4, 14–15, 17, 66, 82, 100, 510, 566
Ego Identity Process Questionnaire, 102, 546, 548
Eichas, K., 7, 340, 347, 564
Elder, G. R., 465
Ellemers, N., 326
Ellison, N. B., 509
Embodied narration, 172–76, 189
Emerging adulthood theory, 6, 53–54. see also adolescence/emerging adulthood
The Emerging Identity Project, 41, 43, 45
Erikson, E. H., 2–5, 17–18, 22, 23, 41, 53–63, 66–68, 73–78, 81–83, 85–87, 89–90, 92, 98, 100, 105, 115–18, 120, 133, 136, 137, 140, 145n1, 150, 199–200, 210, 231, 233, 241, 250, 251, 254, 258, 269, 270, 272, 287–89, 300–302, 337, 339, 349, 355, 357, 358, 407, 455, 462, 465, 473, 478, 479, 510, 530, 531, 535, 540, 542, 564, 568
Erikson, J. M., 67, 73, 76, 77
Espinosa, C., 254
Essentialism, 156, 159, 198, 202–3, 306
Ethnic identity. see racial/ethnic identity
Eudaimonic identity theory, 197, 202–3, 242, 541–42, 551
European Americans, 299, 444
European Union, 324, 332–33
Eurostat, 324, 332–33
Existentialism, 198, 204–5
Exploration
  body image, 407–8
  in breadth, 103, 104, 118, 126
  identity development as process, 116–19
  identity status, 133–35, 137–38
  identity status model, 100, 100t, 102, 103, 117, 200–201, 250, 270, 476
  in-depth, 103, 104, 118, 126
  integrative identity model (Schachter), 234, 239–40
  openness to experience, 99, 101, 105–6, 491, 500–501
  personality development, 492–96, 495f, 499, 500
  ruminative, 103, 104, 118, 135, 161, 395, 501, 543, 545
  school, schooling, 302
  vocational, 322, 324

Exploratory-accommodative approach, 498–99
Extended Objective Measure of Ego-Identity Status (EOM-EIS), 102, 106, 108

Fadjukoff, P., 72
Family relationships
  collaborative vs. individually centered families, 42–43
  cultural neuroscience, 433
  divorce, 466
  family narrative interaction, 42
  identity status model, 548–49
  interaction styles, 210–11
  parenting, 440, 548
  reminiscing, 36–37, 42–43
  risk, resilience, 481–83
  trust issues, 3, 462–63
  work identity, 329
Ferguson, G. M., 410
Ferrari, J. R., 143
Ferrer-Wreder, L., 339, 347
Ferro, A., 154
Fhagen-Smith, P. E., 259–60
Figueredo, A. J., 77
Fika model, 6, 563
Fischer, M. M. J., 263
Five-factor theory, 491, 494
Fivush, R., 6, 35, 36, 82, 83, 90, 159, 217
Flum, H., 6, 117
Fordham, S., 290, 304, 305
Foreclosure
  adaptive resources, 486
  adolescents, 56, 60, 61
  adulthood, 68, 69–72, 74, 75
  characteristics, definitions, 18, 56, 61, 68, 117, 133, 200, 201, 250, 270, 476, 477, 492
  classification, 100–102, 100t
  context, 478–79
  developmental, 117
  developmental changes meta analyses, 60, 61, 108–9
  dynamic systems theory, 139
  ethnic identity, 261
  firm foreclosures, 117
  identity development as process, 117
  identity maturation, 477–78
  identity trajectories, 142
  integrative identity model, 104
  internalizing symptoms, 549
  lifespan identity development, 82, 87
  normative identity style, 441
  psychometric studies, 138
  racial/ethnic identity development, 20
  three-factor model, 106, 107, 107t, 125
  well-being, 481

Foucault, M., 24
Fournier, M. A., 160
Franklin, Benjamin, 91–92
Fraser, E., 103
Freeman, M., 7, 190
Freire, P., 345, 346
French, S. E., 262
Freud, S., 54, 198
Friedan, E., 327
Frisby, C. L., 251, 255
Frisén, A., 102, 134, 144, 407–8, 417, 548
Fuligni, A. J., 447–48
Furlong, A., 534
Fursternberg, F. F., Jr., 461

Gandhi, Mohandes, 3, 53, 89–90, 92
Garbarino, J., 372, 379–80
García-Coll, C., 279
Garfinkel, H., 213
Garmezy, N., 472
Garofalo, R., 550
Gee, J. P., 240
Gendered narrative identity. see also narrative identity
  adolescence (see adolescence)
  autobiographical voice, 35, 40, 48–49
  autonomy, achievement themes, 45
  body image, 407, 410–11, 416–17
  collaborative vs. individually centered families, 42–43
  elaborative reminiscing, 38–42, 39t, 48
  emotional reminiscing, 38–42, 39t, 48
  family narrative interaction, 42
  family reminiscing, 36–37, 42–43
  feminist theory, 36–37, 48
  gender conceptualization, 34
  gender differences, 36–43, 39t
  gendered identity, family reminiscing in, 42–43
  gendered personal narratives emergence, 41
  gender roles, 34, 37
  intergenerational narratives, 41–42, 45–49, 46–47t
  landscape of consciousness, 35, 37–38
  language, 35
  literacy, 35
  parent-preschool reminiscing, gender differences in, 38–40, 39t
  parent reminiscing style generally, 37–38, 48
  power relationships, 36–37
  preadolescence, family reminiscing in, 42–43
  role in identity development generally, 33–34
  role of narrative, 35–36

  self-concept emergence, parental reminiscing style in, 40–41, 48–49
  self-continuity, 34
  social, affiliation themes, 45
  sociocultural theory, 35–36, 49
  voice and silence, 36–37
Gender identity analysis, 218–21, 223, 239
Gender intensification hypothesis, 393–94, 400
Gergen, K. J., 24, 141, 154, 184, 205, 213
Gerson, K., 329–30
Ghavami, N., 274, 280–81
Ghisletta, P., 359
Gibson, M. A., 308
Gillen, M., 8
Glenberg, A. M., 176
Globalization in identity development, 58–60, 293, 566
Goffman, E., 14–15, 154, 529
Gonzalez, E., 8
Goodnow, J. J., 291
Goossens, L., 110, 118, 121, 496, 500–501, 543, 549
Grabe, S., 413
Grant, L., 273
Gray, M. L., 514
Green, K. E., 108
Greene, S. M., 463
Greenhoot, A. F., 502
Grotevant, H. D., 19, 210–11, 495f, 502, 541
Growing Up Today Study, 411
Gutmann, A., 24

Habermas, T., 7, 156, 183–87, 189, 361, 567, 571
Hadassah, 242–43
Hagit, 243
Hale, W. W., III, 109, 550
Hale-Benson, J., 257
Hall, G. S., 18
Hammack, P. L., 9, 63, 91, 141, 288, 358, 363, 366, 372, 373, 384, 567
Hannah, M. T., 77
Harada, T., 8, 427
Harbus, A., 13
Hare, J., 303
Harré, R., 154, 215
Hart, B. I., 395
Harter, S., 61, 84–85, 395
Haslam, S. A., 326
Hauser, S. T., 486
Heer, J., 517
Helms, J. E., 20–21, 252t, 253, 259
Helson, R., 72, 73, 74
Hendrickson, R., 77
Hermans, H. J. M., 205
Herrick, A., 550
Hewitt, J. P., 529

Heyman, R. E., 356
Hidalgo, N. D., 308
Hill, J. P., 393
Hill, P. L., 542
Hispanics. *see* Latina/Latino
Hoare, C. H., 67
Hogan, B., 512
Hohmann-Marriott, B., 457
Hollway, W., 215
Hopper, J., 458
Horney, K., 202
Hoyt, T., 554
Hume, D., 13
Hybrid identity, 59–60, 293–94
Hyde, J. S., 413

Ideal Worker Norm, 328–30
Identities in Talk (Antaki/Widdicombe), 216
Identity: Youth and Crisis (Erikson), 53, 199, 272, 287
Identity capital model, 542
Identity consolidation, 550, 551
Identity crisis, 17–18, 53–54, 56, 58, 61–62, 100–101, 100*t*, 116–17, 301, 339, 393, 476, 480
Identity development as process. *see also* dynamic systems theory; integrative identity model; three-factor model
   accommodation, 121–22, 121*f*
   adulthood, 69
   analysis limitations, 129
   analysis techniques, 127–29, 128*f*
   autonomy, 124
   class analyses, 125
   commitments, 116–20
   context, 120
   coping strategies, 119–20
   cycles, 121–22, 121*f*
   data collection, 125–27
   developmental foreclosures, 117
   developmental processes, 117
   development of commitments, 120
   diaries, 127, 143
   diffusion, 117
   dynamic systems, 119
   ergodicity, 124
   exploration, 116–19
   firm foreclosures, 117
   foreclosures, 117
   identification, 116
   identity crisis, 17–18, 53–54, 56, 58, 61–62, 100–101, 100*t*, 116–17, 301, 339, 393, 476, 480
   identity interviews, 125–27, 137
   interactional process (*see* interactional process)
   intraindividual variability, 124, 127–29
   introjection, 116
   mechanisms, 121–22, 121*f*, 569
   microlevel processes, 120
   quantitative dynamic modeling, 129
   reconsideration of commitment, 104–6, 109, 118, 120, 143, 476, 543
   shifts, sequences, 117–18, 120–21
   standard deviations, 127–28, 128*f*
   State Space Grid (SSG), 128
   storytelling, 127
   systonic pole of identity diffusion, 116–17
   time series analyses, 124–28, 128*f*
   trajectories, 122
   trajectory analysis, 125–26
   trajectory changes, 128
   withdrawal, 121–22, 121*f*
Identity development generally
   concepts, definitions, 540–41, 552, 567–69
   content of identity, 4–5, 120, 569–71
   correlates, 548–50
   critical analyses *vs.* theories, 528–29
   culture, conceptualization of, 7
   development *vs.* socialization, 529
   ego identity, 3–4, 14–15, 17, 66, 82, 100, 510, 566
   epistemological divide, 531
   extensions argument, 8–9
   externalizing, health risk behaviors, 549–50
   healthy identity functions, 551
   identity consolidation, 550, 551
   identity maintenance, 529
   identity synthesis, 4
   individual/subjective focus, 534–35, 534*t*
   interdisciplinary approach to, 530–31, 536
   internalizing symptoms, 549
   internal *vs.* external, 7
   model integration, 550–52
   non-normative, 534–35, 534*t*
   normative, 534–35, 534*t*
   personal identity, 3–4, 15
   personality functioning, 8–9
   perspectives, 531–35, 534*t*
   post modernism, 530–31
   process and content, 4
   psychosexual theory, 54
   psychosocial stages, 17–18, 116, 133, 136, 150–51
   pubertal timing in, 8, 17, 390–92, 396, 397, 400, 401, 411–12
   risk and resilience, 8
   social identity theory, 4, 15, 16–17, 566
   social/interactional focus, 534, 534*t*
   stages, 529
   tensions in perspectives, 565–67
   trust in caregiver as basis of, 3, 462–63
Identity interviews, 125–27, 137
Identity measures generally
   applications, 545–46
   domain specificity, 546–47
   identity interviews, 125–27, 137
   participant classification, 547–48
   quantitative dynamic modeling, 129
   self-report questionnaires, 102–3, 134, 136–37, 140, 143–44, 145n2
   standard deviations, 127–28, 128*f*
   State Space Grid (SSG), 128
Identity politics, 23–24, 372
Identity process models, 103
Identity Status Interview, 60, 61, 68, 101–3, 125, 134, 137, 477, 546
Identity status model
   achievement (*see* achievement)
   alienated achievement, 137
   antecedent conditions, 60
   applications, 70–71
   belonging, group affiliation, 139
   classification, 99–100, 102, 134, 136–37, 142, 145n2
   commitment, 98, 100, 100*t*, 102, 103, 117, 133–38, 200, 201, 250, 270, 476
   concepts, definitions, 133, 136, 137
   concurrent personality variables, 60
   congruency, 111
   consequent conditions, 60
   context, 135, 138–40
   critiques of, 19, 60–61, 543–44
   described, 3–5, 18–19
   developing *vs.* developed countries, 57–59, 63
   developmental assumptions testing, 108–9
   developmental trajectories, 109–10
   diffusion (*see* diffusion)
   dual-cycle process, 18–19, 103, 105, 118–19, 122
   ego identity, 3–4, 14–15, 17, 66, 82, 100, 510, 566
   epigenetic theory, 100
   ethnic identity, 261
   evolutive identity, 137
   exploration, 100, 100*t*, 102, 103, 117, 133–35, 137–38, 200–201, 250, 270, 476
   externalizing, health risk behaviors, 549–50
   family relationships, 548–49
   fidelity, 139
   foreclosure (*see* foreclosure)
   globalization in identity development, 58–60, 293, 566

Identity status model (Cont.)
  group-centered model, 136–38
  identity confusion, 132, 133, 138, 142
  identity crisis, 17–18, 53–54, 56, 58, 61–62, 100–101, 100t, 116–17, 301, 339, 393, 476, 480
  identity formation, 134–38, 144, 145n1
  identity interviews, 125–27, 137
  identity process models, 103
  identity resolution, 138
  identity style, 19
  identity vs. identity confusion, 100, 132
  I/me distinction, 197, 200–201
  individuality, 135, 138–40
  integrative identity model (see integrative identity model)
  internalizing symptoms, 549
  intraindividual changes, 139
  lifespan identity development, 82–84, 88, 92
  lifespan theory, 6, 61–62
  longitudinal studies, 108–10, 138, 140–41
  meta-analyses, 60–61, 108–9, 142
  methodology, 98–101
  modernization of, 539–40
  moratorium (see moratorium)
  narrative inquiry, 137, 139–41
  personality development, 490, 492–96, 495f
  personal vs. master narrative, 63, 91, 288, 358, 363, 366, 503, 567
  person-centered approach applications, 100, 104, 107–8, 110
  person-centered approach characteristics, 98–99, 134
  phylogenetic history, 54–56
  process models, 134–35
  process vs. persons, 6, 19
  psychometric studies, 137–38
  self-report questionnaires, 102–3, 134, 136–37, 140, 143–44, 145n2
  three-factor model (see three-factor model)
  thrill of dissonance diffusions, 137
  trajectories, 137–39, 141–42
  validation testing, 137
  variable-centered approach applications, 100, 104, 107–8, 110, 137
  variable-centered approach characteristics, 98–99, 134
  well-being, 549
Identity Style Measure, 76
Identity styles model
  coping strategies, 119–20
  developmental intervention science, 340
  diffuse/avoidant style, 201, 541
  identity formation processes, 202
  I/me distinction, 197, 201–2
  information-oriented style, 119, 201, 541
  model integration, 551
  modern concepts of, 541
  normative oriented, 119, 201–2, 541
  outcomes, 541
  principles, 119, 201–2
  social environment in, 202
Identity vs. role confusion, 3, 66–68, 72, 75–77, 87
I/me distinction
  aptitudes, 203
  ascription, 197–98, 206
  authenticity, 203
  autobiographical reasoning, 187, 204, 570–71
  choice, 206
  concepts, definitions, 197–99
  content/process correlations, 206
  dialogistic theories, 204–5
  difference and sameness, 14
  essentialism, 156, 159, 198, 202–3, 306
  eudaimonic identity theory, 197, 202–3, 242, 541–42, 551
  existentialism, 198, 204–5
  identification, 206
  identity concepts, definitions, 195–96
  identity status model, 197, 200–201
  identity style paradigm, 197, 201–2
  internal, external, interactional processes, 195–97
  lifespan identity development, 82, 84–85, 88–90, 92
  mind–body dualism, 198
  narrative identity model, 21, 22, 82, 197, 203–4
  parenting, 441–42
  post-modern/social constructionist theory, 205–6
  potentials, 202–3
  psychosocial theory, 197, 199–200
  self as object, 198
  self-awareness, 207
  self-concordance, 203
  self-definition, 198, 203, 207
  self-discovery, self-realization, 202–3
  self-reflection, 204
  social context, 197, 204
  well-being, 203, 206–7
Individuality, style of, 85, 86, 92
Integrative identity model (Luyckx)
  applications, 110
  assessment methodology, 103–4
  commitment making, 103, 104, 118, 119, 126
  dual cycles, 18–19, 103, 105, 118–19, 122
  exploration in breadth, 103, 104, 118, 126
  exploration in-depth, 103, 104, 118, 126
  identification with commitment, 103, 104, 126
  limitations, 135
  person-centered studies, 104
  principles, 103–4, 118, 135, 543–44
  ruminative exploration, 103, 104, 118, 135, 161, 395, 501, 543, 545
  sequences, 118
  validation, 118, 543–44
  variable-centered studies, 104, 118
Integrative identity model (Schachter)
  accountable identity claims, 230–34, 240–43
  antithetical approach, 229–30
  ascriptions, 233–34
  big vs. small stories, 182–83, 185, 186, 203–4, 238–40
  commitment, 234
  consistency constraint, 242–43
  context, 238–40
  discursive identity, 230–34
  disjunctive approach, 229–30
  ego-identity status theory, 232, 234, 238–40
  eudaimonic identity theory, 197, 202–3, 242, 541–42, 551
  exploration, 234, 239–40
  external discursive site, 234–38, 235f
  I/me distinction, 236, 238, 240
  interactional discursive site, 234–38, 235f
  internal approach, 231
  internal discursive site, 234–38, 235f
  justification, 229–30
  language, 237
  lifespan identity formation, 239–40
  positioning (see positioning)
  principles, 230–32
  psychosocial theory, 231–32
  role collaboration, 233–34
  self-affirmation, 234
  self-reflexivity, 232–33
  semiotic mediation, 230
  shared symbolism, 236
  sites of discursive claims, 234–38, 235f
  validation of identity claims, 233, 235–37, 240–43
Interactional processes
  ascriptions, 213–14, 217
  concepts, definitions, 212, 229
  crisis of representation, 213
  developmental contextual model, 211
  discursive positioning, 212, 214–15, 222–25
  dualistic metaphysics, 213

epistemic discursive psychology, 215, 217–18
ethnomethodology, 212–14, 222
factors-and-variables approach, 224
family interaction styles, 210–11
identity development as generally, 120–21, 210–12, 221–25
interior phenomena, 223–24
language, 212–13
limitations, 223–25
microgenesis, 212, 224
microinteractional contexts, 211
narrative identity, 211
positioning (see positioning)
relationality, 213
research methodology, 224
social action, 214
social constructionism, 212–13, 221–22
social epistemology, 213
social identity theory, 211
social-structural identity capital model, 211
Intergenerational narratives, 41–42, 45–49, 46–47t
Intergenerational Study, 71–72
Intersectionality
concepts, definitions, 552–55, 555n2
cultural stereotypes, 274–76, 280–81, 289, 291–94, 553–54
ethnic identity, 553–54
storytelling, 554
Inventory of Psychosocial Balance, 76
Israelis, 91, 141, 288, 370–73

Jaccard, J., 395
Jahromi, P., 108
James, J. B., 77
James, W., 11–15, 17, 21–23, 82, 86, 87, 152, 153, 187, 195, 197, 204, 205, 233, 441, 442
Japan, 331
Jensen, L. A., 63
Johnson, M. K., 322
Jones, L., 376
Jordaan, J. P., 322
Josselson, R., 6, 72, 101–2, 110, 125, 138, 140–43, 145n4
Juang, L. P., 446

Kağitçibaşi, C., 478
Kakihara, F., 447
Kant, I., 13
Kanter, R. M., 329
Kaplan, B., 342
Kasmark, A., 7, 564
Kazdin, A. E., 365
Keijsers, L., 107, 543
Kelley, W. M., 425
Kernberg, O., 142

Kerpelman, J. L., 340, 541
Kiesling, C., 547
Kim, S. Y., 553
King, E. W., 252, 252t
Kinney, D. A., 482
Kitayama, S., 426
Kitzinger, C., 214, 215, 216, 217
Kivnick, H. Q., 67
Klimstra, T. A., 109, 120, 125, 126, 542, 550
Knight, G. P., 260
Köber, C., 7, 183–87, 189, 571
Koepke, S., 483
Kohlberg, L., 54
Kohn, M., 327
Koivisto, P., 486
Kokko, K., 72
Konik, J., 503
Koot, H. M., 550
Koreans, 89
Korobov, N., 126, 127, 171, 228–30, 234, 236, 239, 240, 570
Kostelny, K., 372, 379–80
Kraus, W., 141
Kroger, J., 6, 60, 61, 73–74, 83, 86, 87, 92, 108, 117, 129, 139, 140, 143, 242, 546–47, 567, 569
Kunnen, S., 6, 73, 121, 122, 126, 128, 129, 133, 135, 136, 139–41, 143, 145n2, 569
Kurtines, W., 7

Laclau, E., 215
Ladner, J. A., 280
Lagattuta, K. H., 443, 450
Lam, J., 8
Lamont, M., 327–29
Lapsley, D. K., 447
Lardi Robyn, C., 359
Latina/Latino
cultural stereotypes, 273–74, 290, 292
culture as ethnicity, 253, 290
developmental intervention science, 347, 349
identity confusion, 549–50
lifespan identity development, 85
Lavner, J. A., 457
La Voie, J C., 73
Lawford, H., 497
Leary, M., 5
Lee, S. J., 278
Lee, S-R., 8
Lerner, J. V., 446
Leve, L., 8
Levine, C. G., 19, 230, 241, 530
Lewin, K., 240
Lichtwarck-Aschoff, A., 124, 125
Lifespan identity development
achievement, 82, 87

agency, 89, 145n2
autobiographical authors, 81–83, 89–92
autobiographical memory, 82, 89–91
autobiographical reasoning, 90–91, 190
avoidance goals, 89
bicultural identity integration, 85
class, ethnicity effects, 85, 91
cultural effects, 82–83, 89, 91–92
developmental shifts, 89
diffusion, 82, 87
discontinuity, 85
ego identity, 3–4, 14–15, 17, 66, 82, 100, 510, 566
elaboration in reminiscing, 90
emotion in reminiscing, 90
fidelity, 82, 87, 92
foreclosure, 82, 87
gender differences, 85, 90
generalized other, 84
goals, 84, 88, 89
identity concepts, 81–83
identity status, 82–84, 88, 92 (see also identity status model)
identity vs. role confusion, 87
I/me distinction, 82, 84–85, 88–90, 92
integrative identity model (Schachter), 239–40
life story model, 89
master narratives, 63, 91, 288, 358, 363, 366, 503, 567
maturation, 86
moratorium, 82, 87
motivated agents, 81, 83, 86–89, 92
narrative identity, 89–92 (see also narrative identity model)
operational thought, 88
personality change, 86, 87–88, 91
possible selves concept, 88–89
principles, 6, 61–62, 81, 92
redemptive narratives, 91, 161, 358–59
reputations, 84–86, 88
roles, 84–86, 88
self-continuity, 83–86
self-recognition, 84, 89, 91
self-storytelling, 90
social actors, 81–86, 92
social context, 87
story grammar, 90
style of individuality, 85, 86, 92
traits, 84–86
values, 88
Life story schema, 149, 154–59, 162, 166, 167, 183–86, 476–77, 545
Lifton, R. J., 205
Lilgendahl, J. P. (nee Pals), 8, 22, 127, 154, 161, 485, 491–94, 495f, 497, 499, 501, 545, 565

Linde, C., 157
Locke, J., 13, 152, 167
Lodi-Smith, J., 498
Loevinger, J., 75, 494
Lombardo, J. P., 393
Lukacher, N., 183
Luther, Martin, 53, 54, 87, 89–90, 92
Luyckx, K., 5, 103–4, 109, 110, 118, 121, 124–26, 135, 496, 500–501, 542, 543, 545, 547, 549, 552
Lynch, C. I., 257
Lynch, M. E., 393

MacIntyre, A., 151, 183
Mackavey, W. R., 158
MacLeod, J., 280
Madden-Derdich, D. A., 459
Magnusson, D., 99, 398
Major, B., 34
Malley, J., 158
Manago, A., 9, 566
Mandler, J. M., 90
Mansfield, C. D., 160–61, 359
Mansour, E., 157, 544
Marcia, J. E., 2, 17, 18, 56, 60, 61, 67, 68, 70–71, 75, 76, 77, 83, 87, 88, 98, 100, 101, 103, 105, 106, 108, 111, 115–18, 117, 120, 126, 133–34, 140, 143, 200, 201, 250, 270, 287, 288, 348, 356, 357, 465, 476, 492, 500, 543, 544, 546, 567
Marital dissolution. *see* divorce
Markey, C. N., 407
Marks, S. R., 332
Markus, H., 88–89
Markus, H. R., 426
Marshall, S. K., 551
Martinussen, M., 108, 117, 143, 567
Marwick, A. E., 519
Maslow, A. H., 202
Master narratives, 63, 91, 288, 358, 363, 366, 503, 567
Mathur, V. A., 429
McAdams, D. P., 2, 3, 6, 12, 21, 22, 62, 69–70, 89, 91, 151, 158, 161, 167, 356, 357, 476, 491–94, 495f, 498, 499, 532, 544, 545, 549, 565, 567, 570
McCall, G. J., 15
McCouch, R. J., 377
McCrae, R. R., 491
McKinney, J. P., 446
McLean, K. C., 22, 72, 127, 140, 142, 154, 160–61, 359, 366, 496, 497, 501, 502, 544, 565, 570
McLuhan, M., 508
McWhorter, J., 255, 256, 288
Mead, G. H., 11, 12–18, 22, 23, 84, 228, 231, 236, 237, 529
Meaning-making. *see also* autobiographical reasoning

narrative identity model, 544–45
personality development, 493, 496–98
political conflict, 375–77, 382–83
puberty, 391
Measham, T., 375, 383
Meca, A., 7
Meeus, W. H. J., 6, 19, 103, 104, 105, 106, 107, 108, 109, 110, 117, 118, 125, 133–37, 139, 211, 261, 476, 543, 545, 547, 550, 551
Merrill, N. A., 159
Metz, M., 6, 133, 135, 136, 139–41, 143
Mexican Americans, 85
Miller, J., 416
Misra, S., 516
Missotten, L., 110
Molenaar, P. C. M., 124
Montgomery, M. J., 7, 547, 553
Moratorium
  adolescents, 17–18, 56, 60, 61
  adulthood, 68, 69, 71, 72, 75
  characteristics, definitions, 18, 56, 61, 68, 117, 133–34, 200, 201, 250, 270, 476, 477, 492, 494–96
  classical *vs*. searching, 106, 107, 107t, 125, 543–44
  classification, 100–102, 100t
  developmental changes meta analyses, 60, 61
  divorce, 458
  dynamic systems theory, 139
  emerging adulthood, 494–96
  ethnic identity, 261
  externalizing, health risk behaviors, 549–50
  identity maturation, 477–78
  identity trajectories, 142, 143
  integrative identity model, 104
  lifespan identity development, 82, 87
  psychometric studies, 138
  racial/ethnic identity development, 20
  searching, 106, 107, 107t, 125, 543–44
  three-factor model, 106–7, 107t, 135
Moratorium-achievement moratorium-achievement (MAMA cycles), 68, 129
Mortimer, J. T., 8, 322
Motivated agents, 81, 83, 86–89, 92
Motti, F., 8
Mouffe, C., 215
Mrazek, A., 8
Multidimensional model of racial identity (MMRI), 20, 258
Multigroup Ethnic Identity Measure (MEIM), 254, 261
Murray, Henry, 2
Mustanski, B., 550

Naoi, N., 432
Narrative identity model
  adulthood, 69–70, 72
  agency, 361, 364
  autobiographical memory, 23, 82, 357–58, 358f
  autobiographical reasoning, 167–69, 184–89, 476 (*see also* autobiographical reasoning)
  big stories, 182–83, 185, 186, 203–4, 238–40
  conceptual self (tacit themes of narratives), 153
  contamination stories, 359, 366
  cultural, political situatedness, 23
  culture effects, 358
  depression studies, 359–60
  development as interpretive process, 21
  domain-specificity, 547
  evidence-based identity therapy, 355–56
  externalizing, health risk behaviors, 550
  gendered identity in, 43–48, 44–47t (*see also* gendered narrative identity)
  hierarchical model, 357, 358f
  identity configuration, 22
  I/me distinction, 21, 22, 82, 197, 203–4
  interactional processes, 211
  internalizing symptoms, 549
  language in, 23
  lifespan identity development, 89–92
  life-story construction, 21–22, 358, 361, 364–66
  master narratives, 63, 91, 288, 358, 363, 366, 503, 567
  meaning-making, 544–45
  narrative coherence, 361
  personality development, 490, 492–94, 495f, 496–99, 503
  principles, 69–70, 356–59, 358f, 544–45
  processes, 5, 355
  psychotherapy, 356, 361–66
  redemptive narratives, 91, 161, 358–59
  scripts, 358, 360–61
  self as actor, 22
  self as agent, 22
  self as author, 22
  self as social construct, 23
  self-defining memories, 358–60, 362–64
  self-reflection, 204
  small stories, 182–83, 185, 186, 203–4, 238–40

tacit themes, 169–70, 188
theories generally, 21–23, 532
translational research, 356–57, 364
well-being, 361, 549
Nasir, N., 272, 273, 276
Native Americans, 253, 290, 340
Natsuaki, M., 8
Negro-to-black conversion (nigrescence), 20
Nelson, K., 2, 35
Neuroplasticity, 425, 428, 431
Neuroticism, 86, 491, 492, 496–98, 501, 504, 505
Nguyen, A. M. D., 273
Nichter, M., 417
Nietzsche, F., 183
Nigrescence theory, 258–60, 290
Nord, C. W., 461
Norton, D. L., 202
Nucci, L., 443
Nurius, P., 88–89
Nurmi, J. -E., 486

Obama, Barack, 132, 136, 139, 141, 143, 544
Objectification, 408, 416, 417
Objectification theory, 409–10
Objective Measure of Ego Identity Status (OM-EIS), 140–41
Occupational identity. *see* work identity
Occupy Movement, 291, 332
Ogbu, J. U., 290, 300, 304, 305, 481
Olivardia, R., 410
Olmedo, E., 261
Olsen, J. A., 372
Openness to experience, 99, 101, 105–6, 491, 500–501
Optimal distinctiveness theory, 292–93
Ostrove, J. M., 72, 74
Owens, T. J., 12
Oyserman, D., 273

Pacific Islanders, 275, 277, 290, 302
Packer, M., 212
Paha, C., 156
Palestinians, 24, 91, 141, 370–73
Palkovitz, R., 76
Pals, J. L. *see* Lilgendahl, J. P. (nee Pals)
Parenting
 adaptive control patterns, 446–47
 African-Americans, 444, 447, 450
 agency, 437, 440, 444, 483
 autonomy *vs.* authority, 8, 438, 440–50
 body image, 414–15, 417
 childhood *vs.* adolescence, 437–40, 442–45
 conflict outcomes, 445–48
 conventional domain, 439–41
 decision-making control, 446–48
 domain-specific explanations, 446–47
 ethnic identity, 443–44, 447, 450
 European-Americans, 444
 family relationships, 440, 548
 identity development, 437–39
 I/me distinction, 441–42
 interdependencies, coordinations, 449
 maladaptive control patterns, 447–48
 moral domain/identity, 439–40, 443
 parental control, 449–51
 parental overcontrol, 447–48, 483
 parental undercontrol, 448, 483
 parent–child relationships, 438, 445–49, 548
 parent-preschool reminiscing, gender differences in, 38–40, 39t
 parent reminiscing style generally, 37–38, 48
 peer advice seeking, 448
 peer orientation, 448
 personal domain, 439, 441–45, 448–50
 psychological control, 447
 psychological domain, 439
 secrecy *vs.* disclosure, 445
 self-concept, 437–39, 441, 444
 social-cognitive domain theory, 449
 social domain theory, 439, 449
 social interactions, 437, 443
 styles in risk, resilience, 483
Passeron, C., 302
Pasupathi, M., 7, 22, 127, 153, 154, 157, 183, 186–90, 366, 373, 496, 501, 544, 554, 570
Pennebaker, J. W., 91
Peplau, L. A., 274, 280–81
Perkins, T. S., 292
Personal identity
 cultural stereotypes, 270, 279, 280, 287–88, 566
 development generally, 3–4, 15
 exploration in school, 302
 lifespan development, 86, 87–88, 91
 personal *vs.* master narrative, 63, 91, 288, 358, 363, 366, 503, 567
Personality development
 accommodation, 493, 498–99
 adjustment, 498–99
 adjustment trajectory, 494–99, 495f
 agency, 493
 autobiographical reasoning, 493
 coherence, complexity, 493
 commitment, 492–97, 495f, 499
 communion, 493
 context, 493, 504
 culture, 503, 504
 cumulative continuity model, 491–92, 494
 emerging adulthood, 492, 494–97, 499, 501
 ethnic identity, 503–4
 exploration, 492–96, 495f, 499, 500
 exploratory-accommodative approach, 498–99
 extroversion *vs.* introversion, 501–2
 five-factor theory, 491, 494
 identity concepts, definitions, 490–91
 identity configurations, 503–4
 identity conflict, 503–5
 identity intersections, 502–5
 identity processes, 491–94, 495f
 identity status approach, 490, 492–96, 495f
 maturity, 494–99, 495f
 maturity trajectory, 494
 meaning-making, 493, 496–98
 memory, 497, 501–3
 midlife, 494–99, 495f
 narrative identity approach, 490, 492–94, 495f, 496–99, 503
 neuroticism, 86, 491, 492, 496–98, 501, 504, 505
 openness to experience, 99, 101, 105–6, 491, 500–501
 personality as characteristic adaptations, 492–93
 personality as traits, 491–92
 plasticity, 500–502, 569
 positive, negative events, 494–99, 495f
 redemption, contamination, 493
 resolution, 493, 496–99
 self-change *vs.* self-stability, 493, 496
 self-transformation, 493–94, 498–99
 sentence completion test, 494
 social relationships, 496–98, 501–2
 traits as moderators, 500–505
 transformational processing, 498–99
 well-being, 497–98
Peter, J., 513–14, 517
Pfeifer, J. H., 428
Phenomenological variant of ecological systems theory (P-VEST), 272
Philippe, F. L., 170
Phillips, K. A., 410
Philogène, G., 263
Phinney, J. S., 20, 252t, 253, 254, 261–62, 553, 570
Piaget, J., 54, 121, 258, 569
Pittinsky, T. L., 257
Plasticity
 neuroplasticity, 425, 428, 431
 personality development, 500–502, 569
Pleydell-Pearce, C. W., 153

Pluralism, 23–24
Political conflict
  adaptive processes, 373, 379–80
  adolescence/emerging adulthood, 370–81
  agency, 374–76, 440
  Bosnian youth, 375–77, 381
  collective identity abandonment, 377–78, 381
  Colombia, 377–80
  coping strategies, 373–75, 378–80, 382–84
  dehumanization, 373
  delegitimization, 371, 372
  discrimination, 380–81
  emotional detachment, 374–75
  essentialized identities, 378–82
  goals, emotions, and cognitions, 374–75
  group identity, 371–73
  identity development, 369–70, 373–77, 382–84
  immigrants, refugees, 380–82
  ingroup bias, 370–73, 382
  Israelis, 91, 141, 288, 370–73
  meaning-making, 375–77, 382–83
  meaning-making capacity disruption, 374–75
  multiple identities, 380–81
  narratives, 374, 382, 383
  Palestinians, 24, 91, 141, 370–73
  polarized collective identities, 370–75, 381
  powerlessness, 376–77, 381
  psychological avoidance, numbing, 373–75, 378–79
  psychosocial impacts, 369–70, 377–80
  self as agent, 369–70
  Serbian youth, 376
  societal beliefs, 371–73
  therapeutic interventions, 383–84
  trauma, 374, 383
  victimization, 376–77
  violent acts, 376–81
  war, 375–81
Pope, H. G., 410
Popovska, A., 360
Positioning
  applications, 217–18, 222–23
  discursive, 212, 214–15, 222–25, 230–34
  discursive generally, 214–15, 222–25
  gender identity analysis, 218–21, 223, 239
  identities analysis, 215–17
  membership categories, 216–17
  in narratives, 171–72
  practices, 216–17
  relational, 170–72, 188–89
  as second-order phenomena, 216
  self-positioned resistance, 218–19, 223
  speed-dating, 218–21, 223, 239, 240–41
  validation of identity claims, 233, 235–37, 240–43
Post traumatic stress disorder (PTSD), 3, 369, 374, 563–64
Potter, J., 215, 217
Pratt, M. M., 75–76, 140, 142
Pratt, M. W., 496, 497
Prebble, S. C., 152, 155
Project Competence study, 485
Promotive factors, 475, 484, 485
Protective factors, 475, 484, 485
Protestants, 370
Psychopathology internalization, 389–90, 392–401, 393f, 549
Pubertal timing, 8, 17, 390–92, 396, 397, 400, 401, 411–12
Puberty. *see also* body image
  adrenarche, 390–91
  adult-like behaviors, 398
  adverse outcomes prevention, intervention, 398, 401
  animal models, 396–97
  anxiety, 389–90, 392, 394–97
  biological definition, 390–91
  biopsychosocial model, 392–99, 393f
  body image, 397–98
  cognitive shifts, 394
  context, 393–94, 397–99
  contextual amplification hypothesis, 398–99
  coping strategies, 394–95, 397, 401
  cortisol, 396
  culture differences, 391, 395–96
  depression, 389–90, 392, 394–97, 400
  early maturation, 389–90, 392–99, 393f, 412
  estrogen, estradiol, 396
  false-self behaviors, 395
  gender intensification hypothesis, 393–94, 400
  gender role identity, 390, 392–96, 393f, 400–401
  gonadarche, 390–91
  identity crisis, 393
  masculinity, 394–96
  meaning-making, 391
  menarche rites, 391
  menstruation, 391
  neuroendocrine systems, 390–91, 396–97
  neuroimaging studies, 397
  pituitary gland, 397
  psychopathology internalization, 389–90, 392–401, 393f, 549
  pubertal status, 391
  pubertal tempo, 392
  pubertal timing, 8, 17, 390–92, 396, 397, 400, 401, 411–12
  puberty-initiated mediation hypothesis, 397
  romantic relationships, 399–401
  ruminative response style, 103, 104, 118, 135, 161, 395, 501, 543
  self-silencing, 394–95, 400–401, 417
  social reinforcement, 395–98, 400
  stress regulation, 396–97, 400
  testosterone, 397
  victimization, 398
Pulkkinen, L., 72
Punamaki, R. L., 372
Puritans, 91–92

Q-sort, 72
Quantitative dynamic modeling, 129
Quijada, P. D., 251
Quintana, S. M., 447

Raaijmakers, Q. A. W., 109
Racial/ethnic identity. *see also* cultural stereotypes; culture as ethnicity
  achievement, 20, 261
  African-Americans, 20, 26n1
  autonomy, 20
  belonging, group affiliation, 20
  body image, 413–14
  centrality, 20
  commitment outcomes, 547
  culture as ethnicity, 254–55, 290
  diffusion/foreclosure, 20
  disintegration, 20
  exploration, 339–40
  externalizing, health risk behaviors, 549–50
  ideology, 20
  information processing approaches, 21
  intersectionality, 553–54
  lifespan development, 85, 289
  models generally, 260–62
  moratorium, 20
  negative identity, 19
  Negro-to-black conversion (nigrescence), 20
  parenting, 443–44, 447, 450
  profiles, 261–62, 288, 293–94
  pseudo-independence, 20
  racial identity models, 257–60
  racial identity profiles, 259–60, 288, 293–94
  racial socialization, 253, 260–61, 290
  reintegration, 20
  salience, 20
  theories generally, 19–21
  whites, 20–21

Racial Identity Attitude Scale (RIAS), 259
Radmacher, K., 552
RAP Project, 282n1
Real-time interactions, 123, 123f
Recchia, H., 8
Reconsideration of commitment, 104–6, 109, 118, 120, 143, 476, 543, 545
Redemptive narratives, 91, 161, 358–59
Relational being, 24
Reminiscing. see storytelling
Remy, L., 8
Revill, J., 254
Ricciardelli, L. A., 413
Rice, Condoleeza, 255
Ricoeur, P., 149, 151, 158–59, 183, 188, 203
Risk, resilience
  adaptation indices, 474–75
  adaptive functioning, 475
  adaptive history, 479–80
  adolescent to adult transition, 484, 485
  African-Americans, 481
  agency, 473, 483, 485
  autobiographical reasoning, 161, 476
  concepts, principles, 474–75
  context, 473, 478–79, 482
  coping strategies, 484–85
  dependence–independence, 478
  developmental psychopathology, 472, 479
  developmental tasks, 474–79
  discrimination, 481
  dissociation, 482
  ethnic identity, 473, 477, 480
  factors affecting, 475
  family experiences, 481–83
  identity as resource, 484–86
  identity development, 473–79, 486
  identity maturation, 477–78
  identity synthesis vs. confusion, 476
  immigrant paradox, 481
  individualism–collectivism, 478
  institutionalization, 482, 485
  internal adaptation, 474
  life story construction, 476–77
  multifinality principle, 475, 480
  narrative approach, 473–74, 476–77, 480–81, 484–86
  parenting styles, 483
  personal goals, 484
  positive adaptation, 473, 474, 482–83
  positive identity trajectories, outcome, 475–79
  Project Competence study, 485
  promotive factors, 475, 484, 485
  protective factors, 475, 484, 485
  research generally, 472–73
  resources, 480, 482–86
  risks generally, 480–82
  school experiences, 482
  self-concept, 476
  self-continuity, 477, 485
  self-esteem, 479–80
  self-reflection, 483, 485
  social relationships, 482, 485
  societal-level variables, 481
  status approach, 473–74, 476, 480, 486
  zeitgeist, 473
Roberts, B. W., 73, 491–92, 494, 495f
Robins, R. W., 497
Robinson, T., 277, 281
Rogers, C. R., 202
Rogers, O., 7, 282n1, 286, 287, 291–93, 304, 566
Rogers, T. B., 425
Role-identity theory, 15
Rosenberg, M., 319, 320, 324, 331
Rote, W., 8, 565
Rousseau, C., 375, 383
Rubin, D. C., 162
Rubini, M., 550
Rumbaut, R. G., 300
Ruminative exploration, 103, 104, 118, 135, 161, 395, 501, 543, 545
Russians, 89
Rutter, M., 472

Sabik, N. J., 413
Sacks, H., 213, 234
Saini, M., 459
Sales, J. M., 159
Salgado, J., 205
Salmela-Aro, K., 486
Salmon, K., 161
Sam, D. L., 261–62
Sameness. see difference and sameness
Sameroff, A. J., 481
Samuels, D., 8
Sanders, K., 254
Sankey, A. M., 140–41
Santos, C. E., 281
Sayer, A., 72, 74
Schachter, E., 7, 22, 143, 228–32, 287, 288, 503–4, 554
Schaefer, B. A., 259–60
Schechtman, M., 167
Schneider, B., 321
School, schooling
  academic identities, 300
  academic pipeline problem, 299–300, 310f, 311
  accommodation without assimilation, 304
  acting white, 304–6
  affirmation, 302
  African Americans, 299–302, 304–6
  alienation/belonging, 300, 302–6
  ambivalence, 304–5
  Asian Americans, 299, 300, 302
  aspirational capital, 302, 303, 311
  assimilation, 300
  Bridging Multiple Worlds model, 310–13, 310f
  challenges, 300, 310, 311
  Community Cultural Wealth framework, 302
  continuity, cultural reproduction, 300
  coping strategies, 302–6, 310–12
  cultural, linguistic assimilation, 304
  discrimination/stigma, 302–10
  essentialism, 156, 159, 198, 202–3, 306
  Ethnic Identity Scale, 302
  European Americans, 299
  exploration, 302
  familial capital, 302, 303
  gender differences, 299, 305, 306, 308
  Indigenous Mexican immigrants, 303, 306–10
  Latinos, 299, 300, 302–3, 305–11
  linguistic capital, 302
  mestizos, 307, 308, 311
  Multigroup Ethnic Identity Measure (MEIM-R), 302
  narratives, 302–3
  Native Americans, 299–302
  navigational capital, 302
  oppositional cultural frame of reference, 305
  oppositional identities, 300
  Pacific Islanders, 302
  personal identity exploration, 302
  policy, 307–10, 313–14
  positive identity shift, 309
  psychosocial theory, 301
  race-ethnicity, 300, 304–6
  resistance/opposition, 305
  resistant capital, 302
  resolution (commitment), 302
  social capital theory, 291, 300, 302–3
  social identities, 300–302, 308
  tracking, 303
  upward mobility resources, 302
Schooler, C., 327
Schouten, A. P., 513–14
Schwammlein, E., 511
Schwartz, S. J., 5, 9, 110, 210, 343–46, 467, 483, 500–501, 535, 541–43, 545, 548, 549, 550, 551, 552, 553, 554, 555
Searching moratorium, 106, 107, 107t, 125, 543–44
Seaton, C. L., 76
Seaton, E. K., 261

Self-concept
  adolescence/emerging adulthood, 40, 48–49, 59
  autobiographical reasoning, 153
  body image, 407
  cultural stereotypes, 271–72, 276–77, 292
  difference and sameness, 4, 12
  divorce, 455–56, 464
  emergence, parental reminiscing style in, 40–41, 48–49
  parenting, 437–39, 441, 444
  risk, resilience, 476
  social networking sites, 510, 517
Self-construal theory, 424
Self-continuity
  autobiographical reasoning, 150–62, 167, 184–89
  cumulative continuity model, 491–92, 494
  gendered narrative identity, 34
  lifespan identity development, 83–86
  risk, resilience, 477, 485
  school, schooling, 300
Self-discrepancy theory, 408–9
Self-esteem
  adolescence/emerging adulthood, 41–43, 56–57, 60
  body image, 407, 411, 416
  risk, resilience, 479–80
  social networking sites, 517–19
Self-Examination Interview, 77
Self-report questionnaires, 102–3, 134, 136–37, 140, 143–44, 145n2
Self-silencing, 394–95, 400–401, 417
Self-transformation, 493–94, 498–99
Sellers, R. M., 20, 258, 261, 281
Sen, A., 24
Serafini, T., 551
Serbian youth, 376
Serpe, R. T., 236
Seventh Generation Program, 340
Sexualization, 410–11, 416
Shah, N., 272, 273, 276
Shakespeare, W., 84
Sherman, A. M., 416
Shih, M., 257
Shoda, Y., 356
Sica, L. S., 551
Siegel, P., 360–61
Silverman, W. K., 395
Simmons, J. L., 15
Singer, J. A., 7, 357, 359, 360, 366, 564
Sisters of Nia, 339–40
Sjomeling, M., 257
Skorikov, V. B., 320, 321, 325, 550
Slep, A. M., 356
Slone, M., 373

Small stories, 182–83, 185, 186, 203–4, 238–40
Smetana, J. G., 8, 443, 446, 447, 565
Smith, V., 326
Sneed, J. R., 72, 74
Social actors, 81–86, 92
Social-cognitive domain theory, 449
Social comparison theory, 408
Social domain theory, 439, 449
Social identity, relationships. *see also* family relationships
  culture as ethnicity, 250–51
  identity styles model, 202
  I/me distinction, 197, 204
  lifespan identity development, 87
  narrative identity model, 23
  personality development, 496–98, 501–2
  racial socialization, 253, 260–61, 290
  risk, resilience, 482, 485
  social networking sites, 515
Social identity theory, 4, 15, 16–17, 566
Social networking sites
  agency, 508–9
  alternative perspectives, 514
  autonomy, 510–12, 516–17
  bridging social capital, 514–15
  concepts, definitions, 509–10
  content communities, 509
  context collapse, 519
  customized sociality, 512–17
  displacement hypothesis, 512
  extroversion *vs.* introversion, 518
  Facebook, 509, 511–15, 517–19
  foreclosure, 510
  friendship, 513
  identity development, 510, 513–20
  impression formation, 517
  information overload, 515–16
  Internet technologies, 508
  multiple identities, 519–20
  MySpace, 511, 512, 517, 518
  narcissism, 518
  networked individualism, 510–12, 519
  parental relationship, 515
  personhood, belonging, 511, 515, 516, 518
  photos, 516–17
  popularity as goal, 515
  privacy, 518–19
  relatedness, 510–12
  self-concept, 510, 517
  self-esteem, 517–19
  self-expression, 508–9, 511, 516–20
  self-presentations, 516–18
  social comparison, 515
  social connectedness, 517
  social grooming, 511
  social information, 513–15
  social support, 513–14

Twitter, 509, 511
  virtual worlds, 509
  warranting principle, 517
  well-being, 513–14
  Wikipedia, 509, 511
Soenens, B., 118, 121, 206, 496, 500–501, 543, 549
Sorell, G. T., 547
South Africa, 379, 380
Speed-dating, 218–21, 223, 239, 240–41
Spencer, M. B., 272, 279
Spithorst, H., 127
Standard deviations, 127–28, 128*f*
Starr, C. R., 410
State Space Grid (SSG), 128
Stattin, H., 398
Staudinger, U., 156
Steele, C., 255
Steele, S., 255
Stephan, Y., 417
Stephen, J., 103
Sternberg, L., 456
Stevenson, D., 321
Stewart, A., 72, 74, 503
Stewart, A. J., 72, 158
Stigmatization, 14–15, 251, 253, 288–92, 302–10
Stokols, D., 516
Stone, J., 257
Stone, L. D., 91
Stone, M. R., 485
Storytelling
  big stories, 182–83, 185, 186, 203–4, 238–40
  elaboration in reminiscing, 90
  elaborative reminiscing, 43, 44–45*t*, 46–49, 47*t*
  emotional reminiscing, 43, 44–45*t*, 46–49, 47*t*
  family reminiscing, 36–37, 42–43
  gendered identity, family reminiscing in, 42–43
  identity development as process, 127
  intergenerational narratives, 41–42, 45–49, 46–47*t*
  intersectionality, 554
  life story schema, 149, 154–59, 162, 166, 167, 183–86, 476–77, 545
  narrative identity model, 22–23
  parent-preschool reminiscing, gender differences in, 38–40, 39*t*
  parent reminiscing style generally, 37–38, 48
  personal memory telling, 22
  preadolescence, family reminiscing in, 42–43
  self-concept emergence, parental reminiscing style in, 40–41, 48–49

small stories, 182–83, 185, 186, 203–4, 238–40
tacit themes, 169–70, 188
Strauman, T. J., 356
Strawson, G., 183, 184
Strayer, J., 288
Structural symbolic interactionism, 15–16
Stryker, S., 15–16, 236, 319, 320, 324, 326, 328
Style of individuality, 85, 86, 92
Suárez-Orozco, C., 272
Super, D. E., 322
Sutin, A. R., 497
Syed, M., 289, 477, 502, 503–4, 552, 554, 571
Symbolic interactionism, 14
Systonic pole of identity diffusion, 116–17

Tajfel, H., 12, 16, 211, 287, 300–302
Talleyrand, R. M., 253
Tangney, J., 5
Tashiro, J., 513
Tavernier, R., 549
Taylor, C., 24, 183, 203
Taylor, D. M., 554
Telesford, J., 260
Telzer, E. H, 431, 433
Thomas, Clarence, 255
Thompson, C. E., 252t
Thompson, J. M., 395
Thorne, A., 22, 359, 501
Three-factor model
  achievement, 106, 107, 107t, 125
  applications, 105–6, 110–11
  assessment methodology, 105, 125
  certainty–uncertainty dynamic, 109
  class analyses, 125
  classification, 105–6
  commitment, 104–7, 107t, 109, 119
  consolidators, 110, 125, 500–501
  diffusion, 106, 107, 107t, 125
  dual-cycle process, 18–19, 103, 105, 118–19, 122, 543–44
  early closure, 106, 107, 107t, 125
  entropy, 106
  exploration in breadth, 103, 110, 496, 500–501
  exploration in-depth, 104–6, 109, 110, 118, 476, 500–501
  foreclosure, 106, 107, 107t, 125
  identity clusters, 106
  identity maturation, 109
  identity transitions, 109–10
  limitations, 135
  moratorium, 106–7, 107t, 135
  pathmakers, 110, 125
  person-centered studies, 105–7, 109–10

  principles, 104–5, 118, 135, 543–44
  reconsideration of commitment, 104–6, 109, 118, 120, 143, 476, 543, 545
  searchers, 110, 125
  searching moratorium, 106, 107, 107t, 125, 543–44
  validation studies, 105, 118–19
  variable-centered studies, 105–7, 110
Thrill of dissonance diffusions, 137
Tieu, T. T., 497
Tiggemann, M., 416
Tilton-Weaver, L., 447
Timmerman, M. E., 129
Tippett, L. J., 152, 155
Tisak, M. S., 443
Tompkins, S., 2
Tower of Babel issue, 530, 536, 552
Tracy, J. L., 550
Trimble, J., 261
Tripartite model, 409
Trust issues, 3, 462–63
Tufekci, Z., 519
Tulving, E., 152, 153, 155
Turner, J., 16, 211
Tynes, B., 514

Udall-Weiner, D., 414
Usborne, E., 554
Utrecht-Management of Identity Commitments Scale (U-MICS), 105, 106, 126

Validation of identity claims, 233, 235–37, 240–43
Valkenburg, P. M., 513–14, 517
Valsiner, J., 205, 230
VandenBos, G. R., 251, 252, 252t
Van der Gaag, M., 126–27
Van der Linden, M., 359
Van de Schoot, R., 107, 543
Vandiver, B. J., 259–60
Van Doorn, N., 517
Van Geert, P. L. C., 122
Vansteenkiste, M., 549
Vedder, P., 261–62
Ventura, 287
Vignoles, V. L., 5, 552
Vocational exploration, 322, 324
Vondracek, F. W., 320, 321, 325, 550
Von Eye, A., 446
Vygotsky, L., 35, 212, 221, 228, 231, 236, 237, 272

Wagenbach, P., 414
Wainryb, C., 8, 373, 376
Wallerstein, J. S., 464
Wang, Q., 91
Wängqvist, M., 102, 134, 144, 407–8, 417, 548

Ward, J. V., 277, 281
Wassink, M. E. K., 73
Waterman, A. S., 7, 199, 202, 206, 213, 228–30, 232, 241, 357
Waters, M., 275, 278, 292
Way, N., 7, 286, 287, 291–93, 304, 566
Weight issues, 412–15
Weisz, J. R., 340
Well-being
  achievement, 481
  autobiographical reasoning, 159–62, 185
  body image, 409
  concepts, definitions, 549
  foreclosure, 481
  narrative identity model, 361, 549
  personality development, 497–98
  work identity, 325, 326
Wellman, B., 510, 512
Werner, E. E., 472
Werner, H., 342
Wetherell, M., 531
Whitbourne, S. K., 69, 72, 74, 569
Whiting, B. B., 286
Widdicombe, S., 216
Wiley, R. E., 450
Wilkinson, C., 214, 216, 217
Willoughby, T., 549
Wilson, A., 8
Wittgenstein, L., 212
Wodzicki, K., 511
Wong, C. A., 481
Work identity
  adolescence/emerging adulthood, 322–24
  apprenticeships, 330
  attitudes, 323, 325, 327, 330–31
  collectivism, 330–31
  contexts, 322–26
  cross-cultural variation, 330–32
  development, concepts of, 319–22, 325
  employment relationships, 322–26
  employment-to-population ratio, 331
  family devotion schema, 329
  gender differences, 327–30
  hierarchy of identities, 321, 326
  Ideal Worker Norm, 328–30
  identity formation, 322–25, 332
  identity theory (Stryker), 324–26
  occupational inequality, 332
  organizational affiliation, identity, 326, 327, 331
  precarious employment, 323, 332–33
  retirement, institutionalization of, 332
  role identities, 320–21, 325, 329
  school to work transition, 321, 325

Work identity (*Cont.*)
  self-evaluations, 321, 327
  social class, 326–27
  transition to adulthood, 319, 321, 325
  universality, 326–31
  values, 322, 325–27, 330–31
  vocational exploration, 322, 324
  well-being, 325, 326
  work devotion schema, 329

Worrell, F. C., 251, 259–60, 286, 287, 289–91

Yang, C., 514
YES!, 339–40
Yip, T., 261
Yoder, A., 502
Yosso, T. J., 302
Young, R. A., 140–41

Youth Development Study, 323–25

Zaman, W., 6, 82, 83, 90
Zapata-Gietl, C., 3, 6, 532
Zarrett, N., 77
Zhu, Y., 426
Zucker, A. N., 72
Zurbriggen, E. L., 416

CPSIA information can be obtained at www.ICGtesting.com
Printed in the USA
BVOW09s1951241115

427418BV00004B/2/P